ENGLISH SYNONYMES,

WITH

COPIOUS ILLUSTRATIONS AND EXPLANATIONS,

DRAWN FROM THE BEST WRITERS.

BY GEORGE CRABB, M.A.,

AUTHOR OF THE "UNIVERSAL TECHNOLOGICAL DICTIONARY," AND THE "UNIVERSAL HISTORICAL DICTIONARY."

Tenth Edition.

FROM THE LAST QUARTO EDITION.

NEW YORK:

HARPER & BROTHERS, PUBLISHERS,

329 & 331 PEARL STREET,

FRANKLIN SQUARE.

1853.

PREFACE

TO

THE FIRST EDITION.

It may seem surprising that the English, who have employed their talents successfully in every branch of literature, and in none more than in that of philology, should yet have fallen below other nations in the study of their synonymes: it cannot however be denied that, while the French and Germans have had several considerable works on the subject, we have not a single writer who has treated it in a scientifick manner adequate to its importance: not that I wish by this remark to depreciate the labours of those who have preceded me; but simply to assign it as a reason why I have now been induced to some forward with an attempt to fill up what is considered a chasm in English literature.

In the prosecution of my undertaking, I have profited by every thing which has been written in any language upon the subject; and although I always pursued my own train of thought, yet whenever I met with any thing deserving of notice, I adopted it, and referred it to the author in a note. I had not proceeded far before I found it necessary to restrict myself in the choice of my materials; and accordingly laid it down as a rule not to compare any words together which were sufficiently distinguished from each other by striking features in their signification, such as *abandon* and *quit*, which require a comparison with others, though not necessarily with themselves; for the same reason I thought fit to limit myself, as a rule, to one authority for each word, unless where the case seemed to require farther exemplification.

Although a work of this description does not afford much scope for system and arrangement, yet I laid down to myself the plan of arranging the words according to the extent or universality of their acceptation, placing those first which had the most general sense and application, and the rest in order. By this plan I found myself greatly aided in analyzing their differences, and I trust that the reader will thereby be equally benefited. In the choice of authorities I have been guided by various considerations; namely, the appropriateness of the examples; the classick purity of the author; the justness of the sentiment; and, last of all, the variety of the writers: but I am persuaded that the reader will not be dissatisfied to find that I have shown a decided preference to such authors as Addison, Johnson, Dryden, Pope, Milton, &c. At the same time it is but just to observe that this selection of authorities has been made by an actual perusal of the authors, without the assistance of Johnson's dictionary.

For the sentiments scattered through this work I offer no apology, although I am aware that they will not fall in with the views of many who may be competent to decide on its literary merits. I write not to please or displease any description of persons; but I trust that what I have written according to the dictates of my mind will meet the approbation of those whose good opinion I am most solicitous to obtain. Should any object to the introduction of morality in a work of science, I beg them to consider, that a writer, whose business it was to mark the nice shades of distinction between words closely allied, could not do justice to his subject without entering into all the relations of society, and showing, from the acknowledged sense of many moral and religious terms, what has been the general sense of mankind on many of the most important questions which have agitated the world. My first object certainly has been to assist the philological inquirer in ascertaining the force and comprehension of the English language; yet I should have thought my work but half completed had I made it a mere register of verbal distinctions. While others seize every opportunity unblushingly to avow and zealously to propagate opinions destructive of good order, it would ill become any individual of contrary sentiments to shrink from stating his convictions, when called upon as he seems to be by an occasion like that which has now offered itself. As to the rest, I throw myself on the indulgence of the publick, with the assurance that, having used every endeavour to deserve their approbation, I shall not make an appeal to their candour in vain.

ADVERTISEMENT

TO THE LONDON QUARTO EDITION.

A FOURTH edition of the ENGLISH SYNONYMES having now become desirable, the Author has for some time past occcupied himself in making such additions and improvements, as he deems calculated materially to enhance its value as a work of criticism. The alphabetical arrangement of the words is exchanged for one of a more scientifick character, arising from their alliance in sense or from the general nature of the subjects: thus affording the advantage of a more connected explanation of terms, more or less allied to each other. At the same time the purpose of reference is more fully answered by an index so copious that the reader may immediately turn to the particular article sought for. The subject matter of several articles has been considerably enlarged, and such amplifications admitted as may serve to place the SYNONYMES in a clearer point of view, particularly by comparing them with the corresponding words in the original languages whence they are derived. The English quotations have likewise undergone several alterations both in their number and order, so as to adapt them to the other changes which have been introduced throughout the work.

INDEX.

ENGLISH SYNONYMES

EXPLAINED.

SOUL, MIND.

THESE terms, or the equivalents to them, have been employed by all civilized nations to designate that part of human nature which is distinct from matter. The *Soul*, however, from the German *seele*, &c. and the Greek ζάω, to live, like the *anima* of the Latin, which comes from the Greek ἄνεμος, wind or breath, is represented to our minds by the subtilest or most ethereal of sensible objects, namely, breath or spirit, and denotes properly the quickening or vital principle. *Mind*, on the contrary, from the Greek μένος, which signifies strength, is that sort of power which is closely allied to, and in a great measure dependant upon, corporeal organization: the former is, therefore, the immortal, and the latter the mortal, part of us; the former connects us with angels, the latter with brutes; in this latter we distinguish nothing but the power of receiving impressions from external objects, which we call ideas, and which we have in common with the brutes.

There are minute philosophers, who, from their extreme anxiety after truth, deny that we possess any thing more than what this poor composition of flesh and blood can give us; and yet, methinks, sound philosophy would teach us that we ought to prove the truth of one position, before we assert the falsehood of its opposite; and consequently, that if we deny that we have any thing but what is material in us, we ought first to prove that the material is sufficient to produce the reasoning faculty of man. Now it is upon this very impossibility of finding any thing in matter as an adequate cause for the production of the *soul*, that it is conceived to be an entirely distinct principle. If we had only the mind, that is, an aggregate of ideas or sensible images, such as is possessed by the brutes, it would be no difficulty to conceive of this as purely material, since the act of receiving images is but a passive act, suited to the inactive property of matter: but when the *soul* turns in upon itself, and creates for itself by abstraction, combination, and deduction, a world of new objects, it proves itself to be the most active of all principles in the universe; it then positively acts upon matter instead of being acted upon by it.

But not to lose sight of the distinction drawn between the words *soul* and *mind*, I simply wish to show that the vulgar and the philosophical use of these terms altogether accord, and are both founded on the true nature of things. Poets and philosophers speak of the *soul* in the same strain, as the active and living principle;

> Man's *soul* in a perpetual motion flows,
> And to no outward cause that motion owes.
> DENHAM.

> In bashful coyness, or in maiden pride,
> The soft return conceal'd, save when it stole
> In side-long glances from her downcast eyes,
> Or from her swelling *soul* in stifled sighs.
> THOMSON.

'The soul consists of many faculties, as the understanding, and the will, with all the senses, both outward and inward; or, to speak more philosophically, the *soul* can exert herself in many different ways of action.'—ADDISON. The ancients, though unaided by the light of divine revelation, yet represented the soul as a distinct principle. The Psyche of the Greeks, which was the name they gave to the human *soul*, was feigned to be one of their incorporeal or celestial beings. The *anima* of the Latins was taken precisely in the modern sense of the *soul*, by which it was distinguished from the *animus* or *mind*. Thus the emperour Adrian is said on his dying bed to have addressed his soul in words which clearly denote what he thought of its independent existence.

> Animula vagula, blandula,
> Quæ nunc abibis in loca?
> Hospes comesque corporis,
> Pallidula, rigida, undula,
> Nec (ut soles) dabis joca!

The *mind* being considered as an attribute to the *soul*, is taken sometimes for one faculty, and sometimes for another; as for the understanding, when we say a person is not in his right *mind;*

> I am a very foolish, fond old man;
> I fear I am not in my perfect *mind*.—SHAKSPEARE.

Sometimes for the intellectual power;

> I thought the eternal *mind*
> Had made us masters.—DRYDEN.

Or for the intellectual capacity;

> We say that learning 's endless, and blame fate
> For not allowing life a longer date,
> He did the utmost bounds of knowledge find,
> He found them not so large as was his *mind*.
> COWLEY.

Or for the imagination or conception; 'In the judgment of Aristotle and Bacon, the true poet forms his imitations of nature after a model of ideal perfection, which perhaps has no existence but in his own *mind*.'—BEATTIE.

Sometimes the word *mind* is employed to denote the operations of the thinking faculty, the thoughts or opinions;

> The ambiguous god,
> In these mysterious words his *mind* express'd,
> Some truths revealed, in terms involved the rest.
> DRYDEN.

> The earth was not of my *mind*
> If you suppose, as fearing you, it shook.
> SHAKSPEARE.

Or the will, choice, determination, as in the colloquial phrase to have a *mind* to do a thing; 'All the arguments to a good life will be very insignificant to a man that hath a *mind* to be wicked, when remission of sins may be had on such cheap terms.'—TILLOTSON. 'Our question is, whether all be sin which is done without direction by Scripture, and not whether the Israelites did at any time amiss by following their own *minds* without asking counsel of God.'—HOOKER.

Sometimes it stands for the memory, as in the familiar expressions to call to *mind*, put in *mind*, &c.; 'The king knows their disposition; a small touch will put him in *mind* of them.'—BACON.

> These, and more than I to *mind* can bring,
> Menalcas has not yet forgot to sing.'—DRYDEN.

'They will put him in *mind* of his own waking thoughts, ere these dreams had as yet made their impressions on his fancy.'—ATTERBURY.

> A wholesome law, time out of *mind;*
> Had been confirm'd by fate's decree.'—SWIFT.

Lastly, the *mind* is considered as the seat of all the faculties; 'Every faculty is a distinct taste in the *mind*, and hath objects accommodated to its proper relish.'—ADDISON. And also of the passions or affections;

> E'en from the body's purity, the *mind*
> Receives a secret sympathetick aid.—THOMSON.

'This word, being often used for the *soul* giving life, is attributed abusively to madmen, when we say that they are of a distracted *mind*, instead of a broken understanding; which word *mind* we use also for opinion, as I am of this or that *mind;* and sometimes for men's conditions or virtues, as he is of an honest *mind*, or a man of a just *mind;* sometimes for affection, as I do this for my *mind's* sake,' &c.—RALEIGH.

The *soul*, being the better part of a man, is taken for the man's self, as Horace says, in allusion to his friend Virgil, 'Et serves animæ dimidium meæ:' hence the term is figuratively extended in its application to denote a human being; 'The moral is the case of every *soul* of us.'—L'ESTRANGE. It is a republick; there are in it a hundred burgeois, and about a thousand *souls;* 'The poor *soul* sat singing by a sycamore tree.'—SHAKSPEARE. Or the individual in general;

Join voices, all ye living *souls*. Ye birds
That singing up to heaven-gate ascend
Bear on your wings, and in your notes, his praise.
MILTON.

Also what is excellent, the essential or principal part of a thing, the spirit; 'Thou sun, of this great world both eye and *soul*.'—MILTON. 'He has the very *soul* of bounty.'—SHAKSPEARE.

There is some *soul* of goodness in things evil,
Would men observingly distil it out.—SHAKSPEARE.

INCORPOREAL, UNBODIED, IMMATERIAL, SPIRITUAL.

Incorporeal, from *corpus*, a body, marks the quality of not belonging to the body, or having any properties in common with it; *unbodied* denotes the state of being without the body, or not enclosed in a body; a thing may therefore be *incorporeal* without being *unbodied;* but not *vice versâ;* the soul of man is *incorporeal*, but not *unbodied*, during his natural life;

Th' *unbodied* spirit flies
And lodges where it lights in man or beast.
DRYDEN.

Incorporeal is used in regard to living things, particularly by way of comparison, with *corporeal* or human beings;

Of sense, whereby they hear, see, smell, touch, taste,
Tasting, concoct, digest, assimilate,
And *corporeal* to *incorporeal* turn.—MILTON.

Hence we speak of *incorporeal* agency, or *incorporeal* agents, in reference to such beings as are supposed to act in this world without the help of the body; 'Sense and perception must necessarily proceed from some *incorporeal* substance within us.'—BENTLEY. But *immaterial* is applied to inanimate objects;

O thou great arbiter of life and death,
Nature's immortal, *immaterial* sun!
Thy call I follow to the land unknown.—YOUNG.

Men are *corporeal* as men, spirits are *incorporeal;* the body is the *material* part of man, the soul his *immaterial* part: whatever external object acts upon the senses is *material;* but the action of the mind on itself, and its results are all *immaterial:* the earth, sun, moon, &c. are termed *material;* but the impressions which they make on the mind, that is, our ideas of them, are *immaterial*.

The *incorporeal* and *immaterial* have always a relative sense; the *spiritual* is that which is positive: God is a *spiritual*, not properly an *incorporeal* nor *immaterial* being: the angels are likewise designated, in general, as the *spiritual* inhabitants of Heaven; 'All creatures, as well *spiritual* as *corporeal*, declare their absolute dependance upon the first author of all beings, the only self-existent God.'—BENTLEY. Although, when spoken of in regard to men, they may be denominated *incorporeal;*

Thus *incorporeal* spirits to smallest forms
Reduced their shapes immense.—MILTON.

The epithet *spiritual* has, however, been improperly or figuratively applied to objects in the sense of *immaterial;* 'Echo is a great argument of the *spiritual* essence of sounds; for if it were *corporeal*, the repercussion should be created by like instruments with the original sound.'—BACON.

SPIRITUOUS, SPIRITED, SPIRITUAL, GHOSTLY.

Spirituous signifies having the *spirit* separated from the gross particles of the body, after the manner of *spirituous* liquors; 'The *spirituous* and benign matter most apt for generation.'—SMITH *on Old Age*. *Spirited* is applicable to the animal *spirits* of either men or brutes; a person or a horse may be *spirited;* and also in a moral application in the sense of vivacious, or calculated to rouse the *spirit;* 'Dryden's translation of Virgil is noble and *spirited*.'—POPE. What is *spiritual* is after the manner of a *spirit;* and what is *ghostly* is like a *ghost;* although originally the same in meaning, the former being derived from the Latin *spiritus*, and the latter from the German *geist*, and both signifying what is not corporeal, yet they have acquired a difference of application. *Spiritual* objects are distinguished generally from those of sense; 'Virginity is better than the married life, not that it is more holy, but that it is a freedom from cares, an opportunity to spend more time in *spiritual* employments.'—TAYLOR (*Holy Living*). Hence it is that the word *spiritual* is opposed to the temporal; 'She loves them as her *spiritual* children, and they reverence her as their *spiritual* mother, with an affection far above that of the fondest friend.'—LAW.

Thou art reverend,
Touching thy *spiritual* function, not thy life.
SHAKSPEARE.

Ghostly is more immediately opposed to the carnal or the secular, and is therefore a term of more solemn import than *spiritual;* 'The grace of the *spirit* is much more precious than worldly benefits, and our *ghostly* evils of greater importance than harm which the body feeleth.'—HOOKER. 'To deny me the *ghostly* comfort of my chaplains seems a greater barbarity than is ever used by Christians.'—K. CHARLES.

UNDERSTANDING, INTELLECT, INTELLIGENCE.

Understanding being the Saxon word, is employed to describe a familiar and easy operation of the mind in forming distinct ideas of things. *Intellect*, which is of Latin derivation, is employed to mark the same operation in regard to higher and more abstruse objects. The *understanding* applies to the first exercise of the rational powers: it is therefore aptly said of children and savages that they employ their *understandings* on the simple objects of perception; a child uses his *understanding* to distinguish the dimensions of objects, or to apply the right names to the things that come before his notice; 'By *understanding* I mean that faculty whereby we are enabled to apprehend the objects of knowledge, generals as well as particulars, absent things as well as present, and to judge of their truth or falsehood, good or evil.'—WILKINS.

Intellect, being a matured state of the *understanding*, is most properly applied to the efforts of those who have their powers in full vigour: we speak of *understanding* as the characteristick distinction between man and brute; 'The light within us is (since the fall) become darkness; and the *understanding*, that should be eyes to the blind faculty of the will, is blind itself.'—SOUTH. But human beings are distinguished from each other by the measure of their *intellect;* 'All those arts and inventions which vulgar minds gaze at, the ingenious pursue, and all admire, are but the relicks of an *intellect* defaced with sin and time.'—SOUTH. We may expect the youngest children to employ an *understanding* according to the opportunities which they have of using their senses; one is gratified in seeing great *intellect* in youth.

Intellect and *intelligence* are derived from the same word; but *intellect* describes the power itself, and *intelligence* the exercise of that power: the *intellect* may be hidden, but the *intelligence* brings it to light;

Silent as the ecstatick bliss
Of souls, that by *intelligence* converse.—OTWAY.

Hence we speak of *intelligence* as displayed in the countenance of a child whose looks evince that he has exerted his *intellect*, and thereby proved that it exists Hence it arises that the word *intelligence* has been employed in the sense of knowledge or information, because these are the express fruits of *intelligence:* we must know by means of *intelligence;* but we may be ignorant with a great share of *intellect.*

Understanding and *intelligence* admit of comparison in the sense of acquaintance between two or more persons as to each other's views, and a consequent harmony and concert; but the former term is applied to the ordinary concerns of life, and the harmonious intercourse of men, as in the phrase to be on terms of a good *understanding;* 'He hoped the loyalty of his subjects would concur with him in the preserving a good *understanding* between him and his subjects.'—CLARENDON. *Intelligence,* on the other hand, is particularly applicable to persons who, being obliged to cooperate at a distance from each other, hold a commerce of information, or get to *understand* each other by means of mutual information; 'It was perceived that there had not been in the Catholicks so much foresight as to provide that true *intelligence* might pass between them of what was done.'—HOOKER.

Let all the passages
Be well secured, that no *intelligence*
May pass between the prince and them.—DENHAM.

INTELLECT, GENIUS, TALENT.

Intellect, in Latin *intellectus,* from *intelligo,* to understand, signifying the gift of understanding, as opposed to mere instinct or impulse, is here the generick term, as it includes in its own meaning that of the two others: there cannot be *genius* or *talent* without *intellect;* but there may be *intellect* without *genius* or *talent:* a man of *intellect* distinguishes himself from the common herd of mankind, by the acuteness of his observation, the accuracy of his judgement, the originality of his conceptions, and other peculiar attributes of mental power; *genius,* in Latin *genius,* from *gigno,* to be born, signifying that which is peculiarly born with us, is a particular bent of the *intellect,* which distinguishes a man from every other individual; *talent,* which from *τάλαντον* and *talentum,* a Greek coin exceeding one hundred pounds, is now employed in the figurative language of our Saviour for that particular modus or modification of the *intellect,* which is of practical utility to the possessor. *Intellect* sometimes runs through a family, and becomes as it were an hereditary portion: *genius* is not of so communicable a nature; it is that tone of the thinking faculty which is altogether individual in its character; it is opposed to every thing artificial, acquired, circumstantial, or incidental; it is a pure spark of the Divine flame, which raises the possessor above all his fellow-mortals; it is not expanded, like *intellect,* to many objects; for in its very nature it is contracted within a very short space; and, like the rays of the sun, when concentrated within a focus, it gains in strength what it loses in expansion.

We consider *intellect* as it generally respects speculation and abstraction; but *genius* as it respects the operations of the imagination; *talent* as it respects the exercise or acquirements of the mind. A man of *intellect* may be a good writer; but it requires a *genius* for poetry to be a poet, a *genius* for painting to be a painter, a *genius* for sculpture to be a statuary, and the like: it requires a *talent* to learn languages; it requires a *talent* for the stage to be a good actor; some have a *talent* for imitation, others a *talent* for humour. *Intellect,* in its strict sense, is seen only in a mature state; *genius* or *talent* may be discovered in its earliest dawn: we speak in general of the *intellect* of a man only; but we may speak of the *genius* or *talent* of a youth; *intellect* qualifies a person for conversation, and affords him great enjoyment; 'There was a select set, supposed to be distinguished by superiority of *intellects,* who always passed the evening together.'—JOHNSON. *Genius* qualifies a person for the most exalted efforts of the human mind; 'Thomson thinks in a peculiar train, and always thinks as a man of *genius.*'—JOHNSON. *Talent* qualifies a person for the active duties and employments of life; 'It is commonly thought that the sagacity of these fathers (the Jesuits) in discovering the *talent* of a young student, has not a little contributed to the figure which their order has made in the world.'—BUDGELL.

GIFT, ENDOWMENT, TALENT.

Gift and *endowment* both refer to the act of *giving* and *endowing,* and of course include the idea of something given, and something received: the word *talent* conveys no such collateral idea. When we speak of a *gift,* we refer in our minds to a *giver;*

But Heaven its *gifts* not all at once bestows,
These years with wisdom crowns, with action those.
POPE

When we speak of an *endowment,* we refer in our minds to the receiver; 'A brute arrives at a point of perfection that he can never pass; in a few years he has all the *endowments* he is capable of.'—ADDISON. When we speak of a *talent* (*v. Intellect*) we only think of its intrinsick quality or worth; 'Mr. Locke has an admirable reflection upon the difference of wit and judgement, whereby he endeavours to show the reason why they are not always the *talents* of the same person.'—ADDISON.

The *gift* is either supernatural or natural; the *endowment* is only natural. The primitive Christians received various *gifts* through the inspiration of the Holy Spirit, as the *gift* of tongues, the *gift* of healing, &c. There are some men who have a peculiar *gift* of utterance; beauty of person, and corporeal agility, are *endowments* with which some are peculiarly invested.

The word *gift* excludes the idea of any thing acquired by exertion; it is that which is communicated to us altogether independent of ourselves, and enables us to arrive at that perfection in any art which could not be attained in any other way. Speech is denominated a general *gift,* inasmuch as it is given to the whole human race in distinction from the brutes; but the *gift* of utterance is a peculiar *gift* granted to individuals, in distinction from others, which may be exerted for the benefit of mankind. *Endowments,* though inherent in us, are not independent of exertions; they are qualities which admit of improvement by being used; they are in fact the *gifts* of nature, which serve to adorn and elevate the possessor, when employed for a good purpose. *Talents* are either natural or acquired, or in some measure of a mixed nature; they denote powers without specifying the source from which they proceed; a man may have a *talent* for musick, for drawing, for mimickry, and the like; but this *talent* may be the fruit of practice and experience, as much as of nature.

It is clear from the above that an *endowment* is a *gift,* but a *gift* is not always an *endowment;* and that a *talent* may also be either a *gift* or an *endowment,* but that it is frequently distinct from both. A *gift* or a *talent* is applicable to corporeal as well as spiritual actions; an *endowment* is applicable to corporeal or mental qualities. To write a superiour hand is a *gift,* inasmuch as it is supposed to be unattainable by any force of application and instruction; it is a *talent,* inasmuch as it is a power or property worth our possession; but it is never an *endowment.* On the other hand, courage, discernment, a strong imagination, and the like, are both *gifts* and *endowments;* and when the intellectual *endowment* displays itself in any creative form, as in the case of poetry, musick, or any art, so as to produce that which is valued and esteemed, it becomes a *talent* to the possessor.

ABILITY, CAPACITY.

Ability, in French *habilité,* Latin *habilitas,* comes from *able, habile, habilis,* and *habeo* to have, because possession and power are inseparable. *Capacity,* in French *capacité,* Latin *capacitas,* from *capax* and *capio* to receive, marks the abstract quality of being able to receive or hold.

Ability is to capacity as the genus to the species. *Ability* comprehends the power of doing in general without specifying the quality or degree; *capacity* is a particular kind of *ability.*

Ability may be either physical or mental, *capacity,* when said of persons, is mental only; 'Riches are of no use, if sickness taketh from us the *ability* of enjoying them.'—SWIFT. 'In what I have done, I have rather given a proof of my willingness and desire, than of my *ability* to do him (Shakspeare) justice.'—POPE.

Ability respects action, *capacity* respects thought. *Ability* always supposes something able to be done; 'I look upon an *able* statesman out of business like a huge whale, that will endeavour to overturn the ship unless he has an empty cask to play with.'—STEELE. *Capacity* is a mental endowment, and always supposes something ready to receive or hold; 'The object is too big for our *capacity*, when we would comprehend the circumference of a world.'—ADDISON. Hence we say an *able* commander; an *able* statesman; a man of a *capacious* mind; a great *capacity* of thought.

Ability is in no wise limited in its extent; it may be small or great;

> Of singing thou hast got the reputation,
> Good Thyrsis; mine I yield to thy *ability*.
> My heart doth seek another estimation.—SIDNEY.

Capacity of itself always implies a positive and superiour degree of power; 'Sir Francis Bacon's *capacity* seemed to have grasped all that was revealed in books before.'—HUGHES. Although it may be modified by epithets to denote different degrees; a boy of *capacity* will have the advantage over his school-fellows, particularly if he be classed with those of a dull *capacity*. A person may be *able* to write a letter, who is not *capable* of writing a book; 'St. Paul requireth learning in presbyters, yea, such learning as doth enable them to exhort in doctrine which is sound, and to disprove them that gainsay it. What measure of *ability* in such things shall serve to make men *capable* of that kind of office he doth not determine.'—HOOKER.

Abilities, when used in the plural only, is confined to the signification of mental endowments, and comprehends the operations of thought in general; 'As for me, my *abilities*, if ever I had any, are not what they were.'—ATTERBURY. *Capacity*, on the other hand, is that peculiar endowment, that enlargement of understanding, that exalts the possessor above the rest of mankind; 'We sometimes repine at the narrow limits prescribed to human *capacity*.'—BEATTIE. Many men have the *abilities* for managing the concerns of others, who would not have the *capacity* for conducting a concern of their own. We should not judge highly of that man's *abilities* who could only mar the plans of others, but had no *capacity* for conceiving and proposing any thing better in their stead.

A vivid imagination, a retentive memory, an exuberant flow of language, are *abilities* which may be successfully employed in attracting popular applause; 'I grieve that our senate is dwindled into a school of rhetorick, where men rise to display their *abilities* rather than to deliberate.'—SIR W. JONES. But that *capacity* which embraces a question in all its bearings, which surveys with a discriminating eye the mixed multitude of objects that demand attention, which is accompanied with coolness in reflecting, readiness in combining, quickness in inventing, firmness in deciding, promptitude in action, and penetration in discerning, that is the *capacity* to direct a state, which is the gift of but few; 'An heroick poem requires the accomplishment of some extraordinary undertaking, which requires the duty of a soldier, and the *capacity* and prudence of a general.' —DRYDEN.

ABILITY, FACULTY, TALENT.

The common idea of power is what renders these words synonymous.

Ability, as in the preceding article, signifies that which may be derived either from circumstances or otherwise: *faculty*, in Latin *facultas*, changed from *facilitas* facility, which signifies doableness, or the property of being able to do or bring about effects, is a power derived from nature; 'The vital *faculty* is that by which life is preserved and the ordinary functions of speech preserved; and the animal *faculty* is what conducts the operations of the mind.'—QUINCY. The *faculty* is a permanent possession; it is held by a certain tenure: the *ability* is an incidental possession; it is whatever we have while we have it at our disposal, but it may vary in degree and quality with times, persons, and circumstances; '*Ability* to teach by sermons is a grace which God doth bestow on them whom he maketh sufficient for the commendable discharge of their duty.'—HOOKER. The powers of seeing and hearing are *faculties*; health, strength, and fortune are *abilities*. The *faculty* is some specifick power which is directed to one single object; it is the power of acting according to a given form;

> No fruit our palate courts, or flow'r our smell,
> But on its fragrant bosom nations dwell;
> All formed with proper *faculties* to share
> The daily bounties of their Maker's care.—JENYNS.

The *ability* is in general the power of doing; the *faculty* therefore might, in the strict sense, be considered as a species of *ability*; 'Human *ability* is an unequal match for the violent and unforeseen vicissitudes of the world.'—BLAIR.

A man uses the *faculties* with which he is endowed, he gives according to his *ability*.

Faculty and *talent* both owe their being to nature; but the *faculty* may be either physical or mental; the *talent* is altogether mental: the *faculty* of speech and the rational *faculty* are the grand marks of distinction between man and the brute; 'Reason is a noble *faculty*, and when kept within its proper sphere, and applied to useful purposes, proves a means of exalting human creatures almost to the rank of superiour beings.' —BEATTIE. The *talent* of mimickry, of dramatick acting, and of imitation in general, is what distinguishes one man from the other;

> 'Tis not, indeed, my *talent* to engage
> In lofty trifles, or to swell my page
> With wind and noise.—DRYDEN.

These terms are all used in the plural, agreeably to the above explanation; the *abilities* include, in the aggregate, whatever a man is able to do; hence we speak of a man's *abilities* in speaking, writing, learning, and the like; the *faculties* include all the endowments of body and mind, which are the inherent properties of the being, as when we speak of a man's retaining his *faculties*, or having his *faculties* impaired: *talents* are the particular endowments of the mind, which belong to the individual; hence we say, the *talents* which are requisite for a minister of state are different from those which qualify a man for being a judge.

ABILITY, DEXTERITY, ADDRESS.

Ability is here, as in the preceding articles, the generick term: *dexterity*, says the Abbe Girard,* respects the manner of executing things; it is the mechanical facility of performing an office: *address* refers to the use of means in executing; it signifies properly the mode of *address* or of managing one's self; *dexterity* and *address* are but in fact modes of *ability*.

Dexterity, in Latin *dexteritas*, comes from *dexter*, the right hand, because that it is the member most fitted for *dexterous* execution. *Dexterity* may be acquired; 'His wisdom, by often evading from perils, was turned rather into a *dexterity* to deliver himself from dangers when they pressed him, than into a providence to prevent and remove them afar off.'—BACON. *Address* is the gift of nature; 'It was no sooner dark than she conveyed into his room a young maid of no disagreeable figure, who was one of her attendants, and did not want *address* to improve the opportunity for the advancement of her fortune.—SPECTATOR.

We may have *ability* to any degree (*v. Ability*); 'It is not possible for our small party and small *ability* to extend their operations so far as to be much felt among such numbers.'—COWPER. But *dexterity* and *address* are positive degrees of *ability*; 'It is often observed that the race is won as much by the *dexterity* of the rider as by the vigour and fleetness of the animal.'—EARL OF BATH. 'I could produce innumerable instances from my own observation, of events imputed to the profound skill and *address* of a minister, which in reality were either mere effects of negligence, weakness, humour, or pride, or at best but the natural course of things left to themselves.'—SWIFT.

To form a good government there must be *ability* in the prince or his ministers; *address* in those to whom the detail of operations is intrusted; and *dexterity* in those to whom the execution of orders is confided. With little *ability* and long habit in transacting business, we may acquire a *dexterity* in despatching it, and *address* in giving it whatever turn will best suit our purpose.

Ability enables us to act with intelligence and confidence; *dexterity* lends an air of ease to every action; *address* supplies art and ingenuity in contrivance. To manage the whip with *dexterity*, to carry on an intrigue with *address*, to display some *ability* on the turf, will raise a man high in the rank of the present fashionables

* Vide 'Dexterité, adresse, habilité.

CLEVER, SKILFUL, EXPERT, DEXTEROUS, ADROIT.

Clever, in French *legere*, Latin *levis* light, seems to denote quickness in the mental faculty; *skilful* signifies full of *skill;* and *skill* probably comes from the Latin *scio* to know; *expert*, in French *experte*, Latin *expertus*, participle of *experior* to search or try, signifies searched and tried; *dexterous*, in Latin *dexter*, in Greek δεξιτερὸς, from δεξία the right hand, has the meaning of clever, because the right hand is the most fitted for action; *adroit*, in French *adroite*, Latin *adrectus* or *rectus* right or straight, signifies the quality of doing things in a right manner.

Clever and *skilful* are qualities of the mind; *expert*, *dexterous*, and *adroit*, refer to modes of physical action. *Cleverness* regards in general the readiness to comprehend; *skill* the maturity of the judgement; *expertness* a facility in the use of things; *dexterity* a mechanical facility in the performance of any work; *adroitness* the suitable movements of the body. A person is *clever* at drawing who shows a taste for it, and executes it well without much instruction; he is *skilful* in drawing if he understands it both in theory and practice; he is *expert* in the use of the bow if he can use it with expedition and effect; he is *dexterous* at any game when he goes through the manœuvres with celerity and an unerring hand; he is *adroit* if by a quick, sudden, and well-directed movement of his body, he effects the object he has in view.

Cleverness is mental power employed in the ordinary concerns of life: a person is *clever* in business or amusements;

> My friends bade me welcome, but struck me quite dumb,
> With tidings that Johnson and Burke would not come;
> 'And I knew it," he cried, "both eternally fail,
> The one at the House, and the other with Thrale.
> But no matter; I'll warrant we'll make up the party,
> With two full as *clever* and ten times as hearty."
>
> GOLDSMITH.

Skill is both a mental and corporeal power, exerted in mechanical operations and practical sciences: a physician, a lawyer, and an artist, are *skilful:* one may have a *skill* in divination, or a *skill* in painting. There is nothing more graceful than to see the play stand still for a few moments, and the audience kept in an agreeable suspense, during the silence of a *skilful* actor.'—ADDISON. *Expertness* and *dexterity* require more corporeal than mental power exerted in minor arts and amusements: one is *expert* at throwing the quoit; *dexterous* in the management of horses;

> O'er bar and shelf the watery path they sound,
> With *dext'rous* arm, sagacious of the ground;
> Fearless they combat every hostile wind,
> Wheeling in many tracts with course inclin'd,
> *Expert* to moor where terrours line the road.
>
> FALCONER.

'He applied himself next to the coquette's heart, which he likewise laid open with great *dexterity*.'—ADDISON. *Adroitness* is altogether a corporeal talent, employed only as occasion may require: one is *adroit* at eluding the blows aimed by an adversary; 'Use yourself to carve *adroitly* and genteelly.'—CHESTERFIELD.

Cleverness is rather a natural gift; *skill* is *cleverness* improved by practice and extended knowledge; *expertness* is the effect of long practice; *dexterity* arises from habit combined with agility; *adroitness* is a species of *dexterity* arising from a natural agility and pliability of body.

INABILITY, DISABILITY.

Inability denotes the absence of *ability* (*v. Ability*) in the most general and abstract sense; 'It is not from *inability* to discover what they ought to do that men err in practice.'—BLAIR. *Disability* implies the absence of *ability* only in particular cases: the *inability* lies in the nature of the thing, and is irremediable; the *disability* lies in the circumstances, and may sometimes be removed; weakness, whether physical or mental, will occasion an *inability* to perform a task; there is a total *inability* in an infant to walk and act like an adult: a want of knowledge or of the requisite qualifications may be a *disability;* in this manner minority of age, or an objection to take certain oaths may be a *disability* for filling a publick office; 'Want of age is a legal *disability* to contract a marriage.'—BLACKSTONE.

INCAPABLE, INSUFFICIENT, INCOMPETENT, INADEQUATE.

Incapable, that is, *not* having *capacity* (*v. Ability*); *insufficient*, or *not sufficient*, or *not* having what is *sufficient; incompetent*, or *not competent;* are employed either for persons or things: the first in a general, the last two in a specifick sense: *inadequate* or *not adequate* or equalled, is applied more generally to things.

When a man is said to be *incapable*, it characterizes his whole mind; 'Were a human soul *incapable* of farther enlargements, I could imagine it might fall away insensibly.'—ADDISON. If he be said to have *insufficiency* and *incompetency*, it respects the particular objects to which he has applied his power: he may be *insufficient* or *incompetent* for certain things; but he may have a *capacity* for other things: the term *incapacity*, therefore, implies a direct charge upon the understanding, which is not implied by the *insufficiency* and *incompetency*. An *incapacity* consists altogether of a physical defect: an *insufficiency* and *incompetency* are incidental defects: the former depending upon the age, the condition, the acquisitions, moral qualities, and the like, of the individual; the latter on the extent of his knowledge, and the nature of his studies; where there is direct *incapacity*, a person has no chance of making himself fit for any office or employment; 'It chiefly proceedeth from natural *incapacity*, and general indisposition.'—BROWN. Youth is naturally accompanied with *insufficiency* to fill stations which belong to mature age, and to perform offices which require the exercise of judgement; 'The minister's aptness, or *insufficiency*, otherwise than by reading, to instruct the flock, standeth in this place as a stranger, with whom our Common Prayer has nothing to do.'—HOOKER. A young person is, therefore, still more *incompetent* to form a fixed opinion on any one subject, because he can have made himself master of none; 'Laymen, with equal advantages of parts, are not the most *incompetent* judges of sacred things.'—DRYDEN.

Incapable is applied sometimes to the moral character, to signify the absence of that which is bad; *insufficient* and *incompetent* always convey the idea of a deficiency in that which is at least desirable: it is an honour to a person to be *incapable* of falsehood, or *incapable* of doing an ungenerous action; but to be *insufficient* and *incompetent* are, at all events, qualities not to be boasted of, although they may not be expressly disgraceful. These terms are likewise applicable to things, in which they preserve a similar distinction; infidelity is *incapable* of affording a man any comfort; when the means are *insufficient* for obtaining the ends, it is madness to expect success; it is a sad condition of humanity when a man's resources are *incompetent* to supply him with the first necessaries of life.

Inadequate is relative in its signification, like *insufficient* and *incompetent;* but the relation is different. A thing is *insufficient* which does not suffice either for the wishes, the purposes, or necessities, of any one, in particular or in general cases; thus a quantity of materials may be *insufficient* for a particular building; 'The *insufficiency* of the light of nature is, by the light of Scripture, fully supplied.'—HOOKER. *Incompetency* is an *insufficiency* for general purposes, in things of the first necessity; thus, an income may be *incompetent* to support a family, or perform an office; 'Every speck does not blind a man, nor does every infirmity make one unable to discern, or *incompetent* to reprove, the grosser faults of others.'—GOVERNMENT OF THE TONGUE. *Inadequacy* is still more particular, for it denotes any deficiency which is measured by comparison with the object to which it refers; thus, the strength of an animal may be *inadequate* to the labour which is required, or a reward may be *inadequate* to the service; 'All the attainments possible in our present state are evidently *inadequate* to our capacities of enjoyment.'—JOHNSON.

WIT, HUMOUR, SATIRE, IRONY, BURLESQUE.

Wit, like wisdom, according to its original, from *weissen* to know, signifies knowledge, but it has so extended its meaning as to signify that faculty of the mind by which knowledge or truth is perceived. The first property of *wit*, as an exertion of the intellectual faculty, is that it be spontaneous, and as it were instinctive: laboured or forced *wit* is no *wit*. Reflection and experience supply us with wisdom; study and labour supply us with learning; but *wit* seizes with an eagle eye that which escapes the notice of the deep thinker, and elicits truths which are in vain sought for with any severe effort: '*Wit* lies more in the assemblage of ideas, and putting those together with quickness and variety.'—ADDISON. *Humour* is a pecies of *wit* which flows out of the *humour* of a erson;

> For sure by *wit* is chiefly meant
> Applying well what we invent:
> What *humour* is not, all the tribe
> Of logick-mongers can describe:
> Here nature only acts her part,
> Unhelp'd by practice, books, or art.—SWIFT.

Wit, as distinguished from *humour*, may consist of a single brilliant thought;

> In a true piece of *wit* all things must be,
> Yet all things there agree.—COWLEY.

But *humour* runs in a vein; it is not a striking, but an equable and pleasing flow of *wit*; 'There is a kind of nature, a certain regularity of thought, which must discover the writer (of *humour*) to be a man of sense at the same time that he appears altogether given up to caprice.'—ADDISON. Of this description of *wit* Mr. Addison has given us the most admirable specimens in his writings, who knew best how to explain what *wit* and *humour* were, and to illustrate them by his practice. *Humour* may likewise display itself in actions as well as words, whereby it is more strikingly distinguished from *wit*, which displays itself only in the happy expression of happy thoughts; 'I cannot help remarking that sickness, which often destroys both *wit* and wisdom, yet seldom has power to remove that talent which we call *humour*. Mr. Wycherley showed his in his last compliment paid to his young wife (whom he made promise, on his dying bed, that she would not marry an old man again).'—POPE.

Satire, from *satyr*, probably from *sat* and *ira* abounding in anger, and *irony*, from the Greek εἰρωνία simulation and dissimulation, are personal and censorious sorts of *wit*; the first of which openly points at the object, and the second in a covert manner takes its aim; 'The ordinary subjects of *satire* are such as excite the greatest indignation in the best tempers.'—ADDISON. 'In writings of *humour*, figures are sometimes used of so delicate a nature, that it shall often happen that some people will see things in a direct contrary sense to what the author, and the majority of the readers understand them: to such the most innocent *irony* may appear irreligion.'—CAMBRIDGE. *Burlesque* is rather a species of *humour* than direct *wit* which consists in an assemblage of ideas extravagantly discordant; 'One kind of *burlesque* represents mean persons in the accoutrements of heroes.'—ADDISON. The *satire* and *irony* are the most ill-natured kinds of *wit*; *burlesque* stands in the lowest rank.

TASTE, GENIUS.

Taste, in all probability from the Latin *tactum* and *tango* to touch, seems to designate the capacity to derive pleasure from an object by simply coming in contact with it; 'This metaphor would not have been so general had there not been a conformity between the mental *taste* and that sensitive *taste* which gives a relish of every flavour.'—ADDISON. *Genius* designates the power we have for accomplishing any object; '*Taste* consists in the power of judging, *genius* in the power of executing.'—BLAIR. He who derives particular pleasure from musick may be said to have a *taste* for musick; he who makes very great proficiency in the theory and practice of musick may be said to have a *genius* for it. *Taste* is in some degree an acquired faculty, or at least is dependant on cultivation, as also on our other faculties, for its perfection; 'The cause of a wrong *taste* is a defect of judgement.'—BURKE. *Genius*, from the Latin *gigno* to generate, is a perfectly natural gift which rises to perfection by its own native strength; the former belongs to the critick, and the latter to the poet;

> 'Tis with our judgements as our watches, none
> Go just alike, yet each believes his own;
> In poets as true *genius* is rare,
> True *taste* as seldom is the critick's share.—POPE.

It is obvious, therefore, that we may have a *taste* without having *genius*; but it would not be possible to have *genius* for a thing without having a *taste* for it: for nothing can so effectually give a taste for any accomplishment, as the capacity to learn it, and the susceptibility of all its beauties, which circumstances are inseparable from *genius*.

INGENUITY, WIT.

Both these terms imply acuteness of understanding, and differ mostly in the mode of displaying themselves. *Ingenuity*, in Latin *ingenuitas*, signifies literary freedom of birth, in distinction from slavery, with which condition have been naturally associated nobleness of character and richness in mental endowments, in which latter sense it is allied to *wit*. *Ingenuity* comprehends invention; *wit* comprehends knowledge. *Ingenuity* displays itself in the mode of conducting an argument; 'Men were formerly won over to opinions, by the candour, sense, and *ingenuity* of those who had the right on their side.'—ADDISON. *Wit* is mostly displayed in aptness of expression and illustration; 'When I broke loose from that great body of writers, who have employed their *wit* and parts in propagating vice and irreligion, I did not question but I should be treated as an odd kind of fellow.'—ADDISON. One is *ingenious* in matters either of art or science; one is *witty* only in matters of sentiment: things may, therefore, be *ingenious*, but not *witty*; *witty*, but not *ingenious*, or both *witty* and *ingenious*. A mechanical invention, or any ordinary contrivance, is *ingenious* but not *witty*; an *ingenious*, not a *witty* solution of a difficulty; a flash of *wit*, not a flash of *ingenuity*; a *witty* humour, a *witty* conversation; not an *ingenious* humour or conversation: on the other hand, a conceit is *ingenious*, as it is the fruit of one's own mind; it is *witty*, as it contains point, and strikes on the understanding of others.

SENSE, JUDGEMENT.

Sense, from the Latin *sensus* and *sentio* to feel or perceive, signifies in general the faculty of feeling corporeally, or perceiving mentally; in the first case it is allied to feeling (*v. Feeling*), in the second it is synonymous with *judgement*, which is a special operation of the mind. * The *sense* is that primitive portion of the understanding which renders an account of things through the medium of the senses;

> Then is the soul a nature, which contains
> The power of *sense* within a greater power.
> DAVIES.

And the *judgement*, that portion of the reason which selects or rejects from this account. The *sense* is, so to speak, the reporter which collects the details, and exposes the facts; the *judgement* is the *judge* that passes sentence upon them. According to the strict import of the terms, the *judgement* depends upon the *sense*, and varies with it in degree. He who has no *sense*, has no *judgement*; and he who loses *sense*, loses *judgement*: since *sense* supplies the knowledge of things, and *judgement* pronounces upon them, it is evident that there must be *sense* before there can be *judgement*.

On the other hand, *sense*, when taken to denote the mental faculty of perceiving, may be so distinguished from *judgement*, that there may be *sense* without *judgement*, and *judgement* without *sense*; *sense* is the faculty of perceiving in general; it is applied to abstract science as well as general knowledge: *judgement* is the faculty of determining either in matters of practice or theory. It is the lot of many, therefore, to have *sense* in matters of theory, who have no *judgment* in matters of practice, while others, on the contrary, who have nothing above common *sense*, will have a soundness of *judgement* that is not to be surpassed

Nay, further, it is possible for a man to have good *sense*, and yet not a solid *judgement*: as they are both natural faculties, men are gifted with them as

* Vide Ribaud: "Sens, jugement"

variously as with every other faculty. By good *sense* a man is enabled to discern, as it were intuitively, that which requires another of less *sense* to ponder over and study;

There's something previous ev'n to *taste:* 'tis *sense*,
Good *sense;* which only is the gift of heav'n,
And, though no science, fairly worth the seven;
A light within yourself you must perceive,
Jones and Le Notre have it not to give.—POPE.

By a solid *judgement* a man is enabled to avoid those errours in conduct, which one of a weak *judgement* is always falling into; 'In all instances, where our experience of the past has been extensive and uniform, our *judgement* concerning the future amounts to moral certainty.'—BEATTIE. There is, however, this distinction between *sense* and *judgment*, that the deficiencies of the former may be supplied by diligence and attention; but a defect in the latter is to be supplied by no efforts of one's own. A man may improve his *sense* in proportion as he has the means of information; but a weakness of *judgement*, is an irremediable evil.

When employed as epithets, the term *sensible* and *judicious* serve still more clearly to distinguish the two primitives. A writer or a speaker is said to be *sensible;* 'I have been tired with accounts from *sensible* men, furnished with matters of fact, which have happened within their own knowledge.'—ADDISON. A friend, or an adviser, to be *judicious;* 'Your observations are so *judicious*, I wish you had not been so sparing of them.'—SIR W. JONES. The *sense* displays itself in the conversation, or the communication of one's ideas; the *judgment* in the propriety of one's actions. A *sensible* man may be an entertaining companion; but a *judicious* man, in any post of command, is an inestimable treasure. *Sensible* remarks are always calculated to please and interest *sensible* people; *judicious* measures have a sterling value in themselves, that is appreciated according to the importance of the object. Hence, it is obvious, that to be *sensible* is a desirable thing; but to be *judicious* is an indispensable requisite.

DISCERNMENT, PENETRATION, DISCRIMINATION, JUDGEMENT.

Discernment expresses the judgement or power of *discerning*, which, from the Latin *discerno*, or *dis* and *cerno*, signifies to look at apart, so as to form a true estimate of things; *penetration* denotes the act or power of *penetrating*, from *penetrate*, in Latin *penetratus*, participle of *penetro* and *penitus*, within, signifying to see into the interiour; *discrimination* denotes the act or power of *discriminating*, from *discriminate*, in Latin *discriminatus*, participle of *discrimino*, to make a difference; *judgement* denotes the power of *judging*, from *judge*, in Latin *judico*, compounded of *jus* and *dico*, signifying to pronounce right.

The first three of these terms do not express different powers, but different modes of the same power; namely, the power of seeing intellectually, or exerting the intellectual sight.

Discernment is not so powerful a mode of intellectual vision as *penetration;* the former is a common faculty, the latter is a higher degree of the same faculty; it is the power of seeing quickly, and seeing in spite of all that intercepts the sight, and keeps the object out of view: a man of common *discernment* discerns characters which are not concealed by any particular disguise; 'Great part of the country was abandoned to the spoils of the soldiers, who, not troubling themselves to *discern* between a subject and a rebel, while their liberty lasted, made indifferently profit of both.'—HAYWARD. A man of *penetration* is not to be deceived by any artifice, however thoroughly cloaked or secured, even from suspicion; 'He is as slow to decide as he is quick to apprehend, calmly and deliberately weighing every opposite reason that is offered, and tracing it with a most judicious *penetration*.'—MELMOTH (*Letters of Pliny*).

Discernment and *penetration* serve for the discovery of individual things by their outward marks; *discrimination* is employed in the discovery of differences between two or more objects; the former consists of simple observation, the latter combines also comparison: *discernment* and *penetration* are great aids towards *discrimination;* he who can *discern* the springs of human action, or *penetrate* the views of men, will be most fitted for *discriminating* between the characters of different men; 'Perhaps there is no character through all Shakspeare drawn with more spirit and just *discrimination* than Shylock's.'—HENLEY.

Although *judgement* derives much assistance from the three former operations, it is a totally distinct power: the former only discover the things that are; it acts on external objects by seeing them: the latter is creative; it produces by deduction from that which passes inwardly.* The former are speculative; they are directed to that which is to be known, and are confined to present objects; they serve to discover truth or falsehood, perfections and defects, motives and pretexts: the latter is practical; it is directed to that which is to be done, and extends its views to the future; it marks the relations and connexions of things: it foresees their consequences and effects; 'I love him, I confess, extremely; but my affection does by no means prejudice my *judgement*.')—MELMOTH (*Letters of Pliny*).

Of *discernment*, we say that it is clear; it serves to remove all obscurity and confusion: of *penetration*, we say that it is acute; it pierces every veil which falsehood draws before truth, and prevents us from being deceived: of *discrimination*, we say that it is nice; it renders our ideas accurate, and serves to prevent us from confounding objects: of *judgement*, we say that it is solid or sound; it renders the conduct prudent, and prevents us from committing mistakes, or involving one's self in embarrassments.

When the question is to estimate the real qualities of either persons or things, we exercise *discernment;*

Cool age advances venerably wise,
Turns on all hands its deep *discerning* eyes.—POPE.

When it is required to lay open that which art or cunning has concealed, we must exercise *penetration;* 'A *penetration* into the abstruse difficulties and depths of modern algebra and fluxions, is not worth the labour of those who design either of the three learned professions.'—WATTS. When the question is to determine the proportions and degrees of qualities in persons or things, we must use *discrimination;* 'A satire should expose nothing but what is corrigible, and make a due *discrimination* between those who are, and those who are not, proper objects of it.'—ADDISON. When called upon to take any step, or act any part, we must employ the *judgement;* '*Judgement*, a cool and slow faculty, attends not a man in the rapture of poetical composition.'—DENNIS. *Discernment* is more or less indispensable for every man in private or public station; he who has the most promiscuous dealings with men, has the greatest need of it: *penetration* is of peculiar importance for princes and statesmen: *discrimination* is of great utility for commanders, and all who have the power of distributing rewards and punishments: *judgement* is an absolute requisite for all to whom the execution or management of concerns is intrusted.

REASONABLE, RATIONAL,

Are both derived from the same Latin word *ratio*, reason, which, from *ratus* and *reor*, to think, signifies the thinking faculty.

Reasonable signifies accordant with reason; *rational* signifies having reason in it: the former is more commonly applied in the sense of right reason, propriety, or fairness; the latter is employed in the original sense of the word *reason;* hence we term a man *reasonable* who acts according to the principles of right reason; and a being *rational*, who is possessed of the *rational* or *reasoning* faculty, in distinction from the brutes. It is to be lamented that there are much fewer *reasonable* than there are *rational* creatures. The same distinction exists between them when applied to things; 'A law may be *reasonable* in itself, although a man does not allow it, or does not know the reason of the lawgivers'—SWIFT. 'The evidence which is afforded for a future state is sufficient for a *rational* ground of conduct.'—BLAIR.

* Vide Abbe Girard. "Discernement, jugement"

MENTAL, INTELLECTUAL.

There is the same difference between *mental* and *intellectual* as between *mind* and *intellect:* the *mind* comprehends the thinking faculty in general with all its operations; the *intellect* includes only that part of it which consists in understanding and judgement: *mental* is therefore opposed to corporeal; *intellectual* is opposed to sensual or physical: *mental* exertions are not to be expected from all; *intellectual* enjoyments fall to the lot of comparatively few.

Objects, pleasures, pains, operations, gifts, &c. are denominated *mental;* 'To collect and reposite the various forms of things is far the most pleasing part of *mental* occupation.'—JOHNSON. Subjects, conversation, pursuits, and the like, are entitled *intellectual;*

> Man 's more divine, the master of all these,
> Lord of the wide world, and wide wat'ry seas,
> Endued with *intellectual* sense and soul.
> SHAKSPEARE.

It is not always easy to distinguish our *mental* pleasures from those corporeal pleasures which we enjoy in common with the brutes; the latter are however greatly heightened by the former in whatever degree they are blended: in a society of well-informed persons the conversation will turn principally on *intellectual* subjects.

MEMORY, REMEMBRANCE, RECOLLECTION, REMINISCENCE.

Memory, in Latin *memoria* or *memor*, Greek *μνήμων* and *μνάομαι*, comes, in all probability, from *μένος*, the mind, because *memory* is the principal faculty of the mind; *remembrance*, from the verb *remember*, contracted from *re* and *memoro*, to bring back to the mind, is a verbal substantive, denoting the exercise of that faculty; *recollection*, from *recollect*, compounded of *re* and *collect*, signifies *collecting* again, i. e. carefully, and from different quarters by an effort of the *memory;* *reminiscence*, in Latin *reminiscentia*, from *reminiscor* and *memor*, is the bringing back to the mind what was there before.

Memory is the power of recalling images once made on the mind; *remembrance*, *recollection*, and *reminiscence*, are operations or exertions of this power, which vary in their mode.

The *memory* is a power which exerts itself either independently of the will, or in conformity with the will; but all the other terms express the acts of conscious agents, and consequently are more or less connected with the will. In dreams the *memory* exerts itself, but we should not say that we have then any *remembrance* or *recollection* of objects.

Remembrance is the exercise of *memory* in a conscious agent; it is the calling a thing back to the mind which has been there before, but has passed away; Forgetfulness is necessary to *remembrance*.'—JOHNSON. This may be the effect of repetition or habit, as in the case of a child who *remembers* his lesson after having learned it several times; or of a horse who *remembers* the road which he has been continually passing; or it may be the effect of association and circumstances, by which images are casually brought back to the mind, as happens to intelligent beings continually as they exercise their thinking faculties;

> *Remember* thee!
> Ah, thou poor ghost, while *memory* holds a seat
> In this distracted globe.—SHAKSPEARE.

In these cases *remembrance* is an involuntary act; for things return to the mind before one is aware of it, as in the case of one who hears a particular name, and *remembers* that he has to call on a person of the same name; or of one who, on seeing a particular tree, *remembers* all the circumstances of his youth which were connected with a similar tree.

Remembrance is however likewise a voluntary act, and the consequence of a direct determination, as in the case of a child who strives to *remember* what it has been told by its parent; or of a friend who *remembers* the hour of meeting another friend in consequence of the interest which it has excited in his mind: nay indeed experience teaches us that scarcely any thing in ordinary cases is more under the subservience of the will than the *memory;* for it is now become almost a maxim to say, that one may *remember* whatever one wishes.

The power of *memory*, and the simple exercise of that power in the act of *remembering*, are possessed in common, though in different degrees by man and brute; but *recollection* and *reminiscence* are exercises of the *memory* that are connected with the higher faculties of man, his judgement and understanding. To *remember* is to call to mind that which has once been presented to the mind; but to *recollect* is to *remember* afresh, to *remember* what has been *remembered* before. *Remembrance* busies itself with objects that are at hand; *recollection* carries us back to distant periods: simple *remembrance* is engaged in things that have but just left the mind, which are more or less easily to be recalled, and more or less faithfully to be represented; but *recollection* tries to retrace the faint images of things that have been so long unthought of as to be almost obliterated from the *memory*. In this manner we are said to *remember* in one half hour what was told us in the preceding half hour, or to *remember* what passes from one day to another; but we *recollect* the incidents of childhood; we *recollect* what happened in our native place after many years' absence from it. The *remembrance* is that homely every-day exercise of the *memory* which renders it of essential service in the acquirement of knowledge, or in the performance of one's duties; '*Memory* may be assisted by method, and the decays of knowledge repaired by stated times of *recollection*.'—JOHNSON. The *recollection* is that exalted exercise of the *memory* which affords us the purest of enjoyments, and serves the noblest of purposes; the *recollection* of all the minute incidents of childhood is a more sincere pleasure than any which the present moment can afford.

Reminiscence, if it deserve any notice as a word of English use, is altogether an abstract exercise of the *memory*, which is employed on purely intellectual ideas in distinction from those which are awakened by sensible objects; the mathematician makes use of *reminiscence* in deducing unknown truths from those which he a ready knows; '*Reminiscence* is the retrieving a thing at present forgot, or confusedly *remembered*, by setting the mind to hunt over all its notions.'—SOUTH.

Reminiscence among the disciples of Socrates was the *remembrance* of things purely intellectual, or of that natural knowledge which the souls had had before their union with the body; while the *memory* was exercised upon sensible things, or that knowledge which was acquired through the medium of the senses; therefore the Latins said that *reminiscentia* belonged exclusively to man, because it was purely intellectual, but that *memory* was common to all animals, because it was merely the depot of the senses; but this distinction, from what has been before observed, is only preserved as it respects the meaning of *reminiscence*.

Memory is a generic term, as has been already shown: it includes the common idea of reviving former impressions, but does not qualify the nature of the ideas revived: the term is however extended in its application to signify not merely a power, but also a seat or resting place, as is likewise *remembrance* and *recollection;* but still with this difference, that the *memory* is spacious, and contains every thing; the *remembrance* and *recollection* are partial, and comprehend only passing events: we treasure up knowledge in our *memory;* the occurrences of the preceding year are still fresh in our *remembrance* or *recollection*.

FORGETFULNESS, OBLIVION.

Forgetfulness characterizes the person, or that which is personal; *oblivion* the state of the thing: the former refers to him who *forgets;* 'I have read in ancient authors invitations to lay aside care and anxiety, and give a loose to that pleasing *forgetfulness* wherein men put off their characters of business.'—STEELE. The latter to that which is *forgotten;*

> O'er all the rest, an undistinguished crew,
> Her wing of deepest shade *oblivion* drew.—FALCONER

We blame a person for his *forgetfulness;* but we sometimes bury things in *oblivion*

FANCY, IMAGINATION.

Fancy, considered as a power, simply brings the object to the mind, or makes it appear, from the Latin *phantasia*, and the Greek *φαντασίη* and *φαίνω*, to appear; but *imagination*, from *image*, in Latin *imago*, or *imitago*, or *imitatio*, is a power which presents the images or likenesses of things. The *fancy*, therefore, only employs itself about things without regarding their nature; but the *imagination* aims at tracing a resemblance, and getting a true copy;

> And as *imagination* bodies forth
> The forms of things unknown, the poet's pen
> Turns them to shape.—SHAKSPEARE.

The *fancy* consequently forms combinations, either real or unreal, as chance may direct; but the *imagination* is seldomer led astray. The *fancy* is busy in dreams, or when the mind is in a disordered state; 'There was a certain lady of thin airy shape, who was very active in this solemnity: her name was *Fancy*.'—ADDISON. But the *imagination* is supposed to act when the intellectual powers are in full play. The *fancy* is employed on light and trivial objects, which are present to the senses; the *imagination* soars above all worldly objects, and carries us from the world of matter into the world of spirits, from time present to the time to come. A milliner or mantua-maker may employ her *fancy* in the decorations of a cap or gown;

> Philosophy! I say, and call it He;
> For whatsoe'er the painter's *fancy* be,
> It a male virtue seems to me.—COWLEY.

But the poet's *imagination* depicts every thing grand, every thing bold, and every thing remote; 'Whatever be his subject, Milton never fails to fill the *imagination*.'—JOHNSON.

Although Mr. Addison has thought proper, for his convenience, to use the words *fancy* and *imagination* promiscuously when writing on this subject, yet the distinction, as above pointed out, has been observed both in familiar discourse and in writing. We say that we *fancy*, not that we *imagine*, that we see or hear something; the pleasures of the *imagination*, not of the *fancy*.

IDEA, THOUGHT, IMAGINATION.

Idea, in Latin *idea*, Greek *εἰδέα*, signifies the form or image of an object, from *εἰδέω* to see, that is, the thing seen in the mind. *Thought* literally signifies the thing *thought*, and *imagination* the thing *imagined*.

The *idea* is the simple representation of an object; the *thought* is the reflection; and the *imagination* is the combination of *ideas*: we have *ideas* of the sun, the moon, and all material objects; we have *thoughts* on moral subjects; we have *imaginations* drawn from the *ideas* already existing in the mind. The *ideas* are formed; they are the rude materials with which the *thinking* faculty exerts itself: the *thoughts* arise in the mind by means of association, or recur in the mind by the power of the memory; they are the materials with which the *thinking* faculty employs itself: the *imaginations* are created by the mind's re-action on itself; they are the materials with which the understanding seeks to enrich itself.

The word *idea* is not only the most general in sense, but the most universal in application; *thought* and *imagination* are particular terms used only in connexion with the agent *thinking* or *imagining*. All these words have therefore a distinct office, in which they cannot properly be confounded with each other. *Idea* is used in all cases for the mental representation, abstractedly from the agent that represents them: hence *ideas* are either clear or distinct; *ideas* are attached to words; *ideas* are analyzed, confounded, and the like; in which cases the word *thought* could not be substituted; 'Every one finds that many of the *ideas* which he desired to retain have slipped away irretrievably.'—JOHNSON. The *thought* belongs only to thinking and rational beings: the brutes may be said to have *ideas*, but not *thoughts*: hence *thoughts* are either mean, fine, grovelling, or sublime, according to the nature of the mind in which they exist:

> The warring passions, and tumultuous *thoughts*
> That rage within thee!—ROWE.

Hence we say with more propriety, to indulge a *thought*, than to indulge an *idea*; to express one's *thoughts*, rather than one's *ideas*, on any subject: although the latter term *idea*, on account of its comprehensive use, may without violation of any express rule be indifferently employed in general discourse for *thought*; but the former term does not on this account lose its characteristic meaning.

The *imagination* is not only the fruit of *thought*, but of peculiar *thought*: the *thought* may be another's; the *imagination* is one's own: the *thought* occurs and recurs; it comes and it goes; it is retained or rejected at the pleasure of the *thinking* being: the *imagination* is framed by special desire; it is cherished with the partiality of a parent for its offspring. The *thoughts* are busied with the surrounding objects; the *imaginations* are employed on distant and strange objects; hence the *thoughts* are denominated sober, chaste, and the like; the *imaginations*, wild and extravagant. The *thoughts* engage the mind as circumstances give rise to them; they are always supposed to have a foundation in some thing: the *imaginations*, on the other hand, are often the mere fruit of a disordered brain; they are always regarded as unsubstantial, if not unreal; they frequently owe their origin to the suggestions of the appetites and passions; whence they are termed the *imaginations* of the heart: 'Different climates produce in men, by a different mixture of the humours, a different and unequal course of *imaginations* and passions.'—TEMPLE.

IDEAL, IMAGINARY.

Ideal does not strictly adhere to the sense of its primitive *idea* (*v. Idea*): the *idea* is the representation of a real object in the mind; but *ideal* signifies belonging to the *idea* independent of the reality or the external object. *Imaginary* preserves the signification of its primitive *imagination* (*v. Fancy*, also *v. Idea*), as denoting what is created by the mind itself.

The *ideal* is not directly opposed to, but abstracted from, the reality; 'There is not, perhaps, in all the stores of *ideal* anguish, a thought more painful than the consciousness of having propagated corruption.'—JOHNSON. The *imaginary*, on the other hand, is directly opposed to the reality; it is the unreal thing formed by the *imagination*; 'Superiour beings know well the vanity of those *imaginary* perfections that swell the heart of man.'—ADDISON. *Ideal* happiness is the happiness which is formed in the mind, without having any direct and actual prototype in nature; but it may, nevertheless, be something possible to be realized; it may be above nature, but not in direct contradiction to it: the *imaginary* is that which is opposite to some positive existing reality; the pleasure which a lunatic derives from the conceit of being a king is altogether *imaginary*.

INHERENT, INBRED, INBORN, INNATE.

The *inherent*, from *hæreo* to stick, denotes a permanent quality or property, as opposed to that which is adventitious and transitory. *Inbred* denotes that property which is derived principally from habit or by a gradual process, as opposed to the one acquired by actual efforts. *Inborn* denotes that which is purely natural, in opposition to the artificial. *Inherent* is in its sense the most general; for what is *inbred* and *inborn* is naturally *inherent*; but all is not *inbred* and *inborn* which is *inherent*. Inanimate objects have *inherent* properties; but the *inbred* and *inborn* exist only in that which receives life; solidity is an *inherent*, but not an *inbred* or *inborn* property of matter: a love of truth is an *inborn* property of the human mind: it is consequently *inherent*, in as much as nothing can totally destroy it;

> When my new mind had no infusion known,
> Thou gav'st so deep a tincture of thine own,
> That ever since I vainly try
> To wash away th' *inherent* dye.—COWLEY.

That which is *inbred* is bred or nurtured in us from our birth; hence, likewise, the properties of animals are *inbred* in them, in as much as they are derived through the medium of the breed of which the parent partakes. that which is *inborn* is simply born in us: a property may be *inborn*, but not *inbred*; it cannot, however, be *inbred* and not *inborn*. Habits which are ingrafted into the natural disposition are properly *inbred*; whence the vulgar proverb that 'what is *bred* in the bone will never be out of the flesh;' to denote the influence which parents have on the characters of their children, both physically and morally;

But he, my *inbred* enemy,
Forth issu'd, brandishing his fatal dart,
Made to destroy; I fled, and cry'd out death!
MILTON.

Propensities, on the other hand, which are totally independent of education or external circumstances, are properly *inborn*, as an *inborn* love of freedom;

Despair, and secret shame, and conscious thought
Of *inborn* worth, his lab'ring soul oppress'd.
DRYDEN.

Inborn and *innate*, from the Latin *natus* born, are precisely the same in meaning, yet they differ somewhat in application. Poetry and the grave style have adopted *inborn;* philosophy has adopted *innate:* genius is *inborn* in some men; nobleness is *inborn* in others: there is an *inborn* talent in some men to command, and an *inborn* fitness in others to obey. Mr. Locke and his followers are pleased to say, there is no such thing as *innate* ideas; and if they only mean that there are no sensible impressions on the soul, until it is acted upon by external objects, they may be right: but if they mean to say that there are no *inborn* characters or powers in the soul, which predispose it for the reception of certain impressions, they contradict the experience of the learned and the unlearned in all ages, who believe, and that from close observation on themselves and others, that man has, from his birth, not only the general character, which belongs to him in common with his species, but also those peculiar characteristicks which distinguish individuals from their earliest infancy: all these characters or characteristicks are, therefore, not supposed to be produced, but elicited, by circumstances; and the ideas, which are but the sensible forms that the soul assumes in its connexion with the body, are, on that account, in vulgar language termed *innate;*

Grant these inventions of the crafty priest,
Yet such inventions never could subsist,
Unless some glimmerings of a future state
Were with the mind coeval and *innate*.
JENYNS.

TO CONCEIVE, APPREHEND, SUPPOSE, IMAGINE.

To *conceive*, from the Latin *concipio*, or *con* and *capio* to put together, is to put an image together in the mind, or to form an idea; to *apprehend*, from *apprehendo* to lay hold of, is to seize with the understanding; to *suppose*, in French *supposer*, Latin *supposui*, perfect of *suppono*, or *sub* and *pono* to put one thing in the place of another, is to have one thing in one's mind in lieu of another; to *imagine*, in French *imaginer*, Latin *imagino*, from *imago* an image, signifies to reflect as an image or phantom in the mind.

Conceive, in the strict sense of the word, is the generick, the others the specifick terms: since in *apprehending*, *imagining*, and *supposing*, we always *conceive* or form an idea, but not *vice versâ;* the difference consists in the mode and object of the action: we *conceive* of things as proper or improper, and just or unjust, right or wrong, good or bad, this is an act of the judgement; '*Conceive* of things clearly and distinctly in their own natures; *conceive* of things completely in all their own parts; *conceive* of things comprehensively in all their properties and relations; *conceive* of things extensively in all their kinds; *conceive* of things orderly, or in a proper method.'—WATTS. We *apprehend* the meaning of another; this is by the power of simple perception;

Yet this I *apprehend* not, why to those
Among whom God will deign to dwell on earth
So many and so various laws are given.—MILTON.

Apprehension is considered by logicians as the first power or operation of the mind being employed on the simplest objects; 'Simple *apprehension* denotes no more than the soul's naked intellection of an object, without either composition or deduction.'—GLANVILLE.

Conceiving is applied to objects of any magnitude which are not above the stretch of human power;

O, what avails me now that honour high
To have *conceived* of God, or that salute
Hail highly favour'd, among women blest.—MILTON.

Apprehending is a momentary or sudden act;

I nam'd them as they pass'd, and understood
Their nature, with such knowledge God indued
My sudden *apprehension*.—MILTON.

Conceiving, which is a process of nature, is often slow and gradual, as to *conceive* a design; 'This man *conceived* the duke's death, but what was the motive of that felonious conception is in the clouds.'—WOLTON.

What is *conceived*, is conclusive or at least determinate; 'A state of innocence and happiness is so remote from all that we have ever seen, that although we can easily *conceive* it is possible, yet our speculations upon it must be general and confused.'—JOHNSON. What is *apprehended* may be dubious or indeterminate: hence the term *apprehend* is taken in the sense of fear;

Nothing is a misery,
Unless our weakness *apprehend* it so.

Conceive and *apprehend* are exercises of the understanding; *suppose* and *imagine* of the imagination; but the former commonly rests on some ground of reality, the latter may be the mere offspring of the brain. *Suppose* is used in opposition to positive knowledge; no person *supposes* that, of which he is positively informed; 'It can scarce be *supposed* that the mind is more vigorous when we sleep, than when we are awake.'—HAWKESWORTH. *Imagine* is employed for that which, in all probability, does not exist; we shall not *imagine* what is evident and undeniable; 'The Earl of Rivers did not *imagine* there could exist, in a human form, a mother that would ruin her own son without enriching herself.'—JOHNSON (*Life of Savage*).

TO CONCEIVE, UNDERSTAND, COMPREHEND.

These terms indicate the intellectual operations of forming ideas, that is, ideas of the complex kind in distinction from the simple ideas formed by the act of perception. To *conceive*, is to put together in the mind; to *understand*, is to stand under, or near to the mind; to *comprehend*, from the Latin *com* or *cum* and *prehendo* to take, signifies to seize or embrace in the mind.

Conception is the simplest operation of the three; when we *conceive* we may have but one idea, when we *understand* or *comprehend* we have all the ideas which the subject is capable of presenting. We cannot *understand* or *comprehend* without *conceiving;* but we may often *conceive* that which we neither *understand* nor *comprehend;* 'Whatever they cannot immediately *conceive* they consider as too high to be reached, or too extensive to be *comprehended*.'—JOHNSON.

That which we cannot *conceive* is to us nothing; but the *conception* of it gives it an existence, at least in our minds; but *understanding* or *comprehending* is not essential to the belief of a thing's existence. So long as we have reasons sufficient to *conceive* a thing as possible or probable, it is not necessary either to *understand* or *comprehend* them in order to authorize our belief. The mysteries of our holy religion are objects of *conception*, but not of *comprehension;*

Our finite knowledge cannot *comprehend*
The principles of an abounded sway.—SHIRLEY.

We *conceive* that a thing may be done without *understanding* how it is done; we *conceive* that a thing may exist without *comprehending* the nature of its existence. We *conceive* clearly, *understand* fully, *comprehend* minutely.

Conception is a species of invention; it is the fruit of the mind's operation within itself; 'If, by a more noble and more adequate *conception* that be considered as wit which is at once natural and new, that which, though not obvious, is, upon its first production, acknowledged to be just; if it be that, which he that never found it, wonders how he missed; to wit of this kind the metaphysical poets have seldom risen.'—JOHNSON. *Understanding* and *comprehension* are employed solely on external objects; we *understand* and *comprehend* that which actually exists before us, and presents itself to our observation; 'Swift pays no court to the passions; he excites neither surprise nor admiration; he always *understands* himself, and his readers always *understand* him.'—JOHNSON. *Conceiving* is the office of the imagination, as well as the judgement; *understanding* and *comprehension* are the office of the reasoning faculties exclusively.

* *Conceiving* is employed with regard to matters of taste, to arrangements, designs, and projects; *understanding* is employed on familiar objects which present themselves in the ordinary discourse and business of men; *comprehending* respects principles, lessons, and speculative knowledge in general. The artist *conceives* a design, and he who will execute it must *understand* it; the poet *conceives* that which is grand and sublime, and he who will enjoy the perusal of his *conceptions* must have refinement of mind, and capacity to *comprehend* the grand and sublime. The builder *conceives* plans, the scholar *understands* languages, the metaphysician *comprehends* subtle questions.

A ready *conception* supplies us with a stock of ideas on all subjects; a quick *understanding* catches the intentions of others with half a word; a penetrating mind *comprehends* the abstrusest points. There are human beings involved in such profound ignorance, that they cannot *conceive* of the most ordinary things that exist in civilized life: there are those who, though slow at *understanding* words, will be quick at *understanding* looks and signs: and there are others who, though dull at *conceiving* or *understanding* common matters, will have a power for *comprehending* the abstruser parts of the mathematics.

CONCEPTION, NOTION.

Conception, from *conceive* (*v. To conceive*), signifies the thing *conceived; notion*, in French *notion*, Latin *notio*, from *notus* participle of *nosco* to know, signifies the thing known.

Conception is the mind's own work, what it pictures to itself from the exercise of its own powers; 'Words signify not immediately and primely things themselves, but the *conceptions* of the mind concerning things.'—SOUTH. *Notion* is the representation of objects as they are drawn from observation; 'The story of Telemachus is formed altogether in the spirit of Homer, and will give an unlearned reader a *notion* of that great poet's manner of writing.'—ADDISON. *Conceptions* are the fruit of the imagination; 'It is natural for the imaginations of men who lead their lives in too solitary a manner to prey upon themselves, and form from their own *conceptions* beings and things which have no place in nature.'—STEELE. *Notions* are the result of reflection and experience; 'Considering that the happiness of the other world is to be the happiness of the whole man, who can question, but there is an infinite variety in those pleasures we are speaking of? Revelation, likewise, very much confirms this *notion* under the different views it gives us of our future happiness.'—ADDISON. *Conceptions* are formed; *notions* are entertained. *Conceptions* are either grand or mean, gross or sublime, either clear or indistinct, crude or distinct; *notions* are either true or false, just or absurd. Intellectual culture serves to elevate the *conceptions;* the extension of knowledge serves to correct and refine the *notions*.

Some heathen philosophers had an indistinct *conception* of the Deity, whose attributes and character are unfolded to us in his revelation: the ignorant have often false *notions* of their duty and obligations to their superiours. The unenlightened express their gross and crude *conceptions* of a Superiour Being by some material and visible object: the vulgar *notion* of ghosts and spirits is not entirely banished from the most cultivated parts of England.

PERCEPTION, IDEA, CONCEPTION, NOTION.

Perception expresses either the act of *perceiving* or the impression produced by that act; in this latter sense it is analogous to an *idea* (*v. Idea*). The impression of an object that is present to us is termed a *perception;* the revival of that impression, when the object is removed, is an *idea*. A combination of *ideas* by which any image is presented to the mind is a *conception* (*v. To comprehend*); the association of two or more *ideas*, so as to constitute it a decision, is a *notion*. *Perceptions* are clear or confused, according to the state of the sensible organs, and the *perceptive* faculty; *ideas* are faint or vivid, vague or distinct, according to the nature of the *perception*, *conceptions* are gross or refined according to the number and extent of one's *ideas; notions* are true or false, correct or incorrect, according to the extent of one's knowledge. The *perception* which we have of remote objects is sometimes so indistinct as to leave hardly any traces of the image on the mind; we have in that case a *perception*, but not an *idea*.

What can the fondest mother wish for more,
Ev'n for her darling son, than solid sense,
Perceptions clear, and flowing eloquence.—WYNNE.

If we read the description of any object, we may have an *idea* of it; but we need not have any immediate *perception:* the *idea* in this case being complex, and formed of many images of which we have already had a *perception;* 'Imagination selects *ideas* from the treasures of remembrance.'—JOHNSON.

If we present objects to our minds, according to different images which have already been impressed, we are said to have a *conception* of them: in this case, however, it is not necessary for the objects really to exist; they may be the offspring of the mind's operation within itself; 'It is not a head that is filled with extravagant *conceptions*, which is capable of furnishing the world with diversions of this nature (from humour).'—ADDISON. But with regard to *notions* it is different, for they are formed respecting objects that do really exist, although perhaps the properties or circumstances which we assign to them are not real; 'Those *notions* which are to be collected by reason, in opposition to the senses, will seldom stand forward in the mind, but be treasured in the remoter repositories of the memory.'—JOHNSON. If I look at the moon, I have a *perception* of it; if it disappear from my sight, and the impression remains, I have an *idea* of it; if an object, differing in shape and colour from that or any thing else which I may have seen, present itself to my mind, it is a *conception;* if of this moon I conceive that it is no bigger than what it appears to my eye, this is a *notion*, which in the present instance, assigns an unreal property to a real object.

TO THINK, SUPPOSE, IMAGINE, BELIEVE, DEEM.

To *think*, in Saxon *thincan*, German *denken*, &c. from the Hebrew דן to rule or judge, is the generick term. It expresses, in common with the other terms, the act of having a particular idea in the mind; but it is indefinite as to the mode and the object of the action. To *think* may be the act of the understanding, or merely of the *imagination:* to *suppose* and *imagine* are rather the acts of the *imagination* than of the understanding. To *think*, that is, to have any thought or opinion upon a subject, requires reflection: it is the work of time;

If to conceive how any thing can be
From shape extracted, and locality,
Is hard: what *think* you of the Deity?—JENYNS.

To *suppose* and *imagine* may be the acts of the moment. We *think* a thing right or wrong; we *suppose* it to be true or false; 'It is absurd to *suppose* that while the relations, in which we stand to our fellow-creatures, naturally call forth certain sentiments and affections, there should be none to correspond to the first and greatest of all beings.'—BLAIR. We *imagine* it to be real or unreal. To *think* is employed promiscuously in regard to all objects, whether actually existing or not: to *suppose* applies to those which are uncertain or precarious; *imagine*, to those which are unreal; 'How ridiculous must it be to *imagine* that the clergy of England favour popery, when they cannot be clergymen without renouncing it.'—BEVERIDGE. *Think* and *imagine* are said of that which affects the senses immediately; *suppose* is only said of that which occupies the mind. We *think* that we hear a noise as soon as the sound catches our attention; in certain states of the body or mind we *imagine* we hear noises which were never made: we *think* that a person will come to-day, because he has informed us that he intends to do so; we *suppose* that he will come to-day,

* Vide Abbe Girard: "Entendre, comprendre, concevoir."

at a certain hour, because he came at the same hour yesterday.

When applied to the events and circumstances of life, to *think* may be applied to any time, past, present, or to come, or where no time is expressed: to *suppose* is more aptly applied to a future time; and *imagine* to a past or present time. We *think* that a person has done a thing, is doing it, or will do it; we *suppose* that he will do it; we *imagine* that he has done it, or is doing it. A person *thinks* that he will die; *imagines* that he is in a dangerous way: we *think* that the weather will be fine to-day, we *suppose* that the affair will be decided.

In regard to moral points, in which case the word *deem* may be compared with the others; to *think* is a conclusion drawn from certain premises. I *think* that a man has acted wrong: to *suppose* is to take up an idea arbitrarily or at pleasure; we argue upon a *supposed* case, merely for the sake of argument: to *imagine* is to take up an idea by accident, or without any connexion with the truth or reality; we *imagine* that a person is offended with us, without being able to assign a single reason for the idea; *imaginary* evils are even more numerous than those which are real: to *deem* is to form a conclusion; things are *deemed* hurtful or otherwise in consequence of observation; 'An empty house is by the players *deemed* the most dreadful sign of popular disapprobation.'—HAWKESWORTH.

To *think* and *believe* are both opposite to knowing or perceiving; but to *think* is a more partial action than to *believe:* we *think* as the thing strikes us at the time; we *believe* from a settled deduction: hence, it expresses much less to say that I *think* a person speaks the truth, than that I *believe* that he speaks the truth;

For they can conquer who *believe* they can.—DRYDEN.

I *think*, from what I can recollect, that such and such were the words, is a vague mode of speech, not admissible in a court of law as positive evidence: the natural question which follows upon this is, do you firmly *believe* it? to which, whoever can answer in the affirmative, with the appearance of sincerity, must be admitted as a testimony. Hence it arises, that the word can only be employed in matters that require but little thought in order to come to a conclusion; and *believe* is applicable to things that must be admitted only on substantial evidence. We are at liberty to say that I *think*, or I *believe*, that the account is made out right; but we must say, that I *believe*, not *think*, that the Bible is the word of God.

TO THINK, REFLECT, PONDER, MUSE.

Think, in Saxon *thincan*, German *denken*, &c., comes from the Hebrew דן, to direct, rule, or judge; *reflect*, in Latin *reflecto*, signifies literally to bend back, that is, to bend the mind back on itself; *ponder*, from *pondus* a weight, signifies to weigh; *muse*, from *musa*, a song, signifies to dwell upon with the imagination.

To *think* is a general and indefinite term; to *reflect* is a particular mode of *thinking;* to *ponder* and *muse* are different modes of *reflecting*, the former on grave matters, the latter on matters that interest either the affections or the imagination: we *think* whenever we receive or recall an idea to the mind; but we *reflect* only by recalling, not one only, but many ideas: we *think* if we only suffer the ideas to revolve in succession in the mind: but in *reflecting* we compare, combine, and judge of those ideas which thus pass in the mind: we *think*, therefore, of things past, as they are pleasurable or otherwise; we *reflect* upon them as they are applicable to our present condition: we may *think* on things past, present, or to come; we *reflect, ponder*, and *muse* mostly on that which is past or present. The man *thinks* on the days of his childhood, and wishes them back; the child *thinks* on the time when he shall be a man, and is impatient until it is come; 'No man was ever weary of *thinking*, much less of *thinking* that he had done well or virtuously.'—SOUTH. A man *reflects* on his past follies, and tries to profit by experience; 'Let men but *reflect* upon their own observation, and consider impartially with themselves how few in the world they have known made better by age.'—SOUTH. One *ponders* on any serious concern that affects his destiny;

> Stood on the brink of hell, and look'd awhile,
> *Pond'ring* his voyage.—MILTON.

One *muses* on the happy events of his childhood; 'I was sitting on a sofa one evening, after I had been caressed by Amurath, and my imagination kindled as I *mused*.'—HAWKESWORTH.

TO CONTEMPLATE, MEDITATE, MUSE.

Contemplate, in Latin *contemplatus*, participle of *contemplor*, probably comes from *templum* the temple, that being the place most fitted for *contemplation*. *Meditate*, in Latin *meditatus*, participle of *meditor*, is probably changed from *melitor*, in Greek μελετάω, to modulate, or attune the thoughts, as sounds are harmonized. *Muse* is derived from *musa*, owing to the connexion between the harmony of a song, and the harmony of the thoughts in *musing*.

Different species of reflection are marked by these terms.

We *contemplate* what is present or before our eyes; we *meditate* on what is past or absent; we *muse* on what is present or past.

The heavens, and all the works of the Creator, are objects of *contemplation;* 'I sincerely wish myself with you to *contemplate* the wonders of God in the firmament, rather than the madness of man on the earth.'—POPE. The ways of Providence are fit subjects for *meditation;* 'But a very small part of the moments spent in *meditation* on the past, produce any reasonable caution or salutary sorrow.'—JOHNSON. One *muses* on the events or circumstances which have been just passing.

We may *contemplate* and *meditate* for the future, but never *muse*. In this case the two former terms have the sense of contriving or purposing: what is *contemplated* to be done, is thought of more indistinctly than when it is *meditated* to be done: many things are had in *contemplation* which are never seriously *meditated* upon; 'Life is the immediate gift of God, a right inherent by nature in every individual, and it begins in *contemplation* of law as soon as an infant is able to stir in the mother's womb.'—BLACKSTONE. Between *contemplating* and *meditating* there is oftener a greater difference than between *meditating* and executing;

> Thus plung'd in ills and *meditating* more,
> The people's patience, tried, no longer bore
> The raging monster.—DRYDEN.

Contemplation may be a temporary action directed to a single object; 'There is not any property or circumstances of my being that I *contemplate* with more joy than my immortality.'—BERKELEY. *Meditating* is a permanent and serious action directed to several objects; '*Meditate* till you make some act of piety upon the occasion of what you *meditate*, either get some new arguments against sin, or some new encouragement to virtue.'—TAYLOR. *Musing* is partial and unimportant: *meditation* is a religious duty, it cannot be neglected without injury to a person's spiritual improvement; *musing* is a temporary employment of the mind on the ordinary concerns of life, as they happen to excite an interest for the time;

> *Musing* as wont on this and that,
> Such trifles as I know not what.—FRANCIS.

Contemplative and *musing*, as epithets, have a strong analogy to each other.

Contemplative is a habit of the mind; *musing* is a particular state of the mind. A person may have a *contemplative* turn, or be in a *musing* mood.

TO CONSIDER, REFLECT.

Consider, in French *considerer*, Latin *considero*, a factative, from *consido* to sit down, signifies to make to settle in the mind. *Reflect*, in Latin *reflecto*, compounded of *re* and *flecto*, signifies to turn back, or upon itself, after the manner of the mind.

The operation of thought is expressed by these two words, but it varies in the circumstances of the action.

Consideration is employed for practical purposes, *reflection* for matters of speculation or moral improvement. Common objects call for *consideration;* the workings of the mind itself, or objects purely spiritual, occupy *reflection*. It is necessary to *consider* what is proper to be done, before we take any step; 'It seems necessary, in the choice of persons for greater employments, to *consider* their bodies as well as their minds, and ages and health as well as their abilities.'—TEMPLE. It is consistent with our natures, as rational beings, to *reflect* on what we are, what we ought to be, and what we shall be; 'Whoever *reflects* frequently on the uncertainty of his own duration, will find out that the state of others is not more permanent than his own.'—JOHNSON.

Without *consideration* we shall naturally commit the most flagrant errors; without *reflection* we shall never understand our duty to our Maker, our neighbour, and ourselves.

TO CONSIDER, REGARD.

To consider (*v. To consider*) signifies to take a view of a thing in the mind, which is the result of thought; to *regard* is literally to look back upon, from the French *regarder*, that is, *re* and *garder*, to keep or watch, which is derived from the old German *wahren* to see, of which there are still traces in the words *bewahren* to guard against, *warten* to wait, and the English to *be aware of*.

There is more caution or thought in *considering*; more personal interest in *regarding*. A man may *consider* his reputation so as to be deterred from taking a particular step; if he *regards* his reputation, this *regard* has a general influence on all he does. 'The king had not, at that time, one person about him of his council, who had the least *consideration* of his own honour, or friendship for those who sat at the helm of affairs, the Duke of Lennox excepted.'—CLARENDON.

> If much you note him,
> You offend him; feed and *regard* him not.
> SHAKSPEARE.

A similar distinction exists between these words when not expressly personal: to *consider* a thing in a certain light, is to take a steady view of it; 'I *consider* the soul of man as the ruin of a glorious pile of buildings.'—STEELE. To *regard* a thing is to view it with a certain interest; 'I *regard* trade not only as highly advantageous to the commonwealth in general, but as the most natural and likely method of making a man's fortune.'—BUDGELL.

CONSIDERATION, REASON.

Consideration, or that which enters into a person's consideration, has a reference to the person considering. *Reason*, or that which influences the reason, is taken absolutely: *considerations* are therefore for the most part partial, as affecting particular interests, or dependent on particular circumstances. 'He had been made general upon very partial, and not enough deliberated *considerations*.'—CLARENDON.

Reasons on the contrary may be general, and vary according to the nature of the subject; 'The *reasons* assigned in a law of the 36th year of Edward III. for having pleas and judgements in the English tongue, might have been urged for having the laws themselves in that language.'—TYRWHITT.

When applied to matters of practice the *consideration* influences the particular actions of an individual or individuals; no *consideration* of profit or emolument should induce a person to forfeit his word; 'He was obliged, antecedent to all other *considerations*, to search an asylum.'—DRYDEN.

The *reason* influences a line of conduct; the *reasons* which men assign for their conduct are often as absurd as they are false;

> I mask the business from the common eye
> For sundry weighty *reasons*.—SHAKSPEARE.

In the same manner, when applied to matters of theory, the *consideration* is that which enters into a man's consideration, or which he offers to the consideration of others; 'The folly of ascribing temporal punishments to any particular crimes, may appear from several *considerations*.'—ADDISON. The *reason* is that which flows out of the nature of the thing; 'If it be natural, ought we not rather to conclude that there is some ground or *reason* for those fears, and that nature hath not planted them in us to no purpose?'—TILLOTSON.

TO ARGUE, EVINCE, PROVE.

To *argue*, from the Latin *arguo*, and the Greek ἀργὸς clear, signifies to make clear; to *evince*, in Latin *evinco*, compounded of *vinco* to *prove* or make out, and *e* forth, signifies to bring to light, to make to appear clear; to *prove*, in French *prouver*, in Latin *probo*, from *probus* good, signifies to make good, or make to appear good.

These terms in general convey the idea of *evidence*, but with gradations: *argue* denotes the smallest degree, and *prove* the highest degree. To *argue* is to serve as an indication amounting to probability; to *evince* denotes an indication so clear as to remove doubt; to *prove* marks an evidence so positive as to produce conviction.

It *argues* a want of candour in any man to conceal circumstances in his statement which are any ways calculated to affect the subject in question; 'It is not the being singular, but being singular for something, that *argues* either extraordinary endowments of nature or benevolent intentions to mankind, which draws the admiration and esteem of the world.'—BERKELEY. The tenour of a person's conversation may *evince* the refinement of his mind and the purity of his taste; 'The nature of the soul itself, and particularly its immateriality, has, I think, been *evinced* almost to a demonstration.'—ADDISON. When we see men sacrificing their peace of mind and even their integrity of character to ambition, it *proves* to us how important it is even in early life to check this natural, and in some measure laudable, but still insinuating and dangerous passion;

> What object, what event the moon beneath,
> But *argues* or endears an after-scene?
> To reason *proves*, or weds it to desire?—YOUNG

ARGUMENT, REASON, PROOF.

Argument, from *argue* (*v. To argue*), signifies either the thing that *argues*, or that which is brought forward in *arguing*: *reason*, in French *raison*, Latin *ratio*, from *ratus*, participle of *reor* to think, signifies the thing thought or estimated in the mind by the power of *reason*; *proof*, from to *prove*, signifies the thing that *proves*.

An *argument* serves for defence; a *reason* for justification; a *proof* for conviction. *Arguments* are adduced in support of an hypothesis or proposition; 'When the *arguments* press equally on both sides in matters that are indifferent to us, the safest method is to give up ourselves to neither.'—ADDISON. *Reasons* are assigned in matters of belief and practice;

> The *reasons*, with his friend's experience join'd,
> Encourag'd much, but more disturb'd his mind.
> DRYDEN.

Proofs are collected to ascertain a fact;

> One soul in both, whereof good *proof*
> This day affords.—MILTON.

Arguments are either strong or weak; *reasons* solid or futile; *proofs* clear and positive, or vague and indefinite. We confute an *argument*, overpower a *reason*, and invalidate a *proof*. Whoever wishes to defend Christianity will be in no want of *arguments*; 'This, before revelation had enlightened the world, was the very best *argument* for a future state.'—ATTERBURY. The believer need never be at a loss to give a *reason* for the hope that is in him; 'Virtue and vice are not arbitrary things, but there is a natural and eternal *reason* for that goodness and virtue, and against vice and wickedness.'—TILLOTSON. Throughout the whole of Divine revelation there is no circumstance that is substantiated with such irrefragable *proofs* as the resurrection of our Saviour;

> Are there (still more amazing!) who resist
> The rising thought, who smother in its birth
> The glorious truth, who struggle to be brutes?
> Who fight the *proofs* of immortality?—YOUNG.

CAUSE, REASON, MOTIVE.

Cause is supposed to signify originally the same as case; it means however now, by distinction, the case or thing happening before another as its *cause*; the *reason* is the thing that acts on the reason or understanding; the *motive*, in French *motif*, from the Latin *motus* participle of *moveo* to move, is that which brings into action.

Cause respects the order and connexion of things; *reason* the movements and operations of the mind; *motives* the movements of the mind and body. *Cause* is properly the generick; *reason* and *motive* are specifick: every *reason* or *motive* is a *cause*, but every *cause* is not a *reason* or *motive*.

Cause is said of all inanimate objects; *reason* and *motive* of rational agents: whatever happens in the world, happens from some *cause* mediate or immediate; the primary or first *cause* of all, is God; 'The wise and learned among the very heathens themselves, have all acknowledged some first *cause*, whereupon originally the being of all things dependeth, neither have they otherwise spoken of that *cause*, than as an agent which, knowing what and why it worketh, observeth in working a most exact order or law.'—Hooker. Whatever opinions men hold, they ought to be able to assign a substantial *reason* for them; 'If we commemorate any mystery of our redemption, or article of our faith, we ought to confirm our belief of it by considering all those *reasons* upon which it is built.'—Nelson. For whatever men do they ought to have a sufficient *motive*; 'Every principle that is a *motive* to good actions ought to be encouraged.'—Addison.

As the *cause* gives birth to the effect, so does the *reason* give birth to the conclusion, and the *motive* gives birth to the action. Between *cause* and effect there is a necessary connexion: whatever in the natural world is capable of giving birth to another thing is an adequate *cause*;

Cut off the *causes*, and the effects will cease,
And all the moving madness fall to peace.
Dryden.

But in the moral world there is not a necessary connexion between *reasons* and their results, or *motives* and their actions: the state of the agent's mind is not always such as to be acted upon according to the nature of things; every adequate *reason* will not be followed by its natural conclusion, for every man will not believe who has *reasons* to believe, nor yield to the *reasons* that would lead to a right belief: and every *motive* will not be accompanied with its corresponding action, for every man will not act who has a *motive* for acting, nor act in the manner in which his *motives* ought to dictate: the *causes* of our diseases often lie as hidden as the *reasons* of our opinions, and the *motives* for our actions.

CONCLUSION, INFERENCE, DEDUCTION.

Conclusion, from *conclude*, and the Latin *conclaudo*, or *con* and *cludo* to shut up, signifies literally the winding up of all arguments and reasoning; *inference*, from *infer*, in Latin *infero*, signifies what is brought in; *deduction*, from *deduct*, in Latin *deductus* and *deduco* to bring out, signifies the bringing or drawing one thing from another.

A *conclusion* is full and decisive; an *inference* is partial and indecisive: a *conclusion* leaves the mind in no doubt or hesitation; it puts a stop to all farther reasoning;

I only deal by rules of art,
Such as are lawful, and judge by
Conclusions of astrology.—Hudibras.

Inferences are special *conclusions* from particular circumstances; they serve as links in the chain of reasoning; 'Though it may chance to be right in the *conclusion*, it is yet unjust and mistaken in the method of *inference*.'—Glanville. *Conclusion* in the logical sense is the concluding proposition in a syllogism, drawn from the two others, which are called the premises, and may each of them be *inferences*.

Conclusions are drawn from real facts, *inferences* are drawn from the appearances of things, *deductions* only from arguments or assertions. *Conclusions* are practical; *inferences* ratiocinative; *deductions* are final.

We *conclude* from a person's conduct or declarations what he intends to do, or leave undone;

He praises wine, and we *conclude* from thence
He lik'd his glass, on his own evidence.—Addison.

We *infer* from the appearance of the clouds, or the thickness of the atmosphere, that there will be a heavy fall of rain or snow; 'You might, from the single people departed, make some useful *inferences* or guesses how many there are left unmarried.'—Steele. We *deduce* from a combination of facts, *inferences*, and assertions, that a story is fabricated; 'There is a consequence which seems very naturally *deducible* from the foregoing considerations. If the scale of being rises by such a regular progress so high as man, we may by a parity of reason suppose that it still proceeds gradually through those beings which are of a superior nature to him.'—Addison. Hasty *conclusions* betray a want of judgement, or firmness of mind: contrary *inferences* are frequently drawn from the same circumstances to serve the purposes of party, and support a favourite position; the *deductions* in such cases are not unfrequently true when the *inferences* are false.

BELIEF, CREDIT, TRUST, FAITH.

Belief, from *believe*, in Saxon *gelyfan*, *geleavan*, in German *glauben*, *kilauban*, &c. comes, in all possibility, from *lief*, in German *belieben* to please, and the Latin *libet* it pleaseth, signifying the pleasure or assent of the mind. *Credit*, in French *credit*, Latin *creditus*, participle of *credo*, compounded of *cor* the heart, and *do* to give, signifies also giving the heart. *Trust* is connected with the old word *trow*, in Saxon *treowian*, German *trauen*, old German *thravàhn*, *thruven*, &c. to hold true, and probably from the Greek θάρρειν to have confidence, signifying to depend upon as true. *Faith*, in Latin *fides*, from *fido* to confide, signifies also dependence upon as true.

Belief is the generick term, the others specifick; we *believe* when we *credit* and *trust*, but not always *vice versâ*. *Belief* rests on no particular person or thing; but *credit* and *trust* rest on the authority of one or more individuals. Every thing is the subject of *belief* which produces one's assent: the events of human life are *credited* upon the authority of the narrator: the words, promises, or the integrity of individuals are *trusted*: the power of persons and the virtue of things are objects of *faith*.

Belief and *credit* are particular actions, or sentiments: *trust* and *faith* are permanent dispositions of the mind. Things are entitled to our *belief*; persons are entitled to our *credit*: but people repose a *trust* in others; or have a *faith* in others.

Our *belief* or *unbelief* is not always regulated by our reasoning faculties, or the truth of things: we often *believe* from prejudice and ignorance, things to be true which are very false;

Oh! I've heard him talk
Like the first-born child of love, when every word
Spoke in his eyes, and wept to be *believ'd*,
And all to ruin me.—Southern.

With the bulk of mankind, assurance goes further than any thing else in obtaining *credit*: gross falsehoods, pronounced with confidence, will be *credited* sooner than plain truths told in an unvarnished style;

Oh! I will *credit* my Scamandra's tears!
Nor think them drops of chance like other women's.
Lee.

There are no disappointments more severe than those which we feel on finding that we have *trusted* to men of base principles;

Capricious man! To good or ill inconstant
Too much to fear or *trust* is equal weakness.
Johnson.

Ignorant people have commonly a more implicit *faith* in any nostrum recommended to them by persons of their own class, than in the prescriptions of professional men regularly educated;

For *faith* repos'd on seas and on the flatt'ring sky
Thy naked corpse is doomed on shores unknown to lie
Dryden.

Belief, *trust*, and *faith* have a religious application, which *credit* has not. *Belief* is simply an act of the understanding; *trust* and *faith* are active moving principles of the mind in which the heart is concerned. *Belief* does not extend beyond an assent of the mind to any given proposition; *trust* and *faith* are lively sentiments which impel to action. *Belief* is to *trust* and *faith*, as *cause* to effect: there may be *belief* without either *trust* or *faith*: but there can be no *trust* or *faith* without *belief:* we *believe* that there is a God, who is the creator and preserver of all his creatures; we therefore *trust* in him for his protection of ourselves: we *believe* that Jesus Christ died for the sins of men; we have therefore *faith* in his redeeming grace to save us from our sins.

Belief is common to all religions; 'The Epicureans contented themselves with the denial of a Providence, asserting at the same time the existence of gods in general: because they would not shock the common *belief* of mankind.'—ADDISON. *Trust* is peculiar to the *believers* in Divine revelation; 'What can be a stronger motive to a firm *trust* and reliance on the mercies of our Maker, than the giving us his Son to suffer for us?'—ADDISON. *Faith* is employed by distinction for the Christian *faith;* 'The *faith* or persuasion of a Divine revelation is a Divine *faith*, not only with respect to the object of it, but likewise in respect of the author of it, which is the Divine Spirit.'—TILLOTSON. *Belief* is purely speculative; and *trust* and *faith* are operative: the former operates on the mind; the latter on the outward conduct. *Trust* in God serves to dispel all anxious concern about the future. "*Faith*," says the Apostle, "is dead without works." Theorists substitute *belief* for *faith;* enthusiasts mistake passion for *faith.* True *faith* must be grounded on a right *belief*, and accompanied with a right practice.

FAITH, CREED.

Faith (*v. Belief*) denotes either the principle of trusting, or the thing trusted; *creed*, from the Latin *credo* to believe, denotes the thing believed.

These words are synonymous when taken for the thing trusted in or believed; but they differ in this, that *faith* has always a reference to the principle in the mind; *creed* only respects the thing which is the object of *faith:* the former is likewise taken generally and indefinitely; the latter particularly and definitely, signifying a set form or a code of *faith;* hence we say, to be of the same *faith*, or to adopt the same *creed.* The holy martyrs died for the *faith*, as it is in Christ Jesus; 'St. Paul affirms that a sinner is at first justified and received into the favour of God, by a sincere profession of the Christian *faith.*'—TILLOTSON. Every established form of religion will have its peculiar *creed.* The Church of England has adopted that *creed* which it considers as containing the purest principles of Christian *faith;* 'Supposing all the great points of atheism were formed into a kind of *creed*, I would fain ask whether it would not require an infinitely greater measure of *faith* than any set of articles which they so violently oppose?'—ADDISON.

CONVICTION, PERSUASION.

Conviction, from *convince*, denotes either the act of *convincing* or the state of being *convinced; persuasion*, which, from the Latin *persuadeo*, or *suadeo*, and the Greek ἡδὺς sweet, signifies to make thoroughly agreeable to the taste, expresses likewise the act of *persuading*, or the state of being *persuaded.*

What *convinces* binds; what *persuades* attracts. We *convince* by arguments; it is the understanding which determines: we are *persuaded* by entreaties and personal influence; it is the imagination, the passions, or the will which decide. Our *conviction* respects solely matters of belief or faith; 'When therefore the Apostle requireth ability to *convict* hereticks, can we think he judgeth it a thing unlawful, and not rather needful, to use the principal instrument of their *conviction*, the light of reason.'—HOOKER. Our *persuasion* respects matters of belief or practice; 'I should be glad if I could *persuade* him to write such another critique on any thing of mine, for when he condemns any of my poems, he makes the world have a better opinion of them.'—DRYDEN. We are *convinced* that a thing is true or false; we are *persuaded* that it is either right or wrong, advantageous or the contrary. A person will have half effected a thing who is *convinced* that it is in his power to effect it; he will be easily *persuaded* to do that which favours his own interests.

Conviction respects our most important duties 'Their wisdom is only of this world, to put false colours upon things, to call good evil, and evil good, against the *conviction* of their own consciences.'—SWIFT *Persuasion* is frequently applied to matters of indifference: 'Philoclea's beauty not only *persuaded*, but so *persuaded* that all hearts must yield.'—SIDNEY The first step to true repentance is a thorough *conviction* of the enormity of sin. The cure of people's maladies is sometimes promoted to a surprising degree by their *persuasion* of the efficacy of the remedy.

As *conviction* is the effect of substantial evidence, it is solid and permanent in its nature; it cannot be so easily changed and deceived; *persuasion*, depending on our feelings, is influenced by external objects, and exposed to various changes; it may vary both in the degree and in the object. *Conviction* answers in our minds to positive certainty; *persuasion* answers to probability.

The practical truths of Christianity demand our deepest *conviction;* 'When men have settled in themselves a *conviction* that there is nothing honourable which is not accompanied with innocence; nothing mean but what has guilt in it; riches, pleasures, and honours will easily lose their charms, if they stand between us and our integrity.'—STEELE. Of the speculative truths of Christianity we ought to have a rational *persuasion;* 'Let the mind be possessed with the *persuasion* of immortal happiness annexed to the act, and there will be no want of candidates to struggle for the glorious prerogative.'—CUMBERLAND.

The *conviction* of the truth or falsehood of that which we have been accustomed to condemn or admire cannot be effected without powerful means; but we may be *persuaded* of the propriety of a thing to-day which to-morrow we shall regard with indifference We ought to be *convinced* of the propriety of avoiding every thing which can interfere with the good order of society; we may be *persuaded* of the truth of a person's narrative or not, according to the representation made to us; we may be *persuaded* to pursue any study or lay it aside.

UNBELIEF, INFIDELITY, INCREDULITY

Unbelief (*v. Belief*) respects matters in general; *infidelity*, from *fides* faithful, is *unbelief* as respects Divine revelation; *incredulity* is *unbelief* in ordinary matters *Unbelief* is taken in an indefinite and negative sense; it is the want of *belief* in any particular thing that may or may not be *believed: infidelity* is a more active state of mind; it supposes a violent and total rejection of that which ought to be *believed: incredulity* is also an active state of mind, in which we oppose a *belief* to matters that may be rejected. *Unbelief* does not of itself convey any reproachful meaning; it depends upon the thing disbelieved; we may be *unbelievers* in indifferent as well as the most important matters; but absolutely taken it means one who disbelieves sacred truths; 'Such a universal acquaintance with things will keep you from an excess of credulity and *unbelief;* i. e. a readiness to believe or deny every thing at first hearing.' —WATTS. 'One gets by heart a catalogue of title pages and editions; and immediately, to become conspicuous, declares that he is an *unbeliever*.'—ADDISON. *Infidelity* is taken in the worst sense for a blind and senseless perversity in refusing *belief;* '*Belief* and profession will speak a Christian but very faintly, when thy conversation proclaims thee an *infidel*.'—SOUTH *Incredulity* is often a mark of wisdom, and not unfrequently a mark of the contrary; 'I am not altogether *incredulous* that there may be such candles as are made of salamander's wood, being a kind of mineral which whiteneth in the burning and consumeth not.'—BACON. 'The youth hears all the predictions of the aged with obstinate *incredulity*.'—JOHNSON. The Jews are *unbelievers* in the mission of our Saviour; the Turks are *infidels*, inasmuch as they do not believe in the Bible Deists and Atheists are likewise *infidels*, inasmuch as they set themselves up against Divine revelation; well informed people are always *incredulous* of stories respecting ghosts and apparitions.

DISBELIEF, UNBELIEF

Disbelief properly implies the *believing* that a thing is not, or refusing to *believe* that it is. *Unbelief* expresses properly a *believing* the contrary of what one has *believed* before: *disbelief* is qualified as to its nature by the thing *disbelieved:* 'The belief or *disbelief* of a thing does not alter the nature of the thing.'—TILLOTSON. Our *disbelief* of the idle tales which are told b beggars, is justified by the frequent detection of their falsehood; 'The atheist has not found his post tenable, and is therefore retired into deism, and a *disbelief* of revealed religion only.'—ADDISON. Our Saviour had compassion on Thomas for his *unbelief*, and gave him such evidences of his identity, as dissipated every doubt; 'The opposites to faith are *unbelief* and credulity.'—TILLOTSON.

DOCTRINE, PRECEPT, PRINCIPLE.

Doctrine, in French *doctrine*, Latin *doctrina*, from *doceo* to teach, signifies the thing taught; *precept*, from the Latin *præcipio*, signifies the thing laid down; and *principle*, in French *principe*, Latin *principium*, signifies the beginning of things, that is, their first or original component parts.

The *doctrine* requires a teacher; the *precept* requires a superiour with authority; the *principle* requires only an illustrator. The *doctrine* is always framed by some one; the *precept* is enjoined or laid down by some one; the *principle* lies in the thing itself. The *doctrine* is composed of *principles*; the *precept* rests upon *principles* or *doctrines*. Pythagoras taught the *doctrine* of the metempsychosis, and enjoined many *precepts* on his disciples for the regulation of their conduct, particularly that they should abstain from eating animal food, and be only silent hearers for the first five years of their scholarship: the former of these rules depended upon the preceding *doctrine* of the soul's transmigration to the bodies of animals; the latter rested on that simple *principle* of education, the entire devotion of the scholar to the master.

We are said to believe in *doctrines*; to obey *precepts*; to imbibe or hold *principles*. The *doctrine* is that which enters into the composition of our faith; 'To make new articles of faith and *doctrine* no man thinketh it lawful; new laws of government what church or commonwealth is there which maketh not either at one time or other.'—HOOKER. 'This seditious, unconstitutional *doctrine* of electing kings is now publickly taught, avowed, and printed.'—BURKE. The *precept* is that which is recommended for practice; 'Pythagoras's first rule directs us to worship the gods, as is ordained by law, for that is the most natural interpretation of the *precept*.'—ADDISON. Both are the subjects of rational assent, and suited only to the matured understanding: *principles* are often admitted without examination; and imbibed as frequently from observation and circumstances, as from any direct personal efforts; children as well as men get *principles*; 'If we had the whole history of zeal, from the days of Cain to our times, we should see it filled with so many scenes of slaughter and bloodshed, as would make a wise man very careful not to suffer himself to be actuated by such a *principle*, when it regards matters of opinion and speculation.'—ADDISON.

DOCTRINE, DOGMA, TENET.

The *doctrine* (*v. Doctrine*) originates with the individual who teaches, in application to all subjects; the *doctrine* is whatever is taught or recommended to the belief of others; the *dogma*, from the Greek δόγμα and δοκέω to think, signifies the thing thought, admitted, or taken for granted; this lies with a body or number of individuals; the *tenet*, from the Latin *teneo* to hold or maintain, signifies the thing held or maintained, and is a species of principle (*v. Doctrine*) specifically maintained in matters of opinion by persons in general.

The *doctrine* rests on the authority of the individual by whom it is framed;

> Unpractis'd he to fawn or seek for power
> By *doctrines* fashion'd to the varying hour;
> Far other aims his heart had learn'd to prize,
> More skill'd to raise the wretch'd, than to rise.
> GOLDSMITH.

The *dogma* rests on the authority of the body by whom it is maintained; 'Our poet was a stoick philosopher, and all his moral sentences are drawn from the *dogmas* of that sect.'—DRYDEN. The *tenet* rests on its own intrinsick merits or demerits; 'One of the puritanical *tenets* was the illegality of all games of chance.'—JOHNSON. Many of the *doctrines* of our blessed Saviour are held by faith in him; they are subjects of persuasion by the exercise of our rational powers: the *dogmas* of the Romish church are admitted by none but such as admit its authority: the *tenets* of republicans, levellers, and freethinkers, have been unblushingly maintained both in publick and private.

TENET, POSITION.

The *tenet* (*v. Doctrine*) is the opinion which we hold in our own minds; the *position* is that which we lay down for others. Our *tenets* may be hurtful, our *positions* false. He who gives up his *tenets* readily evinces an unstable mind; he who argues on a false *position* shows more tenacity and subtlety than good sense. The *tenets* of the different denominations of Christians are scarcely to be known or distinguished; they often rest upon such trivial points; 'The occasion of Luther's being first disgusted with the *tenets* of the Romish church, is known to every one, the least conversant with history.'—ROBERTSON. The *positions* which an author lays down must be very definite and clear when he wishes to build upon them any theory or system; 'To the *position* of Tully, that if virtue could be seen, she must be loved, may be added, that if truth could be heard, she must be obeyed.'—JOHNSON.

THEORY, SPECULATION.

Theory, from the Greek θεάομαι to behold, and *speculation*, from the Latin *speculor* to watch for or espy, are both employed to express what is seen with the mind's eye. *Theory* is the fruit of reflection, it serves the purposes of science; practice will be incomplete when the *theory* is false;

> True piety without cessation tost
> By *theories*, the practice past is lost.—DENHAM.

Speculation belongs more to the imagination; it has therefore less to do with realities: it is that which cannot be reduced to practice, and can therefore never be brought to the test of experience; 'In all these things being fully persuaded that what they did, it was obedience to the will of God, and that all men should do the like; there remained after *speculation* practice whereunto the whole world might be framed.'—HOOKER. Hence it arises that *theory* is contrasted sometimes with the practice to designate its insufficiency to render a man complete;

> True Christianity depends on fact,
> Religion is not *theory*, but act.—HARTE.

And *speculation* is put for that which is fanciful or unreal; 'This is a consideration not to be neglected or thought an indifferent matter of mere *speculation*.'—LESLIE. A general who is so only in *theory* will acquit himself miserably in the field; a religionist who is only so in *speculation* will make a wretched Christian.

OPINION, SENTIMENT, NOTION.

Opinion, in Latin *opinio* from *opinor*, and the Greek ἐπινοέω, to think or judge, is the work of the head; *sentiment*, from *sentio* to feel, is the work of the heart; *notion* (vide *Perception*) is a simple operation of the thinking faculty.

We form *opinions*; we have *sentiments*; we get *notions*. *Opinions* are formed on speculative matters; they are the result of reading, experience, or reflection: *sentiments* are entertained on matters of practice; they are the consequence of habits and circumstances: *notions* are gathered upon sensible objects, and arise out of the casualties of hearing and seeing. We have *opinions* on religion as respects its doctrines; we have *sentiments* on religion as respects its practice and its precepts. The unity of the Godhead in the general sense, and the doctrine of the Trinity in the particular sense, are *opinions*; honour and gratitude towards the Deity, the sense of our dependence upon him, and obligations to him, are *sentiments*.

Opinions are more liable to errour than *sentiments*: the former depend upon knowledge, and must therefore be inaccurate; the latter depend rather upon instinct, and a well organized frame of mind; 'Time wears out the fictions of *opinion*, and doth by degrees discover and unmask that fallacy of ungrounded persuasions, but confirms the dictates and *sentiments* of nature.'—WILKINS. *Notions* are still more liable to errour than either; they are the immatured decisions of the uninformed mind on the appearances of things; 'There is nothing made a more common subject of discourse than nature and its laws, and yet few agree in their *notions* about these words.'—CHEYNE.

The difference of *opinion* among men, on the most important questions of human life, is a sufficient evidence that the mind of man is very easily led astray in matters of *opinion;* 'No, cousin, (said Henry IV. when charged by the Duke of Bouillon with having changed his religion) I have changed no religion, but an *opinion*.'—HOWEL. Whatever difference of *opinion* there may be among Christians, there is but one *sentiment* of love and good-will among those who follow the example of Christ, rather than their own passions; 'There are never great numbers in any nation who can raise a pleasing discourse from their own stock of *sentiments* and images.'—JOHNSON. The *notions* of a Deity are so imperfect among savages in general, that they seem to amount to little more than an indistinct idea of some superiour invisible agent; 'Being we are at this time to speak of the proper *notion* of the church, therefore I shall not look upon it as any more than the sons of men.'—PEARSON.

DEITY, DIVINITY.

Deity, from *Deus* a God, signifies a divine person. *Divinity*, from *divinus*, signifies the *divine* essence or power: the *deities* of the heathens had little of *divinity* in them; 'The first original of the drama was religious worship, consisting only of a chorus, which was nothing else but a hymn to a *Deity*.'—ADDISON. The *divinity* of our Saviour is a fundamental article in the Christian faith;

Why shrinks the soul
Back on herself, and startles at destruction?
'Tis the *divinity* that stirs within us.—ADDISON.

CELESTIAL, HEAVENLY.

Celestial and *heavenly* derive their difference in signification from their different origin; they both literally imply belonging to heaven; but the former, from the Latin *cœlestum*, signifies belonging to the *heaven* of heathens; the latter, which has its origin among believers in the true God, has acquired a superiour sense, in regard to *heaven* as the habitation of the Almighty. This distinction is pretty faithfully observed in their application: *celestial* is applied mostly in the natural sense of the *heavens; heavenly* is employed more commonly in a spiritual sense. Hence we speak of the *celestial* globe as distinguished from the terrestrial, of the *celestial* bodies, of Olympus as the *celestial* abode of Jupiter, of the *celestial* deities;

Twice warn'd by the *celestial* messenger,
The pious prince arose, with hasty fear.—DRYDEN.

Unhappy son! (fair Thetis thus replies,
While tears *celestial* trickle from her eyes.)—POPE.

But on the other hand, of the *heavenly* habitation, of *heavenly* joys or bliss, of *heavenly* spirits and the like. There are doubtless many cases in which *celestial* may be used for *heavenly* in the moral sense;

Thus having said, the hero bound his brows
With leafy branches, then perform'd his vows;
Adoring first the genius of the place,
Then Earth, the mother of the *heavenly* race.
DRYDEN.

But there are cases in which *heavenly* cannot so properly be substituted by *celestial;* 'As the love of heaven makes one *heavenly*, the love of virtue virtuous, so doth the love of the world make one become worldly.'—SIDNEY. *Heavenly* is frequently employed in the sense of superexcellent;

But now he seiz'd Briseis' *heav'nly* charms,
And of my valour's prize defrauds my arms.—POPE.

The poets have also availed themselves of the license to use *celestial* in a similar sense, as occasion might serve.

TO ADORE, WORSHIP.

Adore, in French *adorer*, Latin *adoro*, or *ad* and *oro*, signifies literally to pray to. *Worship*, in Saxon *weorthscype*, is contracted from *worthship*, implying either the object that is worth, or the worth itself; whence it has been employed to designate the action of doing suitable homage to the object which has worth and, by a just distinction, of paying homage to our Maker by religious rites.

Adoration, strictly speaking, is the service of the heart towards a Superiour Being, in which we acknowledge our dependence and obedience, by petition and thanksgiving: *worship* consists in the outward form of showing reverence to some supposed superiour being. *Adoration* can with propriety be paid only to the one true God; 'Menander says, that "God, the Lord and Father of all things, is alone worthy of our humble *adoration*, being at once the maker and giver of all blessings."'—CUMBERLAND. But worship is offered by heathens to stocks and stones;

By reason, man a Godhead can discern,
But how he should be *worship'd* cannot learn.
DRYDEN.

We may *adore* our Maker at all times and in all places, whenever the heart is lifted up towards him; but we *worship* him only at stated times, and according to certain rules; 'Solemn and serviceable *worship* we name, for distinction sake, whatsoever belongeth to the church or publick society of God, by way of external *adoration*.'—HOOKER. Outward signs are but secondary in the act of *adoration;* and in divine *worship* there is often nothing existing but the outward form. We seldom *adore* without *worshipping;* but we too frequently *worship* without *adoring*.

TO ADORE, REVERENCE, VENERATE, REVERE.

Adoration has been before considered only in relation to our Maker; it is here employed in an improper and extended application to express, in the strongest possible manner, the devotion of the mind towards sensible objects: *Reverence*, in Latin *reverentia*, reverence or awe, implies to show reverence, from *revereor*, to stand in awe of: *Venerate*, in Latin *veneratus*, participle of *veneror*, probably from *venere* beauty, signifying to hold in very high esteem for its superiour qualities: *revere* is another form of the same verb.

Reverence is equally engendered by the contemplation of superiority in a being, whether of the Supreme Being, as our Creator, or any earthly being as our parent. It differs, however, from *adoration*, in as much as it has a mixture of fear arising from the consciousness of weakness and dependence, or of obligation for favours received; 'The fear acceptable to God, is a filial fear, an awful *reverence* of the Divine Nature, proceeding from a just esteem for his perfections, which produces in us an inclination to his service, and an unwillingness to offend him.'—ROGERS.

To *revere* and *venerate* are applied only to human beings, and that not so much from the relation we stand in to them, as from their characters and endowments; on which account these two latter terms are applicable to inanimate as well as animate objects.

Adoration in this case, as in the former, essentially requires no external form of expression; it is best expressed by the devotion of the individual to the service of him whom he *adores;* '"There is no end of his greatness." The most exalted creature he has made is only capable of *adoring* it; none but himself can comprehend it.'—ADDISON. *Reverencing* our Maker is altogether an inward feeling; but *reverencing* our parents includes in it an outward expression of our sentiments by our deportment towards them;

The war protracted, and the siege delay'd,
Were due to Hector's and this hero's hand;
Both brave alike, and equal in command;
Æneas, not inferiour in the field,
In pious *reverence* to the gods excell'd.—DRYDEN

Revering and *venerating* are confined to the breast of the individual, but they may sometimes display themselves in suitable acts of homage.

Good princes are frequently *adored* by their subjects: it is a part of the Christian character to *reverence* our spiritual pastors and masters, as well as all temporal authorities; 'It seems to be remarkable that death increases our *veneration* for the good, and extenuates our hatred of the bad.'—JOHNSON. We ought to *venerate* all truly good men while living, and to *revere* their memories when they are dead;

And had not men the hoary head *rever'd*,
And boys paid *reverence* when a man appear'd,
Both must have died, though richer skins they wore,
And saw more heaps of acorns in their store.
CREECH.

OFFERING, OBLATION.

Offering, from *offer*, and *oblation*, from *oblatio* and *oblatus* or *oflatus*, come both from *offero* (*v. To offer*): the former is however a term of much more general and familiar use than the latter. *Offerings* are both moral and religious; *oblation*, in the proper sense, is religious only; the money which is put into the sacramental plate is an *offering*; the consecrated bread and wine at the sacrament is an *oblation*. The *offering*, in a religious sense, is whatever one *offers* as a gift by way of reverence to a superiour;

They are polluted *offerings*, more abhorr'd
Than spotted livers in the sacrifice.
SHAKSPEARE.

The winds to heav'n the curling vapours bore,
Ungrateful *off'ring* to the immortal pow'rs,
Whose wrath hung heavy o'er the Trojan tow'rs.
POPE.

The *oblation* is the *offering* which is accompanied with some particular ceremony; 'Many conceive in the *oblation* of Jephtha's daughter, not a natural but a civil kind of death.'—BROWN. The wise men made an *offering* to our Saviour; but not properly an *oblation*; the Jewish sacrifices, as in general all religious sacrifices, were in the proper sense *oblations*. The term *oblation*, in a figurative sense, may be as generally applied as *offering*;

Ye mighty princes, your *oblations* bring,
And pay due honours to your awful king.—PITT.

The kind *oblation* of a falling tear.—DRYDEN.

MALEDICTION, CURSE, IMPRECATION, EXECRATION, ANATHEMA.

Malediction, from *malè* and *dico*, signifies a saying ill, that is, declaring an evil wish against a person: *curse*, in Saxon *kursian*, comes in all probability from the Greek κυρόω, to sanction or ratify, signifying a bad wish declared upon oath, or in a solemn manner: *imprecation*, from *im* and *preco*, signifies a praying down evil upon a person: *execration*, from the Latin *execror*, that is, *è sacris excludere*, signifies the same as to excommunicate, with every form of solemn *imprecation*: *anathema*, in Greek ἀνάθεμα, signifies a setting out, that is, a putting out of a religious community by way of penance.

The *malediction* is the most indefinite and general term, signifying simply the declaration of evil: *curse* is a solemn denunciation of evil: the former is employed mostly by men; the latter by God or man: the rest are species of the *curse* pronounced only by man. The *malediction* is caused by simple anger: the *curse* is occasioned by some grievous offence: men, in the heat of their passions, will utter *maledictions* against any object that offends them; 'With many praises of his good play, and many *maledictions* on the power of chance, he took up the cards and threw them in the fire.'—MACKENZIE. God pronounced a *curse* upon Adam, and all his posterity, after the fall;

But know, that ere your promis'd walls you build,
My *curses* shall severely be fulfill'd.—DRYDEN.

The *curse* differs in the degree of evil pronounced or wished; the *imprecation* and *execration* always imply some positive great evil, and, in fact, as much evil as can be conceived by man in his anger; 'Thus either host their *imprecations* join'd.'—POPE. The *anathema* respects the evil which is pronounced according to the canon law, by which a man is not only put out of the church, but held up as an object of offence. The *malediction* is altogether an unallowed expression of private resentment; the *curse* was admitted, in some cases, according to the Mosaic law; and that, as well as the *anathema*, at one time formed a part of the ecclesiastical discipline of the Christian church; 'The bare *anathemas* of the church fall like so many *bruta fulmina* upon the obstinate and schismatical.'—SOUTH. The *imprecation* formed a part of the heathenish ceremony of religion, whereby they invoked the Diræ to bring down every evil on the heads of their enemies. They had different formulas of speech for different occasions, as to an enemy on his departure; 'Abeas nunquam rediturus.' Mela informs us that the Abrantes, a people of Africa, used to salute the rising and setting sun after this manner.

The *execration* is always the informal expression of the most violent personal anger; 'I have seen in Bedlam a man that has held up his face in a posture of adoration towards heaven to utter *execrations* and blasphemies.'—STEELE.

TEMPLE, CHURCH.

These words designate an edifice destined for the exercise of religion, but with collateral ideas, which sufficiently distinguish them from each other. The *templum* of the *Latin* signified originally an open elevated spot marked out by the augurs with their *lituus*, or sacred wand, whence they could best survey the heavens on all sides; the idea, therefore, of spacious, open, and elevated, enters into the meaning of this word in the same manner as it does in the Hebrew word היכל, derived from הכל, which in the Arabick signifies great and lofty. The Greek ναὸς, from ναίω to inhabit, signifies a dwelling-place, and by distinction the dwelling-place of the Almighty, in which sense the Hebrew word is also taken to denote the high and holy place where Jehovah peculiarly dwelleth, otherwise called the *holy heavens*, Jehovah's dwelling or resting-place; whence St. Paul calls our bodies the *temples* of God when the spirit of God dwelleth in us. The Roman poets used the word *templum* in a similar sense;

——— Cœli tonitralia templa.—LUCRET. (Lib. I.)

Qui templa cœli summa sonitu concutit.
TERENT. (*Eun.*)

Contremuit templum magnum Jovis altitonantis.
ENNIUS.

The word *temple*, therefore, strictly signifies a spacious open place set apart for the peculiar presence and worship of the Divine Being, and is applied with peculiar propriety to the sacred edifices of the Jews.

Church, which, through the medium of the Saxon circe, cyric, and the German *kirche*, is derived from the Greek κυριακὸς, signifying literally what belonged to κύριος, the Lord; whence it became a word among the earliest Christians for the Lord's Supper, the Lord's day, the Lord's house, and also for an assembly of the faithful, and is still used in the two latter meanings; 'That *churches* were consecrated unto none but the Lord only, the very general name chiefly doth sufficiently show; *church* doth signify no other thing than the Lord's house.'—HOOKER. 'The *church* being a supernatural society, doth differ from natural societies in this; that the persons unto whom we associate ourselves in the one, are men simply considered as men; but they to whom we be joined in the other, are God, angels, and holy men.'—HOOKER. The word *church*, having acquired a specifick meaning, is never used by the poets, or in a general application like the word *temple*; 'Here we have no *temple* but the wood, no assembly but horn-beasts.'—SHAKSPEARE. On the other hand, it has a diversity of particular meanings; being taken sometimes in the sense of the ecclesiastical power in distinction from the state, sometimes for holy orders, &c.

TO DEDICATE, DEVOTE, CONSECRATE, HALLOW.

Dedicate, in Latin *dedicatus*, participle from *de* and *dico*, signifies to set apart by a promise; *devote*, in Latin *devotus*, participle from *devoveo*, signifies to vow for an express purpose; *consecrate*, in Latin *consecratus*, from *consecro* or *con* and *sacro*, signifies to make sacred by a special act; *hallow* from *holy*, or the German *heilig*, signifies to make holy.

There is something more positive in the act of *dedicating* than in that of *devoting*; but less so than in that of *consecrating*.

To *dedicate* and *devote* may be employed in both temporal and spiritual matters; to *consecrate* and *hallow* only in the spiritual sense: we may *dedicate* or *devote* any thing that is at our disposal to the service of some object; but the former is employed mostly in regard to superiours, and the latter to persons without distinction of rank: we *dedicate* a house to the service of God;

> Warn'd by the seer, to her offended name
> We raise and *dedicate* this wond'rous frame.
> DRYDEN.

Or we *devote* our time to the benefit of our friends, or the relief of the poor; 'Gilbert West settled himself in a very pleasant house at Wickham in Kent, where he *devoted* himself to piety.'—JOHNSON. We may *dedicate* or *devote* ourselves to an object; but the former always implies a solemn setting apart, springing from a sense of duty; the latter an entire application of one's self from zeal and affection; in this manner he who *dedicates* himself to God abstracts himself from every object which is not immediately connected with the service of God; he who *devotes* himself to the ministry pursues it as the first object of his attention and regard: such a *dedication* of ourself is hardly consistent with our other duties as members of society; but a *devotion* of one's powers, one's time, and one's knowledge to the spread of religion among men is one of the most honourable and sacred kinds of *devotion*.

To *consecrate* is a species of formal *dedication* by virtue of a religious observance; it is applicable mostly to places and things connected with religious works; 'The greatest conqueror in this holy nation did not only compose the words of his divine odes, but generally set them to musick himself; after which his works, though they were *consecrated* to the tabernacle, became the national entertainment.'—ADDISON. *Hallow* is a species of informal *consecration* applied to the same objects: the church is *consecrated; particular days are hallowed;*

> Without the walls a ruin'd temple stands,
> To Ceres *hallowed* once.—DRYDEN.

FORM, CEREMONY, RITE, OBSERVANCE.

Form in this sense respects the *form* or manner of the action; *ceremony*, in Latin *ceremonia*, is supposed to signify the rites of Ceres; *rite*, in Latin *ritus*, is probably changed from *ratus*, signifying a custom that is esteemed; *observance* signifies the thing observed.

All these terms are employed with regard to particular modes of action in civil society. *Form* is here the most general in its sense and application; *ceremony*, *rite*, and *observance* are particular kinds of *form*, suited to particular occasions. *Form*, in its distinct application, respects all modes of acting and speaking, that are adopted by society at large, in every transaction of life; *ceremony* respects those *forms* of outward behaviour which are made the expressions of respect and deference; *rite* and *observance* are applied to national *ceremonies* in matters of religion. A certain *form* is requisite for the sake of order, method, and decorum, in every social matter, whether in affairs of state, in a court of law, in a place of worship, or in the private intercourse of friends. So long as distinctions are admitted in society, and men are agreed to express their sentiments of regard and respect to each other, it will be necessary to preserve the *ceremonies* of politeness which have been established. Every country has adopted certain *rites* founded upon its peculiar religious faith, and prescribed certain *observances* by which individuals could make a publick profession of their faith. Administering oaths by the magistrate is a necessary *form* in law; 'A long table and a square table, or seat about the walls, seem things of *form*, but are things of substance; for at a long table, a few at the upper end, in effect, sway all the business; but in the other *form*, there is more use of the counsellors' opinions that sit lower.'—BACON. Kissing the king's hand is a *ceremony* practised at court;

> And what have kings that privates have not too,
> Save *ceremony*?—SHAKSPEARE.

Baptism is one *rite* of initiation into the Christian church, and confirmation another; prayer, reading the Scriptures, and preaching are different religious *observances*.

As respects religion, the *form* is the established practice, comprehending the *rite*, *ceremony*, and *observance*, but the word is mostly applied to that which is external, and suited for a community; 'He who affirmeth speech to be necessary among all men throughout the world doth not thereby import that all men must necessarily speak one language; even so the necessity of polity and regimen in all churches may be held without holding any one certain *form* to be necessary in them all.'—HOOKER. The *ceremony* may be said either of an individual or a community; the *rite* is said only of a community; the *observance*, more properly of the individual either in publick or private. The *ceremony* of kneeling during the time of prayer is the most becoming posture for a suppliant, whether in publick or private;

> Bring her up to the high altar, that she may
> The sacred *ceremonies* there partake.—SPENSER

The discipline of a Christian church consists in its *rites*, to which every member, either as a layman or a priest, is obliged to conform;

> Live thou to mourn thy love's unhappy fate,
> To bear my mangled body from the foe,
> Or buy it back, and fun'ral *rites* bestow.—DRYDEN.

Publick worship is an *observance* which no Christian thinks himself at liberty to neglect; 'Incorporated minds will always feel some inclination towards exteriour acts and ritual *observances*.'—JOHNSON.

It betrays either gross ignorance or wilful impertinence, in the man who sets at nought any of the established *forms* of society, particularly in religious matters; 'You may discover tribes of men without policy, or laws, or cities, or any of the arts of life; but no where will you find them without some *form* of religion.'—BLAIR. When *ceremonies* are too numerous, they destroy the ease of social intercourse; but the absence of *ceremony* destroys all decency; 'Not to use *ceremonies* at all, is to teach others not to use them again, and so diminish respect to himself.'—BACON. In publick worship the excess of *ceremony* is apt to extinguish the warmth and spirit of devotion; but the want of *ceremony* deprives it of all solemnity.

LORD'S SUPPER, EUCHARIST, COMMUNION, SACRAMENT.

The *Lord's supper* is a term of familiar and general use among Christians, as designating in literal terms the supper of our Lord; that is, either the last solemn supper which he took with his disciples previous to his crucifixion, or the commemoration of that event which conformably to his commands has been observed by the professors of Christianity; 'To the worthy participation of the *Lord's supper*, there is indispensably required a suitable preparation.'—SOUTH. *Eucharist* is a term of peculiar use among the Roman Catholicks, from the Greek ἐυχαρίζω to give thanks, because personal adoration, by way of returning thanks, constitutes in their estimation the chief part of the ceremony; 'This ceremony of feasting belongs most properly both to marriage and to the *eucharist*, as both of them have the nature of a covenant.'—SOUTH. As the social affections are kept alive mostly by the common participation of meals, so is brotherly love, the essence of Christian fellowship, cherished and warmed in the highest degree by the common participation in this holy festival: hence, by distinction, it has been denominated the *communion*; 'One woman he could not bring to the *communion*, and when he reproved or exhorted her, she only answered that she was no scholar.'—JOHNSON. As the vows which are made at the altar of our Lord are the most solemn which a Christian can make, comprehending in them the entire devotion of himself to Christ, the general term *sacrament*, signifying an oath, has been employed by way of emphasis for this ordinance; 'I could not have the consent of the physicians to go to church yesterday; I therefore received the holy *sacrament* at home.'—JOHNSON. The Roman Catholicks have employed the same term to six other ordinances; but the Protestants, who attach a similar degree of sacredness to no other than baptism, annex this appellation only to these two.

MARRIAGE, WEDDING, NUPTIALS.

Marriage, from to *marry*, denotes the act of *marrying*; *wedding* and *nuptials* denote the ceremony of being *married*. As *marry*, in French *marrier*, comes from the Latin *marito* to be joined to a male; hence *marriage* comprehends the act of choosing and being legally bound to a man or a woman: *wedding*, from *wed*, and the Teutonick *wetten*, to promise or betroth, implies the ceremony of *marrying*, inasmuch as it is binding upon the parties. *Nuptials* comes from the Latin *nubo* to veil, because the Roman ladies were veiled at the time of *marriage*: hence the word has been put for the whole ceremony itself. *Marriage* is a general term, which conveys no collateral meaning. *Marriage* is an institution which, by those who have been blessed with the light of Divine revelation, has always been considered as sacred;

> O fatal maid! thy *marriage* is endow'd
> With Phrygian, Latian, and Rutulian blood.
> DRYDEN.

Wedding has always a reference to the ceremony; with some persons, particularly among the lower orders of society, the day of their *wedding* is converted into a day of riot and intemperance; 'Ask any one how he has been employed to-day: he will tell you, perhaps, I have been at the ceremony of taking the manly robe: this friend invited me to a *wedding*; that desired me to attend the hearing of his cause.'—MELMOTH (*Letters of Pliny*). *Nuptials* may either be used in a general or particular import; among the Roman Catholicks in England it is a practice for them to have their *nuptials* solemnized by a priest of their own persuasion as well as by the Protestant clergyman;

> Fir'd with disdain for Turnus dispossess'd,
> And the new *nuptials* of the Trojan guest.—DRYDEN.

MARRIAGE, MATRIMONY, WEDLOCK.

Marriage (*v. Marriage*) is oftener an act than a state; *matrimony* and *wedlock* both describe states.

Marriage is taken in the sense of an act, when we speak of the laws of *marriage*, the day of one's *marriage*, the congratulations upon one's *marriage*, a happy or unhappy *marriage*, &c.; '*Marriage* is rewarded with some honourable distinctions which celibacy is forbidden to usurp.'—JOHNSON. It is taken in the sense of a state, when we speak of the pleasures or pains of *marriage*; but in this latter case, *matrimony*, which signifies a married life abstractedly from all agents or acting persons, is preferable; so likewise, to think of *matrimony*, and to enter into the holy state of *matrimony*, are expressions founded upon the signification of the term. As *matrimony* is derived from *mater* a mother, because *married* women are in general mothers, it has particular reference to the domestick state of the two parties; broils are but too frequently the fruits of *matrimony*, yet there are few cases in which they might not be obviated by the good sense of those who are engaged in them. Hasty *marriages* cannot be expected to produce happiness; young people who are eager for *matrimony* before they are fully aware of its consequences will purchase their experience at the expense of their peace; 'As love generally produces *matrimony*, so it often happens that *matrimony* produces love.'—SPECTATOR.

Wedlock is the old English word for *matrimony*, and is in consequence admitted in law, when one speaks of children born in *wedlock*; agreeably to its derivation it has a reference to the bond of union which follows the *marriage*: hence one speaks of living happily in a state of *wedlock*, of being joined in holy *wedlock*; 'The men who would make good husbands, if they visit publick places, are frighted at *wedlock* and resolve to live single.'—JOHNSON.

FUNERAL, OBSEQUIES.

Funeral, in Latin *funus*, is derived from *funis* a cord, because lighted cords, or torches, were carried before the bodies which were interred by night; the *funeral*, therefore, denotes the ordinary solemnity which attends the consignment of a body to the grave. *Obsequies*, in Latin *exæquiæ*, are both derived from *sequor*, which, in its compound sense, signifies to perform or execute; they comprehend, therefore, *funerals* attended with more than ordinary solemnity.

We speak of the *funeral* as the last sad office which we perform for a friend; it is accompanied by nothing but by mourning and sorrow;

> That pluck'd my nerves, those tender strings of life,
> Which, pluck'd a little more, will toll the bell
> That calls my few friends to my *funeral*.—YOUNG.

We speak of the *obsequies* as the tribute of respect which can be paid to the person of one who was high in station or publick esteem;

> His body shall be royally interr'd.
> I will, myself,
> Be the chief mourner at his *obsequies*.—DRYDEN

The *funeral*, by its frequency, becomes so familiar an object that it passes by unheeded; the *obsequies* which are performed over the remains of the great, attract our notice from the pomp and grandeur with which they are conducted. The *funeral* is performed for one immediately after his decease; but the *obsequies* may be performed at any period afterward, and in this sense is not confined alone to the great;

> Some in the flow'r-strewn grave the corpse have lay'd
> And annual *obsequies* around it paid.—JENYNS.

BURIAL, INTERMENT, SEPULTURE.

Burial, from *bury*, in Saxon *birian*, *birigan*, German *bergen*, signifies, in the original sense, to conceal *Interment*, from *inter*, compounded of *in* and *terra*, signifies the putting into the ground. *Sepulture*, in French *sepulture*, Latin *sepultura*, from *sepultus*, participle of *sepelio* to *bury*, comes from *sepes* a hedge, signifying an enclosure, and probably likewise from the Hebrew שבת to put to rest, or in a state of privacy.

Under *burial* is comprehended simply the purpose of the action; under *interment* and *sepulture*, the manner as well as the motive of the action. We *bury* in order to conceal; 'Among our Saxon ancestors, the dead bodies of such as were slain in the field were not laid in graves; but lying upon the ground were covered with turves or clods of earth, and the more in reputation the persons had been, the greater and higher were the turves raised over their bodies. This some used to call *biriging*, some *beorging* of the dead; all being one thing though differently pronounced, and from whence we yet retain our speech of *burying* the dead, that is, hiding the dead.'—VERSTEGAN *Interment* and *sepulture* are accompanied with religious ceremonies.

**Bury* is confined to no object or place; we *bury* whatever we deposite in the earth, and wherever we please;

> When he lies along
> After your way his tale pronounc'd, shall *bury*
> His reasons with his body.—SHAKSPEARE.

But *interment* and *sepulture* respect only the bodies of the deceased when deposited in a sacred place. *Burial* requires that the object be concealed under ground; *interment* may be used for depositing in vaults. Self-murderers are *buried* in the highways; Christians in general are *buried* in the church-yard;

> If you have kindness left, there see me laid;
> To *bury* decently the injur'd maid
> Is all the favour.—WALLER.

The kings of England were formerly *interred* in Westminster Abbey;

> His body shall be royally *interr'd*,
> And the last funeral pomps adorn his hearse.
> DRYDEN.

Burial is a term in familiar use; *interment* serves frequently as a more elegant expression;

> But good Æneas ordered on the shore
> A stately tomb, whose top a trumpet bore;
> Thus was his friend *interr'd*, and deathless fame
> Still to the lofty cape consigns his name.—DRYDEN.

Sepulture is an abstract term confined to particular cases, as in speaking of the rights and privileges of *sepulture*;

> Ah! leave me not for Grecian dogs to tear.
> The common rites of *sepulture* bestow;
> To sooth a father's and a mother's wo;
> Let their large gifts procure an urn at least,
> And Hector's ashes in his country rest.—POPE

* Vide Trusler: "To bury, inter"

Interment and *sepulture* never depart from their religious import; *bury* is used figuratively for other objects and purposes. A man is said to *bury* himself alive who shuts himself out from the world; he is said to *bury* the talent of which he makes no use, or to *bury* in oblivion what he does not wish to call to mind;

> This is the way to make the city flat
> And *bury* all, which yet distinctly ranges
> In heaps and piles of ruin.—SHAKSPEARE.

Inter is on one occasion applied by Shakspeare also to other objects;

> The evil that men do lives after them,
> The good is oft *interred* with their bones.
> SHAKSPEARE.

BEATIFICATION, CANONIZATION.

These are two acts emanating from the pontifical authority, by which the Pope declares a person, whose life has been exemplary and accompanied with miracles, as entitled to enjoy eternal happiness after his death, and determines in consequence the sort of worship which should be paid to him.

In the act of *beatification* the Pope pronounces only as a private person, and uses his own authority only in granting to certain persons, or to a religious order, the privilege of paying a particular worship to a *beatified* object.

In the act of *canonization*, the Pope speaks as a judge after a judicial examination on the state, and decides the sort of worship which ought to be paid by the whole church.

FEAST, FESTIVAL, HOLIDAY.

Feast, in Latin *festum*, or *festus*, changed most probably from *fesiæ*, or *feriæ*, which, in all probability, comes from the Greek ἱερὸς, sacred, because these days were kept sacred or vacant from all secular labour: *festival* and *holiday*, as the words themselves denote, have precisely the same meaning in their original sense, with this difference, that the former derives its origin from heathenish superstition, the latter owes its rise to the establishment of Christianity in its reformed state.

A *feast*, in the Christian sense of the word, is applied to every day, except Sundays, which are regarded as sacred, and observed with particular solemnity; a *holyday*, or, according to its modern orthography, a *holiday*, is simply a day on which the ordinary business is suspended: among the Roman Catholicks, there are many days which are kept holy, and consequently by them denominated *feasts*, which in the English reformed church are only observed as *holidays*, or days of exemption from publick business; of this description are the Saints' days, on which the publick offices are shut: on the other hand, Christmas, Easter, and Whitsuntide, are regarded in both churches more as *feasts* than as *holidays*.

Feast, as a technical term, is applied only to certain specified *holidays*;

> First, I provide myself a nimble thing,
> To be my page, a varlet of all crafts;
> Next, two new suits for *feasts* and gala days.
> CUMBERLAND.

A *holiday* is an indefinite term, it may be employed for any day or time in which there is a suspension of business; there are, therefore, many *feasts* where there are no *holidays*, and many *holidays* where there are no *feasts*: a *feast* is altogether sacred; a *holiday* has frequently nothing sacred in it, not even in its cause; it may be a simple, ordinary transaction, the act of an individual;

> It happen'd on a summer's *holiday*,
> That to the green wood shade he took his way.
> DRYDEN.

A *festival* has always either a sacred or a serious object; 'In so enlightened an age as the present, I shall perhaps be ridiculed if I hint, as my opinion, that the observation of certain *festivals* is something more than a mere political institution.'—WALPOLE. A *feast* is kept by religious worship; a *holiday* is kept by idleness; 'Many worthy persons urged how great the harmony was between the *holidays* and their attributes (if I may call them so), and what a confusion would follow if Michaelmas-day, for instance, was not to be celebrated when stubble geese are in their highest perfection.'—WALPOLE. A *festival* is kept by mirth and festivity: some *feasts* are *festivals*, as in the case of the carnival at Rome; some *festivals* are *holidays*, as in the case of weddings and publick thanksgivings.

CLERGYMAN, PARSON, PRIEST, MINISTER.

Clergyman, altered from *clerk*, *clericus*, signified any one holding a regular office, and by distinction one who held the holy office; *parson* is either changed from *person*, that is, by distinction the person who spiritually presides over a parish, or contracted from *parochianus*; *priest*, in German, &c. *priester*, is contracted from *presbyter*, in Greek πρεσβυτερος, signifying an elder who holds the sacerdotal office; *minister*, in Latin *minister*, a servant, from *minus*, less or inferior, signifies literally one who performs a subordinate office, and has been extended in its meaning, to signify generally one who officiates or performs an office.

The word *clergyman* applies to such as are regularly bred according to the forms of the national religion, and applies to none else. In this sense we speak of the English, the French, and Scotch *clergy*, without distinction; 'By a *clergyman* I mean one in holy orders.'—STEELE. 'To the time of Edward III. it is probable that the French and English languages subsisted together throughout the kingdom; the higher orders, both of the *clergy* and laity, speaking almost universally French; the lower retaining the use of their native tongue.'—TYRWHITT. A *parson* is a species of *clergyman*, who ranks the highest in the three orders of inferiour *clergy*; that is, *parson*, vicar, and curate; the *parson* being a technical term for the rector, or him who holds the living: in its technical sense it has now acquired a definite use; but in general conversation it is become almost a nickname. The word *clergyman* is always substituted for *parson* in polite society. When *priest* respects the Christian religion it is a species of *clergyman*, that is, one who is ordained to officiate at the altar in distinction from the deacon, who is only an assistant to the *priest*. But the term *priest* has likewise an extended meaning in reference to such as hold the sacerdotal character in any form of religion, as the *priests* of the Jews, or those of the Greeks, Romans, Indians, and the like; 'Call a man a *priest*, or *parson*, and you set him in some men's esteem ten degrees below his own servant.'—SOUTH. A *minister* is one who actually or habitually officiates. *Clergymen* are therefore not always strictly *ministers*; nor are all *ministers clergymen*. If a *clergyman* delegates his functions altogether he is not a *minister*; nor is he who presides over a dissenting congregation a *clergyman*. In the former case, however, it would be invidious to deprive the *clergyman* of the name of *minister* of the gospel, but in the latter case it is a misuse of the term *clergyman* to apply it to any *minister* who does not officiate according to the form of an established religion;

> With leave and honour enter our abodes,
> Ye sacred *ministers* of men and gods.—POPE.

BISHOPRICK, DIOCESS.

Bishoprick, compounded of *bishop* and *rick* or *reich* empire, signifies the empire or government of a bishop: *Diocess*, in Greek διοίχησις, compounded of διὰ and οικέω, signifies an administration throughout.

Both these words describe the extent of an episcopal jurisdiction; the first with relation to the person who officiates, the second with relation to the charge. There may, therefore, be a *bishoprick*, either where there are many *diocesses* or no *diocess*;* but according to the import of the term, there is properly no *diocess* where there is no *bishoprick*. When the jurisdiction is merely titular, as in countries where the Catholick religion is not recognised, it is a *bishoprick*, but not a *diocess*. On the other hand, the *bishoprick* of Rome or that of an archbishop comprehends all the *diocesses* of the subordinate bishops. Hence it arises that when we speak of the ecclesiastical distribution of a country, we term the divisions *bishopricks*; but when we speak

* Girard: "Beatification, canonization."

of the actual office, we term it a *diocess*. England is divided into a certain number of *bishopricks*, not *diocesses*. Every bishop visits his *diocess*, not his *bishoprick*, at stated intervals.

ECCLESIASTICK, DIVINE, THEOLOGIAN.

An *ecclesiastick* derives his title from the office which he bears in the *ecclesia* or church; a *divine* and *theologian* from their pursuit after, or engagement in, *divine* or *theological* matters. An *ecclesiastick* is connected with an episcopacy; a *divine* or *theologian* is not essentially connected with any form of church government.

An *ecclesiastick* need not in his own person perform any office, although he fills a station: a *divine* not only fills a station, but actually performs the office of teaching; a *theologian* neither fills any particular station, nor discharges any specifick duty, but merely follows the pursuit of studying *theology*. An *ecclesiastick* is not always a *divine*, nor a *divine* an *ecclesiastick;* a *divine* is always more or less a *theologian*, but every *theologian* is not a *divine*.

Among the Roman Catholicks all monks, and in the Church of England the various dignitaries who perform the episcopal functions, are entitled *ecclesiasticks;* 'Our old English monks seldom let any of their kings depart in peace, who had endeavoured to diminish the power or wealth of which the *ecclesiasticks* were in those times possessed.'—ADDISON. There are but few denominations of Christians who have not appointed teachers who are called *divines;* 'Nor shall I dwell on our excellence in metaphysical speculations; because, he that reads the works of our *divines* will easily discover how far human subtilty has been able to penetrate.'—JOHNSON. Professors or writers on *theology* are peculiarly denominated *theologians;* 'I looked on that sermon (of Dr. Price's) as the publick declaration of a man much connected with literary caballers, intriguing philosophers, and political *theologians*.'—BURKE.

CLOISTER, CONVENT, MONASTERY.

Cloister, in French * *cloître*, from the word *clos* close, signifies a certain close place in a *convent*, or an enclosure of houses for canons, or in general a religious house; *convent*, from the Latin *conventus*, a meeting, and *convenio* to come together, signifies a religious assembly; *monastery*, in French *monastère*, signifies a habitation for monks, from the Greek *μόνος* alone.

The proper idea of *cloister* is that of seclusion; the proper idea of *convent* is that of community; the proper idea of a *monastery* is that of solitude. One is shut up in a *cloister*, put into a *convent*, and retires to a *monastery*.

Whoever wishes to take an absolute leave of the world, shuts himself up in a *cloister;*

> Some solitary *cloister* will I choose,
> And there with holy virgins live immur'd.
> DRYDEN.

Whoever wishes to attach himself to a community that has renounced all commerce with the world, goes into a *convent;* 'Nor were the new abbots less industrious to stock their *convents* with foreigners.'—TYRWHITT. Whoever wishes to shun all human intercourse retires to a *monastery;* 'I drove my suitor to forswear the full stream of the world, and to live in a nook merely *monastick*.'—SHAKSPEARE.

In the *cloister* our liberty is sacrificed: in the *convent* our worldly habits are renounced, and those of a regular religious community being adopted, we submit to the yoke of established orders: in a *monastery* we impose a sort of voluntary exile upon ourselves; we live with the view of living only to God.

In the ancient and true *monasteries*, the members divided their time between contemplation and labour; but as population increased, and towns multiplied, *monasteries* were, properly speaking, succeeded by *convents*.

In ordinary discourse, *cloister* is employed in an absolute and indefinite manner: we speak of the *cloister* to designate a *monastick* state; as entering a *cloister;* burying one's self in a *cloister;* penances and mortifications are practised in a *cloister;* but it is not the same thing when we speak of the *cloister* of the Benedictines and of their *monastery;* or the *cloister* of the Capuchins and their *convent*.

* Vide Abbe Roubaud: "Cloître, convent, monastère."

CONVERT, PROSELYTE.

Convert, from the Latin *converto*, signifies changed to something in conformity with the views of another; *proselyte*, from the Greek *προσήλυτος* and *προσέρχομαι*, signifies come over to the side of another.

Convert is more extensive in its sense and application than *proselyte: convert* in its full sense includes every change of opinion, without respect to the subject; *proselyte* in its strict sense refers only to changes from one religious belief to another: there are many *converts* to particular doctrines of Christianity, and *proselytes* from the Pagan, Jewish, or Mahomedan, to the Christian faith: there are political as well as religious *converts*, who could not with the same strict propriety be termed *proselytes*.

Conversion is a more voluntary act than *proselytism*, it emanates entirely from the mind of the agent, independent of foreign influence; it extends not merely to the abstract or speculative opinions of the individual, but to the whole current of his feelings and spring of his actions: it is the *conversion* of the heart and soul. *Proselytism* is an outward act, which need not extend beyond the conformity of one's words and actions to a certain rule; *convert* is therefore always taken in a good sense: it bears on the face of it the stamp of sincerity; 'A believer may be excused by the most hardened atheist for endeavouring to make him a *convert*, because he does it with an eye to both their interests.'—ADDISON. *Proselyte* is a term of more ambiguous meaning; the *proselyte* is often the creature and tool of a party; there may be many *proselytes* where there are no *converts;* 'False teachers commonly make use of base, and low, and temporal considerations, of little tricks and devices, to make disciples and gain *proselytes*.'—TILLOTSON.

The *conversion* of a sinner is the work of God's grace, either by his special interposition, or by the ordinary influence of his Holy Word on the heart; it is an act of great presumption, therefore, in those men who rest so strongly on their own particular modes and forms in bringing about this great work: they may without any breach of charity be suspected of rather wishing to make *proselytes* to their own party.

TO TRANSFIGURE, TRANSFORM, METAMORPHOSE.

Transfigure is to make to pass over into another figure; *transform* and *metamorphose* is to put into another form: the former being said mostly of spiritual beings, and particularly in reference to our Saviour; the other two terms being applied to that which has a corporeal form.

Transformation is commonly applied to that which changes its outward form; in this manner a harlequin *transforms* himself into all kinds of shapes and likenesses;

> Something you have heard
> Of Hamlet's *transformation;* so I call it,
> Since not the exteriour, nor the inward man
> Resembles what it was.—SHAKSPEARE.

Sometimes however the word is applied to moral objects: 'Can a good intention, or rather a very wicked one so miscalled, *transform* perjury and hypocrisy into merit and perfection?'—SOUTH. *Metamorphosis* is applied to the form internal as well as external, that is, to the whole nature; in this manner Ovid describes among others, the *metamorphoses* of Narcissus into a flower, and Daphne into a laurel: with the same idea we may speak of a rustick being *metamorphosed*, by the force of art, into a fine gentleman; 'A lady's shift may be *metamorphosed* into billets-doux, and come into her possession a second time.'—ADDISON. *Transfiguration* is frequently taken for a painting of our Saviour's *transfiguration;* 'We have of this gentleman a piece of the *transfiguration*, which I think is held a work second to none in the world.'—STEELE.

PRAYER, PETITION, REQUEST, ENTREATY, SUIT.

Prayer, from the Latin *preco*, and the Greek παρὰ and εὔχομαι to pray, is a general term, including the common idea of application to some person for any favour to be granted; *petition*, from *peto* to seek; *request*, from the Latin *requisitus* and *requiro*, or *re*, and *quæro* to look after, or seek for with desire; *entreaty*, from the French *en* and *traiter*, signifying to act upon; *suit*, from *sue*, in French *suivre*, Latin *sequor* to follow after; denote different modes of *prayer*, varying in the circumstances of the action and the object acted upon.

The *prayer* is made more commonly to the Supreme Being; the *petition* is made more generally to one's fellow-creatures; we may, however, *pray* our fellow-creatures, and *petition* our Creator: the *prayer* is made for every thing which is of the first importance to us as living beings; the *petition* is made for that which may satisfy our desires: hence our *prayers* to the Almighty respect all our circumstances as moral and responsible agents; our *petitions* respect the temporary circumstances of our present existence. When the term *prayer* is applied to one's fellow-creatures it carries with it the idea of earnestness and submission; '*Prayer* among men is supposed a means to change the person to whom we *pray;* but *prayer* to God doth not change him, but fits us to receive the things *prayed* for.'—Stillingfleet.

Torture him with thy softness,
Nor till thy *prayers* are granted set him free.
Otway.

The *petition* and *request* are alike made to our fellow-creatures; but the former is a publick act, in which many express their wishes to the Supreme Authority; the latter is an individual act between men in their private relations; the people *petition* the king or the parliament; a school of boys *petition* their master;

She takes *petitions*, and dispenses laws,
Hears and determines every private cause.
Dryden.

A child makes a *request* to its parent; one friend makes a *request* to another;

Thus spoke Ilioneus; the Trojan crew,
With cries and clamours his *request* renew.
Dryden.

The *request* marks an equality, but the *entreaty* defines no condition; it differs, however, from the former in the nature of the object and the mode of preferring: the *request* is but a simple expression; the *entreaty* is urgent: the *request* may be made in trivial matters; the *entreaty* is made in matters that deeply interest the feelings: we make the *request* of a friend to lend a book; we use every *entreaty* in order to divert a person from the purpose which we think detrimental: one complies with a *request;* one yields to *entreaties*. It was the dying *request* of Socrates, that they would sacrifice a cock to Æsculapius; Regulus was deaf to every *entreaty* of his friends, who wished him not to return to Carthage; 'Arguments, *entreaties*, and promises were employed in order to sooth them (the followers of Cortes).'—Robertson.

The *suit* is a higher kind of *prayer*, varying both in the nature of the subject, and the character of the agent. A gentleman pays his *suit* to a lady; a courtier makes his *suit* to the prince; 'Seldom or never is there much spoke, whenever any one comes to prefer a *suit* to another.'—South.

TO ATONE FOR, EXPIATE.

Atone, or at one, signifies to be in unity, at peace, or good friends; *expiate*, in Latin *expiatus*, participle of *expio*, compounded of *ex* and *pio*, signifies to put out or make clear by an act of piety.

Both these terms express a satisfaction for an offence; but *atone* is general, *expiate* is particular. We may *atone for* a fault by any species of suffering; we *expiate* a crime only by suffering a legal punishment. A female often sufficiently *atones for* her violation of chastity by the misery she entails on herself;

O let the blood, already spilt, *atone*
For the past crimes of curs'd Laomedon.—Dryden

There are too many unfortunate wretches in England who *expiate* their crimes on a gallows;

How sacred ought kings' lives be held,
When but the death of one
Demands an empire's blood for *expiation*.—Lee.

Neither *atonement* nor *expiation* always necessarily require punishment or even suffering from the offender The nature of the *atonement* depends on the will of the individual who is offended; and oftentimes the word implies simply an equivalent given or offered for something; 'I would earnestly desire the story-teller to consider, that no wit or mirth at the end of a story can *atone* for the half hour that has been lost before they come at it.'—Steele. *Expiations* are frequently made by means of performing certain religious rites or acts of piety. Offences between man and man are sometimes *atoned for* by an acknowledgment of errour; but offences towards God require an *expiatory* sacrifice, which our Saviour has been pleased to make of himself, that we, through Him, might become partakers of eternal life. *Expiation*, therefore, in the religious sense, is to *atonement* as the means to the end: *atonement* is often obtained by an *expiation*, but there may be *expiations* where there is no *atonement*.

Atonement replaces in a state of favour; *expiation* produces only a real or supposed exemption from sin and its consequences. Among the Jews and heathens there was *expiation*, but no *atonement;* under the Christian dispensation there is *atonement* as well as *expiation*.

ABSTINENCE, FAST.

Abstinence is a general term, applicable to any object from which we abstain; *fast* is a species of *abstinence*, namely, an abstaining from food; 'Fridays are appointed by the Church as days of *abstinence;* and Good Friday as a day of *fast*.'—Taylor. The general term is likewise used in the particular sense, to imply a partial *abstinence* from particular food; but *fast* signifies an abstinence from food altogether; 'I am verily persuaded that if a whole people were to enter into a course of *abstinence*, and eat nothing but water gruel for a fortnight, it would abate the rage and animosity of parties;' 'Such a *fast* would have the natural tendency to the procuring of those ends for which a *fast* is proclaimed.'—Addison.

TO FORGIVE, PARDON, ABSOLVE, REMIT.

Forgive, compounded of the privative *for* and *give;* and *pardon*, in French *pardonner*, compounded likewise of the privative *par* or *per* and *donner* to give, both signify not to give the punishment that is due, to relax from the rigour of justice in demanding retribution. *Forgive* is the familiar term; *pardon* is adapted to the serious style. Individuals *forgive* each other personal offences; they *pardon* offences against law and morals: the former is an act of Christian charity; the latter an act of clemency: the former is an act that is confined to no condition; the latter is peculiarly the act of a superiour. He who has the right of being offended has an opportunity of *forgiving* the offender:

No more Achilles draws
His conqu'ring sword in any woman's cause.
The gods command me to *forgive* the past,
But let this first invasion be the last.—Pope.

He who has the authority of punishing the offence may pardon; 'A being who has nothing to *pardon* in himself may reward every man according to his works; but he whose very best actions must be seen with a grain of allowance, cannot be too mild, moderate, and *forgiving*.'—Addison. Next to the principle of not taking offence easily, that of *forgiving* real injuries should be instilled into the infant mind: it is the happy prerogative of the monarch that he can extend his *pardon* to all criminals, except to those whose crimes have rendered them unworthy to live: they may be both used in relation to our Maker, but with a similar distinction in sense. God *forgives* the sins of his creatures as a father pitying his children; he *pardons* their sins as a judge extending mercy to criminals, as far as is consistent with justice.

* *Pardon*, when compared with *remission*, is the consequence of offence; it respects principally the person offending; it depends upon him who is offended; it produces reconciliation when it is sincerely granted and sincerely demanded. *Remission* is the consequence of the crime; it has more particular regard to the punishment; it is granted either by the prince or magistrate; it arrests the execution of justice;

With suppliant prayers their powers appease;
The soft Napæan race will soon repent
Their anger, and *remit* the punishment.—DRYDEN.

Remission, like *pardon*, is peculiarly applicable to the sinner with regard to his Maker. *Absolution* is taken in no other sense: it is the consequence of the fault or the sin, and properly concerns the state of the culprit; it properly loosens him from the tie with which he is bound; it is pronounced either by the civil judge or the ecclesiastical minister; it re-establishes the accused or the penitent in the rights of innocence;

Round in his urn the blended balls he rolls,
Absolves the just, and dooms the guilty souls.
DRYDEN.

The *pardon* of sin obliterates that which is past, and restores the sinner to the Divine favour; it is promised throughout Scripture to all men on the condition of faith and repentance; *remission* of sin only averts the Divine vengeance, which otherwise would fall upon those who are guilty of it; it is granted peculiarly to Christians upon the ground of Christ's expiatory sacrifice, which satisfies Divine justice for all offences: *absolution* of sin is the work of God's grace on the heart; it acts for the future as well as the past, by lessening the dominion of sin, and making those free who were before in bondage. The Roman Catholicks look upon *absolution* as the immediate act of the Pope, by virtue of his sacred relationship to Christ; but the Protestants look to Christ only as the dispenser of this blessing to men, and his ministers simply as messengers to declare the Divine will to men.

REPENTANCE, PENITENCE, CONTRITION, COMPUNCTION, REMORSE.

Repentance, from *re* back, and *pœnitet* to be sorry, signifies looking back with sorrow on what one has done amiss; *penitence*, from the same source, signifies simply sorrow for what is amiss. *Contrition*, from *contero* to rub together, or bruise as it were with sorrow; *compunction*, from *compungo* to prick thoroughly; and *remorse*, from *remordeo* to have a gnawing pain; all express modes of *penitence* differing in degree and circumstance.

Repentance refers more to the change of one's mind with regard to an object, and is properly confined to the time when this change takes place; we therefore, strictly speaking, *repent* of a thing but once; we may, however, have *penitence* for the same thing all our lives. *Repentance* may be felt for trivial matters; we may *repent* of going or not going, speaking or not speaking: *penitence* refers only to serious matters; we are *penitent* only for our sins. Errours of judgement will always be attended with *repentance* in a mind that is striving to do right; there is no human being so perfect but that, in the sight of God, he will have occasion to be *penitent* for many acts of commission and omission.

Repentance may be felt for errours which concern only ourselves, or at most offences against our fellow creatures; *penitence*, and the other terms, are applicable only to offences against the moral and divine law, that law which is engraven on the heart of every man. We may *repent* of not having made a bargain that we afterward find would have been advantageous, or we may *repent* of having done any injury to our neighbour; but our *penance* is awakened when we reflect on our unworthiness or sinfulness in the sight of our Maker. This *penitence* is a general sentiment, which belongs to all men as offending creatures; but *contrition*, *compunction*, and *remorse* are awakened by reflecting on particular offences: *contrition* is a continued and severe sorrow, appropriate to one who has been in a continued state of peculiar sinfulness; *compunction* is rather an occasional, but sharp sorrow provoked by a single offence, or a moment's reflection, *remorse* may be temporary, but it is a still sharper pain awakened by some particular offence of peculiar magnitude and atrocity. The prodigal son was a *contrite* sinner; the brethren of Joseph felt great *compunction* when they were carried back with their sacks to Egypt; David was struck with *remorse* for the murder of Uriah.

These four terms depend not so much on the measure of guilt as on the sensibility of the offender Whoever reflects most deeply on the enormity of sin, will be most sensible of *repentance*, when he sees his own liability to offend; 'This is the sinner's hard lot; that the same thing which makes him need *repentance*, makes him also in danger of not obtaining it.'—SOUTH In those who have most offended, and are come to a sense of their own condition, *penitence* will rise to deep *contrition*;

Heaven may forgive a crime to *penitence*,
For heaven can judge if *penitence* be true.—DRYDEN.

'*Contrition*, though it may melt, ought not to sink, or overpower the heart of a Christian.'—BLAIR. There is no man so hardened that he will not some time or other feel *compunction* for the crimes he has committed; 'All men, even the most depraved, are subject more or less to *compunctions* of conscience.'—BLAIR He who has the liveliest sense of the Divine goodness, will feel keen *remorse* whenever he reflects on any thing that he has done, by which he fears to have forfeited the favour of so good a Being;

The heart,
Pierc'd with a sharp *remorse* for guilt, disclaims
The costly poverty of hecatombs,
And offers the best sacrifice itself.—JEFFRY.

CONSCIENTIOUS, SCRUPULOUS.

Conscientious marks the quality of having a nice conscience; *scrupulous*, that of having a scruple. *Conscience*, in Latin *conscientia*, from *consciens*, signifies that by which a man becomes conscious to himself of right and wrong. *Scruple*, in Latin *scrupulus*, a little hard stone, signifies that which gives pain to the mind, as the stone does to the foot in walking.

Conscientious is to *scrupulous* as a whole to a part. A *conscientious* man is so altogether; a *scrupulous* man may have only particular *scruples*: the one is therefore always taken in a good sense; and the other at least in an indifferent, if not a bad sense.

A *conscientious* man does nothing to offend his *conscience*; 'A *conscientious* person would rather distrust his own judgement than condemn his species. He would say, I have observed without attention, or judged upon erroneous maxims; I have trusted to profession when I ought to have attended to conduct.' BURKE.—But a *scrupulous* man has often his *scruples* on trifling or minor points; 'Others by their weakness, and fear, and *scrupulousness*, cannot fully satisfy their own thoughts.'—FULLER. The Pharisees were *scrupulous* without being *conscientious*: we must therefore strive to be *conscientious* without being over *scrupulous*; 'I have been so very *scrupulous* in this particular, of not hurting any man's reputation, that I have forborne mentioning even such authors as I could not name with honour. —ADDISON.

HOLINESS, SANCTITY.

Holiness, which comes from the northern languages, has altogether acquired a Christian signification; it respects the life and temper of a Christian; *sanctity* which is derived from the Latin *sanctus* and *sanctio*, to sanction, has merely a moral signification, which it derives from the *sanction* of human authority.

Holiness is to the mind of a man what sanctity is to his exteriour; with this difference, that *holiness* to a certain degree, ought to belong to every man professing Christianity; but *sanctity*, as it lies in the manners, the outward garb, and deportment, is becoming only to certain persons, and at certain times.

Holiness is a thing not to be affected; it is that genuine characteristick of Christianity which is altogether spiritual, and cannot be counterfeited; 'Habitual preparation for the Sacrament consists in a permanent habit or principle of *holiness*.'—SOUTH. *Sanctity*,

* Vide Abbe Girard: "Absolution, pardon, remission."

on the other hand, is from its very nature exposed to falsehood, and the least to be trusted; when it displays itself in individuals, either by the sorrowfulness of their looks, or the singular cut of their garments, or other singularities of action and gesture, it is of the most questionable nature; but in one who performs the sacerdotal office, it is a useful appendage to the solemnity of the scene, which excites a reverential regard to the individual in the mind of the beholder, and the most exalted sentiments of that religion which he thus adorns by his outward profession; 'About an age ago it was the fashion in England for every one that would be thought religious, to throw as much *sanctity* as possible into his face.'—ADDISON. 'It was an observation of the ancient Romans, that their empire had not increased more by the strength of their arms, than by the *sanctity* of their manners.'—ADDISON.

HOLY, PIOUS, DEVOUT, RELIGIOUS.

Holy is here taken in the sense of *holiness*, as in the preceding article; *pious*, in Latin *pius*, is most probably changed from *dius* or *deus*, signifying regard for the gods; *devout*, in Latin *devotus*, from *devoveo* to engage by a vow, signifies *devoted* or consecrated; *religious*, in Latin *religiosus*, comes from *religio* and *religo*, to bind, because religion binds the mind, and produces in it a fixed principle.

A strong regard to the Supreme Being is expressed by all these epithets; but *holy* conveys the most comprehensive idea; *pious* and *devout* designate most fervour of mind; *religious* is the most general and abstract in its signification. A *holy* man is in all respects heavenly-minded; he is more fit for heaven than earth: *holiness*, to whatever degree it is possessed, abstracts the thoughts from sublunary objects, and fixes them on things that are above; it is therefore a Christian quality, which is not to be attained in its full perfection by human beings, in their present imperfect state, and is attainable by some to a much greater degree than by others. Our Saviour was a perfect pattern of *holiness*; his apostles after him, and innumerable saints and good men, both in and out of the ministry, have striven to imitate his example, by the *holiness* of their life and conversation: in such, however, as have exclusively *devoted* themselves to his service, this *holiness* may shine brighter than in those who are entangled with the affairs of the world; 'The *holiest* man, by conversing with the world insensibly draws something of soil and taint from it.'—SOUTH.

Pious is a term more restricted in its signification, and consequently more extended in its application, than *holy*: *piety* is not a virtue peculiar to Christians, it is common to all believers in a Supreme Being; it is the homage of the heart and the affections to a superiour Being: from a similarity in the relationship between a heavenly and an earthly parent, *devotedness* of the mind has in both cases been denominated *piety*. *Piety* towards God naturally produces *piety* towards parents; for the obedience of the heart, which gives rise to the virtue in the one, seems instantly to dictate the exercise of it in the other. The difference between *holiness* and *piety* is obvious from this, that our Saviour and his apostles are characterized as *holy*, but not *pious*, because *piety* is swallowed up in *holiness*. On the other hand, Jew and Gentile, Christian and Heathen, are alike termed *pious*, when they cannot be called *holy*, because *piety* is not only a more practicable virtue, but because it is more universally applicable to the dependant condition of man; 'In every age the practice has prevailed of substituting certain appearances of *piety* in the place of the great duties of humanity and mercy.'—BLAIR.

Devotion is a species of *piety* peculiar to the worshipper; it bespeaks that devotedness of mind which displays itself in the temple, when the individual seems by his outward services solemnly to *devote* himself, soul and body, to the service of his Maker; '*Devotion* expresses not so much the performance of any particular duty, as the spirit which must animate all *religious* duties.'—BLAIR. *Piety*, therefore, lies in the heart, and may appear externally; but *devotion* does not properly exist except in an external observance: a man *piously* resigns himself to the will of God, in the midst of his afflictions; he prays *devoutly* in the bosom of his family; 'A state of temperance, sobriety, and justice, without *devotion*, is a lifeless insipid condition of virtue.'—ADDISON.

Religious is a term of less import than either of the other terms; it denotes little more than the simple existence of *religion*, or a sense of *religion* in the mind: the *religious* man is so, more in his principles than in his affections; he is *religious* in his sentiments, in as much as he directs all his views according to the will of his Maker; and he is *religious* in his conduct, in as much as he observes the outward formalities of homage that are due to his Maker. A *holy* man fits himself for a higher state of existence, after which he is always aspiring; a *pious* man has God in all his thoughts, and seeks to do his will; a *devout* man bends himself in humble adoration and pays his vows of prayer and thanksgiving; a *religious* man conforms in all things to what the dictates of his conscience require from him, as a responsible being, and a member of society.

When applied to things they preserve a similar distinction: we speak of the *holy* sacrament; of a *pious* discourse, a *pious* ejaculation; of a *devout* exercise, a *devout* air; a *religious* sentiment, a *religious* life, a *religious* education, &c.

HOLY, SACRED, DIVINE.

Holy is here, as in the former article, a term of higher import than either *sacred* or *divine*: *sacred*, in Latin *sacer*, is derived either from the Greek ἅγιος holy or σάος whole, perfect, and the Hebrew *zacah* pure Whatever is most intimately connected with religion and religious worship, in its purest state, is *holy*, is unhallowed by a mixture of inferiour objects, is elevated in the greatest possible degree, so as to suit the nature of an infinitely perfect and exalted Being. Among the Jews, the *holy* of *holies* was that place which was intended to approach the nearest to the heavenly abode, consequently was preserved as much as possible from all contamination with that which is earthly: among Christians, that religion or form of religion is termed *holy*, which is esteemed purest in its doctrine, discipline, and ceremonies, and is applied with equal propriety by the Roman Catholicks and the English Protestants to that which they have in common; 'To fit us for a due access to the *holy* Sacrament, we must add actual preparation to habitual.'—SOUTH. Upon this ground we speak of the church as a *holy* place, of the sacrament as the *holy* sacrament, and the ordinances of the church as *holy*.

Sacred is less than *holy*; the *sacred* derives its sanction from human institutions, and is connected rather with our moral than our religious duties: what is *holy* is altogether spiritual, and abstracted from the earthly; what is *sacred* may be simply the human purified from what is gross and corrupt: what is *holy* must be regarded with awe, and treated with every possible mark of reverence; what is *sacred* must not be violated nor infringed upon. The laws are *sacred*, but not *holy*; a man's word should be *sacred*, though not *holy*: for neither of these things is to be reverenced, but both are to be kept free from injury or external violence. The *holy* is not so much opposed to, as it is set above every thing else; the *sacred* is opposed to the profane the Scriptures are properly denominated *holy*, because they are the word of God, and the fruit of his *Holy* Spirit; but other writings may be termed *sacred* which appertain to religion, in distinction from the profane, which appertain only to worldly matters; 'Common sense could tell them, that the good God could not be pleased with any thing cruel, nor the most *holy* God with any thing filthy and unclean.'—SOUTH. 'Religion properly consists in a reverential esteem of things *sacred*.'—SOUTH.

Divine is a term of even less import than *sacred*; it signifies either belonging to the Deity, or being like the Deity; but from the looseness of its application it has lost in some respects the dignity of its meaning. The *divine* is often contrasted with the human: but there are many human things which are denominated *divine*. Milton's poem is entitled a *divine* poem, not merely on account of the subject, but from the exalted manner in which the poet has treated his subject: what is *divine*, therefore, may be so superlatively excellent as to be conceived of as having the stamp of inspiration from the

Deity, which of course, as it respects human performances, is but a hyperbolical mode of speech.

From the above explanation of these terms, it is clear that there is a manifest difference between them, and yet that their resemblance is sufficiently great for them to be applied to the same objects. We speak of the *Holy* Spirit, and of *Divine* inspiration; by the first of which epithets is understood not only what is superhuman, but what is a constituent part of the Deity: by the second is represented merely in a general manner the source of the inspiration as coming from the Deity, and not from man; 'When a man resteth and assureth himself upon *Divine* protection, he gathereth a force and faith which human nature in itself could not obtain.'—BACON. Subjects are denominated either *sacred* or *divine*, as when we speak of *sacred* poems, or *divine* hymns; *sacred* here characterizes the subjects of the poems, as those which are to be held *sacred;* and *divine* designates the subject of the hymns as not being ordinary or merely human; it is clear, therefore, that what is *holy* is in its very nature *sacred*, but not *vice versâ;* and that what is *holy* and *sacred* is in its very nature *divine;* but the *divine* is not always either *holy* or *sacred.*

GODLIKE, DIVINE, HEAVENLY.

Godlike bespeaks its own meaning, as like *God*, or after the manner of *God; divine*, in Latin *divinus* from *divus* or *Deus*, signifies appertaining to *God; heavenly*, or *heavenlike*, signifies like or appertaining to *heaven.*

Godlike is a more expressive, but less common term than *divine;* the former is used only as an epithet of peculiar praise for a particular object; *divine* is generally employed for that which appertains to a superiour being, in distinction from that which is human. Benevolence is a *godlike* property:

Sure he that made us with such large discourse,
Looking before and after, gave us not
That capability and *godlike* reason,
To rust in us unus'd.—SHAKSPEARE.

The *Divine* image is stamped on the features of man, whence the face is called by Milton 'the human face *Divine*.' 'The benefit of nature's light is not thought excluded as unnecessary, because the necessity of a *divine* light is magnified.'—HOOKER. *Divine* is however frequently used by the poets for what is supe excellent.

Of all that see or read thy comedies,
Whoever in those glasses looks may find
The spots return'd, or graces of his mind;
And by the help of so *divine* an art,
At leisure view and dress his nobler part.
WALLER.

As *divine* is opposed to human, so is *heavenly* to earthly: the *Divine* Being is a term of distinction for the Creator from all other beings; but a *heavenly* being denotes the angels or inhabitants of *heaven*, in distinction from earthly beings or the inhabitants of earth. A *divine* influence is to be sought for only by prayer to the Giver of all good things; but a *heavenly* temper may be acquired by a steady contemplation of *heavenly* things, and an abstraction from those which are earthly. The *Divine* will is the foundation of all moral law and obligation;

Instructed you'd explore
Divine contrivance, and a God adore.—BLACKMORE

Heavenly joys are the fruit of all our labours in this earthly course;

Reason, alas! It does not know itself;
But man, vain man! would with his short-lin'd plummet
Fathom the vast abyss of *heavenly* justice.—DRYDEN.

GODLY, RIGHTEOUS.

Godly is a contraction of *godlike* (*v. Godlike*); *righteous* signifies conformable to *right* or truth.

These epithets are both used in a spiritual sense, and cannot, without an indecorous affectation of religion, be introduced into any other discourse than that which is properly spiritual. *Godliness*, in the strict sense, is that outward deportment which characterizes a heavenly temper; prayer, reading of the Scriptures, publick worship, and every religious act, enters into the signification of *godliness*, which at the same time supposes a temper of mind, not only to delight in, but to profit by such exercises: 'The same church is really holy in this world, in relation to all *godly* persons contained in it, by a real infused sanctity.'—PEARSON. *Righteousness* on the other hand comprehends Christian morality, in distinction from that of the heathen or unbeliever; a *righteous* man does *right*, not only because it is *right*, but because it is agreeable to the will of his Maker, and the example of his Redeemer: *righteousness* is therefore to *godliness* as the effect to the cause; ''T is the gospel's work to reduce man to the principles of his first creation, that is, to be both good and wise. Our ancestors, it seems, were clearly of this opinion. He that was pious and just was reckoned a *righteous* man. *Godliness* and integrity was called and accounted *righteousness.* And in their old Saxon *righteous* was *rightwise*, and *righteousness* was originally *rightwiseness*.'—FELTHAM. The *godly* man goes to the sanctuary and by converse with his Maker assimilates all his affections to the character of that being whom he worships; when he leaves the sanctuary he proves the efficacy of his *godliness* by his righteous converse with his fellow-creatures. It is easy however for men to mistake the means for the end, and to rest with *godliness* without *righteousness*, as too many are apt to do who seem to make their whole duty to consist in an attention to religious observances, and in the indulgence of extravagant feelings; 'It hath been the great design of the devil and his instruments in all ages to undermine religion, by making an unhappy separation and divorce between *godliness* and morality. But let us not deceive ourselves; this was always religion, and the condition of our acceptance with God, to endeavour to be like *God* in purity and holiness, in justice and *righteousness*.'—TILLOTSON.

SECULAR, TEMPORAL, WORLDLY.

Secular in Latin *secularis*, from *seculum* an age or division of time, signifies belonging to time, or this life; *temporal*, in Latin *temporalis*, from *tempus* time, signifies lasting only for a time; *worldly* signifies after the manner of the *world.*

Secular is opposed to ecclesiastical or spiritual, *temporal* and *worldly* are opposed to spiritual or eternal.

The ideas of the *world*, or the outward objects and pursuits of the *world*, in distinction from that whic' is set above the *world*, is implied in common by all th terms; but *secular* is an indifferent term, applicable to the allowed pursuits and concerns of men; *temporal* is used either in an indifferent or a bad sense; and *worldly* mostly in a bad sense, as contrasted with things of more value.

The office of a clergyman is ecclesiastical, but that of a schoolmaster is *secular*, which is frequently vested in the same hands; 'This, in several men's actions of common life, appertaineth unto moral; in publick and politick *secular* affairs, unto civil wisdom.'—HOOKER. The upper house of parliament consists of lords spiritual and *temporal;* 'There is scarce any of those decisions but gives good light, by way of authority or reason, to some questions that arise also between *temporal* dignities, especially to cases wherein some of our subordinate *temporal* titles have part in the controversy.'—SELDEN. *Worldly* interest has a more powerful sway upon the minds of the great bulk of mankind, than their spiritual interests; 'Compare the happiness of men and beasts no farther than it results from *worldly* advantages.'—ATTERBURY. Whoever enters into the holy office of the ministry with merely *secular* views of preferment, chooses a very unfit source of emolument; 'Some saw nothing in what has been done in France but a firm and temperate exertion of freedom, so consistent with morals and piety, as to make it deserving not only of the *secular* applause of dashing Machiavelian politicians, but to make it a fit theme for all the devout effusions of sacred eloquence.'—BURKE A too eager pursuit after *temporal* advantages and *temporal* pleasures is apt to draw the mind away from its regard to those which are eternal; 'The ultimate purpose of government is *temporal*, and that of religion is eternal happiness.'—JOHNSON. *Wordly* applause will weigh very light when set in the balance against the reproach of one's own conscience; '*Worldly* things are of such quality as to lessen upon dividing.'—GROVE

ENTHUSIAST, FANATICK, VISIONARY.

The *enthusiast*, *fanatick*, and *visionary* have disordered imaginations; but the *enthusiast* is only affected inwardly with an extraordinary fervour, the *fanatick* and *visionary* betray that fervour by some outward mark; the former by singularities of conduct, the latter by singularities of doctrine. *Fanaticks* and *visionaries* are therefore always more or less *enthusiasts*; but *enthusiasts* are not always *fanaticks* or *visionaries*. Ἐνθουσιασταὶ among the Greeks, from ἐν in and θεὸς God, signified those supposed to have, or pretending to have, Divine inspiration. *Fanatici* were so called among the Latins, from *fana* the temples in which they spent an extraordinary portion of their time; they, like the ἐνθουσιασταὶ of the Greeks, pretended to revelations and inspirations, during the influence of which they indulged themselves in many extravagant tricks, cutting themselves with knives, and distorting themselves with every species of antick gesture and grimace.

Although we are professors of a pure religion, yet we cannot boast an exemption from the extravagancies which are related of the poor heathens; we have many who indulge themselves in similar practices under the idea of honouring their Maker and Redeemer. There are *fanaticks* who profess to be under extraordinary influences of the spirit; and there are *enthusiasts* whose intemperate zeal disqualifies them for taking a beneficial part in the sober and solemn services of the church. *Visionary* signifies properly one who deals in *visions*, that is, in the pretended appearance of supernatural objects; a species of *enthusiasts* who have sprung up in more modern times. The leaders of sects are commonly *visionaries*, having adopted this artifice to establish their reputation and doctrines among their deluded followers; Mahomet was one of the most successful *visionaries* that ever pretended to divine inspiration; and since his time there have been *visionaries*, particularly in England, who have raised religious parties, by having recourse to the same expedient: of this description was Swedenborg, Huntington, and Brothers.

Fanatick was originally confined to those who were under religious frenzy, but the present age has presented us with the monstrosity of *fanaticks* in irreligion and anarchy; 'They who will not believe that the philosophical *fanaticks* who guide in these matters have long entertained the design (of abolishing religion), are utterly ignorant of their character.'—Burke. *Enthusiast* is a term applied in general to every one who is filled with an extraordinary degree of fervour;

Her little soul is ravish'd, and so pour'd
Into loose ecstasies, that she is placed
Above herself, Musick's *enthusiast*.—Crashaw.

Enthusiasts pretend that they have the gift of prophecy by dreams.'—Pagitt's Heresiography. *Visionary* is a term applied to one who deals in fanciful speculation; 'This account exceeded all the Noctambuli or *visionaries* I have met with.'—Turner. The former may sometimes be innocent, if not laudable, according to the nature of the object; the latter is always censurable: the *enthusiast* has mostly a warm heart; the *visionary* has only a fanciful head. The *enthusiast* will mostly be on the side of virtue even though in an errour; the *visionary* pleads no cause but his own. The *enthusiast* suffers his imagination to follow his heart; the *visionary* makes his understanding bend to his imagination. Although in matters of religion, *enthusiasm* should be cautiously guarded against, yet we admire to see it roused in behalf of one's country and one's friends; 'Cherish true religion as preciously as you will, fly with abhorrence and contempt, superstition and *enthusiasm*.'—Chatham. *Visionaries*, whether in religion, politicks, or science, are dangerous as members of society, and offensive as companions; 'The sons of infamy ridicule every thing as romantick that comes in competition with their present interest, and treat those persons as *visionaries* who dare stand up in a corrupt age, for what has not its immediate reward joined to it.'—Addison.

DREAM, REVERIE.

Dream, in Dutch *drom*, &c. comes either from the Celtic *drem*, a sight, or the Greek δρᾶμα, a fable, or as probably from the word *roam*, signifying to wander, in Hebrew רם to be agitated; *reverie*, in French *reverie*, like the English *rave*, comes from the Latin *rabies*, signifying that which is wandering or incoherent.

Dreams and *reveries* are alike opposed to the reality, and have their origin in the imagination; but the former commonly pass in sleep, and the latter when awake: the *dream* may and does commonly arise when the imagination is in a sound state; the *reverie* is the fruit of a heated imagination; '*Revery* is when ideas float in our mind, without reflection or regard of the understanding.'—Locke. *Dreams* come in the course of nature; *reveries* are the consequence of a peculiar ferment.

When the *dream* is applied to the act of one that is awake, it admits of another distinction from *reverie*. They both designate what is confounded, but the *dream* is less extravagant than the *reverie*. Ambitious men please themselves with *dreams* of future greatness; enthusiasts debase the purity of the Christian religion by blending their own wild *reveries* with the doctrines of the Gospel. He who indulges himself in idle *dreams* lays up a store of disappointment for himself when he recovers his recollection, and finds that it is nothing but a *dream*; 'Gay's friends persuaded him to sell his share of South-sea stock, but he *dreamed* of dignity and splendour, and could not bear to obstruct his own fortune.'—Johnson. A love of singularity operating on an ardent mind will too often lead men to indulge in strange *reveries*; 'I continued to sit motionless, with my eyes fixed upon the curtain, some moments after it fell. When I was roused from my *reverie* I found myself almost alone.'—Hawkesworth.

IRRATIONAL, FOOLISH, ABSURD, PREPOSTEROUS.

Irrational, compounded of *ir* or *in* and *ratio*, signifies contrary to reason, and is employed to express the want of the faculty itself, or a deficiency in the exercise of this faculty; *foolish* denotes the perversion of this faculty; *absurd*, from *surdus*, deaf, signifies that to which one would turn a deaf ear; *preposterous* from *præ* before and *post* behind, signifies literally that side foremost which is unnatural and contrary to common sense.

Irrational is not so strong a term as *foolish*: it is applicable more frequently to the thing than to the person, to the principle than to the practice; 'The schemes of freethinkers are altogether *irrational*, and require the most extravagant credulity to embrace them.'—Addison. *Foolish* on the contrary is commonly applicable to the person as well as the thing, to the practice rather than the principle; 'The same well meaning gentleman took occasion at another time to bring together such of his friends as were addicted to a *foolish* habitual custom of swearing, in order to show them the *absurdity* of the practice.—Addison Skepticism is the most *irrational* thing that exists, the human mind is formed to believe, but not to doubt: he is of all men most *foolish* who stakes his eternal salvation on his own fancied superiority of intelligence and illumination. *Foolish*, *absurd*, and *preposterous*, rise in degree: a violation of common sense is implied by them all, but they vary according to the degree of violence which is done to the understanding: *foolish* is applied to any thing, however trivial, which in the smallest degree offends our understandings: the conduct of children is therefore often *foolish*, but not *absurd* and *preposterous*, which are said only of serious things that are opposed to our judgements: it is *absurd* for a man to persuade another to do that which he in like circumstances would object to do himself;

But grant that those can conquer, these can cheat.
'Tis phrase *absurd* to call a villain great;
Who wickedly is wise or madly brave
Is but the more a fool, the more a knave.—Pope.

It is *preposterous* for a man to expose himself to the ridicule of others, and then be angry with those who will not treat him respectfully; 'By a *preposterous* desire of things in themselves indifferent men forego the enjoyment of that happiness which those things are instrumental to obtain.'—Berkeley

IRRELIGIOUS, PROFANE, IMPIOUS.

As epithets to designate the character of the person, they seem to rise in degree: the *irreligious* is negative; the *profane* and *impious* are positive; the latter being much stronger than the former. The *profani* of the Latins, from *pro* and *fanum*, i. e. *procul a fano*, far from the temple, were those not initiated, who were not permitted to take any part in the sacred mysteries and rites, whence by a natural consequence those who despised what was sacred. All men who are not positively actuated by principles of religion are *irreligious;* 'An officer of the army in Roman Catholick countries, would be afraid to pass for an *irreligious* man if he should be seen to go to bed without offering up his devotions.'—ADDISON. Who, if we include all such as show a disregard to the outward observances of religion, form a too numerous class: *profanity* and *impiety* are however of a still more heinous nature; they consist not in the mere absence of regard for religion, but in a positive contempt of it and open outrage against its laws; the *profane* man treats what is sacred as if it were *profane;* 'These have caused the weak to stumble and the *profane* to blaspheme, offending the one and hardening the other.'—SOUTH. What a believer holds in reverence, and utters with awe, is pronounced with an air of indifference or levity, and as a matter of common discourse, by a *profane* man; he knowing no difference between sacred and *profane;* but as the former may be converted into a source of scandal towards others; 'Fly, ye *profane;* if not, draw near with awe.'—YOUNG. The *impious* man is directly opposed to the *pious* man; the former is filled with defiance and rebellion against his Maker, as the latter is with love and fear; the former curses, while the latter prays; the former is bloated with pride and conceit: the latter is full of humility and self-abasement: we have a picture of the former in the devils, and of the latter in the saints. When applied to things, the term *irreligious* seems to be somewhat more positively opposed to religion: an *irreligious* book is not merely one in which there is no religion, but that also which is detrimental to religion, such as skeptical or licentious writings: the *profane* in this case is not always a term of reproach, but is employed to distinguish what is expressly spiritual in its nature, from that which is temporal: the history of nations is *profane*, as distinguished from the sacred history contained in the Bible: the writings of the heathens are altogether *profane* as distinguished from the moral writings of Christians, or the believers in Divine Revelation. On the other hand, when we speak of a *profane* sentiment, or a *profane* joke, *profane* lips, and the like, the sense is personal and reproachful; 'Nothing is *profane* that serveth to holy things.—RALEGH. *Impious* is never applied but to what is personal, and in the very worst sense; an *impious* thought, an *impious* wish, or an *impious* vow, are the fruits of an *impious* mind;

> Love's great divinity rashly maintains
> Weak *impious* war with an immortal God.
> CUMBERLAND.

TO FORSWEAR, PERJURE, SUBORN.

Forswear is Saxon; *perjure* is Latin; the preposition *for* and *per* are both privative, and the words signify literally to swear contrary to the truth; this is, however, not their only distinction: to *forswear* is applied to all kinds of oaths; to *perjure* is employed only for such oaths as have been administered by the civil magistrate.

A soldier *forswears* himself who breaks his oath of allegiance by desertion; and a subject *forswears* himself who takes an oath of allegiance to his Majesty which he afterward violates;

> False as thou art, and more than false *forsworn!*
> Not sprung from noble blood, nor goddess born;
> Why should I own? what worse have I to fear?
> DRYDEN.

A man *perjures* himself in a court of law who swears to the truth of that which he knows to be false; 'The common oath of the Scythian was by the sword and the fire, for that they accounted those two special divine powers which should work vengeance on the *perjurers*.'—SPENSER. *Forswear* is used only in the proper sense: *perjure* may be used figuratively with regard to lovers' vows; he who deserts his mistress to whom he has pledged his affection is a *perjured* man;

> Be gone, for ever leave this happy sphere;
> For *perjur'd* lovers have no mansions here.—LEE.

Forswear and *perjure* are the acts of individuals; *suborn*, from the Latin *subornare*, signifies to make to *forswear;* a *perjured* man has all the guilt upon himself; but he who is *suborned* shares his guilt with the *suborner;*

> They were *suborn'd;*
> Malcolm and Donalbain, the king's two sons,
> Are stole away and fled.—SHAKSPEARE

DEVIL, DEMON.

Devil, in old German *tiefel*, Saxon *deofl*, Welsh *diafwl*, French *diable*, Italian *diavolo*, Dutch *duyfdel*, Greek διάβολος, from διαβάλλω, to traduce, signifies properly a calumniator, and is always taken in the bad sense, for the spirit which incites to evil, and tempts men through the medium of their evil passions; *demon*, in Latin *dæmon*, Greek δαίμων, from δάω to know, signifies one knowing, that is, having preter natural knowledge, and is taken either in a bad or good sense for the power that acts within us and controls our actions.

Since the *devil** is represented as the father of all wickedness, associations have been connected with the name that render its pronounciation in familiar discourse offensive to the chastened ear; while *demon* is a term of indifferent application, that is commonly substituted in its stead to designate either a good or an evil spirit.

Among Jews and Christians the term *demon* is taken always in a bad sense; but the Greeks and Romans understood by the word *dæmon* any spirit or genius good or evil, but particularly the good spirit or guardian angel, who was supposed to accompany a man from his birth. Socrates professed to be always under the direction of such a *dæmon*, and his example has been followed by other heathen philosophers, particularly those of the Platonick sect. Hence the use of these terms in ordinary discourse, the *devil* being always considered as the supernatural agent, who, by the divine permission, acts on the hearts and minds of men; but a *demon* is applied generally and indefinitely in the sense of any spirit. The *devil* is said in proverbial discourse to be in such things as go contrary to the wish; the *demon* of jealousy is said to possess the mind that is altogether carried away with that passion. Men who wish to have credit for more goodness than they possess, and to throw the load of guilt off themselves, attribute to the *devil* a perpetual endeavour to draw them into the commission of crimes; 'The enemies we are to contend with are not men but *devils*.'—TILLOTSON. Wherever the *demon* of discord has got admittance, there is a farewell to all the comforts of social life; 'My good *demon*, who sat at my right hand during the course of this whole vision, observing in me a burning desire to join that glorious company, told me he highly approved of that generous ardour with which I seemed transported.'—ADDISON.

HERETICK, SCHISMATICK, SECTARIAN OR SECTARY, DISSENTER, NONCONFORMIST.

A *heretick* is the maintainer of *heresy* (*v. Heterodox*); the *schismatick* is the author or promoter of *schism;* the *sectarian* or *sectary* is the member of a *sect;* the *dissenter* is one who *dissents* from the establishment; and the *nonconformist* one who does not *conform* to the establishment. A man is a *heretick* only for matters of faith and doctrine, but he is a *schismatick* in matters of discipline and practice. The *heretick* therefore is not always a *schismatick*, nor the *schismatick* a *heretick*. Whoever holds the doctrines that are common to the Roman Catholick and the reformed Churches, is not a *heretick* in the Protestant sense of the word; although he may in many outward formalities be a *schismatick*. The Calvinists are not *hereticks*, but they are for the most part *schismaticks;* on the other hand, there are many members of the establishment, who hold though they do not avow heretical notions.

* Vide Abbe Girard: "Diable, demon

The *heretick* is considered as such with regard to the Catholick Church, or the whole body of Christians, holding the same fundamental principles; 'When a Papist uses the word *hereticks* he generally means Protestants, when a Protestant uses the word, he generally means any persons wilfully and contentiously obstinate in fundamental errours.'—Watts. But the *schismatick* and *sectarian* are considered as such with regard to particular established bodies of Christians. *Schism*, from the Greek σχίζω, to split, denotes an action, and the *schismatick* is an agent who splits for himself in his own individual capacity: the *sectarian* does not expressly perform a part, he merely holds a relation; he does not divide any thing himself, but belongs to that which is already cut or divided. The *schismatick*, therefore, takes upon himself the whole moral responsibility of the *schism;* but the *sectarian* does not necessarily take an active part in the measures of his *sect:* whatever guilt attaches to *schism* attaches to the *schismatick;* he is a voluntary agent, who acts from an erroneous principle, if not an unchristian temper: the *sectarian* is often an involuntary agent; he follows that to which he has been incidentally attached. It is possible, therefore, to be a *schismatick*, and not a *sectarian;* as also to be a *sectarian*, and not a *schismatick*. Those professed members of the establishment who affect the title of evangelical, and wish to palm upon the Church the peculiarities of the Calvinistick doctrine, and to ingraft their own modes and forms into its discipline, are *schismaticks*, but not *sectarians;* 'The *schismaticks* disturb the sweet peace of our Church.'—Howel. On the other hand, those who by birth and education are attached to a *sect*, are *sectarians*, but not always *schismaticks;* 'In the house of Sir Samuel Luke, one of Cromwell's officers, Butler observed so much of the character of the *sectaries*, that he is said to have written or begun his poem at this time.'—Johnson. Consequently, *schismatick* is a term of much greater reproach than *sectarian*.

The *schismatick* and *sectarian* have a reference to any established body of Christians of any country; but *dissenter* is a term applicable only to the inhabitants of Great Britain, and bearing relation only to the established Church of England: it includes not only those who have individually and personally renounced the doctrines of the Church, but those who are in a state of *dissent* or difference from it. *Dissenters* are not necessarily either *schismaticks* or *sectarians*, for British Roman Catholicks, and the Presbyterians of Scotland, are all *dissenters*, although they are the reverse of what is understood by *schismatick* and *sectarian:* it is equally clear that all *schismaticks* and *sectarians* are not *dissenters*, because every established community of Christians, all over the world, have had individuals, or smaller bodies of individuals, setting themselves up against them: the term *dissenter* being in a great measure technical, it may be applied individually or generally without conveying any idea of reproach; 'Of the *dissenters*, Swift did not wish to infringe the toleration, but he opposed their encroachments.'—Johnson. The same may be said of *nonconformist*, which is a more special term, including only such as do not *conform* to some established or national religion; 'Watts is at least one of the few poets with whom youth and ignorance may be safely pleased; and happy will that reader be, whose mind is disposed, by his verses or his prose, to imitate him in all but his *nonconformity*.'—Johnson. Consequently, all members of the Romish Church, or of the Kirk of Scotland, are excluded from the number of *nonconformists;* while, on the other hand, all British-born subjects, not adhering to these two forms, and at the same time renouncing the established form of their country, are of this number, among whom may be reckoned Independents, Presbyterians, Baptists, Quakers, Methodists, and all other such *sects* as have been formed since the reformation.

HETERODOXY, HERESY.

Heterodoxy, from the Greek ἕτερος and δόξη, signifies another or a different doctrine; *heresy*, from the Greek αἵρεσις a choice, signifies an opinion adopted by individual choice.

* To be of a different persuasion is *heterodoxy;* to have a faith of one's own is *heresy;* the *heterodoxy* characterizes the opinions formed; the *heresy* characterizes the individual forming the opinion: the *heterodoxy* exists independently and for itself; 'All wrong notions in religion are ranked under the general name of *heterodox*.'—Golding. The *heresy* sets itself up against others; '*Heterodoxies*, false doctrines, yea, and *heresies*, may be propagated by prayer as well as preaching.'—Bull. As all division supposes errour either on one side or on both, the words *heterodoxy* and *heresy* are applied only to human opinions, and strictly in the sense of a false opinion, formed in distinction from that which is better founded; but the former respects any opinions, important or otherwise; the latter refers only to matters of importance: the *heresy* is therefore a fundamental errour. There has been much *heterodoxy* in the Christian world at all times, and among these have been *heresies* denying the plainest and most serious truths which have been acknowledged by the great body of Christians since the Apostles.

* Vide Roubaud: "Hérétique, hétérodoxe."

OMEN, PROGNOSTICK, PRESAGE.

All these terms express some token or sign of what is to come; *omen*, in Latin *omen*, probably comes from the Greek οἴομαι to think, because it is what gives rise to much conjecture; *prognostick*, in Greek προγνωςικὸν, from προγνώσκω, to know before, signifies the sign by which one judges a thing before hand, because a *prognostick* is rather a deduction by the use of the understanding; the *presage* is the sentiment of *presaging*, or the thing by which one *presages*.

The *omen* and *prognostick* are both drawn from external objects; the *presage* is drawn from one's own feelings. The *omen* is drawn from objects that have no necessary connexion with the thing they are made to represent; it is the fruit of the imagination, and rests on superstition: the *prognostick*, on the contrary, is a sign which partakes in some degree of the quality of the thing denoted. *Omens* were drawn by the heathens from the flight of birds, or the entrails of beasts; 'Aves dant omina dira.'—Tibullus. And oftentimes from different incidents; thus Ulysses, when landed on his native island, prayed to Jupiter that he would give him a double sign by which he might know that he should be permitted to slay the suitors of his wife; and when he heard the thunder, and saw a maiden supplicating the gods in the temple, he took these for *omens* that he should immediately proceed to put in execution his design; the *omen* was therefore considered as a supernatural sign sent for a particular purpose; 'A signal *omen* stopp'd the passing host.'—Pope. *Prognosticks*, on the other hand, are discovered only by an acquaintance with the objects in which they exist, as the *prognosticks* of a mortal disease are known to none so well as the physician; the *prognosticks* of a storm or tempest are best known to the mariner;

> Though your *prognosticks* run too fast,
> They must be verified at last.—Swift.

In an extended sense, the word *omen* is also applied to objects which serve as a sign, or enable a person to draw a rational inference, which brings it nearer in sense to the *prognostick* and the *presage:* but the *omen* may be used of that which is either good or bad, the *prognostick* mostly of that which is bad. It is an *omen* of our success, if we find those of whom we have to ask a favour in a good humour; 'Hammond would steal from his fellows into places of his privacy there to say his prayers, *omens* of his future pacific temper and eminent devotion.'—Fell. The spirit of discontent which pervades the countenances and discourse of a people is a *prognostick* of some popular commotion;

> Careful observers
> By sure *prognosticks* may foretell a shower.—Swift

Presage, when signifying a sentiment, is commonly applied to what is unfavourable; 'I know but one way of fortifying my soul against these gloomy *presages* that is, by securing to myself the protection of that Being who disposes of events.'—Addison. But when taken for that by which one *presages*, it is understood favourably, or in an indifferent sense. The quickness of powers discoverable in a boy is sometimes a *presage* of his future greatness;

> Ours joy fill'd, and shout
> *Presage* of victory.—MILTON.

TO AUGUR, PRESAGE, FOREBODE, BETOKEN, PORTEND.

Augur, in French *augurer*, Latin *augurium*, comes from *avis* a bird, as an *augury* was originally, and at all times, principally drawn from the song, the flight, or other actions of birds. The *augurium* of the Latins, and the *οἰώνισμα* of the Greeks, was a species of divination practised by the *augurs*, who professed to foretell events, either from the heavenly phenomena, from the chattering or flight of birds, from the sacred chickens, according to the manner of their eating their meat; from quadrupeds, such as wolves, foxes, goats, &c.; or, lastly, from what they called the *diræ*, or the accidents which befell persons, as sneezing, stumbling, spilling salt, or meeting particular objects; whence by a natural extension in the meaning of the term, it has been used to signify any conjecture respecting futurity. *Presage*, in French *présage*, from the Latin *præ* and *sagio* to be instinctively wise, signifies to be thus wise about what is to come; *forebode* is compounded of *fore*, and the Saxon *bodian*, and the English *bid*, to offer or to declare, signifying to pronounce on futurity; *betoken* signifies to serve as a token; *portend*, in Latin *portendo*, compounded of *por* for *pro* and *tendo*, signifies to set or show forth.

To *augur* signifies either to serve or make use of as an *augury*; to *forbode* and *presage* is to form a conclusion in one's own mind: to *betoken* or *portend* is to serve as a sign. Persons or things *augur* or *presage*; persons only *forebode*; things only *betoken* or *portend*. *Auguring* is a calculation of some future event, in which the imagination seems to as much concerned as the understanding: *presaging* rather a conclusion or deduction of what may be from what is; it lies in the understanding more than in the imagination: *foreboding* lies altogether in the imagination. Things are said to *betoken*, which present natural signs; those are said to *portend*, which present extraordinary or supernatural signs.

It *augurs* ill for the prosperity of a country or a state when its wealth has increased so as to take away the ordinary stimulus to industry, and to introduce an inordinate love of pleasure; 'There is always an *augury* to be taken of what a peace is likely to be, from the preliminary steps that are made to bring it about.'—BURKE. We *presage* the future greatness of a man from the indications which he gives of possessing an elevated character; 'An opinion has been long conceived, that quickness of invention, accuracy of judgement, or extent of knowledge, appearing before the usual time, *presage* a short life.'—JOHNSON. A distempered mind is apt to *forebode* every ill from the most trivial circumstances; 'What conscience *forebodes*, revelation verifies, assuring us that a day is appointed when God will render to every man according to his works.'—BLAIR. We see with pleasure those actions in a child which *betoken* an ingenuous temper;

> All more than common menaces an end:
> A blaze *betokens* brevity of life,
> As if bright embers should emit a flame.—YOUNG.

A mariner sees with pain the darkness of the sky which *portends* a storm;

> Skill'd in the wing'd inhabitants of the air,
> What auspices their notes and flights declare,
> O! say—for all religious rites *portend*
> A happy voyage and a prosp'rous end.—DRYDEN

The moralist *augurs* no good to the morals of a nation from the lax discipline which prevails in the education of youth; he *presages* the loss of independence to the minds of men in whom proper principles of subordination have not been early engendered. Men sometimes *forebode* the misfortunes which happen to them, but they oftener *forebode* evils which never come.

TO FORETELL, PREDICT, PROPHESY, PROGNOSTICATE.

To *foretell*, compounded of *fore* and *tell*; *predict*, from *præ* and *dico*; *prophesy*, in French *prophetiser*, Latin *prophetiso*, Greek *προφητεύω*, all signify to tell, expound, or declare what is to happen, and convey the idea of a verbal communication of futurity to others *prognosticate*, from the Greek *προγινώσκω* to know beforehand, to bode or imagine to one's self beforehand, denotes the action of feeling rather than speaking of things to come.

Foretell is the most general in its sense, and familiar in its application; we *foretell* common events; we may *predict* that which is common or uncommon; *prophecies* are for the most part important; *foretelling* is an ordinary gift; one *foretells* by a simple calculation or guess;

> Above the rest, the sun, who never lies,
> *Foretells* the change of weather in the skies.
> DRYDEN.

To *predict* and *prophesy* are extraordinary gifts; one *predicts* either by a superiour degree of intelligence, or by a supernatural power real or supposed; 'The consequences of suffering the French to establish themselves in Scotland, are *predicted* with great accuracy and discernment.'—ROBERTSON. 'In Christ they all meet with an invincible evidence, as if they were not *predictions*, but after relations; and the penmen of them not prophets, but evangelists.'—SOUTH. One *prophesies* by means of inspiration real or supposed;

> An ancient augur *prophesied* from hence,
> "Behold on Latian shores a foreign prince!"
> DRYDEN.

Men of discernment and experience easily *foretell* the events of undertakings which fall under their notice. The priests among the heathens, like the astrologers and conjurers of more modern times, pretended to *predict* events that effected nations and empires. The gift of *prophecy* was one among the number of the supernatural gifts communicated to the primitive Christians by the Holy Ghost. 'No arguments made a stronger impression on these Pagan converts, than the predictions relating to our Saviour, in those old prophetick writings deposited among the hands of the greatest enemies to Christianity.'—ADDISON.

Prediction as a noun is employed for both the verbs *foretell* and *predict*; it is therefore a term of less value than *prophecy*. We speak of a *prediction* being verified, and a *prophecy* fulfilled: the *predictions* of almanack-makers respecting the weather are as seldom verified as the *prophecies* of visionaries and enthusiasts are fulfilled respecting the death of princes or the affairs of governments. To *prognosticate* is an act of the understanding; it is guided by outward symptoms as a rule; it is only stimulated and not guided by outward objects; a physician *prognosticates* the crisis of a disorder by the symptoms discoverable in the patient; 'Who that should view the small beginnings of some persons could imagine or *prognosticate* those vast increases of fortune that have afterward followed them—SOUTH.

CONJECTURE, SUPPOSITION, SURMISE.

Conjecture, in French *conjecture*, Latin *conjectura* from *conjicio* or *con* and *jacio* to throw together, signifies the thing put together or framed in the mind without design or foundation; *supposition*, in French *supposition*, from *suppono*, compounded of *sub* and *pono* to put in the place of a thing, signifies to put one's thoughts in the place of reality; *surmise*, compounded of *sur* or *sub* and *mise*, Latin *missus* participle of *mitto* to send or put forth, has an original meaning similar to the former.

All these terms convey an idea of something in the mind independent of the reality; but *conjecture* is founded less on rational inference than *supposition*; and *surmise* less than either; any circumstance, however trivial, may give rise to a *conjecture*; some reasons are requisite to produce a *supposition*; a particular state of feeling or train of thinking may of itself create a *surmise*.

Although the same epithets are generally applicable to all these terms, yet we may with propriety say that a *conjecture* is idle; a *supposition* false; a *surmise* fanciful.

Conjectures are employed on events, their causes, consequences, and contingencies; 'In the casting of lots, a man cannot, upon any ground of reason, bring the event so much as under *conjecture*.'—SOUTH. *Supposition* is concerned in speculative points; 'This is only an infallibility upon *supposition*, that if a thing be true it is impossible to be false.'—TILLOTSON. *Surmise* is employed on personal concerns; 'To let go private *surmises* whereby the thing is not made better or worse; if just and allowable reasons might lead them to do as they did, then are these censures frustrate.'—HOOKER. The secret measures of government give rise to various *conjectures:* all the *suppositions* which are formed respecting comets seem at present to fall short of the truth: the behaviour of a person will often occasion a *surmise* respecting his intentions and proceedings, let them be ever so disguised. Antiquarians and etymologists deal much in *conjectures;* they have ample scope afforded them for asserting what can be neither proved nor denied; 'Persons of studious and contemplative natures often entertain themselves with the history of past ages, or raise schemes and *conjectures* upon futurity.'—ADDISON. Religionists are pleased to build many *suppositions* of a doctrinal nature on the Scriptures, or, more properly, on their own partial and forced interpretations of the Scriptures; 'Even in that part which we have of the journey to Canterbury, it will be necessary, in the following Review of Chaucer, to take notice of certain defects and inconsistencies, which can only be accounted for upon the *supposition* that the work was never finished by the author.'—TYRWHITT. It is the part of prudence, as well as justice, not to express any *surmises* which we may entertain, either as to the character or conduct of others, which may not redound to their credit; 'Any the least *surmise* of neglect has raised an aversion in one man to another.'—SOUTH.

TO CONJECTURE, GUESS, DIVINE

Conjecturing, in the same sense as before (vide *Conjecture*), in nearly allied to *guessing* and *divining; guess*, in Saxon and Low German *gissen*, is connected with the word *ghost*, and the German *geist*, &c. spirit, signifying the action of a spirit; *divine*, from the Latin *divinus* and *Deus* a God, signifies to think and know as independently as a God.

We *conjecture* that which may be; 'When we look upon such things as equally may or may not be, human reason can then, at the best, but *conjecture* what will be.'—SOUTH. We *guess* that a thing actually is or was;

> Incapable and shallow innocents!
> You cannot *guess* who caused your father's death.
> SHAKSPEARE.

We *conjecture* at the meaning of a person's actions; we *guess* that it is a certain hour. The *conjecturing* is opposed to the full conviction of a thing; the *guessing* is opposed to the certain knowledge of a thing;

> And these discoveries make us all confess
> That sublunary science is but *guess*.—DENHAM.

A child *guesses* at that portion of his lesson which he has not properly learned; a fanciful person employs *conjecture* where he cannot draw any positive conclusion.

To *guess* and *conjecture* both imply, for the most part, the judging or forming an opinion without any grounds; but sometimes they are used for a judgement on some grounds; 'One may *guess* by Plato's writings, that his meaning as to the inferiour deities, was, that they who would have them might, and they who would not might leave them alone; but that himself had a right opinion concerning the true God.'—STILLINGFLEET.

> Now hear the Grecian fraud, and from this one
> *Conjecture* all the rest.—DRYDEN.

To *guess* and *conjecture* are the natural acts of the mind: *divine*, in its proper sense, is a supernatural act; in this sense the heathens affected to *divine* that which was known only to an Omniscient Being; and impostors in our time presume to *divine* in matters that are set above the reach of human comprehension. The term is however employed to denote a species of *guessing* in different matters, as to *divine* the meaning of a mystery;

> Walking they talk'd, and fruitlessly *divin'd*
> What friend the priestess by those words design'd.
> DRYDEN.

TO DOUBT, QUESTION, DISPUTE.

Doubt, in French *douter*, Latin *dubito* from *dubius*, comes from δύω and ἐνδοιάζω, in the same manner as our frequentative *doubt*, signifying to have two opinions; *question*, in Latin *quæstio*, from *quæro*, to inquire, signifies to make a question or inquiry: *dispute*, from the Latin *disputo*, or *dis* asunder and *puto* to think, signifies literally to think differently.

These terms express the act of the mind in staying its decision. The *doubt* lies altogether in the mind; it is a less active feeling than *questioning* or *disputing*: by the former we merely suspend decision; by the latter we actually demand proofs in order to assist us in deciding. We may *doubt* in silence; we cannot *question* or *dispute* without expressing it directly or indirectly.

He who suggests *doubts* does it with caution; he who makes a *question* throws in difficulties with a degree of confidence. *Doubts* insinuate themselves into the mind oftentimes involuntarily on the part of the *doubter; questions* are always made with an express design. We *doubt* in matters of general interest, on abstruse as well as common subjects; we *question* mostly in ordinary matters that are of a personal interest; *disputing* is no less personal than questioning, but the *dispute* respects the opinions or assertions of another; the *question* respects his moral character or qualities; we *doubt* the truth of a position; 'For my part I think the being of a God is so little to be *doubted*, that I think it is almost the only truth we are sure of.'—ADDISON. We *question* the veracity of an author;

> Our business in the field of fight
> Is not to *question*, but to prove our might.—POPE.

The existence of mermaids was *doubted* for a great length of time; but the testimony of creditable persons, who have lately seen them, ought now to put it out of all *doubt*. When the practicability of any plan is *questioned*, it is unnecessary to enter any farther into its merits. When the authority of the person is *disputed* it is in vain for him to offer his advice or opinion;

> Now I am sent, and am not to *dispute*
> My prince's orders, but to execute.

The *doubt* is frequently confined to the individual, the *question* and *dispute* frequently respect others. We *doubt* whether we shall be able to succeed; we *question* another's right to interfere; we *dispute* a person's claim to any honour; we *doubt* whether a thing will answer the end proposed; we *question* the utility of any one making the attempt; we *dispute* the justice of any legal sentence; in this application of the terms *question* and *dispute*, the former expresses a less decisive feeling and action than the latter.

There are many *doubtful* cases in medicine, where the physician is at a loss to decide; there are many *questionable* measures proposed by those who are in or out of power which demand consideration. There are many *disputable* points between man and man which cause much angry feeling and disposition; to *doubt* every thing is more inimical to the cause of truth, than the readiness to believe every thing; a disposition to *question* whatever is said or done by others, is much more calculated to give offence than to prevent deception. A disposition to *dispute* every thing another says or does renders a person very unfit to be dealt with.

DOUBT, SUSPENSE.

The *doubt* respects that which we should believe; the *suspense*, from the Latin *suspensus* and *suspendeo* to hang upon, has regard to that which we wish to know or ascertain. We are in *doubt* for the want of evidence; we are in *suspense* for the want of certainty. The *doubt* interrupts our progress in the attainment of truth; 'Could any difficulty have been proposed, the resolution would have been as early as the proposal; it could not have had time to settle into *doubt*.'—SOUTH. The *suspense* impedes us in the attainment of our objects, or in our motives to action: the former is connected principally with the understanding; the latter acts upon the hopes; it is frequently a state between hope and fear. We have our *doubts* about things that have no regard to time; 'Gold is a wonderful clearer of the understanding; it dissipates every *doubt* and scruple in an instant.'—ADDISON. We are in *suspense* about things that are to happen in future, or that are about to be done; 'The bundle of hay on either side striking his (the ass's) sight and smell in the same proportion, would keep him in perpetual *suspense*.'—Addison. Those are the least inclined to *doubt* who have the most thorough knowledge of a subject; those are the least exposed to the unpleasant feeling of *suspense* who confine their wishes to the present;

Ten days the prophet in *suspense* remain'd,
Would no man's fate pronounce; at last constrain'd
By Ithacus, he solemnly design'd
Me for the sacrifice.—Dryden.

DOUBTFUL, DUBIOUS, UNCERTAIN, PRECARIOUS.

The *doubtful* admits of doubt (*v. Doubt, suspense*): the *dubious* creates suspense. The *doubtful* is said of things in which we are required to have an opinion; the *dubious* respects events and things that must speak for themselves. In *doubtful* cases it is adviseable for a judge to lean to the side of mercy; 'In handling the right of war, I am not willing to intermix matter *doubtful* with that which is out of *doubt*.' —Bacon. While the issue of a contest is *dubious*, all judgment of the parties, or of the case, must be carefully avoided;

His utmost pow'r, with adverse power oppos'd
In *dubious* battle on the plains of heav'n.
Milton.

It is worthy of remark, however, that *doubtful* and *dubious*, being both derivations from the same Latin words *dubito* and *dubius*, are or may be indifferently used in many instances, according as it may suit the verse or otherwise;

The Greeks with slain Tlepolemus retir'd,
Whose fall Ulysses view'd with fury fir'd;
Doubtful if Jove's great son he should pursue,
Or pour his vengeance on the Lycian crew.—Pope.

'At the lower end of the room is to be a side-table for persons of great fame, but *dubious* existence, such as Hercules, Theseus, Æneas, Achilles, Hector, and others.'—Swift.

Doubtful and *dubious* have always a relation to the person forming the opinion on the subject in question; *uncertain* and *precarious* are epithets which designate the qualities of the things themselves. Whatever is uncertain may from that very circumstance be *doubtful* or *dubious* to those who attempt to determine upon them; but they may be designated for their *uncertainty* without any regard to the opinions which they may give rise to.

A person's coming may be *doubtful* or *uncertain;* the length of his stay is oftener described as *uncertain* than as *doubtful*. The *doubtful* is opposed to that on which we form a positive conclusion; the *uncertain* to that which is definite or prescribed. The efficacy of any medicine is *doubtful;* the manner of its operation may be *uncertain*. While our knowledge is limited, we must expect to meet with many things that are *doubtful;* 'In *doubtful* cases reason still determines for the safer side; especially if the case be not only *doubtful*, but also highly concerning, and the venture be a soul, and an eternity.' —South. As every thing in the world is exposed to change, and all that is future is entirely above our control, we must naturally expect to find every thing *uncertain*, but what we see passing before us;

Near old Antandros, and at Ida's foot,
The timber of the sacred grove we cut
And build our fleet, *uncertain* yet to find
What place the gods for our repose assign'd.
Dryden.

Precarious, from the Latin *precarius* and *precor* to pray, signifies granted to entreaty, depending on the will or humor of another, whence it is applicable to whatever is obtained from others. *Precarious* is the highest species of uncertainty, applied to such things as depend on future casualties in opposition to that which is fixed and determined by design. The weather is *uncertain;* the subsistence of a person who has no stated income or source of living must be *precarious*. It is *uncertain* what day a thing may take place, until it is determined; 'Man, without the protection of a superior Being, is secure of nothing that he enjoys, and *uncertain* of every thing he hopes for. —Tillotson. There is nothing more *precarious* than what depends upon the favour of statesmen; 'The frequent disappointments incident to hunting induced men to establish a permanent property in their flocks and herds, in order to sustain themselves in a less *precarious* manner.'—Blackstone.

DEMUR, DOUBT, HESITATION, OBJECTION

The *demur*, the *doubt*, and the *hesitation* are here employed in the sense either of what causes *demur doubt*, and *hesitation*, or of the states of mind themselves; the *objection*, from *objicio*, or *ob* and *jacio* to throw in the way, signifies what is thrown in the way so as to stop our progress.

Demurs are often in matters of deliberation; *doubt* in regard to matters of fact; *hesitation* in matters of ordinary conduct; and *objections* in matters of common consideration. It is the business of one who gives counsel to make *demurs;* it is the business of the inquirer to suggest *doubts;* it is the business of all occasionally to make a *hesitation* who are called upon to decide; it is the business of those to make *objections* whose opinion is consulted. Artabanes made many *demurs* to the proposed invasion of Greece by Xerxes· 'Certainly the highest and dearest concerns of a temporal life are infinitely less valuable than those of an eternal; and consequently ought, without any *demur* at all, to be sacrificed to them whenever they come in competition with them.'—South. *Doubts* have been suggested respecting the veracity of Herodotus as an historian;

Our *doubts* are traitors,
And make us lose, by fearing to attempt
The good we oft might win.—Shakspeare.

It is not proper to ask that which cannot be granted without *hesitation;* 'A spirit of revenge makes him curse the Grecians in the seventh book, when they *hesitate* to accept Hector's challenge.'—Pope. And it is not the part of an amiable disposition to make a *hesitation* in complying with a reasonable request: there are but few things which we either attempt to do or recommend to others that is not liable to some kind of an *objection*.

A *demur* stops the adjustment of any plan or the determination of any question:

But with rejoinders and replies,
Long bills, and answers stuff'd with lies,
Demur, imparlance, and assoign,
The parties ne'er could issue join.—Swift

A *doubt* interrupts the progress of the mind in coming to a state of satisfaction and certainty: they are both applied to abstract questions or such as are of general interest; 'This skeptical proceeding will make every sort of reasoning on every subject vain and frivolous, even that skeptical reasoning itself which has persuaded us to entertain a *doubt* concerning the agreement of our perceptions.'—Burke.

Hesitation and *objection* are more individual and private in their nature. *Hesitation* lies mostly in the state of the will; *objection* is rather the offspring of the understanding. The *hesitation* interferes with the action; 'If every man were wise and virtuous, capable to discern the best use of time and resolute to practise it, it might be granted, I think, without *hesitation*, that total liberty would be a blessing.'—Johnson The *objection* affects the measure or the mode of action; 'Lloyd was always raising *objections* and removing them.'—Johnson.

TO DEMUR, HESITATE, PAUSE.

Demur, in French *demeurer*, Latin *demorari*, signifies to keep back; *hesitate*, in Latin *hæsitatum*, participle of *hæsito*, a frequentative from *hæro*, signifies, first to stick at one thing and then another; *pause*, in Latin *pausa*, from the Greek παύω, to cease, signifies to make a stand.

The idea of stopping is common to these terms, to which signification is added some distinct collateral idea for each: we *demur* from doubt or difficulty; we *hesitate* from an undecided state of mind; we *pause* from *circumstances*. *Demurring* is the act of an equal: we *demur* in giving our assent; *hesitating* is often the ıct of a superiour; we *hesitate* in giving our consent: when a proposition appears to be unjust we *demur* in supporting it on the ground of its injustice; 'In order to banish an evil out of the world that does not only produce great uneasiness to private persons, but has also a very bad influence on the publick, I shall endeavour to show the folly of *demurring*.'—ADDISON. When a request of a dubious nature is made to us we *hesitate* in complying with it; 'I want no solicitations for me to comply where it would be ungenerous for me to refuse; for can I *hesitate* a moment to take upon myself the protection of a daughter of Correllius?'—MELMOTH'S LETTERS OF PLINY. Prudent people are most apt to *demur;* but people of a wavering temper are apt to *hesitate: demurring* may be often unnecessary, but it is seldom injurious; *hesitating* is mostly injurious when it is not necessary; the former is employed in matters that admit of delay; the latter in cases where immediate decision is requisite.

Demurring and *hesitating* are both employed as acts of the mind; *pausing* is an external action: we *demur* and *hesitate* in determining; we *pause* in speaking or doing any thing;

> Think, O think,
> And ere thou plunge into the vast abyss,
> *Pause* on the verge awhile, look down and see
> Thy future mansion.—PORTEUS.

TO SCRUPLE, HESITATE, WAVER, FLUCTUATE.

To *scruple* (*v. Conscientious*) simply keeps us from deciding; the *hesitation*, from the Latin *hæsito*, frequentative of *hæreo* to stick, signifying to stick first at one thing and then another; the *wavering*, from the word *wave*, signifying to move backward and forward like a wave; and *fluctuation*, from the Latin *fluctus* a wave, all bespeak the variable state of the mind: we *scruple* simply from motives of doubt as to the propriety of a thing; we *hesitate* and *waver* from various motives, particularly such as affect our interests. Conscience produces *scruples*, fear produces *hesitation*, passion produces *wavering:* a person *scruples* to do an action which may hurt his neighbour or offend his Maker; he *hesitates* to do a thing which he fears may not prove advantageous to him; he *wavers* in his mind between going or staying, according as his inclinations impel him to the one or the other: a man who does not *scruple* to say or do as he pleases will be an offensive companion, if not a dangerous member of society; 'The Jacobins desire a change, and they will have it if they can; if they cannot have it by English cabal, they will make no sort of *scruple* to have it by the cabal of France.'—BURKE. He who *hesitates* only when the doing of good is proposed, evinces himself a worthless member of society; 'The lords of the congregation did not *hesitate* a moment whether they should employ their whole strength in one generous effort to rescue their religion and liberty from impending destruction.'—ROBERTSON. He who *wavers* between his duty and his inclination, will seldom maintain a long or doubtful contest; 'It is the greatest absurdity to be *wavering* and unsettled without closing with that side which appears the most safe and probable.'—ADDISON.

To *fluctuate* conveys the idea of strong agitation; to *waver*, that of constant motion backward and forward: when applied in the moral sense, to *fluctuate* designates the action of the spirits or the opinions; to *waver* is said only of the will or opinions: he who is alternately merry and sad in quick succession is said to be *fluctuating;* or he who has many opinions in quick succession is said to *fluctuate;* but he who cannot form an opinion, or come to a resolution, is said to *waver*.

Fluctuations and *waverings* are both opposed to a manly character; but the former evinces the uncontrolled influence of the passions, the total want of that equanimity which characterizes the Christian; the latter denotes the want of fixed principle, or the necessary decision of character: we can never have occasion to *fluctuate*, if we never raise our hopes and wishes beyond what is attainable;

> The tempter, but with show of zeal and love
> To man, and indignation at his wrong,
> New part puts on, and as to passion mov'd
> *Fluctuates* disturb'd.—MILTON.

We can never have occasion to *waver*, if we know and feel what is right,and resolve never to swerve from it; 'Let a man, without trepidation or *wavering*, proceed in discharging his duty.'—BLAIR.

TO HESITATE, FAULTER, STAMMER, STUTTER.

Hesitate signifies the same as in the preceding article; *falter* or *faulter* seems to signify to commit a *fault* or blunder, or it may be a frequentative of to fall, signifying to stumble; *stammer*, in the Teutonic *stammern*, comes most probably from the Hebrew סתם to obstruct; *stutter* is but a variation of *stammer*.

A defect in utterance is the idea which is common in the signification of all these terms: they differ either as to the cause or the mode of the action. With regard to the cause, a *hesitation* results from the state of the mind, and an interruption in the train of thoughts; *falter* arises from a perturbed state of feeling; *stammer* and *stutter* arise either from an incidental circumstance, or more commonly from a physical defect in the organs of utterance. A person who is not in the habits of publick speaking, or of collecting his thoughts into a set form, will be apt to *hesitate* even in familiar conversation; he who first addresses a publick assembly will be apt to *falter*. Children who first begin to read will *stammer* at hard words: and one who has an impediment in his speech will *stutter* when he attempts to speak in a hurry.

With regard to the mode or degree of the action, *hesitate* expresses less than *falter: stammer* less than *stutter*.

The slightest difficulty in uttering words constitutes a *hesitation;* a pause or the repetition of a word may be termed *hesitating;* 'To look with solicitude and speak with *hesitation* is attainable at will; but the show of wisdom is ridiculous when there is nothing to cause doubt, as that of valour when there is nothing to be feared.'—JOHNSON. To *falter* supposes a failure in the voice as well as the lips when they refuse to do their office;

> And yet was every *faultering* tongue of man,
> Almighty Father! silent in thy praise,
> Thy works themselves would raise a general voice.
> THOMSON.

Stammering and *stuttering* are confined principally to the useless moving of the mouth;

> Lagean juice
> Will *stamm'ring* tongues and stagg'ring feet produce.
> DRYDEN.

He who *stammers* brings forth sounds, but not the right sounds, without trials and efforts; he who *stutters* remains for some time in a state of agitation without uttering a sound.

QUESTION, QUERY.

The *question* is the thing called in *question*, or that which is sought for by a *question; query* is but a variation of *quære*, from the verb *quæro* to seek or inquire, signifying simply the thing sought for.

Questions and *queries* are both put for the sake of obtaining an answer; but the former may be for a reasonable or unreasonable cause; a *query* is mostly a rational *question:* idlers may put *questions* from mere curiosity; learned men put *queries* for the sake of information.

TO ASK, INQUIRE, QUESTION, INTERROGATE.

Ask, comes from the Saxon *ascian*, low German *esken*, *eschen*, German *heischen*, Danish *adske*, &c. which for the most part signify to wish for, and come from the Greek ἀξιόω to think worthy; whence this word in English has been employed for an expression of our wishes, for the purpose of obtaining what we want from others; *inquire*, Latin *inquiro*, compounded of *in* and *quæro*, signifies to search after; *question*, in Latin is a variation of the same word; *interrogate* Latin *interrogatus*, participle of *interrogo*, compounded of *inter* and *rogo*, signifies to *ask* alternately or an asking between different persons.

We perform all these actions in order to get infor

mation: but we *ask* for general purposes of convenience; we *inquire* from motives of curiosity; we *question* and *interrogate* from motives of discretion. To *ask* respects simply one thing; to *inquire* respects one or many subjects; to *question* and *interrogate* is to *ask* repeatedly, to examine by questioning and interrogating, and in the latter case more authoritatively than in the former.

Indifferent people *ask* of each other whatever they wish to know; 'Upon my *asking* her who it was, she told me it was a very grave elderly gentleman, but that she did not know his name.'—ADDISON. Learners *inquire* the reasons of things which are new to them;

> You have oft *inquir'd*
> After the shepherd that complain'd of love.
> SHAKSPEARE.

Masters *question* their servants, or parents their children, when they wish to ascertain the real state of any case;

> But hark you, Kate,
> I must not henceforth have you *question* me
> Whither I go.—SHAKSPEARE.

Magistrates *interrogate* criminals when they are rought before them; 'Thomson was introduced to the Prince of Wales, and being gayly *interrogated* about the state of his affairs, said, "that they were in a more poetical posture than formerly."'—JOHNSON. It is very uncivil not to answer whatever is *asked* even by the meanest person: it is proper to satisfy every *inquiry*, so as to remove doubt: *questions* are sometimes so impertinent that they cannot with propriety be answered: *interrogations* from unauthorized persons are little better than insults. To *ask* and *interrogate* are always personal acts; to *inquire* and *question* are frequently applied to things, the former in the sense of seeking (*v. Examination*), and the latter in that of doubting (*v. To Doubt*).

EXAMINATION, SEARCH, INQUIRY, RESEARCH, INVESTIGATION, SCRUTINY.

Examination comes from the Latin *examino* and *examen*, the beam by which the poise of the balance is held, because the judgement keeps itself as it were in a balance in *examining; search*, in French *chercher*, is a variation of seek and see; *inquiry* signifies the same as in the preceding article; *research* is an intensive of *search; investigation*, from the Latin *vestigium*, a track, signifies seeking by the tracks or footsteps; *scrutiny*, from the Latin *scrutor*, to search, and *scrutum*, lumber, signifies looking for among lumber and rubbish, i. e. to ransack and turn over.

Examination is the most general of these terms, which all agree in expressing an active effort to find out that which is unknown. The *examination* is made either by the aid of the senses or the understanding, the body or the mind; the *search* is principally a physical action; the *inquiry* is mostly intellectual; we *examine* a face or we *examine* a subject; we *search* a house or a dictionary; we *inquire* into a matter. An *examination* is made for the purpose of forming a judgement; the *search* is made for ascertaining a fact; the *inquiry* is made in order to arrive at truth. To *examine* a person, is either by means of questions to get at his mind, or by means of looks to become acquainted with his person; to *search* a person is by corporeal contact to learn what he has about him. We *examine* the features of those who interest us; officers of justice *search* those who are suspected; but, with the prepositions for or after, the verb *search* may be employed in a moral application; 'If you *search* purely for truth, it will be indifferent to you where you find it.'—BUDGELL. *Examinations* and *inquiries* are both made by means of questions; but the former is an official act for a specifick end, the latter is a private act for purposes of convenience or pleasure. Students undergo *examinations* from their teachers; they pursue their *inquiries* for themselves.

An *examination* or an *inquiry* may be set on foot on any subject: but the *examination* is direct; it is the setting of things before the view, corporeal or mental, in order to obtain a conclusion; 'The body of man is such a subject as stands the utmost test of *examination*.'—ADDISON. The *inquiry* is indirect; it is a circuitous method of coming to the knowledge of what was not known before; '*Inquiries* after happiness are not so necessary and useful to mankind as the arts of consolation.'—ADDISON. The student *examines* the evidences of Christianity, that he may strengthen his own belief; the government institute an *inquiry* into the conduct of subjects. A *research* is an *inquiry* into that which is remote; an *investigation* is a minute *inquiry; a scrutiny* is a strict *examination*. Learned men of inquisitive tempers make their *researches* into antiquity;

> To all inferiour animals 'tis giv'n
> T' enjoy the state allotted them by heav'n;
> No vain *researches* e'er disturb their rest.—JENYNS

Magistrates *investigate* doubtful and mysterious affairs; physicians *investigate* the causes of diseases; 'We have divided natural philosophy into the *investigation* of causes, and the production of effects.'—BACON. Men *scrutinize* the actions of those whom they hold in suspicion; 'Before I go to bed, I make a *scrutiny* what peccant humours have reigned in me that day.'—HOWELL. Acuteness and penetration are peculiarly requisite in making *researches;* patience and perseverance are the necessary qualifications of the *investigator;* a quick discernment will essentially aid the *scrutinizer*.

TO EXAMINE, SEEK, SEARCH, EXPLORE

These words are here considered as they designate the looking upon places or objects, in order to get acquainted with them. To *examine* (*v. Examination*) expresses less than to *seek* and *search:* and these less than to *explore*, which, from the Latin *ex* and *ploro*, signifies to burst forth, whether in lamentation or *examination*.

We *examine* objects that are near; we *seek* those that are remote or not at hand; *search* those that are hidden or out of sight; we *explore* those that are unknown or very distant. The painter *examines* a landscape in order to take a sketch of it;

> Compare each phrase, *examine* ev'ry line,
> Weigh ev'ry word, and ev'ry thought refine.—POPE.

One friend *seeks* another when they have parted;

> I have a venturous fairy, that shall *seek*
> The squirrel's hoard, and fetch thee thence new nuts.
> SHAKSPEARE.

The botanist *searches* after curious plants; the inquisitive traveller *explores* unknown regions; the writer *examines* the books from which he intends to draw his authorities; 'Men will look into our lives, and *examine* our actions, and inquire into our conversations; by these they will judge the truth and reality of our profession.'—TILLOTSON. A person *seeks* an opportunity to effect a purpose;

> Sweet peace, where dost thou dwell?
> I humbly crave
> Let me once know,
> I *sought* thee in a secret cave,
> And ask'd if peace were there.—HERBER

The antiquarian *searches* every corner in which he hopes to find a monument of antiquity;

> Not thou, nor they shall *search* the thoughts that roll
> Up in the close recesses of my soul.—POPE.

The classick *explores* the learning and wisdom of the ancients;

> Hector, he said, my courage bids me meet
> This high achievement, and *explore* the fleet.—POPE.

TO DISCUSS, EXAMINE.

Discuss, in Latin *discussus*, participle of *discutio*, signifies to shake asunder or to separate thoroughly so as to see the whole composition; *examine* has the same signification as in the preceding article, because the judgement holds the balance in examining.

The intellectual operation expressed by these terms is applied to objects that cannot be immediately discerned or understood, but they vary both in mode and degree. *Discussion* is altogether carried on by verbal and personal communication; *examination* proceeds by reading, reflection, and observation; we often examine therefore by *discussion*, which is properly one mode of *examination: a discussion* is always carried on by two or more persons; an *examination* may be carried on by one only: politicks are a frequent though not always a pleasant subject of *discussion* in social meetings; 'A country fellow distinguishes himself as much in the church-yard as a citizen does upon the change; the whole parish politicks being generally *discussed* in that place either after sermon or before the bell rings.'—ADDISON. Complicated questions cannot be too thoroughly *examined;* 'Men follow their inclinations without *examining* whether there be any principles which they ought to form for regulating their conduct.'—BLAIR. *Discussion* serves for amusement rather than for any solid purpose; the cause of truth seldom derives any immediate benefit from it, although the minds of men may become invigorated by a collision of sentiment: *examination* is of great practical utility in the direction of our conduct: all decisions must be partial, unjust, or imprudent, which are made without previous *examination.*

TO PRY, SCRUTINIZE, DIVE INTO.

Pry is in all probability changed from prove, in the sense of try; *scrutinize* comes from the Latin *scrutor* to search thoroughly (*v. Examination*) *dive* expresses the physical action of going under water to the bottom, and figuratively of searching to the bottom.

Pry is taken in the bad sense of looking more narrowly into things than one ought: *scrutinize* and *dive into* are employed in the good sense of searching things to the bottom.

A person who *pries* looks into that which does not belong to him; and too narrowly also into that which may belong to him; it is the consequence of a too eager curiosity or a busy, meddling temper: a person who *scrutinizes* looks into that which is intentionally concealed from him; it is an act of duty flowing out of his office: a person who *dives* penetrates into that which lies hidden very deep; he is impelled to this action by the thirst of knowledge and a laudable curiosity.

A love of *prying* into the private affairs of families makes a person a troublesome neighbour; 'The peaceable man never officiously seeks to *pry* into the secrets of others.'—BLAIR. It is the business of the magistrate to *scrutinize* into all matters which affect the good order of society; 'He who enters upon this *scrutiny* (into the depths of the mind) enters into a labyrinth.' —SOUTH. There are some minds so imbued with a love of science that they delight to *dive into* the secrets of nature;

> In man the more we *dive*, the more we see,
> Heaven's signet stamping an immortal make.
> YOUNG.

CURIOUS, INQUISITIVE, PRYING.

Curious, in French *curieux*, Latin *curiosus*, from *cura* care, signifying full of care; *inquisitive*, in Latin *inquisitus*, from *inquiro* to inquire or search into, signifies a disposition to investigate thoroughly; *prying* signifies the disposition to *pry*, try, or sift to the bottom.

The disposition to interest one's self in matters not of immediate concern to one's self is the idea common to all these terms. *Curiosity* is directed to all objects that can gratify the inclination, taste, or understanding; *inquisitiveness* to such things only as satisfy the understanding.

The *curious* person interests himself in all the works of nature and art; he is *curious* to try effects and examine causes: the *inquisitive* person endeavours to add to his store of knowledge. *Curiosity* employs every means which falls in its way in order to procure gratification; the *curious* man uses his own powers or those of others to serve his purpose; *inquisitiveness* is indulged only by means of verbal inquiry; the *inquisitive* person collects all from others. A traveller is *curious* who examines every thing for himself; 'Sir Francis Bacon says, some have been so *curious* as to remark the times and seasons, when the stroke of an envious eye is most effectually pernicious.' —STEELE. He is *inquisitive* when he minutely questions others. *Inquisitiveness* is therefore to *curiosity* as a part to the whole; whoever is *curious* will naturally be *inquisitive*, and he who is *inquisitive* is so from a species of *curiosity;* but *inquisitiveness* may sometimes be taken in an improper sense for moral objects; 'Checking our *inquisitive* solicitude about what the Almighty hath concealed, let us diligently improve what he hath made known.'—BLAIR.

Curious and *inquisitive* may be both used in a bad sense; *prying* is never used otherwise than in a bad sense. *Inquisitive*, as in the former case, is a mode of *curiosity*, and *prying* is a species of eager *curiosity.* A *curious* person takes unallowed means of learning that which he ought not to wish to know; an *inquisitive* person puts many impertinent and troublesome questions; a *prying* temper is unceasing in its endeavours to get acquainted with the secrets of others. *Curiosity* is a fault common to females; *inquisitiveness* is most general among children; a *prying* temper belongs only to people of low character.

A well-disciplined mind checks the first risings of idle *curiosity:* children should be taught early to suppress an *inquisitive* temper, which may so easily become burdensome to others: those who are of a *prying* temper are insensible to every thing but the desire of unveiling what lies hidden; such a disposition is often engendered by the unlicensed indulgence of *curiosity* in early life, which becomes a sort of passion in riper years; 'By adhering tenaciously to his opinion, and exhibiting other instances of a *prying* disposition, Lord George Sackville had rendered himself disagreeable to the commander-in-chief.'—SMOLLET.

CONCEIT, FANCY.

Conceit comes immediately from the Latin *conceptus*, participle of *concipio* to conceive, or form in the mind; *fancy*, in French *phantasie*, Latin *phantasia*, Greek *φαντασία*, from *φαντάζω* to make appear, and *φαίνω* to appear.

These terms equally express the working of the imagination in its distorted state; but *conceit* denotes a much greater degree of distortion than *fancy;* what we *conceit* is preposterous; what we *fancy* is unreal, or only apparent. *Conceit* applies only to internal objects; it is mental in the operation and the result; it is a species of invention; 'Strong *conceit*, like a new principle, carries all easily with it, when yet above common sense.'—LOCKE. *Fancy* is applied to external objects, or whatever acts on the senses: nervous people are subject to strange *conceits;* timid people *fancy* they hear sounds, or see objects in the dark which awaken terror.

Those who are apt to *conceit* oftener *conceit* that which is painful than otherwise;

> Some have been wounded with *conceit*,
> And died of mere opinion strait.—BUTLER.

Conceiting either that they are always in danger of dying, or that all the world is their enemy. There are however insane people who *conceit* themselves to be kings and queens; and some indeed who are not called insane, who *conceit* themselves very learned while they know nothing, or very wise and clever, while they are exposing themselves to perpetual ridicule for their folly, or very handsome while the world calls them plain, or very peaceable while they are always quarrelling with their neighbours, or very humble while they are tenaciously sticking for their own: it would be well if such *conceits* afforded a harmless pleasure to their authors, but unfortunately they only render them more offensive and disgusting than they would otherwise be.

Those who are apt to *fancy*, never *fancy* any thing to please themselves;

> Desponding fear, of feeble *fancies* full,
> Weak and unmanly, loosens every power.
> THOMSON.

They *fancy* that things are too long or too short, too thick or too thin, too cold or too hot, with a thousand other *fancies* equally trivial in their nature; thereby proving that the slightest aberration of the mind is a serious evil, and productive of evil.

When taken in reference to intellectual objects, *conceit* is mostly in a bad sense; 'Nothing can be more plainly impossible than for a man "to be profitable to God," and consequently nothing can be more absurd than for a man to cherish so irrational a *conceit.*'—ADDISON. But *fancy* may be employed in a good sense; 'My friend, Sir Roger de Coverley, told me t'other day, that he had been reading my paper upon Westminster Abbey, in which, says he, there are a great many ingenious *fancies*.'—ADDISON.

OPINIATED OR OPINIATIVE, CONCEITED, EGOISTICAL.

A fondness for one's opinion bespeaks the *opiniated* man: a fond conceit of one's self bespeaks the *conceited* man: a fond attachment to one's self bespeaks the *egoistical* man: a liking for one's self or one's own is evidently the common idea that runs through these terms; they differ in the mode and in the object.

An *opiniated* man is not only fond of his own *opinion*, but full of his own *opinion*: he has an *opinion* on every thing, which is the best possible *opinion*, and is delivered therefore freely to every one, that they may profit in forming their own *opinions*; 'Down was he cast from all his greatness, as it is pity but all such politick *opiniators* should.'—SOUTH. A *conceited* man has a *conceit* or an idle, fond *opinion* of his own talent; it is not only high in competition with others, but it is so high as to be set above others. The *conceited* man does not want to follow the ordinary means of acquiring knowledge: his *conceit* suggests to him that his talent will supply labour, application, reading and study, and every other contrivance which men have commonly employed for their improvement; he sees by intuition what another learns by experience and observation; he knows in a day what others want years to acquire; he learns of himself what others are contented to get by means of instruction; 'No great measure at a very difficult crisis can be pursued which is not attended with some mischief; none but *conceited* pretenders in publick business hold any other language.'—BURKE. The *egoistical* man makes himself the darling theme of his own contemplation; he admires and loves himself to that degree that he can talk and think of nothing else; his children, his house, his garden, his rooms, and the like, are the incessant theme of his conversation, and become invaluable from the mere circumstance of belonging to him; 'To show their particular aversion to speaking in the first person, the gentlemen of Port Royal branded this form of writing with the name of *egotism*.'—ADDISON.

An *opiniated* man is the most unfit for conversation, which only affords pleasure by an alternate and equable communication of sentiment. A *conceited* man is the most unfit for co-operation, where a junction of talent and effort is essential to bring things to a conclusion; an *egoistical* man is the most unfit to be a companion or friend, for he does not know how to value or like any thing out of himself.

SELF-WILL, SELF-CONCEIT, SELF-SUFFICIENCY.

Self-will signifies the *will* in one's self: *self-conceit*, *conceit* of one's self: *self-sufficiency*, *sufficiency* in one's self. As characteristicks they come very near to each other, but that depravity of the will which refuses to submit to any control either within or without is born with a person, and is among the earliest indications of character; in some it is less predominant than in others, but if not early checked, it is that defect in our natures which will always prevail; *self-conceit* is a vicious habit of the mind which is superinduced on the original character; it is that which determines in matters of judgement; a *self-willed* person thinks nothing of right or wrong: whatever the impulse of the moment suggests, is the motive to action;

> To *wilful* men
> The injuries that they themselves procur'd,
> Must be their schoolmasters.—SHAKSPEARE.

The *self-conceited* person is always much concerned about right and wrong, but it is only that which he conceives to be right and wrong; 'Nothing so haughty and assuming as ignorance, where *self-conceit* bids it set up for infallible.'—SOUTH. *Self-sufficiency* is a species of *self-conceit* applied to action: as a *self-conceited* person thinks of no opinion but his own; a *self-sufficient* person refuses the assistance of every one in whatever he is called upon to do;

> There safe in *self-sufficient* impudence
> Without experience, honesty, or sense,
> Unknowing in her interest, trade, or laws,
> He vainly undertakes his country's cause.—JENYNS.

PRIDE, VANITY, CONCEIT.

Pride is in all probability connected with the word *parade*, and the German *pracht* show or splendour, as it signifies that high-flown temper in a man which makes him paint to himself every thing in himself as beautiful or splendid; *vanity*, in Latin *vanitas*, from *vain* and *vanus*, is compounded of *ve* or *valde* and *inanis*, signifying exceeding emptiness; *conceit* signifies the same as in the preceding article (*v. Conceit, Fancy*).

The valuing of one's self on the possession of any property is the idea common to these terms, but they differ either in regard to the object or the manner of the action. *Pride* is the term of most extensive import and application, and comprehends in its signification not only that of the other two terms, but likewise ideas peculiar to itself.

Pride is applicable to every object, good or bad, high or low, small or great; *vanity* is applicable only to small objects: *pride* is therefore good or bad; *vanity* is always bad, it is always emptiness or nothingness. A man is *proud* who values himself on the possession of his literary or scientifick talent, on his wealth, on his rank, on his power, on his acquirements, or his superiority over his competitors; he is *vain* of his person, his dress, his walk, or any thing that is frivolous. *Pride* is the inherent quality in man; and while it rests on noble objects, it is his noblest characteristick; *vanity* is the distortion of one's nature flowing from a vicious constitution or education: *pride* shows itself variously according to the nature of the object on which it is fixed; a noble *pride* seeks to display itself in all that can command the respect or admiration of mankind; the *pride* of wealth, of power, or of other adventitious properties, commonly displays itself in an unseemly deportment towards others; *vanity* shows itself only by its eagerness to catch the notice of others: '*Vanity* makes men ridiculous, *pride* odious, and ambition terrible.—STEELE.

> 'Tis an old maxim in the schools,
> That *vanity's* the food of fools.—SWIFT.

Pride (says Blair) makes us esteem ourselves: *vanity* makes us desire the esteem of others. But if *pride* is, as I have before observed, self-esteem, or, which is nearly the same thing, self-valuation, it cannot properly be said to make us esteem ourselves. Of *vanity* I have already said that it makes us anxious for the notice and applause of others; but I cannot with Dr. Blair say that it makes us desire the esteem of others, because esteem is too substantial a quality to be sought for by the *vain*. Besides, that which Dr. Blair seems to assign as a leading and characteristick ground of distinction between *pride* and *vanity* is only an incidental property. A man is said to be *vain* of his clothes, if he gives indications that he values himself upon them as a ground of distinction; although he should not expressly seek to display himself to others.

Conceit is that species of self-valuation that respects one's talents only; it is so far therefore closely allied to *pride*; but a man is said to be *proud* of that which he really has, but to be *conceited* of that which he really has not: a man may be *proud* to an excess, of merits which he actually possesses; but when he is *conceited* his merits are all in his own *conceit*; the latter is therefore obviously founded on falsehood altogether; 'The *self-conceit* of the young is the great source of those dangers to which they are exposed.'—BLAIR.

PRIDE, HAUGHTINESS, LOFTINESS, DIGNITY.

Pride is here employed principally as respects the temper of the mind; the other terms are employed either as respects the sentiment of the mind, or the external behaviour.

Pride is here as before (*v. Pride*) a generick term: *haughtiness*, or the spirit of being *haughty* or high spirited (*v. Haughty*); *loftiness*, or the spirit of being lifted up; and *dignity*, or the sense of worth or value, are but modes of *pride*. *Pride*, inasmuch as it consists purely of self-esteem, is a positive sentiment which one may entertain independently of other persons: it lies in the inmost recesses of the human heart, and mingles itself insensibly with our affections and passions; it is our companion by night and by day; in publick or in private; it goes with a man wherever he goes, and stays with him where he stays; it is a never-failing source of satisfaction and self-complacency under every circumstance and in every situation of human life. *Haughtiness* is that mode of *pride* which springs out of one's comparison of one's self with others: the *haughty* man dwells on the inferiority of others; the *proud* man in the strict sense dwells on his own perfections. *Loftiness* is a mode of *pride* which raises the spirit above objects supposed to be inferiour; it does not set a man so much above others as above himself, or that which concerns himself. *Dignity* is a mode of *pride* which exalts the whole man, it is the entire consciousness of what is becoming himself and due to himself.

Pride assumes such a variety of shapes, and puts on such an infinity of disguises, that it is not easy always to recognise it at the first glance; but an insight into human nature will suffice to convince us that it is the spring of all human actions. Whether we see a man professing humility and self-abasement, or a singular degree of self-debasement, or any degree of self-exaltation, we may rest assured that his own *pride* or conscious self-importance is not wounded by any such measures; but that in all cases he is equally stimulated with the desire of giving himself in the eyes of others that degree of importance to which in his own eyes he is entitled; 'Every demonstration of an implacable rancour and an untameable *pride* were the only encouragements we received (from the regicides) to the renewal of our supplications.'—BURKE. *Haughtiness* is an unbending species or mode of *pride* which does not stoop to any artifices to obtain gratification; but compels others to give it what it fancies to be its due; 'Provoked by Edward's *haughtiness*, even the passive Baliol began to mutiny.'—ROBERTSON. *Loftiness* and *dignity* are equally remote from any subtle pliancy, but they are in no less degree exempt from the unamiable characteristick of *haughtiness* which makes a man bear with oppressive sway upon others. A *lofty* spirit and a *dignity* of character preserve a man from yielding to the contamination of outward objects, but leave his judgement and feeling entirely free and unbiassed with respect to others; 'Waller describes Sacharissa as a predominating beauty of *lofty* charms and imperious influence.'—JOHNSON. 'As soon as Almagro knew his fate to be inevitable, he met it with the *dignity* and fortitude of a veteran.'—ROBERTSON.

As respects the external behaviour, a *haughty* carriage is mostly unbecoming; a *lofty* tone is mostly justifiable, particularly as circumstances may require; and a *dignified* air is without qualification becoming the man who possesses real *dignity*.

HAUGHTINESS, DISDAIN, ARROGANCE.

Haughtiness is the abstract quality of haughty, as in the preceding article; *disdain* from the French *dedaigner*, or the privative *de* and *dignus* worthy, signifies thinking a thing to be worthless; *arrogance*, from *arrogate*, or the Latin *ar* or *ad rogo* to ask, signifies claiming or taking to one's self.

Haughtiness (says Dr. Blair) is founded on the high opinion we entertain of ourselves; *disdain*, on the low opinion we have of others; *arrogance* is the result of both, but if any thing, more of the former than the latter. *Haughtiness* and *disdain* are properly sentiments of the mind, and *arrogance* a mode of acting resulting from a state of mind; there may therefore be *haughtiness* and *disdain* which have not betrayed themselves by any visible action; but the sentiment of *arrogance* is always accompanied by its corresponding action: the *haughty* man is known by the air of superiority which he assumes; the *disdainful* man by the contempt which he shows to others: the *arrogant* man by his lofty pretensions.

Haughtiness and *arrogance* are both vicious; they are built upon a false idea of ourselves; 'The same *haughtiness* that prompts the act of injustice will more strongly incite its justification.'—JOHNSON. 'Turbulent, discontented men of quality, in proportion as they are puffed up with personal pride and *arrogance*, generally despise their own order.'—BURKE. *Disdain* may be justifiable when provoked by what is infamous a lady must treat with *disdain* the person who insults her honour; but otherwise it is a highly unbecoming sentiment;

Didst thou not think such vengeance must await
The wretch that, with his crimes all fresh about him,
Rushes, irreverent, unprepar'd, uncall'd,
Into his Maker's presence, throwing back
With insolent *disdain* his choicest gift?—PORTEUS.

HAUGHTY, HIGH, HIGH-MINDED.

Haughty, contracted from high-hearty, in Dutch *hoogharty*, signifies literally high-spirited, and like the word *high*, is derived through the medium of the Northern languages, from the Hebrew גאן to be high.

Haughty characterizes mostly the outward behaviour; *high* respects both the external behaviour, and the internal sentiment; *high-minded* marks the sentiment only, or the state of the mind.

With regard to the outward behaviour, *haughty* is a stronger term than *high*: a *haughty* carriage bespeaks not only a *high* opinion of one's self, but a strong mixture of contempt for others: a *high* carriage denotes simply a *high* opinion of one's self: *haughtiness* is therefore always offensive, as it is burdensome to others; but *height* may sometimes be laudable in as much as it is justice to one's self: one can never give a command in a *haughty* tone without making others feel their inferiority in a painful degree; we may sometimes assume a *high* tone in order to shelter ourselves from insult.

With regard to the sentiment of the mind, *high* denotes either a particular or an habitual state; *high-minded* is most commonly understood to designate an habitual state; the former may be either good or bad according to circumstances; the latter is expressly inconsistent with Christian humility. He is *high* whom virtue ennobles; his *height* is independent of adventitious circumstances, it becomes the poor as well as the rich; he is properly *high* who is set above any mean condescension; *high-mindedness*, on the contrary, includes in it a self-complacency that rests upon one's personal and incidental advantages rather than upon what is worthy of ourselves as rational agents. Superiours are apt to indulge a *haughty* temper which does but excite the scorn and hatred of those who are compelled to endure it;

Let gifts be to the mighty queen design'd,
And mollify with pray'rs her *haughty* mind.
DRYDEN

A *high* spirit is not always serviceable to one in dependent circumstances; but when regulated by discretion, it enhances the value of a man's character; 'Who knows whether indignation may not succeed to terrour, and the revival of *high* sentiments, spurning away the illusion of safety purchased at the expense of glory, may not drive us to a generous despair.'—BURKE. No one can be *high-minded* without thinking better of himself, and worse of others, than he ought to think; 'The wise will determine from the gravity of the case; the irritable, from sensibility to oppression; the *high-minded* from disdain and indignation at abusive power in unworthy hands.—BURKE.

TO CONTEMN, DESPISE, SCORN, DISDAIN

Contemn, in Latin *contemno*, compounded of *con* and *temno*, is probably changed from *tamino*, and is derived from the Hebrew טמא to pollute or render worthless, which is the cause of *contempt; despise*, in Latin *despicio*, compound of *de* and *specio*, signifies to look down upon, which is a strong mark of *contempt; scorn*, varied from our word *shorn*, signifies stripped of all honours and exposed to derision, which situation is the cause of *scorn; disdain* has the same signification as in the preceding article.

The above elucidations sufficiently evince the feeling towards others which gives birth to all these actions. But the feeling of *contempt* is not quite so strong as that of *despising*, nor that of *despising* so strong as those of *scorning* and *disdaining;* the latter of which expresses the strongest sentiment of all. Persons are *contemned* for their moral qualities; they are *despised* on account of their outward circumstances, their characters, or their endowments. Superiours may be *contemned;* inferiours only, real or supposed, are *despised.*

Contempt, as applied to persons, is not incompatible with a Christian temper when justly provoked by their character; but *despising* is distinctly forbidden and seldom warranted. Yet it is not so much our business to *contemn* others as to *contemn* that which is *contemptible;* but we are not equally at liberty to *despise* the person, or any thing belonging to the person, of another. Whatever springs from the free will of another may be a subject of *contempt;* but the casualties of fortune or the gifts of Providence, which are alike independent of personal merit, should never expose a person to be *despised.* We may, however, *contemn* a person for his impotent malice, or *despise* him for his meanness.

Persons are not *scorned* or *disdained,* but they may be treated with *scorn* or *disdain;* they are both improper expressions of *contempt* or *despite;* *scorn* marks the sentiment of a little, vain mind; *disdain* of a haughty and perverted mind. A beautiful woman looks with *scorn* on her whom she *despises* for the want of this natural gift. The wealthy man treats with *disdain* him whom he *despises* for his poverty. There is nothing excites the *contempt* of mankind so powerfully as a mixture of pride and meanness; '*Contempt* and derision are hard words; but in what manner can one give advice to a youth in the pursuit and possession of sensual pleasures, or afford pity to an old man in the impotence and desire of enjoying them.'—Steele. A moment's reflection will teach us the folly and wickedness of *despising* another for that to which by the will of Providence we may the next moment be exposed ourselves; 'It is seldom that the great or the wise suspect that they are cheated and *despised.*'—Johnson. There are silly persons who will *scorn* to be seen in the company of such as have not an equal share of finery

> Infamous wretch!
> So much below my *scorn,* I dare not kill thee.
> Dryden.

And there are weak upstarts of fortune, who *disdain* to look at those who cannot measure purses with themselves;

> Yet not for those,
> For what the potent victor in his rage
> Can else inflict, do I repent or change,
> Though chang'd in outward lustre, that fix'd mind
> And high *disdain* from sense of injur'd merit.
> Milton.

In speaking of things independently of others, or as immediately connected with ourselves, all these terms may be sometimes employed in a good or an indifferent sense.

When we *contemn* a mean action, and *scorn* to conceal by falsehood what we are called upon to acknowledge, we act the part of the gentleman as well as the Christian; 'A man of spirit should *contemn* the praise of the ignorant.'—Steele. And it is inconsistent with our infirm and dependent condition, that we should feel inclined to *despise* any thing that falls in our way;

> Thrice happy they, beneath their northern skies,
> Who that worst fear, the fear of death, *despise;*
> Provoke approaching fate, and bravely *scorn*
> To spare that life which must so soon return.
> Rowe.

Much less are we at liberty to *disdain* to do any thing which our station requires; 'It is in some sort owing to the bounty of Providence that *disdaining* a cheap and vulgar happiness, they frame to themselves imaginary goods, in which there is nothing can raise desire but the difficulty of obtaining them.'—Berkeley. We ought to think nothing unworthy of us, nothing degrading to us, but that which is inconsistent with the will of God: there are, however, too many who affect to *despise* small favours as not reaching their fancied deserts, and others who *disdain* to receive any favour at all, from mistaken ideas of dependence and obligation;

> Virtue *disdains* to lend an ear
> To the mad people's sense of right.—Francis.

CONTEMPTIBLE, CONTEMPTUOUS.

These terms are very frequently, though very erroneously, confounded in common discourse.

Contemptible is applied to the thing deserving *contempt;* *Contemptuous* to that which is expressive of *contempt.* Persons, or what is done by persons, may be either *contemptible* or *contemptuous;* but a thing is only *contemptible.*

A production is *contemptible;* a sneer or look is *contemptuous;* 'Silence, or a negligent indifference, proceeds from anger mixed with scorn, that shows another to be thought by you too *contemptible* to be regarded.'—Addison. 'My sister's principles in many particulars differ; but there has been always such a harmony between us that she seldom smiles upon those who have suffered me to pass with a *contemptuous* negligence.'—Hawkesworth.

CONTEMPTIBLE, DESPICABLE, PITIFUL.

Contemptible is not so strong as *despicable* or *pitiful.*

A person may be *contemptible* for his vanity or weak ness: but he is *despicable* for his servility and baseness of character; he is *pitiful* for his want of manliness and becoming spirit. A lie is at all times *contemptible;* it is *despicable* when it is told for purposes of gain or private interest; it is *pitiful* when accompanied with indications of unmanly fear. It is *contemptible* to take credit to one's self for the good action one has not performed; 'Were every man persuaded from how mean and low a principle this passion (for flattery) is derived, there can be no doubt but the person who should attempt to gratify it would then be as *contemptible* as he is now successful.'—Steele. It is *despicable* to charge another with the faults which we ourselves have committed; 'To put on an artful part to obtain no other but an unjust praise from the undiscerning is of all endeavours the most *despicable.*'—Steele. It is *pitiful* to offend others, and then attempt to screen ourselves from their resentment under any shelter which offers; 'There is something *pitifully* mean in the inverted ambition of that man who can hope for annihilation, and please himself to think that his whole fabrick shall crumble into dust.'—Steele. It is *contemptible* for a man in a superiour station to borrow of his inferiours; it is *despicable* in him to forfeit his word; it is *pitiful* in him to attempt to conceal aught by artifice.

CONTEMPTUOUS, SCORNFUL, DISDAINFUL.

These epithets rise in sense by a regular gradation.

Contemptuous is general, and applied to whatever can express *contempt:* *scornful* and *disdainful* are particular; they apply only to outward marks: one is *contemptuous* who is *scornful* or *disdainful,* but not *vice versâ.*

Words, actions, and looks are *contemptuous;* looks, sneers, and gestures are *scornful* and *disdainful.*

Contemptuous expressions are always unjustifiable: whatever may be the *contempt* which a person's conduct deserves, it is unbecoming in another to give him any indications of the sentiment he feels. *Scornful* and *disdainful* smiles are resorted to by the weakest or the worst of mankind; 'Prior never sacrifices accuracy to haste, nor indulges himself in *contemptuous* negligence or impatient idleness.'—Johnson. 'As soon as Mavia began to look round, and saw the vagabond Mirtillo who had so long absented himself from her circle, she looked upon him with that glance which in the language of oglers is called the *scornful*' Steele.

> In vain he thus attempts her mind to move,
> With tears and prayers and late repenting love;
> *Disdainfully* she looked, then turning round,
> She fix'd her eyes unmov'd upon the ground.
> Dryden.

TO LAUGH AT, RIDICULE.

Laugh, through the medium of the Saxon *hlahan* old German *lahan,* Greek γελάω, comes from the Hebrew צחק with no variation in the meaning; *ridicule,* from Latin *rideo,* has the same original meaning Both these verbs are used here in the improper sense for *laughter,* blended with more or less of contempt but the former displays itself by the natural expression of *laughter;* the latter shows itself by a verbal expression: the former is produced by a feeling of mirth, on observing the real or supposed weakness of another; the latter is produced by a strong sense of the absurd or irrational in another: the former is more immediately directed to the person who has excited the feeling; the latter is more commonly produced by the thing than by persons. We *laugh at* a person to his face; but we *ridicule* his notions by writing or in the course of conversation; we *laugh at* the individual; we *ridicule* that which is maintained by one or many. It is better to *laugh at* the fears of a child than to attempt to restrain them by violence, but it is still better to overcome them if possible by the force of reason; 'Men *laugh at* one another's cost.'—SWIFT. *Ridicule* is not the test of truth; he therefore who attempts to misuse it against the cause of truth, will bring upon himself the contempt of all mankind; but folly can be assailed with no weapon so effectual as *ridicule;* 'It is easy for a man who sits idle at home and has nobody to please but himself, to *ridicule* or censure the common practices of mankind.'—JOHNSON. The philosopher Democritus preferred to *laugh at* the follies of men, rather than weep for them like Heraclitus; infidels have always employed *ridicule* against Christianity, by which they have betrayed not only their want of argument, but their personal depravitv in *laughing* where they ought to be most serious.

LAUGHABLE, LUDICROUS, RIDICULOUS, COMICAL, OR COMICK, DROLL.

Laughable signifies exciting or fit to excite *laughter;* *ludicrous*, in Latin *ludicer* or *ludicrus*, from *ludus* a game, signifies causing game or sport; *ridiculous* exciting or fit to excite *ridicule; comical*, or *comick*, in Latin *comicus*, from the Greek *κωμῳδία* comedy, and *κώμη* a village, because comedies were first performed in villages, signifies after the manner of comedy; *droll*, in French *drôle*, is doubtless connected with the German *rolle* a part, in the phrase *eine rolle spielen* to play a trick or perform a part.

Either the direct action of *laughter* or a corresponding sentiment is included in the signification of all these terms: they differ principally in the cause which produces the feeling; the *laughable* consists of objects in general whether personal or otherwise; the *ludicrous* and *ridiculous* have more or less reference to that which is personal. What is *laughable* may excite simple merriment independently of all personal reference, unless we admit what Mr. Hobbes, and after him Addison, have maintained of all *laughter*, that it springs from pride. But without entering into this nice question, I am inclined to distinguish between the *laughable* which arises from the reflection of what is to our own advantage or pleasure, and that which arises from reflecting on what is to the disadvantage of another. The *droll* tricks of a monkey, or the humorous stories of wit, are *laughable* from the nature of the things themselves; without any apparent allusion, however remote, to any individual but the one whose senses or mind is gratified;

> They'll not show their teeth in way of smile,
> Though Nestor swear the jest be *laughable.*
>
> SHAKSPEARE.

The *ludicrous* and *ridiculous* are however species of the *laughable* which arise altogether from reflecting on that which is to the disadvantage of another. The *ludicrous* lies mostly in the outward circumstances of the individual, or such as are exposed to view and serve as a show; 'The action of the theatre, though modern states esteem it but *ludicrous* unless it be satirical and biting, was carefully watched by the ancients that it might improve mankind in virtue.'—BACON. The *ridiculous* applies to every thing personal, whether external or internal; '*Infelix paupertas* has nothing in it more intolerable than this, that it renders men *ridiculous.*'—SOUTH. The *ludicrous* does not comprehend that which is so much to the desparagement of the individual as the *ridiculous;* whatever there is in ourselves which excites *laughter* in others, is accompanied in their minds with a sense of our inferiority: and consequently the *ludicrous* always produces this feeling; but only in a slight degree compared with the *ridiculous*, which awakens a positive sense of contempt. Whoever is in a *ludicrous* situation is, let it be in ever so small a degree, placed in an inferiour station, with regard to those by whom he is thus viewed; but he who is rendered *ridiculous* is positively degraded. It is possible, therefore, for a person to be in a *ludicrous* situation without any kind of moral demerit, or the slightest depreciation of his moral character; since that which renders his situation *ludicrous* is altogether independent of himself; or it becomes *ludicrous* only in the eyes of incompetent judges. "Let an ambassador," says Mr. Pope, "speak the best sense in the world, and deport himself in the most graceful manner before a prince, yet if the tail of his shirt happen, as I have known it happen to a very wise man, to hang out behind, more people will *laugh* at that than attend to the other." This is the *ludicrous.* The same can seldom be said of the *ridiculous;* for as this springs from positive moral causes, it reflects on the person to whom it attaches in a less questionable shape, and produces positive disgrace. Persons very rarely appear *ridiculous* without being really so; and he who is really *ridiculous* justly excites contempt.

Droll and *comical* are in the proper sense applied to things which cause *laughter*, as when we speak of a *droll* story, or a *comical* incident, or a *comick* song;

> A *comick* subject loves an humble verse,
> Thyestes scorns a low and *comick* style.
>
> ROSCOMMON

'In the Augustine age itself, notwithstanding the censure of Horace, they preferred the low buffoonery and *drollery* of Plautus to the delicacy of Terence.'—WARTON. These epithets may be applied to the person, but not so as to reflect disadvantageously on the individual, like the preceding terms.

TO DERIDE, MOCK, RIDICULE, RALLY, BANTER.

Deride, compounded of *de* and the Latin *rideo;* and *ridicule*, from *rideo*, both signify to laugh at; *mock*, in French *moquer*, Dutch *mocken*, Greek *μωκαω*, signifies likewise to laugh at; *rally* is doubtless connected with *rail*, which is in all probability a contraction of *revile;* and *banter* is possibly a corruption of the French *badiner* to jest.

Strong expressions of contempt are designated by all these terms.

Derision and *mockery* evince themselves by the outward actions in general; *ridicule* consists more in words than actions; *rallying* and *bantering* almost entirely in words. *Deride* is not so strong a term as *mock*, but much stronger than *ridicule.* There is always a mixture of hostility in *derision* and *mockery;* but *ridicule* is frequently unaccompanied with any personal feeling of displeasure. *Derision* is often deep, not loud; it discovers itself in suppressed laughs, contemptuous sneers or gesticulations, and cutting expressions: *mockery* is mostly noisy and outrageous; it breaks forth in insulting buffoonery, and is sometimes accompanied with personal violence: the former consists of real but contemptuous laughter; the latter often of affected laughter and grimace. *Derision* and *mockery* are always personal; *ridicule* may be directed to things as well as persons. *Derision* and *mockery* are a direct attack on the individual, the latter still more so than the former; *ridicule* is as often used in writing as in personal intercourse.

Derision and *mockery* are practised by persons in any station; *ridicule* is mostly used by equals. A person is *derided* and *mocked* for that which is offensive as well as apparently absurd or extravagant; he is *ridiculed* for what is apparently ridiculous. Our Saviour was exposed both to the *derision* and *mockery* of his enemies: they *derided* him for what they dared to think his false pretensions to a superiour mission; they *mocked* him by planting a crown of thorns, and acting the farce of royalty before him.

Derision may be provoked by ordinary circumstances; *mockery* by that which is extraordinary. When the prophet Elijah in his holy zeal *mocked* the false prophets of Baal, or when the children *mocked* the prophet Elisha, the term *deride* would not have suited either for the occasion or the action; but two people may *deride* each other in their angry disputes or unprincipled people may *deride* those whom they cannot imitate, or condemn. *Derision* and *mockery* are altogether incompatible with the Christian temper; *ridicule* is justifiable in certain cases, particularly when it is not personal. When a man renders himself an object of *derision*, it does not follow that any one is justified in *deriding* him;

Satan beheld their plight,
And to his mates thus in *derision* call'd:
O friends, why come not on those victors proud?
MILTON.

Insults are not the means for correcting faults: *mockery* is very seldom used but for the gratification of a malignant disposition; hence it is a strong expression when used figuratively;

Impell'd with steps unceasing to pursue
Some fleeting good that *mocks* me with the view.
GOLDSMITH.

Although *ridicule* is not the test of truth, and ought not to be employed in the place of argument, yet there are some follies too absurd to deserve more serious treatment;

Want is the scorn of every fool,
And wit in rags is turn'd to *ridicule*.—DRYDEN.

Rally and *banter*, like *derision* and *mockery*, are altogether personal acts, in which application they are very analogous to *ridicule*. *Ridicule* is the most general term of the three; we often *rally* and *banter* by *ridiculing*. There is more exposure in *ridiculing*; reproof in *rallying*; and provocation in *bantering*. A person may be *ridiculed* on account of his eccentricities; he is *rallied* for his defects; he is *bantered* for accidental circumstances: the two former actions are often justified by some substantial reason; the latter is an action as puerile as it is unjust, it is a contemptible species of *mockery*. Self-conceit and extravagant follies are oftentimes best corrected by good-natured *ridicule*; a man may deserve sometimes to be *rallied* for his want of resolution; 'The only piece of pleasantry in Paradise Lost, is where the evil spirits are described as *rallying* the angels upon the success of their new invented artillery.'—ADDISON. Those who are of an ill-natured turn of mind will *banter* others for their misfortunes, or their personal defects, rather than not say something to their annoyance; 'As to your manner of behaving towards these unhappy young gentlemen (at College) you describe, let it be manly and easy; if they *banter* your regularity, order, decency, and love of study, *banter* in return their neglect of it.' CHATHAM.

RIDICULE, SATIRE, IRONY, SARCASM.

Ridicule signifies the same as in the preceding article; *satire* and *irony* have the same original meaning as given under the head of *Wit*; *sarcasm*, from the Greek σαρκασμὸς, and σαρκίζω, from σάρξ flesh, signifies literally to tear the flesh.

Ridicule has simple laughter in it; *satire* has a mixture of ill-nature or severity; the former is employed in matters of a shameless or trifling nature, sometimes improperly on deserving objects; 'Nothing is a greater mark of a degenerate and vicious age than the common *ridicule* which passes on this state of life (marriage).'—ADDISON. *Satire* is employed either in personal or grave matters; 'A man resents with more bitterness a *satire* upon his abilities than his practice.' HAWKESWORTH. *Irony* is disguised *satire*; an *ironist* seems to praise that which he really means to condemn; 'When Regan (in King Lear) counsels him to ask her sister forgiveness, he falls on his knees and asks her with a striking kind of *irony* how such supplicating language as this becometh him.'—JOHNSON. *Sarcasm* is bitter and personal *satire*; all the others may be successfully and properly employed to expose folly and vice; but *sarcasm*, which is the indulgence only of personal resentment, is never justifiable; 'The severity of this *sarcasm* stung me with intolerable rage.'—HAWKESWORTH.

TO JEST, JOKE, MAKE GAME, SPORT.

Jest is in all probability abridged from *gesticulate*, because the ancient mimicks used much *gesticulation* in breaking their *jests* on the company; *joke*, in Latin *iocus*, comes in all probability from the Hebrew צחק to laugh; to *make game* signifies here to make the subject of game or play; to *sport* signifies here to *sport* with, or convert into a subject of amusement.

One *jests* in order to make others laugh; one *jokes* in order to please one's self. The *jest* is directed at the object; the *joke* is practised with the person or on the person. One attempts to make a thing laughable or ridiculous by *jesting* about it, or treating it in a *jesting* manner; one attempts to excite good humour in others, or indulge it in one's self by *joking* with them. *Jests* are therefore seldom harmless: *jokes* are frequently allowable. The most serious subject may be degraded by being turned into a *jest*;

But those who aim at ridicule,
Should fix upon some certain rule,
Which fairly hints they are in *jest*.—SWIFT.

Melancholy or dejection of the mind may be conveniently dispelled by a *joke*;

How fond are men of rule and place,
Who court it from the mean and base,
They love the cellar's vulgar *joke*,
And lose their hours in ale and smoke.—GAY.

Court fools and buffoons used formerly to break their *jests* upon every subject by which they thought to entertain their employers: those who know how to *joke* with good-nature and discretion may contribute to the mirth of the company: to *make game* of is applicable only to persons: to *make* a *sport* of or *sport* with, is applied to objects in general, whether persons or things, both are employed like *jest* in the bad sense of treating a thing more lightly than it deserves; 'When Samson's eyes were out, of a public magistrate he was made a public *sport*.'—SOUTH.

To *jest* consists of words or corresponding signs; it is peculiarly appropriate to one who acts a part: to *joke* consists not only of words, but of simple actions, which are calculated to produce mirth; it is peculiarly applicable to the social intercourse of friends: to *make game of* consists more of laughter than any; it has not the ingenuity of the *jest*, nor the good-nature of the *joke*; it is the part of the fool who wishes to make others appear what he himself really is: to *sport* with or to *make sport of*, consists not only of simple actions, but of conduct; it is the errour of a weak mind that does not know how to set a due value on any thing, the fool *sports* with his reputation, when he risks the loss of it for a bauble

TO SCOFF, GIBE, JEER, SNEER.

Scoff comes from the Greek σκώπτω to deride; *gibe* and *jeer* are connected with the word gabble and jabber, denoting an unseemly mode of speech; *sneer* is connected with sneeze and nose, the member by which *sneering* is performed.

Scoffing is a general term for expressing contempt; we may *scoff* either by *gibes*, *jeers*, or *sneers*; or we may *scoff* by opprobrious language and contemptuous looks: to *gibe*, *jeer*, and *sneer*, are personal acts; the *gibe* and *jeer* consist of words addressed to an individual; the former has most of ill-nature and reproach in it;

Where town and country vicars flock in tribes,
Secur'd by numbers from the laymen's *gibes*.—SWIFT.

The latter has more of ridicule or satire in it;

Midas, expos'd to all their *jeers*,
Had lost his art, and kept his ears.—SWIFT.

They are both, however, applied to the actions of vulgar people, who practise their coarse jokes on each other;

Shrewd fellows and such arch wags! A tribe
That meet for nothing but to *gibe*.—SWIFT.

'That *jeering* demeanour is a quality of great offence to others, and danger towards a man's self.'—LORD WENTWORTH. *Scoff* and *sneer* are directed either to persons or things as the object; *gibe* and *jeer* only towards persons: *scoff* is taken only in the proper sense; *sneer* derives its meaning from the literal act of *sneering*: the *scoffer* speaks lightly of that which deserves serious attention;

The fop, with learning at defiance
Scoffs at the pedant and the science.—GAY

The *sneerer* speaks either actually with a *sneer* or as

it were by implication with a *sneer;* 'There is one short passage still remaining (of Alexis the poet's) which conveys a *sneer* at Pythagoras.'—CUMBERLAND. The *scoffers* at religion set at naught all thoughts of decorum, they openly avow the little estimation in which they hold it; the *sneerers* at religion are more sly, but not less malignant; they wish to treat religion with contempt, but not to bring themselves into the contempt they deserve;

And *sneers* as learnedly as they,
Like females o'er their morning tea.—SWIFT

TO DISPARAGE, DETRACT, TRADUCE, DEPRECIATE, DEGRADE, DECRY.

Disparage, compounded of *dis* and *parage*, from *par* equal, signifies to make unequal or below what it ought to be; *detract*, in Latin *detractum*, participle of *detraho*, from *de* and *traho* to draw down, signifies to set a thing below its real value; *traduce*, in Latin *traduco* or *transduco*, signifies to carry from one to another that which is unfavourable; *depreciate*, from the Latin *pretium*, a price, signifies to bring down the price; *degrade*, compounded of *de* and *grade* or *gradus* a step, degree, signifies to bring a degree or step lower than one has been before; *decry* signifies literally to cry down.

The idea of lowering the value of an object is common to all these words, which differ in the circumstances and object of the action. *Disparagement* is the most indefinite in the manner: *detract* and *traduce* are specifick in the forms by which an object is lowered: *disparagement* respects the mental endowments and qualifications: *detract* and *traduce* are said of the moral character; the former, however, in a less specifick manner than the latter. We *disparage* a man's performance by speaking slightingly of it; we *detract* from the merits of a person by ascribing his success to chance; we *traduce* him by handing about tales that are unfavourable to his reputation: thus authors are apt to *disparage* the writings of their rivals; 'It is a hard and nice subject for a man to speak of himself; it grates his own heart to say any thing of *disparagement*, and the reader's ears to hear any thing of praise from him.'—COWLEY. A person may *detract* from the skill of another; 'I have very often been tempted to write invectives upon those who have *detracted* from my works; but I look upon it as a peculiar happiness that I have always hindered my resentments from proceeding to this extremity.'—ADDISON. Or he may *traduce* him by relating scandalous reports; 'Both Homer and Virgil had their compositions usurped by others; both were envied and *traduced* during their lives.'—WALSH.

To *disparage*, *detract*, and *traduce*, can be applied only to persons, or that which is personal; *depreciate*, *degrade*, and *decry*, to whatever is an object of esteem; we *depreciate* and *degrade*, therefore, things as well as persons, and *decry* things: to *depreciate* is, however, not so strong a term as to *degrade;* for the language which is employed to *depreciate* will be mild compared with that used for *degrading:* we may *depreciate* an object by implication, or in indirect terms; but harsh and unseemly epithets are employed for *degrading:* thus a man may be said to *depreciate* human nature, who does not represent it as capable of its true elevation; he *degrades* it who sinks it below the scale of rationality. We may *depreciate* or *degrade* an individual, a language, and the like; we *decry* measures and principles: the two former are an act of an individual; the latter is properly the act of many. Some men have such perverted notions that they are always *depreciating* whatever is esteemed excellent in the world; 'The business of our modish French authors is to *depreciate* human nature, and consider it under its worst appearances.'—ADDISON. They whose interests have stifled all feelings of humanity, have *degraded* the poor Africans, in order to justify the enslaving of them; 'Akenside certainly retained an unnecessary and outrageous zeal for what he called and thought liberty; a zeal which sometimes disguises from the world an envious desire of plundering wealth, or *degrading* greatness.'—JOHNSON. Political partisans commonly *decry* the measures of one party, in order to exalt those of another; 'Ignorant men are very subject to *decry* those beauties in a celebrated work which they have not eyes to discover.'—ADDISON.

TO DISPARAGE, DEROGATE, DEGRADE.

Disparage and *degrade* have the same meaning as given in the preceding article; *derogate*, in Latin *derogatus*, from *derogo* to repeal in part, signifies to take from a thing.

Disparage is here employed, not as the act of persons, but of things, in which case it is allied to *derogate*, but retains its indefinite and general sense as before: circumstances may *disparage* the performances of a writer; or they may *derogate* from the honours and dignities of an individual: it would be a high *disparagement* to an author to have it known that he had been guilty of plagiarism; it *derogates* from the dignity of a magistrate to take part in popular measures. To *degrade* is here, as in the former case, a much stronger expression than the other two: whatever *disparages* or *derogates* does but take away a part from the value; but whatever *degrades* sinks it many degrees in the estimation of those in whose eyes it is *degraded;* in this manner religion is *degraded* by the low arts of its enthusiastick professors; 'Of the mind that can deliberately pollute itself with ideal wickedness, for the sake of spreading the contagion in society, I wish not to conceal or excuse the depravity. Such *degradation* of the dignity of genius cannot be contemplated but with grief and indignation.'—JOHNSON. Whatever may tend to the *disparagement* of a religious profession, does injury to the cause of truth; ''T is no *disparagement* to philosophy, that it cannot deify us.'—GLANVILLE. Whatever *derogates* from the dignity of a man in any office is apt to *degrade* the office itself; 'I think we may say, without *derogating* from those wonderful performances (the Iliad and Æneid), that there is an unquestionable magnificence in every part of Paradise Lost, and indeed a much greater than could have been formed upon any Pagan system.'—ADDISON.

TO ASPERSE, DETRACT, DEFAME, SLANDER, CALUMNIATE.

Asperse, in Latin *aspersus*, participle of *aspergo* to sprinkle, signifies in a moral sense to stain with spots, *detract* has the same signification as given under the head of *disparage; defame*, in Latin *defamo*, compounded of the privative *de* and *fama* fame, signifies to deprive of reputation; *slander* is doubtless connected with the words *slur*, *sully*, and *soil*, signifying to stain with some spot; *calumniate*, from the Latin *calumnia*, and the Hebrew כלם infamy, signifies to load with infamy.

All these terms denote an effort made to injure the character by some representation. *Asperse* and *detract* mark an indirect misrepresentation; *defame*, *slander*, and *calumniate*, a positive assertion.

To *asperse* is to fix a stain on a moral character; to *detract* is to lessen its merits and excellencies. *Aspersions* always imply something bad, real or supposed; *detractions* are always founded on some supposed good in the object that is *detracted:* to *defame* is openly to advance some serious charge against the character: to *slander* is to expose the faults of another in his absence: to *calumniate* is to communicate secretly, or otherwise, circumstances to the injury of another.

Aspersions and *detractions* are never positive falsehoods, as they never amount to more than insinuations; *defamation* is the publick communication of facts, whether true or false: *slander* involves the discussion of moral qualities, and is consequently the declaration of an opinion as well as the communication of a fact: *calumny*, on the other hand, is a positive communication of circumstances known by the narrator at the time to be false. *Aspersions* are the effect of malice and meanness; they are the resource of the basest persons, insidiously to wound the characters of those whom they dare not openly attack: the most virtuous are exposed to the malignity of the *asperser;* 'It is certain, and observed by the wisest writers, that there are women who are not nicely chaste, and men not severely honest, in all families; therefore let those who may be apt to raise *aspersions* upon ours, please to give us an impartial account of their own, and we shall be satisfied.'—STEELE. *Detraction* is the effect of envy: when a man is not disposed or able to follow the example of another, he strives to *detract* from the merit of his actions by questioning the purity of his motives: distinguished persons are the most exposed to the evil tongues of *detractors;* 'What made their enmity the more entertaining to all the rest of their sex was, that in their *detraction* from each other, neither could fall upon terms which did not hit herself as much as her adversary.'—STEELE. *Defamation* is the consequence of personal resentment, or a busy interference with other men's affairs; it is an unjustifiable exposure of their errours or vices, which is often visited with the due vengeance of the law upon the offender; 'What shall we say of the pleasure a man takes in a *defamatory* libel? Is it not a heinous sin in the sight of God?'—ADDISON. *Slander* arises either from a mischievous temper, or a gossipping humour; it is the resource of ignorant and vacant minds, who are in want of some serious occupation: the *slanderer* deals unmercifully with his neighbour, and speaks without regard to truth or falsehood;

> *Slander*, that worst of poisons, ever finds
> An easy entrance to ignoble minds.—HERVEY.

Calumny is the worst of actions, resulting from the worst of motives; to injure the reputation of another by the sacrifice of truth, is an accumulation of guilt which is hardly exceeded by any one in the whole catalogue of vices; 'The way to silence *calumny*, says Bias, is to be always exercised in such things as are praiseworthy.'—ADDISON. *Slanderers* and *calumniators* are so near a-kin, that they are but too often found in the same person: it is to be expected that when the *slanderer* has exhausted all his surmises and censure upon his neighbour, he will not hesitate to *calumniate* him rather than remain silent.

If I speak slightingly of my neighbour, and insinuate any thing against the purity of his principles, or the rectitude of his conduct, I *asperse* him: if he be a charitable man, and I ascribe his charities to a selfish motive, or otherwise take away from the merit of his conduct, I am guilty of *detraction:* if I publish any thing openly that injures his reputation, I am a *defamer:* if I communicate to others the reports that are in circulation to his disadvantage, I am a *slanderer:* if I fabricate any thing myself and spread it abroad, I am a *calumniator.*

TO ABASE, HUMBLE, DEGRADE, DISGRACE, DEBASE.

To *abase* expresses the strongest degree of self-humiliation, from the French *abaisser*, to bring down or make low, which is compounded of the intensive syllable *a* or *ad* and *baisser* from *bas* low, in Latin *basis* the base, which is the lowest part of a column. It is at present used principally in the Scripture language, or in a metaphorical style, to imply the laying aside all the high pretensions which distinguish us from our fellow-creatures, the descending to a state comparatively low and mean; to *humble*, in French *humilier*, from the Latin *humilis* humble, and *humus* the ground, naturally marks a prostration to the ground, and figuratively a lowering the thoughts and feelings. According to the principles of Christianity whoever *abaseth* himself shall be exalted, and according to the same principles whoever reflects on his own littleness and unworthiness will daily *humble* himself before his Maker.

To *degrade* (*v. To disparage*), signifies to lower in the estimation of others. It supposes already a state of elevation either in outward circumstances or in publick opinion; *disgrace* is compounded of the privative *dis* and the noun *grace* or favour. To *disgrace* properly implies to put out of favour, which is always attended more or less with circumstances of ignominy, and reflects contempt on the object; *debase* is compounded of the intensive syllable *de* and the adjective *base*, signifying to make very base or low.

The modest man *abases* himself by not insisting on the distinctions to which he may be justly entitled: the penitent man *humbles* himself by confessing his errours; the man of rank *degrades* himself by a too familiar deportment with his inferiours; he *disgraces* himself by his meanness and irregularities, and *debases* his character by his vices.

We can never be *abased* by abasing ourselves, but we may be *humbled* by unseasonable *humiliations*, or improper concessions; we may be *degraded* by descending from our rank, and *disgraced* by the exposure of our unworthy actions.

The great and good man may be *abased* and *humbled*, but never *degraded* or *disgraced;* his glory follows him in his *abasement* or *humiliation;* his greatness protects him from *degradation*, and his virtue shields him from *disgrace.*

> 'Tis immortality, 'tis that alone
> Amid life's pains, *abasements*, emptiness,
> The soul can comfort.—YOUNG.

> My soul is justly *humbled* in the dust.—ROWE.

It is necessary to *abase* those who will exalt themselves; to *humble* those who have lofty opinions of themselves; 'If the mind be curbed and *humbled* too much in children; if their spirits be *abased* and broken much by too strict a hand over them; they lose all their vigour and industry.'—LOCKE. Those who act inconsistently with their rank and station are frequently *degraded;* but it is more common for others to be unjustly *degraded* through the envy and ill-will of their inferiours; 'It is very disingenuous to level the best of mankind with the worst, and for the faults of particulars to *degrade* the whole species.'—HUGHES. Folly and wickedness bring *disgrace* on courts, where the contrary ought to be found;

> You'd think no fools *disgraced* the former reign,
> Did not some grave examples still remain.—POPE.

The misuse of things for inferiour purposes *debase* their value; 'It is a kind of taking God's name in vain, to *debase* religion with such frivolous disputes.'—HOOKER.

Of all these terms *degrade* and *disgrace* are the most nearly allied to each other; but the former has most regard to the external rank and condition, the latter to the moral estimation and character. Whatever is low and mean is *degrading* for those who are not of mean condition; whatever is immoral is *disgraceful* to all, but most so to those who ought to know better. It is *degrading* for a nobleman to associate with prize-fighters and jockeys; it is *disgraceful* for him to countenance the violation of the laws, which he is bound to protect; it is *degrading* for a clergyman to take part in the ordinary pleasures and occupations of mankind in general; it is *disgraceful* for him to indulge in any levities; Domitian *degraded* himself by the amusement which he chose of catching flies; he *disgraced* himself by the cruelty which he mixed with his meanness; king John of England *degraded* himself by his mean compliances to the pope and the barons, and *disgraced* himself by many acts of injustice and cruelty.

The higher the rank of the individual the greater his *degradation:* the higher his character, or the more sacred his office, the greater his *disgrace*, if he act inconsistently with its dignity: but these terms are not confined to any rank of life; there is that which is *degrading* and *disgraceful* for every person, however low his station; when a man forfeits that which he owes to himself, and sacrifices his independence to his vices, he *degrades* himself; 'When a hero is to be pulled down and *degraded* it is best done in doggerel.'—ADDISON. 'So deplorable is the *degradation* of our nature, that whereas before we bore the image of God, we now only retain the image of men.'—SOUTH. He who forfeits the good opinion of those who know him is *disgraced*, and he who fails to bestow on an object the favour or esteem which it is entitled to *disgraces* it; 'We may not so in any one kind admire her, that we *disgrace* her in any other; but let all her ways be according unto their place and degree adored.'—HOOKER. But although the term *disgrace* when generally applied is always taken in a bad sense, yet in regard to individuals it may be taken in an indifferent sense; it is possible to be *disgraced*, or to lose the favour of a patron, through his caprice, without any fault on the part of the *disgraced* person; 'Philips died honoured and lamented, before any part of his reputation had withered, and before his patron St. John had *disgraced* him.'

Men are very liable to err in their judgements on what is *degrading* and *disgraceful;* but all who are anxious to uphold the station and character in which they have been placed, may safely observe this rule, that nothing can be so *degrading* as the violation of truth and sincerity, and nothing so *disgraceful* as a breach of moral rectitude or propriety.

These terms may be employed with a similar distinction in regard to things; a thing is *degraded* which falls any degree in the scale of general estimation;

All higher knowledge, in her presence, falls
Degraded.—MILTON.

A thing is *disgraced* when it becomes or is made less lovely and desirable than it was;

And where the vales with violets once were crown'd,
Now knotty burrs and thorns *disgrace* the ground.
DRYDEN.

TO ABASH, CONFOUND, CONFUSE.

Abash is an intensive of *abase*, signifying to abase thoroughly in spirit; *confound* and *confuse* are derived from different parts of the same Latin verb *confundo*, and its participle *confusus*. *Confundo* is compounded of *con* and *fundo* to pour together. To *confound* and *confuse* then signify properly to melt together or into one mass what ought to be distinct; and figuratively, as it is here taken, to derange the thoughts in such manner as that they seem melted together.

Abash expresses more than *confound*, and *confound* more than *confuse;* shame contributes greatly to *abashment;* what is sudden and unaccountable serves to *confound;* bashfulness and a variety of emotions give rise to *confusion*.

The haughty man is *abashed* when he is humbled in the eyes of others, or the sinner when he stands convicted; 'If Peter was so *abashed* when Christ gave him a look after his denial; if there was so much dread in his looks when he was a prisoner; how much greater will it be when he sits as a judge.'—SOUTH. The wicked man is *confounded* when his villany is suddenly detected;

Alas! I am afraid they have awak'd,
And 'tis not done: th' attempt, and not the deed,
Confounds us!—SHAKSPEARE.

A modest person may be *confused* in the presence of his superiours; 'The various evils of disease and poverty, pain and sorrow, are frequently derived from others; but shame and *confusion* are supposed to proceed from ourselves, and to be incurred only by the misconduct which they furnish.'—HAWKESWORTH.

Abash is always taken in a bad sense: neither the scorn of fools, nor the taunts of the oppressor, will *abash* him who has a conscience void of offence towards God and man. To be *confounded* is not always the consequence of guilt: superstition and ignorance are liable to be *confounded* by extraordinary phenomena; and Providence sometimes thinks fit to *confound* the wisdom of the wisest by signs and wonders, far above the reach of human comprehension. *Confusion* is at the best an infirmity more or less excusable according to the nature of the cause: a steady mind and a clear head are not easily *confused*, but persons of quick sensibility cannot always preserve a perfect collection of thought in trying situations, and those who have any consciousness of guilt, and are not very hardened, will be soon thrown into *confusion* by close interrogatories.

DISHONOUR, DISGRACE, SHAME.

Dishonour implies the state of being without honour, or the thing which does away honour; *disgrace* signifies the state of disgrace, or that which causes the disgrace (*v. Abase*); *shame* denotes either the feeling of being ashamed, or that which causes this feeling.

Disgrace is more than *dishonour*, and less than *shame*. The *disgrace* is applicable to those who are not sensible of the *dishonour*, and the *shame* for those who are not sensible of the *disgrace*. The tender mind is alive to *dishonour:* those who yield to their passions, or are hardened in their vicious courses, are alike insensible to *disgrace* or *shame*. *Dishonour* is seldom the consequence of any offence, or offered with any intention of punishing; it lies mostly in the consciousness of the individual. *Disgrace* and *shame* are the direct consequences of misconduct: but the former applies to circumstances of less importance than the latter; consequently the feeling of being in *disgrace* is not so strong as that of *shame*. A citizen feels it a *dishonour* not to be chosen to those offices of trust and honour for which he considers himself eligible; it is a *disgrace* to a schoolboy to be placed the lowest in his class; which is heightened into *shame* if it brings him into punishment;

Like a dull actor now,
I have forgot my part, and I am out
Even to a full *disgrace*.—SHAKSPEARE.

'I was secretly concerned to see human nature in so much wretchedness and *disgrace*, but could not forbear smiling to hear Sir Roger advise the old woman to avoid all communications with the devil.'—ADDISON.

The fear of *dishonour* acts as a laudable stimulus to the discharge of one's duty; the fear of *disgrace* or *shame* serves to prevent the commission of vices or crimes. A soldier feels it a *dishonour* not to be placed at the post of danger;

'T is no *dishonour* for the brave to die.—DRYDEN.

But he is not always sufficiently alive to the *disgrace* of being punished, nor is he deterred from his irregularities by the open *shame* to which he is sometimes put in the presence of his fellow-soldiers;

Where the proud theatres disclose the scene
Which interwoven Britons seem to raise,
And show the triumph which their *shame* displays.
DRYDEN.

As epithets these terms likewise rise in sense, and are distinguished by other characteristicks; a *dishonourable* action is that which violates the principles of honour; a *disgraceful* action is that which reflects *disgrace;* a *shameful* action is that of which one ought to be fully *ashamed:* it is very *dishonourable* for a man not to keep his word, or for a soldier not to maintain his post;

He did *dishonourable* find
Those articles which did our state decrease.
DANIEL.

It is very *disgraceful* for a gentleman to associate with those who are his inferiours in station and education; 'Masters must correct their servants with gentleness, prudence, and mercy, not with upbraiding and *disgraceful* language.'—TAYLOR (*Holy Living*). It is very *shameful* for a gentleman to use his rank and influence over the lower orders only to mislead them from their duty;

This all through that great prince's pride did fall,
And came to *shameful* end.—SPENSER.

A person is likewise said to be *dishonourable* who is disposed to bring *dishonour* upon himself; but things only are *disgraceful* or *shameful:* a *dishonourable* man renders himself an outcast among his equals; he must then descend to his inferiours, among whom he may become familiar with the *disgraceful* and the *shameful:* men of cultivation are alive to what is *dishonourable;* men of all stations are alive to that which is for them *disgraceful*, or to that which is in itself *shameful:* the sense of what is *dishonourable* is to the superiour what the sense of the *disgraceful* is to the inferiour; but the sense of what is *shameful* is independent of rank or station, and forms a part of that moral sense which is inherent in the breast of every rational creature. Whoever therefore cherishes in himself a lively sense of what is *dishonourable* or *disgraceful* is tolerably secure of never committing any thing that is *shameful*.

DISCREDIT, DISGRACE, REPROACH, SCANDAL.

Discredit signifies the loss of *credit; disgrace*, the loss of grace, favour, or esteem; *reproach* stands for the thing that deserves to be *reproached;* and *scandal* for the thing that gives *scandal* or offence.

The conduct of men in their various relations with each other may give rise to the unfavourable sentiment which is expressed in common by these terms. Things are said to reflect *discredit*, or *disgrace* to bring *reproach* or *scandal*, on the individual. These terms seem to rise in sense one upon the other: *disgrace* is a stronger term than *discredit; reproach* than *disgrace;* and *scandal* than *reproach*.

Discredit interferes with a man's *credit* or respectability; *disgrace* marks him out as an object of unfavourable distinction; *reproach* makes him a subject of *reproachful* conversation; *scandal* makes him an of offence or even abhorrence. As regularity in hours, regularity in habits or modes of living, regularity in payments, are a *credit* to a family; so is any deviation from this order to its *discredit:* as moral rectitude, kindness, charity, and benevolence, serve to ensure the good-will and esteem of men; so do instances of unfair dealing, cruelty, inhumanity, and an unfeeling temper, tend to the *disgrace* of the offender: as a life of distinguished virtue or particular instances of moral excellence, may cause a man to be spoken of in strong terms of commendation; so will flagrant atrocities or a course of immorality cause his name and himself to be the general subject of *reproach:* as the profession of a Christian with a consistent practice is the greatest ornament which a man can put on: so is the profession with an inconsistent practice the greatest deformity that can be witnessed; it is calculated to bring a *scandal* on religion itself in the eyes of those who do not know and feel its intrinsick excellencies.

Discredit depends much on the character, circumstances, and situation of those who *discredit* and those who are *discredited.* Those who are in responsible situations, and have had confidence reposed in them, must have a peculiar guard over their conduct not to bring *discredit* on themselves: *disgrace* depends on the temper of men's minds as well as collateral circumstances; where a nice sense of moral propriety is prevalent in any community, *disgrace* inevitably attaches to a deviation from good morals. *Reproach* and *scandal* refer more immediately to the nature of the actions than the character of the persons; the former being employed in general matters; the latter mostly in a religious application: it is greatly to the *discredit* of all heads of publick institutions, when they allow of abuses that interfere with the good order of the establishment, or divert it from its original purpose; ''T is the duty of every Christian to be concerned for the reputation or *discredit* his life may bring on his profession.'—ROGERS. 'When a man is made up wholly of the dove without the least grain of the serpent in his composition, he becomes ridiculous in many circumstances of his life, and very often *discredits* his best actions.'—ADDISON. In Sparta the slightest intemperance reflected great *disgrace* on the offender;

> And he whose affluence disdain'd a place,
> Brib'd by a title, makes it a *disgrace.*—BROWN.

In the present age, when the views of men on Christianity and its duties are so much more enlightened than they ever were, it is a *reproach* to any nation to continue to traffick in the blood of its fellow-creatures; 'The cruelty of Mary's persecution equalled the deeds of those tyrants who have been the *reproach* to human nature.'—ROBERTSON. The blasphemous indecencies of which religious enthusiasts are guilty in the excess of their zeal is a *scandal* to all sober-minded Christians;

> His lustful orgies he enlarged
> Even to the hill of *scandal*, by the grove
> Of Moloch homicide.—MILTON.

INFAMOUS, SCANDALOUS.

Infamous, like *infamy* (*v. Infamy*), is applied to both persons and things; *scandalous*, or causing *scandal*, only to things: a character is *infamous*, or a transaction is *infamous;* but a transaction only is *scandalous. Infamous* and *scandalous* are both said of that which is calculated to excite great displeasure in the minds of all who hear it, and to degrade the offenders in the general estimation; but the *infamous* seems to be that which produces greater publicity, and more general reprehension, than the *scandalous*, consequently is that which is more serious in its nature, and a greater violation of good morals. Many of the leaders in the French revolution rendered themselves *infamous* by their violence, their rapine, and their murders; 'There is no crime more *infamous* than the violation of truth.' —JOHNSON. The trick which was played upon the subscribers to the South Sea Company was a *scandalous* fraud, 'It is a very great, though sad and *scandalous* truth, that rich men are esteemed and honoured, while the ways by which they grow rich are abhorred.'—SOUTH

INFAMY, IGNOMINY, OPPROBRIUM.

Infamy is the opposite to good *fame;* it consists in an evil report; *ignominy*, from *nomen* a name, signifies an ill name, a stained name; *opprobrium*, a Latin word, compounded of *op* or *ob* and *probrum*, signifies the highest degree of reproach or stain.

The idea of discredit or disgrace in the highest possible degree is common to all these terms: but *infamy* is that which attaches more to the thing than to the person; *ignominy* is thrown upon the person; and *opprobrium* is thrown upon the agent rather than the action.

The *infamy* causes either the person or thing to be ill spoken of by all; abhorrence of both is expressed by every mouth, and the ill report spreads from mouth to mouth; *ignominy* causes the name and the person to be held in contempt; and to become debased in the eyes of others: *opprobrium* causes the person to be spoken of in severe terms of reproach, and to be shunned as something polluted. The *infamy* of a traitorous proceeding is increased by the addition of ingratitude; the *ignominy* of a publick punishment is increased by the wickedness of the offender; *opprobrium* sometimes falls upon the innocent, when circumstances seem to convict them of guilt.

Infamy is bestowed by the publick voice; it does not belong to one nation or one age, but to every age: the *infamy* of a base transaction, as the massacre of the Danes in England, or of the Hugonots in France, will be handed down to the latest posterity; 'The share of *infamy* that is likely to fall to the lot of each individual in publick acts is small indeed.'—BURKE. *Ignominy* is brought on a person by the act of the magistrate: the publick sentence of the law, and the infliction of that sentence, exposes the name to publick scorn; the *ignominy*, however, seldom extends beyond the individuals who are immediately concerned in it: every honest man, however humble his station and narrow his sphere, would fain preserve his name from being branded with the *ignominy* of either himself, or any of his family, suffering death on the gallows;

> For strength from truth divided, and from just,
> Illaudable naught merits but dispraise,
> And *ignominy.*—MILTON.

Opprobrium is the judgement passed by the publick; it is more silent and even more confined than the *infamy* and the *ignominy;* individuals are exposed to it according to the nature of the imputations under which they lie: every good man would be anxious to escape the *opprobrium* of having forfeited his integrity;

> Nor he their outward only with the skins
> Of beasts, but inward nakedness much more
> *Opprobrious*, with his robe of righteousness
> Arraying, cover'd from his father's sight.
> MILTON.

TO REVILE, VILIFY.

Revile, from the Latin *vilis*, signifies to reflect upon a person, or retort upon him that which is vile: to *vilify*, signifies to make a thing vile, that is, to set it forth as vile.

To *revile* is a personal act, it is addressed directly to the object of offence, and is addressed for the purpose of making the person vile in his own eyes: to *vilify* is an indirect attack which serves to make the object appear vile in the eyes of others. *Revile* is said only of persons, for persons only are *reviled;* but *vilify* is said mostly of things, for things are often *vilified.* To *revile* is contrary to all Christian duty; it is commonly resorted to by the most worthless, and practised upon the most worthy;

> But chief he gloried with licentious style,
> To lash the great, and monarchs to *revile.*—POPE.

To *vilify* is seldom justifiable; for we cannot *vilify* without using improper language; it is seldom resorted to but for the gratification of ill nature: 'There is nobody so weak of invention that cannot make some little stories to *vilify* his enemy.'—ADDISON.

REPROACH, CONTUMELY, OBLOQUY.

Reproach has the same signification as given under *To Blame; contumely*, from *contumeo*, that is, *contra tumeo*, signifies to swell up against; *obloquy*, from *ob* and *loquor*, signifies speaking against or to the disparagement of.

The idea of contemptuous or angry treatment of others is common to all these terms; but *reproach* is the general, *contumely* and *obloquy* are the particular terms. *Reproach* is either deserved or undeserved; the name of Puritan is applied as a term of *reproach* to such as affect greater purity than others; the name of Christian is a name of *reproach* in Turkey; but *reproach* taken absolutely is always supposed to be undeserved, and to be itself a vice;

Has foul *reproach* a privilege from heav'n?—POPE.

Contumely is always undeserved; it is the insolent swelling of a worthless person against merit in distress; our Saviour was exposed to the *contumely* of the Jews; 'The royal captives followed in the train, amid the horrid yells, and frantick dances, and infamous *contumelies*, of the furies of hell.'—BURKE. *Obloquy* is always supposed to be deserved; it is applicable to those whose conduct has rendered them objects of general censure, and whose name therefore has almost become a *reproach*. A man who uses his power only to oppress those who are connected with him will naturally and deservedly bring upon himself much *obloquy*; 'Reasonable moderation hath freed us from being subject unto that kind of *obloquy*, whereby as the church of Rome doth, under the colour of love towards those things which lie harmless, maintain extremely most hurtful corruptions; so we, peradventure might be upbraided, that under colour of hatred towards those things that are corrupt, we are on the other side as extreme, even against most harmless ordinances.'—HOOKER.

REPROACHFUL, ABUSIVE, SCURRILOUS.

Reproachful, when applied to the person, signifies full of *reproaches*; when to the thing, deserving of *reproach*: *abusive* is only applied to the person, signifying after the manner of *abuse*: *scurrilous*, from *scurra* a buffoon, is employed as an epithet either for persons or things, signifying using *scurrility*, or the language of a buffoon. The conduct of a person is *reproachful* in as much as it provokes or is entitled to the *reproaches* of others; the language of a person is *reproachful* when it abounds in *reproaches*, or partakes of the nature of a *reproach*: a person is *abusive* who indulges himself in *abuse* or *abusive* language: and he is *scurrilous* who adopts *scurrility* or *scurrilous* language.

When applied to the same object, whether to the person or to the thing, they rise in sense. the *reproachful* is less than the *abusive*, and this than the *scurrilous*: the *reproachful* is sometimes warranted by the provocation; but the *abusive* and *scurrilous* are always unwarrantable: *reproachful* language may be consistent with decency and propriety of speech, but when the term is taken absolutely, it is generally in the bad sense; 'Honour teaches a man not to revenge a contumelious or *reproachful* word, but to be above it.'—SOUTH. *Abusive* and *scurrilous* language are outrages against the laws of good breeding, if not of morality;

Thus envy pleads a nat'ral claim
To persecute the Muse's fame,
Our poets in all times *abusive*,
From Homer down to Pope inclusive.
SWIFT.

'Let your mirth be ever void of all *scurrility* and biting words to any man.'—SIR HENRY SIDNEY. A parent may sometimes find it necessary to address an unruly son in *reproachful* terms; or one friend may adopt a *reproachful* tone to another; none, however, but the lowest orders of men, and those only when their angry passions are awakened, will descend to *abusive* or *scurrilous* language.

TO REPROBATE, CONDEMN.

To *reprobate*, which is a variation of *reproach*, is much stronger than to *condemn*, which bears the same general meaning as given under *To Blame*; we always *condemn* when we *reprobate*, but not *vice versâ*: to *reprobate* is to *condemn* in strong and reproachful language. We *reprobate* all measures which tend to sow discord in society, and to loosen the ties by which men are bound to each other; 'Simulation (according to my Lord Chesterfield) is by no means to be *reprobated* as a disguise for chagrin or an engine of wit.'—MACKENZIE. We *condemn* all disrespectful language towards superiours;

I see the right, and I approve it too;
Condemn the wrong, and yet the wrong pursue.
TATE.

We *reprobate* only the thing; we *condemn* the person also: any act of disobedience in a child cannot be too strongly *reprobated*; a person must expect to be *condemned* when he involves himself in embarrassments through his own imprudence.

ABUSE, INVECTIVE.

Abuse, which from the Latin *abutor*, signifying to injure by improperly using, is here taken in the metaphorical application for ill-treatment of persons; *invective*, from the Latin *inveho*, signifies to bear upon or against. Harsh and unseemly censure is the idea common to these terms; but the former is employed more properly against the person, the latter against the thing.

Abuse is addressed to the individual, and mostly by word of mouth: *invective* is communicated mostly by writing. *Abuse* is dictated by anger, which throws off all constraint, and violates all decency: *invective* is dictated by party spirit, or an intemperate warmth of feeling in matters of opinion. *Abuse* is always resorted to by the vulgar in their private quarrels: *invective* is the ebullition of zeal and ill-nature in publick concerns.

The more rude and ignorant the man, the more liable he is to indulge in *abuse*; 'At an entertainment given by Pisistratus to some of his intimates, Thrasippus, a man of violent passion, and inflamed with wine, took some occasion, not recorded, to break out into the most violent *abuse* and insult.'—CUMBERLAND. The more restless and opiniated the partisan, whether in religion or politicks, the more ready he is to deal in *invective*; 'This is a true way of examining a libel; and when men consider that no man living thinks better of their heroes and patrons for the panegyrick given them, none can think themselves lessened by their *invective*.'—STEELE. We must expect to meet with *abuse* from the vulgar whom we offend; and if we are in high stations, our conduct will draw forth *invective* from busybodies, whom spleen has converted into oppositionists.

DECLAIM, INVEIGH.

Declaim, in Latin *declamo*, that is, *de* and *clamo*, signifies literally to cry in a set form of words; *inveigh* is taken in the same sense as given in the preceding article.

To *declaim* is to speak either for or against a person; *declaiming* is in all cases a noisy kind of oratory; 'It is usual for masters to make their boys *declaim* on both sides of an argument.'—SWIFT. To *inveigh* signifies always to speak against the object; in this latter application publick men and publick measures are subjects for the *declaimer*; private individuals afford subjects for *inveighing*; the former is under the influence of particular opinions or prejudices; the latter is the fruit of personal resentment or displeasure: patriots (as they are called) are always *declaiming* against the conduct of those in power, or the state of the nation; and not unfrequently they profit by the opportunity of indulging their private pique by *inveighing* against particular members of the government who have disappointed their expectations of advancement. A *declaimer* is noisy; he is a man of words; he makes long and loud speeches; 'Tully (was) a good orator, yet no good poet; Sallust, a good historiographer, but no good *declaimer*.'—FOTHERBY. An *inveigher* is virulent and personal; he enters into private details, and often indulges his malignant feelings under an affected regard for morality; 'Ill-tempered and extravagant *invectives* against papists, made by men, whose persons wanting authority, as much as their speeches do reason, do nothing else but set an edge on our adversaries' sword.'—JACKSON. Although both these words may be applied to moral objects, yet *declamations* are more directed towards the thing, and *invectives* against the person; 'The grave and the merry have equally thought themselves at liberty to conclude, either with *declamatory* complaints, or satirical censures of female folly.'—JOHNSON.

Scarce were the flocks refresh'd with morning dew,
When Damon stretch'd beneath an olive shade,
And wildly staring upward thus *inveigh'd*
Against the conscious gods. —DRYDEN.

TO BLAME, REPROVE, REPROACH, UPBRAID, CENSURE, CONDEMN.

Blame, in French *blamer*, probably from the Greek *βεβλάμμαι*, perfect of the verb *βλάπτω* to hurt, signifying to deal harshly with; *reprove* comes from the Latin *reprobo*, which signifies the contrary of *probo*, to approve; *reproach*, in French *reprocher*, compounded of *re* and *proche*, *proximus* near, signifies to cast back upon a person; *upbraid*, compounded of *up* or *upon*, and *braid* or *breed*, signifies to hatch against one; *censure*, in French *censure*, Latin *censura*, the censorship, or the office of censor; the censor being a Roman magistrate, who took cognizance of the morals and manners of the people, and punished offences against either; *condemn*, in French *condamner*, Latin *condemno*, compounded of *con* and *damno*, from *damnum*, a loss or penalty, signifies to sentence to some penalty.

The expression of one's disapprobation of a person, or of that which he has done, is the common idea in the signification of these terms; but to *blame* expresses less than to *reprove*. We simply charge with a fault in *blaming;* but in *reproving*, severity is mixed with the charge. *Reproach* expresses more than either; it is to *blame* acrimoniously. We need not hesitate to blame as occasion may require; but it is proper to be cautious how we deal out *reproof* where the necessity of the case does not fully warrant it; and it is highly culpable to *reproach* without the most substantial reason.

To *blame* and *reprove* are the acts of a superiour; to *reproach*, *upbraid*, that of an equal: to *censure* and *condemn* leave the relative condition of the parties undefined. Masters *blame* or *reprove* their servants; parents their children; friends and acquaintances *reproach* and *upbraid* each other; persons of all conditions may *censure* or be *censured*, *condemn* or be *condemned*, according to circumstances.

Blame and *reproof* are dealt out on every ordinary occasion; *reproach* and *upbraid* respect personal matters, and always that which affects the moral character; *censure* and *condemnation* are provoked by faults and misconduct of different descriptions. Every fault, however trivial, may expose a person to *blame*, particularly if he perform any office for the vulgar, who are never contented;

Chafe not thyself about the rabble's censure:
They *blame* or praise, but as one leads the other.
PROWDE.

Intentional errours, however small, seem necessarily to call for *reproof*, and yet it is a mark of an imperious temper to substitute *reproof* in the place of admonition, when the latter might possibly answer the purpose; 'In all terms of *reproof*, when the sentence appears to arise from personal hatred or passion, it is not then made the cause of mankind, but a misunderstanding between two persons.'—STEELE. There is nothing which provokes a *reproach* sooner than ingratitude, although the offender is not entitled to so much notice from the injured person;

The prince replies: 'Ah cease, divinely fair,
Nor add *reproaches* to the wounds I bear.'—POPE.

Mutual *upbraidings* commonly follow between those who have mutually contributed to their misfortunes;

Have we not known thee, slave! Of all the host,
The man who acts the least *upbraids* the most.
POPE.

The defective execution of a work is calculated to draw down *censure* upon its author, particularly if he betray a want of modesty;

Though ten times worse themselves, you'll frequent view
Those who with keenest rage will *censure* you.—PITT.

The mistakes of a general, or a minister of state, will provoke condemnation, particularly if his integrity be called in question;

Thus they in mutual accusation spent
The fruitless hours, but neither self-*condemning*.
MILTON.

Blame, *reproof*, and *upbraiding*, are always addressed directly to the individual in person; *reproach*, *censure*, and *condemnation*, are sometimes conveyed through an indirect channel, or not addressed at all to the party who is the object of them. When a master *blames* his servant, or a parent *reproves* his child, or one friend *upbraids* another, he directs his discourse to him to express his disapprobation. A man will always be *reproached* by his neighbours for the vices he commits, however he may fancy himself screened from their observation; 'The very regret of being surpassed in any valuable quality, by a person of the same abilities with ourselves, will *reproach* our own laziness, and even shame us into imitation.'—ROGERS. Writers *censure* each other in their publications;

Men may *censure* thine (weakness)
The gentler, if severely thou exact not
More strength from me, than in thyself was found.
MILTON

The conduct of individuals is sometimes *condemned* by the publick at large; 'They who approve my conduct in this particular are much more numerous than those who *condemn* it.'—SPECTATOR.

Blame, *reproach*, *upbraid*, and *condemn*, may be applied to ourselves; *reproof* and *censure* are applied to others: we *blame* ourselves for acts of imprudence; our consciences *reproach* us for our weaknesses, and *upbraid* or *condemn* us for our sins.

REPREHENSION, REPROOF.

Personal blame or censure is implied by both these terms, but the former is much milder than the latter. By *reprehension* the personal independence is not so sensibly affected as in the case of *reproof:* people of all ages and stations whose conduct is exposed to the investigation of others are liable to *reprehension;* but children only or such as are in a subordinate capacity are exposed to *reproof*. The *reprehension* amounts to little more than passing an unfavourable sentence upon the conduct of another; 'When a man feels the *reprehension* of a friend, seconded by his own heart, he is easily heated into resentment.'—JOHNSON. *Reproof* adds to the *reprehension* an unfriendly address to the offender; 'There is an oblique way of *reproof* which takes off from the sharpness of it.'—STEELE. The master of a school may be exposed to the *reprehension* of the parents for any supposed impropriety: his scholars are subject to his frequent *reproof*.

TO CHECK, CHIDE, REPRIMAND, REPROVE, REBUKE.

Check derives its figurative signification from the *check-mate*, a movement in the game of chess, whereby one stops one's adversary from making a further move; whence to *check* signifies to stop the course of a person, and on this occasion by the exercise of authority; *chide* is in Saxon *cidan*, probably connected with *cyldan* to scold; *reprimand* is compounded of the privative syllable *repri* and *mand*, in Latin *mando* to commend, signifying not to commend; *reprove*, in French *reprouver*, Latin *reprobo*, is compounded of the privative syllable *re* and *probo*, signifying to find the contrary of good, that is, to find bad, to blame; *rebuke* is compounded of *re* and *buke*, in French *bouche* the mouth, signifying to stop the mouth.

The idea of expressing one's disapprobation of a person's conduct is common to all these terms.

A person is *checked* that he may not continue to do what is offensive; he is *chidden* for what he has done that he may not repeat it: impertinent and forward people require to be *checked*, that they may not become intolerable;

I hate when vice can bolt her arguments,
And virtue has no tongue to *check* her pride.
MILTON.

Thoughtless people are *chidden* when they give hurtful proofs of their carelessness; 'What had he to do to *chide* at me?'—SHAKSPEARE.

People are *checked* by actions and looks, as well as words;

> But if a clam'rous vile plebeian rose,
> Him with *reproof* he *check'd*, or tam'd with blows.
> POPE.

They are *chidden* by words only: a timid person is easily *checked;* the want even of due encouragement will serve to damp his resolution: the young are perpetually falling into irregularities which require to be *chidden;*

> His house was known to all the vagrant train,
> He *chid* their wanderings, but reliev'd their pain.
> GOLDSMITH.

To *chide* marks a stronger degree of displeasure than *reprimand*, and *reprimand* than *reprove* or *rebuke;* a person may *chide* or *reprimand* in anger, he *reproves* and *rebukes* with coolness: great offences call forth *chidings;* omissions or mistakes occasion or require a *reprimand;* 'This sort of language was very severely *reprimanded* by the Censor, who told the criminal "that he spoke in contempt of the court."'—ADDISON AND STEELE. Irregularities of conduct give rise to *reproof;* 'He who endeavours only the happiness of him whom he *reproves*, will always have the satisfaction of either obtaining or deserving kindness.'—JOHNSON. Improprieties of behaviour demand *rebuke;* 'With all the infirmities of his disciples he calmly bore; and his *rebukes* were mild when their provocations were great.'—BLAIR.

Chiding and *reprimanding* are employed for offences against the individual, and in cases where the greatest disparity exists in the station of the parties; a child is *chid* by his parent; a servant is *reprimanded* by his master.

Reproving and *rebuking* have less to do with the relation or station of the parties, than with the nature of the offence: wisdom, age, and experience, or a spiritual mission, give authority to *reprove* or *rebuke* those whose conduct has violated any law, human or divine: the prophet Nathan *reproved* king David for his heinous offences against his Maker; our Saviour *rebuked* Peter for his presumptuous mode of speech.

TO ACCUSE, CHARGE, IMPEACH, ARRAIGN.

Accuse, in Latin *accuso*, compounded of *ac* or *ad* and *cuso* or *causa* a cause or trial, signifies to bring to trial; *charge*, from the word *cargo* a burden, signifies to lay a burden; *impeach*, in French *empecher* to hinder or disturb, compounded of *em* or *in* and *pes* the foot, signifies to set one's foot or one's self against another; *arraign*, compounded of *ar* or *ad* and *raign* or *range*, signifies to range, or set at the bar of a tribunal.

The idea of asserting the guilt of another is common to these terms. *Accuse* in the proper sense is applied particularly to crimes, but it is also applied to every species of offence; *charge* may be applied to crimes, but is used more commonly for breaches of moral conduct; we *accuse* a person of murder; we *charge* him with dishonesty.

Accuse is properly a formal action; *charge* is an informal action; criminals are *accused*, and their *accusation* is proved in a court of judicature to be true or false; 'The Countess of Hertford, demanding an audience of the Queen, laid before her the whole series of his mother's cruelty, and exposed the improbability of an *accusation*, by which he was *charged* with an intent to commit a murder that could produce no advantage.'—JOHNSON (*Life of Savage*). Any person may be *charged*, and the *charge* may be either substantiated or refuted in the judgement of a third person; 'Nor was this irregularity the only *charge* which Lord Tyrconnel brought against him. Having given him a collection of valuable books stamped with his own arms, he had the mortification to see them in a short time exposed for sale.'—JOHNSON (*Life of Savage*).

Impeach and *arraign* are both species of *accusing;* the former in application to statesmen and state concerns, the latter in regard to the general conduct or principles; with this difference, that he who *impeaches* only asserts the guilt, but does not determine it; but those who *arraign* also take upon themselves to decide: statesmen are *impeached* for misdemeanours in the administration of government; 'Aristogiton, with revengeful cunning, *impeached* several courtiers and intimates of the tyrant.'—CUMBERLAND. Kings *arraign* governours of provinces and subordinate princes, and in this manner kings are sometimes *arraigned* before mock tribunals: our Saviour was *arraigned* before Pilate; and creatures in the madness of presumption *arraign* their Creator; 'O the inexpressible horrour that will seize upon a poor sinner, when he stands *arraigned* at the bar of Divine justice.'—SOUTH.

TO ACCUSE, CENSURE.

To *accuse* (*v. To Accuse*) is only to assert the guilt of another; to *censure* (*v To Censure*) is to take that guilt for granted. We *accuse* only to make known the offence, to provoke inquiry; we *censure* in order to inflict a punishment. An *accusation* may be false or true; a *censure* mild or severe. It is extremely wrong to *accuse* another without sufficient grounds; 'If the person *accused* maketh his innocence plainly to appear upon his trial, the *accuser* is immediately put to an ignominious death.'—SWIFT. But still worse to *censure* him without the most substantial grounds; 'A statesman, who is possesed of real merit, should look upon his political *censurers* with the same neglect that a good writer regards his criticks.'—ADDISON.

Every one is at liberty to *accuse* another of offences which he knows him for a certainty to have committed; but none can *censure* who are not authorized by their age or station. *Accusing* is for the most part employed for publick offences, or for private offences of much greater magnitude than those which call for *censure;* 'Mr. Locke *accuses* those of great negligence who discourse of moral things with the least obscurity in the terms they make use of.'—BUDGELL. 'If any man measure his words by his heart, and speak as he thinks, and do not express more kindness to every man than men usually have for any man, he can hardly escape the *censure* of the want of breeding.'—TILLOTSON.

TO CENSURE, ANIMADVERT, CRITICISE.

To *censure* (*v. To Accuse*) expresses less than to *animadvert* or *criticise;* one may always *censure* when one *animadverts* or *criticises: animadvert*, in Latin *animadverto*, i. e. *animum verto ad*, signifies to turn the mind towards an object, and, in this case, with the view of finding fault with it: to *criticise*, from the Greek κρίνω to judge, signifies to pass a judgement upon another.

To *censure* and *animadvert* are both personal, the one direct, the other indirect; *criticism* is directed to things, and not to persons only.

Censuring consists in finding some fault real or supposed; it refers mostly to the conduct of individuals. *Animadvert* consists in suggesting some errour or impropriety; it refers mostly to matters of opinion and dispute; *criticism* consists in minutely examining the intrinsick characteristicks, and appreciating the merits of each individually, or the whole collectively; it refers to matters of science and learning.

To *censure* requires no more than simple assertion; its justice or propriety often rests on the authority of the individual; 'Many an author has been dejected at the *censure* of one whom he has looked upon as an idiot.'—ADDISON. *Animadversions* require to be accompanied with reasons; those who *animadvert* on the proceedings or opinions of others must state some grounds for their objections; 'I wish, Sir, you would do us the favour to *animadvert* frequently upon the false taste the town is in, with relation to the plays as well as operas.'—STEELE. *Criticism* is altogether argumentative and illustrative: it takes nothing for granted, it analyzes and decomposes, it compares and combines, it asserts and supports the assertions; 'It is ridiculous for any man to *criticise* on the works of another, who has not distinguished himself by his own performances.'—ADDISON.

The office of the *censurer* is the easiest and least honourable of the three; it may be assumed by ignorance and impertinence, it may be performed for the purpose of indulging an angry or imperious temper. The task of *animadverting* is delicate; it may be resorted to for the indulgence of an overweening self-conceit. The office of a *critick* is both arduous and honourable; it cannot be filled by any one incompetent for the charge without exposing his arrogance and folly o merited contempt.

TO CENSURE, CARP, CAVIL.

Censure has the same general meaning as given in the preceding articles (*v. To Accuse*); *carp*, in Latin *carpo*, signifies to pluck; *cavil*, in French *caviller*, in Latin *cavillor*, from *cavillum* a hollow man, and *cavus* hollow, signifies to be unsound or unsubstantial in speech.

To *censure* respects positive errours; to *carp* and *cavil* have regard to what is trivial or imaginary; the former is employed for errours in persons; the latter for supposed defects in things. *Censures* are frequently necessary from those who have the authority to use them; a good father will *censure* his children when their conduct is *censurable*: but *censure* may likewise be frequently unjust and frivolous; 'From a consciousness of his own integrity, a man assumes force enough to despise the little *censures* of ignorance and malice.'—BUDGELL. *Carping* and *cavilling* are resorted to only to indulge ill-nature or self-conceit; whoever owes another a grudge will be most disposed to *carp* at all he does in order to lessen him in the esteem of others: those who contend more for victory than truth will be apt to *cavil* when they are at a loss for fair argument: party politicians *carp* at the measures of administration; 'It is always thus with pedants; they will ever be *carping*, if a gentleman or man of honour puts pen to paper.'—STEELE. Infidels *cavil* at the evidences of Christianity, because they are determined to disbelieve; 'Envy and *cavil* are the natural fruits of laziness and ignorance, which was probably the reason that in the heathen mythology Momus is said to be the son of Nox and Somnus, of darkness and sleep.'—ADDISON.

ANIMADVERSION, CRITICISM, STRICTURE.

Animadversion (*v. To Censure*) includes censure and reproof; *criticism* implies scrutiny and judgement, whether for or against; and *stricture*, from the Latin *strictura* and *stringo* to touch lightly upon, comprehends a partial investigation mingled with censure. We *animadvert* on a person's opinions by contradicting or correcting them; we *criticise* a person's works by minutely and rationally exposing their imperfections and beauties; we pass *strictures* on publick measures by descanting on them cursorily, and censuring them partially.

Animadversions are too personal to be impartial; consequently they are seldom just; they are mostly resorted to by those who want to build up one system on the ruins of another; but the term is sometimes employed in an indifferent sense; 'These things fall under a province you have partly pursued already, and therefore demand your *animadversion* for the regulating so noble an entertainment as that of the stage.'—STEELE. *Criticism* is one of the most important and honourable departments of literature; a *critick* ought justly to weigh the merits and demerits of authors, but of the two his office is rather to blame than to praise; much less injury will accrue to the cause of literature from the severity than from the laxity of *criticism*; Just *criticism* demands not only that every beauty or blemish be minutely pointed out in its different degree and kind, but also that the reason and foundation of excellencies and faults be accurately ascertained.'—WARTON. *Strictures* are mostly the vehicles of party spleen; like most ephemeral productions, they are too superficial to be entitled to serious notice; but this term is also used in an indifferent sense for cursory *critical* remarks; 'To the end of most plays I have added short *strictures*, containing a general censure of faults or praise of excellence.'—JOHNSON.

COMPLAINT, ACCUSATION.

Both these terms are employed in regard to the conduct of others, but the *complaint*, from the verb to *complain*, is mostly made in matters that personally affect the complainant; the *accusation* (*v. to Accuse*) is made of matters in general, but especially those of a moral nature. A *complaint* is made for the sake of obtaining redress; an *accusation* is made for the sake of ascertaining the fact or bringing to punishment. A *complaint* may be frivolous; an *accusation* false. People in subordinate stations should be careful to give no cause for *complaint*; 'On this occasion (of an interview with Addison), Pope made his *complaint* with frankness and spirit, as a man undeservedly neglected and opposed.'—JOHNSON. The most guarded conduct will not protect any person from the unjust *accusations* of the malevolent; 'With guilt enter distrust and discord, mutual *accusation* and stubborn self-defence.'—JOHNSON.

TO FIND FAULT WITH, BLAME, OBJECT TO.

All these terms denote not simply feeling, but also expressing dissatisfaction with some person or thing. To *find fault with* signifies here to point out a fault, either in some person or thing; to *blame* is said only of the person; *object* is applied to the thing only: we *find fault with* a person for his behaviour; we *find fault with* our seat, our conveyance, and the like; we *blame* a person for his temerity or his improvidence; we *object* to a measure that is proposed. We *find fault with* or *blame* that which has been done; we *object to* that which is to be done.

Finding fault is a familiar action applied to matters of personal convenience or taste; *blame* and *object to*, particularly the latter, are applied to serious objects. *Finding fault* is often the fruit of a discontented temper: there are some whom nothing will please, and who are ever ready to *find fault with* whatever comes in their way; 'Tragi-comedy you have yourself *found fault with* very justly.'—BUDGELL. *Blame* is a matter of discretion; we *blame* frequently in order to correct; 'It is a most certain rule in reason and moral philosophy, that where there is no choice, there can be no *blame*.'—SOUTH. *Objecting to* is an affair either of caprice or necessity; some capriciously *object to* that which is proposed to them merely from a spirit of opposition; others *object to* a thing from substantial reasons; 'Men in all deliberations find ease to be of the negative side, to *object*, and foretel difficulties.'—BACON.

TO OBJECT, OPPOSE.

To *object*, from *ob* and *jacio* to cast, is to cast in the way; to *oppose* is to place in the way; there is, therefore, very little original difference, except that casting is a more momentary and sudden proceeding, placing is a more premeditated action; which distinction, at the same time, corresponds with the use of the terms in ordinary life: to *object* to a thing is to propose or start something against it; but to *oppose* it is to set one's self up steadily against it: one *objects* to ordinary matters that require no reflection; one *opposes* matters that call for deliberation, and afford serious reasons for and against: a parent *objects* to his child's learning the classicks, or to his running about the streets; he *opposes* his marriage when he thinks the connexion or the circumstances not desirable: we *object* to a thing from our own particular feelings; we *oppose* a thing because we judge it improper; capricious or selfish people will *object* to every thing that comes across their own humour; 'About this time, an Archbishop of York *objected* to clerks (recommended to benefices by the Pope), because they were ignorant of English.'—TYRWHITT. Those who *oppose* think it necessary to assign, at least, a reason for their *opposition*;

'T was of no purpose to *oppose*,
She 'd hear to no excuse in prose.—SWIFT.

OBJECTION, DIFFICULTY, EXCEPTION.

The *objection* (*v. Demur*) is here general; it comprehends both the *difficulty* and the *exception*, which are but species of the *objection*: the *objection* and the *difficulty* are started; the *exception is made*: the *objection* to a thing is in general that which renders it less desirable; but the *difficulty* is that which renders it less practicable; there is an *objection* against every scheme which incurs a serious risk; 'I would not desire what you have written to be omitted, unless I had the merit of removing your *objection*.'—POPE. The want of means to begin, or resources to carry on a scheme, are serious *difficulties*; 'In the examination of every great and comprehensive plan, such as that of Christianity *difficulties* may occur.'—BLAIR. In application to moral or intellectual subjects, the *objection* interferes with one's decision; the *difficulty* causes perplexity in the mind; 'They mistake *difficulties* for impossibilities; a pernicious mistake certainly, and the more pernicious, for that men are seldom convinced till their convictions do them no good.'—SOUTH. 'There is ever between all estates a secret war. I know well this speech is the *objection*, and not the decision; and that it is after refuted.'—BACON.

The *objection* and *exception* both respect the nature, the moral tendency, or moral consequences of a thing; but the *objection* may be frivolous or serious; the *exception* is something serious: the *objection* is positive; the *exception* is relatively considered, that is, the thing *excepted* from other things, as not good, and consequently *objected* to. *Objections* are made sometimes to proposals for the mere sake of getting rid of an engagement: those who do not wish to give themselves trouble find an easy method of disengaging themselves, by making *objections* to every proposition; 'Whoever makes such *objections* against an hypothesis, hath a right to be heard, let his temper and genius be what it will.'—BURNET. Lawyers make *exceptions* to charges which are sometimes not sufficiently substantiated: 'When they deride our ceremonies as vain and frivolous, were it hard to apply their *exceptions*, even to those civil ceremonies, which at the coronation, in parliament, and all courts of justice, are used.'—CRANMER. In all engagements entered into, it is necessary to make *exceptions* to the parties, whenever there is any thing *exceptionable* in their characters: the present promiscuous diffusion of knowledge among the poorer orders is very *objectionable* on many grounds; the course of reading, which they commonly pursue, is without question highly *exceptionable*.

TO CONTRADICT, OPPOSE, DENY

To *contradict*, from the Latin *contra* and *dictum*, signifies a speech against a speech; to *oppose*, in French *opposer*, Latin *opposui*, perfect of *oppono* from *op* or *ob* and *pono*, signifies to throw in the way or against a thing; to *deny*, in French *denier*, Latin *denego*, is compounded of *de*, *ne*, and *ago* or *dico*, signifying to say no.

To *contradict*, as the origin of the word sufficiently denotes, is to set up assertion against assertion, and is therefore a mode of opposition, whether used in a general or a particular application. Logicians call those propositions *contradictory* which, in all their terms, are most completely *opposed* to each other; as 'All men are liars;' 'No men are liars.' A *contradiction* necessarily supposes a verbal, though not necessarily a personal, opposition; a person may unintentionally *contradict* himself, as is frequently the case with liars; and two persons may *contradict* each other without knowing what either has asserted; 'The Jews hold that in case two rabbies should *contradict* one another, they were yet bound to believe the *contradictory* assertions of both.'—SOUTH.

But although *contradicting* must be more or less verbal, yet, in an extended application of the term, the *contradiction* may be implied in the action rather than in direct words, as when a person by his good conduct *contradicts* the slanders of his enemies; 'There are many who are fond of *contradicting* the common reports of fame.'—ADDISON. In this application, *contradict* and *oppose* are clearly distinguished from each other. So likewise in personal disputes *contradiction* implies *opposition* only as far as relates to the words; *opposing*, on the other hand, comprehends not only the spirit of the action, but also a great diversity in the mode; we may *contradict* from necessity, or in self-defence; we *oppose* from conviction, or a less honourable nature; we *contradict* by a direct negative; we *oppose* by means of argument or otherwise. It is a breach of politeness ever to *contradict* flatly; it is a violation of the moral law to *oppose* without the most substantial grounds;

> That tongue
> Inspir'd with *contradiction* durst *oppose*
> A third part of the gods.—MILTON.

To *contradict* and to *deny* may be both considered as modes of verbal opposition, but one *contradicts* an assertion, and *denies* a fact; the *contradiction* implies the setting up one person's authority or opinion against that of another; the *denial* implies the maintaining a person's veracity in opposition to the charges or insinuations of others. *Contradicting* is commonly employed in speculative matters; 'If a gentleman is a little sincere in his representations, he is sure to have a dozen *contradicters*.'—SWIFT. *Denying* in matters of personal interest; 'One of the company began to rally him (an infidel) upon his devotion on shipboard, which the other *denied* in so high terms, that it produced the lie on both sides, and ended in a duel.'—ADDISON. *Denying* may, however, be employed as well as *contradicting* in the course of argument; but we *deny* the general truth of the position by *contradicting* the particular assertions of the individuals; 'In the Socratic way of dispute, you agree to every thing your opponent advances; in the Aristotelic, you are still *denying* and *contradicting* some part or other of what he says.'—ADDISON.

When *contradict* respects other persons, it is frequently a mode of *opposition*, as we may most effectually *oppose* a person by *contradicting* what he asserts; but *contradiction* does not necessarily imply *opposition*; the former is simply a mode of action, the latter comprehends both the action and the spirit, with which it is dictated: we *contradict* from necessity or in self-defence; we *oppose*, from conviction or some personal feeling of a less honourable nature. When we hear a friend unjustly charged of an offence, it is but reasonable to *contradict* the charge; objectionable measures may call for *opposition*, but it is sometimes prudent to abstain from *opposing* what we cannot prevent.

Contradict is likewise used in denying what is laid to one's charge; but we may *deny* without *contradicting*, in answer to a question: *contradiction* respects indifferent matters; *denying* is always used in matters of immediate interest.

Contradiction is employed for correcting others; *denying* is used to clear one's self: we may *contradict* falsely when we have not sufficient ground for *contradicting*; and we may *deny* justly when we rebut an unfair charge.

TO DENY, DISOWN, DISCLAIM, DISAVOW.

Deny (*v. To deny*) approaches nearest to the sense of *disown* when applied to persons; *disown*, that is, not to own, on the other hand, bears a strong analogy to *deny* when applied to things.

In the first case *deny* is said with regard to one's knowledge of or connexion with a person; *disowning* on the other hand is a term of larger import, including the renunciation of all relationship or social tie: the former is said of those who are not related; the latter of such only as are related. Peter *denied* our Saviour, 'We may *deny* God in all those acts that are morally good or evil; those are the proper scenes in which we act our confessions or denials of him.'—SOUTH. A parent can scarcely be justified in *disowning* his child let his vices be ever so enormous; a child can never *disown* its parent in any case without violating the most sacred duty.

In the second case *deny* is said in regard to things that concern others as well as ourselves; *disown* only in regard to what is done by one's self or that in which one is personally concerned. A person *denies* that there is any truth in the assertion of another; 'The Earl of Strafford positively *denied* the words.'—CLARENDON. He *disowns* all participation in any affair;

> Then they who brother's better claim *disown*,
> Expel their parents, and usurp the throne.
> DRYDEN.

We may *deny* having seen a thing; we may *disown* that we did it ourselves. Our veracity is often the only thing implicated in a *denial*; our guilt, innocence or honour are implicated in what we *disown*. A witness *denies* what is stated as a fact; the accused party *disowns* what is laid to his charge.

A *denial* is employed only for outward actions or events; that which can be related may be *denied*: *disowning* extends to whatever we can own or possess; we may *disown* our feelings, our name, our connexions, and the like.

Christians *deny* the charges which are brought against the gospel by its enemies; 'If, like Zeno, any one shall walk about and yet *deny* there is any motion in nature, surely that man was constituted for Anti cyra, and were a fit companion for those who, having a conceit they are dead, cannot be convicted unto the society of the living.'—BROWN. The apostles would never *disown* the character which they held as messengers of Christ;

Sometimes lest man should quite his pow'r *disown*,
He makes that power to trembling nations known.
JENYNS.

Disclaim and *disown* are both personal acts respecting the individual who is the agent: to *disclaim* is to throw off a *claim*, as to *disown* is not to admit as one's own; as *claim*, from the Latin *clamo*, signifies to declare with a loud tone what we want as our own; so to *disclaim* is with an equally loud or positive tone, to give up a *claim*: this is a more positive act than to *disown*, which may be performed by insinuation, or by the mere abstaining to own.

He who feels himself disgraced by the actions that are done by his nation, or his family, will be ready to *disclaim* the very name which he bears in common with the offending party;

The thing call'd life, with ease I can *disclaim*,
And think it over-sold to purchase fame.—DRYDEN.

An absurd pride sometimes impels men to *disown* their relationship to those who are beneath them in external rank and condition;

Here Priam's son, Deïphobus, he found:
He scarcely knew him, striving to *disown*
His blotted form, and blushing to be known.
DRYDEN.

An honest mind will *disclaim* all right to praise which it feels not to belong to itself; the fear of ridicule sometimes makes a man *disown* that which would redound to his honour: 'Very few among those who profess themselves Christians, *disclaim* all concern for their souls, *disown* the authority, or renounce the expectations of the gospel.'—ROGERS.

To *disavow* is to *avow* that a thing is not. The *disavowal* is a general declaration; the *denial* is a particular assertion; the former is made voluntarily and unasked for, the latter is always in direct answer to a charge: we *disavow* in matters of general interest where truth only is concerned; we *deny* in matters of personal interest where the character or feelings are implicated.

What is *disavowed* is generally in support of truth; what is *denied* may often be in direct violation of truth: an honest mind will always *disavow* whatever has been erroneously attributed to it; 'Dr. Solander *disavows* some of those narrations (in Hawkesworth's voyages), or at least declares them to be grossly misrepresented.'—BEATTIE. A timid person sometimes *denies* what he knows to be true from a fear of the consequences; 'The king now *denied* his knowledge of the conspiracy against Rizzio, by public proclamations.'—ROBERTSON. Many persons have *disavowed* being the author of the letters which are known under the name of Junius; the real authors who have *denied* their concern in it (as doubtless they have) availed themselves of the subterfuge, that since it was the affair of several, no one individually could call himself the author.

TO CONTROVERT, DISPUTE.

Controvert, compounded of the Latin *contra* and *verto*, signifies to turn against another in discourse, or direct one's self against another.

Dispute, in Latin *disputo*, from *dis* and *puto*, signifies literally to think differently, or to call in question the opinion of another, which is the sense that brings it in closest alliance with *controverting*.

To *controvert* has regard to speculative points; to *dispute* respects matters of fact: there is more of opposition in *controversy*; more of doubt in *disputing*: a sophist *controverts*; a skeptick *disputes*: the plainest and sublimest truths of the Gospel have been all *controverted* in their turn by the self-sufficient inquirer; 'The demolishing of Dunkirk was so eagerly insisted on, and so warmly *controverted*, as had like to have produced a challenge.'—BUDGELL. The authenticity of the Bible itself has been *disputed* by some few individuals; the existence of a God by still fewer;

Now I am sent, and am not to *dispute*
My prince's orders, but to execute.—DRYDEN.

Controversy is worse than an unprofitable task, instead of eliciting truth, it does but expose the failings of the parties engaged; 'How cometh it to pass that we are so rent with mutual contentions, and that the church is so much troubled? If men had been willing to learn, all these *controversies* might have died the very day they were first brought forth.'—HOOKER. *Disputing* is not so personal, and consequently not so objectionable: we never *controvert* any point without seriously and decidedly intending to oppose the notions of another; we may sometimes *dispute* a point for the sake of friendly argument, or the desire of information: theologians and politicians are the greatest *controversialists*; it is the business of men in general to *dispute* whatever ought not to be taken for granted; 'The earth is now placed so conveniently that plants thrive and flourish in it, and animals live; this is matter of fact and beyond all *dispute*.'—BENTLEY. When *dispute* is taken in the sense of verbally maintaining a point in opposition to another, it ceases to have that alliance to the word *controvert*, and comes nearest to the sense of *argue* (*v. Argue*).

INDUBITABLE, UNQUESTIONABLE, INDISPUTABLE, UNDENIABLE, INCONTROVERTIBLE, IRREFRAGABLE.

Indubitable signifies admitting of no doubt (vide *Doubt*); *unquestionable*, admitting of no *question* (*v. Doubt*); *indisputable*, admitting of no *dispute* (*v. To controvert*); *undeniable*, not to be *denied* (*v. To deny, disown*); *incontrovertible*, not to be *controverted* (*v. To controvert*); *irrefragable*, from *frango* to break, signifies not to be *broken*, destroyed, or done away. These terms are all opposed to uncertainty; but they do not imply absolute certainty, for they all express the strong persuasion of a person's mind rather than the absolute nature of the thing: when a fact is supported by such evidence as admits of no kind of doubt, it is termed *indubitable*; 'A full or a thin house will *indubitably* express the sense of a majority.'—HAWKESWORTH. When the truth of an assertion rests on the authority of a man whose character for integrity stands unimpeached, it is termed *unquestionable* authority; 'From the *unquestionable* documents and dictates of the law of nature, I shall evince the obligation lying upon every man to show gratitude.'—SOUTH. When a thing is believed to exist on the evidence of every man's senses, it is termed *undeniable*; 'So *undeniable* is the truth of this (viz. the hardness of our duty), that the scene of virtue is laid in our natural averseness to things excellent.'—SOUTH. When a sentiment has always been held as either true or false, without dispute, it is termed *indisputable*; 'Truth, knowing the *indisputable* claim she has to all that is called reason, thinks it below her to ask that upon courtesy in which she can plead a property.'—SOUTH. When arguments have never been controverted, they are termed *incontrovertible*; 'Our distinction must rest upon a steady adherence to the *incontrovertible* rules of virtue.'—BLAIR. And when they have never been satisfactorily answered, they are termed *irrefragable*; 'There is none who walks so surely, and upon such *irrefragable* grounds of prudence, as he who is religious.'—SOUTH.

TO ARGUE, DISPUTE, DEBATE.

To *argue* is to adduce arguments or reasons in support of one's position: to *dispute*, in Latin *disputo* compounded of *dis* and *puto*, signifies to think differently, in an extended sense, to assert a different opinion; to *debate*, in French *debattre*, compounded of the intensive syllable *de* and *battre*, to beat or fight, signifies to contend for and against.

To *argue* is to defend one's self; *dispute* to oppose another; to *debate* is to *dispute* in a formal manner. To *argue* on a subject is to explain the reasons or proofs in support of an assertion; to *argue* with a person is to defend a position against him; to *dispute* a thing is to advance objections against a position; to *dispute* with a person is to start objections against his positions, to attempt to refute them; a *debate* is a *disputation* held by many. To *argue* does not necessarily suppose a conviction on the part of the *arguer*, that what he defends is true; nor a real difference of opinion in his opponent; for some men have such an itching propensity for an *argument*, that they will attempt to prove what nobody denies; and in some cases the term *argue* may be used in the sense of adducing reasons more for the purpose of producing mutual confirmation and illustration of truth than for the detection of falsehood, or the questioning of opinions;

> Of good and evil much they *argued* then.—MILTON.

To *dispute* always supposes an opposition to some person, but not a sincere opposition to the thing; for we may *dispute* that which we do not deny, for the sake of holding a *dispute* with one who is of different sentiments: to *debate* presupposes a multitude of clashing or opposing opinions. Men of many words *argue* for the sake of talking: men of ready tongues *dispute* for the sake of victory: men in Parliament often *debate* for the sake of opposing the ruling party, or from any other motive than the love of truth.

Argumentation is a dangerous propensity, and renders a man an unpleasant companion in society; no one should set such a value on his opinions as to obtrude the defence of them on those who are uninterested in the question; 'Publick *arguing* oft serves not only to exasperate the minds, but to whet the wits of hereticks.'—DECAY OF PIETY. *Disputation*, as a scholastick exercise, is well fitted to exert the reasoning powers and awaken a spirit of inquiry;

> Thus Rodmond, train'd by this unhallow'd crew,
> The sacred social passions never knew:
> Unskill'd to *argue*, in *dispute* yet loud,
> Bold without caution, without honours proud.
> FALCONER.

Debating in Parliament is by some converted into a trade; he who talks the loudest, and makes the most vehement opposition, expects the greatest applause;

> The murmur ceas'd: then from his lofty throne
> The king invok'd the gods, and thus begun:
> I wish, ye Latins, what ye now *debate*
> Had been resolv'd before it was too late.
> DRYDEN.

TO CONSULT, DELIBERATE, DEBATE.

To *consult*, in French *consulter*, Latin *consulto*, is a frequentative of *consulo*, signifying to counsel together; to *deliberate*, in French *deliberer*, Latin *delibero*, compounded of *de* and *libro*, or *libra* a balance, signifies to weigh as in a balance.

Consultations always require two persons at least; *deliberations* require many, or only a man's self: an individual may *consult* with one or many; assemblies commonly *deliberate*: advice and information are given and received in *consultations*; 'Ulysses (as Homer tells us) made a voyage to the regions of the dead, to *consult* Tiresias how he should return to his country.'—ADDISON. Doubts, difficulties, and objections, are started and removed in *deliberations*; 'Moloch declares himself abruptly for war, and appears incensed with his companions for losing so much time as even to *deliberate* upon it.'—ADDISON. We communicate and hear when we *consult*; we pause and hesitate when we *deliberate*: those who have to co-operate must frequently *consult* together; those who have serious measures to decide upon must coolly *deliberate*.

To *debate* (*v. To argue*) and to *consult* equally mark the acts of pausing or withholding the decision, whether applicable to one or many. To *debate* supposes always a contrariety of opinion; to *deliberate* supposes simply the weighing or estimating the value of the opinion that is offered. Where many persons have the liberty of offering their opinions, it is natural to expect that there will be *debating*;

> To seek sage Nestor now the chief resolves;
> With him in wholesome counsels to *debate*
> What yet remains to safe the sinking state.
> POPE.

When any subject offers that is complicated and questionable, it calls for mature *deliberation*;

> When man's life is in *debate*,
> The judge can ne'er too long *deliberate*.
> DRYDEN.

It is lamentable when passion gets such an ascendency in the mind of any one, as to make him *debate* which course of conduct he shall pursue; the want of *deliberation*, whether in private or publick transactions, is a more fruitful source of mischief than almost any other.

TO OPPOSE, RESIST, WITHSTAND, THWART.

Oppose (*v. To object, oppose*,) is the general term, signifying simply to put in the way; *resist*, signifies literally to stand back, away from, or against; *with* in *withstand* has the force of *re* in *resist*; *thwart*, from the German *quer* cross, signifies to come across.

The action of setting one thing up against another is obviously expressed by all these terms, but they differ in the manner and the circumstances. To *oppose* simply denotes the relative position of two objects, and when applied to persons it does not necessarily imply any personal characteristick: we may *oppose* reason or force to force; or things may be *opposed* to each other which are in an *opposite* direction, as a house to a church. *Resist* is always an act of more or less force when applied to persons; it is mostly a culpable action, as when men *resist* lawful authority; *resistance* is in fact always bad, unless in case of actual self-defence. *Opposition* may be made in any form, as when we *oppose* a person's admittance into a house by our personal efforts; or we *oppose* his admission into a society by a declaration of our opinions. *Resistance* is always a direct action, as when we *resist* an invading army by the sword, or we *resist* the evidence of our senses by denying our assent; or, in relation to things, when wood or any hard substance *resists* the violent efforts of steel or iron to make an impression.

Withstand and *thwart* are modes of *resistance* applicable only to conscious agents. To *withstand* is negative; it implies not to yield to any foreign agency: thus, a person *withstands* the entreaties of another to comply with a request. To *thwart* is positive; it is actively to cross the will of another: thus, humour some people are perpetually *thwarting* the wishes of those with whom they are in connexion. Habitual *opposition*, whether in act or in spirit, is equally senseless; none but conceited or turbulent people are guilty of it;

> So hot th' assault, so high the tumult rose,
> While ours defend, and while the Greeks *oppose*.
> DRYDEN

Oppositionists to government are dangerous members of society, and are ever preaching up *resistance* to constituted authorities;

> To do all our sole delight
> As being the contrary to his high will
> Whom we *resist*.—MILTON.

'Particular instances of second sight have been given with such evidence, as neither Bacon nor Boyle have been able to *resist*.'—JOHNSON. It is a happy thing when a young man can *withstand* the allurements of pleasure;

> For twice five days the good old seer *withstood*
> Th' intended treason, and was dumb to blood.
> DRYDEN.

It is a part of a Christian's duty to bear with patience the untoward events of life that *thwart* his purposes; 'The understanding and will never disagreed (before the fall); for the proposals of the one never *thwarted* the inclinations of the other.'—SOUTH.

TO CONFUTE, REFUTE, DISPROVE, OPPUGN.

Confute and *refute*, in Latin *confuto* and *refuto*, are compounded of *con* against, *re* privative, and *futo*, obsolete for *arguo*, signifying to argue against or to argue the contrary; *disprove*, compounded of *dis* privative and *prove*, signifies to prove the contrary; *oppugn*, in Latin *oppugno*, signifies to fight in order to remove or overthrow.

To *confute* respects what is argumentative; *refute* what is personal; *disprove* whatever is represented or related; *oppugn* whatever is held or maintained.

An argument is *confuted* by proving its fallacy; a charge is *refuted* by proving one's innocence; an assertion is *disproved* by proving that it is false; a doctrine is *oppugned* by a course of reasoning.

Paradoxes may be easily *confuted;* calumnies may be easily *refuted;* the marvellous and incredible stories of travellers may be easily *disproved;* heresies and skeptical notions ought to be *oppugned.*

The pernicious doctrines of skepticks, though often *confuted*, are as often advanced with the same degree of assurance by the free-thinking, and I might say the unthinking few who imbibe their spirit;

> The learned do, by turns, the learn'd *confute*,
> Yet all depart unalter'd by dispute.—ORRERY.

It is the employment of libellists to deal out their malicious aspersions against the objects of their malignity in a manner so loose and indirect as to preclude the possibility of *refutation;* 'Philip of Macedon *refuted* by the force of gold all the wisdom of Athens.'—ADDISON. It would be a fruitless and unthankful task to attempt to *disprove* all the statements which are circulated in a common newspaper,

> Man's feeble race what ills await!
> Labour and penury, the racks of pain,
> Disease, and sorrow's weeping train,
> And death, sad refuge from the storm of fate,
> The fond complaint, my song! *disprove*,
> And justify the laws of Jove.—COLLINS.

It is the duty of ministers of the Gospel to *oppugn* all doctrines that militate against the established faith of Christians; 'Ramus was one of the first *oppugners* of the old philosophy, who disturbed with innovations the quiet of the schools.'—JOHNSON

TO IMPUGN, ATTACK

To *impugn*, from the Latin *in* and *pugno*, signifying to fight against, is synonymous with *attack* only in regard to doctrines or opinions; in which case, to *impugn* signifies to call in question, or bring arguments against; to *attack* is to oppose with warmth. Skepticks *impugn* every opinion, however self-evident or well-grounded they may be: infidels make the most indecent *attacks* upon the Bible, and all that is held sacred by the rest of the world.

He who *impugns* may sometimes proceed insidiously and circuitously to undermine the faith of others: he who *attacks* always proceeds with more or less violence. To *impugn* is not necessarily taken in a bad sense; we may sometimes *impugn* absurd doctrines by a fair train of reasoning: to *attack* is always objectionable, either in the mode of the action, or its object, or in both; it is a mode of proceeding oftener employed in the cause of falsehood than truth: when there are no arguments wherewith to *impugn* a doctrine, it is easy to *attack* it with ridicule and scurrility.

TO ATTACK, ASSAIL, ASSAULT, ENCOUNTER.

Attack, in French *attaquer*, changed from *attacher*, in Latin *attactum*, participle of *attingo*, signifies to bring into close contact; *assail*, *assault*, in French *assailer*, Latin *assilio*, *assaltum*, compounded of *as* or *ad* and *salio*, signifies to leap upon; *encounter*, in French *rencontre*, compounded of *en* or *in* and *contre*, in Latin *contra* against, signifies to run or come against.

Attack is the generick, the rest are specifick terms. To *attack* is to make an approach in order to do some violence to the person; to *assail* or *assault* is to make a sudden and vehement *attack;* to *encounter* is to meet the *attack* of another. One *attacks* by simply offering violence without necessarily producing an effect; one *assails* by means of missile weapons; one *assaults* by direct personal violence; one *encounters* by opposing violence to violence.

Men and animals *attack* or *encounter;* men only, in the literal sense, *assail* or *assault.* Animals *attack* each other with the weapons nature has bestowed upon them; 'King Athelstan *attacked* another body of the Danes at sea near Sandwich, sunk nine of their ships, and put the rest to flight.'—HUME. Those who provoke a multitude may expect to have their houses or windows *assailed* with stones, and their persons *assaulted;*

> So when he saw his flatt'ring arts to fail
> With greedy force he 'gan the fort t' *assail.*
> SPENSER

> And double death did wretched man invade,
> By steel *assaulted*, and by gold betray'd.—DRYDEN.

It is ridiculous to attempt to *encounter* those who are superiour in strength and prowess; 'Putting themselves in order of battle, they *encountered* their enemies.'—KNOWLES.

They are all used figuratively. Men *attack* with reproaches or censures; they *assail* with abuse; they are *assaulted* by temptations; they *encounter* opposition and difficulties. A fever *attacks;* horrid shrieks *assail* the ear; dangers are *encountered.* The reputations of men in publick life are often wantonly *attacked;* 'The women might possibly have carried this Gothick building higher, had not a famous monk, Thomas Conecte by name, *attacked* it with great zeal and resolution.'—ADDISON. Publick men are *assailed* in every direction by the murmurs and complaints of the discontented;

> Not truly penitent, but chief to try
> Her husband, how far urg'd his patience bears,
> His virtue or weakness which way to *assail.*
> MILTON.

They often *encounter* the obstacles which party spirit throws in the way, without reaping any solid advantage to themselves; 'It is sufficient that you are able to *encounter* the temptations which now *assault* you: when God sends trials he may send strength.'—TAYLOR.

ATTACK, ASSAULT, ENCOUNTER, ONSET, CHARGE.

An *attack* and *assault* (*v. To attack*) may be made upon an unresisting object: *encounter*, *onset*, and *charge*, require at least two opposing parties. An *attack* may be slight or indirect; an *assault* must always be direct and mostly vigorous. An attack upon a town need not be attended with any injury to the walls or inhabitants; but an *assault* is commonly conducted so as to effect its capture. *Attacks* are made by robbers upon the person or property of another; *assaults* upon the person only; 'There is one species of diversion which has not been generally condemned, though it is produced by an *attack* upon those who have not voluntarily entered the lists; who find themselves buffetted in the dark, and have neither means of defence nor possibility of advantage.'—HAWKESWORTH. 'We do not find the meeknessof a lamb in a creature so armed for battle and *assault* as the lion.'—ADDISON.

An *encounter* generally respects an unformal casual meeting between single individuals; *onset* and *charge* a regular *attack* between contending armies; *onset* is employed for the commencement of the battle; *charge* for an *attack* from a particular quarter. When knight-errantry was in vogue, *encounters* were perpetually taking place between the knights and their antagonists, who often existed only in the imagination of the combatants: *encounters* were, however, sometimes fierce and bloody, when neither party would yield to the other while he had the power of resistance;

> And such a frown
> Each cast at th' other, as when two black clouds,
> With heav'n's artillery fraught, come rattling on
> Hovering a space, till winds the signal blow,
> To join their dark *encounter* in mid air.—MILTON.

The French are said to make impetuous *onsets*, but not to withstand a continued *attack* with the same perseverance and steadiness as the English;

> *Onsets* in love seem best like those in war,
> Fierce, resolute, and done with all the force.—TATE

A furious and well-directed *charge* from the cavalry will sometimes decide the fortune of the day;

> O my Antonio! I'm all on fire;
> My soul is up in arms, ready to *charge*,
> And bear amid the foe with conqu'ring troops.
> CONGREVE

AGGRESSOR, ASSAILANT.

Aggressor, from the Latin *aggressus*, participle of *aggredior*, compounded of *ag* or *ad*, and *gredior* to step, signifies one stepping up to, falling upon, or attacking; *assailant*, from *assail*, in French *assailer*, compounded of *as* or *ad*, and *salio* to leap upon, signifies one leaping up, or attacking any one vehemently.

The characteristick idea of *aggressor* is that of one going up to another in a hostile manner, and by a natural extension of the sense commencing an attack: the characteristick idea of *assailant* is that of one committing an act of violence on the person.

An *aggressor* offers to do some injury either by word or deed; an *assailant* actually commits some violence: the former commences a dispute, the latter carries it on with a vehement and direct attack. An *aggressor* is blameable for giving rise to quarrels; 'Where one is the *aggressor*, and in pursuance of his first attack kills the other, the law supposes the action, however sudden, to be malicious.'—JOHNSON (*Life of Savage*). An *assailant* is culpable for the mischief he does;

> What ear so fortified and barr'd
> Against the tuneful force of vocal charms,
> But would with transport to such sweet *assailants*
> Surrender its attention ?—MASON.

Were there no *aggressors* there would be no disputes; were there no *assailants* those disputes would not be serious.

An *aggressor* may be an *assailant*, or an *assailant* may be an *aggressor*, but they are as frequently distinct.

TO DISPLEASE, OFFEND, VEX.

Displease naturally marks the contrary of pleasing; *offend*, from the Latin *offendo*, signifies to stumble in the way of; *vex*, in Latin *vexo*, is a frequentative of *veho*, signifying literally to toss up and down.

These words express the act of causing a painful sentiment in th[illegible] by some impropriety, real or supposed, on on[illegible] part. *Displease* is not always applied to that [illegible] personally concerns ourselves; although *offend* an[illegible] *vex* have always more or less of what is personal [illegible] them: a superiour may be *displeased* with one who is under his charge for improper behaviour toward persons in general;

> Meantime imperial Neptune heard the sound
> Of raging billows breaking on the ground;
> *Displeas'd* and fearing for his wat'ry reign,
> He rear'd his awful head above the main.
> DRYDEN.

He will be *offended* with him for disrespectful behaviour toward himself, or neglect of his interests; 'The emperor himself came running to the place in his armour, severely reproving them of cowardice who had forsaken the place, and grievously *offended* with them who had kept such negligent watch.'—KNOLLES. What *displeases* has less regard to what is personal than what *offends*; a supposed intention in the most harmless act may cause offence, and on the contrary the most *offending* action may not give *offence* where the intention of the agent is supposed to be good; 'Nathan's fable of the poor man and his lamb had so good an effect as to convey instruction to the ear of a king without *offending* it.'—ADDISON.

Displease respects mostly the inward state of feeling; *offend* and *vex* have most regard to the outward cause which provokes the feeling: a humoursome person may be *displeased* without any apparent cause; but a captious person will at least have some avowed trifle for which he is *offended*. *Vex* expresses more than *offend*; it marks in fact frequent efforts to *offend*, or the act of *offending* under aggravated circumstances: we often unintentionally *displease* or *offend*; but he who *vexes* has mostly that object in view in so doing: any instance of neglect *displeases*; any marked instance of neglect *offends*; any aggravated instance of neglect *vexes*: the feeling of *displeasure* is more perceptible and vivid than that of *offence*; but it is less durable: the feeling of *vexation* is as transitory as that of *displeasure*, but stronger than either. *Displeasure* and *vexation* betray themselves by an angry word or look; *offence* discovers itself in the whole conduct: our *displeasure* is unjustifiable when it exceeds the measure of another's fault; it is a mark of great weakness to take *offence* at trifles; persons of the greatest irritability are exposed to the most frequent *vexations*; 'Do poor Tom some charity, whom the foul fiend *vexes*.'—SHAKSPEARE. These terms may all be applied to the action of unconscious agents on the mind; 'Foul sights do rather *displease*, in that they excite the memory of foul things, than in the immediate objects. Therefore, in pictures, those foul sights do not much *offend*.'—BACON. 'Gross sins are plainly seen, and easily avoided by persons that profess religion. But the indiscreet and dangerous use of innocent and lawful things, as it does not shock and *offend* our consciences, so it is difficult to make people at all sensible of the danger of it.'—LAW.

> These and a thousand mix'd emotions more,
> From ever-changing views of good and ill,
> Form'd infinitely various, *vex* the mind
> With endless storm.—THOMSON.

As epithets they admit of a similar distinction: it is very *displeasing* to parents not to meet with the most respectful attentions from children, when they give them counsel; and such conduct on the part of children is highly *offensive* to God: when we meet with an *offensive* object, we do most wisely to turn away from it: when we are troubled with *vexatious* affairs, our best and only remedy is patience.

DISLIKE, DISPLEASURE, DISSATISFACTION, DISTASTE, DISGUST.

Dislike signifies the opposite to liking, or being alike to one's self or one's taste; *displeasure*, the opposite to pleasure; *dissatisfaction*, the opposite to satisfaction; *distaste* and *disgust*, from the Latin *gustus* a taste, both signify the opposite to an agreeable taste.

Dislike and *dissatisfaction* denote the feeling or sentiment produced either by persons or things: *displeasure*, that produced by persons mostly; *distaste* and *disgust*, that produced by things only.

In regard to persons, *dislike* is the sentiment of equals and persons unconnected; *displeasure* and *dissatisfaction*, of superiours, or such as stand in some sort of relation to us. Strangers may feel a *dislike* upon seeing each other: parents or masters may feel *displeasure* or *dissatisfaction*: the former sentiment is occasioned by their supposed faults in character; the latter by their supposed defective services. One *dislikes* a person for his assumption, loquacity, or any thing not agreeable in his manners; 'The jealous man is not indeed angry if you *dislike* another; but if you find those faults which are found in his own character, you discover not only your *dislike* of another but of himself.'—ADDISON. One is *displeased* with a person for his carelessness, or any thing wrong in his conduct; 'The threatenings of conscience suggest to the sinner some deep and dark malignity contained in guilt, which has drawn upon his head such high *displeasure* from heaven.'—BLAIR. One is *dissatisfied* with a person on account of the small quantity of work which he has done, or his manner of doing it. *Displeasure* is awakened by whatever is done amiss: *dissatisfaction* is caused by what happens amiss or contrary to our expectation. Accordingly the word *dissatisfaction* is not confined to persons of a particular rank, but to the nature of the connexion which subsists between them. Whoever does not receive what they think themselves entitled to from another are *dissatisfied*. A servant may be *dissatisfied* with the treatment he meets with from his master; and may be said therefore to express *dissatisfaction*, though not *displeasure*; 'I do not like to see any thing destroyed: any void in society. It was therefore with no disappointment or *dissatisfaction* that my observation did not present to me any incorrigible vice in the noblesse of France.'—BURKE.

In regard to things, *dislike* is a casual feeling not arising from any specifick cause. A *dissatisfaction* is connected with our desires and expectations; we *dislike* the performance of an actor from one or many causes, or from no apparent cause; but we are *dissatisfied* with his performance if it fall short of what we were led to expect. In order to lessen the number of our *dislikes* we ought to endeavour not to *dislike* without a cause; and in order to lessen our *dissatisfaction* we ought to be moderate in our expectation.

Dislike, *distaste*, and *disgust* rise on each other in their signification. The *distaste* is more than the *dislike*: and the *disgust* more than the *distaste*. The *dislike* is a partial feeling, quickly produced and quickly subsiding; the *distaste* is a settled feeling, gradually produced, and permanent in its duration: *disgust* is either transitory or otherwise; momentarily or gradually produced, but stronger than either of the two others.

Caprice has a great share in our likes and *dislikes;* 'Dryden's *dislike* of the priesthood is imputed by Langbaine, and I think by Brown, to a repulse which he suffered when he solicited ordination.'—JOHNSON. *Distaste* depends upon the changes to which the constitution physically and mentally is exposed; 'Because true history, through frequent satiety and similitude of things, works a *distaste* and misprision in the minds of men, poesy cheereth and refresheth the soul, chanting things rare and various.'—BACON. *Disgust* owes its origin to the nature of things and their natural operation on the minds of men; 'Vice, for vice is necessary to be shown, should always excite *disgust*.'—JOHNSON. A child likes and *dislikes* his playthings without any apparent cause for the change of sentiment: after a long illness a person will frequently take a *distaste* to the food or the amusements which before afforded him much pleasure: what is indecent or filthy is a natural object of *disgust* to every person whose mind is not depraved. It is good to suppress unfounded *dislikes;* it is difficult to overcome a strong *distaste;* it is advisable to divert our attention from objects calculated to create *disgust*.

DISLIKE, DISINCLINATION.

Dislike is opposed to liking; *disinclination* is the reverse of inclination.

Dislike applies to what one has or does: *disinclination* only to what one does: we *dislike* the thing we have, or *dislike* to do a thing; but we are *disinclined* only to do a thing.

They express a similar feeling, but differing in degree. *Disinclination* is but a small degree of *dislike;* *dislike* marks something contrary; *disinclination* does not amount to more than the absence of an inclination. None but a disobliging temper has a *dislike* to comply with reasonable requests;

> Murmurs rise with mix'd applause,
> Just as they favour or *dislike* the cause.—DRYDEN.

The most obliging disposition may have an occasional *disinclination* to comply with a particular request; 'To be grave to a man's mirth, or inattentive to his discourse, argues a *disinclination* to be entertained by him.'—STEELE.

DISPLEASURE, ANGER, DISAPPROBATION.

Displeasure signifies the feeling of not being pleased with either persons or things; *anger* comes from the Latin *angor* vexation, and *ango* to vex, which is compounded of *an* or *ad* against, and *ago* to act; *disapprobation* is the reverse of approbation.

Between *displeasure* and *anger* there is a difference both in the degree, the cause, and the consequence of the feeling: *displeasure* is always a softened and gentle feeling; *anger* is always a harsh feeling, and sometimes rises to vehemence and madness. *Displeasure* is always produced by some adequate cause, real or supposed; *anger* may be provoked by every or any cause, according to the temper of the individual; 'Man is the merriest species of the creation; all above or below him are serious; he sees things in a different light from other beings, and finds his mirth arising from objects that perhaps cause something like pity or *displeasure* in a higher nature.'—ADDISON. *Displeasure* is mostly satisfied with a simple verbal expression; but *anger*, unless kept down with great force, always seeks to return evil for evil; 'From *anger* in its full import, protracted into malevolence and exerted in revenge, arise many of the evils to which the life of man is exposed.'—JOHNSON. *Displeasure* and *disapprobation* are to be compared in as much as they respect the conduct of those who are under the direction of others: *displeasure* is an act of the will, it is an angry sentiment; 'True repentance may be wrought in the hearts of such as fear God, and yet incur his *displeasure*, the deserved effect whereof is eternal death.'—HOOKER. *Disapprobation* is an act of the judgement, it is an opposite opinion; 'The Queen Regent's brothers knew her secret *disapprobation* of the violent measures they were driving on.'—ROBERTSON. Any mark of self-will in a child is calculated to excite *displeasure;* a mistaken choice in matrimony may produce *disapprobation* in the parent.

Displeasure is always produced by that which is already come to pass; *disapprobation* may be felt upon that which is to take place: a master feels *displeasure* at the carelessness of his servant; a parent expresses his *disapprobation* of his son's proposal to leave his situation: it is sometimes prudent to check our *displeasure;* and mostly prudent to express our *disapprobation:* the former cannot be expressed without inflicting pain; the latter cannot be withheld when required without the danger of misleading.

ANGER, RESENTMENT, WRATH, IRE, INDIGNATION.

Anger has the same original meaning as in the preceding article; *resentment*, in French *ressentiment*, from *ressentir*, is compounded of *re* and *sentir*, signifying to feel again, over and over, or for a continuance; *wrath* and *ire* are derived from the same source, namely, *wrath*, in Saxon *wrath*, and *ire*, in Latin *ira* anger, Greek ἔρις contention, all which spring from the Hebrew חרה heat or anger; *indignation*, in French *indignation*, in Latin *indignatio*, from *indignor*, to think or feel unworthy, marks the strong feeling which base conduct awakens in the mind.

An impatient agitation against any one who acts contrary to our inclinations or opinions is the characteristick of all these terms. *Resentment* is less vivid than *anger*, and *anger* than *wrath*, *ire*, or *indignation*. *Anger* is a sudden sentiment of displeasure; *resentment* is a continued *anger;* *wrath* is a heightened sentiment of *anger*, which is poetically expressed by the word *ire*.

Anger may be either a selfish or a disinterested passion; it may be provoked by injuries done to ourselves, or injustice done to others: in this latter sense of strong displeasure God is *angry* with sinners, and good men may, to a certain degree, be *angry* with those under their control, who act improperly; 'Moralists have defined *anger* to be a desire of revenge for some injury offered.'—STEELE. *Resentment* is a brooding sentiment, altogether arising from a sense of personal injury; it is associated with a dislike of the offender as much as the offence, and is diminished only by the infliction of pain in return; in its rise, progress, and effects, it is alike opposed to the Christian spirit; 'The temperately revengeful have leisure to weigh the merits of the cause, and thereby either to smother their secret *resentments*, or to seek adequate reparations for the damages they have sustained.'—STEELE. *Wrath* and *ire* are the sentiment of a superiour towards an inferiour, and when provoked by personal injuries discovers itself by haughtiness and a vindictive temper;

> Achilles' *wrath*, to Greece the direful spring
> Of woes unnumber'd, heavenly goddess sing.
> POPE.

As a sentiment of displeasure, *wrath* is unjustifiable between man and man; but the *wrath* of God may be provoked by the persevering impenitence of sinners: the *ire* of a heathen god, according to the gross views of Pagans, was but the *wrath* of man associated with greater power; it was altogether unconnected with moral displeasure; the same term is however applied also to the heroes and princes of antiquity;

> The prophet spoke: when with a gloomy frown
> The monarch started from his shining throne;
> Black choler fill'd his breast that boil'd with *ire*,
> And from his eye-balls flash'd the living fire.—POPE.

Indignation is a sentiment awakened by the unworthy and atrocious conduct of others; as it is exempt from personality, it is not irreconcilable with the temper of a Christian; 'It is surely not to be observed without *indignation*, that men may be found of minds mean enough to be satisfied with this treatment; wretches who are proud to obtain the privileges of madmen.'—JOHNSON. A warmth of constitution sometimes gives rise to sallies of *anger;* but depravity of heart breeds *resentment:* unbending pride is a great source of *wrath;* but *indignation* flows from a high sense of honour and virtue.

ANGER, CHOLER, RAGE, FURY.

Anger signifies the same as in the preceding article; *choler*, in French *colère*, Latin *cholera*, Greek χολέρα, comes from χολὴ bile, because the overflowing of the bile is both the cause and consequence of *choler; rage*, in French *rage*, Latin *rabies* madness, and *rabio* to rave like a madman, comes from the Hebrew רבז to tremble or shake with a violent madness; *fury*, in French *furie*, Latin *furor*, comes probably from *fero* to carry away, because one is carried or hurried by the emotions of *fury*.

These words have a progressive force in their signification. *Choler* expresses something more sudden and virulent than *anger; rage* is a vehement ebullition of *anger;* and *fury* is an excess of *rage*. *Anger* may be so stifled as not to discover itself by any outward symptoms; *choler* is discoverable by the paleness of the visage: *rage* breaks forth into extravagant expressions and violent distortions; *fury* takes away the use of the understanding.

Anger is an infirmity incident to human nature; it ought, however, to be suppressed on all occasions; 'The maxim which Periander of Corinth, one of the seven sages of Greece, left as a memorial of his knowledge and benevolence, was χόλου κράτει, be master of thy *anger*.'—JOHNSON. *Choler* is a malady too physical to be always corrected by reflection;

> Must I give way to your rash *choler?*
> Shall I be frighted when a madman stares?
> SHAKSPEARE.

Rage and *fury* are distempers of the soul, which nothing but religion and the grace of God can cure;

> Oppose not *rage*, while *rage* is in its force,
> But give it way awhile and let it waste.
> SHAKSPEARE.

Of this kind is the *fury* to which many men give way among their servants and dependants.'—JOHNSON.

RESENTFUL, REVENGEFUL, VINDICTIVE.

Resentful signifies filled with resentment; *revengeful*, that is, filled with the spirit or desire of revenge; *vindictive*, from *vindico* to avenge or revenge, signifies either given to revenge, or after the manner of revenge.

Resentful marks solely the state or temper of the mind, *revengeful* also extends to the action; a person is *resentful* who retains resentment in his mind without discovering it in any thing but his behaviour; he is *revengeful* if he displays his feeling in any act of revenge or injury toward the offender. *Resentful* people are affected with trifles; 'Pope was as *resentful* of an imputation of the roundness of his back, as Marshal Luxembourg is reported to have been on the sarcasm of King William.'—TYERS. A *revengeful* temper is oftentimes not satisfied with a small portion of revenge;

> If thy *revengeful* heart cannot forgive,
> Lo! here I lend thee this sharp-pointed sword,
> Which hide in this true breast.—SHAKSPEARE.

Revengeful is mostly said of the temper or the person; but *vindictive* or *vindicative*, as it is sometimes written, is said either of the person who is prone to revenge or of the thing which serves the purpose of revenge or punishment; 'Publick revenges are for the most part fortunate; but in private revenges it is not so. *Vindicative* persons live the life of witches, who, as they are mischievous, so end they unfortunate.'—BACON. 'Suits are not reparative, but *vindictive*, when they are commenced against insolvent persons.'—KETTLEWELL.

TO AVENGE, REVENGE, VINDICATE.

Avenge, *revenge*, and *vindicate*, all spring from the same source, namely, the Latin *vindico*, the Greek ἐνδικάζομαι, compounded of ἐν in and δίκη justice, signifying to pronounce justice or put justice in force.

The idea common to these terms is that of taking up some one's cause.

To *avenge* is to punish in behalf of another; to *revenge* is to punish for one's self; to *vindicate* is to defend another

The wrongs of a person are *avenged* or *revenged:* his rights are *vindicated*.

The act of *avenging*, though attended with the infliction of pain, is oftentimes an act of humanity, and always an act of justice; none are the sufferers but such as merit it for their oppression, while those are benefited who are dependent for support: this is the act of God himself, who always *avenges* the oppressed who look up to him for support; and it ought to be the act of all his creatures, who are invested with the power of punishing offenders and protecting the helpless;

> The day shall come, that great *avenging* day,
> When Troy's proud glories in the dust shall lay.
> POPE.

Revenge is the basest of all actions, and the spirit of *revenge* the most diametrically opposed to the Christian principles of forgiving injuries, and returning good for evil; it is gratified only with inflicting pain without any prospect of advantage; 'By a continued series of loose, though apparently trivial gratifications, the heart is often thoroughly corrupted, as by the commission of any one of those enormous crimes which spring from great ambition, or great *revenge*.'—BLAIR. *Vindication* is an act of generosity and humanity; it is the production of good without the infliction of pain: the claims of the widow and orphan call for *vindication* from those who have the time, talent, or ability, to take their cause into their own hands: England can boast of many noble *vindicators* of the rights of humanity, not excepting those which concern the brute creation; 'Injured or oppressed by the world, the good man looks up to a Judge who will *vindicate* his cause'—BLAIR.

ANGRY, PASSIONATE, HASTY, IRASCIBLE.

Anger, signifies either having *anger*, or prone to *anger; passionate*, prone to the *passion* of *anger; hasty*, prone to excess of *haste* from intemperate feeling; *irascible*, able or ready to be made *angry*, from the Latin *ira* anger.

Angry denotes a particular state or emotion of the mind; *passionate* and *hasty* express habits of the mind. An *angry* man is in a state of *anger;* a *passionate* or *hasty* man is habitually prone to be *passionate* or *hasty*. The *angry* has less that is vehement and impetuous in it than the *passionate;* the *hasty* has something less vehement, but more sudden and abrupt in it than either.

The *angry* man is not always easily provoked, nor ready to retaliate; but he often retains his *anger* until the cause is removed; 'It is told by Prior, in a panegyrick on the Duke of Dorset, that his servants used to put themselves in his way when he was *angry*, because he was sure to recompense them for any indignities which he made them suffer.'—JOHNSON. The *passionate* man is quickly roused, eager to repay the offence, and speedily appeased by the infliction of pain of which he afterward probably repents; 'There is in the world a certain class of mortals known, and contentedly known by the name of *passionate* men, who imagine themselves entitled, by that distinction, to be provoked on every slight occasion.'—JOHNSON. The *hasty* man is very soon offended, but not ready to offend in return; his *angry* sentiment spends itself in *angry* words;

> The king, who saw their squadrons yet unmov'd,
> With *hasty* ardour thus the chiefs reprov'd.—POPE.

These three terms are all employed to denote a temporary or partial feeling; *irascible*, on the other hand, is solely employed to denote the temper, and is applied to brutes as well as men; 'We are here in the country surrounded with blessings and pleasures, without any occasion of exercising our *irascible* faculties.'—DIGBY TO POPE.

DISPASSIONATE, COOL.

Dispassionate is taken negatively, it marks merely the absence of passion; *cool* (*v. Cool*) is taken positively, it marks an entire freedom from passion.

Those who are prone to be passionate must learn to be *dispassionate;* those who are of a *cool* temperament will not suffer their passions to be roused. D[illegible].

passionate solely respects angry or irritable sentiments; *cool* respects any perturbed feeling: when we meet with an angry disputant it is necessary to be *dispassionate* in order to avoid quarrels; 'As to violence the lady (Madame D'Acier) has infinitely the better of the gentleman (M. de la Motte). Nothing can be more polite, *dispassionate*, or sensible, than his manner of managing the dispute.'—POPE. In the moment of danger our safety often depends upon our *coolness;* 'I conceived this poem, and gave loose to a degree of resentment, which perhaps I ought not to have indulged, but which in a *cooler* hour I cannot altogether condemn.'—COWPER.

TO DISAPPROVE, DISLIKE.

To *disapprove* is not to approve, or to think not good; to *dislike* is not to like, or to find unlike or unsuitable to one's wishes.

Disapprove is an act of the judgement; *dislike* is an act of the will. To *approve* or *disapprove* is peculiarly the part of a superiour, or one who determines the conduct of others; to *dislike* is altogether a personal act, in which the feelings of the individual are consulted. It is a misuse of the judgement to *disapprove* where we need only *dislike;* 'The poem (Samson Agonistes) has a beginning and an end, which Aristotle himself could not have *disapproved*, but it must be allowed to want a middle.'—JOHNSON. It is a perversion of the judgement to *disapprove*, because we *dislike;* 'The man of peace will bear with many whose opinions or practices he *dislikes*, without an open and violent rupture.'—BLAIR.

DISGUST, LOATHING, NAUSEA.

Disgust has the same signification as given under the head of *Dislike, Displeasure*, &c.; *loathing* signifies the propensity to *loathe* an object; *nausea*, in Latin *nausea*, from the Greek ναῦς a ship, properly denotes sea sickness.

Disgust is less than *loathing*, and that than *nausea.* When applied to sensible objects we are *disgusted* with dirt; we *loathe* the smell of food if we have a sickly appetite; we *nauseate* medicine: and when applied metaphorically, we are *disgusted* with affectation; 'An enumeration of examples to prove a position which nobody denied, as it was from the beginning superfluous, must quickly grow *disgusting.*'—JOHNSON. We *loathe* the endearments of those who are offensive;

> Thus winter falls,
> A heavy gloom oppressive o'er the world,
> Through nature's shedding influence malign,
> The soul of man dies in him, *loathing* life.
> THOMSON.

We *nauseate* all the enjoyments of life, after having made an intemperate use of them, and discovered their inanity;

> Th' irresoluble oil,
> So gentle late and blandishing, in floods
> Of rancid bile o'erflows: what tumults hence,
> What horrors rise, were *nauseous* to relate.
> ARMSTRONG.

OFFENCE, TRESPASS, TRANSGRESSION, MISDEMEANOUR, MISDEED, AFFRONT.

Offence is here the general term, signifying merely the act that *offends*, or runs counter to something else.

Offence is properly indefinite; it merely implies an object without the least signification of the nature of the object; *trespass* and *transgression* have a positive reference to an object *trespassed* upon or *transgressed; trespass* is contracted from *trans* and *pass* that is a passing beyond; and *transgress* from *trans* and *gressus* a going beyond. The *offence* therefore which constitutes a *trespass* arises out of the laws of property; a passing over or treading upon the property of another is a *trespass:* the *offence* which constitutes a *transgression* flows out of the laws of society in general which fix the boundaries of right and wrong; whoever therefore goes beyond or breaks through these bounds is guilty of a *transgression.* The *trespass* is a species of *offence* which peculiarly applies to the land or premises of individuals; *transgression* is a species of moral as well as political evil. Hunters are apt to commit *trespasses* in the eagerness of their pursuit; the passions of men are perpetually misleading them, and causing them to commit various *transgressions;* the term *trespass* is sometimes employed improperly as respects time and other objects; *transgression* is always used in one uniform sense as respects rule and law; we *trespass* upon the time or patience of another;

> Forgive the barbarous *trespass* of my tongue.
> OTWAY.

We *transgress* the moral or civil law;

> To whom with stern regard thus Gabriel spake:
> Why hast thou, Satan, broke the bounds prescrib'd
> To thy *transgressions?*—MILTON.

The *offence* is either publick or private; the *misdemeanour* is properly a private *offence*, although improperly applied for an *offence* against publick law; the *misdemeanour* signifies the wrong *demeanour* or an *offence* in one's *demeanour* against propriety; 'Smaller faults in violation of a publick law are comprised under the name of *misdemeanour.*'—BLACKSTONE. The *misdeed* is always private, it signifies a wrong *deed*, or a *deed* which *offends* against one's duty. Riotous and disorderly behaviour in company are serious *misdemeanours;* every act of drunkenness, lying, fraud, or immorality of every kind, are *misdeeds;*

> Fierce famine is your lot, for this *misdeed*,
> Reduc'd to grind the plates on which you feed.
> DRYDEN

The *offence* is that which affects persons or principles, communities or individuals, and is committed either directly or indirectly against the person; 'Slight provocations and frivolous *offences* are the most frequent causes of disquiet.'—BLAIR. An *affront* is altogether personal and directly brought to bear against the front of the particular person; 'God may some time or other think it the concern of his justice and providence too to revenge the *affronts* put upon the laws of man.'—SOUTH. It is an *offence* against another to speak disrespectfully of him in his absence; it is an *affront* to push past him with violence and rudeness.

Offences are against either God or man; the *trespass* is always an *offence* against man; the *transgression* is against the will of God or the laws of men; the *misdemeanour* is more particularly against the established order of society; the *misdeed* is an *offence* against the Divine Law; the *affront* is an *offence* against good manners.

OFFENDER, DELINQUENT.

The *offender* is he who *offends* in any thing, either by commission or omission; 'When any *offender* is presented into any of the ecclesiastical courts he is cited to appear there.'—BEVERIDGE. The *delinquent*, from *delinquo* to fail, signifies properly he who fails by omission, but the term *delinquency* is extended to a failure by the violation of a law; 'The killing of a deer or boar, or even a hare, was punished with the loss of the *delinquent's* eyes.'—HUME. Those who go into a wrong place are *offenders;* those who stay away when they ought to go are *delinquents:* there are many *offenders* against the Sabbath who commit violent and open breaches of decorum; there are still more *delinquents* who never attend a publick place of worship.

OFFENDING, OFFENSIVE.

Offending signifies either actually *offending* or calculated to *offend; offensive* signifies calculated to *offend* at all times; a person may be *offending* in his manners to a particular individual, or use an *offending* expression on a particular occasion without any imputation on his character;

> And tho' th' *offending* part felt mortal pain,
> Th' immortal part its knowledge did retain.
> DENHAM.

If a person's manners are *offensive*, it reflects both on

his temper and education; 'Gentleness corrects whatever is *offensive* in our manners.'—Blair.

UNOFFENDING, INOFFENSIVE, HARMLESS.

Unoffending denotes the act of not *offending*; *inoffensive* the property of not being disposed or apt to offend; *harmless*, the property of being void of harm. *Unoffending* expresses therefore only a partial state; *inoffensive* and *harmless* mark the disposition and character. A child is *unoffending* as long as he does nothing to offend others; but he may be *offensive* if he discover an unamiable temper, or has unpleasant manners; 'The *unoffending* royal little ones (of France) were not only condemned to languish in solitude and darkness, but their bodies left to perish with disease.'—Seward. A creature is *inoffensive* that has nothing in itself that can offend;

For drink, the grape
She crushes, *inoffensive* must.—Milton.

That is *harmless* which has neither the will nor the power to *harm*; 'When the disciple is questioned about the studies of his master, he makes report of some minute and frivolous researches which are introduced only for the purpose of raising a *harmless* laugh.'—Cumberland. Domestick animals are frequently very *inoffensive*; it is a great recommendation of a quack medicine to say that it is *harmless*.

INDIGNITY, INSULT.

The *indignity*, from the Latin *dignus* worthy, signifying unworthy treatment, respects the feeling and condition of the person offended: the *insult* (*v. Affront*) respects the temper of the offending party. We measure the *indignity* in our own mind; it depends upon the consciousness we have of our own worth: we measure the *insult* by the disposition which is discovered in another to degrade us. Persons in high stations are peculiarly exposed to *indignities*: persons in every station may be exposed to *insults*. The royal family of France suffered every *indignity* which vulgar rage could devise; 'The two caziques made Montezumas' officers prisoners, and treated them with great *indignity*.'—Robertson. Whenever people harbour animosities towards each other, they are apt to discover them by offering *insults* when they have the opportunity; 'Narvaez having learned that Cortez was now advanced with a small body of men, considered this as an *insult* which merited immediate chastisement.'—Robertson. *Indignities* may however be offered to persons of all ranks; but in this case it always consists of more violence than a simple *insult*; it would be an *indignity* to a person of any rank to be compelled to do any office which belongs only to a beast of burden.

It would be an *indignity* to a female of any station to be compelled to expose her person; on the other hand, an *insult* does not extend beyond an abusive expression, a triumphant contemptuous look, or any breach of courtesy.

AFFRONT, INSULT, OUTRAGE.

Affront, in French *affronte*, from the Latin *ad* and *frons*, the forehead, signifies flying in the face of a person; *insult*, in French *insulte*, comes from the Latin *insulto* to dance or leap upon. The former of these actions marks defiance, the latter scorn and triumph; *outrage* is compounded of *out* or *utter* and *rage* or *violence*, signifying an act of extreme violence.

An *affront* is a mark of reproach shown in the presence of others; it piques and mortifies: an *insult* is an attack made with insolence; it irritates and provokes: an *outrage* combines all that is offensive; it wounds and injures. An intentional breach of politeness, or a want of respect where it is due, is an *affront*; 'The person thus conducted, who was Hannibal, seemed much disturbed, and could not forbear complaining to the board of the *affronts* he had met with among the Roman historians.'—Addison. An express mark of disrespect, particularly if coupled with any external indication of hostility, is an *insult*; 'It may very reasonably be expected that the old draw upon themselves the greatest part of those *insults* which they so much lament, and that age is rarely despised but when it is contemptible.'—Johnson When the insult breaks forth into personal violence it is an *outrage*; 'This is the round of a passionate man's life; he contracts debts when he is furious, which his virtue, if he has virtue, obliges him to discharge at the return of reason. He spends his time in *outrage* and reparation.'—Johnson.

Captious people construe every innocent freedom into an *affront*. When people are in a state of animosity, they seek opportunities of offering each other *insults*. Intoxication or violent passion impel men to the commission of *outrages*.

TO AGGRAVATE, IRRITATE, PROVOKE, EXASPERATE, TANTALIZE.

Aggravate, in Latin *aggravatus*, participle of *aggravo*, compounded of the intensive syllable *ag* or *ad* and *gravo* to make heavy, signifies to make very heavy; *irritate*, in Latin *irritatus*, participle of *irrito*, which is a frequentative from *ira*, signifies to excite anger; *provoke*, in French *provoquer*, Latin *provoco*, compounded of *pro* forth, and *voco* to call, signifies to challenge or defy; *exasperate*, Latin *exasperatus*, participle of *exaspero*, is compounded of the intensive syllable *ex* and *asper* rough, signifying to make things exceedingly rough, *tantalize*, in French *tantaliser*, Greek ταντλίζω, comes from *Tantalus*, a king of Phrygia, who, having offended the gods, was destined by way of punishment to stand up to his chin in water with a tree of fair fruit hanging over his head, both of which, as he attempted to allay his hunger and thirst, fled from his touch; whence to *tantalize* signifies to vex by exciting false expectations.

All these words, except the first, refer to the feelings of the mind, and in familiar discourse that also bears the same signification; but otherwise respects the outward circumstances.

The crime of robbery is *aggravated* by any circumstances of cruelty; whatever comes across the feelings *irritates*; whatever awakens anger *provokes*; whatever heightens this anger extraordinarily *exasperates*; whatever raises hopes in order to frustrate them *tantalizes*.

An appearance of unconcern for the offence and its consequences *aggravates* the guilt of the offender; 'As if nature had not sown evils enough in life, we are continually adding grief to grief, and *aggravating* the common calamity by our cruel treatment of one another.'—Addison. A grating harsh sound *irritates* if long continued and often repeated; so also reproaches and unkind treatment *irritate* the mind; 'He *irritated* many of his friends in London so much by his letters, that they withdrew their contributions.'—Johnson (*Life of Savage*). Angry words *provoke*, particularly when spoken with an air of defiance; 'The animadversions of criticks are commonly such as may easily *provoke* the sedatest writer to some quickness of resentment.'—Johnson. When provocations become multiplied and varied they *exasperate*; 'Opposition retards, censure *exasperates*, or neglect depresses.'—Johnson. The weather by its frequent changes *tantalizes* those who depend upon it for amusement; 'Can we think that religion was designed only for a contradiction to nature; and with the greatest and most irrational tyranny in the world to *tantalize*?'—South.

Wicked people *aggravate* their transgressions by violence: susceptible and nervous people are most easily *irritated*; proud people are quickly *provoked*; hot and fiery people are soonest *exasperated*: those who wish for much, and wish for it eagerly, are oftenest *tantalized*.

TO TEASE, VEX, TAUNT, TANTALIZE, TORMENT.

Tease is most probably a frequentative of tear; *vex* has the same signification as given under the head of displease: *taunt* is probably contracted from *tantalize*, the original meaning of which is explained in the preceding article: *torment*, from the Latin *tormentum* and *torqueo* to twist, signifies to give pain by twisting, or griping. The idea of acting upon others so as to produce a painful sentiment is common to all these terms; they differ in the mode of the action, and in the degree of the effect

All these actions rise in importance; to *tease* consists in that which is most trifling; to *torment* in that which is most serious. We are *teased* by a fly that buzzes in our ears; we are *vexed* by the carelessness and stupidity of our servants; we are *taunted* by the sarcasms of others; we are *tantalized* by the fair prospects which only present themselves to disappear again; we are *tormented* by the importunities of troublesome beggars. It is the repetition of unpleasant trifles which *teases*; 'Louisa began to take a little mischievous pleasure in *teasing*.'—CUMBERLAND. It is the crossness and perversity of things which *vex*;

> Still may the dog the wand'ring troops constrain
> Of airy ghosts, and *vex* the guilty train.—DRYDEN.

In this sense things may be said figuratively to be *vexed*;

> And sharpen'd shares shall *vex* the fruitful ground,
> DRYDEN.

It is contemptuous and provoking behaviour which *taunts*,

> Sharp was his voice, which in the shrillest tone,
> Thus with injurious *taunts* attack the throne.
> POPE.

It is the disappointment of awakened expectations which *tantalizes*; 'When the maid (in Sparta) was once sped, she was not suffered to *tantalize* the male part of the commonwealth.'—ADDISON. It is the repetition of grievous troubles which *torments*; 'Truth exerting itself in the searching precepts of self-denial and mortification is *tormenting* to vicious minds.'—SOUTH. We may be *teased* and tormented by that which produces bodily or mental pain; we are *vexed*, *taunted*, and *tantalized* only in the mind. Irritable and nervous people are most easily *teased*; captious and fretful people are most easily *vexed* or *taunted*; sanguine and eager people are most easily *tantalized*: in all these cases the imagination or the bodily state of the individual serves to increase the pain: but persons are *tormented* by such things as inflict positive pain.

VEXATION, MORTIFICATION, CHAGRIN.

Vexation, signifies either the act of vexing, or the feeling of being vexed; *mortification*, the act of mortifying, or the feeling of being mortified; *chagrin*, in French *chagrin*, from *aigrir*, and the Latin *acer* sharp, signifies a sharp feeling.

Vexation springs from a variety of causes, acting unpleasantly on the inclinations or passions of men; *mortification* is a strong degree of *vexation*, which arises from particular circumstances acting on particular passions: the loss of a day's pleasure is a *vexation* to one who is eager for pleasure; the loss of a prize, or the circumstance of coming into disgrace where we expected honour, is a *mortification* to an ambitious person. *Vexation* arises principally from our wishes and views being crossed; *mortification*, from our pride and self-importance being hurt; *chagrin*, from a mixture of the two; disappointments are always attended with more or less of *vexation*, according to the circumstances which give pain and trouble; 'Poverty is an evil complicated with so many circumstances of uneasiness and *vexation*, that every man is studious to avoid it.'—JOHNSON. An exposure of our poverty may be more or less of a *mortification*, according to the value which we set on wealth and grandeur; 'I am *mortified* by those compliments which were designed to encourage me.'—POPE. A refusal of a request will produce more or less of *chagrin* as it is accompanied with circumstances more or less *mortifying* to our pride; 'It was your purpose to balance my *chagrin* at the inconsiderable effect of that essay, by representing that it obtained some notice.'—HILL.

CRIME, MISDEMEANOUR.

Crime (*v. Crime*) is to *misdemeanour* (*v. Offence*), as the genus to the species: a *misdemeanour* is in the technical sense a minor *crime*. Housebreaking is under all circumstances a *crime*; but shoplifting or pilfering amounts only to a *misdemeanour*.

Corporeal punishments are most commonly annexed to *crimes*; pecuniary punishments frequently to *misdemeanours*. In the vulgar use of these terms, *misdemeanour* is moreover distinguished from *crime*, by not always signifying a violation of publick law, but only of private morals; in which sense the term *crime* implies what is done against the state;

> No *crime* of thine our present sufferings draws,
> Not thou, but Heav'n's disposing will the cause
> POPE.

The *misdemeanour* is that which offends individuals or small communities; 'I mention this for the sake of several rural squires, whose reading does not rise so high as to "the present state of England," and who are often apt to usurp that precedency which by the laws of their country is not due to them. Their want of learning, which has planted them in this station may in some measure excuse their *misdemeanour*.'—ADDISON.

CRIME, VICE, SIN.

Crime, in Latin *crimen*, Greek κρῖμα, signifies a judgement, sentence, or punishment; also the cause of the sentence or punishment, in which latter sense it is here taken: *vice*, in Latin *vitium*, from *vito* to avoid, signifies that which ought to be avoided: *sin*, in Saxon *synne*, Swedish *synd*, German *sunde*, old German *sunta*, *sunto*, &c. Latin *sontes*, Greek σίντης, from σίνω to hurt, signifies the thing that hurts: *sin* being of all things the most hurtful.

A *crime* is a social offence; a *vice* is a personal offence: every action which does injury to others, either individually or collectively, is a *crime*; that which does injury to ourselves is a *vice*.

A *crime* consists in the violation of human laws; 'The most ignorant heathen knows and feels that, when he has committed an unjust and cruel action, he has committed a *crime* and deserves punishment.'—BLAIR. *Vice* consists in the violation of the moral law; 'If a man makes his *vices* publick, though they be such as seem principally to affect himself (as drunkenness or the like), they then become, by the bad example they set, of pernicious effects to society.'—BLACKSTONE. *Sin* consists in the violation of the Divine law; 'Every single gross act of *sin* is much the same thing to the conscience that a great blow or fall is to the head; it stuns and bereaves it of all use of its senses for a time.'—SOUTH. *Sin*, therefore, comprehends both *crime* and *vice*; but there are many *sins* which are not *crimes* nor *vices*: *crimes* are tried before a human court, and punished agreeably to the sentence of the judge; *vices* and *sins* are brought before the tribunal of the conscience; the former are punished in this world, the latter will be punished in the world to come, by the sentence of the Almighty: treason is one of the most atrocious *crimes*: drunkenness one of the most dreadful *vices*; religious hypocrisy one of the most heinous *sins*.

Crimes cannot be atoned for by repentance; society demands reparation for the injury committed: vices continue to punish the offender as long as they are cherished: *sins* are pardoned through the atonement and mediation of our blessed Redeemer, on the simple condition of sincere repentance. *Crimes* and *vices* disturb the peace and good order of society, they affect men's earthly happiness only; *sin* destroys the soul, both for this world and the world to come: *crimes* sometimes go unpunished; but *sin* carries its own punishment with it: murderers who escape the punishment due to their *crimes* commonly suffer the torments which attend the commission of such flagrant *sins*. *Crimes* are particular acts; *vices* are habitual acts of commission; *sins* are acts of commission or omission, habitual or particular: personal security, respect for the laws, and regard for one's moral character, operate to prevent the commission of *crimes* or *vices*; the fear of God deters from the commission of sin.

A *crime* always involves a violation of a law; a *vice*, whether in conduct or disposition, always diminishes moral excellence and involves guilt; a *sin* always supposes some perversity of will in an accountable agent Children may commit *crimes*, but we may trust that in the divine mercy they will not all be imputed to them as *sins*. Of *vices*, however, as they are habitual, we have no right to suppose that any exception will be made in the account of our *sins*.

Crimes vary with times and countries; *vices* may be more or less pernicious; but *sin* is as unchangeable in its nature as the Being whom it offends. Smuggling and forgery are *crimes* in England, which in other countries are either not known or not regarded: the *vice* of gluttony is not so dreadful as that of drunkenness; every *sin* as an offence against an infinitely good and wise Being, must always bear the same stamp of guilt and enormity.

By the affectation of some writers in modern times, the word *crime* has been used in the singular to denote, in the abstract sense, a course of criminal conduct, but the innovation is not warranted by the necessity of the case, the word being used in the plural number, in that sense, as to be encouraged in the commission of *crimes*, not of crime.

CRIMINAL, GUILTY.

Criminal, from *crime*, signifies belonging or relating to a *crime; guilty*, from *guilt*, signifies having *guilt: guilt* comes from the German *gelten* to pay, and *gelt* a fine, debt, or from *guile* and *beguile*, according to Horne Tooke; '*Guilt* is ge-wigled *guiled, guil'd, guilt;* the past participle of ge-wiglian and to find *guilt* in any one, is to find that he has been *guiled*, or as we now say, *beguiled*, as wicked means witched or bewitched.'—(*Diversions of Purley*.)

Criminal respects the character of the offence; 'True modesty avoids every thing that is *criminal;* false modesty every thing that is unfashionable.'—ADDISON. *Guilty* respects the fact of committing the offence, or more properly the person committing it;

> Guilt hears appall'd with deeply troubled thought;
> And yet not always on the *guilty* head
> Descends the fated flash.—THOMSON.

The *criminality* of a person is estimated by all the circumstances of his conduct which present themselves to observation; his *guilt* requires to be proved by evidence. The *criminality* is not a matter of question, but of judgement; the *guilt* is often doubtful, if not positively concealed. The higher the rank of a person, the greater his *criminality* if he does not observe an upright and irreproachable conduct; 'If this perseverance in wrong often appertains to individuals, it much more frequently belongs to publick bodies; in them the disgrace of errour, or even the *criminality* of conduct, belongs to so many, that no one is ashamed of the part which belongs to himself.'—WATSON. Where a number of individuals are concerned in any unlawful proceeding, the difficulty of attaching the *guilt* to the real offender is greatly increased; 'When these two are taken away, the possibility of *guilt*, and the possibility of innocence, what restraint can the belief of the creed lay upon any man?'—HAMMOND.

Criminality attaches to the aider, abettor, or encourager; but *guilt*, in the strict sense only, to the perpetrator of what is bad. A person may therefore sometimes be *criminal* without being *guilty*. He who conceals the offences of another may, under certain circumstances, be more *criminal* than the *guilty* person himself. On the other hand, we may be *guilty* without being *criminal:* the latter designates something positively bad, but the former is qualified by the object of the *guilt*. Those only are denominated *criminal* who offend seriously, either against publick law or private morals; but a person may be said to be *guilty*, either of the greatest or the smallest offences. He who contradicts another abruptly in conversation is *guilty* of a breach of politeness, but he is not *criminal*.

Criminal is moreover applied as an epithet to the things done; *guilty* is mostly applied to the person doing. We commonly speak of actions, proceedings, intentions, and views, as *criminal;* but of the person, the mind, or the conscience, as *guilty*. It is very *criminal* to sow dissension among men; although there are too many who from a busy temper are *guilty* of this offence.

CRIMINAL, CULPRIT, MALEFACTOR, FELON, CONVICT.

All these terms are employed for a publick offender; but the first conveys no more than this general idea; while the others comprehend some accessory idea in their signification: *criminal* (*v. Criminal, Guilty*) is a general term, and the rest are properly species of *criminals: culprit*, from the Latin *culpa*, and *prehensus* taken in a fault, signifies the *criminal* who is directly charged with his offence: *malefactor*, compounded of the Latin terms *male* and *factor*, signifies an evil-doer, that is, one who does evil, in distinction from him who does good: *felon*, from *felony*, in Latin *felonia* a capital *crime*, comes from the Greek φηλώσις an imposture because fraud and villany are the prominent features of every capital offence: *convict*, in Latin, *convictus*, participle of *convinco* to convince or prove, signifies one proved or found guilty.

When we wish to speak in general of those who by offences against the laws or regulations of society have exposed themselves to punishment, we denominate them *criminals;* 'If I attack the vicious, I shall only set upon them in a body, and will not be provoked by the worst usage I can receive from others, to make an example of any particular *criminal*.'—ADDISON. When we consider persons as already brought before a tribunal, we call them *culprits;*

> The jury then withdrew a moment,
> As if on weighty points to comment,
> And right or wrong resolved to save her,
> They gave a verdict in her favour.
> The *culprit* by escape grown bold,
> Pilfers alike from young and old.—MOORE

When we consider men in regard to the moral turpitude of their character, as the promoters of evil rather than of good, we entitle them *malefactors;*

> For this the *malefactor* goat was laid
> On Bacchus' altar, and his forfeit paid.—DRYDEN.

When we consider men as offending by the grosser violations of the law, they are termed *felons;* 'He (Earl Ferrers) expressed some displeasure at being executed as a common *felon*, exposed to the eyes of such a multitude.'—SMOLLET. When we consider men as already under the sentence of the law, we denominate them *convicts;*

> Attendance none shall need, nor train, where none
> Are to behold the judgement, but the judged;
> Those two: the third best absent is condemn'd
> *Convict* by flight, and rebel to all law,
> Conviction to the serpent none belongs.—MILTON

The punishments inflicted on *criminals* vary according to the nature of their crimes, and the spirit of the laws by which they are judged: a guilty conscience will give a man the air of a *culprit* in the presence of those who have not authority to be either his accusers or judges: it gratified the malice of the Jews to cause our blessed Saviour to be crucified between two *malefactors:* it is an important regulation in the internal economy of a prison, to have *felons* kept distinct from each other, particularly if their crimes are of an atrocious nature: it has not unfrequently happened, that when the sentence of the law has placed *convicts* in the lowest state of degradation, their characters have undergone so entire a reformation, as to enable them to attain a higher pitch of elevation than they had ever enjoyed before.

CULPABLE, FAULTY.

Culpable, in Latin *culpabilis*, from *culpa* a fault or blame, signifies worthy of blame, fit to be blamed; *faulty*, from *fault*, having *faults*.

We are *culpable* from the commission of one *fault;* we are *faulty* from the number of *faults: culpable* is a relative term; *faulty* is absolute; we are *culpable* with regard to a superiour whose intentions we have not fulfilled; we are *faulty* whenever we commit any *faults*. A master pronounces his servant *culpable* for not having attended to his commands; 'In the common business of life, we find the memory of one like that of another, and honestly impute omissions not to involuntary forgetfulness, but *culpable* inattention.'—JOHNSON. An indifferent person pronounces another as *faulty* whose *faults* have come under his notice; 'In the consideration of human life the satirist never falls upon persons who are not glaringly *faulty*.'—STEELE. It is possible therefore to be *faulty* without being *culpable*, but not *vice versâ*.

GUILTLESS, INNOCENT, HARMLESS.

Guiltless, without *guilt*, is more than *innocent: innocence*, from *noceo* to hurt, extends no farther than the quality of not hurting by any direct act; *guiltless* comprehends the quality of not intending to hurt: it is possible, therefore, to be *innocent* without being *guiltless*, though not *vice versâ;* he who wishes for the death of another is not *guiltless*, though he may be *innocent* of the crime of murder. *Guiltless* seems to regard a man's general condition; *innocent* his particular condition: no man is *guiltless* in the sight of God, for no man is exempt from the guilt of sin; but he may be *innocent* in the sight of men, or *innocent* of all such intentiona offences as render him obnoxious to his fellow-creatures. *Guiltlessness* was that happy state of perfection which men lost at the fall;

> Ah! why should all mankind
> For one man's fault thus *guiltless* be condemn'd,
> If *guiltless*? But from me what can proceed
> But all corrupt?—MILTON.

Innocence is that relative or comparative state of perfection which is attainable here on earth: the highest state of *innocence* is an ignorance of evil; 'When Adam sees the several changes of nature about him, he appears in a disorder of mind suitable to one who had forfeited both his *innocence* and his happiness.'—ADDISON.

Guiltless is in the proper sense applicable only to the condition of man; and when applied to things, it still has a reference to the person;

> But from the mountain's grassy side
> A *guiltless* feast I bring;
> A scrip with fruits and herbs supplied,
> And water from the spring.—GOLDSMITH.

Innocent is equally applicable to persons or things; a person is *innocent* who has not committed any injury, or has not any direct purpose to commit an injury; or a conversation is *innocent* which is free from what is hurtful. *Innocent* and *harmless* both recommend themselves as qualities negatively good; they designate an exemption either in the person or thing from injury, and differ only in regard to the nature of the injury: *innocence* respects moral injury, and *harmless* physical injury: a person is *innocent* who is free from moral impurity and wicked purposes; he is *harmless* if he have not the power or disposition to commit any violence; a diversion is *innocent* which has nothing in it likely to corrupt the morals; 'A man should endeavour to make the sphere of his *innocent* pleasures as wide as possible, that he may retire into them with safety.'—ADDISON. A game is *harmless* which is not likely to inflict any wound, or endanger the health;

> Full on his breast the Trojan arrow fell,
> But *harmless* bounded from the plated steel.
> ADDISON.

IMPERFECTION, DEFECT, FAULT, VICE.

Imperfection denotes either the abstract quality of *imperfect*, or the thing which constitutes it *imperfect*; *defect* signifies that which is deficient or falls short, from the Latin *deficio* to fall short; *fault*, from fail, signifies that which fails; *vice*, signifies the same as explained under the head of *Crime*.

These terms are applied either to persons or things. An *imperfection* in a person arises from his want of *perfection*, and the infirmity of his nature; there is no one without some point of *imperfection* which is obvious to others, if not to himself: he may strive to diminish it, although he cannot expect to get altogether rid of it: a *defect* is a deviation from the general constitution of man; it is what may be natural to the man as an individual, but not natural to man as a species; in this manner we may speak of a *defect* in the speech, or a *defect* in temper. The *fault* and *vice* rise in degree and character above either of the former terms; they both reflect disgrace more or less on the person possessing them; but the *fault* always characterizes the agent, and is said in relation to an individual; the *vice* characterizes the action, and may be considered abstractedly: hence we speak of a man's *faults* as the things we may condemn in him; but we may speak of the *vices* of drunkenness, lying, and the like, without any immediate reference to any one who practises these *vices*. When they are both employed for an individual, their distinction is obvious: the *fault* may lessen the amiability or excellence of the character; the *vice* is a stain; a single act destroys its purity, an habitual practice is a pollution.

In regard to things the distinction depends upon the preceding explanation in a great measure, for we can scarcely use these words without thinking on man as a moral agent, who was made the most perfect of all creatures, and became the most *imperfect*; and from our *imperfection* has arisen, also, a general *imperfection* throughout all the works of creation. The word *imperfection* is therefore the most unqualified term of all: there may be *imperfection* in regard to our Maker; or there may be *imperfection* in regard to what we conceive of *perfection*: and in this case the term simply and generally implies whatever falls short in any degree or manner of *perfection*; 'It is a pleasant story that we, forsooth, who are the only *imperfect* creatures in the universe, are the only beings that will not allow of *imperfection*.'—STEELE. *Defect* is a positive degree of *imperfection*: it is contrary both to our ideas of *perfection* or our particular intention: thus, there may be a *defect* in the materials of which a thing is made; or a *defect* in the mode of making it: the term *defect*, however, whether said of persons or things, characterizes rather the object than the agent; 'This low race of men take a particular pleasure in finding an eminent character levelled to their condition by a report of its *defects*, and keep themselves in countenance, though they are excelled in a thousand virtues, if they believe that they have in common with a great person any one *fault*.'—ADDISON. *Fault*, on the other hand, when said of things, always refers to the agent: thus we may say there is a *defect* in the glass, or a *defect* in the spring; but there is a *fault* in the workmanship, or a *fault* in the putting together, and the like *Vice*, with regard to things, is properly a serious or radical *defect*; the former lies in the constitution of the whole, the latter may lie in the parts; the former lies in essentials, the latter lies in the accidents; there may be a *defect* in the shape or make of a horse; but the *vice* is said in regard to his soundness or unsoundness, his docility or indocility; 'I did myself the honour this day to make a visit to a lady of quality, who is one of those who are ever railing at the *vices* of the age.'—STEELE.

IMPERFECTION, WEAKNESS, FRAILTY, FAILING, FOIBLE.

Imperfection (v. *Imperfection*) has already been considered as that which in the most extended sense abridges the moral *perfection* of man; the rest are but modes of *imperfection*, varying in degree and circumstances; 'You live in a reign of human infirmity, where every one has *imperfections*.'—BLAIR. *Weakness* is a positive and strong degree of *imperfection*, which is opposed to strength; it is what we do not so necessarily look for, and therefore distinguishes the individual who is liable to it; 'The folly of allowing ourselves to delay what we know cannot finally be escaped, is one of the general *weaknesses* which, to a greater or less degree, prevail in every mind.'—JOHNSON. *Frailty* is another strong mode of *imperfection* which characterizes the fragility of man, but not of all men; it differs from *weakness* in respect to the object. A *weakness* lies more in the judgement or in the sentiment; *frailty* lies more in the moral features of an action; 'There are circumstances which every man must know will prove the occasions of calling forth his latent *frailties*.'—BLAIR. It is a *weakness* in a man to yield to the persuasions of any one against his better judgement; it is a *frailty* to yield to intemperance or illicit indulgences. *Failings* and *foibles* are the smallest degrees of *imperfection* to which the human character is liable: we have all our *failings* in temper, and our *foibles* in our habits and our prepossessions; and he, as Horace observes, is the best who has the fewest; 'Never allow small *failings* to dwell on your attention so much as to deface the whole of an amiable character.'—BLAIR. 'Witty men have sometimes sense enough to know their own *foibles*, and therefore they craftily shun the attacks of an argument.'—WATTS. For our *imperfections* we must seek superiour aid: we must be most on our guard against those *weaknesses* to which the softness or susceptibility of our minds may most expose us, and against those *frailties* into which the violence of our evil passions may bring us: toward the *failings* and *foibles* of others we may be indulgent, but should be ambitious to correct them in ourselves.

TO FAIL, FALL SHORT, BE DEFICIENT.

Fail, in French *faillir*, German, &c. *fehlen*, like the word fall, comes from the Latin *fallo* to deceive, and the Hebrew רפל to fall or decay.

To *fail* marks the result of actions or efforts; a person *fails* in his undertaking: *fall short* designates either the result of actions, or the state of things; a person *falls short* in his calculation, or in his account; the issue *falls short* of the expectation: to *be deficient* marks only the state or quality of objects; a person is *deficient* in good manners. People frequently *fail* in their best endeavours for want of knowing how to apply their abilities; 'I would not willingly laugh but to instruct; or, if I sometimes *fail* in this point, when my mirth ceases to be instructive, it shall never cease to be innocent.'—ADDISON. When our expectations are immoderate, it is not surprising if our success *falls short* of our hopes and wishes; 'There is not in my opinion any thing more mysterious in nature than this instinct in animals, which thus rises above reason, and *falls* infinitely *short* of it.'—ADDISON. There is nothing in which people discover themselves to be more *deficient* than in keeping ordinary engagements;

While all creation speaks the pow'r divine,
Is it *deficient* in the main design?—JENYNS.

To *fail* and *be deficient* are both applicable to the characters of men; but the former is mostly employed for the moral conduct, the latter for the outward behaviour: hence a man is said to *fail* in his duty, in the discharge of his obligations, in the performance of a promise, and the like; but to be *deficient* in politeness, in attention to his friends, in his address, in his manner of entering a room and the like.

FAILURE, FAILING.

The *failure* (*v. To fail*) bespeaks the action, or the result of the action; the *failing* is the habit, or the habitual *failure*: the *failure* is said of one's undertakings, or in any point generally in which one *fails*; 'Though some violations of the petition of rights may perhaps be imputed to him (Charles I.), these are more to be ascribed to the necessity of his situation, than to any *failure* in the integrity of his principles.'—HUME. The *failing* is said of one's moral character; 'There is scarcely any *failing* of mind or body, which instead of producing shame and discontent, its natural effects, has not one time or other gladdened vanity with the hope of praise.'—JOHNSON. The *failure* is opposed to the success; the *failing* to the perfection. The merchant must be prepared for *failures* in his speculations; the statesman for *failures* in his projects, the result of which depends upon contingencies that are above human control. With our *failings*, however, it is somewhat different; we must never rest satisfied that we are without them, nor contented with the mere consciousness that we have them.

FAILURE, MISCARRIAGE, ABORTION

Failure (*v. To fail*) has always a reference to the agent and his design; *miscarriage*, that is, the carrying or going wrong, is applicable to all sublunary concerns, without reference to any particular agent; *abortion*, from the Latin *aborior*, to deviate from the rise, or to pass away before it be come to maturity, is in the proper sense applied to the process of animal nature, and in the figurative sense, to the thoughts and designs which are conceived in the mind.

Failure is more definite in its signification, and limited in its application; we speak of the *failures* of individuals, but of the *miscarriages* of nations or things: the *failure* reflects on the person so as to excite towards him some sentiment, either of compassion, displeasure, or the like; 'He that attempts to show, however modestly, the *failures* of a celebrated writer, shall surely irritate his admirers.'—JOHNSON. The *miscarriage* is considered mostly in relation to the course of human events; 'The *miscarriages* of the great designs of princes are recorded in the histories of the world.'—JOHNSON. The *failure* of Xerxes' expedition reflected disgrace upon himself; but the *miscarriage* of military enterprises in general are attributable to the elements, or some such untoward circumstance. The *abortion*, in its proper sense, is a species of *miscarriage*, and in application a species of *failure*, as it applies only to the designs of conscious agents; but it does not carry the mind back to the agent, for we speak of the *abortion* of a scheme with as little reference to the schemer, as when we speak of the *miscarriage* of an expedition; 'All *abortion* is from infirmity and defect.'—SOUTH.

INSOLVENCY, FAILURE, BANKRUPTCY.

All these terms are properly used in the mercantile world, but are not excluded also in a figurative sense from general application. *Insolvency*, from *in* privative, and *solvo* to pay, signifying not to pay, denotes a state, namely, the state of not being able to pay what one owes; *failure*, from to *fail*, signifies the act of *failing* in one's business, or a cessation of business for want of means to carry it on; *bankruptcy*, from the two words *banca rupta*, or a broken bank, denotes the effect of a *failure*, namely, the breaking up of the capital and credit by which a concern is upheld. The word *bankruptcy* owes its origin to the Italians, by whom it is called *bancorotto*, because originally the money-changers of Italy had benches at which they conducted their business, and when any one of them *failed* his bench was broken. These terms are seldom confined to one person, or description of persons. As an incapacity to pay debts is very frequent among others besides men of business, *insolvency* is said of any such persons; a gentleman may die in a state of *insolvency* who does not leave effects sufficient to cover all demands;

Even the dear delight
Of sculpture, paint, intaglios, books and coins,
Thy breast, sagacious prudence! shall connect
With filth and beggary, nor disdain to link
With black *insolvency*.—SHENSTONE.

Although *failure* is here specifically taken for a *failure* in business, yet there may be a *failure* in one particular undertaking without any direct *insolvency*: a *failure* may likewise only imply a temporary *failure* in payment, or it may imply an entire *failure* of the concern; 'The greater the whole quantity of trade, the greater of course must be the positive number of *failures*, while the aggregate success is still in the same proportion.'—BURKE. As a *bankruptcy* is a legal transaction, which entirely dissolves the firm under which any business is conducted, it necessarily implies a *failure* in the full extent of the term; yet it does not necessarily imply an *insolvency*; for some men may, in consequence of a temporary *failure*, be led to commit an act of *bankruptcy*, who are afterward enabled to give a full dividend to all their creditors; 'By an act of *insolvency* all persons who are in too low a way of dealing to be bankrupts, or not in a mercantile state of life, are discharged from all suits and imprisonments, by delivering up all their estates and effects.'—BLACKSTONE. But from the entire state of destitution which a *bankruptcy* involves in it, the term is generally taken for the most hopeless state of want; 'Perkin gathered together a power neither in number nor in hardiness contemptible; but in their fortunes to be feared, being *bankrupts*, and many of them felons.'—BACON. It is also used figuratively; 'Sir, if you spend word for word with me I shall make your wit *bankrupt*.—SHAKSPEARE.

ERROUR, FAULT.

Errour, from *erro* to wander or go astray, respects the act; *fault*, from *fail*, respects the agent: the *errour* may lay in the judgement, or in the conduct; but the *fault* lies in the will or intention: the *errours* of youth must be treated with indulgence: but their *faults* must on all accounts be corrected; *errour* is said of that which is individual and partial;

Bold is the task when subjects, grown too wise,
Instruct a monarch where his *errour* lies.—POPE.

Fault is said of that which is habitual; 'Other *faults* are not under the wife's jurisdiction, and should if possible escape her observation, but jealousy calls upon her particularly for its cure.'—ADDISON. It is an *errour* to use intemperate language at any time; it is a *fault* in the temper of some persons who cannot restrain their anger.

ERROUR, MISTAKE, BLUNDER.

Errour, as in the preceding article, marks the act of wandering, or the state of being gone astray; a *mistake* is a taking amiss or wrong; *blunder* is not improbably changed from blind, and signifies any thing done blindly.

Errour in its universal sense is the general term, since every deviation from what is right in rational agents is termed *errour*, which is strictly opposed to truth: *errour* is the lot of humanity; into whatever we attempt to do or think *errour* will be sure to creep: the term therefore is of unlimited use; the very mention of it reminds us of our condition: we have *errours* of judgement; *errours* of calculation; *errours* of the head; and *errours* of the heart; 'Idolatry may be looked upon as an *errour* arising from mistaken devotion.'—ADDISON. The other terms designate modes of *errour*, which mostly refer to the common concerns of life: *mistake* is an *errour* of choice; *blunder* an *errour* of action: children and careless people are most apt to make *mistakes;* 'It happened that the king himself passed through the gallery during this debate, and smiling at the *mistake* of the dervise, asked him how he could possibly be so dull as not to distinguish a palace from a caravansary.'—ADDISON. Ignorant, conceited and stupid people commonly commit *blunders:* 'Pope allows that Dennis had detected one of those *blunders* which are called bulls.'—JOHNSON. A *mistake* must be rectified; in commercial transactions it may be of serious consequence: a *blunder* must be set right; but *blunderers* are not always to be set right; and *blunders* are frequently so ridiculous as only to excite laughter.

TO DEVIATE, WANDER, SWERVE, STRAY.

Deviate, from the Latin *devius*, and *de via*, signifies literally to turn out of the way; *wander*, in German *wandern*, or *wandeln*, a frequentative of *wenden* to turn, signifies to turn frequently; *swerve*, probably from the German *schweifen* to ramble, *schweben* to soar, &c. signifies to take an unsteady, wide, and indirect course; *stray* is probably a change from *erro* to wander.

Deviate always supposes a direct path; *wander* includes no such idea. The act of *deviating* is commonly faulty, that of *wandering* is indifferent: they may frequently exchange significations; the former being justifiable by necessity; and the latter arising from an unsteadiness of mind. *Deviate* is mostly used in the moral acceptation; *wander* may be used in either sense. A person *deviates* from any plan or rule laid down; he *wanders* from the subject in which he is engaged. As no rule can be laid down which will not admit of an exception, it is impossible but the wisest will find it necessary in their moral conduct to *deviate* occasionally; yet every wanton *deviation* from an established practice evinces a culpable temper on the part of the *deviator;* 'While we remain in this life we are subject to innumerable temptations, which, if listened to, will make us *deviate* from reason and goodness.'—SPECTATOR. Those who *wander* into the regions of metaphysicks are in great danger of losing themselves; it is with them as with most *wanderers*, that they spend their time at best but idly;

> Our aim is happiness; 't is yours, 't is mine;
> He said; 't is the pursuit of all that live,
> Yet few attain it, if 't was e'er attain'd;
> But they the widest *wander* from the mark,
> Who thro' the flow'ry paths of sauntering joy
> Seek this coy goddess.—ARMSTRONG.

To *swerve* is to *deviate* from that which one holds right; to *stray* is to *wander* in the same bad sense: men *swerve* from their duty to consult their interest;

> Nor number, nor example, with him wrought,
> To *swerve* from truth.—MILTON.

The young *stray* from the path of rectitude to seek that of pleasure;

> Why have I *stray'd* from pleasure and repose,
> To seek a good each government bestows?
> GOLDSMITH.

TO DIGRESS, DEVIATE.

Both in the original and the accepted sense, these words express going out of the ordinary course: but *digress* is used only in particular, and *deviate* in genera cases. We *digress* only in a narrative whether written or spoken; we *deviate* in actions as well as in words, in our conduct as well as in writings.

Digress is mostly taken in a good or indifferent sense; 'The *digressions* in the Tale of a Tub, relating to Wotton and Bentley, must be confessed to discover want of knowledge or want of integrity.'—JOHNSON. *Deviate* in an indifferent or bad sense; 'A resolution was taken (by the authors of the Spectator) of courting general approbation by general topicks; to this practice they adhered with few *deviations*.'—JOHNSON. Although frequent *digressions* are faulty, yet occasionally it is necessary to *digress* for the purposes of explanation: every *deviation* is bad, which is not sanctioned by the necessity of circumstances.

TO WANDER, TO STROLL, RAMBLE, ROVE, ROAM, RANGE.

Wander signifies the same as in the article *Deviate; stroll* is probably an intensive of to *roll*, that is, to go in a planless manner, *ramble* from the Latin *re* and *ambulo*, is to walk backward and forward; and *rove* is probably a contraction of *ramble; roam* is connected with our word *room*, space, signifying to go in a wide space, and the Hebrew רום, to be violently moved backward and forward; *range*, from the noun *range*, a rank, row, or extended space, signifies to go over a great space, but within certain limits. The idea of going in an irregular and free manner is common to al these terms.

To *wander* is to go out of the path that has been already marked out;

> But far about they *wander* from the grave
> Of him, whom his ungentle fortune urg'd
> Against his own sad breast to lift the hand
> Of impious violence.—THOMSON.

Sometimes *wandering* may be an involuntary action a person may *wander* to a great distance, or for an in definite length of time; in this manner a person *wanders* who has lost himself in a wood; or it may be a planless course;

> I will go lose myself,
> And *wander* up and down to view the city.
> SHAKSPEARE.

To *stroll* is to go in a fixed path, but *strolling* is a voluntary action, limited at our discretion; thus, when a person takes a walk, he sometimes *strolls* from one path into another, as he pleases; 'I found by the voice of my friend who walked by me, that we had insensibly *strolled* into the grove sacred to the widow.'—ADDISON. To *ramble* is to *wander* without any object, and consequently with more than ordinary irregularity: in this manner he who sets out to take a walk, without knowing or thinking where he shall go, *rambles* as chance directs; 'I thus *rambled* from pocket to pocket until the beginning of the civil wars.—ADDISON. To *rove* is to *wander* in the same planless manner, but to a wider extent; a fugitive who does not know his road, *roves* about the country in quest of some retreat;

> Where is that knowledge now, that regal thought
> With just advice and timely counsel fraught?
> Where now, O judge of Israel, does it *rove?*
> PRIOR.

To *roam* is to *wander* from the impulse of a disordered mind; in this manner a lunatick who has broken loose may *roam* about the country; so likewise a person who travels about, because he cannot rest in quiet at home, may also be said to *roam* in quest of peace;

> She looks abroad, and prunes herself for flight,
> Like an unwilling inmate longs to *roam*
> From this dull earth, and seek her native home.
> JENYNS.

To *range* is the contrary of to *roam;* as the latter indicates a disordered state of mind, the former indicates composure and fixedness; we *range* within certain limits, as the hunter *ranges* the forest, the shepherd *ranges* the mountains;

> The stag too singled from the herd, where long
> He *rang'd* the branching monarch of the shades
> Before the tempest drives.—THOMSON.

BLEMISH, DEFECT, FAULT.

Blemish is probably changed from the word *blame*, signifying that which causes blame; *defect* and *fault* have the same signification as given under the head of *imperfection*.

Blemish respects accidents or incidental properties of an object: *defect* consists in the want of some specifick propriety in an object; *fault* conveys the idea not only of something wrong, but also of its relation to the author. There is a *blemish* in fine china; a *defect* in the springs of a clock; and a *fault* in the contrivance. An accident may cause a *blemish* in a fine painting; 'There is another particular which may be reckoned among the *blemishes*, or rather, the false beauties, of our English tragedy: I mean those particular speeches which are commonly known by the name of rants.'—ADDISON. The course of nature may occasion a *defect* in a person's speech; 'It has been often remarked, though not without wonder, that a man is more jealous of his natural than of his moral qualities; perhaps it will no longer appear strange, if it be considered that natural *defects* are of necessity, and moral of choice.'—HAWKESWORTH. The carelessness of the workman is evinced by the *faults* in the workmanship; 'The resentment which the discovery of a *fault* or folly produces must bear a certain proportion to our pride.'—JOHNSON. A *blemish* may be easier remedied than a *defect* is corrected, or a *fault* repaired.

BLEMISH, STAIN, SPOT, SPECK, FLAW.

Blemish comes immediately from the French *blêmir* to grow pale, but probably in an indirect manner from blame; *stain*, in French *teindre*, old French *desteindre*, comes from the Latin *tingo* to die; *spot* is not improbably connected with the word *spit*, Latin *sputum*, and the Hebrew ספח, to adhere as something extraneous; *speck*, in Saxon *specce*, probably comes from the same Hebrew root; *flaw*, in Saxon *floh*, *fliece*, German *fleck*, low German *flak* or *plakke*, a spot or a fragment, a piece, most probably from the Latin *plaga*, Greek πληγή a strip of land, or a stripe, a wound in the body.

In the proper sense *blemish* is the generick term, the rest are specifick: a *stain*, a *spot*, *speck*, and *flaw*, are *blemishes*, but there are likewise many *blemishes* which are neither *stains*, *spots*, *specks*, nor *flaws*.

Whatever takes off from the seemliness of appearance is a *blemish*. In works of art, the slightest dimness of colour, or want of proportion, is a *blemish*. A *stain* and *spot* sufficiently characterize themselves, as that which is superfluous and out of its place. A *speck* is a small *spot*; and a *flaw*, which is confined to hard substances, mostly consists of a faulty indenture on the outer surface. A *blemish* tarnishes; a *stain* spoils; a *spot*, *speck*, or *flaw*, disfigures. A *blemish* is rectified, a *stain* wiped out, a *spot* or *speck* removed.

These terms are also employed figuratively. Even an imputation of what is improper in our moral conduct is a *blemish* in our reputation; 'It is impossible for authors to discover beauties in one another's works: they have eyes only for *spots* and *blemishes*.'—ADDISON. The failings of a good man are so many *spots* in the bright hemisphere of his virtue: there are some vices which affix a *stain* on the character of nations, as well as of the individuals who are guilty of them;

> By length of time,
> The scurf is worn away of each committed crime;
> No *speck* is left of their habitual *stains*,
> But the pure æther of the soul remains.—DRYDEN.

A *blemish* or a *spot* may be removed by a course of good conduct, but a *stain* is mostly indelible: it is as great a privilege to have an *unblemished* reputation, or a *spotless* character, as it is a misfortune to have the *stain* of bad actions affixed to our name: 'There are many who applaud themselves for the singularity of their judgement, which has searched deeper than others, and found a *flaw* in what the generality of mankind have admired.'—ADDISON.

DEFECTIVE, DEFICIENT.

Defective expresses the quality or property of having a *defect* (*v. Blemish*); *deficient* is employed with regard to the thing itself that is wanting. A book may be *defective*, in consequence of some leaves being *deficient*. A *deficiency* is therefore often what constitutes a *defect*. Many things, however, may be *defective* without having any *deficiency*, and *vice versâ*. What ever is misshapen, and fails, either in beauty or utility, is *defective*; that which is wanted to make a thing complete is *deficient*. It is a *defect* in the eye when it is so constructed that things are not seen at their proper distances; 'Providence, for the most part, sets us upon a level; if it renders us perfect in one accomplishment, it generally leaves us *defective* in another'—ADDISON. There is a *deficiency* in a tradesman's accounts, when one side falls short of the other; 'If there be a *deficiency* in the speaker, there will not be sufficient attention and regard paid to the thing spoken.'—SWIFT.

Things only are said to be *defective*; but persons may be termed *deficient* either in attention, in good breeding, in civility, or whatever else the occasion may require. That which is *defective* is most likely to be permanent; but a *deficiency* may be only occasional, and easily rectified.

BAD, WICKED, EVIL.

Bad, in Saxon *bad*, *baed*, in German *bös*, is probably connected with the Latin *pejus* worse, and the Hebrew יבש to be ashamed; *wicked* is probably changed from *witched* or *bewitched*, that is, possessed with an evil spirit; *bad* respects moral and physical qualities in general; *wicked* only moral qualities; *evil*, in German *üebel*, from the Hebrew חבל pain, signifies that which is the prime cause of pain; *evil* therefore, in its full extent, comprehends both *badness* and *wickedness*.

Whatever offends the taste and sentiments of a rational being is *bad*: food is *bad* when it disagrees with the constitution; the air is *bad* which has any thing in it disagreeable to the senses or hurtful to the body; books are *bad* which only inflame the imagination or the passions; 'Whatever we may pretend, as to our belief, it is the strain of our actions that must show whether our principles have been good or *bad*.'—BLAIR. Whatever is wicked offends the moral principles of a rational agent: any violation of the law is *wicked*, as law is the support of human society; an act of injustice or cruelty is *wicked*, as it opposes the will of God and the feelings of humanity;

> For when th' impenitent and *wicked die*,
> Loaded with crimes and infamy;
> If any sense at that sad time remains,
> They feel amazing terrour, mighty pains.
> POMFRET.

Evil is either moral or natural, and may be applied to every object that is contrary to good; but the term is employed only for that which is in the highest degree *bad* or *wicked*;

> And what your bounded view, which only saw
> A little part, deem'd *evil*, is no more;
> The storms of wintry time will quickly pass,
> And one unbounded spring encircle all.—THOMSON.

When used in relation to persons, both refer to the morals, but *bad* is more general than *wicked*; a *bad* man is one who is generally wanting in the performance of his duty; a *wicked* man is one who is chargeable with actual violations of the law, human or Divine; such a one has an *evil* mind. A *bad* character is the consequence of immoral conduct; but no man has the character of being *wicked* who has not been guilty of some known and flagrant vices: the inclinations of the best are *evil* at certain times

BADLY, ILL.

Badly, in the manner of *bad* (*v. Bad*); *ill*, in Swedish *ill*, Icelandick *ilur*, Danish *ill*, &c. is supposed by Adelung, and with some degree of justice, not to be a contraction of evil, but to spring from the Greek οὐλὸς destructive, and ολλύω to destroy.

These terms are both employed to modify the actions or qualities of things, but *badly* is always annexed to the action, and *ill* to the quality: as to do any thing *badly*, the thing is *badly* done; an *ill*-judged scheme, an *ill*-contrived measure an *ill*-disposed person.

DEPRAVITY, DEPRAVATION, CORRUPTION.

Depravity, from the Latin *pravitas* and *pravus*, in Greek *ῥαιβὸς*, and the Hebrew רע to be disordered, or put out of its established order, signifying the quality of not being straight; *depravation*, in Latin *depravatio*, signifies the act of making depraved; *corruption*, in Latin *corruptio*, *corrumpo*, from *rumpo* to break, marks the disunion and decomposition of the parts.

* All these terms are applied to objects which are contrary to the order of Providence, but the term *depravity* characterizes the thing as it is; the terms *depravation* and *corruption* designate the making or causing it to be so: *depravity* therefore excludes the idea of any cause; *depravation* always refers us to the cause or external agency: hence we may speak of *depravity* as natural, but we speak of *depravation* and *corruption* as the result of circumstances: there is a *depravity* in man, which nothing but the grace of God can correct; 'Nothing can show greater *depravity* of understanding than to delight in the show when the reality is wanting.'—JOHNSON. The introduction of obscenity on the stage tends greatly to the *depravation* of morals; bad company tends to the *corruption* of a young man's morals; 'The *corruption* of our taste is not of equal consequence with the *depravation* of our virtue.'—WARTON.

Depravity or *depravation* implies crookedness, or a distortion from the regular course; *corruption* implies a dissolution as it were in the component parts of bodies.

Cicero says that *depravity* is applicable only to the mind and heart; but we say a *depraved* taste, and *depraved* humours in regard to the body. A *depraved* taste loathes common food, and longs for that which is unnatural and hurtful. *Corruption* is the natural process by which material substances are disorganized.

In the figurative application of these terms they preserve the same signification. *Depravity* is characterized by being directly opposed to order, and an established system of things; *corruption* marks the vitiation or spoiling of things, and the ferment that leads to destruction. *Depravity* turns things out of their ordinary course; *corruption* destroys their essential qualities. *Depravity* is a vicious state of things, in which all is deranged and perverted; *corruption* is a vicious state of things, in which all is sullied and polluted. That which is *depraved* loses its proper manner of acting and existing; 'The *depravation* of human will was followed by a disorder of the harmony of nature.'—JOHNSON. That which is *corrupted* loses its virtue and essence; 'We can discover that where there is universal innocence, there will probably be universal happiness; for why should afflictions be permitted to infest beings who are not in danger of *corruption* from blessings?'—JOHNSON.

The force of irregular propensities and distempered imaginations produces a *depravity* of manners; the force of example and the dissemination of bad principles produce *corruption*. A judgement not sound or right is *depraved;* a judgement debased by that which is vicious is *corrupted*. What is *depraved* requires to be reformed: what is *corrupted* requires to be purified. *Depravity* has most regard to apparent and excessive disorders; *corruption* to internal and dissolute vices. "Manners," says Cicero, "are *corrupted* and *depraved* by the love of riches." Port Royal says that God has given up infidels to the wandering of a *corrupted* and *depraved* mind. These words are by no means a pleonasm or repetition, because they represent two distinct images; one indicates the state of a thing very much changed in its substance: the other the state of a thing very much opposed to regularity. "Good God! (says Masillon the preacher), what a dreadful account will the rich and powerful have one day to give'; since, besides their own sins, they will have to account before Thee for publick disorder, *depravity* of morals, and the *corruption* of the age!' Publick disorders bring on naturally *depravity* of morals; and sins of vicious practices naturally give birth to *corruption*. *Depravity* is more or less open; it revolts the sober upright understanding; *corruption* is more or less disguised in its operations, but fatal in its effects the former sweeps away every thing before it like a torrent; the latter infuses itself into the moral frame like a slow poison.

That is a *depraved* state of morals in which the gross vices are openly practised in defiance of all decorum; 'The greatest difficulty that occurs in analyzing his (Swift's) character, is to discover by what *depravity* of intellect he took delight in revolving ideas from which almost every other mind shrinks with disgust.'—JOHNSON. That is a *corrupt* state of society in which vice has secretly insinuated itself into all the principles and habits of men, and concealed its deformity under the fair semblance of virtue and honour;

> Peace is the happy natural state of man;
> War his *corruption*, his disgrace.—THOMSON.

The manners of savages are most likely to be *depraved;* those of civilized nations to be *corrupt*, when luxury and refinement are risen to an excessive pitch. Cannibal nations present us with the picture of human *depravity;* the Roman nation, during the time of the emperors, affords us an example of almost universal *corruption.*

From the above observations, it is clear that *depravity* is best applied to those objects to which common usage has annexed the epithets of right, regular, fine, &c.; and *corruption* to those which may be characterized by the epithets of sound, pure, innocent, or good. Hence we say *depravity* of mind and *corruption* of heart; *depravity* of principle and *corruption* of sentiment or feeling: a *depraved* character; a *corrupt* example; a *corrupt* influence; 'No *depravity* of the mind has been more frequently or justly censured than ingratitude.'—JOHNSON. 'I have remarked in a former paper, that credulity is the common failing of inexperienced virtue, and that he who is spontaneously suspicious may be justly charged with radical *corruption*.'—JOHNSON.

In reference to the arts or belles lettres we say either *depravity* or *corruption* of taste, because taste has its rules, is liable to be disordered, is or is not conformable to natural order, is regular or irregular; and on the other hand it may be so intermingled with sentiments and feelings foreign to its own native purity as to give it justly the title of *corrupt.*

The last thing worthy of notice respecting the two words *depravity* and *corruption*, is that the former is used for man in his moral capacity; but the latter for man in a political capacity: hence we speak of human *depravity*, but the *corruption* of government; 'The *depravity* of mankind is so easily discoverable, that nothing but the desert or the cell can exclude it from notice.'—JOHNSON. 'Every government, say the politicians, is perpetually degenerating toward *corruption*.'—JOHNSON.

* Vide Roubaud: "Depravation, corruption."—Trussler: "Depravity, corruption."

WICKED, UNJUST, INIQUITOUS, NEFARIOUS

Wicked (*v. Bad*) is here the generick term; *iniquitous*, from *iniquus* unjust, signifies that species of *wickedness* which consists in violating the law of right between man and man; *nefarious*, from the Latin *nefas* wicked or abominable, is that species of *wickedness* which consists in violating the most sacred obligations. The term *wicked*, being indefinite, is commonly applied in a milder sense than *iniquitous;* and *iniquitous* than *nefarious:* it is *wicked* to deprive another of his property unlawfully, under any circumstances;

> In the corrupted currents of this world,
> Offence's gilded hand may shove by justice;
> And oft 't is seen, the *wicked* prize itself
> Buys out the law.—SHAKSPEARE.

It is *iniquitous* if it be done by fraud and circumvention; and *nefarious* if it involves any breach of trust, or is in direct violation of any known law: any undue influence over another, in the making of his will, to the detriment of the rightful heir, is *iniquitous;* 'Lucullus found that the province of Pontus had fallen under great disorders and oppressions from the *iniquity* of usurers and publicans.—PRIDEAUX. Any underhand dealing of a servant to defraud his master is *nefarious*, or any conspiracy to defraud or injure others is called *nefarious;* 'That unhallowed villany *nefariously* attempted upon the person of our agent.'—MILTON.

TO CONTAMINATE, DEFILE, POLLUTE, TAINT, CORRUPT.

Contaminate, in Latin *contaminatus*, participle of *contamino*, comes from the Hebrew טמח to pollute; *defile*, compounded of *de* and *file* or *vile*, signifies to make vile; *pollute*, in Latin *pollutus*, participle of *polluo*, compounded of *per* and *luo* or *lavo* to wash or dye, signifies to infuse thoroughly; *taint*, in French *teint*, participle of *teindre*, in Latin *tingo*, signifies to dye or stain; *corrupt*, signifies the same as in the preceding article.

Contaminate is not so strong an expression as *defile* or *pollute*; but it is stronger than *taint*; these terms are used in the sense of injuring purity: *corrupt* has the idea of destroying it. Whatever is impure *contaminates*, what is gross and vile in the natural sense *defiles* and in the moral sense *pollutes*; what is contagious or infectious *corrupts*; and what is *corrupted* may *taint* other things. Improper conversation or reading *contaminates* the mind of youth; 'The drop of water after its progress through all the channels of the street is not more *contaminated* with filth and dirt, than a simple story after it has passed through the mouths of a few modern tale-bearers.'—HAWKESWORTH. Lewdness and obscenity *defile* the body and *pollute* the mind;

When from the mountain tops with hideous cry
And clatt'ring wings the hungry harpies fly,
They snatch the meat, *defiling* all they find,
And parting leave a loathsome stench behind.
DRYDEN.

Her virgin statue with their bloody hands
Polluted, and profan'd her holy bands.—DRYDEN.

Loose company *corrupts* the morals; 'All men agree that licentious poems do, of all writings, soonest *corrupt* the heart.'—STEELE. The coming in contact with a *corrupted* body is sufficient to give a *taint*;

Your teeming ewes shall no strange meadows try,
Nor fear a rot from *tainted* company.—DRYDEN.

If young people be admitted to a promiscuous intercourse with society, they must unavoidably witness objects that are calculated to *contaminate* their thoughts if not their inclinations. They are thrown in the way of seeing the lips of females *defiled* with the grossest indecencies, and hearing or seeing things which cannot be heard or seen without *polluting* the soul: it cannot be surprising if after this their principles are found to be *corrupted* before they have reached the age of maturity.

CONTACT, TOUCH.

Contact, Latin *Contactus*, participle of *contingo*, compounded of *con* and *tango* to touch together, is distinguished from the simple word *touch*, not so much in sense as in grammatical construction; the former expressing a state, and referring to two bodies actually in that state; the latter on the other hand implying the abstract act of *touching*: we speak of things coming or being in *contact*, but not of the *contact* instead of the *touch* of a thing: the poison which comes from the poison-tree is so powerful in its nature, that it is not necessary to come in *contact* with it in order to feel its baneful influence; 'We are attracted towards each other by general sympathy, but kept back from *contact* in private interest.'—JOHNSON. Some insects are armed with stings so inconceivably sharp, that the smallest *touch* possible is sufficient to produce a puncture into the flesh; 'O death! where is now thy sting? O grave! where is thy victory? Where are the terrours with which thou hast so long affrighted the nations? At the *touch* of the Divine rod, thy visionary horrours are fled.'—BLAIR.

CONTAGION, INFECTION.

Both these terms imply the power of communicating something bad, but *contagion*, from the Latin verb *contingo* to come in contact, proceeds from a simple touch; and *infection*, from the Latin verb *inficio* or *in* and *facio* to put in, proceeds by receiving something inwardly, or having it infused.

Some things act more properly by *contagion*, others by *infection*: the more powerful diseases, as the plague or yellow fever, are communicated by *contagion*; they are therefore denominated *contagious*; the less virulent disorders, as fevers, consumptions, and the like, are termed *infectious*, as they are communicated by the less rapid process of *infection*: the air is *contagious* or *infectious* according to the same rule of distinction: when heavily overcharged with noxious vapours and deadly disease, it is justly entitled *contagious*, but in ordinary cases *infectious*. In the figurative sense, vice is for the same obvious reason termed *contagious*; 'If I send my son abroad, it is scarcely possible to keep him from the reigning *contagion* of rudeness.'—LOCKE. Bad principles are denominated *infectious*;

But we who only do infuse,
The rage in them like bouté-feus,
'T is our example that instils
In them the *infection* of our ills.—BUTLER.

Some young people, who are fortunate enough to shun the *contagion* of bad society, are, perhaps, caught by the *infection* of bad principles, acting as a slow poison on the moral constitution.

CONTAGIOUS, EPIDEMICAL, PESTILENTIAL.

Contagious signifies having *contagion* (*v. Contagion*); *epidemical*, in Latin *epidemicus*, Greek ἐπιδήμιος, that is ἐπί and δῆμος among the people, signifies universally spread; *pestilential*, from the Latin *pestis* the plague, signifies having the plague, or a similar disorder.

The *contagious* applies to that which is capable of being caught, and ought not, therefore, to be touched; the *epidemical* to that which is already caught or circulated, and requires, therefore, to be stopped; the *pestilential* to that which may breed an evil, and is, therefore, to be removed: diseases are *contagious* or *epidemical*; the air or breath is *pestilential*.

They may all be applied morally or figuratively in the same sense.

We endeavour to shun a *contagious* disorder, that it may not come near us; we endeavour to purify a *pestilential* air, that it may not be inhaled to our injury; we endeavour to provide against *epidemical* disorders, that they may not spread any farther.

Vicious example is *contagious*;

No foreign food the teeming ewes shall fear,
No touch *contagious* spread its influence here.
WARTON.

Certain follies or vices of fashion are *epidemical* in almost every age; 'Among all the diseases of the mind, there is not one more *epidemical* or more pernicious than the love of flattery.'—STEELE. The breath of infidelity is *pestilential*;

Capricious, wanton, bold, and brutal lust
Is meanly selfish; when resisted, cruel;
And like the blast of *pestilential* winds,
Taints the sweet bloom of nature's fairest forms.
MILTON.

BLAMELESS, IRREPROACHABLE, UNBLEMISHED, UNSPOTTED, OR SPOTLESS.

Blameless signifies literally void of *blame* (*v. To blame*); *irreproachable*, that is, not able to be *reproached* (*v. To blame*); *unblemished*, that is, without *blemish* (*v. Blemish*); *unspotted*, that is, without *spot* (*v. Blemish*).

Blameless is less than *irreproachable*; what is *blameless* is simply free from *blame*, but that which is *irreproachable* cannot be *blamed*, or have any *reproach* attached to it. It is good to say of a man that he leads a *blameless* life, but it is a high encomium to say, that he leads an *irreproachable* life: the former is but the negative praise of one who is known only for his harmlessness; the latter is but positive commendation of a man who is well known for his integrity in the different relations of society;

The sire of Gods, and all th' ethereal train,
On the warm limits of the farthest main,
Now mix with mortals, nor disdain to grace
The feasts of Æthiopia's *blameless* race.—POPE.

Take particular care that your amusements be of an *irreproachable* kind.'—BLAIR.

Unblemished and *unspotted* are applicable to many objects, besides that of personal conduct; and when applied to this, their original meaning sufficiently points out their use in distinction from the two former. We may say of a man that he has an *irreproachable* or an *unblemished* reputation, and *unspotted* or *spotless* purity of life;

But now those white *unblemish'd* manners, whence
The fabling poets took their golden age,
Are found no more amid these iron times.
THOMSON.

But the good man, whose soul is pure,
Unspotted, regular, and free
From all the ugly stains of lust and villany,
Of mercy and of pardon sure,
Looks through the darkness of the gloomy night,
And sees the dawning of a glorious day.
POMFRET.

Hail, rev'rend priest! To Phœbus' awful dome
A suppliant I from great Atrides come.
Unransom'd here, receive the *spotless* fair,
Accept the hecatomb the Greeks prepare.—POPE.

TO PRAISE, COMMEND, APPLAUD, EXTOL.

Praise comes from the German *preisen* to value, and our own word *price*, signifying to give a value to a thing; *commend*, in Latin *commendo*, compounded of *com* and *mando*, signifies to commit to the good opinion of others; *applaud* (*v. Applause*); *extol*, in Latin *extollo*, signifies to lift up very high.

All these terms denote the act of expressing approbation. The *praise* is the most general and indefinite; it may rise to a high degree, but it generally implies a lower degree: we *praise* a person generally; we *commend* him particularly: we *praise* him for his diligence, sobriety, and the like; we *commend* him for his performances, or for any particular instance of prudence or good conduct. To *applaud* is an ardent mode of *praising*; we *applaud* a person for his nobleness of spirit: to *extol* is a reverential mode of *praising*; we *extol* a man for his heroick exploits. *Praise* is confined to no station, though with most propriety bestowed by superiours or equals: *commendation* is the part of a superiour; a parent *commends* his child for an act of charity: *applause* is the act of many as well as of one; theatrical performances are the frequent subjects of publick *applauses*: *extol* is the act of inferiours, who declare thus decidedly their sense of a person's superiority.

In the scale of signification *commend* stands the lowest, and *extol* the highest; we *praise* in stronger terms than we *commend*: to *applaud* is to *praise* in loud terms; to *extol* is to *praise* in strong terms;

The servile rout their careful Cæsar *praise*,
Him they *extol*; they worship him alone.
DRYDEN.

He who expects *praise* will not be contented with simple *commendation*: *praise*, when sincere, and bestowed by one whom we esteem, is truly gratifying: but it is a dangerous gift for the receiver; happy that man who has no occasion to repent the acceptance of it;

How happy them we find,
Who know by merit to engage mankind,
Prais'd by each each tongue, by ev'ry heart belov'd,
For virtues practis'd, and for arts improv'd.—JENYNS.

Commendation is always sincere, and may be very beneficial by giving encouragement; 'When schoolboys write verse, it may indeed suggest an expectation of something better hereafter, but deserves not to be *commended* for any real merit of their own.'—COWPER.

Applause is noisy; it is the sentiment of the multitude, who are continually changing;

While from both benches, with redoubled sounds,
Th' *applause* of lords and commoners abounds.
DRYDEN.

APPLAUSE, ACCLAMATION, PLAUDIT.

Applause, from the Latin *applaudo*, signifies literally to clap the hands or stamp the feet to a thing; *acclamation*, from *acclamo*, signifies a crying out to a thing. These two words answer to the *plausus* and *acclamatio* of the Romans, which were distinguished from each other in the same manner; but the *plausus* was an artful way of moving the hands so as to produce an harmonious sound by way of *applause*, particularly in the theatre;

Datus in theatro,
Cum tibi *plausus*.—HORACE.

In medio plausa, *plausus* tunc arte carebat.—OVID

Stantiaque in *plausum* tota theatra juvent.
PROPERTIUS.

The word *plausus* was sometimes used in the sense of *applause* expressed by words; the *acclamatio* was an expression by the voice only, but it was either a mark of approbation or disapprobation; favourable *acclamations* were denominated *laudationes et bona vota*, the unfavourable were *exsecrationes et convicia*, all which were expressed by a certain prescribed modulation of the voice. *Plaudit*, or, as it was originally written, *plaudite*, is the imperative of the verb *plaudo*, and was addressed by the actors to the spectators at the close of the performance by way of soliciting their applause;

Si plausoris eges aulæa manentis, et usque
Sessuri, donec cantor, vos plaudite, dicat.
HORACE.

Hence the term *plaudit* denotes a single act of *applause*, but is now mostly employed figuratively;

True wisdom must our actions so direct
Not only the last *plaudit* to expect.—DENHAM.

These terms express a publick demonstration; the former by means of a noise with the hands or feet; the latter by means of shouts and cries: the former being employed as a testimony of approbation; the latter as a sanction, or an indication of respect. An actor looks for *applause*; a speaker looks for *acclamation*.

What a man does calls forth *applause*, but the person himself is mostly received with *acclamations*. At the hustings popular speeches meet with *applause*, and favourite members are greeted with loud *acclamations*:

Amid the loud *applauses* of the shore
Gyas outstripp'd the rest and sprung before.
DRYDEN.

'When this illustrious person (the duke of Marlborough) touched on the shore, he was received by the *acclamations* of the people.'—STEELE.

ENCOMIUM, EULOGY, PANEGYRICK.

Encomium, in Greek ἐγκώμιον, signified a set form of verses, used for the purposes of praise; *eulogy*, in Greek εὐλογία, from εὖ and λόγος, signifies well spoken, or a good word for any one; *panegyrick*, in Greek πανηγυρικὸς, from πᾶς the whole, and ἄγυρις an assembly, signifies that which is spoken before an assembly, a solemn oration.

The idea of praise is common to all these terms: but the first seems more properly applied to the thing, or the unconscious object; the second to the person in general, or to the characters and actions of men in general; the third to the person of some particular individual: thus we bestow *encomiums* upon any work of art, or production of genius, without reference to the performer; we bestow *eulogies* on the exploits of a hero, who is of another age or country; but we write *panegyricks* either in a direct address, or in direct reference to the person who is *panegyrized*: the *encomium* is produced by merit, real or supposed; the *eulogy* may spring from admiration of the person *eulogized*; the *panegyrick* may be mere flattery, resulting from servile dependence: great *encomiums* have been paid by all persons to the constitution of England; 'Our lawyers are, with justice, copious in their *encomiums* on the common law.'—BLACKSTONE. Our naval and military heroes have received the *eulogies* of many besides their own countrymen; 'Sallust would say of Cato, "That he had rather be than appear good:" but indeed this *eulogium* rose no higher than to an inoffensiveness.'—STEELE. Authors of no mean reputation have condescended to deal out their *panegyricks* pretty freely in dedications to their patrons;

On me, when dunces are satirick,
I take it for a *panegyrick*.—SWIFT.

LAUDABLE, PRAISEWORTHY COMMENDABLE.

Laudable, from the Latin *laudo* to praise, is in sense literally *praiseworthy*, that is, *worthy of praise*, or to be praised (*v. To praise*); *commendable* signifies entitled to *commendation*.

Laudable is used in a general application; *praiseworthy* and *commendable* are applied to individuals: things are *laudable* in themselves; they are *praiseworthy* or *commendable* in this or that person.

That which is *laudable* is entitled to encouragement and general approbation; an honest endeavour to be useful to one's family or one's self is at all times *laudable*, and will ensure the support of all good people. What is *praiseworthy* obtains the respect of all men: as all have temptations to do that which is wrong, the performance of one's duty is in all cases *praiseworthy*; but particularly so in those cases where it opposes one's interests and interferes with one's pleasures. What is *commendable* is not equally important with the two former; it entitles a person only to a temporary or partial expression of good will and approbation: the performance of those minor and particular duties which belong to children and subordinate persons is in the proper sense *commendable*.

It is a *laudable* ambition to wish to excel in that which is good; 'Nothing is more *laudable* than an inquiry after truth.'—ADDISON. It is very *praiseworthy* in a child to assist its parent as occasion may require; 'Ridicule is generally made use of to laugh men out of virtue and good sense by attacking every thing *praiseworthy* in human life.'—ADDISON. Silence is *commendable* in a young person when he is reproved; 'Edmund Waller was born to a very fair estate by the parsimony or frugality of a wise father and mother, and he thought it so *commendable* an advantage that he resolved to improve it with his utmost care'—CLARENDON.

TO CONTEND, STRIVE, VIE.

Contend, in Latin *contendo*, compounded of *con* or *contra* and *tendo* to bend one's steps, signifies to exert one's self against any thing; *strive*, in Dutch *streven*, low German *strevan*, high German *streben*, is probably a frequentative of the Latin *strepo* to make a bustle; *vie* is probably changed from *view*, signifying to look at with the desire of excelling.

Contending requires two parties; *strive* either one or two. There is no *contending* where there is not an opposition; but a person may *strive* by himself.

Contend and *strive* differ in the object as well as mode: we *contend* for a prize; we *strive* for the mastery: we *contend* verbally; but we never *strive* without an actual effort, and labour more or less severe. We may *contend* with a person at a distance; but *striving* requires the opponent, when there is one, to be present. Opponents in matters of opinion *contend* for what they fancy to be the truth; sometimes they *contend* for trifles;

> Mad as the seas and the winds, when both *contend*
> Which is the master.—SHAKSPEARE.

Combatants *strive* to overcome their adversaries, either by dint of superiour skill or strength. In *contention* the prominent idea is the mutual efforts of two or more persons for the same object; but in *striving* the prominent idea is the efforts of one to attain an object; hence the terms may sometimes be employed in one and the same connexion, and yet expressing these collateral ideas;

> Mad as the winds
> When for the empire of the main they *strive*.
> DENNIS.

Contend is frequently used in a figurative sense, in application to things; *strive* very seldom. We *contend* with difficulties; and in the spiritual application, we may be said to *strive* with the spirit.

Vie has more of *striving* than *contending* in it; we *strive* to excel when we *vie*, but we do not *strive* with any one; there is no personal collision or opposition: those we *vie* with may be as ignorant of our persons as our intentions. The term *vie* is therefore frequently applied to unconscious objects;

> Shall a form
> Of elemental dross, of mould'ring clay,
> *Vie* with these charms imperial?
> MASON (*on Truth*)

Vying is an act of no moment, but *contending* and *striving* are always serious actions: neighbours often *vie* with each other in the finery and grandeur of their house, dress, and equipage.

COMPETITION, EMULATION, RIVALRY.

Competition, from the Latin *competo*, compounded of *com* or *con* and *peto*, signifies to sue or seek together, to seek for the same object; *emulation*, in Latin *emulatio*, from *æmulor*, and the Greek ἅμιλλα a contest, signifies the spirit of contending; *rivalry*, from the Latin *rivus* the bank of a stream, signifies the undivided or common enjoyment of any stream which is the natural source of discord.

Competition expresses the relation of a competitor, or the act of seeking the same object; *emulation* expresses a disposition of the mind toward particular objects; *rivalry* expresses both the relation and the disposition of a rival. *Emulation* is to *competition* as the motive to the action; *emulation* produces *competitors*, but it may exist without it; 'Of the ancients enough remains to excite our *emulation* and direct our endeavours.'—JOHNSON.

Competition and *emulation* have the same marks to distinguish them from *rivalry*. *Competition* and *emulation* have honour for their basis; *rivalry* is but a desire for selfish gratification. A *competitor* strives to surpass by honest means; he cannot succeed so well by any other; 'It cannot be doubted but there is as great a desire of glory in a ring of wrestlers or cudgel players as in any other more refined *competition* for superiority.'—HUGHES. A *rival* is not bound by any principle; he seeks to supplant by whatever means seem to promise success; 'Those, that have been raised by the interest of some great minister, trample upon the steps by which they rise, to *rival* him in his greatness, and at length step into his place.'—SOUTH. An unfair *competitor* and a generous *rival* are equally unusual and inconsistent. *Competition* animates to exertion; *rivalry* provokes hatred:* *competition* seeks to merit success; *rivalry* is contented with obtaining it; 'To be no man's *rival* in love, or *competitor* in business, is a character which, if it does not recommend you as it ought to benevolence among those whom you live with, yet has it certainly this effect, that you do not stand so much in need of their approbation as if you aimed at more.'—STEELE. *Competitors* may sometimes become *rivals* in spirit, although *rivals* will never become *competitors*.

It is further to be remarked, that *competition* supposes some actual effort for the attainment of a specifick object set in view: *rivalry* may consist of a continued wishing for and aiming at the same general end without necessarily comprehending the idea of close action. *Competitors* are in the same line with each other, *rivals* may work toward the same point at a great distance from each other. Literary prizes are the objects of *competition* among scholars; 'The prize of beauty was disputed till you were seen, but now all pretenders have withdrawn their claims; there is no *competition* but for the second place.'—DRYDEN. The affections of a female are the object of *rivals*;

> Oh, love! thou sternly dost thy power maintain,
> And wilt not bear a *rival* in thy reign,
> Tyrants and thou all fellowship disdain.—DRYDEN

William the Conqueror and Harold were *competitors* for the crown of England; Æneas and Turnus were *rivals* for the hand of Lavinia. In the games which were celebrated by Æneas in honour of his father Anchises, the naval *competitors* were the most eager in the contest. Juno, Minerva, and Venus, were *rival* goddesses in their pretensions to beauty.

TO CONTEND, CONTEST, DISPUTE.

To *contend* signifies generally to strive one against another; to *contest*, from the Latin *contestor*, to call one witness againt another; and *dispute*, from *disputo*

* Vide Abbe Roubaud: "Emulation, rivalité."

to think differently, or maintain a different opinion, are different modes of *contending*. We may *contend* for or *dispute* a prize, but the latter is a higher form of expression, adapted to the style of poetry;

Permit me not to languish out my days,
But make the best exchange of life for praise.
This arm, this lance, can well *dispute* the prize
DRYDEN.

We cannot *contest* or *dispute* without *contending*, although we may *contend* without *contesting* or *disputing*. To *contend* is confined to the idea of setting one's self up against another; to *contest* and *dispute* must include some object *contested* or *disputed*. *Contend* is applied to all matters, either of personal interest or speculative opinion; *contest* always to the former; *dispute* mostly to the latter. We *contend* with a person, and *contest* about a thing;

'Tis madness to *contend* with strength Divine
DRYDEN.

During the present long and eventful *contest* between England and France, the English have *contended* with their enemies as successfully by land as by sea. Trifling matters may give rise to *contending*; serious points only are *contested*. *Contentions* are always conducted personally, and in general verbally; *contests* are carried on in different manners according to the nature of the object. The parties themselves mostly decide *contentions*; but *contested* matters mostly depend upon others to decide.

For want of an accommodating temper, men are frequently *contending* with each other about little points of convenience, advantage, or privilege, which they ought by mutual consent to share, or voluntarily to resign;

Death and nature do *contend* about them
Whether they live or die.—SHAKSPEARE.

When seats in parliament or other posts of honour are to be obtained by suffrages, rival candidates *contest* their claims to publick approbation; 'As the same causes had nearly the same effects in the different countries of Europe, the several crowns either lost or acquired authority, according to their different success in the *contest*.'—HUME.

When we assert the right, and support this assertion with reasons, we *contend* for it;

'T is thus the spring of youth, the morn of life,
Rears in our minds the rival seeds of strife;
Then passion riots, reason then *contends*,
And on the conquest every bliss depends.
SHENSTONE.

But we do not *contest* until we take serious measures to obtain what we *contend* for;

The poor worm
Shall prove her *contest* vain. Life's little day
Shall pass, and she is gone. While I appear
Flush'd with the bloom of youth through heav'n's
eternal year.—MASON (*on Truth*).

Contend is to *dispute* as a part to the whole: two parties *dispute* conjointly; they *contend* individually. Each *contends* for his own opinion, which constitutes the *dispute*. Theological *disputants* often *contend* with more warmth than discretion for their favourite hypothesis; 'The question which our author would *contend for*, if he did not forget it, is what persons have a right to be obeyed.'—LOCKE. With regard to claims, it is possible to *dispute* the claim of another without *contending* for it for ourselves; 'Until any point is determined to be a law, it remains *disputable* by any subject.'—SWIFT.

CONTENTION, STRIFE.

Though derived from the preceding verbs (*v. To contend, strive*), have a distinct meaning in which they are analogous. The common idea to them is that of opposing one's self to another with an angry humour.

Contention is mostly occasioned by the desire of seeking one's own. *Strife* springs from a quarrelsome temper. Greedy and envious people deal in *contention*, the former because they are fearful lest they should not get enough; the latter because they are fearful lest others should get too much;

With these four more of lesser fame
And humble rank, attendant came;
Hypocrisy with smiling grace,
And Impudence, with brazen face,
Contention bold, with iron lungs,
And Slander, with her hundred tongues.
MOORE

Where bad tempers that are under no control come in frequent collision, perpetual *strife* will be the consequence; 'A solid and substantial greatness of soul looks down with a generous neglect on the censures and applauses of the multitude, and places a man beyond the little noise and *strife* of tongues.'—ADDISON.

TO DIFFER, VARY, DISAGREE, DISSENT.

Differ, in Latin *differo* or *dis* and *fero*, signifies to make into two; *vary*, in Latin *vario* to make various, from *varus* a spot or speckle, because that destroys the uniformity in the appearance of things; to *disagree* is literally not to *agree*; and *dissent*, in Latin *dissentio* or *dis* and *sentio*, is to think or feel apart or differently.

Differ, *vary*, and *disagree*, are applicable either to persons or things; *dissent* to persons only. First as to persons; to *differ* is the most general and indefinite term, the rest are but modes of *difference*: we may *differ* from any cause, or in any degree; we *vary* only in small matters; thus persons may *differ* or *vary* in their statements. There must be two at least to *differ*; and there may be an indefinite number: one may *vary*, or an indefinite number may *vary*; two or a specifick number *disagree*: thus two or more may *differ* in an account which they give; one person may *vary* at different times in the account which he gives; and two particular individuals *disagree*: we may *differ* in matters of fact or speculation; we *vary* only in matters of fact; we *disagree* mostly in matters of speculation. Historians may *differ* in the representation of an affair, and authors may *differ* in their views of a particular subject; narrators *vary* in certain circumstances; two particular philosophers *disagree* in accounting for a phenomenon.

To *disagree* is the act of one man with another: to *dissent* is the act of one or more in relation to a community; thus two writers on the same subject may *disagree* in their conclusions, because they set out from *different* premises; men *dissent* from the established religion of their country according to their education and character.

When applied to the ordinary transactions of life, *differences* may exist merely in opinion, or with a mixture of more or less acrimonious and discordant feeling; *variances* arise from a collision of interests; *disagreements* from asperity of humour; *dissensions* from a clashing of opinions; *differences* may exist between nations, and may be settled by cool discussions; 'The ministers of the different potentates conferred and conferred; but the peace advanced so slowly, that speedier methods were found necessary, and Bolingbroke was sent to Paris to adjust *differences* with less formality.'—JOHNSON. When *variances* arise between neighbours, their passions often interfere to prevent accommodations;

How many bleed
By shameful *variance* betwixt man and man.
THOMSON.

When members of a family consult interest or humour rather than affections, there will be necessarily *disagreements*; 'On his arrival at Geneva, Goldsmith was recommended as a travelling tutor to a young gentleman who had been unexpectedly left a sum of money by a near relation. This connexion lasted but a short time: they *disagreed* in the south of France and parted.'—JOHNSON. When many members of a community have an equal liberty to express their opinions, there will necessarily be *dissensions*;

When Carthage shall contend the world with Rome,
Then is your time for faction and debate,
For partial favour and permitted hate:
Let now your immature *dissension* cease.
DRYDEN.

In regard to things, *differ* is said of two things with respect to each other; *vary* of one thing in respect to itself: thus two tempers *differ* from each other, and a person's temper *varies* from time to time. Things *differ* in their essences, they *vary* in their accidents: thus the genera and species of things *differ* from each other, and the individuals of each species *vary*; 'We do not know in what reason and instinct consist, and therefore cannot tell with exactness in what they *differ*.'—JOHNSON. 'Trade and commerce might doubtless be still *varied* a thousand ways, out of which would arise such branches as have not been touched.'—JOHNSON. *Differ* is said of every thing promiscuously, but *disagree* is only said of such things as might agree; thus two trees *differ* from each other by the course of things, but two numbers *disagree* which are intended to agree; 'The several parts of the same animal *differ* in their qualities.'—ARBUTHNOT.

> That mind and body often sympathize
> Is plain; such is this union nature ties;
> But then as often too they *disagree*,
> Which proves the soul's superiour progeny.
> JENYNS.

DIFFERENCE, DISPUTE, ALTERCATION, QUARREL.

The *difference* is that on which one differs, or the state of differing (*v. To differ*); the *dispute* that on which one disputes, or the act of disputing; *altercation*, in Latin *altercatio* and *alterco*, from *alterum* and *cor* another mind, signifies expressing another opinion; *quarrel*, in French *querelle*, from the Latin *queror* to complain, signifies having a complaint against another.

All these terms are here taken in the general sense of a *difference* on some personal question; the term *difference* is here as general and indefinite as in the former case (*v. To differ, vary*): a *difference*, as distinguished from the others, is generally of a less serious and personal kind; a *dispute* consists not only of angry words, but much ill blood and unkind offices; an *altercation* is a wordy *dispute*, in which *difference* of opinion is drawn out into a multitude of words on all sides; *quarrel* is the most serious of all *differences*, which leads to every species of violence: the *difference* may sometimes arise from a misunderstanding, which may be easily rectified; *differences* seldom grow to *disputes* but by the fault of both parties; *altercations* arise mostly from pertinacious adherence to, and obstinate defence of, one's opinions; *quarrels* mostly spring from injuries real or supposed: *differences* subsist between men in an individual or publick capacity: they may be carried on in a direct or indirect manner; 'Ought less *differences* altogether to divide and estrange those from one another, whom such ancient and sacred bands unite?'—BLAIR. *Disputes* and *altercations* are mostly conducted in a direct manner between individuals; 'I have often been pleased to hear *disputes* on the Exchange adjusted between an inhabitant of Japan and an alderman of London.'—ADDISON. 'In the house of Peers the bill passes through the same forms as in the other house, and if rejected no more notice is taken, but it passes *sub silensio* to prevent unbecoming *altercation*.'—BLACKSTONE. *Quarrels* may arise between nations or individuals, and be carried on by acts of offence directly or indirectly;

> Unvex'd with *quarrels*, undisturb'd with noise,
> The country king his peaceful realm enjoys.
> DRYDEN.

DISSENSION, CONTENTION, DISCORD, STRIFE.

Dissension, *contention*, and *strife*, mark the act or state of dissenting, of contending and striving; *discord* derives its signification from the harshness produced in musick by the clashing of two strings which do not suit with each other; whence, in the moral sense, the chords of the mind, which come into an unsuitable collision, produce a *discord*.

A collision of opinions produces *dissension*; a collision of interests produces *contention*; a collision of humours produces *discord* (*v. Contention*). A love of one's own opinion, combined with a disregard for the opinions of others, gives rise to *dissension*; selfishness is the main cause of *contention*; and an ungoverned temper that of *discord*.

Dissension is peculiar to bodies or communities of men; *contention* and *discord* to individuals. A Christian temper of conformity to the general will of those with whom one is in connexion would do away *dissension*; 'At the time the poem we are now treating of was written, the *dissensions* of the barons, who were then so many petty princes, ran very high.'—ADDISON. A limitation of one's desire to that which is attainable by legitimate means would put a stop to *contention*; 'Because it is apprehended there may be great *contention* about precedence, the proposer humbly desires the assistance of the learned.'—SWIFT. A correction of one's impatient and irritable humour would check the progress of *discord*;

> But shall celestial *discord* never cease?
> 'T is better ended in a lasting peace.—DRYDEN.

Dissension tends not only to alienate the minds of men from each other, but to dissolve the bonds of society;

> Now join your hands, and with your hands your hearts,
> That no *dissension* hinder government.
> SHAKSPEARE.

Contention is accompanied by anger, ill-will, envy, and many evil passions; 'The ancients made *contention* the principle that reigned in the chaos at first, and then love: the one to express the divisions, and the other the union of all parties in the middle and common bond.'—BURNET. *Discord* interrupts the progress of the kind affections, and bars all tender intercourse;

> See what a scourge is laid upon your hate
> That heav'n finds means to kill your joys with love!
> And I, for winking at your *discords* too,
> Have lost a brace of kinsmen.—SHAKSPEARE.

Where there is *strife*, there must be *discord*; but there may be *discord* without *strife*: *discord* consists most in the feeling; *strife* consists most in the outward action. *Discord* evinces itself in various ways; by looks, words, or actions;

> Good Heav'n! what dire effects from civil *discord* flow.—DRYDEN.

Strife displays itself in words or acts of violence

> Let men their days in senseless *strife* employ,
> We in eternal peace and constant joy.—POPE.

Discord is fatal to the happiness of families; *strife* is the greatest enemy to peace between neighbours: *discord* arose between the goddesses on the apple being thrown into the assembly; Homer commences his poem with the *strife* that took place between Agamemnon and Achilles.

Discord may arise from mere difference of opinion; *strife* is in general occasioned by some matter of personal interest: *discord* in the councils of a nation is the almost certain forerunner of its ruin; the common principles of politeness forbid *strife* among persons of good breeding.

QUARREL, BROIL, FEUD, AFFRAY OR FRAY.

Quarrel (*v. Difference*) is the general and ordinary term; *broil*, *feud*, and *affray*, are particular terms; *broil*, from *brawl*, is a noisy *quarrel*; *feud*, from the German *fehde*, and the English *fight*, is an active *quarrel*; *affray* or *fray*, from the Latin *frico* to rub, signifying the collision of the passions, is a tumultuous *quarrel*.

The idea of a variance between two parties is common to these terms; but the former respects the complaints and charges which are reciprocally made; *broil* respects the confusion and entanglement which arises from a contention and collision of interests; *feud* respects the hostilities which arise out of the variance. There are *quarrels* where there are no *broils*, and there are *broils* where there are no *feuds*; but there are no *broils* and *feuds* without *quarrels*: the *quarrel* is not always openly conducted between the parties; it may sometimes be secret, and sometimes manifest itself only in a coolness of behaviour: the *broil* is a noisy kind of *quarrel*, it always breaks out in loud, and mostly reproachful language: *feud* is a deadly kind of *quarrel* which is heightened by mutual aggravations and insults. *Quarrels* are very lamentable when they take place between members of the same family; 'The dirk or broad dagger, I am afraid, was of more use in private *quarrels* than in battles.'—JOHNSON. *Broils* are very frequent among profligate and restless people who live together;

Ev'n haughty Juno, who with endless *broils*,
Earth, seas, and heav'n, and Jove himself turmoils,
At length aton'd, her friendly pow'r shall join
To cherish and advance the Trojan line.—DRYDEN.

Feuds were very general in former times between different families of the nobility; 'The poet describes (in the poem of Chevy-Chase) a battle occasioned by the mutual *feuds* which reigned in the families of an English and Scotch nobleman.'—ADDISON.

A *quarrel* is indefinite, both as to the cause and the manner in which it is conducted; an *affray* is a sudden violent kind of *quarrel*: a *quarrel* may subsist between two persons from a private difference; an *affray* always takes place between many upon some publick occasion: a *quarrel* may be carried on merely by words; an *affray* is commonly conducted by acts of violence: many angry words pass in a *quarrel* between two hasty people; 'The *quarrel* between my friends did not run so high as I find your accounts have made it.'—STEELE. Many are wounded, if not killed in *affrays*, when opposite parties meet; 'The provost of Edinburgh, his son, and several citizens of distinction, were killed in the *fray*.'—ROBERTSON.

TO JANGLE, JAR, WRANGLE.

A verbal contention is expressed by all these terms, but with various modifications; *jangle* seems to be an onomatopoeia, for it conveys by its own discordant sound an idea of the discordance which accompanies this kind of war of words; *jar* and war are in all probability but variations of each other, as also *jangle* and *wrangle*. There is in *jangling* more of cross questions and perverse replies than direct differences of opinion; 'Where the judicatories of the church were near an equality of the men on both sides, there were perpetual *janglings* on both sides.'—BURNET. Those *jangle* who are out of humour with each other; there is more of discordant feeling and opposition of opinion in *jarring*: those who have no good will to each other will be sure to *jar* when they come in collision; and those who indulge themselves in *jarring* will soon convert affection into ill will; 'There is no *jar* or contest between the different gifts of the spirit.'—SOUTH. Married people may destroy the good humour of the company by *jangling*, but they destroy their domestick peace and felicity by *jarring*. To *wrangle* is technically, what to *jangle* is morally: those who dispute by a verbal opposition only are said to *wrangle*; and the disputers who engage in this scholastick exercise are termed *wranglers*; most disputations amount to little more than *wrangles*;

Peace, factious monster! born to vex the state,
With *wrangling* talents form'd for foul debate.
POPE.

TO COMBAT, OPPOSE.

Combat, from the French *combattre* to fight together, is used figuratively in the same sense with regard to matters of opinion; *oppose*, in French *opposer*, Latin *opposui* perfect of *oppono*, compounded of *ob* and *pono* to place one's self in the way, signifies to set one's self up against another.

Combat is properly a species of *opposing*; one always *opposes* in *combatting*, though not *vice versâ*. To *combat* is used in regard to speculative matters; *oppose* in regard to private and personal concerns as well as matters of opinion. A person's positions are *combatted*, his interests or his measures are *opposed*. The Christian *combats* the erroneous doctrines of the infidel with no other weapon than that of argument;

When fierce temptation, seconded within
By traitor appetite, and armed with darts
Tempered in hell, invades the throbbing breast,
To *combat* may be glorious, and success
Perhaps may crown us, but to fly is safe.—COWPER.

The sophist *opposes* Christianity with ridicule and misrepresentation;

Though various foes against the truth combine,
Pride above all *opposes* her design.—COWPER.

The most laudable use to which knowledge can be converted is to *combat* errour wherever it presents itself; but there are too many, particularly in the present day, who employ the little pittance of knowledge which they have collected, to no better purpose than to *oppose* every thing that is good, and excite the same spirit of *opposition* in others.

COMBATANT, CHAMPION.

Combatant, from to *combat*, marks any one that engages in a *combat*; *champion*, in French *champion*, Saxon *cempe*, German *kaempe*, signifies originally a soldier or fighter, from the Latin *campus* a field of battle.

A *combatant* fights for himself and for victory; a *champion* fights either for another, or in another's cause. The word *combatant* has always relation to some actual engagement; *champion* may be employed for one ready to be engaged, or in the habits of being engaged. The *combatants* in the Olympic games used to contend for a prize; the Roman gladiators were *combatants* who fought for their lives: when knight errantry was in fashion there were *champions* of all descriptions, *champions* in behalf of distressed females, *champions* in behalf of the injured and oppressed, or *champions* in behalf of aggrieved princes.

The mere act of fighting constitutes a *combatant*; the act of standing up in another's defence at a personal risk, constitutes the *champion*. Animals have their *combats*, and consequently are *combatants*; but they are seldom *champions*. In the present day there are fewer *combatants* than *champions* among men. We have *champions* for liberty, who are the least honourable and the most questionable members of the community; they mostly contend for a shadow, and court persecution, in order to serve their own purposes of ambition. *Champions* in the cause of Christianity are not less ennobled by the object for which they contend, than by the disinterestedness of their motives in contending; they must expect in an infidel age, like the present, to be exposed to the derision and contempt of their self-sufficient opponents; 'Conscious that I do not possess the strength, I shall not assume the importance, of a *champion*, and as I am not of dignity enough to be angry, I shall keep my temper and my distance too, skirmishing like those insignificant gentry, who play the part of teasers in the Spanish bull-fights while bolder *combatants* engage him at the point of his horns.'—CUMBERLAND.

ENEMY, FOE, ADVERSARY, OPPONENT, ANTAGONIST.

Enemy, in Latin *inimicus*, compounded of *in* privative, and *amicus* a friend, signifies one that is unfriendly; *foe*, in Saxon *fah*, most probably from the old Teutonic *fian* to hate, signifies one that bears a hatred; *adversary*, in Latin *adversarius*, from *adversus* against, signifies one that takes part against another; *adversarius* in Latin was particularly applied to one who contested a point in law with another; *opponent*, in Latin *opponens*, participle of *oppono* or *obpono* to place in the way, signifies one pitted against another; *antagonist*, in Greek ἀνταγώνιϛος, compounded of ἀντὶ against, and ἀγωνίζομαι to contend, signifies one struggling against another.

An *enemy* is not so formidable as a *foe*; the former may be reconciled, but the latter always retains a deadly hatred. An *enemy* may be so in spirit, in action, or in relation; a *foe* is always so in spirit, if not in action likewise: a man may be an *enemy* to himself, though not a *foe*. Those who are national or political *enemies* are often private friends, but a *foe* is never any thing but a *foe*. A single act may create an *enemy*, but continued warfare creates a *foe*.

Enemies are either publick or private, collective or personal; in the latter sense the word *enemy* is most analogous in signification to that of *adversary*, *opponent*, *antagonist*. * *Enemies* seek to injure each other commonly from a sentiment of hatred; the heart is always more or less implicated; 'Plutarch says very finely, that a man should not allow himself to hate even his *enemies*.'—ADDISON. *Adversaries* set up their claims, and frequently urge their pretensions with angry strife; but interest or contrariety of opinion more than sentiment stimulates to action; 'Those disputants (the persecutors) convince their *adversaries*

* Vide Abbe Girard: "Ennemi adversaire, antagoniste."

with a sorites commonly called a pile of fagots.'—ADDISON. *Opponents* set up different parties, and treat each other sometimes with acrimony; but their differences do not necessarily include any thing personal; 'The name of Boyle is indeed revered, but his works are neglected; we are contented to know that he conquered his *opponents*, without inquiring what cavils were produced against him.'—JOHNSON. *Antagonists* are a species of *opponents* who are in actual engagement: emulation and direct exertion, but not anger, is concerned in making the *antagonist;* 'Sir Francis Bacon observes that a well written book, compared with its rivals and *antagonists*, is like Moses's serpent that immediately swallowed up those of the Egyptians.'—ADDISON. *Enemies* make war, aim at destruction, and commit acts of personal violence: *adversaries* are contented with appropriating to themselves some object of desire, or depriving their rival of it; cupidity being the moving principle, and gain the object: *opponents* oppose each other systematically and perpetually; each aims at being thought right in their disputes: tastes and opinions are commonly the subjects of debate, self-love oftener than a love of truth is the moving principle: *antagonists* engage in a trial of strength; victory is the end; the love of distinction or superiority the moving principle; the contest may lie either in mental or physical exertion; may aim at superiority in a verbal dispute or in a manual combat. There are nations whose subjects are born *enemies* to those of a neighbouring nation: nothing evinces the radical corruption of any country more than when the poor man dares not show himself as an *adversary* to his rich neighbour without fearing to lose more than he might gain: the ambition of some men does not rise higher than that of being the *opponent* of ministers: Scaliger and Petavius among the French were great *antagonists* in their day, as were Boyle and Bentley among the English; the Horatii and Curiatii were equally famous *antagonists* in their way.

Enemy and *foe* are likewise employed in a figurative sense for moral objects: our passions are our *enemies*, when indulged; envy is a *foe* to happiness.

ENMITY, ANIMOSITY, HOSTILITY.

Enmity lies in the heart; it is deep and malignant: *animosity*, from *animus*, a spirit, lies in the passions; it is fierce and vindictive: *hostility*, from *hostis* a political enemy, lies in the action; it is mischievous and destructive.

Enmity is something permanent; *animosity* is partial and transitory: in the feudal ages, when the darkness and ignorance of the times prevented the mild influence of Christianity, *enmities* between particular families were handed down as an inheritance from father to son; in free states, party spirit engenders greater *animosities* than private disputes.

Enmity is altogether personal: *hostility* mostly respects publick measures, *animosity* respects either one or many individuals. *Enmity* often lies concealed in the heart; *animosity* mostly betrays itself by some open act of *hostility*. He who cherishes *enmity* towards another is his own greatest enemy; 'In some instances, indeed, the *enmity* of others cannot be avoided without a participation in their guilt; but then it is the *enmity* of those with whom neither wisdom nor virtue can desire to associate.'—JOHNSON. He who is guided by a spirit of *animosity* is unfit to have any command over others; 'I will never let my heart reproach me with having done any thing towards increasing those *animosities* that extinguish religion, deface government, and make a nation miserable.'—ADDISON. He who proceeds to wanton *hostility* often provokes an enemy where he might have a friend; 'Erasmus himself had, it seems, the misfortune to fall into the hands of a party of Trojans who laid on him with so many blows and buffets, that he never forgot their *hostilities* to his dying day.'—ADDISON.

ADVERSE, CONTRARY, OPPOSITE.

Adverse, in French *adverse*, Latin *adversus*, participle of *adverto*, compounded of *ad* and *verto*, signifies turning towards or against; *contrary*, in French *contraire*, Latin *contrarius*, comes from *contra* against; *opposite*, in Latin *oppositus*, participle of *oppono*, is compounded of *ob* and *pono*, signifying placed in the way.

Adverse respects the feelings and interests of persons; *contrary* regards their plans and purposes; *opposite* relates to the situation of persons and nature of things;

> And as Ægæon, when with heav'n he strove,
> Stood *opposite* in arms to mighty Jove.—DRYDEN.

Fortune is *adverse;* an event turns out *contrary* to what was expected; sentiments are *opposite* to each other. An *adverse* wind comes across our wishes and pursuits; 'The periodical winds which were then set in were distinctly *adverse* to the course which Pizarro proposed to steer.'—ROBERTSON. A *contrary* wind lies in an opposite direction; *contrary* winds are mostly *adverse* to some one who is crossing the ocean; *adverse* winds need not always be directly *contrary*.

Circumstances are sometimes so *adverse* as to baffle the best concerted plans. Facts often prove directly *contrary* to the representations given of them; 'As I should be loth to offer none but instances of the abuse of prosperity, I am happy in recollecting one very singular example of the *contrary* sort.'—CUMBERLAND. People with *opposite* characters cannot be expected to act together with pleasure to either party. *Adverse* events interrupt the peace of mind; *contrary* accounts invalidate the testimony of a narration; *opposite* principles interrupt the harmony of society.

COMPARISON, CONTRAST.

Comparison, from *compare*, and the Latin *comparo* or *com* and *par* equal, signifies the putting together of things that are equal; *contrast*, in French *contraster*, Latin *contrasto* or *contra* and *sto* to stand, or *sisto* to place against, signifies the placing of one thing opposite to another.

Likeness in the quality and difference in the degree are requisite for a *comparison;* likeness in the degree and opposition in the quality are requisite for a *contrast:* things of the same colour are *compared;* those of an opposite colour are *contrasted:* a *comparison* is made between two shades of red: a *contrast* between black and white.

Comparison is of a practical utility, it serves to ascertain the true relation of objects; *contrast* is of utility among poets, it serves to heighten the effect of opposite qualities: things are large or small by *comparison;* things are magnified or diminished by *contrast:* the value of a coin is best learned by *comparing* it with another of the same metal; 'They who are apt to remind us of their ancestors only put us upon making *comparisons* to their own disadvantage.'—SPECTATOR.

The generosity of one person is most strongly felt when *contrasted* with the meanness of another;

> In lovely *contrast* to this glorious view,
> Calmly magnificent then will we turn
> To where the silver Thames first rural grows.
> THOMSON.

ADVERSE, INIMICAL, HOSTILE, REPUGNANT.

Adverse signifies the same as in the preceding article; *inimical*, from the Latin *inimicus* an enemy, signifies belonging to an enemy; which is also the meaning of *hostile*, from *hostis* an enemy; *repugnant*, in Latin *repugnans*, from *repugno*, or *re* and *pugno* to fight against, signifies warring with.

Adverse may be applied to either persons or things; *inimical* and *hostile* to persons or things personal; *repugnant* to things only: a person is *adverse* or a thing is *adverse* to an object; a person, or what is personal, is either *inimical* or *hostile* to an object; one thing is *repugnant* to another. We are *adverse* to a proposition; or circumstances are *adverse* to our advancement. Partizans are *inimical* to the proceedings of government, and *hostile* to the possessors of power. Slavery is *repugnant* to the mild temper of Christianity.

Adverse expresses simple dissent or opposition; *inimical* either an acrimonious spirit or a tendency to injure; *hostile* a determined resistance; *repugnant* a direct relation of variance. Those who are *adverse* to any undertaking will not be likely to use the endeavours which are essential to ensure its success; 'Only two soldiers were killed on the side of Cortes, and two officers with fifteen privates of the *adverse* faction.'—

ROBERTSON. Those who dissent from the establishment, are *inimical* to its forms, its discipline, or its doctrine; 'God hath shown himself to be favourable to virtue, and *inimical* to vice and guilt.'—BLAIR. Many are so *hostile* to the religious establishment of their country as to aim at its subversion;

> Then with a purple veil involve your eyes,
> Lest *hostile* faces blast the sacrifice.—DRYDEN.

The restraints which it imposes on the wandering and licentious imagination is *repugnant* to the temper of their minds; 'The exorbitant jurisdiction of the (Scotch) ecclesiastical courts were founded on maxims *repugnant* to justice.'—ROBERTSON.
Sickness is *adverse* to the improvement of youth. The dissensions in the Christian world are *inimical* to the interests of religion, and tend to produce many *hostile* measures. Democracy is *inimical* to good order, the fomenter of *hostile* parties, and *repugnant* to every sound principle of civil society.

ADVERSE, AVERSE.

Adverse (*v. Adverse*), signifying turned against or over against, denotes simply opposition of situation; *averse*, from *a* and *versus*, signifying turned from or away from, denotes an active removal or separation from. *Adverse* is therefore as applicable to inanimate as to animate objects, *averse* only to animate objects. When applied to conscious agents *adverse* refers to matters of opinion and sentiment, *averse* to those affecting our feelings. We are *adverse* to that which we think wrong; 'Before you were a tyrant I was your friend, and am now no otherwise your enemy than every Athenian must be who is *adverse* to your usurpation.'—CUMBERLAND. We are *averse* to that which opposes our inclinations, our habits, or our interests; 'Men relinquish ancient habits slowly, and with reluctance. They are *averse* to new experiments, and venture upon them with timidity.'—ROBERTSON. Sectarians profess to be *adverse* to the doctrines and discipline of the establishment, but the greater part of them are still more *averse* to the wholesome restraints which it imposes on the imagination.

AVERSE, UNWILLING, BACKWARD, LOATH, RELUCTANT.

Averse signifies the same as in the preceding article; *unwilling* literally signifies not willing; *backward*, having the will in a *backward* direction; *loath* or *loth*, from to *loath*, denotes the quality of loathing; *reluctant*, from the Latin *re* and *lucto* to struggle, signifies struggling with the will against a thing.

Averse is positive, it marks an actual sentiment of dislike; *unwilling* is negative, it marks the absence of the will; *backward* is a sentiment between the two, it marks the leaning of a will against a thing; *loath* and *reluctant* mark strong feelings of *aversion*. *Aversion* is an habitual sentiment; *unwillingness* and *backwardness* are mostly occasional; *loath* and *reluctant* always occasional.

Aversion must be conquered; *unwillingness* must be removed; *backwardness* must be counteracted, or urged forward; *loathing* and *reluctance* must be overpowered. One who is *averse* to study will never have recourse to books; but a child may be *unwilling* or *backward* to attend to his lessons from partial motives, which the authority of the parent or master may correct; he who is *loath* to receive instruction will always remain ignorant; he who is *reluctant* in doing his duty will always do it as a task.

A miser is *averse* to nothing so much as to parting with his money;

> Of all the race of animals, alone,
> The bees have common cities of their own;
> But (what 's more strange) their modest appetites,
> *Averse* from Venus, fly the nuptial rites.—DRYDEN.

The miser is even *unwilling* to provide himself with necessaries, but he is not *backward* in disposing of his money when he has the prospect of getting more;

> I part with thee,
> As wretches that are doubtful of hereafter
> Part with their lives, *unwilling*, *loath*, and fearful,
> And trembling at futurity.—ROWE.

'All men, even the most depraved, are subject more or less to compunctions of conscience; but *backward* at the same time to resign the gains of dishonesty, or the pleasures of vice.'—BLAIR. Friends are *loath* to part who have had many years' enjoyment in each other's society;

> E'en thus two friends condemn'd
> Embrace, and kiss, and take ten thousand leaves,
> *Loather* a hundred times to part than die.
> SHAKSPEARE.

One is *reluctant* in giving unpleasant advice;

> From better habitations spurn'd,
> *Reluctant* dost thou rove,
> Or grieve for friendship unreturn'd,
> Or unregarded love?—GOLDSMITH.

Lazy people are *averse* to labour: those who are not paid are *unwilling* to work; and those who are paid less than others are *backward* in giving their services: every one is *loath* to give up a favourite pursuit, and when compelled to it by circumstances they do it with *reluctance*.

AVERSION, ANTIPATHY, DISLIKE, HATRED, REPUGNANCE.

Aversion denotes the quality of being averse (*vide Averse*); *antipathy*, in French *antipathie*, Latin *antipathia*, Greek ἀντιπαθεία, compounded of ἀντὶ against, and παθεία feeling, signifies a feeling against; *dislike*, compounded of the privative *dis* and *like*, signifies not to like or be attached to; *hatred*, in German *hass*, is supposed by Adelung to be connected with *heiss* hot, signifying heat of temper; *repugnance*, in French *repugnance*, Latin *repugnantia* and *repugno*, compounded of *re* and *pugno*, signifies the resistance of the feelings to an object.

Aversion is in its most general sense the generick term to these and many other similar expressions, in which case it is opposed to attachment: the former denoting an alienation of the mind from an object; the latter a knitting or binding of the mind to objects: it has, however, more commonly a partial acceptation, in which it is justly comparable with the above words. *Aversion* and *antipathy* apply more properly to things: *dislike* and *hatred* to persons; *repugnance* to actions, that is, such actions as one is called upon to perform.

Aversion and *antipathy* seem to be less dependent on the will, and to have their origin in the temperament or natural taste, particularly the latter, which springs from causes that are not always visible; and lies in the physical organization. *Antipathy* is in fact a natural *aversion* opposed to sympathy: *dislike* and *hatred* are on the contrary voluntary, and seem to have their root in the angry passions of the heart; the former is less deep-rooted than the latter, and is commonly awakened by slighter causes; *repugnance* is not an habitual and lasting sentiment, like the rest; it is a transitory but strong *dislike* to what one is obliged to do.

An unfitness in the temper to harmonize with an object produces *aversion*: a contrariety in the nature of particular persons and things occasions *antipathies*, although some pretend that there are no such mysterious incongruities in nature, and that all *antipathies* are but *aversions* early engendered by the influence of fear and the workings of imagination; but under this supposition we are still at a loss to account for those singular effects of fear and imagination in some persons which do not discover themselves in others: a difference in the character, habits, and manners, produces *dislike*: injuries, quarrels, or more commonly the influence of malignant passions, occasion *hatred*: a contrariety to one's moral sense, or one's humours, awakens *repugnance*.

People of a quiet temper have an *aversion* to disputing or argumentation; those of a gloomy temper have an *aversion* to society; 'I cannot forbear mentioning a tribe of egotists, for whom I have always had a mortal *aversion*; I mean the authors of memoirs who are never mentioned in any works but their own.'—ADDISON. *Antipathies* mostly discover themselves in early life, and as soon as the object comes within the view of the person affected; 'There is one species of terrour which those who are unwilling to suffer the reproach of cowardice have wisely dignified with the name of *antipathy*. A man has indeed no dread of harm from an insect or a worm, but his *antipathy* turns nim pale whenever they approach him.'—JOHNSON. Men of different sentiments in religion or politicks, if not of amiable temper, are apt to contract *dislikes* to each other by frequent irritation in discourse; 'Every man whom business or curiosity has thrown at large into the world, will recollect many instances of fondness and *dislike*, which have forced themselves upon him without the intervention of his judgement.'—JOHNSON. When men of malignant tempers come in collision, nothing but a deadly *hatred* can ensue from their repeated and complicated aggressions towards each other; 'One punishment that attends the lying and deceitful person is the *hatred* of all those whom he either has, or would have deceived. I do not say that a Christian can lawfully hate any one, and yet I affirm that some may very worthily deserve to be *hated*.'—SOUTH. Any one who is under the influence of a misplaced pride is apt to feel a *repugnance* to acknowledge himself in an errour; 'In this dilemma Aristophanes conquered his *repugnance*, and determined upon presenting himself on the stage for the first time in his life.'—CUMBERLAND.

Aversions produce an anxious desire for the removal of the object *disliked: antipathies* produce the most violent physical revulsion of the frame, and vehement recoiling from the object; persons have not unfrequently been known to faint away at the sight of insects for whom this *antipathy* has been conceived: *dislikes* too often betray themselves by distant and uncourteous behaviour: *hatred* assumes every form which is black and horrid: *repugnance* does not make its appearance until called forth by the necessity of the occasion.

Aversions will never be so strong in a well-regulated mind, that they cannot be overcome when their cause is removed, or they are found to be ill-grounded; sometimes they lie in a vicious temperament formed by nature or habit, in which case they will not easily be destroyed: a slothful man will find a difficulty in overcoming his *aversion* to labour, or an idle man his *aversion* to steady application. *Antipathies* may be indulged or resisted: people of irritable temperaments, particularly females, are liable to them in a most violent degree; but those who are fully persuaded of their fallacy, may do much by the force of conviction to diminish their violence. *Dislikes* are often groundless, or have their origin in trifles, owing to the influence of caprice or humour: people of sense will be ashamed of them, and the true Christian will stifle them in their birth, lest they grow into the formidable passion of *hatred*, which strikes at the root of all peace; being a mental poison that infuses its venom into all the sinuosities of the heart, and pollutes the sources of human affection. *Repugnance* ought always to be resisted whenever it prevents us from doing what either reason, honour, or duty require.

Aversions are applicable to animals as well as men: dogs have a particular *aversion* to beggars, most probably from their suspicious appearance; in certain cases likewise we may speak of their *antipathies*, as in the instance of the dog and the cat: according to the schoolmen there existed also *antipathies* between certain plants and vegetables; but these are not borne out by facts sufficiently strong to warrant a belief of their existence. *Dislike* and *hatred* are sometimes applied to things, but in a sense less exceptionable than in the former case: *dislike* does not express so much as *aversion*, and *aversion* not so much as *hatred*: we ought to have a *hatred* for vice and sin, an *aversion* to gossipping and idle talking, and a *dislike* to the frivolities of fashionable life.

TO HATE, DETEST.

Hate has the same signification as in the preceding article; *detest*, from *detestor* or *de* and *testor*, signifies to call to witness against. The difference between these two words consists more in sense than application. To *hate* is a personal feeling directed toward the object independently of its qualities; to *detest* is a feeling independent of the person, and altogether dependent upon the nature of the thing. What one *hates*, one *hates* commonly on one's own account; what one *detests*, one *detests* on account of the object: hence it is that one *hates*, but not *detests*, the person who has done an injury to one's self; and that one *detests*, rather than *hates*, the person who has done injuries to others. Joseph's brethren *hated* him because he was more beloved than they;

> Spleen to mankind his envious heart possest,
> And much he *hated* all, but most the best.—POPE

We *detest* a traitor to his country because of the enormity of his offence;

> Who dares think one thing, and another tell,
> My heart *detests* him as the gates of hell.—POPE.

In this connexion, to *hate* is always a bad passion; to *detest* always laudable: but when both are applied to inanimate objects, to *hate* is bad or good according to circumstances; to *detest* always retains its good meaning. When men *hate* things because they interfere with their indulgences, as the wicked *hate* the light, it is a bad personal feeling, as in the former case; but when good men are said to *hate* that which is bad, it is a laudable feeling justified by the nature of the object. As this feeling is, however, so closely allied to *detestation*, it is necessary farther to observe that *hate*, whether rightly or wrongly applied, seeks the injury or destruction of the object; but *detest* is confined simply to the shunning of the object, or thinking of it with very great pain. God *hates* sin, and on that account punishes sinners; conscientious men *detest* all fraud, and therefore cautiously avoid being concerned in it

HATEFUL, ODIOUS.

Hateful, signifies literally full of that which is apt to excite *hatred; odious*, from the Latin *odi* to *hate*, has the same sense originally.

These epithets are employed in regard to such objects as produce strong aversion in the mind; but when employed as they commonly are upon familiar subjects, they indicate an unbecoming vehemence in the speaker. The *hateful* is that which we ourselves *hate*; but the *odious* is that which makes us *hateful* to others. *Hateful* is properly applied to whatever violates general principles of morality: lying and swearing are *hateful* vices: *odious* applied to such things as affect the interests of others, and bring *odium* upon the individual; a tax that bears particularly hard and unequally is termed *odious*; or a measure of government that is thought oppressive is denominated *odious*. There is something particularly *hateful* in the meanness of cringing sycophants;

> Let me be deemed the *hateful* cause of all,
> And suffer, rather than my people fall.—POPE.

Nothing brought more *odium* on King James than his attempts to introduce popery; 'Projectors and inventors of new taxes being *hateful* to the people, seldom fail of bringing *odium* on their master.'—DAVENANT.

HATRED, ENMITY, ILL WILL, RANCOUR.

These terms agree in this particular, that those who are under the influence of such feelings derive a pleasure from the misfortune of others; but *hatred*, (*v. Aversion*) expresses more than *enmity*, (*v. Enemy*,) and this is more than *ill will*, which signifies merely willing ill or evil to another. *Hatred* is not contented with merely wishing *ill* to others, but derives its whole happiness from their misery or destruction; *enmity* on the contrary is limited in its operations to particular circumstances: *hatred*, on the other hand, is frequently confined to the feeling of the individual; but *enmity* consists as much in the action as the feeling. He who is possessed with *hatred* is happy when the object of his passion is miserable, and is miserable when he is happy; but the *hater* is not always instrumental in causing his misery or destroying his happiness: he who is inflamed with *enmity*, is more active in disturbing the peace of his *enemy*; but oftener displays his temper in trifling than in important matters. *Ill will*, as the word denotes, lies only in the mind, and is so indefinite in its signification, that it admits of every conceivable degree. When the will is evilly directed towards another, in ever so small a degree, it constitutes *ill will*. *Rancour*, in Latin *rancor*, from *ranceo* to grow stale, signifying staleness, mustiness, is a species of bitter, deep-rooted *enmity*, that has lain so long in the mind as to become thoroughly corrupt.

Hatred is opposed to love; the object in both cases occupies the thoughts: the former torments the possessor; the latter delights him;

Phœnician Dido rules the growing state,
Who fled from Tyre to shun her brother's *hate.*
DRYDEN.

Enmity is opposed to friendship; the object in both cases interests the passions: the former the bad, and the latter the good passions or the affections: the possessor is in both cases busy either in injuring or forwarding the cause of him who is his *enemy* or friend;

That space the evil one abstracted stood
From his own evil, and for the time remain'd
Stupidly good, of *enmity* disarm'd.—MILTON.

Ill will is opposed to good will; it is either a general or a particular feeling; it embraces many or few, a single individual or the whole human race: he is least unhappy who bears least *ill will* to others; he is most happy who bears true good will to all; he is neither happy or unhappy who is not possessed of the one or the other; 'For your servants neither use them so familiarly as to lose your reverence at their hands, nor so disdainfully as to purchase yourself their *ill will.*'—WENTWORTH.

There is a farther distinction between these terms; that *hatred* and *ill will* are oftener the fruit of a depraved mind, than the consequence of any external provocation; *enmity* and *rancour*, on the contrary, are mostly produced by particular circumstances of offence or commission; the best of men are sometimes the objects of *hatred* on account of their very virtues, which have been unwittingly to themselves the causes of producing this evil passion; good advice, however kindly given, may probably occasion *ill will* in the mind of him who is not disposed to receive it kindly; an angry word or a party contest is frequently the causes of *enmity* between irritable people, and of *rancour* between resentful and imperious people;

Oh lasting *rancour!* oh insatiate *hate*,
To Phrygia's monarch, and the Phrygian state.
POPE.

TO ABHOR, DETEST, ABOMINATE, LOATH.

These terms equally denote a sentiment of aversion; *abhor*, in Latin *abhorreo*, compounded of *ab* from and *horreo* to stiffen with horrour, signifies to start from, with a strong emotion of horrour; *detest* (*v. To hate, detest*); *abominate*, in Latin *abominatus*, participle of *abominor*, compounded of *ab* from or against, and *ominor* to wish ill luck, signifies to hold in religious abhorrence, to detest in the highest possible degree; *loath*, in Saxon *lathen*, may possibly be a variation of load, in the sense of overload, because it expresses the nausea which commonly attends an overloaded stomach. In the moral acceptation, it is a strong figure of speech to mark the abhorrence and disgust which the sight of offensive objects produces.

What we *abhor* is repugnant to our moral feelings; what we *detest* contradicts our moral principle; what we *abominate* does equal violence to our religious and moral sentiments; what we *loath* acts upon us physically and mentally.

Inhumanity and cruelty are objects of *abhorrence;* crimes and injustice of *detestation;* impiety and profaneness of *abomination;* enormous offenders of *loathing.*

The tender mind will *abhor* what is base and atrocious;

The lie that flatters I *abhor* the most.—COWPER.

The rigid moralist will *detest* every violent infringement on the rights of his fellow creatures;

'This thirst of kindred blood my sons *detest.*
DRYDEN.

The conscientious man will *abominate* every breach of the Divine law; 'The passion that is excited in the fable of the Sick Kite is terrour; the object of which is the despair of him who perceives himself to be dying, and has reason to fear that his very prayer is an *abomination.*'—HAWKESWORTH. The agonized mind *loaths* the sight of every object which recalls to its recollection the subject of its distress;

No costly lords the sumptuous banquet deal,
To make him *loath* his vegetable meal.
GOLDSMITH

Revolving in his mind the stern command,
He longs to fly, and *loaths* the charming land.
DRYDEN.

The chaste Lucretia *abhorred* the pollution to which she had been exposed and would have *loathed* the sight of the atrocious perpetrator: Brutus *detested* the oppression and the oppressor.

ABOMINABLE,* DETESTABLE, EXECRABLE

The primitive idea of these terms, agreeable to their derivation, is that of badness in the highest degree, conveying by themselves the strongest signification and excluding the necessity for every other modifying epithet.

The *abominable* thing excites aversion; the *detestable* thing, hatred and revulsion; the *execrable* thing, indignation and horrour.

These sentiments are expressed against what is *abominable* by strong ejaculations, against what is *detestable* by animadversion and reprobation, and against what is *execrable* by imprecations and anathemas.

In the ordinary acceptation of these terms, they serve to mark a degree of excess in a very bad thing; *abominable* expressing less than *detestable*, and that less than *execrable.* This gradation is sufficiently illustrated in the following example. Dionysius, the tyrant, having been informed that a very aged woman prayed to the gods every day for his preservation, and wondering that any of his subjects should be so interested for his safety, inquired of this woman respecting the motives of her conduct, to which she replied, "In my infancy I lived under an *abominable* prince, whose death I desired; but when he perished, he was succeeded by a *detestable* tyrant worse than himself. I offered up my vows for his death also, which were in like manner answered; but we have since had a worse tyrant than he. This *execrable* monster is yourself, whose life I have prayed for, lest, if it be possible, you should be succeeded by one even more wicked."

The exaggeration conveyed by these expressions has given rise to their abuse in vulgar discourse, where they are often employed indifferently to serve the humour of the speaker; 'This *abominable* endeavour to suppress or lessen every thing that is praiseworthy is as frequent among the men as among the women.'—STEELE. 'Nothing can atone for the want of modesty, without which beauty is ungraceful, and wit *detestable.*'—STEELE.

All vote to leave that *execrable* shore,
Polluted with the blood of Polydore.—DRYDEN.

TO BRAVE, DEFY, DARE, CHALLENGE.

Brave, from the epithet *brave* (*v. Brave*), signifies to act the *brave; defy*, in French *defier*, is probably charged from *defaire* to undo, signifying to make nothing or set at nought; *dare*, in Saxon *dearran*, *dyrran*, Franconian, &c. *odurren*, *thorren*, Greek θάρσειν, signifies to be bold, or have the confidence to do a thing; *challenge* is probably changed from the Greek καλέω to call.

We *brave* things; we *dare* and *challenge* persons, we *defy* persons or their actions: the sailor *braves* the tempestuous ocean, and very often *braves* death itself in its most terrifick form; he *dares* the enemy whom he meets to the engagement; he *defies* all his boastings and vain threats.

Brave is sometimes used in a bad sense; *defy* and *dare* commonly so. There is much idle contempt and affected indifference in *braving;* much insolent resistance to authority in *defying;* much provocation and affront in *daring:* a bad man *braves* the scorn and reproach of all the world; he *defies* the threats of his superiours to punish him; he *dares* them to exert their power over him.

Brave and *defy* are dispositions of mind which display themselves in the conduct; *dare* and *challenge* are modes of action; we *brave* a storm by meeting its violence, and bearing it down with superiour force: we *defy* the malice of our enemies by pursuing that line of conduct which is most calculated to increase its bitter-

* Vide Abbe Roubaud's Synonymes: "Abominable, detestable, execrable."

ness. To *brave*, conveys the idea of a direct and personal application of force to force; *defying* is carried on by a more indirect and circuitous mode of procedure: men *brave* the dangers which threaten them with evil, and in a figurative application things are said to *brave* resistance; 'Joining in proper union the amiable and the estimable qualities, in one part of our character we shall resemble the flower that smiles in spring; in another the firmly-rooted tree, that *braves* the winter storm.'—BLAIR. Men *defy* the angry will which opposes them;

The soul, secur'd in her existence, smiles
At the drawn dagger, and *defies* its point.—ADDISON.

To *dare* and *challenge* are both direct and personal; but the former consists either of actions, words, or looks; the latter of words only. We *dare* a number of persons indefinitely; we *challenge* an individual, and very frequently by name.

Daring arises from our contempt of others; *challenging* arises from a high opinion of ourselves: the former is mostly accompanied with unbecoming expressions of disrespect as well as aggravation; the latter is mostly divested of all angry personality. Metius the Tuscan *dared* Titus Manlius Torquatus, the son of the Roman consul, to engage with him in contradiction to his father's commands. Paris was persuaded to *challenge* Menelaus in order to terminate the Grecian war.

We *dare* only to acts of violence; we *challenge* to any kind of contest in which the skill or power of the parties are to be tried. It is folly to *dare* one of superiour strength if we are not prepared to meet with the just reward of our impertinence;

Troy sunk in flames I saw (nor could prevent),
And Ilium from its old foundations rent—
Rent like a mountain ash, which *dar'd* the winds,
And stood the sturdy strokes of lab'ring hinds.
DRYDEN.

Whoever has a confidence in the justice of his cause, needs not fear to challenge his opponent to a trial of their respective merits; 'The Platos and Ciceros among the ancients; the Bacons, Boyles, and Lockes, among our own countrymen, are all instances of what I have been saying, namely, that the greatest persons in all ages have conformed to the established religion of their country; not to mention any of the divines, however celebrated, since our adversaries *challenge* all those as men who have too much interest in this case to be impartial evidences.'—BUDGELL.

BRAVERY, COURAGE, VALOUR, GALLANTRY.

Bravery denotes the abstract quality of *brave*, which through the medium of the northern languages comes from the Greek βραβεῖον the reward of victory; *courage*, in French *courage*, from *cœur*, in Latin *cor* the heart, which is the seat of *courage; valour*, in French *valeur*, Latin *valor*, from *valeo* to be strong, signifies by distinction strength of mind; *gallantry*, from the Greek ἀγαλλω to adorn or make distinguished for splendid qualities.

Bravery lies in the blood; *courage* lies in the mind: the latter depends on the reason; the former on the physical temperament: the first is a species of instinct: the second is a virtue: a man is *brave* in proportion as he is without thought; he has *courage* in proportion as he reasons or reflects.

Bravery seems to be something involuntary, a mechanical movement that does not depend on one's self; *courage* requires conviction, and gathers strength by delay; it is a noble and lofty sentiment: the force of example, the charms of musick, the fury and tumult of battle, the desperation of the conflict, will make cowards *brave;* the *courageous* man wants no other incentives than what his own mind suggests.

Bravery is of utility only in the hour of attack or contest; *courage* is of service at all times and under all circumstances: *bravery* is of avail in overcoming the obstacle of the moment; *courage* seeks to avert the distant evil that may possibly arrive. *Bravery* is a thing of the moment that is or is not, as circumstances may favour; it varies with the time and season: *courage* exists at all times and on all occasions. The *brave* man who fearlessly rushes to the mouth of the cannon may tremble at his own shadow as he passes through a churchyard or turn pale at the sight of blood: the *courageous* man smiles at imaginary dangers, and prepares to meet those that are real.

It is as possible for a man to have *courage* without *bravery*, as to have *bravery* without *courage:* Cicero betrayed his want of *bravery* when he sought to shelter himself against the attacks of Cataline; he displayed his *courage* when he laid open the treasonable purposes of this conspirator to the whole senate, and charged him to his face with the crimes of which he knew him to be guilty.

Valour is a higher quality than either *bravery* or *courage*, and seems to partake of the grand characteristicks of both; it combines the fire of *bravery* with the determination and firmness of *courage: bravery* is most fitted for the soldier and all who receive orders; *courage* is most adapted for the general and all who give commands; *valour* for the leader and framer of enterprises, and all who carry great projects into execution: *bravery* requires to be guided; *courage* is equally fitted to command or obey; *valour* directs and executes. *Bravery* has most relation to danger; *courage* and *valour* include in them a particular reference to action: the *brave* man exposes himself; the *courageous* man advances to the scene of action which is before him; the *valiant* man seeks for occasions to act.

Courage may be exercised in ordinary cases; *valour* displays itself most effectually in the achievement of heroic exploits. A consciousness of duty, a love of one's country, a zeal for the cause in which one is engaged, an over-ruling sense of religion, the dictates of a pure conscience, always inspire *courage:* an ardent thirst for glory, and an insatiable ambition, render men *valiant.*

The *brave* man, when he is wounded, is proud of being so, and boasts of his wounds; the *courageous* man collects the strength which his wounds have left him, to pursue the object which he has in view; the *valiant* man thinks less of the life he is about to lose, than of the glory which has escaped him. The *brave* man, in the hour of victory, exults and triumphs: he discovers his joy in boisterous war shouts. The *courageous* man forgets his success in order to profit by its advantages. The *valiant* man is stimulated by success to seek after new trophies. *Bravery* sinks after a defeat: *courage* may be damped for a moment, but is never destroyed; it is ever ready to seize the first opportunity which offers to regain the lost advantage: *valour*, when defeated on any occasion, seeks another in which more glory is to be acquired.

The three hundred Spartans who defended the Straits of Thermopylæ were *brave;*

This *brave* man, with long resistance,
Held the combat doubtful.—ROWE.

Socrates drinking the hemlock, Regulus returning to Carthage, Titus tearing himself from the arms of the weeping Berenice, Alfred the Great going into the camp of the Danes, were *courageous;*

"Oh! When I see him arming for his honour,
His country, and his gods, that martial fire
That mounts his *courage*, kindles even me.
DRYDEN.

Hercules destroying monsters, Perseus delivering Andromeda, Achilles running to the ramparts of Troy, and the knights of more modern date who have gone in quest of extraordinary adventures, are all entitled to the peculiar appellation of *valiant;*

True *valour*, friends, on virtue founded strong,
Meets all events alike.—MALLETT.

Gallantry is extraordinary *bravery*, or *bravery* on extraordinary occasions. The *brave* man goes willingly where he is commanded; the *gallant* man leads on with vigour to the attack. *Bravery* is common to vast numbers and whole nations; *gallantry* is peculiar to individuals or particular bodies: the *brave* man *bravely* defends the post assigned him; the *gallant* man volunteers his services in cases of peculiar danger; a man may feel ashamed in not being considered *brave;* he feels a pride in being looked upon as *gallant* To call a hero *brave* adds little or nothing to his cha racter; 'The *brave* unfortunate are our best acquaintance.'—FRANCIS. But to entitle him *gallant* adds a lustre to the glory he has acquired;

Death is the worst; a fate which all must try,
And for our country 't is a bliss to die.
The *gallant* man, though slain in fight he be,
Yet leaves his nation safe, his children free.
POPE.

We cannot speak of a British tar without thinking of *bravery;* of his exploits without thinking of *gallantry.*

COURAGE, FORTITUDE, RESOLUTION.

Courage signifies the same as in the preceding article; *fortitude,* in French *fortitude,* Latin *fortitudo,* is the abstract noun from *fortis* strong; *resolution,* from the verb *resolve,* marks the habit of *resolving.*

Courage respects action, *fortitude* respects passion: a man has *courage* to meet danger, and *fortitude* to endure pain.

Courage is that power of the mind which bears up against the evil that is in prospect; *fortitude* is that power which endures the pain that is felt: the man of *courage* goes with the same coolness to the mouth of the cannon, as the man of *fortitude* undergoes the amputation of a limb.

Horatius Cocles displayed his *courage* in defending a bridge against the whole army of the Etruscans: Caius Mucius displayed no less *fortitude* when he thrust his hand into the fire in the presence of King Porsenna, and awed him as much by his language as his action.

Courage seems to be more of a manly virtue; *fortitude* is more distinguishable as a feminine virtue: the former is at least most adapted to the male sex, who are called upon to act, and the latter to females, who are obliged to endure: a man without *courage* would be as ill prepared to discharge his duty in his intercourse with the world, as a woman without *fortitude* would be to support herself under the complicated trials of body and mind with which she is liable to be assailed.

We can make no pretensions to *courage* unless we set aside every personal consideration in the conduct we should pursue; 'What can be more honourable than to have *courage* enough to execute the commands of reason and conscience?'—COLLIER. We cannot boast of *fortitude* where the sense of pain provokes a murmur or any token of impatience: since life is a chequered scene, in which the prospect of one evil is most commonly succeeded by the actual existence of another, it is a happy endowment to be able to ascend the scaffold with *fortitude,* or to mount the breach with *courage* as occasion may require;

With wonted *fortitude* she bore the smart,
And not a groan confess'd her burning heart.—GAY.

Resolution is a minor species of *courage;* it is *courage* in the minor concerns of life: *courage* comprehends under it a spirit to advance; *resolution* simply marks the will not to recede: we require *courage* to bear down all the obstacles which oppose themselves to us; we require *resolution* not to yield to the first difficulties that offer: *courage* is an elevated feature in the human character which adorns the possessor; *resolution* is that common quality of the mind which is in perpetual request; the want of which degrades a man in the eyes of his fellow-creatures. *Courage* comprehends the absence of all fear, the disregard of all personal convenience, the spirit to begin and the determination to pursue what has been begun; *resolution* consists of no more than the last quality of *courage,* which respects the persistance in a conduct; 'The unusual extension of my muscles on this occasion made my face ache to such a degree, that nothing but an invincible *resolution* and perseverance could have prevented me from falling back to my monosyllables.'—ADDISON. *Courage* is displayed on the most trying occasions; *resolution* is never put to any severe test; *courage* always supposes some danger to be encountered; *resolution* may be exerted in merely encountering opposition and difficulty: we have need of *courage* in opposing a formidable enemy; we have need of *resolution* in the management of a stubborn will.

AUDACITY, EFFRONTERY, HARDIHOOD OR HARDINESS, BOLDNESS.

Audacity, from *audacious,* in French *audacieux,* Latin *audax* and *audeo* to dare, signifies literally the quality of daring; *effrontery,* compounded of *ef, en,* or *in,* and *frons* a face, signifies the standing face to face *hardihood* or *hardiness,* from *hardy* or *hard,* signifies a capacity to endure or stand the brunt of difficulties, opposition, or shame; *boldness,* from *bold,* in Saxon *bald,* is in all probability changed from bald, that is, uncovered, open-fronted, without disguise, which are the characteristicks of *boldness.*

The idea of disregarding what others regard is common to all these terms. *Audacity* expresses more than *effrontery:* the first has something of vehemence or defiance in it; the latter that of cool unconcern: *hardihood* expresses less than *boldness;* the first has more of determination, and the second more of spirit and enterprise. *Audacity* and *effrontery* are always taken in a bad sense: *hardihood* in an indifferent, if not a bad sense; *boldness* in a good, bad, or indifferent sense.

* *Audacity* marks haughtiness and temerity; 'As knowledge without justice ought to be called cunning rather than wisdom, so a mind prepared to meet danger, if excited by its own eagerness and not the publick good, deserves the name of *audacity* rather than of fortitude.'—STEELE. *Effrontery* is the want of all modesty, a total shamelessness; 'I could never forbear to wish that while vice is every day multiplying seducements, and stalking forth with more hardened *effrontery,* virtue would not withdraw the influence of her presence.'—JOHNSON. *Hardihood* indicates a firm resolution to meet consequences; 'I do not find any one so *hardy* at present as to deny that there are very great advantages in the enjoyment of a plentiful fortune.'—BUDGELL. *Boldness* denotes a spirit to commence action, or in a less favourable sense to be heedless and free in one's speech; 'A *bold* tongue and a feeble arm are the qualifications of Drances in Virgil.'—ADDISON. An *audacious* man speaks with a loftv tone, without respect and without reflection; h. haughty demeanour makes him forget what is due to his superiours. *Effrontery* discovers itself by an insolent air; a total unconcern for the opinions of those present, and a disregard of all the forms of civil society. A *hardy* man speaks with a resolute tone, which seems to brave the utmost evil that can result from what he says. A *bold* man speaks without reserve, undaunted by the quality, rank, or haughtiness of those whom he addresses;

Bold in the council board,
But cautious in the field, he shunn'd the sword.
DRYDEN.

It requires *audacity* to assert false claims, or vindicate a lawless conduct in the presence of accusers and judges; it requires *effrontery* to ask a favour of the man whom one has basely injured, or to assume a placid unconcerned air in the presence of those by whom one has been convicted of flagrant atrocities; it requires *hardihood* to assert as a positive fact what is dubious or suspected to be false; it requires *boldness* to maintain the truth in spite of every danger with which one is threatened, or to assert one's claims in the presence of one's superiours.

Audacity makes a man to be hated; but it is not always such a base metal in the estimation of the world as it ought to be; it frequently passes current for *boldness* when it is practised with success. *Effrontery* makes a man despised; it is of too mean and vulgar a stamp to meet with general sanction: it is odious to all but those by whom it is practised, as it seems to run counter to every principle and feeling of common honesty. *Hardihood* is a die on which a man stakes his character for veracity; it serves the purpose of disputants, and frequently brings a man through difficulties which, with more deliberation and caution, might have proved his ruin. *Boldness* makes a man universally respected though not always beloved: a *bold* man is a particular favourite with the fair sex, with whom timidity passes for folly, and *boldness* of course for great talent or a fine spirit.

Audacity is the characteristick of rebels; *effrontery*

* Vide Girard: "Hardiesse, audace, effronterie"

that of villains; *hardihood* is serviceable to gentlemen of the bar; *boldness* is indispensable in every great undertaking.

DARING, BOLD.

Daring signifies having the spirit to *dare; bold* has the same signification as given under the head of *audacity.*

These terms may be both taken in a bad sense; but *daring* much oftener than *bold.* In either case *daring* expresses much more than *bold;* he who is *daring* provokes resistance, and courts danger; but the *bold* man is contented to overcome the resistance that is offered to him. A man may be *bold* in the use of words only; he must be daring in actions: a man is *bold* in the defence of truth: '*Boldness* is the power to speak or to do what we intend without fear or disorder.'—LOCKE. A man is *daring* in military enterprise;

> Too *daring* prince! ah! whither dost thou run,
> Ah! too forgetful of thy wife and son.—POPE.

STRENUOUS, BOLD.

Strenuous, in Latin *strenuus,* from the Greek ςρηνὴς undaunted, untamed, from ςρηνιάω to be without all rein or control; *bold, v. Audacity.*

Strenuous expresses much more than *bold; boldness* is a prominent idea, but it is only one idea which enters into the signification of *strenuousness;* it combines likewise fearlessness, activity, and ardour. An advocate in a cause may be *strenuous,* or merely *bold:* in the former case he omits nothing that can be either said or done in favour of the cause, he is always on the alert, he heeds no difficulties or danger; but in the latter case he only displays his spirit in the undisguised declaration of his sentiments. *Strenuous* supporters of any opinion are always strongly convinced of the truth of that which they support, and warmly impressed with a sense of its importance; 'While the good weather continued, I strolled about the country, and made many *strenuous* attempts to run away from this odious giddiness.'—BEATTIE. But the *bold* supporter of an opinion may be impelled rather with the desire of showing his *boldness* than maintaining his point;

> Fortune befriends the *bold.*—DRYDEN.

ARMS, WEAPONS.

Arms, from the Latin *arma,* is now properly used for instruments of offence, and never otherwise except by a poetick license of *arms* for armour; but *weapons,* from the German *waffen,* may be used either for an instrument of offence or defence. We say fire *arms,* but not fire *weapons;* and *weapons* offensive or defensive, not *arms* offensive or defensive. *Arms* likewise, agreeably to its origin, is employed for whatever is intentionally made as an instrument of offence; *weapon,* according to its extended and indefinite application, is employed for whatever may be accidentally used for this purpose: guns and swords are always *arms;*

> Louder, and yet more loud, I hear th' alarms
> Of human cries distinct and clashing *arms.*
> DRYDEN.

Stones, and brickbats, and pitchforks, may be occasionally *weapons;*

> The cry of Talbot serves me for a sword;
> For I have loaded me with many spoils,
> Using no other *weapon* than his name.
> SHAKSPEARE.

ARMY, HOST.

An *army* is an organized body of *armed* men; a *host,* from *hostis* an enemy, is properly a body of *hostile* men.

An *army* is a limited body; a *host* may be unlimited, and is therefore generally considered a very large body.

The word *army* applies only to that which has been formed by the rules of art for purposes of war;

> No more applause would on ambition wait,
> And laying waste the world be counted great;
> But one goodnatured act more praises gain,
> Than *armies* overthrown and thousands slain.
> JENYNS.

Host has been extended in its application not only to bodies, whether of men or angels, that were assembled for purposes of offence, but also in the figurative sense to whatever rises up to assail;

> He it was whose guile,
> Stirr'd up with envy and revenge, deceiv'd
> The mother of mankind, what time his pride
> Had cast him out of heav'n with all his *host*
> Of rebel angels.—MILTON.

> Yet true it is, survey we life around,
> Whole *hosts* of ills on every side are found.
> JENYNS

BATTLE, COMBAT, ENGAGEMENT.

Battle, in French *bataille,* comes from the Latin *batuo,* Hebrew עבת to twist, signifying a beating; *combat,* from the French *combattre,* i. e. *com* or *cum* together, and *battre* to beat or fight, signifies literally a *battle* one with the other; *engagement* signifies the act of being engaged or occupied in a contest.

* *Battle* is a general action requiring some preparation: *combat* is only particular, and sometimes unexpected. Thus the action which took place between the Carthaginians and the Romans, or Cæsar and Pompey, were *battles;* but the action in which the Horatii and the Curiatii, decided the fate of Rome, as also many of the actions in which Hercules was engaged, were *combats.* The *battle* of Almanza was a decisive action between Philip of France and Charles of Austria, in their contest for the throne of Spain, in the *combat* between Menelaus and Paris, Homer very artfully describes the seasonable interference of Venus to save her favourite from destruction; 'The most curious reason of all (for the wager of *battle*) is given in the Mirror, that it is allowable upon warrant of the *combat* between David for the people of Israel of the one party, and Goliath for the Philistines of the other party.'—BLACKSTONE.

The word *combat* has more relation to the act of fighting than that of *battle,* which is used with more propriety simply to denominate the action. In the *battle* between the Romans and Pyrrhus, King of Epirus, the *combat* was obstinate and bloody; the Romans seven times repulsed the enemy, and were as often repulsed in their turn. In this latter sense *engagement* and *combat* are analogous, but the former has a specifick relation to the agents and parties *engaged,* which is not implied in the latter term. We speak of a person being present in an *engagement;* wounded in an *engagement;* or having fought desperately in an *engagement:* on the other hand; to *engage* in a *combat;* to challenge to single *combat: combats* are sometimes begun by the accidental meeting of avowed opponents; in such *engagements* nothing is thought of but the gratification of revenge.

Battles are fought between armies only; they are gained or lost: *combats* are entered into between individuals, whether of the brute or human species, in which they seek to destroy or excel: *engagements* are confined to no particular member, only to such as are *engaged:* a general *engagement* is said of an army when the whole body is *engaged;* partial *engagements* respect only such as are fought by small parties or companies of an army. History is mostly occupied with the details of *battles;*

> A *battle* bloody fought,
> Where darkness and surprise made conquest cheap.
> DRYDEN.

In the history of the Greeks and Romans, we have likewise an account of the *combats* between men and wild beasts, which formed their principal amusement;

> This brave man with long resistance,
> Held the *combat* doubtful.—ROWE.

It is reported of the German women, that whenever their husbands went to *battle* they used to go into the thickest of the *combat* to carry them provisions or dress

* Girard "Bataille, combat."

their wounds; and that sometimes they would take part in the *engagement;* 'The Emperor of Morocco commanded his principal officers, that if he died during the *engagement*, they should conceal his death from the army.'—ADDISON. The word *combat* is likewise sometimes taken in a moral application; 'The relation of events becomes a moral lecture, when the *combat* of honour is rewarded with virtue.'—HAWKESWORTH.

CONFLICT, COMBAT, CONTEST.

Conflict, in Latin *conflictus*, participle of *confligo* compounded of *con* and *fligo*, in Greek φλίγω Æolic for φλίβω to flip or strike, signifies to strike against each other. This term is allied to *combat* and *conflict* in the sense of striving for the superiority; but they differ both in the manner and spirit of the action.

A *conflict* has more of violence in it than a *combat*, and a *combat* than a *contest*.

A *conflict* and *combat*, in the proper sense, are always attended with a personal attack; *contest* consists mostly of a striving for some common object.

A *conflict* is mostly sanguinary and desperate, it arises from the undisciplined operations of the bad passions, animosity, and brutal rage; it seldom ends in any thing but destruction: a *combat* is often a matter of art and a trial of skill; it may be obstinate and lasting, though not arising from any personal resentment, and mostly terminates with the triumph of one party and the defeat of the other: a *contest* is interested and personal; it may often give rise to angry and even malignant sentiments, but is not necessarily associated with any bad passion; it ends in the advancement of one to the injury of the other.

The lion, the tiger, and other beasts of the forest, have dreadful *conflicts* whenever they meet; which seldom terminate but in the death of one if not both of the antagonists: it would be well if the use of the word were confined to the irrational part of the creation; but there have been wars and party-broils among men, which have occasioned *conflicts* the most horrible and destructive that can be conceived;

It is my father's face,
Whom in this *conflict*, I unawares have kill'd.
SHAKSPEARE.

That *combats* have been mere trials of skill is evinced by the *combats* in the ancient games of the Greeks and Romans, as also in the justs and tournaments of later date; but in all applications of the term, it implies a set *engagement* between two or more particular individuals;

Elsewhere he saw, where Troilus defied
Achilles, an unequal *combat* tried.—DRYDEN.

Contests are as various as the pursuits and wishes of men: whatever is an object of desire for two parties becomes the ground of a *contest;* ambition, interest, and party-zeal are always busy in furnishing men with objects for a *contest;* on the same ground, the attainment of victory in a battle, or of any subordinate point during an engagement, become the object of *contest;* 'When the ships grappled together, and the *contest* became more steady and furious, the example of the King and so many gallant nobles, who accompanied him, animated to such a degree the seamen and soldiers, that they maintained every where a superiority.'—HUME.

In a figurative sense these terms are applied to the movements of the mind, the elements or whatever seems to oppose itself to another thing, in which sense they preserve the same analogy: violent passions have their *conflicts;* ordinary desires their *combats;* motives their *contests:* it is the poet's part to describe the *conflicts* between pride and passion, rage and despair, in the breast of the disappointed lover; 'Happy is the man who in the *conflict* of desire between God and the world, can oppose not only argument to argument but pleasure to pleasure.'—BLAIR. Reason will seldom come off victorious in its *combat* with ambition, avarice, a love of pleasure, or any predominant desire, unless aided by religion; 'The noble *combat* that, 'twixt joy and sorrow, was fought in Paulina! She had one eye declined for the loss of her husband, another elevated that the oracle was fulfilled.'—SHAKSPEARE. Where there is a *contest* between the desire of following one's will and a sense of propriety, the voice of a prudent friend may be heard and heeded; 'Soon afterward the death of the king furnished a general subject for poetical *contest*.'—JOHNSON.

TO CONFRONT, FACE.

Confront, from the Latin *frons* a forehead, implies to set *face* to *face;* and *face*, from the noun *face*, signifies to set the *face* towards any object. The former of these terms is always employed for two or more persons with regard to each other; the latter for a single individual with regard to objects in general.

Witnesses are *confronted;* a person *faces* danger, or *faces* an enemy. when people give contrary evidence it is sometimes necessary, in extra-judicial matters, to *confront* them, in order to arrive at the truth;

Whereto serves mercy,
But to *confront* the visage of offence?
SHAKSPEARE.

The best test which a man can give of his courage, is to evince his readiness for *facing* his enemy whenever the occasion requires;

The rev'rend charioteer directs the course,
And strains his aged arm to lash the horse:
Hector they *face;* unknowing how to fear,
Fierce he drove on.—POPE.

TO BEAT, STRIKE, HIT.

Beat, in French *battre*, Latin *battuo*, comes from the Hebrew *habat* to beat; *Strike*, in Saxon *strican*, Danish *stricker*, &c. from the Latin *strictum*, participle of *stringo* to brush or sweep along, signifies literally to pass one thing along the surface of another; *hit*, in Latin *ictus*, participle of *ico*, comes from the Hebrew *necat* to strike.

To *beat* is to redouble blows; to *strike* is to give one single blow; but the bare touching in consequence of an effort constitutes *hitting*. We never beat but with design, nor *hit* without an aim, but we may strike by accident. It is the part of the strong to *beat;* of the most vehement to *strike;* of the most sure sighted to *hit*.

Notwithstanding the declamations of philosophers as they are pleased to style themselves, the practice of *beating* cannot altogether be discarded from the military or scholastick discipline. The master who *strikes* his pupil hastily is oftener impelled by the force of passion than of conviction. *Hitting* is the object and delight of the marksman; it is the utmost exertion of his skill to *hit* the exact point at which he aims. In an extended application of these terms, *beating* is, for the most part, an act of passion, either from anger or sorrow;

Young Sylvia *beats* her breast, and cries aloud
For succour from the clownish neighbourhood,
DRYDEN.

Striking is an act of decision, as to *strike* a blow;

Send thy arrows forth
Strike, strike these tyrants and avenge my tears.
CUMBERLAND.

Hitting is an act of design, as to *hit* a mark; 'No man is thought to become vicious by sacrificing the life of an animal to the pleasure of *hitting* a mark. It is howevercertain that by this act more happiness is destroyed than produced.'—HAWKESWORTH.

Blow probably derives the meaning in which it is here taken from the action of the wind, which it resembles when it is violent; *stroke*, from the word *strike*, denotes the act of striking.

Blow is used abstractedly to denote the effect of violence; *stroke* is employed relatively to the person producing that effect A *blow* may be received by the carelessness of the receiver, or by a pure accident; 'The advance of the human mind towards any object of laudable pursuit may be compared to the progress of a body driven by a *blow*.'—JOHNSON. *Strokes* are dealt out according to the design of the giver; 'Penetrated to the heart with the recollection of his behaviour, and the unmerited pardon he had met with, Thrasyppus was proceeding to execute vengeance on himself, by rushing on his sword, when Pisistratus again interposed, and seizing his hand, stopped the *stroke.*'—Cumberland. Children are always in the way of getting *blows* in the course of their play; and of receiving *strokes* by way of chastisement.

A *blow* may be given with the hand, or with any flat substance; a *stroke* is rather a long drawn *blow* given with a long instrument, like a stick. *Blows* may be given with the flat part of a sword, and *strokes* with a stick.

Blow is seldom used but in the proper sense; *stroke* sometimes figuratively, as a *stroke* of death, or a stroke of fortune: 'This declaration was a *stroke* which Evander had neither skill to elude, nor force to resist.' —Hawkesworth.

TO BEAT, DEFEAT, OVERPOWER, ROUT, OVERTHROW.

Beat is here figuratively employed in the sense of the former section; *defeat*, from the French *defaire*, implies to undo; *overpower*, to have the power over any one; *rout*, from the French *mettre en deroute* is to turn from one's route, and *overthrow* to throw over or upside down.

Beat respects personal contests between individuals or parties; *defeat*, *rout*, *overpower*, and *overthrow*, are employed mostly for contests between numbers. A general is *beaten* in important engagements: he is *defeated* and may be *routed* in partial attacks; he is *overpowered* by numbers, and *overthrown* in set engagements. The English pride themselves on *beating* their enemies by land as well as by sea, whenever they come to fair engagements, but the English are sometimes *defeated* when they make too desperate attempts, and sometimes they are in danger of being *overpowered:* they have scarcely ever been *routed* or *overthrown*.

To *beat* is an indefinite term expressive of no particular degree: the being *beaten* may be attended with greater or less damage. To be *defeated* is a specifick disadvantage, it is a failure in a particular object of more or less importance. To be *overpowered* is a positive loss; it is a loss of the power of acting which may be of longer or shorter duration: to be *routed* is a temporary disadvantage; a *rout* alters the *route* or course of proceeding, but does not disable: to be *overthrown* is the greatest of all mischiefs, and is applicable only to great armies and great concerns, an *overthrow* commonly decides the contest;

Beat is a term which reflects more or less dishonour on the general or the army or on both;

Turnus, I know you think me not your friend,
Nor will I much with your belief contend;
I beg your greatness not to give the law
In other realms, but *beaten* to withdraw.
Dryden.

Defeat is an indifferent term; the best generals may sometimes be *defeated* by circumstances which are above human control; 'Satan frequently confesses the omnipotence of the Supreme Being, that being the perfection he was forced to allow him, and the only consideration which could support his pride under the shame of his *defeat.*'—Addison. *Overpowering* is coupled with no particular honour to the winner, nor disgrace to the loser; superiour power is oftener the result of good fortune than of skill. The bravest and finest troops may be *overpowered* in cases which exceed human power; 'The veterans who defended the walls, were soon *overpowered* by numbers.'—Robertson. A *rout* is always disgraceful, particularly to the army; it always arises from want of firmness; 'The *rout* (at the battle of Pavia) now became universal, and resistance ceased in almost every part but where the king was in person.'—Robertson. An *overthrow* is fatal rather than dishonourable; it excites pity rather than contempt; 'Milton's subject is rebellion against the Supreme Being; raised by the highest order of created beings; the *overthrow* of their host is the punishment of their crime.'—Johnson.

TO DEFEAT, FOIL, DISAPPOINT, FRUSTRATE.

To *defeat* has the same meaning as given under the article *To beat; foil* may probably come from *fail*, and the Latin *fallo* to deceive, signifying to make to fail; *frustrate*, in Latin *frustratus*, from *frustra* in vain, signifies to make vain; *disappoint*, from the privative *dis* and the verb *appoint*, signifies literally to do away what has been appointed.

Defeat and *foil* are both applied to matters of enterprise; but that may be *defeated* which is only planned, and that is *foiled* which is in the act of being executed. What is rejected is *defeated:* what is aimed at or purposed is *frustrated:* what is calculated on is *disappointed*. The best concerted schemes may sometimes be easily *defeated:* where art is employed against simplicity the latter may be easily *foiled:* when we aim at what is above our reach, we must be *frustrated* in our endeavours: when our expectations are extravagant, it seems to follow of course, that they will be *disappointed*.

Design or accident may tend to *defeat*, design only to *foil*, accident only to *frustrate* or *disappoint*. The superiour force of the enemy, or a combination of untoward events which are above the control of the commander, will serve to *defeat* the best concerted plans of the best generals; 'The very purposes of wantonness are *defeated* by a carriage which has so much boldness.' —Steele. Men of upright minds can seldom *foil* the deep laid schemes of knaves; 'The devil haunts those most where he hath greatest hopes of success; and is too eager and intent upon mischief to employ his time and temptations where he hath been so often *foiled.*'—Tillotson. When we see that the perversity of men is liable to *frustrate* the kind intentions of others in their behalf, it is wiser to leave them to their folly;

Let all the Tuscans, all th' Arcadians join,
Nor these nor those shall *frustrate* my design.
Dryden.

The cross accidents of human life are a fruitful source of *disappointments* to those who suffer themselves to be affected by them; 'It seems rational to hope that minds qualified for great attainments should first endeavour their own benefit. But this expectation, however plausible, has been very frequently *disappointed*. —Johnson.

TO BAFFLE, DEFEAT, DISCONCERT, CONFOUND.

Baffle, in French *baffler*, from *buffle* an ox, signifies to lead by the nose as an ox, that is, to amuse or disappoint; *defeat*, in French *défait*, participle of *défaire*, is compounded of the privative *de* and *faire* to do, signifying to undo; *disconcert* is compounded of the privative *dis* and *concert*, signifying to throw out of concert or harmony, to put into disorder; *confound*, in French *confondre*, is compounded of *con* and *fondre* to melt or mix together in general disorder.

When applied to the derangement of the mind or rational faculties, *baffle* and *defeat* respect the powers of argument, *disconcert* and *confound* the thoughts and feelings: *baffle* expresses less than *defeat; disconcert* less than *confound;* a person is *baffled* in argument who is for the time discomposed and silenced by the superiour address of his opponent: he is *defeated* in argument if his opponent has altogether the advantage of him in strength of reasoning and justness of sentiment: a person is *disconcerted* who loses his presence of mind for a moment, or has his feelings any way discomposed; he is *confounded* when the powers of thought and consciousness become torpid or vanish.

A superiour command of language or a particular degree of effrontery will frequently enable one person to *baffle* another who is advocating the cause of truth; 'When the mind has brought itself to close thinking, it may go on roundly. Every abstruse problem, every intricate question will not *baffle*, discourage, or break it.'—Locke. Ignorance of the subject, or a want of ability, may occasion a man to be *defeated* by his adversary, even when he is supporting a good cause; 'He that could withstand conscience is frighted at infamy, and shame prevails when reason is *defeated.*'—Johnson. Assurance is requisite to prevent any one from being *disconcerted* who is suddenly detected in any disgraceful proceeding; 'She looked in the glass while she was speaking to me, and without any confusion adjusted her tucker: she seemed rather pleased than *disconcerted* at being regarded with earnestness.'—Hawkesworth. Hardened effrontery sometimes keeps the daring villain from being *confounded* by any events, however awful; 'I could not help inquiring of the clerks if they knew this lady, and was greatly *founded* when they told me with an air of secrecy that she was my cousin's mistress.'—HAWKESWORTH.

When applied to the derangement of plans, *baffle* expresses less than *defeat; defeat* less than *confound;* and *disconcert* less than all. Obstinacy, perseverance, skill, or art, *baffles;* force or violence *defeats;* awkward circumstances *disconcert;* the visitation of God *confounds*. When wicked men strive to obtain their ends, it is a happy thing when their adversaries have sufficient skill and address to *baffle* all their arts, and sufficient power to *defeat* all their projects;

Now shepherds! To your helpless charge be kind,
Baffle the raging year, and fill their pens
With food at will.—THOMSON.

'He finds himself naturally to dread a superiour Being, that can *defeat* all his designs and disappoint all his hopes.'—TILLOTSON. Sometimes when our best endeavours fail in our own behalf, the devices of men are *confounded* by the interposition of heaven;

So spake the Son of God; and Satan stood
A while as mute, *confounded* what to say.
MILTON.

It frequently happens even in the common transactions of life that the best schemes are *disconcerted* by the trivial casualties of wind and weather; 'The King (William) informed of these dangerous discontents hastened over to England; and by his presence, and the vigorous measures which he pursued, *disconcerted* all the schemes of the conspirators.'—HUME. The obstinacy of a disorder may *baffle* the skill of the physician; the imprudence of the patient may *defeat* the object of his prescriptions: the unexpected arrival of a superiour may *disconcert* the unauthorized plan of those who are subordinate: the miraculous destruction of his army *confounded* the project of the King of Assyria.

TO CONQUER, VANQUISH, SUBDUE, OVERCOME, SURMOUNT.

Conquer, in French *conquerir*, Latin *conquiro*, compounded of *con* and *quæro*, signifies to seek or try to gain an object; *vanquish*, in French *vaincre*, Latin *vinco*, Greek (*per metathesin*) νικάω, comes from the Hebrew נצח to destroy; *subdue*, from the Latin *subdo*, signifies to give or put under; *overcome*, compounded of *over* and *come*, signifies to come over or get the mastery over one: *surmount*, in French *surmonter*, compounded of *sur* over and *monter* to mount, signifies to rise above any one.

Persons or things are *conquered* or *subdued:* persons only are *vanquished*. An enemy or a country is *conquered;* a foe is *vanquished;* people are *subdued*.

We *conquer* an enemy or a country by whatever means we gain the mastery over him or it. The idea of something gained is most predominant: 'He (Ethelwolf) began his reign with making a partition of his dominions, and delivering over to his eldest son Athelstan, the new *conquered* provinces of Essex, Kent, and Sussex.'—HUME. We *vanquish* him, when by force we make him yield; 'A few troops of the *vanquished*, had still the courage to turn upon their pursuers.'—HUME. We *subdue* him by whatever means we check in him the spirit of resistance; 'The Danes, surprised to see an army of English, whom they considered as totally *subdued*, and still more astonished to hear that Alfred was at their head, made but a faint resistance.'—HUME. A Christian tries to *conquer* his enemies by kindness and generosity; a warriour tries to *vanquish* them in the field; a prudent monarch tries to *subdue* his rebellious subjects by a due mixture of clemency and rigour.

One may be *vanquished* in a single battle; one is *subdued* only by the most violent and persevering measures. William the First *conquered* England by *vanquishing* his rival Harold; after which he completely *subdued* the English.

Alexander having *vanquished* all the enemies that opposed him, and *subdued* all the nations with whom he warred, fancied that he had *conquered* the whole world, and is said to have wept at the idea that there were no more worlds to *conquer*.

In an extended and moral application these terms are nearly allied to *overcome* and *surmount*. That is *conquered* and *subdued* which is in the mind; that is *overcome* and *surmounted* which is either internal or external. We *conquer* and *overcome* what makes no great resistance; we *subdue* and *surmount* what is violent and strong in its opposition; dislikes, attachments, and feelings in general, either for or against, are *conquered;* unruly and tumultuous passions are to be *subdued;* a man *conquers* himself;

Real glory
Springs from the silent *conquest* of ourselves.
THOMSON.

He *subdues* his spirit or his passions; 'Socrates and Marcus Aurelius are instances of men, who, by the strength of philosophy having *subdued* their passions, are celebrated for good husbands.'—SPECTATOR.

One *conquers* by ordinary means and efforts; one *subdues* by extraordinary means. Antipathies when cherished in early life are not easily *conquered* in riper years: nothing but a prevailing sense of religion, and a perpetual fear of God, can ever *subdue* the rebellious wills and propensities.

It requires for the most part determination and force to *overcome;* patience and perseverance to *surmount*. Prejudices and prepossessions are *overcome;* obstacles and difficulties are *surmounted;* 'Actuated by some high passion, a man conceives great designs, and *surmounts* all difficulties in the execution.'—BLAIR. It too frequently happens that those who are eager to *overcome* their prejudices, in order to dispose themselves for the reception of new opinions, fall into greater errours than those they have abandoned. Nothing truly great has ever been effected where great difficulties have not been encountered: it is the characterístick of genius to *surmount* every difficulty: Alexander conceived that he could *overcome* nature herself, and Hannibal succeeded in this very point: there were scarcely any obstacles which she opposed to him that he did not *surmount* by prowess and perseverance.

Whoever aims at Christian perfection must strive with God's assistance to *conquer* avarice, pride, and every inordinate propensity; to *subdue* wrath, anger, lust, and every carnal appetite; to *overcome* temptations, and to *surmount* trials and impediments which obstruct his course.

To *conquer* and *overcome* may sometimes be indifferently applied to the same objects; but the former has always a reference to the thing gained, the latter to the resistance which is opposed, hence we talk of *conquering* a prejudice as far as we bring it under the power of the understanding; we *overcome* it as far as we successfully oppose its influence: this illustration will serve to show the propriety of using these words distinctly in other cases where they cannot be used in differently;

Equal success hath set these champions high,
And both resolv'd to *conquer* or to die.—WALLER.

The patient mind by yielding *overcomes*.—PHILIPS.

To *vanquish* in the moral application bears the same meaning as in the proper application, signifying to *overcome* in a struggle or combat; thus a person may be said to be *vanquished* by any ruling passion which gets the better of his conscience; 'There are two parts in our nature. The inferiour part is generally much stronger, and has always the start of reason; which, if it were not aided by religion, would almost universally be *vanquished*.'—BERKELEY.

TO OVERBEAR, BEAR DOWN, OVERPOWER, OVERWHELM, SUBDUE.

To *overbear* is to *bear* one's self *over* another, that is, to make another *bear* one's weight;

Crowding on the last the first impel;
Till *overborne* with weight the Cyprians fell.
DRYDEN.

To *bear down* is literally to bring down by *bearing* upon; 'The residue were so disordered as they could not conveniently fight or fly, and not only justled and *bore down* one another, but in their confused tumbling back, brake a part of the avant-guard.'—HAYWARD. To *overpower* is to get the *power* over an object; 'After the death of Crassus, Pompey found himself outwitted by Cæsar; he broke with him, *overpowered* him in the senate, and caused many unjust decrees to pass against him.'—DRYDEN. To *overwhelm*, from *whelm* or *wheel*, signifies to turn one quite round as well as over.

What age is this, where honest men,
Plac'd at the helm,
A sea of some foul mouth or pen
Shall *overwhelm*.—Jonson.

To *subdue* (*v. To conquer*) is literally to bring or put underneath;

Nothing could have *subdued* nature
To such a lowness, but his unkind daughters.
Shakspeare.

A man *overbears* by carrying himself higher than others, and putting to silence those who might claim an equality with him; an *overbearing* demeanour is most conspicuous in narrow circles where an individual, from certain casual advantages, affects a superiority over the members of the same community. To *bear down* is an act of greater violence: one *bears down* opposition; it is properly the opposing force to force, until one side yields: there may be occasions in which *bearing down* is fully justifiable and laudable. Mr. Pitt was often compelled to *bear down* a factious party which threatened to overturn the government. *Overpower*, as the term implies, belongs to the exercise of power which may be either physical or moral: one may be *overpowered* by another, who in a struggle gets him into his power; or one may be *overpowered* in an argument, when the argument of one's antagonist is such as to bring one to silence. One is *overborne* or *borne down* by the exertion of individuals; one is *overpowered* by the active efforts of individuals, or by the force of circumstances; one is *overwhelmed* by circumstances or things only: one is *overborne* by another of superiour influence; one is *borne down* by the force of his attack; one is *overpowered* by numbers, by entreaties, by looks, and the like; one is *overwhelmed* by the torrent of words, or the impetuosity of the attack. In the moral or extended application *overbear* and *bear down* both imply force or violence, but the latter even more than the former. One passion may be said to *overbear* another, or to *overbear* reason; 'The duty of fear, like that of other passions, is not to *overbear* reason, but to assist it.'—Johnson. Whatever *bears down* carries all before it;

Contention like a horse
Full of high feeding, madly hath broken loose,
And *bears down* all before him.—Shakspeare.

Overpower and *overwhelm* denote a partial superiority; *subdue* denotes that which is permanent and positive: we may *overpower* or *overwhelm* for a time, or to a certain degree; but to *subdue* is to get an entire and lasting superiority. *Overpower* and *overwhelm* are said of what passes between persons nearly on a level; but *subdue* is said of those who are, or may be, reduced to a low state of inferiority: individuals or armies are *overpowered* or *overwhelmed;* individuals or nations are *subdued:* we may be *overpowered* in one engagement, and *overpower* our opponent in another; we may be *overwhelmed* by the suddenness and impetuosity of the attack, yet we may recover ourselves so as to renew the attack; but when we are *subdued* all power of resistance is gone.

To *overpower*, *overwhelm*, and *subdue*, are applied either to the moral feelings or to the external relations of things; but the two former are the effects of external circumstances; the latter follows from the exercise of the reasoning powers: the tender feelings are *overpowered*, or the senses may be *overpowered;* 'All colours that are more luminous (than green) *overpower* and dissipate the animal spirits which are employed in sight.'—Addison. The mind is *overwhelmed* with shame, horrour, and other painful feelings; 'How trifling an apprehension is the shame of being laughed at by fools, when compared with that everlasting shame and astonishment which shall *overwhelm* the sinner when he shall appear before the tribunal of Christ.'—Rogers.

Such implements of mischief as shall dash
To pieces, and *overwhelm* whatever stands
Adverse.—Milton.

The unruly passions are *subdued* by the force of religious contemplation, or the fortitude is *subdued* by pain;

For what avails
Valour or strength, though matchless, quell'd with pain,
Which all *subdues?*—Milton.

A person may be so *overpowered*, on seeing a dying friend, as to be unable to speak; he may be so *overwhelmed* with grief, upon the death of a near and dear relative, as to be unable to attend to his ordinary avocations; the angry passions have been so completely *subdued* by the influence of religion on the heart, that instances have been known of the most irascible tempers being converted into the most mild and forbearing.

TO SUBJECT, SUBJUGATE, SUBDUE.

Subdue, *v. To conquer*.

To *subject*, signifying to make *subject*, is here the generick term: to *subjugate*, from *jugum* a yoke, signifying to bring under a yoke: and *subdue*, signifying as in the preceding article to bring under, are specifick terms. We may *subject* either individuals or nations; but we *subjugate* only nations. We *subject* ourselves to reproof, to inconvenience, or to the influence of our passions;

Think not, young warriours, your diminish'd name
Shall lose of lustre, by *subjecting* rage
To the cool dictates of experienced age.—Dryden.

Where there is no awe, there will be no *subjection*.
South.

One nation *subjugates* another: *subjugate* and *subdue* are both employed with regard to nations that are compelled to submit to the conqueror: but *subjugate* expresses even more than *subdue*, for it implies to bring into a state of permanent submission; whereas to *subdue* may be only a nominal and temporary subjection. Cæsar *subjugated* the Gauls, for he made them subjects to the Roman empire;

O fav'rite virgin, that hast warm'd the breast
Whose sov'reign dictates *subjugate* the east.
Prior.

Alexander *subdued* the Indian nations, who revolted after his departure;

Thy son (nor is th' appointed season far,)
In Italy shall wage successful war,
Till, after every foe *subdu'd*, the sun
Thrice through the signs his annual race shall run.
Dryden.

INVINCIBLE, UNCONQUERABLE, INSUPERABLE, INSURMOUNTABLE.

Invincible signifies not to be vanquished (*v. To conquer*): *unconquerable*, not to be conquered: *insuperable*, not to be overcome: *insurmountable*, not to be surmounted. Persons or things are in the strict sense *invincible* which can withstand all force; but as in this sense nothing created can be termed *invincible*, the term is employed to express strongly whatever can withstand human force in general: on this ground the Spaniards termed their Armada *invincible;* 'The Americans believed at first, that while cherished by the parental beams of the sun, the Spaniards were *invincible*.'—Robertson. The qualities of the mind are termed *unconquerable* when they are not to be gained over or brought under the control of one's own reason, or the judgement of another: hence obstinacy is with propriety denominated *unconquerable* which will yield to no foreign influence; 'The mind of an ungrateful person is *unconquerable* by that which conquers all things else, even by love itself.'—South. The particular disposition of the mind or turn of thinking is termed *insuperable*, inasmuch as it baffles our resolution or wishes to have it altered: an aversion is *insuperable* which no reasoning or endeavour on our own part can overcome; 'To this literary word (metaphysicks) I have an *insuperable* aversion.'—Beattie. Things are denominated *insurmountable*, inasmuch as they baffle one's skill or efforts to get over them, or put them out of one's way: an obstacle is *insurmountable* which in the nature of things is irremoveable; 'It is a melancholy reflection, that while one is plagued with acquaintance at the corner of every street, real friends should be separated from each other by *insurmountable* bars.'—Gibbon. Some people have an *insuperable* antipathy to certain animals; some persons are of so modest and timid a character, that the necessity of addressing strangers is with them an *insuperable* objection to using any endeavours for their own advance ment; the difficulties which Columbus had to encounter in his discovery of the New World, would have appeared *insurmountable* to any mind less determined and persevering.

SUBJECT, SUBORDINATE, INFERIOUR, SUBSERVIENT.

Subject, in Latin *subjectus*, participle of *subjicio* or *sub* and *jacio* to throw under, signifies thrown and cast under; *subordinate*, compounded of *sub* and *order*, signifies to be in an order that is under others; *inferiour*, in Latin *inferior*, comparative of *inferus* low, which probably comes from *infero* to cast into, because we are cast into places that are low; *subservient*, compounded of *sub* and *servio*, signifies serving under something else.

These terms may either express the relation of persons to persons, or of things to persons and things. *Subject* in the first case respects the exercise of power; *subordinate* is said of the station and office; *inferiour*, either of a man's outward circumstances or of his merits and qualifications; *subservient*, of one's relative services to another, but mostly in a bad sense. According to the law of nature, a child should be *subject* to his parents; according to the law of God and man he must be *subject* to his prince; 'Esau was never *subject* to Jacob, but founded a distinct people, and government, and was himself prince over them.'—LOCKE. The good order of society cannot be rightly maintained unless there be some to act in a *subordinate* capacity; 'Whether dark presages of the night proceed from any latent power of the soul, during her abstraction, or from any operation of *subordinate* spirits, has been a dispute.'—ADDISON. Men of *inferiour* talent have a part to act which, in the aggregate, is of no less importance than that which is sustained by men of the highest endowments; 'A great person gets more by obliging his *inferiour* than by disdaining him.'—SOUTH. Men of no principle or character will be most *subservient* to the base purposes of those who pay them best; 'Wicked spirits may, by their cunning, carry farther in a seeming confederacy or *subserviency* to the designs of a good angel.'—DRYDEN. It is the part of the prince to protect the *subject*, and of the *subject* to love and honour the prince; it is the part of the exalted to treat the *subordinate* with indulgence; and of the latter to show respect to those under whom they are placed; it is the part of the superiour to instruct, assist, and encourage the *inferiour*; it is the part of the latter to be willing to learn, ready to obey, and prompt to execute. It is not necessary for any one to act the degrading part of being *subservient* to another.

In the second instance *subject* preserves the same sense as before, particularly when it expresses the relation of things to persons; *subordinate* designates the degree of relative importance between things: *inferiour* designates every circumstance which can render things comparatively higher or lower; *subservient* designates the relative utility of things under certain circumstances, but seldom in the bad sense. All creatures are *subject* to man; 'Contemplate the world as *subject* to the Divine dominion.'—BLAIR. Matters of *subordinate* consideration ought to be entirely set out of the question, when any grand object is to be obtained; 'The idea of pain in its highest degree is much stronger than the highest degree of pleasure, and preserves the same superiority through all the *subordinate* gradations.'—BURKE. Things of *inferiour* value must necessarily sell for an *inferiour* price; 'I can myself remember the time when in respect of musick our reigning taste was in many degrees *inferiour* to the French.'—SHAFTESBURY. There is nothing so insignificant but it may be made *subservient* to some purpose; 'Though a writer may be wrong himself, he may chance to make his errours *subservient* to the cause of truth.'—BURKE. The word *subject* when expressing the relation of things to things has the meaning of *liable*, as in the following article.

SUBJECT, LIABLE, EXPOSED, OBNOXIOUS.

Subject is here considered as expressing the relation of things to things, in distinction from its signification in the preceding article; *liable*, compounded of *lie* and *able*, signifies ready to lie near or lie under; *exposed*, in Latin *expositus*, participle of *expono*, compounded of *ex* and *pono*, signifies set out, set within the view or reach; *obnoxious*, in Latin *obnoxius*, compounded of *ob* and *noxia* mischief, signifies in the way of mischief.

All these terms are applied to those circumstances in human life by which we are affected independently of our own choice. Direct necessity is included in the term *subject;* whatever we are obliged to suffer, that we are subject to; we may apply remedies to remove the evil, but often in vain; 'The devout man aspires after some principles of more perfect felicity, which shall not be *subject* to change or decay.'—BLAIR. *Liable* conveys more the idea of casualties; we may suffer that which we are *liable* to, but we may also escape the evil if we are careful; 'The sinner is not only *liable* to that disappointment of success which so often frustrates all the designs of men, but *liable* to a disappointment still more cruel, of being successful and miserable at once.'—BLAIR. *Exposed* conveys the idea of a passive state into which we may be brought, either through our own means or through the instrumentality of others; we are *exposed* to that which we are not in a condition to keep off from ourselves; it is frequently not in our power to guard against the evil;

> On the bare earth *expos'd* he lies,
> With not a friend to close his eyes.—DRYDEN.

Obnoxious conveys the idea of a state into which we have altogether brought ourselves; we may avoid bringing ourselves into the state, but we cannot avoid the consequences which will ensue from being thus involved;

> And much he blames the softness of his mind,
> *Obnoxious* to the charms of womankind.—DRYDEN.

We are *subject* to disease, or *subject* to death; this is the irrevocable law of our nature: tender people are *liable* to catch cold; all persons are *liable* to make mistakes: a person is *exposed* to insults who provokes the anger of a low-bred man: a minister sometimes renders himself *obnoxious* to the people, that is, puts himself in the way of their animosity.

To *subject* and *expose*, as verbs, are taken in the same sense: a person *subjects* himself to impertinent freedoms by descending to indecent familiarities with his inferiours; 'If the vessels yield, it *subjects* the person to all the inconveniences of an erroneous circulation.'—ARBUTHNOT. He *exposes* himself to the derision of his equals by an affectation of superiority;

> Who here
> Will envy whom the highest place *exposes*
> Foremost to stand against the Thunderer's aim.
> MILTON

OBNOXIOUS, OFFENSIVE.

Obnoxious, from the intensive syllable *ob* and *noxious*, signifies exceedingly *noxious* and causing offence, or else liable to offence from others by reason of its *noxiousness;* *offensive* signifies simply liable to give offence. *Obnoxious* is, therefore, a much more comprehensive term than *offensive;* for an *obnoxious* man both suffers from others and causes sufferings to others: an *obnoxious* man is one whom others seek to exclude; an *offensive* man may possibly be endured; gross vices, or particularly odious qualities, make a man *obnoxious;* 'I must have leave to be grateful to any one who serves me, let him be ever so *obnoxious* to any party.'—POPE. Rude manners and perverse tempers make men *offensive;* 'The understanding is often drawn by the will and the affections from fixing its contemplation on an *offensive* truth.'—SOUTH. A man is *obnoxious* to many, and *offensive* to individuals: a man of loose Jacobinical principles will be *obnoxious* to a society of loyalists; a child may make himself *offensive* to his friends.

TO HUMBLE, HUMILIATE, DEGRADE.

Humble and *humiliate* signify to make *humble* or bring low; *degrade* has the same signification as given under *Abase*.

Humble is commonly used as the act either of persons or things; a person may *humble* himself or he may be *humbled:* *humiliate* is employed to characterize things; a thing is *humiliating* or an *humiliation*. No man *humbles* himself by the acknowledgement of a fault;

Deep horrour seizes ev'ry human breast,
Their pride is *humbled*, and their fear confess'd.
DRYDEN.

It is a great *humiliation* for a person to be dependent on another for a living when he has it in his power to obtain it for himself; 'A long habit of *humiliation* does not seem a very good preparative to manly and vigorous sentiments.'—BURKE. To *humble* is to bring down to the ground; it supposes a certain eminence, either created by the mind, or really existing in the outward circumstances: to *degrade* is to let down lower; it supposes steps for ascending or descending. He who is most elevated in his own esteem may be most *humbled;* misfortunes may *humble* the proudest conqueror;

The mistress of the world, the seat of empire,
The nurse of heroes, the delight of gods,
That *humbled* the proud tyrants of the earth.
ADDISON.

He who is most elevated in the esteem of others, may be the most *degraded;* envy is ever on the alert to *degrade;* 'Who but a tyrant (a name expressive of every thing which can vitiate and *degrade* human nature,) could think of seizing on the property of men unaccused and unheard ?'—BURKE. A lesson in the school of adversity is *humbling* to one who has known nothing but prosperity: terms of peace are *humiliating:* low vices are peculiarly *degrading* to a man of rank.

HUMBLE, LOWLY, LOW.

Humble (*v. Humble, modest*) is here compared with the other terms as it respects both persons and things. A person is said to be *humble* on account of the state of his mind; he is said to be *lowly* and *low* either on account of his mind or his outward circumstances. An *humble* person is so in his principles and in his conduct; a *lowly* person is so in the tone of his feelings, or in his station and walk of life; a *low* person is so either in his sentiments, in his actions, or in his rank and condition.

Humility should form a part of the character, as it is opposed to arrogance and assumption; it is most consistent with the fallibility of our nature;

Sleep is a god too proud to wait in palaces,
And yet so *humble* too as not to scorn
The meanest country cottages.—COWLEY.

Lowliness should form a part of our temper, as it is opposed to an aspiring and lofty mind; it is most consistent with the temper of our Saviour, who was meek and *lowly* of mind;

Where purple violets lurk,
With all the *lowly* children of the shade.
THOMSON.

The *humble* and *lowly* are always taken in a good sense; but the *low* either in a bad or an indifferent sense. A *lowly* man, whether as it respects his mind or his condition, is so without any moral debasement; but a man who is *low* in his condition is likewise conceived to be *low* in his habits and his sentiments, which is being near akin to the vicious. The same distinction is preserved in applying these terms to inanimate or spiritual objects. An *humble* roof, an *humble* office, an *humble* station, are associated with the highest moral worth;

The example of the heavenly lark,
Thy fellow poet, Cowley, mark!
Above the skies let thy proud musick sound,
Thy *humble* nest build upon the ground.
COWLEY.

A *low* office, a *low* situation, a *low* birth, seem to exclude the idea of worth;

To be worst,
The *lowest*, most dejected thing of fortune
Stands still in esperance.—SHAKSPEARE.

HUMBLE, MODEST, SUBMISSIVE.

Humble, in Latin *humilis* low, comes from *humus* the ground, which is the lowest position; *modest*, in Latin *modestus*, from *modus* a measure, signifies keeping a measure; *submissive*, in Latin *submissus*, participle of *submitto*, signifies put under.

These terms designate a temper of mind, the reverse of self-conceit or pride. The *humble* is so with regard to ourselves or others: *modesty* is that which respects ourselves only: *submissiveness* that which respects others. A man is *humble* from a sense of his comparative inferiority to others in point of station and outward circumstances; or he is *humble* from a sense of his imperfections, and a consciousness of not being what he ought to be; 'In God's holy house, I prostrate myself in the *humblest* and decentest way of genuflection I can imagine.'—HOWE. A man is *modest* in as much as he sets but little value on his qualifications acquirements, and endowments;

Of boasting more than of a tomb afraid
A soldier should be *modest* as a maid.—YOUNG.

Humility is a painful sentiment; for when it respects others it is coupled with fear, when it respects our own unworthiness it is coupled with sorrow: *modesty* is a peaceful sentiment; it serves to keep the whole mind in due bounds.

When *humility* and *modesty* show themselves in the outward conduct, the former bows itself down, the latter shrinks: an *humble* man gives freely to others from a sense of their desert: a *modest* man demands nothing for himself, from an unconsciousness of desert in himself; 'Sedition itself is *modest* in the dawn, and only toleration may be petitioned, where nothing less than empire is designed.'—SOUTH.

Between *humble* and *submissive* there is this prominent feature of distinction, that the former marks a temper of mind, the latter a mode of action: the former is therefore often the cause of the latter, but not so always: we may be *submissive* because we are *humble:* but we may likewise be *submissive* from fear, from interested motives, from necessity, from duty, and the like:

And potent Rajahs, who themselves preside
O'er realms of wide extent! But here *submissive*
Their homage pay; alternate kings and slaves!
SOMERVILLE.

And on the other hand, we may be *humble* without being *submissive*, when we are not brought into connexion with others. A man is *humble* in his closet when he takes a review of his sinfulness: he is *submissive* to a master whose displeasure he dreads.

As *humility* may display itself in the outward conduct, it approaches still nearer to *submissive* in application: hence we say an *humble* air, and a *submissive* air; the former to denote a man's sense of his own comparative littleness, the latter to indicate his readiness to submit to the will of another: a man therefore carries his *humble* air about with him to all his superiours, nay, indeed, to the world at large; but he puts on his *submissive* air only to the individual who has the power of controlling him. Upon the same principle, if I *humbly* ask a person's pardon, or *humbly* solicit any favour, I mean to express a sense of my own unworthiness, compared with the individual addressed: but when a counsellor *submissively* or with *submission* addresses a judge on the bench, it implies his willingness to *submit* to the decision of the bench: or if a person *submissively* yields to the wishes of another, it is done with an air that bespeaks his readiness to conform his actions to a prescribed rule;

She should be *humble*, who would please;
And she must suffer, who can love.—PRIOR.

LOW, MEAN, ABJECT.

Low (*v. Humble*) is a much stronger term than *mean;* for what is *low* stands more directly opposed to what is high, but what is *mean* is intermediate: *mean*, in German *gemein*, &c. comes from the Latin *communis* common. The *low* is applied only to a certain number or description; but *mean*, like common, is applicable to the great bulk of mankind. A man of *low* extraction falls below the ordinary level; he is opposed to a nobleman;

Had I been born a servant, my *low* life
Had steady stood from all these miseries.
RANDOLPH.

A man of *mean* birth does not rise above the ordinary level; he is upon a level with the majority;

For t is the mind that makes the body rich;
And as the sun breaks through the darkest clouds,
So honour 'peareth in the *meanest* habit.
SHAKSPEARE.

When employed to designate character, they preserve the same distinction; the *low* is that which is positively sunk in itself;

Yet sometimes nations will decline so *low*
From virtue.—MILTON.

But the *mean* is that which is comparatively *low* in regard to the outward circumstances and relative condition of the individual. Swearing and drunkenness are *low* vices; boxing, cudgelling, and wrestling, are *low* games; a misplaced economy in people of property is *mean;* a condescension to those who are beneath us, for our own petty advantages, is *meanness;* 'We fast not to please men, nor to promote any *mean,* worldly interest.'—SMALRIDGE. A man is commonly *low* by birth, education, or habits; but *meanness* is a defect of nature which sinks a person in spite of every external advantage.

The *low* and *mean* are qualities whether of the condition or the character: but *abject* is a peculiar state into which a man is thrown; a man is in the course of things *low;* he is voluntarily *mean* and involuntarily *abject;* the word *abject,* from the Latin *abjicio* to cast down, signifying literally brought very low. *Lowness* discovers itself in one's actions and sentiments; the *mean* and *abject* in one's spirit; the latter being much more powerful and oppressive than the former: the *mean* man stoops in order to get: the *abject* man crawls in order to submit: the *lowest* man will sometimes have a consciousness of what is due to himself; he will even rise above his condition; the *mean* man sacrifices his dignity to his convenience; he is always below himself; the *abject* man altogether forgets that he has any dignity; he is kept down by the pressure of adverse circumstances. The condition of a servant is *low;* his manners, his words, and his habits, will be *low;* but by good conduct he may elevate himself in his sphere of life: a nobleman is in station the reverse of *low:* but if he will stoop to the artifices practised by the vulgar in order to carry a point, we denominate it *mean,* if it be but trifling; otherwise it deserves a stronger epithet. The slave is, in every sense of the word *abject;* as he is bereft of that quality which sets man above the brute, so, in his actions, he evinces no higher impulse than what guides brutes: whether a man be a slave to another's will or to any passion, such as fear or superstition, he is equally said to be *abject;* 'There needs no more be said to extol the excellence and power of his (Waller's) wit, than that it was of magnitude enough to cover a world of very great faults, that is, a narrowness in his nature to the *lowest* degree, an *abjectness* and want of courage, an insinuating and servile flattering,' &c.—CLARENDON.

TO REDUCE, LOWER.

Reduce is to bring down, and *lower* to make *low* or *lower,* which proves the close connexion of these words in their original meaning; it is, however, only in their improper application that they have any further connexion. *Reduce* is used in the sense of lessen, when applied to number, quantity, price, &c.: *lower* is used in the same sense when applied to price, demands, terms, &c.: the former, however, occurs in cases where circumstances as well as persons are concerned; the latter only in cases where persons act: the price of corn is *reduced* by means of importation; a person *lowers* his price or his demand, when he finds them too high. As a moral quality, the former is much stronger than the latter: a man is said to be *reduced* to an abject condition; but to be *lowered* in the estimation of others, to be *reduced* to a state of slavery, to be *lowered* in his own eyes; 'The regular metres then in use may be *reduced,* I think, to four.'—TYRWHITT. 'It would be a matter of astonishment to me, that any critic should be found proof against the beauties of Agamemnon so as to *lower* its author to a comparison with Sophocles or Euripides.'—CUMBERLAND.

BASE, VILE, MEAN.

Base, in French *bas* low, from the Latin *basis* the foundation or lowest part, is the most directly opposed to the elevated; *vile,* in French *vil,* Latin *vilis,* Greek φαῦλος, worthless, of no account, is literally opposed to the worthy; *mean* and *middle,* from the Latin *medius,* signify moderate, not elevated, of little value.

Base is a stronger term than *vile,* and *vile* than *mean.* *Base* marks a high degree of moral turpitude; *vile* and *mean* denote in different degrees the want of all value or esteem. What is *base* excites our abhorrence, what is *vile* provokes disgust, what is *mean* awakens contempt. *Base* is opposed to magnanimous; *vile* to noble; *mean* to generous. Ingratitude is *base,* it does violence to the best affections of our nature flattery is *vile;* it violates truth in the grossest manner for the lowest purposes of gain; compliances are *mean* which are derogatory to the rank or dignity of the individual.

The *base* character violates the strongest moral obligations; the *vile* character blends low and despicable arts with his vices; the *mean* character acts inconsistently with his honour or respectability. Depravity of mind dictates *base* conduct; lowness of sentiment or disposition leads to *vileness;* a selfish temper engenders *meanness.* The schoolmaster of Falerii was guilty of the *basest* treachery in surrendering his helpless charge to the enemy; the Roman general, therefore, with true nobleness of mind treated him as a *vile* malefactor: sycophants are in the habits of practising every *mean* artifice to obtain favour.

The more elevated a person's rank, the greater is his *baseness* who abuses his influence to the injury of those who repose confidence in him;

Scorns the *base* earth and crowd below,
And with a soaring wing still mounts on high.
CREECH.

The lower the rank of the individual, and the more atrocious his conduct, the *viler* is his character;

That all the petty kings him envy'd,
And worshipp'd be like him and deify'd,
Of courtly sycophants and caitiffs *vile.*
GILBERT WEST

The more respectable the station of the person, and the more extended his wealth, the greater is his *meanness* when he descends to practices fitted only for his inferiours; 'There is hardly a spirit upon earth so *mean* and contracted as to centre all regards on its own interest exclusive of the rest of mankind.'—BERKELEY.

MODEST, BASHFUL, DIFFIDENT.

Modest, in Latin *modestus,* from *modus* a measure, signifies setting a measure, and in this case setting a measure to one's estimate of one's self; *bashful* signifies ready to be *abashed; diffident,* from the Latin *diffido* or *dis* privative, and *fido* to trust, signifies literally not trusting, and in this case not trusting to one's self.

Modesty is a habit or principle of the mind; *bashfulness* is a state of feeling: *modesty* is at all times becoming; *bashfulness* is only becoming in females, or very young persons, in the presence of their superiours: *modesty* discovers itself in the absence of every thing assuming, whether in look, word, or action;

Her face, as in a nymph display'd
A fair fierce boy, or in a boy betray'd
The blushing beauties of a *modest* maid.
DRYDEN.

Bashfulness betrays itself by a downcast look, and a timid air: a *modest* deportment is always commendable a *bashful* temper is not desirable; 'Mere *bashfulness,* without merit, is awkwardness.'—ADDISON. *Modesty* does not necessarily discover itself by any external mark; but *bashfulness* always shows itself in the manner; 'A man truly *modest* is as much so when he is alone as in company.'—BUDGELL.

Modesty is a proper distrust of ourselves; *diffidence* is a culpable distrust. *Modesty,* though opposed to assurance, is not incompatible with a confidence in ourselves; *diffidence* altogether unmans a person, and disqualifies him for his duty: a person is generally *modest* in the display of his talents to others; but a *diffident* man cannot turn his talents to their proper use: '*Diffidence* and presumption both arise from the want of knowing, or rather endeavouring to know, ourselves —STEELE.

PASSIVE, SUBMISSIVE.

Passive, in Latin *passivus* from *patior*, and the Greek πάσχω to suffer, signifying disposed to suffer, is mostly taken in the bad sense of suffering indignity from another; *submissive* (*v. Humble*) is mostly taken in a good sense for submitting to another, or suffering one's self to be directed by another; to be *passive* therefore is to be *submissive* to an improper degree.

When men attempt unjustly to enforce obedience from a mere love of rule, it betrays a want of proper spirit to be *passive*, or to submit quietly to the imposition; 'I know that we are supposed (by the French revolutionists) a dull, sluggish race, rendered *passive* by finding our situation tolerable.'—Burke. When men lawfully enforce obedience, it is none but the unruly and self-willed who will not be *submissive*;

> He in delight
> Both of her beauty and *submissive* charms,
> Smil'd with superiour love.—Milton.

PATIENCE, RESIGNATION, ENDURANCE.

Patience applies to any troubles or pains whatever, small or great; *resignation* is employed only for those of great moment, in which our dearest interests are concerned: *patience* when compared with *resignation* is somewhat negative; it consists in the abstaining from all complaint or indication of what one suffers: but *resignation* consists in a positive sentiment of conformity to the existing circumstances, be they what they may. There are perpetual occurrences which are apt to harass the temper, unless one regards them with patience; 'Though the duty of *patience* and subjection, where men suffer wrongfully, might possibly be of some force in those times of darkness; yet modern Christianity teaches that then only men are bound to suffer when they are not able to resist.'—South. The misfortunes of some men are of so calamitous a nature, that if they have not acquired the *resignation* of Christians, they must inevitably sink under them; 'My mother is in that dispirited state of *resignation* which is the effect of a long life, and the loss of what is dear to us.'—Pope.

Patience applies only to the evils that actually hang over us; but there is a *resignation* connected with a firm trust in Providence which extends its views to futurity, and prepares us for the worst that may happen.

As *patience* lies in the manner and temper of suffering, and *endurance* in the act: we may have *endurance* and not *patience*: for we may have much to *endure* and consequently *endurance*: but if we do not *endure* it with an easy mind and without the disturbance of our looks and words, we have not *patience*: on the other hand we may have *patience* but not *endurance*: for our *patience* may be exercised by momentary trifles, which are not sufficiently great or lasting to constitute *endurance*;

> There was never yet philosopher
> That could *endure* the tooth-ache patiently.
> Shakspeare.

PATIENT, PASSIVE.

Patient comes from *patiens*, the active participle of *patior* to suffer; *passive* comes from the *passive* participle of the same verb; hence the difference between the words: *patient* signifies suffering from an active principle, a determination to suffer; *passive* signifies suffered or acted upon for want of power to prevent. The former, therefore, is always taken in an indifferent or good sense; the latter in an indifferent or bad sense. When physically applied *patient* denotes the act of receiving impressions from external agents; 'Wheat, which is the best sort of grain, of which the purest bread is made, is *patient* of heat and cold.'—Ray. *Passive* implies the state of being acted upon by external agents;

> High above the ground
> Their march was, and the *passive* air upbore
> Their nimble tread.—Milton.

In the moral application the distinction is the same; but *patience* is always a virtue, as it signifies the suffering quietly that which cannot be remedied; as there are many such evils incident to our condition, it has been made one of the first Christian duties: *passiveness* is considered as a weakness, if not a vice; it is the enduring that from others which we ought not to endure.

TO SUFFER, BEAR, ENDURE, SUPPORT.

Suffer, in Latin *suffero*, compounded of *sub* and *fero*, signifies bearing up or firm underneath; *bear* in Saxon *baran*, old German *beran*, Latin *pario*, and Hebrew ברא to create; *endure*, in Latin *induro*, signifies to harden or be hardened; *support*, from the Latin *sub* and *porto*, signifies to carry up or to carry from underneath ourselves, or to receive the weight.

To *suffer* is a passive and involuntary act; it denotes simply the being a receiver of evil; it is therefore the condition of our being: to *bear* is positive and voluntary; it denotes the manner in which we receive the evil. 'Man,' says the Psalmist, 'is born to *suffering* as the sparks fly upwards;' hence the necessity for us to learn to *bear* all the numerous and diversified evils to which we are obnoxious; 'Let a man be brought into some such severe and trying situation as fixes the attention of the publick on his behaviour. The first question which we put concerning him is not, what does he *suffer?* but how does he *bear* it? If we judge him to be composed and firm, resigned to providence, and *supported* by conscious integrity, his character rises, and his miseries lessen in our view.'—Blair.

To *bear* is a single act of the resolution, and relates only to common ills; we *bear* disappointments and crosses: to *endure* is a continued and powerful act of the mind; we *endure* severe and lasting pains both of body and mind; we *endure* hunger and cold; we *endure* provocations and aggravations; it is a making of ourselves, by our own act, insensible to external evils; 'How miserable his state who is condemned to *endure* at once the pangs of guilt and the vexations of calamity.'—Blair. The first object of education should be to accustom children to *bear* contradictions and crosses, that they may afterward be enabled to *endure* every trial and misery.

To *bear* and *endure* signify to receive becomingly the weight of what befalls ourselves: to *support* signifies to *bear* either our own or another's evils; for we may either *support* ourselves, or be *supported* by others: but in this latter case we *bear* from the capacity which is within ourselves: but we *support* ourselves by foreign aid, that is, by the consolations of religion, the participation and condolence of friends, and the like. As the body may be early and gradually trained to *bear* cold, hunger, and pain, until it is enabled to *endure* even excruciating agonies: so may the mind be brought, from *bearing* the roughnesses of others' tempers with equanimity, or the unpleasantnesses which daily occur with patience, to *endure* the utmost scorn and provocation which human malice can invent: but whatever a person may *bear* or *endure* of personal inconvenience, there are *sufferings* arising from the wounded affections of the heart which by no efforts of our own we shall be enabled to *support*: in such moments we feel the unspeakable value of religion, which puts us in possession of the means of *supporting* every sublunary pain;

> With inward consolations recompens'd
> And oft *supported*.—Milton.

The words *suffer* and *endure* are said only of persons and personal matters; to *bear* and *support* are said also of things, signifying to receive a weight: in this case they differ principally in the degree of weight received. To *bear* is said of any weight, large or small, and either of the whole or any part of the weight; *support* is said of a great weight and the whole weight. The beams or the foundation *bear* the weight of a house; but the pillars upon which it is raised, or against which it leans, *support* the weight.

OBEDIENT, SUBMISSIVE, OBSEQUIOUS.

Obedient signifies ready to obey, and *submissive* the disposition to submit; *obsequious*, in Latin *obsequius*, from *obsequor*, or the intensive *ob* and *sequor* to follow, signifies following diligently, or with intensity of mind.

One is *obedient* to the command, *submissive* to the power or the will, *obsequious* to the person. *Obedience* is always taken in a good sense: one ought always to be *obedient* where *obedience* is due: *submission* is relatively good; it may, however, be indifferent or bad, one may be *submissive* from interested motives, or meanness of spirit, which is a base kind of *submission;* but to be *submissive* for conscience sake is the bounden duty of a Christian: *obsequiousness* is never good; it is an excessive concern about the will of another, which has always interest for its end.

Obedience is a course of conduct conformable either to some specifick rule, or the express will of another; *submission* is often a personal act, immediately directed to the individual. We show our *obedience* to the law by avoiding the breach of it; we show our *obedience* to the will of God, or of our parent, by making that will the rule of our life; 'The *obedience* of men is to imitate the *obedience* of angels, and rational beings on earth are to live unto God as rational beings in heaven live unto him.'—LAW. On the other hand we show *submission* to the person of the magistrate; we adopt a *submissive* deportment by a downcast look and a bent body;

Her at his feet, *submissive* in distress,
He thus with peaceful words uprais'd.—MILTON.

Obedience is founded upon principle, and cannot be feigned;

In vain thou bidst me to forbear,
Obedience were rebellion here.—COWLEY.

Submission is a partial bending to another, which is easily affected in our outward behaviour;

In all *submission* and humility,
York doth present himself unto your highness.
SHAKSPEARE.

The understanding and the heart produce the *obedience;* but force, or the necessity of circumstances, give rise to the *submission.*

Obedience and *submission* suppose a restraint on one's own will, in order to bring it into accordance with that of another; but *obsequiousness* is the consulting the will or pleasure of another: we are *obedient* from a sense of right;

What gen'rous Greek, *obedient* to thy word,
Shall form an ambush, or shall lift the sword.
POPE.

We are *submissive* from a sense of necessity; 'The natives (of Britain) disarmed, dispirited, and *submissive,* had lost all desire, and even idea, of their former liberty.'—HUME. We are *obsequious* from a desire of gaining favour; 'Adore not so the rising son, that you forget the father, who raised you to this height; nor be you so *obsequious* to the father, that you give just cause to the son to suspect that you neglect him.'—BACON. A love of God is followed by *obedience* to his will; they are coincident sentiments that reciprocally act on each other, so as to serve the cause of virtue: a *submissive* conduct is at the worst an involuntary sacrifice of our independence to our fears or necessities, the evil of which is confined principally to the individual who makes the sacrifice; but *obsequiousness* is a voluntary sacrifice of all that is noble in man to base gain, the evil of which extends far and wide: the *submissive* man, however mean he may be in himself, does not contribute to the vices of others: but the *obsequious* man has no scope for his paltry talent, but among the weak and wicked, whose weakness he profits by, and whose wickedness he encourages.

DUTIFUL, OBEDIENT, RESPECTFUL.

Dutiful signifies full of a sense of duty, or full of what belongs to duty; *obedient,* ready to obey; *respectful,* full of respect.

The *obedient* and *respectful* are but modes of the *dutiful:* we may be *dutiful* without being either *obedient* or *respectful;* but we are so far *dutiful* as we are either *obedient* or *respectful. Duty* denotes what is due from one being to another; it is independent of all circumstances: *obedience* and *respect* are relative *duties* depending upon the character and station of individuals: as we owe to no one on earth so much as to our parents, we are said to be *dutiful* to no earthly being besides; and in order to deserve the name of *dutiful,* a child during the period of his childhood, ought to make a parent's will to be his aw, and at no future period ought that will ever to be an object of indifference; 'For one cruel parent we meet with a thousand *undutiful* children.'—ADDISON. We may be *obedient* and *respectful* to others besides our parents, although to them *obedience* and *respect* are in the highest degree and in the first case due; yet servants are enjoined to be *obedient* to their masters, wives to their husbands, and subjects to their king; 'The *obedience* of children to their parents is the basis of all government, and set forth as the measure of that *obedience* which we owe to those whom Providence has placed over us.'—ADDISON.

Respectful is a term of still greater latitude than either, for as the characters of men as much as their stations demand *respect,* there is a *respectful* deportment due towards every superiour; 'Let your behaviour towards your superiours in dignity, age, learning, or any distinguished excellence, be full of *respect* and deference.'—CHATHAM.

DUTY, OBLIGATION.

Duty, as we see in the preceding section, consists altogether of what is right or due from one being to another; *obligation,* from the Latin *obligo* to bind, signifies the bond or necessity which lies in the thing.

All *duty* depends upon moral *obligation* which subsists between man and man, or between man and his Maker; in this abstract sense, therefore, there can be no *duty* without a previous *obligation,* and where there is an *obligation* it involves a *duty;* but in the vulgar acceptation, *duty* is applicable to the conduct of men in their various relations; *obligation* only to particular circumstances or modes of action: we have *duties* to perform as parents and children, as husbands and wives, as rulers and subjects, as neighbours and citizens;

The ways of Heav'n, judg'd by a private breast,
Is often what's our private interest,
And therefore those who would that will obey
Without their interest must their *duty* weigh.
DRYDEN.

The debtor is under an *obligation* to discharge debt; and he who has promised is under an *obligation* to fulfil his promise: a conscientious man, therefore, never loses sight of the *obligations* which he has at different times to discharge; 'No man can be under an *obligation* to believe any thing, who hath not sufficient means whereby he may be assured that such a thing is true.'—TILLOTSON.

The *duty* is not so peremptory as the *obligation;* the *obligation* is not so lasting as the *duty*. our affections impel us to the discharge of *duty;* interest or necessity impels us to the discharge of an *obligation:* it may therefore osmetimes happen that the man whom a sense of *duty* cannot actuate to do that which is right, will not be able to withstand the *obligation* under which he has laid himself.

TO COMPLY, CONFORM, YIELD, SUBMIT

The original meaning of *comply* and *yield* will be explained under the head of *Accede; conform,* compounded of *con* and *form,* signifies to put into the same *form; submit,* in Latin *submitto,* compounded of *sub* and *mitto,* signifies to put under, that is to say, to put one's self under another person.

Compliance and *conformity* are voluntary; *yielding* and *submission* are involuntary.

Compliance is an act of the inclination; *conformity* an act of the judgement: *compliance* is altogether optional; we *comply* with a thing or not at pleasure: *conformity* is binding on the conscience; it relates to matters in which there is a right and a wrong. *Compliance* with the fashions and customs of those we live with is a natural propensity of the human mind that may be mostly indulged without impropriety; 'I would not be thought in any part of this relation to reflect upon Signor Nicolini, who in acting this part only *complies* with the wretched taste of his audience.'—ADDISON. *Conformity* in religious matters, though not to be enforced by human authority, is not on that account less binding on the consciences of every member in the community; the neglect of this duty on trivial grounds involves in it the violation of more than one branch of the moral law; 'Being of a lay profession, I humbly *conform* to the constitutions of the church and my spiritual superiours, and I hold this obedience to be an acceptable sacrifice to God.'—HOWEL. *Compliances* are sometimes culpable, but *conformity* at least in the exteriour, is always a duty; 'The actions to which the world solicits our *compliance* are sins which forfeit eternal expectations.'

Compliance and *conformity* are produced by no external action on the mind: they flow spontaneously from the will and understanding; *yielding* is altogether the result of foreign agency. We *comply* with a wish as soon as it is known; it accords with our feelings so to do. we *yield* to the entreaties of others; it is the effect of persuasion, a constraint upon the inclination. We *conform* to the regulations of a community, it is a matter of discretion; we *yield* to the superiour judgement or power of another, we have no choice or alternative. We *comply* cheerfully; we *conform* willingly; we *yield* reluctantly.

To *yield* is to give way to another, either with one's will, one's judgement, or one's outward conduct: *submission* is the giving up of one's self altogether; it is the substitution of another's will for one's own. *Yielding* is partial; we may *yield* in one case or in one action, though not in another: *submission* is general; it includes a system of conduct.

We *yield* when we do not resist; this may sometimes be the act of a superiour: we *submit* only by adopting the measures and conduct proposed to us; this is always the act of an inferiour. *Yielding* may be produced by means more or less gentle, by enticing or insinuating arts, or by the force of argument; *submission* is made only to power or positive force: one *yields* after a struggle; one *submits* without resistance: we *yield* to ourselves or others; we *submit* to others only: it is a weakness to *yield* either to the suggestions of others or our own inclinations to do that which our judgements condemn; it is a folly to *submit* to the caprice of any one where there is not a moral obligation: it is obstinacy not to *yield* when one's adversary has the advantage; it is sinful not to *submit* to constituted authorities; 'There has been a long dispute for precedency between the tragick and the heroick poets. Aristotle would have the latter *yield* the past to the former, but Mr. Dryden and many others would never *submit* to this decision.' —ADDISON.

A cheerful *compliance* with the request of a friend is the sincerest proof of friendship;

Let the king meet *compliance* in your looks,
A free and ready *yielding* to his wishes.—ROWE.

The wisest and most learned of men have ever been the readiest to *conform* to the general sense of the community in which they live;

Among mankind so few there are
Who will *conform* to philosophick fare.—DRYDEN.

The harmony of social life is frequently disturbed by the reluctance which men have to *yield* to each other; 'That *yieldingness*, whatever foundations it might lay to the disadvantage of posterity, was a specifick to preserve us in peace for his own time.'—LORD HALIFAX. The order of civil society is frequently destroyed by the want of proper *submission* to superiours; 'Christian people *submit* themselves to *conformable* observances of the lawful and religious constitutions of their spiritual rulers.'—WHITE.

COMPLAINT, YIELDING, SUBMISSIVE.

As epithets from the preceding verbs, serve to designate a propensity to the respective actions mostly in an excessive or improper degree.

A *compliant* temper *complies* with every wish of another good or bad,

Be silent and *complying*; you'll soon find
Sir John without a medicine will be kind.
HARRISON.

A *yielding* temper leans to every opinion right or wrong; 'A peaceable temper supposes *yielding* and condescending manners.'—BLAIR. A *submissive* temper *submits* to every demand, just or unjust; 'When force and violence and hard necessity have brought the yoke of servitude upon a people's neck, religion will supply them with a patient and *submissive* spirit.'—FLEETWOOD.

A *compliant* person wants command of feeling; a *yielding* person wants fixedness of principle; a *submissive* person wants resolution: a *compliant* disposition will be imposed upon by the selfish and unreasonable; a *yielding* disposition is most unfit for commanding; a *submissive* disposition exposes a person to the exactions of tyranny.

TO ACCEDE, CONSENT, COMPLY, ACQUIESCE, AGREE.

Accede, in Latin *accedo*, compounded of *ac* or *ad* and *cedo* to go or come, signifies to come or fall into a thing; *consent*, in French *consentir*, Latin *consentio*, compounded of *con* together and *sentio* to feel, signifies to feel in unison with another; *comply* comes probably from the French *complaire*, Latin *complaceo*, signifying to be pleased in unison with another; *acquiesce*, in French *acquiescer*, Latin *acquiesco*, compounded of *ac* or *ad* and *quiesco*, signifies to be easy about or contented with a thing; *agree*, in French *agréer*, is most probably derived from the Latin *gruo*, in the word *congruo*, signifying to accord or suit.

We *accede* to what others propose to us by falling in with their ideas: we *consent** to what others wish by authorizing it: we *comply* with what is asked of us by allowing it, or not hindering it. we *acquiesce* in what is insisted by accepting it, and conforming to it. we *agree* to what is proposed by admitting and embracing it.

We object to those things to which we do not *accede*: we refuse those things to which we do not *consent*, or with which we will not *comply*: we oppose those things in which we will not *acquiesce*: we dispute that to which we will not *agree*.

To *accede* is the unconstrained action of an equal; it is a matter of discretion: *consent* and *comply* suppose a degree of superiority, at least the power of preventing; they are acts of good nature or civility; *acquiesce* implies a degree of submission, it is a matter of prudence or necessity: *agree* indicates an aversion to disputes; it respects the harmony of social intercourse.

Members of any community ought to be willing to *accede* to what is the general will of their associates, 'At last persuasion, menaces, and the impending pressure of necessity, conquered her virtue, and she *acceded* to the fraud.'—CUMBERLAND. Parents should never be induced to *consent* to any thing which may prove injurious to their children;

My poverty, but not my will *consents*.—SHAKSPEARE

People ought not to *comply* indiscriminately with what is requested of them; 'Inclination will at length come over to reason, though we can never force reason to *comply* with inclination.'—ADDISON. In all matters of difference it is a happy circumstance when the parties will *acquiesce* in the judgement of an umpire; 'This we ought to *acquiesce* in, that the Sovereign Being, the great Author of Nature, has in him all possible perfection.'—ADDISON. Differences will soon be terminated when there is a willingness to *agree*; 'We *agreed* to adopt the infant as the orphan son of a distant relation of our own name.'—CUMBERLAND.

TO AGREE, COINCIDE, CONCUR.

In the former section *agree* is compared with terms that are employed only for things; in the present case it is compared with words as they are applied to persons only.

Agree implies a general sameness; *coincide*, from *co* together and the Latin *incido* to fall, implies a meeting in a certain point; *concur*, from *con* together, and *curro* to run, implies a running in the same course, an acting together on the same principles.

Agree denotes a state of rest; *coincide* and *concur* a state of motion, either towards or with another.

Agreement is either the voluntary or involuntary act of persons in general; *coincidence* is the voluntary but casual act of individuals, the act of one falling into the opinion of another; *concurrence* is the intentional positive act of individuals, it is the act of one authorizing the opinions and measures of another.

Men of like education and temperament *agree* upon most subjects;

Since all *agree*, who both with judgement read,
'T is the same sun, and does himself succeed.
TATE

People cannot expect others to *coincide* with them

* Vide Abbe Girard: "Consentir, acquiescer, adherer, tomber d'acord

when they advance extravagant positions; 'There is not perhaps any couple whose dispositions and relish of life are so perfectly similar as that their wills constantly *coincide*.'—HAWKESWORTH. The wiser part of mankind are backward in *concurring* in any schemes which are not warranted by experience; 'The plan being thus concerted, and my cousin's *concurrence* obtained, it was immediately put in execution.'—HAWKESWORTH.

When *coincide* and *concur* are considered in their application to things, the former implies simply meeting at a point, the latter running towards a point; the former seems to exclude the idea of design, the latter that of chance: two sides of different triangles *coincide* when they are applied to each other so as to fall on the same points; two powers *concur* when they both act so as to produce the same result.

A *coincidence* of circumstances is sometimes so striking and singular that it can hardly be attributed to pure accident; 'A *coincidence* of sentiment may easily happen without any communication, since there are many occasions in which all reasonable men will nearly think alike.'—JOHNSON. A *concurrence* of circumstances, which seemed all to be formed to combine, is sometimes notwithstanding purely casual; 'Eminence of station, greatness of effect, and all the favours of fortune, must *concur* to place excellence in publick view.'—JOHNSON.

AGREEMENT, CONTRACT, COVENANT, COMPACT, BARGAIN.

Agreement signifies what is agreed to (*v. To agree*); *contract*, in French *contracte*, from the Latin *contractus*, participle of *contraho* to bring close together or bind, signifies the thing thus contracted or bound; *covenant*, in French *covenante*, Latin *conventus*, participle of *convenio* to meet together at a point, signifies the point at which several meet, that is, the thing agreed upon by many; *compact*, in Latin *compactus*, participle of *compingo* to bind close, signifies the thing to which people bind themselves close; *bargain*, from the Welsh *bargan* to contract or deal for, signifies the act of dealing, or the thing dealt for.

An *agreement* is general, and applies to transactions of every description, but particularly such as are made between single individuals; in cases where the other terms are not so applicable; a *contract* is a binding *agreement* between individuals; a simple *agreement* may be verbal, but a *contract* must be written and legally executed: *covenant* and *compact* are *agreements* among communities; the *covenant* is commonly a national and publick transaction; the *compact* respects individuals as members of a community, or communities with each other: the *bargain*, in its proper sense, is an *agreement* solely in matters of trade; but applies figuratively in the same sense to other objects.

The simple consent of parties constitutes an *agreement;* a seal and signature are requisite for a *contract;* a solemn engagement on the one hand, and faith in that engagement on the other hand, enter into the nature of a *covenant;* a tacit sense of mutual obligation in all the parties gives virtue to a *compact;* an assent to stipulated terms of sale may form a *bargain*.

Friends make an *agreement* to meet at a certain time; 'Frog had given his word that he would meet the above-mentioned company at the Salutation, to talk of this *agreement*.'—ARBUTHNOT (*History of John Bull*). Two tradesmen enter into a *contract* to carry on a joint trade; 'It is impossible to see the long scrolls in which every *contract* is included, with all their appendages of seals and attestations, without wondering at the depravity of those beings, who must be restrained from violation of promise, by such formal and publick evidences.'—JOHNSON. The people of England made a *covenant* with King Charles I. entitled the solemn covenant;

> These flashes of blue lightning gave the sign
> Of *covenants* broke; three peals of thunder join.
> DRYDEN.

In the society of Freemasons, every individual is bound to secrecy by a solemn *compact;* 'In the beginnings and first establishment of speech, there was an implicit *compact* among men, founded upon common use and consent, that such and such words or voices, actions or gestures, should be means or signs whereby they would express or convey their thoughts one to another.'—SOUTH. The trading part of the community are continually striking *bargains;* 'We see men frequently dexterous and sharp enough in making a *bargain*, who, if you reason with them about matters of religion, appear perfectly stupid.—LOCKE.

AGREEABLE, PLEASANT, PLEASING.

The first two of these epithets approach so near in sense and application, that they can with propriety be used indifferently, the one for the other; yet there is an occasional difference which may be clearly defined; the *agreeable* is that which agrees with or suits the character, temper, and feelings of a person: the *pleasant* that which pleases; the *pleasing* that which is adapted to please.

Agreeable expresses a feeling less vivid than *pleasant:* people of the soberest and gravest character may talk of passing *agreeable* hours, or enjoying *agreeable* society, if those hours were passed *agreeably* to their turn of mind, or that society which suited their taste; 'To divert me, I took up a volume of Shakspeare, where I chanced to cast my eye upon a part in the tragedy of Richard the Third, which filled my mind with an *agreeable* horrour.'—STEELE. The young and the gay will prefer *pleasant* society, where vivacity and mirth prevail, suitable to the tone of their spirits;

> *Pleasant* the sun
> When first on this delightful land he spreads
> His orient beams.—MILTON.

A man is *agreeable* who by a soft and easy address contributes to the amusement of others; a man is *pleasant* who to this softness adds affability and communicativeness.

Pleasing marks a sentiment less vivid and distinctive than either;

> Nor this alone t' indulge a vain delight,
> And make a *pleasing* prospect for the sight.
> DRYDEN

A *pleasing* voice has something in it which we like, an *agreeable* voice strikes with positive pleasure upon the ear. A *pleasing* countenance denotes tranquillity and contentment; it satisfies us when we view it. a *pleasant* countenance bespeaks happiness; it gratifies the beholder, and invites him to behold.

TO AGREE, ACCORD, SUIT.

Agree (*v. To agree*) is here used in application to things in which it is allied; to *accord*, in French *accorder*, from the Latin *chorda* the string of a harp, signifies the same as to attune or join in tune; and *suit*, from the Latin *secutus*, participle of *sequor* to follow, signifies to be in a line, in the order as it ought to be.

An *agreement* between two things requires an entire sameness; an *accordance* supposes a considerable resemblance; a *suitableness* implies an aptitude to coalesce.

Opinions *agree*, feelings *accord*, and tempers *suit*.

Two statements *agree* which are in all respects alike: that *accords* with our feelings, which produces pleasurable sensations; that *suits* our taste, which we wish to adopt, or in adopting gives us pleasure.

Where there is no *agreement* in the essentials of any two accounts, their authenticity may be greatly questioned: if a representation of any thing *accords* with what has been stated from other quarters, it serves to corroborate: it is advisable that the ages and stations as well as tempers of the parties should be *suitable*, who look forward for happiness in a matrimonial connexion.

Where there is no *agreement* of opinion, there can be no assimilation of habit; where there is no *accordance* of sound, there can be no harmony; where there is no *suitability* of temper, there can be no co-operation.

When opinions do not *agree*, men must *agree* to differ: the precepts of our Saviour *accord* with the tenderest as well as the noblest feelings of our nature: when the humours and dispositions of people do not *suit*, they do wisely not to have any intercourse with each other;

The laurel and the myrtle sweets *agree*.—DRYDEN.

'Metre aids and is adapted to the memory; it *accords* to musick, and is the vehicle of enthusiasm.'—CUMBERLAND. 'Rollo followed, in the partition of his states, the customs of the feudal law, which was then universally established in the southern countries of Europe, and which suited the peculiar circumstances of the age.'—HUME.

CONSONANT, ACCORDANT, CONSISTENT.

Consonant, from the Latin *consonans*, participle of *con* and *sono* to sound together, signifies to sound, or be, in unison or harmony; *accordant*, from *accord* (*v. To Agree*), signifies the quality of according; *consistent*, from the Latin *consistens*, participle of *consisto*, or *con* and *sisto* to place together, signifies the quality of being able to stand in unison together.

Consonant is employed in matters of representation; *accordant* in matters of opinion or sentiment; *consistent* in matters of conduct. A particular passage is *consonant* with the whole tenour of the Scriptures; a particular account is *accordant* with all one hears and sees on a subject; a person's conduct is not always *consistent* with his station.

The *consonance* of the whole Scriptures, in the Old and New Testaments, with regard to the character, dignity, and mission of our Blessed Saviour, has justly given birth to that form which constitutes the established religion of England; 'Our faith in the discoveries of the Gospel will receive confirmation from discerning their *consonance* with the natural sentiments of the human heart.'—BLAIR. The *accordance* of the prophecies respecting our Saviour with the event of his birth, life, and sufferings, are incontestable evidences of his being the true Messiah; 'The difference of good and evil in actions is not founded on arbitrary opinions or institutions, but in the nature of things, and the nature of man; it *accords* with the universal sense of the human mind.'—BLAIR. The *consistency* of a man's practice with his profession is the only criterion of his sincerity;

Keep one *consistent* plan from end to end.—ADDISON.

Consonant is opposed to dissonant; *accordant* to discordant; *consistent* to inconsistent. *Consonance* is not so positive a thing as either *accordance* or *consistency*, which respect real events, circumstances, and actions. *Consonance* mostly serves to prove the truth of any thing, but *dissonance* does not prove its falsehood until it amounts to direct *discordance* or *inconsistency*. There is a *dissonance* in the accounts given by the four Evangelists of our Saviour, which serves to prove the absence of all collusion and imposture, since there is neither *discordance* nor *inconsistency* in what they have related or omitted.

TO CONCILIATE, RECONCILE.

Conciliate, in Latin *conciliatus*, participle of *concilio*; and *reconcile*, in Latin *reconcilio*, both come from *concilium* a council, denoting unity and harmony. *Conciliate* and *reconcile* are both employed in the sense of uniting men's affections, but under different circumstances.

The *conciliator* gets the good will and affections for himself; the *reconciler* unites the affections of two persons to each other. The *conciliator* may either gain new affections, or regain those which are lost; the *reconciler* always renews affections which have been once lost. The best means of *conciliating* esteem is by *reconciling* all that are at variance.

Conciliate is mostly employed for men in publick stations; 'The preacher may enforce his doctrines in the style of authority, for it is his profession to summon mankind to their duty; but an uncommissioned instructer will study to *conciliate* while he attempts to correct.'—CUMBERLAND. *Reconcile* is indifferently employed for those in publick or private stations; 'He (Hammond) not only attained his purpose of uniting distant parties to each other, but, contrary to the usual fate of *reconcilers*, gained them to himself.'—FELL. Men in power have sometimes the happy opportunity of *conciliating* the good will of those who are most averse to their authority, and thus *reconciling* them to measures which would otherwise be odious.

Kindness and condescension serve to *conciliate*; a friendly influence, or a well-timed exercise of authority, is often successfully exerted in *reconciling*. *Conciliate* is employed only for persons, or that which is personal; but *reconciling* is also employed in the sense of bringing a person's thoughts or feelings in unison with the things that he has not liked before, or might be expected not to like: 'It must be confessed a happy attachment, which can *reconcile* the Laplander to his freezing snows, and the African to his scorching sun.'—CUMBERLAND.

COMPATIBLE, CONSISTENT.

Compatible, compounded of *com* or *cum* with, and *patior* to suffer, signifies a fitness to be suffered together; *consistent*, in Latin *consistens*, participle of *consisto*, compounded of *con* and *sisto*, to place, signifies the fitness to be placed together.

Compatibility has a principal reference to plans and measures; *consistency* to character, conduct, and station. Every thing is *compatible* with a plan which does not interrupt its prosecution; every thing is *consistent* with a person's station by which it is neither degraded nor elevated. It is not *compatible* with the good discipline of a school to allow of foreign interference; 'Whatever is *incompatible* with the highest dignity of our nature should indeed be excluded from our conversation.'—HAWKESWORTH. It is not *consistent* with the elevated and dignified character of a clergyman to engage in the ordinary pursuits of other men; 'Truth is always *consistent* with itself, and needs nothing to help it out.'—TILLOTSON.

INCONSISTENT, INCONGRUOUS, INCOHERENT.

Inconsistent, from *sisto* to place, marks the unfitness of being placed together; *incongruous*, from *congruo* to suit, marks the unsuitableness of one thing to another; *incoherent*, from *hæreo* to stick, marks the incapacity of two things to coalesce or be united to each other.

Inconsistency attaches either to the actions or sentiments of men; *incongruity* attaches to the modes and qualities of things; *incoherency* to words or thoughts: things are made *inconsistent* by an act of the will; a man acts or thinks *inconsistently*, according to his own pleasure; 'Every individual is so unequal to himself that man seems to be the most wavering and *inconsistent* being in the universe.'—HUGHES. *Incongruity* depends upon the nature of the things; there is some thing very *incongruous* in blending the solemn and decent service of the church with the extravagant rant of Methodism; 'The solemn introduction of the Phœnix, in the last scene of Sampson Agonistes, is *incongruous* to the personage to whom it is ascribed.'—JOHNSON. *Incoherence* marks the want of coherence in that which ought to follow in a train; extemporary effusions from the pulpit are often distinguished most by their *incoherence*; 'Be but a person in credit with the multitude, he shall be able to make rambling *incoherent* stuff pass for high rhetorick.'—SOUTH.

CONFORMABLE, AGREEABLE, SUITABLE.

Conformable signifies able to *conform* (*v. To comply*), that is, having a sameness of form; *agreeable*, the quality of being able to *agree* (*v. To agree*); *suitable*, able to *suit* (*v. To agree*).

Conformable is employed for matters of obligation; *agreeable* for matters of choice; *suitable* for matters of propriety and discretion: what is *conformable* accords with some prescribed form or given rule of others; 'A man is glad to gain numbers on his side, as they serve to strengthen him in his opinions. It makes him believe that his principles carry conviction with them, and are the more likely to be true, when he finds they are *conformable* to the reason of others as well as to his own.'—ADDISON. What is *agreeable* accords with the feelings, tempers, or judgements of ourselves or others; 'As you have formerly offer d some arguments for the soul's immortality, *agree* [illegible] both to reason and the Christian doctrine I belie e your readers will not be displeased to see how the sa[illegible] great truth shines in the pomp of Roman eloquence.'—HUGHES. What is *suitable* accords with outward circumstances; 'I think banging a cushion gives a man too warlike or perhaps too theatrical a figure to be *suitable* to a Christian congregation.'—SWIFT. It is the business of those who act for others to act *conformably* to their directions; it is the part of a friend to act *agreeably* to the wishes of a friend; it is the part of every man to act *suitably* to his station.

The decisions of a judge must be strictly *conformable* to the letter of the law; he is seldom at liberty to consult his views of equity: the decision of a partisan is always *agreeable* to the temper of his party: the style of a writer should be *suitable* to his subject.

Conformable is most commonly employed for matters of temporary moment; *agreeable* and *suitable* are mostly said of things which are of constant value: we make things *conformable* by an act of discretion; they are *agreeable* or *suitable* by their own nature: a treaty of peace is made *conformable* to the preliminaries; a legislator must take care to frame laws *agreeably* to the Divine law; it is of no small importance for every man to act *suitably* to the character he has assumed.

TO FIT, SUIT, ADAPT, ACCOMMODATE, ADJUST.

Fit signifies to make or be *fit; suit* to make or be *suitable; adapt*, from *aptus* fit, to make *fit* for a specifick purpose; *accommodate*, to make commodious; *adjust*, to make a thing such as it is desired to be.

To *fit* and *suit* are used in the literal sense of applying things to each other as they are intended: but *fit* is employed mostly in regard to material and familiar objects. A tailor *fits* on a coat, or a coat *fits* when it is made right to the body;

'Then meditates the mark; and couching low,
Fits the sharp arrow to the well-strung bow.—POPE.

Suit is employed for intellectual or moral objects; '*Suit* the action to the word, the word to the action, with this special observance, that you o'erstep not the modesty of nature.'—SHAKSPEARE. So also intransitively;

Ill *suits* it now the joys of love to know,
Too deep my anguish, and too wild my wo.—POPE.

In an extended application of the terms to *fit* is intransitively used for what is morally *fit* in the nature of things;

Nor *fits* it to prolong the feast
Timeless, indecent, but retire to rest.—POPE.

Whence we speak of the *fitness* of things; *suit* is applied either transitively or intransitively in the sense of agree, as a thing *suits* a person's taste, or one thing *suits* with another; 'The matter and manner of their tales, and of their telling, are so *suited* to their different educations and humours, that each would be improper in any other.'—DRYDEN.

Her purple habit sits with such a grace
On her smooth shoulders, and so *suits* her face.
DRYDEN.

The one intense, the other still remiss,
Cannot well *suit* with either, but soon prove
Tedious alike.—MILTON.

To *adapt* is a species of *fitting;* to *accommodate* is a species of *suiting;* both applied to the intellectual and moral actions of conscious beings. *Adaptation* is an act of the judgement; *accommodation* is an act of the will: we *adapt* by an exercise of discretion; we *accommodate* by a management of the humours: the *adaptation* does not interfere with our interests; but the *accommodation* always supposes a sacrifice: we *adapt* our language to the understandings of our hearers; 'It is not enough that nothing offends the ear, but a good poet will adapt the very sounds as well as words to the things he treats of.'—POPE. We *accommodate* ourselves to the humours of others; 'He had altered many things, not that they were not natural before, but that he might *accommodate* himself to the age in which he lived.'—DRYDEN. The mind of an infinitely wise Creator is clearly evinced in the world, by the universal *adaptation* of means to their ends; 'It is in his power so to *adapt* one thing to another, as to fulfil his promise of making all things work together for good to those who love him.'—BLAIR. A spirit of *accommodation* is not merely a characteristick of politeness; it is of sufficient importance to be ranked among the Christian duties; 'It is an old observation which has been made of politicians, who would rather ingratiate themselves with their sovereigns, than promote his real service, that they *accommodate* their counsels to his inclinations.'—ADDISON. The term *adapt* is sometimes applied to things of a less familiar nature; 'It may not be a useless inquiry, in what respects the love of novelty is peculiarly *adapted* to the present state.'—GROVE. 'Adhesion may be in part ascribed, either to some elastical motion in the pressed glass, or to the exquisite *adaptation* of the almost innumerable, though very small asperities of the one, and the numerous little cavities of the other, whereby the surfaces do lock in with one another, or are as it were clasped together.'—BOYLE.

Accommodate and *adjust* are both applied to the affairs of men which require to be kept or put in right order; but the former implies the keeping as well as putting in order; the latter simply the putting in order. Men *accommodate* each other, that is, make things commodious for each other; but they *adjust* things either for themselves or for others. Thus they *accommodate* each other in pecuniary matters; or they *adjust* the ceremonial of a visit. On this ground we may say that a difference is either *accommodated* or *adjusted:* for it is *accommodated*, inasmuch as the parties yield to each other; it is *adjusted*, inasmuch as that which was wrong is set right; 'When things were thus far *adjusted*, towards a peace, all other differences were soon *accommodated*.'—ADDISON.

TO FIT, EQUIP, PREPARE, QUALIFY.

To *fit* signifies to adopt means in order to make *fit*, and conveys the general sense of all the other terms, which differ principally in the means and circumstances of *fitting:* to *equip*, probably from the old barbarous Latin *eschipare* to furnish or adorn ships, is to *fit* out by furnishing the necessary materials: to *prepare*, from the Latin *præparo*, compounded of *præ* and *paro* to get before hand, is to take steps for the purpose of *fitting* in future: to *qualify*, from the Latin *qualifico*, or *facio* and *qualis* to make a thing as it should be, is to *fit* or furnish with the moral requisites.

To *fit* is employed for ordinary cases; to *equip* only for expeditions; they may be both employed in application to the same objects with this distinction, a vessel is *equipped* when it is furnished with every thing requisite for a voyage; it is *fitted* by simply putting those things to it which have been temporarily removed;

With long resounding cries they urge the train,
To *fit* the ships and launch into the main.—POPE

The word *equip* is also applied figuratively in the same sense; 'The religious man is *equipped* for the storm as well as the calm in this dubious navigation of life.'—BLAIR. To *fit* is for an immediate purpose; to *prepare* is for a remote purpose. A person *fits* himself for taking orders when he is at the university: he *prepares* himself at school before he goes to the university. To *fit* is to adopt positive and decisive measures; to *prepare* is to use those which are only precarious: a scholar *fits* himself for reading Horace by reading Virgil with attention; he *prepares* for an examination by going over what he has already learned.

To *fit* is said of every thing, both in a natural and a moral sense: to *qualify* is used only in a moral sense. *Fit* is employed mostly for acquirements which are gained by labour: *qualify* for those which are gained by intellectual exertion; a youth *fits* himself for a mechanical business by working at it; a youth *qualifies* himself for a profession by following a particular course of studies.

COMPETENT, FITTED, QUALIFIED.

Competent, in Latin *competens*, participle of *competo* to agree or suit, signifies suitable; *fitted* signifies made fit; *qualified*, participle of *qualify*, from the Latin *qualis* and *facio*, signifies made as it ought to be.

Competency mostly respects the mental endowments and attainments; *fitness* the disposition and character; *qualification* the artificial acquirements. A person is *competent* to undertake an office; *fitted* or *qualified* to fill a situation.

Familiarity with any subject aided by strong mental endowments gives *competency:* suitable habits and temper constitute the *fitness:* acquaintance with the business to be done, and expertness in the mode of performing it, constitutes the *qualification:* none should pretend to give their opinions on serious subjects who are not *competent* judges; none but lawyers are *competent* to decide in cases of law; none but medical men are *competent* to prescribe medicines; none but divines of sound learning, as well as piety, to determine on doctrinal questions; 'Man is not *competent* to decide upon the good or evil of many events which befall him in this life.'—CUMBERLAND. Men of sedentary and studious habits, with a serious temper, are most *fitted* to be clergymen; 'What is more obvious and ordinary than a mole? and yet what more palpable argument of Providence than it? The members of her body are so exactly *fitted* to her nature and manner of life.'—ADDISON. Those who have the most learning and acquaintance with the Holy Scriptures are the best *qualified* for the important and sacred office of instructing the people; 'Such benefits only can be bestowed as others are capable to receive, and such pleasures imparted as others are *qualified* to enjoy.'—JOHNSON.

Many are *qualified* for managing the concerns of others, who would not be *competent* to manage a concern for themselves. Many who are *fitted* from their turn of mind for any particular charge, may be unfortunately *incompetent* for want of the requisite *qualifications.*

FIT, APT, MEET.

Fit, from the Latin *fit* it is made, signifying made for the purpose, is either an acquired or a natural property; *apt*, in Latin *aptus*, from the Greek ἅπτω to connect, is a natural property; *meet*, from to meet or measure, signifying measured, is a moral quality. A house is *fit* for the accommodation of the family according to the plan of the builder;

He lends him vain Goliah's sacred word,
The *fittest* help just fortune could afford.—COWLEY.

The young mind is *apt* to receive either good or bad impressions; 'If you hear a wise sentence or an *apt* phrase commit it to your memory.'—SIR HENRY SIDNEY. *Meet* is a term of rare use, except in spiritual matters or in poetry; it is *meet* to offer our prayers to the Supreme Disposer of all things;

My image not imparted to the brute
Whose fellowship therefore not *unmeet* for thee,
Good reason was thou freely shouldst dislike.
MILTON.

CONCORD, HARMONY.

The idea of union is common to both these terms, but under different circumstances. *Concord*, in French *concorde*, Latin *concordia*, from *con* and *cor*, having the same heart and mind, is generally employed for the union of wills and affections; *harmony*, in French *harmonie*, Latin *harmonia*, Greek ἁρμονία, from ἄρω to fit or suit, signifying the state of fitting or suiting, respects the aptitude of minds to coalesce.

There may be *concord* without *harmony*, and *harmony* without *concord*. Persons may live in *concord* who are at a distance from each other;

Kind *concord*, heavenly born! whose blissful reign
Holds this vast globe in one surrounding chain
Soul of the world.—TICKEL.

Harmony is mostly employed for those who are in close connexion, and obliged to co-operate;

In us both one soul
Harmony to behold in wedded pair!
More grateful than harmonious sounds to the ear.
MILTON.

Concord should never be broken by relations under any circumstances; *harmony* is indispensable in all members of a family that dwell together. Interest will sometimes stand in the way of brotherly *concord;* a love of rule, and a dogmatical temper, will sometimes disturb the *harmony* of a family. *Concord* is as essential to domestick happiness, as *harmony* is to the peace of society and the uninterrupted prosecution of business. What *concord* can there be between kindred who despise each other? what *harmony* between the rash and the discreet? These terms are both applied to musick; but *concord* solely respects the agreement of twor or more sounds;

The man that hath no musick in himself,
Nor is not mov'd with *concord* of sweet sounds,
Is fit for treasons, villanies, and spoils.
SHAKSPEARE.

But *harmony* respects the effect of an aggregate number of sounds; '*Harmony* is a compound idea made up of different sounds united.'—WATTS. *Harmony* has also a farther application to objects in general to denote their adaptation to each other;

The *harmony* of things
As well as that of sounds, from *discord* springs.
DENHAM.

'If we consider the world in its subserviency to man, one would think it was made for our use; but if we consider it in its natural beauty and *harmony*, one would be apt to conclude it was made for our pleasure.'—ADDISON.

MELODY, HARMONY, ACCORDANCE

Melody, in Latin *melodia*, from *melos*, in Greek μέλος a verse, and the Hebrew מלה a word or a verse; *harmony*, in Latin *harmonia*, Greek ἁρμονία concord, from ἄρω *apto* to fit or suit, signifies the agreement of sounds; *accordance* denotes the act or state of according (*v. To agree*).

Melody signifies any measured or modulated sounds measured after the manner of verse into distinct members or parts; *harmony* signifies the suiting or adapting different modulated sounds to each other; *melody* is therefore to *harmony* as a part to the whole: we must first produce *melody* by the rules of art; the *harmony* which follows must be regulated by the ear: there may be *melody* without *harmony*, but there cannot be *harmony* without *melody:* we speak of simple *melody* where the modes of musick are not very much diversified; but we cannot speak of *harmony* unless there be a variety of notes to fall in with each other.

A voice is *melodious* inasmuch as it is capable of producing a regularly modulated note; it is *harmonious* inasmuch as it strikes agreeably on the ear, and produces no discordant sounds. The song of a bird is *melodious* or has *melody* in it, inasmuch as there is a concatenation of sounds in it which are admitted to be regular, and consequently agreeable to the musical ear;

Lend me your song, ye nightingales! Oh pour
The mazy-running soul of *melody*
Into my varied verse.—THOMSON.

There is *harmony* in a concert of voices and instruments;

Now the distemper'd mind
Has lost that concord of *harmonious* powers,
Which forms the soul of happiness.—THOMSON.

Accordance is strictly speaking the property on which both *melody* and *harmony* is founded: for the whole of musick depends on an *accordance* of sounds;

The musick
Of man's fair composition best *accords*
When 't is in concert.—SHAKSPEARE.

The same distinction marks *accordance* and *harmony* in the moral application. There may be occasional *accordance* of opinion or feeling; but *harmony* is an entire *accordance* in every point.

CORRESPONDENT, ANSWERABLE, SUITABLE.

Correspondent, in French *correspondant*, from the Latin *cum* and *respondeo* to answer, signifies to answer in unison or in uniformity; *answerable* and *suitable* from *answer* and *suit*, mark the quality or capacity of *answering* or *suiting*. *Correspondent* supposes a greater agreement than *answerable*, and *answerable* requires a greater agreement than *suitable*. Things that *correspond* must be alike in size, shape, colour and every minute particular; those that *answer* must be fitted for the same purpose; those that *suit* must have nothing disproportionate or discordant. In the artificial disposition of furniture, or all matters of art and ornament, it is of considerable importance to have some things made to *correspond*, so that they may be placed in *suitable* directions to *answer* to each other.

In the moral application, actions are said to *correspond* with professions; the success of an undertaking to *answer* the expectation; particular measures to *suit* the purpose of individuals. It ill *corresponds* with a profession of friendship to refuse assistance to a friend in the time of need; 'As the attractive power in bodies is the most universal principle which produceth innumerable effects, so the *corresponding* social appetite in human souls is the great spring and source of moral actions.'—BERKELEY. Wild schemes undertaken without thought, will never *answer* the expectations of the projectors; 'All the features of the face and tones of the voice *answer* like strings upon musical instruments to the impressions made on them by the mind.'—HUGHES. It never *suits* the purpose of the selfish and greedy to contribute to the relief of the necessitous; 'When we consider the infinite power and wisdom of the Maker, we have reason to think that it is *suitable* to the magnificent harmony of the universe, that the species of creatures should also by gentle degrees ascend upward from us.'—ADDISON.

ASSENT, CONSENT, APPROBATION, CONCURRENCE.

Assent, in Latin *assentio*, is compounded of *as* or *ad* and *sentio* to think, signifying to bring one's mind or judgement to a thing; *approbation* in Latin *approbatio*, is compounded of *ad* and *probo* to prove, signifying to make a thing out good: *consent* and *concurrence* are taken in the same sense as in the preceding articles.

Assent respects the judgement; *consent* respects the will. We assent to what we think true; we *consent* to the wish of another by agreeing to it and allowing it. Some men give their hasty *assent* to propositions which they do not fully understand; 'Precept gains only the cold *approbation* of reason, and compels an *assent* which judgement frequently yields with reluctance, even when delay is impossible.'—HAWKESWORTH. Some men give their hasty *consent* to measures which are very injudicious.

What in sleep thou didst abhor to dream,
Waking thou never wilt *consent* to do.—MILTON.

It is the part of the true believer not merely to *assent* to the Christian doctrines, but to make them the rule of his life: those who *consent* to a bad action are partakers in the guilt of it.

Approbation is a species of *assent; concurrence* of *consent*. To *approve* is not merely to *assent* to a thing that is right, but to feel it positively; to have the will and judgement in accordance; *concurrence* is the *consent* of many. *Approbation* respects the practical conduct of men in their intercourse with each other; *assent* is given to speculative truths, abstract propositions, or direct assertions. It is a happy thing when our actions meet with the *approbation* of others; but it is of little importance if we have not at the same time an *approving* conscience;

That not past me, but
By learned *approbation* of my judges.
SHAKSPEARE.

We may often *assent* to the premises of a question or proposition, without admitting the deductions drawn from them; 'Faith is the *assent* to any proposition not thus made out by the deduction of reason, but upon the credit of the proposer.'—LOCKE.

Concurrence respects matters of general concern, as *consent* respects those of individual interest. No bill in the house of parliament can pass for a second reading without the *concurrence* of a majority; 'Tarquin the Proud was expelled by a universal *concurrence* of nobles and people.'—SWIFT. No parent should be induced by persuasion to give his *consent* to what his judgement disapproves; 'I am far from excusing or denying that compliance: for plenary *consent* it was not.' —KING CHARLES.

Assent is opposed to contradiction or denial; *consent* to refusal; *approbation* to dislike or blame; *concurrence* to opposition: but we may sometimes seem to give our *assent* to what we do not expressly contradict, or seem to *approve* what we do not blame; and we are supposed to *consent* to a request when we do not positively refuse it. We may *approve* or disapprove of a thing without giving an intimation either of our *approbation* or the contrary: but *concurrence* cannot be altogether a negative action; it must be signified by some sign, although that need not necessarily be a word.

The *assent* of some people to the most important truths is so tame, that it might with no great difficulty be converted into a contradiction; 'The evidence of God's own testimony added unto the natural *assent* of reason, concerning the certainty of them, doth not a little comfort and confirm the same.'—HOOKER. He who is anxious to obtain universal *approbation*, or even to escape censure, will find his fate depictured in the story of the old man and his ass; 'There is as much difference between the *approbation* of the judgement and the actual volitions of the will with relation to the same object, as there is between a man's viewing a desirable thing with his eye and his reaching after it with his hand.'—SOUTH. According to the old proverb, 'Silence gives *consent*:' 'Whatever be the reason, it appears by the common *consent* of mankind that the want of virtue does not incur equal contempt with the want parts.'—HAWKESWORTH. It is not uncommon for ministerial men to give their *concurrence* in parliament to the measures of administration by a silent vote, while those of the opposite party spout forth their opposition to catch the applause of the multitude; 'Sir Matthew Hale mentions one case wherein the Lords may alter a money bill (that is, from a greater to a less time)—here he says the bill need not be sent back to the Commons for their *concurrence*.'—BLACKSTONE.

TO CONSENT, PERMIT, ALLOW

Consent has the same meaning as given under the head of *Accede; permit*, in French *permettre*, Latin *permitto*, compounded of *per* and *mitto*, signifies to send or let go past; *allow*, in French *allouer*, compounded of *ad* and *louer*, in German *loben*, low German *laven*, &c. from the Latin *laudare* to praise, signifies to give one's assent to a thing.

The idea of determining the conduct of others by some authorized act of one's own is common to these terms, but under various circumstances. They express either the act of an equal or a superiour.

As the act of an equal we *consent* to that in which we have an interest; we *permit* or *allow* what is for the accommodation of others: we *allow* by abstaining to oppose; we *permit* by a direct expression of our will; contracts are formed by the *consent* of the parties who are interested;

When thou canst truly call these virtues thine,
Be wise and free, by heaven's *consent* and mine.
DRYDEN.

The proprietor of an estate *permits* his friends to sport on his ground: 'You have given me your *permission* for this address, and encouraged me by your perusal and approbation.'—DRYDEN. A person *allows* of passage through his premises; 'I was by the freedom *allowable* among friends tempted to vent my thoughts with negligence.'—BOYLE. It is sometimes prudent to *consent; complaisant to *permit; good natured or weak to *allow*.

When applied to superiours, *consent* is an act of private authority; *permit* and *allow* are acts of private or publick authority: in the first case, *consent* respects matters of serious importance; *permit* and *allow* regard those of an indifferent nature: a parent *consents* to the establishment of his children; he *permits* them to read certain books: he *allows* them to converse with him familiarly.

We must pause before we give our *consent;* it is an express sanction to the conduct of others; it involves our own judgement, and the future interests of those who are under our control;

Though what thou tell'st some doubt within me move,
But more desire to hear, if thou *consent*
The full relation.—MILTON.

This is not always so necessary in *permitting* and *allowing;* they are partial actions, which require no more than the bare exercise of authority, and involve no other consequences than the temporary pleasure of the parties concerned. Publick measures are *permitted* and *allowed*, but never *consented* to. The law *permits* or *allows;* or the person who is authorized *permits* or *allows. Permit* in this case retains its positive sense; *allow* its negative sense, as before. Government *permits* individuals to fit out privateers in time of war; After men have acquired as much as the law *permits* them, they have nothing to do but to take care of the publick.'—SWIFT. When magistrates are not vigilant, many things will be done which are not *allowed;* 'They referred all laws, that were to be passed in Ireland, to be considered, corrected, and *allowed* by the state of England.'—SPENSER. A judge is not *permitted* to pass any sentence, but what is strictly conformable to law: every man who is accused is *allowed* to plead his own cause, or intrust it to another, as he thinks fit.

All these terms may be used in a general sense with the same distinction;

O no! our reason was not vainly lent!
Nor is a slave, but by its own *consent.*—DRYDEN.

Shame, and his conscience,
Will not *permit* him to deny it.—RANDOLPH.

'I think the strictest moralists *allow* forms of address to be used, without much regard to their literal acceptation.'—JOHNSON.

TO ADMIT, ALLOW, PERMIT, SUFFER, TOLERATE.

Admit, in French *admettre*, Latin *admitto*, compounded of *ad* and *mitto*, signifies to send or to suffer to pass into; to *allow*, in French *allouer*, compounded of the intensive syllable *al* or *ad* and *louer*, in German *loben*, old German *laubzan*, low German *laven*, Swedish *lofwa*, Danish *lover*, &c. Latin *laus* praise, *laudare* to praise, signifies to give praise or approbation to a thing; *permit*, in French *permettre*, Latin *permitto*, is compounded of *per* through or away, and *mitto* to send or let go, signifying to let it go its way; *suffer*, in French *souffrir*, Latin *suffero*, is compounded of *sub* and *fero*, signifying to bear with; *tolerate*, in Latin *toleratus*, participle of *tolero*, from the Greek τλάω to sustain, signifies also to bear or bear with.

The actions denoted by the first three terms are more or less voluntary; those of the last two are involuntary; *admit* is less voluntary than *allow;* and that than *permit*. We *admit* what we profess not to know, or seek not to prevent; we *allow* what we know, and tacitly consent to; we *permit* what we authorize by a formal consent; we *suffer* and *tolerate* what we object to, but do not think proper to prevent. We *admit* of things from inadvertence, or the want of inclination to prevent them; we *allow* of things from easiness of temper, or the want of resolution to oppose them; we *permit* things from a desire to oblige or a dislike to refuse; we *suffer* things for want of ability to remove them; we *tolerate* things from motives of discretion.

What is *admitted, allowed, suffered,* or *tolerated*, has already been done; what is *permitted* is desired to be done. To *admit, suffer*, and *tolerate*, are said of what ought to be avoided; *allow* and *permit* of things good, bad, or indifferent. *Suffer* is employed mostly with regard to private individuals; *tolerate* with respect to the civil power. It is dangerous to *admit* of familiarities from persons in a subordinate station, as they are apt to degenerate into impertinent freedoms, which though not *allowable* cannot be so conveniently resented: in this case we are often led to *permit* what we might otherwise prohibit: it is a great mark of weakness and blindness in parents to *suffer* that in their children which they condemn in others: opinions, however absurd, in matters of religion, must be *tolerated* by the civil authority when they have acquired such an ascendancy that they cannot be prevented without great violence.

A well-regulated society will be careful not to *admit* of any deviation from good order, which may afterward become injurious as a practice; 'Both Houses declared that they could *admit* of no treaty with the king, till he took down his standard and recalled his proclamations, in which the parliament supposed themselves to be declared traitors.'—HUME. It frequently happens that what has been *allowed* from indiscretion is afterward claimed as a right; 'Plutarch says very finely, that a man should not *allow* himself to hate even his enemies.'—ADDISON. No earthly power can *permit* that which is prohibited by the Divine law;

Permit our ships a shelter on your shores,
Refitted from your woods with planks and oars,
That if our prince be safe, we may renew
Our destin'd course, and Italy pursue.—DRYDEN.

When abuses are *suffered* to creep in, and to take deep root in any established institution, it is difficult to bring about a reform without endangering the existence of the whole; 'No man can be said to enjoy health, who is only not sick, without he feel within himself a light some and invigorating principle, which will not *suffer* him to remain idle.—SPECTATOR. When abuses are not very grievous, it is wiser to *tolerate* them than run the risk of producing a greater evil; 'No man ought to be *tolerated* in an habitual humour, whim, or particu larity of behaviour, by any who do not wait upon him for bread.'—STEELE.

TO ADMIT, ALLOW, GRANT.

Admit and *allow* are here taken mostly in applica tion to things that the mind assents to, and in this sense they are closely allied to the word *grant*, which, like the words *guarantee, warrant*, and *guard*, come from the German *währen* to see or look to, &c. signifying here to take consideration of.

We *admit* the truth of a position; *allow* the propriety of a remark; *grant* what is desired. Some men will not readily *admit* the possibility of overcoming bad habits; 'Though the fallibility of man's reason, and the narrowness of his knowledge, are very liberally confessed, yet the conduct of those who so willingly *admit* the weakness of human nature, seems to discover that this acknowledgment is not sincere.'—JOHNSON. It is ungenerous not to *allow* that some credit is due to those who effect any reformation in themselves; 'The zealots in atheism are perpetually teasing their friends to come over to them, although they *allow* that neither of them shall get any thing by the bargain.'—ADDISON. It is necessary, before any argument can be commenced, that something should be taken for *granted* on both sides; 'I take it at the same time for *granted* that the immortality of the soul is sufficiently established by other arguments'—STEELE.

TO ASK, BEG, REQUEST.

Ask (*v. To ask, inquire*) is here taken to denote an expression of our wishes generally for what we want from another; *beg* is contracted from the word *beggar*, and the German *begehren* to desire vehemently; *request* in Latin *requisitus*, participle of *requiro*, is com pounded of *re* and *quæro* to seek or look after with indications of desire to possess.

The expression of a wish to some one to have something is the common idea comprehended in these terms. As this is the simple signification of *ask*, it is the generick term; the other two are specifick: we *ask* in *begging* and *requesting*, but not *vice versâ*.

Asking is peculiar to no rank or station; in consequence of our mutual dependence on each other, it is requisite for every man to *ask* something of another: the master *asks* of the servant, the servant *asks* of the master; the parent *asks* of the child, the child *asks* of the parent. *Begging* marks a degree of dependence which is peculiar to inferiours in station: we *ask* for matters of indifference; we *beg* that which we think is of importance: a child *asks* a favour of his parent; a poor man *begs* the assistance of one who is able to afford it: that is asked for which is easily granted; that is *begged* which is with difficulty obtained. To *ask* therefore requires no effort; but to *beg* is to *ask* with importunity; those who by merely *asking* find themselves unable to obtain what they wish will have recourse to *begging*.

As *ask* sometimes implies a demand, and *beg* a vehemence of desire, or strong degree of necessity, politeness has adopted another phrase, which conveys neither the imperiousness of the one, nor the urgency of the other; this is the word *request*. *Asking* carries with it an air of superiority; *begging* that of submission; *requesting* has the air of independence and equality. *Asking* borders too nearly on an infringe ment of personal liberty; *begging* imposes a constrain by making an appeal to the feelings: *requests* leave the liberty of granting or refusing unencumbered. It is the character of impertinent people to *ask* without considering the circumstances and situation of the person *asked;* they seem ready to take without permission that which is *asked* if it be not granted;

Let him pursue the promis'd Latian shore,
A short delay is all I *ask* him now,
A pause of grief, an interval from wo.—DRYDEN.

Selfish and greedy people *beg* with importunity, and in a tone that admits of no refusal;

But we must *beg* our bread in climes unknown,
Beneath the scorching or the frozen zone.—DRYDEN.

Men of good breeding tender their *requests* with moderation and discretion; they *request* nothing but what they are certain can be conveniently complied with;

But do not you my last *request* deny,
With yon perfidious man your int'rest try.
DRYDEN.

Ask is altogether exploded from polite life, although *beg* is not. We may *beg* a person's acceptance of any thing; we may *beg* him to favour or honour us with his company; but we can never talk of *asking* a person's acceptance, or *asking* him to do us an honour. *Beg* in such cases indicates a condescension which is sometimes not unbecoming, but on ordinary occasion *request* is with more propriety substituted in its place.

TO BEG, DESIRE.

Beg in its original sense as before given (*v. To ask, beg*) signifies to *desire; desire*, in French *desir*, Latin *desidero*, comes from *desido* to fix the mind on an object.

To *beg*, marks the wish; to *desire*, the will and determination.

Beg is the act of an inferiour, or one in subordinate condition; *desire* is the act of a superiour: we *beg* a thing as a favour; we *desire* it as a right; children *beg* their parents to grant them an indulgence;

She 'll hang upon his lips, and *beg* him tell
The story of my passion o'er again.—SOUTHERN.

Parents *desire* their children to attend to their business; 'Once, when he was without lodging, meat, or clothes, one of his friends left a message, that he *desired* to see him about nine in the morning. Savage knew that it was his intention to assist him; but was very much disgusted that he should presume to prescribe the hour of his attendance, and I believe refused to see him.'—JOHNSON.

TO BEG, BESEECH, SOLICIT, ENTREAT, SUPPLICATE, IMPLORE, CRAVE.

Beg is here taken as before (*v. To ask, beg*); *beseech*, compounded of *be* and *seech*, or *seek*, is an intensive verb, signifying to seek strongly; *solicit*, in French *soliciter*, Latin *solicito*, is probably compounded of *solum* or *totum*, and *cito* to cite, summon, appeal to, signifying to rouse altogether; *entreat*, compounded of *en* or *in* and *treat*, in French *traiter*, Latin *tracto* to manage, signifies to act upon; *supplicate*, in Latin *supplicatus*, participle of *supplico*, compounded of *sup* or *sub* and *plico* to fold, signifies to bend the body down in token of submission or distress in order to awaken notice; *implore*, in French *implorer*, Latin *imploro*, compounded of *im* or *in* and *ploro* to weep or lament, signifies to act upon by weeping; *crave*, in Saxon *cravian*, signifies to long for earnestly.

All these terms denote a species of asking, varied as to the person, the object, and the manner; the first four do not mark such a state of dependence in the agent as the last three: to *beg* denotes a state of want; to *beseech*, *entreat*, and *solicit*, a state of urgent necessity; *supplicate* and *implore*, a state of abject distress; *crave*, the lowest state of physical want: one *begs* with importunity; *beseeches* with earnestness; *entreats* by the force of reasoning and strong representation; one *solicits* by virtue of one's interest; *supplicates* by an humble address; *implores* by every mark of dejection and humiliation.

Begging is the act of the poor when they need assistance: *beseeching* and *entreating* are resorted to by friends and equals, when they want to influence or persuade, but *beseeching* is more urgent; *entreating* more argumentative: *solicitations* are employed to obtain favours, which have more respect to the circumstances than the rank of the solicitor: *supplicating* and *imploring* are resorted to by sufferers for the relief of their misery, and are addressed to those who have the power of averting or increasing the calamity: *craving* is the consequence of longing; it marks an earnestness of *supplication*: an abject state of suffering dependence.

Those who have any object to obtain commonly have recourse to *begging;*

What more advance can mortals make in sin,
So near perfection, who with blood begin?
Deaf to the calf that lies beneath the knife,
Looks up, and from the butcher *begs* her life.
DRYDEN.

A kind parent will sometimes rather *beseech* an undutiful child to lay aside his wicked courses, than plunge him deeper into guilt by an ill-timed exercise of authority; 'Modesty never rages, never murmurs, never pouts when it is ill-treated; it pines, it *beseeches*, it languishes.'—STEELE. When we are *entreated* to do an act of civility, it is a mark of unkindness to be heedless to the wishes of our friends;

I have a wife, whom I protest I love;
I would she were in heav'n, so she could
Entreat some pow'r to change this currish Jew.
SHAKSPEARE.

Gentlemen in office are perpetually exposed to the *solicitations* of their friends, to procure for themselves or their connexions places of trust and emolument; 'As money collected by subscription is necessarily received in small sums, Savage was never able to send his poems to the press, but for many years continued his *solicitation*, and squandered whatever he obtained.'—JOHNSON. A slave *supplicates* his master for pardon, whom he has offended; 'Savage wrote to Lord Tyrconnel, not in a style of *supplication* and respect; but of reproach, menace, and contempt.'—JOHNSON. An offender *implores* mercy for the mitigation, if not the remission, of his punishment;

Is 't then so hard, Monimia, to forgive
A fault, where humble love, like mine, *implores* thee?
OTWAY.

A poor wretch, suffering with hunger, *craves* a morsel of bread;

For my past crimes, my forfeit life receive.
No pity for my sufferings here I *crave*,
And only hope forgiveness in the grave.
ROWE'S JANE SHORE.

SOLICITATION, IMPORTUNITY.

Solicitation (*v. To beg*) is general; *importunity*, from the Latin *importunus*, or *in* and *portus*, signifies a running into harbour after the manner of distressed mariners, is a vehement and troublesome form of *solicitation*. *Solicitation* is itself indeed that which gives trouble to a certain extent, but it is not always unreasonable: there may be cases in which we may yield to the *solicitations* of friends, to do that which we have no objection to be obliged to do: but *importunity* is that *solicitation* which never ceases to apply for that which it is not agreeable to give. We may sometimes be urgent in our *solicitations* of a friend to accept some proffered honour; the *solicitation* however, in this case, although it may even be troublesome, yet it is sweetened by the motive of the action: the *importunity* of beggars is often a politick means of extorting money from the passenger; 'Although the devil cannot compel a man to sin, yet he can follow a man with continual *solicitations*.'—SOUTH. The torment of expectation is not easily to be borne, when the heart has no rival engagements to withdraw it from the *importunities* of desire.'—JOHNSON.

PRESSING, URGENT, IMPORTUNATE.

Pressing and *urgent*, from to *press* and *urge*, are applied as qualifying terms, either to persons or things, *importunate*, from the verb to *importune*, which probably signifies to wish to get into port, to land at some port, is applied only to persons. In regard to *pressing*, it is said either of one's demands, one's requests or one's exhortations; *urgent* is said of one's solicitations or entreaties; *importunate* is said of one's begging or applying for. The *pressing* has more of violence in it; it is supported by force and authority; it is employed in matters of right, and appeals to the understanding; 'Mr. Gay, whose zeal in your concern is worthy a friend, writes to me in the most *pressing* terms about it.'—POPE. The *urgent* makes an appeal to one's feelings; it is more persuasive, and is employed in matters of favour; 'Neither would he have done it at all but at my *urgency*.'—SWIFT. The *importunate* has some of the force, but none of the authority or obligation of the *pressing;* it is employed in matters of personal gratification: 'Sleep may be put off from time to time, yet the demand is of so *importunate* a nature as not to remain long unsatisfied.'—JOHNSON. When applied to things, *pressing* is as much more forcible than *urgent*, as in the former case; we speak of a *pressing* necessity, an *urgent* case. A creditor will be *pressing* for his money when he fears to lose it; one friend is *urgent* with another to intercede in his behalf; beggars are commonly *importunate* with the hope of teasing persons out of their money.

TO DESIRE, WISH, LONG FOR, HANKER AFTER, COVET.

Desire, in Latin *desidero*, comes from *desido* to rest or fix upon with the mind; *wish*, in German *wünschen*, comes from *wonne* pleasure, signifying to take pleasure in a thing; *long*, from the German *langen* to reach after, signifies to seek after with the mind; *hanker*, *hanger*, or *hang*, signifies to hang on an object with one's mind; *covet* is changed from the Latin *cupio* to desire.

The *desire* is imperious, it demands gratification; 'When men have discovered a passionate *desire* of fame in the ambitious man (as no temper of mind is more apt to show itself,) they become sparing and reserved in their commendations.'—ADDISON. The *wish* is less vehement, it consists of a strong inclination; 'It is as absurd in an old man to *wish* for the strength of youth, as it would be in a young man to *wish* for the strength of a bull or a horse.'—STEELE. *Longing* is an impatient and continued species of desire;

Extended on the fun'ral couch he lies,
And soon as morning paints the eastern skies,
The sight is granted to thy *longing* eyes.—POPE.

Hankering is a *desire* for that which is set out of one's reach; 'The wife is an old coquette that is always *hankering after* the diversions of the town.'—ADDISON. *Coveting* is a *desire* for that which belongs to another, or what it is in his power to grant; 'You know Chaucer has a tale, where a knight saves his head by discovering it was the thing which all women most *coveted*.'—GAY. We *desire* or *long for* that which is near at hand, or within view; we *wish* for and *covet* that which is more remote, or less distinctly seen; we *hanker after* that which has been once enjoyed: a discontented person *wishes* for more than he has; he who is in a strange land *longs* to see his native country; vicious men *hanker after* the pleasures which are denied them; ambitious men *covet* honours, avaricious men *covet* riches.

Desires ought to be moderated; *wishes* to be limited; *longings*, *hankerings*, and *covetings* to be suppressed: uncontrolled *desires* become the greatest torments; unbounded *wishes* are the bane of all happiness; ardent *longings* are mostly irrational, and not entitled to indulgence; *coveting* is expressly prohibited by the Divine law.

Desire, as it regards others, is not less imperative than when it respects ourselves; it lays an obligation on the person to whom it is expressed: a *wish* is gentle and unassuming; it appeals to the good nature of another: we act by the *desire* of a superiour, and according to the *wishes* of an equal: the *desire* of a parent will amount to a command in the mind of a dutiful child: his *wishes* will be anticipated by the warmth of affection.

TO WILL, WISH.

The *will* is that faculty of the soul which is the most prompt and decisive; it immediately impels to action: the *wish* is but a gentle motion of the soul towards a thing. We can *will* nothing but what we can effect, we may *wish* for many things which lie above our reach. The *will* must be under the entire control of reason, or it will lead a person into every mischief; 'A good inclination is but the first rude draught of virtue: but the finishing strokes are from the *will*.'—SOUTH. *Wishes* ought to be under the direction of reason; or otherwise they may greatly disturb our happiness: 'The *wishing* of a thing is not properly the *willing* of it; it imports no more than an idle, unoperative, complacency in, and desire of, the object.'—SOUTH.

WILLINGLY, VOLUNTARILY, SPONTANEOUSLY.

To do a thing *willingly* is to do it with a good-will; to do a thing *voluntarily* is to do it of one's own accord: the former respects one's *willingness* to comply with the wishes of another; we do what is asked of us, it is a mark of good nature: the latter respects our freedom from foreign influence; we do that which we like to do; it is a mark of our sincerity. It is pleasant to see a child do his task *willingly;*

Food not of angels, yet accepted so,
As that more *willingly* thou couldst not seem,
At heav'n's high feasts t' have fed.—MILTON.

It is pleasant to see a man *voluntarily* engage in any service of publick good; 'Thoughts are only criminal when they are first chosen, and then *voluntarily* continued.'—JOHNSON. *Spontaneously* is but a mode of the *voluntary*, applied, however, more commonly to inanimate objects than to the will of persons: the ground produces *spontaneously*, when it produces without culture; and words flow *spontaneously*, which require no effort on the part of the speaker to produce them;

Of these none uncontroll'd and lawless rove,
But to some destin'd end *spontaneous* move.
JENYNS

If, however, applied to the will, it bespeaks in a stronger degree the totally unbiassed state of the agent's mind: the *spontaneous* effusions of the heart are more than the *voluntary* services of benevolence. The *willing* is opposed to the *unwilling*, the *voluntary* to the mechanical or *involuntary*, the *spontaneous* to the reluctant or the artificial.

TO LEAN, INCLINE, BEND.

Lean and *incline* both come from the Latin *clino*, and Greek κλίνω to bow or bend; *bend* is connected with the German *wenden* to turn, and the English *wind*, &c.

In the proper sense *lean* and *incline* are both said of the position of bodies; *bend* is said of the shape of bodies: that which *leans* rests on one side, or in a sideward direction; that which *inclines*, *leans* or turns only in a slight degree: that which *bends* forms a curvature; it does not all *lean* the same way: a house *leans* when the foundation gives way; a tree may grow so as *incline* to the right or the left, or a road may *incline* this or that way; a tree or a road *bends* when it turns out of the straight course.

In the improper sense the judgement *leans*, the will *inclines*, the will or conduct *bends*, in consequence of some outward action. A person *leans* to this or that side of a question which he favours; he *inclines* or is *inclined* to this or that mode of conduct; he *bends* to the will of another. It is the duty of a judge to *lean* to the side of mercy as far as is consistent with justice;

Like you a courtier born and bred,
Kings *lean'd* their ear to what I said.—GAY.

Whoever *inclines* too readily to listen to the tales of distress which are continually told to excite compassion, will find himself in general deceived;

Say what you want: the Latins you shall find,
Not forc'd to goodness, but by will *inclin'd*.—DRYDEN.

An *unbending* temper is the bane of domestick felicity;

And as on corn when western gusts descend,
Before the blast the lofty harvest *bend*.—POPE.

BENT, BIAS, INCLINATION, PREPOSSESSION.

Bias, in French *Biais*, signifies a weight fixed on one side of a bowl in order to turn its course that way towards which the *bias* leans, from the Greek *βία* force; *inclination*, in French *inclination*, Latin *inclinatio*, from *inclino*, Greek *κλίνω*, signifies a leaning towards; *prepossession*, compounded of *pre* and *possession*, signifies the taking *possession* of the mind previously, or beforehand.

All these terms denote a preponderating influence on the mind. *Bent* is applied to the will, affection, and power in general; *bias* solely to the judgement; *inclination* and *prepossession* to the state of the feelings. The *bent* includes the general state of the mind, and the object on which it fixes a regard;

Servile *inclinations*, and gross love,
The guilty *bent* of vicious appetite.—HAVARD.

Bias, the particular influential power which sways the judging faculty; 'The choice of man's will is indeed uncertain, because in many things free; but yet there are certain habits and principles in the soul that have some kind of sway upon it, apt to *bias* it more one way than another.'—SOUTH. The one is absolutely considered with regard to itself; the other relatively to its results and the object it acts upon.

Bent is sometimes with regard to *bias*, as cause is to effect; we may frequently trace in the particular *bent* of a person's likes and dislikes the principal *bias* which determines his opinions. *Inclination* is a faint kind of *bent; prepossession* is a weak species of *bias*: an *inclination* is a state of something, namely, a state of the feelings: *prepossession* is an actual something, namely, the thing that *prepossesses*.

We may discover the *bent* of a person's mind in his gay or serious moments; in his occupations, and in his pleasures; in some persons it is so strong, that scarcely an action passes which is not more or less influenced by it, and even the exteriour of a man will be under its control: in all disputed matters the support of a party will operate more or less to *bias* the minds of men for or against particular men, or particular measures: when we are attached to the party that espouses the cause of religion and good order, this *bias* is in some measure commendable and salutary: a mind without *inclination* would be a blank, and where *inclination* is, there is the groundwork for *prepossession*. Strong minds will be strongly *bent*, and labour under a strong *bias*; but there is no mind so weak and powerless as not to have its *inclinations*, and none so perfect as to be without its *prepossessions*: the mind that has virtuous *inclinations* will be *prepossessed* in favour of every thing that leans to virtue's side; it were well for mankind that this were the only *prepossession*; but in the present mixture of truth and errour, it is necessary to guard against *prepossessions* as dangerous anticipations of the judgement; if their object be not perfectly pure, or their force be not qualified by the restrictive powers of the judgement, much evil springs from their abuse;

'T is not indulging private *inclination*,
The selfish passions, that sustains the world,
And lends its Ruler grace.—THOMSON.

I take it for a rule, that in marriage the chief business is to acquire a *prepossession* in favour of each other.'—STEELE.

INCLINATION, TENDENCY, PROPENSITY, PRONENESS.

All these terms are employed to designate the state of the will towards an object: *inclination* (*v. Bent*) denotes its first movement towards an object: *tendency*, from to *tend*, is a continued *inclination*: *propensity*, from the Latin *propensus* and *propendeo* to hang forward, denotes a still stronger leaning of the will; and *prone*, from the Latin *pronus* downward, characterizes an habitual and fixed state of the will towards an object. The *inclination* expresses the leaning but not the direction of that leaning; it may be to the right or to the left, upwards or downwards; consequently we may have an *inclination* to that which is good or bad, high or low; *tendency* does not specify any particular direction; but from the idea of pressing, which it conveys, it is appropriately applied to those things which degenerate or lead to what is bad; excessive strictness in the treatment of children has a *tendency* to damp the spirit: *propensity* and *proneness* both designate a downward direction, and consequently refer only to that which is bad and low; a person has a *propensity* to drinking, and a *proneness* to lying

Inclination is always at the command of the understanding; it is our duty therefore to suppress the first risings of any *inclination* to extravagance, intemperance, or any irregularity; 'Partiality is properly the understanding's judging according to the *inclination* of the will.'—SOUTH. As *tendency* refers to the thing rather than the person, it is our business to avoid that which has a *tendency* to evil; 'Every immoral act, in the direct *tendency* of it, is certainly a step downwards.'—SOUTH. The *propensity* will soon get the mastery of the best principles, and the firmest resolution; it is our duty therefore to seek all the aids which religion affords to subdue every *propensity*; 'Such is the *propensity* of our nature to vice, that stronger restraints than those of mere reason are necessary to be imposed on man.'—BLAIR. *Proneness* to evil is inherent in our nature which we derive from our first parents; it is the grace of God which alone can lift us up above this grovelling part of ourselves; 'Every commission of sin imprints upon the soul a further disposition and *proneness* to sin.'—SOUTH.

BIAS, PREPOSSESSION, PREJUDICE.

Bias (*v. Bent, Bias*) marks the state of the mind; *prepossession* applies either to the general or particular state of the feelings; *prejudice* is employed only for opinions. *Prejudice*, in French *préjudice*, Latin *præjudicium*, compounded of *præ* before, and *judicium* judgement, signifies a judgement before hand, that is, before examination. Children may receive an early *bias* that influences their future character and destiny: *prepossessions* spring from casualties; they do not exist in young minds: *prejudices* are the fruits of a contracted education. Physical infirmities often give a strong *bias* to serious pursuits; 'It should be the principal labour of moral writers to remove the *bias* which inclines the mind rather to prefer natural than moral endowments.'—HAWKESWORTH. *Prepossessions* created by outward appearances are not always fallacious: 'A man in power, who can, without the ordinary *prepossessions* which stop the way to the true knowledge and service of mankind, overlook the little distinctions of fortune, raise obscure merit, and discountenance successful indesert, has, in the minds of knowing men, the figure of an angel rather than a man.'—STEELE. It is at present the fashion to brand every thing with the name of *prejudice*, which does not coincide with the lax notions of the age 'It is the work of a philosopher to be every day subduing his passions, and laying aside his *prejudices*. I endeavour at least to look upon men and their actions only as an impartial spectator.'—SPECTATOR. A *bias* may be overpowered, a *prepossession* overcome, and a *prejudice* corrected or removed.

We may be *biassed* for or against, we are always *prepossessed* in favour, and mostly *prejudiced* against.

COVETOUSNESS, CUPIDITY, AVARICE

Covetousness, from *covet*, and *cupido* to desire, signifies having a desire; *cupidity* is a more immediate derivative from the Latin *cupiditas*, and signifies the same thing; *avarice*, from *aveo* to long for, signifies by distinction a longing for money.

All these terms are employed to express an illicit desire after objects of gratification; but *covetousness* is applied to property in general; *cupidity* and *avarice* only to money or possessions. A child may display its *covetousness* in regard to the playthings which fall in its way; a man shows his *cupidity* in regard to the gains that fall in his way; we should therefore be careful to check a *covetous* disposition in early life, lest it show itself in the more hateful character of *cupidity* in advanced years. *Covetousness* is the natural disposition for having or getting; *cupidity* is the acquired disposition. As the love of appropriation is an innate characteristick in man, that of accumulating or wanting to accumulate, which constitutes *covetousness*, will show itself, in some persons, among the first indications of character; 'Nothing lies on our hands with such uneasiness as time. Wretched and thoughtless creatures! In the only place where *covetousness* were a virtue, we turn prodigals.—ADDISON. Where the prospect of amassing great wealth is set before a man, as in the case of a governour of a distant province, it will evince great virtue in him, if his *cupidity* be not excited; 'If prescription be once shaken, no species of property is secure, when it once becomes an object large enough to tempt the *cupidity* of indigent power.'—BURKE.

The *covetous* man seeks to add to what he has: the *avaricious* man only strives to retain what he has; the *covetous* man sacrifices others to indulge himself; the *avaricious* man will sometimes sacrifice himself to indulge others: for generosity, which is opposed to *covetousness*, is sometimes associated with *avarice*; 'At last Swift's *avarice* grew too powerful for his kindness; he would refuse (his friends) a bottle of wine.'—JOHNSON.

AVARICIOUS, MISERLY, PARSIMONIOUS, NIGGARDLY.

Avaricious, from the Latin *aveo* to desire, signifies in general longing for, but by distinction longing for money; *miserly* signifies like a *miser* or *miserable man*, for none are so miserable as the lovers of money; *parsimonious*, from the Latin *parco* to spare or save, signifies literally saving; *niggardly* is a frequentative of nigh or close, signifies very nigh.

The *avaricious* man and the *miser* are one and the same character, with this exception, that the *miser* carries his passion for money to a still greater excess. An *avaricious* man shows his love of money in his ordinary dealings; but the *miser* lives upon it, and suffers every privation rather than part with it. An *avaricious* man may sometimes be indulgent to himself, and generous to others; 'Though the apprehensions of the aged may justify a cautious frugality, they can by no means excuse a sordid *avarice*.'—BLAIR. The *miser* is dead to every thing but the treasure which he has amassed;

As some lone *miser* visiting his store,
Bends at his treasure, counts, recounts it o'er;
Hoards after hoards his rising raptures fill,
Yet still he sighs, for hoards are wanting still;
Thus to my breast alternate passions rise,
Pleas'd with each bliss that Heav'n to man supplies.
Yet oft a sigh prevails and sorrows fall,
To see the hoard of human bliss so small.
GOLDSMITH.

Parsimonious and *niggardly* are the subordinate characteristicks of *avarice*. The *avaricious* man indulges his passion for money by *parsimony*, that is, by saving out of himself, or by *niggardly* ways in his dealings with others. He who spends a farthing on himself, where others with the same means spend a shilling, does it from *parsimony*; 'Armstrong died in September, 1779, and to the surprise of his friends left a considerable sum of money, saved by great *parsimony* out of a very moderate income.'—JOHNSON. He who looks to every farthing in the bargains he makes, gets the name of a *niggard*; 'I have heard Dodsley, by whom Akenside's "*Pleasures of the Imagination*" was published, relate, that when the copy was offered him, he carried the work to Pope, who, having looked into it, advised him not to make a *niggardly* offer, for this was no every day writer.'—JOHNSON. *Avarice* sometimes cloaks itself under the name of prudence: it is, as Goldsmith says, often the only virtue which is left a man at the age of seventy-two. The *miser* is his own greatest enemy, and no man's friend; his ill-gotten wealth is generally a curse to him by whom it is inherited. A man is sometimes rendered *parsimonious* by circumstances; he who first saves from necessity but too often ends with saving from inclination. The *niggard* is an object of contempt, and sometimes hatred; every one fears to lose by a man who strives to gain from all.

ŒCONOMICAL, SAVING, SPARING, THRIFTY, PENURIOUS, NIGGARDLY.

The idea of not spending is common to all these terms; but *œconomical* signifies not spending unnecessarily or unwisely; *saving* is keeping and laying by with care; *sparing* is keeping out of that which ought to be spent; *thrifty* or *thriving* is accumulating by means of *saving*: *penurious* is suffering as from *penury* by means of *saving*; *niggardly*, after the manner of a *niggard*, nigh or close person, is not spending or letting go, but in the smallest possible quantities.

To be *œconomical* is a virtue in those who have but narrow means; 'I cannot fancy that a shopkeeper's wife in Cheapside has a greater tenderness for the fortune of her husband than a citizen's wife in Paris; or that Miss in a boarding-school is more an *œconomist* in dress than Mademoiselle in a nunnery.'—GOLDSMITH All the other epithets however are employed in a sense more or less unfavourable; he who is *saving* when young, will be covetous when old; he who is *sparing* will generally be *sparing* out of the comforts of others; he who is *thrifty* commonly adds the desire of getting with that of *saving*; he who is *penurious* wants no thing to make him a complete miser; he who is *niggardly* in his dealings will be mostly avaricious in his character; 'I may say of fame as Falstaff did of honour, "if it comes it comes unlook'd for, and there is an end on't." I am content with a bare *saving* game.'—POPE.

Youth is not rich, in time it may be poor,
Part with it, as with money, *sparing*.—YOUNG.

'Nothing is *penuriously* imparted, of which a more liberal distribution would increase real felicity.'—JOHNSON.

Who by resolves and vows engag'd does stand,
For days that yet belong to fate,
Does like an *unthrift* mortgage his estate
Before it falls into his hands.—COWLEY.

No *niggard* nature; men are prodigals.—YOUNG.

ŒCONOMY, FRUGALITY, PARSIMONY

Œconomy, from the Greek οἰκονομία, implies management; *frugality*, from the Latin *fruges* fruits, implies temperance; *parsimony* (*v. Avaricious*) implies simply forbearing to spend, which is in fact the common idea included in these terms; but the *œconomical* man spares expense according to circumstances; he adapts his expenditure to his means, and renders it by contrivance as effectual to his purpose as possible; 'War and *œconomy* are things not easily reconciled, and the attempt of leaning towards *parsimony* in such a state may be the worst *œconomy* in the world.'—BURKE. The *frugal* man spares expense on himself or on his indulgences; he may however be liberal to others while he is *frugal* towards himself; 'I accept of your invitation to supper, but I must make this agreement beforehand, that you dismiss me soon, and treat me *frugally*.'—MELMOTH (*Letters of Pliny*). The *parsimonious* man saves from himself as well as others; he has no other object than saving. By *œconomy*, a man may make a limited income turn to the best account for himself and his family; by *frugality* he may with a limited income be enabled to do much good to others; by *parsimony* he may be enabled to accumulate great sums out of a narrow income: hence it is that we recommend a plan for being *œconomical*; we recommend a diet for being *frugal*; we condemn a habit or a character for being *parsimonious*.

ŒCONOMY, MANAGEMENT.

Œconomy (*v. Œconomy*) has a more comprehensive meaning than *management*; for it includes the system of science and of legislation as well as that of domestick arrangements; as the *œconomy* of agriculture; the internal *œconomy* of a government; political, civil, or religious *œconomy*; or the *œconomy* of one's house hold; 'Your *œconomy* I suppose begins now to be settled; your expenses are adjusted to your revenue.'—JOHNSON. *Management*, on the contrary, is an action that is very seldom abstracted from its agent, and is always taken in a partial sense, namely, as a part of *œconomy*. The internal *œconomy* of a family depends principally on the prudent *management* of the female: the *œconomy* of every well-regulated community requires that all the members should keep their station, and preserve a strict subordination;

Oh spare this waste of being half divine,
And vindicate th' *œconomy* of heav'n.—YOUNG.

The *management* of particular branches of civil *œconomy* should belong to particular individuals; 'What incident can show more *management* and address in the poet (Milton), than this of Sampson's refusing the summons of the idolaters, and obeying the visitation of God's spirit.'—CUMBERLAND.

AVIDITY, GREEDINESS, EAGERNESS,

Are epithets expressive of a strong desire; *avidity*, in Latin *aviditas*, from *aveo* to desire, expresses very strong desire; *greediness*, from the German *gierig*, and *begehren* to desire, signifies the same; *eagerness*, from *eager*, and the Latin *acer* sharp, signifies acuteness of feeling.

Avidity is in mental desires what *greediness* is in animal appetites: *eagerness* is not so vehement, but more impatient than *avidity* or *greediness*. *Avidity* and *greediness* respect simply the desire of possessing; *eagerness* the general desire of attaining an object. An opportunity is seized with *avidity*; or a person gratifies his *avidity*; 'I have heard that Addison's *avidity* did not satisfy itself with the air of renown, but that with great *eagerness* he laid hold on his proportion of the profits.'—JOHNSON. The miser grasps at money with *greediness*, or the glutton devours with *greediness*. A person runs with *eagerness* in order to get to the place of destination: a soldier fights with *eagerness* in order to conquer: a lover looks with *eager* impatience for a letter from the object of his affection;

> Bid the sea listen, when the *greedy* merchant,
> To gorge its ravenous jaws, hurls all his wealth,
> And stands himself upon the splitting deck
> For the last plunge.—LEE.

Avidity is employed in an adverbial form to qualify an action: we seize with *avidity*. *Greediness* marks the abstract quality or habit of the mind; it is the characteristick of low and brutal minds: *eagerness* denotes the transitory state of a feeling; a person discovers his *eagerness* in his looks.

TO GIVE, GRANT, BESTOW, ALLOW.

Give, in Saxon *gifan*, German *geben*, &c. is derived by Adelung from the old word *gaff* the hollow of the hand, because the hand was commonly used in pledging or giving, whence this word is allied to the Greek ἐγγυάω to pledge or promise, and γυιὸν a limb; *grant* is probably contracted from *guarantee*, and the French *garantir*, signifying to assure any thing to a person by one's word or deed; *bestow* is compounded of *be* and *stow*, which in English and the northern languages signifies to place, whence to *bestow* signifies to dispose according to one's wishes and convenience; *allow* is here taken in the same general sense as in the article *To admit, allow*.

The idea of communicating to another what is our own, or in our power, is common to these terms; this is the whole signification of *give*; but *grant*, *bestow*, and *allow* include accessory ideas in their meaning. To *grant* is to *give* at one's pleasure; to *bestow* is to *give* with a certain degree of necessity. *Giving* is confined to no object; whatever property we transfer into the hands of another, that we *give*; we *give* money, clothes, food, or whatever is transferable: *granting* is confined to such objects as afford pleasure or convenience; they may consist of transferable property or not; *bestowing* is applied to such objects only as are necessary to supply wants, which always consist of that which is transferable. We *give* what is liked or not liked, asked for or unasked for; we *grant* that only which is wished for and requested. One may *give* poison or medicine; one may *give* to a beggar, or to a friend; one *grants* a sum of money by way of loan: we *give* what is wanted or not wanted; we *bestow* that only which is expressly wanted: we *give* with an idea of a return or otherwise; we *grant* voluntarily, without any prospect of a return; we *give* for a permanency or otherwise; we *bestow* only in particular cases which require immediate notice. Many *give* things to the rich only to increase the number of their superfluities, and they *give* to the poor to relieve their necessities; they *bestow* their alms on an indigent sufferer.

To *give* has no respect to the circumstances of the action or the agent; it is applicable to persons of all conditions: to *grant* bespeaks not only the will but the power and influence of the *grantor*; to *bestow* bespeaks the necessitous condition of the receiver. Children may *give* to their parents and parents to their children, kings to their subjects or subjects to their kings; but monarchs only *grant* to their subjects, or parents to their children; and superiours in general *bestow* upon their dependants that which they cannot provide for themselves.

In an extended application of the terms to moral objects or circumstances, they strictly adhere to the same line of distinction. We *give* our consent; we *give* our promise; we *give* our word; we *give* credit; we *give* in all cases that which may be simply transferred from one to another;

> Happy when both to the same centre move,
> When kings *give* liberty, and subjects love.
> DENHAM.

Liberties, rights, privileges, favours, indulgences, permissions, and all things are *granted*, which are in the hands only of a few, but are acceptable to many;

> The gods will *grant*
> What their unerring wisdom sees they want
> DRYDEN.

Blessings, care, concern, and the like, are *bestowed* upon those who are dependent upon others for whatever they have.

Give and *bestow* are likewise said of things as well as of persons; *grant* is said only of persons. *Give* is here equally general and indefinite; *bestow* conveys the idea of *giving* under circumstances of necessity and urgency. One *gives* a preference to a particular situation; one *gives* a thought to a subject that is proposed; one *gives* time and labour to any matter that engages one's attention; 'Milton afterward *give* us a description of the morning, which is wonderfully suitable to a divine poem.'—ADDISON. But one *bestows* pains on that which demands particular attention; one *bestows* a moment's thought on one particular subject, out of the number which engage attention; 'After having thus treated at large of Paradise Lost, I could not think it sufficient to have celebrated this poem, in the whole, without descending to particulars: I have therefore *bestowed* a paper on each book.'—ADDISON.

That is *granted* which is desired, if not directly asked for; that is *bestowed* which is wanted as a matter of necessity; that is *allowed* which may be expected, if not directly required.

What is *granted* is perfectly gratuitous on the part of the giver, it is a pure favour, and lays the receiver under an obligation; what is *bestowed* is occasional, altogether depending on the circumstances and disposition of both giver and receiver; what is *allowed* is a gift stipulated as to time and quantity, which as to continuance depends upon the will of the giver.

It is as improper to *grant* a person more than he asks, as it is to ask a person for more than he can *grant*. Alms are very ill *bestowed* which only serve to encourage beggary and idleness; many of the poor are *allowed* a small sum weekly from the parish.

A *grant* comprehends in it something more important than an *allowance*, and passes between persons in a higher station; what is *bestowed* is of less value than either. A father *allows* his son a yearly sum for his casual expenses, or a master *allows* his servant a maintenance; 'Martial's description of a species of lawyers is full of humour: "Men that hire out their words and anger, that are more or less passionate as they are paid for it, and *allow* their client a quantity of wrath proportionable to the fee which they receive from him."'—ADDISON. Kings *grant* pensions to their officers; governments *grant* subsidies to one another

> If you in pity *grant* this one request,
> My death shall glut the hatred of his breast.
> DRYDEN.

Relief is *bestowed* on the indigent; 'Our Saviour doth plainly witness that there should not be as much as a cup of cold water *bestowed* for his sake without reward.'—HOOKER.

In a figurative acceptation that is *granted* which is given by way of favour or indulgence; that is *bestowed* which is done in justice, or by way of reward or necessity; that is *allowed* which is done by way of courtesy or compliance.

In former times the kings of England *granted* certain privileges to some towns, which they retain to this day; 'All the land is the queen's, unless there be some *grant* of any part thereof to be showed from her majesty.'—SPENSER. Those who are hasty in ap plauding frequently *bestow* their commendations on very undeserving objects;

> So much the more thy diligence *bestow*,
> In depth of winter to defend the snow.—DRYDEN.

A candid man *allows* merit even in his rivals; 'I shall be ready to *allow* the pope as little power here as you please.'—SWIFT.

TO GIVE, AFFORD, SPARE.

Give is here the generick term, as in the preceding article; *afford*, probably changed from *afferred*, from the Latin *affero*, or *ad* and *fero*, signifies literally to bring to a person; *spare*, in German *sparen*, Latin *parco*, and Hebrew פרק to preserve, signifies here to lay up for a particular purpose. These words are allied to each other in the sense of sending forth: but the former denotes an unqualified and unconditional action; the latter bears a relation to the circumstances of the agent. A person is said to *give* money without any regard to the state of his finances: he is said to *afford* what he *gives*, when one wishes to define his pecuniary condition; 'Nothing can *give* that to another which it hath not itself.'—BRAMHALL. 'The same errours run through all families, where there is wealth enough to afford that their sons may be good for nothing.'—SWIFT. The same idea runs through the application of these terms to all other cases, in which inanimate things are made the agents;

> Are these our great pursuits? Is this to live,
> These all the hopes this much-lov'd world can *give*?
> JENYNS.

'Our paper manufacture takes into use several mean materials, which could be put to no other use, and *affords* work for several hands in the collection of them, which are incapable of any other employment.'—ADDISON. When we say a thing *gives* satisfaction, we simply designate the action; when we say it *affords* pleasure, we refer to the nature and properties of the thing thus specified; the former is employed only to declare the fact, the latter to characterize the object. Hence, in certain cases, we should say, this or that posture of the body *gives* ease to a sick person; but, as a moral sentiment, we should say, nothing *affords* such ease to the mind as a clear conscience; 'This is the consolation of all good men, unto whom the ubiquity *affordeth* continual comfort and security.'—BROWN. (*Vulg. Err.*) Upon the same grounds the use of these terms is justified in the following cases; to *give* rise; or *give* birth; to *give* occasion: to *afford* an opportunity; to *afford* a plea or a pretext; to *afford* ground, and the like.

To *afford* and *spare* both imply the deducting from one's property with convenience, but *afford* respects solely expenses which are no more than commensurate with our income; *spare* is said of things in general, which we may part with without any sensible diminution of our comfort. There are few so destitute that they cannot *afford* something for the relief of others, who are more destitute;

> Accept whate'er Æneas can *afford*,
> Untouch'd thy arms, untaken by thy sword.
> DRYDEN.

He who has two things of a kind may easily *spare* one; 'How many men, in the common concerns of life, lend sums of money which they are not able to *spare*.'—ADDISON.

TO GIVE, PRESENT, OFFER, EXHIBIT.

These terms have a common signification, inasmuch as they designate the manual act of transferring something from one's self to another. The first is here as elsewhere (*v. To give, grant*) the most indefinite and extensive in its meaning; it denotes the complete act:* the latter two refer rather to the preliminaries of *giving*, than to the act itself. What is *given* is actually transferred: what is *presented*, that is made a *present* to any one; what is *offered* is brought in the way of a person, or put in the way of being transferred: we *present* in *giving*, and *offer* in order to *give*; but it may be that we may *give* without presenting or offering; and, on the other hand, we may *present* or *offer* without *giving*.

To *give* is the familiar term which designates the ordinary transfer of property: to *present* is a term of respect; it includes in it the formality and ceremony of setting before another that which we wish to *give*: to *offer* is an act of humility or solemnity: it bespeaks the movement of the heart, which impels to the making a transfer or *gift*. We *give* to our domesticks; we *present* to princes; we *offer* to God: we *give* to a person what we wish to be received; we *present* to a person what we think agreeable; we *offer* what we think acceptable: what is *given* is supposed to be ours;

> Of seven smooth joints a mellow pipe I have,
> Which with his dying breath Damœtas *gave*.
> DRYDEN.

What we *offer* is supposed to be at our command;

> Alexis will thy homely gifts disdain;
> Nor, shouldst thou *offer* all thy little store,
> Will rich Iolas yield, but *offer* more.—DRYDEN.

What we *present* need not be either our own or at our command; 'It fell out at the same time, that a very fine colt, which promised great strength and speed, was *presented* to Octavius: Virgil assured them that he would prove a jade: upon trial, it was found as he had said.'—WALSH. We *give* a person not only our external property, but our esteem, our confidence, our company, and the like; an ambassador *presents* his credentials at court; a subject *offers* his services to his king.

They bear the same relation to each other when applied to words or actions, instead of property; we speak of *giving* a person an assurance, or a contradiction: of *presenting* an address, and *offering* an apology: of *giving* a reception, *presenting* a figure, or *offering* an insult. They may likewise be extended in their application, not only to personal and individual actions, but also to such as respect the publick at large: we *give* a description in writing, as well as by word of mouth; one *presents* the publick with the fruit of one's labours; we *offer* remarks on such things as attract notice, and call for animadversion.

These terms may also be employed to designate the actions of unconscious agents, by which they are characterized: in this sense they come very near to the word *exhibit*, which, from *exhibeo*, signifies to hold or put forth. Here the word *give* is equally indefinite and general, denoting simply to send from itself, and applies mostly to what proceeds from another thing, by a natural cause: thus, a thing is said to *give* pain, or to *give* pleasure;

> The apprehension of the good
> *Gives* but the greater feeling to the worse.
> SHAKSPEARE.

Things are said to *present* or *offer*, that is, in the sense of setting them to view; others only by the figure of personification: thus, a town is said to *present* a fine view, or an idea *presents* itself to the mind;

> Its pearl the rock *presents*, its gold the mine.
> JENYNS.

An opportunity *offers*, that is, *offers* itself to our notice:

> True genuine dulness mov'd his pity,
> Unless it *offer'd* to be witty.—SWIFT.

To *exhibit* is properly applied in this sense of setting forth to view; but expresses likewise the idea of attracting notice also: that which is *exhibited* is more striking than what is *presented* or *offered*; thus a poem is said to *exhibit* marks of genius; 'The recollection of the past becomes dreadful to a guilty man. It *exhibits* to him a life thrown away on vanities and follies.'—BLAIR.

TO INTRODUCE, PRESENT.

To *introduce*, from the Latin *introduco*, signifies literally to bring within or into any place; to *present* (*v. To give*) signifies to bring into the *presence* of. As they respect persons, the former passes between equals, the latter only among persons of rank and power: one literary man is *introduced* to another by means of a common friend: he is *presented* at court by a nobleman.

As these terms respect things, we say that subjects

* Vide Girard: "Donner, presenter, offrir."

are *introduced* in the course of conversation; 'The endeavours of freethinkers tend only to *introduce* slavery and errour among men.'—BERKELEY. Men's particular views upon certain subjects are *presented* to the notice of others through the medium of publication, or objects are *presented* to the view;

> Now every leaf, and every moving breath,
> *Presents* a foe, and every foe a death.
> DENHAM.

ALLOWANCE, STIPEND, SALARY, WAGES, HIRE, PAY.

All these terms denote a stated sum paid according to certain stipulations. *Allowance*, from *allow* (*v. To admit, allow*), signifies the thing *allowed; stipend*, in Latin *stipendium*, from *stipes* a piece of money, signifies money *paid: salary*, in French *salaire*, Latin *salarium*, comes from *sal* salt, which was originally the principal *pay* for soldiers; *wages*, in French *gage*, Latin *vadium*, from the Hebrew יגע, labour, signifies that which is *paid* for labour; *hire* expresses the sum for which one is *hired*, and *pay* the sum that is to be *paid*.

An *allowance* is gratuitous; it ceases at the pleasure of the donor; 'Sir Richard Steele was officiously informed, that Mr. Savage had ridiculed him: by which he was so much exasperated that he withdrew the *allowance* which he had paid him.'—JOHNSON. All the rest are the requital for some supposed service; they cease with the engagement made between the parties. A *stipend* is more fixed and permanent than a *salary;* and that than *wages, hire*, or *pay:* a *stipend* depends upon the fulfilling of an engagement, rather than on the will of an individual; a *salary* is a matter of contract between the giver and receiver, and may be increased or diminished at will.

An *allowance* may be given in any form, or at any stated times; a *stipend* and *salary* are paid yearly, or at even portions of a year; *wages, hire*, and *pay*, are estimated by days, weeks, or months, as well as years.

An *allowance* may be made by, with, and to persons of all ranks, a *stipend* and *salary* are assignable only to persons of respectability;

> Is not the care of souls a load sufficient?
> Are not your holy *stipends* paid for this?
> DRYDEN.

'Several persons, out of a *salary* of five hundred pounds, have always lived at the rate of two thousand.'—SWIFT. *Wages* are given to labourers; 'The peasant and the mechanick, when they have received the *wages* of the day, and procured their strong beer and supper, have scarce a wish unsatisfied.'—HAWKESWORTH. *Hire* is given to servants;

> I have five hundred crowns,
> The thrifty *hire* I sav'd under your father.
> SHAKSPEARE.

Pay is given to soldiers or such as are employed under government;

> Come on, brave soldiers, doubt not of the day;
> And that once gotten, doubt not of large *pay*.
> SHAKSPEARE.

GIFT, PRESENT, DONATION, BENEFACTION.

Gift is derived from to *give*, in the sense of what is communicated to another gratuitously of one's property; *present* is derived from to *present*, signifying the thing *presented* to another; *donation*, from the French *donation*, and the Latin *dono* to present or *give*, is a species of *gift*.

The *gift* is an act of generosity or condescension; it contributes to the benefit of the receiver: the *present* is an act of kindness, courtesy, or respect; it contributes to the pleasure of the receiver. The *gift* passes from the rich to the poor, from the high to the low, and creates an obligation: the *present* passes either between equals, or from the inferiour to the superiour. Whatever we receive from God, through the bounty of his Providence, we entitle a *gift;*

> The *gifts* of heav'n my following song pursues,
> Aerial honey and ambrosial dews.—DRYDEN.

Whatever we receive from our friends, or whatever princes receive from their subjects, are entitled *presents;*

> Have what you ask, your *presents* I receive;
> Land, where and when you please, with ample leave.
> DRYDEN

We are told by all travellers that it is a custom in the east, never to approach a great man without a *present;* the value of a *gift* is often heightened by being given opportunely. The value of a *present* often depends upon the value we have for the giver; the smallest *present* from an esteemed friend is of more worth in our eyes, than the costliest *presents* that monarchs receive

The *gift* is private, and benefits the individual; the *donation* is publick, and serves some general purpose: what is given to relieve the necessities of any poor person, is a *gift;* what is given to support an institution is a *donation*. The clergy are indebted to their patrons for the livings which are in their *gift;*

> And she shall have them, if again she sues,
> Since you the giver and the *gift* refuse.—DRYDEN.

It has been the custom of the pious and charitable, in all ages, to make *donations* for the support of alms-houses, hospitals, infirmaries, and such institutions as serve to diminish the sum of human misery; 'The ecclesiasticks were not content with the *donations* made them by the Saxon princes and nobles.'—HUME.

Benefaction and *donation* both denote an act of charity, but the former comprehends more than the latter; a *benefaction* comprehends acts of personal service in general towards the indigent: *donation* respects simply the act of giving and the thing given. *Benefactions* are for private use; *donations* are for publick service. A *benefactor* to the poor does not confine himself to the distribution of money; he enters into all their necessities, consults their individual cases, and suits his *benefactions* to their exigencies; his influence, his counsel, his purse, and his property, are employed for their good his *donations* form the smallest part of the good which he does; 'The light and influence that the heavens bestow upon this lower world, though the lower world cannot equal their *benefaction*, yet with a kind of grateful return, it reflects those rays that it cannot recompense.'—SOUTH. 'Titles and lands given to God are never, and plates, vestments, and other sacred utensils, are seldom consecrated; yet certain it is that after the *donation* of them to the church, it is as really a sacrilege to steal them as it is to pull down a church.'—SOUTH.

TO DEVISE, BEQUEATH.

Devise, compounded of *de* and *vise* or *visus*, participle of *video* to see or show, signifies to point out specifically; *bequeath*, compounded of *be* and *queath*, in Saxon *cuesan*, from the Latin *quæso* to say, signifies to give over to a person by saying or by word of mouth.

To *devise* is a formal, to *bequeath* is an informal assignment of our property to another on our death. We devise only by a legal testament; 'The right of inheritance or descent to his children and relations seems to have been allowed much earlier than the right of *devising* by testament.'—BLACKSTONE. We may *bequeath* simply by word of mouth, or by any expression of our will: we can *devise* only that which is property in the eye of the law; we may *bequeath* in the moral sense any thing which we cause to pass over to another: a man *devises* his lands; he *bequeaths* his name or his glory to his children;

> With this, the Medes to lab'ring age *bequeath*
> New lungs.—DRYDEN.

WILL, TESTAMENT.

A *will* is any written document which contains the last *will* of a man in regard to the disposal of his property; this may be either a formal or an informal instrument in the eye of the law; 'Do men make their last *wills* by word of mouth only?'—STEPHENS A *testament*, on the other hand, is a formal instrument regularly drawn up, and duly attested, according to the forms of law; 'He bringeth arguments from the love which the testator always bore him, imagining that these, or the like proofs, will convict a *testament* to have that in it which other men can nowhere by reading find.'—HOOKER.

BENEFICENT, BOUNTIFUL OR BOUNTEOUS, MUNIFICENT, GENEROUS, LIBERAL.

Beneficent, from *benefacio*, signifies doing well or good, that is, by distinction for others: *bountiful* signifies full of *bounty* or goodness, from the French *bonté*, Latin *bonitas; munificent*, in Latin *munificus*, from *munus* and *facio*, signifies the quality of making presents; *generous*, in French *genereux*, Latin *generosus*, of high blood, noble extraction, and consequently of a noble character; *liberal*, in French *liberal*, Latin *liberalis*, from *liber* free, signifies the quality of being like a free man in distinction from a bondman, and by a natural association being of a free disposition, ready to communicate.

Beneficent respects every thing done for the good of others: *bounty*, *munificence*, and *generosity*, are species of *beneficence: liberality* is a qualification of all. The first two denote modes of action: the latter three either modes of action or modes of sentiment. The sincere well-wisher to his fellow-creatures is *beneficent* according to his means; he is *bountiful* in providing for the comfort and happiness of others; he is *munificent* in dispensing favours; he is *generous* in imparting his property; he is *liberal* in all he does.

Beneficence and *bounty* are characteristicks of the Deity as well as of his creatures: *munificence*, *generosity*, and *liberality*, are mere human qualities. *Beneficence* and *bounty* are the peculiar characteristicks of the Deity: with him the will and the act of doing good are commensurate only with the power: he was *beneficent* to us as our Creator, and continues his *beneficence* to us by his daily preservation and protection; to some, however, he has been more *bountiful* than to others, by providing them with an unequal share of the good things of this life.

The *beneficence* of a man is regulated by the *bounty* of Providence: to whom much is given, from him much will be required. Instructed by his word, and illumined by that spark of benevolence which was infused into their souls with the breath of life, good men are ready to believe that they are but stewards of all God's gifts, holden for the use of such as are less *bountifully* provided for; 'The most *beneficent* of all beings is He who hath an absolute fulness of perfection in himself, who gave existence to the universe, and so cannot be supposed to want that which he communicated.'—GROVE. Good men will desire, as far as their powers extend, to imitate this feature of the Deity by bettering with their *beneficent* counsel and assistance the condition of all who require it, and by gladdening the hearts of many with their *bountiful* provisions;

> Hail! Universal Lord, be *bounteous* still
> To give us only good.—MILTON.

Princes are *munificent*, friends are *generous*, patrons *liberal*. *Munificence* is measured by the quality and quantity of the thing bestowed: *generosity* by the extent of the sacrifice made; *liberality* by the warmth of the spirit discovered. A monarch displays his *munificence* in the presents which he sends by his ambassadors to another monarch. A *generous* man will waive his claims, however powerful they may be, when the accommodation or relief of another is in question. A *liberal* spirit does not stop to inquire the reason for giving, but gives when the occasion offers.

Munificence may spring either from ostentation or a becoming sense of dignity; 'I esteem a habit of benignity greatly preferable to *munificence*.'—STEELE after CICERO. *Generosity* may spring either from a generous temper, or an easy unconcern about property; 'We may with great confidence and equal truth affirm, that since there was such a thing as mankind in the world, there never was any heart truly great and *generous*, that was not also tender and compassionate.'—SOUTH. *Liberality* of conduct is dictated by nothing but a warm heart and an expanded mind: 'The citizen, above all other men, has opportunities of arriving at the highest fruit of wealth, to be *liberal* without the least expense of a man's own fortune.'—STEELE. *Munificence* is confined simply to giving, but we may be *generous* in assisting, and *liberal* in rewarding.

BENEVOLENCE, BENEFICENCE.

Benevolence is literally well-willing; *beneficence* is literally well doing. The former consists of intention, the latter of action: the former is the cause, the latter the result. *Benevolence* may exist without *beneficence*; but *beneficence* always supposes *benevolence*: a man is not said to be *beneficent* who does good from sinister views. The *benevolent* man enjoys but half his happiness if he cannot be *beneficent;* yet there will still remain to him an ample store of enjoyment in the contemplation of others' happiness: the man who is gratified only with that happiness which he himself is the instrument of producing, is not entitled to the name of *benevolent;* 'The pity which arises on sight of persons in distress, and the satisfaction of mind which is the consequence of having removed them into a happier state, are instead of a thousand arguments to prove such a thing as a disinterested *benevolence*.'—GROVE.

As *benevolence* is an affair of the heart, and *beneficence* of the outward conduct, the former is confined to no station, no rank, no degree of education or power: the poor may be *benevolent* as well as the rich, the unlearned as well as the learned, the weak as well as the strong: the latter on the contrary is controlled by outward circumstances, and is therefore principally confined to the rich, the powerful, the wise, and the learned; 'He that banishes gratitude from among men, by so doing stops up the stream of *beneficence:* for though, in conferring kindness, a truly generous man doth not aim at a return, yet he looks to the qualities of the person obliged.'—GROVE.

BENEVOLENCE, BENIGNITY, HUMANITY KINDNESS, TENDERNESS.

Benevolence is well-willing; *benignity*, in Latin *benignitas*, from *bene* and *gigno*, signifies the quality or disposition for producing good; *humanity*, in French *humanité*, Latin *humanitas*, from *humanus* and *homo*, signifies the quality of belonging to man, or having what is common to man; *kindness*, the disposition to be kind, or the act which marks that disposition; *tenderness*, a tender feeling.

Benevolence and *benignity* lie in the will; *humanity* lies in the heart; *kindness* and *tenderness* in the affections; *benevolence* indicates a general good will to all mankind; *benignity* a particular good will, flowing out of certain relations; *humanity* is a general tone of feeling; *kindness* and *tenderness* are particular modes of feeling.

Benevolence consists in the wish or intention to do good: it is confined to no station or object: the *benevolent* man may be rich or poor, and his *benevolence* will be exerted wherever there is an opportunity of doing good: *benignity* is always associated with power, and accompanied with condescension.

Benevolence in its fullest sense is the sum of moral excellence, and comprehends every other virtue; when taken in this acceptation, *benignity*, *humanity*, *kindness*, and *tenderness*, are but modes of *benevolence*.

Benevolence and *benignity* tend to the communicating of happiness; *humanity* is concerned in the removal of evil. *Benevolence* is common to the Creator and his creatures; it differs only in degree; the former has the knowledge and power as well as the will to do good; man often has the will to do good without having the power to carry it into effect; 'I have heard say, that Pope Clement XI. never passes through the people, who always kneel in crowds and ask his benediction, but the tears are seen to flow from his eyes. This must proceed from an imagination that he is the father of all these people, and that he is touched with so extensive a *benevolence*, that it breaks out into a passion of tears.'—STEELE. *Benignity* is ascribed to the stars, to heaven, or to princes; ignorant and superstitious people are apt to ascribe their good fortune to the *benign* influence of the stars rather than to the gracious dispensations of Providence; 'A constant *benignity* in commerce with the rest of the world, which ought to run through all a man's actions, has effects more useful to those whom you oblige, and is less ostentatious in yourself.'—STEELE. *Humanity* belongs to man only; it is his peculiar characteristick, and ought at all times to be his boast; when he throws off this, his distinguishing badge, he loses every thing valuable in him; it is a virtue that is indispensable in his present suffering condition: *humanity* is as universal in its application as *benevolence;* wherever there is distress, *humanity* flies to its relief; *humanity* is, however, not merely an attribute of man; it is also the peculiar feeling for one's fellow-creatures which exists in some men in a greater degree than in others; 'The greatest wits I have conversed with are men eminent for their *humanity*.'—ADDISON. *Kindness* and *tenderness* are partial modes of affection, confined to those who know or are related to each other: we are kind to friends and acquaintances, *tender* towards those who are near and dear: *kindness* is a mode of affection most fitted for social beings; it is what every one can show, and every one is pleased to receive; '*Beneficence*, would the followers of Epicurus say, is all founded in weakness; and whatever be pretended, the *kindness* that passeth between men and men is by every man directed to himself. This it must be confessed is of a piece with that hopeful philosophy which, having patched man up out of the four elements, attributes his being to chance.'—GROVE. *Tenderness* is a state of feeling that is sometimes praiseworthy: the young and the weak demand *tenderness* from those who stand in the closest connexion with them, but this feeling may be carried to an excess so as to injure the object on which it is fixed; 'Dependence is a perpetual call upon *humanity*, and a greater incitement to *tenderness* and pity than any other motive whatsoever.'—ADDISON.

There are no circumstances or situation in life which preclude the exercise of *benevolence:* next to the pleasure of making others happy, the *benevolent* man rejoices in seeing them so: the *benign* influence of a *benevolent* monarch extends to the remotest corner of his dominions: *benignity* is a becoming attribute for a prince, when it does not lead him to sanction vice by its impunity; it is highly to be applauded in him as far as it renders him forgiving of minor offences, gracious to all who are deserving of his favours, and ready to afford a gratification to all whom it is in his power to serve: the multiplied misfortunes to which all men are exposed afford ample scope for the exercise of *humanity*, which, in consequence of the unequal distribution of wealth, power, and talent, is peculiar to no situation of life; even the profession of arms does not exclude *humanity* from the breasts of its followers; and when we observe men's habits of thinking in various situations, we may remark that the soldier, with arms by his side, is commonly more *humane* than the partisan with arms in his hands. *Kindness* is always an amiable feeling, and in a grateful mind always begets *kindness;* but it is sometimes ill bestowed upon selfish people, who requite it by making fresh exactions: *tenderness* is frequently little better than an amiable weakness, when directed to a wrong end, and fixed on an improper object; the false *tenderness* of parents has often been the ruin of children.

BENEFIT, FAVOUR, KINDNESS, CIVILITY.

Benefit signifies here that which benefits; *favour*, in French *faveur*, Latin *favor* and *faveo* to bear good will, signifies the act flowing from good will; *kindness* signifies an action that is kind; *civility*, that which is civil (*v. Civil*).

The idea of an action gratuitously performed for the advantage of another is common to these terms.

Benefits and *favours* are granted by superiours; *kindnesses* and *civilities* pass between equals.

Benefits serve to relieve actual wants: the power of conferring and the necessity of receiving them, constitute the relative difference in station between the giver and the receiver: *favours* tend to promote the interest or convenience: the power of giving and the advantage of receiving are dependent on local circumstances, more than on difference of station. *Kindnesses* and *civilities* serve to afford mutual accommodation by a reciprocity of kind offices on the many and various occasions which offer in human life: they are not so important as either *benefits* or *favours*, but they carry a charm with them which is not possessed by the former. *Kindnesses* are more endearing than *civilities*, and pass mostly between those who are known to each other: *civilities* may pass between strangers.

Dependence affords an opportunity for conferring *benefits;* partiality gives rise to *favours: kindnesses* are the result of personal regard: *civilities* of general benevolence. A master confers his *benefits* on such of his domesticks as are entitled to encouragement for their fidelity. Men in power distribute their *favours* so as to increase their influence. Friends, in their intercourse with each other, are perpetually called upon to perform *kindnesses* for each other. There is no man so mean that he may not have it in his power to show *civilities* to those who are above him.

Benefits tend to draw those closer to each other who by station in life are set at the greatest distance from each other: affection is engendered in him who *benefits;* and devoted attachment in him who is *benefited;* 'I think I have a right to conclude that there is such a thing as *generosity* in the world. Though if I were under a mistake in this, I should say as Cicero in relation to the immortality of the soul, I willingly err; for the contrary notion naturally teaches people to be ungrateful by possessing them with a persuasion concerning their benefactors, that they have no regard to them in the *benefits* they bestow.'—GROVE. *Favours* increase obligation beyond its due limits; if they are not asked and granted with discretion, they may produce servility on the one hand, and haughtiness on the other; 'A *favour* well bestowed is almost as great an honour to him who confers it, as to him who receives it. What, indeed, makes for the superiour reputation of the patron in this case is, that he is always surrounded with specious pretences of unworthy candidates.'—STEELE. *Kindnesses* are the offspring and parent of affection; they convert our multiplied wants into so many enjoyments; 'Ingratitude is too base to return a *kindness*, and too proud to regard it.'—SOUTH. *Civilities* are the sweets which we gather in the way as we pass along the journey of life: 'A common *civility* to an impertinent fellow often draws upon one a great many unforeseen troubles.'—STEELE.

BENEFIT, SERVICE, GOOD OFFICE.

These terms, like the former (*v. Benefit, favour*), agree in denoting some action performed for the good of another, but they differ in the principle on which the action is performed.

A *benefit* (*v. Benefit, favour*) is perfectly gratuitous, it produces an obligation: a *service* (*v. Advantage*) is not altogether gratuitous; it is that at least which may be expected, though it cannot be demanded: a *good office* is between the two; it is in part gratuitous, and in part such as one may reasonably expect.

Benefits flow from superiours, and *services* from inferiours or equals; but *good offices* are performed by equals only. Princes confer *benefits* on their subjects; subjects perform *services* for their princes; neighbours do *good offices* for each other. *Benefits* are sometimes the reward of *services: good offices* produce a return from the receiver.

Benefits consist of such things as serve to relieve the difficulties, or advance the interests, of the receiver: *services* consist in those acts which tend to lessen the trouble, or increase the ease and convenience of the person served: *good offices* consist in the employ of one's credit, influence, and mediation for the advantage of another: it is a species of voluntary service.

Humanity leads to *benefits;* the zeal of devotion or friendship renders *services;* general good-will dictates *good offices*.

It is a great *benefit* to assist an embarrassed tradesman out of his difficulty; 'I have often pleased myself with considering the two kinds of *benefits* which accrue to the publick from these my speculations, and which, were I to speak after the manner of logicians, I should distinguish into the material and formal.'—ADDISON. It is a great *service* for a soldier to save the life of his commander, or for a friend to open the eyes of another to see his danger; 'Cicero, whose learning and *services* to his country are so well known, was inflamed by a passion for glory to an extravagant degree.'—HUGHES. It is a *good office* for any one to interpose his mediation to settle disputes, and heal divisions; 'There are several persons who have many pleasures and entertainments in their possession which they do not enjoy It is therefore a kind and good *office* to acquaint them with their own happiness.'—STEELE.

It is possible to be loaded with *benefits* so as to affect one's independence of character. *Services* are some times a source of dissatisfaction and disappointment when they do not meet with the remuneration or return which they are supposed to deserve. *Good offices* tend to nothing but the increase of good will. Those who perform them are too independent to expect a return, and those who receive them are too sensible of their value not to seek an opportunity of making a return.

TO OFFER, BID, TENDER, PROPOSE.

Offer signifies the same as before (*v. To Offer, exhibit*); *bid*, in Saxon *besdan*, *bidden* to offer, old German *buden*, low German *bedan*, high German *bieten*, &c. comes in all probability from the Latin *vito* and *invito*, from *in* and *viam*, signifying to call into the way or measure of another; *tender*, like the word *tend*, from *tendo* to stretch, signifies to stretch forth by way of *offering*; *propose*, in Latin *proposui*, perfect of *propono* to place or set before, likewise characterizes a mode of *offering*.

Offer is employed for that which is literally transferable, or for that which is indirectly communicable: *bid* and *tender* belong to *offer* in the first sense; *propose* belongs to *offer* in the latter sense. To *offer* is a voluntary and discretionary act; the *offer* may be accepted or rejected at pleasure; to *bid* and *tender* are specifick modes of *offering* which depend on circumstances: one *bids* with the hope of its being accepted; one *tenders* from a prudential motive, and in order to serve specifick purposes. We *offer* money to a poor person, it is an act of charity or good nature; or we *offer* a reward by way of inducing another to do a thing, which is an act of discretion;

Nor should thou *offer* all thy little store,
Will rich Iolas yield but *offer* more.—DRYDEN.

Should all these *offers* for my friendship call,
'T is he that *offers*, and I scorn them all.—POPE.

We *bid* a price for the purchase of a house, it is a commercial dealing subject to the rules of commerce; 'To give interest a share in friendship, is to sell it by inch of candle; he that *bids* most shall have it; and when it is mercenary, there is no depending upon it.' —COLLIER. We *tender* a sum of money by way of payment, it is a matter of prudence in order to fulfil an obligation; 'Aulus Gellius tells a story of one Lucius Neratius who made it his diversion to give a blow to whomsoever he pleased, and then *tender* them the legal forfeiture.'—BLACKSTONE. By the same rule one *offers* a person the use of one's horse; one *bids* a sum at an auction; one *tenders* one's services to the government.

To *offer* and *propose* are both employed in matters of practice or speculation; but the former is a less definite and decisive act than the latter; we *offer* an opinion by way of promoting a discussion; we *propose* a plan for the deliberation of others. Sentiments which differ widely from those of the major part of the present company ought to be *offered* with modesty and caution; 'Our author *offers* no reason.'—LOCKE. We should not *propose* to another what we should be unwilling to do ourselves; 'We *propose* measures for securing to the young the possession of pleasure (by connecting with it religion).'—BLAIR. We commonly *offer* by way of obliging; we commonly *propose* by way of arranging or accommodating. It is an act of puerility to *offer* to do more than one is enabled to perform; it does not evince a sincere disposition for peace to *propose* such terms as we know cannot be accepted; 'Upon the *proposal* of an agreeable object, a man's choice will rather incline him to accept than refuse it.' SOUTH.

TO INVEST, ENDUE OR ENDOW.

To *invest*, from *vestio*, signifies to clothe with any thing; *endue* or *endow*, from the Latin *induo*, signifies to put on any thing. One is *invested* with that which is external: one is *endued* with that which is internal. We *invest* a person with an office or a dignity: one *endues* a person with good qualities. The *investment* is a real external action; but *endue* may be merely fictitious or mental. The king is *invested* with supreme authority; 'A strict and efficacious constitution, indeed, which *invests* the church with no power at all, but where men will be so civil as to obey it.'—SOUTH. A lover *endues* his mistress with every earthly perfection; 'As in the natural body, the eye does not speak, nor the tongue see; so neither in the spiritual, is every one *endued* also with the gift and spirit of government.' —SOUTH. *Endow* is but a variation of *endue*, and yet it seems to have acquired a distinct office: we may say that a person is *endued* or *endowed* with a good understanding; but as an act of the imagination *endow* is not to be substituted for *endue*: for we do not say that it *endows* but *endues* things with properties.

TO CONFER, BESTOW.

Confer, in French *conferer*, Latin *confero*, compounded of *con* and *fero*, signifies to bring something towards a person, or place it upon him, in which sense it is allied to *bestow* (*v. To give, grant*).

Conferring is an act of authority; *bestowing* that of charity or generosity. Princes and men in power *confer*; people in a private station *bestow*. Honours, dignities, privileges, and rank, are the things *conferred*; 'The *conferring* this honour upon him, would increase the credit he had.'—CLARENDON. Favours, kindnesses, and pecuniary relief, are the things *bestowed*; 'You always exceed expectations as if yours was not your own, but to *bestow* on wanting merit.'—DRYDEN.

Merit, favour, interest, caprice, and intrigue, give rise to *conferring*; necessity, solicitation, and private affection, lead to *bestowing*. England affords more than one instance in which the highest honours of the state have been *conferred* on persons of distinguished merit, though not of elevated birth: it is the characteristick of Christianity, that it inspires its followers with a desire of *bestowing* their goods on the poor and necessitous.

It is not easy to *confer* a favour on the unthankful. the value of a kindness is greatly enhanced by the manner in which it is *bestowed*;

On him *confer* the poet's sacred name,
Whose lofty voice declares the heavenly flame.
ADDISON.

'It sometimes happens, that even enemies and envious persons *bestow* the sincerest marks of esteem when they least design it.'—STEELE.

TO MINISTER, ADMINISTER, CONTRIBUTE.

To *minister*, from the noun *minister*, in the sense of a servant, signifies to act in subservience to another, either in a good, bad, or indifferent sense: we *minister* to the caprices or indulgences of another when we encourage them unnecessarily; or, we *minister* to one who is entitled to our services; *administer* is taken in the good sense of serving another to his advantage: thus the good Samaritan *administered* to the comfort of the man who had fallen among thieves; *contribute*, from the Latin *contribuo*, or *con* and *tribuo* to bestow, signifying to bestow for the same end, or for some particular purpose, is taken in either a good or bad sense; we may *contribute* to the relief of the indigent, or we may *contribute* to the follies and vices of others.

It is the part of the Christian minister to *minister* to the spiritual wants of the flock intrusted to his charge; 'Those good men who take such pleasure in relieving the miserable for Christ's sake, would not have been less forward to *minister* unto Christ himself.'—ATTERBURY. It is the part of every Christian to *administer*, as far as lies in his power, comfort to those who are in want, consolation to the afflicted, advice to those who ask for it, and require it; help to those who are feeble, and support to those who cannot uphold themselves. On the same ground we speak of grace or spiritual gifts being *administered*; 'By the universal *administration* of grace, begun by our blessed Saviour, enlarged by his Apostles, carried on by their immediate successors, and to be completed by the rest to the world's end; all types that darkened this faith are enlightened.'—SPRATT. It is the part of all who are in high stations to *contribute* to the dissemination of religion and morality among their dependants; but there are, on the contrary, many who *contribute* to the spread of immorality, and a contempt of all sacred things, by the most pernicious example of irreligion in themselves; 'Parents owe their children not only material subsistence for their body, but much more spiritual *contributions* for their mind.'—DIGBY. As expressing the act of unconscious agents, they bear a similar distinction;

He flings the pregnant ashes through the air,
And speaks a mighty prayer,
Both which the *minist'ring* winds around all Egypt bear.—COWLEY.

Thus do our eyes, as do all common mirrors,
Successively reflect succeeding images;
Not what they would, but must! a star or toad,
Just as the hand of chance *administers*.
CONGREVE.

May from my bones a new Achilles rise,
That shall infest the Trojan colonies
With fire, and sword, and famine, when, at length,
Time to our great attempts *contributes* strength.
DENHAM.

TO CONDUCE, CONTRIBUTE.

To *conduce*, from the Latin *conduco*, or *con* and *duco*, signifying to bring together for the same end, is applied to that which serves the full purpose; to *contribute*, as in the preceding article, is applied to that only which serves as a subordinate instrument: the former is always taken in a good sense, the latter in a bad or good sense. Exercise *conduces* to the health; it *contributes* to give vigour to the frame.

Nothing *conduces* more to the well-being of any community than a spirit of subordination among all ranks and classes: 'It is to be allowed that doing all honour to the superiority of heroes above the rest of mankind, must needs *conduce* to the glory and advantage of a nation.'—STEELE. A want of firmness and vigilance in the government or magistrates *contributes* greatly to the spread of disaffection and rebellion; 'The true choice of our diet, and our companions at it, seems to consist in that which *contributes* most to cheerfulness and refreshment.'—FULLER.

Schemes of ambition never *conduce* to tranquillity of mind. A single failure may *contribute* sometimes to involve a person in perpetual trouble.

TAX, CUSTOM, DUTY, TOLL, IMPOST, TRIBUTE, CONTRIBUTION.

Tax, in French *taxe*, Latin *taxo*, from the Greek τάσσω, τάξω, to dispose or put in order, signifies what is disposed in order for each to pay; *custom* signifies that which is given under certain circumstances, according to *custom; duty*, that which is given as a due or debt; *toll*, in Saxon *toll*, &c. Latin *telonium*, from the Greek τέλος a custom, signifies a particular kind of *custom* or due.

Tax is the most general of these terms, and applies to or implies whatever is paid by the people to the government, according to a certain estimate: the *customs* are a species of tax which are less specifick than other *taxes*, being regulated by *custom* rather than any definite law; the *customs* apply particularly to what was *customarily* given by merchants for the goods which they imported from abroad: the *duty* is a species of *tax* more positive and binding than the *custom*, being a specifick estimate of what is *due* upon goods, according to their value; hence it is not only applied to goods that are imported, but also to many other articles of inland produce; *toll* is that species of *tax* which serves for the repair of roads and havens.

The preceding terms refer to that which is levied by authority on the people; but they do not directly express the idea of levying or paying; *impost*, on the contrary, signifies literally that which is imposed; and *tribute* that which is paid or yielded: the former, therefore exclude that idea of coercion which is included in the latter. The *tax* is levied by the consent of many; the *impost* is imposed by the will of one; and the *tribute* is paid at the demand of one or a few; the *tax* serves for the support of the nation; the *impost* and the *tribute* serve to enrich a government. Conquerors lay heavy *imposts* upon the conquered countries; distant provinces pay a *tribute* to the princes to whom they owe allegiance. *Contribution* signifies the *tribute* of many in unison, or for the same end; in this general sense it includes all the other terms; for *taxes* and *imposts* are alike paid by many for the same purpose; but as the predominant idea in *contribution* is that of common consent, it supposes a degree of freedom in the agent which is incompatible with the exercise of authority expressed by the other terms hence the term is with more propriety applied to those cases in which men voluntarily unite in giving towards any particular object; as charitable *contributions*, or *contributions* in support of a war; but it may be taken in the general sense of a forced payment, as in speaking of military *contribution*.

TAX, RATE, ASSESSMENT.

Tax, agreeably to the above explanation (*v. Tax*), and *rate*, from the Latin *ratus* and *reor* to think or estimate, both derive their principal meaning from the valuation or proportion according to which any sum is demanded from the people; but the *tax* is imposed directly by the government for publick purposes, as the land *tax*, the window *tax*, and the like; and the *rate* is imposed indirectly for the local purposes of each parish, as the church *rates*, the poor *rates*, and the like. The *tax* or *rate* is a general rule or ratio, by which a certain sum is raised upon a given number of persons; the *assessment* is the application of that rule to the individual.

The house-duty is a *tax* upon houses, according to their real or supposed value; the poor's *rate* is a *rate* laid on the individual likewise, according to the value of his house, or the supposed rent which he pays; the *assessment* in both these, is the valuation of the house, which determines the sum to be paid by each individual: it is the business of the minister to make the *tax;* of the parish officers to make the *rate;* of the commissioners or assessors to make the *assessment;* the former has the publick to consider; the latter the individual. An equitable *tax* must not bear harder upon one class of the community than another: an equitable *assessment* must not bear harder upon one inhabitant than another.

TO ALLOT, ASSIGN, APPORTION, DISTRIBUTE.

Allot is compounded of the Latin *al* or *ad* and the word *lot*, which owes its origin to the Saxon and other northern languages. It signifies literally to set apart as a particular lot; *assign*, in French *assigner*, Latin *assigno*, is compounded of *as* or *ad* and *signo* to sign, or mark to, or for, signifying to mark out for any one, *apportion* is compounded of *ap* or *ad* and *portion*, signifying to *portion* out for a certain purpose; *distribute*, in Latin *distributus*, participle of *dis* and *tribuo*, signifies to bestow or portion out to several.

To *allot* is to dispose on the ground of utility for the sake of good order; to *assign* is to communicate according to the merit of the object; to *apportion* is to regulate according to the due proportion; to *distribute* is to give in several distinct portions.

A portion of one's property is *allotted* to charitable purposes, or a portion of one's time to religious meditation; 'Every one that has been long dead, has a due proportion of praise *allotted* him, in which, while he lived, his friends were too profuse, and his enemies too sparing.'—ADDISON. A prize is *assigned* to the most meritorious, or an honourable post to those whose abilities entitle them to distinction; I find by several hints in ancient authors, that when the Romans were in the height of power and luxury they *assigned* out of their vast dominions an island called Anticyra, as a habitation for madmen.'—STEELE. A person's business is *apportioned* to the time and abilities he has for performing it; 'Of the happiness and misery of our present condition, part is *distributed* by nature and part is in a great measure *apportioned* by ourselves.'—JOHNSON. A person's alms ought to be *distributed* among those who are most indigent;

From thence the cup of mortal man he fills,
Blessings to these, to those *distributes* ills.—POPE

When any complicated undertaking is to be performed by a number of individuals, it is necessary to *allot* to each his distinct task. It is the part of a wise prince to *assign* the highest offices to the most worthy, and to *apportion* to every one of his ministers an employment suited to his peculiar character and qualifi tations; the business of the state thus *distributed* will proceed with regularity and exactitude.

TO ALLOT, APPOINT, DESTINE.

To *allot* is taken in a similar sense as in the preceding article; *appoint*, in French *appointer*, Latin *appono*, that is, *ap* or *ad* and *pono* to place, signifies to put in a particular place, or in a particular manner; *destine*, in Latin *destino*, compounded of *de* and *stino*, *sto* or *sisto*, signifies to place apart.

Allot is used only for things, *appoint* and *destine* for persons or things. A space of ground is *allotted* for cultivation; a person is *appointed* as steward or governour; a youth is *destined* for a particular profession. *Allotments* are mostly made in the time past or present; they are made for a special purpose, and according to a given design, whence we may speak of the allotments of Providence; 'It is unworthy a reasonable being to spend any of the little time *allotted* us without some tendency, direct or oblique, to the end of our existence.'—JOHNSON. *Appointments* respect either the present or the future; they mostly regard matters of human prudence; 'Having notified to my good friend, Sir Roger, that I should set out for London the next day, his horses were ready at the *appointed* hour.'—STEELE. *Destinations* always respect some distant purposes, and include preparatory measures; they may be either the work of God or man; 'Look round and survey the various beauties of the globe, which Heaven has *destined* for man, and consider whether a world thus exquisitely framed could be meant for the abode of misery and pain.'—JOHNSON. A conscientious man *allots* a portion of his annual income to the relief of the poor; when publick meetings are held it is necessary to *appoint* a particular day for the purpose: our plans in life are defeated by a thousand contingencies: the man who builds a house is not certain he will live to use it for the purpose for which it was *destined*.

DESTINY, FATE, LOT, DOOM.

Destiny, from *destine* (*v. To appoint*) signifies either the power that *destines*, or the thing *destined; fate*, in Latin *fatum*, participle of *for* to speak or decree, signifies that which is decreed, or the power that decrees; *lot*, in German *loos*, signifies a ticket, die, or any other thing by which the casual distribution of things is determined; and in an extended sense, it expresses the portion thus assigned by chance; *doom*, in Saxon *dome*, Danish *döm*, most probably like the word *deem*, comes from the Hebrew דן to judge, signifying the thing judged, spoken, or decreed.

All these terms are employed with regard to human events which are not under one's control: among the heathens *destiny* and *fate* were considered as deities, who each in his way could direct human affairs, and were both superiour even to Jupiter himself: the *Destinies*, or Parcæ as they were termed, presided only over life and death; but *fate* was employed in ruling the general affairs of men. Since revelation has instructed mankind in the nature and attributes of the true God, these blind powers are now not acknowledged to exist in the overruling providence of an all-wise and an all-good Being; the terms *destiny* and *fate* therefore have now only a relative sense, as to what happens without the will or control of the individual who is the subject of it.

Destiny is used in regard to one's station and walk in life; *fate* in regard to what one suffers; *lot* in regard to what one gets or possesses; and *doom* is that portion of one's *destiny* or *fate* which depends upon the will of another: *destiny* is marked out; *fate* is fixed; a *lot* is assigned; a *doom* is passed.

It was the *destiny* of Julius Cæsar to act a great part in the world, and to establish a new form of government at Rome; it was his *fate* at last to die by the hands of assassins, the chief of whom had been his avowed friends; had he been contented with an humbler *lot* than that of an empire, he might have enjoyed honours, riches, and a long life; his *doom* was sealed by the last step which he took in making himself emperor: it is not permitted for us to inquire into our future *destiny;* it is our duty to submit to our *fate*, to be contented with our *lot*, and prepared for our *doom:* a parent may have great influence over the *destiny* of his child, by the education he gives to him or the principles he instils into his mind;

> If death be your design—at least, said she,
> Take us along to share your *destiny*.—DRYDEN.

There are many who owe their unhappy *fate* entirely to the want of early habits of piety;

> The gods these armies and this force employ,
> The hostile gods conspire the *fate* of Troy.—POPE

Riches and poverty may be assigned to us as our *lot*, but the former will not ensure us happiness, nor the latter prevent us from being happy if we have a contented temper;

> To labour is the *lot* of man below,
> And when Jove gave us life, he gave us wo.
> POPE

Criminals must await the *doom* of an earthly judge; but all men, as sinners, must meet the *doom* which is prepared for them at the awful day of judgement;

> Oh! grant me, gods! ere Hector meets his *doom*,
> All I can ask of Heav'n, an early tomb.—POPE.

It is the *destiny* of some men to be always changing their plan of life; it is but too frequently the *fate* of authors to labour for the benefit of mankind, and to reap nothing for themselves but poverty and neglect; it is the *lot* but of very few, to enjoy what they themselves consider a competency.

DESTINY, DESTINATION.

Both *destiny* and *destination* are used for the thing *destined;* but the former is said in relation to a man's important concerns, the latter only of particular circumstances; in which sense it may likewise be employed for the act of *destining*.

Destiny is the point or line marked out in the walk of life; *destination* is the place fixed upon in particular: as every man has his peculiar *destiny*, so every traveller has his particular *destination*. *Destiny* is altogether set above human control; no man can determine, though he may influence the *destiny* of another: *destination* is, however, the specifick act of an individual, either for himself or another: we leave the *destiny* of a man to develope itself; but we may inquire about his own *destination*, or that of his children: it is a consoling reflection that the *destinies* of short-sighted mortals, like ourselves, are in the hands of One who both can and will overrule them to our advantage if we place full reliance in Him:

> At the pit of Acheron
> Meet one i' th' morning; thither he
> Will come to know his *destiny*.—SHAKSPEARE.

In the *destination* of children for their several professions or callings, it is of importance to consult their particular turn of mind, as well as inclination; 'Moore's original *destination* appears to have been for trade' JOHNSON.

TO SENTENCE, DOOM, CONDEMN.

To *sentence*, or pass *sentence*, is to give a final opinion or decision which is to influence the fate of an object; *condemn*, from *damnum* a loss, is to pass such a *sentence* as shall be to the hurt of an object: *doom*, which is a variation from *damnum*, has the same meaning.

Sentence is the generick, the two others specifick terms. *Sentence* and *condemn* are used in the juridical as well as the moral sense; *doom* is employed in the moral sense only. In the juridical sense, *sentence* is indefinite; *condemn* is definite: a criminal may be sentenced to a mild or severe punishment; he is always *condemned* to that which is severe; he is *sentenced* to imprisonment, or transportation, or death: he is *condemned* to the galleys, to transportation for life, or to death.

In the moral application they are in like manner distinguished. To *sentence* is a softer term than to *condemn*, and this is less than to *doom*. *Sentence* applies to inanimate objects; *condemn* and *doom* only to persons or that which is personal. An author is *sentenced* by the decision of the publick to suffer neglect; a thing is *sentenced* to be thrown away which is esteemed as worthless; we may be *condemned* to hear the prating of a loquacious person; we may be *doomed* to spend our lives in penury and wretchedness. *Sentence*, particularly when employed as a noun, may even be favourable to the interests of a person; *condemn* is always prejudicial, either to his interest, his comfort, or his reputation; *doom* is always destructive of his happiness, it is that which always runs most counter to the wishes of an individual. It is of importance for an author, that a critick should pronounce a favourable *sentence* on his works; 'Let him set out some of Luther's works; that by them we may pass *sentence* upon his doctrines.'—Atterbury. But, in the signification of a *sentence* passed by a judge, it is, when absolutely taken, always in a bad sense; 'At the end of the tenth book the poet ioins this beautiful circumstance, that they offered up their penitential prayers on the very place where their judge appeared to them when he pronounced their *sentence*.'—Addison. Immoral writers are justly *condemned* to oblivion or perpetual infamy; 'Liberty (Thomson's Liberty) called in vain upon her votaries to read her praises, her praises were *condemned* to harbour spiders and gather dust.'—Johnson. Some of the best writers have been *doomed* to experience neglect in their life time; 'Even the abridger, compiler, and translator, though their labours cannot be ranked with those of the diurnal biographer, yet must not be rashly *doomed* to annihilation.'—Johnson.

A *sentence* and *condemnation* is always the act of some person or conscious agent: *doom* is sometimes the fruit of circumstances. Tarquin the Proud was *sentenced* by the Roman people to be banished from Rome: Regulus was *condemned* to the most cruel death by the Carthaginians; many writers have been *doomed* to pass their lives in obscurity and want, whose works have acquired for them lasting honours after their death.

CHANCE, FORTUNE, FATE.

Chance, probably contracted from the Latin *cadens* falling, is here considered as the cause of what falls out; *fortune*, in French *fortune*, Latin *fortuna*, from *fors* chance, in Hebrew גרל; *fate* signifies the same as in the preceding article. These terms have served at all times as cloaks for human ignorance, and before mankind were favoured by the light of Divine Revelation, they had an imaginary importance which has now happily vanished.

Believers in Divine Providence no longer conceive the events of the world as left to themselves, or as under the control of any unintelligent or unconscious agent, but ascribe the whole to an overruling mind, which, though invisible to the bodily eye, is clearly to be traced by the intellectual eye, wherever we turn ourselves. In conformity however to the preconceived notions attached to these words, we now employ them in regard to the agency of secondary causes. But how far a Christian may use them without disparagement to the majesty of the Divine Being, it is not so much my business to inquire, as to define their ordinary acceptation; 'Some there are who utterly proscribe the name of *chance* as a word of impious and profane signification: and indeed if it be taken by us in that sense in which it was used by the heathens, so as to make any thing casual in respect of God himself, their exception ought to be admitted. But to say a thing is a *chance* or casualty as it relates to second causes, is not profaneness, but a great truth.'—South.

In this ordinary sense, *chance* is the generick, *fortune* and *fate* are specifick terms: *chance* applies to all things personal or otherwise: *fortune* and *fate* are mostly said of that which is personal.

Chance neither forms orders nor designs: neither knowledge nor intention is attributed to it; its events are uncertain and variable;

> *Chance* aids their daring with unhop'd success.
> Dryden.

Fortune forms plans and designs, but without choice; we attribute to it an intention without discernment; it is said to be blind; 'We should learn that none but intellectual possessions are what we can properly call our own. All things from without are but borrowed. What *fortune* gives us is not ours, and whatever she gives she can take away.'—Steele. *Fate* forms plans and chains of causes; intention, knowledge, and power are attributed to it: its views are fixed, its results decisive;

> Since *fate* divides then, since I must lose thee,
> For pity's sake, for love's, oh! suffer me,
> Thus languishing, thus dying, to approach thee;
> And sigh my last adieu upon thy bosom.—Trapp.

A person goes as *chance* directs him when he has no express object to determine his choice one way or other; his *fortune* favours him, if without any expectation he gets the thing he wishes; his *fate* wills it, if he reaches the desired point contrary to what he intended.

Men's success in their undertakings depends oftener on *chance* than on their ability: we are ever ready to ascribe to ourselves what we owe to our good *fortune*; it is the *fate* of some men to fail in every thing they undertake.

When speaking of trivial matters, this language is unquestionably innocent, and any objection to their use must spring from an over scrupulous conscience.

If I suffer my horse to direct me in the road I take to London, I may fairly attribute it to *chance* if I take the right instead of the left; if I meet with an agreeable companion by the way I shall not hesitate to call it my good *fortune* that led me to take one road in preference to another; if in spite of any previous intention to the contrary, I should be led to take the same road repeatedly, and as often to meet with an agreeable companion, I shall immediately say that is my *fate* to meet with an agreeable companion whenever I go to London.

CHANCE, PROBABILITY.

Chance signifies the same as in the preceding article; *probability*, in French *probabilité*, Latin *probabilitas*, from *probabilis* and *probo* to prove, signifies the quality of being able to be proved or made good.

These terms are both employed in forming an estimate of future events; but the *chance* is either for or against, the *probability* is always for a thing. *Chance* is but a degree of *probability*; there may in this latter case be a *chance* where there is no *probability*. A *chance* affords a possibility; many *chances* are requisite to constitute a *probability*.

What has been once may, under similar circumstances, be again; for that there is a *chance*; what has fallen to one man may fall to another; so far he has a *chance* in his favour; but in all the *chances* of life there will be no *probability* of success, where a man does not unite industry with integrity;

> Thus equal deaths are dealt with equal *chance*,
> By turns they quit their ground, by turns advance.
> Dryden.

Chance cannot be calculated upon; it is apt to produce disappointment: *probability* justifies hope; it is sanctioned by experience; '"There never appear," says Swift, "more than five or six men of genius in an age, but if they were united the world could not stand before them." It is happy therefore for mankind that of this union there is no *probability*.'—Johnson.

CHANCE, HAZARD.

Chance signifies the same as in the preceding article, *hazard* comes from the oriental *zar* and *tzar*, signifying any thing bearing an impression, particularly the dice used in *chance* games, which is called by the Italians *zara*, and by the Spaniards *azar*.

Both these terms are employed to mark the course of future events, which is not discernible by the human eye. With the Deity there is neither *chance* nor *hazard*; his plans are the result of omniscience: but the designs and actions of men are all dependent on *chance* or *hazard*. *Chance* may be favourable or unfavourable, more commonly the former; *hazard* is always unfavourable: it is properly a species of *chance*. There is a *chance* either of gaining or losing: there is a *hazard* of losing. In most speculations the *chance* of succeeding scarcely outweighs the *hazard* of losing;

> Against ill *chances* men are ever merry,
> But heaviness foreruns the good event.
> Shakspeare.

'Though wit and learning are certain and habitual perfections of the mind, yet the declaration of them which alone brings the repute, is subject to a thousand *hazards*.'—SOUTH

TO HAZARD, RISK, VENTURE.

Hazard signifies the same as in the preceding article; *risk* may be traced to the French *risque*, the Italian *rischio*, and the Spanish *riesgo*, and has been further traced by Meursius to the barbarous Greek word *ῥίζηκον* fortune or chance, but its more remote derivation is uncertain; *venture* is the same as adventure.

All these terms denote actions performed under an uncertainty of the event; but *hazard* bespeaks a want of design and choice on the part of the agent; to risk implies a choice of alternatives; to *venture*, a calculation and balance of probabilities: one *hazards* and *risks* under the fear of an evil; one *ventures* with the hope of a good. He who *hazards* an opinion or an assertion does it from presumptuous feelings and upon slight grounds; chances are rather against him than for him that it may prove erroneous;

> They list with women each degenerate name
> Who dares not *hazard* life for future fame.
> DRYDEN.

He who *risks* a battle does it often from necessity; he who chooses the least of two evils, although the event is dubious, yet he fears less from a failure than from inaction; 'If the adventurer *risques* honour, he *risques* more than the knight.'—HAWKESWORTH. He who *ventures* on a mercantile speculation does it from a love of gain; he flatters himself with a favourable event, and acquires boldness from the prospect; 'Socrates, in his discourse before his death, says, he did not know whether his body shall (would) remain after death, but he thought so, and had such hopes of it that he was very willing to *venture* his life upon these hopes.'—TILLOTSON.

There are but very few circumstances to justify us in *hazarding*; there may be several occasions which render it necessary to *risk*, and very many cases in which it may be advantageous to *venture*.

DANGER, PERIL, HAZARD.

Danger, in French *danger*, comes from the Latin *damnum* a loss or damage, signifying the chance of a loss; *peril*, in French *peril*, comes from *pereo*, which signifies either to go over, or to perish, and *periculum*, which signifies literally that which is undergone; designating a critical situation, a rude trial, which may terminate in one's ruin; *hazard* signifies the same as in the preceding article.

The idea of chance or uncertainty is common to all these terms; but the two former may sometimes be foreseen and calculated upon; the latter is purely contingent. *Danger* and *peril* are applied to a positive evil; *hazard* may simply respect the loss of a good; risks are voluntarily run from the hope of good: there may be many *dangers* included in a *hazard*; and there cannot be a *hazard* without some *danger*.

A general *hazards* a battle, in order to disengage himself from a difficulty; he may by this step involve himself in imminent *danger* of losing his honour or his life; but it is likewise possible that by his superiour skill he may set both out of all *danger*: we are hourly exposed to *dangers* which no human foresight can guard against, and are frequently induced to engage in enterprises at the *hazard* of our lives, and of all that we hold dear;

> One was their care, and their delight was one;
> One common *hazard* in the war they shared.
> DRYDEN.

Dangers are far and near, ordinary and extraordinary; they meet us if we do not go in search of them;

> Proud of the favours mighty Jove has shown,
> On certain *dangers* we too rashly run.—POPE.

Perils are always distant and extraordinary; we must go out of our course to expose ourselves to them: in the quiet walk of life as in the most busy and tumultuous, it is the lot of man to be surrounded by *danger*; he has nothing which he is not in *danger* of losing; and knows of nothing which he is not in *danger* of suffering: the mariner and the traveller who go in search of unknown countries put themselves in the way of undergoing *perils* both by sea and land;

> From that dire deluge through the watery waste,
> Such length of years, such various *perils* past,
> At last escaped, to Latium we repair.—DRYDEN.

The same distinction exists between the epithets that are derived from these terms.

It is *dangerous* for a youth to act without the advice of his friends; it is *perilous* for a traveller to explore the wilds of Africa: it is *hazardous* for a merchant to speculate in time of war: experiments in matters of policy or government are always *dangerous*;

> Hear this and tremble! all who would be great,
> Yet know not what attends that *dang'rous*, wretched state.—JENYNS.

A journey through deserts that are infested with beasts of prey is *perilous*;

> The grisly boar is singled from his herd,
> A match for Hercules; round him they fly
> In circles wide, and each in passing sends
> His feather'd death into his brawny sides;
> But *perilous* th' attempt.—SOMERVILLE.

A military expedition conducted with inadequate means is *hazardous*; 'The previous steps being taken, and the time fixed for this *hazardous* attempt, Admiral Holmes moved with his squadron farther up the river, about three leagues above the place appointed for the disembarkation, that he might deceive the enemy' – SMOLLET.

TO HAPPEN, CHANCE.

To *happen*, that is, to fall out by a *hap*, is to *chance* (*v. Chance, fortune*) as the genus to the species; whatever *chances happens*, but not *vice versâ*. *Happen* respects all events without including any collateral idea; *chance* comprehends, likewise, the idea of the cause and order of events: whatever comes to pass *happens*, whether regularly in the course of things, or particularly, and out of the order; whatever *chances happens* altogether without concert, intention, and often without relation to any other thing. Accidents *happen* daily which no human foresight could prevent; the newspapers contain an account of all that *happens* in the course of the day or week;

> With equal mind what *happens* let us bear,
> Nor joy, nor grieve too much for things beyond our care.
> DRYDEN.

Listeners and busy bodies are ready to catch every word that *chances* to fall in their hearing; 'An idiot *chancing* to live within the sound of a clock, always amused himself with counting the hour of the day whenever the clock struck; but the clock being spoiled by accident, the idiot continued to count the hour without the help of it.'—ADDISON.

ACCIDENT, CHANCE.

Accident, in French *accident*, Latin *accidens*, participle of *accido* to happen, compounded of *ac* or *ad* and *cado* to fall, signifies the thing falling out; *chance* (*v. Chance, fortune.*)

Accident is said of things that have been; *chance* of things that are to be. That is an *accident* which is done without intention: that is a *chance* which cannot be brought about by the use of means. It is an *accident* when a house falls: it is a *chance* when and how it may fall; 'That little *accident* of Alexander's taking a fancy to bathe himself caused the interruption of his march; and that interruption gave occasion to that great victory that founded the third monarchy of the world.'—SOUTH. 'Surely there could not be a greater *chance* than that which brought to light the Powder-Treason.'—SOUTH.

Accidents cannot be prevented: *chances* cannot be calculated upon. *Accidents* may sometimes be remedied; *chances* can never be controlled: *accidents* give rise to sorrow, they mostly occasion mischief; *chances* give rise to hope; they often produce disappointment: it is wise to dwell upon neither.

ACCIDENT, CONTINGENCY, CASUALTY.

Accident signifies the same as in the preceding article; *contingency*, in French *contingence*, Latin *contingens*, participle of *contingo*, compounded of *con* and *tango* to touch one another, signifies the falling out or happening together; or the thing that happens in conjunction with another; *casualty*, in French *casualté*, from the Latin *casualis* and *cado* to fall or happen, signifies what happens in the course of events.

These words imply whatever takes place independently of our intentions. *Accidents* express more than *contingencies;* the former comprehend events with their causes and consequences; the latter respect collateral actions, or circumstances appended to events; *casualties* have regard simply to circumstances. *Accidents* are frequently occasioned by carelessness, and *contingencies* by trivial mistakes; but *casualties* are altogether independent of ourselves.

The overturning a carriage is an *accident;* our situation in a carriage, at the time, is a *contingency*, which may occasion us to be more or less hurt; the passing of any one at the time is a *casualty*. We are all exposed to the most calamitous *accidents;* 'This natural impatience to look into futurity, and to know what *accidents* may happen to us hereafter, has given birth to many ridiculous arts and inventions.'—Addison. The happiness or misery of every man depends upon a thousand *contingencies;* 'Nothing less than infinite wisdom can have an absolute command over fortune; the highest degree of it which man can possess is by no means equal to fortuitous events, and to such *contingencies* as may rise in the prosecution of our affairs.'—Addison. The best concerted scheme may be thwarted by *casualties*, which no human foresight can prevent; 'Men are exposed to more *casualties* than women, as battles, sea-voyages, with several dangerous trades and professions.—Addison.

ACCIDENTAL, INCIDENTAL, CASUAL, CONTINGENT.

Accidental belonging to or after the manner of an accident (*v. Accident*): *incidental*, from *incident*, in Latin *incidens* and *incido* or *in* and *cado* to fall upon, signifies belonging to a thing by chance; *casual* after the manner of a chance or casualty; and *contingent*, after the manner of a contingency.

Accidental is opposed to what is designed or planned, *incidental* to what is premeditated, *casual* to what is constant and regular, *contingent* to what is definite and fixed. A meeting may be *accidental*, an expression *incidental*, a look, expression, &c. *casual*, an expense or circumstance *contingent*. We do not expect what is *accidental;* we do not suspect or guard against what is *incidental;* we do not heed what is *casual;* we are not prepared for what is *contingent*. Many of the most fortunate and important occurrences in our lives are *accidental;* many remarks, seemingly *incidental*, do in reality conceal a settled intent, 'This book fell *accidentally* into the hands of one who had never seen it before.'—Addison. 'The distempers of the mind may be figuratively classed under the several characters of those maladies which are *incidental* to the body.'—Cumberland. A *casual* remark in the course of conversation will sometimes make a stronger impression on the minds of children than the most eloquent and impressive discourse or repeated counsel; 'Savage lodged as much by *accident* and passed the night sometimes in mean houses, which are set open at night to any *casual* wanderers.'—Johnson. In the prosecution of any plan we ought to be prepared for the numerous *contingencies* which we may meet with to interfere with our arrangements; 'We see how a *contingent* event baffles man's knowledge and evades his power.'—South.

EVENT, INCIDENT, ADVENTURE, OCCURRENCE.

Event, in Latin *eventus*, participle of *envenio* to come out, signifies that which falls out or turns up; *incident*, in Latin *incidens*, from *incido*, signifies that which falls in or forms a collateral part of any thing (*v. Accidental*); *adventure*, from the Latin *advenio* to come to, signifies what comes to or befalls one; *occurrence*, from the Latin *occurro*, signifies that which runs or comes in the way.

These terms are expressive of what passes in the world, which is the sole signification of the term *event;* while to that of the other terms are annexed some accessary ideas: an *incident* is a personal *event:* an *accident* an unpleasant *event;* an *adventure* an extraordinary *event;* an *occurrence* an ordinary or domestick *event:* *event* in its ordinary and unlimited acceptation excludes the idea of chance; *accident* excludes that of design; *incident*, *adventure*, and *occurrence*, are applicable in both cases.

Events affect nations and communities as well as individuals; *incidents* and *adventures* affect particular individuals; *accidents* and *occurrences* affect persons or things particularly or generally, individually or collectively: the making of peace, the loss of a battle, or the death of a prince, are national *events;* a marriage or a death are domestick *events;* 'These *events*, the permission of which seems to accuse his goodness now, may, in the consummation of things, both magnify his goodness and exalt his wisdom.'—Addison. The forming a new acquaintance and the revival of an old one are *incidents* that have an interest for the parties concerned; 'I have laid before you only small *incidents* seemingly frivolous, but they are principally evils of this nature which make marriages unhappy.'—Steele. An escape from shipwreck, an encounter with wild beasts or savages, are *adventures* which individuals are pleased to relate, and others to hear;

For I must love, and am resolv'd to try
My fate, or failing in the *adventure*, die.—Dryden.

A fire, the fall of a house, the breaking of a limb are *accidents* or *occurrences;* a robbery or the death of individuals are properly *occurrences* which afford subjects for a newspaper, and excite an interest in the reader; 'I think there is somewhere in Montaigne mention made of a family book, wherein all the *occurrences* that happened from one generation of that house to another were recorded.'—Steele.

Event, when used for individuals, is always of greater importance than an *incident*. The settlement of a young person in life, the adoption of an employment, or the taking a wife, are *events*, but not *incidents;* while on the other hand the setting out on a journey or the return, the purchase of a house or the despatch of a vessel, are characterized as *incidents* and not *events*.

It is farther to be observed that *incident*, *event*, and *occurrence* are said only of that which is supposed really to happen: *incidents* and *adventures* are often fictitious; in this case the *incident* cannot be too important, nor the *adventure* too marvellous. History records the *events* of nations; plays require to be full of *incident* in order to render them interesting; 'No person, no *incident* in the play, but must be of use to carry on the main design.'—Dryden. Romances and novels derive most of their charms from the extravagance of the *adventures* which they describe; 'To make an episode, "take any remaining *adventure* of your former collection," in which you could no way involve your hero, or any unfortunate *accident* that was too good to be thrown away.'—Pope. Periodical works supply the publick with information respecting daily *occurrences*.

CIRCUMSTANCE, INCIDENT, FACT.

Circumstance, in Latin *circumstantia*, from *circum* and *sto*, signifies what stands about a thing or belongs to it as its accident; *incident* signifies the same as before; *fact*, in Latin *factum*, participle of *facio* to do, signifies the thing done.

Circumstance is a general term; *incident* and *fact* are species of *circumstances*. *Incident* is what happens; *fact* is what is done; *circumstance* is not only what happens and is done, but whatever is or belongs to a thing. To every thing are annexed *circumstances* either of time, place, age, colour, or other collateral appendages which change its nature. Every thing that moves and operates is exposed to *incidents*, effects are produced, results follow, and changes are brought about; these are *incidents:* whatever moves and operates does, and what it produces is done or is the *fact:* when the artificer performs any work of art, it depends not only on his skill, but on the excellence of his tools, the time he employs, the particular frame of his mind, the place where he works, with a variety of other *circumstances* whether he will succeed in producing any thing masterly. Newspapers abound with the various *incidents* which occur in the animal or the vegetable world, some of which are surprising and singular; they likewise contain a number of *facts* which serve to present a melancholy picture of human depravity.

Circumstance is as often employed with regard to the operations of things, in which case it is most analogous to *incident* and *fact:* it may then be employed for the whole affair, or any part of it whatever, that can be distinctly considered. *Incidents* and *facts* either are *circumstances*, or have *circumstances* belonging to them. A remarkably abundant crop in any particular part of a field is for the agriculturist a singular *circumstance* or *incident;* this may be rendered more surprising if associated with unusual sterility in other parts of the same field. A robbery may either be a *fact* or a *circumstance;* its atrocity may be aggravated by the murder of the injured parties; the savageness of the perpetrators, and a variety of *circumstances*.

Circumstance comprehends in its signification whatever may be said or thought of any thing: 'You very often hear people after a story has been told with some entertaining *circumstances*, tell it again with particulars that destroy the jest.'—STEELE. *Incident* carries with it the idea of whatever may befall or be said to befall any thing; 'It is to be considered that Providence in its economy regards the whole system of time and things together, so that we cannot discover the beautiful connexion between *incidents* which lie widely separate in time.'—ADDISON. *Fact* includes in it nothing but what really is or is done; 'In describing the achievements and institutions of the Spaniards in the New World, I have departed in many instances from the accounts of preceding historians, and have often related *facts* which seem to have been unknown to them.'—ROBERTSON. A narrative therefore may contain many *circumstances* and *incidents* without any *fact*, when what is related is either fictitious or not positively known to have happened: it is necessary for a novel or play to contain much *incident*, but no *facts*, in order to render it interesting; history should contain nothing but *facts*, as authenticity is its chief merit.

CIRCUMSTANCE, SITUATION.

Circumstance signifies the same as in the preceding article; *situation*, in French *situation*, comes from the Latin *situs*, and the Hebrew שות to place, signifying what is placed in a certain manner.

Circumstance is to *situation* as a part to a whole; many *circumstances* constitute a *situation;* a *situation* is an aggregate of *circumstances*. A person is said to be in *circumstances* of affluence who has an abundance of every thing essential for his comfort; he is in an easy *situation* when nothing exists to create uneasiness.

Circumstance respects that which externally affects us; *situation* is employed both for the outward *circumstances* and the inward feelings. The success of any undertaking depends greatly on the *circumstances* under which it is begun; 'As for the ass's behaviour in such nice *circumstances*, whether he would starve sooner than violate his neutrality to the two bundles of hay, I shall not presume to determine.'—ADDISON. The particular *situation* of a person's mind will give a cast to his words or actions; 'We are not at present in a proper *situation* to judge of the councils by which Providence acts.'—ADDISON. *Circumstances* are critical, a *situation* is dangerous.

CIRCUMSTANTIAL, PARTICULAR, MINUTE.

Circumstantial, from *circumstance*, signifies consisting of *circumstances; particular*, in French *particulier*, from the word *particle*, signifies consisting of particles; *minute*, in French *minute*, Latin *minutus*, participle of *minuo* to diminish, signifies diminished or reduced to a very small point.

Circumstantial expresses less than *particular*, and that less than *minute*. A *circumstantial* account contains all leading events; a *particular* account includes every event and movement however trivial; a *minute* account omits nothing as to person, time, place, figure, form, and every other trivial *circumstance* connected with the events. A narrative may be *circumstantial, particular*, or *minute;* an inquiry, investigation, or description may be *particular* or *minute*, a detail may be *minute*. An event or occurrence may be *particular*, a *circumstance* or *particular* may be *minute*. We may be generally satisfied with a *circumstantial* account of ordinary events; but whatever interests the feelings cannot be detailed with too much *particularity* or *minuteness;* 'Thomson's wide expansion of general views and his enumeration of *circumstantial* varieties, would have been obstructed and embarrassed by the frequent intersections of the sense which are the necessary effects of the rhyme.'—JOHNSON. 'I am extremely troubled at the return of your deafness; you cannot be too *particular* in the accounts of your health to me.'—POPE. When Pope's letters were published and avowed, as they had relation to recent facts, and persons either then living or not yet forgotten, they may be supposed to have found readers, but as the facts were *minute*, and the characters little known, or little regarded, they awakened no popular kindness or resentment.'—JOHNSON.

CONJUNCTURE, CRISIS.

Conjuncture, in Latin *conjunctura*, from *conjungo* to join together, signifies the joining together of circumstances; *crisis*, in Latin *crisis*, Greek κρίσις a judgement, signifies in an extended sense whatever decides or turns the scale.

Both these terms are employed to express a period of time marked by the state of affairs. A *conjuncture* is a joining or combination of corresponding circumstances tending towards the same end; 'Every virtue requires time and place, a proper object, and a fit *conjuncture* of circumstances for the due exercise of it.'—ADDISON. A *crisis* is the high-wrought state of any affair which immediately precedes a change;

> Thought he, this is the lucky hour,
> Wines work, when vines are in the flower;
> This *crisis* then I will set my rest on,
> And put her boldly to the question.—BUTLER.

A *conjuncture* may be favourable, a *crisis* alarming.

An able statesman seizes the *conjuncture* which promises to suit his purpose, for the introduction of a favourite measure: the abilities, firmness, and perseverance of Alfred the Great, at one important *crisis* of his reign, saved England from destruction.

EXIGENCY, EMERGENCY.

Necessity is the idea which is common to the signification of these terms: the former, from the Latin *exigo* to demand, expresses what the case demands; and the latter, from *emergo*, to arise out of, denotes what rises out of the case.

The *exigency* is more common, but less pressing; the *emergency* is imperious when it comes, but comes less frequently: a prudent traveller will never carry more money with him than what will supply the *exigencies* of his journey; and in case of an *emergency* will rather borrow of his friends than risk his property; 'Savage was again confined to Bristol, where he was every day hunted by bailiffs. In this *exigence* he once more found a friend who sheltered him in his house.'—JOHNSON. When it was formerly the fashion to husband a lie and to trump it up in some extraordinary *emergency*, it generally did execution; but at present every man is on his guard.'—ADDISON.

ENTERPRISING, ADVENTUROUS.

These terms mark a disposition to engage in that which is extraordinary and hazardous: but *enterprising*, from *enterprise* (*v. Attempt*), is connected with the understanding; and *adventurous*, from *adventure*, venture or trial, is a characteristick of the passions. The *enterprising* character conceives great projects, and pursues objects that are difficult to be obtained; the *adventurous* character is contented with seeking that which is new, and placing himself in dangerous and unusual situations. An *enterprising* spirit belongs to the commander of an army, or the ruler of a nation; an *adventurous* disposition is sometimes to be found in men of low degree, but was formerly attributed for the most part to knights; Robinson Crusoe was a man of an *adventurous* turn;

> At land and sea, in many a doubtful fight
> Was never known a more *adventurous* knight,
> Who oftener drew his sword, and always for the right
> DRYDEN.

Peter the Great possessed, in a peculiar manner, an *enterprising* genius; 'Sir Walter Raleigh, who had anew forfeited the king's friendship, by an intrigue with a maid of honour, and who had been thrown into prison for this misdemeanour, no sooner recovered his liberty than he was pushed by his active and *enterprising* genius to attempt some great action.'—HUME. *Enterprising* characterizes persons only: but *adventurous* is also applied to things, to signify containing *adventures;* as a journey, or a voyage, or a history, may be denominated *adventurous:* also in the sense of hazardous;

But 't is enough
In this late age, *advent'rous* to have touch'd
Light on the numbers of the Samian sage;
High heaven forbids the bold presumptuous strain.
THOMSON.

TO HOLD, CONTAIN.

These terms agree in sense, but differ in application. To *hold* (*v. To hold, keep*) is the familiar term employed only for material objects; *contain*, in French *contenir*, Latin *contineo*, compounded of *con* and *teneo*, signifying to keep together in one place, is a term of more noble use, being applied to moral or spiritual objects.

To *hold* is to occupy a space, whether enclosed or open: to *contain* is to fill an enclosed space; hence it is that these words may both be applied to the same objects A cask is said to *hold*, or in more polished language it is said to *contain* a certain number of gallons. A coach *holds* or *contains* a given number of persons; a room *holds* a given quantity of furniture; a house or city *contains* its inhabitants. *Hold* is applied figuratively and in poetry in a similar sense;

Death only this mysterious truth unfolds,
The mighty soul how small a body *holds*.
DRYDEN.

Contain is applied in its proper sense to spiritual as material objects;

But man, the abstract
Of all perfection, which the workmanship
Of heav'n hath modell'd, in himself *contains*
Passions of several qualities.—FORD.

CAPACITY, CAPACIOUSNESS.

Capacity is the abstract of *capax*, receiving or apt to hold, and is therefore applied to the contents of hollow bodies: *capaciousness* is the abstract of *capacious*, and is therefore applied to the plane surface comprehended within a given space. Hence we speak of the *capacity* of a vessel, and the *capaciousness* of a room.

Capacity is an indefinite term simply designating fitness to hold or receive; but *capaciousness* denotes something specifically large. Measuring the *capacity* of vessels belongs to the science of mensuration: the *capaciousness* of rooms is to be observed by the eye. They are marked by the same distinction in their moral application: men are born with various *capacities;* some are remarkable for the *capaciousness* of their minds.

TO COMPRISE, COMPREHEND, EMBRACE, CONTAIN, INCLUDE.

Comprise, through the French *compris*, participle of *comprendre*, comes from the same source as *comprehend* (*v. Comprehensive*); *embrace*, in French *embrasser*, from *em* or *in* and *bras* the arm, signifies literally to enclose in the arms; *contain* has the same signification as in the preceding article; *include*, in Latin *includo*, compounded of *in* and *cludo* or *claudo*, signifies to shut in or within a given space.

Persons or things *comprise* or *include;* things only *comprehend*, *embrace*, and *contain:* a person *comprises* a certain quantity of matter within a given space; he *includes* one thing within another: an author *comprises* his work within a certain number of volumes, and *includes* in it a variety of interesting particulars.

When things are spoken of, *comprise*, *comprehend*, and *embrace*, have regard to the aggregate value, quantity, or extent: *include*, to the individual things which form the whole: *contain*, either to the aggregate or to the individual, being in fact a term of more ordinary application than any of the others. *Comprise* and *contain* are used either in the proper or the figurative sense; *comprehend*, *embrace*, and *include*, in the figurative sense only: a stock *comprises* a variety of articles; a library *comprises* a variety of books; the whole is *comprised* within a small compass:

What, Egypt, do thy pyramids *comprise?*
What greatness in the high-raised folly lies!
SEWELL.

Rules *comprehend* a number of particulars; laws *comprehend* a number of cases; countries *comprehend* a certain number of districts or divisions; terms *comprehend* a certain meaning; 'That particular scheme which *comprehends* the social virtues may give employment to the most industrious temper, and find a man in business more than the most active station of life.'—ADDISON. A discourse *embraces* a variety of topicks; a plan, project, scheme, or system, *embraces* a variety of objects;

The virtues of the several soils I sing,
Mæcenas, now the needful succour bring;
Not that my song in such a scanty space
So large a subject fully can *embrace*.—DRYDEN.

A house *contains* one, two, or more persons; a city *contains* a number of houses; a book *contains* much useful matter; a society *contains* very many individuals; 'All a woman has to do in this world is *contained* within the duties of a daughter, a sister, a wife, and a mother.'—STEELE. A society *includes* none but persons of a certain class; or it *includes* some of every class; 'The universal axiom in which all complaisance is *included* is, that *no man should give any preference to himself*.'—JOHNSON.

Their arms and fishing tackle *comprise* the personal effects of most savages; all the moral law of a Christian is *comprised* under the word charity: Sweden *comprehends* Finland and Lapland: London is said to *contain* above a million of inhabitants: bills of mortality are made out in most large parishes, but they *include* only such persons as die of diseases; a calculator of expenses will always fall short of his estimate who does not *include* the minor contingencies which usually attach to every undertaking.

It is here worthy of observation, that in the last two examples from Steele and Johnson the words *comprehend* and *comprise* would, according to established usage, have been more appropriate than *contain* and *include*.

COMPREHENSIVE, EXTENSIVE.

Comprehensive respects quantity, *extensive* regards space; that is *comprehensive* that *comprehends* much, that is *extensive* that *extends* into a wide field: a *comprehensive* view of a subject includes all branches of it; an *extensive* view of a subject enters into minute details: the *comprehensive* is associated with the concise; the *extensive* with the diffuse: it requires a capacious mind to take a *comprehensive* survey of any subject; it is possible for a superficial thinker to enter very *extensively* into some parts, while he passes over others.

Comprehensive is employed only with regard to intellectual objects; 'It is natural to hope that a *comprehensive* is likewise an elevated soul, and that whoever is wise is also honest.'—JOHNSON. *Extensive* is used both in the proper and the improper sense: the signification of a word is *comprehensive*, or the powers of the mind are *comprehensive:* a plain is *extensive*, or a field of inquiry is *extensive;* 'The trade carried on by the Phœnicians of Sidon and Tyre was more *extensive* and enterprising than that of any state in the ancient world.'—ROBERTSON.

TO ENCLOSE, INCLUDE.

From the Latin *includo* and its participle *inclusus* are derived *enclose* and *include;* the former to express the proper, and the latter the improper signification: a yard is *enclosed* by a wall; particular goods are *included* in a reckoning: the kernel of a nut is *enclosed* in a shell, or a body of men are *enclosed* within walls;

With whom she marched straight against her foes,
And them unawares besides the Severne did *enclose*
SPENSER

Morality as well as faith is *included* in Christian perfection; 'The idea of being once present is *included* in the idea of its being past.'—GROVE.

TO CIRCUMSCRIBE, ENCLOSE.

Circumscribe, from the Latin *circum* about, and *scribo* to write, marks simply the surrounding with a line; *enclose*, from the Latin *inclusus*, participle of *includo*, compounded of *in* and *claudo* to shut, marks a species of confinement.

The extent of any place is drawn out to the eye by a *circumscription*: 'Who can imagine that the existence of a creature is to be *circumscribed* by time, whose thoughts are not?'—ADDISON. The extent of a place is limited to a given point by an *enclosure*;

> Remember on that happy coast to build,
> And with a trench *enclose* the fruitful field.
> DRYDEN.

A garden is *circumscribed* by any ditch, line, or posts, that serve as its boundaries; it is *enclosed* by a wall or fence. An *enclosure* may serve to *circumscribe*, but that which barely *circumscribes* will seldom serve to *enclose*.

TO SURROUND, ENCOMPASS, ENVIRON, ENCIRCLE.

Surround, in old French *surronder*, signifies, by means of the intensive syllable *sur* over, to go all round; *encompass*, compounded of *en* or *in* and *compass*, signifies to bring within a certain compass formed by a circle; so likewise *environ*, from the Latin *gyrus*, and the Greek γυρὸς a curve, and also *encircle*, signify to bring within a circle.

Surround is the most literal and general of all these terms, which signify to enclose any object either directly or indirectly. We may *surround* an object by standing at certain distances all round it; in this manner a town, a house, or a person, may be *surrounded* by other persons, or an object may be *surrounded* by enclosing it in every direction, and at every point; in this manner a garden is *surrounded* by a wall;

> But not to me returns
> Day, or the sweet approach of ev'n or morn,
> But cloud instead, and ever-during dark
> *Surrounds* me.—MILTON.

To *encompass* is to surround in the latter sense, and applies to objects of a great or indefinite extent: the earth is *encompassed* by the air, which we term the atmosphere: towns are *encompassed* by walls;

> Where Orpheus on his lyre laments his love,
> With beasts *encompass'd*, and a dancing grove.
> DRYDEN.

To *surround* is to go round an object of any form, whether square or circular, long or short; but to *environ* and to *encircle* carry with them the idea of forming a circle round an object; thus a town or a valley may be *environed* by hills, a basin of water may be *encircled* by trees, or the head may be *encircled* by a wreath of flowers;

> Of fighting elements, on all sides round
> *Environ'd*.—MILTON.

> As in the hollow breast of Apennine,
> Beneath the shelter of *encircling* hills,
> A myrtle rises, far from human eye,
> So flourish'd, blooming, and unseen by all,
> The sweet Lavinia.—THOMSON.

In an extended or moral sense we are said to be *surrounded* by objects which are in great numbers, and in different directions about us: thus a person living in a particular spot where he has many friends may say he is *surrounded* by his friends; so likewise a particular person may say that he is *surrounded* by dangers and difficulties: but in speaking of man in a general sense, we should rather say he is *encompassed* by dangers, which expresses in a much stronger manner our peculiarly exposed condition.

CIRCLE, SPHERE, ORB, GLOBE.

Circle, in Latin *circulus*, Greek κικλος, in all probability comes from the Hebrew חוג a circle; *sphere*, in Latin *sphæra*, Greek σφαῖρα, from σπεῖρα a line, signifies that which is contained within a prescribed line; *orb*, in Latin *orbis*, from *orbo* to circumscribe with a *circle*, signifies the thing that is circumscribed; *globe*, in Latin *globus*, in all probability comes from the Hebrew גל a rolled heap.

Rotundity of figure is the common idea expressed by these terms; but the *circle* is that figure which is represented on a plane superficies; the others are figures represented by solids. We draw a *circle* by means of compasses; the *sphere* is a round body, conceived to be formed according to the rules of geometry by the circumvolution of a *circle* round about its diameter; hence the whole frame of the world is denominated a *sphere*. An *orb* is any body which describes a *circle*; hence the heavenly bodies are termed *orbs*;

> Thousands of suns beyond each other blaze,
> *Orbs* roll o'er *orbs*, and glow with mutual rays.
> JENYNS.

A *globe* is any solid body, the surface of which is in every part equidistant from the centre; of this description is the terrestrial *globe*.

The term *circle* may be applied in the improper sense to any round figure, which is formed or supposed to be formed by circumscribing a space; simple rotundity constituting a *circle*: in this manner a *circle* may be formed by real objects, as persons, or by moral objects, as pleasures;

> Might I from fortune's bounteous hand receive
> Each boon, each blessing in her power to give;
> E'en at this mighty price I 'd not be bound
> To tread the same dull *circle* round and round.
> The soul requires enjoyments more sublime,
> By space unbounded, undestroy'd by time.
> JENYNS.

To the idea of *circle* is annexed that of extent around, in the signification of a *sphere*, as a *sphere* of activity whether applied in the philosophical sense to natural bodies, or in the moral sense to men;

> Or if some stripes from Providence we feel,
> He strikes with pity, and but wounds to heal;
> Kindly, perhaps, sometimes afflicts us here,
> To guide our views to a sublimer *sphere*.—JENYNS

Hollowness, as well as rotundity, belongs to an *orb*; hence we speak of the *orb* of a wheel. Of a *globe* solidity is the peculiar characteristick; hence any ball, like the ball of the earth, may be represented as a *globe*;

> Thus roaming with advent'rous wing the *globe*,
> From scene to scene excursive, I behold
> In all her workings, beauteous, great, or new
> Fair nature.—MALLET.

CIRCUIT, TOUR, ROUND.

Circuit, in French *circuit*, Latin *circuitus*, participle of *circumeo*, signifies either the act of going round, or the extent gone; *tour* is but a variation of turn, signifying a mere turn of the body in travelling; *round* marks the track *round*, or the space gone *round*.

A *circuit* is made for a specifick end of a serious kind; a *tour* is always made for pleasure; a *round*, like a *circuit*, is employed in matters of business; but of a more familiar and ordinary kind. A judge goes his *circuit* at particular periods of time: gentlemen, in times of peace, consider it as an essential part of their education to make what is termed the grand *tour*: tradesmen have certain *rounds* which they take on certain days;

> 'T is night! the season when the happy take
> Repose, and only wretches are awake;
> Now discontented ghosts begin their *rounds*,
> Haunt ruin'd buildings and unwholesome grounds.
> OTWAY.

We speak of making the *circuit* of a place; of taking a *tour* in a given county; or going a particular *round*. A *circuit* is wide or narrow; a *tour* and a *round* is great or little. A *circuit* is prescribed as to extent: a *tour* is optional; a *round* is prescribed or otherwise. *Circuit* is seldom used but in a specifick sense;

> Th' unfledg'd commanders and the martial train,
> First make the *circuit* of the sandy plain.—DRYDEN

Tour is seldom employed but in regard to travelling; Goldsmith's *tour* through Europe we are told was made for the most part on foot.'—JOHNSON. *Round* may be taken figuratively, as when we speak of going one's *round* of pleasure; 'Savage had projected a perpetual *round* of innocent pleasure in Wales, of which he suspected no interruption from pride, or ignorance, or brutality.'—JOHNSON.

TO BOUND, LIMIT, CONFINE, CIRCUMSCRIBE, RESTRICT.

Bound comes from the verb *bind*, signifying that which *binds* fast or close to an object; *limit*, from the Latin *limes* a landmark, signifies to draw a line which is to be the exteriour line or limit; *confine* signifies to bring within *confines* (*v. Border*); *circumscribe* has the same signification as given under the head of *Circumscribe; restrict*, in Latin *restrictum*, participle of *restringo*, compounded of *re* and *stringo*, signifies to keep fast back.

The first four of these terms are employed in the proper sense of parting off certain spaces.

Bound applies to the natural or political divisions of the earth: countries are *bounded* by mountains and seas; kingdoms are often *bounded* by each other; Spain is *bounded* on one side by Portugal, on another side by the Mediterranean, and on the third by the Pyrenees. *Limit* applies to any artificial boundary: as landmarks in fields serve to show the *limits* of one man's ground from another; so may walls, palings, hedges, or any other visible sign, be converted into a *limit*, to distinguish one spot from another, and in this manner a field is said to be *limited*, because it has *limits* assigned to it. To *confine* is to bring the *limits* close together; to part off one space absolutely from another: in this manner we *confine* a garden by means of walls. To *circumscribe* is literally to surround: in this manner a circle may *circumscribe* a square: there is this difference however between *confine* and *circumscribe*, that the former denotes not only visible *limits*, but such as may also prevent egress and ingress; whereas the latter, which is only a line, is but a simple mark that *limits*.

From the proper acceptation of these terms we may easily perceive the ground on which their improper acceptation rests: to *bound* is an action suited to the nature of things or to some given rule; in this manner our views are *bounded* by the objects which intercept our sight: we *bound* our desires according to principles of propriety. To *limit*, *confine*, and *circumscribe*, all convey the idea of control which is more or less exercised. To *limit*, whether it be said of persons *limiting* things, or persons being *limited* by things, is an affair of discretion or necessity; we *limit* our expenses because we are *limited* by circumstances. *Confine* conveys the same idea to a still stronger degree: what is *confined* is not only brought within a *limit* but is kept to that *limit* which it cannot pass: in this manner a person *confines* himself to a diet which he finds absolutely necessary for his health, or he is *confined* in the size of his house, in the choice of his situation, or in other circumstances equally uncontrollable: hence the term *confined* expresses also the idea of the *limits* being made narrow as well as impassable or unchangeable. To *circumscribe* is figuratively to draw a line round; in this manner we are *circumscribed* in our pecuniary circumstances when our sphere of action is brought within a line by the want of riches. In as much as all these terms convey the idea of being acted upon involuntarily, they become allied to the term *restrict*, which simply expresses the exercise of control on the will: we use *restriction* when we *limit* and *confine*, but we may *restrict* without *limiting* or *confining*: to *limit* and *confine* are the acts of things upon persons, or persons upon persons; but *restrict* is only the act of persons upon persons: we are *limited* or *confined* only to a certain degree, but we may be *restricted* to an indefinite degree: the *limiting* and *confining* depend often on ourselves; the *restriction* depends upon the will of others: a person *limits* himself to so many hours' work in a day; an author *confines* himself to a particular branch of a subject; a person is *restricted* by his physician to a certain portion of food in the day: to be *confined* to a certain spot is irksome to one who has always had his liberty; but to be *restricted* in all his actions would be intolerable.

Our greatest happiness consists in *bounding* our desires to our condition;

> My passion is too strong
> In reason's narrow *bounds* to be *confin'd*.
> WANDESFORD.

It is prudent to *limit* our exertions, when we find them prejudicial to our health; 'The operations of the mind are not, like those of the hands, *limited* to one individual object, but at once extended to a whole species.'—BARTLET. It is necessary to *confine* our attention to one object at a time; 'Mechanical motions or operations are *confined* to a narrow circle of low and little things.'—BARTLET. It is unfortunate to be *circumscribed* in our means of doing good;

> Therefore must his choice be *circumscrib'd*
> Unto the voice and yielding of that body,
> Whereof he 's head.—SHAKSPEARE.

It is painful to be *restricted* in the enjoyment of innocent pleasure; 'It is not necessary to teach men to thirst after power; but it is very expedient that by moral instructions they should be taught, and by their civil institutions they should be compelled, to put many *restrictions* upon the immoderate exercise of it.'—BLACKSTONE.

Bounded is opposed to *unbounded*, *limited* to extended, *confined* to expanded, *circumscribed* to ample, *restricted* to unshackled.

BORDER, EDGE, RIM OR BRIM, BRINK, MARGIN, VERGE.

Border, in French *bord* or *bordure*, Teutonick *bord*, is probably connected with *bret*, and the English *board*, from *brytan*, in Greek πρίζειν to split; *edge*, in Saxon *ege*, low German *egge*, high German *ecke* a point, Latin *acies*, Greek ἀκή sharpness, signifies a sharp point; *rim*, in Saxon *rima*, high German *rahmen* a frame, *riemen* a thong, Greek ῥῦμα a tract, from ῥέω to draw, signifies a line drawn round; *brim*, *brink*, are but variations of *rim; margin*, in French *margin*, Latin *margo*, probably comes from *mare* the sea, as it is mostly connected with water; *verge*, from the Latin *virga*, signifies a rod, but is here used in the improper sense for the extremity of an object.

Of these terms *border* is the least definite point, *edge* the most so; *rim* and *brink* are species of *edge; margin* and *verge* are species of *border*. A *border* is a stripe, an *edge* is a line. The *border* lies at a certain distance from the *edge*, the *edge* is the exteriour termination of the surface of any substance; 'Methought the shilling that lay upon the table reared itself upon its *edge*, and turning its face towards me opened its mouth.'—ADDISON. Whatever is wide enough to admit of any space round its circumference may have a *border;*

> So the pure limpid stream, when with foul stains
> Of rushing torrents and descending rains,
> Works itself clear, and as it runs refines,
> Till by degrees the crystal mirror shines,
> Reflects each flower that on its *border* grows.
> ADDISON.

Whatever comes to a narrow extended surface has an *edge*. Many things may have both a *border* and an *edge;* of this description are caps, gowns, carpets, and the like; others have a *border* but no *edge*, as lands; and others have an *edge* but no *border*, as a knife or a table.

A *rim* is the *edge* of any vessel;

> But Merion's spear o'ertook him as he flew,
> Deep in the belly's *rim* an entrance found
> Where sharp the pang, and mortal is the wound.
> POPE.

The *brim* is the exteriour *edge* of a cup; a *brink* is the *edge* of any precipice or deep place;

> As I approach the precipice's *brink*,
> So steep, so terrible, appears the depth.
> LANSDOWNE.

A *margin* is the *border* of a book or a piece of water

> By the sea's *margin* on the watery strand
> Thy monument, Themistocles, shall stand.
> CUMBERLAND.

A *verge* is the extreme *border* of a place;

To the earth's utmost *verge* I will pursue him;
No place, though e'er so holy, shall protect him.
ROWE.

BOUNDLESS, UNBOUNDED, UNLIMITED, INFINITE.

Boundless, or without *bounds*, is applied to infinite objects which admit of no *bounds* to be made or conceived by us; *unbounded*, or not *bounded*, is applied to that which might be *bounded; unlimited*, or not *limited*, applies to that which might be *limited; infinite*, or not *finite*, applies to that which in its nature admits of no *bounds*.

The ocean is a *boundless* object so long as no *bounds* to it have been discovered, or no *bounds* are set to it in our imagination;

And see the country far diffus'd around
One *boundless* blush, one white empurpled shower
Of mingled blossoms.—THOMSON.

Desires are often *unbounded*, which ought always to be *bounded;*

The soul requires enjoyments more sublime,
By space *unbounded*, undestroy'd by time.
JENYNS.

Power is sometimes *unlimited* when it would be better *limited;* 'Gray's curiosity was *unlimited*, and his judgement cultivated.'—JOHNSON. Nothing is *infinite* but that Being from whom all *finite* beings proceed; 'In the wide fields of nature the sight wanders up and down without confinement, and is fed with an *infinite* variety of images.'—ADDISON.

BOUNDS, BOUNDARY.

Bounds and *boundary*, from the verb *bound* (*v. To bound*), signify the line which sets a *bound*, or marks the extent to which any spot of ground reaches. The term *bounds* is employed to designate the whole space including the outer line that *confines: boundary* comprehends only this outer line. *Bounds* are made for a local purpose; *boundary* for a political purpose: the master of a school prescribes the *bounds* beyond which the scholar is not to go;

So when the swelling Nile contemns her *bounds*,
And with extended waste the valleys drowns,
At length her ebbing streams resign the field,
And to the pregnant soil a tenfold harvest yield.
CIBBER.

The parishes throughout England have their *boundaries*, which are distinguished by marks; fields have likewise their *boundaries*, which are commonly marked out by a hedge or a ditch; 'Alexander did not in his progress towards the East advance beyond the banks of the rivers that fall into the Indus, which is now the Western *boundary* of the vast continent of India.'—ROBERTSON.

Bounds are temporary and changeable; *boundaries* permanent and fixed: whoever has the authority of prescribing *bounds* for others, may in like manner contract or extend them at pleasure; the *boundaries* of places are seldom altered, but in consequence of great political changes.

In the figurative sense *bound* or *bounds* is even more frequently used than *boundary:* we speak of setting *bounds* or keeping within *bounds;* but of knowing a *boundary:* it is necessary occasionally to set *bounds* to the inordinate appetites of the best disposed children; 'There are *bounds* within which our concern for worldly success must be confined.'—BLAIR. Children cannot be expected to know the exact *boundary* for indulgence; 'It is the proper ambition of heroes in literature to enlarge the *boundaries* of knowledge by discovering and conquering new regions of the intellectual world.'—JOHNSON.

LIMIT, EXTENT.

Limit is a more specifick and definite term than *extent;* by the former we are directed to the point where any thing ends; by the latter we are led to no particular point, but to the whole space included; the *limits* are in their nature something finite; the *extent* is either finite or infinite: we therefore speak of that which exceeds the *limits*, or comes within the *limits;* and of that which comprehends the *extent*, or is according to the *extent:* a plenipotentiary or minister must not exceed the *limits* of his instruction; when we think of the immense *extent* of this globe, and that it is among the smallest of an infinite number of worlds, the mind is lost in admiration and amazement: it does not fall within the *limits* of a periodical work to enter into historical details; 'Whatsoever a man accounts his treasure answers all his capacities of pleasure. It is the utmost *limit* of enjoyment.'—SOUTH. A complete history of any country is a work of great *extent;* 'It is observable that, either by nature or habit, our faculties are fitted to images of a certain *extent*.'—JOHNSON

TERM, LIMIT, BOUNDARY.

* *Term*, in Latin *terminus*, from the Greek *τέρμα* an end, is the point that ends, and that to which we direct our steps: *limit*, from the Latin *limes* a landmark, is the line which we must not pass: *boundary*, from to *bound*, is the obstacle which interrupts our progress, and prevents us from passing.

We are either carried towards or away from the *term;* we either keep within *limits*, or we overstep them; we contract or extend a *boundary*.

The *term* and the *limit* belong to the thing; by them it is ended; they include it in the space which it occupies, or contain it within its sphere; the *boundary* is extraneous of it. The Straits of Gibraltar was the *term* of Hercules' voyages: it was said with more eloquence than truth, that the *limits* of the Roman empire were those of the world: the sea, the Alps, and the Pyrenees, are the natural *boundaries* of France. We mostly reach the *term* of our prosperity when we attempt to pass the *limits* which Providence has assigned to human efforts: human ambition often finds a *boundary* set to its gratification by circumstances which were the most unlooked for, and apparently the least adapted to bring about such important results.

We see the *term* of our evils only in the term of our life;

No *term* of time this union shall divide.—DRYDEN.

Our desires have no *limits;* their gratification only serves to extend our prospects indefinitely; 'The wall of Antoninus was fixed as the *limit* of the Roman empire.'—GIBBON. Those only are happy whose fortune is the *boundary* of their desires; 'Providence has fixed the *limits* of human enjoyment by immoveable *boundaries*.'—JOHNSON.

CONTRACTED, CONFINED, NARROW.

Contracted, from the verb *contract*, in Latin *contractus*, participle of *contraho* to draw or come close together, signifies either the state or quality of being shrunk up, lessened in size, or brought within a smaller compass; *confined* marks the state of being *confined; narrow* is a variation of near, signifying the quality of being near, close, or not extended.

Contraction arises from the inherent state of the object; *confined* is produced by some external agent: a limb is *contracted* from disease; it is *confined* by a chain: we speak morally of the *contracted* span of a man's life, and the *confined* view which he takes of a subject.

Contracted and *confined* respect the operation of things; *narrow*, their qualities or accidents: whatever is *contracted* or *confined* is more or less *narrow;* but many things are *narrow* which have never been *contracted* or *confined;* what is *narrow* is therefore more positively so than either *contracted* or *confined:* a *contracted* mind has but few objects on which it dwells to the exclusion of others; 'Notwithstanding a *narrow*, *contracted* temper be that which obtains most in the world, we must not therefore conclude this to be the genuine characteristick of mankind'—GROVE. A *confined* education is *confined* to few points of knowledge or information; 'In its present habitation, the soul is plainly *confined* in its operations.'—BLAIR. 'The presence of every created being is *confined* to a certain measure of space, and consequently his observation is stinted to a certain number of objects.'—ADDISON. A *narrow* soul is hemmed in by a single selfish passion. 'Resentments are not easily dislodged from *narrow* minds.'—CUMBERLAND

* Vide Girard; "Termes, limites, bornes."

TO ABRIDGE, CURTAIL, CONTRACT.

Abridge, in French *abréger*, Latin *abbreviare*, is compounded of the intensive syllable *ab* and *breviare*, from *brevis* short, signifying to make short; *curtail*, in French *courte* short, and *tailler* to cut, signifies to diminish in length by cutting; *contract*, in Latin *contractus*, participle of *contraho*, is compounded of *con* and *traho*, signifying to draw close together.

By *abridging*, in the figurative as well as the literal sense, the quality is diminished; by *curtailing*, the magnitude or number is reduced; by *contracting*, a thing is brought within smaller compass. Privileges are *abridged*, pleasures *curtailed*, and powers *contracted*.

When the liberty of a person is too much *abridged*, the enjoyments of life become *curtailed*, as the powers of acting and thinking, according to the genuine impulse of the mind, are thereby considerably *contracted*; 'This would very much *abridge* the lover's pains in this way of writing a letter, as it would enable him to express the most useful and significant words with a single touch of the needle.'—ADDISON. 'I remember several ladies who were once very near seven feet high, that at present want some inches of five: how they came to be thus *curtailed* I cannot learn.'—ADDISON. 'He that rises up early and goes to bed late only to receive addresses is really as much tied and *abridged* in his freedom as he that waits all that time to present one.'—SOUTH. 'God has given no man a body as strong as his appetites; but has corrected the boundlessness of his voluptuous desires, by stinting his strength and *contracting* his capacities.'—SOUTH

CONFINEMENT, IMPRISONMENT, CAPTIVITY.

Confinement signifies the act of confining, or the state of being confined; *imprisonment*, compounded of *im* and *prison*, French *prison*, from *pris*, participle of *prendre*, Latin *prehendo* to take, signifies the act or state of being taken or laid hold of; *captivity*, in French *captivité*, Latin *captivitas* from *capio* to take, signifies likewise the state of being, or being kept in possession by another.

Confinement is the generick, the other two specifick terms. *Confinement* and *imprisonment* both imply the abridgement of one's personal freedom, but the former specifies no cause which the latter does. We may be *confined* in a room by ill health, or *confined* in any place by way of punishment: but we are never *imprisoned* but in some specifick place appointed for the *confinement* of offenders, and always on some supposed offence. We are *captives* by the rights of war, when we fall into the hands of the enemy.

Confinement does not specify the degree or manner as the other terms do; it may even extend to the restricting of the body of its free movements. *Imprisonment* simply *confines* the person within a certain extent of ground, or the walls of a *prison*; '*Confinement* of any kind is dreadful: let your imagination acquaint you with what I have not words to express, and conceive, if possible, the horrours of *imprisonment*, attended with reproach and ignominy.'—JOHNSON. *Captivity* leaves a person at liberty to range within a whole country or district;

> There in *captivity* he lets them dwell
> The space of seventy years; then brings them back,
> Rememb'ring mercy.—MILTON.

> For life, being weary of these worldly bars,
> Never lacks power to dismiss itself;
> In that each bondman, in his own hand, bears
> The power to cancel his *captivity*:
> But I do think it cowardly and vile.—SHAKSPEARE.

Confinement is so general a term, as to be applied to animals and even to inanimate objects; *imprisonment* and *captivity* are applied in the proper sense to persons only, but they admit of a figurative application. Poor stray animals, who are found trespassing on unlawful ground, are doomed to a wretched *confinement*, rendered still more hard and intolerable by the want of food: the *confinement* of plants within too narrow a space will stop their growth for want of air;

> But now my sorrows, long with pain supprest,
> Burst their *confinement* with impetuous sway.
> YOUNG.

There is many a poor *captive* in a cage who, like Sterne's starling, would say, if it could, "I want to get out."

FINITE, LIMITED.

Finite, from *finis* an end, is the natural property of things; and *limited*, from *limes* a boundary, is the artificial property: the former is opposite only to the *infinite*; but the latter, which lies within the *finite*, is opposed to the *unlimited* or the *infinite*. This world is *finite*, and space *infinite*; 'Methinks this single consideration of the progress of a *finite* spirit to perfection will be sufficient to extinguish all envy in inferiour natures, and all contempt in superiour.'—ADDISON. The power of a prince is sometimes *limited*; 'Those complaints which we are apt to make of our *limited* capacity and narrow view, are just as unreasonable as the childish complaints of our not being formed with a microscopick eye.'—BLAIR. It is not in our power to extend the bounds of the *finite*, but the *limited* is mostly under our control. We are *finite* beings, and our capacities are variously *limited* either by nature or circumstances.

TO RESERVE, RETAIN.

Reserve, from the Latin *servo* to keep, signifies to keep back; and *retain*, from *teneo* to hold, signifies to hold back; they in some measure, therefore, have the same distinction as hold and keep, mentioned in a former article.

To *reserve* is an act of more specifick design; we *reserve* that which is the particular object of our choice: to *retain* is a simple exertion of our power; we *retain* that which is once come into our possession. To *reserve* is employed only for that which is allowable; we *reserve* a thing, that is, keep it back with care for some future purpose; 'Augustus caused most of the prophetick books to be burnt, as spurious, *reserving* only those which bore the name of some of the sybils for their authors.'—PRIDEAUX. To *retain* is often an unlawful act, as when a debtor *retains* in his hands the money which he has borrowed; sometimes it is simply an unreasonable act; 'They who have restored painting in Germany, not having seen any of those fair relicks of antiquity, have *retained* much of that barbarous method.'—DRYDEN.

Reserve, whether in the proper or improper application, is employed only as the act of a conscious agent; *retain* is often the act of an unconscious agent: we *reserve* what we have to say on a subject until a more suitable opportunity offers; 'Conceal your esteem and love in your own breast, and *reserve* your kind looks and language for private hours.'—SWIFT. The mind *retains* the impressions of external objects, by its peculiar faculty, the memory; certain substances are said to *retain* the colour with which they have been dyed; 'Whatever ideas the mind can receive and contemplate without the help of the body, it is reasonable to conclude it can *retain* without the help of the body too.'—LOCKE. 'The beauties of Homer are difficult to be lost, and those of Virgil to be *retained*.'—JOHNSON.

RESERVE, RESERVATION.

Reserve and *reservation*, from *servo* to keep, both signify a keeping back, but differ as to the object and the circumstance of the action. *Reserve* is applied in a good sense to any thing natural or moral which is kept back to be employed for a better purpose on a future occasion: *reservation* is an artful keeping back for selfish purposes: there is a prudent *reserve* which every man ought to maintain in his discourse with a stranger; equivocators deal altogether in mental *reservation*; 'There is no maxim in politicks more indisputable than that a nation should have many honours in *reserve* for those who do national services.'—ADDISON. 'There be three degrees of this hiding and veiling of a man's self: first *reservation* and secrecy; second dissimulation in the negative; and the third simulation.'—BACON.

TO KEEP, PRESERVE, SAVE.

To *keep* has the same original meaning here as explained under the article *To hold, keep*; to *preserve*, compounded of *pre* and the Latin *servo* to *keep*, signifies to *keep* away from all mischief; *save* signifies to *keep* safe.

The idea of having in one's possession is common to all these terms: which is, however, the simple meaning of *keep*: to *preserve* is to *keep* with care and free from all injury, to *save* is to *keep* laid up in a safe place, and free from destruction. Things are *kept* at all times, and under all circumstances; they are *preserved* in circumstances of peculiar difficulty and danger; they are *saved* in the moment in which they are threatened with destruction; things are *kept* at pleasure; 'We are resolved to *keep* an established church, an established monarchy, an established aristocracy, and an established democracy, each in the degree it exists and no greater.'—Burke. Things are *preserved* by an exertion of power; 'A war to *preserve* national independence, property, and liberty, from certain universal havock, is a war just and necessary'—Burke. Things are *saved* by the use of extraordinary means; 'If any thing defensive can possibly *save* us from the disasters of a regicide peace, Mr. Pitt is the man to save us.'—Burke. The shepherd *keeps* his flock by simply watching over them; children are sometimes wonderfully *preserved* in the midst of the greatest dangers; things are frequently *saved* in the midst of fire, by the exertions of those present.

KEEPING, CUSTODY.

Keeping is as before the most general term; *custody*, in Latin *custodia* and *custos*, comes in all probability from *cura* care, because care is particularly required in *keeping*. The *keeping* amounts to little more than having purposely in one's possession; but *custody* is a particular kind of *keeping*, for the purpose of preventing an escape: inanimate objects may be in one's *keeping*; but prisoners or that which is in danger of getting away, is placed in *custody*: a person has in his *keeping* that which he values as the property of an absent friend; 'Life and all its enjoyments would be scarce worth the *keeping*, if we were under a perpetual dread of losing them.'—Spectator. The officers of justice get into their *custody* those who have offended against the laws, or such property as has been stolen; 'Prior was suffered to live in his own house under the *custody* of a messenger, until he was examined before a committee of the Privy Council.'—Johnson.

TO SAVE, SPARE, PRESERVE, PROTECT.

To *save* signifies the same as in the preceding article; *spare*, in German *sparen*, comes from the Latin *pareo*, and the Hebrew פרק to free; to *preserve* signifies the same as in the preceding article; and *protect*, the same as under the article *To defend, protect.*

The idea of keeping free from evil is common to all these terms, and the peculiar signification of the term *save*; they differ either in the nature of the evil kept off, or the circumstances of the agent: we may be *saved* from every kind of evil; but we are *spared* only from those which it is in the power of another to inflict: we may be *saved* from falling, or *saved* from an illness; a criminal is *spared* from the punishment, or we may be *spared* by Divine Providence in the midst of some calamity: we may be *saved* and *spared* from any evils, large or small; we are *preserved* and *protected* mostly from evils of magnitude; we may be *saved* either from the inclemency of the weather, or the fatal vicissitudes of life, or from destruction here and hereafter;

> A wondrous ark
> To *save* himself and household from amidst
> A world devote to universal wreck.—Milton.

We may be *spared* the pain of a disagreeable meeting, or we may be *spared* our lives;

> Let Cæsar spread his conquests far,
> Less pleased to triumph than to *spare*.—Johnson.

We are *preserved* from ruin, or *protected* from oppression; 'Cortes was extremely solicitous to *preserve* the city of Mexico as much as possible from being destroyed.'—Robertson.

> How poor a thing is man, whom death itself
> Cannot *protect* from injuries.—Randolph.

12*

To *save* and *spare* apply to evils that are actual and temporary; *preserve* and *protect* to those which are possible or permanent: we may be *saved* from drowning, or we may *save* a thing instead of throwing it away;

> Attilius sacrific'd himself to *save*
> That faith which to his barb'rous foes he gave.
> Denham.

A person may be *spared* from the sentence of the law, or *spared* a pain;

> *Spare* my sight the pain
> Of seeing what a world of tears it costs you.
> Dryden

We *preserve* with care that which is liable to injury, or *protect* ourselves against the attacks of robbers.

To *save* may be the effect of accident or design; to *spare* is always the effect of some design or connexion; to *preserve* and *protect* are the effect of a special exertion of power; the latter in a still higher degree than the former: we may be *preserved*, by ordinary means, from the evils of human life; but we are *protected* by the government, or by Divine Providence, from the active assaults of those who aim at doing us mischief

TO DEFEND, PROTECT, VINDICATE.

To *defend*, which signifies literally to keep off any evil (*v. To guard*), is closely allied to *protect*, which comes from the Latin *protectum*, participle of *protego*, compounded of *pro* and *tego*, signifies to put any thing before a person as a covering, and also to *vindicate*, which comes from the Latin *vindico* and the Greek ἐνδικέω to avenge by bringing an offender to justice.

Defend is a general term; it defines nothing with regard to the degree and manner of the action: *protect* is a particular and positive term, expressing an action of some considerable importance. Persons may *defend* others without distinction of rank or station: none but superiours *protect* their inferiours. *Defence* is an occasional action; *protection* is a permanent action. A person may be *defended* in any particular case of actual danger or difficulty; he is *protected* from what may happen as well as what does happen. *Defence* respects the evil that threatens; 'A master may justify an assault in *defence* of his servant, and a servant in *defence* of his master.'—Blackstone. *Protection* involves the supply of necessities and the affording of comforts; 'They who *protected* the weakness of our infancy are entitled to our *protection* in their old age.'—Blackstone.

Defence requires some active exertion either of body or mind; *protection* may consist only of the extension of power in behalf of any particular. A *defence* is successful or unsuccessful; a *protection* weak or strong. A soldier *defends* his country; a counsellor *defends* his client: 'Savage (on his trial for the murder of Sinclair) did not deny the fact, but endeavoured to justify it by the necessity of *self-defence*, and the hazard of his own life if he had lost the opportunity of giving the thrust' Johnson. A prince *protects* his subjects;

> First give thy faith and plight, a prince's word,
> Of sure *protection* by thy power and sword;
> For I must speak what wisdom would conceal,
> And truth invidious to the great reveal.—Pope.

Henry the Eighth styled himself *defender* of the faith (that is of the Romish faith) at the time that he was subverting the whole religious system of the Catholicks: Oliver Cromwell styled himself *protector* at the time that he was overturning the government.

In a figurative and extended sense, things may either *defend* or *protect* with a similar distinction: a coat *defends* us from the inclemencies of the weather;

> How shall the vine with tender leaves *defend*
> Her teeming clusters when the rains descend?
> Dryden.

Houses are a *protection* not only against the changes of the seasons, but also against the violence of men;

> Some to the holly hedge
> Nestling repair, and to the thicket some:
> Some to the rude *protection* of the thorn
> Commit their feeble offspring.—Thomson.

To *vindicate* is a *species* of *defence* only in the moral sense of the word. Acts of importance are *defended*; those of trifling import are commonly *vindicated*

Cicero *defended* Milo against the charge of murder, in which he was implicated by the death of Clodius; a child or a servant *vindicates* himself when any blame is attached to him. *Defence* is employed either in matters of opinion or conduct; *vindicate* only in matters of conduct. No absurdities are too great to want occasional *defenders* among the various advocates to free inquiry; 'While we can easily *defend* our character, we are no more disturbed at an accusation, than we are alarmed by an enemy whom we are sure to conquer.'—JOHNSON. He who *vindicates* the conduct of another should be fully satisfied of the innocence of the person whom he *defends*; 'In this poem (the Epistle to Dr. Arbuthnot), Pope seems to reckon with the publick. He *vindicates* himself from censures, and with dignity rather than arrogance, enforces his claims to kindness and respect.'—POPE.

DEFENDANT, DEFENDER.

The *defendant* defends himself (*v. To defend*;) the *defender* defends another. We are *defendants* when any charge is brought against us which we wish to refute; 'Of what consequence could it be to the cause whether the counsellor did or did not know the *defendant?*'—SMOLLET. We are *defenders* when we undertake to rebut or refute the charge brought against another; 'The abbot of Paisley was a warm partizan of France, and a zealous *defender* of the established religion.'—ROBERTSON.

DEFENDER, ADVOCATE, PLEADER.

A *defender* exerts himself in favour of one that wants support: an *advocate*, in Latin *advocatus*, from *advoco* to call to one's aid, signified originally one who was called into court to speak in behalf of his friend, and who if he pleaded his cause was styled *patronus*; 'Qui defendit alterum in judicio, aut *patronus* dicitur, si orator est; aut *advocatus* si aut jus suggerit, aut præsentiam suam commodat amico.'—ASCONIUS IN CIC. A *pleader*, from *plea* or *excuse*, signifies one who brings forward *pleas* in favour of him that is accused. These terms are now employed more in a general than a technical sense, which brings them into still closer alliance with each other. A *defender* attempts to keep off the threatened injury by rebutting the attack of another: an *advocate* states that which is to the advantage of the person or thing *advocated*: a *pleader* throws in *pleas* and extenuations: he blends entreaty with argument. Oppressed or accused persons and disputed opinions require *defenders*; 'But the time was now come when Warburton was to change his opinion, and Pope was to find a *defender* in him who had contributed so much to the exaltation of his rival.'—JOHNSON. That which falls in with the humours of men will always have *advocates*; 'It is said that some endeavours were used to incense the queen against Savage, but he found *advocates* to obviate at least part of their effect.' —JOHNSON. The unfortunate and the guilty require *pleaders*;

> Next call the *pleader* from his learned strife,
> To the calm blessings of a learned life.
> HORNECK.

St. Paul was a bold *defender* of the faith which is in Christ Jesus. Epicurus has been charged with being the *advocate* for pleasure in its gross and sensual sense, whence the *advocates* for sensual indulgences have been termed Epicureans. Vetruvia and Volumnia, the wife and mother of Coriolanus, were *pleaders* in behalf of the Roman republick, too powerful for him to be able to refuse their request.

DEFENSIBLE, DEFENSIVE.

Defensible is employed for the thing that is *defended*: *defensive* for the thing that *defends*. An opinion or a line of conduct is *defensible*; a weapon or a military operation is *defensive*. The *defensible* is opposed to the *indefensible*; and the *defensive* to the *offensive*.

It is the height of folly to attempt to *defend* that which is *indefensible*; 'Impressing is only *defensible* from publick necessity, to which all private considerations must give way.'—BLACKSTONE. It is sometimes prudent to act on the *defensive*, when we are not in a condition to commence the *offensive*; 'A king circumstanced as the present king (of France) has no generous interest that can excite him to action. At best his conduct will be passive and *defensive*.'—BURKE.

TO GUARD, DEFEND, WATCH.

Guard is but a variation of *ward* and *guarantee*, &c., which comes from the Teutonick *wahren* to look to; *watch* and *wake*, through the medium of the northern languages, are derived from the Latin *vigil* watchful, *vigeo* to flourish, and the Greek ἀγάλλω to exult or be in spirits.

Guard seems to include in it the idea of both *defend* and *watch*, inasmuch as one aims to keep off danger, by personal efforts; *guard* comprehends the signification of *defend*, inasmuch as one employs one's powers to keep off the danger. *Guard* comprehends the idea of *watch*, inasmuch as one employs one's eyes to detect the danger; one *defends* and *watches*, therefore, when one *guards*; but one does not always *guard* when one *defends* or *watches*.

To *defend* is employed in a case of actual attack; to *guard* is to *defend* by preventing the attack: the soldier *guards* the palace of the king in time of peace;

> Fix'd on defence, the Trojans are not slow
> To *guard* their shore from an expected foe.
> DRYDEN.

He *defends* the power and kingdom of his prince in time of war, or the person of the king in the field of battle;

> Forthwith on all sides to his aid was run,
> By angels many and strong, who interpos'd
> *Defence*.—MILTON.

One *guards* in cases where resistance is requisite, and attack is threatened; one *watches* in cases where an unresisting enemy is apprehended: soldiers or armed men are employed to *guard* those who are in custody: children are set to *watch* the corn which is threatened by the birds: hence it is that those are termed *guards* who surround the person of the monarch, and those are termed *watchmen* who are employed by night, to *watch* for thieves and give the alarm, rather than make any attack.

In the improper application they have a similar sense: modesty *guards* female honour; it enables her to present a bold front to the daring violator; 'Modesty is not only an ornament, but also a *guard* to virtue.'—ADDISON. Clothing *defends* against the inclemency of the weather;

> And here th' access a gloomy grove *defends*,
> And here th' unnavigable lake extends.—DRYDEN

Watching is frequently employed not merely to prevent an external evil, but also for the attainment of some object of desire; thus a person *watches* an opportunity to escape, or *watches* the countenance of another;

> But see the well-plum'd hearse comes nodding on
> Stately and slow, and properly attended
> By the whole sable tribe, that painful *watch*
> The sick man's door, and live upon the dead.
> BLAIR.

The love of his subjects is the king's greatest safe *guard*; walls are no *defence* against an enraged multitude; it is necessary for every man to set a *watch* upon his lips, lest he suffer that to escape from him of which he may afterward repent.

GUARD, SENTINEL.

These terms are employed to designate those who are employed for the protection of either persons or things; but the *sentinel*, in French *sentinelle*, is properly a species of *guard*, namely, a military *guard* in the time of a campaign: any one may be set as *guard* over property, who is empowered to keep off every intruder by force; but the *sentinel* acts in the army as the watch in the police, rather to observe the motions of the enemy, than to repel any force;

> Fast as he could, he sighing quits the walls,
> And thus descending on the *guards* he calls.
> POPE.

'One of the *sentinels* who stood on the stage to prevent disorder, burst into tears.'—STEELE. In the moral acceptation of the terms, the *guard* acts in ordinary cases, where there is no immediate danger, but the *sentinel* where one is surrounded with danger; Conscience is the *sentinel* of virtue.'—JOHNSON.

GUARD, GUARDIAN.

These words are derived from the verb to *guard* (*v. To guard*); but they have acquired a distinct office.

Guard is used either in the literal or figurative sense; *guardian* only in the improper sense. *Guard* is applied either to persons or things; *guardian* only to persons. In application to persons, the *guard* is temporary; the *guardian* is fixed and permanent: the *guard* only *guards* against external evils; the *guardian* takes upon him the office of parent, counsellor, and director: when a house is in danger of being attacked, a person may sit up as a *guard;* when the parent is dead, the *guardian* supplies his place: we expect from a *guard* nothing but human assistance; but from our *guardian* angel we may expect supernatural assistance;

> Him Hermes to Achilles shall convey,
> *Guard* of his life, and partner of his way.
> POPE.

> Ye guides and *guardians* of our Argive race!
> Come all! let gen'rous rage your arms employ,
> And save Patroclus from the dogs of Troy.
> POPE.

In an extended application they preserve a similar distinction; 'He must be trusted to his own conduct, since there cannot always be a *guard* upon him, except what you put into his own mind by good principles.'—LOCKE. 'It then becomes the common concern of all that have truth at heart, and more especially of those who are the appointed *guardians* of the Christian faith, to be upon the watch against seducers.' WATERLAND.

TO GUARD AGAINST, TAKE HEED.

Both these terms simply express care on the part of the agent; but the former is used with regard to external or internal evils, the latter only with regard to internal or mental evils: in an enemy's country it is essential to be particularly on one's *guard*, for fear of a surprise; in difficult matters, where we are liable to err, it is of importance to *take heed* lest we run from one extreme to another: young men, on their entrance into life, cannot be too much on their *guard against* associating with those who would lead them into expensive pleasures; 'One would take more than ordinary care to *guard* one's self *against* this particular imperfection (changeableness), because it is that which our nature very strongly inclines us to.'—ADDISON. In slippery paths, whether physically or morally understood, it is necessary to *take heed* how we go; '*Take heed* of that dreadful tribunal where it will not be enough to say that I thought this or I heard that.'—SOUTH.

TO APOLOGIZE, DEFEND, JUSTIFY, EXCULPATE, EXCUSE, PLEAD.

Apologize, from the French *apologie*, Greek ἀπολογία, and ἀπολογέομαι, compounded of ἀπὸ from or away, and λέγω to speak, signifies to do away by speaking; *defend*, in French *defendre*, Latin *defendo*, compounded of *de* and *fendo*, signifies to keep or ward off; *justify*, in French *justifier*, Latin *justifico*, compounded of *justus* and *facio*, signifies to make or set right, that is, to set one's self right with others; *exculpate*, in Latin *exculpatus*, participle of *exculpo*, compounded of *ex* and *culpa*, signifies to get out of a fault; *excuse*, in French *excuser*, Latin *excuso*, compounded of *ex* and *causa*, signifies to get out of any cause or affair; *plead*, in French *plaider*, may either come from *placitum* or *placendum*, or be contracted from *appellatum*.

There is always some imperfection supposed or real which gives rise to an *apology;** with regard to persons it presupposes a consciousness of impropriety, if not of guilt; we *apologize* for an errour by acknowledging ourselves guilty of it: a *defence* presupposes a consciousness of innocence more or less; we *defend* ourselves against a charge by proving its fallacy: a *justification* is founded on the conviction not only of entire innocence, but of strict propriety; we *justify* our conduct against any imputation by proving that it was blameless: *exculpation* rests on the conviction of innocence with regard to the fact; we *exculpate* our selves from all blame by proving that we took no part in the transaction: *excuse* and *plea* are not grounded on any idea of innocence; they are rather appeals for favour resting on some collateral circumstance which serves to extenuate; a *plea* is frequently an idle or unfounded *excuse*, a frivolous attempt to lessen displeasure; we *excuse* ourselves for a neglect by alleging indisposition; we *plead* for forgiveness by solicitation and entreaty.

An *apology* mostly respects the conduct of individuals with regard to each other as equals: it is a voluntary act springing out of a regard to decorum, or the good opinion of others. To avoid misunderstandings it is necessary to *apologize* for any omission that wears the appearance of neglect. A *defence* respects matters of higher importance; the violation of laws or publick morals; judicial questions decided in a court, or matters of opinion which are offered to the decision of the publick: no one *defends* himself, but he whose conduct or opinions are called in question. A *justification* is applicable to all moral cases in common life, whether of a serious nature or otherwise: it is the act of individuals towards each other according to their different stations: no one can demand a *justification* from another without a sufficient authority, and no one will attempt to *justify* himself to another whose authority he does not acknowledge: men *justify* themselves either on principles of honour, or from the less creditable motive of concealing their imperfections from the observation and censure of others. An *exculpation* is the act of an inferiour, it respects the violations of duty towards a superiour; it is dictated by necessity, and seldom the offspring of any higher motive than the desire to screen one's self from punishment: *exculpation* regards offences only of commission; *excuse* is employed for those of omission as well as commission: we *excuse* ourselves oftener for what we have not done, than for what we have done; it is the act of persons in all stations, and arises from various motives dishonourable or otherwise: a person may often have substantial reasons to *excuse* himself from doing a thing, or for not having done it; an *excuse* may likewise sometimes be the refuge of idleness and selfishness. To *plead* is properly a judicial act, and extended in its sense to the ordinary concerns of life; it is mostly employed for the benefit of others, rather than ourselves.

Excuse and *plea*, which are mostly employed in an unfavourable sense, are to *apology*, *defence*, and *exculpation*, as the means to an end: an *apology* is lame when, instead of an honest confession of an unintentional errour, an idle attempt is made at *justification:* a *defence* is poor when it does not contain sufficient to invalidate the charge: a *justification* is nugatory when it applies to conduct altogether wrong: an *excuse* or a *plea* is frivolous or idle, which turns upon some false hood, misrepresentation, or irrelevant point.

There are some men who are contented to be the *apologists* for the vices of others; 'But for this practice (detraction), however vile, some have dared to *apologize* by contending that the report by which they injured an absent character was true.'—HAWKESWORTH. No man should hold precepts secretly which he is not prepared to *defend* openly; 'Attacked by great injuries, the man of mild and gentle spirit will feel what human nature feels, and will *defend* and resent as his duty allows him.'—BLAIR. It is a habit with some people contracted in early life to *justify* themselves on every

* According to the vulgar acceptation of the term, this imperfection is always presumed to be real in the thing for which we *apologize;* but the bishop of Landaff did not use the term in this sense when he wrote his "*Apology* for the Bible;" by which, bearing in mind the original meaning of the word, he wished to imply an attempt to do away the alleged imperfections of the Bible, or to do away the objections made to it. Whether the learned prelate might not have used a less classical, but more intelligible expression for such a work, is a question which, happily for mankind, it is not necessary now to decide.

occasion, from a reluctance which they feel to acknowledge themselves in an errour;

Whatever private views and passions *plead*,
No cause can *justify* so black a deed.
THOMSON.

When several are involved in a general charge each seeks to *exculpate* himself 'A good child will not seek to *exculpate* herself at the expense of the most revered characters.'—RICHARDSON. A *plea* of incapacity is often set up to *excuse* remissness, which is in fact but the refuge of idleness and indolence; 'The strength of he passions will never be accepted as an *excuse* for omplying with them.'—SPECTATOR. It is the boast of Englishmen that, in their courts of judicature, the poor man's *plea* will be heard with as much attention as that of his rich neighbour; 'Poverty on this occasion *pleads* her cause very notably, and represents to her old landlord that should she be driven out of the country, all their trades, arts, and sciences would be driven out with her.'—ADDISON.

TO EXCUSE, PARDON.

We *excuse* (*v. To apologize*) a person or thing by exempting him from blame; we *pardon* (from the prepositive *par* or *per* and *dono* to give) by giving up or not insisting on the punishment of another for his offence.

We *excuse* a small fault, we *pardon* a great fault: we *excuse* that which personally affects ourselves; we *pardon* that which offends against morals: we may *excuse* as equals; we can *pardon* only as superiours. We exercise good nature in *excusing:* we exercise generosity or mercy in *pardoning*. Friends *excuse* each other for the unintentional omission of formalities;

I will not quarrel with a slight mistake
Such as our nature's frailty may *excuse*.
ROSCOMMON.

It is the privilege of the prince to *pardon* criminals whose offences will admit of *pardon;*

But infinite in *pardon* is my judge.—MILTON.

The violation of good manners is *inexcusable* in those who are cultivated; falsehood is *unpardonable* even in a child.

VENIAL, PARDONABLE.

Venial, from the Latin *venia* pardon or indulgence, is applied to what may be tolerated without express disparagement to the individual, or direct censure; but the *pardonable* is that which may only escape severe censure, but cannot be allowed; garrulity is a *venial* offence in old age; 'While the clergy are employed in extirpating mortal sins, I should be glad to rally the world out of indecencies and *venial* transgressions.'—CUMBERLAND. Levity in youth is *pardonable* in single instances; 'The weaknesses of Elizabeth were not confined to that period of life when they are more *pardonable*.'—ROBERTSON.

TO EXONERATE, EXCULPATE.

Exonerate, from *onus* a burthen, signifies literally to take off a burthen, either physically, as in the sense of relieving the body from a burthen;

This tyrant God, the belly! Take that from us
With all its bestial appetites, and man,
Exonerated man, shall be all soul.'—CUMBERLAND.

Or in the moral application of relieving from the burthen of a charge or of guilt; to *exculpate*, from *culpa* a fault or blame, is to throw off the blame: the first is the act of another; the second is one's own act: we *exonerate* him upon whom a charge has lain, or who has the load of guilt; we *exculpate* ourselves when there is any danger of being blamed: circumstances may sometimes tend to *exonerate;* the explanation of some person is requisite to *exculpate:* in a case of dishonesty the absence of an individual at the moment when the act was committed will altogether *exonerate* him from suspicion; it is fruitless for any one to attempt to *exculpate* himself from the charge of faithlessness who is detected in conniving at the dishonesty of others; 'By this fond and easy acceptance of *exculpatory* comment, Pope testified that he had not intentionally attacked religion.'—JOHNSON.

TO EXTENUATE, PALLIATE.

Extenuate, from the Latin *tenuis* thin, small, signifies literally to make small; *palliate*, in Latin *palliatus*, participle of *pallio*, from *pallium* a cloak, signifies to throw a cloak over a thing so that it may not be seen.

These terms are both applicable to the moral conduct, and express the act of lessening the guilt of any impropriety. To *extenuate* is simply to lessen guilt without reference to the means: to *palliate* is to lessen it by means of art. To *extenuate* is rather the effect of circumstances: to *palliate* is the direct effort of an individual. Ignorance in the offender may serve as an *extenuation* of his guilt, although not of his offence: 'Savage endeavoured to *extenuate* the fact (of having killed Sinclair), by urging the suddenness of the whole action.'—JOHNSON. It is but a poor *palliation* of a man's guilt, to say that his crimes have not been attended with the mischief which they were calculated to produce; 'Mons. St. Evremond has endeavoured to *palliate* the superstitions of the Roman Catholick religion.'—ADDISON.

TO ABSOLVE, ACQUIT, CLEAR.

Absolve, in Latin *absolvo*, is compounded of *ab* from and *solvo* to loose, signifying to loose from that with which one is bound; *acquit*, in French *acquitter*, is compounded of the intensive syllable *ac* or *ad*, and *quit*, *quitter*, in Latin *quietus* quiet, signifying to make easy by the removal of a charge; to *clear* is to make clear

These three words convey an important distinction between the act of the Creator and the creature.

To *absolve* is the free act of an omnipotent and merciful being towards sinners; to *acquit* is the act of an earthly tribunal towards supposed offenders; by *absolution* we are released from the bondage of sin, and placed in a state of favour with God; by an *acquittal* we are released from the charge of guilt, and reinstated in the good estimation of our fellow-creatures.

Absolution is obtained not from our own merits, but the atoning merits of a Redeemer; *acquittal* is an act of justice due to the innocence of the individual. *Absolution* is the work of God only; by him alone it can be made known to the penitent offender;

Yet to be secret makes not sin the less;
'T is only hidden from the vulgar view,
Maintains indeed the reverence due to princes,
But not *absolves* the conscience from the crime.
DRYDEN

Acquittal is the work of man only; by him alone it is pronounced; 'The fault of Mr. Savage was rather negligence than ingratitude; but Sir Richard Steele must likewise be *acquitted* of severity; for who is there that can patiently bear contempt from one whom he has relieved and supported?'—JOHNSON

Although but few individuals may have occasion for *acquittal;* yet we all stand in daily and hourly need of *absolution* at the hands of our Creator and Redeemer

One is *absolved* (*v. To absolve*) from an oath, *acquitted* of a charge, and *cleared* from actual guilt, that is, made clearly free.

No one can *absolve* from an oath but he to whom the oath is made; no one can *acquit* another of a charge but he who has the right of substantiating the charge; yet any one may *clear* himself or another from guilt, or the suspicion of guilt, who has adequate proofs of innocence to allege.

The Pope has assumed to himself the right of *absolving* subjects at pleasure from their oath of allegiance to their sovereign; but as an oath is made to God only, it must be his immediate act to cancel the obligation which binds men's consciences;

Compell'd by threats to take that bloody oath,
And the act ill, I am *absolv'd* by both.'—WALLER.

It is but justice to *acquit* a man of blame, who is enabled to *clear* himself from the appearance of guilt; 'Those who are truly learned will *acquit* me in this point, in which I have been so far from offending, that I have been scrupulous perhaps to a fault in quoting the authors of several passages which I have made my own.'—ADDISON. 'In vain we attempt to *clear* our conscience by affecting to compensate for fraud or cruelty by acts of strict religious homage towards God.'—BLAIR.

TO GUARANTEE, BE SECURITY, BE RESPONSIBLE, WARRANT.

Guarantee and *warrant* are both derived from the Teutonick *wahren* to look to; to be *security* is to be that which makes secure; and to be *responsible*, from the Latin *respondeo* to answer, is to take upon one's self to answer for another.

Guarantee is a term of higher import than the others: one *guarantees* for others in matters of contract and stipulation: *security* is employed in matters of right and justice; one may be *security* for another, or give *security* for one's self: *responsibility* is employed in moral concerns; we take the *responsibility* upon ourselves: *warrant* is employed in civil and commercial concerns; we *warrant* for that which concerns ourselves.

We *guarantee* by virtue of our power and the confidence of those who accept the *guarantee;* it is given by means of a word, which is accepted as a pledge for the future performance of a contract; governments, in order to make peace, frequently *guarantee* for the performance of certain stipulations by powers of minor importance; 'The people of England, then, are willing to trust to the sympathy of regicides, the *guarantee* of the British monarchy.'—BURKE. We are *security* by virtue of our wealth and credit; the *security* is not confined to a simple word, it is always accompanied with some legitimate act that binds, it regards the payment of money for another; tradesmen are frequently *security* for others who are not supposed sufficiently wealthy to answer for themselves; 'Richard Cromwell desired only *security* for the debts he had contracted.' -BURNET. We are *responsible* by virtue of one's office and relation; the *responsibility* binds for the reparation of injuries; teachers are *responsible* for the good conduct of the children intrusted to their care: one *warrants* by virtue of one's knowledge and situation: 'What a dreadful thing is a standing army, for the conduct of the whole or of any part of which no one is *responsible*.'—BURKE. The *warrant* binds to make restitution; the seller *warrants* his articles on sale to be such as are worth the purchase, or in case of defectiveness to be returned; and in a moral application things are said to *warrant* or justify a person in forming conclusions or pursuing a line of conduct; 'No man's mistake will be able to *warrant* an unjust surmise, much less justify a false censure.'—SOUTH. A king *guarantees* for the transfer of the lands of one prince, on his decease, into the possession of another; when men have neither honour nor money, they must get others to be *security* for them, if any can be found sufficiently credulous; in England masters are *responsible* for all the mischiefs done by their servants; a tradesman who stands upon his reputation will be careful not to *warrant* any thing which he is not assured will stand the trial.

ANSWERABLE, RESPONSIBLE, ACCOUNTABLE, AMENABLE.

Answerable signifies ready or able to answer for; *responsible*, from *respondeo* to *answer*, has a similar meaning in its original sense; *accountable*, from *account*, signifies able or ready to give an *account; amenable*, from the French *amener* to lead, signifies liable to be led.

We are *answerable* for a demand; *responsible* for a trust; *accountable* for our proceedings; and *amenable* to the laws. When a man's credit is firmly established he will have occasions to be *answerable* for those in less flourishing circumstances: every one becomes *responsible* more or less in proportion to the confidence which is reposed in his judgement and integrity: we are all *accountable* beings, either to one another, or at least to the great Judge of all; when a man sincerely wishes to do right, he will have no objection to be *amenable* to the laws of his country.

An honest man will not make himself *answerable* for any thing which it is above his ability to fulfil; 'That he might render the execution of justice strict and regular, Alfred divided all England into counties, these counties he subdivided into hundreds, and the hundreds into tithings. Every householder was *answerable* for the behaviour of his family and his slaves, and even of his guests if they lived above three days in his house.'—HUME. A prudent man will avoid a too heavy *responsibility*; 'As a person's *responsibility* bears respect to his reason, so do human punishments bear respect to his *responsibility;* infants and boys are chastised by the hand of the parent or the master: rational adults are *amenable* to the laws.'—CUMBERLAND. An upright man never refuses to be *accountable* to any who are invested with proper authority, 'We know that we are the subjects of a Supreme Righteous Governour, to whom we are *accountable* for our conduct.'—BLAIR. A conscientious man makes himself *amenable* to the wise regulations of society.

FENCE, GUARD, SECURITY

Fence, from the Latin *fendo* to fend or keep off, serves to prevent the attack of an external enemy; *guard*, which is but a variety of *ward*, from the old German *wahren* to look to, and *wachen* to watch, signifies that which keeps from any danger; *security* implies that which secures or prevents injury, mischief, and loss.

The *fence* in the proper sense is an inanimate object; the *guard* is a living agent; the former is of permanent utility, the latter acts to a partial extent: in the figurative sense they retain the same distinction. Modesty is a *fence* to a woman's virtue; the love of the subject is the monarch's greatest *safeguard.* There are prejudices which favour religion and subordination, that act as *fences* against the introduction of licentious principles into the juvenile or enlightened mind; 'Whatever disregard certain modern refiners of morality may attempt to throw on all the instituted means of public religion, they must in their lowest view be considered as the out-guards and *fences* of virtuous conduct.'—BLAIR. A proper sense of an overruling providence will serve as a *guard* to prevent the admission of improper thoughts; 'Let the heart be either wounded by sore distress, or agitated by violent emotions: and you shall presently see that virtue without religion is inadequate to the government of life. It is destitute of its proper *guard*, of its firmest support, of its chief encouragement.'—BLAIR. The *guard* only stands at the entrance, to prevent the ingress of evil: the *security* stops up all the avenues, it locks up with firmness. A *guard* serves to prevent the ingress of every thing that may have an evil intention or tendency: the *security* rather secures the possession of what one has, and prevents a loss. A king has a *guard* about his person to keep off all violence. The *security* may either *secure* against the loss of property or against the loss of any external advantage or moral benefit; 'The Romans do not seem to have known the secret of paper money or *securities* upon mortgages.'—ARBUTHNOT.

DEPOSITE, PLEDGE, SECURITY.

Deposite is a general term from the Latin *depositus*, participle of *depono* to lay down, or put into the hands of another, signifying that which is laid down or given in charge, as a guarantee for the performance of an engagement; *pledge*, comes probably from *plico*, signifying what engages by a tie or envelope; *security* signifies that which makes *secure*.

The *deposite* has most regard to the confidence we place in another; the *pledge* has most regard to the *security* we give for ourselves; *security* is a species of *pledge*. A *deposite* is always voluntarily placed in the hands of an indifferent person; a *pledge* and *security* are required from the parties who are interested. A person may make a *deposite* for purposes of charity or convenience; he gives a *pledge* or *security* for a temporary accommodation, or the relief of a necessity. Money is *deposited* in the hands of a friend in order to execute a commission: a *pledge* is given as an equivalent for that which has been received: a *security* is given by way of *security* for the performance.

A *deposite* may often serve the purpose of a *security;* but it need not contain any thing so binding as either a *pledge* or a *security;* both of which involve a loss on the non-fulfilment of a certain contract. A *pledge* is given for matters purely personal; a *security* is given in behalf of another.

Deposites are always transportable articles, consisting either of money, papers, jewels, or other valuables: a *pledge* is seldom pecuniary, but it is always some article of positive value, as estates, furniture, and the like, given at the moment of forming the contra *security* is always pecuniary, but it often consists of a promise, and not of any immediate resignation of one's property. *Deposites* are made and *securities* given by the wealthy; *pledges* are commonly given by those who are in distress.

These words bear a similar distinction in the figurative application; 'It is without reason we praise the wisdom of our constitution, in putting under the discretion of the crown the awful trust of war and peace, if the ministers of the crown virtually return it again into our hands. The trust was placed there as a sacred *deposite*, to secure us against popular rashness in plunging into wars.'—BURKE.

These garments once were his, and left to me,
The *pledges* of his promised loyalty.—DRYDEN.

'It is possible for a man, who hath the appearance of religion, to be wicked and a hypocrite; but it is impossible for a man who openly declares against religion, to give any reasonable *security* that he will not be false and cruel.'—SWIFT.

EARNEST, PLEDGE.

In the proper sense, the *earnest* (*v. Eager*) is given as a token of our being in *earnest* in the promise we have made; the *pledge*, in all probability from *plico* to fold or implicate, signifies a security by which we are engaged to indemnify for a loss.

The *earnest* has regard to the confidence inspired; the *pledge* has regard to the bond or tie produced: when a contract is only verbally formed, it is usual to give *earnest*; whenever money is advanced, it is common to give a *pledge*.

In the figurative application the terms bear the same analogy: a man of genius sometimes, though not always, gives an *earnest* in youth of his future greatness;

Nature has wove into the human mind
This anxious care for names we leave behind,
T' extend our narrow views beyond the tomb,
And give an *earnest* of a life to come.—JENYNS.

Children are the dearest *pledges* of affection between parents;

Fairest of stars, last in the train of night,
If better thou belong not to the dawn,
Sure *pledge* of day that crown'st the smiling morn,
With thy bright circlet praise him in thy sphere.
MILTON.

TO APPOINT, ORDER, PRESCRIBE, ORDAIN.

To *appoint* (*v. Allot*) is either the act of an equal or superiour: we *appoint* a meeting with any one at a given time and place; a king *appoints* his ministers. To *order*, in French *ordre*, Latin *ordino* to arrange, dispose, *ordo* order, Greek ὄρχος a row of trees, which is the symbol of order, is the act of one invested with a partial authority: a customer *orders* a commodity from his tradesman: a master gives his *orders* to his servant. To *prescribe*, in Latin *prescribo*, compounded of *pre* before, and *scribo* to write, signifying to draw a line for a person, is the act of one who is superiour by virtue of his knowledge: a physician *prescribes* to his patient. To *ordain*, which is a variation of *order*, is an act emanating from the highest authority: kings and councils *ordain*; but their *ordinances* must be conformable to what is *ordained* by the Divine Being.

Appointments are made for the convenience of individuals or communities; but they may be altered or annulled at the pleasure of the contracting parties;

Majestic months
Set out with him to their *appointed* race.—DRYDEN.

Orders are dictated by the superiour only, but they presuppose a discretionary obligation on the part of the individual to whom they are given; 'Upon this new fright an *order* was made by both Houses for disarming all papists.'—CLARENDON. *Prescriptions* are binding on none but such as voluntarily admit their authority; 'It will be found a work of no small difficulty, to dispossess a vice from that heart, where long possession begins to plead *prescription*.'—SOUTH. *Ordinances* leave no choice to those on whom they are imposed to accept or reject them: the *ordinances* of man are not less binding than those of God, so long as they do not expressly contradict the Divine law; 'It seemeth hard to plant any sound *ordinance*, or reduce them (the Irish) to a civil government; since all their ill customs are permitted unto them.'—SPENSER.

Appointments are kept, *orders* executed or obeyed, *prescriptions* followed, *ordinances* submitted to. It is a point of politeness or honour, if not of direct moral obligation, to keep the *appointments* which we have made. Interest will lead men to execute the *orders* which they receive in the course of business: duty obliges them to obey the *orders* of their superiours. It is a nice matter to *prescribe* to another without hurting his pride: this principle leads men often to regard the counsels of their best friends as *prescriptions*: with children it is an unquestionable duty to follow the *prescriptions* of those whose age, station, or experience, authorize them to *prescribe*; 'Sir Francis Bacon, in his Essay upon Health, has not thought it improper to *prescribe* to his reader a poem or a prospect, where he particularly dissuades him from knotty or subtle disquisitions.'—ADDISON. God has *ordained* all things for our good; it rests with ourselves to submit to his *ordinances* and be happy; 'It was perhaps *ordained* by Providence to hinder us from tyrannizing over one another, that no individual should be of such importance as to cause by his retirement or death any chasm in the world.'—JOHNSON. Sometimes the word *order* is taken in the sense of direct and regulate, which brings it still nearer to the word *ordain*. God is said to *ordain*, as an act of power; he is said to *order*, as an act of wisdom; 'The whole course of things is so *ordered*, that we neither by an irregular and precipitate education become men too soon; nor by a fond and trifling indulgence be suffered to continue children for ever.'—BLAIR.

TO DICTATE, PRESCRIBE.

Dictate, from the Latin *dictatus* and *dictum*, a word, signifies to make a word for another; and *prescribe* literally signifies to write down for another (*v. To appoint*), in which sense the former of these terms is used technically for a principal who gets his secretary to write down his words as he utters them; and the latter for a physician who writes down for his patient what he wishes him to take as a remedy. They are used figuratively for a species of counsel given by a superiour: to *dictate* is however a greater exercise of authority than to *prescribe*.

To *dictate* amounts even to more than to command, it signifies commanding with a tone of unwarrantable authority, or still oftener a species of commanding by those who have no right to command; it is therefore mostly taken in a bad sense. To *prescribe* partakes altogether of the nature of counsel, and nothing of command; it serves as a rule to the person *prescribed*, and is justified by the superiour wisdom and knowledge of the person *prescribing*; it is therefore always taken in an indifferent or a good sense. He who *dictates* speaks with an adventitious authority; he who *prescribes* has the sanction of reason.

To *dictate* implies an entire subserviency in the person *dictated* to: to *prescribe* carries its own weight with it in the nature of the thing *prescribed*. Upstarts are ready to *dictate* even to their superiours on every occasion that offers. 'The physician and divine are often heard to *dictate* in private company with the same authority which they exercise over their patients and disciples.'—BUDGELL. Modest people are often fearful of giving advice lest they should be suspected of *prescribing*; 'In the form which is *prescribed* to us (the Lord's Prayer), we only pray for that happiness which is our chief good, and the great end of our existence, when we petition the Supreme for the coming of his kingdom.'—ADDISON.

DICTATE, SUGGESTION.

Dictate signifies the thing *dictated*, and has an imperative sense as in the former case (*v. To dictate*) *suggestion* signifies the thing *suggested*, and conveys the idea of being secretly or in a gentle manner proposed.

The *dictate* comes from the conscience, the reason or the passion; *suggestions* spring from the mind, the will, or the desire. *Dictate* is taken either in a good or bad sense; *suggestion* mostly in a bad sense. It is the part of a Christian at all times to listen to the *dictates* of conscience; it is the characteristick of a weak mind to follow the *suggestions* of envy. A man renounces the character of a rational being who yields to the *dictates* of passion ; 'When the *dictates* of honour are contrary to those of religion and equity, they are the greatest depravations of human nature.'—ADDISON. Whoever does not resist the *suggestions* of his own evil mind is very far gone in corruption, and will never be able to bear up long against temptation ; 'Did not conscience *suggest* this natural relation between guilt and punishment; the mere principle of approbation or disapprobation, with respect to moral conduct, would prove of small efficacy.'—BLAIR.

Dictate is employed only for what passes inwardly; *suggestion* may be used for any action on the mind by external objects. No man will err essentially in the ordinary affairs of life who is guided by the *dictates* of plain sense. It is the lot of sinful mortals to be drawn to evil by the *suggestions* of Satan as well as their own evil inclinations.

COMMAND, ORDER, INJUNCTION, PRECEPT, MANDATE.

Command, compounded of *com* and *mando*, *manudo*, or *dare in manus* to give into the hand, signifies giving or appointing as a task; a *command* is imperative; it is the strongest exercise of authority; *order*, which in the extended sense of regularity, implies what is done in the way of *order*, or for the sake of regularity; an *order* is instructive ; it is an expression of the wishes: *injunction*, in French *injunction*, from *in* and *jungo*, signifies literally to join or bring close to; figuratively to impress on the mind ; an *injunction* is decisive ; it is a greater exercise of authority than *order*, and less than *command: precept*, in French *précepte*, Latin *præceptum*, participle of *præcipio*, compounded of *præ* and *capio* to put or lay before, signifies the thing proposed to the mind; a *precept* is a moral law; it is binding on the conscience. The three former of these are personal in their application; the latter is general: a *command*, an *order*, and an *injunction*, must be addressed to some particular individual; a *precept* is addressed to all.

Command and *order* exclusively flow from the will of the speaker in the ordinary concerns of life; *injunction* has more regard to the conduct of the person addressed ; *precept* is altogether founded on the moral obligations of men to each other. A *command* is just or unjust; an *order* is prudent or imprudent; an *injunction* is mild or severe; a *precept* is general or particular.

Command and *order* are affirmative ; *injunction* or *precept* are either affirmative or negative: the *command* and the *order* oblige us to do a thing; the *injunction* and *precept* oblige us to do it, or leave it undone. A sovereign issues his *commands*, which the well-being of society requires to be instantly obeyed;

'Tis Heav'n *commands* me, and you urge in vain:
Had any mortal voice the *injunction* laid,
Nor augur, seer, or priest, had been obey'd.—POPE.

A master gives his *orders*, which it is the duty of the servant to execute;

A stepdame too I have, a cursed she,
Who rules my henpeck'd sire, and *orders* me.
DRYDEN.

This done, Æneas *orders* for the close,
The strife of archers with contending bows.
DRYDEN.

A father lays an *injunction* on his children, which they with filial regard ought to endeavour to follow; 'The duties which religion *enjoins* us to perform towards God are those which have oftenest furnished matter to the scoffs of the licentious.'—BLAIR. The moralist lays down his *precepts*, which every rational creature is called upon to practise;

We say not that these ills from virtue flow;
Did her wise *precepts* rule the world, we know
The golden ages would again begin.—JENYNS.

Mandate, in Latin *mandatum*, participle of *mando*, has the same original meaning as *command*, but is employed to denote a *command* given by publick authority; whence the *commands* of princes, or the *commands* of the church, are properly denominated *mandates ;* 'The necessities of the times cast the power of the three estates upon himself, that his *mandates* should pass for laws, whereby he laid what taxes he pleased.' —HOWELL.

COMMANDING, IMPERATIVE, IMPERIOUS, AUTHORITATIVE.

Commanding, which signifies having the force of a *command* (*v. To command*), is either good or bad according to circumstances; a *commanding* voice is necessary for one who has to command; but a *commanding* air is offensive when it is affected ;

Oh ! that my tongue had every grace of speech,
Great and *commanding* as the breath of kings.
ROWE.

Imperative from *impero*, to command, signifying simply in the imperative mood, is applied to things, and used in an indifferent sense; *imperious*, which signifies literally in the tone or way of command, is used for persons or things in the bad sense: any direction is *imperative* which comes in the shape of a command, and circumstances are likewise *imperative*, which act with the force of a *command;* 'Quitting the dry *imperative* style of an act of Parliament he (Lord Somers) makes the Lords and Commons fall to a pious legislative ejaculation.'—BURKE. Persons are *imperious* who exercise their power oppressively;

Fear not, that I shall watch, with servile shame,
Th' *imperious* looks of some proud Grecian dame.
DRYDEN.

In this manner underlings in office are *imperious* necessity is *imperious* when it leaves us no choice in our conduct. *Authoritative*, which signifies having authority, or in the way of authority, is mostly applied to persons or things personal in the good sense only ; magistrates are called upon to assume an *authoritative* air when they meet with any resistance ; '*Authoritative* instructions, mandates issued, which the member (of Parliament) is bound blindly and implicitly to vote and argue for, though contrary to the clearest conviction of his judgement and conscience; these are things utterly unknown to the laws of this land.'—BURKE.

IMPERIOUS, LORDLY, DOMINEERING, OVERBEARING.

All these epithets imply an unseemly exercise or affectation of power or superiority. *Imperious*, from *impero* to command, characterizes either the disposition to command without adequate authority, or to convey one's commands in an offensive manner: *lordly*, signifying like a *lord*, characterizes the manner of acting the *lord:* and *domineering*, from *dominus* a *lord*, denotes the manner of ruling like a *lord*, or rather of attempting to rule: hence a person's temper or his tone is denominated *imperious ;* his air or deportment is *lordly ;* his tone is *domineering*. A woman of an *imperious* temper commands in order to be obeyed: she commands with an *imperious* tone in order to enforce obedience ; 'He is an *imperious* dictator of the principles of vice, and impatient of all contradiction.'—MORE. A person assumes a *lordly* air in order to display his own importance: he gives orders in a *domineering* tone in order to make others feel their inferiority. There is always something offensive in *imperiousness ;* there is frequently something ludicrous in that which is *lordly ;* and a mixture of the ludicrous and offensive in that which is *domineering :* the *lordly* is an affectation of grandeur where there are the fewest pretensions;

Lords are *lordliest* in their wine.—MILTON.

The *domineering* is an affectation of authority where it least exists; 'He who has sunk so far below himself as to have given up his assent to a *domineering* errour is fit for nothing but to be trampled on.'—SOUTH *Lordly* is applied even to the brutes who set themselves up above those of their kind ; *domineering* is applied to servants and ignorant people, who have the opportunity of commanding without knowing how to command. A turkey-cock struts about the yard in a *lordly* style; an upper servant *domineers* over all that are under him.

The first three of these terms are employed for such as are invested with some sort of power, or endowed with some sort of superiority, however trifling; but *overbearing* is employed for men in the general relations of society, whether superiours or equals. A man of an *imperious* temper and some talent will frequently be so *overbearing* in the assemblies of his equals as to awe the rest into silence, and carry every measure of his own without contradiction; 'I reflected within myself how much society would suffer if such insolent *overbearing* characters as Leontine were not held in restraint.'—CUMBERLAND. As the petty airs of superiority here described are most common among the uncultivated part of mankind, we may say that the *imperious* temper shows itself peculiarly in the domestick circle; that the *lordly* air shows itself in publick; that the *domineering* tone is most remarkable in the kitchen; and the *overbearing* behaviour in villages.

TO COMMISSION, AUTHORIZE, EMPOWER.

Commission, from *commit*, signifies the act of *committing*, or putting into the hands of another; to *authorize* signifies to give *authority;* to *empower*, to put in possession of the *power* to do any thing.

The idea of transferring some business to another is common to these terms; the circumstances under which this is performed constitute the difference. We *commission* in ordinary cases; we *authorize* and *empower* in extraordinary cases. We *commission* in matters where our own will and convenience are concerned; we *authorize* in matters where our personal *authority* is requisite; and we *empower* in matters where the *authority* of the law is required. A *commission* is given by the bare communication of one's wishes; we *authorize* by a positive and formal declaration to that intent; we *empower* by the transfer of some legal document. A person is *commissioned* to make a purchase;

> *Commission'd* in alternate watch they stand,
> The sun's bright portals and the skies command.
> POPE.

One is *authorized* to communicate what has been intrusted to him as a secret, or people are *authorized* to act any given part; 'A more decisive proof cannot be given of the full conviction of the British nation that the principles of the Revolution did not *authorize* them to elect kings at pleasure, than their continuing to adopt a plan of hereditary Protestant succession in the old line.'—BURKE. One is *empowered* to receive money;

> *Empower'd* the wrath of gods and men to tame,
> E'en Jove rever'd the venerable dame.—POPE.

When *commissions* pass between equals, the performance of them is an act of civility; but they are frequently given by sovereigns to their subjects; *authorizing* and *empowering* are as often directed to inferiours, they are frequently acts of justice and necessity. Judges and ambassadors receive *commissions* from their prince; 'Princes do not use to send their viceroys unfurnished with patents clearly signifying their *commission*.'—SOUTH. Servants and subordinate persons are sometimes *authorized* to act in the name of their employers; magistrates *empower* the officers of justice to apprehend individuals or enter houses. We are *commissioned* by persons only; we are *authorized* sometimes by circumstances; we are *empowered* by law.

INFLUENCE, AUTHORITY, ASCENDANCY OR ASCENDANT, SWAY.

Influence, from the Latin *influo* to flow in upon or cause to flow in upon, signifies the power of acting on an object so as to direct or move it; *authority*, in Latin *auctoritas*, from *auctor* the author or prime mover of a thing, signifies that power which is vested in the prime mover; *ascendancy* or *ascendant*, from *ascend*, signifies having the upper hand; *sway*, like our word *swing* and the German *schweben*, comes in all probability from the Hebrew זוז to move, signifying also the power to move an object.

These terms imply power, under different circumstances: *influence* is altogether unconnected with any right to direct; *authority* includes the idea of right necessarily: superiority of rank, talent, or property, personal attachment, and a variety of circumstances give *influence;* it commonly acts by persuasion, and employs engaging manners, so as to determine in favour of what is proposed: superiour wisdom, age, office, and relation, give *authority;* it determines of itself, and requires no collateral aid: *ascendancy* and *sway* are modes of *influence*, differing only in degree; they both imply an excessive and improper degree of *influence* over the mind, independent of reason; the former is, however, more gradual in its process, and consequently more confirmed in its nature; the latter may be only temporary, but may be more violent. A person employs many arts, and for a length of time, to gain the *ascendancy;* but he exerts a *sway* by a violent stretch of power. It is of great importance for those who have *influence*, to conduct themselves consistently with their rank and station; 'The *influence* of France as a republick is equal to a war.'—BURKE Men are apt to regard the warnings and admonitions of a true friend as an odious assumption of *authority;* 'Without the force of *authority* the power of soldiers grows pernicious to their master.'—TEMPLE. Some men voluntarily give themselves up to the *ascendancy* which a valet or a mistress has gained over them, while the latter exert the most unwarrantable *sway* to serve their own interested and vicious purposes; 'By the *ascendant* he had in his understanding, and the dexterity of his nature, he could persuade him very much.'—CLARENDON 'France, since her revolution, is under the *sway* of a sect whose leaders, at one stroke, have demolished the whole body of jurisprudence.'—BURKE.

Influence and *ascendancy* are said likewise of things as well as persons: true religion will have an *influence* not only on the outward conduct of a man, but the inward affections of his heart; 'Religion hath so great an *influence* upon the felicity of man, that it ought to be upheld, not only out of a dread of divine vengeance in another world, but out of regard to temporal prosperity.'—TILLOTSON. That man is truly happy in whose mind religion has the *ascendancy* over every other principle; 'If you allow any passion, even though it be esteemed innocent, to acquire an absolute *ascendant*, your inward peace will be impaired.'—BLAIR.

POWER, STRENGTH, FORCE, AUTHORITY, DOMINION.

Power, in French *pouvoir*, comes from the Latin *possum* to be able; *strength* denotes the abstract quality of *strong; authority* signifies the same as in the preceding article; *dominion*, from *dominus* a lord, signifies the power of a lord or the exercise of that *power; force*, from the Latin *fortis* strong, signifies the abstract quality of *strength*.

Power is the generick and universal term, comprehending in it that simple principle of nature which exists in all subjects. *Strength* and *force* are modes of *power*. These terms are all used either in a physical or moral application. *Power* in the physical sense respects whatever causes motion; 'Observing in ourselves that we can at pleasure move several parts of our bodies which were at rest; the effects also that natural bodies are able to produce in one another, occurring every moment to our senses, we both these ways get the idea of *power*.'—LOCKE. *Strength* respects that species of *power* that lies in the vital and muscular parts of the body;

> Not founded on the brittle *strength* of bones.
> MILTON.

Strength, therefore, is internal, and depends upon the internal organization of the frame; *power*, on the external circumstances. A man may have *strength* to move, but not the *power* if he be bound with cords. Our *strength* is proportioned to the health of the body, and the firmness of its make; our *power* may be increased by the help of instruments.

Power may be exerted or otherwise; *force* is *power* exerted, or active; bodies have a *power* of resistance while in a state of rest, but they are moved by a certain *force* from other bodies;

> A ship which hath struck sail, doth run,
> By *force* of that *force* which before it won.
> DONNE

The word *power* is used technically for the moving *force;* 'By understanding the true difference between the weight and the *power*, a man may add such a fitting supplement to the *strength* of the *power*, that it shall move any conceivable weight, though it should never so much exceed that *force* which the *power* is naturally endowed with.'—WILKINS.

In a moral acceptation *power*, *strength*, and *force*, may be applied to the same objects with a similar distinction, thus we may speak of the *power* of language generally, the *strength* of a person's expressions to convey the state of his own mind; and the *force* of terms as to their extent of meaning and fitness to convey the ideas of those who use them. In this case it is evident that *strength* and *force* are here employed as particular properties, but *strength* is the *power* actually exerted, and *force* the *power* which may be exerted.

Power is either publick or private, which brings it in alliance with *authority*. Civil *power* includes in it all that which enables us to have any influence or control over the actions, persons, property, &c. of others;

Hence thou shalt prove my might, and curse the hour,
Thou stoodst a rival of imperial *pow'r*.—Pope.

Authority is confined to that species of *power* which is derived from some legitimate source; '*Power* arising from *strength* is always in those who are governed, who are many; but *authority* arising from opinion is in those who govern, who are few.'—Temple. *Power* exists independently of all right; *authority* is founded only on right. A king has often the *power* to be cruel, but he has never the *authority* to be so. Subjects have sometimes the *power* of overturning the government, but they can in no case have the *authority*. *Power* may be abused; *authority* may be exceeded. A sovereign abuses his *power*, who exercises it for the misery of his subjects; he exceeds his *authority*, if he deprive them of any right from mere caprice or humour.

Power may be seized either by fraud or force; *authority* is derived from some present law, or delegated by a higher *power*. Despotism is an assumed *power*, it acknowledges no law but the will of the individual; it is, therefore, exercised by no *authority:* the sovereign holds his *power* by the law of God; for God is the source of all *authority*, which is commensurate with his goodness, his *power*, and his wisdom: man, therefore, exercises the supreme *authority* over man, as the minister of God's *authority;* he exceeds that *authority* if he do any thing contrary to God's will. Subjects have a delegated *authority* which they receive from a superiour; if they act for themselves, without respect to the will of that superiour, they exert a *power* without *authority*. In this manner a prime minister acts by the *authority* of the king, to whom he is responsible. A minister of the gospel performs his functions by the *authority* of the gospel, as it is interpreted and administered by the church; but when he acts by an individual or particular interpretation, it is a self-assumed *power*, but not *authority*. Social beings, in order to act in concert, must act by laws and the subordination of ranks, whether in religion or politicks; and he who acts solely by his own will, in opposition to the general consent of competent judges, exerts a *power*, but is without *authority*. Hence those who officiate in England as ministers of the gospel, otherwise than according to the form and discipline of the Established Church, act by an assumed *power*, which, though not punishable by the laws of man, must, like other sins, be answered for at the bar of God.

It lies properly with the supreme *power* to grant privileges, or take them away; but the same may be done by one in whom the *authority* is invested. *Authority* in this sense is applied to the ordinary concerns of life, where the line of distinction is always drawn, between what we can and what we ought to do. There is *power* where we can or may act; there is *authority* only where we ought to act. In all our dealings with others, it is necessary to consider in every thing, not what we have the *power* of doing, but what we have the *authority* to do. In matters of indifference, and in what concerns ourselves only, it is sufficient to have the *power* to act, but in all important matters we must have the *authority* of the divine law: a man may have the *power* to read or leave it alone; but he cannot dispose of his person in all respects, without *authority*. In what concerns others, we must act by their *authority*, if we wish to act conscientiously; when the secrets of another are confided to us, we have the *power* to divulge them, but not the *authority*, unless it be given by him who intrusted them.

Instructers are invested by parents with *authority* over their children; and parents receive their *authority* from nature, that is, the law of God; this paternal *authority*, according to the Christian system, extends to the education, but not to the destruction, of their offspring. The heathens, however, claimed and exerted a *power* over the lives of their children. By my superiour *strength* I may be enabled to exert a *power* over a man, so as to control his action; of his own accord he gives me *authority* to dispose of his property; so in literature, men of established reputation, of classical merit, and known veracity, are quoted as *authorities* in support of any position.

Power is indefinite as to degree; one may have little or much *power:* *dominion* is a positive degree of *power*. A monarch's *power* may be limited by various circumstances; a despot exercises *dominion* over all his subjects, high and low. One is not said to get a *power* over any object, but to get an object into one's *power:* on the other hand, we get a *dominion* over an object; thus some men have a *dominion* over the consciences of others;

And each of these must will, perceive, design
And draw confus'dly in a diff'rent line,
Which then can claim *dominion* o'er the rest,
Or stamp the ruling passion in the breast.
Jenyns

POWERFUL, POTENT, MIGHTY.

Powerful, or full of *power*, is also the original meaning of *potent;* but *mighty* signifies having *might*. *Powerful* is applicable to strength as well as *power:* a *powerful* man is one who by his size and make can easily overpower another: and a *powerful* person is one who has much in his *power;* 'It is certain that the senses are more *powerful* as the reason is weaker.'—Johnson. *Potent* is used only in this latter sense, in which it expresses a larger extent of *power;*

Now, flaming up the heavens, the *potent* sun
Melts into limpid air the high-raised clouds.
Thomson.

A *potent* monarch is much more than a *powerful* prince; *mighty* expresses a still higher degree of *power;* *might* is *power* unlimited by any consideration or circumstance; 'He who lives by a *mighty* principle within, which the world about him neither sees nor understands, he only ought to pass for godly.'—South. A giant is called *mighty* in the physical sense, and that genius is said to be *mighty* which takes every thing within its grasp; the Supreme Being is entitled either *Omnipotent* or *Almighty;* but the latter term seems to convey the idea of boundless extent more forcibly than the former.

EMPIRE, REIGN, DOMINION.

Empire in this case conveys the idea of power,* or an exercise of sovereignty; in this sense it is allied to the word *reign*, which, from the verb to *reign*, signifies the act of *reigning;* and to the word *dominion*, which signifies the same as in the preceding article.

Empire is used more properly for people or nations; *reign* for the individuals who hold the power: hence we say the *empire* of the Assyrians, or of the Turks; the *reign* of the Cæsars or the Paleologi. The most glorious epoch of the *empire* of the Babylonians is the *reign* of Nebuchadnezzar; that of the *empire* of the Persians is the *reign* of Cyrus; that of the *empire* of the Greeks is the *reign* of Alexander; that of the Romans is the *reign* of Augustus; these are the four great *empires* foretold by the prophet Daniel.

All the epithets applied to the word *empire*, in this sense, belong equally to *reign;* but all which are applied to *reign* are not suitable in application to *empire*. We may speak of a *reign* as long and glorious; but not of an *empire* as long and glorious, unless the idea be expressed paraphrastically. The *empire* of the Romans was of longer duration than that of the Greeks; but the glory of the latter was more brilliant, from the rapidity of its conquests: the *reign* of King George III. was one of the longest and most eventful recorded in history.

Empire and *reign* are both applied in the proper sense to the exercise of publick authority;

* Vide Abbe Girard: "Empire, règne."

The sage historick muse
Should next conduct us through the deeps of time,
Show us how *empire* grew, declin'd, and fell.
THOMSON.

Dominion applies to the personal act, whether of a sovereign or a private individual: a sovereign may have *dominion* over many nations by the force of arms, but he holds his *reign* over one nation by the force of law;

He who, like a father, held his *reign*,
So soon forgot, was wise and just in vain.—POPE.

Hence the word *dominion* may, in the proper sense, be applied to the power which man exercises over the brutes, over inanimate objects, or over himself: but if *empire* and *reign* be applied to any thing but civil government, or to nations, it is only in the improper sense: thus a female may be said to hold her *empire* among her admirers; or fashions may be said to have their *reign*. In this application of the terms, *empire* is something wide and all-commanding;

Let great Achilles, to the gods resign'd,
To reason yield the *empire* of his mind.—POPE.

Reign is that which is steady and settled;

The frigid zone,
Where for relentless months continual night
Holds o'er the glittering waste her starry *reign*.
THOMSON.

Dominion is full of control and force; 'By timely caution those desires may be repressed to which indulgence would give absolute *dominion*.'—JOHNSON.

PRINCE, MONARCH, SOVEREIGN, POTENTATE.

Prince, in French *prince*, Latin *princeps*, from *primus*, signifies the chief or the first person in the nation; *monarch*, from the Greek *μόνος* alone, and *ἀρχὴ* government, signifies one having sole authority; *sovereign* is probably changed from *superregnum; potentate*, from *potens* powerful, signifies one having supreme power.

Prince is the generick term, the rest are specifick terms; every *monarch, sovereign*, and *potentate*, is a *prince*, but not *vice versâ*. The term *prince* is indefinite as to the degree of power: a *prince* may have a limited or despotick power; but in its restricted sense this title denotes a smaller degree of power than any of the other terms: the term *monarch* does not define the extent of the power, but simply that it is undivided as opposed to that species of power which is lodged in the hands of many: *sovereign* and *potentate* indicate the highest degree of power; but the former is employed only as respects the nation that is governed, the latter respects other nations: a *sovereign* is supreme over his subjects; a *potentate* is powerful by means of his subjects. Every man having independent power is a *prince*, let his territory be ever so inconsiderable; Germany is divided into a number of small states, which are governed by petty *princes; '*Of all the *princes* who had swayed the Mexican sceptre, Montezuma was the most haughty.'—ROBERTSON. Every one reigning by himself in a state of some considerable magnitude, and having an independent authority over his subjects is a *monarch;* kings and emperours therefore are all *monarchs;* 'The Mexican people were warlike and enterprising, the authority of the *monarch* unbounded.'—ROBERTSON. Every *monarch* is a *sovereign*, whose extent of dominion and number of subjects rises above the ordinary level; 'The Peruvians yielded a blind submission to their *sovereigns*.'—ROBERTSON. He is a *potentate* if his influence either in the cabinet or the field extends very considerably over the affairs of other nations; 'How mean must the most exalted *potentate* upon earth appear to that eye which takes in innumerable orders of spirits.'—ADDISON. Although we know that *princes* are but men, yet in estimating their characters we are apt to expect more of them than what is human. It is the great concern of every *monarch* who wishes for the welfare of his subjects to choose good counsellors: whoever has approved himself a faithful subject may approach his *sovereign* with a steady confidence in having done his duty: the *potentates* of the earth may sometimes be intoxicated with their power and their triumphs but in general they have too many mementoes of their common infirmity, to forget that they are but mortal men.

ABSOLUTE, DESPOTICK, ARBITRARY, TYRANNICAL.

Absolute in Latin *absolutus*, participle of *absolvo*, signifies absolved or set at liberty from all restraint as it regards persons; unconditional, unlimited, as it regards things; *despotick*, from *despot*, in Greek *δεσπότης* a master or lord, implies being like a lord, uncontrolled; *arbitrary*, in French *arbitraire*, from the Latin *arbitrium* will, implies belonging to the will of one independent of that of others; *tyrannical* signifies being like a tyrant.

Absolute power is independent of and superiour to all other power: an *absolute* monarch is uncontrolled not only by men but things; he is above all law except what emanates from himself;

Unerring power!
Supreme and *absolute*, of these your ways
You render no account.—LYLLO.

When *absolute* power is assigned to any one according to the constitution of a government, it is *despotick. Despotick* power is therefore something less than *absolute* power: a prince is *absolute* of himself: he is *despotick* by the consent of others.

In the early ages of society monarchs were *absolute*, and among the Eastern nations they still retain the *absolute* form of government, though much limited by established usage. In the more civilized stages of society the power of *despots* has been considerably restricted by prescribed laws, in so much that *despotism* is now classed among the regular forms of government; 'Such a history as that of Suetonius is to me an unanswerable argument against *despotick* power.'—ADDISON. This term may also be applied figuratively; 'Whatever the will commands, the whole man must do; the empire of the will over all the faculties being absolutely overruling and *despotick*.'—SOUTH.

Arbitrary and *tyrannical* do not respect the power itself, so much as the exercise of power: the latter is always taken in a bad sense, the former sometimes in an indifferent sense. With *arbitrariness* is associated the idea of caprice and selfishness; for where is the individual whose uncontrolled will may not oftener be capricious than otherwise? With *tyranny* is associated the idea of oppression and injustice. Among the Greeks the word *τύραννος* a tyrant, implied no more than what we now understand by *despot*, namely, a possessor of unlimited power: but from the natural abuse of such power, it has acquired the signification now attached to it, namely, of exercising power to the injury of another;

Our sects a more *tyrannick* power assume,
And would for scorpions change the rod of Rome.
ROSCOMMON.

Absolute power should be granted to no one man or body of men; since there is no security that it will not be exercised *arbitrarily;* 'An honest private man often grows cruel and abandoned, when converted into an *absolute* prince.'—ADDISON. In *despotick* governments the *tyrannical* proceedings of the subordinate officers are often more intolerable than those of the Prince

POSITIVE, ABSOLUTE. PEREMPTORY.

Positive, in Latin *positivus*, from *pono* to put or place signifies placed or fixed, that is, fixed or established in the mind; *absolute* (*v. Absolute*) signifies uncontrolled by any external circumstances; *peremptory*, in Latin *peremptorius*, from *perimo* to take away, signifies removing all further question.

Positive is said either of a man's convictions or temper of mind, or of his proceedings; *absolute* is said of his mode of proceeding, or his relative circumstances, *peremptory* is said of his proceeding. *Positive*, as respects a man's conviction, has been spoken of under the article of *confident* (*v. Confident*); in the latter sense it bears the closest analogy to *absolute* or *peremptory:* a *positive* mode of speech depends upon a *positive* state of mind; 'The diminution or ceasing of pain does not operate like *positive* pleasure.'—BURKE. An *absolute* mode of speech depends upon the uncontrollable authority of the speaker; 'Those parts of the moral world which have not an *absolute*, may yet have a relative beauty, in respect of some other parts concealed from us.'—ADDISON. A *peremptory* mode of speech depends upon the disposition and relative circumstances of the speaker; 'The Highlander gives to every question an answer so prompt and *peremptory*, that skepticism is dared into silence.'—JOHNSON. A decision is *positive;* a command *absolute* or *peremptory:* what is *positive* excludes all question; what is *absolute* bars all resistance; what is *peremptory* removes all hesitation: a *positive* answer can be given only by one who has *positive* information; an *absolute* decree can issue only from one vested with *absolute* authority; a *peremptory* refusal can be given only by one who has the will and the power of deciding it without any controversy.

As adverbs, *positively*, *absolutely*, and *peremptorily*, have an equally close connexion: a thing is said to be *positively* known, or *positively* determined upon, or *positively* agreed to; it is said to be *absolutely* necessary, *absolutely* true or false, *absolutely* required; it is not to be *peremptorily* decided, *peremptorily* declared, *peremptorily* refused.

Positive and *absolute* are likewise applied to moral objects with the same distinction as before: the *positive* expresses what is fixed in distinction from the relative that may vary; the absolute is that which is independent of every thing: thus, pleasure and pains are *positive;* names in logic are *absolute;* cases in grammar are *absolute.*

ROYAL, REGAL, KINGLY.

Royal and *regal* from the Latin *rex* a king, though of foreign origin, have obtained more general application than the corresponding English term *kingly*. *Royal* signifies belonging to a king, in its most general sense; *regal* in Latin *regalis*, signifies appertaining to a king, in its particular application; *kingly* signifies properly like a king. A *royal* carriage, a *royal* residence, a *royal* couple, a *royal* salute, *royal* authority, all designate the general and ordinary appurtenances to a king.

> He died, and oh! may no reflection shed
> Its pois'nous venom on the *royal* dead.—PRIOR.

Regal government, *regal* state, *regal* power, *regal* dignity, denote the peculiar properties of a king;

> Jerusalem combined must see
> My open fault and *regal* infamy.—PRIOR.

Kingly always implies what is becoming a king, or after the manner of a king; a *kingly* crown is such as a king ought to wear; a *kingly* mien, that which is after the manner of a king;

> Scipio, you know how Massanissa bears
> His *kingly* post at more than ninety years.
> DENHAM.

EMPIRE, KINGDOM.

Although these two words obviously refer to two species of states, where the princes assume the title of either emperour or king, yet the difference between them is not limited to this distinction.

* The word *empire* carries with it the idea of a state that is vast, and composed of many different people; that of *kingdom* marks a state more limited in extent, and united in its composition. In *kingdoms* there is a uniformity of fundamental laws; the difference in regard to particular laws or modes of jurisprudence being merely variations from custom, which do not affect the unity of political administration. From this uniformity, indeed, in the functions of government, we may trace the origin of the words *king* and *kingdom:* since there is but one prince or sovereign ruler, although there may be many employed in the administration. With *empires* it is different: one part is sometimes governed by fundamental laws, very different from those by which another part of the same *empire* is governed; which diversity destroys the unity of government, and makes the union of the state to consist in the submission of certain chiefs to the commands of a superiour general or chief. From this very right of commanding, then, it is evident that the words *empire* and *emperour* derive their origin; and hence it is that there may be many princes or sovereigns, and *kingdoms*, in the same *empire*.

* Vide Abbe Bauzee: "Empire, royaume."

As a farther illustration of these terms, we need only look to their application from the earliest ages in which they were used, down to the present period. The word *king* had its existence long prior to that of *emperour*, being doubtless derived, through the channel of the northern languages, from the Hebrew כהן a priest, since in those ages of primitive simplicity, before the lust of dominion had led to the extension of power and conquest, he who performed the sacerdotal office was unanimously regarded as the fittest person to discharge the civil functions for the community. So in like manner among the Romans the corresponding word *rex*, which comes from *rego*, and the Hebrew רעה to feed, signifies a pastor or shepherd, because he who filled the office of king acted both spiritually and civilly as their guide. Rome therefore was first a *kingdom*, while it was formed of only one people: it acquired the name of *empire* as soon as other nations were brought into subjection to it, and became members of it; not by losing their distinctive character as nations, but by submitting themselves to the supreme command of their conquerors.

For the same reason the German *empire* was so denominated, because it consisted of several states independent of each other, yet all subject to one ruler o emperor; so likewise the Russian *empire*, the Ottomar *empire*, and the Mogul *empire*, which are composed of different nations: and on the other hand the *kingdom* of Spain, of Portugal, of France, and of England, all of which, though divided into different provinces, were nevertheless, one people, having but one ruler. While France, however, included many distinct countries within its jurisdiction, it properly assumed the name of an *empire;* and England having by a legislative act united to itself a country distinct both in its laws and customs, has likewise, with equal propriety, been denominated the British *empire*.

A *kingdom* can never reach to the extent of an *empire*, for the unity of government and administration which constitutes its leading feature cannot reach so far, and at the same time requires more time than the simple exercise of superiority, and the right of receiving certain marks of homage, which suffice to form an *empire*. Although a *kingdom* may not be free, yet an *empire* can scarcely be otherwise than despotick in its form of government. Power, when extended and ramified, as it must unavoidably be in an *empire*, derives no aid from the personal influence of the sovereign, and requires therefore to be dealt out in portions far too great to be consistent with the happiness of the subject.

TERRITORY, DOMINION.

Both these terms respect a portion of country under a particular government; but the word *territory* brings to our minds the land which is included; *dominion* conveys to our minds the power which is exercised: *territory* refers to that which is in its nature bounded; *dominion* may be said of that which is boundless. A petty prince has his *territory;* the monarch of a great empire has *dominions*.

It is the object of every ruler to guard his *territory* against the irruptions of an enemy; 'The conquered *territory* was divided among the Spanish invaders, according to rules which custom had introduced.'—ROBERTSON. Ambitious monarchs are always aiming to extend their *dominions;*

> And while the heroick Pyrrhus shines in arms,
> Our wide *dominions* shall the world o'errun.
> TRAPP.

STATE, REALM, COMMONWEALTH.

The *state* is that consolidated part of a nation in which lies its power and greatness; the *realm*, from *royaume* a kingdom, is any state whose government is monarchical; the *commonwealth* is the grand body of a nation, consisting both of the government and people, which forms the *commonwealth* or *commonweal* of a nation.

The ruling idea in the sense and application of the

word *state* is that of government in its most abstract sense; affairs of *state* may either respect the internal regulations of a country, or it may respect the arrangements of different *states* with each other. The term *realm* is employed for the nation at large, but confined to such nations as are monarchical and aristocratical; peers of the *realm* sit in the English Parliament by their own right. The term *commonwealth* refers rather to the aggregate body of men, and their possessions, rather than to the government of a country: it is the business of the minister to consult the interests of the *commonwealth*.

The term *state* is indefinitely applied to all communities, large or small, living under any form of government: a petty principality in Germany, and the whole German or Russian empire, are alike termed *states*; 'No man that understands the *state* of Poland, and the United Provinces, will be able to range them under any particular names of government that have been invented.'—TEMPLE. *Realm* is a term of dignity in regard to a nation; France, Germany, England, Russia, are, therefore, with most propriety termed *realms*, when spoken of either in regard to themselves or in general connexions;

Then Saturn came, who fled the power of Jove,
Robb'd of his *realms*, and banish'd from above.
DRYDEN.

Commonwealth, although not appropriately applied to any nation, is most fitted for republicks, which have hardly fixedness enough in themselves to deserve the name of *state*;

Civil dissension is a viperous worm,
That gnaws the bowels of the *commonwealth*.
SHAKSPEARE.

CREDIT, FAVOUR, INFLUENCE.

Credit, from the Latin *creditus*, participle of *credo* to believe or trust, marks the state of being believed or trusted; *favour*, from the Latin *faveo*, and probably *favus* a honey comb, marks an agreeable or pleasant state of feeling; *influence* signifies the same as in the preceding article.

These terms denote the state we stand in with regard to others as flowing out of their sentiments towards ourselves: *credit* arises out of esteem; *favour* out of good-will or affection; *influence* out of either *credit* or *favour*: *credit* depends most on personal merit; *favour* may depend on the caprice of him who bestows it.

The *credit* which we have with others is marked by their confidence in our judgement; by their disposition to submit to our decisions; by their reliance in our veracity, or assent to our opinions: the *favour* we have with others is marked by their readiness to comply with our wishes; their subserviency to our views; attachment to our society: men of talent are ambitious to gain *credit* with their sovereigns, by the superiority of their counsel; weak men or men of ordinary powers are contented with being the *favourites* of princes, and enjoying their patronage and protection. *Credit* redounds to the honour of the individual, and stimulates him to noble exertions; it is beneficial in its results to all mankind, individually or collectively; 'Truth itself shall lose its *credit*, if delivered by a person that has none.'—SOUTH. *Favour* redounds to the personal advantage, the selfish gratification of the individual; it is apt to inflame pride, and provoke jealousy; 'Halifax, thinking this a lucky opportunity of securing immortality, made some advances of *favour*, and some overtures of advantage to Pope, which he seems to have received with sullen coldness.'—JOHNSON. The honest exertion of our abilities is all that is necessary to gain *credit*; there will always be found those who are just enough to give *credit* where *credit* is due: *favour*, whether in the gaining or maintaining, requires much finesse and trick; much management of the humours of others; much control of one's own humours; what is thus gained with difficulty is often lost in a moment, and for a trifle. *Credit*, though sometimes obtained by falsehood, is never got without exertion; but *favour*, whether justly or unjustly bestowed, often comes by little or no effort on the part of the receiver: a clergyman gains *credit* with his parishioners by the consistency of his conduct, the gravity of his demeanour, and the strictness of his life; the *favour* of the populace is gained by arts which men of upright minds would disdain to employ.

Credit and *favour* are the gifts of others; *influence* is a possession which we derive from circumstances: there will always be *influence* where there is *credit* or *favour*, but it may exist independently of either: we have *credit* and *favour* for ourselves; we exert *influence* over others: *credit* and *favour* serve one's own purposes; *influence* is employed in directing others: weak people easily give *credit*, or bestow their *favour*, by which an *influence* is gained over them to bend them to the will of others; the *influence* itself may be good or bad, according to the views of the person by whom it is exerted; 'What motive could induce Murray to murder a prince without capacity, without followers, without *influence* over the nobles, whom the queen, by her neglect, had reduced to the lowest state of contempt.'—ROBERTSON.

GRACE, FAVOUR.

Grace, in French *grace*, Latin *gratia*, comes from *gratus* kind, because a *grace* results from pure kindness independently of the merit of the receiver; but *favour* is that which is granted voluntarily and without hope of recompense independently of all obligation.

Grace is never used but in regard to those who have offended and made themselves liable to punishment; *favour* is employed for actual good. An *act of grace* is a term employed to denote that act of the government by which insolvent debtors are released; but otherwise the term is in most frequent use among Christians to denote that merciful influence which God exerts over his most unworthy creatures from the infinite goodness of his Divine nature; it is to his special *grace* that we attribute every good feeling by which we are prevented from committing sin;

But say I could repent and could obtain,
By act of *grace*, my former state, how soon
Would height recall high thoughts.—MILTON.

The term *favour* is employed indiscriminately with regard to man or his Maker; those who are in power have the greatest opportunity of conferring *favours*; 'A bad man is wholly the creature of the world. He hangs upon its *favour*.'—BLAIR. But all we receive at the hands of our Maker must be acknowledged as a *favour*. The Divine *grace* is absolutely indispensable for men as sinners; the Divine *favour* is perpetually necessary for men as his creatures dependent upon him for every thing.

FAVOURABLE, PROPITIOUS, AUSPICIOUS.

Favourable, disposed to *favour*, or after the manner of *favour*, is the general term; *propitious* and *auspicious* are species of the *favourable*; *propitious*, in Latin *propitius*, comes from *prope* near, because the heathens solicited their deities to be near or present to give them aid in favour of their designs; whence *propitious* signifies *favourable* as it springs from the design of an agent: *auspicious*, in French *auspice*, Latin *auspicium* and *auspex*, compounded of *avis* and *spicio* to behold, signifies *favourable* according to the auspices; what is *propitious* or *auspicious*, therefore, is always *favourable*, but not *vice versâ*: the *favourable* properly characterizes both persons and things; the *propitious*, in the proper sense, characterizes the person only; *auspicious* is said of things only: as applied to persons, an equal may be *favourable*: a superiour only is *propitious*: the one may be *favourable* only in inclination; the latter is *favourable* also in granting timely *assistance*. Cato was *favourable* to Pompey; the gods were *propitious* to the Greeks: we may all wish to have our friends *favourable* to our projects;

Famous Plantagenet! most gracious prince,
Lend *favourable* ear to our requests.—SHAKSPEARE.

None but heathens expect to have a blind destiny *propitious*. In the improper sense, *propitious* may be applied to things with a similar distinction: whatever is well disposed to us, and seconds our endeavours, or serves our purpose, is *favourable*; 'You have indeed every *favourable* circumstance for your advancement that can be wished.'—MELMOTH (*Letters of Cicero*)

Whatever efficaciously protects us, speeds our exertions, and decides our success, is *propitious* to us:

> But ah! what use of valour can be made,
> When Heaven's *propitious* powers refuse their aid.
> DRYDEN.

On ordinary occasions, a wind is said to be *favourable* which carries us to the end of our voyage; but it is said to be *propitious* if the rapidity of our passage forwards any great purpose of our own. Those things are *auspicious* which are casual, or only indicative of good; persons are *propitious* to the wishes of another who listen to their requests and contribute to their satisfaction. A journey is undertaken under *auspicious* circumstances, where every thing incidental, as weather, society, and the like, bid fair to afford pleasure;

> Still follow where *auspicious* fates invite,
> Caress the happy, and the wretched slight.
> Sooner shall jarring elements unite,
> Than truth with gain, than interest with right.
> LEWIS.

A journey is undertaken under *propitious* circumstances when every thing favours the attainment of the object for which it was begun;

> Who loves a garden loves a greenhouse too:
> Unconscious of a less *propitious* clime,
> There blooms exotic beauty.—COWPER.

Whoever has any request to make ought to seize the *auspicious* moment when the person of whom it is asked is in a pleasant frame of mind; a poet in his invocation requests the muse to be *propitious* to him, or the lover conjures his beloved to be *propitious* to his vows.

TO LEAD, CONDUCT, GUIDE.

Lead, in Saxon *lädden*, *läden*, Danish *lede*, Swedish *leda*, low German *leiden*, high German *leiten*, is most probably connected with the obsolete German *leit*, *leige*, a way or road, Swedish *led*, Saxon *late*, &c. signifying properly to show or direct in the way; *conduct*, in Latin *conductus*, participle of *conduco*, signifies to carry a person with one, or to make a thing go according to one's will; *guide*, in French *guider*, Saxon *witan* or *wisan*, German, &c. *weisen* to show, Latin *video* to see or show, signifies properly to point out the way.

These terms are all employed to denote the influence which one person has over the movements or actions of another; but the first implies nothing more than personal presence and direction or going before, the last two convey also the idea of superiour intelligence; those are *led* who either cannot or will not go alone, those are *conducted* and *guided* who do not know the road; in the literal sense it is the hand that *leads*, the head that *conducts*, and the eye that *guides*; one *leads* an infant; *conducts* a person to a given spot; and *guides* a traveller,

> His *guide*, as faithful from that day
> As Hesperus that *leads* the sun his way.
> FAIRFAX.

'We waited some time in expectation of the next worthy, who came in with a great retinue of historians, whose names I could not learn, most of them being natives of Carthage. The person thus *conducted*, who was Hannibal, seemed much disturbed.' ADDISON.

> Can knowledge have no bound, but must advance
> So far to make us wish for ignorance?
> And rather in the dark to grope our way
> Than *led* by a false *guide* to err by day?—DENHAM.

A general *leads* an army, inasmuch as he goes before it into the field of battle; he *conducts* an army, inasmuch as he directs its movements by his judgement and skill; he is himself *guided*, inasmuch as he follows the *guide* who points out the road. The coachman *leads* his horses in or out of the stable; he *guides* them when they are in a carriage; the pilot *conducts* a vessel; the steersman *guides* it.

These words bear the same analogy in the moral or figurative application; the personal influence of another *leads*; the understanding *conducts*; authority or law *guides*. Men are *led* into mistakes by listening to evil counsellors. The word is also applied in the same sense to circumstances; 'Human testimony is not so proper to *lead* us into the knowledge of the essence of things, as to acquaint us with the existence of things.' —WATTS. But sometimes the word *lead* is taken in the sense of draw or move into action, as men are said to be *led* by their passions into errours; 'What I say will have little influence on those whose ends *lead* them to wish the continuance of the war.'—SWIFT. *Conducting* in the moral sense is applied mostly to things; one *conducts* a lawsuit or a business; 'He so *conducted* the affairs of the kingdom, that he made the reign of a prince most happy to the English.'—LORD LYTTLETON. *Guiding*, which comes nearest to *leading* in this application, conveys the idea of serving as a rule; an attentive perusal of the Scriptures is sufficient to *guide* us in the way of salvation; 'The brutes are *guided* by instinct and know no sorrow; the angels have knowledge and they are happy.'—STEELE. 'Upon those, or such like secular maxims, when nothing but interest *guides* men, they many times conclude that the slightest wrongs are not to be put up with.'-KETTELWELL.

TO CONDUCT, MANAGE, DIRECT.

Conducting, as in the preceding article, requires most wisdom and knowledge: *managing*, from the French *menager* and *mener*, and the Latin *manus* a hand, supposes most action; *direction*, from the Latin *directus*, participle of *dirigo* or *di* and *rego*, signifies to regulate distinctly, which supposes most authority. A lawyer *conducts* the cause intrusted to him; a steward *manages* the mercantile concerns for his employer; a superintendent *directs* the movements of all the subordinate agents.

Conducting is always applied to affairs of the first importance; 'The general purposes of men in the *conduct* of their lives, I mean with relation to this life only, end in gaining either the affection or esteem of those with whom they converse.'—STEELE. *Management* is a term of familiar use to characterize a familiar employment; 'Good delivery is a graceful *management* of the voice, countenance, and gesture.'—STEELE. 'I have sometimes amused myself with considering the several methods of *managing* a debate, which have obtained in the world.'—ADDISON. *Direction* makes up in authority what it wants in importance; it falls but little short of the word *conduct*; 'To *direct* a wanderer in the right way is to light another man's candle by one's own, which loses none of its light by what the other gains.'—GROVE. A *conductor* conceives and plans as well as executes: 'If he did not entirely project the union and regency, none will deny him to have been the chief conductor in both.'—ADDISON. A *manager*, for the most part simply acts or executes, except in a subordinate capacity, or in mean concerns; 'A skilful *manager* of the rabble, so long as they have but ears to hear, need never inquire whether they have understanding.'—SOUTH. A *director* commands; 'Himself stood *director* over them, with nodding or stamping, showing he did like or mislike those things he did not understand.'—SIDNEY. It is necessary to *conduct* with wisdom; to *manage* with diligence and attention; to *direct* with promptitude, precision, and clearness. A minister of state requires peculiar talents to *conduct*, with success, the various and complicated concerns which are connected with his office: he must exercise much skill in *managing* the various characters and clashing interests with which he becomes connected: and possess much influence to *direct* the multiplied operations by which the grand machine of government is kept in motion.

When a general undertakes to *conduct* a campaign he will intrust the *management* of minor concerns to persons on whom he can rely; but he will *direct* in person whatever is likely to have any serious influence on his success.

TO DIRECT, DISPOSE, REGULATE.

We *direct* for the instruction of individuals. We *regulate* for the good order or convenience of many We *dispose* for the benefit of one or many

To *direct* (*v. To conduct*) is personal, it supposes authority; to *regulate*, from the Latin *regula* a rule, signifying to settle according to a rule, is general, it supposes superiour information. An officer *directs* the movements of his men in military operations;

Canst thou with all a monarch's cares opprest!
Oh Atreus' son! canst thou indulge thy rest?
Ill fits a chief, who mighty nations guides,
Directs in council, and in war presides.—POPE.

The steward or master of the ceremonies *regulates* the whole concerns of an entertainment;

Ev'n goddesses are women: and no wife
Has power to *regulate* her husband's life.
DRYDEN.

The *director* is often a man in power; the *regulator* is always the man of business; the latter is frequently employed to act under the former. The Bank of England has its *directors*, who only take part in the administration of the whole; the *regulation* of the subordinate part, and of the details of business, is intrusted to the superiour clerks.

To *direct* is mostly used with regard to others; to *regulate*, frequently with regard to ourselves. One person *directs* another according to his better judgement; he *regulates* his own conduct by principles or circumstances; 'Strange disorders are bred in the minds of those men whose passions are not *regulated* by reason.'—ADDISON. But sometimes the word *direct* is taken in the sense of giving a direction towards an object, and it is then distinguished from *regulate*, which signifies to determine the measure and other circumstances; 'It is the business of religion and philosophy not so much to extinguish our passions, as to *regulate* and *direct* them to valuable, well-chosen objects.'—ADDISON.

To *dispose*, from *dispono*, or *dis* and *pono*, signifying to put apart for a particular use, supposes superiour power, like the word *direct*, and superiour wisdom, like that of *regulate*; whence the term has been applied to the Supreme Being, who is styled the '*Disposer* of all events;' and in the same sense, it is used by the poets in reference to the heathen gods;

Endure, and conquer; Jove will soon *dispose*
To future good, our past and present woes.
DRYDEN.

BEHAVIOUR, CONDUCT, CARRIAGE, DEPORTMENT, DEMEANOUR.

Behaviour comes from *behave*, compounded of *be* and *have*, signifying to have one's self, or have self-possession; *conduct*, in Latin *conductus*, participle of *conduco*, compounded of *con* or *cum* and *duco* to lead along, signifies leading one's self along; *carriage*, the abstract of *carry* (*v. To bear, carry*), signifies the act of carrying one's body, or one's self; *deportment*, from the Latin *deporto* to carry; and *demeanour*, from the French *demener* to lead, have the same original sense as the preceding.

Behaviour respects corporeal or mental actions; *conduct*, mental actions; *carriage*, *deportment*, and *demeanour*, are different species of behaviour. *Behaviour* respects all actions exposed to the notice of others: *conduct* the general line of a person's moral proceedings: we speak of a person's *behaviour* at table, or in company, in a ball room, in the street, or in publick; of his *conduct* in the management of his private concerns, in the direction of his family, or in his different relations with his fellow-creatures. *Behaviour* applies to the minor morals of society; *conduct* to those of the first moment: in our intercourse with others we may adopt a civil or polite, a rude or boisterous *behaviour*; in our serious transactions we may adopt a peaceable, discreet, or prudent, a rash, dangerous, or mischievous *conduct*. Our *behaviour* is good or bad; our *conduct* is wise or foolish: by our *behaviour* we may render ourselves agreeable, or otherwise; by our *conduct* we may command esteem, or provoke contempt: the *behaviour* of young people in society is of particular importance; it should, above all things, be marked with propriety in the presence of superiours and elders; 'The circumstance of life is not that which gives us place, but our *behaviour* in that circumstance is what should be our solid distinction.'—STEELE. The youth who does not learn betimes a seemly *behaviour* in company, will scarcely know how to *conduct* himself judiciously on any future occasion; 'Wisdom is no less necessary in religious and moral than in civil *conduct*.'—BLAIR.

Carriage respects simply the manner of carrying the body; *deportment* includes both the action and the *carriage* of the body in performing the action; *demeanour* respects only the moral character or tendency of the action; *deportment* is said only of those exteriour actions that have an immediate reference to others; *demeanour*, of the general *behaviour* as it relates to the circumstances and situation of the individual: the *carriage* is that part of *behaviour*, which is of the first importance to attend to in young persons. The *carriage* should neither be haughty nor servile; to be graceful, it ought to have a due mixture of dignity and condescension: the *deportment* of a man should be suited to his station; an humble *deportment* is becoming in inferiours; a stately and forbidding *deportment* is very unbecoming in superiours; the *demeanour* of a man should be suited to his situation; the suitable *demeanour* of a judge on the bench, or of a clergy man in the pulpit, or when performing his clerical functions, adds much to the dignity and solemnity of the office itself.

The *carriage* marks the birth and education: an awkward *carriage* stamps a man as vulgar; a graceful *carriage* evinces refinement and culture; 'He that will look back upon all the acquaintances he has had in his whole life, will find he has seen more men capable of the greatest employments and performances, than such as could in the general bent of their *carriage* act otherwise than according to their own complexion and humour.'—STEELE. The *deportment* marks the existing temper of the mind; whoever is really impressed with the solemnity and importance of publick worship will evince his impressions by a gravity of *deportment*; females should guard against a light *deportment*, as highly prejudicial to their reputation 'The mild *demeanour*, the modest *deportment*, are valued not only as they denote internal purity and innocence, but as forming in themselves the most amiable and engaging part of the female character.'—MACKENZIE. The *demeanour* marks the habitual temper of the mind, or in fact the real character; we are often led to judge favourably of an individual from the first glance, whose *demeanour* on close examination does not leave such favourable impressions; 'I have been told the same even of Mahometans, with relation to the propriety of their *demeanour* in the conventions of their erroneous worship.'—STEELE.

CARRIAGE, GAIT, WALK.

Carriage, from the verb to *carry* (*v. To bear, carry*), signifies the act of *carrying* in general, but here that of *carrying* the body; *gait*, from go, signifies the manner of going with the body; *walk* signifies the manner of *walking*.

Carriage is here the most general term; it respects the manner of *carrying* the body, whether in a state of motion or rest: *gait* is the mode of *carrying* the limbs and body whenever we move: *walk* is the manner of *carrying* the body when we move forward to *walk*.

A person's *carriage* is somewhat natural to him; it is often an indication of character, but admits of great change by education; we may always distinguish a man as high or low, either in mind or station, by his *carriage*; 'Upon her nearer approach to Hercules, she stepped before the other lady, who came forward with a regular composed *carriage*.'—ADDISON. *Gait* is artificial; we may contract a certain *gait* by habit; the *gait* is therefore often taken for a bad habit of going, as when a person has a limping *gait*, or an unsteady *gait*;

Lifeless her *gait*, and slow, with seeming pain,
She dragg'd her loit'ring limbs along the plain.
SHENSTONE.

Walk is less definite than either, as it is applicable to the ordinary movements of men: there is a good, a bad, or an indifferent *walk;* but it is not a matter of ndifference which of these kinds of *walk* we have; it is the great art of the dancing-master to give a good *walk;*

In length of train descends her sweeping gown,
And by her graceful *walk*, the queen of love is known.
DRYDEN.

MANNERS, MORALS.

Manners (v. *Air*, *manner*) respect the minor forms of acting with others and towards others; *morals* include the important duties of life: *manners* have, therefore, been denominated minor *morals*. By an attention to good *manners* we render ourselves good companions; by an observance of good *morals* we become good members of society: the former gains the good will of others, the latter their esteem. The *manners* of a child are of more or less importance, according to his station in life; his *morals* cannot be attended to too early, let his station be what it may; 'In the present corrupted state of human *manners*, always to assent and to comply, is the very worst maxim we can adopt. It is impossible to support the purity and dignity of Christian *morals*, without opposing the world on various occasions.'—BLAIR.

AIR, MANNER.

Air, in Latin *aer*, Greek ἀὴρ, comes from the Hebrew אור, because it is the vehicle of light; hence in the figurative sense, in which it is here taken, it denotes an appearance: *manner*, in French *manière*, comes probably from *mener* to lead or direct, signifying the direction of one's movements.

An *air* is inherent in the whole person; a *manner* is confined to the action or the movement of a single limb. A man has the *air* of a common person; it discovers itself in all his *manners*. An *air* has something superficial in its nature; it strikes at the first glance; 'The *air* she gave herself was that of a romping girl.' —STEELE. *Manner* has something more solid in it; it developes itself on closer observation; 'The boy is well fashioned, and will easily fall into a graceful *manner*.'—STEELE. Some people have an *air* about them which displeases; but their *manners* afterward win upon those who have a farther intercourse with them. Nothing is more common than to suffer ourselves to be prejudiced by a person's *air*, either in his favour or otherwise: the *manners* of a man will often contribute to his advancement in life, more than his real merits.

An *air* is indicative of a state of mind; it may result either from a natural or habitual mode of thinking: a *manner* is indicative of the education; it is produced by external circumstances. An *air* is noble or simple, it marks an elevation or simplicity of character: a *manner* is rude, rustic, or awkward, for want of culture, good society, and good example. We assume an *air*, and affect a *manner*. An assumed *air* of importance exposes the littleness of the assumer, which might otherwise pass unnoticed: the same *manners* which are becoming when natural, render a person ridiculous when they are affected. A prepossessing *air* and engaging *manners* have more influence on the heart than the solid qualities of the mind.

AIR, MIEN, LOOK.

Air signifies the same as in the preceding article; *mien*, in German *miene*, comes, as Adelung supposes, from *mahnen* to move or draw, because the lines of the face, which constitute the *mien* in the German sense, are drawn together: *look* signifies properly a mode of looking or appearing.

The exteriour of a person is comprehended in the sense of all these words. *Air* depends not only on the countenance, but the stature, carriage, and action: *mien* respects the whole outward appearance, not excepting the dress: *look* depends altogether on the face and its changes. *Air* marks any particular state of the mind; 'The truth of it is, the *air* is generally nothing else but the inward disposition of the mind made visible.'—ADDISON. *Mien* denotes any state of the outward circumstances;

How sleek their *looks*, how goodly is their *mien*,
When big they strut behind a double chin.
DRYDEN.

Look denotes any individual movement of the mind;

How in the *looks* does conscious guilt appear
ADDISON.

We may judge by a person's *air*, that he has a confident and fearless mind: we may judge by his sorrowful *mien*, that he has substantial cause for sorrow; and by sorrowful *looks*, that he has some partial or temporary cause for sorrow.

We talk of doing any thing with a particular *air;* of having a *mien;* of giving a *look*. An innocent man will answer his accusers with an *air* of composure; a person's whole *mien* sometimes bespeaks his wretched condition; a *look* is sometimes given to one who acts in concert, by way of intimation.

TO ADMONISH, ADVISE.

Admonish, in Latin *admoneo*, is compounded of the intensive *ad* and *moneo* to advise, signifying to put seriously in mind; *advise* compounded of the Latin *ad* and *visus*, participle of *video* to see, signifies to make to see, or to show.

Admonish mostly regards the past; *advise* respects the future. We *admonish* a person on the errours he has committed, by representing to him the extent and consequences of his offence; we *advise* a person as to his future conduct, by giving him rules and instructions. Those who are most liable to transgress require to be *admonished;*

He of their wicked ways
Shall them *admonish*, and before them set
The paths of righteousness.—MILTON.

Those who are most inexperienced require to be *advised;* 'My worthy friend, the clergyman, told us, that he wondered any order of persons should think themselves too considerable to be *advised*.'—ADDISON. *Admonition* serves to put people on their guard against evil; *advice* to direct them in the choice of good.

ADMONITION, WARNING, CAUTION.

Admonition signifies the act of admonishing, or that by which one admonishes: *warning*, in Saxon *warnien*, German *warnen*, probably from *wahren* to perceive, signifies making to see; *caution*, from *caveo* to beware, signifies the making beware.

A guarding against evil is common to these terms; but *admonition* expresses more than *warning*, and that more than *caution*.

An *admonition* respects the moral conduct; it comprehends reasoning and remonstrance: *warning* and *caution* respect the personal interest or safety; the former comprehends a strong forcible representation of the evil to be dreaded; the latter a simple apprisal of a future contingency. *Admonition* may therefore frequently comprehend *warning;* and *warning* may comprehend *caution*, though not *vice versâ*. We *admonish* a person against the commission of any offence; we *warn* him against danger; we *caution* him against any misfortune.

Admonitions and *warnings* are given by those who are superiour in age and station; *cautions* by any who are previously in possession of information. Parents give *admonitions;* ministers of the gospel give *warnings:* indifferent persons give *cautions*. It is necessary to *admonish* those who have once offended to abstain from a similar offence; 'At the same time that I am talking of the cruelty of urging people's faults with severity, I cannot but bewail some which men are guilty of for want of *admonition*.'—STEELE. It is necessary to *warn* those of the consequences of sin who seem determined to persevere in a wicked course;

Not e'en Philander had bespoke his shroud,
Nor had he cause—a *warning* was denied.
YOUNG.

It is necessary to *caution* those against any false step who are going in a strange path;

You *caution'd* me against their charms,
But never gave me equal arms;

Your lessons found the weakest part,
Aim'd at the head, but reach'd the heart.—SWIFT.

Admonitions are given by persons only; *warnings* and *cautions* are given by things. The young are *admonished* by the old: the death of friends or relatives serves as a *warning* to the survivors; the unfortunate accidents of the careless serve as a *caution* to others to avoid the like errour. *Admonitions* should be given with mildness and gravity; *warnings* with impressive force and warmth; *cautions* with clearness and precision. The young require frequent *admonitions;* the ignorant and self-deluded solemn *warnings;* the inexperienced timely *cautions*.

Admonitions ought to be listened to with sorrowful attention; *warnings* should make a deep and lasting impression; *cautions* should be borne in mind: but *admonitions* are too often rejected, *warnings* despised, and *cautions* slighted.

ADVICE, COUNSEL, INSTRUCTION.

Advice signifies that which is advised (*v. Advice*); *counsel*, in French *conseil*, Latin *consilium*, comes from *consilio*, compounded of *con* and *salio* to leap together, signifying to run or act in accordance; and in an extended sense implies deliberation, or the thing deliberated upon, determined, and prescribed; *instruction*, in French *instruction*, Latin *instructio*, comes from *in* and *struo* to dispose or regulate, signifying the thing laid down.

The end of all the actions implied by these words is the communication of knowledge, and all of them include the accessary idea of superiority, either of age, station, knowledge, or talent. *Advice* flows from superiour professional knowledge, or an acquaintance with things in general; *counsel* regards superiour wisdom, or a superiour acquaintance with moral principles and practice; *instruction* respects superiour local knowledge in particular transactions. A medical man gives *advice* to his patient; a father gives *counsel* to his children; a counsellor gives *advice* to his client in points of law; he receives *instructions* from him in matters of fact.

Advice should be prudent and cautious; *counsel*, sage and deliberative; *instructions*, clear and positive. *Advice* is given on all the concerns of life, important or otherwise; 'In what manner can one give *advice* to a youth in the pursuit and possession of pleasure?'—STEELE. *Counsel* is employed for grave and weighty matters; 'Young persons are commonly inclined to slight the remarks and *counsels* of their elders.'—JOHNSON. *Instruction* is used on official occasions;

To serve by way of guide or direction
See this despatch'd with all the haste thou canst;
Anon I'll give thee more *instruction*.
SHAKSPEARE.

Men of business are best able to give *advice* in mercantile transactions. In all measures that involve our future happiness, it is prudent to take the *counsel* of those who are more experienced than ourselves. An ambassador must not act without *instructions* from his court.

A wise king will not act without the *advice* of his ministers. A considerate youth will not take any serious step without the *counsel* of his better informed friends. All diplomatick persons are guided by particular *instructions* in carrying on negotiations.

Advice and *counsel* are often given unasked and undesired, but *instructions* are always required for the regulation of a person's conduct in an official capacity. The term *instruction* may however be also applied morally and figuratively for that which serves to guide one in his course of life;

On ev'ry thorn delightful wisdom grows,
In ev'ry stream a sweet *instruction* flows.—YOUNG.

TO INFORM, INSTRUCT, TEACH.

The communication of knowledge in general is the common idea by which these words are connected with each other. *Inform* is the general term; the other two are specifick. To *inform* is the act of persons in all conditions; to *instruct* and *teach* are the acts of superiours, either on one ground or another: one *informs* by virtue of an accidental superiority or priority of knowledge; one *instructs* by virtue of superiour knowledge or superiour station: one *teaches* by virtue of superiour knowledge, rather than of station: diplomatick agents *inform* their governments of the political transactions in which they have been concerned; government *instructs* its different functionaries and officers in regard to their mode of proceeding; professors and preceptors *teach* those who attend a publick school to learn

To *inform* is applicable to matters of general interest; we may *inform* ourselves or others on every thing which is a subject of inquiry or curiosity; and the *information* serves either to amuse or to improve the mind; 'While we only desire to have our ignorance *informed*, we are most delighted with the plainest diction.'—JOHNSON To *instruct* is applicable to matters of serious concern, or that which is practically useful; it serves to set us right in the path of life. A parent *instructs* his child in the course of conduct he should pursue; a good child profits by the *instruction* of a good parent to make him wiser and better for the time to come;

Not Thracian Orpheus should transcend my lays,
Nor Linus, crown'd with never fading bays;
Though each his heav'nly parent should inspire,
The Muse *instruct* the voice, and Phœbus tune the lyre.
DRYDEN.

To *teach* respects matters of art and science; the learner depends upon the *teacher* for the formation of his mind, and the establishment of his principles; 'He that *teaches* us any thing which we knew not before is undoubtedly to be reverenced as a master.'—JOHNSON. Every one ought to be properly *informed* before he pretends to give an opinion; the young and inexperienced must be *instructed* before they can act; the ignorant must be *taught*, in order to guard them against errour. Truth and sincerity are all that is necessary for an *informant;* general experience and a perfect knowledge of the subject in question are requisite for the *instructer;* fundamental knowledge is requisite for a *teacher*. Those who give *information* upon the authority of others are liable to mislead; those who *instruct* others in doing that which is bad, scandalously abuse the authority that is reposed in them; those who pretend to *teach* what they themselves do not understand, mostly betray their ignorance sooner or later.

To *inform* and to *teach* are employed for things as well as persons; to *instruct* only for persons: books and reading *inform* the mind; history or experience *teaches* mankind; 'The long speeches rather confounded than *informed* his understanding.'—CLARENDON. 'Nature is no sufficient *teacher* what we should do that we may attain unto life everlasting.'—HOOKER

TO INFORM, MAKE KNOWN, ACQUAINT, APPRIZE.

The idea of bringing to the knowledge of one or more persons is common to all these terms. *Inform*, from the Latin *informo* to fashion the mind, comprehends this general idea only, without the addition of any collateral idea; it is therefore the generick term, and the rest specifick: to *inform* is to communicate what has lately happened, or the contrary; but to *make known* is to bring to light what has long been *known* and purposely concealed: to *inform* is to communicate directly or indirectly to one or many;

Our ruin, by thee *inform'd*, I learn.—MILTON.

To *make known* is mostly to communicate indirectly to many: one *informs* the publick of one's intentions by means of an advertisement in one's own name; one *makes known* a fact through a circuitous channel, and without any name;

But fools, to talking ever prone,
Are sure to *make* their follies *known*.—GAY.

To *inform* may be either a personal address or otherwise; to *acquaint* and *apprize* are immediate and personal communications. One *informs* the government, or any publick body, or one *informs* one's friends; one *acquaints* or *apprizes* only one's friends, or particular individuals: one is *informed* of that which either concerns the *informant*, or the person *informed;* one *acquaints* a person with, or *apprizes* him of such things as peculiarly concern himself, but the latter in more specifick circumstances than the former: one *informs* a correspondent by letter of the day on which he may expect to receive his order, or of one's own wishes with regard to an order;

> I have this present evening from my sister,
> Been well *informed* of them, and with cautions.
> SHAKSPEARE.

One *acquaints* a father with all the circumstances that respect his son's conduct; 'If any man lives under a minister that doth not act according to the rules of the gospel, it is his own fault in that he doth not *acquaint* the bishop with it.'—BEVERIDGE. One *apprizes* a friend of a bequest that has been made to him; 'You know, without my telling you, with what zeal I have recommended you to Cæsar, although you may not be *apprized* that I have frequently written to him upon that subject.'—MELMOTH (*Letters of Cicero*). One *informs* the magistrate of any irregularity that passes; one *acquaints* the master of a family with the misconduct of his servants: one *apprizes* a person of the time when he will be obliged to appear. *Inform* is used figuratively, but the other terms mostly in the proper sense; 'Religion *informs* us that misery and sin were produced together.'—JOHNSON.

INFORMANT, INFORMER.

These two epithets, from the verb to inform, have acquired by their application an important distinction. The *informant* being he who informs for the benefit of others, and the *informer* to the molestation of others. What the *informant* communicates is for the benefit of the individual, and what the *informer* communicates is for the benefit of the whole. The *informant* is thanked for his civility in making the communication; the *informer* undergoes a great deal of odium, but is thanked by not one, not even by those who employ him. We may all be *informants* in our turn, if we know of any thing of which another may be informed; 'Aye (says our Artist's *informant*), but at the same time he declared you (Hogarth) were as good a portrait painter as Vandyke.'—PILKINGTON. None are *informers* who do not inform against the transgressors of any law; 'Every member of society feels and acknowledges the necessity of detecting crimes, yet scarce any degree of virtue or reputation is able to secure an *informer* from publick hatred.'—JOHNSON.

INFORMATION, INTELLIGENCE, NOTICE, ADVICE.

Information (*v. To inform*) signifies the thing of which one is informed: *Intelligence*, from the Latin *intelligo* to understand, signifies that by which one is made to understand: *notice*, from the Latin *notitia*, is that which brings a circumstance to our knowledge: *Advice* (*v. Advice*) signifies that which is made known. These terms come very near to each other in signification, but differ in application: *information* is the most general and indefinite of all; the three others are but modes of *information*. Whatever is communicated to us is *information*, be it publick or private, open or concealed;

> There, centring in a focus round and neat,
> Let all your rays of *information* meet.—COWPER.

Notice, *intelligence*, and *advice*, are mostly publick, but particularly the former. *Information* and *notice* may be communicated by word of mouth or by writing; *intelligence* is mostly communicated by writing or printing; *advices* are mostly sent by letter: *information* is mostly an informal mode of communication; *notice*, *intelligence*, and *advice*, are mostly formal communications. A servant gives his master *information*, or one friend sends another *information* from the country; magistrates or officers give *notice* of such things as it concerns the publick to know and to observe; spies give *intelligence* of all that passes under their notice; or *intelligence* is given in the publick prints of all that passes worthy of notice; 'My lion, whose jaws are at all hours open to *intelligence*, informs me that there are a few enormous weapons still in being.'—STEELE. A military commander sends *advice* to his government of the operations which are going forward under his direction; or one merchant gives *advice* to another of the state of the market; 'As he was dictating to his hearers with great authority, there came in a gentleman from Garraway's, who told us that there were several letters from France just come in, with *advice* that the king was in good health.'—ADDISON.

Information, as calculated to influence men's actions, ought to be correct: those who are too eager to know what is passing, are often misled by false *information*. *Notice*, as it serves either to warn or direct ought to be timely;

> At his years
> Death gives short *notice*.—THOMSON.

No law of general interest is carried into effect without timely *notice* being given. *Intelligence*, as the first intimation of an interesting event, ought to be early; *advices*, as entering into details, ought to be clear and particular; official *advices* often arrive to contradict non-official *intelligence*.

Information and *intelligence*, when applied as characteristicks of men, have a farther distinction: the man of *information* is so denominated only on account of his knowledge; but a man of *intelligence* is so denominated on account of his understanding as well as experience and information. It is not possible to be *intelligent* without *information*; but we may be well *informed* without being remarkable for *intelligence*: a man of *information* may be an agreeable companion, and fitted to maintain conversation; but an *intelligent* man will be an instructive companion, and most fitted for conducting business.

ACQUAINTANCE, FAMILIARITY, INTIMACY.

Acquaintance comes from *acquaint*, which is compounded of the intensive syllable *ac* or *ad* and *quaint*, in old French *coint*, Teut. *gekannt* known, signifying known to one; *familiarity* comes from *familiar*, in Latin *familiaris* and *familia*, signifying known as one of the family; *intimacy*, from *intimate*, in Latin *intimatus*, participle of *intimo* to love entirely, from *intimus* innermost, signifies known to the innermost recesses of the heart.

These terms mark different degrees of closeness in the social intercourse; *acquaintance* expressing less than *familiarity*; and that less than *intimacy*; 'A slight knowledge of any one constitutes an *acquaintance*; to be *familiar* requires an *acquaintance* of some standing; *intimacy* supposes such an *acquaintance* as is supported by friendship.'—TRUSLER.

Acquaintance springs from occasional intercourse; *familiarity* is produced by a daily intercourse, which wears off all constraint, and banishes all ceremony; *intimacy* arises not merely from frequent intercourse, but unreserved communication. An *acquaintance* will be occasionally a guest; 'An *acquaintance* is a being who meets us with a smile and salute, who tells us with the same breath that he is glad and sorry for the most trivial good and ill that befalls us.'—HAWKESWORTH. One that is on terms of *familiarity* has easy access to our table; 'His *familiars* were his entire friends, and could have no interested views in courting his *acquaintance*.'—STEELE. An *intimate* lays claim to a share at least of our confidence; 'At an entertainment given by Pisistratus to some of his *intimates*, Thrasippus took some occasion, not recorded, to break out into the most violent abuse.'—CUMBERLAND. An *acquaintance* with a person affords but little opportunity for knowing his character; *familiarity* puts us in the way of seeing his foibles, rather than his virtues; but *intimacy* enables us to appreciate his worth; 'Those who are apt to be *familiar* on a slight *acquaintance*, will never acquire any degree of *intimacy*.'—TRUSLER.

A simple *acquaintance* is the most desirable footing on which to stand with all persons, however deserving

> *Acquaintance* grew; th' *acquaintance* they improve
> To friendship; friendship ripen'd into love.
> EUSDEN.

If it have not the pleasures of *familiarity* or *intimacy*, it can claim the privilege of being exempted from their pains. "Too much *familiarity*," according to the old proverb, "breeds contempt." The unlicensed freedom which commonly attends *familiarity* affords but too ample scope for the indulgence of the selfish and unamiable passions; 'That *familiarity* produces neglect has been long observed.'—JOHNSON. *Intimacies* begun in love often end in hatred, as ill chosen friends commonly become the bitterest enemies. A man may have a thousand acquaintance, and not one whom he should make his *intimate;* 'The *intimacy* between the father of Eugenio and Agrestis produced a tender friendship between his sister and Amelia.'—HAWKESWORTH.

These terms may be applied to things as well as persons, in which case they bear a similar analogy. An *acquaintance* with a subject is opposed to entire ignorance upon it; *familiarity* with it is the consequence of frequent repetition; and *intimacy* of a steady and thorough research; 'With Homer's heroes we have more than historical *acquaintance:* we are made *intimate* with their habits and manners.'—CUMBERLAND. 'The frequency of envy makes it so *familiar*, that it escapes our notice.'—JOHNSON. In our intercourse with the world we become daily *acquainted* with fresh subjects to engage our attention. Some men have by extraordinary diligence acquired a considerable *familiarity* with more than one language and science; but few, if any, can boast of having possessed an *intimate acquaintance* with all the particulars of even one language or science. When we can translate the authors of any foreign language, we may claim an *acquaintance* with it; when we can speak, or write it freely, we may be said to be *familiar* with it; but an *intimate acquaintance* comprehends a thorough critical *intimacy* with all the niceties and subtleties of its structure.

TO KNOW, BE ACQUAINTED WITH.

To *know* is a general term; to *be acquainted with* is particular (*v. Acquaintance*). We may know things or persons in various ways; we may *know* them by name only; or we may know their internal properties or characters; or we may simply *know* their figure; we may *know* them by report; or we may *know* them by a direct intercourse: one is *acquainted with* either a person or a thing, only in a direct manner, and by an immediate intercourse in one's own person. We *know* a man to be good or bad, virtuous or vicious, by being a witness to his actions;

> Is there no temp'rate region can be *known*,
> Between their frigid and our torrid zone?
> Could we not wake from that lethargick dream,
> But to be restless in a worse extreme.—DENHAM.

We become *acquainted with* a person by frequently being in his company; 'But how shall I express my anguish for my little boy, who became *acquainted with* sorrow as soon as he was capable of reflection.'—MELMOTH (*Letters of Cicero*).

KNOWLEDGE, SCIENCE, LEARNING, ERUDITION.

Knowledge, from *know*, in all probability comes from the Latin *nosco*, and the Greek γινώσκω; *science*, in Latin *scientia*, from *scio*, Greek ἴσημι to know, and שכה to see or perceive; *learning*, from *learn*, signifies the thing *learned; erudition*, in Latin *eruditio*, comes from *erudio* to bring out of a state of rudeness or ignorance.

Knowledge is a general term which simply implies the thing *known: science, learning*, and *erudition*, are modes of *knowledge* qualified by some collateral idea: *science* is a systematick species of *knowledge* which consists of rule and order; *learning* is that species of *knowledge* which one derives from schools, or through the medium of personal instruction; *erudition* is scholastick *knowledge* obtained by profound research: *knowledge* admits of every possible degree, and is expressly opposed to ignorance; *science, learning*, and *erudition*, are positively high degrees of *knowledge*.

The attainment of *knowledge* is, of itself, a pleasure, independent of the many extrinsick advantages which it brings to every individual, according to the station of life in which he is placed; the pursuits of *science* have a peculiar interest for men of a peculiar turn: those who thirst after general *knowledge* may not have a reach of intellect to take the comprehensive survey of nature, which is requisite for a *scientifick* man. *Learning* is less dependent on the genius, than on the will of the individual; men of moderate talents have overcome the deficiencies of nature, by labour and perseverance, and have acquired such stores of *learning* as have raised them to a respectable station in the republick of letters. Profound *erudition* is obtained but by few; a retentive memory, patient industry, and deep penetration, are requisites for one who aspires to the title of an *erudite* man.

Knowledge, in the unqualified and universal sense, is not always a good: Pope says, "A little knowledge is a dangerous thing:" it is certain we may have a *knowledge* of evil as well as good, and as our passions are ever ready to serve us an ill turn, they will call in our imperfect or superficial *knowledge* to their aid;

> Can *knowledge* have no bound, but must advance
> So far, to make us wish for ignorance.—DENHAM.

Science is more exempt from this danger; but the *scientifick* man who forgets to make experience his guide, as many are apt to do in the present day, will wander in the regions of idle speculation, and sink in the quicksands of skepticism;

> O sacred poesy, thou spirit of Roman arts,
> The soul of *science*, and the queen of souls.
> B. JONSON.

Learning is more generally and practically useful to the morals of men than *science;* while it makes us acquainted with the language, the sentiments, and manners of former ages: it serves to purify the sentiments, to enlarge the understanding, and exert the powers; but the pursuit of that *learning* which consists merely in the *knowledge* of words or in the study of editions, is even worse than a useless employment of the time; 'As *learning* advanced, new works were adopted into our language, but I think with little improvement of the art of translation.'—JOHNSON. *Erudition* is always good, it does not merely serve to ennoble the possessor, but it adds to the stock of important *knowledge;* it serves the cause of religion and morality, and elevates the views of men to the grandest objects of inquiry; 'Two of the French clergy with whom I passed my evenings were men of deep *erudition*.'—BURKE.

LETTER, EPISTLE.

According to the origin of these words, *letter*, in Latin *litera*, signifies any document composed of written *letters;* and *epistle*, in Greek ἐπιςολὴ from ἐπιςέλλω to send, signifies a *letter* sent or addressed to any one; consequently the former is the generick, the latter the specifick term. *Letter* is a term altogether familiar, it may be used for whatever is written by one friend to another in domestick life, or for the publick documents of this description, which have emanated from the pen of writers, as the *letters* of Madame de Savigny, the *letters* of Pope or of Swift, and even those which were written by the ancients, as the *letters* of Cicero, Pliny, and Seneca: but in strict propriety these are entitled *epistles*, as a term most adapted to whatever has received the sanction of ages, and by the same rule, likewise, whatever is pecularly solemn in its contents has acquired the same epithet, as the *epistles* of St. Paul, St. Peter, St. John, St. Jude; and by an analogous rule, whatever poetry is written in the *epistolary* form is denominated an *epistle* rather than a *letter*, whether of ancient or modern date, as the *epistles* of Horace, or the *epistles* of Boileau; and finally, whatever is addressed by way of dedication is denominated a dedicatory *epistle*. Ease and a friendly familiarity should characterize the *letter:* sentiment and instruction are always conveyed by an *epistle*.

LETTERS, LITERATURE, LEARNING.

Letters and *literature* signify knowledge, derived through the medium of written *letters* or books, that is, information: *learning* (*v. Knowledge*) is confined to that which is communicated, that is, scholastick knowledge. The term men of *letters*, or the republick of *letters*, comprehends all who devote themselves to the cultivation of their minds; 'To the greater part of mankind the duties of life are inconsistent with much study; and the hours which they would spend upon *letters* must be stolen from their occupations and families.'—JOHNSON. *Literary* societies have for their object the diffusion of general information: *learned* societies propose to themselves the higher object of extending the bounds of science, and increasing the sum of human knowledge. Men of *letters* have a passport for admittance into the higher circles; literary men can always find resources for themselves in their own society: *learned* men, or men of *learning*, are more the objects of respect and admiration than of imitation; 'He that recalls the attention of mankind to any part of *learning* which time has left behind it, may be truly said to advance the *literature* of his own age.'—JOHNSON.

CHARACTER, LETTER.

Character comes from the Greek χαρακτὴρ, signifying an impression or mark, from χαράσσω to imprint or stamp: *letter*, in French *lettre*, Latin *litera*, is probably contracted from *legitera*, signifying what is legible.

Character is to *letter* as the genus to the species: every *letter* is a *character;* but every *character* is not a *letter*. *Character* is any printed mark that serves to designate something; a *letter* is a species of *character* which is the constituted part of a word. Shorthand and hieroglyphicks consist of *characters*, but not of letters.

Character is employed figuratively, but *letter* is not. A grateful person has the favours which are conferred upon him written in indelible *characters* upon his heart; 'A disdainful, a subtle, and a suspicious temper, is displayed in *characters* that are almost universally understood.'—HAWKESWORTH.

SCHOLAR, DISCIPLE, PUPIL.

Scholar and *disciple* are both applied to such as learn from others: but the former is said only of those who learn the rudiments of knowledge; the latter of one who acquires any art or science from the instruction of another; the *scholar* is opposed to the teacher, the *disciple* to the master: children are always *scholars;* adult persons may be *disciples*.

Scholars chiefly employ themselves in the study of words; *disciples*, as the *disciples* of our Saviour, in the study of things: we are the *scholars* of any one under whose care we are placed, or from whom we learn any thing, good or bad; 'The Romans confessed themselves the *scholars* of the Greeks.'—JOHNSON. We are the *disciples* only of distinguished persons or such as communicate either knowledge or opinions, useful or otherwise; 'We are not the *disciples* of Voltaire.'—BURKE. Children are sometimes too apt *scholars* in learning evil from one another.

A *pupil* is a species of *scholar* who is under the immediate and personal superintendance of the person from whom he receives his instruction. The Latin word *pupillus* signifies a fatherless child, or a man child under age and in ward, in which sense it is also sometimes used for the term ward; but in the ordinary acceptation of the term it now comprehends the idea of instruction more than that of wardship and superintendence;

My master sues to her, and she hath taught her suitor,
He being her *pupil*, to become her tutor.
SHAKSPEARE.

SCHOOL, ACADEMY.

The Latin term *schola* signifies a loitering place, a place for desultory conversation or instruction, from the Greek σχολὴ leisure; hence it has been extended to any place where instruction is given, particularly that which is communicated to youth, which being an easy task to one who is familiar with this subject is considered as a relaxation rather than a labour; *academy* derives its name from the Greek ἀκαδημία the name of a publick place in Athens, where the philosopher Plato first gave his lectures, which afterward became a place of resort for learned men; hence societies of learned men have since been termed *academics*.

The leading idea in the word *school* is that of instruction given and doctrine received: in the word *academy* is that of association among those who have already learned: hence we speak in the literal sense of the *school* where young persons meet to be taught, or in the extended and moral sense of the old and new *school*, the Pythagorean *school*, the philosophical *school*, and the like; 'The world is a great *school* where deceit, in all its forms, is one of the lessons that is first learned.'—BLAIR. But the *academy* of arts or sciences, the French *academy*, being members of any *academy*, and the like; As for other *academies* such as those for painting, sculpture, or architecture, we have not so much as heard the proposal.'—SHAFTESBURY.

EDUCATION, INSTRUCTION, BREEDING.

Instruction and *breeding* are to *education* as parts to a whole; *instruction* respects the communication of knowledge, and *breeding* the manners or outward conduct; but *education* comprehends not only both these but the formation of the mind, the regulation of the heart and the establishment of the principles: good *instruction* makes one wiser; good breeding makes one more polished and agreeable; good *education* makes one really good. A want of *education* will always be to the injury if not to the ruin of the sufferer: a want of *instruction* is of more or less inconvenience, according to circumstances: a want of *breeding* only unfits a man for the society of the cultivated. *Education* belongs to the period of childhood and youth; 'A mother tells her infant that two and two make four, the child remembers the proposition, and is able to count four for all the purposes of life, till the course of his *education* brings him among philosophers, who fright him from his former knowledge, by telling him that four is a certain aggregate of units.' —JOHNSON. *Instruction* may be given at different ages: 'To illustrate one thing by its resemblance to another, has been always the most popular and efficacious art of *instruction*.'—JOHNSON. *Good breeding* is best learned in the early part of life; 'My *breeding* abroad hath shown me more of the world than yours has done.'—WENTWORTH.

IGNORANT, ILLITERATE, UNLEARNED, UNLETTERED.

Ignorant, in Latin *ignorans*, from the privative *ig* or *in* and *noro*, or the Greek γινώσκω, signifies no knowing things in general, or not knowing any particular circumstance; *unlearned*, *illiterate*, and *unlettered*, are compared with *ignorant* in the general sense

Ignorant is a comprehensive term; it includes want of knowledge to any degree from the highest to the lowest, and consequently includes the other terms, *illiterate*, *unlearned*, and *unlettered*, which express different forms of *ignorance;*

He said, and sent Cyllenius with command
To free the ports and ope the Punic land
To Trojan guests; lest, *ignorant* of fate,
The queen might force them from her town and state.
DRYDEN.

Ignorance is not always to one's disgrace, since it is not always one's fault; the term is not therefore directly reproachful: the poor *ignorant* savage is an object of pity, rather than condemnation; but when *ignorance* is coupled with self-conceit and presumption, it is a perfect deformity: hence the word *illiterate*, which is used only in such cases as to become a term of reproach: an *ignorant* man who sets up to teach others, is termed an *illiterate* preacher; and quacks, whether in religion or medicine, from the very nature of their calling, are altogether an *illiterate* race of men. The words *unlearned* and *unlettered* are exempt from such unfavourable associations. A modest man, who makes no pretensions to learning, may suitably apologize for his supposed deficiencies by saying he is an *unlearned* or *unlettered* man; the former is, however, a term of more familiar use than the latter. A man may be described either as generally *unlearned*, or as *unlearned* in particular sciences or arts; as *unlearned* in history; *unlearned* in philosophy; 'Because this doctrine may have appeared to the *unlearned* light and whimsical, I must take leave to unfold the wisdom and antiquity of my first proposition in these my essays, to wit, that "every worthless man is a dead man."'—ADDISON. We say of a person that he is *unlearned* in the ways of the world: and a poet may describe his muse as *unlettered;* 'Ajax, the haughty chief, the *unlettered* soldier, had no way of making his anger known, but by gloomy sullenness.'—JOHNSON.

TO ILLUMINATE, ILLUMINE, ENLIGHTEN.

Illuminate, in Latin, *illuminatus*, participle of *illumino*, and *enlighten*, from the noun *light*, both denote the communication of light; the former in the natural, the latter in the moral sense. We *illuminate* by means of artificial lights; the sun *illuminates* the world by its own *light;*

> Reason our guide, what can she more reply,
> Than that the sun *illuminates* the sky ?—PRIOR.

Preaching and instruction *enlighten* the minds of men; 'But if neither you nor I can gather so much from these places, they will tell us it is because we are not inwardly *enlightened*.'—SOUTH. *Illumine* is but a poetick variation of *illuminate;* as, the Sun of Righteousness *illumined* the benighted world;

> What in me is dark
> *Illumine;* what is low, raise and support.
> MILTON.

Illuminations are employed as publick demonstrations of joy: no nation is now termed *enlightened* but such as have received the light of the Gospel.

CULTIVATION, CULTURE, CIVILIZATION, REFINEMENT.

Cultivation, from the Latin *cultus*, denotes the act of *cultivating*, or state of being *cultivated; culture* signifies the state only of being *cultivated; civilization* signifies the act of *civilizing*, or state of being *civilized; refinement* denotes the act of *refining*, or the state of being *refined.*

Cultivation is with more propriety applied to the thing that grows; *culture* to that in which it grows. The cultivation of flowers will not repay the labour unless the soil be prepared by proper *culture*. In the same manner, when speaking figuratively, we say the *cultivation* of any art or science; the *cultivation* of one's taste or inclination, may be said to contribute to one's own skill, or the perfection of the thing itself; but the mind requires *culture* previously to this particular exertion of the powers; 'Notwithstanding this faculty (of taste) must be in some measure born with us, there are several methods of *cultivating* and improving it.'—ADDISON.

> But tho' Heav'n
> In every breath has sown these early seeds
> Of love and admiration, yet in vain
> Without fair *culture's* kind parental aid.
> AKENSIDE.

Civilization is the first stage of *cultivation; refinement* is the last: we *civilize* savages by divesting them of their rudeness, and giving them a knowledge of such arts as are requisite for *civil* society; we *cultivate* people in general by calling forth their powers into action and independent exertion; we *refine* them by the introduction of the liberal arts.

The introduction of Christianity has been the best means of *civilizing* the rudest nations. The *cultivation* of the mind in serious pursuits tends to *refine* the sentiments without debilitating the character; but the *cultivation* of the liberal arts may be pursued to a vicious extent, so as to introduce an excessive *refinement* of feeling that is incompatible with real manliness;

> To *civilize* the rude unpolish'd world
> And lay it under the restraint of laws,
> To make man mild and sociable to man,
> To *cultivate* the wild licentious savage
> With wisdom, discipline, and lib'ral arts,
> Th' embellishments of life! Virtues like these
> Make human nature shine.—ADDISON.

Poetry makes a principal amusement among unpolished nations, but in a country verging to the extremes of *refinement*, painting and musick come in for a share.' GOLDSMITH.

Cultivation is applied either to persons or things; *civilization* is applied to men collectively, *refinement* to men individually: we may *cultivate* the mind or any of its operations; or we may *cultivate* the ground or any thing that grows upon the ground; we *civilize* nations; we *refine* the mind or the manners.

SUAVITY, URBANITY.

Suavity is literally sweetness; and *urbanity* the refinement of the city, in distinction with the country: inasmuch, therefore, as a polite education tends to soften the mind and the manners, it produces *suavity;* but *suavity may* sometimes arise from natural temper, and exist therefore without *urbanity;* although there cannot be *urbanity* without *suavity*. By the *suavity* of our manners we gain the love of those around us; by the *urbanity* of our manners we render ourselves agreeable companions; 'The virtue called *urbanity* by the moralists, or a courtly behaviour, consists in a desire to please the company.'—POPE. Hence also arises another distinction that the term *suavity* may be applied to other things, as the voice, or the style; 'The *suavity* of Menander's style might be more to Plutarch's taste than the irregular sublimity of Aristophanes.'—CUMBERLAND. *Urbanity* is applied to manners only.

CIVIL, POLITE.

Civil, in French *civile*, Latin *civilis*, from *civis*, citizen, signifies belonging to or becoming a citizen; *polite*, in French *poli*, Latin *politus*, participle of *polio* to polish, signifies literally polished.

These two epithets are employed to denote different modes of acting in social intercourse; *polite* expresses more than *civil;* it is possible to be *civil* without being *polite: politeness* supposes *civility* and something in addition.

Civility is confined to no rank, age, condition, or country; all have an opportunity with equal propriety of being *civil*, but it is not so with *politeness;* this requires a certain degree of equality, at least the equality of education; it would be contradictory for masters and servants, rich and poor, learned and unlearned, to be *polite* to each other. *Civility* is a Christian duty; there are times when every man ought to be *civil* to his neighbour: *politeness* is rather a voluntary devotion of ourselves to others; among the inferiour orders *civility* is indispensable; an *uncivil* person in a subordinate station is an obnoxious member of society;

> He has good nature,
> And I have good manners,
> His sons too are *civil* to me, because
> I do not pretend to be wiser than they.—OTWAY.

Among the higher orders, *politeness* is often a substitute; and where the form and spirit are combined, it supersedes the necessity of *civility: politeness* is the sweetener of human society; it gives a charm to every thing that is said and done; 'The true effect of genuine *politeness* seems to be rather ease than pleasure.'—JOHNSON.

Civility is contented with pleasing when the occasion offers; *politeness* seeks the opportunity to please, it prevents the necessity of asking by anticipating the wishes; it is full of delicate attentions, and is an active benevolence in the minor concerns of life.

Civility is anxious not to offend, but it often gives pain from ignorance or errour: *politeness* studies all the circumstances and situations of men; it enters into their characters, suits itself to their humours, and even yields indulgently to their weaknesses; its object is no less to avoid giving pain than to study to afford pleasure.

Civility is dictated by the desire of serving, *politeness* by that of pleasing: *civility* often confines itself to the bare intention of serving; *politeness* looks to the action and its consequences: when a peasant is *civil* he often does the reverse of what would be desired of him; he takes no heed of the wants and necessities of others: *politeness* considers what is due to others and from others; it does nothing superfluously; men of good breeding think before they speak, and move before they act. It is necessary to be *civil* without being troublesome, and *polite* without being affected.

Civility requires nothing but goodness of intention; it may be associated with the coarsest manners, the grossest ignorance, and the total want of all culture: *politeness* requires peculiar properties of the head and the heart, natural and artificial; much goodness and gentleness of character, an even current of feeling, quickness and refined delicacy of sentiment, a command of temper, a general insight into men and manners, and a thorough acquaintance with the forms of society.

Civility is not incompatible with the harshest expressions of one's feelings; it allows the utterance of all a man thinks without regard to person, time, or season; it lays no restraint upon the angry passions: *politeness* enjoins upon us to say nothing to another which we would not wish to be said to ourselves: it lays at least a temporary constraint on all the angry passions, and prevents all turbulent commotions.

Civility is always the same; whatever is once *civil*

is always so, and acknowledged as such by all persons; hence the term *civil* may be applied figuratively in the same sense;

> I heard a mermaid on a dolphin's back,
> Uttering such dulcet and harmonious sounds,
> That the rude sea grew *civil* at her song.
> SHAKSPEARE.

Politeness varies with the fashions and times; what is *polite* in one age or in one country may be *unpolite* in another; 'A *polite* country squire shall make you as many bows in half an hour as would serve a courtier for a week.'—ADDISON.

If *civility* be not a splendid virtue, it has at least the recommendation of being genuine and harmless, having nothing artificial in it: it admits of no gloss, and will never deceive; it is the true expression of good will, the companion of respect in inferiours, of condescension in superiours, of humanity and kindness in equals: *politeness* springs from education, is the offspring of refinement, and consists much in the exteriour: it often rests contented with the bare imitation of virtue, and is distinguished into true and false; in the latter case [illegible] may be abused for the worst of purposes, and serve [illegible] mask to conceal malignant passions under t[illegible] ance of kindness; hence it is possible to [illegible]n form without being *civil*, or any thing else [illegible]od.

CIVIL, OBLIGING, COMPLAISANT.

Civil (*v. Civil, polite*); *obliging*, from *oblige*, signifies either doing what *obliges*, or ready to *oblige*; *complaisant*, in French *complaisant*, comes from *complaire* to please, signifying ready to please.

Civil is more general than *obliging*: one is always *civil* when one is *obliging*, but one is not always *obliging* when one is *civil*: *complaisance* is more than either, it refines upon both; it is a branch of *politeness* (*v. Civil, polite*).

Civil regards the manner as well as the action, *obliging* respects the action, *complaisant* includes all the circumstances of the action: to be *civil* is to please by any word or action; 'Pride is never more offensive than when it condescends to be *civil*.'—CUMBERLAND. To be *obliging* is to perform some actual service;

> The shepherd home
> Hies merry-hearted, and by turns relieves
> The ruddy milkmaid of her brimming pail,
> The beauty whom perhaps his witless heart
> Sincerely loves, by that best language shown
> Of cordial glances, and *obliging* deeds.
> THOMSON.

To be *complaisant* is to do a service in the time and manner that is most suitable and agreeable; 'I seem'd so pleased with what every one said, and smiled with so much *complaisance* at all their pretty fancies, that though I did not put one word into their discourse, I have the vanity to think they looked upon me as very agreeable company.'—ADDISON. *Civility* requires no effort; to be *obliging* always costs the agent some trouble; *complaisance* requires attention and observation; a person is *civil* in his reply, *obliging* in lending assistance, *complaisant* in his attentions to his friends.

One is habitually *civil*; *obliging* from disposition; *complaisant* from education and disposition: it is necessary to be *civil* without being free, to be *obliging* without being *officious*, to be *complaisant* without being servile.

COURTEOUS, COMPLAISANT, COURTLY.

Courteous, from *court*, denotes properly belonging to a *court*, and by a natural extension of the sense, suitable to a *court*; *complaisant* (*v. Complaisance*).

Courteous in one respect comprehends in it more than *complaisant*; it includes the manner as well as the action; it is, properly speaking, polished *complaisance*: on the other hand, *complaisance* includes more of the disposition in it than *courteousness*; it has less of the polish, but more of the reality of kindness.

Courteousness displays itself in the address and the manners;

> And then I stole all *courtesy* from Heav'n,
> And dress'd myself in such humility,
> That I did pluck allegiance from men's hearts.
> SHAKSPEARE

Complaisance displays itself in direct good offices, particularly in complying with the wishes of others; 'To comply with the notions of mankind is in some degree the duty of a social being; because by compliance only he can please, and by pleasing only he can become useful; but as the end is not to be lost for the sake of the means, we are not to give up virtue for *complaisance*.'—JOHNSON. *Courteousness* is most suitable for strangers; *complaisance* for friends or the nearest relatives: among well-bred men, and men of rank, it is an invariable rule to address each other *courteously* on all occasions whenever they meet, whether acquainted or otherwise; there is a degree of *complaisance* due between husbands and wives, brothers and sisters, and members of the same family, which cannot be neglected without endangering the harmony of their intercourse.

Courtly, though derived from the same word as *courteous*, is in some degree opposed to it in point of sense; it denotes a likeness to a *court*, but not a likeness which is favourable; *courtly* is to *courteous* as the form to the reality; the *courtly* consists of the exteriour only, the latter of the exteriour combined with the spirit; the former therefore seems to convey the idea of insincerity when contrasted with the latter, which must necessarily suppose the contrary: a *courtly* demeanour, or a *courtier-like* demeanour may be suitable on certain occasions; but a *courteous* demeanour is always desirable;

> In our own time (excuse some *courtly* strains)
> No whiter page than Addison's remains.—POPE.

Courtly may likewise be employed in relation to things; but *courteous* has always respect to persons: we may speak of a *courtly* style, or *courtly* grandeur; but we always speak of *courteous* behaviour, *courteous* language, and the like.

> Yes, I know
> He had a troublesome old-fashion'd way
> Of shocking *courtly* ears with horrid truth.
> THOMSON

POLITE, POLISHED, REFINED, GENTEEL

Polite (*v. Civil*) denotes a quality; *polished*, a state: he who is *polite* is so according to the rules of *politeness*; he who is *polished* is *polished* by the force of art: a *polite* man is, in regard to his behaviour, a finished gentleman. A rude person may be more or less *polished*, or freed from rudeness; 'In rude nations the dependence of children on their parents is of shorter continuance than in *polished* societies.'—ROBERTSON. *Refined* rises in sense, both in regard to *polite* and *polished*: a man is indebted to nature, rather than to art, for his *refinement*; but his *politeness*, or his *polish*, are entirely the fruit of education. *Politeness* and *polish* do not extend to any thing but externals; *refinement* applies as much to the mind as the body: rules of conduct, and good society, will make a man *polite*; 'A pedant among men of learning and sense is like an ignorant servant giving an account of *polite* conversation.'—STEELE. Lessons in dancing will serve to give a *polish*; *refined* manners or principles will naturally arise out of *refinement* of mind and temper; 'What is honour but the height and flower of morality, and the utmost *refinement* of conversation?'—SOUTH.

As *polish* extends only to the exteriour, it is less liable to excess than *refinement*: when the language, the walk, and deportment of a man is *polished*, he is divested of all that can make him offensive in social intercourse; but if the temper of a man be *refined* beyond a certain boundary, he loses the nerve of character which is essential for maintaining his dignity against the rude shocks of human life.

Genteel, in French *gentil*, Latin *gentilis*, signified literally one belonging to the same gens or family, the next akin to whom the estate would fall, if there were no children; hence by an extended application it denoted to be of a good family, and the term *gentility* now respects rank in life; in distinction from *politeness*, which respects the refinement of the mind and outward behaviour, a *genteel* education is suited to the station of a gentleman; 'A lady of genius will give a *genteel* air to her whole dress by a well-fancied suit of knots, as a judicious writer gives a spirit to a whole sentence by a single expression.'—GAY. A *polite* education fits for polished society and conversation, and raises the individual among his equals;

> In this isle remote,
> Our painted ancestors were slow to learn,
> To arms devote, in the *politer* arts,
> Nor skilled, nor studious.—Somerville.

There may be *gentility* without *politeness;* and *vice versâ.* A person may have *genteel* manners, a *genteel* carriage, a *genteel* mode of living as far as respects his general relation with society; but a *polite* behaviour and a *polite* address, which qualify him for every relation in society, and enable him to shine in connexion with all orders of men, is independent of either birth or wealth; it is in part a gift of nature, although it is to be acquired by art.

A person's equipage, servants, house, and furniture, may be such as to entitle a man to the name of *genteel*, although he is wanting in all the forms of real good-breeding. Fortune may sometimes frown upon the polished gentleman, whose *politeness* is a recommendation to him wherever he goes.

AFFABLE, COURTEOUS.

Affable, in French *affable*, Latin *affabilis*, from *af* or *ad*, and *for* to speak, signifies a readiness to speak to any one; *courteous*, in French *courtois*, from the word court, signifies after the refined manner of a court.

We are *affable* by a mild and easy address towards all, without distinction of rank, who have occasion to speak to us; we are *courteous* by a refined and engaging air to our equals or superiours who address themselves to us.

The *affable* man invites to inquiry, and is ready to gratify curiosity; 'It is impossible for a publick minister to be so open and easy to all his old friends as he was in his private condition; but this may be helped out by an *affability* of address.'—L'Estrange. The *courteous* man encourages to a communication of our wants, and discovers in his manners a willingness to relieve them;

> Whereat the Elfin knight with speeches gent
> Him first saluted, who, well as he might,
> Him fair salutes again, as seemeth *courteous* knight.
> West.

Affability results from good nature, and *courteousness* from fine feeling; it is necessary to be *affable* without familiarity, and *courteous* without officiousness.

COMPLAISANCE, DEFERENCE, CONDESCENSION.

Complaisance, from *com* and *plaire* to please, signifies the act of complying with, or pleasing others; *deference*, in French *déference*, from the Latin *defero* to bear down, marks the inclination to defer, or acquiesce in the sentiments of another in preference to one's own; *condescension* marks the act of *condescending* from one's own height to yield to the satisfaction of others, rather than rigourously to exact one's rights.

The necessities, the conveniences, the accommodations and allurements of society, of familiarity, and of intimacy, lead to *complaisance;* it makes sacrifices to the wishes, tastes, comforts, enjoyments, and personal feelings of others; '*Complaisance* renders a superiour amiable, an equal agreeable, and an inferiour acceptable.'—Addison. Age, rank, dignity, and personal merit, call for *deference:* it enjoins compliance with respect to our opinions, judgements, pretensions, and designs; 'Tom Courtly never fails of paying his obeisance to every man he sees, who has title or office to make him conspicuous; but his *deference* is wholly given to outward consideration.'—Steele. The infirmities, the wants, the defects and foibles of others, call for *condescension:* it relaxes the rigour of authority, and removes the distinction of rank or station; 'The same noble *condescension* which never dwells but in truly great minds, and such as Homer would represent that of Ulysses to have been, discovers itself likewise in the speech which he made to the ghost of Ajax.'—Addison.

Complaisance is properly the act of an equal; *deference* that of an inferiour; *condescension* that of a superiour. *Complaisance* is due from one well-bred person to another; *deference* is due to all superiours in age, knowledge, or station, whom one approaches; *condescension* is due from all superiours to such as are dependent on them for comfort and enjoyment.

All these qualities spring from a refinement of humanity; but *complaisance* has most of genuine kindness in its nature; *deference* most of respectful submission; *condescension* most of easy indulgence. *Complaisance* has unalloyed pleasure for its companion; it is pleased with doing: it is pleased with seeing that it has pleased; it is pleasure to the giver and pleasure to the receiver. *Deference* is not unmixed with pain; it fears to offend, or to fail in the part it has to perform; it is mingled with a consciousness of inferiority, and a fear of appearing lower than it deserves to be thought. *Condescension* is not without its alloy; it is accompanied with the painful sentiment of witnessing inferiority, and the no less painful apprehension of not maintaining its own dignity.

Complaisance is busied in anticipating and meeting the wishes of others; it seeks to amalgamate one's own will with that of another: *deference* is busied in yielding submission, doing homage, and marking one's sense of another's superiority: *condescension* employs itself in not opposing the will of others; in yielding to their gratification, and laying aside unnecessary distinction of superiority. *Complaisance* among strangers is often the forerunner of the most friendly intercourse: it is the characteristick of self-conceit to pay *deference* to no one, because it considers no one as having superiour worth: it is the common characteristick of ignorant and low persons when placed in a state of elevation, to think themselves degraded by any act of *condescension.*

IMPERTINENT, RUDE, SAUCY, IMPUDENT, INSOLENT.

Impertinent, in Latin *in* and *pertinens* not belonging to one, signifies being or wanting to do what it does not belong to one to be or do; *rude*, in Latin *rudis* rude, and *raudus* a ragged stone, in the Greek ῥάβδος a rough stick, signifies literally unpolished; and in an extended sense, wanting all culture; *saucy* comes from sauce, and the Latin *salsus*, signifying literally salt; and in an extended sense, stinging like salt; *impudent* (*v. Assurance*); *insolent*, from the Latin *in* and *solens*, contrary to custom, signifies being or wanting to be contrary to custom.

Impertinent is allied to *rude*, as respects one's general relations in society, without regard to station; it is allied to *saucy*, *impudent*, and *insolent*, as respects the conduct of inferiours.

He who does not respect the laws of civil society in his intercourse with individuals, and wants to assume to himself what belongs to another, is *impertinent:* if he carry this *impertinence* so far as to commit any violent breach of decorum in his behaviour, he is *rude.* *Impertinence* seems to spring from a too high regard of one's self: *rudeness* from an ignorance of what is due to others. An *impertinent* man will ask questions for the mere gratification of curiosity; a *rude man* will stare in one's face in order to please himself. An *impertinent* man will take possession of the best seat without regard to the right or convenience of another: a *rude* man will burst into the room of another, or push against his person, in violation of all ceremony.

Impertinent, in comparison with the other terms, *saucy*, *impudent*, and *insolent*, is the most general and indefinite: whatever one does or says that is not compatible with our station is *impertinent; saucy* is a sharp kind of *impertinence; impudent* an unblushing kind of *impertinence; insolence* is an outrageous kind of *impertinence*, it runs counter to all established order: thus, the terms seem to rise in sense. A person may be *impertinent* in words or actions: he is *saucy* in words or looks: he is *impudent* or *insolent* in words, tones, gesture, looks, and every species of action. A person's *impertinence* discovers itself in not giving the respect which is due to his superiours in general, strangers, or otherwise; as when a common person sits down in the presence of a man of rank: *sauciness* discovers itself towards particular individuals, in certain relations; as in the case of servants who are *saucy* to their masters, or children who are *saucy* to their teachers: *impudence* and *insolence* are the strongest degrees of *impertinence;* but the former is more particularly said of such things as reflect disgrace upon the offender, and spring from a low depravity of mind, such as the abuse of one's superiours, and a vulgar defiance of those to whom one owes obedience and respect: *insolence*, on the contrary, originates from a haughtiness of spirit, and a misplaced pride, which breaks out into a contemptuous disregard of the station of those by whom one is offended; as in the case of a servant who should offer to strike his master, or of a criminal who sets a magistrate at defiance; 'It is publickly whispered as a piece of *impertinent* pride in me, that I have hitherto been *saucily* civil to every body, as if I thought nobody good enough to quarrel with.'—Lady M. W. Montagu.

My house should no such *rude* disorders know,
As from high drinking consequently flow.
Pomfret.

Whether he knew the thing or no,
His tongue externally would go;
For he had *impudence* at will.—Gay.

He claims the bull with lawless *insolence*,
And having seiz'd his horns, accosts the prince.
Dryden.

Self-conceit is the grand source of *impertinence*, it makes persons forget themselves; the young thereby forget their youth; the servant forgets his relationship to his master; the poor and ignorant man forgets the distance between himself and those who are elevated by education, rank, power, or wealth: *impertinent* persons, therefore, act towards their equals as if they were inferiours, and towards their superiours as if they were their equals: an angry pride that is offended with reproof commonly provokes *sauciness:* an insensibility to shame, or an unconsciousness of what is honourable either in one's self or others, gives birth to *impudence:* uncontrolled passions, and bloated pride, are the ordinary stimulants to *insolence*.

ABRUPT, RUGGED, ROUGH.

Abrupt, in Latin *abruptus*, participle of *abrumpo*, to break off, signifies the state of being broken off; *rugged*, in Saxon *hrugge*, comes from the Latin *rugosus* full of wrinkles; *rough* is in Saxon *reoh*, high German *rauh*, low German *rug*, Dutch *ruig*, in Latin *rudis* uneven.

These words mark different degrees of unevenness. What is *abrupt* has greater cavities and protuberances than what is *rugged;* what is *rugged* has greater irregularities than what is *rough*. In the natural sense *abrupt* is opposed to what is unbroken, *rugged* to what is even, and *rough* to what is smooth. A precipice is *abrupt*, a path is *rugged*, a plank is *rough;*

The precipice *abrupt*,
Projecting horrour on the blackened flood,
Softens at thy return.—Thomson's Summer.

'The evils of this life appear like rocks and precipices, *rugged* and barren at a distance; but at our nearer approach we find them little fruitful spots.'—Spectator.

Not the *rough* whirlwind, that deforms
Adria's black gulf, and vexes it with storms,
The stubborn virtue of his soul can move.
Francis.

The *abruptness* of a body is generally occasioned by a violent concussion and separation of its parts; *ruggedness* arises from natural, but less violent causes; *roughness* is mostly a natural property, although sometimes produced by friction.

In the figurative sense the distinction is equally clear. Words and manners are *abrupt* when they are sudden and unconnected; the temper is *rugged* which is exposed to frequent ebullitions of angry humour; actions are *rough* when performed with violence and incaution.

An *abrupt* behaviour is the consequence of an agitated mind;

My lady craves
To know the cause of your *abrupt* departure.
Shakspeare.

A *rugged* disposition is inherent in the character; The greatest favours to such a one neither soften nor win upon him; neither melt nor endear him, but leave him as hard, *rugged*, and unconcerned as ever.'—South. A *rough* deportment arises from an undisciplined state of feeling; 'Kind words prevent a good deal of that perverseness, which *rough* and imperious usage often produces in generous minds.'—Locke.

An habitual steadiness and coolness of reflection is best fitted to prevent or correct any *abruptness* of manners; a cultivation of the Christian temper cannot fail of smoothing down all *ruggedness* of humour; an intercourse with polished society will inevitably refine down all *roughness* of behaviour.

COARSE, ROUGH, RUDE.

Coarse, probably from the Gothick *kaurids* heavy, answering to our word *gross*, and the Latin *gravis;* *rough*, in Saxon *hruh*, German *rauh*, *roh*, &c. is probably a variation of *rude* (*v. Impertinent*).

These epithets are equally applied to what is not polished by art. In the proper sense *coarse* refers to the composition and materials of bodies, as *coarse* bread, *coarse* meat, *coarse* cloth; *rough* respects the surface of bodies, as *rough* wood and *rough* skin; *rude* respects the make or fashion of things, as a *rude* bark, a *rude* utensil. *Coarse* is opposed to fine, *rough* to smooth, *rude* to polished.

In the figurative application they are distinguished in a similar manner: *coarse* language is used by persons of naturally *coarse* feeling; 'The fineness and delicacy of perception which the man of taste requires, may be more liable to irritation than the *coarser* feelings of minds less cultivated.'—Craig. *Rough* language is used by those whose tempers are either naturally or occasionally *rough;*

This is some fellow,
Who, having been prais'd for bluntness, doth affect
A saucy *roughness*.—Shakspeare.

Rude language is used by those who are ignorant of any better; 'Is it in destroying and pulling down that skill is displayed? the shallowest understanding, the *rudest* hand, is more than equal to that task.'—Burke.

GROSS, COARSE.

Gross derives its meaning in this application from the Latin *crassus* thick from fat, or that which is of common materials; *coarse* (*v. Coarse.*)

These terms are synonymous in the moral application. *Grossness* of habit is opposed to delicacy, *coarseness* to softness and refinement. A person becomes *gross* by an unrestrained indulgence of his sensual appetites; particularly in eating and drinking; he is *coarse* from the want of polish either as to his mind or manners. A *gross* sensualist approximates very nearly to the brute; he sets aside all moral considerations; he indulges himself in the open face of day in defiance of all decency: a *coarse* person approaches nearest to the savage, whose roughness of humour and inclination have not been refined down by habits of restraining his own will, and complying with the will of another. A *gross* expression conveys the idea of that which should be kept from the view of the mind, which shocks the moral feeling, a *coarse* expression conveys the idea of an unseemly sentiment in the mind of the speaker. The representation of the Deity by any sensible image is *gross*, because it gives us a low and grovelling idea of the Supreme; the doing a kindness, and making the receiver at the same time sensible of your superiority and his dependence, indicates great *coarseness* in the character of the person granting the favour; 'A certain preparation is requisite for the enjoyment of devotion in its whole extent; not only must the life be reformed from *gross* enormities, but the heart must have undergone that change which the Gospel demands.'—Blair. 'The refined pleasures of a pious mind are, in many respects, superiour to the *coarse* gratifications of sense.'—Blair.

TO AMEND, CORRECT, REFORM, RECTIFY, EMEND, IMPROVE, MEND, BETTER.

Amend, in Latin *emendo*, from *menda* a fault in transcribing, signifies to remove this fault; *correct*, in Latin *correctus*, participle of *corrigo*, compounded of *con* and *rego*, signifies to set in order, to set to rights; *reform*, compounded of *re* and *form*, signifies to reform afresh, or put into a new form; *rectify*, in Latin *rectifico*, compounded of *rectus* and *facio*, signifies to make or put right; *emend* is the immediate derivative of the Latin *emendo; improve* comes from the Latin *in* and *probo* to prove or try, signifying to make any thing good, or better than it was, by trials or after experiments; *mend* is a contraction of *emend; better* is properly to make *better*.

To *amend*, *correct*, *rectify*, and *emend*, imply the lessening of evil; to *improve*, *reform*, and *better*, the increase of good. We *amend* the moral conduct, *correct* errors, *reform* the life, *rectify* mistakes, *emend* the readings of an author, *improve* the mind, *mend* or *better* the condition. What is *amended* is mostly that which is wrong in ourselves: what is *reformed* or *corrected* is that which is faulty in ourselves or in others; what is *rectified* is mostly wrong in that which has been done; that which is *improved* may relate either to an individual or to indifferent objects.

To *mend* and *better* are common terms, employed only on familiar occasions, corresponding to the terms *amend* and *improve*. Whatever is wrong must be *amended;* whatever is faulty must be *corrected;* whatever is altogether insufficient for the purpose must be *reformed;* whatever errour escapes by an oversight must be *rectified;* whatever is obscure or incorrect must be *amended*.

What has been torn may be *mended;*

> The wise for cure on exercise depend,
> God never made his work for man to *mend*.
> DRYDEN.

What admits of change may be *improved* or *bettered;* 'I then *bettered* my condition a little, and lived a whole summer in the shape of a bee.'—ADDISON. When a person's conduct is any way culpable, it ought to be *amended;* 'The interest which the corrupt part of mankind have in hardening themselves against every motive to *amendment*, has disposed them to give to contradictions, when they can be produced against the cause of virtue, that weight which they will not allow them in any other case.'—JOHNSON. When a person's habits and principles are vicious, his character ought to be *reformed;* 'Indolence is one of the vices from which those whom it once infects are seldom *reformed*.'—JOHNSON. When a man has any particular faulty habit, it ought to be *corrected;* 'Presumption will be easily *corrected;* but timidity is a disease of the mind more obstinate and fatal.'—JOHNSON. When we commit mistakes we should not object to have them *rectified;* 'That sorrow which dictates no caution, that fear which does not quicken our escape, that austerity which fails to *rectify* our affections, are vain and unavailing.'—JOHNSON. 'Some had read the manuscript, and *rectified* its inaccuracies.'—JOHNSON. The *emendations* of criticks frequently involve an author in still greater obscurity; 'That useful part of learning which consists in *emendations*, knowledge of different readings, and the like, is what in all ages persons extremely wise and learned have had in great veneration.'—ADDISON. Whoever wishes to advance himself in life must endeavour to *improve* his time and talents. 'While a man, infatuated with the promises of greatness, wastes his hours and days in attendance and solicitation, the honest opportunities of *improving* his condition pass by without his notice.'—ADDISON.

The first step to *amendment* is a consciousness of errour in ourselves: busy politicians are ever ready to propose a *reform* in the constitution of their country, but they forget the *reformation* which is requisite in themselves: the *correction* of the temper is of the first moment, in order to live in harmony with others: in order to avoid the necessity of *rectifying* what has been done amiss, we must strive to do every thing with care: criticks *emend* the productions of the pen, and ingenious artists *improve* the inventions of art.

Correct respects ourselves or others; *rectify* has regard to one's self only; *correct* is either an act of authority or discretion; *rectify* is an act of discretion only. What is *corrected* may vary in its magnitude or importance, and consequently may require more or less trouble; what is *rectified* is always of a nature to be altered without great injury or effort. Habitual or individual faults are *corrected;* 'Desire is *corrected* when there is a tenderness or admiration expressed which partakes of the passion. Licentious language has something brutal in it which disgraces humanity.'—STEELE. Individual mistakes are *rectified;* 'A man has frequent opportunities of mitigating the fierceness of a party; of softening the envious, quieting the angry, and *rectifying* the prejudiced.'—ADDISON. A person *corrects* himself or another of a bad habit in speaking or pronouncing; he *rectifies* any errour in his accounts. Mistakes in writing must be *corrected* for the advantage of the scholar; mistakes in pecuniary transactions cannot be too soon *rectified* for the satisfaction of all parties.

Reform like *rectify* is used only for one's self when it respects personal actions: but *reform* and *correct* are likewise employed for matters of general interest. *Correct* in neither case amounts to the same as *reform*. A person *corrects* himself of particular habits; he *reforms* his whole life; what is *corrected* undergoes a change, more or less slight; what is *reformed* assumes a new form and becomes a new thing. *Correction* is always advisable: it is the removal of an evil; *reform* is equally so as it respects a man's own conduct; but as it respects publick matters, it is altogether of a questionable nature; a man cannot begin too soon to *reform* himself, nor too late to attempt *reforming* the constitution of society. The abuses of government may always be advantageously *corrected* by the judicious hand of a wise minister; *reforms* in a state are always attended with a certain evil, and promise but an uncertain good; they are never recommended but by the young, the thoughtless, the busy, or the interested. The *reformation* of laws is the peculiar province of the prince;

> Edward and Henry, now the boast of fame,
> And virtuous Alfred, a more sacred name,
> After a life of generous toils endur'd,
> The Gauls subdu'd, or property secur'd,
> Ambition humbled, mighty cities storm'd,
> Or laws establish'd, and the world *reformed*.
> POPE.

CORRECT, ACCURATE.

Correct is equivalent to *corrected* (*v. To Amend*,) or set to rights. *Accurate* (*v. Accurate*) implies properly done with care, or by the application of care. *Correct* is negative in its sense; *accurate* is positive; it is sufficient to be free from fault to be *correct;* it must contain every minute particular to be *accurate*. Information is *correct* which contains nothing but facts; 'Sallust the most elegant and *correct* of all the Latin historians, observes, that in his time when the most formidable states of the world were subdued by the Romans, the republick sunk into those two opposite vices of a quite different nature, luxury and avarice.'—ADDISON. Information is *accurate* when it contains a vast number of details; 'Those ancients who were the most *accurate* in their remarks on the genius and temper of mankind, have with great exactness allotted inclinations and objects of desire to every stage of life.'—STEELE.

What is *incorrect* is allied to falsehood; what is *inaccurate* is general and indefinite.

According to the dialect of modern times, in which gross vices are varnished over with smooth names, a liar is said to speak *incorrectly;* this is however not only an *inaccurate* but an *incorrect* mode of speech, for a lie is a direct violation of truth, and the *incorrect* is only a deviation from it to greater or less extent

JUSTNESS, CORRECTNESS.

Justness, from *jus* law (*v. Justice*), is the conformity to established principle: *correctness*, from *rectus* right or straight (*v. Correct*), is the conformity to a certain mark or line: the former is used in the moral or improper sense only; the latter is used either in the proper or improper sense. We estimate the value of remarks by their *justness*, that is, their accordance to certain admitted principles; 'Few men, possessed of the most perfect sight, can describe visual objects with more spirit and *justness* than Mr. Blacklock the poet, born blind.'—BURKE. *Correctness* of outline is of the first importance in drawing; *correctness* of dates enhances the value of a history; 'I do not mean the popular eloquence which cannot be tolerated at the bar, but that *correctness* of style and elegance of method which at once pleases and persuades the hearer.'—SIR WM. JONES It has been *justly* observed by the moralists of antiquity, that money is the root of all evil; partisans seldom state *correctly* what they see and hear.

ACCURATE, EXACT, PRECISE.

Accurate, in French *accurate*, Latin *accuratus*, participle of *accuro*, compounded of the intensive *ac* or *ad*, and *curo*, to take care of, signifies done with great care; *exact*, in French *exacte*, Latin *exactus*, participle of *exigo*, to finish or complete, denotes the quality of completeness, the absence of defect; *precise*, in French *précis*, Latin *præcisus*, participle of *præcido*, to cut by rule, signifies the quality of doing by rule.

A man is *accurate* when he avoids faults; *exact*, when he attends to every minutia, and leaves nothing undone; *precise*, when he does it according to a certain measure. These epithets, therefore, bear a comparative relation to each other; *exact* expresses more than *accurate*, and *precise* more than *exact*. An account is *accurate* in which there is no misrepresentation; it is *exact* when nothing essential is omitted; it is *precise* when it contains particular details of time, place, and circumstance.

Accuracy is indispensable in all our concerns, be they ever so ordinary; 'An eminent artist who wrought up his pictures with the greatest *accuracy*, and gave them all those delicate touches which are apt to please the nicest eye, is represented as tuning a theorbo.'—ADDISON. *Exactness* is of peculiar importance in matters of economy and taste; 'This lady is the most *exact* economist, without appearing busy.'—CONGREVE. In some cases, where great results flow from trifling causes, the greatest *precision* becomes requisite: we may, however, be too *precise* when we dwell on unimportant particulars; but we never can be too *accurate* or *exact*. Hence the epithet *precise* is sometimes taken in the unfavourable sense for affectedly exact; 'An apparent desire of admiration, a reflection upon their own merit, and a *precise* behaviour in their general conduct, are almost inseparable accidents in beauties.'—HUGHES. An *accurate* man will save himself much trouble; an *exact* man will gain himself much credit; and a *precise* man will take much pains only to render himself ridiculous. Young people should strive to do every thing *accurately*, which they think worth doing at all, and thus they will learn to be *exact* or *precise*, as occasion may require.

Accuracy, moreover, concerns our mechanical labours, and the operations of our senses and understandings; 'An aptness to jumble things together, wherein can be found any likeness, hinders the mind from *accurate* conceptions of them.'—LOCKE. *Exactness* respects our dealings with others, or our views of things; 'Angels and spirits, in their several degrees of elevation above us, may be endowed with more comprehensive faculties; and some of them, perhaps, have perfect and *exact* views of all finite beings that come under their consideration.'—LOCKE. *Precision* is applied to our habits and manners in society, or to our representations of things; 'A definition is the only way whereby the *precise* meaning of moral words can be known.'—LOCKE. We write, we see, we think, we judge *accurately*; we are *exact* in our payments; we are *precise* in our modes of dress. Some men are very *accurate* in their particular line of business, who are not very *exact* in fulfilling their engagements, nor very *precise* in the hours which they keep.

EXACT, NICE, PARTICULAR, PUNCTUAL.

Exact (*v. Accurate*); *nice*, in Saxon *nise*, comes in all probability from the German *geniessen*, &c. to enjoy, signifying a quick and discriminating taste; *particular* signifies here directed to a *particular* point; *punctual*, from the Latin *punctum* a point, signifies keeping to a point.

Exact and *nice* are to be compared in their application, either to persons or things; *particular* and *punctual* only in application to persons. To be *exact*, is to arrive at perfection; to be *nice*, is to be free from faults; to be *particular*, is to be *nice* in certain *particulars*; to be *punctual*, is to be *exact* in certain points. We are *exact* in our conduct or in what we do; *nice* and *particular* in our mode of doing it; *punctual* as to the time and season for doing it. It is necessary to be *exact* in our accounts; to be *nice* as an artist in the choice and distribution of colours; to be *particular* as a man of business, in the number and the details of merchandises that are to be delivered out; to be *punctual* in observing the hour or the day that has been fixed upon for keeping appointments.

Exactness and *punctuality* are always taken in a good sense; they designate an attention to that which cannot be dispensed with; they form a part of one's duty; *niceness* and *particularity* are not always taken in the best sense; they designate an excessive attention to things of inferiour importance; to matters of taste and choice. Early habits of method and regularity will make a man very *exact* in the performance of all his duties, and *particularly punctual* in his payments; 'What if you and I inquire how money matters stand between us? With all my heart, I love *exact* dealing; and let Hocus audit.'—ARBUTHNOT. 'The trading part of mankind suffer by the want of *punctuality* in the dealings of persons above them.'—STEELE. An over *niceness* in the observance of mechanical rules often supplies the want of genius; or a *niceness* in regard to one's diet is the mark of an epicure;

> Nor be so *nice* in taste myself to know,
> If what I swallow, be a thrush or no.—DRYDEN
>
> Thus criticks, of less judgement than caprice
> Curious, not knowing, not *exact*, but *nice*.—POPE.

It is the mark of a contracted mind to amuse itself with *particularities* about the dress, the person, the furniture, and the like. On the other hand, it is desirable for a person to be *particular* in the account he is called upon to give of any transaction: 'I have been the more *particular* in this inquiry, because I hear there is scarce a village in England that has not a Moll White in it.'—ADDISON.

When *exact* and *nice* are applied to things, the former expresses more than the latter; we speak of an *exact* resemblance, and a *nice* distinction. The *exact* point is that which we wish to reach; 'We know not so much as the true names of either Homer or Virgil, with any *exactness*.'—WALSH. The *nice* point is that which it is difficult to keep; 'Every age a man passes through, and way of life he engages in, has some particular vice or imperfection naturally cleaving to it, which it will require his *nicest* care to avoid.'—BUDGELL.

REFORM, REFORMATION.

Reform has a general, and *reformation* a particular application: whatever undergoes such a change as to give a new form to an object occasions a *reform*; when such a change is produced in the moral character, it is termed a *reformation*: the concerns of a state require occasional *reform*; which, when administered with discretion, may be of great benefit, otherwise of great injury; 'He was anxious to keep the distemper of France from the least countenance in England, where he was sure some wicked persons had shown a strong disposition to recommend an imitation of the French spirit of *reform*.'—BURKE. The concerns of an individual require *reformation*; 'Examples are pictures, and strike the senses, nay, raise the passions, and call in those (the strongest and most general of all motives) to the aid of *reformation*.'—POPE. When *reform* and *reformation* are applied to the moral character, the former has a more extensive signification than the latter: the term *reform* conveying the idea of a complete amendment; *reformation* implying only the process of amending or improving.

A *reform* in one's life and conversation will always be accompanied with a corresponding increase of happiness to the individual: when we observe any approaches to *reformation*, we may cease to despair of the individual who gives the happy indications.

TO RECLAIM, REFORM.

Reclaim, from *clamo* to call, signifies to call back to its right place that which has gone astray; *reform* signifies the same as in the preceding article.

A man is *reclaimed* from his vicious courses by the force of advice or exhortation; he may be *reformed* by various means, external or internal.

A parent endeavours to *reclaim* a child, but too often in vain; 'Scotland had nothing to dread from a princess of Mary's character, who was wholly occupied in endeavouring to *reclaim* her heretical subjects.'—Ro

BERTSON. A hardened offender is seldom *reformed*, nor is a corrupt state easy to be *reformed;*

A monkey, to *reform* the times,
Resolv'd to visit foreign climes.—GAY.

PROGRESS, PROFICIENCY, IMPROVEMENT.

Progress (*v. Proceeding*) is a generick term, the rest are specifick; *proficiency*, from the Latin *proficio*, compounded of *pro* and *facio*, signifies a profited state, that is to say, a *progress* already made; and *improvement*, from the verb *improved*, signifies an improved condition, that is, *progress* in that which *improves*. The *progress* here, as in the former paragraph, marks the step or motion onward, and the two others the point already reached; but the term *progress* is applied either in the proper or improper sense, that is, either to those travelling forward, or to those going on stepwise in any work; *proficiency* is applied in the proper sense, to the ground gained in an art, and *improvement* to what is gained in science or arts: when idle people set out about any work, it is difficult to perceive that they make any *progress* in it from time to time;

Solon, the sage, his *progress* never ceas'd,
But still his learning with his days increas'd.
DENHAM.

Those who have a thorough taste for either musick or drawing will make a *proficiency* in it which is astonishing to those who are unacquainted with the circumstances; 'When the lad was about nineteen, his uncle desired to see him, that he might know what *proficiency* he had made.'—HAWKESWORTH. The *improvement* of the mind can never be so effectually and easily obtained as in the period of childhood; 'The metrical part of our poetry, in the time of Chaucer, was capable of more *improvement*.'—TYRWHITT.

PROGRESS, PROGRESSION, ADVANCE, ADVANCEMENT.

A forward motion is designated by these terms: but *progress* and *progression* simply imply this sort of motion; *advance* and *advancement* also imply an approximation to some object: we may make a *progress* in that which has no specifick termination, as a *progress* in learning, which may cease only with life; 'I wish it were in my power to give a regular history of the *progress* which our ancestors have made in this species of versification.'—TYRWHITT. The *advance* is only made to some limited point or object in view; as an *advance* in wealth or honour, which may find a termination within the life; 'The most successful students make their *advances* in knowledge by short flights.'—JOHNSON.

Progress and *advance* are said of that which has been passed over; but *progression* and *advancement* may be said of that which one is passing: the *progress* is made, or a person is in *advance;* he is in the act of *progression* or *advancement:* a child makes a *progress* in learning by daily attention; the *progression* from one stage of learning to another is not always perceptible;

And better thence again, and better still,
In infinite *progression*.—THOMSON.

It is not always possible to overtake one who is in *advance;* sometimes a person's *advancement* is retarded by circumstances that are altogether contingent; 'I have lived to see the fierce *advancement*, the sudden turn, and the abrupt period, of three or four enormous friendships.'—POPE. The first step in any destructive course still prepares for the second, and the second for the third, after which there is no stop, but the *progress* is infinite.

CORRECTION, DISCIPLINE, PUNISHMENT.

As *correction* and *discipline* have commonly required *punishment* to render them efficacious, custom has affixed to them a strong resemblance in their application, although they are distinguished from each other by obvious marks of difference. The prominent idea in *correction* (*v. To correct*), is that of making right what has been wrong. In *discipline*, from the Latin *disciplina* and *disco* to learn, the leading idea is that of instructing or regulating. In *punishment*, from the Latin *punio*, and the Greek *ποίνη* pain, the leading idea is that of inflicting pain.

Children are the peculiar subjects of *correction;* *discipline* and *punishment* are confined to no age. A wise parent *corrects* his child;

Wilt thou, pupil-like,
Take thy *correction* mildly, kiss the rod?
SHAKSPEARE.

A master maintains *discipline* in his school; a general preserves *discipline* in his army; 'The imaginations of young men are of a roving nature, and their passions under no *discipline* or restraint.'—ADDISON. Whoever commits a fault is liable to be *punished* by those who have authority over him; if he commits a crime he subjects himself to be *punished* by law.

Correction and *discipline* are mostly exercised by means of chastisement, for which they are often employed as a substitute; *punishment* is inflicted in any way that gives pain. *Correction* and *discipline* are both of them personal acts of authority exercised by superiours over inferiours, but the former is mostly employed by one individual over another: the latter has regard to a number who are the subjects of it directly or indirectly: *punishment* has no relation whatever to the agent by which the action is performed; it may proceed alike from persons or things. A parent who spares the due *correction* of his child, or a master who does not use a proper *discipline* in his school, will alike be *punished* by the insubordination and irregularities of those over whom they have a control;

When by just vengeance impious mortals perish,
The gods behold their *punishment* with pleasure.
ADDISON

TO CHASTEN, TO CHASTISE.

Chasten, *chastise*, both come through the French *châtier*, from the Latin *castigo*, which is compounded of *castus* and *ago* to make pure.

Chasten has most regard to the end, *chastise* to the means; the former is an act of the Deity, the latter a human action: God *chastens* his faithful people to cleanse them from their transgressions; parents *chastise* their children to prevent the repetition of faults: afflictions are the means which the Almighty adopts for *chastening* those whom he wishes to make more obedient to his will;

I follow thee, safe guide! the path
Thou leadst me; and to the hand of Heaven submit,
However *chastening*.—MILTON.

Stripes are the means by which offenders are *chastised;* 'Bad characters are dispersed abroad with profusion; I hope for example's sake, and (as punishments are designed by the civil power) more for the delivering of the innocent, than the *chastising* of the guilty.'—HUGHES. To *chasten* is also sometimes taken in the sense of making *chaste* by a course of discipline, either moral, literary, or religious, as to *chasten* the fancy, or to *chasten* the style; 'By repairing sometimes to the house of mourning, you would *chasten* the looseness of fancy.'—BLAIR.

STRICT, SEVERE.

Strict, from *strictus*, bound or confined, characterizes the thing which binds or keeps in control: *severe* (*v. Austere*) characterizes in the proper sense the disposition of the person to inflict pain, and in an extended application the thing which inflicts pain. The term *strict* is, therefore, taken always in the good sense; *severe* is good or bad, according to circumstances: he who has authority over others must be *strict* in enforcing obedience, in keeping good order, and a proper attention to their duties; but it is possible to be very *severe* in punishing those who are under us, and yet very lax in all matters that our duty demands of us;

Lycurgus then, who bow'd beneath the force
Of *strictest* discipline, *severely* wise,
All human passions.—THOMSON.

FINE, MULCT, PENALTY, FORFEITURE.

Fine, from the Latin *finis* the end or purpose, signifies by an extended application, satisfaction by way of amends for an offence; *mulct*, in Latin *mulcta*, comes from *mulgeo* to draw or wipe, because an offence is wiped off by money; *penalty*, in Latin *pœnalitus*, from *pœna* a pain, signifies what gives pain by way of punishment; *forfeiture*, from *forfeit*, in French *forfait*, from *forfaire*, signifies to do away or lose by doing wrong.

The *fine* and *mulct* are always pecuniary; a *penalty* may be pecuniary; a *forfeiture* applies to any loss of personal property: the *fine* and *mulct* are imposed; the *penalty* is inflicted or incurred; the *forfeiture* is incurred.

The violation of a rule or law is attended with a *fine* or *mulct*, but the former is a term of general use; the latter is rather a technical term in law: a criminal offence incurs a *penalty*: negligence of duty occasions the *forfeiture*.

A *fine* or *mulct* serves either as punishment to the offender, or as an amends for the offence;

> Too dear a *fine*, ah much lamented maid!
> For warring with the Trojans thou hast paid.
> DRYDEN.

> For to prohibit and dispense,
> To find out or to make offence,
> To set what characters they please,
> And *mulcts* on sin, or godliness,
> Must prove a pretty thriving trade.—BUTLER.

A *penalty* always inflicts some kind of pain as a punishment on the offender; 'It must be confessed, that as for the laws of men, gratitude is not enjoined by the sanction of *penalties*.'—SOUTH. A *forfeiture* is attended with loss as a punishment to the delinquent; 'The Earl of Hereford, being tried secundum leges Normannorum, could only be punished by a *forfeiture* of his inheritance.'—TYRWHITT. 'In the Roman law, if a lord manumits his slave, gross ingratitude in the person so made free *forfeits* his freedom.'—SOUTH. Among the Chinese, all offences are punished with *fines* or flogging; the Roman Catholicks were formerly subject to *penalties* if detected in the performance of their religious worship: societies subject their members to *forfeitures* for the violation of their laws.

TO BANISH, EXILE, EXPEL.

Banish, in French *bannir*, German *bannen*, signified to put out of a community by a ban or civil interdict, which was formerly either ecclesiastical or civil; *exile*, in French *exiler*, from the Latin *exilium* banishment, and *exul* an exile, compounded of *extra* and *solum* the soil, signifies to put away from one's native soil or country; *expel*, in Latin *expello*, compounded of *ex* and *pello* to drive, signifies to drive out.

The idea of exclusion, or of a coercive removal from a place, is common to these terms: *banishment* includes the removal from any place, or the prohibition of access to any place, where one has been, or whither one is in the habit of going; *exile* signifies the removal from one's home: to *exile*, therefore, is to *banish*, but to *banish*, is not always to *exile*:* the Tarquins were *banished* from Rome; Coriolanus was *exiled*.

Banishment follows from a decree of justice; *exile* either by the necessity of circumstances or an order of authority: *banishment* is a disgraceful punishment inflicted by tribunals upon delinquents; *exile* is a disgrace incurred without dishonour: *exile* removes us from our country: *banishment* drives us from it ignominiously: it is the custom in Russia to *banish* offenders to Siberia; Ovid was *exiled* by an order of Augustus.

Banishment is an action, a compulsory exercise of power over another, which must be submitted to;

> O *banishment!* Eternal *banishment!*
> Ne'er to return! Must we ne'er meet again!
> My heart will break.—OTWAY.

Exile is a state into which we may go voluntarily; many Romans chose to go into *exile* rather than await the judgement of the people, by whom they might have been *banished;*

> Arms, and the man I sing, who forc'd by fate,
> And haughty Juno's unrelenting hate,
> *Expell'd* and *exil'd*, left the Trojan shore.—DRYDEN

Banishment and *expulsion* both mark a disgraceful and coercive exclusion, but *banishment* is authoritative; it is a publick act of government: *expulsion* is simply coercive; it is the act of a private individual, or a small community; 'The *expulsion* and escape of Hippias at length set Athens free.'—CUMBERLAND. *Banishment* always supposes a removal to a distant spot, to another land; *expulsion* never reaches beyond a particular house or society: *expulsion* from the university, or any publick school, is the necessary consequence of discovering a refractory temper, or a propensity to insubordination.

Banishment and *expulsion* are likewise used in a figurative sense, although *exile* is not: in this sense, *banishment* marks a distant and entire removal; *expulsion* a violent removal: we *banish* that which it is not prudent to retain; we *expel* that which is noxious. Hopes are *banished* from the mind when every prospect of success has disappeared; fears are *banished* when they are altogether groundless;

> If sweet content is *banish'd* from my soul,
> Life grows a burden and a weight of wo.
> GENTLEMAN.

Envy, hatred, and every evil passion, should be *expelled* from the mind as disturbers of its peace: harmony and good humour are best promoted by *banishing* from conversation all subjects of difference in religion and politicks; good morals require that every unseemly word should be *expelled* from conversation; 'In all the tottering imbecility of a new government, and with a parliament totally unmanageable, his Majesty (King William III.) persevered. He persevered to *expel* the fears of his people by his fortitude; to steady their fickleness by his constancy.'—BURKE.

PREVAILING, PREVALENT, RULING, OVERRULING, PREDOMINANT.

Prevailing and *prevalent* both come from the Latin *prevaleo* to be strong above others; *ruling*, *overruling*, and *predominant* (from *dominor* to *rule*), signify *ruling* or bearing greater sway than others.

Prevailing expresses the actual state or quality of a particular object: *prevalent* marks the quality of *prevailing*, as it affects objects in general. The same distinction exists between *overruling* and *predominant*. A person has a *prevailing* sense of religion; 'The evils naturally consequent upon a *prevailing* temptation are intolerable.'—SOUTH. Religious feeling is *prevalent* in a country or in a community. The *prevailing* idea at present is in favour of the legitimate rights of sovereigns: a contrary principle has been very *prevalent* for many years; 'The conduct of a peculiar providence made the instruments of that great design *prevalent* and victorious, and all those mountains of opposition to become plains.'—SOUTH. *Prevailing* and *prevalent* mark simply the existing state of superiority: *ruling* and *predominant* express this state, in relation to some other which it has superseded or reduced to a state of inferiority. An opinion is said to be *prevailing* as respects the number of persons by whom it is maintained: a principle is said to be *ruling* as respects the superiour influence which it has over the conduct of men more than any other;

> Whate'er thou shalt ordain, thou *ruling* pow'r,
> Unknown and sudden be the dreadful hour.
> ROWE.

An argument is *overruling* that bears down every other, and Providence is said to be *overruling* when it determines things contrary to the natural course of events; 'Nor can a man independently of the *overruling* influence of God's blessing and care, call himself one penny richer.'—SOUTH. Particular disorders are *prevalent* at certain seasons of the year, when they affect the generality of persons: a particular taste or fashion is *predominant* which supersedes all other tastes or fashions. Excessive drinking is too *prevalent* a practice in England: virtue is certainly *predominant* over vice in this country, if it be in any country; 'The doctrine of not owning a foreigner to be a king was held and taught by the Pharisees, a *predominant* sect of the Jews.'—PRIDEAUX.

* Vide Roubaud: "Exiler, bannir."

TO OVERBALANCE, OUTWEIGH, PREPONDERATE.

To *overbalance* is to throw the balance over on one side; to *outweigh* is to exceed in weight; to *preponderate*, from *præ* before, and *pondus* a weight, signifies also to exceed in weight.

Although these terms approach so near to each other in their original meaning, yet they have now a different application: in the proper sense, a person *overbalances* himself who loses his balance and goes on one side; a heavy body *outweighs* one that is light, when they are put into the same pair of scales. *Overbalance* and *outweigh* are likewise used in the improper application; *preponderate* is never used otherwise: things are said to *overbalance* which are supposed to turn the scale to one side or the other; they are said to *outweigh* when they are to be weighed against each other; they are said to *preponderate* when one weighs every thing else down: the evils which arise from innovations in society commonly *overbalance* the good; 'Whatever any man may have written or done, his precepts or his valour will scarcely *overbalance* the unimportant uniformity which runs through his time.' —JOHNSON. The will of a parent should *outweigh* every personal consideration in the mind of a child;

If endless ages can *outweigh* an hour,
Let not the laurel but the palm inspire.—YOUNG.

Children can never be unmindful of their duty to their parents where the power of religion *preponderates* in the heart; 'Looks which do not correspond with the heart cannot be assumed without labour, nor continued without pain; the motive to relinquish them must, therefore, soon *preponderate*.'—HAWKESWORTH.

TO OVERRULE, SUPERSEDE.

To *overrule* is literally to get the superiority of rule; and to *supersede* is to get the upper or superiour seat; but the former is employed only as the act of persons or things personified; the latter is also applied to things as the agents: a man may be *overruled* in his domestick government, or he may be *overruled* in a publick assembly, or he may be *overruled* in the cabinet; 'When fancy begins to be *overruled* by reason, and corrected by experience, the most artful tale raises but little curiosity.'—JOHNSON. Large works in general *supersede* the necessity of smaller ones, by containing that which is superiour both in quantity and quality; or one person *supersedes* another in an office; 'Christoval received a commission empowering him to *supersede* Cortes.'—ROBERTSON.

CHIEF, CHIEFTAIN, LEADER, HEAD.

Chief and *chieftain* signify he who is *chief; leader*, from to *lead*, and *head*, from the *head*, sufficiently designate their own signification.

Chief respects precedency in civil matters; *leader* regards the direction of enterprises: *chieftain* is employed for the superiour in military rank: and *head* for the superiour in general concerns.

Among savages the *chief* of every tribe is a despotick prince within his own district. Factions and parties in a state, like savage tribes, must have their *leaders*, to whom they are blindly devoted, and by whom they are instigated to every desperate proceeding. Robbers have their *chieftains*, who plan and direct every thing, having an unlimited power over the band. The *heads* of families were, in the primitive ages, the *chiefs*, who in conjunction regulated the affairs of state.

Chiefs have a permanent power, which may descend by inheritance to branches of the same families;

No *chief* like thee, Menestheus, Greece could yield,
To marshal armies in the dusty field.—POPE.

Leaders and *chieftains* have a deputed power with which they are invested, as the time and occasion require; 'Their constant emulation in military renown dissolved not that inviolable friendship which the ancient Saxons professed to their *chieftain* and to each other.'—HUME. 'Savage alleged that he was then dependent upon the Lord Tyrconnel, who was an implicit follower of the ministry; and, being enjoined by him, not without menaces, to write in praise of his *leader*, he had not sufficient resolution to sacrifice the pleasure of affluence to that of integrity.'—JOHNSON. *Heads* have a natural power springing out of the nature of their birth, rank, talents, and situation; it is not hereditary, but it may be successive, as the father is the *head* of his family, and may be succeeded by his son; a *head* is also sometimes temporary and partial, as the *head* of a party; 'As each is more able to distinguish himself as the *head* of a party, he will less readily be made a follower or associate.'—JOHNSON.

Chiefs ought to have superiority of birth combined with talents for ruling; *leaders* and *chieftains* require a bold and enterprising spirit; *heads* should have talents for directing.

CHIEF, PRINCIPAL, MAIN.

Chief, in French *chef*, from the Latin *caput* the head, signifies belonging to the uppermost part; *principal*, in French *principal*, Latin *principalis*, comes from *princeps* a chief or prince, signifying belonging to a prince; *main*, from the Latin *magnus*, signifies in a great degree.

Chief respects order and rank; *principal* has regard to importance and respectability; *main* to degree or quantity. We speak of a *chief* clerk; a commander in *chief*: the *chief* person in a city: but the *principal* people in a city; the *principal* circumstances in a narrative, and the *main* object.

The *chief* cities, as mentioned by geographers, are those which are classed in the first rank;

What is man,
If his *chief* good and market of his time
Be but to sleep and feed? A beast, no more!
SHAKSPEARE.

The *principal* cities generally include those which are the most considerable for wealth and population these, however, are not always technically comprehended under the name of *chief* cities; 'The right which one man has to the actions of another is generally borrowed, or derived from one or both of these two great originals, production or possession, which two are certainly the *principal* and most undoubted rights that take place in the world.'—SOUTH. The *main* end of man's exertions is the acquirement of wealth; 'To the accidental or adventitious parts of Paradise Lost, some slight exceptions may be made; but the *main* fabrick is immoveably supported.'—JOHNSON.

ESPECIALLY, PARTICULARLY, PRINCIPALLY, CHIEFLY.

Especially and *particularly* are exclusive or superlative in their import; they refer to one object out of many that is superiour to all: *principally* and *chiefly* are comparative in their import; they designate in general the superiority of some objects over others *Especially* is a term of stronger import than *particularly*, and *principally* expresses something less general than *chiefly*: we ought to have God before our eyes at all times, but *especially* in those moments when we present ourselves before him in prayer; 'All love has something of blindness in it, but the love of money *especially*.'—SOUTH. The heat is very oppressive in all countries under the torrid zone, but *particularly* in the deserts of Arabia, where there is a want of shade and moisture; '*Particularly* let a man dread every gross act of sin.'—SOUTH. It is *principally* among the higher and lower orders of society that we find vices of every description to be prevalent; 'Neither Pythagoras nor any of his disciples were, properly speaking, practitioners of physick, since they applied themselves *principally* to the theory.'—JAMES Patriots who declaim so loudly against the measures of government do it *chiefly* (may I not say solely?) with a view to their own interest; 'The reformers gained credit *chiefly* among persons in the lower and middle classes.'—ROBERTSON.

TO GOVERN, RULE, REGULATE.

Govern, in French *gouverner*, comes from the Latin *guberno*, Greek κυβερνάω, which properly signify to govern a ship, and are in all probability derived from the Hebrew גבר to prevail or be strong: *rule* and *regulate* signify to bring under a *rule*, or make by *rule*.

The exercise of authority enters more or less into the signification of these terms; but to *govern* implies the exercise likewise of judgement and knowledge.

To *rule* implies rather the unqualified exercise of power, the making the will the *rule;* a king *governs* his people by means of wise laws and an upright administration: a despot *rules* over a nation according to his arbitrary decision; if he have no principle his *rule* becomes an oppressive tyranny: of Robespierre it has been said, that if he did not know how to *govern*, he aimed at least at *ruling*.

These terms are applied either to persons or things: persons *govern* or *rule* others; or they *govern*, *rule*, or *regulate* things.

In regard to persons, *govern* is always in a good sense, but *rule* is sometimes taken in a bad sense; it is naturally associated with an abuse of power: to *govern* is so perfectly discretionary, that we speak of *governing* ourselves; but we speak only of *ruling* others: nothing can be more lamentable than to be *ruled* by one who does not know how to govern himself;

Slaves to our passions we become, and then
It becomes impossible to *govern* men.—WALLER.

It is the business of a man to *rule* his house by keeping all its members in due subjection to his authority; it is the duty of a person to *rule* those who are under him in all matters wherein they are incompetent to *govern* themselves;

Marg'ret shall now be queen, and *rule* the king,
But I will *rule* both her, the king, and realm.
SHAKSPEARE.

To *govern*, necessarily supposes the adoption of judicious means; but *ruling* is confined to no means but such as will obtain the end of subjecting the will of one to that of another; a woman is said to *rule* by obeying; an artful and imperious woman will have recourse to various stratagems to elude the power to which she ought to submit, and render it subservient to her own purposes.

In application to things, *govern* and *rule* admit of a similar distinction: a minister *governs* the state, and a pilot *governs* the vessel; the movements of the machine are in both cases directed by the exercise of the judgement;

Whence can this very motion take its birth,
Not sure from matter, from dull clods of earth?
But from a living spirit lodg'd within,
Which *governs* all the bodily machine.—JENYNS.

A person *rules* the times, seasons, fashions, and the like; it is an act of the individual will;

When I behold a factious band agree,
To call it freedom when themselves are free;
Each wanton judge new penal statutes draw;
Laws grind the poor, and rich men *rule* the law;
I fly from petty tyrants to the throne.—GOLDSMITH.

Regulate is a species of *governing* simply by judgement; the word is applicable to things of minor moment, where the force of authority is not so requisite: one *governs* the affairs of a nation, or a large body where great interests are involved; we *regulate* the concerns of an individual, or we *regulate* in cases where good order or convenience only is consulted; '*Regulate* the patient in his manner of living.'—WISEMAN. So likewise in regard to ourselves, we *govern* our passions, but we *regulate* our affections.

These terms are all properly used to denote the acts of conscious agents, but by a figure of personification they may be applied to inanimate or moral objects: the price of one market *governs* the price of another, or *governs* the seller in his demand; 'The chief point which he is to carry always in his eye, and by which he is to *govern* all his counsels, designs, and actions.' —ATTERBURY. Fashion and caprice *rule* the majority, or particular fashions *rule;*

Distracting thoughts by turns his bosom *rul'd*,
Now fir'd by wrath, and now by reason cool'd.
POPE.

One clock may *regulate* many others; 'Though a sense of moral good and evil be deeply impressed on the heart of man, it is not of sufficient power to *regulate* his life.'—BLAIR.

GOVERNMENT, ADMINISTRATION.

Both these terms may be employed either to designate the act of *governing* and *administering*, or the persons *governing* and *administering*. In both cases *government* has a more extensive meaning than *administration:* the *government* includes every exercise of authority; the *administration* implies only that exercise of authority, which consists in putting the laws or will of another in force: hence, when we speak of the *government*, as it respects the persons, it implies the whole body of constituted authorities; and the *administration*, only that part which puts in execution the intentions of the whole: the *government* of a country, therefore, may remain unaltered, while the *administration* undergoes many changes; '*Government* is an art above the attainment of an ordinary genius.'—SOUTH. It is the business of the *government* to make treaties of peace and war; and without a *government* it is impossible for any people to negociate; 'What are we to do if the *government* and the whole community are of the same description?'—BURKE. It is the business of the *administration* to *administer* justice, to regulate the finances, and to direct all the complicated concerns of a nation; without an *administration* all publick business would be at a stand; 'In treating of an invisible world, and the *administration* of *government* there carried on by the Father of spirits, particulars occur which appear incomprehensible.'—BLAIR.

GOVERNMENT, CONSTITUTION.

Government is here as in the former article (*v. Government*) the generick term; *constitution* the specifick. *Government* implies generally the act of *governing* or exercising authority under any form whatever; *constitution* implies any *constituted* or fixed form of *government:* we may have a *government* without a *constitution;* we cannot have a *constitution* without a *government*. In the first formation of society *government* was placed in the hands of individuals who exercised authority according to discretion rather than any fixed rule or law: here then was *government* without a *constitution:* as time and experience proved the necessity of some established form, and the wisdom of enlightened men discovered the advantages and disadvantages of different forms, *government* in every country assumed a more definite shape, and became the *constitution* of the country; hence then the union of *government* and *constitution*. *Governments* are divided by political writers into three classes, monarchical, aristocratick, and republican: but these three general forms have been adopted with such variations and modifications as to render the *constitution* of every country something peculiar to itself; 'Free *governments* have committed more flagrant acts of tyranny than the most perfect despotick *governments* which we have ever known.'—BURKE. 'The physician of the state who, not satisfied with the cure of distempers, undertakes to regenerate *constitutions*, ought to show uncommon powers.'—BURKE.

Political squabblers have always chosen to consider *government* in its limited sense as including only the supreme or executive authority, and the *constitution* as that which is set up by the authority of the people; but this is only a forced application of a general term to serve the purposes of party. *Constitution*, according to its real signification, does not convey the idea of the source of power any more than *government;* the *constitution* may with as much propriety be formed or *constituted* by the monarch as *government* is exercised by the monarch; and of this we may be assured, that what is to be formed specifically by any person or persons so as to become *constituted* must be framed by something more authoritative than a rabble. The *constitution* may, as I have before observed, be the work of time, for most of the *constitutions* in Europe, whether republican or monarchical, are indebted to time and the natural course of events for their establishment; but in our own country the case has been so far different that by the wisdom and humanity of those in *government* or power, a *constitution* has been expressly formed, which distinguishes the English nation from all others Hence the word *constitution* is applied by distinction to the English form of *government;* and since this *constitution* has happily secured the rights and liberties of the people by salutary laws, a vulgar errour has arisen that the *constitution* is the work of the people, and by a natural consequence it is maintained that the people, if they are not satisfied with their *constitution*, have the right of introducing changes; a dangerous errour which cannot be combated with too much steadfastness. It must be obvious to all who reflect on this subject that the *constitution*, as far as it is assignable to the efforts of any man or set of men, was never the work of the people; but of the *government* or those who held the supreme power.

This view of the matter is calculated to lessen the jealousies of the people towards their *government*, and to abate that overweening complacency with which they are apt to look upon themselves, and their own imaginary work; for it is impossible but that they must regard with a more dispassionate eye the possesosrs of power, when they see themselves indebted to those in power for the most admirable *constitution* ever framed.

The *constitution* is in danger, is the watchword of a party who want to increase the power of the people; but every one who is acquainted with history, and remembers that before the *constitution* was fully formed it was the people who overturned the *government*, will perceive that much more is to be apprehended by throwing any weight into the scale of the popular side of *government*, than by strengthening the hands of the executive *government*. The *constitution* of England has arrived at the acme of human perfection; it ensures to every man as much as he can wish; it deprives no man of what he can consistently with the publick peace expect; it has within itself adequate powers for correcting every evil and abuse as it may arise, and is fully competent to make such modifications of its own powers as the circumstances may require. Every good citizen therefore will be contented to leave the *government* of the country in the hands of those constituted authorities as they at present exist, fully assured that if they have not the wisdom and the power to meet every exigency, the evil will not be diminished by making the people our legislators.

UNRULY, UNGOVERNABLE, REFRACTORY.

Unruly marks the want of disposition to be ruled: *ungovernable*, an absolute incapacity to be governed: the former is a temporary or partial errour, the latter is an habitual defect in the temper: a volatile child will be occasionally *unruly;* any child of strong passions will become *ungovernable* by excessive indulgence: we say that our wills are *unruly*, and our tempers are *ungovernable;* 'How hardly is the restive *unruly* will of man first tamed and broke to duty.'—SOUTH.

Heav'ns, how unlike their Belgic sires of old!
Rough, poor, content, *ungovernably* bold.
GOLDSMITH.

The *unruly* respects that which is to be ruled or turned at the instant, and is applicable therefore to the management of children: *ungovernable* respects that which is to be put into a regular course, and is applicable therefore either to the management of children or the direction of those who are above the state of childhood; a child is *unruly* in his actions, and *ungovernable* in his conduct. *Refractory*, which from the Latin *refringo* to break open, marks the disposition to break every thing down before it, is the excess of the *unruly* with regard to children: the *unruly* is however negative; but the *refractory* is positive: an *unruly* child objects to be ruled; a *refractory* child sets up a positive resistance to all rule: an *unruly* child may be altogether silent and passive; a *refractory* child always commits himself by some act of intemperance in word or deed: he is *unruly* if in any degree he gives trouble in the *ruling;* he is *refractory* if he refuses altogether to be ruled. This term *refractory* may also be applied to the brutes; 'I conceive (replied Nicholas) I stand here before you, my most equitable judges, for no worse a crime than cudgelling my *refractory* mules. CUMBERLAND.

TUMULTUOUS, TURBULENT, SEDITIOUS, MUTINOUS.

Tumultuous describes the disposition to make a noise; those who attend the play-houses, particularly the lower orders, are frequently *tumultuous;* 'Many civil broils and *tumultuous* rebellions, they fairly overcame, by reason of the continual presence of their king, whose only presence oftentimes constrains the unruly people from a thousand evil occasions.'—SPENSER (*on Ireland*). *Turbulent* marks a hostile spirit of resistance to authority; when prisoners are dissatisfied they are frequently *turbulent;* 'Men of ambitious and *turbulent* spirits, that were dissatisfied with privacy, were allowed to engage in matters of state.'—BENTLEY. *Seditious* marks a spirit of resistance to government; during the French revolution the people were often disposed to be *seditious;* 'Very many of the nobility in Edinburgh, at that time, did not appear yet in this *seditious* behaviour.'—CLARENDON.—*Mutinous* marks a spirit of resistance against officers either in the army or navy; a general will not fail to quell the first risings of a *mutinous* spirit;

Lend me your guards, that if persuasion fail,
Force may against the *mutinous* prevail.—WALLER

Electioneering mobs are always *tumultuous;* the young and the ignorant are so averse to control that they are easily led by the example of an individual to be *turbulent;* among the Romans the people were in the habit of holding *seditious* meetings, and sometimes the soldiery would be *mutinous.*

TUMULTUOUS, TUMULTUARY

Tumultuous signifies having tumult; *tumultuary*, disposed for tumult: the former is applied to object in general; the latter to persons only: in *tumultuous* meetings the voice of reason is the last thing that is heard;

But, O! beyond description happiest he
Who ne'er must roll on life's *tumultuous* sea.
PRIOR.

It is the natural tendency of large and promiscuous assemblies to become *tumultuary;* 'With *tumultuary*, but irresistible violence, the Scotch insurgents fell upon the churches in that city (Perth).'—ROBERTSON.

INSURRECTION, SEDITION, REBELLION, REVOLT.

Insurrection, from *surgo* to rise up, signifies rising up against any power that is; *sedition*, in Latin *seditio* compounded of *se* and *itio*, signifies a going apart, that is, the people going apart from the government; *rebellion*, in Latin *rebellio*, from *rebello*, signifies turning upon or against in a hostile manner; *revolt*, in French *revolter*, is most probably compounded of *re* and *volter*, from *volvo* to roll, signifying to roll or turn back from, to turn against.

The term *insurrection* is general; it is used in a good or bad sense, according to the nature of the power against which one rises up; *sedition* and *rebellion* are more specifick; they are always taken in the bad sense of unallowed opposition to lawful authority. There may be an *insurrection* against usurped power, which is always justifiable; but *sedition* and *rebellion* are levelled against power universally acknowledged to be legitimate. *Insurrection* is always open; it is a rising up of many in a mass; but it does not imply any concerted, or any specifically active measure; a united spirit of opposition, as the moving cause, is all that is comprehended in the meaning of the term; 'Elizabeth enjoyed a wonderful calm (excepting some short gusts of *insurrection* at the beginning) for near upon forty-five years together.'—HOWELL. *Sedition* is either secret or open, according to circumstances; in popular governments it will be open and determined; in monarchical governments it is secretly organized; 'When the Roman people began to bring in plebeians to the office of chiefest power and dignity, then began those *seditions* which so long distempered, and at length ruined, the state.'—TEMPLE. *Rebellion* is the consummation of *sedition;* the scheme of opposition which has been digested in secrecy breaks out into open hostilities, and becomes *rebellion;*

If that *rebellion*
Came like itself, in base and abject routs,
You reverend father, and these noble lords,
Had not been here to dress the ugly forms
Of base and bloody *insurrection*.—SHAKSPEARE.

The *insurrection* which was headed by Wat Tyler, in the time of Richard II. was an unhappy instance of widely extended delusion among the common people; the *insurrection* in Madrid, in the year 1808, against the infamous usurpation of Buonaparte, has led to the most important results that ever sprung from any commotion. Rome was the grand theatre of *seditions*, which were set on foot by the Tribunes: England has been disgraced by one *rebellion*, which ended in the death of its king.

Sedition is common to all forms of government, but flourishes most in republicks, since there it can scarcely be regarded as a political or moral offence: *rebellion* exists properly in none but monarchical states; in which the allegiance that men owe to their sovereign requires to be broken with the utmost violence, in order to be shaken off. *Insurrections* may be made by nations against a foreign dominion, or by subjects against their government: *sedition* and *rebellion* are carried on by subjects only against their government: *revolt* is carried on only by nations against a foreign dominion; upon the death of Alexander the Great most of his conquered countries *revolted* from his successors; 'He was greatly strengthened, and the enemy as much enfeebled by daily *revolts*.'—RALEIGH.

Revolt is also applied to moral objects in the same sense; 'Our self-love is ever ready to *revolt* from our better judgement, and join the enemy within.'—STEELE.

FACTION, PARTY.

* These two words equally suppose the union of many persons, and their opposition to certain views different from their own. But *faction*, from *factio* making, denotes an activity and secret machination against those whose views are opposed; and *party*, from the verb to part or split, expresses only a division of opinion.

The term *party* has of itself nothing odious, that of *faction* is always so. Any man, without distinction of rank, may have a *party* either at court or in the army, in the city or in literature, without being himself immediately implicated in raising it; but *factions* are always the result of active efforts; one may have a *party* for one's merit from the number and ardour of one's friends; but a *faction* is raised by busy and turbulent spirits for their own purposes. Rome was torn by the intestine *factions* of Cæsar and Pompey; France, from the commencement of the revolution to the period of Buonaparte's usurpation, was successively governed by some ruling *faction* which raised itself upon the ruins of that which it had destroyed. *Factions* are not so prevalent in England as *parties*, owing to the peculiar excellence of the constitution; but there are not wanting *factious* spirits who, if they could overturn the present balance of power which has been so happily obtained, would have an opportunity of practising their arts alternately on the high and low, and carrying on their schemes by the aid of both. *Faction* is the demon of discord, armed with the power to do endless mischief, and intent alone on destroying whatever opposes its progress. Wo to that state into which it has found an entrance; 'It is the restless ambition of a few artful men that thus breaks a people into *factions*, and draws several well-meaning persons to their interest by a specious concern for their country.'—ADDISON. *Party* spirit may show itself in noisy debate; but while it keeps within the legitimate bounds of opposition, it is an evil that must be endured; 'As men formerly became eminent in learned societies by their parts and acquisitions, they now distinguish themselves by the warmth and violence with which they espouse their respective *parties*.'—ADDISON.

FACTIOUS, SEDITIOUS.

Factious, in Latin *factiosus* from *facio* to do, signifies the same as busy or intermeddling; ready to take an active part in matters of one's own immediate concern; *seditious*, in Latin *seditiosus*, signifies prone to sedition (*v. Insurrection*).

Factious is an epithet to characterize the tempers of men; *seditious* characterizes their conduct: the *factious* man attempts to raise himself into importance, he aims at authority, and seeks to interfere in the measures of government; the *seditious* man attempts to excite others, and to provoke their resistance to established authority: the first wants to be a law-giver; the second does not hesitate to be a law-breaker: the first wants to direct the state; the second to overturn it: the *factious* man is mostly in possession of either power, rank, or fortune; the *seditious* man is seldom elevated in station or circumstances above the mass of the people. The Roman tribunes were in general little better than *factious* demagogues; such, in fact, as abound in all republicks: Wat Tyler was a *seditious* disturber of the peace. *Factious* is mostly applied to individuals;

He is a traitor, let him to the Tower,
And crop away that *factious* pate of his.
SHAKSPEARE

Seditious is employed for bodies of men: hence we speak of a *factious* nobleman, a *seditious* multitude; 'France is considered (by the ministry) as merely a foreign power, and the *seditious* English only as a domestick faction.'—BURKE.

OBSTINATE, CONTUMACIOUS, STUBBORN, HEADSTRONG, HEADY

Obstinate, in Latin *obstinatus*, participle of *obstino*, from *ob* and *stino*, *sto* or *sisto*, signifies standing in the way of another; *contumacious*, prone to *contumacy* (*v. Contumacy*); *stubborn*, or *stoutborn*, stiff or immoveable by nature; *headstrong*, strong in the head or the mind; and *heady*, full of one's own head.

Obstinacy is a habit of the mind; *contumacy* is either a particular state of feeling or a mode of action: *obstinacy* consists in an attachment to one's own mode of acting; *contumacy* consists in a swelling contempt of others: the *obstinate* man adheres tenaciously to his own ways, and opposes reason to reason: the *contumacious* man disputes the right of another to control his actions, and opposes force to force. *Obstinacy* interferes with a man's private conduct, and makes him blind to right reason; *contumacy* is a crime against lawful authority; the *contumacious* man sets himself against his superiours: when young people are *obstinate* they are bad subjects of education;

But man we find the only creature
Who, led by folly, combats nature;
Who, when she loudly cries, forbear
With *obstinacy* fixes there.—SWIFT.

When people are *contumacious* they are troublesome subjects to the king; 'When an offender is cited to appear in any ecclesiastical court, and he neglects to do it, he is pronounced *contumacious*.'—BEVERIDGE.

The *stubborn* and the *headstrong* are species of the *obstinate*: the former lies altogether in the perversion of the will; the latter in the perversion of the judgement: the *stubborn* person wills what he wills; the *headstrong* person thinks what he thinks. *Stubbornness* is mostly inherent in the nature: a *headstrong* temper is commonly associated with violence and impetuosity of character. *Obstinacy* discovers itself in persons of all ages and stations; a *stubborn* and *headstrong* disposition betray themselves mostly in those who are bound to conform to the will of another.

The *obstinate* keep the opinions which they have once embraced in spite of all proof; but they are not hasty in forming their opinions, nor adopt them without a choice: the *headstrong* seize the first opinions that offer, and act upon them in spite of all remonstrance;

We, blindly by our *headstrong* passions led,
Are hot for action.—DRYDEN.

The *stubborn* follow the ruling will or bent of the mind, without regard to any opinions: they are not to be turned by force or persuasion;

From whence he brought them to these salvage parts,
And with science mollified their *stubborn* hearts.
SPENSER.

* Vide Beauzée: "Faction, parti."

If an *obstinate* child be treated with some degree of indulgence, there may be hopes of correcting his failing; but a *stubborn* and a *headstrong* child are troublesome subjects of education, who will baffle the utmost skill and patience: the former is insensible to all reason; the latter has blinded the little reason which he possesses: the former is unconscious of every thing, but the simple will and determination to do what he does; the latter is so preoccupied with his own favourite ideas as to set every other at nought: force serves mostly to confirm both in their perverse resolution of persistance. *Heady* is applied as an epithet to the thing rather than the person; '*Heady* confidence promises victory without contest.'—JOHNSON.

CONTUMACY, REBELLION.

Contumacy, from the Latin *contumax*, compounded of *contra* and *tumeo* to swell, signifies the swelling one's self by way of resistance; *rebellion*, in Latin *rebellio*, from *rebello*, or *re* and *bello* to war in return, signifies carrying on war against those to whom we owe, and have before paid, a lawful subjection.

Resistance to lawful authority is the common idea included in the signification of both these terms, but *contumacy* does not express so much as *rebellion*: the *contumacious* resist only occasionally; the *rebel* resists systematically: the *contumacious* stand only on certain points, and oppose the individual; the *rebel* sets himself up against the authority itself: the *contumacious* thwart and contradict, they never resort to open violence; the *rebel* acts only by main force: *contumacy* shelters itself under the plea of equity and justice; 'The censor told the criminal that he spoke in contempt of the court, and that he should be proceeded against for *contumacy*.'—ADDISON. *Rebellion* sets all law and order at defiance; 'The mother of Waller was the daughter of John Hampden of Hampden, in the same county, and sister to Hampden the zealot of *rebellion*.'—JOHNSON.

DISAFFECTION, DISLOYALTY.

Disaffection is general; *disloyalty* is particular, being a species of *disaffection*. Men are disaffected to the government; *disloyal* to their prince.

Disaffection may be said with regard to any form of government; *disloyalty* only with regard to a monarchy. Although both terms are commonly employed in a bad sense, yet the former does not always convey the unfavourable meaning which is attached to the latter. A man may have reasons to think himself justified in *disaffection*; but he will never attempt to offer any thing in justification of *disloyalty*. A usurped government will have many *disaffected* subjects with whom it must deal leniently;

Yet, I protest, it is no salt desire
Of seeing countries shifting for a religion!
Nor any *disaffection* to the state
Where I was bred, and unto which I owe
My dearest plots, hath brought me out.
BEN JONSON.

The best king may have *disloyal* subjects, upon whom he must exercise the rigour of the law; 'Milton being cleared from the effects of his *disloyalty*, had nothing required from him but the common duty of living in quiet.'—JOHNSON. Many were *disaffected* to the usurpation of Oliver Cromwell, because they would not be *disloyal* to their king.

GUIDE, RULE.

Guide, signifies either the person that *guides*, or the thing that *guides*; *rule* is only the thing that *rules* or regulates; *guide* is to *rule* as the genus to the species; every *rule* is a *guide* to a certain extent; but the *guide* is often that which exceeds the *rule*. The *guide*, in the moral sense, as in the proper sense, goes with us, and points out the exact path; it does not permit us to err either to the right or left: the *rule* marks out a line, beyond which we may not go; but it leaves us to trace the line, and consequently to fail either on the one side or other.

The Bible is our best *guide* for moral practice; 'You must first apply to religion as the *guide* of life, before you can have recourse to it as the refuge of sorrow.'—BLAIR. Its doctrines as interpreted in the articles of the established church are the best *rule* of faith for every Christian; 'There is something so wild and yet so solemn, in Shakspeare's speeches of his ghosts and fairies, and the like imaginary persons, that we cannot forbear thinking them natural, though we have no *rule* by which to judge them.'—ADDISON.

AXIOM, MAXIM, APHORISM, APOPHTHEGM, SAYING, ADAGE, PROVERB, BY-WORD SAW.

Axiom, in French *axiome*, Latin *axioma*, comes from the Greek ἀξίοω to think worthy, signifying the thing valued; *maxim*, in French *maxime*, in Latin *maximus* the greatest, signifies that which is most important; *aphorism*, from the Greek ἀφορισμὸς a short sentence, and αφορίζω to distinguish, signifies that which is set apart; *apophthegm*, in Greek ἀπόφθεγμα, from ἀποφθέγγομαι to speak pointedly, signifies a pointed saying; *saying* signifies literally what is said, that is, said habitually; *adage*, in Latin *adagium*, probably compounded of *ad* and *ago*, signifies that which is fit to be acted upon; *proverb*, in French *proverbe*, Latin *proverbium*, compounded of *pro* and *verbum*, signifies that expression which stands for something particular; *by-word* signifies a word by the by, or by the way, in the course of conversation; *saw* is but a variation of say, put for saying.

A given sentiment conveyed in a specifick sentence, or form of expression, is the common idea included in the signification of these terms. The *axiom* is a truth of the first value; a self-evident proposition which is the basis of other truths. A *maxim* is a truth of the first moral importance for all practical purposes. An *aphorism* is a truth set apart for its pointedness and excellence. *Apophthegm* is, in respect to the ancients, what *saying* is in regard to the moderns; it is a pointed sentiment pronounced by an individual, and adopted by others. *Adage* and *proverb* are vulgar sayings, the former among the ancients, the latter among the moderns. A *by-word* is a casual saying, originating in some local circumstance. The *saw*, which is a barbarous corruption of *saying*, is a *saying* formerly current among the ignorant.

Axioms are in science what *maxims* are in morals; self-evidence is an essential characteristick in both; the *axiom* presents itself in so simple and undeniable a form to the understanding as to exclude doubt, and the necessity for reasoning. The *maxim*, though not so definite in its expression as the *axiom*, is at the same time equally parallel to the mind of man, and of such general application, that it is acknowledged by all moral agents who are susceptible of moral truth; it comes home to the common sense of all mankind. * "Things that are equal to one and the same thing are equal to each other,"—"Two bodies cannot occupy the same space at the same time," are *axioms* in mathematicks and metaphysicks. "Virtue is the true source of happiness,"—"The happiness of man is the end of civil government," are *axioms* in ethicks and politicks. "To err is human, to forgive divine,"—"When our vices leave us, we flatter ourselves that we leave them," are among the number of *maxims*. Between *axioms* and *maxims* there is this obvious difference to be observed; that the *axiom* is unchangeable both in matter and manner, and admits of little or no increase in number; the *maxim* may vary with the circumstances of human life, and admit of considerable extension; 'Those authors are to be read at schools, that supply most *axioms* of prudence, most principles of moral truth.'—JOHNSON. 'It was my grandfather's *maxim, that a young man seldom makes much money, who is out of his time before two and twenty*.'—JOHNSON.

Aphorism is a speculative principle, either in science or morals, which is presented in a few words to the understanding: it is the substance of a doctrine, and many *aphorisms* may contain the abstract of a science. Of this description are the *aphorisms* of Hippocrates, and those of Lavater in physiognomy; 'As this one *aphorism, Jesus Christ is the Son of God*, is virtually and eminently the whole Gospel; so to confess or deny

* Vide Roubaud: "Axiome, maxime, apophthègme aphorisme."

it is virtually to embrace or reject the whole round and series of Gospel truths.'—SOUTH.

Sayings and *apophthegms* differ from the preceding, in as much as they always carry the mind back to the person speaking; there is always one who says when there is a *saying* or an *apophthegm*, and both acquire a value as much from the person who utters them, as from the thing that is uttered: when Leonidas was asked why brave men prefer honour to life, his answer became an *apophthegm;* namely, that they hold life by fortune, and honour by virtue; 'It is remarkable that so near his time so much should be known of what Pope has written, and so little of what he has said. One *apophthegm* only stands upon record. When an objection raised against his inscription for Shakspeare was defended by the authority of Patrick, he replied, that he would allow the publisher of a dictionary to know the meaning of a single word, but not of two words together.'—JOHNSON. Of this description also are the *apophthegms* comprised by Plutarch; so likewise in modern times, the *sayings* of Franklin's Old Richard, or those of Dr. Johnson: these are happy effusions of the mind which men are fond of treasuring; 'The little and short *sayings* of wise and excellent men are of great value, like the dust of gold, or the least sparks of diamonds.'—TILLOTSON.

The *adage* and *proverb* are habitual, as well as general *sayings*, not repeated as the *sayings* of one, but of all; not adopted for the sake of the person, but for the sake of the thing; and they have been used in all ages for the purpose of conveying the sense of mankind on ordinary subjects. The *adage* of former times is the *proverb* of the present times; if there be any difference between them, it lies in this, that the former are the fruit of knowledge and long experience, the latter of vulgar observations; the *adage* is therefore more refined than the *proverb*. Adversity is our best teacher, according to the Greek *adage*, "What hurts us instructs us,"—"Old birds are not to be caught with chaff," is a vulgar *proverb;* 'It is in praise and commendation of men, as it is in gettings and gains; the *proverb* is true that light gains make heavy purses: for light gains come thick, whereas great come now and then.'—BACON.

Quoth Hudibras, thou offer'st much,
But art not able to keep touch,
Mira de lente, as 'tis I, the *adage*,
Id est, to make a leek a cabbage.—BUTLER.

By-words rarely contain any important sentiment; they mostly consist of familiar similes, nick-names, and the like, as the Cambridge *by-word* of Hobson's choice, signifying that or none: the name of Nazarene was a *by-word* among the Jews, for a Christian; 'I knew a pretty young girl in a country village, who, overfond of her own praise, became a property to a poor rogue in the parish, who was ignorant of all things but fawning.—Thus Isaac extols her out of a quartern of *cut and dry* every day she lives, and though the young woman is really handsome, she and her beauty are become a *by-word*, and all the country round, she is called nothing but *Isaac's best Virginia*.' —ARBUTHNOT. A *saw* is vulgar in form, and vulgar in matter: it is the partial *saying* of particular neighbourhoods, originating in ignorance and superstition: of this description are the *sayings* which attribute particular properties to animals or to plants, termed old women's *saws;* 'If we meet this dreadful and portentous energy with poor commonplace proceedings, with trivial *maxims*, paltry old *saws*, with doubts, fears, and suspicions; down we go to the bottom of the abyss, and nothing short of omnipotence can save us.'—BURKE.

MAXIM, PRECEPT, RULE, LAW.

Maxim (*v. Axiom*), is a moral truth that carries its own weight with itself; *precept* (*v. Command*), *rule* (*v. Guide*), and *law*, from *lex* and *lego*, signifying the thing specially chosen or marked out, all borrow their weight from some external circumstance: the *precept* derives its authority from the individual delivering it; in this manner the *precepts* of our Saviour have a weight which gives them a decided superiority over every thing else: the *rule* acquires a worth from its fitness for guiding us in our proceeding: the *law*, which is a species of *rule*, derives its weight from the sanction of power. *Maxims* are often *precepts* inasmuch as they are communicated to us by our parents they are *rules* inasmuch as they serve as a rule for our conduct; they are *laws* inasmuch as they have the sanction of conscience. We respect the *maxims* of antiquity as containing the essence of human wisdom; 'I think I may lay it down as a *maxim*, that every man of good common sense may, if he pleases, most certainly be rich.'—BUDGELL. We reverence the *precepts* of religion as the foundation of all happiness; 'Philosophy has accumulated *precept* upon *precept* to warn us against the anticipation of future calamities.'—JOHNSON. We regard the *rules* of prudence as preserving us from errours and misfortunes; 'I know not whether any *rule* has yet been fixed by which it may be decided when poetry can properly be called easy.'—JOHNSON. We respect the *laws* as they are the basis of civil society;

God is thy *law*, thou mine.—MILTON.

LAWFUL, LEGAL, LEGITIMATE, LICIT

Lawful, from *law*, and the French *loi*, comes from the Latin *lex*, in the same manner as *legal* or *legitimate*, all signifying in the proper sense belonging to *law*. They differ therefore according to the sense of the word *law;* *lawful* respects the *law* in general, defined or undefined; *legal* respects only civil *law*, which is defined; and *legitimate* respects the laws or rules of science as well as civil matters in general. *Licit*, from the Latin *licet* to be allowed, is used only to characterize the moral quality of actions: the *lawful* property implies conformable to or enjoined by *law;* the *legal* what is in the form or after the manner of *law*, or binding by *law:* it is not *lawful* to coin money with the king's stamp; a marriage is not *legal* in England which is not solemnized according to the rites of the established church: men's passions impel them to do many things which are *unlawful* or *illicit;* their ignorance leads them into many things which are *illegal* or *illegitimate*. As a good citizen and a true Christian, every man will be anxious to avoid every thing which is *unlawful:* it is the business of the lawyer to define what is *legal* or *illegal:* it is the business of the critick to define what is *legitimate* verse in poetry; it is the business of the linguist to define the *legitimate* use of words; it is the business of the moralist to point out what is *licit* or *illicit*. As usurpers have no *lawful* authority, no one is under any obligation to obey them; 'According to this spiritual doctor of politicks, if his Majesty does not owe his crown to the choice of his people, he is no *lawful* king.'—BURKE. When a claim to property cannot be made out according to the established *laws* of the country it is not *legal;* 'Swift's mental powers declined till (1741) it was found necessary that *legal* guardians should be appointed to his person and fortune.'—JOHNSON. The cause of *legitimate* sovereigns is at length brought to a happy issue; it is to be hoped that men will never be so unwise as ever to revive the question; 'Upon the whole I have sent this my offspring into the world in as decent a dress as I was able; a *legitimate* one, I am sure it is.'—MOORE. The first inclination to an *illicit* indulgence should be carefully suppressed; 'The King of Prussia charged some of the officers, his prisoners, with maintaining an *illicit* correspondence.'—SMOLLETT.

JUDGE, UMPIRE, ARBITER, ARBITRATOR.

Judge, in Latin *judico* and *judex*, from *jus* right, signifies one pronouncing the law or determining right; *umpire* is most probably a corruption from empire, signifying one who has authority; *arbiter* and *arbitrator*, from *arbitror* to think or determine, signifying one who decides.

Judge is the generick term, the others are specifick terms. The *judge* determines in all matters disputed or undisputed; he pronounces, what is *law* now as well as what will be *law* for the future; the *umpire* and *arbiter* are only *judges* in particular cases that admit of dispute: there may be *judges* in literature, in arts and civil matters;

Palæmon shall be *judge* how ill you rhyme.
DRYDEN.

Umpires and *arbiters* are only *judges* in civil or pri

vate matters. The *judge* pronounces, in matters of dispute, according to a written law or a prescribed rule; 'I am not out of the reach of people who oblige me to act as their *judge* or their *arbitrator*.'—MELMOTH (*Letters of Pliny*). The *umpire* decides in all matters of contest; and the *arbiter* or *arbitrator* in all matters of litigation, according to his own judgement. The *judge* acts under the appointment of government; the *umpire* and *arbitrator* are appointed by individuals: the former is chosen for his skill; he adjudges the palm to the victor according to the merits of the case: the latter is chosen for his impartiality; he consults the interests of both by equalizing their claims.

The office of an English *judge* is one of the most honourable in the state; he is the voice of the legislator, and the organ for dispensing justice; he holds the balance between the king and the subject: the characters of those who have filled this office have been every way fitted to raise it in the estimation of all the world. An *umpire* has no particular moral duty to discharge, nor important office; but he is of use in deciding the contested merits of individuals; among the Romans and Greeks, the *umpire* at their games was held in high estimation; but the term may be used in poetry in a higher sense;

> To pray'r, repentance, and obedience due,
> Mine ear shall not be slow, mine eye not shut,
> And I will place within them as a guide,
> My *umpire* conscience.—MILTON.

The office of an *arbiter*, although not so elevated as that of a *judge* in its literal sense, has often the important duty of a Christian peace-maker; and as the determinations of an *arbiter* are controlled by no external circumstances, the term is applied to monarchs, and even to the Creator as the sovereign *Arbiter* of the world;

> You once have known me
> 'Twixt warring monarchs and contending states,
> The glorious *arbiter*.—LEWIS.

JUSTICE, EQUITY.

* *Justice*, from *jus* right, is founded on the laws of society: *equity*, from *æquitas* fairness, rightness, and equality, is founded on the laws of nature.

Justice is a written or prescribed law, to which one is bound to conform and make it the rule of one's decisions: *equity* is a law in our hearts; it conforms to no rule but to circumstances, and decides by the consciousness of right and wrong. The proper object of *justice* is to secure property; the proper object of *equity* is to secure the rights of humanity. *Justice* is exclusive, it assigns to every one his own: it preserves the subsisting inequality between men: *equity* is communicative; it seeks to *equalize* the condition of men by a fair distribution.

Justice forbids us doing wrong to any one; and requires us to repair the wrongs we have done to others: *equity* forbids us doing to others what we would not have them do to us; it requires us to do to others what in similar circumstances we would expect from them.

The obligations to *justice* are imperative: the observance of its laws is enforced by the civil power, and the breach of them is exposed to punishment: the obligations to *equity* are altogether moral; we are impelled to it by the dictates of conscience; we cannot violate it without exposing ourselves to the Divine displeasure. *Justice* is inflexible, it follows one invariable rule, which can seldom be deviated from consistently with the general good; *equity*, on the other hand, varies with the circumstances of the case, and is guided by discretion; *justice* may, therefore, sometimes run counter to *equity*, when the interests of the individual must be sacrificed to those of the community; and *equity* sometimes tempers the rigour of *justice*, by admitting of reasonable deviations from the literal interpretations of its laws; 'We see in contracts, and other dealings, which daily pass between man and man, that, to the utter undoing of some, many things by strictness of law may be done, which *equity* and honest meaning forbiddeth. Not that the law is unjust, but imperfect, nor *equity* against but above law; binding men's consciences in things which law cannot reach unto.'—HOOKER. The tranquillity of society, and the security of the individual, are ensured by *justice*; the harmony and good will of one man towards another are cherished by *equity*: when *justice* requires any sacrifices which are not absolutely necessary for the preservation of this tranquillity and security, it is a useless breach of *equity*: on the other hand, when a regard to *equity* leads to the direct violation of any law, it ceases to be either *equity* or justice. The rights of property are alike to be preserved by both *justice* and *equity*: but the former respects only those general and fundamental principles which are universally admitted in the social compact, and comprehended under the laws; the latter respects those particular principles which belong to the case of individuals: *justice* is, therefore, properly a virtue belonging only to a large and organized society: *equity* must exist wherever two individuals come in connexion with each other. When a father disinherits his son, he does not violate *justice*, although he does not act consistently with *equity*; the disposal of his property is a right which is guaranteed to him by the established laws of civil society; but the claims which a child has by nature over the property of his parent become the claims of *equity*, which the latter is not at liberty to set at nought without the most substantial reasons. On the other hand, when Cyrus adjudged the coat to each boy as it fitted him, without regard to the will of the younger from whom the large coat had been taken, it is evident that he committed an act of *injustice*, without performing an act of *equity*; since all violence is positively *unjust*, and what is positively *unjust*, can never be *equitable*: whence it is clear that *justice*, which respects the absolute and unalienable rights of mankind, can at no time be superseded by what is supposed to be *equity*; although *equity* may be conveniently made to interpose where the laws of *justice* are either too severe or altogether silent. On this ground, supposing I have received an injury, *justice* demands reparation; it listens to no palliation, excuse, or exception: but supposing the reparation which I have a right to demand involves the ruin of him who is more unfortunate than guilty, can I in *equity* insist on the demand? *Justice* is that which publick law requires: *equity* is that which private law or the law of every man's conscience requires; 'They who supplicate for mercy from others, can never hope for *justice* through themselves.'—BURKE.

> Ev'ry rule of *equity* demands
> That vice and virtue from the Almighty's hands
> Should due rewards and punishments receive.
> JENYNS

INJUSTICE, INJURY, WRONG.

Injustice, signifying the abstract quality of unjust, *injury*, from *injuria*, or *in* privative, and *jus* right, signifying any act that is contrary to right; and *wrong*, signifying the thing that is *wrong*, are all opposed to the right; but the *injustice* lies in the principle, the *injury* in the action that *injures*. There may, therefore, be *injustice* where there is no specifick *injury*; and, on the other hand, there may be *injury* where there is no *injustice*. When we think worse of a person than we ought to think, we do him an act of *injustice*; but we do not, in the strict sense of the word, do him an *injury*: on the other hand, if we say any thing to the discredit of another, it will be an *injury* to his reputation if it be believed; but it may not be an *injustice*, if it be strictly conformable to truth, and that which one is compelled to say.

The violation of justice, or a breach of the rule of right, constitutes the *injustice*; but the quantum of ill which falls on the person constitutes the *injury*. Sometimes a person is dispossessed of his property by fraud or violence, this is an act of *injustice*; but it is not an *injury*, if, in consequence of this act, he obtains friends who make it good to him beyond what he has lost: on the other hand, a person suffers very much through the inadvertence of another, which to him is a serious *injury*, although the offender has not been guilty of *injustice*; 'A lie is properly a species of *injustice*, and a violation of the right of that person to whom the false speech is directed.'—SOUTH.

> Law suits I'd shun with as much studious care,
> As I would dens where hungry lions are:

* Vide Roubaud: 'Justice, equité.'

And rather put up *injuries* than be
A plague to him who'd be a plague to me.
POMFRET.

A *wrong* partakes both of *injustice* and *injury;* it is in fact an *injury* done by one person to another, in express violation of justice. The man who seduces a woman from the path of virtue does her the greatest of all *wrongs*. One repents of *injustice*, repairs *injuries* and redresses *wrongs;*

The humble man when he receives a *wrong*,
Refers revenge to whom it doth belong.—WALLER.

PRINCIPLE, MOTIVE.

The *principle* (*v. Doctrine*) may sometimes be the *motive;* but often there is a *principle* where there is no *motive*, and there is a *motive* where there is no *principle*. The *principle* lies in conscious and unconscious agents; the *motive* only in conscious agents: all nature is guided by certain *principles;* its movements go forward by certain *principles:* man is put into action by certain *motives;* the *principle* is the prime *moving* cause of every thing that is set in motion; the *motive* is the prime *moving* cause that sets the human machine into action. The *principle* in its restricted sense comes still nearer to the *motive*, when it refers to the opinions which we form: the *principle* in this case is that idea which we form of things, so as to regulate our conduct: 'The best legislators have been satisfied with the establishment of some sure, solid, and ruling *principle* in government.'—BURKE. The *motive* is that idea which simply impels to action; 'The danger of betraying our weakness to our servants, and the impossibility of concealing it from them, may be justly considered as one *motive* to a regular life.'—JOHNSON. The former is therefore something permanent, and grounded upon the exercise of our reasoning powers; the latter is momentary, and arises simply from our capacity of thinking: bad *principles* lead a man into a bad course of life; bad *motives* lead him to the commission of actions bad or good.

DIRECTION, ORDER.

Direction (*v. To direct*) contains most of instruction in it: *order* (*v. To command*) most of authority. *Directions* should be followed; *orders* obeyed. It is necessary to *direct* those who are unable to act for themselves: it is necessary to *order* those whose business it is to execute the *orders*. To servants and children the *directions* must be clear, simple, and precise;

Then meet me forthwith at the notary's,
Give him *direction* for this merry bond.
SHAKSPEARE.

To tradespeople the *orders* may be particular or general; 'To execute laws is a royal office: to execute *orders* is not to be a king.'—BURKE.

Directions extend to the moral conduct of others, as well as the ordinary concerns of life; 'A general *direction* for scholastick disputers is never to dispute upon mere trifles.'—WATTS. *Orders* are confined to the personal convenience of the individual;

Give *order* to my servants, that they take
No note of our being absent.—SHAKSPEARE.

A parent *directs* a child as to his behaviour in company, or as to his conduct when he enters life; a teacher *directs* his pupil in the choice of books, or in the distribution of his studies: the master gives *orders* to his attendants to be in waiting for him at a certain hour; or he gives *orders* to his tradesmen to provide what is necessary.

DIRECTION, ADDRESS, SUPERSCRIPTION.

Direction marks that which directs; *address* is that which addresses: *superscription*, from *super* and *scribo*, signifies that which is written over something else.

Although these terms may be used promiscuously for each other, yet they have a peculiarity of signification by which their proper use is defined: the *direction* may serve to direct to places as well as to persons: the *address* is never used but in direct application to the person: the *superscription* has more respect to the thing than the person. The *direction* may be written or verbal; the *address* in this sense is always written; the *superscription* must not only be written, but either on or over some other thing: a *direction* is given to such as go in search of persons and places, it ought to be clear and particular; 'There could not be a greater chance than that which brought to light the powder treason, when Providence, as it were, snatched a king and a kingdom out of the very jaws of death only by the mistake of a word in the *direction* of a letter.'—SOUTH. An *address* is put either on a card, and a letter, or in a book; it ought to be suitable to the station and situation of the person *addressed;* 'We think you may be able to point out to him the evil of succeeding; if it be solicitation, you will tell him where to *address* it.'—LORD CHESTERFIELD. A *superscription* is placed at the head of other writings, or over tombs and pillars, it ought to be appropriate; 'Deceit and hypocrisy carry in them more of the express image and *superscription* of the devil than any bodily sins whatsoever.'—SOUTH

INSIGHT, INSPECTION.

The *insight* is what we receive; the *inspection* is what we give: one gets a view into a thing by the *insight;* one takes a view over a thing by an *inspection*. The *insight* serves to increase our own knowledge; the *inspection* enables us to instruct others. An inquisitive traveller tries to get an *insight* into the manners, customs, laws, and government of the countries which he visits; 'Angels both good and bad have a full *insight* into the activity and force of natural causes.'—SOUTH. By *inspection* a master discovers the errours which are committed by his scholars, and sets them right; 'Something no doubt is designed; but what that is, I will not presume to determine from an *inspection* of men's hearts.'—SOUTH.

INSPECTION, SUPERINTENDENCY, OVERSIGHT.

The office of looking into the conduct of others is expressed by all these terms; but the former comprehends little more than the preservation of good order; the two latter include the arrangement of the whole.

The monitor of a school has the *inspection* of the conduct of his schoolfellows, but the master has the *superintendence* of the school. The officers of an army *inspect* the men, to see that they observe all the rules that have been laid down to them; 'This author proposes that there should be examiners appointed to *inspect* the genius of every particular boy.'—BUDGELL. A general or superiour officer has the *superintendence* of any military operation; 'When female minds are imbittered by age or solitude, their malignity is generally exerted by a spiteful *superintendence* of trifles.'—JOHNSON. Fidelity is peculiarly wanted in an *inspector*, judgement and experience in a *superintendent*. *Inspection* is said of things as well as persons; *oversight* only of persons: one has the *inspection* of books in order to ascertain their accuracy: one has the *oversight* of persons to prevent irregularity: there are *inspectors* of the customs, and *overseers* of the poor.

TO INSTITUTE, ESTABLISH, FOUND, ERECT.

Institute, in Latin *institutus*, participle of *instituo*, from *in* and *statuo* to place or appoint, signifies to dispose or fix a specifick end; *establish* (*v. To fix*); *found* (*v To found*); *erect* (*v. To build*).

To *institute* is to form according to a certain plan, to *establish* is to fix in a certain position what has been formed; to *found* is to lay the foundation; to *erect* is to make *erect*. Laws, communities, and particular orders, are *instituted;* schools, colleges, and various societies, are *established;* in the former case something new is supposed to be framed; in the latter case it is supposed only to have a certain situation assigned to it. The order of the Jesuits was *instituted* by Ignatius de Loyola: schools were *established* by Alfred the Great in various parts of his dominions. The act of *instituting* comprehends design and method; that of *establishing* includes the idea of authority. The inquisition was *instituted* in the time of Ferdinand; the Church of England is *established* by authority. To *institute* is always the immediate act of some agent; to *establish* is sometimes the effect of circumstances. Men of pub lick spirit *institute* that which is for the publick good; a communication or trade between certain places becomes *established* in course of time. An *institution* is properly of a publick nature, but *establishments* are as often private: there are charitable and literary *institutions*, but domestick *establishments*; 'The leap years were fixed to their due times according to Julius Cæsar's *institution*.'—PRIDEAUX. 'The French have outdone us in these particulars by the *establishment* of a society for the invention of proper inscriptions (for their medals).'—ADDISON. To *found* is a species of *instituting* which borrows its figurative meaning from the nature of buildings, and is applicable to that which is formed after the manner of a building: a publick school is *founded* when its pecuniary resources are formed into a fund or *foundation*; 'After the flood which depopulated Attica, it is generally supposed no king reigned over it till the time of Cecrops, the *founder* of Athens.'—CUMBERLAND. To *erect* is a species of *founding*, for it expresses in fact a leading particular in the act of *founding*; 'Princes as well as private persons have *erected* colleges, and assigned liberal endowments to students and professors.'—BERKELEY. Nothing can be *founded* without being *erected*; although some things may be *erected* without being expressly *founded* in the natural sense; a house is both *founded* and *erected*: a monument is *erected* but not *founded*: so in the figurative sense, a college is *founded* and consequently *erected*: but a tribunal is *erected*, but not *founded*.

TO CONSTITUTE, APPOINT, DEPUTE.

To *constitute*, in Latin *constitutus*, participle of *constituo*, that is *con* and *statuo* to place together, signifies here to put or place for a specifick purpose, in which sense it is allied to *appoint* as explained under the head of *allot*, and also *depute*, which from the French *deputer*, Latin *deputo*, compounded of *de* and *puto* to esteem or assign, signifies to assign a certain office to a person.

The act of choosing some person or persons for an office, is comprehended under all these terms: to *constitute* is a more solemn act than *appoint*, and this than *depute*. To *constitute* is the act of a body; to *appoint* and *depute*, either of a body or an individual: a community *constitutes* any one their leader; a monarch *appoints* his ministers, an assembly *deputes* some of its members.

To *constitute* implies the act of making as well as choosing; the office as well as the person is new: in *appointing*, the person but not the office is new. A person may be *constituted* arbiter or judge as circumstances may require; a successor is *appointed* but not *constituted*.

Whoever is *constituted* is invested with supreme authority derived from the highest sources of human power; 'Where there is no *constituted* judge, as between independent states there is not, the vicinage itself is the natural judge.'—BURKE. Whoever is *appointed* derives his authority from the authority of others, and has consequently but limited power: no individual can *appoint* another with authority equal to his own; 'The accusations against Columbus gained such credit in a jealous court, that a commissioner was *appointed* to repair to Hispaniola, and to inspect into his conduct.'—ROBERTSON. Whoever is *deputed* has private and not publick authority; his office is partial, often confined to the particular transaction of an individual, or a body of individuals; 'If the Commons disagree to the amendments, a conference usually follows between members *deputed* from each house.'—BLACKSTONE. According to the Romish religion, the Pope is *constituted* supreme head of the Christian church throughout the whole world; governours are *appointed* to distant provinces, persons are *deputed* to present petitions or make representations to government.

It has been the fashion of the present day to speak contemptuously of all *constituted* authorities: the *appointments* made by government are a fruitful source of discontent for those who follow the trade of opposition: a busy multitude, when agitated by political discussions, are ever ready to form societies and send *deputations*, in order to communicate their wishes to their rulers.

AMBASSADOR, ENVOY, PLENIPOTENTIARY DEPUTY.

Ambassador is supposed to come from the low Latin *ambasciator* a waiter, although this does not accord with the high station which ambassadors have always held; *envoy*, from the French *envoyer* to send, signifies one sent; *plenipotentiary*, from the Latin *plenus* and *potens*, signifies one invested with full powers; *deputy*, signifies one deputed.

Ambassadors, *envoys*, and *plenipotentiaries*, speak and act in the name of their sovereigns, with this difference, that the first are invested with the highest authority, acting in all cases as their representatives; the second appear only as simple authorized ministers acting for another, but not always representing him; the third are a species of *envoy* used by courts only on the occasion of concluding peace or making treaties: *deputies* are not deputed by sovereigns, although they may be *deputed* to sovereigns; they have no power to act or speak, but in the name of some subordinate community, or particular body. The functions of the first three belong to the minister, those of the latter to the agent.

An *ambassador* is a resident in a country during a state of peace; he must maintain the dignity of his court by a suitable degree of splendour; 'Prior continued to act without a title till the Duke of Shrewsbury returned next year to England, and then he assumed the style and dignity of an *ambassador*.'—JOHNSON. An *envoy* may be a resident, but he is more commonly employed on particular occasions; address in negotiating forms an essential in his character; 'We hear from Rome, by letters dated the 20th of April, that the count de Mellos, *envoy* from the king of Portugal, had made his publick entry into that city with much state and magnificence.'—STEELE. A *plenipotentiary* is not so much connected with the court immediately, as with persons in the same capacity with himself; he requires to have integrity, coolness, penetration, loyalty, and patriotism; 'The conferences began at Utrecht on the 1st of January, 1711-12, and the English *plenipotentiaries* arrived on the fifteenth.'—JOHNSON. A *deputy* has little or no responsibility; and still less intercourse with those to whom he is *deputed*; he needs no more talent than is sufficient to maintain the respectability of his own character, and that of the body to which he belongs; 'They add that the *deputies* of the Swiss cantons were returned from Soleure, where they were assembled at the instance of the French *ambassador*.'—STEELE.

DELEGATE, DEPUTY.

Delegate, in Latin *delegatus*, from *delego*, signifies one commissioned; *deputy*, in Latin *deputatus*, from *deputo*, signifies one to whom a business is assigned.

A *delegate* has a more active office than a *deputy*; he is appointed to execute some positive commission, and officiates in the place of another;

> Elect by Jove, his *delegate* of sway,
> With joyous pride the summons I'd obey.—POPE.

A *deputy* may often serve only to supply the place or answer in the name of one who is absent; 'Every member (of parliament), though chosen by one particular district, when elected and returned serves for the whole realm; and therefore he is not bound, like a *deputy* in the United Provinces, to consult with his constituents on any particular point.'—BLACKSTONE. *Delegates* are mostly appointed in publick transactions; *deputies* are chosen either in publick or private matters: *delegates* are chosen by particular bodies for purposes of negotiation either in regard to civil or political affairs; *deputies* are chosen either by individuals or small communities to officiate on certain occasions of a purely civil nature: the Hans towns in Germany used formerly to send *delegates* to the Diet at Ratisbon;

> Let chosen *delegates* this hour be sent,
> Myself will name them, to Pelides' tent.—POPE.

When Calais was going to surrender to Edward III. King of England, *deputies* were sent from the townsmen to implore his mercy: 'The assembling of persons *deputed* from people at great distances is a trouble to them that are sent and a charge to them that send.'—TEMPLE. *Delegate* is sometimes also used figuratively in the same sense;

But this
And all the much transported muse can sing,
Are to thy beauty, dignity, and use,
Unequal far, great *delegated* source
Of light, and life, and grace, and joy below.
THOMSON.

Deputy is also extended in its application to other objects; 'He exerciseth dominion over them as the vicegerent and deputy of Almighty God.'—HALE.

TO NEGOTIATE, TREAT FOR OR ABOUT, TRANSACT.

The idea of conducting business with others is included in the signification of all these terms; but they differ in the mode of conducting it, and the nature of the business to be conducted. *Negotiate*, in the Latin *negotiatus*, participle of *negotior*, from *negotium*, is applied in the original mostly to merchandise or traffick, but it is now more commonly employed in the complicated concerns of governments and nations. *Treat*, from the Latin *tracto*, frequentative of *traho* to draw, signifies to turn over and over or set forth in all ways: these two verbs, therefore, suppose deliberation: but *transact*, from *transactus*, participle of *transago*, to carry forward or bring to an end, supposes more direct agency than consultation or deliberation: this latter is therefore adapted to the more ordinary and less entangled concerns of commerce. *Negotiations* are conducted by many parties, and involve questions of peace or war, dominions, territories, rights of nations, and the like; 'I do not love to mingle speech with any about news or worldly *negotiations* in God's holy house.'—HOWEL. *Treaties* are often a part of *negotiations*; they are seldom conducted by more than two parties, and involve only partial questions, as in *treaties* about peace, about commerce, about the boundaries of any particular state, or between families about domestick concerns; 'You have a great work in hand, for you write to me that you are upon a *treaty* of marriage.'—HOWEL. A congress carries on *negotiations* for the establishment of good order among the ruling powers of Europe; individual states *treat* with each other, to settle their particular differences. To *negotiate* mostly respects political concerns, except in the case of *negotiating* bills: to *treat*, as well as *transact*, is said of domestick and private concerns: we *treat* with a person about the purchase of a house; we *transact* business with a person either by paying or receiving money, or in any matter of mutual interest; 'We are permitted to know nothing of what is *transacting* in the regions above us.'—BLAIR.

As nouns, *negotiation* expresses rather the act of deliberating than the thing deliberated: *treaty* includes the ideas of the terms proposed, and the arrangement of those terms: *transaction* expresses the idea of something actually done and finished, and in that sense may often be the result of a *negotiation* or *treaty*; 'It is not the purpose of this discourse to set down the particular *transactions* of this *treaty*.'—CLARENDON. *Negotiations* are sometimes very long pending before the preliminary terms are even proposed, or any basis is defined; *treaties* of commerce are entered into by all civilized countries, in order to obviate misunderstandings, and enable them to preserve an amicable intercourse; the *transactions* which daily pass in a great metropolis, like that of London, are of so multifarious a nature, and so infinitely numerous, that the bare contemplation of them fills the mind with astonishment. *Negotiations* are long or short; *treaties* are advantageous or the contrary; *transactions* are honourable or dishonourable.

MISSION, MESSAGE, ERRAND.

Message, from the Latin *missus*, participle of *mitto* to send, signifies the thing for which one is sent; *mission*, signifies the state of being sent, or thing for which one is sent; *errand*, from *erro* to wander, or go to a distance, signifies the thing for which one goes to a distance.

Between *mission* and *message* the difference consists as much in the application as the sense. The *mission* is always a subject of importance, and the situation one of trust and authority, whence it is with propriety applied to our Saviour;

Her son tracing the desert wild,
All his great work to come before him set,
How to begin, how to accomplish best,
His end of being on earth, and *mission* high.
MILTON.

The subject of a *message* is of inferiour importance, and is commonly intrusted to inferiour persons.

The *message* is properly any communication which is conveyed; the *errand* sent from one person to another is that which causes one to go: servants are the bearers of *messages*, and are sent on various *errands*. The *message* may be either verbal or written; the *errand* is limited to no form, and to no circumstance: one delivers the *message*, and goes the *errand*. Sometimes the *message* may be the *errand*, and the *errand* may include the *message*: when that which is sent consists of a notice or intimation to another, it is a *message*; and if that causes any one to go to a place, it is an *errand*: thus it is that the greater part of *errands* consist of sending *messages* from one person to another. Both the terms *message* and *errand* are employed by the poets in reference to higher objects, but they preserve the same distinction;

The scenes where ancient bards th' inspiring breath
Ecstatick felt, and, from this world retir'd,
Convers'd with angels and immortal forms,
On gracious *errands* bent.—THOMSON.

Sometimes, from her eyes,
I did receive fair speechless *messages*.
SHAKSPEARE.

MINISTER, AGENT.

Minister comes from *minus* less, as *magister* comes from *magis* more; the one being less, and the other greater, than others: the *minister*, therefore, is literally one that acts in a subordinate capacity; and the *agent*, from *ago* to act, is the one that takes the acting part: they both perform the will of another, but the *minister* performs a higher part than the *agent*: the *minister* gives his counsel, and exerts his intellectual powers in the service of another; but the *agent* executes the orders or commission given him: a *minister* is employed by government in political affairs; an *agent* is employed by individuals in commercial and pecuniary affairs, or by government in subordinate matters: a *minister* is received at court, and serves as a representative for his government; an *agent* generally acts under the directions of the *minister* or some officer of government: ambassadors or plenipotentiaries, or the first officers of the state, are *ministers*; but those who regulate the affairs respecting prisoners, the police, and the like, are termed *agents*.

FORERUNNER, PRECURSOR, MESSENGER, HARBINGER.

Forerunner and *precursor* signify literally the same thing, namely, one *running before*; but the term *forerunner* is properly applied only to one who runs before to any spot to communicate intelligence; and it is figuratively applied to things which in their nature, or from a natural connexion, precede others; *precursor* is only employed in this figurative sense: thus imprudent speculations are said to be the *forerunners* of a man's ruin; 'Loss of sight is the misery of life, and usually the *forerunner* of death.'—SOUTH. The ferment which took place in men's minds was the *precursor* of the French revolution; 'Gospeller was a name of contempt given by the papists to the Lollards, the puritans of early times, and the *precursors* of protestantism.'—JOHNSON.

Messenger signifies literally one bearing *messages*: and *harbinger*, from the Teutonick *herbinger*, signifies a provider of a *herbege* or *inn* for princes.

Both terms are employed for persons: but the *messenger* states what has been or is; the *harbinger* announces what is to be. Our Saviour was the *messenger* of glad tidings to all mankind; the prophets were the *harbingers* of the Messiah. A *messenger* may be employed on different offices; a *harbinger* is a *messenger* who acts in a specifick office. The angels are represented as *messengers* on different occasions;

His words are bonds, his oaths are oracles,
His tears pure *messengers* sent from his heart
SHAKSPEARE.

John the Baptist was the *harbinger* of our Saviour, who prepared the way of the Lord;

> Sin, and her shadow death; and misery,
> Death's *harbinger*.—MILTON.

TO INTERCEDE, INTERPOSE, MEDIATE, INTERFERE, INTERMEDDLE.

Intercede signifies literally going between; *interpose*, placing one's self between; *mediate*, coming in the middle; *interfere*, setting one's self between; and *intermeddle*, meddling or mixing among.

One *intercedes* between parties that are unequal; one *interposes* between parties that are equal: one *intercedes* in favour of that party which is threatened with punishment; one *interposes* between parties that threaten each other with evil: we *intercede* with the parent in favour of the child who has offended, in order to obtain pardon for him; one *interposes* between two friends who are disputing, to prevent them from going to extremities. One *intercedes* by means of persuasion; it is an act of courtesy or kindness in the *interceded* party to comply: one *interposes* by an exercise of authority; it is a matter of propriety or necessity in the parties to conform. The favourite of a monarch *intercedes* in behalf of some criminal, that his punishment may be mitigated; 'Virgil recovered his estate by Mæcenas's *intercession*.'—DRYDEN. The magistrates *interpose* with their authority, to prevent the broils of the disorderly from coming to serious acts of violence;

> Those few you see escap'd the storm, and fear,
> Unless you *interpose*, a shipwreck here.—DRYDEN.

To *mediate* and *intercede* are both conciliatory acts; the *intercessor* and *mediator* are equals or even inferiours; to *interpose* is an act of authority, and belongs most commonly to a superiour: one *intercedes* or *interposes* for the removal of evil; one *mediates* for the attainment of good: Christ is our *Intercessor*, to avert from us the consequences of our guilt; he is our *Mediator*, to obtain for us the blessings of grace and salvation. An *intercessor* only pleads: a *mediator* guarantees; he takes upon himself a responsibility. Christ is our *Intercessor*, by virtue of his relationship with the Father: he is our *Mediator*, by virtue of his atonement; by which act he takes upon himself the sins of all who are truly penitent.

To *intercede* and *interpose* are employed on the highest and lowest occasions; to *mediate* is never employed but in matters of the greatest moment. As earthly offenders we require the *intercession* of a fellow mortal; as offenders against the God of Heaven, we require the *intercession* of a Divine Being: without the timely *interposition* of a superiour, trifling disputes may grow into bloody quarrels; without the *interposition* of Divine Providence, we cannot conceive of any thing important as taking place; to settle the affairs of nations, *mediators* may afford a salutary assistance; 'It is generally better (in negotiating) to deal by speech than by letter, and by the *mediation* of a third than by a man's self.'—BACON. To bring about the redemption of a lost world, the Son of God condescended to be *Mediator*.

All these acts are performed for the good of others: but *interfere* and *intermeddle* are of a different description: one may *interfere* for the good of others, or to gratify one's self; one never *intermeddles* but for selfish purposes: the first three terms are, therefore, always used in a good sense; the fourth in a good or bad sense, according to circumstances; the last always in a bad sense.

To *interfere* has nothing conciliating in it like *intercede*, nothing authoritative in it like *interpose*, nothing responsible in it like *mediate*; it may be useful, or it may be injurious; it may be authorized or unauthorized; it may be necessary, or altogether impertinent: when we *interfere* so as to make peace between men, it is useful; but when we *interfere* unreasonably, it often occasions differences rather than removes them; 'Religion *interferes* not with any rational pleasure.'—SOUTH.

Intercede, and the other terms, are used in cases where two or more parties are concerned; but *interfere* and *intermeddle* are said of what concerns only one individual; one *interferes* and *intermeddles* rather in the concern, than between the persons; and, on that account, it becomes a question of some importance to decide when we ought to *interfere* in the affairs of another: with regard to *intermeddle*, it always is the unauthorized act of one who is busy in things that ought not to concern him; 'The sight *intermeddles* not with that which affects the smell.'—SOUTH.

INTERMEDIATE, INTERVENING.

Intermediate signifies being in the midst, between two objects; *intervening* signifies coming between, the former is applicable to space and time; the latter either to time or circumstances.

The *intermediate* time between the commencement and the termination of a truce is occupied with preparations for the renewal of hostilities; 'A right opinion is that which connects truth by the shortest train of *intermediate* propositions.'—JOHNSON. *Intervening* circumstances sometimes change the views of the belligerent parties, and dispose their minds to peace; 'Hardly would any transient gleams of *intervening* joy be able to force its way through the clouds, if the successive scenes of distress through which we are to pass were laid before our view.'—BLAIR.

INTERVENTION, INTERPOSITION.

The *intervention*, from *inter* between, and *venio* to come, is said of inanimate objects; the *interposition*, from *inter* between, and *pono* to place, is said only of rational agents. The light of the moon is obstructed by the *intervention* of the clouds; the life of an individual is preserved by the *interposition* of a superiour: human life is so full of contingencies, that when we have formed our projects we can never say what may *intervene* to prevent their execution; 'Reflect also on the calamitous *intervention* of picture-cleaners (to originals).'—BARRY. When a man is engaged in an unequal combat, he has no chance of escaping but by the timely *interposition* of one who is able to rescue him;

> Death ready stands to *interpose* his dart.'—MILTON.

TO BIND, OBLIGE, ENGAGE

Bind, through the medium of the northern languages, comes from the Latin *vincio*, and the Greek σφίγγω; to *oblige*, in French *obliger*, Latin *obligo*, compounded of *ob* and *ligo*, signifies to tie up; *engage*, in French *engager*, compounded of *en* or *in* and *gage* a pledge, signifies to *bind* by means of a pledge.

Bind is more forcible and coercive than *obliges*; *oblige* than *engage*. We are *bound* by an oath, *obliged* by circumstances, and *engaged* by promises.

Conscience *binds*, prudence or necessity *obliges*, honour and principle *engage*. A parent is *bound* no less by the law of his conscience, than by those of the community to which he belongs, to provide for his helpless offspring. Politeness *obliges* men of the world to preserve a friendly exteriour towards those for whom they have no regard. When we are *engaged* in the service of our king and country, we cannot shrink from our duty without exposing ourselves to the infamy of all the world.

We *bind* a man by fear of what may befall him; we *oblige* him by some immediately urgent motive; we *engage* him by alluring offers, and the prospect of gain. A debtor is *bound* to pay by virtue of a written instrument in law;

> Who can be *bound* by any solemn vow,
> To do a murd'rous deed?—SHAKSPEARE.

He is *obliged* to pay in consequence of the importunate demands of the creditor; 'No man is commanded or *obliged* to obey beyond his power.'—SOUTH. He is *engaged* to pay in consequence of a promise given; 'While the Israelites were appearing in God's house, God himself *engages* to keep and defend theirs.'—SOUTH. A *bond* is the strictest deed in law; an *obligation* binds under pain of a pecuniary loss; an *engagement* is mostly verbal, and rests entirely on the rectitude of the parties.

TO BIND, TIE.

Bind, in Saxon *binden*, German, &c. *binden*, come from the Latin *vincio*, Greek σφίγγω, and is connected with the word *wind:* *tie*, in Saxon *tian*, is very probably connected with the low German *tehen*, high German *ziehen* to draw, the English *tug* or *tow*, and the Latin *duco* to draw.

The species of fastening denoted by these two words differ both in manner and degree. *Binding* is performed by circumvolution round a body; *tying*, by involution within itself. Some bodies are *bound* without being *tied;* others are *tied* without being *bound:* a wounded leg is *bound* but not *tied;*

Now are our brows *bound* with victorious wreaths,
Our stern alarms are chang'd to merry meetings.
SHAKSPEARE.

A string is *tied* but not *bound;*

A fluttering dove upon the top they *tie*,
The living mark at which their arrows fly
DRYDEN.

A riband may sometimes be *bound* round the head, and *tied* under the chin. *Binding* therefore serves to keep several things in a compact form together; *tying* may serve to prevent one single body separating from another: a criminal is *bound* hand and foot; he is *tied* to a stake.

Binding and *tying* likewise differ in degree; *binding* serves to produce adhesion in all the parts of a body; *tying* only to produce contact in a single part; thus when the hair is *bound*, it is almost enclosed in an envelope: when it is *tied* with a string, the ends are left to hang loose.

A similar distinction is preserved in the figurative use of the terms. A *bond* of union is applicable to a large body with many component parts; a *tie* of affection marks an adhesion between individual minds;

As nature's *ties* decay;
As duty, love, and honour fail to sway;
Fictitious *bonds*, the *bonds* of wealth and law,
Still gather strength, and force unwilling awe.
GOLDSMITH.

CHAIN, FETTER, BAND, SHACKLE.

Chain, in French *chaine*, Latin *catena*, probably contracted from *captena*, comes from *capio*, signifying that which takes or holds; *fetter*, in German *fessel*, comes from *fassen* to lay hold of; *band*, from *bind*, signifies that which *binds;* *shackle*, in Saxon *scacul*, from *shake*, signifies that which makes a creature shake or move irregularly by confining the legs.

All these terms designate the instrument by which animals or men are confined. *Chain* is general and indefinite; all the rest are species of *chains:* but there are many *chains* which do not come under the other names; a *chain* is indefinite as to its make; it is made generally of iron rings, but of different sizes and shapes: *fetters* are larger, they consist of many stout *chains:* *bands* are in general any thing which confines the body or the limbs; they may be either *chains* or even cords: *shackle* is that species of *chain* which goes on the legs to confine them; malefactors of the worst order have *fetters* on different parts of their bodies, and *shackles* on their legs.

These terms may all be used figuratively. The substantive *chain* is applied to whatever hangs together like a *chain*, as a *chain* of events; but the verb to *chain* signifies to confine as with a *chain:* thus the mind is *chained* to rules, according to the opinions of the free-thinkers, when men adhere strictly to rule and order; and to represent the slavery of conforming to the establishment, they tell us we are *fettered* by systems;

Almighty wisdom never acts in vain,
Nor shall the soul, on which it has bestow'd
Such powers, e'er perish like an earthly clod;
But purg'd at length from foul corruption's stain,
Freed from her prison, and unbound her *chain*,
She shall her native strength and native skies regain.
JENYNS.

'Legislators have no rule to *bind* them but the great principles of justice and equity. These they are *bound* to obey and follow; and rather to enlarge and enlighten law by the liberality of legislative reason than to *fetter* their higher capacity by the narrow constructions of subordinate artificial justice.'—BURKE.

Band in the figurative sense is applied, particularly in poetry, to every thing which is supposed to serve the purpose of a *band;* thus love is said to have its silken *bands;*

Break his *bands* of sleep asunder,
And rouse him like a rattling peal of thunder
DRYDEN.

Shackle, whether as a substantive or a verb, retains the idea of controlling the movements of the person, not in his body only, but also in his mind and in his moral conduct; thus, a man who commences life with a borrowed capital is *shackled* in his commercial concerns by the interest he has to pay, and the obligations he has to discharge; 'It is the freedom of the spirit that gives worth and life to the performance. But a servant commonly is less free in mind than in condition; his very will seems to be in *bonds* and *shackles*.'—SOUTH.

DEBT, DUE.

Debt and *due* are both derived from the same verb. *Debt* comes from *debitus*, participle of the Latin verb *debeo:* and *due*, in French *du*, participle of *devoir* comes likewise from *debeo* to owe.

Debt is used always as a substantive; *due*, either as a substantive or an adjective. A person contracts *debts*, and receives his *due*. The *debt* is both obligatory and compulsory; it is a return for something equivalent in value, and cannot be dispensed with; what is *due* is obligatory, but not always compulsory A *debtor* may be compelled to discharge his *debts;* but it is not always in the power of a man even to claim that which is his *due*. *Debt* is generally used in a mercantile sense; *due* either in a mercantile or moral sense. A *debt* is determined by law: what is *due* is fixed often by principles of equity and honour. He who receives the stipulated price of his goods receives his *debt;* he who receives praise and honour, as a reward of good actions, receives his *due;*

The ghosts rejected are th' unhappy crew,
Depriv'd of sepulchres and fun'ral *due*.
DRYDEN.

Debt may sometimes be used figuratively, as, to pay the *debt* of nature; 'Though Christ was as pure and undefiled, without the least spot of sin, as purity and innocence itself; yet he was pleased to make himself the greatest sinner in the world by imputation, and render himself a surety responsible for our *debts*' SOUTH.

PROMISE, ENGAGEMENT, WORD.

Promise, in Latin *promissus*, from *promitto*, compounded of *pro* before, and *mitto* to set or fix, that is, to fix beforehand; *engagement* is that which engages a person, or places him under an *engagement;* *word*, that is, the word given.

The *promise* is specifick, and consequently more binding than the *engagement:* we *promise* a thing in a set form of words, that are clearly and strictly understood; we *engage* in general terms, that may admit of alteration: a *promise* is mostly unconditional; an *engagement* is frequently conditional. In *promises* the faith of an individual is admitted upon his *word*, and built upon as if it were a deed; in *engagements* the intentions of an individual for the future are all that are either implied or understood: on the fulfilment of *promises* often depend the most important interests of individuals; 'An acre of performance is worth the whole world of *promise*.'—HOWEL. An attention to *engagements* is a matter of mutual convenience in the ordinary concerns of life; 'The *engagements* I had to Dr. Swift were such as the actual services he had done me, in relation to the subscription for Homer, obliged me to.'—POPE. A man makes a *promise* of payment, and upon his *promise* it may happen that many others depend upon the fulfilment of their *promises;* when *engagements* are made to visit or meet others, an inattention to such *engagements* causes great trouble. As a *promise* and *engagement* can be made only by *words*, the *word* is often put for either, or for both, as the case requires: he who breaks his *word* in small matters cannot be trusted when he gives his *word* in matters of consequence;

Æneas was our prince, a juster lord,
Or nobler warriour, never drew a sword;
Observant of the right, religious of his *word*.
DRYDEN.

TO IMPLICATE, INVOLVE.

Implicate, from *plico* to fold, denotes to fold into a thing; and *involve*, from *volvo* to roll, signifies to roll into a thing: by which explanation we perceive, that to *implicate* marks something less entangled than to *involve:* for that which is folded may be folded only once, but that which is rolled, is rolled many times. In application therefore to human affairs, people are said to be *implicated* who have taken ever so small a share in a transaction; but they are *involved* only when they are deeply concerned: the former is likewise especially applied to criminal transactions, the latter to those things which are in themselves troublesome: thus a man is *implicated* in the guilt of robbery, who should stand by and see it done, without interfering for its prevention; as law-suits are of all things the most intricate and harassing, he who is engaged in one is said to be *involved* in it, or he who is in debt in every direction is strictly said to be *involved* in debt; 'Those who cultivate the memory of our Revolution, will take care how they are *involved* with persons who, under pretext of zeal towards the Revolution and constitution, frequently wander from their true principles.'—BURKE. When *implication* is derived from the verb *imply*, signifying the act of implying, it departs altogether from the meaning of *involve;* 'That which can exalt a wife only by degrading a husband, will appear on the whole not worth the acquisition, even though it could be made without provoking jealousy by the *implication* of contempt.'—HAWKESWORTH.

TO DISENGAGE, DISENTANGLE, EXTRICATE.

To *disengage* is to make free from an *engagement; disentangle* to get rid of an *entanglement; extricate*, in Latin *extricatus*, from *ex* and *trica* a hair, or noose, signifies to get as it were out of a noose. As to *engage* signifies simply to bind, and *entangle* signifies to bind in an involved manner; to *disentangle* is naturally applied to matters of greater difficulty and perplexity than to *disengage:* and as the term *extricate* includes the idea of that which would hold fast and keep within a tight involvement, it is employed with respect to matters of the greatest possible embarrassment and intricacy. We may be *disengaged* from an oath; *disentangled* from pecuniary difficulties; *extricated* from a suit at law: it is not right to expect to be *disengaged* from all the duties which attach to men as members of society; 'In old age the voice of nature calls you to leave to others the bustle and contest of the world, and gradually to *disengage* yourself from a burden which begins to exceed your strength.'—BLAIR. He who enters into disputes about contested property must not expect to be soon *disentangled* from the law; 'Savage seldom appeared to be melancholy but when some sudden misfortune had fallen upon him, and even then in a few moments he would *disentangle* himself from his perplexity.'—JOHNSON. When a general has committed himself by coming into too close a contact with a very superiour force, he may think himself fortunate if he can *extricate* himself from his awkward situation with the loss of half his army; 'Nature felt its inability to *extricate* itself from the consequences of guilt; the Gospel reveals the plan of Divine interposition and aid.'—BLAIR.

TO UNFOLD, UNRAVEL, DEVELOPE.

To *unfold* is to open that which has been folded; to *unravel* is to open that which has been *ravelled* or tangled; to *develope* is to open that which has been wrapped in an *envelope*. The application of these terms therefore to moral objects is obvious: what has been *folded* and kept secret is *unfolded;* in this manner a hidden transaction is *unfolded*, by being related circumstantially;

And to the sage-instructing eye *unfold*
The various twine of light.—THOMSON.

What has been entangled in any mystery or confusion is *unravelled:* in this manner a mysterious transaction is *unravelled*, if every circumstance is fully accounted for; 'You must be sure to *unravel* all your designs to a jealous man.'—ADDISON. What has been wrapped up so as to be entirely shut out from view is *developed;* in this manner the plot of a play or novel, or the character and talent of a person, are *developed;* 'The character of Tiberius is extremely difficult to *develope* CUMBERLAND.

COMPLEXITY, COMPLICATION, INTRICACY.

Complexity and *complication*, in French *complication*, Latin *complicatio* and *complico*, compounded of *com* and *plico*, signifies a folding one within another; *intricacy*, in Latin *intricatio* and *intrico*, compounded of *in* and *trico* or *trices*, the small hairs which are used to ensnare birds, signifies a state of entanglement by means of many involutions.

Complexity expresses the abstract quality or state, *complication* the act: they both convey less than *intricacy; intricate* is that which is very *complicated*.

Complexity arises from a multitude of objects, and the nature of these objects; *complication* from an involvement of objects; and *intricacy* from a winding and confused involution. What is *complex* must be decomposed; what is *complicated* must be developed; what is *intricate* must be unravelled. A proposition is *complex;* affairs are *complicated;* the law is *intricate*.

Complexity puzzles; *complication* confounds; *intricacy* bewilders. A clear head is requisite for understanding the *complex;* keenness and penetration are required to lay open that which is *complicated;* a comprehensive mind, coupled with coolness and perseverance of research, are essential to disentangle the *intricate*. A *copmlex* system may have every perfection but the one that is requisite, namely, a fitness to be reduced to practice. *Complicated* schemes of villany commonly frustrate themselves. They require unity of design among too many individuals of different stations, interests, and vices, to allow of frequent success with such heterogeneous combinations. The *intricacy* of the law is but the natural attendant on human affairs; every question admits of different illustrations as to their causes, consequences, analogies, and bearings; it is likewise dependent on so many cases infinitely ramified as to impede the exercise of the judgement in the act of deciding.

The *complexity* of the subject often deters young persons from application to their business;

Through the disclosing deep
Light my blind way; the mineral strata there
Thrust blooming, thence the vegetable world;
O'er that the rising system more *complex*
Of animals, and higher still the mind.
THOMSON.

There is nothing embarrasses a physician more than a *complication* of disorders, where the remedy for one impedes the cure for the other; 'Every living creature, considered in itself, has many very *complicated* parts that are exact copies of some other parts which it possesses, and which are *complicated* in the same manner.' —ADDISON. Some affairs are involved in such a degree of *intricacy*, as to exhaust the patience and perseverance of the most laborious; 'When the mind, by insensible degrees, has brought itself to attention and close thinking, it will be able to cope with difficulties. Every abstruse problem, every *intricate* question, will not baffle or break it.'—LOCKE.

COMPOUND, COMPLEX.

Compound comes from the present of *compono*, as *compose* (*v. To compose*) comes from *composui* the preterite of the same verb; *complex* (*v. Complexity*).

The *compound* consist of similar and whole bodies put together; the *complex* consists of various parts linked together: adhesion is sufficient to constitute a *compound;* involution is requisite for the *complex*. We distinguish the wholes that form the *compound;* we separate the parts that form the *complex*. What is *compound* may consist only of two; what is *complex* consists always of several.

Compound and *complex* are both commonly opposed to the simple; but the former may be opposed to the single, and the latter to the simple. Words are *compound*, sentences are *complex;* 'Inasmuch as man is a *compound* and a mixture of flesh as well as spirit, the soul during its abode in the body does all things by the mediation of these passions, and inferiour affections.'—SOUTH.

With such perfection fram'd,
Is this *complex* stupendous scheme of things.
THOMSON.

TO COMPOUND, COMPOSE.

Compound (*v. Compound*) is used in the physical sense only; *compose* in the proper or the moral sense. Words are *compounded* by making two or more into one; sentences are *composed* by putting words together so as to make sense. A medicine is *compounded* of many ingredients; society is *composed* of various classes; 'The simple beauties of nature, if they cannot be multiplied, may be *compounded*.'—BATHURST. 'The heathens, ignorant of the true source of moral evil, generally charged it on the obliquity of matter. This notion, as most others of theirs, is a *composition* of truth and errour.'—GROVE.

TO COMPEL, FORCE, OBLIGE, NECESSITATE.

Compel, Latin *compello* or *pello* to drive, signifies to drive for a specifick purpose or to a point; *force*, in French *force*, comes from the Latin *fortis* strong; *force* being nothing but the exertion of strength; *oblige*, in French *obliger*, Latin *obligo*, compounded of *ob* and *ligo*, signifies to bind down. These three terms mark an external action on the will, but *compel* expresses more than *oblige*, and less than *force*. *Necessitate* is to make necessary.

Compel and *force* act much more directly and positively than *oblige* or *necessitate;* and the latter indicates more of physical strength than the former. We are *compelled* by outward or inward motives; we are *obliged* more by motives than any thing else; we are *forced* sometimes by circumstances, though oftener by plain strength; we are *necessitated* solely by circumstances. An adversary is *compelled* to yield who resigns from despair of victory; he is *forced* to yield if he stand in fear of his life; he is *obliged* to yield if he cannot withstand the entreaties of his friends; he is *necessitated* to yield if he want the strength to continue the contest.

An obstinate person must be compelled to give up his point;

You will *compel* me then to read the will.
SHAKSPEARE.

A turbulent and disorderly man must be *forced* to go where the officers of justice choose to lead him;

With fates averse, the rout in arms resort
To *force* their monarch, and insult the court.
DRYDEN.

An unreasonable person must be obliged to satisfy a ust demand; 'He that once owes more than he can pay is often *obliged* to bribe his creditors to patience, by increasing his debt.'—JOHNSON. We are all occasionally *necessitated* to do that which is not agreeable to us; 'I have sometimes fancied that women have not a retentive power, or the faculty of suppressing their thoughts, but that they are *necessitated* to speak every thing they think.'—ADDISON.

Pecuniary want *compels* men to do many things inconsistent with their station;

He would the ghosts of slaughter'd soldiers call,
These his dread wands did to short life *compel*,
And *forc'd* the fate of battles to foretell.—DRYDEN.

Honour and religion *oblige* men scrupulously to observe their word one to another; 'The church hath been thought fit to be called Catholick, in reference to the universal obedience which it prescribeth; both in respect of the persons *obliging* men of all conditions; and in relation to the precepts requiring the performance of all the evangelical commands.'—PEARSON. Hunger *forces* men to eat that which is most loathsome to the palate. The fear of a loss *necessitates* a man to give up a favourite project.

FORCE, VIOLENCE.

Force signifies here the exertion of strength in a particular manner, which brings it very near to the meaning of *violence*, which, from the Latin *violentia* and *vis* force, comes from the Greek *βία* strength.

Force, which expresses a much less degree of exertion than *violence*, is ordinarily employed to supply the want of a proper will, *violence* is used to counteract an opposing will. The arm of justice must exercise *force* in order to bring offenders to a proper account; one nation exercises *violence* against another in the act of carrying on war. *Force* is mostly conformable to reason and equity, or employed in self defence;

Our host expell'd, what farther *force* can stay
The victor troops from universal sway?
DRYDEN

Violence is always resorted to for the attainment of that which is unattainable by law; 'He sees his distress to be the immediate effect of human *violence* or oppression; and is obliged at the same time to consider it as a Divine judgement.'—BLAIR. All who are invested with authority have occasion to use *force* at certain times to subdue the unruly will of those who should submit: *violence* and rapine are inseparable companions: a robber could not subsist by the latter without exercising the former.

In an extended and figurative application to things, these terms convey the same general idea of exerting strength. That is said to have *force* that acts with *force;* and that to have *violence* that acts with *violence*. A word, an expression, or a remark, has *force* or is *forcible;* a disorder, a passion, a sentiment, has *violence* or is *violent*. *Force* is always something desirable; *violence* is always something hurtful. We ought to listen to arguments which have *force* in them; we endeavour to correct the *violence* of all angry passions.

VIOLENT, FURIOUS, BOISTEROUS, VEHEMENT, IMPETUOUS.

Violent signifies having force; *furious* having *fury*, *boisterous* in all probability comes from *bestir*, signifying ready to *bestir* or come into motion; *vehement*, in Latin *vehemens*, compounded of *veho* and *mens*, signifies carried away by the mind or the force of passion; *impetuous*, that is, having an *impetus*.

Violent is here the most general term, including the idea of force or violence, which is common to them all; it is as general in its application as in its meaning. When *violent* and *furious* are applied to the same objects, the latter expresses a higher degree of the former: thus a *furious* temper is *violent* to an excessive degree: a *furious* whirlwind is *violent* beyond measure;

The *furious* pard,
Cow'd and subdu'd, flies from the face of man.
SOMERVILLE.

Violent and *boisterous* are likewise applied to the same objects; but the *boisterous* refers only to the *violence* of the motion or noise: hence we say that a wind is *violent*, inasmuch as it acts with great force upon all bodies; it is *boisterous*, inasmuch as it causes the great motion of bodies: a *violent* person deals in *violence* of every kind; a *boisterous* person is full of *violent* action;

Ye too, ye winds! that now begin to blow
With *boisterous* sweep, I raise my voice to you.
THOMSON.

Violent, *vehement*, and *impetuous*, are all applied to persons, or that which is personal: a man is *violent* in his opinions, *violent* in his measures, *violent* in his resentments; 'This gentleman (Mr. Steele) among a thousand others, is a great instance of the fate of all who are carried away by party spirit of any side; I wish all *violence* may succeed as ill.'—POPE. He is *vehement* in his affections or passions, *vehement* in love, *vehement* in zeal, *vehement* in pursuing an object, *vehement* in expression; 'If there be any use of gesticulation, it must be applied to the ignorant and rude, who will be more affected by *vehemence* than delighted by propriety.'—JOHNSON. *Violence* transfers itself to some external object on which it acts with force; but *vehemence* respects that species of *violence* which is confined to the person himself: we may dread *violence*, because it is always liable to do mischief; we ought to suppress our *vehemence*, because it is injurious to ourselves: a *violent* partisan renders himself obnoxious to others; a man who is *vehement* in any cause puts it out of his own power to be of use. *Impetuosity* is rather the extreme of *violence* or *vehemence*: an *impetuous* attack is an excessively *violent* attack: an *impetuous* character is an excessively *vehement* character;

The central waters round *impetuous* rush'd.
THOMSON.

BUSTLE, TUMULT, UPROAR.

Bustle is probably a frequentative of *busy; tumult*, in French *tumulte*, Latin *tumultus*, compounded probably of *tumor multus*, signifies much swelling and perturbation; *uproar*, compounded of *up* and *roar*, marks the act of setting up a roar or clamour, or the state of its being so set up.

Bustle has most of hurry in it; *tumult* most of disorder and confusion; *uproar* most of noise.

The hurried movements of one, or many, cause a *bustle;* disorderly struggles of many constitute a *tumult;* the loud elevation of many opposing voices produces an *uproar*.

Bustle is frequently not the effect of design, but the natural consequence of many persons coming together; 'They who live in the *bustle* of the world are not, perhaps, the most accurate observers of the progressive change of manners in that society in which they pass their time.'—ABERCROMBY. *Tumult* commonly arises from a general effervescence in the minds of a multitude;

Outlaws of nature! yet the great must use 'em
Sometimes as necessary tools of *tumult*.—DRYDEN.

Uproar is the consequence either of general anger or mirth; 'Amid the *uproar* of other bad passions, conscience acts as a restraining power.'—BLAIR.

A crowded street will always be in a *bustle*. Contested elections are always accompanied with great *tumult*. Drinking parties make a considerable *uproar*, in the indulgence of their intemperate mirth.

TO COERCE, RESTRAIN.

Coerce, in Latin *coerceo*, that is, *con* and *arceo*, signifies to drive into conformity with any person or thing; *restrain*, in Latin *restringo*, i. e. *re* and *stringo*, signifies to bind hard.

Coercion is a species of *restraint:* we always *restrain* or intend to *restrain* when we *coerce;* but we do not always *coerce* when we *restrain: coercion* always comprehends the idea of force, *restraint* that of simply keeping under or back: *coercion* is always an external application; *restraint* either external or internal: a person is *coerced* by others only; he may be *restrained* by himself as well as others.

Coercion acts by a direct application, it opposes force to resistance; *restraint* acts indirectly to the prevention of an act: the law *restrains* all men in their actions more or less; it *coerces* those who attempt to violate it: the unruly will is *coerced;* the improper will is *restrained: coercion* is exercised; *restraint* is imposed: punishment, threats, or any actual exercise of authority, *coerces;* 'Without *coercive* power all government is but toothless and precarious, and does not so much command as beg obedience.'—SOUTH. Fear, shame, or a remonstrance from others, *restrains;* 'The enmity of some men against goodness is so violent and implacable, that no innocency, no excellence of goodness, how great soever, can *restrain* their malice.'—TILLOTSON. The innovators of the present age are for having all *coercion* laid aside in the management of children, in lieu of which a system of reasoning is to be adopted; could they persuade the world to adopt their fanciful scheme, we may next expect to hear that all *restraint* on the inclinations ought to be laid aside as an infringement of personal liberty.

COGENT, FORCIBLE, STRONG.

Cogent, from the Latin *cogo* to compel; and *forcible*, from the verb to *force*, have equally the sense of acting by *force; strong* is here figuratively employed for that species of strength which is connected with the mind.

Cogency applies to reasons individually considered *force* and *strength* to modes of reasoning or expression: *cogent* reasons impel to decisive conduct; *strong* conviction is produced by *forcible* reasoning conveyed in *strong* language: changes of any kind are so seldom attended with benefit to society, that a legislator will be cautious not to adopt them without the most *cogent* reasons; 'Upon men intent only upon truth, the art of an orator has little power; a credible testimony, or a *cogent* argument, will overcome all the art of modulation and all the violence of contortion.'—JOHNSON The important truths of Christianity cannot be presented from the pulpit too *forcibly* to the minds of men; 'The ingenious author just mentioned, assured me that the Turkish satires of Ruhi Bag-dadi were very *forcible*.'—SIR WM. JONES.

Accuracy and *strength* are seldom associated in the same mind; those who accustom themselves to *strong* language are not very scrupulous about the correctness of their assertions; 'Such is the censure of Dennis. There is, as Dryden expresses it, perhaps "too much horse-play in his raillery;" but if his jests are coarse his arguments are *strong*.'—JOHNSON.

CONSTRAINT, COMPULSION.

Constraint, from *constrain*, Latin *constringo*, compounded of *con* and *stringo*, signifies the act of straining or tying together; *compulsion* signifies the act of compelling.

There is much of binding in *constraint;* of violence in *compulsion: constraint* prevents from acting agreeably to the will: *compulsion* forces to act contrary to the will: a soldier in the ranks moves with much *constraint*, and is often subject to much *compulsion* to make him move as is desired. *Constraint* may arise from outward circumstances; *compulsion* is always produced by some active agent: the forms of civil society lay a proper *constraint* upon the behaviour of men so as to render them agreeable to each other;

Commands are no *constraints*. If I obey them
I do it freely.—MILTON.

The arm of the civil power must ever be ready to *compel* those who will not submit without *compulsion:* 'Savage declared that it was not his design to fly from justice; that he intended to have appeared (to appear) at the bar without *compulsion*.'—JOHNSON. In the moments of relaxation, the actions of children should be as free from *constraint* as possible, which is one means of lessening the necessity for *compulsion* when they are called to the performance of their duty.

CONSTRAINT, RESTRAINT, RESTRICTION

The meaning of *constraint* is given in the preceding article; that of *restraint* as given under *To coerce, restrain; restriction* is but a variation of *restraint*.

Constraint respects the movements of the body only; *restraint* those of the mind and the outward actions: when they both refer to the outward actions, we say a person's behaviour is *constrained;* his feelings are *restrained:* he is *constrained* to act or not to act, or to act in a certain manner; he is *restrained* from acting at all, if not from feeling: the conduct is *constrained* by certain prescribed rules, by discipline and order; it is *restrained* by particular motives whoever learns a mechanical exercise is *constrained* to move his body in a certain direction; the fear of detection often *restrains* persons from the commission of vices more than any sense of their enormity.

The behaviour of children must be more *constrained* in the presence of their superiours than when they are by themselves: the angry passions should at all times be *restrained*. A person who is in the slightest degree *constrained* to do a good action, does good only by halves; 'When from *constraint* only the offices of seeming kindness are performed, little dependence can be placed on them.'—BLAIR. The inordinate passions and propensities of men are *restrained* by nothing so effectually as religion; 'What *restraints* do they lie under who have no regards beyond the grave?'—BERKELEY. Whoever is *restrained* by shame only may seek gratification under the shelter of concealment.

Restrain and *restrict*, though but variations from the same verb, have acquired a distinct acceptation: the former applies to the desires, as well as the outward conduct; the latter only to the outward conduct. A person *restrains* his inordinate appetite; or he is *restrained* by others from doing mischief: he is *restricted* in the use of his money. *Restrain* is an act of power; but *restrict* is an act of authority or law: the will or the actions of a child are *restrained* by the parent;

> Tully, whose powerful eloquence awhile
> *Restrain'd* the rapid fate of rushing Rome.
> THOMSON.

A patient is *restricted* in his diet by a physician, or any body of people may be *restricted* by laws; 'Though the Egyptians used flesh for food, yet they were under greater *restrictions*, in this particular, than most other nations.'—JAMES.

STRAIN, SPRAIN, STRESS, FORCE.

Strain and *sprain* are without doubt variations of the same word, namely, the Latin *stringo* to pull tight, or to stretch; they have now, however, a distinct application: to *strain* is to extend a thing beyond its ordinary length by some extraordinary effort; to *sprain* is to *strain* it so as to put out of its place, or extend to an injurious length: the ankle and the wrist are liable to be *sprained* by a contusion; the back and other parts of the body may be *strained* by over-exertion.

Strain and *stress* are kindred terms, as being both variations of stretch and *stringo;* but they differ now very considerably in their application: figuratively we speak of *straining* a nerve, or *straining* a point, to express making great exertions, even beyond our ordinary powers; and morally we speak of laying a *stress* upon any particular measure or mode of action, signifying to give a thing importance: the *strain* may be put for the course of sentiment which we express, and the manner of expressing it; the *stress* may be put for the efforts of the voice in uttering a word or syllable: a writer may proceed in a *strain* of panegyric or invective; a speaker or a reader lays a *stress* on certain words by way of distinguishing them from others. To *strain* is properly a species of *forcing;* we may *force* in a variety of ways, that is, by the exercise of *force* upon different bodies, and in different directions; but to *strain* is to exercise *force* by stretching or prolonging bodies; thus to *strain* a cord is to pull it to its full extent; but we may speak of *forcing* any hard substance in, or *forcing* it out, or *forcing* it through, or *forcing* it from a body: a door or a lock may be *forced* by violently breaking them: but a door or a lock may be *strained* by putting the hinges or the spring out of its place. So likewise, a person may be said to *force* himself to speak, when by a violent exertion he gives utterance to his words; but he *strains* his throat or his voice when he exercises the *force* on the throat or lungs so as to extend them, or he *strains* his powers of thinking; 'There was then (before the fall) no poring, no struggling with memory, no *straining* for invention.'—SOUTH. *Force* and *stress* as nouns are in like manner comparable when they are applied to the mode of utterance. we must use a certain *force* in the pronunciation of every word; this therefore is indefinite and general; but the *stress* is that particular and strong degree of *force* which is exerted in the pronunciation of certain words; 'Was ever any one observed to come out of a tavern fit for his study, or indeed for any thing requiring *stress*.'—SOUTH.

> Oppose not rage, while rage is in its *force*.
> SHAKSPEARE.

STRESS, STRAIN, EMPHASIS, ACCENT.

Stress and *strain* signify the same as in the preceding article; *emphasis*, from the Greek φαίνω to appear, signifies making to appear; *accent*, in Latin *accentus*, from *cano* to sing, signifies to suit the tune or tone of the voice.

Stress and *strain* are general both in sense and application: the former still more than the latter: *emphasis* and *accent* are modes of the *stress*. *Stress* is applicable to all bodies, the powers of which may be tried by exertion; as the *stress* upon a rope, upon a shaft of a carriage, a wheel or spring in a machine: the *strain* is an excessive *stress*, by which a thing is thrown out of its course; there may be a *strain* in most cases where there is a *stress:* but *stress* and *strain* are to be compared with *emphasis* and *accent*, particularly in the exertion of the voice, in which case the *stress* is a strong and special exertion of the voice, on one word, or one part of a word, so as to distinguish it from another; but the *strain* is the undue exertion of the voice beyond its usual pitch, in the utterance of one or more words; we lay a *stress* on our words for the convenience of others; but when we *strain* the voice it is as much to the annoyance of others as it is hurtful to ourselves; 'Singing differs from vociferation in this, that it consists in a certain harmony; nor is it performed with so much *straining* of the voice.'—JAMES. The *stress* may consist in an elevation of voice, or a prolonged utterance; 'Those English syllables which I call long ones receive a peculiar *stress* of voice from their acute or circumflex accent, as in quickly, dôwry.'—FOSTER. The *emphasis* is that species of *stress* which is employed to distinguish one word or syllable from another: the *stress* may be accidental; but the *emphasis* is an intentional *stress:* ignorant people and children are often led to lay the *stress* on little and unimportant words in a sentence; speakers sometimes find it convenient to mark particular words, to which they attach a value, by the *emphasis* with which they utter them; '*Emphasis* not so much regards the time as a certain grandeur, whereby some letter, syllable, word, or sentence, is rendered more remarkable than the rest by a more vigorous pronunciation and a longer stay upon it.'—HOLDER. The *stress* may be casual or regular, on words or syllables; the *accent* is that kind of regulated *stress* which is laid on one syllable to distinguish it from another: there are many words in our own language, such as subject, object, present, and the like, where, to distinguish the verb from the noun, the *accent* falls on the last syllable for the former, and on the first syllable for the latter; 'The correctness and harmony of English verse depends entirely upon its being composed of a certain number of syllables, and its having the *accents* of those syllables properly placed.'—TYRWHITT.

In reference to the use of words, these terms may admit of a farther distinction: for we may lay a *stress* or *emphasis* on a particular point of our reasoning, in the first case, by enlarging upon it longer than on other points; or, in the second case, by the use of stronger expressions or epithets; 'After such a mighty *stress*, so irrationally laid upon two slight, empty words ('self-consciousness' and 'mutual consciousness') have they made any thing, but the author himself (Sherlock on the Trinity) better understood?'—SOUTH. 'The idle, who are neither wise for this world nor the next, are *emphatically* called, by Dr. Tillotson, "Fools at large."'—SPECTATOR. The *strain* or *accent* may be employed to designate the tone or manner in which we express ourselves, that is, the spirit of our discourse: in familiar language we talk of a person's proceeding in a *strain* of panegyric, or of censure; 'An assured hope of future glory raises him to a pursuit of a more than ordinary *strain* of duty and perfection.'—SOUTH. In poetry persons are said to pour forth their complaints in tender *accents;*

> For thee my tuneful *accents* will I raise.—DRYDEN

TO REPRESS, RESTRAIN, SUPPRESS.

To *repress* is to press back or down: to *restrain* is to strain back or down. the former is the general, the latter is the specifick term: we always *repress* when we *restrain*, but not *vice versâ*. *Repress* is used mostly for pressing down, so as to keep that inward which wants to make its appearance: *restrain* is an habitual *repression* by which it is kept in a state of lowness: a person is said to *repress* his feelings when he does not give them vent either by his words or actions; he is said to *restrain* his feelings when he never lets them rise beyond a certain pitch: good morals, as well as good manners, call upon us to *repress* every unseemly expression of joy in the company of those who are not in a condition to partake of our joy; it is prudence as well as virtue to *restrain* our appetites by an habitual forbearance, that they may not gain the ascendancy. One cannot too quickly *repress* a rising spirit of resistance in any community, large or small; 'Philosophy has often attempted to repress insolence by asserting that all conditions are levelled by death.'—JOHNSON. One cannot too early *restrain* the irregularities of childhood; 'He that would keep the power of sin from running out into act, must *restrain* it from conversing with the object.'—SOUTH. The innocent vivacity of youth should not be *repressed;* but their wildness and intemperance ought to be *restrained.*

To *repress* is simply to keep down or to keep from rising to excess. To *suppress* is to keep under or to keep from appearing in publick or coming into notice. A judicious parent *represses* every tumultuous passion in a child; 'Her forwardness was *repressed* with a frown by her mother or aunt.'—JOHNSON. A judicious commander *suppresses* a rebellion by a timely and resolute exercise of authority; 'Every rebellion, when it is *suppressed*, makes the subject weaker and the prince stronger.'—DAVIES. To *repress* a feeling is to keep it down so that it may not increase in force; so likewise to *repress* violence either of feeling or conduct;

Such kings
Favour the innocent, *repress* the bold,
And, while they flourish, make an age of gold,
WALLER.

'Some, taking dangers to be the only remedy against dangers, endeavoured to set up the sedition again, but they were speedily *repressed*, and thereby the sedition *suppressed* wholly.'—HAYWARD. To *suppress* a feeling is not to give it expression, to *suppress* a work, &c. is not to give it publication, or withdraw it from farther publication;

With him Palemon kept the watch at night,
In whose sad bosom many a sigh *supprest*
Some painful secret of the soul confest.
FALCONER.

You may depend upon the *suppression* of these verses.'—POPE.

TO STIFLE, SUPPRESS, SMOTHER.

Stifle is a frequentative of *stuff*, in Latin *stipo*, and Greek ςύφω to make tight or close; *suppress* signifies the same as in the preceding article; *smother*, as a frequentative of smut or smoke, signifies to cover with smut or smoke.

Stifle and *smother* in their literal sense will be more properly considered under the article of *Suffocate*, &c. (*v. To suffocate*); they are here taken in a moral application.

The leading idea of all these terms is that of keeping out of view: *stifle* is applicable to the feelings only; *suppress* to the feelings or to outward circumstances; *smother* to outward circumstances only: we *stifle* resentment; we *suppress* anger: the former is an act of some continuance; the latter is the act of the moment: we *stifle* our resentment by abstaining to take any measures of retaliation; 'You excel in the art of *stifling* and concealing your resentment.'—SWIFT. We *suppress* the rising emotion of anger, so as not to give it utterance or even the expression of a look; 'They foresaw the violence with which this indignation would burst out after being so long *suppressed*.'—ROBERTSON. It requires time and powerful motives to *stifle*, but only a single effort to *suppress;* nothing but a long course of vice can enable a man to *stifle* the admonitions and reproaches of conscience;

Art, brainless art! our furious charioteer,
(For nature's voice *unstifled* would recall)
Drives headlong to the precipice of death.
YOUNG.

A sense of prudence may sometimes lead a man to *suppress* the joy which an occurrence produces in his mind;

Well did'st thou, Richard, to *suppress* thy voice;
For had the passions of thy heart burst out,
I fear we should have seen decipher'd there
More rancorous spight, more furious raging broils.
SHAKSPEARE.

In regard to outward circumstances, we say that a book is *suppressed* by the authority of government; that vice is *suppressed* by the exertions of those who have power: an affair is *smothered* so that it shall not become generally known, or that the fire is *smothered* under the embers; 'Great and generous principles not being kept up and cherished, but *smothered* in sensual delights, God suffers them to sink into low and inglorious satisfaction.'—SOUTH.

TO SUFFOCATE, STIFLE, SMOTHER, CHOKE

Suffocate, in Latin *suffocatus*, participle of *suffoco*, is compounded of *sub* and *faux*, signifying to stop up the throat; *stifle* is a frequentative of *stuff*, that is, to stuff excessively; *smother* is a frequentative of *smoke;* *choke* is probably a variation of *cheek*, in Saxon *ceac*, because strangulation is effected by a compression of the throat under the cheek-bone.

These terms express the act of stopping the breath; but under various circumstances and by various means; *suffocation* is produced by every kind of means, external or internal, and is therefore the most general of these terms;

A *suffocating* wind the pilgrim smites
With instant death.—THOMSON.

Stifling proceeds by internal means, that is, by the admission of foreign bodies into the passages which lead to the respiratory organs, and in this sense is employed figuratively;

When my heart was ready with a sigh to cleave,
I have, with mighty anguish of my soul,
Just at the birth *stifled* this still-born sigh.
SHAKSPEARE.

We may be *suffocated* by excluding the air externally, as by gagging, confining closely, or pressing violently: we may be *suffocated* or *stifled* by means of vapours, close air, or smoke. To *smother* is to *suffocate* by the exclusion of air externally, as by covering a person entirely with bedclothes: to *choke* is a mode of *stifling* by means of bodies disproportionately large, as a piece of food lodging in the throat or the larynx, in which sense they may both be used figuratively; 'The love of jealous men breaks out furiously (when the object of their loves is taken from them) and throws off all mixture of suspicion which *choked* and *smothered* it before.'—ADDISON.

TO CHECK, CURB, CONTROL.

All these terms express a species of restraining.

Check and *curb* are figurative expressions borrowed from natural objects. *Check*, from *check* or *check-mate* in the game of chess, signifies as a verb to exert a restrictive power; *curb*, from the *curb*, by which horses are kept in, signifies in like manner, a coercive restraining; *control* is probably contracted from *counter-roll*, that is, to turn against an object, to act against it.

To *check* is to throw obstacles in the way, to impede the course; to *curb* is to bear down by the direct exercise of force, to prevent from action; to *control* is to direct and turn the course: the actions of men are *checked;* their feelings are *curbed;* their actions or feelings are *controlled.*

External means are employed in *checking* or *controlling;* external or internal means are employed in *curbing:* men *check* and *control* others; they *curb* themselves or others; young people ought always to be *checked* whenever they discover a too forward temper in the presence of their superiours or elders; 'Devotion, when it does not lie under the *check* of reason, is apt to degenerate into enthusiasm.'—ADDISON. It is necessary to *curb* those who are of an impetuous temper;

The point of honour has been deem'd of use,
To teach good manners, and to *curb* abuse;
Admit it true, the consequence is clear,
Our polished manners are a mask we wear.
COWPER.

It is necessary to keep youth under *control*, until they have within themselves the restrictive power of judgement to *curb* their passions, and *control* their inordinate appetites;

Whatever private views and passions plead,
No cause can justify so black a deed;
These, when the angry tempest clouds the soul,
May darken reason and her course *control.*
THOMSON

unlimited power cannot with propriety be intrusted to any body of individuals; there ought in every state to be a legitimate means of *checking* those who show a disposition to exercise an undue authority; but to invest the people with this office is in fact giving back, into the hands of the community, that which for the wisest purposes was taken from them by the institution of government: it is giving a restraining power to those who themselves are most in want of being restrained; whose ungovernable passions require to be *curbed* by the iron arm of power, whose unruly wills require all he influence of wisdom and authority to *control* them.

TO FORBID, PROHIBIT, INTERDICT, PROSCRIBE.

The *for* in *forbid*, from the German *ver*, is negative, signifying to bid not to do; the *pro* in *prohibit*, and *inter* in *interdict*, have both a similarly negative sense: the former verb, from *habeo* to have, signifies to have or hold that a thing shall not be done, to restrain from doing; the latter, from *dico* to say, signifies to say that a thing shall not be done.

Forbid is the ordinary term; *prohibit* is the judicial term; *interdict* the moral term.

To *forbid* is a direct and personal act, to *prohibit* is an indirect action that operates by means of extended influence: both imply the exercise of power or authority of an individual; but the former is more applicable to the power of an individual, and the latter to the authority of government. A parent *forbids* his child marrying when he thinks proper; 'The father of Constantia was so incensed at the father of Theodosius that he *forbade* the son his house.'—ADDISON. The government *prohibits* the use of spirituous liquors; 'I think that all persons (that is, quacks) should be *prohibited* from curing their incurable patients by act of parliament.'—HAWKESWORTH. *Interdict* is a species of *forbidding* applied to more serious concerns; we may be *interdicted* the use of wine by a physician; 'It is not to be desired that morality should be considered as *interdicted* to all future writers.'—JOHNSON.

A thing is *forbidden* by a command; it is *prohibited* by a law: hence that which is immoral is *forbidden* by the express word of God; that which is illegal is *prohibited* by the laws of man. We are *forbidden* in the Scripture from even indulging a thought of committing evil; it is the policy of every government to *prohibit* the importation and exportation of such commodities as are likely to affect the internal trade of the country.* To *forbid* or *interdict* are opposed to command; to *prohibit*, to allow. As nothing is *forbidden* to Christians which is good and just in itself, so nothing is commanded that is hurtful and unjust; the same cannot be said of the Mahometan or any other religion. As no one is *prohibited* in our own country from writing that which can tend to the improvement of mankind; so on the other hand he is not allowed to indulge his private malignity by the publication of injurious personalities.

Forbid and *interdict*, as personal acts, are properly applicable to persons only, but by an improper application are extended to things; *prohibit*, however, in the general sense of restraining, is applied with equal propriety to things as to persons: shame *forbids* us doing a thing;

> Life's span *forbids* us to extend our cares,
> And stretch our hopes beyond our years.
> CREECH.

Law, authority, and the like, *prohibit*; 'Fear *prohibits* endeavours by infusing despair of success.'—JOHNSON. Nature *interdicts*;

> Other ambition nature *interdicts*.—YOUNG.

Proscribe, in Latin *proscribo*, signified originally to offer for sale, and also to outlaw a person, but is now employed either in the political or moral sense of condemning capitally or utterly, whence it has been extended in its application to signify the absolutely *forbidding* to be used or held as to *proscribe* a name or a doctrine; 'Some utterly *proscribe* the name of chance, as a word of impious and profane signification.'—SOUTH.

* Vide Trusler: "To forbid, prohibit."

TO DECIDE, DETERMINE, CONCLUDE UPON

The idea of bringing a thing to an end is common to the signification of all these words; but *decide* expresses more than *determine*, and *determine* more than *conclude upon*; to *decide*, from the Latin *decido*, compounded of *de* and *cædo*, signifying to cut off or cut short a business; and *determine*, from the Latin *determino*, compounded of *de* and *terminus* a term or boundary, signifying to fix the boundary, are both employed in matters relating to ourselves or others; *conclude*, from the Latin *concludo*, signifying to make the mind up to a thing, is employed in matters that respect the parties only who *conclude*. As it respects others, to *decide* is an act of greater authority than to *determine*: a parent *decides* for his child; a subordinate person may *determine* sometimes for those who are under him in the absence of his superiours. In all cases, to *decide* is an act of greater importance than to *determine*. The nature and character of a thing is *decided* upon: its limits or extent are *determined* on. A judge *decides* on the law and equity of the case; the jury *determine* as to the guilt or innocence of the person. An individual *decides* in his own mind on any measure, and the propriety of adopting it; he *determines* in his own mind, as to how, when, and where it shall be commenced.

One *decides* in all matters of question or dispute; one *determines* in all matters of fact. We *decide* in order to have an opinion; we *determine* in order to act. In complicated cases, where arguments of apparently equal weight are offered by men of equal authority, it is difficult to *decide*;

> With mutual blood th' Ausonian soil is dyed,
> While on its borders each their claim *decide*.
> DRYDEN

When equally feasible plans are offered for our choice, we are often led to *determine* upon one of them from trifling motives; 'Revolutions of state, many times make way for new institutions and forms; and often *determine* in either setting up some tyranny at home, or bringing in some conquest from abroad.'—TEMPLE

To *determine* and *conclude* are equally practical: but *determine* seems to be more peculiarly the act of an individual; *conclude* may be the act of one or of many. We *determine* by an immediate act of the will: we *conclude on* a thing by inference and deduction. Caprice may often influence in *determining*; but nothing is *concluded on* without deliberation and judgement. Many things may be *determined* on which are either never put into execution, or remain long unexecuted;

> Eve! now expect great tidings, which perhaps
> Of us will soon *determine*, or impose
> New laws to be observ'd.—MILTON.

What is *concluded on* is mostly followed by immediate action. To *conclude on* is properly to come to a final *determination*;

> Is it *concluded* he shall be protector?
> It is *determined*, not *concluded* yet;
> But so it must be, if the king miscarry.
> SHAKSPEARE.

TO DETERMINE, RESOLVE.

To *determine* (*v. To decide*) is more especially an act of the judgement; *to *resolve* (*v. Courage*) is an act of the will: the former requires examination and choice; we *determine* how or what we shall do: the latter requires a firm spirit; we *resolve* that we will do what we have *determined* upon. Our *determinations* should be prudent, that they may not cause repentance; our *resolutions* should be fixed, in order to prevent variation. There can be no co-operation with a man who is *undetermined*; it will be dangerous to co-operate with a man who is *irresolute*.

In the ordinary concerns of life we have frequent occasion to *determine* without *resolving*; in the discharge of our moral duties, or the performance of any office, we have occasion to *resolve* without *determining*. A master *determines* to dismiss his servant; the servant *resolves* on becoming more diligent. Personal convenience or necessity gives rise to the *determination*; a sense of duty, honour, fidelity, and the like, gives birth to the *resolution*. A traveller *determines* to take a certain route; a learner *resolves* to conquer ever

* Vide Abbe Girard: "Decision, resolution."

difficulty in the acquirement of learning. Humour or change of circumstances occasions a person to alter his *determination;* timidity, fear, or defect in principle, occasions the *resolution* to waver. Children are not capable of *determining;* and their best *resolutions* fall before the gratification of the moment. Those who *determine* hastily are frequently under the necessity of altering their *determinations;* 'When the mind hovers among such a variety of allurements, one had better settle on a way of life that is not the very best we might have chosen, than grow old without *determining* our choice.'—ADDISON. There are no *resolutions* so weak as those that are made on a sick bed: the return of health is quickly succeeded by a recurrence to our former course of life; 'The *resolution* of dying to end our miseries does not show such a degree of magnanimity, as a *resolution* to bear them, and submit to the dispensations of Providence.'—ADDISON.

In matters of science, *determine* is to fix the mind, or to cause it to rest in a certain opinion; to *resolve* is to lay open what is obscure, to clear the mind from doubt and hesitation. We *determine* points of question; we *resolve* difficulties. It is more difficult to *determine* in matters of rank or precedence than in cases where the solid and real interests of men are concerned; 'We pray against nothing but sin, and against evil in general (in the Lord's prayer), leaving it with Omniscience to *determine* what is really such.'—ADDISON. It is the business of the teacher to *resolve* the difficulties which are proposed by the scholar; 'I think there is no great difficulty in *resolving* your doubts. The reasons for which you are inclined to visit London are, I think, not of sufficient strength to answer the objections.'—JOHNSON. Every point is not proved which is *determined;* nor is every difficulty *resolved* which is answered.

TO SOLVE, RESOLVE.

Solve and *resolve* both come from the Latin *solvo*, in Greek λύω, in Hebrew שׁל to loosen.

Between *solve* and *resolve* there is no considerable difference either in sense or application: the former seems merely to speak of unfolding, in a general manner, that which is wrapped up in obscurity: to *resolve* is rather to unfold it by the particular method of carrying one back to first principles; we *solve* a problem, and *resolve* a difficulty;

> Something yet of doubt remains,
> Which only thy *solution* can *resolve.*—MILTON.

DECIDED, DETERMINED, RESOLUTE.

A man who is *decided* (*v. To decide*) remains in no doubt: he who is *determined* is uninfluenced by the doubts or questions of others: he who is *resolute* (*v. To determine, resolve*) is uninfluenced by the consequences of his actions. A *decided* character is at all times essential for a prince or a minister, but particularly so in an unsettled period like the present; a *determined* character is essential for a commander, or any one who has to exercise authority; a *resolute* character is essential for one who has engaged in dangerous enterprises. Pericles was a man of a *decided* temper, which was well fitted to direct the affairs of government in a season of turbulence and disquietude; 'Almost all the high-bred republicans of my time have, after a short space, become the most *decided* thorough-paced courtiers.'—BURKE. Titus Manlius Torquatus displayed himself to be a man of a *determined* character, when he put to death his victorious son for a breach of military discipline;

> A race *determined*, that to death contend;
> So fierce these Greeks their last retreats defend.
> POPE.

Brutus, the murderer of Cæsar, was a man of a *resolute* temper; 'Most of the propositions we think, reason, discourse, nay, act upon, are such as we cannot have undoubted knowledge of their truth; yet some of them border so near upon certainty that we make no doubt at all about them; but assent to them as firmly, and act according to that assent as *resolutely*, as if they were infallibly demonstrated.'—LOCKE.

DECIDED, DECISIVE.

Decided marks that which is actually *decided: decisive* that which appertains to *decision*.

Decided is employed for persons or things; *decisive* only for things. A person's aversion or attachment is *decided;* a sentence, a judgement, or a victory, is *decisive*. A man of a *decided* character always adopts *decisive* measures. It is right to be *decidedly* averse to every thing which is immoral: we should be cautious not to pronounce *decisively* on any point where we are not perfectly clear and well grounded in our opinion. In every popular commotion it is the duty of a good subject to take a *decided* part in favour of law and order; 'A politick caution, a guarded circumspection, were among the ruling principles of our forefathers in their most *decided* conduct.'—BURKE. Such is the nature of law, that, if it were not *decisive*, it would be of no value; 'The sentences of superiour judges are final, *decisive*, and irrevocable.'—BLACKSTONE.

DECISION, JUDGEMENT, SENTENCE.

Decision signifies literally the act of *deciding*, or the thing *decided* upon (*v. To decide*); *judgement* signifies the act of *judging* or *determining* in general (*v. To decide*); *sentence*, in Latin *sententia*, signifies the opinion held or maintained.

These terms, though very different in their original meaning, are now employed so that the two latter are species of the former; a final conclusion of any business is comprehended in them all: but the *decision* conveys none of the collateral ideas which are expressed by *judgement* and *sentence:* a *decision* has no respect to the agent; it may be said of one or many; it may be the *decision* of a court of law, of the nation, of the publick, of a particular body of men, or of a private individual: but a *judgement* is given in a publick court, or among private individuals: a *sentence* is passed in a court of law, or at the bar of the publick.

A *decision* specifies none of the circumstances of the action; it may be a legal or an arbitrary *decision;* it may be a *decision* according to one's caprice, or after mature deliberation: a *judgement* is always passed either in a court of law, and consequently by virtue of authority; or it is passed by an individual by the authority of his own *judgement:* a *sentence* is always passed by the authority of law, or the will of the publick.

A *decision* respects matters of dispute or litigation; it puts an end to all question; 'The *decisions* of the judges, in the several courts of justice, are the principal and most authoritative evidence that can be given of the existence of such a custom as shall form a part of the common law.'—BLACKSTONE. A *judgement* respects the guilt or innocence, the moral excellence or defects, of a person; 'It is the greatest folly to seek the praise or approbation of any being besides the Supreme Being; because no other being can make a right *judgement* of us.'—ADDISON. A *sentence* respects the punishment or consequent fate of the object: 'The guilty man has an honour for the judge, who with justice pronounces against him the *sentence* of death itself.'—STEELE. Some questions are of so complicated a nature, that it is not possible to bring them to a *decision:* men are forbidden by the Christian religion to be severe in their *judgements* on one another; the works of an author must sometimes await the *sentence* of impartial posterity before their value can be duly appreciated.

FINAL, CONCLUSIVE.

Final, in French *final*, Latin *finalis*, from *finis* the end, signifies having an end; *conclusive*, as in the preceding article, signifies shutting up, or coming to a conclusion.

Final designates simply the circumstance of being the last; *conclusive* the mode of finishing or coming to the last: a determination is *final* which is to be succeeded by no other; 'Neither with us in England hath there been (till very lately) any *final* determination upon the right of authors at the common law.'—BLACKSTONE. A reasoning is *conclusive* that puts a stop to farther question; 'I hardly think the example of Abraham's complaining, that, unless he had some children of his body, his steward Eliezer of Damascus would be his heir, is quite *conclusive* to show that he made him so by will.'—BLACKSTONE. The *final* is arbitrary; it depends upon the will to make it so or not; the *conclusive* is relative; it depends upon the circumstances and the understanding: a person gives a *final* answer at option; but, in order to make an answer *conclusive*, it must be satisfactory to all parties.

CONCLUSIVE, DECISIVE, CONVINCING.

Conclusive applies either to practical or argumentative matters; *decisive* to what is practical only; *convincing* to what is argumentative only.

It is necessary to be *conclusive* when we deliberate, and *decisive* when we command. What is *conclusive* puts an end to all discussion, and determines the judgement; 'I will not disguise that Dr. Bentley, whose criticism is so *conclusive* for the forgery of those tragedies quoted by Plutarch, is of opinion "Thespis himself published nothing in writing."'—CUMBERLAND. What is *decisive* puts an end to all wavering, and determines the will; 'Is it not somewhat singular that Young preserved, without any palliation, this preface (to his Satire on Women) so bluntly *decisive* in favour of laughing at the world, in the same collection of his works which contains the mournful, angry, gloomy, *Night Thoughts*?'—CROFT. Negotiators have sometimes an interest in not speaking *conclusively*; commanders can never retain their authority without speaking *decisively*; *conclusive*, when compared to *convincing*, is general; the latter is particular: an argument is *convincing*, a chain of reasoning *conclusive*. There may be much that is *convincing*, where there is nothing *conclusive*: a proof may be *convincing* of a particular circumstance; but *conclusive* evidence will bear upon the main question; 'That religion is essential to the welfare of man, can be proved by the most *convincing* arguments.'—BLAIR.

CRITERION, STANDARD.

Criterion, in Greek κριτήριον, from κρίνω to judge, signifies the mark or rule by which one may judge; *standard*, from the verb to *stand*, signifies the point at which one must *stand*, or beyond which one must not go.

The *criterion* is employed only in matters of judgement; the *standard* is used in the ordinary concerns of life. The former serves for determining the characters and qualities of things; the latter for defining quantity and measure. The language and manners of a person is the best *criterion* for forming an estimate of his station and education;

> But have we then no law besides our will,
> No just *criterion* fix'd to good or ill?
> As well at noon we may obstruct our sight,
> Then doubt if such a thing exists as light.
> JENYNS.

In order to produce a uniformity in the mercantile transactions of mankind, one with another, it is the custom of government to set up a certain *standard* for the regulation of coins, weights, and measures.

The word *standard* may likewise be used figuratively in the same sense. The Bible is a *standard* of excellence, both in morals and religion, which cannot be too closely followed. It is impossible to have the same *standard* in the arts and sciences, because all our performances fall short of perfection, and will admit of improvement;

> Rate not th' extension of the human mind,
> By the plebeian *standard* of mankind.—JENYNS.

TO CONFIRM, CORROBORATE.

Confirm, in French *confirmer*, Latin *confirmo*, which is compounded of *con* and *firmo* or *firmus*, signifying to make additionally *firm*; *corroborate*, in Latin *corroboratus*, participle of *corroboro*, compounded of *cor* or *con* and *roboro* to strengthen, signifies to add to the strength.

The idea of strengthening is common to these terms, but under different circumstances: *confirm* is used generally; *corroborate* only in particular instances.

What *confirms* serves to *confirm* the minds of others: 'There is an Abyssinian here who knew Mr. Bruce at Givender. I have examined him, and he *confirms* Mr. Bruce's account.'—SIR WM. JONES. What *corroborates* strengthens one's self; 'The secrecy of this conference very much favours my conjecture, that Augustus made an attempt to persuade Tiberius from holding on the empire; and the length of time it took up *corroborates* the probability of that conjecture.'—CUMBERLAND. A testimony may be *confirmed* or *corroborated*; but all doubt is removed by a *confirmation*; the persuasion is strengthened by a *corroboration*: when the truth of a person's assertions is called in question, it is fortunate for him when circumstances present themselves that *confirm* the truth of what he has said, or, if he have respectable friends, to *corroborate* his testimony.

TO CONFIRM, ESTABLISH.

Confirm (*v. To confirm, corroborate*); *establish*, from the word *stable*, signifies to make stable or able to stand.

The idea of strengthening is common to these as to the former terms, but with a different application: *confirm* respects the state of a person's mind, and whatever acts upon the mind; *establish* is employed with regard to whatever is external: a report is *confirmed*; a reputation is *established*: a person is *confirmed* in the persuasion or belief of any truth or circumstance;

> Trifles, light as air,
> Are to the jealous, *confirmations* strong
> As proofs of Holy Writ.—SHAKSPEARE.

A thing is *established* in the publick estimation, or a principle is *established* in the mind; 'The silkworm, after having spun her task, lays her eggs and dies; but a man can never have taken in his full measure of knowledge, has not time to subdue his passions, or *establish* his soul in virtue, and come up to the perfection of his nature, before he is hurried off the stage.'—ADDISON.

The mind seeks its own means of *confirming* itself; things are *established* either by time or authority: no person should be hasty in giving credit to reports that are not fully *confirmed*, nor in giving support to measures that are not *established* upon the surest grounds: a reciprocity of good offices serves to *confirm* an alliance, or a good understanding between people and nations; interest or reciprocal affection serve to *establish* an intercourse between individuals, which has perhaps, been casually commenced.

UNDETERMINED, UNSETTLED, UNSTEADY, WAVERING.

Undetermined (*v. To determine*,) is a temporary state of the mind; *unsettled* is commonly more lasting; we are *undetermined* in the ordinary concerns of life; we are *unsettled* in matters of opinion: we may be *undetermined* whether we shall go or stay; we are *unsettled* in our faith or religious profession; 'Uncertain and *unsettled* as Cicero was, he seems fired with the contemplation of immortality.'—PEARSE.

Undetermined and *unsettled* are applied to particular objects; *unsteady* and *wavering* are habits of the mind: to be *unsteady* is, in fact, to be habitually *unsettled* in regard to all objects. An *unsettled* character is one that has no settled principles: an *unsteady* character has an unfitness in himself to settle; 'You will find soberness and truth in the proper teachers of religion, and much *unsteadiness* and vanity in others.'—EARL WENTWORTH. *Undetermined* describes one uniform state of mind, namely, the want of determination: *wavering* describes a changeable state, namely, the state of determining variously at different times. *Undetermined* is always taken in an indifferent, *wavering* mostly in a bad, sense: we may frequently be *undetermined* from the nature of the case, which does not present motives for determining; 'We suffer the last part of life to steal from us in weak hopes of some fortuitous occurrence or drowsy equilibrations of *undetermined* counsel.'—JOHNSON. A person is mostly *wavering* from a defect in his character, in cases where he might determine;

> Yet such, we find, they are as can control
> The servile actions of our *wav'ring* soul.
> PRIOR.

A parent may with reason be *undetermined* as to the line of life which he shall choose for his son: men of soft and timid characters are always *wavering* in the most trivial, as well as the most important, concerns of life.

CONSTANCY, STABILITY, STEADINESS, FIRMNESS.

Constancy, in French *constance*, Latin *constantia*, from *constans* and *consto*, compounded of *con* and *sto* to stand by or close to a thing, signifies the quality of adhering to the thing that has been once chosen; *stability*, in French *stabilité*, Latin *stabilitas*, from *stabilis* and *sto* to stand, signifies the abstract quality of being able to stand; *steadiness*, from *steady* or *staid*, Saxon *stetig*, high German *stätig*, Greek *στᾶθος* and *ἵστημι* to stand, signifies a capacity for standing; *firmness*, signifies the abstract quality of firm.

Constancy respects the affections; *stability* the opinions; *steadiness* the action or the motives of action; *firmness* the purpose or resolution.

* *Constancy* prevents from changing, and furnishes the mind with resources against weariness or disgust of the same object; it preserves and supports an attachment under every change of circumstances; 'Without *constancy* there is neither love, friendship, nor virtue in the world.'—Addison. *Stability* prevents from varying, it bears up the mind against the movements of levity or curiosity, which a diversity of objects might produce; 'With God there is no variableness, with man there is no *stability*. Virtue and vice divide the empire of his mind, and wisdom and folly alternately rule him.'—Blair. *Steadiness* prevents from deviating; it enables the mind to bear up against the influence of humour, which temperament or outward circumstances might produce; it fixes on one course and keeps to it; 'A manly *steadiness* of conduct is the object we are always to keep in view.'—Blair. *Firmness* prevents from yielding; it gives the mind strength against all the attacks to which it may be exposed; it makes a resistance, and comes off triumphant; 'A corrupted and guilty man can possess no true firmness of heart.'—Blair.

Constancy, among lovers and friends, is the favourite theme of poets; the world has, however, afforded but few originals from which they could copy their pictures: they have mostly described what is desirable rather than what is real. *Stability* of character is essential for those who are to command; for how can they govern others who cannot govern their own thoughts? *Steadiness* of deportment is a great recommendation to those who have to obey: how can any one perform his part well who suffers himself to be perpetually interrupted? *Firmness* of character is indispensable in the support of principles: there are many occasions in which this part of a man's character is likely to be put to a severe test.

Constancy is opposed to fickleness; *stability* to changeableness; *steadiness* to flightiness; *firmness* to pliancy.

FIRM, FIXED, SOLID, STABLE.

Firm, in French *ferme*, Latin *firmus*, comes from *fero* to bear, signifying the quality of bearing, upholding, or keeping; *fixed* denotes the state of being *fixed: solid*, in Latin *solidus*, comes from *solum* the ground, which is the most solid thing existing; *stable*, in Latin *stabilis*, from *sto*, signifies the quality of being able to stand.

That is *firm* which is not easily shaken; that is *fixed* which is fastened to something else, and not easily torn; that is *solid* which is able to bear, and does not easily give way; that is *stable* which is able to make a stand against resistance, or the effects of time. A pillar which is *firm* on its base, *fixed* to a wall made of *solid* oak, is likely to be *stable*. A man stands *firm* in battle who does not flinch from the attack: he is *fixed* to a spot by the order of his commander. An army of *firm* men form a *solid* mass, and, by their heroism, may deserve the most *stable* monument that can be erected;

> In one *firm* orb the bands were rang'd around,
> A cloud of heroes blacken'd all the ground.
> Pope.

* Girard: "Stabilité, constance, fermeté."

> Unmov'd and silent, the whole war they wait,
> Serenely dreadful, and as *fix'd* as fate.—Pope.

In the moral sense, *firmness* respects the purpose, or such actions as depend on the purpose; *fixed* is used either for the mind, or for outward circumstances; *solid* is applicable to things in general, in an absolute sense; *stable* is applicable to things in a relative sense. Decrees are more or less *firm*, according to the source from which they spring; none are *firm*, compared with those which arise from the will of the Almighty:

> The man that's resolute and just
> *Firm* to his principles and trust,
> Nor hopes nor fears can bind.—Walsh.

Laws are *fixed* in proportion as they are connected with a constitution in which it is difficult to innovate, 'One loves *fixed* laws, and the other arbitrary power.'—Temple. That which is *solid* is so of its own nature, but does not admit of degrees: a *solid* reason has within itself an independent property, which can not be increased or diminished;

> But these fantastick errours of our dream
> Lead us to *solid* wrong.—Cowley.

That which is *stable* is so by comparison with that which is of less duration; the characters of some men are more *stable* than those of others; youth will not have so *stable* a character as manhood; 'The prosperity of no man on earth is *stable* and assured.'—Blair.

A friendship is *firm* when it does not depend upon the opinion of others: it is *fixed* when the choice is made and grounded in the mind; it is *solid* when it rests on the only *solid* basis of accordancy in virtue and religion; it is *stable* when it is not liable to decrease or die away with time.

HARD, FIRM, SOLID.

The close adherence of the component parts of a body constitutes *hardness*. The close adherence of different bodies to each other constitutes *firmness* (*v. Fixed*). That is *hard* which will not yield to a closer compression; that is *firm* which will not yield so as to produce a separation. Ice is *hard*, as far as it respects itself, when it resists every pressure; it is *firm*, with regard to the water which it covers, when it is so closely bound as to resist every weight without breaking.

Hard and *solid* respect the internal constitution of bodies, and the adherence of the component parts; but *hard* denotes a much closer degree of adherence than *solid:* the *hard* is opposed to the soft; the *solid* to the fluid: every *hard* body is by nature *solid;* although every *solid* body is not *hard*. Wood is always a *solid* body, but it is sometimes *hard*, and sometimes soft; water, when congealed, is a *solid* body, and admits of different degrees of *hardness*.

In the improper application, *hardness* is allied to insensibility: *firmness* to fixedness; *solidity* to substantiality: a *hard* man is not to be acted upon by any tender motives; a *firm* man is not to be turned from his purpose; a *solid* man holds no purposes that are not well founded. A man is *hardened* in that which is bad, by being made insensible to that which is good: a man is *confirmed* in any thing good or bad, by being rendered less disposed to lay it aside; his mind is *consolidated* by acquiring fresh motives for action.

TO FIX, FASTEN, STICK.

Fix (*v. To fix, settle*); *fasten* is to make *fast; stick* is to make to *stick*.

Fix is a generick term; *fasten* and *stick* are but modes of *fixing*: we *fix* whatever we make to remain in a given situation; we *fasten* if we *fix* it firmly: we *stick* when we *fix* a thing by means of *sticking*. A post is *fixed* in the ground; it is *fastened* to a wall by a nail; it is *stuck* to another board by means of glue. Shelves are *fixed:* a horse is *fastened* to a gate: bills are *stuck* up. What is *fixed* may be removed in various ways;

> On mules and dogs the infection first began,
> And fast the vengeful arrows *fix'd* in man.—Pope.

What is *fastened* is removed by main force;

As the bold hound that gives the lion chase,
With beating bosom, and with eager pace,
Hangs on his haunch, or *fastens* on his heels,
Guards as he turns, and circles as he wheels.
POPE.

What is *stuck* must be separated by contrivance;

Some lines more moving than the rest,
Stuck to the point that pierc'd her breast.—SWIFT.

TO FIX, SETTLE, ESTABLISH.

To *fix*, in Latin *fixum*, perfect of *figo*, and in Greek πήγω, signifies simply to make to keep its place; *settle*, which is a frequentative of *set*, signifies to make to sit or be at rest; *establish*, from the Latin *stabilis*, signifies to make stable or keep its ground.

Fix is the general and indefinite term; to *settle* and *establish* are to *fix* strongly. *Fix* and *settle* are applied either to material or spiritual objects, *establish* only to moral objects. A post may be *fixed* in the ground in any manner, but it requires time for it to *settle*;

Hell heard the insufferable noise, hell saw
Heaven running from heav'n, and would have fled
Affrighted, but that fate had *fix'd* too deep
Her dark foundations.—MILTON.

Warm'd in the brain the brazen weapon lies,
And shades eternal *settle* o'er his eyes.—POPE.

A person may either *fix* himself, *settle* himself, or *establish* himself: the first case refers simply to his taking up his abode, or choosing a certain spot; the second refers to his permanency of stay; and the third to the business which he raises or renders permanent.

The same distinction exists between these words in their farther application to the conduct of men. We may *fix* one or many points, important or unimportant, it is a mere act of the will; we *settle* many points of importance; it is an act of deliberation: thus we *fix* the day and hour of doing a thing; we *settle* the affairs of our family;

While wavering councils thus his mind engage,
Fluctuates in doubtful thought the Pylian sage,
To join the host or to the gen'ral haste,
Debating long, he *fixes* on the last.—POPE.

Justice submitted to what Abra pleas'd,
Her will alone could *settle* or revoke,
And law was *fixed* by what she latest spoke.
PRIOR.

So likewise to *fix* is properly the act of one; to *settle* may be the joint act of many: thus a parent *fixes* on a business for his child, or he *settles* the marriage contract with another parent. To *fix* and *settle* are personal acts, and the objects are mostly of a private nature, but to *establish* is an indirect action, and the object mostly of a public nature: thus we *fix* our opinions; we *settle* our minds; or we are instrumental in *establishing* laws, institutions, and the like. It is much to be lamented that any one should remain *unsettled* in his faith; and still more so, that the best form of faith is not universally *established*; 'A pamphlet that talks of slavery, France, and the pretender; they desire no more; it will *settle* the wavering and confirm the doubtful.'—SWIFT. 'I would *establish* but one general rule to be observed in all conversation, which is this, that men should not talk to please themselves, but those that hear them.'—STEELE.

TO FIX, DETERMINE, SETTLE, LIMIT.

To *fix*, as in the preceding article, is here the general term; to *determine* (*v. To decide*); to *settle* (*v. To fix*); to *limit* (*v. To bound*); are here modes of *fixing*. They all denote the acts of conscious agents, but differ in the object and circumstances of the action: we may *fix* any object by any means, and to any point, we may *fix* material objects or spiritual objects, we may either *fix* by means of our senses, or our thoughts; but we can *determine* only by means of our thoughts. To *fix*, in distinction from the rest, is said in regard to a single point or a line; but to *determine* is always said of one or more points, or a whole: we *fix* where a thing shall begin; but we *determine* where it shall begin, and where it shall end, which way, and how far it shall go, and the like: thus, we may *fix* our eye upon a star, or we *fix* our minds upon a particular branch of astronomy; 'In a rotund, whether it be a building or a plantation, you can no where *fix* a boundary.'—BURKE. We *determine* the distance of the heavenly bodies, or the specific gravity of bodies, and the like, upon philosophical principles. So in morals we may *fix* our minds on an object; but we *determine* the mode of accomplishing it; 'Your first care must be to acquire the power of *fixing* your thoughts.'—BLAIR. 'More particularly to *determine* the proper season for grammar, I do not see how it can be made a study, but as an introduction to rhetorick.'—LOCKE.

Determine is to *settle* as a means to the end; we commonly *determine* all subordinate matters, in order to *settle* a matter finally: thus, the *determination* of a single cause will serve to settle all other differences. 'One had better *settle* on a way of life that is not the very best we might have chosen, than grow old without *determining* our choice.'—ADDISON. The *determination* respects the act of the individual who *fixes* certain points and brings them to a term; the *settlement* respects simply the conclusion of the affair, or the termination of all dispute and question; 'Religion *settles* the pretensions and otherwise interfering interests of mortal men.'—ADDISON.

How can we bind or *limit* his decree
But what our ear has heard or eye may see?
PRIOR.

To *determine* and *limit* both signify to *fix* boundaries; but the former respects, for the most part, such boundaries or terms as are formed by the nature of things; 'No sooner have they climbed that hill, which thus *determines* their view at a distance, but a new prospect is opened.'—ATTERBURY.

No mystic dreams could make their fates appear,
Though now *determin'd* by Tydides' spear.—POPE.

Limit, on the other hand, is the act of a conscious agent employed upon visible objects, and the process of the action itself is rendered visible, as when we *limit* a price, or *limit* our time, &c.

TO COMPOSE, SETTLE.

Compose, in Latin *composui*, perfect of *compono* to put together, signifies to put in due order; in which sense it is allied to *settle*.

We *compose* that which has been disjointed and separated, by bringing it together again; we *settle* that which has been disturbed and put in motion, by making it rest: we *compose* the thoughts which have been deranged and thrown into confusion;

Thy presence did each doubtful heart *compose*,
And factions wonder'd that they once arose.
TICKELL.

We *settle* the mind which has been fluctuating and distracted by contending desires;

Perhaps my reason may but ill defend
My *settled* faith, my mind with age impair'd.
SHENSTONE.

The mind must be *composed* before we can think justly; it must be *settled* before we can act consistently.

We *compose* the differences of others: we *settle* our own differences with others: it is difficult to *compose* the quarrels of angry opponents, or to *settle* the disputes of obstinate partisans.

COMPOSED, SEDATE.

Composed expresses the state of being *composed* (*v. To compose*); *sedate*, in Latin *sedatus*, participle of *sedo* to settle, signifies the quality of being settled.

Composed respects the air and looks externally, and the spirits internally; *sedate* relates to the deportment or carriage externally, and the fixedness of the purpose internally: *composed* is opposed to ruffled or hurried, *sedate* to buoyant or volatile.

Composure is a particular state of the mind; *sedateness* is an habitual frame of mind; a part of the character: a *composed* mien is very becoming in the season of devotion; 'Upon her nearer approach to Hercules she stepped before the other lady, who came forward with a regular *composed* carriage.'—ADDISON.

A *sedate* carriage is becoming in youth who are engaged in serious concerns;

Let me associate with the serious night,
And contemplation, her *sedate* compeer.
THOMSON.

TO ASK, OR ASK FOR, CLAIM, DEMAND.

To *ask*, is here taken for something more than a simple expression of wishes, as denoted in the article under *To ask, beg; claim*, in Latin *clamo* to cry after, signifies to express an imperious wish for; *demand*, in French *demander*, Latin *demando*, compounded of *de* and *mando*, signifies to call for imperatively.

Ask, in the sense of *beg*, is confined to the expression of wishes on the part of the *asker*, without involving any obligation on the part of the person *asked;* all granted in this case is voluntary, or complied with as a favour: but *ask for* in the sense here taken is involuntary, and springs from the forms and distinctions of society. *Ask* is here, as before, generick or specifick; *claim* and *demand* are specifick; in its specifick sense it conveys a less peremptory sense than either *claim* or *demand*. To *ask for* denotes simply the expressed wish to have what is considered as due;

Virtue, with them, is only to abstain
From all that nature *asks*, and covet pain.
JENYNS.

To *claim* is to assert a right, or to make it known;

My country *claims* me all, *claims* ev'ry passion.
MARTYN.

To *demand* is to insist on having without the liberty of a refusal;

Even mountains, vales,
And forests, seem impatient to *demand*
The promis'd sweetness. THOMSON.

Asking respects obligation in general, great or small; *claim* respects obligations of importance. *Asking for* supposes a right, not questionable; *claim* supposes a right hitherto unacknowledged; *demand* supposes either a disputed right, or the absence of all right, and the simple determination to have: a tradesman *asks for* what is owing to him as circumstances may require; a *person* claims the property he has lost; people are sometimes pleased to make *demands*, the legality of which cannot be proved. What is lent must be *asked for* when it is wanted; whatever has been lost and is found must be recovered by a *claim;* whatever a selfish person wants, he strives to obtain by a *demand*, whether just or unjust.

TO DEMAND, REQUIRE.

To *demand*, is here taken in the same sense as in the preceding article; *require*, in Latin *requiro*, compounded of *re* and *quæro*, signifies to seek for, or to seek to get back.

We *demand* that which is owing and ought to be given; we *require* that which we wish and expect to have done. A *demand* is more positive than a *requisition;* the former admits of no question; the latter is liable to be both questioned and refused: the creditor makes a *demand* on the debtor; the master *requires* a certain portion of duty from his servant: it is unjust to *demand* of a person what he has no right to give;

Hear, all ye Trojans! all ye Grecian bands,
What Paris, author of the war, *demands*.
POPE.

It is unreasonable to *require* of a person what it is not in his power to do;

Now, by my sov'reign and his fate I swear,
Renown'd for faith in peace, and force in war,
Oft our alliance other lands desir'd,
And what we seek of you, of us *requir'd*.
DRYDEN.

A thing is commonly *demanded* in express words; it is *required* by implication: a person *demands* admittance when it is not voluntarily granted; he *requires* respectful deportment from those who are subordinate to him.

In the figurative application the same sense is preserved: things of urgency and moment *demand* immediate attention; 'Surely the retrospect of life and the extirpation of lusts and appetites, deeply rooted and widely spread, may be allowed to *demand* some secession from business and folly.'—JOHNSON. Difficult matters *require* a steady attention;

Oh then how blind to all that truth *requires*,
Who think it freedom when a part aspires.
GOLDSMITH

RIGHT, CLAIM, PRIVILEGE.

Right signifies in this sense what it is *right* for one to possess, which is in fact a word of large meaning: for since the *right* and the wrong depend upon inde terminable questions, the *right* of having is equally indeterminable in some cases with every other species of *right*. A *claim* (*v. To ask for*) is a species of *right* to have that which is in the hands of another; the *right* to ask another for it. The *privilege* is a species of *right* peculiar to particular individuals or bodies.

Right, in its full sense, is altogether an abstract thing which is independent of human laws and regulations; *claims* and *privileges* are altogether connected with the establishments of civil society.

Liberty, in the general sense, is an unalienable *right* which belongs to man as a rational and responsible agent; it is not a *claim*, for it is set above all question, and all condition; nor is it a *privilege*, for it cannot be exclusively granted to one being, nor unconditionally be taken away from another.

Between the right and the power there is often as wide a distinction as between truth and falsehood; we have often a *right* to do that which we have no power to do, and the power to do that which we have no *right* to do; slaves have a *right* to the freedom which is enjoyed by all other creatures of the same species with themselves, but they have not the power to use this freedom as others do. In England men have the power of thinking for themselves as they please: but, by the abuse which they make of this power, we see that, in many cases, they have not the *right*, unless we admit the contradiction that men have a *right* to do what is wrong; they have the power therefore of exercising this *right* only, because no other person has the legal *right* of controlling them;

In ev'ry street a city bard
Rules, like an alderman, his ward:
His undisputed *rights* extend
Through all the lane from end to end.—SWIFT.

We have often a *claim* to a thing, which it is not in our power to substantiate; and, on the other hand, *claims* are set up in cases which are totally unfounded on any *right;*

Whence is this pow'r, this fondness of all arts,
Serving, adorning life through all its parts;
Which names impos'd, by letters mark'd those names,
Adjusted properly by legal *claims?*—JENYNS.

Privileges are *rights* granted to individuals, depending either upon the will of the granter, or the circumstances of the receiver, or both; *privileges* are therefore partial *rights*, transferable at the discretion of persons indivi dually or collectively;

A thousand bards thy *rights* disown,
And with rebellious arm pretend,
An equal *privilege* to descend.—SWIFT

PRIVILEGE, PREROGATIVE, EXEMPTION IMMUNITY.

Privilege, in Latin *privilegium*, compounded of *privus* and *lex*, signifies a law made in favour of any individual or set of individuals; *prerogative*, comes from the Latin *prærogativi*, so called from *præ* and *rogo* to ask, because certain Roman tribes, so called, were first asked whom they would have to be consuls: hence applied in our language to the right of determining or choosing first in many particulars; *exemption*, from the verb to *exempt*, and *immunity*, from the Latin *immunis* free, are both employed for the object from which one is *exempt* or free.

Privilege and *prerogative* consist of positive advan tages; *exemption* and *immunity* of those which are negative: by the former we obtain an actual good, by the latter the removal of an evil.

Privilege, in its most extended sense, comprehends all the rest: for every *prerogative*, *exemption*, and *immunity*, are *privileges*, inasmuch as they rest upon certain laws or customs, which are made for the benefi of certain individuals; but in the restricted sense the *privilege* is used only for the subordinate parts of society, and the *prerogative* for the superiour orders; as they respect the publick, *privileges* belong to, or are granted to, the subject: *prerogatives* belong, to the crown. It is the *privilege* of a member of parliament to escape arrest for debt; it is the *prerogative* of the crown to be irresponsible for the conduct of its ministers: as respects private cases it is the *privilege* of females to have the best places assigned to them; it is the *prerogative* of the male to address the female.

Privileges are applied to every object which it is desirable to have; 'As the aged depart from the dignity, so they forfeit the *privileges* of gray hairs.'—Blair. *Prerogative* is confined to the case of making one's election, or exercising any special power; 'By the worst of usurpations, a usurpation on the *prerogatives* of nature, you attempt to force tailors and carpenters into the state.'—Burke. *Exemption* is applicable to cases in which one is exempted from any tribute, or payment; 'Neither nobility nor clergy (in France) enjoyed any *exemption* from the duty on consumable commodities.'—Burke. *Immunity*, from the Latin *munus* an office, is peculiarly applicable to cases in which one is freed from a service: but it is figuratively applied to a *privileged* freedom from any thing painful; 'You claim an *immunity* from evil which belongs not to the lot of man.'—Blair. All chartered towns or corporations have *privileges*, *exemptions*, and *immunities:* it is the *privilege* of the city of London to shut its gates against the king.

PRETENSION, CLAIM.

Pretension (*v. To affect*) and *claim* (*v. To ask for*) both signify an assertion of rights, but they differ in the nature of the rights. The first refers only to the rights which are calculated as such by an individual; the latter to those which exist independently of his supposition: there cannot therefore be a *pretension* without one to pretend, but there may be a *claim* without any immediate *claimant:* thus we say a person rests his *pretension* to the crown upon the ground of being descended from the former king; in hereditary monarchies there is no one who has any *claim* to the crown except the next heir in succession. The *pretension* is commonly built upon one's personal merits, or the views of one's own merits;

> But if to unjust things thou dost pretend,
> Ere they begin, let thy *pretensions* end.
> Denham.

The *claim* rests upon the laws of civil society; 'Will he not therefore, of the two evils, choose the least, by submitting to a master who hath no immediate *claim* upon him, rather than to another who hath already revived several *claims* upon him?'—Swift. A person makes high *pretensions* who estimates his merits and consequent deserts at a high rate; he judges of his *claims* according as they are supported by the laws of his country or the circumstances of the case: the *pretension*, when denied, can never be proved; the *claim*, when proved, can always be enforced. One is in general willing to dispute the *pretensions* of men who make themselves judges in their own cause; but one is not unwilling to listen to any *claims* which are modestly preferred. Those who make a *pretension* to the greatest learning are commonly men of shallow information; 'It is often charged upon writers, that, with all their *pretensions* to genius and discoveries, they do little more than copy one another.'—Johnson. Those who have the most substantial *claims* to the gratitude and respect of mankind are commonly found to be men of the fewest *pretensions;*

> Poets have undoubted right to *claim*,
> If not the greatest, the most lasting name.
> Congreve.

PRETENCE, PRETENSION, PRETEXT, EXCUSE.

Pretence comes from *pretend* (*v. To affect*) in the sense of setting forth any thing independent of ourselves. *Pretension* comes from the same verb in the sense of setting forth any thing that depends upon ourselves. The *pretence* is commonly a misrepresentation; the *pretension* is frequently a miscalculation; the *pretence* is set forth to conceal what is bad in one s self; the *pretension* is set forth to display what is good: the former betrays one's falsehood, the latter one's conceit or self-importance; the former can never be employed in a good sense, the latter may sometimes be employed in an indifferent sense: a man of bad character may make a *pretence* of religion by adopting an outward profession;

> Ovid had warn'd her to beware
> Of strolling gods, whose usual trade is,
> Under *pretence* of taking air,
> To pick up sublunary ladies.—Swift.

Men of the least merit often make the highest *pretensions;*

> Each thinks his own the best *pretension.*—Gay.

The *pretence* and *pretext* alike consist of what is unreal; but the former is not so great a violation of truth as the latter: the *pretence* may consist of truth and falsehood blended; the *pretext*, from *prætego* to cloak or cover over, consists altogether of falsehood: the *pretence* may sometimes serve only to conceal or palliate a fault; the *pretext* serves to hide something seriously culpable or wicked: a child may make indisposition a *pretence* for idleness;

> Let not the Trojans, with a feigned *pretence*
> Of proffer'd peace, delude the Latian prince.
> Dryden.

A thief makes his acquaintance with the servants a *pretext* for getting admittance into houses; 'Justifying perfidy and murder for publick benefit, publick benefit would soon become the *pretext*, and perfidy and murder the end.'—Burke.

The *pretence* and *excuse* (*v. To apologise*) are both set forth to justify one's conduct in the eyes of others; but the *pretence* always conceals something more or less culpable, and by a greater or less violation of truth; the *excuse* may sometimes justify that which is justifiable, and with strict regard to truth. To oblige one's self, under the *pretence* of obliging another, is a despicable trick; 'I should have dressed the whole with greater care; but I had little time, which I am sure you know to be more than pretence.'—Wake. Illness is an allowable *excuse* to justify any omission in business;

> Nothing but love this patience could produce,
> And I allow your rage that kind *excuse.*
> Dryden.

Although the *excuse* for the most part supposes what is groundless, yet it is moreover distinguished from the *pretence*, that it never implies an intentional falsehood; 'The last refuge of a guilty person is to take shelter under an *excuse*.'—South.

TO AFFECT, PRETEND TO.

Affect is here taken in the same sense as in the following article; *pretend*, in Latin *prætendo*, that is, *præ* and *tendo*, signifies to hold or stretch one thing before another by way of a blind.

These terms are synonymous* only in the bad sense of setting forth to others what is not real: we *affect* by putting on a false air; we *pretend* by making a false declaration. Art is employed in *affecting;* assurance and self-complacency in *pretending*. A person *affects* not to hear what it is convenient for him not to answer; he *pretends* to have forgotten what it is convenient for him not to recollect. One *affects* the manners of a gentleman, and *pretends* to gentility of birth. One *affects* the character and habits of a scholar; one *pretends* to learning.

To *affect* the qualities which we have not spoils those which we have;

> Self, quite put off, *affects* with too much art
> To put on Woodward in each mangled part.
> Churchill.

To *pretend* to attainments which we have not made, obliges us to have recourse to falsehoods in order to escape detection; 'There is something so natively great and good in a person that is truly devout, that an awkward man may as well *pretend* to be genteel as a hypocrite to be pious.'—Steele.

* Vide Trussler, "To affect, pretend to."

TO AFFECT, ASSUME.

Affect, in this sense, derives its origin immediately from the Latin *affecto* to desire after eagerly, signifying to aim at or aspire after; *assume*, in Latin *assumo*, compounded of *as* or *ad* and *sumo* to take, signifies to take to one's self.

To *affect* is to use forced efforts to appear to have some quality; to *assume* is to appropriate something to one's self. One *affects* to have fine feelings, and *assumes* great importance.

Affectation springs from the desire of appearing better than we really are; *assumption* from the thinking ourselves better than we really are. We *affect* the virtues which we have not: 'It has been from age to age an *affectation* to love the pleasures of solitude, among those who cannot possibly be supposed qualified for passing life in that manner.'—SPECTATOR. We *assume* the character which does not belong to us;

> Laughs not the heart when giants, big with pride,
> *Assume* the pompous port, the martial part?
> CHURCHILL.

An *affected* person is always thinking of others; an *assuming* person thinks only of himself. The *affected* man strives to gain applause by appearing to be what he is not; the *assuming* man demands respect upon the ground of what he supposes himself to be. Hypocrisy is often the companion of *affectation*; self-conceit always that of *assumption*.

To *affect* is mostly taken in a bad sense, but sometimes in an indifferent sense; to *assume* may be sometimes an indifferent action at least, if not justifiable. Men always *affect* that which is admired by others, in order to gain their applause; 'In conversation the medium is neither to *affect* silence nor eloquence.'—STERNE. Men sometimes *assume* an appearance, a name, or an authority, which is no more than their just right;

> This when the various god had urg'd in vain,
> He strait *assum'd* his native form again.—POPE.

TO APPROPRIATE, USURP, ARROGATE, ASSUME, ASCRIBE.

Appropriate, in French *approprier*, compounded of *ap* or *ad* and *propriatus*, participle of *proprio*, an old verb, from *proprius* proper or own, signifies to make one's own: *usurp*, in French *usurper*, Latin *usurpo*, from *usus* use, is a frequentative of *utor*, signifying to make use of as if it were one's own; *arrogate*, in Latin *arrogatus*, participle of *arrogo*, signifies to ask or claim to for one's self; *assume*, in French *assumer*, Latin *assumo*, compounded of *as* or *ad* and *sumo* to take, signifies to take to one's self; *ascribe*, in Latin *ascribo*, compounded of *as* or *ad* and *scribo* to write, signifies here to write down to one's own account.

The idea of taking something to one's self by an act of one's own, is common to all these terms.

To *appropriate* is to take to one's self either with or without right; to *usurp* is to take to one's self by violence, or in violation of right. *Appropriating* is applied in its proper sense to goods or possessions;

> To themselves *appropriating*
> The spirit of God, promis'd alike, and giv'n
> To all believers.—MILTON.

Usurping is properly applied to power, publick or private; a *usurper* exercises the functions of government without a legitimate sanction; 'Not having the natural superiority of fathers, their power must be *usurped*, and then unlawful; or if lawful, then granted or consented unto by them over whom they exercise the same, or else given them extraordinarily from God.'—HOOKER. *Appropriation* is a matter of convenience; it springs from a selfish concern for ourselves, and a total unconcern for others: *usurpation* is a matter of self-indulgence; it springs from an inordinate ambition that is gratified only at the expense of others. *Appropriation* seldom requires an effort: a person *appropriates* that which casually falls into his hands. *Usurpation* mostly takes place in a disorganized state of society; when the strongest prevail, the most artful and the most vicious individual invests himself with the supreme authority. *Appropriation* is generally an act of injustice: *usurpation* is always an act of violence. To *usurp* is applied figuratively in the same sense; 'If any passion has so much *usurped* our understanding, as not to suffer us to enjoy advantages with the moderation prescribed by reason, it is not too late to apply this remedy: when we find ourselves sinking under sorrow, we may then usefully revolve the uncertainty of our condition, and the folly of lamenting that from which, if it had staid a little longer, we should ourselves have been taken away.'—JOHNSON. To *appropriate* may be applied in the sense of assigning to others their own, as well as taking to one's self; 'Things sanctified were thereby in such sort *appropriated* unto God, as that they might never afterward be made common.'—HOOKER. But in this sense it has nothing in common with the word *usurp*.

Arrogate, *assume*, and *ascribe*, denote the taking to one's self, but do not, like *appropriate* and *usurp*, imply taking from another. *Arrogate* is a more violent action than *assume*, and *assume* than *ascribe*. *Arrogate* and *assume* are employed either in the proper or figurative sense, *ascribe* only in the figurative sense. We *arrogate* distinctions, honours, and titles; we *assume* names, rights, privileges.

In the moral sense we *arrogate* pre-eminence, *assume* importance, *ascribe* merit. To *arrogate* is a species of moral *usurpation*; it is always accompanied with haughtiness and contempt for others: that is *arrogated* to one's self to which one has not the smallest title: an *arrogant* temper is one of the most odious features in the human character; it is a compound of folly and insolence; 'After having thus *ascribed* due honour to birth and parentage, I must however take notice of those who *arrogate* to themselves more honours than are due to them on this account.'—ADDISON. To *assume* is a species of moral *appropriation*; its objects are of a less serious nature than those of *arrogating*; and it does less violence to moral propriety: we *assume* in trifles, we *arrogate* only in important matters; 'It very seldom happens that a man is slow enough in *assuming* the character of a husband, or a woman quick enough in condescending to that of a wife.'—ADDISON. To *ascribe* is oftener an act of vanity than of injustice: many men are entitled to the merit which they *ascribe* to themselves; but by this very act they lessen the merit of their best actions; 'Sometimes we *ascribe* to ourselves the merit of good qualities, which, if justly considered, should cover us with shame.'—CRAIG. A conscientious man will *appropriate* nothing to himself which he cannot unquestionably claim as his own; 'A voice was heard from the clouds declaring the intention of this visit, which was to restore and *appropriate* to every one what was his due.'—ADDISON.

Usurpers, who violate the laws both of God and man, are as much to be pitied as dreaded: they generally pay the price of their crimes in a miserable life, and a still more miserable death. Nothing exposes a man to greater ridicule than *arrogating* to himself titles and distinctions which do not belong to him. Although a man may sometimes innocently *assume* to himself the right of judging for others, yet he can never, with any degree of justice, *assume* the right of oppressing them. Self-complacence leads many to *ascribe* great merit to themselves for things which are generally regarded as trifling.

Arrogating as an action, or *arrogance* as a disposition, is always taken in a bad sense: the former is always dictated by the most preposterous pride; the latter is associated with every unworthy quality. *Assumption*, as an action, varies in its character according to circumstances; it may be either good, bad, or indifferent: it is justifiable in certain exigencies to *assume* a command where there is no one else able to direct: it is often a matter of indifference what name a person *assumes* who does so only in conformity to the will of another; but it is always bad to *assume* a name as a mask to impose upon others.

As a disposition *assumption* is always bad, but still not to the same degree as *arrogance*. An *arrogant* man renders himself intolerable to society, an *assuming* man makes himself offensive: *arrogance* is the characteristick of men; *assumption* is peculiar to youths: an *arrogant* man can be humbled only by silent contempt; 'Humility is expressed by the stooping and bending of the head; *arrogance* when it is lifted up, or, as we say, tossed up.'—DRYDEN. An *assuming* youth must be checked by the voice of authority; 'This makes him over-forward in business, *assuming* in conversation, and peremptory in answers.—COLLIER.

ARROGANCE, PRESUMPTION.

Arrogance signifies either the act of *arrogating* or the disposition to *arrogate; presumption*, from *presume*, Latin *præsumo*, compounded of *præ* before, and *sumo* to take or put, signifies the disposition to put one's self forward.

Arrogance is the act of the great; *presumption* that of the little: the *arrogant* man takes upon himself to be above others; 'I must confess I was very much surprised to see so great a body of editors, criticks, commentators, and grammarians, meet with so very ill a reception They had formed themselves into a body, and with a great deal of *arrogance* demanded the first station in the column of knowledge; but the goddess, instead of complying with their request, clapped them into liveries.'—Addison. The *presumptuous* man strives to be on a level with those who are above him; 'In the vanity and *presumption* of youth, it is common to allege the consciousness of innocence as a reason for the contempt of censure.'—Hawkesworth. *Arrogance* is commonly coupled with haughtiness: *presumption* with meanness: men *arrogantly* demand as a right the homage which has perhaps before been voluntarily granted; the creature *presumptuously* arraigns the conduct of the Creator, and murmurs against the dispensations of his providence.

TO APPROPRIATE, IMPROPRIATE.

To *appropriate* (*v. To appropriate*) is to consign to some particular use;

> Some they *appropriated* to the gods,
> And some to publick, some to private ends.
> Roscommon.

But in a more particular manner to take to one's own private use; 'Why should people engross and *appropriate* the common benefits of fire, air, and water to themselves.'—L'Estrange. To *impropriate* is in some cases used in this latter sense; 'For the pardon of the rest, the king thought it not fit it should pass by Parliament; the better, being matter of grace, to *impropriate* the thanks to himself.'—Bacon. But for the most part this word has been employed to denote the lawless *appropriation* of the church lands by the laity, which took place at the Reformation; 'Those *impropriated* livings, which have now no settled endowment, and are therefore called not vicarages, but perpetual or sometimes arbitrary curacies; they are such, as belonged formerly to those orders who could serve the cure of them in their own persons.'—Wharton.

PRELUDE, PREFACE.

Prelude, from the Latin *præ* before and *ludo* to play, signifies the game that precedes another; *preface*, from the Latin *for* to speak, signifies the speech that precedes.

The idea of a preparatory introduction is included in both these terms, but the former consists of actions; the latter of words; the throwing of stones and breaking of windows is the *prelude* on the part of a mob to a general riot; 'At this time there was a general peace all over the world, which was a proper *prelude* for ushering in his coming who was the Prince of peace.'—Prideaux. An apology for one's ill-behaviour is sometimes the *preface* to soliciting a remission of punishment;

> As no delay
> Of *preface* brooking through his zeal of right.
> Milton.

The *prelude* is mostly preparatory to that which is in itself actually bad: the *preface* is mostly preparatory to something supposed to be objectionable. Intemperance in liquor is the *prelude* to every other extravagance; when one wishes to ensure compliance with a request that may possibly be unreasonable, it is necessary to pave the way by some suitable *preface*.

TO PREMISE, PRESUME.

Premise, from *præ* and *mitto*, signifies set down beforehand; *presume*, from *præ* and *sumo* to take, signifies to take beforehand.

Both these terms are employed in regard to our previous assertions or admissions of any circumstance; the former is used for what is theoretical or belongs to opinions; the latter is used for what is practical or belongs to facts: we *premise* that the existence of a Deity is unquestionable when we argue respecting his attributes; 'Here we must first *premise* what it is to enter into temptation.'—South. We *presume* that a person has a firm belief in divine revelation when we exhort him to follow the precepts of the Gospel; 'In the long Iambic metre, it does not appear that Chaucer ever composed at all; for I *presume* no one can imagine that he was the author of Gamelyn.'—Tyrwhitt. No argument can be pursued until we have *premised* those points upon which both parties are to agree: we must be careful not to *presume* upon more than what we are fully authorized to take for certain.

PECULIAR, APPROPRIATE, PARTICULAR.

Peculiar, in Latin *peculiaris*, comes from *pecus* cattle; that is, the cattle which belonged to the slave or servant, in distinction from the master; and the epithet, therefore, designates in a strong manner private property, belonging exclusively to one's self; *appropriate* signifies *appropriated* (*v. To ascribe*); *particular* (*v. Particular*).

Peculiar is said of that which belongs to persons or things; *appropriate* is said of that which belongs to things only: the faculty of speech is *peculiar* to man, in distinction from all other animals; 'I agree with Sir William Temple, but not that the thing itself is *peculiar* to the English, because the contrary may be found in many Spanish, Italian, and French productions.'—Swift. An address may be *appropriate* to the circumstances of the individual who makes it; 'Modesty and diffidence, gentleness and meekness, were looked upon as the *appropriate* virtues of the sex.'—Johnson. *Peculiar* designates simple property; *appropriate* designates the right of propriety; there are advantages and disadvantages *peculiar* to every situation; the excellence of a discourse depends often on its being *appropriate* to the season *Peculiar* and *particular* are both employed to distinguish objects; but the former distinguishes the object by showing its connexion with, or alliance to, others; *particular* distinguishes it by a reference to some acknowledged circumstance; hence we may say that a person enjoys *peculiar* privileges or *particular* privileges: in this case *peculiar* signifies such as are confined to him, and enjoyed by none else;

> Great father Bacchus, to my song repair,
> For clust'ring grapes are thy *peculiar* care.
> Dryden.

Particular signifies such as are distinguished in degree and quality from others of the kind; 'This is true of actions considered in their general nature or kind, but not considered in their *particular* individual instances.'—South.

TO ASCRIBE, ATTRIBUTE, IMPUTE.

Ascribe signifies the same as in the article under *To Appropriate, Usurp; attribute*, in Latin *attributus*, participle of *attribuo*, compounded of *ad* and *tribuo*, signifies to bestow upon, or attach to a thing what belongs to it; *impute*, compounded of *im* or *in* and *pute*, Latin *puto* to think, signifies to think or judge what is in a thing.

To *ascribe* is to assign any thing to a person as his property, his possession, or the fruit of his labour, &c.; to *attribute* is to assign things to others as their causes; to *impute* is to assign qualities to persons. Milton *ascribes* the first use of artillery to the rebel angels; the loss of a vessel is *attributed* to the violence of the storm; the conduct of the captain is *imputed* to his want of firmness. The letters of Junius have been falsely *ascribed* to many persons in succession, as the author to this day remains concealed, and out of the reach of even probable conjecture; the oracles of the heathens are *ascribed* by some theologians to the devil; 'Holiness is *ascribed* to the pope; majesty to kings; serenity or mildness to princes; excellence or perfection to ambassadors; grace to archbishops; honour to peers.'—Addison. The death of Alexander the Great is *attributed* to his intemperance; generosity has been *imputed* to him from his conduct on certain occasions, but particularly in his treatment of the Persian princesses, the relatives of Darius; 'Perhaps it may appear upon examination that the most polite ages are the least virtuous. This may be *attributed* to the folly of admitting wit and learning as merit in themselves, without considering the application of them.'—STEELE. 'Men in their innovations should follow the example of time, which innovateth, but quietly, and by degrees scarce to be perceived, for otherwise what is new and unlooked for, ever mends some and impairs others; and he that is hurt for a wrong *imputeth* it to the author.'—BACON.

Ascribe is mostly used in a favourable or indifferent sense; *impute* is either favourable or unfavourable. In the doxology of the church ritual, all honour, might, majesty, dominion, and power, are *ascribed* to the three persons in the Holy Trinity: the actions of men are often so equivocal that it is difficult to decide whether praise or blame ought to be *imputed* to them; 'I made it by your persuasion, to satisfy those who *imputed* it to folly.'—TEMPLE. 'We who are adepts in astrology can *impute* it to several causes in the planets, that this quarter of our great city is the region of such as either never had, or have lost, the use of reason.'—STEELE.

QUALITY, PROPERTY, ATTRIBUTE.

Quality, in Latin *qualitas*, from *qualis* such, signifies such as a thing really is; *property*, which is changed from *propriety* and *proprius* proper or one's own, signifies belonging to a thing as an essential ingredient; *attribute*, in Latin *attributus*, participle of *attribuo* to bestow upon, signifies the things bestowed upon or assigned to another.

The *quality* is that which is inherent in the object and co-existent; 'Humility and patience, industry and temperance, are very often the good *qualities* of a poor man.'—ADDISON. The *property* is that which belongs to it for the time being; 'No man can have sunk so far into stupidity, as not to consider the *properties* of the ground on which he walks, of the plants on which he feeds, or of the animals that delight his ear.'—JOHNSON. The *attribute* is the *quality* which is assigned to any object;

> Man o'er a wider field extends his views,
> God through the wonder of his works pursues,
> Exploring thence his *attributes* and laws,
> Adores, loves, imitates, th' Eternal Cause.
> JENYNS.

We cannot alter the *quality* of a thing without altering the whole thing; but we may give or take away *properties* from bodies at pleasure, without entirely destroying their identity; and we may ascribe *attributes* at discretion.

PRESUMPTIVE, PRESUMPTUOUS, PRESUMING.

Presumptive comes from *presume*, in the sense of supposing or taking for granted; *presumptuous*, *presuming* (*v. Arrogance*), come from the same verb in the sense of taking upon one's self, or taking to one's self any importance: the former is therefore employed in an indifferent, the latter in a bad acceptation: a *presumptive* heir is one *presumed* or expected to be heir; *presumptive* evidence is evidence founded on some *presumption* or supposition; so likewise *presumptive* reasoning; 'There is no qualification for government but virtue and wisdom, actual or *presumptive*.'—BURKE. A *presumptuous* man, a *presumptuous* thought, a *presumptuous* behaviour, all indicate an unauthorized *presumption* in one's own favour; 'See what is got by those *presumptuous* principles which have brought your leaders (of the revolution) to despise all their predecessors.'—BURKE. *Presumptuous* is a stronger term than *presuming*, because it has a more definite use; the former designates the express quality of *presumption*, the latter the inclination; a man is *presumptuous* when his conduct partakes of the nature of *presumption*; he is *presuming* inasmuch as he shows himself disposed to *presume*; hence we speak of a *presumptuous* language, not a *presuming* language; a *presuming* temper, not a *presumptuous* temper. In like manner when one says it is *presumptuous* in a man to do any thing, this expresses the idea of *presumption* much more forcibly than to say it is *presuming* in him to do it. It would be *presumptuous* in a man to address a monarch in the language of familiarity and disrespect; it is *presuming* in a common person to address any one who is superiour in station with familiarity and disrespect.

TO DENY, REFUSE.

Deny, in Latin *denego*, or *nego*, that is, *ne* or *non* and *ago*, signifies to say no to a thing; *refuse*, in Latin *refusus*, from *re* and *fundo* to pour, signifies to throw back that which is presented.

To *deny* respects matters of fact or knowledge; to *refuse* matters of wish or request. We *deny* what immediately belongs to ourselves; we *refuse* what belongs to another. We *deny* as to the past; we *refuse* as to the future: we *deny* our participation in that which has been; we *refuse* our participation in that which may be: to *deny* must always be expressly verbal; a *refusal* may sometimes be signified by actions or looks as well as words. A *denial* affects our veracity; a *refusal* affects our good-nature.

To *deny* is likewise sometimes used in regard to one's own gratifications as well as to one's knowledge, in which case it is still more analogous to *refuse*, which regards the gratifications of another. In this case we say we *deny* a person a thing, but we *refuse* his request, or *refuse* to do a thing;

> Jove to his Thetis nothing could *deny*,
> Nor was the signal vain that shook the sky.
> POPE.

> O sire of Gods and men! Thy suppliant hear;
> *Refuse* or grant; for what has Jove to fear?
> POPE.

Some Christians think it very meritorious to *deny* themselves their usual quantity of food at certain times; they are however but sorry professors of Christianity if they *refuse* at the same time to give of their substance to the poor. Instances are not rare of misers who have *denied* themselves the common necessaries of life, and yet have never *refused* to relieve those who were in distress, or assist those who were in trouble.

Deny is sometimes the act of unconscious agents; *refuse* is always a personal and intentional act. We are sometimes *denied* by circumstances the consolation of seeing our friends before they die;

> Inquire you how these pow'rs we shall attain?
> 'T is not for us to know; our search is vain;
> Can any one remember or relate
> How he existed in the embryo state?
> That light's *deny'd* to him which others see,
> He knows perhaps you 'll say—and so do we
> JENYNS.

TO REFUSE, DECLINE, REJECT, REPEL, REBUFF.

Refuse signifies, as in the preceding article, simply to pour, that is, to send back, which is the common idea of all these terms; to *decline*, in Latin *declino*, is literally to turn aside; to *reject*, from *jacio* to throw, is to cast back; *repel*, from *pello* to drive, to drive back; to *rebuff*, from *buff* or *puff*, signifies to puff one back, send off with a puff.

Refuse is an unqualified action, it is accompanied with no expression of opinion; *decline* is a gentle and indirect mode of refusal; *reject* is a direct mode, and conveys a positive sentiment of disapprobation: we *refuse* what is asked of us, for want of inclination to comply;

> But all her arts are still employ'd in vain;
> Again she comes, and is *refus'd* again.
> DRYDEN.

We *decline* what is proposed from motives of discretion 'Melissa, though she could not boast the apathy of Cato, wanted not the more prudent virtue of Scipio, and gained the victory by *declining* the contest.'—JOHNSON. We *reject* what is offered to us, because it does not fall in with our views;

> Why should he then *reject* a suit so just?—DRYDEN.

We *refuse* to listen to the suggestions of our friends, 'Having most affectionately set life and death before them, and conjured them to choose one and avoid the other, he still leaves unto them, as to free and rational agents, a liberty to *refuse* all his calls, to let his talents lie by them unprofitable.'—HAMMOND We *decline* an offer of service; 'Could Caroline have been captivated with the glories of this world, she had them all laid before her; but she generously *declined* them, because she saw the acceptance of them was inconsistent with religion.'—ADDISON. We *reject* the insinuations of the interested and evil-minded; 'Whether it be a divine revelation or no, reason must judge, which can never permit the mind to *reject* a greater evidence, to embrace what is less evident.'—LOCKE. To *refuse* is properly the act of an individual; to *reject* is said of that which comes from any quarter: requests and petitions are *refused* by those who are solicited; opinions, propositions, and counsels, are *rejected* by particular communities: the king *refuses* to give his assent to a bill; 'If he should choose the right casket, you should *refuse* to perform his father's will, if you should *refuse* to accept him.'—SHAKSPEARE. The parliament *rejects* a bill; 'The House was then so far from being possessed with that spirit, that the utmost that could be obtained, upon a long debate upon that petition (for the total extirpation of episcopacy) was, that it should not be *rejected*.'—CLARENDON.

To *repel* is to *reject* with violence; to *rebuff* is to *refuse* with contempt. We *refuse* and *reject* that which is either offered, or simply presents itself, for acceptance: but we *repel* and *rebuff* that which forces itself into our presence, contrary to our inclination: we *repel* the attack of an enemy, or we *repel* the advances of one who is not agreeable;

Th' unwearied watch their listening leaders keep,
And, couching close, *repel* invading sleep.—POPE.

We *rebuff* those who put that in our way that is offensive. Importunate persons must necessarily expect to meet with *rebuffs*, and are in general less susceptible of them than others; delicate minds feel a *refusal* as a *rebuff;*

At length *rebuff'd*, they leave their mangled prey
DRYDEN.

TO TAKE, RECEIVE, ACCEPT.

To *take*, which in all probability comes from the Latin *tactum*, participle of *tango* to touch, is a general term; *receive*, from *re* and *capio* to take back, and *accept*, from *ac* or *ad* and *capio* to take to one's self, are specifick.

To *take* signifies to make one's own by coming in exclusive contact with it; to *receive* is to take under peculiar circumstances. We *take* either from things or persons; we *receive* from persons only: we *take* a book from the table; we *receive* a parcel which is sent us: we *take* either with or without the consent of the person; we *receive* it with his consent, or according to his wishes;

Each *takes* his seat, and each *receives* his share.
POPE.

A robber *takes* money when he can find it; a friend *receives* the gift of a friend.

To *receive* is an act of right, we *receive* what is our own; to *accept* is an act of courtesy, we *accept* what is offered by another. To *receive* simply excludes the idea of refusal; to *accept* includes the idea of consent: we may *receive* with indifference or reluctance; but we *accept* with willingness: the idea of *receiving* is included in that of *accepting*, but not *vice versâ:* what we *receive* may either involve an obligation or not; what we *accept* always involves the return of like courtesy at least: he who *receives* a debt is under no obligation, but he who *receives* a favour is bound by gratitude;

The sweetest cordial we *receive* at last
Is conscience of our virtuous actions past.
DENHAM.

He who *accepts* a present will feel himself called upon to make some return;

Unransom'd here *receive* the spotless fair,
Accept the hecatomb the Greeks prepare.—POPE.

RECEIPT, RECEPTION.

Receipt comes from *receive*, in its application to inanimate objects, which are taken into possession; *reception* comes from the same verb, in the sense of treating persons at their first arrival: in the commercial intercourse of men, the *receipt* of goods or money must be acknowledged in writing; 'If a man will keep but of even hand, his ordinary expenses ought to be but to half of his *receipts*.'—BACON. In the friendly intercourse of men, their *reception* of each other will be polite or cold, according to the sentiments entertained towards the individual; 'I thank you and Mrs. Pope for my kind *reception*.'—ATTERBURY.

TO CHOOSE, PREFER

Choose, in French *choisir*, German *kiesen*, from the French *cher*, Celtick *choe* dear or good, signifies to hold good; *prefer*, in French *preferer*, Latin *præfero*, compounded of *præ* and *fero* to take before, signifies to take one thing rather than another.

* To *choose* is to *prefer* as the genus to the species: we always *choose* in *preferring*, but we do not always *prefer* in *choosing*. To *choose* is to take one thing from among others; to *prefer* is to take one thing before or rather than another. We sometimes *choose* from the bare necessity of *choosing;* but we never *prefer* without making a positive and voluntary *choice*.

When we *choose* from a specifick motive, the acts of *choosing* and *preferring* differ in the nature of the motive. The former is absolute, the latter relative. We *choose* a thing for what it is, or what we esteem it to be of itself; we *prefer* a thing for what it has, or what we suppose it has, superiour to another; 'Judgement was wearied with the perplexity of *choice* where there was no motive for *preference*.'—JOHNSON.

Utility and convenience are grounds for *choosing*, comparative merit occasions the *preference:* we *choose* something that is good, and are contented with it until we see something better which we *prefer*.

We calculate and pause in *choosing;* we decide in *preferring;* the judgement determines in making the *choice;* the will determines in giving the *preference*. We *choose* things from an estimate of their merits or their fitness for the purpose proposed; we *prefer* them from their accordance with our tastes, habits, and pursuits. Books are *chosen* by those who wish to read; romances and works of fiction are *preferred* by general readers; learned works by the scholar.

One who wants instruction *chooses* a master, but he will mostly *prefer* a teacher whom he knows to a perfect stranger. Our *choice* is good or bad according to our knowledge; our *preference* is just or unjust, according as it is sanctioned by reason.

Our *choice* may be directed by our own experience or that of others; our *preference* must be guided by our own feelings. We make our *choice;* we give our *preference:* the first is the settled purpose of the mind, it fixes on the object; the latter is the inclining of the will, it yields to the object.

Choosing must be employed in all the important concerns of life; 'There is nothing of so great importance to us, as the good qualities of one to whom we join ourselves for life. When the *choice* is left to friends, the chief point under consideration is an estate; where the parties *choose* for themselves, their thoughts turn most upon the person.—ADDISON. *Preferring* is admissible in subordinate matters only; 'When a man has a mind to venture his money in a lottery, every figure of it appears equally alluring; and no manner of reason can be given why a man should *prefer* one to the other before the lottery is drawn.'—ADDISON. There is but one thing that is right, and that ought to be *chosen* when it is discovered: there are many indifferent things that may suit our tastes and inclinations; these we are at liberty to *prefer*. But to *prefer* what we ought not to *choose* is to make our reason bend to our will. Our Saviour said of Mary that she chose the better part: had she consulted her feelings she would have *preferred* the part she had rejected. The path of life should be *chosen;* but the path to be taken in a walk may be *preferred*. It is advisable for a youth in the *choice* of a profession to consult what he *prefers*, as he has the greatest chance

* The Abbe Girard, under the article *choisir, preferer*, has reversed this rule; but as I conceive, from a confusion of thought, which pervades the whole of his illustration on these words. The Abbe Roubaud has controverted his positions with some degree of accuracy. I have, however, given my own view of the matter in distinction from either.

of succeeding when he can combine his pleasure with his duty. A friend should be *chosen:* a companion may be *preferred.* A wife should be *chosen;* but unfortunately lovers are most apt to give a *preference* in a matter where a good or bad *choice* may determine one's happiness or misery for life. A wise prince is careful in the *choice* of his ministers; but a weak prince has mostly favourites whom he *prefers.*

TO CHOOSE, PICK, SELECT.

Choose signifies the same as in the preceding article; *pick*, in German *picken*, or *bicken*, French *bicquer*, Dutch *becken*, Icelandick *picka*, Swedish *piacka*, comes very probably from the old German *bag*, *bich*, to stick, corresponding to the Latin *figo* to fix, signifying to fix upon; *select*, Latin *selectus*, participle of *seligo*, that is, *lego* to gather or put, and *se* apart.

Choose is as in the former case the generick; the others are specifick terms: *pick* and *select* are expressly different modes of *choosing.* We always *choose* when we *pick* and *select;* but we do not always *pick* and *select* when we *choose.*

To *choose* may be applied to two or more things; to *pick* and *select* can be used only for several things. We may *choose* one book out of two, but we *pick* and *select* out of a library or a parcel; *pick* may be said of one or many; *select* only of many.

To *choose* does not always spring from any particular design or preference; 'My friend, Sir Roger, being a good churchman, has beautified the inside of his church with several texts of his own *choosing.*'—Addison. To *pick* and *select* signify to *choose* with care. What is *picked* and *selected* is always the best of its kind, but the former is commonly something of a physical nature; the latter of a moral or intellectual description. Soldiers are sometimes *picked* to form a particular regiment; 'I know, by several experiments, that those little animals (the ants) take great care to provide themselves with wheat when they can find it, and always *pick* out the best.'—Addison. Pieces are *selected* in prose or verse for general purposes; 'The chief advantage which these fictions have over real life is, that their authors are at liberty, though not to invent, yet to *select* objects.'—Johnson.

TO CHOOSE, ELECT.

Both these terms are employed in regard to persons appointed to an office; the former in a general, the latter in a particular sense.

Choosing (*v. To choose, prefer*) is either the act of one man or of many; *election*, from *eligo*, or *e* and *lego*, signifying to take or gather out of or from, is always that of a number: it is performed by the concurrence of many voices.

A prince *chooses* his ministers; the constituents *elect* members of parliament. A person is *chosen* to serve the office of sheriff; he is *elected* by the corporation to be mayor.

Choosing is an act of authority; it binds the person *chosen: election* is a voluntary act; the *elected* have the power of refusal. People are obliged to serve in some offices when they are *chosen*, although they would gladly be exempt;

> Wise were the kings who never *chose* a friend,
> Till with full cups they had unmask'd his soul,
> And seen the bottom of his deepest thoughts.
> Roscommon.

The circumstance of being *elected* is an honour after which men eagerly aspire; and for the attainment of which they risk their property, and use the most strenuous exertions; 'This prince, in gratitude to the people, by whose consent he was chosen, elected a hundred senators out of the commoners.'—Swift.

ELIGIBLE, PREFERABLE.

Eligible, or fit to be elected, and *preferable*, fit to be preferred, serve as epithets in the sense of choose and prefer (*v. To choose, prefer*); what is *eligible* is desirable in itself, what is *preferable* is more desirable than another. There may be many *eligible* situations, out of which perhaps there is but one *preferable.* Of persons however we say rather that they are *eligible* to an office than *preferable;* 'The middle condition is the most *eligible* to the man who would improve himself in virtue.'—Addison. The saying of Plato is, that labour is as *preferable* to idleness as brightness to rust!'—Hughes.

OPTION, CHOICE.

Option is immediately of Latin derivation, and is consequently a term of less frequent use than the word *choice*, which has been shown (*v. To choose*) to be of Celtick origin. The former term, from the Greek ὀπτόμαι to see or consider, implies an uncontrolled act of the mind; the latter a simple leaning of the will. We speak of *option* only as regards one's freedom from external constraint in the act of *choosing:* one speaks of *choice* only as the simple act itself. The *option* or the power of *choosing* is given; the *choice* itself is made: hence we say a thing is at a person's *option*, or it is his own option, or the *option* is left to him, in order to designate his freedom of *choice* more strongly than is expressed by the word *choice* itself; 'While they talk we must make our *choice*, they or the jacobins. We have no other *option.*'—Burke.

TO GATHER, COLLECT.

To *gather*, in Saxon *gatherian*, probably contracted from *get here*, signifies simply to bring to one spot. To *collect*, from *colligo* or *col*, *cum*, and *lego* to gather into one place, annexes also the idea of binding or forming into a whole; we *gather* that which is scattered in different parts: thus stones are *gathered* into a heap; vessels are *collected* so as to form a fleet. *Gathering* is a mere act of necessity or convenience;

> As the small ant (for she instructs the man,
> And preaches labour) *gathers* all she can.
> Creech.

Collecting is an act of design or choice;

> The royal bee, queen of the rosy bower,
> *Collects* her precious sweets from every flower
> C. Johnson.

We *gather* apples from a tree, or a servant *gathers* the books from the table; the antiquarian *collects* coins, or the bibliomaniac *collects* rare books.

ACCEPTABLE, GRATEFUL, WELCOME.

Acceptable signifies worthy to be accepted; *grateful*, from the Latin *gratus* pleasing, signifies altogether pleasing; it is that which recommends itself. The *acceptable* is a relative good; the *grateful* is positive: the former depends upon our external condition, the latter on our feelings and taste: a gift is *acceptable* to a poor man, which would be refused by one less needy than himself; 'I cannot but think the following letter from the Emperor of China to the Pope of Rome, proposing a coalition of the Chinese and Roman Churches, will be *acceptable* to the curious.'—Steele. Harmonious sounds are always *grateful* to a musical ear;

> The kids with pleasure browze the bushy plain:
> The showers are *grateful* to the swelling grain
> Dryden.

Acceptable and *welcome* both apply to external circumstances, and are therefore relatively employed; but *acceptable* is confined to such things as are offered for our choice; but *welcome*, signifying come well or in season, refers to whatever happens according to our wishes: we may not always accept that which is *acceptable*, but we shall never reject that which is *welcome:* it is an insult to offer any thing by way of a gift to another which is not *acceptable;* it is a *grateful* task to be the bearer of *welcome* intelligence to our friends; 'Whatever is remote from common appearances is always *welcome* to vulgar as to childish credulity.'—Johnson

ACCEPTANCE, ACCEPTATION.

Though both derived from the verb accept, have this difference, that the former is employed to express the abstract action generally; the latter only in regard to particular objects. A book, or whatever else is offered to us, may be worthy of our *acceptance* or not; 'It is not necessary to refuse benefits from a bad man, when the *acceptance* implies no approbation of his crimes.'—JOHNSON. A word acquires its *acceptation* from the manner in which it is generally accepted by the learned; 'On the subject of dress I may add by way of caution that the ladies would do well not to forget themselves. I do not mean this in the common *acceptation* of the phrase, which it may be sometimes convenient and proper to do.'—MACKENZIE.

TO ADMIT,* RECEIVE.

Admit, in French *admettre*, Latin *admitto*, compounded of *ad* and *mitto*, signifies to send or suffer to pass into; *receive*, in French *recevoir*, Latin *recipio*, compounded of *re* and *capio*, signifies to take back or to one's self.

To *admit* is a general term, the sense of which depends upon what follows; to *receive* has a complete sense in itself: we cannot speak of *admitting*, without associating with it an idea of the object to which one is *admitted*; but *receive* includes no relative idea of the *receiver* or the *received*.

Admitting is an act of relative import; *receiving* is always a positive measure: a person may be *admitted* into a house, who is not prevented from entering;

> Somewhat is sure design'd by fraud or force;
> Trust not their presents, nor *admit* the horse.
> DRYDEN.

A person is *received* only by the actual consent of some individual;

> He star'd and roll'd his haggard eyes around;
> Then said, 'Alas! what earth remains, what sea
> Is open to *receive* unhappy me?—DRYDEN.

We may be *admitted* in various capacities; we are *received* only as guests, friends, or inmates. Persons are *admitted* to the tables, and into the familiarity or confidence of others;

> The Tyrian train, *admitted* to the feast,
> Approach, and on the painted couches rest.
> DRYDEN.

Persons are hospitably *received* by those who wish to be their entertainers;

> Pretending to consult
> About the great *reception* of their king
> Thither to come.—MILTON.

We *admit* willingly or reluctantly; we *receive* politely or rudely. Foreign ambassadors are *admitted* to an audience, and *received* at court. It is necessary to be cautious not to *admit* any one into our society, who may not be agreeable and suitable companions; but still more necessary not to *receive* any one into our houses whose character may reflect disgrace on ourselves.

Whoever is *admitted* as a member of any community should consider himself as bound to conform to its regulations: whoever is *received* into the service of another should study to make himself valued and esteemed. A winning address, and agreeable manners, gain a person *admittance* into the genteelest circles: the talent for affording amusement, procures a person a good *reception* among the mass of mankind.

When applied to unconscious agents there is a similar distinction between these terms: ideas are *admitted* into the mind by means of association and the like; 'There are some ideas which have *admittance* only through one sense, which is peculiarly adapted to *receive* them.'—LOCKE. Things are *received* by others in consequence of their adaptation to each other;

> The thin-leav'd arbute hazel-grafts *receives*,
> And planes huge apples bare, that bore but leaves.
> DRYDEN.

ADMITTANCE, ACCESS, APPROACH.

Admittance marks the act or liberty of admitting (*v. To admit, receive*); *access*, from *accedo* to approach or come up to, marks the act or liberty of approaching; *approach*, from *ap* or *ad* and *proximus* nearest, signifies coming near or drawing near.

We get *admittance* into a place or a society; we have *access* to a person; and make an *approach* either towards a person or a thing.

* Girard: "Amettre, recevoir.'

Admittance may be open or excluded; *access* and *approach* may be free or difficult.

We have *admittance* when we enter; we have *access* to him whom we address. There can be no *access* where there is no *admittance*; but there may be *admittance* without *access*. Servants or officers may grant us *admittance* into the palaces of princes; 'As my pleasures are almost wholly confined to those of the sight, I take it for a peculiar happiness that I have always had an easy and familiar *admittance* to the fair sex.'—STEELE. The favourites of princes have *access* to their persons; 'Do not be surprised, most holy father, at seeing, instead of a coxcomb to laugh at, your old friend who has taken this way of *access* to admonish you of your own folly.'—STEELE.

Access and *admittance* are here considered as the acts of conscious agents; *approach* is as properly the act of unconscious as conscious agents. We may speak of the *approach* of an army, or the *approach* of a war;

> 'T is with our souls
> As with our eyes, that after a long darkness
> Are dazzled at th' *approach* of sudden light.

Admittance may likewise sometimes be taken figuratively, as when we speak of the *admittance* of ideas into the mind.

ADMITTANCE, ADMISSION.

These words differ according to the different acceptations of the primitive from which they are both derived; the former being taken in the proper sense or familiar style, and the latter in the figurative sense or in the grave style.

The *admittance* to publick places of entertainment is on particular occasions difficult; 'Assurance never failed to get *admittance* into the houses of the great.'—MOORE. The *admission* of irregularities, however trifling in the commencement, is mostly attended with serious consequences; 'The gospel has then only a free *admission* into the assent of the understanding, when it brings a passport from a rightly disposed will.'—SOUTH.

IMPERVIOUS, IMPASSABLE, INACCESSIBLE

Impervious, from the Latin *in*, *per*, and *via*, signifies not having a way through; *impassable*, not to be passed through; *inaccessible*, not to be approached. A wood is *impervious* when the trees, branches, and leaves are entangled to such a degree as to admit of no passage at all;

> The monster, Cacus, more than half a beast,
> This hold *impervious* to the sun possess'd.
> DRYDEN.

A river is *impassable* that is so deep that it cannot be forded.

> But lest the difficulty of passing back
> Stay his return perhaps over this gulf
> *Impassable*, *impervious*, let us try
> Advent'rous work.—MILTON.

A rock or a mountain is *inaccessible* the summit of which is not to be reached by any path whatever;

> At least our envious foe hath fail'd who thought
> All like himself rebellious, by whose aid
> This *inaccessible* high strength, the seat
> Of Deity Supreme, us dispossess'd,
> He trusted to have seiz'd.—MILTON.

What is *impervious* is for a permanency; what is *impassable* is commonly so only for a time: roads are frequently *impassable* in the winter that are *passable* in the summer, while a thicket is *impervious* during the whole of the year: *impassable* is likewise said only of that which is to be passed by living creatures, but *impervious* may be extended to inanimate objects; a wood may be *impervious* to the rays of the sun

TO APPROACH, APPROXIMATE.

Approach, in French *approcher*, compound of *ap* or *ad* and *proche*, or in Latin *prope* near, signifies to come near; *approximate*, compounded of *ap* and *proximus* to come nearest or next, signifies either to draw near or bring near.

To *approach* is intransitive only; a person *approaches* an object; 'Lambs push at those that *approach* them with their heads before the first budding of a horn appears.'—ADDISON. To *approximate* is both transitive and intransitive; a person *approximates* two objects; 'Shakspeare *approximates* the remote and far.'—JOHNSON.

To *approach* denotes simply the moving of an object towards another, but to *approximate* denotes the gradual moving of two objects towards each other: that which *approaches* may come into immediate conjunction; 'Comets, in their *approaches* towards the earth, are imagined to cause diseases, famines, and other such like judgements of God.'—DERHAM. But bodies may *approximate* for some time before they form a junction, or may never form a junction; 'The *approximations* and recesses of some of the little stars I speak of, suit not with the observations of some very ancient astronomers.'—DERHAM. An equivocation *approaches* to a lie. Minds *approximate* by long intercourse.

TO HOLD, KEEP, DETAIN, RETAIN.

Hold, in Saxon *healden*, Teutonick *holden;* is probably connected with the verb to have, in Latin *habeo*, &c.; *keep* in all probability comes from *capio* to lay hold of; *detain* and *retain* both come from the Latin *teneo* to hold; the first signifies, by virtue of the particle *de*, to hold from another; the second, by virtue of the particle *re*, signifies to *hold* back for one's self.

To *hold* is a physical act; it requires a degree of bodily strength, or at least the use of the limbs; to *keep* is simply to have by one at one's pleasure. The mode of the action is the leading idea in the signification of *hold;* the durability of the action is the leading idea in the word *keep:* we may *hold* a thing only for a moment: but what we *keep* we *keep* for a time. On the other hand, we may *keep* a thing by *holding*, although we may *keep* it by various other means: we may therefore *hold* without *keeping*, and we may *keep* without *holding*. A servant *holds* a thing in his hand for it to be seen, but he does not *keep* it; he gives it to his master who puts it into his pocket, and consequently *keeps*, but does not *hold* it. A thing may be *held* in the hand, or *kept* in the hand; in the former case, the pressure of the hand is an essential part of the action, but in the latter case it is simply a contingent part of the action: the hand *holds*, but the person *keeps* it.

What is *held* is fixed in position, but what is *kept* is left loose or otherwise, at the will of the individual. Things are *held* by human beings in their hands, by beasts in their claws or mouths, by birds in their beaks; things are *kept* by human beings either about their persons or in their houses, according to convenience;

France, thou mayst hold a serpent by the tongue,
A fasting tiger safer by the tooth,
Than keep in peace that hand which thou dost *hold*.
SHAKSPEARE.

Detain and *retain* are modes of *keeping:* the former signifies *keeping* back what belongs to another; the latter signifies *keeping* a long time for one's own purpose. A person may be either *held, kept, detained*, or *retained:* when he is *held* he is *held* contrary to his will by the hand of another; as suspected persons are *held* by the officers of justice, that they may not make their escape: he is *kept*, if he stops in any place, by the desire of another; as a man is *kept* in prison until his innocence is proved; or a child is *kept* at school, until he has finished his education: he is *detained* if he be *kept* away from any place to which he is going, or from any person to whom he belongs: as the servant of another is *detained* to take back a letter; or one is *detained* by business, so as to be prevented attending to an appointment: a person is *retained*, who is *kept* for a continuance in the service, the favour, or the power of another; as some servants are said to be *retained* while others are dismissed;

Too late it was for satyr to be told,
Or ever hope recover her again;
In vain he seeks, that having, cannot *hold*.
SPENSER.

That I may know what *keeps* you here with me.
DRYDEN.

He has described the passion of Calypso, and the indecent advances she made to *detain* him from his country.'—BROOME. 'Having the address to *retain* the conquest she (Roxalana) had made, she kept possession of his (Solyman's) love without any rival for many years.'—ROBERTSON.

These words bear a similar analogy to each other in an extended application. A money-lender *holds* the property of others in pledge; the idea of a temporary and partial action is here expressed by *hold*, in distinction from *keep*, which is used to express something definite and permanent; 'Assuredly it is more shame for a man to lose that which he *holdeth*, than to fail in getting that which he never had.'—HAYWARD. The money-lender *keeps* the property as his own, if the borrower forfeits it by breach of contract;

This charge I *keep* until my appointed day
Of rendering up.—MILTON.

When a person purchases any thing, he is expected to *keep* it, or pay the value of the thing ordered, if the tradesman fulfil his part of the engagement. What is *detained* is *kept* either contrary to the will, or without the consent, of the possessor: when things are suspected to be stolen, the officers of justice have the right of *detaining* them until inquiry be instituted;

Haste! goddess, haste! the flying host *detain*
Nor let one sail be hoisted on the main.—POPE.

What is *retained* is continued to be *kept;* it supposes, however, some alteration in the terms or circumstances under which it is *kept;* a person *retains* his seat in a coach, notwithstanding he finds it disagreeable; or a lady *retains* some of the articles of millinery, which are sent for her choice, but she returns the rest;

Let me *retain*
The name, and all th' addition to a king.
SHAKSPEARE.

All are used in a moral application except *detain;* in this case they are marked by a similar distinction. A person is said to *hold* an office, by which simple possession is implied; he may *hold* it for a long or a short time, at the will of others, or by his own will, which are not marked: he *keeps* a situation, or he *keeps* his post, by which his continuance in the situation, or at the post, are denoted: he *retains* his office, by which is signified that he might have given it up, or lost it, had he not been led to continue in it. In like manner, with regard to one's sentiments, feelings, or external circumstances, a man is said to *hold* certain opinions, which are ascribed to him as a part of his creed; 'It is a certain sign of a wise government, when it can *hold* men's hearts by hopes.'—BACON. A person *keeps* his opinions when no one can induce him to give them up; 'The proof is best when men *keep* their authority towards their children, but not their purse.'—BACON. He *retains* his old attachments, notwithstanding the lapse of years, and change of circumstances, which have intervened, and were naturally calculated to wean him; 'Ideas are *retained* by renovation of that impression which time is always wearing away.'—JOHNSON.

TO HOLD, OCCUPY, POSSESS.

Hold has the same general meaning as in the preceding article; *occupy*, in Latin *occupo*, or *oc* and *capio* to hold or keep, signifies to keep so that it cannot be held by others; *possess*, in Latin *possideo*, or *potis* and *sedeo*, signifies to sit as master of.

We *hold* a thing for a long or a short time; we *occupy* it for a permanence: we *hold* it for ourselves or others; we *occupy* it only for ourselves: we *hold* it for various purposes; we *occupy* only for the purpose of converting it to our private use. Thus a person may *hold* an estate, or, which is the same thing, the title deeds to an estate pro tempore, for another person's benefit: but he *occupies* an estate if he enjoys the fruit of it. On the other hand, to *occupy* is only to *hold* under a certain compact; but to *possess* is to *hold* as one's own. The tenant *occupies* the farm when he *holds* it by a certain lease, and cultivates it for his subsistence: but the landlord *possesses* the farm who *possesses* the right to let it, and to receive the rent.

We may *hold* by force, or fraud, or right;

He (the eagle) drives them from his fort the towering seat,
For ages of his empire which in peace
Unstain'd he *holds*.'—THOMSON

We *occupy* either by force or right; 'If the title of *occupiers* be good in a land unpeopled, why should it be bad accounted in a country peopled thinly.'—RALEIGH.

We *possess* only by right;

But now the feather'd youth their former bounds
Ardent disdain, and weighing oft their wings,
Demand the free *possession* of the sky.
THOMSON.

Hence we say figuratively, to *hold* a person in esteem or contempt, to *occupy* a person's attention, to *occupy* a place, &c. or to *possess* one's affection;

I, as a stranger to my heart and me,
Hold thee from this for ever.—SHAKSPEARE.

'He must assert infinite generations before that first deluge, and then the earth could not receive them, but the infinite bodies of men must *occupy* an infinite space.'—BENTLEY.

Of fortune's favour long *possess'd*,
He was with one fair daughter only bless'd.
DRYDEN.

TO HOLD, SUPPORT, MAINTAIN.

Hold is here, as in the former article, a term of very general import; to *support*, from *sub* and *porto* to carry, signifying to bear the weight of a thing; and to *maintain*, from the French *maintenir*, and the Latin *manus* a hand, and *teneo* to hold, signifying to hold firmly, are particular modes of holding.

Hold and *support* are employed in the proper sense, *maintain* in the improper sense. To *hold* is a term unqualified by any circumstance; we may *hold* a thing in any direction, *hold* up or down, straight or crooked: *support* is a species of *holding* up; to *hold* up, however, is a personal act, or a direct effort of the individual; to *support* may be an indirect and a passive act; he who *holds* any thing up keeps it in an upright posture, by the exertion of his strength; he who *supports* a thing only bears its weight, or suffers it to rest upon himself: persons or voluntary agents can *hold* up; inanimate objects may *support:* a servant *holds* up a child that it may see; a pillar *supports* a building.

Hold, *maintain*, and *support* are likewise employed still farther in a moral application, as it respects the different opinions and circumstances of men; opinions are *held* and *maintained* as one's own; they are *supported* when they are another's. We *hold* and *maintain* when we believe; we *support* the belief or doctrine of another, or what we ourselves have asserted and *maintained* at a former time. What is *held* is *held* by the act of the mind within one's self; what is *maintained* and *supported* is openly declared to be *held*. To *hold* marks simply the state of one's own mind; 'It was a notable observation of a wise father, that those which *held* and persuaded pressure of consciences were commonly interested therein themselves for their own ends.'—BACON. To *maintain* indicates the effort which one makes to inform others of this state; 'If any man of quality will *maintain* upon Edward, Earl of Gloucester, that he is a manifold traitor, let him appear.'—SHAKSPEARE. To *support* indicates the efforts which one makes to justify that state. We *hold* an opinion only as it regards ourselves; we *maintain* and *support* it as it regards others; that is, we *maintain* it either with others, for others, or against others: we *support* it in an especial manner against others: we *maintain* it by assertion; we *support* it by argument. Bad principles do harm only to the individual when they are *held;* they will do harm to all over whom our influence extends when we *maintain* them; they may do harm to all the world, when we undertake to *support* them. Good principles need only be *held*, or at most *maintained*, unless where adversaries set themselves up against them, and render it necessary to *support* them. Infidel principles have been *held* occasionally by individuals in all ages, but they were never *maintained* with so much openness and effrontery at any time, as at the close of the eighteenth century, when *supporters* of such principles were to be found in every tap-room.

Hold is applied not only to principles and opinions, but also to sentiments; *maintain* and *support* are confined either to abstract and speculative opinions, or to the whole mind: we *hold* a thing dear or cheap, we *hold* it in abhorrence, or we *hold* it sacred. 'As Chaucer is the father of English poetry, so I *hold* him in the same degree of veneration as the Grecians *held* Homer or the Romans Virgil.'—DRYDEN. We *maintain* or *support* truth or errour; we *maintain* an influence over ourselves, or *maintain* a cause;

Who then is free? The wise, who well *maintains*
An empire o'er himself.—FRANCIS.

We *support* our resolution or our minds; 'Nothing can *support* the minds of the guilty from drooping.'—SOUTH.

TO HAVE, POSSESS.

Have, in German *haben*, Latin *habeo*, not improbably from the Hebrew אבה to desire, or אהב he loved, because those who have most, desire most, or because men love worldly possessions above every thing else; *possess* has the same meaning as in the preceding article; *have* is the general, *possess* is the particular term: *have* designates no circumstance of the action; *possess* expresses a particular species of having.

To *have* is sometimes to *have* in one's hand or within one's reach; but to *possess* is to *have* as one's own: a clerk *has* the money which he has fetched for his employer; the latter *possesses* the money, which he *has* the power of turning to his use. To *have* is sometimes to *have* the right to, to belong; to *possess* is to *have* by one and at one's command: a debtor *has* the property which he has surrendered to his creditor; but he cannot be said to *possess* it, because he *has* it not within his reach, and at his disposal:* we are not necessarily masters of that which we *have;* although we always are of that which we *possess:* to *have* is sometimes only temporary; to *possess* is mostly permanent: we *have* money which we are perpetually disposing of; we *possess* lands which we keep for a permanency: a person *has* the good graces of those whom he pleases; he *possesses* the confidence of those who put every thing in his power: the stoutest heart may *have* occasional alarms, but will never lose its self-possession: a husband *has* continual torments who is *possessed* by the demon of jealousy: a miser *has* goods in his coffers, but he is not master of them; they *possess* his heart and affections: we *have* things by halves when we share them with others; we *possess* them only when they are exclusively ours and we enjoy them undividedly;

That I spent, that I *had;*
That I gave, that I *have;*
That I left, that I lost.
EPITAPH ON A CHARITABLE MAN

A lover *has* the affections of his mistress by whom he is beloved; he *possesses* her whole heart when she loves him only: one *has* an interest in a mercantile concern in which he is a partner; the lord of a manor *possesses* all the rights annexed to that manor; 'The various objects that compose the world were by nature formed to delight our senses; and as it is this alone that makes them desirable to an uncorrupted taste, a man may be said naturally to *possess* them when he *possesseth* those enjoyments which they are fitted by nature to yield.'—BERKELEY.

TO LAY OR TAKE HOLD OF, CATCH, SEIZE, SNATCH, GRASP, GRIPE.

To *lay* or *take hold of* is here the generick expression. it denotes simply getting into the possession, which is the common idea in the signification of all these terms, which differ chiefly in regard to the motion in which the action is performed. To *catch* is to *lay hold of* with an effort. To *seize* is to *lay hold of* with violence. To *snatch* is to *lay hold of* by a sudden and violent effort. One is said to *lay hold of* that on which he places his hand; he *takes hold of* that which he secures in his hand. We *lay hold of* any thing when we see it falling; we *take hold of* any thing when we wish to lift it up; 'Sometimes it happens that a corn slips out of their paws when they (the ants) are climbing up; they *take hold of* it again when they can find it, otherwise they look for another.'—ADDISON. We *catch* the thing which attempts to escape; 'One great genius

* Vide Abbe Girard: "Avoir, posséder

often *catches* the flame from another.'—ADDISON. We *seize* a thing when it makes resistance;

> Furious he said, and tow'rd the Grecian crew,
> (*Seiz'd* by the crest) th' unhappy warriour drew.
> POPE.

We *snatch* that which we are particularly afraid of not getting otherwise;

> The hungry harpies fly,
> They *snatch* the meat, defiling all they find.
> DRYDEN.

A person, who is fainting, *lays hold of* the first thing which comes in his way; a sick person or one that wants support *takes hold* of another's arm in walking; various artifices are employed to *catch* animals; the wild beasts of the forest *seize* their prey the moment they come within their reach; it is the rude sport of a schoolboy to *snatch* out of the hand of another that which he is not willing to let go.

To *lay hold of* is to get in the possession. To *grasp* and to *gripe* signify to have or keep in the possession: an eagerness to keep or not to let go is expressed by that of *grasping;*

> Like a miser 'midst his store,
> Who *grasps* and *grasps* till he can hold no more.
> DRYDEN.

A fearful anxiety of losing and an earnest desire of keeping is expressed by the act of *griping;*

> They *gripe* their oaks; and every panting breast
> Is rais'd by turns with hope, by turns with fear depress'd.
> DRYDEN.

When a famished man *lays hold of* food, he *grasps* it, from a convulsive kind of fear lest it should leave him; when a miser *lays hold of* money he *gripes* it from the love he bears to it; and the fear he has that it will be taken from him.

OCCUPANCY, OCCUPATION,

Are words which derive their meaning from the different acceptations of the primitive verb *occupy:* the former being used to express the state of holding or possessing any object; the latter to express the act of taking possession of, or keeping in possession. He who has the *occupancy* of land enjoys the fruits of it; 'As *occupancy* gave the right to the temporary use of the soil; so it is agreed on all hands, that *occupancy* gave also the original right to the permanent property in the substance of the earth itself.'—BLACKSTONE. The *occupation* of a country by force of arms is of little avail, unless one has an adequate force to maintain one's ground; 'The unhappy consequences of this temperament is, that my attachment to any *occupation* seldom outlives its novelty.'—COWPER.

POSSESSOR, PROPRIETOR, OWNER, MASTER.

The *possessor* has the full power, if not the right, of the present disposal over the object of possession; 'I am convinced that a poetick talent is a blessing to its *possessor*.'—SEWARD. The *proprietor* and *owner* has the unlimited right of transfer, but not always the power of immediate disposal. The *proprietor* and the *owner* are the same in signification, though not in application; the first term being used principally in regard to matters of importance; the latter on familiar occasions: the *proprietor* of an estate is a more suitable expression than the *owner* of an estate;

> Death! great *proprietor* of all! 'T is thine
> To tread out empire and to quench the stars.
> YOUNG.

The *owner* of a book is a more becoming expression than the *proprietor;* 'One cause of the insufficiency of riches (to produce happiness) is, that they very seldom make their *owner* rich.'—JOHNSON. The *possessor* and the *master* are commonly the same person, when those things are in question which are subject to *possession;* but the terms are otherwise so different in their original meaning, that they can scarcely admit of comparison: the *possessor* of a house is naturally the *master* of the house; and, in general, whatever a man *possesses*, that he has in his power, and is consequently *master* of; but we may have, legally, the right of *possessing* a thing, over which we have actually no power of control: in this case, we are nominally *possessor*, but virtually not *master*. A minor, or insane person, may be both *possessor* and *proprietor* of that over which he has no control; a man is, therefore, on the other hand, appropriately denominated *master*, not *possessor* of his actions;

> There, Cæsar, grac'd with both Minervas, shone,
> Cæsar, the world's great *master*, and his own.
> POPE.

TO SUSTAIN, SUPPORT, MAINTAIN.

The idea of exerting one's self to keep an object from sinking is common to all these terms, which vary either in the mode or the object of the action. To *sustain*, from the Latin *sustineo*, i. e. *sus* or *sub* and *teneo* to hold, signifying to hold from underneath; and *support*, from *sub* and *porto* to bear, signifying to bear from underneath, are passive actions, and imply that we bear the weight of something pressing upon us; *maintain* (*v. To assert*) is active, and implies that we exert ourselves so as to keep it from pressing upon us. We *sustain* a load; we *support* a burden; we *maintain* a contest. The principal difficulty in an engagement is often to *sustain* the first shock of the attack;

> With labour spent, no longer can he wield
> The heavy falchion, or *sustain* the shield,
> O'erwhelm'd with darts.—DRYDEN.

A soldier has not merely to *support* the weight of his arms, but to *maintain* his post; 'Let this *support* and comfort you, that you are the father of ten children, among whom there seems to be but one soul of love and obedience.'—LYTTLETON. What is *sustained* is often temporary; what is *supported* is mostly permanent: a loss or an injury is *sustained;* pain, distress, and misfortunes, are *supported:* *maintain*, on the other hand, is mostly something of importance or advantage; credit must always be *maintained;*

> As compass'd with a wood of spears around,
> The lordly lion still *maintains* his ground,
> So Turnus fares.—DRYDEN.

We must *sustain* a loss with tranquillity; we must *support* an affliction with equanimity; we must *maintain* our own honour, and that of the community to which we belong, by the rectitude of our conduct.

STAFF, STAY, PROP, SUPPORT.

From *staff* in the literal sense (*v. Staff*) comes *staff* in the figurative application: any thing may be denominated a *staff* which holds up after the manner of a *staff*, particularly as it respects persons; bread is said to be the *staff* of life; one person may serve as a *staff* to another. The *staff* serves in a state of motion; 'Let shame and confusion then cover me if I do not abhor the intolerable anxiety I well understand to wait inseparably upon that *staff* of going about beguilefully to supplant any man.'—LORD WENTWORTH. The *stay* and *prop* are employed for objects in a state of rest: the *stay* makes a thing *stay* for the time being, it keeps it from falling; it is equally applied to persons and things; we may be a *stay* to a person who is falling by letting his body rest against us; in the same manner buttresses against a wall, and shores against a building, serve the purpose of a *stay*, while it is under repair. For the same reason that part of a female's dress which serves as a *stay* to the body is denominated *stays;* the *prop* keeps a thing up for a permanency; every pillar on which a building rests is a *prop;* whatever therefore requires to be raised from the ground, and kept in that state, may be set upon *props;* between the *stay* and the *prop* there is this obvious distinction, that as the *stay* does not receive the whole weight, it is put so as to receive it indirectly, by leaning against the object; but the *prop*, for a contrary reason, is put upright underneath the object so as to receive the weight directly: the derivation of this word *prop*, from the Dutch *proppe* a plug, and the German *pfropfen* a cork, does not seem to account very clearly for its present use in English.

Stay and *prop* may be figuratively extended in their application with the same distinction in their sense; a crust of bread may serve as a *stay* to the stomach

> If hope precarious, and of things when gain'd
> Of little moment, and as little *stay*,
> Can sweeten toils and dangers into joys,
> When then that hope which nothing can defeat?
>
> YOUNG.

A person's money may serve as a *prop* for the credit of another. *Support* is altogether taken in the moral and abstract sense: whatever *supports*, that is, bears the weight of an object, is a *support*, whether in a state of motion like a *staff*, or in a state of rest like a *stay*; whether to bear the weight in part like a *stay*, or altogether like a *prop*, it is still a *support*: but the term is likewise employed on all occasions in which the other terms are not admissible. Whatever *supports* existence, whether directly or indirectly, is a *support*: food is the *support* of the animal body; labour or any particular employment is likewise one's *support*, or the indirect means of gaining the *support*; hope is the *support* of the mind under the most trying circumstances; religion, as the foundation of all our hopes, is the best and surest *support* under affliction;

> Whate'er thy many fingers can entwine,
> Proves thy *support* and all its strength is thine,
> Tho' nature gave not legs, it gave thee hands,
> By which thy *prop*, thy prouder cedar stands.
>
> DENHAM.

STAFF, STICK, CRUTCH

Staff, in Low German *staff*, &c., in Latin *stipes*, in Greek ςύπη, comes from ςύφω *stipo* to fix; *stick* signifies that which can be stuck in the ground; *crutch*, as changed from *cross*, is a *staff* or *stick* which has a cross bar at the top.

The ruling idea in a *staff* is that of firmness and fixedness; it is employed for leaning upon: the ruling idea in the *stick* is that of sharpness with which it can penetrate, it is used for walking and ordinary purposes; the ruling idea in the *crutch* is its form, which serves the specifick purpose of support in case of lameness; a *staff* can never be small, but a *stick* may be large; a *crutch* is in size more of a *staff* than a common *stick*.

LIVELIHOOD, LIVING, SUBSISTENCE, MAINTENANCE, SUPPORT, SUSTENANCE.

The means of *living* or supporting life is the idea common to all these terms, which vary according to the circumstances of the individual and the nature of the object which constitutes the means: the *livelihood* is the thing sought after by the day; a labourer earns a *livelihood* by the sweat of his brow: *living* is obtained by more respectable and less severe efforts than the two former; tradesmen obtain a good *living* by keeping shops; artists procure a *living* by the exercise of their talents; 'A man may as easily know where to find one to teach to debauch, whore, game, and blaspheme, as to teach him to write or cast accounts; 't is the very profession and *livelihood* of such people, getting their *living* by those practices for which they deserve to forfeit their lives.'—SOUTH. A *subsistence* is obtained by irregular efforts of various descriptions; beggars meet with so much that they obtain something better than a precarious and scanty *subsistence*: 'Just the necessities of a bare *subsistence* are not to be the only measure of a parent's care for his children.'—SOUTH. *Maintenance*, *support*, and *sustenance*, differ from the other three inasmuch as they do not comprehend what one gains by one's own efforts, but by the efforts of others: the *maintenance* is that which is permanent; it supplies the place of a living: the *support* may be casual, and vary in degree: the object of most publick charities is to afford a *maintenance* to such as cannot obtain a *livelihood* or *living* for themselves; 'The Jews, in Babylonia, honoured Hyrcanus their king, and supplied him with a *maintenance* suitable thereto.'—PRIDEAUX. It is the business of the parish to give *support*, in time of sickness and distress, to all who are legal parishioners; 'If it be a curse to be forced to toil for the necessary *support* of life, how does he heighten the curse who toils for superfluities.'—SOUTH. The *maintenance* and *support* are always granted; but the *sustenance* is that which is taken or received: the former comprehends the means of obtaining food; the *sustenance* comprehends that which sustains the body which supplies the place of food; 'Besides, man has a claim also to a promise for his *support* and *sustenance* which none have ever missed of who come up to the conditions of it.'—SOUTH.

LIVING, BENEFICE.

Living signifies literally the pecuniary resource by which one lives; *benefice*, from *benefacio*, signifies whatever one obtains as a benefit: the former is applicable to any situation of life, but particularly to that resource which a parish affords to the clergyman; the latter is applicable to no other object: we speak of the *living* as a resource immediately derived from the parish, in distinction from a curacy, which is derived from an individual; 'In consequence of the Pope's interference, the best *livings* were filled by Italian, and other foreign, clergy.'—BLACKSTONE. We speak of a *benefice* in respect to the terms by which it is held, according to the ecclesiastical law: there are many *livings* which are not *benefices*, although not *vice versâ*; 'Estates held by feudal tenure, being originally gratuitous donations, were at that time denominated *beneficia*; their very name, as well as constitution, was borrowed, and the care of the souls of a parish thence came to be denominated a *benefice*.'—BLACKSTONE.

TO BE, EXIST, SUBSIST.

Be, with its inflections, is to be traced through the northern and Oriental languages to the Hebrew יה the name of God, and הוא to *be*. From the derivation of *exist*, as given under the article *To Exist, Live*, arises the distinction in the use of the two words. To *be* is applicable either to the accidents of things, or to the substances or things themselves; to *exist* only to substances or things that stand or *exist* of themselves. * We say of qualities, of forms, of actions, of arrangement, of movement, and of every different relation, whether real, ideal, or qualificative, that they *are*; 'He does not understand either vice or virtue who will not allow that life without the rules of morality is a wayward uneasy *being*.'—STEELE. We say of matter, of spirit, of body, and of all substances, that they *exist*; 'When the soul is freed from all corporeal alliance, then it truly *exists*.'—HUGHES AFTER XENOPHON. Man *is* man, and will *be* man under all circumstances and changes of life: he *exists* under every known climate and variety of heat or cold in the atmosphere.

Being and *existence* as nouns have this farther distinction, that the former is employed not only to designate the abstract state of *being*, but is metaphorically employed for the sensible object that *is*; the latter is confined altogether to the abstract sense. Hence we speak of human *beings*; *beings* animate or inanimate, the Supreme *Being*: but the *existence* of a God; *existence* of innumerable worlds; the *existence* of evil. *Being* may in some cases be indifferently employed for *existence*, particularly in the grave style; when speaking of animate objects, as the *being* of a God; our frail *being*; and when qualified in a compound form is preferable, as our *well-being*.

Subsist is properly a species of *existing*; from the Latin prepositive *sub*, signifying for a time, it denotes temporary or partial *existence*. Every thing *exists* by the creative and preservative power of the Almighty; that which *subsists* depends for its *existence* upon the chances and changes of this mortal life;

> Forlorn of thee,
> Whither shall I betake me? where *subsist*?
>
> MILTON.

To *exist* therefore designates simply the event of *being* or *existing*; to *subsist* conveys the accessory ideas of the mode and duration of *existing*. Man *exists* while the vital or spiritual part of him remains; he *subsists* by what he obtains to support life. Friendships *exist* in the world, notwithstanding the prevalence of selfishness; but it cannot *subsist* for any length of time between individuals in whom this base temper prevails.

* Vide Abbe Girard: "Etre exister subsister"

TO BE, BECOME, GROW.

Be (*v. To be, exist*); *become* signifies to *come* to *be*, that is, to *be* in course of time; *grow* is, in all probability, changed from the Latin *crevi*, perfect of *cresco* to increase or grow.

Be (*v. To be, exist*) is positive; *become*, that is to *come* to *be*, or to *be* in course of time is relative: a person *is* what he *is* without regard to what he *was*; he *becomes* that which he *was* not before;

> To *be* or not to *be*? that is the question.
> SHAKSPEARE.

We judge of a man by what he *is*, but we cannot judge of him by what he will *become*: this year he *is* immoral and irreligious, but by the force of reflection on himself he may *become* the contrary in another year: 'About this time Savage's nurse, who had always treated him as her own son, died; and it was natural for him to take care of those effects which by her death were, as he imagined, *become* his own.'—JOHNSON.

To *become* includes no idea of the mode or circumstance of *becoming*; to *grow* is to *become* by a gradual process: a man may *become* a good man from a vicious one, in consequence of a sudden action on his mind; but he *grows* in wisdom and virtue by means of an increase in knowledge and experience;

> Authors, like coins, *grow* dear, as they *grow* old.
> POPE.

TO EXIST, LIVE.

Exist, in French *exister*, Latin *existo*, compounded of *e* or *ex* and *sisto*, signifies to place or stand by itself or of itself; *live*, through the medium of the Saxon *libban*, and the other northern dialects, comes in all probability from the Hebrew לב the heart, which is the seat of animal life.

Existence is the property of all things in the universe; *life*, which is the inherent power of motion, is the particular property communicated by the Divine Being to some parts only of his creation: *exist*, therefore, is the general, and *live* the specifick, term: whatever *lives*, *exists* according to a certain mode; but many things *exist* without *living*: when we wish to speak of things in their most abstract relation, we say they *exist*;

> Can any now remember or relate
> How he *existed* in an embryo state?—JENYNS.

When we wish to characterize the form of *existence* we say they *live*; 'Death to such a man is rather to be looked upon as the period of his mortality, than the end of his *life*.'—MELMOTH (*Letters of Pliny*).

Existence, in its proper sense, is the attribute which we commonly ascribe to the Divine Being, and it is that which is immediately communicable by himself; *life* is that mode of *existence* which he has made to be communicable by other objects besides himself: *existence* is taken only in its strict and proper sense, independent of all its attributes and appendages; but *life* is regarded in connexion with the means by which it is supported, as animal life, or vegetable life. In like manner, when speaking of spiritual objects, *exist* retains its abstract sense, and *live* is employed to denote an active principle: animosities should never *exist* in the mind; and every thing which is calculated to keep them *alive* should be kept at a distance.

TO OUTLIVE, SURVIVE.

To *outlive* is literally to live out the life of another, to live longer: to *survive*, in French *survivre*, is to live after: the former is employed to express the comparison between two lives; the latter to denote a protracted existence beyond any given term: one person is said properly to *outlive* another who enjoys a longer life; but we speak of surviving persons or things, in an indefinite or unqualified manner: it is not a peculiar blessing to *outlive* all our nearest relatives and friends; 'A man never *outlives* his conscience, and that for this cause only, he cannot *outlive* himself.'—SOUTH. No man can be happy in *surviving* his honour; 'Of so vast, so lasting, so *surviving* an extent is the malignity of a great guilt.'—SOUTH.

TO DELIVER, RESCUE, SAVE.

To *deliver*, in French *delivrer*, compounded of *de* and *livrer*, in Latin *libero*, signifies literally to make free; to *rescue*, contracted from the French *re* and *secourir*, and indirectly from the Latin *re* and *curro* to run, signifies to run to a person's assistance in the moment of difficulty; to *save* is to make safe.

The idea of taking or keeping from danger is common to these terms; but *deliver* and *rescue* signify rather the taking from, *save* the keeping from danger: we *deliver* and *rescue* from the evil that is; we *save* from evils that may be, as well as from those that are. *Deliver* and *rescue* do not convey any idea of the means by which the end is produced; *save* commonly includes the idea of some superiour agency: a man may be *delivered* or *rescued* by any person without distinction; he is commonly *saved* by a superiour.

Deliver is an unqualified term, it is applicable to every mode of the action or species of evil; to *rescue* is a species of *delivering*, namely, *delivering* from the power of another: to *save* is applicable to the greatest possible evils: a person may be *delivered* from a burden, from an oppression, from disease, or from danger by any means; 'In our greatest fears and troubles we may ease our hearts by reposing ourselves upon God, in confidence of his support and *deliverance*'—TILLOTSON. A prisoner is *rescued* from the hands of an enemy;

> My household gods, companions of my woes,
> With pious care I *rescu'd* from our foes.—DRYDEN

A person is *saved* from destruction;

> Now shameful flight alone can *save* the host,
> Our blood, our treasure, and our glory lost.—POPE.

'He who feareth God and worketh righteousness, and perseveres in the faith and duties of our religion, shall certainly be *saved*.'—ROGERS.

DELIVERANCE, DELIVERY,

Are drawn from the same verb (*v. To deliver*) to express its different senses of taking from or giving to; the former denotes the taking of something from one's self: the latter implies giving something to another.

To wish for a *deliverance* from that which is hurtful or painful is to a certain extent justifiable;

> Whate'er befalls your life shall be my care,
> One death, or one *deliverance*, we will share.
> DRYDEN.

The careful *delivery* of property into the hands of the owner will be the first object of concern with a faithful agent; 'With our Saxon ancestors the *delivery* of a turf was a necessary solemnity to establish the conveyance of lands.'—BLACKSTONE.

TO FREE, SET FREE, DELIVER, LIBERATE

To *free* is properly to make *free*, in distinction from *set free*; the first is employed in what concerns our selves, and the second in that which concerns another. A man *frees* himself from an engagement; he *sets* another *free* from his engagement: we *free* or *set* ourselves *free*, from that which has been imposed upon us by ourselves or by circumstances; we are *delivered* or *liberated* from that which others have imposed upon us; the former from evils in general, the latter from the evil of confinement. I *free* myself from a burden; I *set* my own slave *free* from his slavery; I *deliver* another man's slave from a state of bondage; I *liberate* a man from prison. A man *frees* an estate from rent, service, taxes, and all incumbrances; a king *sets* his subjects *free* from certain imposts or tribute, he *delivers* them from a foreign yoke, or he *liberates* those who have been taken in war. We *free* either by an act of the will, or by contrivance and method; we *set free* by an act of authority; we *deliver* or *liberate* by active measures and physical strength. A man *frees* himself from impertinence by escaping the company of the impertinent; he *sets* others *free* from all apprehensions by assuring them of his protection; he *delivers* them out of a perilous situation by his presence of mind. A country is *freed* from the horrours of a revolution by the vigorous councils of a determined statesman; in this manner was England *freed* from a counterpart of the French evolution by the vigour of the government; a country is *set free* from the exactions and hardships of usurpation and tyranny by the mild influence of established government: in this manner is Europe *set free* from the iron yoke of the French usurper by its ancient rulers. A country is *delivered* from the grasp and oppression of the invader; in this manner has Spain been *delivered*, by the wisdom and valour of an illustrious British general at the head of a band of British heroes.

When applied in a moral sense *free* is applied to sin, or any other moral evil;

She then
Sent Iris down to *free* her from the strife
Of labouring nature, and dissolve her life.
DRYDEN.

Set free is employed for ties, obligation, and responsibility;

When heav'n would kindly *set* us *free*,
And earth's enchantment end;
It takes the most effectual means,
And robs us of a friend.—YOUNG.

Deliver is employed for external circumstances; 'However desirous Mary was of obtaining *deliverance* from Darnley's caprices, she had good reasons for rejecting the method by which they proposed to accomplish it.'—ROBERTSON. God, as our Redeemer, *frees* us from the bondage and consequences of sin, by the dispensations of his atoning grace; but he does not *set* us *free* from any of our moral obligations or moral responsibility as *free* agents; as our Preserver he *delivers* us from dangers and misfortunes, trials and temptations.

FREE, LIBERAL.

Free is here considered as it respects actions and sentiments. In all its acceptations *free* is a term of dispraise, and *liberal* that of commendation. To be *free*, signifies to act or think at will; to be *liberal* is to act according to the dictates of an enlarged heart and an enlightened mind. A clown or a fool may be *free* with his money, and may squander it away to please his humour, or gratify his appetite; but the nobleman and the wise man will be *liberal* in rewarding merit, in encouraging industry, and in promoting whatever can contribute to the ornament, the prosperity, and improvement of his country. A man who is *free* in his sentiments thinks as he pleases; the man who is *liberal* thinks according to the extent of his knowledge. The *free*-thinking man is wise in his own conceit, he despises the opinions of others; the *liberal*-minded thinks modestly on his own personal attainments, and builds upon the wisdom of others.

The *free*thinker circumscribes all knowledge within the conceptions of a few superlatively wise heads; 'The *free*thinkers plead very hard to think *freely*: they have it; but what use do they make of it? Do their writings show a greater depth of design, or more just and correct reasoning, than those of other men?'—BERKELEY. 'Their pretensions to be *free*thinkers is no other than rakes have to be *free*livers, and savages to be *free*men.'—ADDISON. The *liberal*-minded is anxious to enlarge the boundaries of science by making all the thinking world in all ages to contribute to the advancement of knowledge;

For me, for whose well-being
So amply, and with hands so *liberal*,
Thou hast provided all things.—MILTON.

The desire of knowledge discovers a *liberal* mind.'—BLAIR. With the *free*thinker nothing is good that is old or established; with the *liberal* man nothing is good because it is new, nothing bad because it is old. Men of the least knowledge and understanding are the most *free* in their opinions, in which description of men this age abounds above all others; such men are exceedingly anxious to usurp the epithet *liberal* to themselves; but the good sense of mankind will prevail against partial endeavours, and assign this title to none but men of comprehensive talents, sound judgements, extensive experience, and deep erudition.

It seems as if *freedom* of thought was that aberration of the mind which is opposed to the two extremes of superstition and bigotry; and that *liberality* is the happy medium. The *free*thinker holds nothing sacred, and is attached to nothing but his own conceits; the superstitious man holds too many things sacred, and is attached to every thing that favours this bent of his mind. A *free*thinker accommodates his duties to his inclinations: he denies his obligation to any thing which comes across the peculiar fashion of his sentiment. A man of *free* sentiments rejects the spirit of Christianity, with the letter or outward formality; the superstitious man loses the spirit of Christianity in his extravagant devotion to its outward formalities.

On the other hand bigotry and *liberality* are opposed to each other, not in regard to what they believe, so much as in regard to the nature of their belief. The bigoted man so narrows his mind to the compass of his belief as to exclude every other object; the *liberal* man directs his views to every object which does not directly interfere with his belief. It is possible for the bigoted and the *liberal* man to have the same faith but the former mistakes its true object and tendency namely, the improvement of his rational powers, which the latter pursues.

It is evident, therefore, from the above, that the *free*thinker, the superstitious man, and the bigot, are alike the offspring of ignorance; and that *liberality* is the handmaid of science, and the daughter of truth. Of all the mental aberrations *freedom* of thinking is the most obnoxious, as it is fostered by the pride of the heart, and the vanity of the imagination. In superstition we sometimes see the anxiety of a well-disposed mind to discharge its conscience: with bigotry we often see associated the mild virtues which are taught by Christianity; but in the *free*thinker we only see the bad passions and the unruly will set *free* from all the constraints of outward authority, and disengaged from the control of reason and judgement: in such a man the amiable qualities of the natural disposition become corrupted, and the evil humours triumph

FREE, FAMILIAR.

Free has already been considered as it respects the words, actions, and sentiments (*v. Free*); in the present case it is coupled with *familiarity*, inasmuch as they respect the outward behaviour or conduct in general of men one to another.

To be *free* is to be disengaged from all the constraints which the ceremonies of social intercourse impose; to be *familiar* is to be upon the footing of a *familiar*, of a relative, or one of the same family. Neither of these terms can be admitted as unexceptionable; but *freedom* is that which is in general totally unauthorized; *familiarity* sometimes shelters itself under the sanction of long, close, and friendly intercourse.

Free is a term of much more extensive import than *familiar;* a man may be *free* towards another in a thousand ways; but he is *familiar* towards him only in his manners and address. A man who is *free* looks upon every thing as his which he chooses to make use of; a *familiar* man only wants to share with another and to stand upon an equal footing. A man who is *free* will take possession of another man's house or room in his absence, and will make use of his name or his property as it suits his convenience; his *freedom* always turns upon that which contributes to his own indulgence; 'Being one day very *free* at a great feast, he suddenly broke forth into a great laughter.'—HAKEWELL. A man who is *familiar* will smile upon you, take hold of your arm, call you by some friendly or common name, and seek to enjoy with you all the pleasures of social intercourse; his *familiarity* always turns upon that which will increase his own importance; 'Kalandar streight thought he saw his niece Parthenia, and was about in such *familiar* sort to have spoken unto her; but she in grave and honourable manner, gave him to understand he was mistaken.'—SIDNEY. There cannot be two greater enemies to the harmony of society than *freedom* and *familiarity;* both of which it is the whole business of politeness to destroy; for no man can be *free* without being in danger of infringing upon what belongs to another, nor *familiar* without being in danger of obtruding himself to the annoyance of others.

When these words are used figuratively in reference to things, they do not bear that objectionable feature;

Free and *familiar* with misfortune grow,
Be us'd to sorrow, and inur'd to wo.—PRIOR

FREE, EXEMPT.

To *free* is as general in its signification as in the preceding articles; to *exempt*, in Latin *exemptus*, participle of *eximo*, signifies set out or disengaged from a part.

The condition and not the conduct of men is here considered. *Freedom* is either accidental or intentional; the *exemption* is always intentional: we may be *free* from disorders, or *free* from troubles; we are *exempt*, that is *exempted* by government, from serving in the militia. *Free* is applied to every thing from which any one may wish to be *free*; but *exempt*, on the contrary, to those burdens which we should share with others: we may be *free* from imperfections, *free* from inconveniencies, *free* from the interruptions of others;

O happy, if he knew his happy state,
The swain who, *free* from bus'ness and debate,
Receives his easy food from nature's hand!
DRYDEN.

A man is *exempt* from any office or tax; 'To be *exempt* from the passions with which others are tormented, is the only pleasing solitude.'—ADDISON. We may likewise be said to be *exempt* from troubles when speaking of these as the dispensations of Providence to others.

FREEDOM, LIBERTY.

Freedom, the abstract noun of *free*, is taken in all the senses of the primitive; *liberty*, from the Latin *liber* free, is only taken in the sense of *free* from external constraint, from the action of power.

Freedom is personal and private; *liberty* is publick. The *freedom* of the city is the privilege granted by any city to individuals; the *liberty* of the city are the immunities enjoyed by the city. By the same rule of distinction we speak of the *freedom* of the will, the *freedom* of manners, the *freedom* of conversation, or the *freedom* of debate; 'The ends for which men unite in society, and submit to government, are to enjoy security to their property, and *freedom* to their persons, from all injustice or violence.'—BLAIR. 'I would not venture into the world under the character of a man who pretends to talk like other people, until I had arrived at a full *freedom* of speech.'—ADDISON. We speak of the *liberty* of conscience, the *liberty* of the press, the *liberty* of the subject; 'The *liberty* of the press is a blessing when we are inclined to write against others, and a calamity when we find ourselves overborne by the multitude of our assailants.'—JOHNSON. A slave obtains his *freedom*;

O *freedom!* first delight of human kind!
Not that which bondmen from their masters find,
The privilege of doles.—DRYDEN.

A captive obtains his *liberty*.

Freedom serves moreover to qualify the action; *liberty* is applied only to the agent: hence we say, to speak or think with *freedom*; but to have the *liberty* of speaking, thinking, or acting. *Freedom* and *liberty* are likewise employed for the private conduct of individuals towards each other; but the former is used in a qualified good sense, the latter in an unqualified bad sense. A *freedom* may sometimes be licensed or allowed; *liberty* is always taken in a bad sense. A *freedom* may be innocent and even pleasant; a *liberty* always does more or less violence to the decencies of life, or the feelings of individuals. There are little *freedoms* which may pass between youth of different sexes, so as to heighten the pleasures of society; but a modest woman will be careful to guard against any *freedoms* which may admit of misinterpretation, and resent every *liberty* offered to her as an insult.

TO GIVE UP, DELIVER, SURRENDER, YIELD, CEDE, CONCEDE.

We *give up* (*v. To give, grant*) that which we wish to retain; we *deliver* that which we wish not to retain. *Deliver* does not include the idea of a transfer; but *give up* implies both the *giving* from, and the *giving* to: we *give up* our house to the accommodation of our friends; 'A popish priest threatens to excommunicate a Northumberland esquire if he did not *give up* to him the church lands.'—ADDISON. We *deliver* property into the hands of the owner; 'It is no wonder that they who at such a time could be corrupted to frame and *deliver* such a petition, would not be reformed by such an answer.'—DRYDEN. We may *give up* with reluctance, and *deliver* with pleasure; 'Such an expectation will never come to pass; therefore I will e'en *give* it up and go and fret myself.'—COLLIER.

On my experience, Adam, freely taste,
And fear of death *deliver* to the winds.—MILTON

To *give up* is a colloquial substitute for either *surrender* or *yield*; as it designates no circumstance of the action, it may be employed in familiar discourse, in almost every case for the other terms: where the action is compulsory, we may either say an officer *gives up* or *surrenders* his sword; when the action is discretionary, we may either say he *gives up*, or *yields* a point of discussion: *give up* has, however, an extensiveness of application which gives it an office distinct from either *surrender* or *yield*. When we speak of familiar and personal subjects, *give up* is more suitable than *surrender*, which is confined to matters of publick interest or great moment, unless when taken figuratively: a man *gives up* his place, his right, his claim, and the like; he *surrenders* a fortress, a vessel, or his property to his creditors, or figuratively he *surrenders* his judgement or opinions. When *give up* is compared with *yield*, they both respect personal matters; but the former expresses a much stronger action than the latter: a man *gives up* his whole judgement to another; he *yields* to the opinion of another in particular cases: he *gives* himself *up* to sensual indulgencies; he *yields* to the force of temptation; 'The peaceable man will *give up* his favourite schemes: he will *yield* to an opponent rather than become the cause of violent embroilments.'—BLAIR. 'The young, half-seduced by persuasion, and half-compelled by ridicule, *surrender* their convictions, and consent to live as they see others around them living.'—BLAIR.

Cede, from the Latin *cedo* to give, is properly to *surrender* by virtue of a treaty: we may *surrender* a town as an act of necessity; but the *cession* of a country is purely a political transaction: thus, generals frequently *surrender* such towns as they are not able to defend; and governments *cede* such countries as they find it not convenient to retain. To *concede*, which is but a variation of *cede*, is a mode of *yielding* which may be either an act of discretion or courtesy; as when a government *concedes* to the demands of the people certain privileges, or when an individual *concedes* any point in dispute for the sake of peace: 'As to the magick power which the devil imparts for these *concessions* of his votaries, theologians have different opinions.'—CUMBERLAND.

TO GIVE UP, ABANDON, RESIGN, FOREGO.

These terms differ from the preceding (*v. To give up*), inasmuch as they designate actions entirely free from foreign influence. A man *gives up*, *abandons*, and *resigns*, from the dictates of his own mind, independent of all control from others. To *give up* and *abandon* both denote a positive decision of the mind; but the former may be the act of the understanding or the will, the latter is more commonly the act of the will and the passions: to *give up* is applied to familiar cases; *abandon* to matters of importance: one *gives up* an idea, an intention, a plan, and the like; 'Upon his friend telling him, he wondered he *gave up* the question, when he had visibly the better of the dispute; I am never ashamed, says he, to be confuted by one who is master of fifty legions.'—ADDISON. One *abandons* a project, a scheme, a measure of government;

For Greece we grieve, *abandoned* by her fate,
To drink the dregs of thy unmeasur'd hate.
POPE.

To *give up* and *resign* are applied either to the outward actions, or merely to the inward movements; but the former is active, it determinately fixes the conduct; the latter seems to be rather passive, it is the leaning of the mind to the circumstances: a man *gives up* his situation by a positive act of his choice; he *resigns* his office when he feels it inconvenient to hold it: so, likewise, we *give up* what we expect or lay claim to; 'He declares himself to be now satisfied to the contrary, in which he has *given up* the cause.—DRYDEN. We *resign* what we hope or wish for;

The praise of artful numbers I *resign*,
And hang my pipe upon the sacred pine.—DRYDEN.

In this sense, *forego*, which signifies to let go or let pass by, is comparable with *resign*, inasmuch as it expresses a passive action; but we *resign* that which we have, and we *forego* that which we might have: thus, we *resign* the claims which we have already made; we *forego* the claim if we abstain altogether from making it: the former may be a matter of prudence: the latter is always an act of virtue and forbearance;

Desirous to *resign* and render back
All I receiv'd.—MILTON.

'What they have enjoyed with great pleasure at one time, has proved insipid or nauseous at another; and they see nothing in it, for which they should *forego* a present enjoyment.'—LOCKE.

Then, pilgrim, turn, thy cares *forego;*
All earth-born cares are wrong.—GOLDSMITH.

When applied reflectively, to *give up* is used either in a good, bad, or indifferent sense; *abandon* always in a bad sense; *resign* always in a good sense: a man may *give* himself *up*, either to studious pursuits, to idle vagaries, or vicious indulgencies; he *abandons* himself to gross vices; he *resigns* himself to the will of Providence, or to the circumstances of his condition: a man is said to be *given up* to his lusts who is without any principle to control him in the gratification; he is said to be *abandoned*, when his outrageous conduct bespeaks an entire insensibility to every honest principle; he is said to be *resigned* when he discovers composure and tranquillity in the hour of affliction.

TO ABANDON, DESERT, FORSAKE, RELINQUISH.

The idea of leaving or separating one's self from an object is common to these terms, which differ in the circumstances or modes of leaving. The two former are more solemn acts than the two latter. *Abandon*, from the French *abandonner*, is a concretion of the words *donner à ban*, to give up to a publick ban or outlawry. To *abandon* then is to expose to every misfortune which results from a formal and publick denunciation; to set out of the protection of law and government; and to deny the privileges of citizenship; *desert*, in Latin *desertus*, participle of *desero*, that is, *de* privative and *sero* to sow, signifies to lie unsown, unplanted, cultivated no longer. To *desert* then is to leave off cultivating; and as there is something of idleness and improvidence in ceasing to render the soil productive, ideas of disapprobation accompany the word in all its metaphorical applications. He who leaves off cultivating a farm usually removes from it; hence the idea of removal and blameworthy removal, which usually attaches to the term; *forsake*, in Saxon *forsecan*, is compounded of the primitive *for* and sake, *seek*, *secan*, signifying to seek no more, to leave off seeking that which has been an object of search; *relinquish*, in Latin *relinquo*, is compounded of *re* or *retro* behind, and *linquo* to leave, that is, to leave what we would fain take with us, to leave with reluctance.

To *abandon* is totally to withdraw ourselves from an object; to lay aside all care and concern for it; to leave it altogether to itself: to *desert* is to withdraw ourselves at certain times when our assistance or cooperation is required, or to separate ourselves from that to which we ought to be attached: to *forsake* is to withdraw our regard for and interest in an object, to keep at a distance from it; to *relinquish* is to leave that which has once been an object of our pursuit.

Abandon and *desert* are employed for persons or things; *forsake* for persons or places; *relinquish* for things only.

With regard to persons these terms express moral culpability in a progressive ratio downwards: *abandon* comprehends the violation of the most sacred ties, *desert*, a breach of honour and fidelity; *forsake*, a rupture of the social bond.

We *abandon* those who are entirely dependent for protection and support; they are left in a helpless state exposed to every danger; a child is *abandoned* by its parent; 'He who *abandons* his offspring or corrupts them by his example, perpetrates a greater evil than a murderer.'—HAWKESWORTH. We *desert* those with whom we have entered into a coalition; they are left to their own resources: a soldier *deserts* his comrades; a partisan *deserts* his friends; 'After the death of Stella, Swift's benevolence was contracted, and his severity exasperated: he drove his acquaintance from his table, and wondered why he was *deserted*.'—JOHNSON. We *forsake* those with whom we have been in habits of intimacy; they are deprived of the pleasures and comforts of society; a man *forsakes* his companions; a lover *forsakes* his mistress, or a husband his wife;

Forsake me not thus, Adam!—MILTON.

We are bound by every law human and divine not to *abandon;* we are called upon by every good principle not to *desert;* we are impelled by every kind feeling not to *forsake*. Few animals except man will *abandon* their young until they are enabled to provide for themselves. Interest, which is but too often the only principle that brings men together, will lead them to *desert* each other in the time of difficulty. We are enjoined in the gospel not to *forsake* the poor and needy.

When *abandoned* by our dearest relatives, *deserted* by our friends, and *forsaken* by the world, we have always a resource in our Maker.

With regard to things (in which sense the word *relinquish* is synonymous) the character of *abandoning* varies with the circumstances and motives of the action, according to which it is either good, bad, or indifferent; *deserting* is always taken in an unfavourable or bad sense; the act of *forsaking* is mostly indifferent, but implies a greater or less breach of some tie; that of *relinquishing* is prudent or imprudent.

A captain may *abandon* his vessel when he has no means of saving it, except at the risk of his life;

He boldly spake, sir knight, if knight thou be,
Abandon this forestalled place at erst,
For fear of further harm, I counsel thee.
SPENSER

———neglected nature pines
Abandoned.—COWPER.

An upright statesman will never *desert* his post when his country is in danger, nor a true soldier *desert* his colours; 'He who at the approach of evil betrays his trust, or *deserts* his post, is branded with cowardice.'—HAWKESWORTH. Birds will mostly *forsake* their nests when they discover them to have been visited, and most animals will *forsake* their haunts when they find themselves discovered; 'Macdonald and Macleod of Skie have lost many tenants and labourers, but Raarsa has not yet been *forsaken* by any of its inhabitants.'—JOHNSON. So likewise figuratively; 'When learning, abilities, and what is excellent in the world, *forsake* the church, we may easily foretell its ruin without the gift of prophecy.'—SOUTH. Men often inadvertently *relinquish* the fairest prospects in order to follow some favourite scheme which terminates in their ruin; 'Men are wearied with the toil which they bear, but cannot find in their hearts to *relinquish* it.'—STEELE.

Having *abandoned* their all, they *forsook* the place which gave them birth, and *relinquished* the advantages which they might have obtained from their rank and family.

TO ABANDON, RESIGN, RENOUNCE, ABDICATE.

The idea of giving up is common to these terms, which signification, though analogous to the former, admits, however, of a distinction; as in the one case we separate ourselves from an object, in the other we send or cast it from us. In this latter sense the terms *abandon* and *resign* have been partially considered in the preceding articles; *renounce*, in Latin *renuncio*, from *nuncio* to tell or declare, is to declare off from a thing; *abdicate*, from *dico* to speak, signifies likewise to call or cry off from a thing.

We *abandon* and *resign* by giving up to another; we *renounce* by sending away from ourselves; we *abandon* a thing by transferring our power over to another; in this manner a debtor *abandons* his goods to his creditors: we *resign* a thing by transferring our possession of it to another; in this manner we *resign* a place to a friend: we *renounce* a thing by simply ceasing to hold it; in this manner we *renounce* a claim or a profession. As to *renounce* signified originally to give up by word of mouth, and to *resign* to give up by signature, the former is consequently a less formal action than the latter: we may *renounce* by implication; we *resign* in direct terms: we *renounce* the pleasures of the world when we do not seek to enjoy them; we *resign* a pleasure, a profit, or advantage, of which we expressly give up the enjoyment.

To *abdicate* is a species of informal resignation. A monarch *abdicates* his throne who simply declares his will to cease to reign; but a minister *resigns* his office when he gives up the seals by which he held it.

A humane commander will not *abandon* a town to the rapine of the soldiers;

> The passive Gods beheld the Greeks defile
> Their temples, and *abandon* to the spoil
> Their own abodes.—DRYDEN.

The motives for *resignations* are various. Discontent, disgust, and the love of repose, are the ordinary inducements for men to *resign* honourable and lucrative employments; 'It would be a good appendix to "the art of living and dying," if any one would write "the art of growing old," and teach men to *resign* their pretensions to the pleasures of youth.'—STEELE. Men are not so ready to *renounce* the pleasures that are within their reach, as to seek after those which are out of their reach; 'For ministers to be silent in the cause of Christ is to *renounce* it, and to fly is to desert it.'—SOUTH. The *abdication* of a throne is not always an act of magnanimity, it may frequently result from caprice or necessity; 'Much gratitude is due to the nine from their favoured poets, and much hath been paid: for even to the present hour they are invoked and worshipped by the sons of verse, while all the other deities of Olympus have either *abdicated* their thrones, or been dismissed from them with contempt.'—CUMBERLAND. Charles the Fifth *abdicated* his crown, and his minister *resigned* his office on the very same day, when both *renounced* the world with its allurements and its troubles.

We *abandon* nothing but that over which we have had an entire and lawful control; we *abdicate* nothing but that which we have held by a certain right; but we may *resign* or *renounce* that which may be in our possession only by an act of violence. A usurper cannot *abandon* his people, because he has no people over whom he can exert a lawful authority; still less can he *abdicate* a throne, because he has no throne to *abdicate*, but he may *resign* supreme power, because power may be unjustly held; or he may *renounce* his pretensions to a throne, because pretensions may be fallacious or extravagant.

Abandon and *resign* are likewise used in a reflective sense; the former to express an involuntary or culpable action, the latter that which is voluntary and proper. The soldiers of Hannibal *abandoned* themselves to effeminacy during their winter quarters at Cumæ; 'It is the part of every good man's religion to *resign* himself to God's will.'—CUMBERLAND.

TO ABSTAIN, FORBEAR, REFRAIN.

Abstain, in French *abstenir*, Latin *abstineo*, is compounded of *ab* or *abs* from and *teneo* to keep, signifying to keep one's self from a thing; *forbear* is compounded of the preposition for, or from, and the verb to bear or carry, signifying to carry or take one's self from a thing; *refrain*, in French *refrèner*, Latin *refærno*, is compounded of *re* back and *fræno*, from *frænum* a bridle, signifying to keep back as it were by a bridle, to bridle in.

The first of these terms marks the leaving a thing, and the two others the omission of an action. We *abstain* from any object by not making use of it; we *forbear* to do or *refrain* from doing a thing by not taking any part in it.

Abstaining and *forbearing* are outward actions, but *refraining* is connected with the operations of the mind. We may *abstain* from the thing we desire, or *forbear* to do the thing which we wish to do; but we can never *refrain* from any action without in some measure losing our desire to do it.

We *abstain* from whatever concerns our food and clothing; we *forbear* to do what we may have particular motives for doing; *refrain* from what we desire to do, or have been in the habits of doing.

It is a part of the Mahometan faith to *abstain* from the use of wine; but it is a Christian duty to *forbear* doing an injury even in return for an injury: and to *refrain* from all swearing and evil speaking.

Abstinence is a virtue when we *abstain* from that which may be hurtful to ourselves or injurious to another; 'Though a man cannot *abstain* from being weak, he may from being vicious.'—ADDISON. *Forbearance* is essential to preserve peace and good will between man and man. Every one is too liable to offend, not to have motives for *forbearing* to deal harshly with the offences of his neighbour; 'By *forbearing* to do what may be innocently done, we may add hourly new vigour and resolution, and secure the power of resistance when pleasure or interest shall lend their charms to guilt.'—JOHNSON. If we *refrain* from uttering with the lips the first dictates of an angry mind, we shall be saved much repentance in future; 'If we conceive a being, created with all his faculties and senses, to open his eyes in a most delightful plain, to view for the first time the serenity of the sky, the splendour of the sun, the verdure of the fields and woods, the glowing colours of the flowers, we can hardly believe it possible that he should *refrain* from bursting into an ecstacy of joy, and pouring out his praises to the Creator of those wonders.'—SIR WILLIAM JONES.

ABSTINENT, SOBER, ABSTEMIOUS, TEMPERATE.

The first of these terms is generick, the rest specifick; *Abstinent* (v. *To abstain*) respects every thing that acts on the senses, and in a limited sense applies particularly to solid food; *sober*, from the Latin *sobrius*, or *sebrius*, that is, *sine ebrius*, not drunk, implies an abstinence from excessive drinking; *abstemious*, from the Latin *abstemius*, compounded of *abs* and *temetum* wine, implies the abstaining from wine or strong liquor in general; *temperate*, in Latin *temperatus*, participle of *tempero* to moderate or regulate, implies a well regulated abstinence in all manner of sensual indulgence.

We may be *abstinent* without being *sober*, *sober* without being *abstemious*, and all together without being *temperate*.

An *abstinent* man does not eat or drink so much as he could enjoy; a *sober* man may drink much without being affected.* An *abstemious* man drinks nothing strong. A *temperate* man enjoys all in a due proportion.

A particular passion may cause us to be *abstinent*, either partially or totally: *sobriety* may often depend upon the strength of the constitution, or be prescribed by prudence: necessity may dictate *abstemiousness*, but nothing short of a well disciplined mind will enable us to be *temperate*. Diogenes practised the most rigorous *abstinence*: some men have unjustly obtained a character for *sobriety*, whose habit of body has enabled them to resist the force of strong liquor even when taken to excess: it is not uncommon for persons to practise *abstemiousness* to that degree, as not to drink any thing but water all their lives: Cyrus was distinguished by his *temperance* as his other virtues; he shared all hardships with his soldiers, and partook of their frugal diet.

Unlimited *abstinence* is rather a vice than a virtue, for we are taught to enjoy the things which Providence has set before us; 'To set the mind above the appetites is the end of *abstinence*, which one of the fathers observes to be not a virtue, but the groundwork of virtue.'—JOHNSON. *Sobriety* ought to be highly esteemed among the lower orders, where the *abstinence* from vice is to be regarded as positive virtue; 'Cratinus carried his love of wine to such an excess, that he got the name of φιλοποτος, launching out in praise of drinking, and rallying all *sobriety* out of countenance.'—CUMBERLAND. *Abstemiousness* is sometimes the only means of preserving health;

> The strongest oaths are straw
> To th' fire i' th' blood; be more *abstemious*,
> Or else good night your vow.—SHAKSPEARE.

Habitual *temperance* is the most efficacious means of keeping both body and mind in the most regular state; 'If we consider the life of these ancient sages, a great

* Vide Trusler: "Sober, temperate, abstemious'

part of whose philosophy consisted in a *temperate* and *abstemious* course of life, one would think the life of a philosopher and the life of a man were of two different dates.'—ADDISON.

MODESTY, MODERATION, TEMPERANCE, SOBRIETY.

Modesty, in French *modestie*, Latin *modestia*, and *moderation*, in Latin *moderatio* and *moderor*, both come from *modus* a measure, limit, or boundary: that is, forming a measure or rule; *temperance*, in Latin *temperantia*, from *tempus* time, signifies fixing a time or term (*v. Abstinent*); *sobriety* (*v. Abstinent*).

Modesty lies in the mind, and in the tone of feeling; *moderation* respects the desires: *modesty* is a principle that acts discretionally; *moderation* is a rule or line that acts as a restraint on the views and the outward conduct.

Modesty consists in a fair and medium estimate of one's character and qualification; it guards a man against too high an estimate; it recommends to him an estimate below the reality: *moderation* consists in a suitable regulation of one's desires, demands, and expectations; it consequently depends very often on *modesty* as its groundwork: he who thinks *modestly* of his own acquirements, his own performances, and his own merits, will be *moderate* in his expectations of praise, reward, and recompense: he, on the other hand, who overrates his own abilities and qualifications, will equally overrate the use he makes of them, and consequently be *immoderate* in the price which he sets upon his services: in such cases, therefore, *modesty* and *moderation* are to each other as cause and effect; but there may be *modesty* without *moderation*, and *moderation* without *modesty*. *Modesty* is a sentiment confined to one's self as the object, and consisting solely of one's judgement of what one is, and what one does. *Moderation*, as is evident from the above, extends to objects that are external of ourselves: *modesty*, rather than *moderation*, belongs to an author; *moderation*, rather than *modesty*, belongs to a tradesman, or a man who has gains to make and purposes to answer; 'I may *modestly* conclude, that whatever errours there may be in this play, there are not those which have been objected to it.'—DRYDEN.

Equally inur'd
By *moderation* either state to bear,
Prosperous or adverse.—MILTON.

Modesty shields a man from mortification and disappointments, which assail the self-conceited man in every direction: a *modest* man conciliates the esteem even of an enemy and a rival; he disarms the resentments of those who feel themselves most injured by his superiority; he makes all pleased with him by making them at ease with themselves: the self-conceited man, on the contrary, sets the whole world against himself, because he sets himself against every body; every one is out of humour with him, because he makes them ill at ease with themselves while in his company;

There 's a proud *modesty* in merit!—DRYDEN.

Moderation protects a man equally from injustice on the one hand, and imposition on the other: he who is *moderate* himself makes others so; for every one finds his advantage in keeping within that bound which is as convenient to himself as to his neighbour: the world will always do this homage to real goodness, that they will admire it if they cannot practise it, and they will practise it to the utmost extent that their passions will allow them. *Modesty*, as a female virtue, has regard solely to the conduct of females with the other sex, and is still more distinguished from *moderation* than in the former case.

Moderation is the measure of one's desires, one's habits, one's actions and one's words; *temperance* is the adaptation of the time or season for particular feelings, actions, or words: a man is said to be *moderate* in his principles, who adopts the medium or middle course of thinking; it rather qualifies the thing than the person: he is said to be *temperate* in his anger, if he do not suffer it to break out into any excesses; *temperance* characterizes the person rather than the thing; 'These are the tenets which the *moderatest* of the Romanists will not venture to affirm.'—SMALRIDGE.

She 's not forward, but *modest* as the dove,
She 's not hot, but *temperate* as the morn.
SHAKSPEARE.

A *moderate* man in politicks endeavours to steer clear of all party spirit, and is consequently so *temperate* in his language as to provoke no animosity; 'Few harangues from the pulpit, except in the days of your league in France, or in the days of our solemn league and covenant in England, have ever breathed less of the spirit of *moderation* than this lecture in the Old Jewry.'—BURKE. '*Temperate* mirth is not extinguished by old age.'—BLAIR. *Moderation* in the enjoyment of every thing is essential in order to obtain the purest pleasure: and *temperance*, which absolutely taken is habitual *moderation*, is always attended with the happiest effects to one's constitution; as, on the contrary, any deviation from *temperance*, even in a single instance, is always punished with bodily pain and sickness.

Temperance and *sobriety* have already been considered in their proper application, which will serve to illustrate their improper application (*v. Abstinent*). *Temperance* is an action; it is the *tempering* of our words and actions to the circumstances: *sobriety* is a state in which one is exempt from every stimulus to deviate from the right course; as a man who is intoxicated with wine runs into excesses, and loses that power of guiding himself which he has when he is *sober* or free from all intoxication, so is he who is intoxicated with any passion, in like manner, hurried away into irregularities which a man in his right senses will not be guilty of: *sobriety* is, therefore, the state of being in one's right or *sober* senses; and *sobriety* is with regard to *temperance*, as a cause to the effect; *sobriety* of mind will not only produce *moderation* and *temperance*, but extend its influence to the whole conduct of a man in every relation and circumstance, to his internal sentiments and his external behaviour: hence we speak of *sobriety* in one's mien or deportment, *sobriety* in one's dress and manners, *sobriety* in one's religious opinions and observances; 'The vines give wine to the drunkard as well as to the *sober* man.'—TAYLOR. 'Another, who had a great genius for tragedy, following the fury of his natural temper, made every man and woman in his plays stark raging mad, there was not a *sober* person to be had.'—DRYDEN.

Spread thy close curtains, love-performing night,
Thou *sober*-suited matron, all in black.—SHAKSPEARE.

CHASTITY, CONTINENCE, MODESTY.

Chastity, in French *chastité*, Latin *castitas*, comes from *castus* pure, and the Hebrew קדש sacred; *continence*, in French *continence*, Latin *continentia*, from *continens* and *contineo*, signifies the act of keeping one's self within bounds.

These two terms are equally employed in relation to the pleasures of sense: both are virtues, but sufficiently distinct in their characteristicks.

* *Chastity* prescribes rules for the indulgence of these pleasures; *continence* altogether interdicts their use. *Chastity* extends its views to whatever may bear the smallest relation to the object which it proposes to regulate; it controls the thoughts, words, looks, attitudes, food, dress, company, and in short the whole mode of living: *continence* simply confines itself to the privations of the pleasures themselves: it is possible, therefore, to be *chaste* without being *continent*, and *continent* without being *chaste*.

Chastity is suited to all times, ages, and conditions; *continence* belongs only to a state of celibacy: the Christian religion enjoins *chastity*, as a positive duty on all its followers; the Romish religion enjoins *continence* on its clerical members: old age renders men *continent*, although it seldom makes them *chaste*:

It fails me here to write of *chastity*,
That fairest virtue far above the rest.—SPENSER.

'When Pythagoras enjoined on his disciples an abstinence from beans, it has been thought by some an injunction only of *continency*.'—BROWN (*Vulgar Errors*).

Chastity and *continence* have special regard to the outward conduct; *modesty* goes farther, it is an habitual frame of mind, which prescribes a limit to all the desires. When *modesty* shows itself by an external sign, it is to be seen mostly in the behaviour; but *chastity* shows itself more commonly in the conduct. We

* Beauzée: "Chastité, continence"

speak of a *modest* blush, not of a *chaste* blush. When the term *chastity* is applied to the mind it denotes a chastened mind, or a chastened tone of feeling, which has been evidently acquired; but *modesty* results from the natural character, or from early formed habits. *Modesty* is the peculiar characteristick of a virtuous female, and is the safeguard of virtue. When a woman has laid aside her *modesty*, she will not long retain her *chastity;* 'Of the general character of women, which is *modesty*, he has taken a most becoming care: for his amorous expressions go no farther than virtue may allow.'—DRYDEN.

MODERATION, MEDIOCRITY.

Moderation (*v. Modesty*) is the characteristick of the person; *mediocrity*, implying the mean or medium, characterizes the condition: *moderation* is a virtue of no small importance for beings who find excess in every thing to be an evil;

Such *moderation* with thy bounty join,
That thou may'st nothing give that is not thine.
DENHAM.

Mediocrity in external circumstances is exempt from all the evils which attend either poverty or riches; '*Mediocrity* only of enjoyment is allowed to man.'—BLAIR.

MEAN, MEDIUM.

Mean is but a contraction of *medium*, which signifies in Latin the middle path. The term *mean* is used abstractedly in all speculative matters: there is a *mean* in opinions between the two extremes; this *mean* is doubtless the point nearest to truth, and has been denominated the *golden mean*, from its supposed excellence;

The man within the golden *mean*,
Who can his boldest wish contain,
Securely views the ruin'd cell
Where sordid want and sorrow dwell.
FRANCIS.

Medium is employed in practical matters; computations are often erroneous from being too high or too low: the *medium* is in this case the one most to be preferred. The moralist will always recommend the *mean* in all opinions that widely differ from each other: our passions always recommend to us some extravagant conduct either of insolent resistance or mean compliance; but discretion recommends the *medium* or middle course in such matters. This term is however mostly used to denote any intervening object, which may serve as a middle point; 'He who looks upon the soul through its outward actions, often sees it through a deceitful *medium*.'—ADDISON.

BECOMING, DECENT, SEEMLY, FIT, SUITABLE.

Becoming, from *become*, compounded of *be* and *come*, signifies coming in its place; *decent*, in French *decent*, in Latin *decens*, participle of *deceo*, from the Greek δόκει, and the Chaldee דכא to beseem, signifies the quality of beseeming and befitting; *seemly*, compounded of *seem* to appear, and *ly* or *like*, signifies likely or pleasant in appearance; *fit* and *suitable* are explained under the article *Fit*.

What is *becoming* respects the manner of being in society, such as it ought to be, as to person, time, and place. *Decency* regards the manner of displaying one's self, so as to be approved and respected. *Seemliness* is very similar in sense to *decency:* but its application is confined only to such things as immediately strike the observer. *Fitness* and *suitableness* relate to the disposition, arrangement, and order of either being or doing, according to persons, things, or circumstances.

The *becoming* consists of an exteriour that is pleasing to the view: *decency* involves moral propriety; it is regulated by the fixed rules of good breeding: *seemliness* is *decency* in the minor morals, or in our behaviour to or in the presence of others: *fitness* is regulated by local circumstances, and *suitableness* by the established customs and usages of society. The dress of a woman is *becoming* when it renders her person more agreeable to the eye; it is *decent* if it in no wise offend modesty; it is *unseemly* if in any degree, however trivial, it violates decorum; it is *fit* if it be what the occasion requires; it is *suitable* if it be according to the rank and character of the wearer. What is *becoming* varies for every individual; the age, the complexion, the stature, and the habits of the person must be consulted in order to obtain the appearance which is *becoming;* what *becomes* a young female, or one of fair complexion, may not *become* one who is farther advanced in life, or who has dark features: *decency* and *seemliness* are one and the same for all; all civilized nations have drawn the exact line between the *decent* and *indecent*, although fashion may sometimes draw females aside from this line, and cause them to be *unseemly* if not expressly *indecent: fitness* varies with the seasons, or the circumstances of persons; what is *fit* for the winter is *unfit* for the summer, or what is *fit* for dry weather is *unfit* for the wet; what is *fit* for town is not *fit* for the country; what is *fit* for a healthy person is not *fit* for one that is infirm: *suitableness* accommodates itself to the external circumstances and conditions of persons; the house, the furniture, and equipage of a prince, must be *suitable* to his rank; the retinue of an ambassador must be *suitable* to the character which he has to maintain, and to the wealth, dignity, and importance of the nation, whose monarch he represents; 'Raphael, amid his tenderness and friendship for man, shows such a dignity and condescension in all his speech and behaviour, as are *suitable* to a superiour nature.'—ADDISON.

Gravity *becomes* a judge, or a clergyman, at all times: an unassuming tone is *becoming* in a child when he addresses his superiours; 'Nothing ought to be held laudable or *becoming*, but what nature itself should prompt us to think so.'—STEELE. *Decency* requires a more than ordinary gravity when we are in the house of mourning or prayer; it is *indecent* for a child on the commission of a fault to affect a careless unconcern in the presence of those whom he has offended; 'A Gothick bishop, perhaps, thought it proper to repeat such a form in such particular shoes or slippers; another fancied it would be very *decent* if such a part of publick devotions was performed with a mitre on his head.'—ADDISON. *Seemliness* is an essential part of good manners; to be loud in one's discourse, to use expressions not authorized in cultivated society, or to discover a captious or tenacious temper in one's social intercourse with others are *unseemly* things;

I am a woman lacking wit
To make a *seemly* answer to such persons.
SHAKSPEARE.

There is a *fitness* or *unfitness* in persons for each other's society: education *fits* a person for the society of the noble, the wealthy, the polite, and the learned. There is also a *fitness* of things for persons according to their circumstances; 'To the wiser judgement of God it must be left to determine what is *fit* to be bestowed, and what to be withheld.'—BLAIR. There is a *suitableness* in people's tempers for each other; such a *suitability* is particularly requisite for those who are destined to live together: selfish people, with opposite taste and habits, can never be *suitable* companions; 'He creates those sympathies and *suitableness* of nature that are the foundation of all true friendship, and by his providence brings persons so affected together'—SOUTH.

DECENCY, DECORUM.

Though *decency* and *decorum* are both derived from the same word (*v. Becoming*), they have acquired a distinction in their sense and application. *Decency* respects a man's conduct; *decorum* his behaviour: a person conducts himself with *decency;* he behaves with *decorum*.

Indecency is a vice; it is the violation of publick or private morals: *indecorum* is a fault; it offends the feelings of those who witness it. Nothing but a depraved mind can lead to *indecent* practices: indiscretion and thoughtlessness may sometimes give rise to that which is *indecorous*. *Decency* enjoins upon all relatives, according to the proximity of their relationship, to show certain marks of respect to the memory of the dead; 'Even religion itself, unless *decency* be the handmaid which waits upon her, is apt to make people appear guilty of sourness and ill-humour.'—SPECTATOR. Regard for the feelings of others enjoins a certain outward *decorum* upon every one who attends a funeral; 'I will admit that a fine woman of a certain rank cannot have too many real vices; but at the same time I do insist upon it, that it is essentially her interest not to have the appearance of any one. This *decorum*, I confess, will conceal her conquests: but on the other hand, if she will be pleased to reflect that those conquests are known sooner or later, she will not upon an average find herself a loser.'—CHESTERFIELD.

IMMODEST, IMPUDENT, SHAMELESS.

Immodest signifies the want of *modesty; impudent* and *shameless* signify without *shame*.

The *immodest* is less than either the *impudent* or *shameless*: an *immodest* girl lays aside the ornament of her sex, and puts on another garb that is less becoming; but her heart need not be corrupt until she becomes *impudent*: she wants a good quality when she is *immodest*; she is possessed of a positively bad quality when she is *impudent*. There is always hope that an *immodest* woman may be sensible of her errour, and amend; but of an *impudent* woman there is no such chance, she is radically corrupt; 'Musick diffuses a calm all around us, and makes us drop all those *immodest* thoughts which would be a hindrance to us in the performance of the great duty of thanksgiving.'—SPECTATOR. 'I am at once equally fearful of sparing you, and of being too *impudent* a corrector.'—POPE.

Impudent may characterize the person or the thing: *shameless* characterizes the person. A person's air, look, and words, are *impudent*, when contrary to all modesty: the person himself is *shameless* who is devoid of all sense of *shame*;

The sole remorse his greedy heart can feel
Is if one life escapes his murdering steel;
Shameless by force or fraud to work his way,
And no less prompt to flatter than betray.
CUMBERLAND.

INDECENT, IMMODEST, INDELICATE.

Indecent is the contrary of *decent* (*v. Becoming*), *immodest* the contrary of *modest* (*v. Modest*), *indelicate* the contrary of *delicate* (*v. Fine*).

Indecency and *immodesty* violate the fundamental principles of morality: the former however in external matters, as dress, words, and looks; the latter in conduct and disposition. A person may be *indecent* for want of either knowing or thinking better; but a female cannot be habitually *immodest* without radical corruption of principle. *Indecency* may be a partial, *immodesty* is a positive and entire breach of the moral law. *Indecency* belongs to both sexes; *immodesty* is peculiarly applicable to the misconduct of females; 'The Dubistan contains more ingenuity and wit, more *indecency* and blasphemy, than I ever saw collected in one single volume.'—SIR WM. JONES.

Immodest words admit of no defence,
For want of decency is want of sense.
ROSCOMMON.

Indecency is less than *immodesty*, but more than *indelicacy*: they both respect the outward behaviour; but the former springs from illicit or uncurbed desire; *indelicacy* from the want of education. It is a great *indecency* for a man to marry again very quickly after the death of his wife; but a still greater *indecency* for a woman to put such an affront on her deceased husband: it is a great *indelicacy* in any one to break in upon the retirement of such as are in sorrow and mourning. It is *indecent* for females to expose their persons as many do whom we cannot call *immodest* women; it is *indelicate* for females to engage in masculine exercises; 'Your papers would be chargeable with something worse than *indelicacy*, did you treat the detestable sin of uncleanness in the same manner as you rally self-love.'—SPECTATOR.

TO ABJURE, RECANT, RETRACT, REVOKE, RECALL.

Abjure, in Latin *abjuro*, is compounded of the privative *ab* and *juro* to swear, signifying to swear to the contrary or give up with an oath; *recant*, in Latin *recanto*, is compounded of the privative *re* and *canto* to sing or declare, signifying to unsay, to contradict by a counter declaration; *retract*, in Latin *retractus*, participle of *retraho*, is compounded of *re* back and *traho* to draw, signifying to draw back what has been let go; *revoke* and *recall* have the same original sense as *recant*, with this difference only, that the word *call*, which is expressed also by *voke*, or in Latin *voco*, implies an action more suited to a multitude than the word *canto* to sing, which may pass in solitude.

We *abjure* a religion, we *recant* a doctrine, we *retract* a promise, we *revoke* a command, we *recall* an expression.

What has been solemnly professed is renounced by *abjuration*;

The pontiff saw Britannia's golden fleece,
Once all his own, invest her worthier sons!
Her verdant valleys, and her fertile plains,
Yellow with grain, *abjure* his hateful sway.
SHENSTONE.

What has been publickly maintained as a settled point of belief is given up by *recanting*; 'A false satire ought to be *recanted* for the sake of him whose reputation may be injured.'—JOHNSON. What has been pledged so as to gain credit is contradicted by *retracting*; 'When any scholar will convince me that these were futile and malicious tales against Socrates, I will *retract* all credit in them, and thank him for the conviction.'—CUMBERLAND. What has been pronounced by an act of authority is rendered null by *revocation*; 'What reason is there, but that those grants and privileges should be *revoked* or reduced to their first intention.'—SPENSER. What has been misspoken through inadvertence or mistake is rectified by *recalling* the words;

'T is done, and since 't is done 't is past *recall*,
And since 't is past recall must be forgotten.
DRYDEN.

Although Archbishop Cranmer *recanted* the principles of the reformation, yet he soon after *recalled* his words, and died boldly for his faith. Henry IV. of France *abjured* Calvinism, but he did not *retract* the promise which he had made to the Calvinists of his protection. Louis XIV. drove many of his best subjects from France by *revoking* the edict of Nantes.

Interest but too often leads men to *abjure* their faith; the fear of shame or punishment leads them to *recant* their opinions; the want of principle dictates the *retracting* of one's promise; instability is the ordinary cause for *revoking* decrees; a love of precision commonly induces a speaker or writer to *recall* a false expression.

TO ABOLISH, ABROGATE, REPEAL, REVOKE, ANNUL, CANCEL.

Abolish, in French *abolir*, Latin *aboleo*, is compounded of *ab* and *oleo* to lose the smell, signifying to lose every trace of former existence; *abrogate*, in French *abroger*, Latin *abrogatus*, participle of *abrogo*, compounded of *ab* and *rogo* to ask, signifies literally to ask away, or to ask that a thing may be done away; in allusion to the custom of the Romans, among whom no law was valid unless the consent of the people was obtained by asking, and in like manner no law was unmade without asking their consent; *repeal*, in French *rappeler*, from the Latin words *re* and *appello*, signifies literally to call back or unsay what has been said, which is in like manner the original meaning of *revoke*; *annul*, in French *annuller*, comes from *nulle*, in Latin *nihil*, signifying to reduce to nothing; *cancel*, in French *canceller*, comes from the Latin *cancello* to cut crosswise, signifying to strike out crosswise, that is, to cross out.

Abolish is a more gradual proceeding than *abrogate* or any of the other actions. Disuse *abolishes*; a positive interference is necessary to *abrogate*. The former is employed with regard to customs: the latter with regard to the authorized transactions of mankind; 'The long-continued wars between the English and the Scots, had then raised invincible jealousies and hate, which long continued peace hath since *abolished*.'—SIR JOHN HAYWARD. 'Solon *abrogated* all Draco's sanguinary laws, except those that affected murder'—CUMBERLAND.

Laws are *repealed* or *abrogated;* but the former of these terms is mostly in modern use, the latter is applied to the proceedings of the ancients. Edicts are *revoked.* Official proceedings, contracts, &c. are *annulled.* Deeds, bonds, obligations, debts, &c. are *cancelled.*

The introduction of new customs will cause the *abolition* of the old. 'On the parliament's part it was proposed that all the bishops, deans, and chapters might be immediately taken away and *abolished.*'—Clarendon. None can *repeal*, but those that have the power to make laws; 'If the Presbyterians should obtain their ends, I could not be sorry to find them mistaken in the point which they have most at heart, by the *repeal* of the test; I mean the benefit of employments.'—Swift. The *revocation* of any edict is the individual act of one who has the power to publish it; 'When we *abrogate* a law as being ill made, the whole cause for which it has been made still remaining, do we not herein *revoke* our own deed, and upbraid ourselves with folly?'—Hooker. To *annul* may be the act of superiour authority, or an agreement between the parties from whom the act emanated; a reciprocal obligation is *annulled* by the mutual consent of those who have imposed it on each other; but if the obligation be an authoritative act, the *annulment* must be so too;

I will *annul*
By the high power with which the laws invest me,
Those guilty forms in which you have entrapp'd,
Basely entrapp'd, to thy detested nuptials,
My queen betroth'd.—Thomson

To *cancel* is the act of an individual towards another on whom he has a legal demand; an obligation may be *cancelled*, either by a resignation of right on the part of the one to whom it belonged, or a satisfaction of the demand on the part of the obliged person;

This hour makes friendships which he breaks the next,
And every breach supplies a vile pretext,
Basely to *cancel* all concessions past,
If in a thousand you deny the last.
Cumberland.

A change of taste, aided by political circumstances, has caused the *abolition* of justs and tournaments and other military sports in Europe. The Roman people sometimes *abrogated* from party spirit what the magistrates enacted for the good of the republick; the same restless temper would lead many to wish for the *repeal* of the most salutary acts of our parliament.

Caprice, which has often dictated the proclamation of a decree in arbitrary governments, has occasioned its *revocation* after a short interval.

It is sometimes prudent to *annul* proceedings which have been decided upon hastily.

A generous man may be willing to *cancel* a debt; but a grateful man preserves the debt in his mind, and will never suffer it to be *cancelled.*

TO BLOT OUT, EXPUNGE, RASE OR ERASE, EFFACE, CANCEL, OBLITERATE.

Blot is in all probability a variation of *spot*, signifying to cover over with a *blot; expunge*, in Latin *expungo*, compounded of *ex* and *pungo* to prick, signifies to put out by pricking with the pen; *erase*, comes from the Latin *erasus*, participle of *erado*, that is, *e* and *rado* to scratch out; *efface*, in French *effacer*, compounded of the Latin *e* and *facio* to make, signifies literally to make or put out; *cancel*, in French *canceller*, Latin *cancello*, from *cancelli* lattice-work, signifies to strike out with cross lines; *obliterate*, in Latin *obliteratus*, participle of *oblitero*, compounded of *ob* and *litera*, signifies to cover over letters.

All these terms obviously refer to characters that are impressed on bodies; the first three apply in the proper sense only to that which is written with the hand, and bespeak the manner in which the action is performed. Letters are *blotted out*, so that they cannot be seen again; they are *expunged*, so as to signify that they cannot stand for any thing; they are *erased*, so that the space may be reoccupied with writing. The last three are extended in their application to other characters formed on other substances: *efface* is general, and does not designate either the manner or the object: inscriptions on stone may be *effaced*, which are rubbed off so as not to be visible: *cancel* is principally confined to written or printed characters; they are *cancelled* by striking through them with the pen; in this manner, leaves or pages of a book are *cancelled* which are no longer to be used as a part of a work: *obliterate* is said of all characters, but without defining the mode in which they are put out; letters are *obliterated*, which are in any way made illegible.

Efface applies to images, or the representations of things; in this manner the likeness of a person may be *effaced* from a statue; *cancel* respects the subject which is written or printed; *obliterate* respects the single letters which *constitute* words.

Effacing is the consequence of some direct action on the thing which is *effaced;* in this manner writing may be *effaced* from a wall by the action of the elements: *cancel* is the act of a person, and always the fruit of design: *obliterate* is the fruit of accident and circumstances in general; time itself may *obliterate* characters on a wall or on paper.

The metaphorical use of these terms is easily deducible from the preceding explanation; what is figuratively described, as written in a book, may be said to be *blotted;* thus our sins are *blotted out* by the atoning blood of Christ, and in the same manner things may be *blotted out* from the mind or the recollection; 'If virtue is of this amiable nature, what can we think of those who can look upon it with an eye of hatred and ill-will, and can suffer themselves, from their aversion for a party, to *blot out* all the merit of the person who is engaged in it.'—Addison. When the contents of a book are in part rejected, they are aptly described as being *expunged;* in this manner, the free-thinking sects *expunge* every thing from the Bible which does not suit their purpose, or they *expunge* from their creed what does not humour their passions; 'I believe that any person who was of age to take a part in publick concerns forty years ago (if the intermediate space were *expunged* from his memory) would hardly credit his senses when he should hear that an army of two hundred thousand men was kept up in this island.'—Burke. When the memory is represented as having characters impressed, they are said to be *erased*, when they are, as it were, directly taken out and occupied by others; in this manner, the recollection of what a child has learned is easily *erased* by play; and with equal propriety sorrows may be said to *efface* the recollection of a person's image from the mind;

Yet the best blood by learning is refin'd,
And virtue arms the solid mind;
While vice will stain the noblest race,
And the paternal stamp *efface.*—Oldisworth

From the idea of striking out or *cancelling* a debt in an account book, a debt of gratitude, or an obligation, is said to be *cancelled;*

Yet these are they the world pronounces wise;
The world, which *cancels* nature's right and wrong,
And new casts wisdom.—Young.

As the lineaments of the face correspond to written characters, we may say that all traces of his former greatness are *obliterated;* 'The transferring of the scene from Sicily to the Court of King Arthur, must have had a very pleasing effect, before the fabulous majesty of that court was quite *obliterated.*'—Tyrwhitt.

FORSAKEN, FORLORN, DESTITUTE.

To be *forsaken*, (*v. To abandon*) is to be deprived of the company and assistance of others; to be *forlorn*, from the German *verlohren* lost, is to be *forsaken* in time of difficulty, to be without a guide in an unknown road; to be *destitute*, from the Latin *destitutus*, is to be deprived of the first necessaries of life.

To be *forsaken* is a partial situation; to be *forlorn* and *destitute* are permanent conditions. We may be *forsaken* by a fellow-traveller on the road; we are *forlorn* when we get into a deserted path, with no one to direct us; we are *destitute* when we have no means of subsistence, nor the prospect of obtaining the means. It is particularly painful to be *forsaken* by the friend of our youth, and the sharer of our fortunes.

But fearful for themselves, my countrymen
Left me *forsaken* in the Cyclops' den.
DRYDEN.

The orphan, who is left to travel the road of life without counsellor or friend, is of all others in the most *forlorn* condition; 'Conscience made them (Joseph's brethren) recollect, that they who had once been deaf to the supplications of a brother, were now left friendless and *forlorn*.'—BLAIR. If poverty be added to forlornness, a man's misery is aggravated by his becoming *destitute*; 'Friendless and *destitute*, Dr. Goldsmith was exposed to all the miseries of indigence in a foreign country.'—JOHNSON.

PROFLIGATE, ABANDONED, REPROBATE.

Profligate, in Latin *profligatus*, participle of *profligo*, compounded of the intensive *pro* and *fligo* to dash or beat, signifies completely ruined and lost to every thing; *abandoned* signifies given up to one's lusts and vicious indulgences; *reprobate* (*v. To reprove*) signifies one thoroughly rejected.

These terms, in their proper acceptation, expresses the most wretched condition of fortune into which it is possible for any human being to be plunged, and consequently in their improper application they denote that state of moral desertion and ruin which cannot be exceeded in wickedness or depravity. A *profligate* man has lost all by his vices, consequently to his vices alone he looks for the regaining those goods of fortune which he has squandered; as he has nothing to lose, and every thing to gain in his own estimation, by pursuing the career of his vices, he surpasses all others in his unprincipled conduct; 'Aged wisdom can check the most forward, and abash the most *profligate*.'—BLAIR. An *abandoned* man is altogether *abandoned* to his passions, which, having the entire sway over him, naturally impel him to every excess; 'To be negligent of what any one thinks of you, does not only show you arrogant but *abandoned*.'—HUGHES. The *reprobate* man is one who has been reproved until he becomes insensible to reproof, and is given up to the malignity of his own passions;

And here let those who boast in mortal things,
Learn how their greatest monuments of fame,
And strength, and art, are easily outdone
By *reprobate* spirits.—MILTON.

The *profligate* man is the greatest enemy to society; the *abandoned* man is a still greater enemy to himself; the *profligate* man lives upon the publick, whom he plunders or defrauds; the *abandoned* man lives for the indulgence of his own unbridled passions; the *reprobate* man is little better than an outcast both by God and man: unprincipled debtors, gamesters, sharpers, swindlers, and the like, are *profligate* characters; whoremasters, drunkards, spendthrifts, seducers, and debauchees of all descriptions, are *abandoned* characters; although the *profligate* and *abandoned* are commonly the same persons, yet the young are in general *abandoned*, and those more hackneyed in vice are *profligate*: none can be *reprobate* but those who have been long inured to *profligate* courses.

HEINOUS, FLAGRANT, FLAGITIOUS, ATROCIOUS.

Heinous, in French *heinous*, Greek *αἶνος* or *δεινὸς* terrible; *flagrant*, in Latin *flagrans* burning, is a figurative expression for what is excessive and violent in its nature; *flagitious*, in Latin *flagitiosus*, from *flagitium* infamy, signifies peculiarly infamous; *atrocious*, in Latin *atrox* cruel, from *ater* black, signifies exceedingly black.

These epithets, which are applied to crimes, seem to rise in degree. A crime is *heinous* which seriously offends against the laws of men; a sin is *heinous* which seriously offends against the will of God; 'There are many authors who have shown wherein the malignity of a lie consists, and set forth in proper colours the *heinousness* of the offence.'—ADDISON. An offence is *flagrant* which is in direct defiance of established opinions and practice; 'If any flagrant deed occur to smite a man's conscience, on this he cannot avoid resting with anxiety and terrour.'—BLAIR. An act is *flagitious* if it be a gross violation of the moral law, or coupled with any grossness; 'It is recorded of Sir Matthew Hale, that he for a long time concealed the consecration of himself to the stricter duties of religion, lest by some *flagitious* action he should bring piety into disgrace.'—JOHNSON. A crime is *atrocious* which is attended with any aggravating circumstances; 'The wickedness of a loose or profane author is more *atrocious* than that of the giddy libertine.'—JOHNSON. Lying is a *heinous* sin; gaming and drunkenness are *flagrant* breaches of the Divine law; the murder of a whole family is in the fullest sense *atrocious*.

BARE, NAKED, UNCOVERED.

Bare, in Saxon *bare*, German *bar*, Hebrew פרץ to lay bare; *naked*, in Saxon *naced*, German *nacket* or *nakt*, low German *naakt*, Swedish *nakot*, Danish *nogen*, &c. comes from the Latin *nudus*, compounded of *ne* not, and *dutus* or *indutus* clothed, and the Greek *δύω* to clothe.

Bare marks the condition of being without some necessary appendage; 'Though the lords used to be covered while the commons were *bare*, yet the commons would not be *bare* before the Scottish commissioners; and so none were covered.'—CLARENDON. *Naked* denotes the absence of an external covering or something essential; *bare* is therefore often substituted for *naked* although not *vice versâ*: we speak of *bareheaded*, *barefoot*, to expose the *bare* arm; but a figure is said to be *naked*, or the body is *naked*.

When applied to other objects, *bare* conveys the idea of want in general; *naked* simply the want of something exteriour: when we speak of sitting upon the *bare* ground, of laying any place *bare*, of *bare* walls, a *bare* house, the idea of want in essentials is strongly conveyed; but *naked* walls, *naked* fields, a *naked* appearance, all denote something wanting to the eye. *bare* in this sense is frequently followed by the object that is wanted; *naked* is mostly employed as an adjunct; a tree is *bare* of leaves; this constitutes it a *naked* tree; 'The story of Æneas, on which Virgil founded his poem, was very *bare* of circumstances.'—ADDISON.

Why turn'st thou from me? I'm alone already;
Methinks I stand upon a *naked* beach,
Sighing to winds and to the seas complaining.
OTWAY.

They preserve the same analogy in their figurative application: a *bare* sufficiency is that which scarcely suffices; 'Christ and the Apostles did most earnestly inculcate the belief of his Godhead, and accepted men upon the *bare* acknowledgement of this.'—SOUTH. The *naked* truth is that which has nothing about it to intercept the view of it from the mind;

The truth appears so *naked* on my side,
That any purblind eye may find it out.
SHAKSPEARE.

Sometimes the word *naked* may be applied in the exact sense of *bare* to imply the want of some necessary addition, when it expresses the idea more strongly than *bare*; 'Not that God doth require nothing unto happiness at the hands of men, saving only a *naked* belief, for hope and charity we may not exclude.'—HOOKER.

Naked and *uncovered* bear a strong resemblance to each other; to be *naked* is in fact to have the body *uncovered*, but many things are *uncovered* which are not *naked*: nothing is said to be *naked* but what in the nature of things, or according to the usages of men ought to be covered;

He pitying how they stood
Before him *naked* to the air, that now
Must suffer change;—
As father of his family, he clad
Their *nakedness* with skins of beasts.—MILTON

Every thing is *uncovered* from which the covering is removed; 'In the eye of that Supreme Being to whom our whole internal frame is *uncovered*, dispositions hold the place of actions.'—BLAIR. According to our natural sentiments of decency, or our acquired sentiments of propriety, we expect to see the *naked* body covered with clothing, the *naked* tree covered with leaves; the *naked* walls covered with paper or paint: and the *naked* country covered with verdure or habitations: on the other hand, plants are left *uncovered* to receive the benefit of the sun or rain: furniture or articles of use or necessity are left *uncovered* to suit the convenience of the user: or a person may be *uncovered*, in the sense of *bare-headed*, on certain occasions.

BARE, SCANTY, DESTITUTE.

Bare (*v. Bare, naked*): *scanty*, from to *scant*, signifies the quality of *scanting; scant* is most probably changed from the Latin *scindo* to clip or cut; *destitute*, in Latin *destitutus*, participle of *destituo*, compounded of *de* privative and *statuo* to appoint or provide for, signifies unprovided for or wanting.

All these terms denote the absence or deprivation of some necessary. *Bare* and *scanty* have a relative sense: *bare* respects what serves for ourselves; *scanty* that which is provided by others. A subsistence is *bare*; a supply is *scanty*. An imprudent person will estimate as a *bare* competence what would supply an economist with superfluities; 'Were it for the glory of God, that the clergy should be left as *bare* as the apostles when they had neither staff nor scrip, God would, I hope, endue them with the self-same affection.'—Hooker. A hungry person will consider as a *scanty* allowance what would more than suffice for a moderate eater; 'So *scanty* is our present allowance of happiness, that in many situations life could scarcely be supported, if hope were not allowed to relieve the present hour, by pleasures borrowed from the future.'—Johnson.

Bare is said of those things which belong to the corporeal sustenance; *destitute* is said of one's outward circumstances in general. A person is *bare* of clothes or money; he is *destitute* of friends, of resources, or of comforts; '*Destitute* of that faithful guide, the compass, the ancients had no other method of regulating their course than by observing the sun and stars.'—Robertson.

BARE, MERE.

Bare (*v. Bare, naked*); *mere*, in Latin *merus* mere, properly *solus* alone, from the Greek μείρω to divide, signifies separated from others.

Bare is used in a positive sense: *mere*, negatively. The *bare* recital of some events brings tears. The *mere* circumstance of receiving favours ought not to bind any person to the opinions of another.

The *bare* idea of being in the company of a murderer is apt to awaken horrour in the mind; 'He who goes no farther than *bare* justice, stops at the beginning of virtue.'—Blair. The *mere* attendance at a place of worship is the smallest part of a Christian's duty; 'I would advise every man, who would not appear in the world a *mere* scholar or philosopher, to make himself master of the social virtue of complaisance.'—Addison.

SCARCITY, DEARTH.

Scarcity (*v. Rare*) is a generick term to denote the circumstance of a thing being *scarce: dearth*, which is the same as dearness, is a mode of *scarcity* applied in the literal sense to provisions mostly, as provisions are mostly dear when they are *scarce*; the word *dearth* therefore denotes *scarcity* in a high degree: whatever men want, and find it difficult to procure, they complain of its *scarcity*; when a country has the misfortune to be visited with a famine, it experiences the frightfullest of all *dearths*.

RARE, SCARCE, SINGULAR.

Rare, in Latin *rarus*, comes from the Greek ἀραιὸς thin; *scarce*, in Dutch *schaers* sparing, comes from *scheren* to cut or clip, signifying cut close; *singular* (*v. Particular*.)

Rare and *scarce* both respect number and quantity, which admits of expansion or diminution: *rare* is a thinned number, a diminished quantity; *scarce* is a short quantity.

Rare is applied to matters of convenience or luxury; *scarce* to matters of utility or necessity: that which is *rare* becomes valuable, and fetches a high price; that which is *scarce* becomes precious, and the loss of it is seriously felt. The best of every thing is in its nature *rare*; there will never be a superfluity of such things, there are, however, some things, as particularly curious plants, or particular animals, which, owing to circumstances, are always *rare:* that which is most in use, will, in certain cases, be *scarce*; when the supply of an article fails, and the demand for it continues, it naturally becomes *scarce*. An aloe in blossom is a *rarity*, for nature has prescribed such limits to its growth as to give but very few of such flowers; 'A perfect union of wit and judgement is one of the *rarest* things in the world.'—Burke. The paintings of Raphael, and other distinguished painters, are daily becoming more *scarce*, because time will diminish their quantity, although not their value; 'When any particular piece of money grew very *scarce*, it was often recoined by a succeeding emperour.'—Addison.

What is *rare* will often be *singular*, and what is *singular* will often, on that account, be *rare*; but they are not necessarily applied to the same object: fewness is the idea common to both; but *rare* is said of that of which there might be more; but *singular* is applied to that which is single, or nearly single, in its kind. The *rare* is that which is always sought for; the *singular* is not always that which one esteems: a thing is *rare* which is difficult to be obtained; a thing is *singular* for its peculiar qualities, good or bad; 'We should learn, by reflecting on the misfortunes which have attended others, that there is nothing *singular* in those which befall ourselves.'—Melmoth (*Letters of Cicero*). Indian plants are many of them *rare* in England, because the climate will not agree with them; the sensitive plant is *singular*, as its quality of yielding to the touch distinguishes it from all other plants.

Scarce is applied only in the proper sense to physical objects; *rare* and *singular* are applicable to moral objects. One speaks of a *rare* instance of fidelity of which many like examples cannot be found; of a *singular* instance of depravity, when a parallel case can *scarcely* be found.

SIMPLE, SINGLE, SINGULAR.

Simple, in Latin *simplex* or *sine plicâ* without a fold, is opposed to the complex, which has many folds, or to the compound which has several parts involved or connected with each other; 'To make the compound for the rich metal *simple*, is an adulteration or counterfeiting.'—Bacon. *Single* and *singular* (*v. One*) are opposed, one to double, and the other to multifarious;

> Mankind with other animals compare,
> *Single* how weak and impotent they are
> Jenyns.

'These busts of the emperours and empresses are all very scarce, and some of them almost *singular* in their kind.'—Addison. We may speak of a *simple* circumstance as independent of any thing; of a *single* instance or circumstance as unaccompanied by any other: and a *singular* instance as one that rarely has its like In the moral application to the person, *simplicity*, as far as it is opposed to duplicity in the heart, can never be excessive; but when it lies in the head, so that it cannot penetrate the folds and doublings of other persons, it is a fault; 'Nothing extraneous must cleave to the eye in the act of seeing; its bare object must be as naked as truth, as *simple* and unmixed as sincerity.'—South. *Singleness* of heart and intention is that species of *simplicity* which is altogether to be admired; *singularity* may be either good or bad according to circumstances; to be *singular* in virtue is to be truly good; but to be *singular* in manner is affectation, which is at variance with genuine *simplicity*, if not directly opposed to it; 'From the union of the crowns to the Revolution in 1688, Scotland was placed in a political situation the most *singular* and most unhappy'—Robertson.

SOME, ANY.

Some, probably contracted from so a one or such a one, is altogether restrictive in its sense: *any*, from a one, is altogether universal and indefinite. *Some* applies to one particular part in distinction from the rest. *any* to every individual part without distinction. *Some* think this, and others that: *any* person might believe if he would; *any* one can conquer his passions who calls in the aid of religion. In consequence of this distinction in sense, *some* can only be used in particular affirmative propositions; but *any*, which is equivalent to all, may be either in negative, interrogative, or hypothetical propositions: *some* say so: does *any* one believe it? He will not give to *any*.

SOLITARY, SOLE, ONLY, SINGLE.

Solitary and *sole* are both derived from *solus* alone or whole; *only*, that is onely, signifies the quality of unity; *single* is an abbreviation of singular (*v. Simple*).

All these terms are more or less opposed to several or many. *Solitary* and *sole* signify one left by itself; the former mostly in application to particular sensible objects, the latter in regard mostly to moral objects: a *solitary* shrub expresses not only one shrub, but one that has been left to itself;

> The cattle in the fields and meadows green,
> Those rare and *solitary*, these in flocks.—MILTON.

The *sole* cause or reason signifies that reason or cause which stands unsupported by any thing else; 'All things are but insipid to a man in comparison of that one, which is the *sole* minion of his fancy.'—SOUTH. *Only* does not include the idea of desertion or deprivation, but it comprehends that of want or deficiency: to say of a person that he has *only* one shilling in his pocket, means to imply, that he wants more or ought to have more. *Single* signifies simply one or more detached from others, without conveying any other collateral idea: a *single* sheet of paper may be sometimes more convenient than a double one; a *single* shilling may be all that is necessary for the present purpose: there may be *single* ones, as well as a *single* one; but the other terms exclude the idea of there being any thing else,

> Thy fear
> Will save us trial, what the least can do,
> *Single* against the wicked.—MILTON.

A *solitary* act of generosity is not sufficient to characterize a man as generous: with most criminals the *sole* ground of their defence rests upon their not having learned to know and do better: harsh language and severe looks are not the *only* means of correcting the faults of others: *single* instances of extraordinary talents now and then present themselves in the course of an age.

In the adverbial form, *solely*, *only*, and *singly* are employed with a similar distinction. The disasters which attend an unsuccessful military enterprise are seldom to be attributed *solely* to the incapacity of the general: there are many circumstances both in the natural and moral world which are to be accounted for *only* by admitting a providence as presented to us in Divine revelation: there are many things which men could not effect *singly* that might be effected by them conjointly

ONE, SINGLE, ONLY.

Unity is the common idea of all these terms; and at the same time the whole signification of *one*, which is opposed to none; *single*, in Latin *singulus* each or one by itself, probably contracted from *sine angulo* without an angle, because what is entirely by itself cannot form an angle, signifies that *one* which is abstracted from others, and is particularly opposed to two, or a double which may form a pair; *only*, contracted from *onely*, signifying in the form of unity, is employed for that of which there is no more. A person has *one* child, is a positive expression that bespeaks its own meaning: a person has a *single* child, conveys the idea that there ought to be or might be more, that more was expected, or that once there were more: a person has an *only* child, implies that he never had more;

> For shame, Rutilians, can you bear the sight
> Of *one* exposed for all, in *single* fight?—DRYDEN.

> Homely but wholesome roots
> My daily food, and water from the nearest spring
> My *only* drink.—FILMER.

BESIDES, MOREOVER.

Besides that is, by the *side*, next to, marks simply the connexion which subsists between what goes before and what follows; *moreover*, that is, more than all else, marks the addition of something particular to what has already been said.

Thus in enumerating the good qualities of an individual, we may say, "he is *besides* of a peaceable disposition." On concluding any subject of question we may introduce a farther clause by a *moreover:* "*Moreover* we must not forget the claims of those who will suffer by such a change;" 'Now, the best way in the world for a man to seem to be any thing, is really to be what he would seem to be. *Besides*, that it is many times as troublesome to make good the pretence of a good quality as to have it.'—TILLOTSON. 'It being granted that God governs the world, it will follow also that he does it by means suitable to the natures of the things that he governs; and *moreover* man being by nature a free, moral agent, and so capable of deviating from his duty, as well as performing it, it is necessary that he should be governed by laws' —SOUTH.

BESIDES, EXCEPT.

Besides (*v. Moreover*), which is here taken as a preposition, expresses the idea of addition; *except* expresses that of exclusion.

There were many there *besides* ourselves; no one *except* ourselves will be admitted; '*Besides* impiety discontent carries along with it as its inseparable concomitants, several other sinful passions.'—BLAIR. 'Neither jealousy nor envy can dwell with the Supreme Being. He is a rival to none, he is an enemy to none, *except* to such as, by rebellion against his laws seek enmity with him.'—BLAIR.

UNLESS, EXCEPT.

Unless, which is equivalent to *if less*, if not, or if one fail, is employed only for the particular case; but *except* has always a reference to some general rule, of which an *exception* is hereby signified: I shall not do it *unless* he ask me; no one can enter *except* those who are provided with tickets; '*Unless* money can be borrowed, trade cannot be carried on.'—BLACKSTONE. 'If a wife continues in the use of her jewels till her husband's death, she shall afterward retain them against his executors and administrators, and all other persons *except* creditors.'—BLACKSTONE.

HOWEVER, YET, NEVERTHELESS, NOTWITHSTANDING.

These conjunctions are in grammar termed adversative, because they join sentences together that stand more or less in opposition to each other. *However* is the most general and indefinite; it serves as a conclusive deduction drawn from the whole.

The truth is *however* not yet all come out: by which is understood that much of the truth has been told, and much *yet* remains to be told: so likewise in similar sentences; I am not, *however*, of that opinion; where it is implied either that many hold the opinion, or much may be said of it; but be that as it may, I am not of that opinion: *however* you may rely on my assistance to that amount; that is, at all events, let whatever happen, you may rely on so much of my assistance: *however*, as is obvious from the above examples, connects not only one single proposition, but many propositions either expressed or understood; '*However* it is but just sometimes to give the world a representation of the bright side of human nature.'—HUGHES. *Yet*, *nevertheless*, and *notwithstanding*, are mostly employed to set two specifick propositions either in contrast or direct opposition to each other; the two latter are but species of the former, pointing out the opposition in a more specifick manner.

There are cases in which *yet* is peculiarly proper; others in which *nevertheless*, and others in which *notwithstanding*, is preferable. *Yet* bespeaks a simple contrast; Addison was not a good speaker, *yet* he was an admirable writer; Johnson was a man of uncouth manners, *yet* he had a good heart and a sound head; 'He had not that reverence for the queen as might have been expected from a man of his wisdom and breeding; *yet* he was impertinently solicitous to know what her Majesty said of him in private.'—CLAREN

DON. *Nevertheless* and *notwithstanding* could not in these cases have been substituted. *Nevertheless* and *notwithstanding* are mostly used to imply effects or consequences opposite to what might naturally be expected to result. He has acted an unworthy part; *nevertheless* I will be a friend to him as far as I can; that is, although he has acted an unworthy part, I will be no less his friend as far as lies in my power; 'There will always be something that we shall wish to have finished, and be *nevertheless* unwilling to begin.'—JOHNSON. *Notwithstanding* all I have said, he still persists in his own imprudent conduct, that is, all I have said *notwithstanding* or not restraining him from it, he still persists. He is still rich *notwithstanding* his loss; that is, his loss *notwithstanding*, or *not standing* in the way of it, he is still rich; '*Notwithstanding* there is such infinite room between man and his Maker for the creative power to exert itself in, it is impossible that it ever should be filled up.'—ADDISON. From this resolution of the terms, more than from any specifick rule, we may judge of their distinct applications, and clearly perceive that in such cases as those above-cited the conjunctions *nevertheless* and *notwithstanding* could not be substituted for each other, nor *yet* for either: in other cases, *however*, where the objects are less definitely pointed out, they may be used indifferently. The Jesuits piqued themselves always upon their strict morality, and *yet* (*notwithstanding*, or *nevertheless*) they admitted of many things not altogether consonant with moral principle: you know that these are but tales, *yet* (*notwithstanding*, *nevertheless*) you believe them.

ALL, WHOLE.

All and *whole* are derived from the same source, that is, in German *all* and *heil* whole or sound, Dutch *all*, *hel*, or *heel*, Saxon *al*, *wal*, Danish *al*, *ald*, Greek ὅλος, Hebrew כל.

All respects a number of individuals; *whole* respects a single body with its components: we have not *all*, if we have not the *whole* number; we have not the *whole*, if we have not *all* the parts of which it is composed. It is not within the limits of human capacity to take more than a partial survey of *all* the interesting objects which the *whole* globe contains.

When applied to spiritual objects in a general sense, *all* is preferred to *whole*; but when the object is specifick, *whole* is preferable: thus we say, *all* hope was lost; but, our *whole* hope rested in this; 'It will be asked how the drama moves if it be not credited. It is credited with *all* the credit due to a drama.'—JOHNSON. 'The *whole* story of the transactions between Edward Harold and the Duke of Normandy is told so differently by ancient writers, that there are few important passages of the English history liable to so great uncertainty.'—HUME.

ALL, EVERY, EACH.

All is collective; *every* single or individual; *each* distributive.

All and *every* are universal in their signification: *each* is restrictive: the former are used in speaking of great numbers; the latter is applicable to small numbers. *All* men are not born with the same talent, either in degree or kind; but *every* man has a talent peculiar to himself: a parent divides his property among his children, and gives to *each* his due share; 'Harold by his marriage broke *all* measures with the Duke of Normandy.'—HUME. '*Every* man's performances, to be rightly estimated, must be compared to the state of the age in which he lived.'—JOHNSON. 'Taken singly and individually, it might be difficult to conceive how *each* event wrought for good. They must be viewed in their consequences and effects.'—BLAIR.

NUMEROUS, NUMERAL, NUMERICAL.

Numerous signifies literally containing a number, and is taken to denote a great many or a great number; *numeral* and *numerical* both imply belonging to number. *Numeral* is applied to a class of words in grammar, as a *numeral* adjective, or a *numeral* noun: *numerical* is applied to whatever other objects respect number: as a *numerical* difference, where the difference subsists between any two numbers, or is expressed by numbers.

SPECIAL, SPECIFICK, PARTICULAR.

Special, in Latin *specialis*, signifies belonging to the species; *particular*, belonging to a particle or small part; *specifick*, in Latin *specificus*, from *species* a species, and *facio* to make, signifies making a species. The *special* is that which comes under the general; the *particular* is that which comes under the *special*: hence we speak of a *special* rule; but a *particular* case; 'God claims it as a *special* part of his prerogative to have the entire disposal of riches.'—SOUTH. *Particular* and *specifick* are both applied to the properties of individuals; but *particular* is said of the contingent circumstances of things, *specifick* of their inherent properties; every plant has something *particular* in itself different from others, it is either longer or shorter, weaker or stronger; 'Every state has a *particular* principle of happiness, and this principle may in each be carried to a mischievous excess.'—GOLDSMITH. The *specifick* property of a plant is that which it has in common with its species; 'The imputation of being a fool is a thing which mankind, of all others, is the most impatient of, it being a blot upon the prime and *specifick* perfection of human nature.'—SOUTH. *Particular* is, therefore, a term adapted to loose discourse; *specifick* is a scientifick term which describes things minutely.

The same may be said of *particularize* and *specify*: we *particularize* for the sake of information; we *specify* for the sake of instruction: in describing a man's person and dress we *particularize* if we mention every thing singly which can be said upon it; in delineating a plan it is necessary to *specify* time, place, distance, materials, and every thing else which may be connected with the carrying of it into execution.

PARTICULAR, INDIVIDUAL.

Particular (*v. Peculiar*); *individual*, in French *individuel*, Latin *individuus*, signifies that which cannot be divided.

Both these terms are employed to express one object; but *particular* is much more specifick than *individual*: the *particular* confines us to one object only of many but *individual* may be said of any one object among many. A *particular* object cannot be misunderstood for any other, while it remains *particular*; but the *individual* object can never be known from other *individual* objects, while it remains only *individual*. *Particular* is a term used in regard to *individuals*, and is opposed to the general: *individual* is a term used in regard to collectives; and is opposed to the whole or that which is divisible into parts; 'Those *particular* speeches, which are commonly known by the name of rants, are blemishes in our English tragedy.'—ADDISON.

> To give thee being, I lent
> Out of my side to thee, nearest my heart,
> Substantial life, to have thee by my side,
> Henceforth an *individual* solace dear.—MILTON

ALONE, SOLITARY, LONELY.

Alone, compounded of *all* and *one*, signifies altogether one, or single; that is, by one's self; *solitary*, in French *solitaire*, Latin *solitarius*, from *solus* alone, signifies the quality of being *alone*; *lonely* signifies in the manner of *alone*.

Alone marks the state of a person; *solitary* the quality of a person or thing; *lonely* the quality of a thing only. A person walks *alone*, or takes a *solitary* walk in a *lonely* place.

Whoever likes to be much *alone* is of a *solitary* turn;

> Here we stand *alone*,
> As in our form distinct, pre-eminent.—YOUNG.

Wherever a man can be most and oftenest *alone*, that is a *solitary* or *lonely* place; 'I would wish no man to deceive himself with opinions which he has not thoroughly reflected upon in his *solitary* hours.'—CUMBERLAND

Within an ancient forest's ample verge
There stands a *lonely*, but a healthful dwelling,
Built for convenience and the use of life.—ROWE.

ALSO, LIKEWISE, TOO.

Also, compounded of *all* and *so*, signifies literally all in the same manner; *likewise*, compounded of *like* and *wise* or manner, signifies in like manner; *too*, a variation of the numeral *two*, signifies what may be added or joined to another thing from its similarity.

These adverbial expressions obviously convey the same idea of including or classing certain objects together upon a supposed ground of affinity. *Also* is a more general term, and has a more comprehensive meaning, as it implies a sameness in the whole; 'Let us only think for a little of that reproach of modern times, that gulf of time and fortune, the passion for gaming, which is so often the refuge of the idle sons of pleasure, and often *also* the last resource of the ruined.' —BLAIR. *Likewise* is more specifick and limited in its acceptation; 'All the duties of a daughter, a sister, a wife, and a mother, may be well performed, though a lady should not be the finest woman at an opera. They are *likewise* consistent with a moderate share of wit, a plain dress, and a modest air.'—STEELE.

Too is still more limited than either, and refers only to a single object; 'Long life is of all others the most general, and seemingly the most innocent object of desire. With respect to this, *too*, we so frequently err, that it would have been a blessing to many to have had their wish denied.'—BLAIR.

"He *also* was among the number" may convey the idea of totality both as respects the person and the event: "he writes *likewise* a very fine hand" conveys the idea of similar perfection in his writing as in other qualifications: "he said so *too*," signifies he said so in addition to the others; he said it *likewise* would imply that he said the same thing, or in the same manner.

SOLITARY, DESERT, DESOLATE.

Solitary is derived from the Latin *solus* alone; *desert* is the same as *deserted; desolate*, in Latin *desolatus*, signifies made *solitary*.

All these epithets are applied to places, but with different modifications of the common idea of solitude which belongs to them. The *solitary* simply denotes the absence of all beings of the same kind: thus a place is *solitary* to a man, where there is no human being but himself; and it is *solitary* to a brute, when there are no brutes with which it can hold society; 'The first time we behold the hero (Ulysses), we find him disconsolately sitting on the *solitary* shore, sighing to return to Ithaca.'—WHARTON. *Desert* conveys the idea of a place made *solitary* by being shunned, from its unfitness as a place of residence; all *deserts* are places of such wildness as seems to frighten away almost all inhabitants;

A peopled city made a *desert* place.—DRYDEN.

Desolate conveys the idea of a place made *solitary*, or bare of inhabitants, and all traces of habitation, by violent means; every country may become *desolate* which is exposed to the inroads of a ravaging army;

Supporting and supported, polish'd friends
And dear relations mingle into bliss;
But this the rugged savage never felt,
E'n *desolate* in crowds.—THOMSON.

TO RECEDE, RETREAT, RETIRE, WITHDRAW, SECEDE.

To *recede* is to go back; to *retreat* is to draw back; the former is a simple action, suited to one's convenience; the latter is a particular action, dictated by necessity: we *recede* by a direct backward movement; we *retreat* by an indirect backward movement: we *recede* a few steps in order to observe an object more distinctly; we *retreat* from the position we have taken, in order to escape danger: whoever can advance can *recede*; but in general those only *retreat* whose advance is not free: *receding* is the act of every one; *retreating* is peculiarly the act of soldiers, or those who make hostile movements. To *retire* and *withdraw* originally signify the same as *retreat*, that is, draw back or off; but they agree in application mostly with *recede*: to *recede* is to go back from a given spot; but to *retire* and *withdraw* have respect to the place or the presence of the persons: we may *recede* on an open plain; but we *retire* or *withdraw* from a room, or from some company. In this application *withdraw* is the more familiar term: *retire* may likewise be used for an army; but it denotes a much more leisurely action than *retreat*: a general *retreats*, by compulsion, from an enemy; but he may *retire* from an enemy's country when there is no enemy present.

Recede, retire, withdraw, and *retreat*, are also used in a moral application; *secede* is used only in this sense: a person *recedes* from his engagement, which is seldom justifiable; or he may *recede* from his pretensions, which is mostly commendable; 'We were soon brought to the necessity of *receding* from our imagined equality with our cousins.'—JOHNSON. A person *retires* from business when he ceases to carry it on any longer; '*Retirement* from the world's cares and pleasures has been often recommended as useful to repentance.'—JOHNSON. A person *withdraws* from a society either for a time or altogether; 'A temptation may *withdraw* for awhile, and return again.'—SOUTH. As life is religiously considered as a warfare with the world, they are said to *retreat* from the contest who do not enter into its pleasures; 'How certain is our ruin, unless we sometimes *retreat* from this pestilential region (the world of pleasure).'—BLAIR. To *secede* is a public act: men *secede* from a religious or political body: *withdraw* is a private act; they *withdraw* themselves as individual members from any society; 'Pisistratus and his sons maintained their usurpations during a period of sixty-eight years, including those of Pisistratus's *secessions* from Athens.'—CUMBERLAND.

PRIVACY, RETIREMENT, SECLUSION.

Privacy literally denotes the abstract quality of *private*; but when taken by itself it signifies the state of being *private*: *retirement* literally signifies the abstract act of *retiring*: and *seclusion* that of *secluding* one's self: but *retirement* by itself frequently denotes a state of being retired, or a place of *retirement*; *seclusion*, a state of being *secluded*: hence we say a person lives in *privacy*, in *retirement*, in *seclusion*: *privacy* is opposed to publicity; he who lives in *privacy*, therefore, is one who follows no publick line, who lives so as to be little known;

Fly with me to some safe, some sacred *privacy*.
ROWE

Retirement is opposed to openness or freedom of access he, therefore, who lives in *retirement*, withdraws from the society of others, he lives by himself; 'In our *retirements* every thing disposes us to be serious.'—ADDISON *Seclusion* is the excess of *retirement*; he who lives in *seclusion* bars all access to himself; he shuts himself from the world;

What can thy imag'ry of sorrow mean?
Secluded from the world, and all its care,
Hast thou to grieve or joy, to hope or fear?
PRIOR

Privacy is most suitable for such as are in circumstances of humiliation, whether from their misfortune or their fault: *retirement* is peculiarly agreeable to those who are of a reflective turn; but *seclusion* is chosen only by those who labour under some strong affection of the mind, whether of a religious or physical nature.

TO ABDICATE, DESERT

The following celebrated speech of Lord Somers, in 1688, on King James's vacating the throne, may be admitted as a happy elucidation of these two important words; but I am not inclined to think that they come sufficiently close in signification to render any comparison necessary.

"What is appointed me to speak to is your Lordships' first amendment by which the word *abdicated* in the Commons' vote is changed into the word *deserted*, and I am to acquaint your Lordships what some of the grounds are that induced the Commons to insist on the word *abdicated*, and not to agree to your amendment.

"The first reason your Lordships are pleased to deliver for your changing the word is, that the word *abdicated* your Lordships do not find is a word known to the common law of England, and therefore ought not to be used. The next is that the common application of the word amounts to a voluntary express renunciation, which is not in this case, nor will follow from the premises.

"My Lords, as to the first of these reasons, if it be an objection that the word *abdicated* hath not a known sense in the common law of England, there is the same objection against the word *deserted;* so that your Lordships' first reason hath the same force against your own amendment, as against the term used by the Commons.

"The words are both Latin words, and used in the best authors, and both of a known signification; their meaning is very well understood, though it be true their meaning is not the same. The word *abdicate* doth naturally and properly signify, entirely to renounce, throw off, disown, relinquish any thing or person, so as to have no further to do with it; and that whether it be done by express words or in writing (which is the sense your Lordships put upon it, and which is properly called resignation or cession), or by doing such acts as are inconsistent with the holding and retaining of the thing, which the Commons take to be the present case, and therefore make choice of the word *abdicate*, as that which they thought did above all others express that meaning. And in this latter sense it is taken by others; and that this is the true signification of the word I shall show your Lordships out of the best authors.

"The first I shall mention is Grotius, De Jure Belli et Pacis, l. 2, c. 4, § 4. Venit enim hoc non ex jure civili, sed ex jure naturali, quo quisque suum potest *abdicare*, et ex naturali præsumptione, quâ voluisse quis creditur quod sufficienter significavit. And then he goes on: Recusari hæreditas, non tantum verbis sed etiam re, potest, et quovis indicio voluntatis.

"Another instance which I shall mention, to show that for *abdicating* a thing it is sufficient to do an act which is inconsistent with retaining it, though there be nothing of express renunciation, is out of Calvin's Lexicon Juridicum, where he says, Generum *abdicat* qui sponsam repudiat. Here is an *abdication* without express words, but it is by doing such an act as doth sufficiently signify his purpose.

"The next author I shall quote is Brissonius, De Verborum Significatione, who hath this passage: Homo liber qui seipsum vendit *abdicat* se statu suo. That is, he who sells himself hath thereby done such an act as cannot consist with his former state of freedom, and is thereby said properly se *abdicasse* statu suo.

"Budæus, in his Commentaries Ad Legem Secundam de Origine Juris, expounds the words in the same sense. *Abdicare* se magistratu est idem quod abire penitus magistratu. He that goes out of his office of magistracy, let it be in what manner he will, has *abdicated* the magistracy.

"And Grotius, in his Book de Jure Belli et Pacis, l. 1, c. 4, § 9, seems to expound the word *abdicare* by *manifeste habere pro derelicto;* that is, he who hath *abdicated* any thing hath so far relinquished it, that he hath no right of return to it. And that is the sense the Commons put upon the word. It is an entire alienation of the thing *abdicated*, and so stands in opposition to *dicare*. *Dicat* qui proprium aliquot facit, *abdicat* qui alienat: so says Pralejus in his Lexicon Juris. It is therefore insisted on as the proper word by the Commons.

"But the word *deserted* (which is the word used in the amendment made by your Lordships) hath not only a very doubtful signification, but in the common acceptance both of the civil and canon law, doth signify only a bare withdrawing, a temporary quitting of a thing, and neglect only, which leaveth the party at liberty of returning to it again. *Desertum* pro neglecto, says Spigelius in his Lexicon. But the difference between *deserere* and *derelinquere* is expressly laid down by Bartolus on the 8th law of the 58th title of the 11th book of the Code, and his words are these: Nota diligenter ex hac lege, quod aliud est agrum *deserere*, aliud *derelinquere;* qui enim *derelinquit* ipsum ex pœnitentiâ non revocare, sed qui *deserit*, intra biennium potest.

"Whereby it appears, my lords, that is called *desertion* which is temporary and relievable; that is called *dereliction* where there is no power or right to return.

"So in the best Latin authors, and in the civil law *deserere exercitum* is used to signify soldiers leaving their colours; and in the canon law to *desert* a benefice signifies no more than to be a non-resident.

"In both cases the party hath not only a right of returning, but is bound to return again; which, my Lords, as the Commons do not take to be the present case, so they cannot think that your Lordships do, because it is expressly said, in one of your reasons given in defence of the last amendment, that your Lordships have been and are willing to secure the nation against the return of King James, which your Lordships would in justice do, if you did look upon it to be no more than a negligent withdrawing, which leaveth a liberty to the party to return.

"For which reasons, my Lords, the Commons cannot agree to the first amendment, to insert the word *deserted* instead of *abdicated;* because it doth not in any sort come up to their sense of the thing, so they apprehend it doth not reach your Lordships' meaning as it is expressed in your reasons, whereas they look upon the word *abdicated* to express properly what is to be inferred from that part of the vote to which your Lordships have agreed, viz. 'That King James II., by going about to subvert the constitution, and by breaking the original contract between king and people, and by violating the fundamental laws, and withdrawing himself out of the kingdom, hath thereby renounced to be a king according to the constitution.' By avowing to govern according to a despotick power unknown to the constitution, and inconsistent therewith, he hath renounced to be a king according to the law; such a king as he swore to be at the coronation; such a king to whom the allegiance of an English subject is due; and hath set up another kind of dominion; which is to all intents an *abdication* or abandoning of his legal title as fully as if it had been done by express words.

"And, my Lords, for these reasons the Commons do insist upon the word *abdicated*, and cannot agree to the word *deserted*."

Without all this learned verbosity it will be obvious to every person that the two words are widely distinct from each other; *abdication* being a pure act of discretion for which a man is answerable to himself only: but *desertion* an act which involves more or less a breach of moral obligation.

TO DISMISS, DISCHARGE, DISCARD.

Dismiss, in Latin *dimissus*, participle of *dimitto*, compounded of *di* and *mitto*, signifies to send asunder or away; *discharge*, signifies to release from a charge; *discard*, in Spanish *descartar*, compounded of *des* and *cartar*, signifies to lay cards out or aside, to cast them off.

The idea of removing to a distance is included in all these terms; but with various collateral circumstances. *Dismiss* is the general term; *discharge* and *discard* are modes of dismissing: *dismiss* is applicable to persons of all stations, but is used more particularly for the higher orders: *discharge* on the other hand is confined to those in a subordinate station. A clerk, or an officer, or a minister, is *dismissed;* 'In order to an accommodation, they agreed upon this preliminary, that each of them should immediately *dismiss* his privy counsellor.'—ADDISON. A menial servant or a soldier is *discharged;* 'Mr. Pope's errands were so frequent and frivolous that the footman in time avoided and neglected him, and the Earl of Oxford *discharged* some of his servants for their obstinate refusal of his messages.'—JOHNSON.

Neither *dismiss* nor *discharge* define the motive of the action; they are used indifferently for that which is voluntary, or the contrary: *discard*, on the contrary, always marks a *dismissal* that is not agreeable to the party *discarded*. A person may request to be *dismissed* or *discharged*, but never to be *discarded*. The *dismissal* or *discharge* frees a person from the obligation or necessity of performing a certain duty;

> *Dismiss* the people then, and give command
> With strong repast to hearten every band.—POPE.

The *discarding* throws him out of a desirable rank or station: 'I am so great a lover of whatever is French, that I lately *discarded* an humble admirer because he neither spoke that tongue nor drank claret.'—BUDGELL.

They are all applied to things in the moral sense, and with the same distinction: we are said to *dismiss* our fears, to *discharge* a duty, and to *discard* a sentiment from the mind:

> Resume your courage, and *dismiss* your care.
> DRYDEN.

If I am bound to pay money on a certain day, I *discharge* the obligation if I pay it before twelve o'clock at night.'—BLACKSTONE. 'Justice *discards* party friendship and kindred.'—ADDISON.

TO LET, LEAVE, SUFFER.

Let, through the medium of the Gothick *letan*, and other changes in the French *laisser*, German *lassen*, &c. comes in all probability from the Latin *laxo*, to loosen, or set loose, free; *leave* (*v. To leave*); *suffer*, from the Latin *suffero* to bear with, signifies not to put a stop to.

The removal of hindrance or constraint on the actions of others, is implied by all these terms; but *let* is a less formal action than *leave*, and this than *suffer*. I *let* a person pass in the road by getting out of his way: I *leave* a person to decide on a matter according to his own discretion, by declining to interfere: I *suffer* a person to go his own way, over whom I am expected to exercise a control. It is in general most prudent to *let* things take their own course; 'Where there is a certainty and an uncertainty, *let* the uncertainty go, and hold to that which is certain.'—SAUNDERSON. In the education of youth, the greatest art lies in *leaving* them to follow the natural bent of their minds and turn of disposition without at the same time *suffering* them to do any thing prejudicial to their character or future interests;

> This crime I could not *leave* unpunished.
> DENHAM.

If Pope had *suffered* his heart to be alienated from her, he could have found nothing that might fill her place.'—JOHNSON.

TO LEAVE, QUIT, RELINQUISH.

Leave, in Saxon *leafve*, in old German *laube*, Latin *linquo*, Greek λείπω, signifies either to *leave* or be wanting, because one is wanting in the place which one *leaves*; *quit*, in French *quitter*, from the Latin *quietus* rest, signifies to rest or remain, to give up the hold of; the sense of *relinquish* is given under the head of *Abandon*.

We *leave* that to which we may intend to return; we *quit* that to which we return no more: we may *leave* a place voluntarily or otherwise; but we *relinquish* it unwillingly. We *leave* persons or things; we *quit* and *relinquish* things only. I *leave* one person in order to speak to another; I *leave* my house for a short time;

> Why *leave* we not the fatal Trojan shore,
> And measure back the seas we cross'd before?
> POPE.

I *quit* it not to return to it; 'At last he (Savage) *quitted* the house of his friend.'—JOHNSON.

They preserve the same distinction in the moral application. A prudent man *leaves* all questions about minor matters in religion and politics to men of busy, restless tempers; 'We have no better materials to compound the priesthood of, than the mass of mankind, which, corrupted as it is, those who receive orders, must have some vices to *leave* behind them.'—SWIFT. It is a source of great pleasure to a contemplative mind to revisit the scenes of early childhood, which have been long *quitted* for the busy scenes of active life;

> The sacred wrestler, till a blessing's giv'n,
> *Quits* not his hold, but halting, conquers heav'n.
> WALLER.

A miser is loath to *relinquish* the gain which has added so greatly to his stores and his pleasures; 'Although Charles *relinquished* almost every power for the crown, he would neither give up his friends to punishment, nor desert what he esteemed his religious duty.'—HUME.

TO LEAVE, TAKE LEAVE, BID FAREWELL, OR ADIEU.

Leave is here general as before (*v. To leave*); it expresses simply the idea of separating one's self from an object, whether for a time or otherwise; to *take leave* and *bid farewell* imply a separation for a perpetuity.

To *leave* is an unqualified action, it is applied to objects of indifference, or otherwise, but supposes in general no exercise of one's feelings. We *leave* persons as convenience requires;

> Self alone, in nature rooted fast,
> Attends us first and *leaves* us last.—SWIFT.

We *leave* them on the road, in the field, in the house, or wherever circumstances direct; we *leave* them with or without speaking; to *take leave* is a parting ceremony between friends, on their parting for a considerable time; 'Now I am to *take leave* of my readers, I am under greater anxiety than I have known for the work of any day since I undertook this province.'—STEELE. To *bid farewell* or *adieu* is a still more solemn ceremony, when the parting is expected to be final. When applied to things, we *leave* such as we do not wish to meddle with; we *take leave* of those things which were agreeable to us, but which we find it prudent to give up; and we *bid farewell* to those for which we still retain a great attachment; 'Anticipate the awful moment of your *bidding* the world an eternal *farewell*.'—BLAIR. It is better to *leave* a question undecided, than to attempt to decide it by altercation or violence; it is greater virtue in a man to *take leave* of his vices, than to let them *take leave* of him; when a man engages in schemes of ambition, he must *bid adieu* to all the enjoyments of domestick life.

LEAVE, LIBERTY, PERMISSION, LICENSE.

Leave has here the sense of freedom granted, because what is left to itself is left free; *liberty*, in Latin *libertas*, from *liber* free, denotes the state of being free from external restraint; *permission* signifies the act of *permitting*, or the thing *permitted*; *license*, in Latin *licentia*, from *licet* to be lawful, signifies the state of being *permitted* by law, or the act of the law in *permitting*.

Leave and *liberty* are either given or taken: *permission* is taken only; *license* is granted, and that in a special manner: *leave* is employed only on familiar occasions; 'I must have *leave* to be grateful to any one who serves me, let him be ever so obnoxious to any party.'—POPE. *Liberty* is given in more important matters; 'I am for the full *liberty* of diversion (for children), as much as you can be.'—LOCKE. The master gives leave to his servant to go out for his pleasure; a gentleman gives his friends the *liberty* of shooting on his grounds; *leave* is taken in indifferent matters, particularly as it respects *leave* of absence, *liberty* is taken by a greater, and in general an unauthorized stretch of one's powers, and is, therefore, an infringement on the rights of another. What is done without the *leave* may be done without the knowledge, though not contrary to the will, of another; but *liberties* which are taken without offering an apology are always calculated to give offence.

Leave is granted by private individuals, but *license* is granted by publick authority: a parent gives *leave* to a child to take a walk; the government grants *licenses* for selling different commodities. The word *license* is however sometimes used figuratively;

> Leaving the wits the spacious air,
> With *license* to build castles there.—SWIFT.

Leave and *permission* are said to be asked for, but not *liberty*: we beg *leave* to offer our opinions; we request *permission*, but not *liberty*, to speak; 'The repeated *permissions* you give me of dealing freely with you will, I hope, excuse what I have done.'—POPE.

LEAVINGS, REMAINS, RELICKS.

Leavings are the consequence of a voluntary ac they signify what is left: *remains* are what follow in the course of things; they are what *remain*; the former is therefore taken in the bad sense to signify what has been left as worthless; the latter is never taken in this bad sense. When many persons of good taste have the liberty of choosing, it is fair to expect that the *leavings* will be worth little or nothing, after all have made their choice;

> Scales, fins, and bones, the *leavings* of the feast.
> SOMERVILLE.

By the *remains* of beauty which are discoverable in the face of a female, we may be enabled to estimate what her personal charms had been;

> So midnight tapers waste their last *remains.*
> SOMERVILLE.

Remains signify literally what *remains: relicks*, from the Latin *relinquo* to leave, that which is left. The former is a term of general and familiar application; the latter is specifick. What *remains* after the use or consumption of any thing is termed the *remains;* what is left of any thing after a lapse of years is the *relick* or *relicks.* There are *remains* of buildings mostly after a conflagration; there are *relicks* of antiquity in most monasteries and old churches.

Remains are of value, or not, according to the circumstances of the cases; *relicks* always derive a value from the person to whom they were supposed originally to belong. The *remains* of a person, that is, what corporeally *remains* of a person, after the extinction of life, will be respected by his friend;

> Upon these friendly shores, and flow'ry plains,
> Which hide Anchises, and his blest *remains.*
> DRYDEN.

A bit of a garment that belonged, or is supposed to have belonged, to some saint, will be a precious *relick* in the eyes of a superstitious Roman Catholick; 'All those arts, rarities, and inventions, which the ingenious pursue, and all admire, are but the *relick* of an intellect defaced with sin and time.'—SOUTH. All nations have agreed to respect the *remains* of the dead; religion, under most forms, has given a sacredness to *relicks* in the eyes of its most zealous votaries; the veneration of genius, or the devotedness of friendship, has in like manner transferred itself, from the individual himself, to some object which has been his property or in his possession, and thus fabricated for itself *relicks* equally precious.

LOOSE, VAGUE, LAX, DISSOLUTE, LICENTIOUS.

Loose, in German *los*, &c., Latin *laxus*, Greek ἀλάσσειν, and Hebrew חלץ to make free; *vague*, in Latin *vagus*, signifies wandering; *lax*, in Latin *laxus*, has a similar origin with *loose; dissolute*, in Latin *dissolutus*, participle of *dissolvo*, signifies *dissolved* or set free; *licentious*, i. e. having the *license* or power to do as one pleases (*v. Leave, liberty*).

Loose is the generick, the rest are specifick terms; they are all opposed to that which is bound or adheres closely: *loose* is employed either for moral or intellectual subjects; *vague* only for intellectual objects: *lax* sometimes for what is intellectual, but oftener for the moral; *dissolute* and *licentious* only in moral matters: whatever wants a proper connexion, or linking together of the parts, is *loose;* whatever is scattered and remotely separated is *vague:* a style is *loose* where the words and sentences are not made to coalesce, so as to form a regularly connected series; assertions are *vague* which have but a remote connexion with the subject referred to: by the same rule, *loose* hints thrown out at random may give rise to speculation and conjecture, but cannot serve as the ground of any conclusion; ignorant people are apt to credit every *vague* rumour, and to communicate it as a certainty.

Opinions are *loose*, either inasmuch as they want logical precision, or as they fail in moral strictness; 'Because conscience and the fear of swerving from that which is right, maketh them diligent observers of circumstances, the *loose* regard whereof is the nurse of vulgar folly.'—HOOKER. Suggestions and surmises are in their nature *vague*, as they spring from a very remote channel, or are produced by the wanderings of the imagination; 'That action which is *vague* and indeterminate will at last settle into habit, and habitual peculiarities are quickly ridiculous.'—JOHNSON. Opinions are *lax*, inasmuch as they have a tendency to lessen the moral obligation, or to *loosen* moral ties; 'In this general depravity of manners and *laxity* of principles, pure religion is no where more strongly inculcated (than in our universities).'—JOHNSON. *Loose* notions arise from the unrestrained state of the will, from the influence of the unruly passions; *lax* notions from the errour of the judgement; *loose* principles affect the moral conduct of individuals; *lax* principles affect the speculative opinions of men, either as individuals or in society: one is *loose* in practice, and *lax* in speculation or in discipline: the *loose* man sins against his conscience; he sets himself free from that to which he knows that he ought to submit; the *lax* man errs, but he affects to defend his errour. A *loose* man injures himself, but a *lax* man injures society at large. *Dissoluteness* is the excess of *looseness; licentiousness* is the consequence of *laxity*, or the freedom from external constraint.

Looseness of character, if indulged, soon sinks into *dissoluteness* of morals; and *laxity* of discipline is quickly followed by *licentiousness* of manners.

A young man of *loose* character makes light of moral obligations in general; 'The most voluptuous and *loose* person breathing, were he but tied to follow his dice and his courtships every day, would find it the greatest torment that could befall him.'—SOUTH. A man of *dissolute* character commits every excess, and totally disregards every restraint; 'As the life of Petronius Arbiter was altogether *dissolute*, the indifference which he showed at the close of it is to be looked upon as a piece of natural carelessness rather than fortitude.' —ADDISON. In proportion as a commander is *lax* in the punishment of offences, an army will become *licentious;* in proportion as the administration of law becomes *lax*, the age will become *licentious;* 'Moral philosophy is very agreeable to the paradoxical and *licentious* spirit of the age.'—BEATTIE.

SLACK, LOOSE.

Slack, in Saxon *slaec*, low German *slack*, French *lache*, Latin *laxus*, and *loose*, in Saxon *laes*, both come from the Hebrew חלץ to make free or *loose;* they differ more in application than in sense: they are both opposed to that which is close bound; but *slack* is said only of that which is tied, or that with which any thing is tied; while *loose* is said of any substances, the parts of which do not adhere closely: a rope is *slack* in opposition to the tight rope, which is stretched to its full extent; and in general cords or strings are said to be *slack* which fail in the requisite degree of tightness; but they are said to be *loose* in an indefinite manner, without conveying any collateral idea: thus the string of an instrument is denominated *slack* rather than *loose;* on the other hand, *loose* is said of many bodies to which the word *slack* cannot be applied: a garment is *loose*, but not *slack;* the leg of a table is *loose*, but not *slack.* In the moral application that which admits of extension lengthways is denominated *slack;* and that which fails in consistency and close adherence is *loose:* trade in general is said to be *slack*, or the sale of a particular article to be *slack;* but an engagement is said to be *loose*, and principles *loose.*

> Rebellion now began, for lack
> Of zeal and plunder, to grow *slack.*—HUDIBRAS
>
> Nor fear that he who sits so *loose* to life,
> Should too much shun its labours and its strife.
> DENHAM

TO RELAX, REMIT.

The general idea of diminution is that which allies these words to each other; but they differ very widely in their original meaning, and somewhat in their ordinary application; *relax*, from the word *lax* or loose, signifies to make loose, and in its moral use to lessen any thing in its degree of tightness or rigour; to *remit*, from *re* and *mitto* to send back, signifies to take off in part or entirely that which has been imposed; that is, to lessen in quantity. In regard to our attempts to act, we may speak of *relaxing* in our endeavours, and *remitting* our labours or exertions;

> No more the smith his dusky brow shall clear,
> *Relax* his ponderous strength, and lean to hear.
> GOLDSMITH
>
> How often have I blessed the coming day,
> When toil *remitting* lent its turn to play.
> GOLDSMITH

in regard to our dealings with others, we may speak of *relaxing* in discipline, *relaxing* in the severity or strictness of our conduct, of *remitting* a punishment or *remitting* a sentence. The discretionary power of showing mercy when placed in the hands of the sovereign, serves to *relax* the rigour of the law; 'The statute of mortmain was at several times *relaxed* by the legislature.'—SWIFT. When the punishment seems to be disproportioned to the magnitude of the offence, it is but equitable to *remit* it. 'The magistrate can often, where the publick good demands not the execution of the law, *remit* the punishment of criminal offences by his own authority.'—LOCKE.

TO CEASE, LEAVE OFF, DISCONTINUE, DESIST.

Cease, in French *cesser*, Latin *cesso*, from *cessi* perfect of *cedo* to yield, signifies to give up or put an end to: to *leave off* is literally to separate one's self from an action or course of conduct; *discontinue*, with the privative *dis*, expresses the opposite of *continue: desist*, from the Latin *desisto*, or *de* and *sisto*, signifies literally to take one's self off from a thing.

To *cease* is neuter; to *leave off* and *discontinue* are active: we *cease* from doing a thing; we *leave off* or *discontinue* a thing. *Cease* is used either for particular actions or general habits; *leave off* more usually and properly for particular actions; *discontinue* for general habits. A restless, spoiled child never *ceases* crying until it has obtained what it wants; it is a mark of impatience not to *cease* lamenting when one is in pain; 'A successful author is equally in danger of the diminution of his fame, whether he continues or *ceases* to write.'—JOHNSON. A labourer *leaves off* his work at any given hour; 'As harsh and irregular sound is not harmony; so neither is banging a cushion, oratory; therefore, in my humble opinion, a certain divine of the first order would do well to *leave* this *off*.'—SWIFT. A delicate person *discontinues* his visits when they are found not to be agreeable; 'I would cheerfully have borne the whole expense of it, if my private establishment of native readers and writers, which I cannot with convenience *discontinue* at present, did not require more than half of the monthly expense, which the completion of a Digest would in my opinion demand.'—SIR WM. JONES.

It should be our first endeavour to *cease* to do evil. It is never good to *leave off* working while there is any thing to do, and time to do it in. The *discontinuing* of a good practice without adequate grounds evinces great instability of character.

To *cease* is said of that which flows out of the nature of things; to *leave off*, *discontinue*, and *desist*, are always the acts of conscious agents. To *leave off* and *discontinue* are voluntary acts, *desist* is involuntary; it is prudent to *desist* from using our endeavours when we find them ineffectual; it is natural for a person to *leave off* when he sees no farther occasion to continue his labour; 'The laird of Raarsa has sometimes disputed the chieftainry of the clan with Macleod of Skie; but being much inferiour in extent of possessions, has, I suppose, been forced to *desist*.'—JOHNSON.

CESSATION, STOP, REST, INTERMISSION.

Cessation, from the verb to *cease*, marks the condition of leaving off; *stop*, from to *stop*, marks that of being *stopped* or prevented from going on; *rest*, from to *rest*, marks the state of being quiet; and *intermission*, from *intermit*, marks that of *ceasing* occasionally.

To *cease* respects the course of things; whatever does not go on has *ceased;* things *cease* of themselves: *stop* respects some external action or influence; nothing *stops* but what is supposed to be *stopped* or hindered by another: *rest* is a species of *cessation* that regards labour or exertion; whatever does not move or exert itself is at *rest: intermission* is a species of *cessation* only for a time or at certain intervals.

That which *ceases* or *stops* is supposed to be at an end; *rest* or *intermission* supposes a renewal. A *cessation* of hostilities is at all times desirable: to put a *stop* to evil practices is sometimes the most difficult and dangerous of all undertakings: *rest* after fatigue is indispensable, for labour without *intermission* exhausts the frame. The rain *ceases*, a person or a ball *stops* running, the labourer *rests* from his toil, a fever is *intermittent*. There is nothing in the world which does not *cease* to exist at one period or another;

Who then would court the pomp of guilty power,
When the mind sickens at the weary show,
And flies to temporary death for ease?
When half our life's *cessation* of our being.

STEELE.

Death *stops* every one sooner or later in his career; 'In all those motions and operations which are incessantly going on throughout nature, there is no *stop* nor interruption.'—BLAIR. Whoever is vexed with the cares of getting riches will find no *rest* for his mind or body; 'The refreshing *rest* and peaceful night are the portion of him only who lies down weary with honest labour.'—JOHNSON. He will labour without *intermission* oftentimes only to heap troubles on himself; 'Whether the time of *intermission* is spent in company or in solitude, in necessary business or involuntary levities, the understanding is equally abstracted from the object of inquiry.'—JOHNSON.

INTERVAL, RESPITE.

Interval, in Latin *intervallum*, signifies literally the space between the stakes which formed a Roman intrenchment; and, by an extended application, it signifies any space; *respite*, probably contracted from *respirit*, signifies a breathing again.

Every *respite* requires an *interval;* but there are many *intervals* where there is no *respite*. The term *interval* respects time only; *respite* includes the idea of action within that time which may be more or less agreeable; *intervals* of ease are a *respite* to one who is oppressed with labour; 'Any uncommon exertion of strength, or perseverance in labour, is succeeded by a long *interval* of languor.'—JOHNSON. The *interval* which is sometimes granted to a criminal before his execution is in the properest sense a *respite;* 'Give me leave to allow myself no *respite* from labour.'—SPECTATOR.

REPRIEVE, RESPITE.

Reprieve comes in all probability from the French *repris*, participle of *reprendre*, and the Latin *reprehendo*, signifying to take back or take off that which has been laid on; *respite* signifies the same as in the preceding article.

The idea of a release from any pressure or burden is common to these terms; but the *reprieve* is that which is granted; the *respite* sometimes comes to us in the course of things: we gain a *reprieve* from any punishment or trouble which threatens us; we gain a *respite* from any labour or weight that presses upon us. A criminal gains a *reprieve* when the punishmeut of death is commuted for that of transportation; a debtor may be said to obtain a *reprieve* when, with a prison before his eyes, he gets such indulgence from his creditors as sets him free; there is frequently no *respite* for persons in a subordinate station, when they fall into the hands of a hard taskmaster; Sisyphus is feigned by the poets to have been condemned to the toil of perpetually rolling a stone up a hill as fast as it rolled back, from which toil he had no *respite;*

All that I ask is but a short *reprieve*,
Till I forget to love and learn to grieve,
Some pause and *respite* only I require,
Till with my tears I shall have quench'd my fire.

DRYDEN.

INCESSANTLY, UNCEASINGLY, UNINTERRUPTEDLY, WITHOUT INTERMISSION.

The want of continuity, not of duration, is denoted by these terms; *incessantly* is the most general and indefinite of all; it signifies without ceasing, but may be applied to things which admit of certain intervals: *unceasingly* is definite, and signifies never ceasing, it cannot therefore be applied to what has any cessation. In familiar discourse, *incessantly* is a hyperbolick mode of speech, by which one means to denote the absence of those ordinary intervals which are to be expected; as when one says a person is *incessantly* talking; by which is understood, that he does not allow himself the ordinary intervals of rest from talking;

Surfeat, misdiet, and unthrifty waste,
Vaine feastes, and ydle superfluite,
All those this sence's fort assayle *incessantly*.
SPENSER.

Unceasingly, on the other hand, is more literally employed for a positive want of cessation; a noise is said to be *unceasing* which literally never ceases; or complaints are *unceasing* which are made without any pauses or intervals;

Impell'd with steps *unceasing*, to pursue
Some fleeting good that mocks me with the view.
GOLDSMITH.

Incessantly and *unceasingly* are said of things which act of themselves; *uninterruptedly* is said of that which depends upon other things: it rains *incessantly* marks a continued operation of nature, independent of every thing; but to be *uninterruptedly* happy marks one's freedom from every foreign influence which is unfriendly to one's happiness;

She draws a close incumbent cloud of death,
Uninterrupted by the living winds.—THOMSON.

Incessantly and the other two words are employed either for persons or things; *without intermission* is however mostly employed for persons: things act and react *incessantly* upon one another; a man of a persevering temper goes on labouring without *intermission*, until he has effected his purpose; 'For any one to be always in a laborious, hazardous posture of defence, *without intermission*, must needs be intolerable.'—SOUTH.

ALWAYS, AT ALL TIMES, EVER.

Always, compounded of *all* and *ways*, is the same as, under all circumstances, through all the ways of life, that is, uninterruptedly; *at all times*, means, without distinction of time; *ever* implies, for a perpetuity, without end.

A man must be *always* virtuous, that is, whether in adversity or prosperity; 'Human life never stands still for any long time. It is by no means a fixed and steady object, like the mountain or the rock, which you *always* find in the same situation.'—BLAIR. A man must be *at all times* virtuous, that is, in his going in and coming out, his rising up and his lying down, by day and by night; 'Among all the expressions of good nature, I shall single out that which goes under the general name of charity, as it consists in relieving the indigent; that being a trial of this kind which offers itself to us almost *at all times*, and in every place.'—ADDISON. A virtuous man will be *ever* happy, that is, in this life, and the life to come; 'Have you forgotten all the blessings you have continued to enjoy *ever* since the day that you came forth a helpless infant into the world.'—BLAIR.

TO STAND, STOP, REST, STAGNATE.

To *stand*, in German *stehen*, &c. Latin *sto*, Greek Ἵςημι to stand, Hebrew שות to settle; *stop*, in Saxon *stoppan*, &c. conveys the ideas of pressing, thickening, like the Latin *stipa*, and the Greek ςείβειν; whence it has been made in English to express immoveability; *rest* is contracted from the Latin *resisto* or *re* and *sisto* to place or stand back; *stagnate*, in Latin *stagnatus*, participle of *stagno*, comes from *stagnum* a pool, and that either from *sto* to *stand*, because waters *stand* perpetually in a pool, or from the Greek ςεγνὸς an enclosure, because a pool is an enclosure for waters.

The absence of motion is expressed by all these terms; *stand* is the most general of all; to *stand* is simply not to move; to *stop* is to cease to move: we *stand* either for want of inclination or power to move; but we *stop* from a disinclination to go on: to *rest* is to *stop* from an express dislike to motion; we may *stop* for purposes of convenience, or because we have no farther to go, but we *rest* from fatigue; to *stagnate* is only a species of *standing* as respects liquids; water may both *stand* and *stagnate;* but the former implies a temporary, the latter a permanent state: water *stands* in a puddle, but it *stagnates* in a pond or in any confined space.

All these terms admit of an extended application; business *stands* still, or there is a *stand* in business;

Whither can we run,
Where make a *stand?*—DRYDEN.

A mercantile house *stops*, or *stops* payment, or a person *stops* in his career; 'I am afraid should I put a *stop* now to this design, now that it is so near being compleated, I shall find it difficult to resume it.'—MELMOTH (*Pliny*). An affair *rests* undecided, or *rests* in the hands of a person;

Who *rests* of immortality assur'd
Is safe, whatever ills are here endur'd.—JENYNS.

Trade *stagnates;* 'This inundation of strangers, which used to be confined to the summer, will *stagnate* all the winter.'—GIBBON. *Stand*, *stop*, and *rest*, are likewise employed transitively, but with a wide distinction in the sense; to *stand* in this case is to set one's self up to resist; as to *stand* the trial, to *stand* the test: to *stop* has the sense of hinder; as to *stop* a person who is going on, that is, to make him *stop:* to *rest* is to make a thing *rest* or *lean;* a person *rests* his argument upon the supposed innocence of another

TO CHECK, STOP.

Check, from the German *Schach* chess, derives its figurative signification of restraining the movements, from *checkmate*, a movement in that game whereby one *stops* one adversary from carrying his game any farther; to *stop* (*v. Cessation*) is to cause not to move at all: the growth of a plant is *checked* when it does not grow so fast as usual; its growth is *stopped* when it ceases altogether to grow: the water of a river is *stopped* by a dam; the rapidity of its course is *checked* by the intervention of rocks and sands.

When applied to persons, to *check* is always contrary to the will of the sufferer; but to *stop* is often a matter of indifference, if not directly serviceable: one is *checked* in his career of success by some untoward event; 'Shall neither the admonitions which you receive from the visible inconstancy of the world, nor the declarations of the Divine displeasure, be sufficient to *check* your thoughtless career?'—BLAIR. One is *stopped* on a journey by the meeting of a friend;

Embosom'd in the deep where Holland lies,
Methinks her patient sons before me stand,
Where the broad ocean leans against the land,
And sedulous to *stop* the coming tide,
Lift the tall rampire's artificial pride.—GOLDSMITH.

In a moral application these terms bear a similar analogy; *check* has the import of diminishing; *stop* that of destroying or causing to cease: many evils may be easily *checked*, to which it would not be easy to put an effectual *stop*.

TO HINDER, STOP.

Hinder, from *hind* or *behind*, signifies to *hinder* by going behind or pulling one behind; to *stop* is to make to stand.

Hindering refers solely to the prosecution of an object: *stop* refers simply to the cessation of motion; we may be *hindered*, therefore, by being *stopped;* but we may also be *hindered* without being expressly *stopped*, and we may be *stopped* without being *hindered*. If the *stoppage* do not interfere with any other object in view, it is a *stoppage*, but not a *hindrance;* as when we are *stopped* by a friend while walking for pleasure;

A signal omen *stopp'd* the passing host,
Their martial fury in their wonder lost.—POPE.

But if *stopped* by an idler in the midst of urgent business, so as not to be able to proceed according to our business, this is both a *stoppage* and a *hindrance*. On the other hand, if we are interrupted in the regular course of our proceeding, but not compelled to stand still or give up our business for any time, this may be a *hindrance*, but not a *stoppage:* in this manner, the conversation of others, in the midst of our business, may considerably retard its progress, and so far *hinder*, but not expressly put a *stop* to the whole concern; 'Is it not the height of wisdom and goodness too, to *hinder* the consummation of those soul-wasting sins, by obliging us to withstand them in their first infancy?'—SOUTH.

TO HINDER, PREVENT, IMPEDE, OBSTRUCT

Hinder signifies the same as in the preceding article, *prevent*, from *præ* before and *venio* to come, signifies to *hinder* by coming before, or to cross another by the anticipation of his purpose; *impede*, in Latin from *in* and *pedes* the feet, signifies to come between his feet and entangle him in his progress; 'Impedire profectionem aut certe tardare.'—CICERO. *Obstruct*, from *ob* and *struo*, signifies to set up something in one's way, to block up the passage.

Hinder is the most general of these terms, as it conveys little more than the idea which is common to them all, namely, that of keeping one from his purpose. To *hinder* is commonly said of that which is rendered impossible for the time being, or merely delayed; *prevent* is said of that which is rendered altogether impracticable. A person is *hindered* by the weather and his various engagements from reaching a place at the time he intended; he is *prevented* but not *hindered* by ill health from going thither at all. If a friend calls, he *hinders* me from finishing the letter which I was writing; if I wish to *prevent* my son from reading any book, I keep it out of his way; 'It is much easier to keep ourselves void of resentment, than to restrain it from excess when it has gained admission. To use the illustration of an excellent author, we can *prevent* the beginnings of some things, whose progress afterward we cannot *hinder*.'—HOLLAND.

To *hinder* is an act of the moment, it supposes no design; *prevent* is a premeditated act, deliberated upon, and adopted for general purposes: the former is applied only to the movements of any particular individual, the latter to events and circumstances. I *hinder* a person who is running, if I lay hold of his arm and make him walk; it is the object of every good government to *prevent* offences rather than to punish offenders. In ordinary discourse these words fall very much into one another, when the circumstances of the case do not sufficiently define, whether the action in hand be altogether suspended, or only suspended for a time; but the above explanation must make it very clear, that *hinder*, in its proper sense and application, is but a temporary act, and *prevent* is a decisive and permanent act.

To *impede* and *obstruct* is a species of *hindering* which is said rather of things than of persons; *hinder* is said of both; but *hinder* is commonly employed in regard to trifling matters, or such as retard a person's proceedings in the smallest degree; *impede* and *obstruct* are acts of greater importance, or produce a still greater degree of delay. A person is *hindered* in his work, although neither *impeded* nor *obstructed;* but the quantity of artillery and baggage which is attached to an army will greatly *impede* it in its march; and the trees which are thrown across the roads will *obstruct* its march.

Whatever causes a person to do a thing slower than he wishes is a *hindrance;* whatever binds him so that he cannot move freely forward is an *impediment;* whatever acts upon the path or passage so as to *prevent* him from moving forward is an *obstruction.* Every *impediment* and *obstruction* is a *hindrance*, though not *vice versâ.* A person is *hindered* in the thing he is about if he be called off to do something else; ill health *impedes* a person's progress in learning; any foreign body lodging in the vessels of the human body *obstructs* the course of the fluids, and consequently brings on serious diseases. *Hindrances* always suppose the agency of a person, either of the one who *hinders*, or the one who is *hindered;* but *impediments* and *obstructions* may be employed with regard to the operations of nature on inanimate objects. Cold *impedes* the growth of plants; a dam *obstructs* the course of water; 'Truth was provoked to see herself thus baffled and *impeded* by an enemy whom she looked on with contempt.'—JOHNSON.

> This path you say is hid in endless night,
> 'T is self-conceit alone *obstructs* your sight.
>
> JENYNS.

DIFFICULTY, OBSTACLE, IMPEDIMENT.

Difficulty, in Latin *difficultas* and *difficilis*, compounded of the privative *dis* and *facilis* easy, from *facio* to do, signifies the thing not easy to be done; *obstacle*, in Latin *obstaculum*, from *obsto* to stand in the way, signifies the thing that stands in the way between a person and the object he has in view; *impediment*, in Latin *impedimentum*, from *impedio* compounded of *in* and *pedes*, signifies something that entangles the feet.

All these terms include in their signification that which interferes either with the actions or views of men: the *difficulty** lies most in the nature and circumstances of the thing itself; the *obstacle* and *impediment* consist of that which is external or foreign: a *difficulty* interferes with the completion of any work; an *obstacle* interferes with the attainment of any end; an *impediment* interrupts the progress, and prevents the execution of one's wishes: a *difficulty* embarrasses, it suspends the powers of acting or deciding; an *obstacle* opposes itself, it is properly met in the way, and intervenes between us and our object; an *impediment* shackles and puts a stop to our proceedings: we speak of encountering a *difficulty*, surmounting an *obstacle*, and removing an *impediment:* the disposition of the mind often occasions more *difficulties* in negociations than the subjects themselves; 'Truth has less of trouble and *difficulty*, of entanglement and perplexity, of danger and hazard in it.'—TILLOTSON. The eloquence of Demosthenes was the greatest *obstacle* which Philip of Macedon experienced in his political career; 'One *obstacle* must have stood not a little in the way of that preferment after which Young seems to have panted. Though he took orders, he never entirely shook off politicks.'—CROFT. Ignorance of the language is the greatest *impediment* which a foreigner experiences in the pursuit of any object out of his own country; 'The necessity of complying with times, and of sparing persons, is the great *impedimen* of biography.'—JOHNSON.

* Vide Abbe Girard: "Difficulté, obstacle, empêchement."

TO PREVENT, ANTICIPATE.

To *prevent* (*v. To hinder*) is literally to come beforehand, and *anticipate*, from *ante* and *capio* to take beforehand: the former is employed for actual occurrences; the latter as much for calculations as for actions: *prevent* is the act of one being towards another; *anticipate* is the act of a being either towards himself or another. God is said to *prevent* us, if he interposes with his grace to divert our purposes towards that which is right; '*Prevent* us, O Lord, in all our doings with thy most gracious favour.'—COMMON PRAYER. We *anticipate* the happiness which we are to enjoy in future; and so in like manner we may *anticipate* our pains;

> Why should we
> *Anticipate* our sorrows? 'T is like those
> Who die for fear of death.—DENHAM.

We also *anticipate* what a person is going to say by saying the same thing before him. The term *prevent*, when taken in this its strict and literal sense, is employed only as the act of the Divine Being;

> But I do think it most cowardly and vile,
> For fear of what might fall, so to *prevent*
> The time of life.—SHAKSPEARE.

Anticipate, on the contrary, is taken only as the act of human beings towards each other or themselves; 'He that has *anticipated* the conversation of a wit will wonder to what prejudice he owes his reputation.'—JOHNSON. These words may, however, be farther allied to each other, when under the term *prevention* in its vulgar acceptation is included the idea of hindering another in his proceedings; in which case to *anticipate* is a species of *prevention;* that is, to *prevent* another from doing a thing by doing it one's self, 'I am far from pretending to instruct the profession, or *anticipating* their directions to such as are under their government.'—ARBUTHNOT.

TO PREVENT, OBVIATE, PRECLUDE.

To *prevent* (*v. To hinder*) is here as in the former case the generick term, the others are specifick. What one *prevents* does not happen at all: what one *obviates* ceases to happen in future; we *prevent* those evils which we know will come to pass if not *prevented:* we *obviate* those evils which we have already felt; that is, we *prevent* their repetition. Crimes and calamities are *prevented;* difficulties, objections, inconveniences, and troubles, are *obviated.* When crowds collect in vast numbers in any small spot, it is not easy to *prevent* mischief: wise precautions may be adopted to *obviate* the inconvenience which necessarily attends a great crowd.

Prevent and *obviate* are the acts of either conscious or unconscious agents: *preclude* is the act of unconscious agents only: one *prevents* or *obviates* a thing by the use of means, or else the things themselves *prevent* and *obviate*, as when we say, that a person *prevents* another from coming, or illness *prevents* him from coming; a person *obviates* a difficulty by a contrivance, a certain arrangement or change *obviates* every difficulty. We intentionally *prevent* a person from doing that which we disapprove of; his circumstances *preclude* him from enjoying certain privileges. *Prevent* respects that which is either good or bad; *obviate* respects that which is always bad; *preclude* respects that which is good or desirable: ill-health *prevents* a person from pursuing his business; employment *prevents* a young person from falling into bad practices;

Ev'ry disease of age we may *prevent*,
Like those of youth, by being diligent.—DENHAM.

Admonition often *obviates* the necessity of punishments; 'The imputation of folly, if it is true, must be suffered without hope; but that of immorality may be *obviated* by removing the cause.'—HAWKESWORTH. Want of learning or of a regular education often *precludes* a man from many of the political advantages which he might otherwise enjoy; 'Has not man an inheritance to which all may return, who are not so foolish as to continue the pursuit after pleasure till every hope is *precluded?*'—HAWKESWORTH.

TO RETARD, HINDER.

To *retard*, from the Latin *tardus* slow, signifying to make slow, is applied to the movements of any object forward: as in the Latin 'Impetum inimici *tardare*.'—CICERO. To *hinder* (*v. To hinder*) is applied to the person moving or acting: we *retard* or make slow the progress of any scheme towards completion; 'Nothing has tended more to *retard* the advancement of science than the disposition in vulgar minds to vilify what they cannot comprehend.'—JOHNSON. We *hinder* or keep back the person who is completing the scheme; 'The very nearness of an object sometimes *hinders* the sight of it.'—SOUTH. We *retard* a thing therefore often by *hindering* the person; but we frequently *hinder* a person without expressly *retarding*, and on the contrary the thing is *retarded* without the person being *hindered*. The publication of a work is sometimes *retarded* by the *hindrances* which an author meets with in bringing it to a conclusion; but a work may be *retarded* through the idleness of printers and a variety of other causes which are independent of any *hindrance*. So in like manner a person may be *hindered* in going to his place of destination; but we do not say that he is *retarded*, because it is only the execution of an object, and not the simple movements of the person which are *retarded*.

TO DELAY, DEFER, POSTPONE, PROCRASTINATE, PROLONG, PROTRACT, RETARD.

Delay, compounded of *de* and *lay*, signifies to lay or keep back; *defer*, compounded of *de* and *fer*, in Latin *fero*, signifies to put off; *postpone*, compounded of *post* and *pone*, from the Latin *pono* to place, signifies to place behind or after; *procrastinate*, from *pro* and *cras* to-morrow, signifies to put off till to-morrow; *prolonging*, answering to the *prolatio* of the Latins, signifies the lengthening the period of time for beginning or ending a thing; *protract*, from *traho* to draw, signifies to draw out the time; and *retard* to make a thing hang in hand.

To *delay* is simply not to commence action; to *defer* and *postpone* are to fix its commencement at a more distant period: we may *delay* a thing for days, hours, and minutes; we *defer* or *postpone* it for months or weeks. *Delays* mostly arise from faults in the person *delaying;* they are seldom reasonable or advantageous; *differing* and *postponing* are discretionary acts, which are justified by the circumstances: indolent people are most prone to *delay;*

From thee both old and young with profit learn,
The bounds of good and evil to discern;
Unhappy he who does this work adjourn,
And to to-morrow would the search *delay;*
His lazy morrow will be like to-day.—DRYDEN.

When a plan is not maturely digested, it is prudent to *defer* its execution until every thing is in an entire state of preparation. *Procrastination* is a culpable *delay* arising solely from the fault of the *procrastinator;* 'Cum plerisque in rebis gerendis tarditas et *procrastinatio* odiosa est, tum hoc bellum indiget celeritatis.'—CICERO. It is the part of a dilatory man to *procrastinate* that which it is both his interest and duty to perform;

Procrastination is the thief of time.—YOUNG

To *defer* is used without regard to any particular time or object; to *postpone* has always relation to something else: it is properly to *defer* until the completion of some period or event: a person may *defer* his visit from month to month; he *postpones* his visit until the commencement of a new year: a tardy debtor *delays* the settlement of his accounts; a merchant *defers* the shipment of any goods in consequence of the receipt of fresh intelligence; 'Never *defer* that till to-morrow which you can do to-day.'—BUDGELL. A merchant *postpones* the shipment until after the arrival of the expected fleet; 'When I *postponed* to another summer my journey to England, could I apprehend that I never should see her again!'—GIBBON.

We *delay* the execution of a thing; we *prolong* or *protract* the continuation of a thing: we *retard* the termination of a thing: we may *delay* answering a letter, *prolong* a contest, *protract* a lawsuit, and *retard* a publication;

Perhaps great Hector then had found his fate,
But Jove and destiny *prolong'd* his date.—POPE.

To this Euryalus: "You plead in vain,
And but *protract* the cause you cannot gain."
VIRGIL

I see the layers then
Of mingled moulds of more retentive earths,
That while the stealing moisture they transmit,
Retard its motion and forbid its waste.
THOMSON.

TO PROROGUE, ADJOURN.

Prorogue, from the Latin *prorogo*, signifies to put off, and is used in the general sense of deferring for an indefinite period; 'A *prorogation* is the continuance of Parliament from one session to another.'—BLACKSTONE.

Adjourn, from *journée* the day, signifies only to put off for a day or some short period; 'An *adjournment* is no more than a continuance of the session from one day to another.'—BLACKSTONE. *Prorogueing* is applied to national assemblies only; *adjourning* is applicable to any meeting.

SLOW, DILATORY, TARDY, TEDIOUS.

Slow is doubtless connected with sluther and slide, which kind of motion when walking is the *slowest* and the laziest; *dilatory*, from the Latin *defero* to defer, signifies prone to defer; *tardy* is but a variation of the Latin *tardus* slow; *tedious*, from the Latin *tædit* to be weary, signifies causing weariness.

Slow is a general and unqualified term applicable to the motion of any object or to the motions and actions of persons in particular, and to their dispositions also; *dilatory* relates to the temper only of persons: we are *slow* in what we are about;

The powers above are *slow*
In punishing, and should not we resemble them?
DRYDEN.

We are *dilatory* in setting about a thing; 'A *dilatory* temper is unfit for a place of trust.'—ADDISON. *Slow* is applied to corporeal or mental actions; a person may be *slow* in walking, or *slow* in conceiving: *tardy* applies more to what is mental than to what is corporeal; we are *tardy* in our proceedings or our progress; we are *tardy* in making up accounts or in concluding a treaty;

Death he has oft accus'd
Of *tardy* execution, since denounc'd
The day of his offence.—MILTON.

We may be *slow* with propriety or not, to our own inconvenience or that of others; when we are *tedious* we are always so improperly: "'To be *slow* and sure" is a vulgar proverb, but a great truth; by this we do ourselves good, and inconvenience no one; but he who is *tedious* is *slow* to the annoyance of others; a prolix writer must always be *tedious*, for he keeps the reader long in suspense before he comes to the conclusion of a period;

Her sympathizing lover takes his stand
High on th' opponent bank, and ceaseless sings
The *tedious* time away.—THOMSON.

TO LINGER, TARRY, LOITER, LAG, SAUNTER.

Linger, from *longer*, signifies to make the time longer in doing a thing; *tarry*, from *tardus* slow, is to make the thing slow; *loiter* may probably come from *lentus* slow; *lag*, from *lie*, signifies to lie back; *saunter* is derived from *sancta terra* the Holy Land; because, in the time of the crusades, many idle persons were going backwards and forwards: hence idle, planless going, comes to be so denominated.

Suspension of action or slow movement enters into the meaning of all these terms: to *linger* is to stop altogether, or to move but slowly forward, and to *tarry* is properly to suspend one's movement: the former proceeds from reluctance to leave the spot on which we stand; the latter from motives of discretion: he will naturally *linger* who is going to leave the place of his nativity for an indefinite period; in which sense it is figuratively applied to life and other objects;

'T is long since I, for my celestial wife,
Loath'd by the Gods, have dragg'd a *ling'ring* life.
DRYDEN.

Those who have much business to transact will be led to *tarry* long in a place; 'Herod having *tarried* only seven days at Rome for the dispatch of his business, returned to his ships at Brundusium.'—PRIDEAUX. To *loiter* is to move slowly and reluctantly; but, from a bad cause, a child *loiters* who is unwilling to go to school; 'Rapid wits *loiter*, or faint, and suffer themselves to be surpassed by the even and regular perseverance of slower understandings.'—JOHNSON. To *lag* is to move slower than others; to stop while they are going on; this is seldom done for a good purpose: those who *lag* have generally some sinister and private end to answer;

I shall not *lag* behind, nor err
The way, thou leading.—MILTON.

To *saunter* is altogether the act of an idler; those who have no object in moving either backward or forward, will *saunter* if they move at all; 'She walks all the morning *sauntering* about the shop, with her arms through her pocket holes.'—JOHNSON.

TO HASTEN, ACCELERATE, SPEED, EXPEDITE, DESPATCH.

Hasten, in French *hatir*, and in the Northern languages *hasten*, &c., is most probably connected with *heiss* hot, expressing what is vivid and active; *accelerate*, from *celer* quick, signifies literally to quicken for a specifick purpose; *speed*, from the Greek *σπουδάζω*, signifies to carry on diligently; *expedite*, in Latin *expedio*, from *ex* and *pes*, signifies literally to remove obstacles; *despatch*, in French *depecher*, from *pes* a foot, signifies also putting off, or clearing away impediments.

Quickness in movement and action is the common idea in all these terms, which vary in the nature of the movement and the action. To *hasten* expresses little more than the general idea of quickness in moving towards a point; thus, he *hastens* who runs to get to the end of his journey: *accelerate* expresses moreover the idea of bringing something to a point; thus, every mechanical business is *accelerated* by the order and distribution of its several parts; 'Let the aged consider well, that by every intemperate indulgence they *accelerate* decay.'—BLAIR. *Accelerate* may be employed, like the word *hasten*, for corporeal and familiar actions: the tailor *accelerates* any particular work that he has in hand by putting on additional hands, or a compositor *accelerates* the printing of a work by doing his part with correctness. The word *speed* includes not only quick but forward movement. He who goes with *speed* goes effectually forward, and comes to his journey's end the soonest. This idea is excluded from the term *haste*, which may often be a planless unsuitable quickness. Hence the proverb, "The more *haste*, the worst *speed*;"

Where with like *haste*, though several ways they run,
Some to undo, and some to be undone.—DENHAM.

Expedite and *despatch* are terms of higher import, in application to the most serious concerns in life; but to *expedite* expresses a process, a bringing forward towards an end: *despatch* implies a putting an end to, a making a clearance. We do every thing in our power to *expedite* a business: we *despatch* a great deal of business within a given time. *Expedition* is requisite for one who executes; 'The coachman was ordered to drive on, and they hurried with the utmost *expedition* to Hyde Park Corner.'—JOHNSON. *Despatch* is most important for one who determines and directs; 'And as, in races, it is not the large stride, or high lift, that makes the *speed*; so, in business, the keeping close to the matter, and not taking of it too much at once, procureth *despatch*.'—BACON. An inferiour officer must proceed with *expedition* to fulfil the orders, or execute the purposes of his commander; a general or minister of state *despatches* the concerns of planning, directing, and instructing. Hence it is we speak only of *expediting* a thing; but we may speak of *despatching* a person, as well as a thing.

Every man *hastens* to remove his property in case of fire. Those who are anxious to bring any thing to an end will do every thing in their power to *accelerate* its progress. Those who are sent on any pressing errand will do great service by using *speed*. The success of a military progress depends often on the *expedition* with which it is conducted. In the counting-house and the cabinet, *despatch* is equally important; as we cannot do more than one thing at a time, it is of importance to get that quickly concluded to make way for another.

TO HASTEN, HURRY.

Hasten signifies the same as in the preceding article *hurry*, in old French *harier*, probably comes from the Hebrew חרר to be inflamed, or be in a *hurry*.

To *hasten* and *hurry* both imply to move forward with quickness in any matter; but the former may proceed with some design and good order, but the latter always supposes perturbation and irregularity. We *hasten* in the communication of good news, when we make efforts to convey it in the shortest time possible; 'Homer, to preserve the unity of action, *hastens* into the midst of things, as Horace has observed.'—ADDISON. We *hurry* to get to an end, when we impatiently and inconsiderately press forward without making choice of our means;

Now 't is nought
But restless *hurry* through the busy air,
Beat by unnumber'd wings.—THOMSON.

To *hasten* is opposed to delay or a dilatory mode of proceeding; it is frequently indispensable to *hasten* in the affairs of human life: to *hurry* is opposed to deliberate and cautious proceeding; it must always be prejudicial and unwise to *hurry*: men may *hasten*; children *hurry*.

As epithets, *hasty* and *hurried* are both employed in the bad sense; but *hasty* implies merely an overquickness of motion which outstrips consideration; *hurried* implies a disorderly motion which springs from a distempered state of mind. Irritable people use *hasty* expressions; they speak before they think: deranged people walk with *hurried* steps; they follow the blind impulse of undirected feeling.

QUICKNESS, SWIFTNESS, FLEETNESS, CELERITY, RAPIDITY, VELOCITY.

These terms are all applied to the motion of bodies, of which *quickness*, from *quick*, denotes the general and simple idea that characterizes all the rest. *Quickness* is near akin to life, and is directly opposed to slowness; 'Impatience of labour ceases those who are most distinguished for *quickness* of apprehension.'—JOHNSON. *Swiftness*, in all probability from the German *schweifen* to roam.; and *fleetness*, from flee or fly; express higher degrees of *quickness*. *Celerity*, probably from *celer* a horse; *velocity*, from *volo* to fly; and *rapidity*, from *rapio*, to seize or hurry along, differ more in application than in degree. *Quick* and *swift* are applicable to any objects; men are *quick* in moving, *swift* in running: dogs hear *quickly*, and run *swiftly:* a mill goes *quickly* or *swiftly* round, according to the force of the wind;

> Above the bounding billows *swift* they flew,
> Till now the Grecian camp appear'd in view.
> POPE.

Fleetness is the peculiar characteristick of winds or horses; a horse is *fleet* in the race, and is sometimes described to be as *fleet* as the winds;

> For fear, though *fleeter* than the wind,
> Believes 't is always left behind.—BUTLER.

That which we wish to characterize as particularly *quick* in our ordinary operations, we say is done with *celerity;* in this manner our thoughts are said to pass with *celerity* from one object to another; 'By moving the eye we gather up with great *celerity* the several parts of an object, so as to form one piece.'—BURKE. Those things are said to move with *rapidity* which seem to hurry every thing away with them; a river or stream moves with *rapidity;* time goes on with a *rapid* flight;

> Mean time the radiant sun, to mortal sight
> Descending *swift*, roll'd down the *rapid* light.
> POPE.

Velocity signifies the *swiftness* of flight, which is a motion that exceeds all others in *swiftness:* hence, we speak of the *velocity* of a ball shot from a cannon, or of a celestial body moving in its orbit; sometimes these words *rapidity* and *velocity*, are applied in the improper sense by way of emphasis to the very *swift* movements of other bodies: in this manner the wheel of a carriage is said to move *rapidly:* and the flight of an animal or the progress of a vessel before the wind, is compared to the flight of a bird in point of *velocity;* Lightning is productive of grandeur which it chiefly owes to the *velocity* of its motion.'—BURKE.

DILIGENT, EXPEDITIOUS, PROMPT.

All these terms mark the quality of quickness in a commendable degree; *diligent* (from *diligo* to love (*v. Active, diligent*) marks the interest one takes in doing something; he is * *diligent* who loses no time, who keeps close to the work; *expeditious*, from the Latin *expedio* to despatch, marks the desire one has to complete the thing begun. He who is *expeditious* applies himself to no other thing that offers; he finishes every thing in its turn; *prompt*, from the Latin *promo* to draw out or make ready, marks one's desire to get ready; he is *prompt* who works with spirit so as to make things ready.

Idleness, dilatoriness, and slowness, are the three defects opposed to these three qualities. The *diligent* man has no reluctance in commencing or continuing the labour, the *expeditious* man never leaves it till it is finished; the *prompt* man brings it quickly to an end. It is necessary to be *diligent* in the concerns which belong to us; 'We must be *diligent* in our particular calling and charge, in that province and station which God has appointed us, whatever it be.'—TILLOTSON. We must be *expeditious* in any business that requires to be terminated; 'The regent assembled an army with his usual *expedition*, and marched to Glasgow.'—ROBERTSON. We must be *prompt* in the execution of orders that are given to us;

* Vide Abbe Girard: "Diligent, expeditif, prompt."

> To him she hasted, in her face excuse
> Came prologue, and apology too *prompt*,
> Which, with bland words at will, she thus address'd
> MILTON

DIRECTLY, IMMEDIATELY, INSTANTLY, INSTANTANEOUSLY.

Directly signifies in a direct or straight manner; *immediately* without any medium or intervention; *instantly* and *instantaneously*, in the space of an instant.

Directly is most applicable to the actions of men; *immediately* and *instantly* to either actions or events. *Directly* refers to the interruptions which may intentionally delay the commencement of any work: *immediately* in general refers to the space of time that intervenes. A diligent person goes *directly* to his work; he suffers nothing to draw him aside: good news is *immediately* spread abroad upon its arrival; nothing intervenes to retard it. *Immediately* and *instantly*, or *instantaneously*, both mark a quick succession of events, but the latter in a much stronger degree than the former. *Immediately* is negative; it expresses simply that nothing intervenes; *instantly* is positive, signifying the very existing moment in which the thing happens. A person who is of a willing disposition goes or runs *immediately* to the assistance of another; but the ardour of affection impels him to fly *instantly* to his relief, as he sees the danger. A surgeon does not proceed *directly* to dress a wound; he first examines it in order to ascertain its nature; 'Besides those things which *directly* suggest the idea of danger, and those which produce a similar effect from a mechanical cause. I know of nothing sublime which is not some modification of power.'—BURKE. Men of lively minds immediately see the source of their own errours; 'Admiration is a short-lived passion, that *immediately* decays upon growing familiar with the object.'—ADDISON People of delicate feelings are *instantly* alive to the slightest breach of decorum;

> Sleep *instantly* fell upon me.—MILTON.

A course of proceeding is *direct*, the consequences are *immediate*, and the effects *instantaneous;* 'A painter must have an action, not successive, but *instantaneous;* for the time of a picture is a single moment.'—JOHNSON.

SOON, EARLY, BETIMES.

All these words are expressive of time; but *soon* respects some future period in general; *early*, or *ere*, before, and *betimes*, or by the time, before a given time, respect some particular period at no great distance. A person may come *soon* or *early;* in the former case he may not be long in coming from the time that the words are spoken; in the latter case he comes before the time appointed. He who rises *soon* does nothing extraordi nary; but he who rises *early* or *betimes* exceeds the usual hour considerably. *Soon* is said mostly of particular acts, and is always dated from the time of the person speaking, if not otherwise expressed; come *soon* signifies after the present moment;

> But *soon*, too *soon!* the lover turns his eyes;
> Again she falls--again she dies—she dies.—POPE

Early and *betimes*, if not otherwise expressed, have always respect to some specifick time appointed; come *early*, will signify a visit, a meeting, and the like; a thing *betimes* will signify before the thing to be done is wanted: in this manner both are employed for the actions of youth. An *early* attention to religious duties will render them habitual and pleasing; 'Pope, not being sent *early* to school, was taught to read by an aunt.'—JOHNSON. We must begin *betimes* to bring the stubborn will into subjection; 'Happy is the man who *betimes* acquires a relish for holy solitude.'—HORNE.

CURSORY, HASTY, SLIGHT, DESULTORY.

Cursory, from the Latin *curro*, signifies run over or done in running; *hasty* applies to that done in *haste;* *slight* is a variation of light; *desultory*, from *desilio* to leap, signifies leaped over.

Cursory includes both *hasty* and *slight;* it includes *hasty* inasmuch as it expresses a quick motion; it includes *slight* inasmuch as it conveys the idea of a partial action. A view may be either *cursory* or *hasty*, as the former is taken by design, the latter from care lessness. A view may be either *cursory* or *slight;* but the former is not so imperfect as the latter. An author will take a *cursory* view of those points which are not necessarily connected with his subject; 'Savage mingled in *cursory* conversation with the same steadiness of attention as others apply to a lecture.'—JOHNSON. An author who takes a *hasty* view of a subject will mislead by his errours; 'The emperour Macrinus had once resolved to abolish these rescripts (of the emperors), and retain only the general edicts. He could not bear that the *hasty* and crude answers of such princes as Commodus and Caracalla should be reverenced as laws.'—BLACKSTONE. He who takes a *slight* view of a subject will disappoint by the shallowness of his information; 'The wits of Charles's time had seldom more than *slight* and superficial views.'—JOHNSON. Between *cursory* and *desultory* there is the same difference as between running and leaping; we run in a line, but we leap from one part to another; so remarks that are *cursory* have still more or less connexion, but remarks that are *desultory* are without any coherence; 'If compassion ever be felt from the brute instinct of uninstructed nature, it will only produce effects *desultory* and transient.'—JOHNSON.

RASHNESS, TEMERITY, HASTINESS, PRECIPITANCY.

Rashness denotes the quality of being *rash*, which, like the German *rasch*, and our word *rush*, comes from the Latin *ruo*, expressing hurried and excessive motion; *temerity*, in Latin *temeritas*, from *temerè*, possibly comes from the Greek *τήμερον* at the moment, denoting the quality of acting by the impulse of the moment; *hastiness* denotes the quality of being hasty, or impelled by an impatient feeling; *precipitancy*, from the Latin *præ* and *capio*, signifies the quality or disposition of taking things before they ought to be taken.

Rashness and *temerity* have a close alliance with each other in sense; but they have a slight difference, which is entitled to notice: *rashness* is a general and indefinite term, in the signification of which an improper celerity is the leading idea: this celerity may arise either from a vehemence of character, or a temporary ardour of the mind: in the signification of *temerity*, the leading idea is want of consideration, springing mostly from an overweening confidence, or a presumption of character. *Rashness* is, therefore, applied to our corporeal as well as moral actions, as the jumping into a river, without being able to swim, or the leaping over a hedge, without being an expert horseman;

Nature to youth hot *rashness* doth dispense,
But with cold prudence age doth recompense.
DENHAM.

Temerity is applied to our moral actions only, particularly such as require deliberation, and a calculation of consequences; 'All mankind have a sufficient plea for some degree of restlessness, and the fault seems to be little more than too much *temerity* of conclusion in favour of something not experienced.'—JOHNSON. *Hastiness* and *precipitancy* are but modes or characteristicks of *rashness*, and consequently employed only in particular cases, as *hastiness* in regard to our movements, and *precipitancy* in regard to our measures;

And hurry through the woods with *hasty* step,
Rustling and full of hope.—SOMERVILLE.

'As the chymist, by catching at it too soon, lost the philosophical elixir, so *precipitancy* of our understanding is an occasion of errour.'—GLANVILLE.

TO ABIDE, SOJOURN, DWELL, RESIDE, INHABIT.

Abide, in Saxon *abitan*, old German *beiten*, comes from the Arabick or Persian *but*, or *bit*, to pass the night, that is, to make a partial stay; *sojourn*, in French *sejourner*, from *sub* and *diurnus* in the daytime, signifies to pass the day, that is, a certain portion of one's time, in a place; *dwell*, from the Danish *dwelger* to abide, and the Saxon *dwelian*, Dutch *dwalen* to wander, conveys the idea of a moveable habitation, such as was the practice of living formerly in tents. At present it implies a perpetual stay, which is expressed in common discourse by the word live, for passing one's life; *reside*, from the Latin *re* and *sideo* to sit down, conveys the full idea of a settlement; *inhabit*, from the Latin *habito*, a frequentative of *habeo*, signifies to have or occupy for a permanency.

The length of stay implied in these terms is marked by a certain gradation.

Abide denotes the shortest stay; to *sojourn* is of longer continuance; *dwell* comprehends the idea of perpetuity, but *reside* and *inhabit* are partial and local—we *dwell* only in one spot, but we may *reside* at or *inhabit* many places.

These words have likewise a reference to the state of society.

Abide and *sojourn* relate more properly to the wandering habits of men in a primitive state of society. *Dwell*, as implying a stay under a cover, is universal in its application; for we may *dwell* either in a palace, a house, a cottage, or any shelter. *Live*, *reside*, and *inhabit* are confined to a civilized state of society; the former applying to the abodes of the inferiour orders, the latter to those of the higher classes. The word *inhabit* is never used but in connexion with the place *inhabited*.

The Easterns *abode* with each other, *sojourned* in a country, and *dwelt* in tents. The Angels *abode* with Lot one night; 'From the first to the last of man's *abode* on earth, the discipline must never be relaxed of guarding the heart from the dominion of passion.'—BLAIR. Abraham *sojourned* in the land of Canaan; 'By the Israelites' *sojourning* in Egypt, God made way for their bondage there, and their bondage for a glorious deliverance through those prodigious manifestations of the Divine power.'—SOUTH. The Israelites *dwelt* in the land of Goshen;

Hence from my sight! Thy father cannot bear thee;
Fly with thy infamy to some dark cell,
Where on the confines of eternal night,
Mourning, misfortunes, cares, and anguish *dwell*.
MASSINGER.

Savages either *dwell* in the cavities which nature has formed for them, or in some rude structure erected for a temporary purpose; but as men increase in cultivation they build places for themselves which they can *inhabit;* 'By good company, in the place which I have the misfortune to *inhabit*, we understand not always those from whom good can be learned.'—JOHNSON. The poor have their cottages in which they can live; the wealthy provide themselves with superb buildings in which they *reside;* 'Being obliged to remove my *habitation*, I was led by my evil genius to a convenient house in the street where the nobility *reside*.'—JOHNSON.

TO CONTINUE, REMAIN, STAY.

Continue, from the Latin *contineo*, or *con* and *teneo* to hold together, signifies to keep together without intermission; *remain*, in Latin *remaneo*, is compounded of *re* or *retro* and *maneo*, Greek *μένω*, Hebrew עמד to tarry. *Maneo* signifies literally to tarry in a place during the night; whence the Latins called those places *Mansiones*, where travellers passed a night; 'In Mamurrharum urbe manemus.'—HORACE. *Remaneo* signified literally to tarry behind; 'Ii qui per valetudinis causam remanserant;' *stay* is but a variation of the word *stand*.

The idea of confining one's self to something is common to all these terms; but *continue* applies often to the sameness of action, and *remain* to sameness of place or situation; the former has most of the active sense in it, and expresses a state of action; the latter is altogether neuter, and expresses a state of rest. We speak of *continuing* a certain course, of *continuing* to do, or *continuing* to be any thing; but of *remaining* in a position, in a house, in a town, in a condition, and the like; 'Mr. Pryn was sent to a castle in the island of Jersey, Dr. Bastwick to Scilly, and Mr. Burton to Guernsey, where they *remained* unconsidered, and truly I thought unpitied, (for they were men of no virtue or merit) for the space of two years.'—CLARENDON.

There is more of will in *continuing:* more of necessity and circumstances in *remaining*. A person *continues* in office as long as he can perform it with satisfaction to himself, and his employers; 'I have seen some Roman Catholick authors who tell us, that vicious writers *continue* in purgatory so long as the influence of their writings *continues* upon posterity.'—ADDISON. A sentinel *remains* at his post or station. *Continue* is opposed to cease; *remain* is opposed to go. Things *continue* in motion; they *remain* stationary. The females among the brutes will sometimes *continue* to feed their young, long after they are able to provide for themselves; many persons are restored to life after having *remained* several hours in a state of suspended animation.

Remain and *stay* are both perfectly neuter in their sense, but *remain* is employed for either persons or things; *stay* in this sense is used for persons only. It is necessary for some species of wood to *remain* long in the water in order to be seasoned;

I will be true to thee, preserve thee ever,
The sad companion of this faithful breast:
While life and thought *remain*.—ROWE.

Some persons are of so restless a temper, that they cannot *stay* long in a place without giving symptoms of uneasiness;

Where'er I go, my soul shall *stay* with thee;
'T is but my shadow that I take away.—DRYDEN.

When *remain* is employed for persons, it is often involuntary, if not compulsory; *stay* is altogether voluntary. Soldiers must *remain* where they are stationed. Friends *stay* at each other's houses as visiters. Former times afford many instances of servants *continuing* faithful to their employers, even in the season of adversity: but so much are times altered, that at present, domesticks never *remain* long enough in their places to create any bond of attachment between master and servant. Their time of *stay* is now limited to weeks and months, instead of being extended to years.

To *remain* is frequently taken in the sense of being left from other things, to *stay* in that of supporting, in which they are perfectly distinct from each other, and also from *continue*.

TO CONTINUE, PERSEVERE, PERSIST, PURSUE, PROSECUTE.

To *continue* signifies the same as in the preceding article; to *persevere*, in French *persevérer*, Latin *perseverare*, compounded of *per* and *severus* strict and steady, signifies to be steady throughout or to the end; 'Ad ultimum *perseverare*.'—LIVY. *Persist*, in French *persister*, Latin *persisto*, compounded of *per* and *sisto* or *sto*, signifies to stand by or to a thing; 'In proposito *persistere*.'—CICERO. *Pursue* and *prosecute*, in French, *poursuivre*, come from the Latin *sequor* to follow, that is, *prosequor* and its participle *prosecutus*, corresponding with *prosequor*, signifying to follow after or keep on with.

The idea of not laying aside is common to these terms, which is the sense of *continue* without any other addition; the other terms, which are all species of *continuing*, include likewise some collateral idea which distinguishes them from the first, as well as from each other. *Continue* is comparable with *persevere* and *persist* in the neuter sense; with *pursue* and *prosecute* in the active sense. To *continue* is simply to do as one has done hitherto; 'Abdallah *continuing* to extend his former improvements, beautified this whole prospect with groves and fountains.'—ADDISON. To *persevere* is to *continue* without wishing to change, or from a positive desire to attain an object; 'If we *persevere* in studying to do our duty towards God and man, we shall meet with the esteem, love, and confidence of those who are around us.'—BLAIR. To *persist* is to *continue* from a determination or will not to cease. The act of *continuing*, therefore, specifies no characteristick of the agent; that of *persevering* or *persisting* marks a direct temper of mind; the former is always used in a good sense, the latter in an indifferent or bad sense; 'If they *persist* in pointing their batteries to particular persons, no laws of war forbid the making reprisals.'—ADDISON. The Latins have not observed this last distinction between *perseverare* and *persistere*, for they say, 'In errore *perseverare*.'—CICERO. 'In eâdem impudentiâ *persistere*.'—LIVY. And probably in imitation of them, examples are to be found in English authors of *persevere* in a bad sense, and *persist* in a good sense; but modern writers have uniformly observed the distinction. We *continue* from habit or casualty: we *persevere* from reflection and the exercise of one's judgement: we *persist* from attachment. It is not the most exalted virtue to *continue* in a good course, merely because we have been in the habits of so doing; what is done from habit, merely without any fixed principle, is always exposed to change from the influence of passion or evil counsel: there is real virtue in the act of *perseverance*, without which many of our best intentions would remain unfulfilled, and our best plans would be defeated; those who do not *persevere* can do no essential good; and those who do *persevere* often effect what has appeared to be impracticable; of this truth the discoverer of America is a remarkable proof, who in spite of every mortification, rebuff, and disappointment, *persevered* in calling the attention of monarchs to his project, until he at length obtained the assistance requisite for effecting the discovery of a new world.

Persevere is employed only in matters of some moment, in things of sufficient importance to demand a steady purpose of the mind; *persist* is employed in the ordinary business of life, as well as on more important occasions; a learner *perseveres* in his studies, in order to arrive at the necessary degree of improvement; 'Patience and *perseverance* overcome the greatest difficulties.'—RICHARDSON. A child *persists* in making a request, until he has obtained the object of his desire; 'The Arians themselves which were present, subscribed also (to the Nicene creed), not that they meant sincerely and in deed to forsake their errour; but only to escape deprivation and exile, which they saw they could not avoid, openly *persisting* in their former opinions, when the greater part had concluded against them, and that with the emperor's royal assent.'—HOOKER. There is always wisdom in *perseverance*, even though unsuccessful; there is mostly folly, caprice, or obstinacy in *persistance*: how different the man who *perseveres* in the cultivation of his talents, from him who only *persists* in maintaining falsehoods or supporting errours!

Continue, when compared with *persevere* or *persist*, is always coupled with modes of action; but in comparison with *pursue* or *prosecute*, it is always followed by some object: we *continue* to do, *persevere*, or *persist* in doing something: but we *continue*, *pursue*, or *prosecute* some object which we wish to bring to perfection by additional labour.

Continue is here equally indefinite, as in the former case; *pursue* and *prosecute* both comprehend collateral ideas respecting the disposition of the agent, and the nature of the object: to *continue* is to go on with a thing as it has been begun; to *pursue* and *prosecute* is to *continue* by some prescribed rule, or in some particular manner: a work is *continued*; a plan, measure, or line of conduct is *pursued*; an undertaking or a design is *prosecuted*: we may continue the work of another in order to supply a deficiency; we may *pursue* a plan that emanates either from ourselves or another: we *prosecute* our own work only in order to obtain some peculiar object; *continue*, therefore, expresses less than *pursue*, and this less than *prosecute*: the history of England has been *continued* down to the present period by different writers; Smollett has *pursued* the same plan as Hume, in the *continuation* of his history; Captain Cook *prosecuted* his work of discovery in three several voyages.

We *continue* the conversation which has been interrupted; we *pursue* the subject which has engaged our attention; we *pursue* a journey after a certain length of stay; we *prosecute* any particular journey which is important either on account of its difficulties or its object.

To *continue* is in itself altogether an indifferent action; to *pursue* is always a commendable action; to *prosecute* rises still higher in value it is a mark of great instability not to *continue* any thing that we begin; 'After having petitioned for power to resist temptation, there is so great an incongruity in not *continuing* the struggle, that we blush at the thought, and *persevere*, lest we lose all reverence for ourselves.'—HAWKESWORTH. It betrays a great want of prudence and discernment not to *pursue* some plan on every occasion which requires method;

Look round the habitable world, how few
Know their own good, or, knowing it, *pursue*.
DRYDEN.

Will ye not now the pair of sages praise,
Who the same end *pursu'd* by several ways?
DRYDEN.

It is the characteristick of a *persevering* mind to *prosecute* whatever it has deemed worthy to enter upon; 'There will be some study which every man more zealously *prosecutes*, some darling subject on which he is principally pleased to converse.'—JOHNSON.

TO INSIST, PERSIST.

Both these terms, being derived from the Latin *sisto* to stand, express the idea of resting or keeping to a thing; but *insist* signifies to rest on a point, and *persist*, from *per* through or by (*v. To continue*), signifies to keep on with a thing to carry it through. We *insist* on a matter by maintaining it; we *persist* in a thing by continuing to do it; we *insist* by the force of authority or argument; we *persist* by the mere act of the will. A person *insists* on that which he conceives to be his right: or he *insists* on that which he conceives to be right: but he *persists* in that which he has no will to give up. To *insist* is therefore an act of discretion: to *persist* is mostly an act of folly or caprice; the former is always taken in a good or indifferent sense; the latter mostly in a bad sense, at least in colloquial discourse. A parent ought to *insist* on all matters that are of essential importance to his children; 'This natural tendency of despotick power to ignorance and barbarity, though not *insisted* upon by others, is, I think, an inconsiderable argument against that form of government.'—ADDISON. A spoiled child *persists* in its follies from perversity of humour; 'So easy it is for every man living to err, and so hard to wrest from any man's mouth the plain acknowledgment of errour, that what hath been once inconsiderately defended, the same is commonly *persisted* in as long as wit, by whetting itself, is able to find out any shift, be it never so slight, whereby to escape out of the hands of present contradiction.'—HOOKER.

TENACIOUS, PERTINACIOUS.

To be *tenacious* is to hold a thing close, to let it go with reluctance; to be *pertinacious* is to hold it out in spite of what can be advanced against it, the prepositive syllable *per* having an intensive force. A man of *tenacious* temper insists on trifles that are supposed to affect his importance; a *pertinacious* temper insists on every thing which is apt to affect his opinions. *Tenacity* and *pertinacity* are both foibles, but the former is sometimes more excusable than the latter.

We may be *tenacious* of that which is good, as when a man is *tenacious* of whatever may affect his honour; 'So *tenacious* are we of the old ecclesiastical modes, that very little alteration has been made in them since the fourteenth or fifteenth century; adhering to our old settled maxim, never entirely, nor at once, to depart from antiquity.'—BURKE. We cannot be *pertinacious* in any thing but our opinions, and that too in cases where they are least defensible: 'The most *pertinacious* and vehement demonstrator may be wearied in time by continual negation.'—JOHNSON. It commonly happens that people are most *tenacious* of being thought to possess that in which they are most deficient, and most *pertinacious* in maintaining that which is absurd. A liar is *tenacious* of his reputation for truth; 'Men are *tenacious* of the opinions that first possess them.'—LOCKE. Sophists, freethinkers, and skepticks, are the most *pertinacious* objectors to whatever is established; 'One of the dissenters appeared to Dr. Sanderson to be so bold, so troublesome, and illogical in the dispute, as forced him to say, that he had never met with a man of more *pertinacious* confidence and less abilities.'—WALTON.

CONTINUAL, PERPETUAL, CONSTANT.

Continual, in French *continuel*, Latin *continuus*, from *contineo* to hold or keep together, signifies keeping together without intermission; *perpetual*, in French *perpétuel*, Latin *perpetualis*, from *perpeto*, compounded of *per* and *peto* to seek thoroughly, signifies going on every where and at all times; *constant*, in Latin *constans*, or *con* and *sto*, signifies the quality of standing to a thing, or standing close together.

What is *continual* admits of no interruption: what is *perpetual* admits of no termination. There may be an end to that which is *continual* and there may be intervals in that which is *perpetual*. Rains are *continual* in the tropical climates at certain seasons; complaints among the lower orders are *perpetual*, but they are frequently without foundation. There is a *continual* passing and repassing in the streets of the metropolis during the day;

Open your ears, for which of you will stop
The vent of hearing when loud rumour speaks·
Upon my tongue *continual* slanders ride,
The which in every language I pronounce.
SHAKSPEARE.

The world, and all that it contains, are subject to *perpetual* change; 'If affluence of fortune unhappily concur to favour the inclinations of the youthful, amusements and diversions succeed in a *perpetual* round.'—BLAIR.

The *continual* is that which admits of no interruption, the *constant* is that which admits of no change. The last twenty-five years have presented to the world a *continual* succession of events, that have exceeded in importance those going before; the French revolution and the atrocities attendant upon it have been the *constant* theme of execration with the well-disposed part of mankind. To an intelligent parent it is a *continual* source of pleasure to watch the progress of his child in the acquirement of knowledge, and the development of his faculties;

'Tis all blank sadness, or *continual* tears.—POPE.

It will be the *constant* endeavour of a parent to train him up in principles of religion and virtue, while he is cultivating his talents, and storing his mind with science;

The world's a scene of changes, and to be
Constant in nature were inconstancy.—COWLEY.

Continual is used in the proper sense only, *constant* is employed in the moral sense o denote the temper of the mind (*v. Constancy*).

CONTINUAL, CONTINUED.

Both these terms mark length of duration, but the former admits of a certain degree of interruption, which the latter does not. What is *continual* may have frequent pauses; what is *continued* ceases only to terminate. Rains are *continual*; noises in a tumultuous street are *continual*: the bass in musick is said to be *continued*; the mirth of a drunken party is one *continued* noise. *Continual* interruptions abate the vigour of application and create disgust: *in countries situated near the poles, there is one *continued* darkness for the space of five or six months; during which time the inhabitants are obliged to leave the place.

Continual respects the duration of actions or circumstances only; *continued* is likewise applied to the extent or course of things: rumours are *continual*; talking, walking, running, and the like, are *continual*;

And gulphy Simoïs rolling to the main,
Helmets and shields and godlike heroes slain:
These turn'd by Phœbus from their wonted ways,
Delug'd the rampire nine *continual* days.—POPE.

A line, a series, a scene, or a stream of water, &c. is *continued*:

Our life is one *continued* toil for fame.'—MARTYN.

'By too intense and *continued* application, our feeble powers would soon be worn out.'—BLAIR.

CONTINUANCE, CONTINUATION, DURATION.

Continuance is said of the time that a thing *continues* (*v. To continue*); *continuation* expresses the act of *continuing* what has been begun. The *continuance* of any particular practice may be attended with serious consequence; 'Their duty depending upon fear, the one was of no greater *continuance* than the other.'—HAYWARD. The *continuation* of a work depends on the abilities and will of the workmen, 'The Roman poem is but the second part of the Ilias, the *continuation* of the same story.'—RAY. Authors

* Vide Trussler: "Continual, continued."

have however not always observed this distinction; Providence seems to have equally divided the whole mass of mankind into different sexes, that every woman may have her husband, and that both may equally contribute to the *continuance* of the species.'—STEELE. 'The Pythagorean transmigration, the sensual habitations of the Mahometan, and the shady realms of Pluto, do all agree in the main point, the *continuation* of our existence.'—BERKELEY.

Continuance and *duration*, in Latin *duratio*, from *duro* to harden, or figuratively to last, are both employed for time; things may be of long *continuance*, or of long *duration:* but *continuance* is used only with regard to the action; *duration* with regard to the thing and its existence. Whatever is occasionally done, and soon to be ended, is not for a *continuance;* whatever is made, and soon destroyed, is not of long *duration;* there are many excellent institutions in England which promise to be of no less *continuance* than of utility; 'That pleasure is not of greater *continuance*, which arises from the prejudice or malice of its hearers.'—ADDISON. *Duration* is with us a relative term; things are of long or short *duration:* by comparison, the *duration* of the world and all sublunary objects is nothing in regard to eternity; 'Mr. Locke observes, "that we get the idea of time and *duration*, by reflecting on that train of ideas which succeed one another in our minds."'—ADDISON.

CONTINUATION, CONTINUITY.

Continuation, as may be seen above (*v. Continuance*), is the act of *continuing; continuity* is the quality of *continuing:* the former is employed in the figurative sense for the duration of events and actions; the latter in the physical sense for the adhesion of the component parts of the bodies. The *continuation* of a history up to the existing period of the writer is the work of every age, if not of every year; 'The sun ascending into the northern signs begetteth first a temperate heat, which by his approach unto the solstice he intendeth; and by *continuation* the same even upon declination.'—BROWN (*Vulgar Errours*). There are bodies of so little *continuity* that they will crumble to pieces on the slightest touch; 'A body always perceives the passages by which it insinuates; feels the impulse of another body where it yields thereto: perceives the separation of its *continuity*, and for a time resists it; in fine, perception is diffused through all nature.'—BACON.

The sprightly breast demands
Incessant rapture; life, a tedious load,
Deny'd its *continuity* of joy.—SHENSTONE.

DURABLE, LASTING, PERMANENT.

Durable is said of things that are intended to remain a shorter time than those which are *lasting;* and *permanent* expresses less than *durable; durable*, from the Latin *durus* hard, respects the textures of bodies, and marks the capacity to hold out; *lasting*, from the verb to *last*, or the adjective *last*, signifies to remain the *last* or longest, and is applicable only to that which is supposed of the longest *duration*. *Permanent*, from the Latin *permaneo*, signifies remaining to the end.

Durable is naturally said of material substances; and *lasting* of those which are spiritual; although in ordinary discourse sometimes they exchange offices: *permanent* applies more to the affairs of men.

That which perishes quickly is not *durable:* that which ceases quickly is not *lasting;* that which is only for a time is not *permanent*. Stone is more *durable* than iron, and iron than wood: in the feudal times animosities between families used to be *lasting:* a clerk has not a *permanent* situation in an office. However we may boast of our progress in the arts, we appear to have lost the art of making things as *durable* as they were made in former times; 'If writings be thus *durable*, and may pass from age to age, through the whole course of time, how careful should an author be of not committing any thing to print that may corrupt posterity.'—ADDISON. The writings of the moderns will many of them be as *lasting* monuments of human genius as those of the ancients; 'I must desire my fair readers to give a proper direction to their being admired; in order to which they must endeavour to make themselves the objects of a reasonable and *lasting* admiration.'—ADDISON. One who is of a contented, moderate disposition will generally prefer a *permanent* situation with small gains to one that is very lucrative but temporary and precarious; 'Land comprehends all things in law of a *permanent*, substantial nature.'—BLACKSTONE.

DURABLE, CONSTANT.

Durability is the property of things; *constancy* (*v. Constancy*) is the property of either persons or things. The *durable* is that which lasts long. The *constant* is that which continues without interruption. No *durable* connexions can be formed which are founded on vicious principles; 'Some states have suddenly emerged, and even in the depths of their calamity have laid the foundation of a towering and *durable* greatness.'—BURKE. Some persons are never happy but in a *constant* round of pleasures; 'Since we cannot promise ourselves *constant* health, let us endeavour at such a temper, as may be our best support in the decay of it.'—STEELE. What is *durable* is so from its inherent property, but what is *constant*, in regard to persons or things, arises from the temper of the mind; 'He showed his firm adherence to religion as modelled by our national constitution, and was *constant* to its offices in devotion, both in publick and in his family.'—ADDISON.

DURATION, TIME.

In the philosophical sense, according to Mr. Locke, *time* is that mode of *duration* which is formed in the mind by its own power of observing and measuring passing objects.

In the vulgar sense in which *duration* is synonymous with time, it stands for the time of *duration*, and is more particularly applicable to the objects which are said to last; *time* being employed in general for whatever passes in the world.

Duration comprehends the beginning and end of any portion of *time*, that is the how long of a thing; *time* is employed more frequently for the particular portion itself, namely, the *time* when: we mark the *duration* of a sound from the *time* of its commencement to the *time* that it ceases: the *duration* of a prince's reign is an object of particular concern to his subjects if he be either very good or the reverse; the *time* in which he reigns is marked by extraordinary events. An historian computes the *duration* of reigns and of events in order to determine the antiquity of a nation; 'I think another probable conjecture (respecting the soul's immortality) may be raised from our appetite to *duration* itself.'—STEELE. An historian fixes the exact *time* when each person begins to reign and when he dies, in order to determine the number of years that each reigned; 'The *time* of the fool is long because he does not know what to do with it; that of the wise man, because he distinguishes every moment of it with useful or amusing thoughts.'—ADDISON.

TIME, SEASON, TIMELY, SEASONABLE.

Time is here the generick term; it is taken either for the whole or the part: *season* is any given portion of *time*. We speak of *time* when the simple idea of *time* only is to be expressed, as the *time* of the day, or the *time* of the year; the *season* is spoken in reference to some circumstances; the year is divided into four parts, called the *seasons*, according to the nature of the weather: hence, in general, that *time* is called the *season* which is suitable for any particular purpose, youth is the *season* for improvement. It is a matter of necessity to choose the *time;* it is an affair of wisdom to choose the *season;* 'You will often want religion in *times* of most danger.'—CHATHAM. 'Piso's behaviour towards us in this *season* of affliction has endeared him to us.'—MELMOTH (*Letters of Cicero*).

The same distinction exists between the epithets *timely* and *seasonable* as their primitives. The former signifies within the time, that is, before the time is past; the latter according to the season or what the season requires. A *timely* notice prevents that which would otherwise happen; 'It imports all men, especially bad men, to think on the judgement, that by a *timely* repentance they may prevent the woful effects of it'—SOUTH. A *seasonable* hint seldom fails of its effect because it is *seasonable;* What you call a bold, is not only the kindest, but the most *seasonable* proposal you could have made.'—LOCKE. We must not expect to have a *timely* notice of death, but must be prepared to die at any time; an admonition to one who is on a sick-bed is very *seasonable*, when given by a minister of religion or a friend. The opposites of these terms are *untimely* or *ill-timed* and *unseasonable: untimely* is directly opposed to *timely*, signifying before the time appointed; as an *untimely* death; but *ill-timed* is indirectly opposed, signifying in the wrong *time;* as an *ill-timed* remark.

TIME, PERIOD, AGE, DATE, ÆRA, EPOCHA.

Time (*v. Time*) is, as before, taken either from *time* in general, or *time* in particular; all the other terms are taken for particular portions of *time*. *Time*, in the sense of a particular portion of *time*, is used indefinitely, and in cases where the other terms are not so proper; 'There is a *time* when we should not only number our days, but our hours.'—YOUNG.

Time included within any given points is termed a *period*, from the Greek περίοδος, signifying a course, round, or any revolution: thus, the *period* of day, or of night, is the space of *time* comprehended between the rising and setting, or setting and rising of the sun; the *period* of a year comprehends the space which the earth requires for its annual revolution. So, in an extended and moral application, we have stated *periods* in our life for particular things: during the *period* of infancy a child is in a state of total dependence on its parents; a *period* of apprenticeship has been appointed for youth to learn different trades; 'Some experiment would be made how by art to make plants more lasting than their ordinary *period;* as to make a stalk of wheat last a whole year.'—BACON. This term is employed not only to denote the whole intervening space of *time*, but also the particular concluding point, which makes it equivalent in sense to the termination of the existence of any body, as to put a *period* to one's existence, for to kill one's self, or be killed;

> But the last *period*, and the fatal hour,
> Of Troy is come.—DENHAM.

The *age* is a species of *period* comprehending the life of a man, and consequently referring to what is done by men living within that *period:* hence we speak of the different *ages* that have existed since the commencement of the world, and characterize this or that *age* by the particular degrees of vice or virtue, genius, and the like, for which it is distinguished; 'The story of Haman only shows us what human nature has too generally appeared to be in every *age*.'—BLAIR.

The *date* is that *period* of *time* which is reckoned from the *date* or commencement of a thing to the *time* that it is spoken of: hence we speak of a thing as being of a long or a short *date*, that is, of being of long or short duration; 'Plantations have one advantage in them which is not to be found in most other works, as they give a pleasure of a more lasting *date*.'—ADDISON.

Æra, in Latin *æra*, probably from *æs* brass, signifying coin with which one computes; and *epocha*, from the Greek ἐποχὴ, from ἐπέχω to stop, signifying a resting place; both refer to points of *time* rendered remarkable by events: but the term *æra* is more commonly employed in the literal sense for points of computation in chronology, as the Christian *æra;* 'That *period* of the Athenian history which is included within the *æra* of Pisistratus, and the death of Menander the comic poet, may justly be styled the literary *age* of Greece.'—CUMBERLAND. The term *epocha* is indefinitely employed for any *period* distinguished by remarkable events: the grand rebellion is an *epocha* in the history of England; 'The institution of this library (by Pisistratus) forms a signal *epocha* in the annals of literature.'—CUMBERLAND.

TIMESERVING, TEMPORIZING.

Timeserving and *temporizing* are both applied to the conduct of one who adapts himself servilely to the time and season; but a *timeserver* is rather active, and a *temporizer* passive. A *timeserver* avows those opinions which will serve his purpose: the *temporizer* forbears to avow those which are likely for the time being to hurt him. The former acts from a desire of gain, the latter from a fear of loss. *Timeservers* are of all parties, as they come in the way; 'Ward had complied during the late times, and held in by taking the covenant: so he was hated by the high men as a *timeserver*.'—BURNETT. *Temporizers* are of no party, as occasion requires; 'Feeble and *temporizing* measures will always be the result, when men assemble to deliberate in a situation where they ought to act.'—ROBERTSON. Sycophant courtiers must always be *timeservers:* ministers of state are frequently *temporizers*.

INSTANT, MOMENT.

Instant, from *sto* to stand, signifies the point of time that stands over us, or as it were over our heads; *moment*, from the Latin *momentum*, is any small particle, particularly a small particle of time.

The *instant* is always taken for the time present; the *moment* is taken generally for either past, present, or future. A dutiful child comes the *instant* he is called; a prudent person embraces the favourable *moment*. When they are both taken for the present time, the *instant* expresses a much shorter space than the *moment;* when we desire a person to do a thing this *instant*, it requires haste; if we desire him to do it this *moment*, it only admits of no delay. *Instantaneous* relief is necessary on some occasions to preserve life; 'Some circumstances of misery are so powerfully ridiculous, that neither kindness nor duty can withstand them; they force the friend, the dependant, or the child, to give way to *instantaneous* motions of merriment.'—JOHNSON. A *moment's* thought will furnish a ready wit with a suitable reply; 'I can easily overlook any present *momentary* sorrow, when I reflect that it is in my power to be happy a thousand years hence.'—BERKELEY.

TEMPORARY, TRANSIENT, TRANSITORY FLEETING.

Temporary, from *tempus* time, characterizes that which is intended to last only for a time, in distinction from that which is permanent; offices depending upon a state of war are *temporary*, in distinction from those which are connected with internal policy; 'By the force of superiour principles the *temporary* prevalence of passions may be restrained.'—JOHNSON. *Transient*, that is, passing, or in the act of passing, characterizes what in its nature exists only for the moment; a glance is *transient;* 'Any sudden diversion of the spirits, or the justling in of a *transient* thought, is able to deface the little images of things (in the memory).'—SOUTH. *Transitory*, that is, apt to pass away, characterizes every thing in the world which is formed only to exist for a time, and then to pass away; thus our pleasures, and our pains, and our very being, are denominated *transitory;* 'Man is a *transitory* being.'—JOHNSON. *Fleeting*, which is derived from the verb to *fly* and *flight*, is but a stronger term to express the same idea as *transitory;*

> Thus when my *fleeting* days at last,
> Unheeded, silently are past,
> Calmly I shall resign my breath,
> In life unknown, forgot in death.—SPECTATOR

COEVAL, COTEMPORARY.

Coeval, from the Latin *ævum* an age, signifies of the same age; *cotemporary*, from *tempus*, signifies of the same time.

An age is a specifically long space of time; a time is indefinite; hence the application of the terms to things in the first case, and to persons in the second: the dispersion of mankind and the confusion of languages were *coeval* with the building of the tower of Babel; 'The passion of fear seems *coeval* with our nature.'—CUMBERLAND. Addison was *cotemporary* with Swift and Pope; 'If the elder Orpheus was the disciple of Linus, he must have been of too early an age to have been *cotemporary* with Hercules: for Orpheus is placed eleven ages before the siege of Troy.'—CUMBERLAND.

DAILY, DIURNAL.

Daily, from *day* and *like*, signifies after the manner or in the time of the *day; diurnal*, from *dies* day, signifies belonging to the *day*.

Daily is the colloquial term, which is applicable to whatever passes in the *day* time; *diurnal* is the scientifick term, which applies to what passes within or belongs to the astronomical *day:* the physician makes *daily* visits to his patients;

All creatures else forget their *daily* care,
And sleep, the common gift of nature, share.
DRYDEN.

The earth has a *diurnal* motion on its own axis;

Half yet remains unsung, but narrow bound
Within the visible *diurnal* sphere.—MILTON.

NIGHTLY, NOCTURNAL.

Nightly, immediately from the word *night*, and *nocturnal*, from *nox* night, signify belonging to the night, or the night season; the former is therefore more familiar than the latter: we speak of *nightly* depredations to express what passes every night, or *nightly* disturbances, *nocturnal* dreams, *nocturnal* visits;

Yet not alone, while thou
Visit'st my slumbers *nightly*, or when morn
Purples the east.—MILTON.

Or save the sun his labour, and that swift
Nocturnal and diurnal rhomb suppos'd
Invisible else above all stars, the wheel
Of day and night.—MILTON.

OFTEN, FREQUENTLY.

Often, or in its contracted form *oft*, comes in all probability through the medium of the northern languages, from the Greek ἄψ again, and signifies properly repetition of action; *frequently*, from *frequent* crowded or numerous, respects a plurality or number of objects.

An ignorant man *often* uses a word without knowing what it means; ignorant people *frequently* mistake the meaning of the words they hear. A person goes out very *often* in the course of a week; he has *frequently* six or seven persons to visit him in the course of that time. * By doing a thing *often* it becomes habitual; we *frequently* meet the same persons in the route which we *often* take;

Often from the careless back
Of herds and flocks a thousand tugging bills
Pluck hair and wool.—THOMSON.

Here *frequent* at the visionary hour,
When musing midnight reigns or silent noon,
Angelick harps are in full concert heard.
THOMSON.

OLD, ANCIENT, ANTIQUE, ANTIQUATED, OLD-FASHIONED, OBSOLETE.

Old, in German *alt*, Low German *old*, &c., comes from the Greek ἕωλος of yesterday; *ancient*, in French *ancien*, and *antique*, *antiquated*, all come from the Latin *antiquus*, and *antea* before, signifying in general before our time; *old-fashioned* signifies after an *old fashion; obsolete*, in Latin *obsoletus*, participle of *obsoleo*, signifies literally out of use.

Old respects what has long existed and still exists; *ancient* what existed at a distant period, but does not necessarily exist at present; *antique*, that which has been long *ancient*, and of which there remain but faint traces: *antiquated*, *old-fashioned*, and *obsolete* that which has ceased to be any longer used or esteemed. A *fashion* is *old* when it has been long in use; 'The Venetians are tenacious of *old* laws and customs to their great prejudice.'—ADDISON. A custom is *ancient* when its use has long been passed;

But sev'n wise men the *ancient* world did know,
We scarce know sev'n who think themselves not so.
DENHAM.

A bust or statue is *antique* which is the work of the ancients, or made after the manner of the ancient works of art;

Under an oak, whose *antique* root peeps out
Under the brook that brawls along this wood,
A poor sequester'd stag,
That from the hunters' aim had ta'en a hurt,
Did come to languish.—SHAKSPEARE.

A person is *antiquated* whose appearance is grown out of date; 'Whoever thinks it necessary to regulate his conversation by *antiquated* rules, will be rather despised for his futility than caressed for his politeness. —JOHNSON. Manners which are gone quite out of *fashion* are *old-fashioned;* 'The swords in the arsenal of Venice are *old-fashioned* and unwieldy.'—ADDISON. A word or custom is *obsolete* which is grown out of use; '*Obsolete* words may be laudably revived, when they are more sounding or more significant than those in practice.'—DRYDEN.

The *old* is opposed to the new: some things are the worse for being *old;* other things are the better *Ancient* and *antique* are opposed to modern: all things are valued the more for being *ancient* or *antique;* hence we esteem the writings of the *ancients* above those of the moderns. The *antiquated* is opposed to the customary and established; it is that which we cannot like, because we cannot esteem it: the *old-fashioned* is opposed to the fashionable: there is much in the *old-fashioned* to like and esteem; there is much that is ridiculous in the fashionable: the *obsolete* is opposed to the current; the *obsolete* may be good; the current may be vulgar and mean.

FRESH, NEW, NOVEL, RECENT, MODERN.

Adelung supposes the German word *frisch* to be derived from *frieren* to freeze, as the idea of coolness is prevalent in its application to the air; it is therefore figuratively applied to that which is in its first pure and best state; *new*, in German *neu*, comes from the Latin *novus*, and the Greek *νεος*; *recent*, in Latin *recens*, is supposed to come from *re* and *candeo* to whiten or give a fair colour to, because what is *new* looks so much fairer than what is old.

The *fresh* is properly opposed to the stale, as the *new* is to the old: the *fresh* has undergone no change; the *new* has not been long in being. Meat, beer, and provisions in general, are said to be *fresh;* so likewise a person is said to be *fresh* who is in his full vigour;

Lo! great Æneas rushes to the fight,
Sprung from a god, and more than mortal bold;
He *fresh* in youth, and I in arms grown old.
POPE.

That which is substantial and durable, as houses, clothes, books, or, in the moral sense, pleasures, &c. are said to be *new;*

Seasons but change *new* pleasures to produce,
And elements contend to serve our use.—JENYNS.

Novel is to *new* as the species to the genus: every thing *novel* is *new;* but all that is *new* is not *novel:* what is *novel* is mostly strange and unexpected; but what is *new* is usual and expected: the freezing of the river Thames is a *novelty;* the frost in every winter is something *new* when it first comes: that is a *novel* sight which was either never seen before, or seen but seldom; that is a *new* sight which is seen for the first time: the entrance of the French king into the British capital was a sight as *novel* as it was interesting; 'We are naturally delighted with *novelty*.'—JOHNSON. The entrance of a king into the capital of France was a *new* sight, after the revolution which had so long existed;

'T is on some evening, sunny, grateful, mild,
When nought but balm is beaming through the woods,
With yellow lustre bright, that the *new* tribes
Visit the spacious heav'ns.—THOMSON.

Recent is taken only in the improper application; the other two admit of both applications in this case: the *fresh* is said in relation to what has lately preceded; *new* is said in relation to what has not long subsisted; *recent* is used for what has just passed in distinction from that which has long gone by. A person is said to give *fresh* cause of offence who has already offended;

That love which first was set, will first decay,
Mine of a *fresher* date will longer stay.—DRYDEN

* Vide Trusler: "Often, frequently."

A thing receives a *new* name in lieu of the one which it has long had; 'Do not all men complain how little we know, and how much is still unknown? And can we ever know more, unless something *new* be discovered?'—BURNET. A *recent* transaction excites an interest which cannot be excited by one of earlier date; 'The courage of the Parliament was increased by two *recent* events which had happened in their favour.'—HUME. *Fresh* intelligence arrives every day; it quickly succeeds the events: that intelligence which is *recent* to a person at a distance is already old to one who is on the spot. *Fresh* circumstances continually arise to confirm reports; *new* changes continually take place to supersede the things that were established.

New is said of every thing which has not before existed, or not in the same form as before; *modern*, from the low Latin *modernus*, changed as is supposed from *hodiernus* belonging to the day, is said of that which is *new* or springs up in the present day or age. A book is *new* which has never been used; it is *modern* if it has never been published before; so in like manner principles are *new* which have not been broached before; but they are *modern* inasmuch as they are first offered in the day in which we live; 'Some of the ancient and likewise divers of the *modern* writers, that have laboured in natural magick, have noted a sympathy between the sun and certain herbs.'—BACON.

TO REVIVE, REFRESH, RENOVATE, RENEW.

Revive, from the Latin *vivo* to live, signifies to bring to life again; to *refresh*, to make fresh again; to *renew* and *renovate*, to make new again. The restoration of things to their primitive state is the common idea included in these terms; the difference consists in their application. *Revive*, *refresh*, and *renovate* are applied to animal bodies; *revive* expressing the return of motion and spirits to one who was for the time lifeless; *refresh* expressing the return of vigour to one in whom it has been diminished; the air *revives* one who is faint; a cool breeze *refreshes* one who flags from the heat. *Revive* and *refresh* respect only the temporary state of the body; *renovate* respects its permanent state, that is, the health of the body; one is *revived* and *refreshed* after a partial exhaustion; one's health is *renovated* after having been considerably impaired.

Revive is applied likewise in the moral sense; 'Herod's rage being quenched by the blood of Mariamne, his love to her again *revived*.'—PRIDEAUX. *Refresh* and *renovate* mostly in the proper sense;

> Nor less thy world, Columbus! drinks, *refresh'd*,
> The lavish moisture of the melting year.
> THOMSON.

> All nature feels the *renovating* force
> Of winter.—THOMSON.

Renew only in the moral sense;

> The last great age, foretold by sacred rhymes,
> *Renews* its finished course.—THOMSON.

A discussion is said to be *revived*, or a report to be *revived*; a clamour is said to be *renewed*, or entreaties to be *renewed*: customs are *revived* which have lain long dormant, and as it were dead; practices are *renewed* that have ceased for a time.

FOREFATHERS, PROGENITORS, ANCESTORS.

Forefathers signifies our *fathers before* us, and includes our immediate parents; *progenitors*, from *pro* and *gigno*, signifies those begotten before us, exclusive of our immediate parents; *ancestors*, contracted from *antecessors* or those going before, is said of those from whom we are remotely descended.

Forefathers is a partial and familiar term for the preceding branches of any family; 'We passed slightly over three or four of our immediate *forefathers* whom we knew by tradition.'—ADDISON. *Progenitors* is a higher term in the same sense, applied to families of distinction: we speak of the *forefathers* of a peasant, but the *progenitors* of a nobleman;

> Each in his narrow cell for ever laid,
> The rude *forefathers* of the hamlet sleep.—GRAY.

Suppose a gentleman, full of his illustrious family, should see the whole line of his *progenitors* pass in review before him; with how many varying passions would he behold shepherds, soldiers, princes, and beggars, walk in the procession of five thousand years?' —ADDISON. *Forefathers* and *progenitors*, but particularly the latter, are said mostly of individuals, and respect the regular line of succession in a family; *ancestors* is employed collectively as well as individually and regards simply the order of succession: we may speak of the *ancestors* of a nation as well as of any particular person; 'It is highly laudable to pay respect to men who are descended from worthy *ancestors*.'—ADDISON. This term may also be applied figuratively;

> O majestick night!
> Nature's great *ancestor*!—YOUNG.

SENIOR, ELDER, OLDER.

These are all comparatives expressive of the same quality, and differ therefore less in sense than in application.

Senior is employed not only in regard to the extent of age, but also to duration either in office or any given situation; *elder* is employed only in regard to age: an officer in the army is a *senior* by virtue of having served longer than another; a boy is a *senior* in a school either by virtue of his age, his standing in the school, or his situation in the class; 'Cratinus was *senior* in age to both his competitors Eupolis and Aristophanes.'—CUMBERLAND. When age alone is to be expressed, *elder* is more suitable than *senior*; the *elder* children or the *elder* branches of a family are clearly understood to include those who have priority of age.

Senior and *elder* are both employed as substantives; *older* only as an adjective: hence we speak of the *seniors* in a school, or the *elders* in an assembly; but an *older* inhabitant, an *older* family;

> The Spartans to their highest magistrate
> The name of *elder* did appropriate.—DENHAM.

> Since oft
> Man must compute that age he cannot feel,
> He scarce believes he's *older* for his years.—YOUNG.

Elder has only a partial use; *older* is employed in general cases: in speaking of children in the same family we may say, the *elder* son is heir to the estate; he is *older* than his brother by ten years.

ELDERLY, AGED, OLD.

These three words rise by gradation in their sense, *aged* denotes a greater degree of *age* than *elderly*; and *old* still more than either.

The *elderly* man has passed the meridian of life; 'I have a race of orderly, *elderly*, persons of both sexes, at my command.'—SWIFT. The *aged* man is fast approaching the term of human existence;

> A godlike race of heroes once I knew,
> Such as no more these *aged* eyes shall view.—POPE.

The *old* man has already reached this term, or has exceeded it;

> The field of combat fills the young and bold,
> The solemn council best becomes the *old*.—POPE.

In conformity, however, to the vulgar prepossession against *age* and its concomitant infirmities, the term *elderly* or *aged* is always more respectful than *old*, which latter word is often used by way of reproach, and can seldom be used free from such an association, unless qualified by an epithet of praise as good or venerable.

FORMERLY, IN TIMES PAST, OR OLD TIMES, DAYS OF YORE, ANCIENTLY, OR ANCIENT TIMES.

Formerly supposes a less remote period than *in times past*; and that less remote than *in days of yore* and *anciently*. The first two may be said of what happens within the age of man; the last two are extended to many generations and ages. Any individual may use the word *formerly* with regard to himself: thus we enjoyed our health better *formerly* than now; 'Men were *formerly* disputed out of their doubts.'—ADDISON. An old man may speak of *times past*, as when he says he does not enjoy himself as he did *in times past* *Old times*, *days of yore*, and *anciently*, are more applicable to nations than to individuals; and all these express different degrees of *remoteness*. As to our present period, the age of Queen Elizabeth may be called *old times*:

> In *times of old*, when time was young,
> And poets their own verses sung,
> A verse could draw a stone or beam.—SWIFT.

The days of Alfred, and still later, the *days of yore*;

> Thus Edgar proud in *days of yore*,
> Held monarchs labouring at the oar.—SWIFT.

The earliest period in which Britain is mentioned may be called *ancient times*;

> In *ancient* times the sacred plough employ'd
> The kings and awful fathers of mankind.
> THOMSON.

GENERATION, AGE.

Generation is said of the persons who live during any particular period; and *age* is said of the period itself. Those who are born at the same time constitute the *generation*; that period of time which comprehends the age of man is the *age*: there may therefore be many *generations* spring up in the course of an *age*: a fresh *generation* is springing up every day, which in the course of an *age* pass away, and are succeeded by fresh *generations*.

We consider man in his *generation* as the part which he has to perform; 'I often lamented that I was not one of that happy *generation* who demolished the convents.'—JOHNSON. We consider the *age* in which we live as to the manners of men and the events of nations; 'Throughout every *age*, God hath pointed his peculiar displeasure against the confidence of presumption, and the arrogance of prosperity.'—BLAIR.

LAST, LATEST, FINAL, ULTIMATE.

Last and *latest*, both from *late*, in German *letze*, come from the Greek λδισθος and λειπω to leave, signifying left or remaining; *final*, (*v. Final*); *ultimate* comes from *ultimus* the last.

Last and *ultimate* respect the order of succession: *latest* respects the order of time; *final* respects the completion of an object. What is *last* or *ultimate* is succeeded by nothing else: what is *latest* is not succeeded by any great interval of time; what is *final* requires to be succeeded by nothing else. The *last* is opposed to the first; the *ultimate* is distinguished from that which might follow; the *latest* is opposed to the earliest; the *final* is opposed to the introductory or beginning. A person's last words are those by which one is guided; 'The supreme Author of our being has so formed the soul of man that nothing but himself can be its *last*, adequate, and proper happiness.'—ADDISON. A man's *ultimate* object is distinguished from that more remote one which may possibly be in his mind: 'The *ultimate* end of man is the enjoyment of God, beyond which he cannot form a wish.'—GROVE. A conscientious man remains firm to his principles to his *latest* breath; a pleasant comedy which paints the manners of the age is a durable work, and is transmitted to the *latest* posterity.'—HUME. The *final* determination of difficult matters requires caution; '*Final* causes lie more bare and open to our observation, as there are often a greater variety that belong to the same effect.'—ADDISON. Jealous people strive not to be the *last* in any thing; the *latest* intelligence which a man gets of his country is acceptable to one who is in distant quarters of the globe; it requires resolution to take a *final* leave of those whom one holds near and dear.

LASTLY, AT LAST, AT LENGTH.

Lastly, like *last* (*v. Last*), respects the order of succession: *at last* or *at length* refer to what has preceded. When a sermon is divided into many heads, the term *lastly* comprehends the *last* division. When an affair is settled after much difficulty it is said to be *at last* settled; and if it be settled after a protracted continuance, it is said to be settled *at length*; '*Lastly*, opportunities do sometimes offer in which a man may wickedly make his fortune without fear of temporal damage. In such cases what restraint do they lie under who have no regard beyond the grave?'—BLAIR. '*At last* being satisfied they had nothing to fear they brought out all their corn every day.'—ADDISON. 'A neighbouring king made war upon this female republick several years with various success, and *at length* over threw them in a very great battle.'—ADDISON.

ETERNAL, ENDLESS, EVERLASTING.

The *eternal* is set above time, the endless lies within time, it is therefore by a strong figure that we apply *eternal* to any thing sublunary; although *endless* may with propriety be applied to that which is heavenly. That is properly *eternal* which has neither beginning nor end; that is *endless* which has a beginning, but no end. God is, therefore, an *eternal*, but not an *endless* being;

> Distance immense between the pow'rs that shine
> Above, *eternal*, deathless, and divine,
> And mortal man!—POPE.

There is an *eternal* state of happiness or misery, which awaits all men, according to their deeds in this life; the joys or sorrows of men may be said to be *endless* as regards this life;

> The faithful Mydon, as he turn'd from fight
> His flying coursers, sunk to *endless* night.—POPE.

That which is *endless* has no cessation; that which is *everlasting* has neither interruption or cessation. The *endless* may be said of existing things; the *everlasting* naturally extends itself into futurity: hence we speak of *endless* disputes, an *endless* warfare, an *everlasting* memorial, an *everlasting* crown of glory;

> Back from the car he tumbles to the ground,
> And *everlasting* shades his eyes surround.—POPE

REST, REMAINDER, REMNANT, RESCUE.

Rest evidently comes from the Latin *resto*, which is compounded of *re* and *sto*, signifying to stand or remain back; *remainder* literally signifies what remains after the first part is gone; *remnant* is but a variation of *remainder*; and *residue*, from *resideo*, signifies what keeps back by settling.

All these terms express that part which is separated from the other and left distinct: *rest* is the most general, both in sense and application; the others have a more specifick meaning and use: the *rest* may be either that which is left behind by itself or that which is set apart as a distinct portion: the *remainder*, *remnant*, and *residue* are the quantities which remain when the other parts are gone. The *rest* is said of any part indefinitely without regard to what has been taken or is gone;

> A last farewell!
> For since a last must come, the *rest* are vain,
> Like gasps in death which but prolong our pain.
> DRYDEN.

But the remainder commonly regards the part which has been left after a part has been taken: 'If he to whom ten talents have been committed, has squandered away five, he is concerned to make a double improvement of the *remainder*.'—ROGERS. A person may be said to sell some and give away the *rest*: when a number of hearty persons sit down to a meal, the *remainder* of the provisions, after all have been satisfied, will not be considerable. *Rest* is applied either to persons or things; *remainder* only to things: some were of that opinion, but the *rest* did not agree to it: the *remainder* of the paper was not worth preserving. *Remnant*, from *remanens* in Latin, is a species of *remainder*, applicable in the proper sense only to cloth or whatever remains unsold out of whole pieces: as a *remnant* of cotton, linen, and the like; but it may be taken figuratively. *Residue* is another species of *remainder*, employed in less familiar matters; the *remainder* is applied to that which remains after a consumption or removal has taken place: the *residue* is applied to that which remains after a division has taken place: hence we speak of the *remainder* of the corn, the *remainder* of the books, and the like: but the *residue* of the property, the *residue* of the effects, and the like. The *remainder*, *remnant*, and *residue* may all be applied either to moral or less familiar objects with a similar distinction: 'Whatever you take from amusements or indo lence will be repaid you a hundred fold for all the *remainder* of your days.'—CHATHAM.

> For this, far distant from the Latian coast,
> She drove the *remnant* of the Trojan host.
> DRYDEN.

> The rising deluge is not stopp'd with dams,
> But wisely managed, its divided strength
> Is sluiced in channels, and securely drained;
> And while its force is spent, and unsupply'd,
> The *residue*, with mounds may be restrain'd.
> SHAKSPEARE.

TO SUBSIDE, ABATE, INTERMIT.

A settlement after agitation is the peculiar meaning of *subside*, from the Latin *sub* and *sedeo*, signifying to settle to the bottom. *That* which has been put into commotion *subsides;* heavy particles *subside* in a fluid that is at rest, and tumults are said to *subside;* 'It was not long before this joy *subsided* in the remembrance of that dignity from which I had fallen.'—HAWKESWORTH. A diminution of strength characterizes the meaning of *abate*, which, from the French *abattre*, signifies to come down in quantity: that which has been high in action may *abate;* the rain *abates* after it has been heavy; and a man's anger *abates;*

> But first to heav'n thy due devotions pay,
> And annual gifts on Ceres' altar lay,
> When winter's rage *abates*.—DRYDEN.

Alternate action and rest is implied in the word *intermit*, from the Latin *inter* between, and *mitto* to put, signifying to leave a space or interval of rest between labour or action; 'Certain Indians, when a horse is running in his full career, leap down, gather any thing from the ground, and immediately leap up again, the horse not *intermitting* his course.'—WILKINS.

TO FOLLOW, SUCCEED, ENSUE.

Follow comes probably through the medium of the northern languages from the Greek ὁλκὸς a trace, or ἕλκω to draw; *succeed*, in Latin *succedo*, compounded of *sub* and *cedo* to walk after; *ensue*, in French *ensuivre*, Latin *insequor*, signifies to follow close upon the back or at the heels.

Follow and *succeed* are said of persons and things; *ensue* of things only: *follow* denotes the going in order, in a trace or line; *succeed* denotes the going or being in the same place immediately after another: many persons may *follow* each other at the same time; but only one individual properly *succeeds* another. *Follow* is taken literally for the motion of one physical body in relation to another; *succeed* is taken in the moral sense for taking the situation or office of another: people *follow* each other in a procession, or one *follows* another to the grave; a king *succeeds* to a throne, or a son *succeeds* to the inheritance of his father.

To *follow* in relation to things is said either simply of the order in which they go, or of such as go according to a connexion between them; to succeed implies simply to take the place after another; to *ensue* is to *follow* by a necessary connexion: people who die quickly one after the other are said to *follow* each other to the grave; a youth of debauchery is *followed* by a diseased old age; 'If a man of a good genius for fable were to represent the nature of pleasure and pain in that way of writing, he would probably join them together after such a manner that it would be impossible for the one to come into any place without being *followed* by the other.'—ADDISON. As in a natural tempest one wave of the sea *follows* another in rapid succession, so in the moral tempest of political revolutions one mad convulsion is quickly *succeeded* by another;

> Ulysses hastens with a trembling heart,
> Before him steps, and bending draws the dart:
> Forth flows the blood; an eager pang *succeeds*,
> Tydides mounts, and to the navy speeds.—POPE.

Nothing can *ensue* from popular commotions but bloodshed and misery;

> Nor deem this day, this battle, all you lose;
> A day more black, a fate more vile *ensues:*
> Impetuous Hector thunders at the wall,
> The hour, the spot, to conquer or to fall.—POPE.

Follow is used in abstract propositions: *ensue* is used in specifick cases: sin and misery *follow* each other as cause and effect; quarrels too often ensue from the conversations of violent men who differ either in religion or politicks.

TO FOLLOW, PURSUE.

The idea of going after any thing in order to reach or obtain it is common to these terms, but under different circumstances: one *follows* (*v. To follow*) a person mostly with a friendly intention; one *pursues* (*v. To continue*) with a hostile intention: a person *follows* his fellowt-raveller whom he wishes to overtake;

> "Now, now," said he, "my son, no more delay,
> I yield, I *follow* where Heav'n shows the way."
> DRYDEN.

The officers of justice *pursue* the criminal whom they wish to apprehend;

> The same Rutilians who with arms *pursue*
> The Trojan race are equal foes to you.—DRYDEN.

So likewise the huntsmen and hunters *follow* the dogs in the chase; the dogs *pursue* the hare. In application to things, *follow* is taken more in the passive, and *pursue* more in the active sense: a man *follows* the plan of another, and *pursues* his own plan; he *follows* his inclination, and *pursues* an object; 'The felicity is when any one is so happy as to find out and *follow* what is the proper bent of his genius.'—STEELE.

> Look round the habitual world, how few
> Know their own good, or, knowing it, *pursue*.
> DRYDEN

HUNT, CHASE.

The leading idea in the word *hunt* is that of searching after; the leading idea in the word *chase* is that of driving away, or before one. In the strict sense, the *hunt* is made for objects not within sight; the *chase* is made after such objects only as are within sight: we may *hunt*, therefore, without *chasing;* we may *chase* without *hunting:* a person *hunts* after, but does not *chase*, that which is lost; a boy *chases*, rather than *hunts* a butterfly;

> Come hither, boy! we 'll *hunt* to-day
> The bookworm, ravening beast of prey
> PARNELL

> Greatness of mind and fortune too
> Th' Olympic trophies show;
> Both their several parts must do
> In the noble *chase* of fame.—COWLEY.

When applied to field sports, the *hunt* commences as soon as the huntsman begins to look for the game; the *chase* commences as soon as it is found: on this ground, perhaps it is, that *hunt* is used in familiar discourse, to designate the specifick act of taking this amusement; and *chase* is used only in particular cases where the peculiar idea is to be expressed: a fox *hunt*, or a stag *hunt*, is said to take place on a particular day; or that there has been no *hunting* this season, or that the *hunt* has been very bad: but we speak, on the other hand, of the pleasures of the *chase;* or say that the *chase* lasted very long; the animal gave a long *chase*.

FOREST, CHASE, PARK,

* Are all habitations for animals of venery: but the *forest* is of the fairest magnitude and importance, it being a franchise and the property of the king; the *chase* and *park* may be either publick or private property. The *forest* is so formed of wood, and covers such an extent of ground, that it may be the haunt of wild beasts; of this description are the forests in Germany: the *chase* is an indefinite and open space that is allotted expressly for the *chase* of particular animals, such as deer; the *park* is an enclosed space that serves for the preservation of domestick animals.

SUCCESSION, SERIES, ORDER.

Succession signifies the act or state of *succeeding* (*v. To follow*); *series*, (*v. Series*); *order* (*v. To place*).

Succession (*v. To follow*) is a matter of necessity or casualty: things *succeed* each other, or they are taken

* Vide Trusler: "Forest, chase, park."

in *succession* either arbitrarily or by design: the *series* (*v. Series*) is a connected *succession*; the *order* is the *ordered* or arranged *succession*. We observe the *succession* of events as a matter of curiosity; 'We can conceive of time only by the *succession* of ideas one to another.'—HAWKESWORTH. We trace the *series* of events as a matter of intelligence; 'A number of distinct fables may contain all the topicks of moral instruction; yet each must be remembered by a distinct effort of the mind, and will not recur in a *series*, because they have no connexion with each other.'—HAWKESWORTH. We follow the *order* which the historian has pursued as a matter of judgement; 'In all verse, however familiar and easy, the words are necessarily thrown out of the *order* in which they are commonly used.'—HAWKESWORTH. The *succession* may be slow or quick; the *series* may be long or short; the *order* may be correct or incorrect. The present age has afforded a quick *succession* of events, and presented us with a *series* of atrocious attempts to disturb the peace of society under the name of liberty. The historian of these times needs only pursue the *order* which the events themselves point out.

SUCCESSIVE, ALTERNATE.

What is *successive* follows directly; what is *alternate* follows indirectly. A minister preaches *successively* who preaches every Sunday uninterruptedly at the same hour; but he preaches *alternately* if he preaches on one Sunday in the morning, and the other Sunday in the afternoon at the same place. The *successive* may be accidental or intentional; the *alternate* is mostly intentional: it may rain for three *successive* days, or a fair may be held for three *successive* days; 'Think of a hundred solitary streams peacefully gliding between amazing cliffs on one side and rich meadows on the other, gradually swelling into noble rivers, *successively* losing themselves in each other, and all at length terminating in the harbour of Plymouth.'—GIBBON. Trees are placed sometimes in *alternate* order, when every other tree is of the same size and kind; 'Suffer me to point out one great essential towards acquiring facility in composition; viz. the writing *alternately* in different measures.'—SEWARD.

NATURALLY, IN COURSE, CONSEQUENTLY, OF COURSE.

The connexion between events, actions, and things, is expressed by all these terms. *Naturally* signifies according to the *nature* of things, and applies therefore to the connexion which subsists between events according to the original constitution or inherent properties of things: *in course* signifies *in* the *course* of things, that is, in the regular order that things ought to follow: *consequently* signifies by a *consequence*, that is, by a necessary law of dependence, which makes one thing follow another: *of course* signifies on account *of* the *course* which things most commonly or even necessarily take. Whatever happens *naturally*, happens as we expect it; whatever happens *in course*, happens as we approve of it; whatever follows *consequently*, follows as we judge it right; whatever follows *of course*, follows as we see it necessarily. Children *naturally* imitate their parents: people *naturally* fall into the habits of those they associate with: both these circumstances result from the *nature* of things: whoever is made a peer of the realm, takes his seat in the upper house *in course*; he requires no other qualification to entitle him to this privilege, he goes thither according to the established course of things; *consequently*, as a peer, he is admitted without question; this is a decision of the judgement by which the question is at once determined: *of course* none are admitted who are not peers; this flows necessarily out of the constituted law of the land.

Naturally and *in course* describe things as they are; *consequently* and *of course* represent them as they must be; *naturally* and *in course* state facts or realities; *consequently* and *of course* state the inferences drawn from those facts, or *consequences* resulting from them; a mob is *naturally* disposed to riot, and *consequently* it is dangerous to appeal to a mob for its judgement; the nobility attend at court *in course*, that is, by virtue of their rank, soldiers leave the town *of course* at assize or election times, that is, because the law forbids them to remain. *Naturally* is opposed to the artificial or forced; *in course* is opposed to the irregular: *naturally* excludes the idea of design or purpose; *in course* includes the idea of arrangement and social order: the former is applicable to every thing that has an independent existence; the latter is applied to the constituted order of society: the former is, therefore, said of every object, animate or inanimate, having *natural* properties, and performing *natural* operations; the latter only of persons and their establishment. Plants that require much air *naturally* thrive most in an open country; 'Egotists are generally the vain and shallow part of mankind; people being *naturally* full of themselves when they have nothing else in them.'—ADDISON. Members of a society, who do not forfeit their title by the breach of any rule or law, are readmitted *in course*, after ever so long an absence; 'Our Lord foresaw, that all the Mosaic orders would cease *in course* upon his death.'—BEVERIDGE.

Consequently is either a speculative or a practical inference; *of course* is always practical. We know that all men must die, and *consequently* we expect to share the common lot of humanity: we see that our friends are particularly engaged at a certain time; *consequently* we do not interrupt them by calling upon them; 'The forty-seventh proposition of the first book of Euclid is the foundation of trigonometry, and *consequently* of navigation.'—BARTLETT. When a man does not fulfil his engagements, he cannot *of course* expect to be rewarded, as if he had done his duty; 'What do trust and confidence signify in a matter *of course* and formality?'—STILLINGFLEET. *In course* applies to what one does or may do; *of course* applies to what one must do or leave undone. Children take possession of their patrimony *in course* at the death of their parents: while the parents are living, children *of course* derive support or assistance from them.

SUBSEQUENT, CONSEQUENT, POSTERIOUR.

Subsequent, in Latin *subsequens*, from *sub* and *sequor* signifies following next in order; *consequent*, in Latin *consequens*, from *con* and *sequor*, i. e. following in connexion; *posteriour*, from *postea* afterward, signifies literally that which is after.

These terms are all applied to events as they follow one another, but *subsequent* and *consequent* respect the order of events. *Subsequent* simply denotes this order without any collateral idea: one event is said to be *subsequent* to another at any given time; 'This article is introduced as *subsequent* to the treaty of Munster, made about 1648, when England was in the utmost confusion.'—SWIFT. *Consequent* denotes the connexion between two events, one of which follows the other as the effect of a cause; 'This satisfaction or dissatisfaction, *consequent* upon a man's acting suitably or unsuitably to conscience, is a principle not easily to be worn out.'—SOUTH. *Posteriour* respects the time of events; Hesiod was *posteriour* to Homer: and also the place of things; 'Where the anteriour body giveth way as fast as the *posteriour* cometh on, it maketh no noise, be the motion never so great.'—BACON.

ANTECEDENT, PRECEDING, FOREGOING, PREVIOUS ANTERIOUR, PRIOR, FORMER.

Antecedent, in Latin *antecedens*, that is, *ante* and *cedens* going before; *preceding*, in Latin *præcedens* going before; *foregoing*, literally going before; *previous*, in Latin *prævius*, that is, *præ* and *via* making a way before; *anteriour*, the comparative of the Latin *ante* before; *prior*, in Latin *prior*, comparative of *primus* first; *former*, in English the comparative of first.

Antecedent, *preceding*, *foregoing*, *previous*, are employed for what goes or happens before; *anteriour*, *prior*, *former*, for what is, or exists before.

* *Antecedent* marks priority of order, place, and position, with this peculiar circumstance, that it denotes the relation of influence, dependence and connexion established between two objects: thus, in logic the premises are called the *antecedent*, and the conclu-

* Vide Roubaud: "Antérieur, antécédent, précédent"

sion the consequent; in theology or politicks, the *antecedent* is any decree or resolution which influences another decree or action; in mathematicks, it is that term from which any induction can be drawn to another; in grammar, the *antecedent* is that which requires a particular regimen from its consequent.

Antecedent and *preceding* both denote *priority* of time, or the order of events; but the former in a more vague and indeterminate manner than the latter. A *preceding* event is that which happens immediately before the one of which we are speaking; whereas *antecedent* may have events or circumstances intervening; 'The seventeen centuries since the birth of Christ are *antecedent* to the eighteenth, or the one we live in; but it is the seventeenth only which we call the *preceding* one.'—TRUSLER. 'Little attention was paid to literature by the Romans in the early and more martial ages. I read of no collections of books *antecedent* to those made by Æmilius Paulus, and Lucullus.'—CUMBERLAND. 'Letters from Rome, dated the thirteenth instant, say, that on the *preceding* Sunday, his Holiness was carried in an open chair from St. Peter's to St. Mary's.'—STEELE. An *antecedent* proposition may be separated from its consequent by other propositions; but a *preceding* proposition is closely followed by another. In this sense *antecedent* is opposed to *posteriour; preceding* to *succeeding*.

Preceding respects simply the succession of times and things; but *previous* denotes the succession of actions and events, with the collateral idea of their connexion with and influence upon each other: we speak of the *preceding* day, or the *preceding* chapter, merely as the day or chapter that goes before; but when we speak of a *previous* engagement or a *previous* inquiry, it supposes an engagement or inquiry preparatory to something that is to follow. *Previous* is opposed to subsequent:

A boding silence reigns
Dead through the dun expanse, save the dull sound
That from the mountain, *previous* to the storm,
Rolls o'er the muttering earth.—THOMSON.

Foregoing is employed to mark the order of things narrated or stated; as when we speak of the *foregoing* statement, the *foregoing* objections, or the *foregoing* calculation, &c.; *foregoing* is opposed to following; 'Consistently with the *foregoing* principles we may define original and native poetry to be the language of the violent passions, expressed in exact measure.'—SIR W. JONES.

Anteriour, *prior*, and *former* have all a relative sense, and are used for things that are more before than others: *anteriour* is a technical term to denote forwardness of position, as in anatomy; the *anteriour* or fore part of the skull, in contradistinction to the hind part; so likewise the *anteriour* or fore front of a building, in opposition to the back front; 'If that be the *anteriour* or upper part wherein the senses are placed, and that the posteriour and lower part, which is opposite thereunto, there is no inferiour or former part in this animal: for the senses being placed at both extremes make both ends *anteriour*, which is impossible.'—BROWN. *Prior* is used in the sense of *previous* when speaking of comparatively two or more things, when it implies anticipation; a *prior* claim invalidates the one that is set up; a *prior* engagement prevents the forming of any other that is proposed; 'Some accounts make Thamyris the eighth epick poet *prior* to Homer, an authority to which no credit seems due.'—CUMBERLAND. *Former* is employed either with regard to times, as *former* times, in contradistinction to later periods, or with regard to propositions, when the *former* or first thing mentioned is opposed to the latter or last mentioned; '*Former* follies pass away and are forgotten. Those which are present strike observation and sharpen censure.'—BLAIR.

PRIORITY, PRECEDENCE, PRE-EMINENCE, PREFERENCE.

Priority denotes the abstract quality of being before others; *precedence*, from *præ* and *cedo*, signifies the state of going before; *pre-eminence* signifies being more eminent or elevated than others; *preference* signifies being put before others. *Priority* respects simply the order of succession, and is applied to objects either in a state of motion or rest: *precedence* signifies *priority* in going, and depends upon a right or privilege; *pre-eminence* signifies *priority* in being, and depends upon merit; *preference* signifies *priority* in placing, and depends upon favour. The *priority* is applicable rather to the thing than the person; it is not that which is sought for, but that which is to be had: age frequently gives *priority* where every other claim is wanting; 'A better place, a more commodious seat, *priority* in being helped at table, &c., what is it but sacrificing ourselves in such trifles to the convenience and pleasures of others?'—EARL CHATHAM. The immoderate desire for *precedence* is often nothing but a childish vanity; it is a distinction that flows out of rank and power: a nobleman claims a *precedence* on all occasions of ceremony; 'Ranks will then (in the next world) be adjusted, and *precedency* set aright.'—ADDISON. The love of *pre eminence* is laudable, inasmuch as it requires a degree of moral worth which exceeds that of others; a general aims at *pre-eminence* in his profession; 'It is the concern of mankind, that the destruction of order snould not be a claim to rank; that crimes should not be the only title to *pre-eminence* and honour.'—BURKE. Those who are anxious to obtain the best for themselves, are eager to have the *preference*: we seek for the *preference* in matters of choice; 'You will agree with me in giving the *preference* to a sincere and sensible friend.'—GIBBON.

TO EXCEED, SURPASS, EXCEL, TRANSCEND, OUTDO.

Exceed, from the Latin *excedo*, compounded of *ex* and *cedo* to pass out of, or beyond the line, is the general term. *Surpass*, compounded of *sur* over, and *pass*, is one species of exceeding. *Excel*, compounded of *ex* and *cello* to lift, or move over, is another species.

Exceed, in its limited acceptation, conveys no idea of moral desert; *surpass* and *excel* are always taken in a good sense. It is not so much persons as things which *exceed;* both persons and things *surpass;* persons only *excel*. One thing *exceeds* another, as the success of an undertaking *exceeds* the expectations of the undertaker, or a man's exertions *exceed* his strength;

Man's boundless *avarice* exceeds,
And on his neighbours round about him feeds.
WALLER.

One person *surpasses* another, as the English have *surpassed* all other nations in the extent of their naval power; or one thing *surpasses* another, as poetry *surpasses* painting in its effects on the imagination; 'Dryden often *surpasses* expectation, and Pope never falls below it.'—JOHNSON. One person *excels* another; thus formerly the Dutch and Italians *excelled* the English in painting;

To him the king: How much thy years *excel*
In arts of counsel, and in speaking well.—POPE.

We may *surpass* without any direct or immediate effort; we cannot *excel* without effort. Nations as well as individuals will *surpass* each other in particular arts and sciences, as much from local and adventitious circumstances, as from natural genius and steady application; no one can expect to *excel* in learning, whose indolence gets the better of his ambition. The derivatives *excessive* and *excellent* have this obvious distinction between them, that the former always signifies *exceeding* in that which ought not to be *exceeded*, and the latter *exceeding* in that where it is honourable to *exceed:* he who is habitually *excessive* in any of his indulgencies, must be insensible to the *excellence* of a temperate life.

Transcend, from *trans* beyond, and *scendo* or *scando* to climb, signifies climbing beyond; and *outdo* signifies doing out of the ordinary course: the former, like *surpass*, refers rather to the state of things; and *outdo*, like *excel*, to the exertions of persons: the former rises in sense above *surpass;* but the latter is only employed in particular cases, that is, to *excel* in action: *excel* is however confined to that which is good; *outdo* to that which is good or bad. The genius of Homer *transcends* that of almost every other poet;

Auspicious prince, in arms a mighty name,
But yet whose actions far *transcend* your fame.
DRYDEN.

Heliogabalus *outdid* every other emperor in extravagance; 'The last and crowning instance of our love to our enemies is to pray for them. For by this a man would fain to *outdo* himself.'—SOUTH.

EXCELLENCE, SUPERIORITY.

Excellence is an absolute term; *superiority* is a relative term: many may have *excellence* in the same degree, but they must have *superiority* in different degrees; *superiority* is often superiour *excellence*, but in many cases they are applied to different objects.

There is a moral *excellence* attainable by all who have the will to strive after it;

> Base envy withers at another's joy,
> And hates that *excellence* it cannot reach.
> THOMSON.

There is an intellectual and physical *superiority* which is above the reach of our wishes, and is granted to a few only; 'To be able to benefit others is a condition of freedom and *superiority*.'—TILLOTSON.

PRIMARY, PRIMITIVE, PRISTINE, ORIGINAL.

Primary, from *primus*, signifies belonging to or like the first; *primitive*, from the same, signifies according to the first; *pristine*, in Latin *pristinus*, from *prius*, signifies in former times; *original* signifies containing the *origin*.

The *primary* denotes simply the order of succession, and is therefore the generick term; *primitive*, *pristine*, and *original* include also the idea of some other relation to the thing that succeeds, and are therefore modes of the *primary*. The *primary* has nothing to come before it; in this manner we speak of the *primary* cause as the cause which precedes secondary causes: the *primitive* is that after which other things are formed; in this manner a *primitive* word is that after which, or from which, the derivatives are formed: the *pristine* is that which follows the *primitive*, so as to become customary; there are but few specimens of the *pristine* purity of life among the professors of Christianity: the *original* is that which either gives birth to the thing or belongs to that which gives birth to the thing; the *original* meaning of a word is that which was given to it by the makers of the word. The *primary* subject of consideration is that which should precede all others; 'Memory is the *primary* and fundamental power, without which there could be no other intellectual operation.'—JOHNSON. The *primitive* state of society is that which was formed without a model, but might serve as a model;

> Meanwhile our *primitive* great sire to meet
> His godlike guest walks forth.—MILTON.

The *pristine* simplicity of manners may serve as a just pattern for the imitation of present times;

> While with her friendly clay he deign'd to dwell,
> Shall she with safety reach her *pristine* seat.
> PRIOR.

The *original* state of things is that which is coeval with the things themselves; 'As to the share of power each individual ought to have in the state, that I must deny to be among the direct *original* rights of man.' —BURKE.

SECOND, SECONDARY, INFERIOUR.

Second and *secondary* both come from the Latin *secundus*, changed from *sequundus* and *sequor* to follow, signifying the order of succession. The former simply expresses this order; but the latter includes the accessory idea of comparative demerit; a person stands *second* in a list, or a letter is *second* which immediately succeeds the first;

> Fond, foolish man! With fear of death surpris'd,
> Which either should be wish'd for or despis'd;
> This, if our souls with bodies death destroy,
> That, if our souls a *second* life enjoy.—DENHAM.

A consideration is *secondary*, or of *secondary* importance, which is opposed to that which holds the first rank; 'Many, instead of endeavouring to form their own opinions, content themselves with the *secondary* knowledge which a convenient bench in a coffee-house can supply.'—JOHNSON. *Secondary* and *inferiour* both designate some lower degree of a quality: but *secondary* is only applied to the importance or value of things; *inferiour* is applied generally to all qualities: a man of business reckons every thing as *secondary* which does not forward the object he has in view; 'Whensoever there is moral right on the one hand, no *secondary* right can discharge it.'—L'ESTRANGE. Men of *inferiour* abilities are disqualified by nature for high and important stations, although they may be more fitted for lower stations than those of greater abilities;

> Hast thou not made me here thy substitute,
> And these *inferiour* far beneath me set?
> MILTON.

Sometimes *second* is taken in the sense of *inferiour* when applied to any particular object compared with another;

> Who am alone
> From all eternity; for none I know
> *Second* to me, or like.—MILTON.

THEREFORE, CONSEQUENTLY, ACCORDINGLY.

Therefore, that is, for this reason, marks a deduction; *consequently*, that is, in *consequence*, marks a *consequence*; *accordingly*, that is, according to some thing, implies an agreement or adaptation. *Therefore* is employed particularly in abstract reasoning; *consequently* is employed either in reasoning or in the narrative style; *accordingly* is used principally in the narrative style. Young persons are perpetually liable to fall into errour through inexperience; they ought *therefore* the more willingly to submit themselves to the guidance of those who can direct them; 'If you cut off the top branches of a tree, it will not *therefore* cease to grow.'—HUGHES. The French nation was reduced to a state of moral anarchy during the revolution; *consequently* nothing but time and good government could bring the people back to the use of their sober senses; 'Reputation is power; *consequently* to despise is to weaken.'—SOUTH. Every preparation was made, and every precaution was taken; *accordingly* at the fixed hour they proceeded to the place of destination; 'The pathetick, as Longinus observes, may animate the sublime; but is not essential to it. *Accordingly*, as he further remarks, we very often find that those who excel most in stirring up the passions, very often want the talent of writing in the sublime manner.'—ADDISON.

PREVIOUS, PRELIMINARY, PREPARATORY, INTRODUCTORY.

Previous, in Latin *prævius*, compounded of *præ* and *via*, signifies leading the way or going before; *preliminary*, from *præ* and *limen* a threshold, signifies belonging to the threshold or entrance; *preparatory* and *introductory* signify belonging to a preparation or introduction.

Previous denotes simply the order of succession: the other terms, in addition to this, convey the idea of connexion between the objects which succeed each other. *Previous* applies to actions and proceedings in general; as a *previous* question, a *previous* inquiry, a *previous* determination; 'One step by which a temptation approaches to its crisis is a *previous* growing familiarity of the mind with the sin which a man is tempted to.'—SOUTH. *Preliminary* is employed only for matters of contract; a *preliminary* article, a *preliminary* condition, are what precede the final settlement of any question; 'I have discussed the nuptial *preliminaries* so often, that I can repeat the forms in which jointures are settled and pin-money secured.'—JOHNSON. *Preparatory* is employed for matters of arrangements; the disposing of men in battle is *preparatory* to an engagement; the making of marriage deeds and contracts is *preparatory* to the final solemnization of the marriage; 'Æschylus is in the practice of holding the spectator in suspense by a *preparatory* silence in his chief person.' —CUMBERLAND. *Introductory* is employed for matters of science or discussion; as remarks are *introductory* to the main subject in question; compendiums of grammar, geography, and the like, as *introductory* to larger works, are useful for young people; 'Consider your selves as acting now, under the eye of God, an *introductory* part to a more important scene.'—Blair. Prudent people are careful to make every *previous* inquiry before they seriously enter into engagements with strangers: it is impolitick to enter into details until all *preliminary* matters are fully adjusted: one ought never to undertake any important matter without first adopting every *preparatory* measure that can facilitate its prosecution: in complicated matters it is necessary to have something *introductory* by way of explanation.

SERIES, COURSE.

Series, which is also *series* in Latin, comes from *sero* or *necto* to knit together, and the Greek σειρὰ a chain, and signifies the order and connexion, in which things follow each other; *course*, in Latin *cursus*, from the verb *curro*, signifies here the direction in which things run one after another.

There is always a *course* where there is a *séries*, but not *vice versâ*. Things must have some sort of connexion with each other in order to form a *series*, but they need simply to follow in order to form a *course;* thus a *series* of events respects those which flow out of each other, a *course* of events, on the contrary, respects those which happen unconnectedly within a certain space: so in like manner, the numbers of a book, which serve to form a whole, are a *series;* and a number of lectures following each other at a given time are a *course:* hence, likewise, the technical phrase infinite *series* in algebra.

COURSE, RACE, PASSAGE.

Course, from *curro* to run, signifies either the act of running, or the space run over; *race*, from *run*, signifies the same; *passage*, from to *pass*, signifies either the act of passing or the space passed over.

With regard to the act of going, *course* is taken absolutely and indefinitely; *race* relates to the object for which we run; *passage* relates to the place passed over: thus a person may be swift in *course*, obtain a *race*, and have an easy *passage;*

Him neither rocks can crush, nor steel can wound
When Ajax fell not on th' ensanguined ground;
In standing fight he mates Achilles' force,
Excell'd alone in swiftness in the *course*.—Pope.

Unhappy man whose death our hands shall grace,
Fate calls thee hence, and finish'd is thy *race*.
Pope.

Between his shoulders pierced the following dart,
And held its *passage* through the panting heart.
Pope.

We pursue whatever *course* we think proper: we run the *race* that is set before us. *Course* is taken absolutely by itself; *race* is considered in relation to others: a man pursues a certain *course* according to discretion; he runs a *race* with another by way of competition. *Course* has a more particular reference to the space that is gone over; *race* includes in it more particularly the idea of the mode of going: we speak of going in, or pursuing a particular *course;* but always of running a *race*,

Course is as often used in the improper as the proper sense; *race* is seldom used figuratively, except in a spiritual application: man's success and respectability in life depend much upon the *course* of moral conduct which he pursues;

So Mars omnipotent invades the plain
(The wide destroyer of the race of man);
Terrour, his best loved son, attends his *course*,
Arm'd with stern boldness, and enormous force.
Pope.

The Christian's *course* in this world is represented in Scripture as a *race* which is set before him;

Remote from towns he ran his godly *race*,
Nor e'er had changed, nor wish'd to change, his place.
Goldsmith.

Course may be used in connexion with the object passed over or not; *passage* is seldom employed but in the direct connexion; we speak of a person's *course* in a place, or simply of his *course;* but we always speak of a person's *passage* through a place;

Direct against which open'd from beneath,
Just o'er the blissful seat of paradise,
A *passage* down to earth, a *passage* wide.
Milton

Course and *passage* are used for inanimate, as well as animate objects; *race* is used for those only which are animate: a river has its *course*, and sometimes it is a dangerous *passage* for vessels; the horse or man runs the *race*.

WAY, ROAD, ROUT OR ROUTE, COURSE.

Way has the same signification as given under the head of *way; road* comes no doubt from *ride*, signifying the place where one rides; *route* or *rout* comes in all probability from *rotundus* round, signifying the round which one goes; *course*, from the Latin *cursus*, signifies the place where one walks or runs. *Way* is here the generick term; it is the path which a person chooses at pleasure for himself;

He stood in the gate, and asked of ev'ry one
Which *way* she took, and whither she was gone.
Dryden.

The *road* is the regular and beaten *way*, whether taken in a proper or improper sense; 'At our first sally into the intellectual world, we all march together along one straight and open *road*.'—Johnson. The *route* is any *way* or *road* chosen for a particular purpose, either of pleasure or business. An army or a company go a certain *route;* 'Cortes (after his defeat at Mexico) was engaged in deep consultation with his officers concerning the *route* which they ought to take in their retreat.'—Robertson. The *course* is chosen in the unbeaten track: foot passengers are seen to take a certain *course* over fields;

Then to the stream when neither friends nor force,
Nor speed, nor art avail, he shapes his *course*.
Denham.

WAY, MANNER, METHOD, MODE, COURSE, MEANS.

All those words denote the steps which are pursued from the beginning to the completion of any work. The way is both general and indefinite; it is either taken by accident or chosen by design. Whoever attempts to do that which is strange to him, will at first do it in an awkward *way;* 'His way of expressing and applying them, not his invention of them we must admire.'—Addison. The *manner* and the *method* are both species of the *way*. The *manner* is that which a person chooses for a particular occasion; the *manner* of conferring a favour is often more than the favour itself; 'My mind is taken up in a more melancholy *manner*.'—Atterbury. The *method* is that which a person conceives in his own mind; experience supplies men in the end with a suitable method of carrying on their business. The *method* is said of that which requires contrivance; the *mode*, of that which requires practice and habitual attention; the former being applied to matters of art, and the latter to mechanical actions: the master has a good *method* of teaching to write; the scholar has a good or bad *mode* of holding his pen; '*Modes* of speech, which owe their prevalence to modish folly, die away with their inventors.'—Johnson. The *course* and the *means* are the *way* which we pursue in our moral conduct; the *course* is the *course* of measures which are adopted to produce a certain result; 'All your sophisters cannot produce any thing better adapted to preserve a rational and manly freedom than the *course* that we have pursued.'—Burke. The *means* collectively for the *course* which lead to a certain end; 'The most wonderful things are brought about in many instances by *means* the most absurd and ridiculous.'—Burke. In order to obtain legal redress, we must pursue a certain *course* in law; law is one *means* of gaining redress, which must be adopted when all other *means* fail.

SYSTEM, METHOD.

System, in Latin *systema*, Greek σύστημα, from συνίστημι or σὺν and ἵστημι to stand together, signifies that which is put together so as to form a whole; *method*, in Latin *methodus*, from the Greek μετὰ and ὁδὸς a way, signifies by distinction the way by which any thing is effected

System expresses more than *method*, which is but a part of *system: system* is an arrangement of many single or individual objects according to some given rule, so as to make them coalesce. *Method* is the manner of this arrangement, or the principle upon which this arrangement takes place. The term *system* however applies to a complexity of objects, but arrangement, and consequently *method*, may be applied to every thing that is to be put into execution. All sciences must be reduced to *system;* for without *system* there is no science;

If a better *system*'s thine,
Impart it frankly, or make use of mine.—FRANCIS.

All business requires *method;* and without *method* little can be done to any good purpose; 'The great defect of the Seasons is the want of *method*, but for this I know not that there was any remedy.'—JOHNSON.

ORDER, METHOD, RULE.

Order is applied in general to every thing that is disposed (*v. To dispose*); *method* (*v. System*) and *rule* (*v. Guide*) are applied only to that which is done; the *order* lies in consulting the time, the place, and the object, so as to make them accord; the *method* consists in the right choice of means to an end; the *rule* consists in that which will keep us in the right way. Where there is a number of objects there must be *order* in the disposition of them: there must be *order* in a school as to the arrangement both of the pupils and of the business: where there is work to carry on, or any object to obtain, or any art to follow, there must be *method* in the pursuit; a tradesman or merchant must have *method* in keeping his accounts; a teacher must have a *method* for the communication of instruction; 'It will be in vain to talk to you concerning the *method* I think best to be observed in schools.'—LOCKE. The *rule* is the part of the *method;* it is that on which the *method* rests; there cannot be *method* without *rule*, but there may be *rule* without *method;* the *method* varies with the thing that is to be done; the *rule* is that which is permanent and serves as a guide under all circumstances. We adopt the *method* and follow the *rule*. A painter adopts a certain *method* of preparing his colours according to the *rules* laid down by his art; 'A *rule* that relates even to the smallest part of our life, is of great benefit to us, merely as it is a *rule*.'—LAW.

Order is said of every complicated machine, either of a physical or a moral kind: the *order* of the universe, by which every part is made to harmonize to the other part, and all individually to the whole collectively, is that which constitutes its principal beauty: as rational beings we aim at introducing the same *order* into the moral scheme of society: *order* is therefore that which is founded upon the nature of things, and seems in its extensive sense to comprehend all the rest; 'The *order* and *method* of nature is generally very different from our measures and proportions.'—BURKE. *Method* is the work of the understanding, mostly as it is employed in the mechanical process; sometimes, however, as respects intellectual objects; *rule* is said either as it respects mechanical and physical actions or moral conduct.

The *order* of society is preserved by means of government, or authority: laws or *rules* are employed by authority as instruments in the preservation of *order:* no work should be performed, whether it be the building a house, or the writing a book, without *method;* this *method* will be more or less correct, as it is formed according to definite *rules*.

The term *rule* is, however, as before observed, employed distinctly from either *order* or *method*, for it applies to the moral conduct of the individual. The Christian religion contains *rules* for the guidance of our conduct in all the relations of human society;

Their story I revolv'd; and reverent own'd
Their polish'd arts of *rule*, their human virtues.
MALLET.

As epithets, *orderly*, *methodical*, and *regular*, are applied to persons and even to things, according to the above distinction of the nouns: an *orderly* man, or an *orderly* society, is one that adheres to the established *order* of things: the former in his domestick habits, the latter in their publick capacity, their social meetings, and their social measures;

Then to their dams
Lets in their young, and wondrous *orderly*,
With manly haste, dispatch this house-wifery.
CHAPMAN.

A *methodical* man is one who adopts *methods* in all he sets about; such a one may sometimes run into the extreme of formality, by being precise where precision is not necessary. We cannot however speak of a *methodical* society, for *method* is altogether a personal quality. A man is *regular*, inasmuch as he follows a certain *rule* in his moral actions, and thereby preserves a uniformity of conduct: a *regular* society is one founded by certain prescribed *rules*.

A *disorderly* person in a family discomposes its domestick economy: a man who is *disorderly* in his business throws every thing into confusion. It is of peculiar importance for a person to be *methodical* who has the superintendence of other people's labour: much time is lost and much fruitless trouble occasioned by the want of *method;* 'To begin *methodically*, I should enjoin you travel; for absence doth remove the cause, removing the object.'—SUCKLING. *Regularity* of life is of as much more importance than *order* and *method*, as a man's durable happiness is of more importance than the happiness of the moment: the *orderly* and *methodical* respect only the transitory modes of things; but the *regular* concerns a man both for body and soul; 'He was a mighty lover of regularity and *order*, and managed his affairs with the utmost exactness.'—ATTERBURY.

These terms are in like manner applied to that which is personal; we say, an *orderly* proceeding, or an *orderly* course for what is done in due order: a *regular* proceeding, or a *regular* course, which goes on according to a prescribed rule; a *methodical* grammar, a *methodical* delineation, and the like, for what is done according to a given *method*.

CLASS, ORDER, RANK, DEGREE.

Class, in French *classe*, Latin *classis*, very probably from the Greek κλάσις, a fraction, division, or class; *order*, in French *ordre*, Latin *ordo*, comes from the Greek ὄρχος a row, which is a species of order; *rank*, in German *rang*, is connected with *row*, &c.; *degree*, in French *degré*, comes from the Latin *gradus* a step.

Class is more general than *order; degree* is more specifick than *rank*.

Class and *order* are said of the body who are distinguished; *rank* and *degree* of the distinction itself: men belong to a certain *class* or *order;* they hold a certain *rank;* they are of a certain *degree:* among the Romans all the citizens were distinctly divided into *classes* according to their property; but in the modern constitution of society, *classes* are distinguished from each other on general, moral, or civil grounds; there are reputable or disreputable *classes;* the labouring *class*, the *class* of merchants, mechanicks, &c.; 'We are by our occupations, education, and habits of life, divided almost into different species. Each of these *classes* of the human race has desires, fears, and conversation, vexations and merriment, peculiar to itself.' —JOHNSON. *Order* has a more particular signification; it is founded upon some positive civil privilege or distinction; the general orders are divided into higher, lower, or middle, arising from the unequal distribution of wealth and power; the particular *orders* are those of the nobility, of the clergy, of freemasonry, and the like; 'Learning and knowledge are perfections in us, not as we are men, but as we are reasonable creatures, in which *order* of beings the female world is upon the same level with the male.'—ADDISON. *Rank* distinguishes one individual from another; it is peculiarly applied to the nobility and the gentry: although every man in the community holds a certain *rank* in relation to those who are above or below him; 'Young women of humble *rank*, and small pretensions, should be particularly cautious how a vain ambition of being noticed by their superiours betrays them into an attempt at displaying their unprotected persons on a stage.'—CUMBERLAND. *Degree* like *rank* is applicable to the individual, but only in particular cases; literary and scientifick *degrees* are conferred upon superiour merit in different departments of science; there are likewise *degrees* in the same *rank*, whence we speak of men of high and low *degree;*

Then learn, ye fair! to soften splendour's ray,
Endure the swain, the youth of low *degree*.
SHENSTONE.

During the French revolution the most worthless *class*, from all *orders*, obtained the supremacy only to destroy all *rank* and *degree*, and sacrifice such as possessed any wealth, power, *rank*, or *degree*.

TO CLASS, ARRANGE, RANGE.

To *class*, from the noun *class*, signifies to put in a *class; arrange* and *range* are both derived from the word *rank*, signifying to put in a certain rank or order.

The general qualities and attributes of things are to be considered in *classing;* their fitness to stand by each other must be considered in *arranging* them; their capacity for forming a line is the only thing to be attended to in *ranging* them.

Classification serves the purposes of science; *arrangement* those of decoration and ornament; *ranging* those of general convenience; men are *classed* into different bodies, according to some certain standard of property, power, education, occupation, &c.; 'We are all ranked and *classed* by him who seeth into every heart.'—BLAIR. Furniture is *arranged* in a room according as it answers either in colour, shade, convenience of situation, &c.; 'In vain you attempt to regulate your expense, if into your amusements, or your society, disorder has crept. You have admitted a principle of confusion which will defeat all your plans, and perplex and entangle what you sought to *arrange*.' —BLAIR. Men are *ranged* in order whenever they make a procession, or our ideas are *ranged* in the mind; 'A noble writer should be born with this faculty, (a strong imagination) so as to be well able to receive lively ideas from outward objects, to retain them long, and to *range* them together in such figures and representations as are most likely to hit the fancy of the reader.'—ADDISON. *Classification* is concerned with mental objects; *arrangement* with either physical or mental objects; *ranging* mostly with physical objects: knowledge, experience, and judgement are requisite in *classing;* taste and practice are indispensable in *arranging;* care only is wanted in *ranging*. When applied to spiritual objects, *arrangement* is the ordinary operation of the mind, requiring only methodical habits: *classification* is a branch of philosophy which is not attainable by art only; it requires a mind peculiarly methodical by nature, that is capable of distinguishing things by their generick and specifick differences; not separating things that are alike; nor blending things that are different: books are *classed* in a catalogue according to their contents; they are *arranged* in a shop according to their size or price; they are *ranged* on a counter for convenience: ideas are *classed* by the logician into simple and complex, abstract and concrete: they are *arranged* by the power of reflection in the mind of the thinker: words are *classed* by the grammarian into different parts of speech; they are suitably *arranged* by the writer in different parts of a sentence; a man of business *arranges* his affairs so as to suit the time and season for every thing; a shopkeeper *arranges* his goods so as to have a place for every thing, and to know its place; he *ranges* those things before him, of which he wishes to command a view: a general *arranges* his men for the battle; a drill sergeant *ranges* his men when he makes them exercise.

TO DISPOSE, ARRANGE, DIGEST.

To *dispose* signifies the same here as in the preceding article; to *arrange*, from *ar* or *ad* and *range* is to put in a certain range or order; to *digest*, in Latin *digestus*, participle of *digero* or *dis* and *gero*, signifies to gather apart with design.

The idea of a systematick laying apart is common to all and proper to the word *dispose*.

We *dispose* when we *arrange* and *digest;* but we do not always *arrange* and *digest* when we *dispose:* they differ in the circumstances and object of the action. There is less thought employed in *disposing* than in *arranging* and *digesting;* we may *dispose* ordinary matters by simply assigning a place to each; in this manner trees are *disposed* in a row, but we *arange* and *digest* by an intellectual effort; in the first case by putting those together which ought to go together; and in the latter case by both separating that which is dissimilar, and bringing together that which is similar; in this manner books are *arranged* in a library according to their size or their subject; the materials for a literary production are *digested;* or the laws of the land are *digested*. What is not wanted should be neatly *disposed* in a suitable place;

Then near the altar of the darting king,
Dispos'd in rank their hecatomb they bring.
POPE.

Nothing contributes so much to beauty and convenience as the *arrangement* of every thing according to the way and manner in which they should follow; 'There is a proper *arrangement* of the parts in elastick bodies, which may be facilitated by use.'—CHEYNE. When writings are involved in great intricacy and confusion, it is difficult to *digest* them; 'The marks and impressions of diseases, and the changes and devastations they bring upon the internal parts, should be very carefully examined and orderly *digested* in the comparative anatomy we speak of.'—BACON.

In an extended and moral application of these words, we speak of a person's time, talent, and the like, being *disposed* to a good purpose;

Thus while she did her various power *dispose*,
The world was free from tyrants, wars, and woes.
PRIOR.

We speak of a man's ideas being properly *arranged*, 'When a number of distinct images are collected by these erratick and hasty surveys, the fancy is busied in *arranging* them.'—JOHNSON. We speak of a work being *digested* into a form;

Chosen friends, with sense refin'd
Learning *digested* well.—THOMSON.

On the *disposition* of a man's time and property will depend in a great measure his success in life; on the *arrangement* of accounts greatly depends his facility in conducting business; on the habit of *digesting* our thoughts depends in a great measure the correctness of thinking.

DISPOSAL, DISPOSITION.

These words derive their different meanings from the verb to *dispose* (*v. To dispose*), to which they owe their common origin.

Disposal is a personal act; it depends upon the will of the individual: *disposition* is an act of the judgement; it depends upon the nature of the things.

The removal of a thing from one's self is involved in a *disposal;* the good order of the things is comprehended in their *disposition*. The *disposal* of property is in the hands of the rightful owner; the success of a battle often depends upon the right *disposition* of an army; 'In the reign of Henry the Second, if a man died without wife or issue, the whole of his property was at his own *disposal*.'—BLACKSTONE. 'In case a person made no *disposition* of such of his goods as were testable, he was and is said to die intestate.'—BLACKSTONE.

APPAREL, ATTIRE, ARRAY.

Apparel, in French *appareil*, like the word *apparatus*, comes from the Latin *apparatus* or *adparatus*, signifying the thing fitted or adapted for another; *attire*, compounded of *at* or *ad* and *tire*, in French *tirer*, Latin *traho* to draw, signifies the thing drawn or put on; *array* is compounded of *ar* or *ad* and *ray* or *row*, signifying the state of being in a row, or being in order.

These terms are all applicable to dress or exterior decoration. *Apparel* is the dress of every one; *attire* is the dress of the great; *array* is the dress of particular persons on particular occasions: it is the first object of every man to provide himself with *apparel* suitable to his station; 'It is much, that this depraved custom of painting the face should so long escape the penal laws, both of the church and state, which have been very severe against luxury in *apparel*.'—BACON. The desire of shining forth in gaudy *attire* is the property of little minds;

A robe of tissue, stiff with golden wire,
An upper vest, once Helen's rich *attire*.
DRYDEN

On festivals and solemn occasions, it may be proper for those who are to be conspicuous to set themselves out with a comely *array;*

> She seem'd a virgin of the Spartan blood,
> With such *array* Harpalyce bestrode
> Her Thracian courser.—DRYDEN.

Apparel and *attire* respect the quality and fashion of the thing; but *array* has regard to the disposition of the things with their neatness and decorum: *apparel* may be costly or mean; *attire* may be gay or shabby; but *array* will never be otherwise than neat or comely.

TO PLACE, DISPOSE, ORDER.

To *place* is to assign a *place* (*v. Place*) to a thing: to *dispose* is to *place* according to a certain rule; to *order* is to *place* in a certain *order.*

Things are often *placed* from the necessity of being *placed* in some way or another: they are *disposed* so as to appear to the best advantage.

Books are *placed* on a shelf or in a cupboard to be out of the way; they are *disposed* on shelves according to their size: chairs are *placed* in different parts of a room; prints are tastefully *disposed* round a room.

Material objects only are *placed*, in the proper sense of the term. Sticks are *placed* at certain distances for purposes of convenience; persons or things are *placed* in particular situations;

> Our two first parents, yet the only two
> Of mankind in the happy garden *plac'd.*—MILTON.

If I have a wish that is prominent above the rest, it is to see you *placed* to your satisfaction near me.'—SHENSTONE. It may also be applied in the improper sense to spiritual objects.

Material or spiritual objects are *dispos'd;*

> And last the reliques by themselves *dispose*,
> Which in a brazen urn the priests enclose.
> DRYDEN.

Spiritual objects only are *ordered.*

To *dispose* in the improper sense is a more partial action than to *order:* one *disposes* for particular occasions; one *orders* for a permanency and in complicated matters: our thoughts may be *disposed* to seriousness in certain cases; our thoughts and wills ought to be *ordered* aright at all times. An author *disposes* his work agreeably to the nature of his subject; a tradesman *orders* his business so as to do every thing in good time.

PLACE, SITUATION, STATION, POSITION, POST.

Place, in German *platz*, comes from *platt* even or open; *situation*, in Latin *situs*, comes from the Hebrew שות to put; *station*, from the Latin *status* and *sto* to stand, signifies the manner or place in which an object stands or is put; *position*, in Latin *positio* or *positus*, comes from the same source as *situs.*

Place is the abstract or general term that comprehends the idea of any given space that may be occupied: *station* is the *place* where one stands or is fixed: *situation* and *position* respect the object as well as the *place*, that is, they signify how the object is put, as well as where it is put. A *place* or a *station* may be either vacant or otherwise; a *situation* and a *position* necessarily suppose some occupied *place.* A *place* is either assigned or not assigned, known or unknown, real or supposed; 'Surely the church is a *place* where one day's truce ought to be allowed to the dissensions and animosities of mankind.'—BURKE. A *station* is a specifically assigned *place;*

> The planets in their *station* listening stood.
> MILTON.

We choose a *place* according to our convenience, and we leave it again at pleasure; but we take up our *station*, and hold it for a given period. One inquires for a *place* which is known only by name; the *station* is appointed for us, and is therefore easily found out. Travellers wander from *place* to *place;* soldiers have always some *station.*

The terms *place* and *situation* are said of objects animate or inanimate; *station* only of animate objects, or objects figuratively considered as such; *position* only of inanimate objects: a person chooses a *place*, a thing occupies a *place*, or has a *place* set apart for it: a *station* or stated *place* must always be assigned to each person who has to act in concert with others; 'The seditious remained within their *station*, which, by reason of the nastiness of the beastly multitude, might more fitly be termed a kennel than a camp.'—HAYWARD. A person chooses a *situation* according to his convenience; 'A *situation* in which I am as unknown to all the world as I am ignorant of all that passes in it would exactly suit me.'—COWPER. A *situation* or *position* is chosen for a thing to suit the convenience of an individual: the former is said of things as they stand with regard to others; the latter of things as they stand with regard to themselves. The *situation* of a house comprehends the nature of the *place*, whether on high or low ground; and also its relation to other objects, that is, whether higher or lower, nearer or more distant: the *position* of a window in a house is considered as to whether it is by the side or in front; the *position* of a book is considered as to whether it stands leaning or upright, with its face or back forward. *Situation* is moreover said of things that come thither of themselves; *position* mostly of those things that have been put there at will. The *situation* of some tree or rock, on some elevated *place*, is agreeable to be looked at, or to be looked from; 'Prince Cesarini has a palace in a pleasant *situation*, and set off with many beautiful walks.'—ADDISON. The faulty *position* of a letter in writing sometimes spoils the whole performance; 'By varying the *position* of my eye, and moving it nearer to or farther from the direct beam of the sun's light, the colour of the sun's reflected light constantly varied upon the speculum as it did upon my eye.'—NEWTON.

Place, situation, and *station* have an improper signification in respect to men in civil society, that is, either to their circumstances or actions. *Post* has no other sense when applied to persons. *Place* is as indefinite as before; it may be taken for that share which we personally have in society either generally, as when every one is said to fill a *place* in society; or particularly for a specifick share of its business, so as to fill a *place* under government: *situation* is that kind of *place* which specifies either our share in its business, but with a higher import than the general term *place*, or a share in its gains and losses, as the prosperous or adverse *situation* of a man: a *station* is that kind of *place* which denotes a share in its relative consequence, power, and honour; in which sense every man holds a certain *station;* the *post* is that kind of *place* in which he has a specifick share in the duties of society: the *situation* comprehends many duties; but the *post* includes properly one duty only; the word being figuratively employed from the *post*, or particular spot which a soldier is said to occupy. A clerk in a counting-house fills a *place:* a clergyman holds a *situation* by virtue of his office; 'Though this is a *situation* of the greatest ease and tranquillity in human life, yet this is by no means fit to be the subject of all men's petitions to God.'—ROGERS. A clergyman is in the *station* of a gentleman by reason of his education, as well as his *situation;* 'It has been my fate to be engaged in business much and often, by the *stations* in which I have been placed.'—ATTERBURY. A faithful minister will always consider that his *post* where good is to be done; 'I will never, while I have health, be wanting to my duty in my *post.*'—ATTERBURY.

PLACE, SPOT, SITE.

A particular or given space is the idea common to these terms; but the former is general and indefinite, the latter specifick. *Place* is limited to no size nor quantity, it may be large: but *spot* implies a very small *place*, such as by a figure of speech is supposed to be no larger than a *spot:* the term *place* is employed upon every occasion; the term *spot* is confined to very particular cases: we may often know the *place* in a general way where a thing is, but it is not easy after a course of years to find out the exact *spot* on which it has happened. The *place* where our Saviour was buried is to be seen and pointed out, but not the very *spot* where he lay;

> O, how unlike the *place* from whence they fell!
> MILTON.

My fortune leads to traverse realms alone,
And find no *spot* of all the world my own.
GOLDSMITH.

The *site* is the *spot* on which any thing stands or is situated; it is more commonly applied to a building or any *place* marked out for a specifick purpose; as the *site* on which a camp had been formed;

Before my view appear'd a structure fair,
Its *site* uncertain if on earth or air.—POPE.

BACK, BACKWARD, BEHIND.

Back and *backward* are used only as adverbs; *behind* either as an adverb or a preposition. Hence we say to go *back* or *backward*, to go *behind* or *behind* the wall.

Back denotes the situation of being, and the direction of going; *backward*, simply the manner of going: a person stands *back*, who does not wish to be in the way; he goes *backward*, when he does not wish to turn his *back* to an object;

So rag'd Tydides, boundless in his ire,
Drove armies *back*, and made all Troy retire.
POPE.

Whence many wearied e'er they had o'erpast
The middle stream (for they in vain have tried)
Again return'd astounded and aghast,
No one regardful look would ever *backward* cast.
GILBERT WEST.

Back marks simply the situation of a place, *behind* the situation of one object with regard to another: a person stands *back*, who stands in the *back* part of any place; he stands *behind*, who has any one in the front of him: the *back* is opposed to the front, *behind* to before;

Forth flew this hated fiend, the child of Rome,
Driv'n to the verge of Albion, lingered there.
Then, with her James receding, cast *behind*
One angry frown, and sought more servile climes.
SHENSTONE (*on Cruelty*).

AFTER, BEHIND.

After respects order; *behind* respects position. One runs *after* a person, or stands *behind* his chair; *after* is used either figuratively or literally: *behind* is used only literally. Men hunt *after* amusements; misfortunes come *after* one another: a garden lies *behind* a house; a thing is concealed *behind* a bush;

Good *after* ill, and *after* pain delight,
Alternate, like the scenes of day and night.
DRYDEN.

He first, and close *behind* him followed she,
For such was Proserpine's severe decree.—DRYDEN.

UNDER, BELOW, BENEATH.

Under, like hind in behind, and the German *unter*, *hinter*, &c., are all connected with the preposition *in* implying the relation of enclosure; *below* denotes the state of being low; and *beneath* from the German *nieder*, and the Greek νερθε or ἔνερθε downwards, has the same original signification. It is evident, therefore, from the above, that the preposition *under* denotes any situation of retirement or concealment; *below* any situation of inferiority or lowness; and *beneath*, the same, only in a still greater degree. We are covered or sheltered by that which we stand *under*; we excel or rise above that which is *below* us; we look down upon that which is *beneath* us: we live *under* the protection of government; the sun disappears when it is *below* the horizon; we are apt to tread upon that which is altogether *beneath* us; 'The Jewish writers in their chronological computations often shoot *under* or over the truth at their pleasure.'—PRIDEAUX. 'All sublunary comforts imitate the changeableness, as well as feel the influence, of the planet they are *under*.'—SOUTH.

Our minds are here and there, *below*, above;
Nothing that 's mortal can so quickly move.
DENHAM.

'How can any thing better be expected than rust and canker when men will rather dig their treasure from *beneath* than fetch it from above.'—SOUTH.

ABOVE, OVER, UPON, BEYOND.

When an object is *above* another, it exceeds it in height; when it is *over* another, it extends along its superiour surface; when it is *upon* another, it comes in contact with its superiour surface; when it is *beyond* another, it lies at a greater distance. Trees frequently grow *above* a wall, and sometimes the branches hang *over* the wall or rest *upon* it, but they seldom stretch much *beyond* it;

So when with crackling flames a caldron fries,
The bubbling waters from the bottom rise,
Above the brim they force their fiery way;
Black vapours climb aloft and cloud the day.
DRYDEN.

The geese fly *o'er* the barn, the bees in arms
Drive headlong from their waxen cells in swarms.
DRYDEN.

As I did stand my watch *upon* the hill
I look'd toward Birnam, and anon methought
The wood began to move.—SHAKSPEARE

He that sees a dark and shady grove
Stays not, but looks *beyond* it on the sky.
HERBERT

In the figurative sense the first is mostly employed to convey the idea of superiority, the second of authority, the third of immediate influence, and the fourth of extent. Every one should be *above* falsehood, but particularly those who are set *over* others, who may have an influence *on* their minds *beyond* all calculation.

SITUATION, CONDITION, STATE, PREDICAMENT, PLIGHT, CASE.

Situation (*v. Place*) is said generally of objects as they respect others; *condition* (*v. Condition*) as they respect themselves. Whatever affects our property our honour, our liberty, and the like, constitutes our *situation*; 'The man who has a character of his own is little changed by varying his *situation*.'—MRS. MONTAGUE. Whatever affects our person immediately is our *condition*: a person who is unable to pay a sum of money to save himself from a prison is in a bad *situation*: a traveller who is left in a ditch robbed and wounded is in a bad *condition*; 'It is indeed not easy to prescribe a successful manner of approach to the distressed or necessitous, whose *condition* subjects every kind of behaviour equally to miscarriage.'—JOHNSON. The *situation* and *condition* are said of that which is contingent and changeable; the *state*, from the Latin *sto* to stand, signifying the point that is stood upon, is said of that which is comparatively stable or established. A tradesman is in a good *situation* who is in the way of carrying on a good trade: his affairs are in a good *state* if he is enabled to answer every demand and to keep up his credit. Hence it is that we speak of the *state* of health, and the *state* of the mind; not the *situation* or *condition*, because the body and mind are considered as to their general frame, and not as to any relative or particular circumstances; so likewise we say a *state* of infancy, a *state* of guilt, a *state* of innocence, and the like; but not either a *situation* or a *condition*; 'Patience itself is one virtue by which we are prepared for that *state* in which evil shall be no more.'—JOHNSON.

When speaking of bodies there is the same distinction in the terms, as in regard to individuals. An army may be either in a *situation*, a *condition*, or a *state*. An army that is on service may be in a critical *situation*, with respect to the enemy and its own comparative weakness; it may be in a deplorable *condition* if it stand in need of provisions and necessaries. an army that is at home will be in a good or bad *state*, according to the regulations of the commander-in chief. Of a prince who is threatened with invasion from foreign enemies, and with a rebellion from his subjects, we should not say that his *condition*, but his *situation*, was critical. Of a prince, however, who like Alfred was obliged to fly, and to seek safety in disguise and poverty, we should speak of his hard *condition*: the *state* of a prince cannot be spoken of, but the *state* of his affairs and government may; hence, likewise, *state* may with most propriety be said of a nation: but *situation* seldom, unless in respect to other nations, and *condition* never. On the other hand when speaking of the poor, we seldom employ the term *situation*, because they are seldom considered as a body in relation to other bodies: we mostly speak of their *condition* as better or worse, according as they have more or less of the comforts of life; and of their *state* as regards their moral habits.

These terms may likewise be applied to inanimate objects; and upon the same grounds, a house is in a good *situation* as respects the surrounding objects; it is in a good or bad *condition* as respects the painting, cleaning, and exteriour, altogether; it is in a bad *state*, as respects the beams, plaster, roof, and interiour structure, altogether. The hand of a watch is in a different *situation* every hour; the watch itself may be in a bad *condition* if the wheels are clogged with dirt; but in a good *state* if the works are altogether sound and fit for service.

Situation and *condition* are either permanent or temporary. The *predicament*, from the Latin *predico* to assert or declare, signifies to commit one's self by an assertion; and when applied to circumstances, it expresses a temporary embarrassed *situation* occasioned by an act of one's own: hence we always speak of bringing ourselves into a *predicament*;

The offender's life lies in the mercy
Of the duke only 'gainst all other voice,
In which *predicament* I say thou stand'st.
SHAKSPEARE.

Plight, contracted from the Latin *plicatus*, participle of *plico* to fold, signifies any circumstance in which one is disagreeably entangled; and *case* (*v. Case*) signifies any thing which may befall us, or into which we fall mostly, though not necessarily contrary to our inclination. Those two latter terms therefore denote a species of temporary *condition*; for they both express that which happens to the object itself, without reference to any other. A person is in an unpleasant *situation* who is shut up in a stage coach with disagreeable company. He is in an awkward *predicament* when attempting to please one friend he displeases another. He may be in a wretched *plight* if he is overturned in a stage at night, and at a distance from any habitation;

Satan beheld their *plight*
And to his mates thus in derision call'd.—MILTON.

He will be in evil *case* if he is compelled to put up with a spare and poor diet; 'Our *case* is like that of a traveller upon the Alps, who should fancy that the top of the next hill must end his journey, because it terminates his prospect.'—ADDISON.

CASE, CAUSE.

Case, in Latin *casus*, from *cado* to fall, chance, happen, signifies the thing falling out; *cause*, in French *cause*, Latin *causa*, is probably changed from *case*, and the Latin *casus*.

The *case* is matter of fact; the *cause* is matter of question: a *case* involves circumstances and consequences; a *cause* involves reasons and arguments: a *case* is something to be learned; a *cause* is something to be decided.

A *case* needs only to be stated; a *cause* must be defended: a *cause* may include *cases*, but not *vice versâ*: in all *causes* that are to be tried, there are many legal *cases* that must be cited: 'There is a double praise due to virtue when it is lodged in a body that seems to have been prepared for the reception of vice: in many such *cases* the soul and body do not seem to be fellows.'—ADDISON. Whoever is interested in the *cause* of humanity will not be heedless of those *cases* of distress which are perpetually presenting themselves; 'I was myself an advocate so long, that I never mind what advocates say, but what they prove, and I can only examine proofs in *causes* brought before me.'—SIR WILLIAM JONES

CONDITION, STATION.

Condition, in French *condition*, Latin *conditio*, from *condo* to build or form, signifies properly the thing formed; and in an extended sense, the manner and circumstances under which a thing is formed; *station*, in French *station*, Latin *statio*, from *sto* to stand, signifies the standing place or point.

Condition has most relation to the circumstances, education, birth, and the like; *station* refers rather to the rank, occupation, or mode of life which one pursues. Riches suddenly acquired are calculated to make a man forget his original *condition*; 'The common charge against those who rise above their original *condition*, is that of pride.'—JOHNSON. There is nothing which men are more apt to forget than the duties of their *station*; 'The last day will assign to every one a *station* suitable to the dignity of his character.'—ADDISON.

The *condition* of men in reality is often so different from what it appears, that it is extremely difficult to form an estimate of what they are, or what they have been. It is the folly of the present day, that every man is unwilling to keep the *station* which has been assigned to him by Providence. The rage for equality destroys every just distinction in society; the low aspire to be, in appearance, at least, equal with their superiours; and those in elevated *stations* do not hesitate to put themselves on a level with their inferiours.

TO PUT, PLACE, LAY, SET.

Put is in all probability contracted from *positus*, participle of *pono* to *place*; *place* signifies the same as in the preceding articles; *lay*, in Saxon *legan*, German *legen*, Latin *loco*, and Greek *λέγομαι*, signifies to cause to lie; *set*, in German *setzen*, Latin *sisto*, from *sto* to stand, signifies to cause to stand.

Put is the most general of all these terms;

The labourer cuts
Young slips, and in the soil securely *puts*.—DRYDEN.

Place, *lay*, and *set* are but modes of *putting*; one *puts*, but the way of *putting* it is not defined; we may *put* a thing into one's room, one's desk, one's pocket, and the like; but to *place* is to *put* in a specifick manner, and for a specifick purpose; one *places* a book on a shelf as a fixed place for it, and in a position most suitable to it;

Then youths and virgins, twice as many, join
To *place* the dishes, and to serve the wine.
DRYDEN.

To *lay* and *set* are still more specifick than *place*; the former being applied only to such things as can be made to *lie*;

Here some design a mole, while others there
Lay deep foundations for a theatre.—DRYDEN.

And *set* only to such as can be made to stand: a book may be said to be *laid* on the table when placed in a downward position: and *set* on a shelf when *placed* on one end; we *lay* ourselves down on the ground; we *set* a trunk upon the ground;

Ere I could
Give him that parting kiss, which I had *set*
Between two charming words, comes in my father.
SHAKSPEARE

TO LIE, LAY.

By a vulgar errour these words have been so confounded as to deserve some notice. To *lie* is neuter, and designates a state: to *lay* is active, and denotes an action on an object; it is properly to cause to *lie*: a thing *lies* on the table; some one *lays* it on the table: he *lies* with his fathers; they *laid* him with his fathers. In the same manner, when used idiomatically, we say, a thing *lies* by us until we bring it into use: we *lay* it by for some future purpose: we *lie* down in order to repose ourselves; we *lay* money down by way of deposite: the disorder *lies* in the constitution; we *lay* the ill treatment of others to heart: we *lie* with the person with whom we sleep; we *lay* a wager with a person when we stake our money against his; 'Ants bite off all the buds before they *lay* it up, and, therefore, the corn that has *lain* in their nests will produce nothing.'—ADDISON. 'The church admits none to holy orders without *laying* upon them the highest obligations imaginable.'—BEVERIDGE.

TO DISORDER, DERANGE, DISCONCERT, DISCOMPOSE.

Disorder signifies to put out of order; *derange*, from *de* and *range* or *rank*, signifies to put out of the rank in which it was placed; *disconcert*, to put out of the concert or harmony; *discompose*, to put out of a state of composure.

All these terms express the idea of putting out of order; but the three latter vary as to the mode or object of the action. The term *disorder* is used in a perfectly indefinite form, and might be applied to any object. As every thing may be in order, so may every thing be *disordered;* yet it is seldom used except in regard to such things as have been in a natural order. *Derange* and *disconcert* are employed in speaking of such things as have been put into an artificial order. To *derange* is to *disorder* that which has been systematically arranged, or put in a certain range; and to *disconcert* is to *disorder* that which has been put together by concert or contrivance: thus the body may be *disordered;* a man's affairs or papers *deranged;* a scheme *disconcerted.* To *discompose* is a species of *derangement* in regard to trivial matters: thus a tucker, a frill, or a cap may be *discomposed.* The slightest change of diet will *disorder* people of tender constitutions: misfortunes are apt to *derange* the affairs of the most prosperous: the unexpected return of a master to his home *disconcerts* the schemes which have been formed by the domesticks: those who are particular as to their appearance are careful not to have any part of their dress *discomposed.*

When applied to the mind *disorder* and *derange* are said of the intellect; *disconcert* and *discompose* of the ideas or spirits: the former denoting a permanent state; the latter a temporary or transient state. The mind is said to be *disordered* when the faculty of ratiocination is in any degree interrupted; 'Since devotion itself may *disorder* the mind, unless its heats are tempered with caution or prudence, we should be particularly careful to keep our reason as cool as possible.'—ADDISON. The intellect is said to be *deranged* when it is brought into a positive state of incapacity for action: persons are sometimes *disordered* in their minds for a time by particular occurrences, who do not become actually *deranged;* 'All passion implies a violent emotion of mind; of course it is apt to *derange* the regular course of our ideas.'—BLAIR. A person is said to be *disconcerted* who suddenly loses his collectedness of thinking; 'There are men whose powers operate only at leisure and in retirement; and whose intellectual vigour deserts them in conversation; whom merriment confuses, and objection *disconcerts.*'—JOHNSON. A person is said to be *discomposed* who loses his regularity of feeling;

But with the changeful temper of the skies,
As rains condense, and sunshine rarefies,
So turn the species in their alter'd minds,
Compos'd by calms, and *discompos'd* by winds.
DRYDEN.

A sense of shame is the most apt to *disconcert:* the more irritable the temper the more easily one is *discomposed.*

DERANGEMENT, INSANITY, LUNACY, MADNESS, MANIA.

Derangement, from the verb to *derange*, implies the first stage of disorder in the intellect; *insanity*, or unsoundness, implies positive disease, which is more or less permanent; *lunacy* is a violent sort of *insanity*, which was supposed to be influenced by the moon; *madness* and *mania*, from the Greek *μαίνομαι* to rage, implies *insanity* or *lunacy* in its most furious and confirmed stage. *Deranged* persons may sometimes be perfectly sensible in every thing but particular subjects. *Insane* persons are sometimes entirely restored. *Lunaticks* have their lucid intervals, and *maniacks* their intervals of repose.

Derangement may sometimes be applied to the temporary confusion of a disturbed mind, which is not in full possession of all its faculties: *madness* may sometimes be the result of violently inflamed passions: and *mania* may be applied to any vehement attachment which takes possession of the mind; 'The locomotive *mania* of an Englishman circulates his person, and of course his cash, into every quarter of the kingdom.'—CUMBERLAND

MADNESS, PHRENSY, RAGE, FURY.

Madness (*v. Derangement*); *phrensy*, in Latin *phrenesis*, Greek *φρενῖτις* from *φρὴν* the mind, signifies a disordered mind; *rage*, in French *rage*, Latin *rabies; fury*, in Latin *furor*, comes in all probability from *feror* to be carried, because *fury* carries a person away.

Madness and *phrensy* are used in the physical and moral sense; *rage* and *fury* only in the moral sense: in the first case, *madness* is a confirmed derangement in the organ of thought; *phrensy* is only a temporary derangement from the violence of fever: the former lies in the system, and is, in general, incurable; the latter is only occasional, and yields to the power of medicine.

In the moral sense of these terms the cause is put for the effect, that is, *madness* and *phrensy* are put for that excessive violence of passion by which they are caused; and as *rage* and *fury* are species of this passion, namely, the angry passion, they are therefore to *madness* and *phrensy* sometimes as the cause is to the effect: the former, however, are so much more violent than the latter, as they altogether destroy the reasoning faculty, which is not expressly implied in the signification of the latter terms. Moral *madness* differs both in degree and duration from *phrensy:* if it spring from the extravagance of *rage*, it bursts out into every conceivable extravagance, but is only transitory; if it spring from disappointed love, or any other disappointed passion, it is as permanent as direct physical *madness;*

'T was no false heraldry when *madness* drew
Her pedigree from those who too much knew.
DENHAM.

Phrensy is always temporary, but even more impetuous than *madness;* in the *phrensy* of despair men commit acts of suicide: in the *phrensy* of distress and grief, people are hurried into many actions fatal to themselves or others;

What *phrensy*, shepherd, has thy soul possessed?
DRYDEN.

Rage refers more immediately to the agitation that exists within the mind; *fury* refers to that which shows itself outwardly: a person contains or stifles his *rage;* but his *fury* breaks out into some external mark of violence: *rage* will subside of itself; *fury* spends itself: a person may be choked with *rage;* but his *fury* finds a vent: an *enraged* man may be pacified; a *furious* one is deaf to every remonstrance,

Desire not
To allay my *rages* and revenges with
Your colder reasons.—SHAKSPEARE.

Rage, when applied to persons, commonly signifies highly inflamed anger; but it may be employed for inflamed passion towards any object which is specified, as a *rage* for musick, a *rage* for theatrical performances, a fashionable *rage* for any whim of the day. *Fury*, though commonly signifying *rage* bursting out, yet may be any impetuous feeling displaying itself in extravagant action: as the Divine *fury* supposed to be produced upon the priestess of Apollo, by the inspiration of the god, and the Bacchanalian *fury*, which expression depicts the influence of wine upon the body and mind;

Confin'd their *fury* to those dark abodes.—DRYDEN

In the improper application, to inanimate objects, the words *rage* and *fury* preserve a similar distinction the *rage* of the heat denotes the excessive height to which it is risen; the *fury* of the winds indicates their violent commotion and turbulence: so in like manner the *raging* of the tempest characterizes figuratively its burning anger; and the *fury* of the flames marks their impetuous movements, their wild and rapid spread.

TO CONFOUND, TO CONFUSE.

Confound and *confuse* are both derived from different parts of the same verb, namely, *confundo* and its participle *confusus*, signifying to pour or mix together without design that which ought to be distinct.

Confound has an active sense; *confuse* a neuter or reflective sense: a person *confounds* one thing with another;

I to the tempest make the poles resound,
And the conflicting elements *confound.*—Dryden.

Objects become *confused*, or a person *confuses* himself: it is a common errour among ignorant people to *confound* names, and among children to have their ideas *confused* on commencing a new study;

A *confus'd* report passed through my ears;
But full of hurry, like a morning dream,
It vanished in the bus'ness of the day.—Lee.

The present age is distinguished by nothing so much as by *confounding* all distinctions, which is a great source of *confusion* in men's intercourse with each other, both in publick and private life.

CONFUSION, DISORDER.

Confusion signifies the state of being *confounded* or *confused* (*v. To confound*); *disorder*, compounded of the privative *dis* and *order*, signifies the reverse of order.

Confusion is to *disorder* as the species to the genus: *confusion* supposes the absence of all order; *disorder* the derangement of order: there is always *disorder* in *confusion*, but not always *confusion* in *disorder*: a routed army, or a tumultuous mob, will be in *confusion* and will create *confusion*:

Now seas and earth were in *confusion* lost,
A world of waters, and without a coast.
Dryden.

A whisper or an ill-timed motion of an individual constitutes *disorder* in a school, or in an army that is drawn up; 'When you behold a man's affairs through negligence and misconduct involved in *disorder*, you naturally conclude that his ruin approaches.'—Blair.

DIFFERENCE, VARIETY, DIVERSITY, MEDLEY.

Difference signifies the cause or the act of differing: *variety*, from *various* or *vary*, in Latin *varius*, probably comes from *varus* a speck or speckle, because this is the best emblem of *variety*; *diversity*, in Latin *diversitas*, comes from *diverto*, compounded of *di* and *verto*, signifying the quality of being asunder; *medley* comes from the word *meddle*, which is but a change from *mingle*, *mix*, &c.

Difference and *variety* seem to lie in the things themselves; *diversity* and *medley* are created either by accident or design: a *difference* may lie in two objects only; a *variety* cannot exist without an assemblage: a *difference* is discovered by means of a comparison which the mind forms of objects to prevent confusion; *variety* strikes on the mind, and pleases the imagination with many agreeable images; it is opposed to dull uniformity: the acute observer traces *differences*, however minute, in the objects of his research, and by this means is enabled to class them under their general or particular heads; 'Where the faith of the Holy Church is one, a *difference* between customs of the church doth no harm.'—Hooker. * Nature affords such an infinite *variety* in every thing which exists, that if we do not perceive it, the fault is in ourselves; 'Homer does not only outshine all other poets in the *variety*, but also in the novelty, of his characters.'—Addison. *Diversity* arises from an assemblage of objects naturally contrasted; 'The goodness of the Supreme Being is no less seen in the *diversity*, than in the multitude of living creatures.'—Addison. A *medley* is produced by an assemblage of objects so ill suited as to produce a ludicrous effect; 'What unnatural motions and counter-ferments must such a *medley* of intemperance produce in the body?'—Addison.

Diversity exists in the tastes or opinions of men; a *medley* is produced by the concurrence of such tastes or opinions as can in no wise coalesce: where the minds of men are disengaged from the control of authority, there will be a great *diversity* of opinions; where a number of men come together with *different* habits, we may expect to find a *medley* of characters; good taste may render a *diversity* of colour agreeable to the eye; caprice or bad taste will be apt to form a ridiculous *medley* of colours and ornaments. A *diversity* of sounds heard at a suitable distance in the stillness of the evening, will have an agreeable effect on the ear; a *medley* of noises, whether heard near or at a distance, must always be harsh and offensive.

* Vide Abbe Girard: "Différence, diversité, varieté, bizarrure"

DIFFERENCE, DISTINCTION.

Difference (*v. Difference*) lies in the thing; *distinction* (*v. To abstract*) is the act of the person; the former is, therefore, to the latter as the cause to the effect; the *distinction* rests on the *difference*; those are equally bad logicians who make a *distinction* without a *difference*, or who make no *distinction* where there is a *difference*. Sometimes *distinction* is put for the ground of *distinction*, which brings it nearer in sense to *difference*, in which case the former is a species of the latter: a *difference* is either external or internal; a *distinction* is always external: we have *differences* in character, and *distinctions* in dress: the *difference* between profession and practice, though very considerable, is often lost sight of by the professors of Christianity; in the sight of God, there is no rank or *distinction* that will screen a man from the consequences of unrepented sins;

O son of Tydeus, cease! be wise, and see
How vast the *diff'rence* of the gods and thee.
Pope.

'When I was got into this way of thinking, I presently grew conceited of the argument, and was just preparing to write a letter of advice to a member of parliament, for opening the freedom of our towns and trades for taking away all manner of *distinctions* between the natives and foreigners.'—Steele.

DIFFERENT, DISTINCT, SEPARATE.

Difference (*v. To differ, vary*) is opposed to similitude; there is no *difference* between objects absolutely alike: *distinctness* (*v. To abstract*) is opposed to identity; there can be no *distinction* where there is only one and the same being: *separation* is opposed to unity; there can be no *separation* between objects that coalesce or adhere: things may be *different* and not *distinct*, or *distinct* and not *different*: *different* is said altogether of the internal properties of things; *distinct* is said of things as objects of vision, or as they appear either to the eye or the mind: when two or more things are seen only as one, they may be *different*, but they are not *distinct*; but whatever is seen as two or more things, each complete in itself, is *distinct*, although it may not be *different*: two roads are said to be *different* which run in *different* directions, but they may not be *distinct* when seen on a map: on the other hand, two roads are said to be *distinct* when they are observed as two roads to run in the same direction, but they need not in any particular to be *different*: two stars of *different* magnitudes may, in certain directions, appear as one, in which case they are *different*, but not *distinct*; two books on the same subject, and by the same author, but not written in continuation of each other, are *distinct* books, but not *different*;

No hostile arms approach your happy ground;
Far *diff'rent* is my fate.—Dryden.

What is *separate* must in its nature be generally *distinct*; but every thing is not *separate* which is *distinct*: when houses are *separate* they are obviously *distinct*; but they may frequently be *distinct* when they are not positively *separated*: the *distinct* is marked out by some external sign, which determines its beginning and its end; the *separate* is that which is set apart, and to be seen by itself: *distinct* is a term used only in determining the singularity or plurality of objects; the *separate* only in regard to their proximity or to distance from each other; we speak of having a *distinct* household, but of living in *separate* apartments; of dividing one's subject into *distinct* heads or of making things into *separate* parcels: the body and soul are *different*, inasmuch as they have *different* properties; they are *distinct* inasmuch as they have marks by which they may be *distinguished*, and at death they will be *separate*;

His *sep'rate* troops let every leader call,
Each strengthen each, and all encourage all;
What chief or soldier of the num'rous band,
Or bravely fights or ill obeys command,
When thus *distinct* they war, soon shall be known.
POPE.

DIFFERENT, SEVERAL, DIVERS, SUNDRY, VARIOUS.

All these terms are employed to mark a number (*v. To differ, vary*): but *different* is the most indefinite of all these terms, as its office is rather to define the quality than the number, and is equally applicable to few and many; it is opposed to singularity, but the other terms are employed positively to express many. *Several*, from to *sever*, signifies split or made into many; they may be either *different* or alike: there may be *several* different things, or *several* things alike; but there cannot be *several* divers things, for the word *divers* signifies properly many *different*. *Sundry*, from *asunder* or apart, signifies many things scattered or at a distance, whether as it regards time or space. *Various* expresses not only a greater number, but a greater *diversity* than all the rest.

The same thing often affects *different* persons *differently*: an individual may be affected *several* times in the same way; or particular persons may be affected at *sundry* times and in *divers* manners; the ways in which men are affected are so *various* as not to admit of enumeration: it is not so much to understand *different* languages as to understand *several different* languages; 'It is astonishing to consider the *different* degrees of care that descend from the parent to the young, so far as is absolutely necessary for the leaving a posterity.'—ADDISON. 'The bishop has *several* courts under him, and may visit at pleasure every part of his diocess.'—BLACKSTONE. *Divers* modes have been suggested and tried for the good education of youth, but most of too theoretical a nature to admit of being reduced successfully to practice; 'In the frame and constitution of the ecclesiastical polity, there are *divers* ranks and degrees.'—BLACKSTONE. An incorrect writer omits *sundry* articles that belong to a statement;

Fat olives of *sundry* sorts appear,
Of *sundry* shapes their unctuous berries bear.
DRYDEN.

We need not wonder at the misery which is introduced into families by extravagance and luxury, when we notice the infinitely *various* allurements for spending money which are held out to the young and the thoughtless; 'As land is improved by sowing it with *various* seeds, so is the mind by exercising it with different studies.'—MELMOTH (*Letters of Pliny*).

DIFFERENT, UNLIKE.

Different is positive, *unlike* is negative: we look at what is *different*, and draw a comparison; but that which is *unlike* needs no comparison: a thing is said to be *different* from every other thing, or *unlike* to any thing seen before; which latter mode of expression obviously conveys less to the mind than the former; 'How *different* is the view of past life in the man who is grown old in knowledge and wisdom from that of him who is grown old in ignorance and folly.'—ADDISON.

How far *unlike* those chiefs of race divine,
How vast the diff'rence of their deeds and mine.
POPE.

TO CHANGE, ALTER, VARY.

Change, in French *changer*, is probably derived from the middle Latin *cambio* to *exchange*, signifying to take one thing for another; *alter*, from the Latin *alter* another, signifies to make a thing otherwise; *vary*, in Latin *vario* to make various, comes in all probability from *varus* a spot or speckle, which destroys uniformity of appearance in any surface.

We *change* a thing by putting another in its place; we *alter* a thing by making it different from what it was before; we *vary* it by *altering* it in different manners and at different times. We *change* our clothes whenever we put on others: the tailor *alters* clothes which are found not to fit; and he *varies* the fashion of making them whenever he makes new. A man *changes* his habits, *alters* his conduct, and *varies* his manner of speaking and thinking, according to circumstances; 'The general remedy of those who are uneasy without knowing the cause is *change* of place'—JOHNSON.

All things are but *alter'd*, nothing dies:
And here and there th' unbodied spirit flies;
By time, or force, or sickness, dispossess'd,
And lodges, where it lights, in man or beast.
DRYDEN.

'In every work of the imagination, the disposition of parts, the insertion of incidents, and use of decorations, may be *varied* a thousand ways with equal pro priety.'—JOHNSON.

A thing is *changed* without *altering* its kind; it is *altered* without destroying its identity; and it is *varied* without destroying the similarity. We *change* our habitation, but it still remains a habitation; we *alter* our house, but it still remains the same house; we *vary* the manner of painting and decoration, but it may strongly resemble the manner in which it has been before executed.

CHANGE, VARIATION, VICISSITUDE.

Change (*v. To change, alter*) is both to *vicissitude* and *variation* as the genus to the species. Every *variation* or *vicissitude* is a *change*, but every *change* is not a *variation* or *vicissitude*; *vicissitude*, in French *vicissitude*, Latin *vicissitudo*, from *vicissim* by turns, signifies changing alternately.

Change consists simply in ceasing to be the same: *variation* consists in being different at different times; *vicissitude* in being alternately or reciprocally different and the same. All created things are liable to *change*; old things pass away, all things become new: the humours of men, like the elements, are exposed to perpetual *variations*: human affairs, like the seasons, are subject to frequent *vicissitudes*.

Changes in governments or families are seldom attended with any good effect; 'How strangely are the opinions of men altered by a *change* in their condi tion.'—BLAIR. *Variations* in the state of the atmosphere are indicated by the barometer or thermometer; 'One of the company affirmed to us he had actually enclosed the liquor, found in a coquette's heart, in a small tube made after the manner of a weather-glass; but that instead of acquainting him with the *varia tions* of the atmosphere, it showed him the qualities of those persons who entered the room where it stood.'—ADDISON. *Vicissitudes* of a painful nature are less dangerous than those which elevate men to an unusual state of grandeur. By the former they are brought to a sense of themselves; by the latter they are carried beyond themselves;

It makes through heaven
Grateful *vicissitude*, like day and night.

VARIATION, VARIETY.

Variation denotes the act of *varying* (*v. To change*); *variety* denotes the quality of *varying*, or the thing *varied*. The astronomer observes the *variations* in the heavens; the philosopher observes the *variations* in the climate from year to year; 'The idea of *variation* (as a constituent in beauty), without attending so accurately to the manner of *variation*, has led Mr. Hogarth to consider angular figures as beautiful.'—BURKE. *Variety* is pleasing to all persons, but to none so much as the young and the fickle: there is an infinite *variety* in every species of objects animate or inanimate; 'As to the colours usually found in beautiful bodies, it may be difficult to ascertain them, because in the several parts of nature there is an infinite *variety*.'—BURKE.

INDISTINCT, CONFUSED.

Indistinct is negative; it marks simply the want of *distinctness*; *confused* is positive; it marks a positive degree of *indistinctness*. A thing may be *indistinct* without being *confused*; but it cannot be *confused* without being *indistinct*: two things may be *indistinct*, or not easily distinguished from each other but many things, or parts of the same things, are *confused:* two letters in a word may be *indistinct;* but the whole writings or many words are *confused;* sounds are *indistinct* which reach our ears only in part; but they are *confused* if they come in great numbers and out of all order. We see objects *indistinctly* when we cannot see all the features by which they would be distinguished from all objects; 'When a volume of travels is opened, nothing is found but such general accounts as leave no *distinct* idea behind them.'—JOHNSON. We see an object *confusedly* when every part is so blended with the other that no one feature can be distinguished; 'He that enters a town at night and surveys it in the morning, then hastens to another place, may please himself for a time with a hasty change of scene and a *confused* remembrance of palaces and churches.'—JOHNSON. By means of great distance objects become *indistinct;* from a defect in sight objects become more *confused.*

TO MIX, MINGLE, BLEND, CONFOUND.

Mix is in German *mischen*, Latin *misceo*, Greek μίσγω, Hebrew מזג; *mingle*, in Greek μιγνύω, is but a variation of *mix; blend*, in German *blenden* to dazzle, comes from *blind*, signifying to see confusedly, or confuse objects in a general way; *confound*, (*v. Confound*).

Mix is here a general and indefinite term, signifying simply to put together: but we may *mix* two or several things; we *mingle* several objects: things are *mixed* so as to lose all distinction; but they may be *mingled* and yet retain a distinction: liquids *mix* so as to become one, and individuals *mix* in a crowd so as to be lost;

> Can imagination boast,
> Amid its gay creation, hues like hers,
> Or can it *mix* them with that matchless skill,
> And lose them in each other?—THOMSON.

Things are *mingled* together of different sizes if they lie in the same spot, but they may still be distinguished;

> There as I pass'd with careless steps and slow,
> The *mingling* notes came soften'd from below.
> GOLDSMITH.

To *blend* is only partially to *mix*, as colours *blend* which fall into each other: to *confound* is to *mix* in a wrong way, as objects of sight are *confounded* when they are erroneously taken to be joined.

To *mix* and *mingle* are mostly applied to material objects, except in poetry: to *blend* and *confound* are mental operations, and principally employed on spiritual subjects: thus, events and circumstances are *blended* together in a narrative;

> But happy they! the happiest of their kind,
> Whom gentler stars unite, and in one fate
> Their hearts, their fortunes, and their beings *blend.*
> THOMSON.

The ideas of the ignorant are *confounded* in most cases, but particularly when they attempt to think for themselves;

> And long the gods, we know,
> Have grudg'd thee, Cæsar, to the world below,
> Where fraud and rapine, right and wrong, *confound.*
> DRYDEN.

MIXTURE, MEDLEY, MISCELLANY.

Mixture is the thing *mixed* (*v. To mix*); *medley*, from *meddle* or *middle*, signifies what comes between another; *miscellany*, in Latin *miscellaneus*, from *misceo* to *mix*, signifies also a *mixture*.

The *mixture* is general; whatever objects can be *mixed* will form a *mixture;* a *medley* is a *mixture* of things not fit to be *mixed:* and a *miscellany* is a *mixture* of many different things. Flour, water, and eggs may form a *mixture*, in the proper sense; but if to these were added all sorts of spices, it would form a *medley;* 'In great villanies, there is often such a *mixture* of the fool, as quite spoils the whole project of the knave.'—SOUTH.

> More oft in fools' and madmen's hands than sages,
> She seems a *medley* of all ages.—SWIFT.

Miscellany is a species of mixture applicable only to intellectual subjects: the *miscellaneous* is opposed to that which is systematically arranged: essays are *miscellaneous* in distinction from works on one particular subject; 'A writer, whose design is so comprehensive and *miscellaneous* as that of an essayist, may accommodate himself with a topick from every scene of life.—JOHNSON.

PROMISCUOUS, INDISCRIMINATE.

Promiscuous, in Latin *promiscuus*, from *promisceo* or *pro* and *misceo* to mingle, signifies thoroughly mingled; *indiscriminate*, from the Latin *in* privative and *discrimen* a difference, signifies without any difference.

Promiscuous is applied to any number of different objects mixed together;

> Victors and vanquish'd join *promiscuous* cries
> POPE.

Indiscriminate is only applied to the action in which one does not discriminate different objects: a multitude is termed *promiscuous*, as characterizing the thing; the use of different things for the same purpose, or of the same things for different purposes, is termed *indiscriminate*, as characterizing the person: things become *promiscuous* by the want of design in any one; they are *indiscriminate* by the fault of any one: plants of all descriptions are to be found *promiscuously* situated in the beds of a garden: it is folly to level any charge *indiscriminately* against all the members of any community or profession; 'From this *indiscriminate* distribution of misery, moralists have always derived one of their strongest moral arguments for a future state.'—JOHNSON.

IRREGULAR, DISORDERLY, INORDINATE, INTEMPERATE.

Irregular, that is literally *not regular*, marks merely the absence of a good quality; *disorderly*, that is literally out of order, marks the presence of a positively bad quality. What is *irregular* may be so from the nature of the thing; what is *disorderly* is rendered so by some external circumstance. Things are planted *irregularly* for want of design: the best troops are apt to be *disorderly* in a long march. *Irregular* and *disorderly* are taken in a moral as well as a natural sense; *inordinate*, which signifies also put out of order, is employed only in the moral sense. What is *irregular* is contrary to the rule that is established, or ought to be; what is *disorderly* is contrary to the order that has existed; what is *inordinate* is contrary to the order that is prescribed; what is *intemperate* is contrary to the temper or spirit that ought to be encouraged. Our habits are *irregular* which are not conformable to the laws of social society; 'In youth there is a certain *irregularity* and agitation by no means unbecoming.'—MELMOTH (*Letters of Pliny*). Our practices will be *disorderly* when we follow the blind impulse of passion; 'The minds of bad men are *disorderly*.'—BLAIR. Our desires will be *inordinate* when they are not under the control of reason guided by religion; '*Inordinate* passions are the great disturbers of life.'—BLAIR. Our indulgencies will be *intemperate* when we consult nothing but our appetites: 'Persuade but the covetous man not to deify his money, the *intemperate* man to abandon his revels, and I dare undertake all their giant-like objections shall vanish.'—SOUTH. Young people are apt to contract *irregular* habits if not placed under the care of discreet and sober people, and made to conform to the regulations of domestick life: children are naturally prone to become *disorderly*, if not perpetually under the eye of a master: it is the lot of human beings in all ages and stations to have *inordinate* desires, which require a constant check so as to prevent *intemperate* conduct of any kind.

SEQUEL, CLOSE.

Sequel is a species of *close;* it is that which follows by way of termination; but the *close* is simply that which *closes*, or puts an end to any thing. There cannot be a *sequel* without a *close*, but there may be a *close* without a *sequel*. A story may have either a *sequel* or a *close;* when the end is detached from the beginning so as to follow, it is a *sequel;* if the beginning and end are uninterrupted, it is simply a *close*.

When a work is published in distinct parts, those which follow at the end may be termed the *sequel:* if it appears all at once, the concluding pages are the *close*. The same distinction between these words is preserved in their figurative application;

> If black scandal or foul-fac'd reproach
> Attend the *sequel* of your imposition,
> Your meer enforcement shall acquittance me.
> SHAKSPEARE.

> Speedy death,
> The *close* of all my miseries, and the balm.
> MILTON.

TO END, CLOSE, TERMINATE.

To bring any thing to its last point is the common idea in the signification of these terms.

To *end* is the simple action of putting an *end* to, without any collateral idea; it is therefore the generick term. To *close* is to *end* gradually, or by shutting in, hence we speak of *closing* the rear, or of a scene *closing;*

> Orestes, Acamas, in front appear,
> And Œnomaus and Thoon *close* the rear.—POPE.

To *terminate* is to *end* in a specifick manner, hence we speak with propriety of a road or a line *terminating;* 'As I had a mind to know how each of these roads *terminated*, I joined myself with the assembly that were in the flower and vigour of their age, and called themselves the band of lovers.'—ADDISON. They preserve this distinction in the moral application. There are persons even in civilized countries so ignorant as, like the brutes, to *end* their lives as they began them, without one rational reflection;

> Greece in her single heroes strove in vain,
> Now hosts oppose thee, and thou must be slain:
> So shall my days in one sad tenour run,
> And *end* with sorrows as they first begun.—POPE.

The Christian *closes* his career of active duty only with the failure of his bodily powers;

> One frugal supper did our studies *close*.—DRYDEN.

A person *ends* a dispute, or puts an *end* to it, by yielding the subject of contest; he *terminates* the dispute by entering into a compromise; 'The wisdom of this world, its designs and efficacy, *terminate* on this side heaven.'—SOUTH.

END, EXTREMITY.

Both these words imply the last of those parts which constitute a thing; but the *end* designates that part generally; the *extremity* marks the particular point. The *extremity* is from the Latin *extremus* the very last *end*, that which is outermost. Hence the *end* may be said of that which bounds any thing; but *extremity* of that which extends farthest from us: we may speak of the *ends* of that which is circular in its form, or of that which has no specifick form;

> Now with full force the yielding horn he bends,
> Drawn to an arch, and joins the doubling *ends*.—POPE.

We speak of the *extremities* of that only which is supposed to project lengthwise; 'Our female projectors were all the last summer so taken up with the improvement of their petticoats, that they had not time to attend to any thing else; but having at length sufficiently adorned their lower parts, they now begin to turn their thoughts upon the other *extremity*.'—ADDISON.

The *end* is opposed to the beginning; the *extremity* to the centre or point from which we reckon. When a man is said to go to the *end* of a journey or to the *end* of the world, the expression is in both cases indefinite and general; but when he is said to go to the *extremities* of the earth or the *extremities* of a kingdom, the idea of relative distance is manifestly implied.

He who goes to the *end* of a path may possibly have a little farther to go in order to reach the *extremity*. In the figurative application *end* and *extremity* differ so widely as not to render any comparison needful.

EXTREMITY, EXTREME.

Extremity is used in the proper or the improper sense; *extreme* in the improper sense: we speak of the *extremity* of a line or an avenue, the *extremity* of distress, but the *extreme* of the fashion.

In the moral sense, *extremity* is applicable to the outward circumstances; *extreme* to the opinions and conduct of men: in matters of dispute between individuals it is a happy thing to guard against coming to *extremities*; 'Savage suffered the utmost *extremities* of poverty, and often fasted so long that he was seized with faintness.'—JOHNSON. It is the characteristick of volatile tempers to be always in *extremes*, either the *extreme* of joy or the *extreme* of sorrow; 'The two *extremes* to be guarded against are despotism, where all are slaves, and anarchy, where all would rule and none obey.'—BLAIR.

CLOSE, COMPACT.

Close, in French *clos*, comes from the Latin *clausus* participle of *claudo* to shut; *compact*, in Latin *compactus*, participle of *compingo* to fix or join, signifies jointed close together.

Proximity is expressed by both these terms; the former in a general and the latter in a restricted sense. Two bodies may be *close* to each other, but a body is *compact* with regard to itself.

Contact is not essential to constitute *closeness;* but a perfect adhesion of all the parts of a body is essential to produce *compactness*. Lines are *close* to each other that are separated but by a small space;

> To right and left the martial wings display
> Their shining arms, and stand in *close* array;
> Though weak their spears, though dwarfish be their height,
> *Compact* they move, the bulwark of the fight.
> SIR WM. JONES.

Things are rolled together in a *compact* form that are brought within the smallest possible space; 'Without attraction the dissevered particles of the chaos could never convene into such great *compact* masses as the planets.'—BENTLEY.

CLOSE, NEAR, NIGH.

Close signifies the same as in the preceding article; *near* and *nigh* are in Saxon *near*, *neah*, German, *nah*, &c.

Close is more definite than *near:* houses stand *close* to each other which are almost joined; men stand *close* when they touch each other;

> Th' unwearied watch their listening leaders keep,
> And couching *close*, repel invading sleep.—POPE.

Objects are *near* which are within sight; persons are *near* each other when they can converse together *Near* and *nigh*, which are but variations of each other, in etymology, admit of little or no difference in their use; the former however is the most general. People live *near* each other who are in the same street; they live *close* to each other when their houses are adjoining;

> O friend! Ulysses' shouts invade my ear;
> Distress'd he seems, and no assistance *near*.—POPE.

> From the red field their scatter'd bodies bear,
> And *nigh* the fleet a funeral structure rear.—POPE.

Close is annexed as an adjective; *near* is employed only as an adverb or preposition. We speak of *close* ranks or *close* lines; but not *near* ranks or *near* lines

STRAIT, NARROW.

Strait, which is otherwise spelled *straight*, from the Latin *strictus* bound, signifies bound tight, that is, brought into a small compass: *narrow*, which is a variation of near, expresses a mode of nearness or closeness. *Strait* is a particular term; *narrow* is general: *straitness* is an artificial mode of *narrowness;* a coat is *strait* which is made to compress the body within a small compass: *narrow* is either the artificial or the natural property of a body; as a *narrow* ribbon, or a *narrow* leaf.

That which is *strait* is so by the means of other bodies; that which is so of itself, as a piece of water confined close on each side by land, is called a *strait;* 'They are afraid to meet her if they have missed the church; but then they are more afraid to see her if they are laced as *strait* as they can possibly be'

LAW. Whatever is bounded by sides that are near each other is *narrow;* thus a piece of land whose pro- onged sides are at a small distance from each other is *narrow;*

No *narrow* frith
He had to pass.—MILTON.

The same distinction applies to these terms in their moral use: a person in *straitened* circumstances is kept, by means of his circumstances, from incurring even necessary expenses; a person who is in *narrow* circumstances is represented as having but a small extent of property.

DISTANT, FAR, REMOTE.

Distant is employed as an adjunct or otherwise; *far* is used only as an adverb. We speak of *distant* objects, or objects being *distant;* but we speak of things only as being *far.*

Distant, in Latin *distans* compounded of *di* and *stans* standing asunder, is employed only for bodies at rest; *far,* in German *fern,* most probably from *gefahren,* participle of *fahren,* in Greek πόρειν to go, signifies gone or removed away, and is employed for bodies either stationary or otherwise; hence we say that a thing is *distant,* or it goes, runs, or flies *far.*

Distant is used to designate great space; *far* only that which is ordinary: the sun is ninety-four millions of miles *distant* from the earth; a person lives not very *far* off, or a person is *far* from the spot.

Distant is used absolutely to express an intervening space. *Remote,* in Latin *remotus,* participle of *removeo* to remove, rather expresses the relative idea of being gone out of sight. A person is said to live in a *distant* country or in a *remote* corner of any country.

These terms bear a similar analogy in the figurative application; when we speak of a *remote* idea it designates that which is less liable to strike the mind than a *distant* idea. A *distant* relationship between individuals is never altogether lost sight of; when the connexion between objects is very *remote* it easily escapes observation; 'It is a pretty saying of Thales, "Falsehood is just as *far distant* from truth as the ears from the eyes," by which he would intimate that a wise man would not easily give credit to the reports of actions which he has not seen.'—SPECTATOR.

O might a parent's careful wish prevail,
Far, far from Ilion should thy vessels sail,
And thou from camps *remote* the danger shun,
Which now, alas! too nearly threats my son.
POPE.

SHORT, BRIEF, CONCISE, SUCCINCT, SUMMARY.

Short, in French *court,* German *kurz,* Latin *curtus,* Greek κυρτὸς; *brief,* in Latin *brevis,* in Greek βραχὺς; *concise,* in Latin *concisus,* signifies cut into a small body; *succinct,* in Latin *succinctus,* participle of *succingo,* signifies brought within a small compass, *summary, v. Abridgement.*

Short is the generick, the rest are specifick terms: every thing which admits of dimensions may be *short,* as opposed to the long, that is, either naturally or artificially; the rest are species of artificial *shortness,* or that which is the work of art: hence it is that material, as well as spiritual, objects may be termed *short;* but the *brief, concise, succinct,* and *summary,* are intellectual or spiritual only. We may term a stick, a letter, or a discourse, *short;* 'The widest excursions of the mind are made by *short* flights frequently repeated.'—JOHNSON. We speak of *brevity* only in regard to the mode of speech; 'Premeditation of thought, and *brevity* of expression, are the great ingredients of that reverence that is required to a pious and acceptable prayer.'—SOUTH. *Conciseness* and *succinctness* apply to the matter of speech; 'Aristotle has a dry *conciseness,* that makes one imagine one is perusing a table of contents.'—GRAY.

Let all your precepts be *succinct* and clear,
That ready wits may comprehend them soon.
ROSCOMMON.

Summary regards the mode either of speaking or action;

Nor spend their time to show their reading,
She 'd have a *summary* proceeding.—SWIFT.

The *brief* is opposed to the prolix; the *concise* and *succinct* to the diffuse; the *summary* to the circumstantial or ceremonious. It is a matter of comparatively little importance whether a man's life be long or *short;* but it deeply concerns him that every moment be well spent. *Brevity* of expression ought to be consulted by speakers, even more than by writers; *conciseness* is of peculiar advantage in the formation of rules for young persons: and *succinctness* is a requisite in every writer, who has extensive materials to digest: a *summary* mode of proceeding may have the advantage of saving time, but it has the disadvantage of incorrectness, and often of injustice.

TO CLOSE, SHUT.

Close is to make close; *shut* is in Saxon *scuttan,* Dutch *schutten,* Hebrew סתם to stop up.

Close is to *shut,* frequently as the means to the end. To *close* signifies simply to put together; to *shut* signifies to put together so *close* that no opening is left. The eyes are *shut* by *closing* the eyelids; the mouth is *shut* by *closing* the lips. The idea of bringing near or joining is prominent in the signification of *close;* that of fastening or preventing admittance in the word *shut.* By the figure of metonymy, *close* may be often substituted for *shut;* as we may speak of *closing* the eyes or the mouth; *closing* a book or a door in the sense of *shutting,* particularly in poetry;

Soon shall the sire Seraglio's horrid gates
Close like the eternal bars of death upon thee.
JOHNSON

On the other hand, the poets may sometimes use *shut* where *close* would be more appropriate;

Behold, fond man!
See here thy pictur'd life: pass some few years
Thy flowering spring, thy summer's ardent strength,
Thy sober autumn fading into age,
And pale conluding winter comes at last,
And *shuts* the scene.—THOMSON.

In ordinary discourse, however, these words are very distinct.

Many things are *closed* which are not to be *shut,* and are *shut* which cannot be *closed.* Nothing can be *closed* but what consists of more than one part; nothing can be *shut* but what has or is supposed to have a cavity. A wound is *closed,* but cannot be *shut;* a window or a box is *shut,* but not *closed.*

When both are applied to hollow bodies, *close* implies a stopping up of the whole, *shut* an occasional stoppage at the entrance. What is *closed* remains *closed;* what is *shut* may be opened. A hole in a road, or a passage through any place is *closed;* a gate, a window, or a door, is *shut.*

TO CLOSE, FINISH, CONCLUDE.

To *close* signifies literally to make close, or bring as near together as they ought to be, and in an extended sense, to bring things to the point where they ought to end; to *finish,* from the Latin *finis* an end, and *conclude,* from *con* and *cludo* or *claudo* to shut, have the same general and literal meaning as *close.*

To *close* is to bring to an end; to *finish* is to make an end: we *close* a thing by ceasing to have any thing more to do with it; we *finish* it by really having no more to do to it. We *close* an account with a person with whom we mean to have no farther transactions; we *finish* the business which we have begun.

It is sometimes necessary to *close* without *finishing,* but we cannot *finish* without *closing.* The want of time will compel a person to *close* his letter before he has *finished* saying all he wishes. It is a laudable desire in every one to wish to *close* his career in life honourably, and to *finish* whatever he undertakes to the satisfaction of himself and others.

To *conclude* is a species of *finishing,* that is to say, *finishing* in a certain manner; we always *finish* when we *conclude,* but we do not always *conclude* when we *finish.* A history is *closed* at a certain reign; it is *finished* when brought to the period proposed; it is *concluded* with a recapitulation of the leading events.

Close and *finish* are employed generally, and in the ordinary transactions of life; the former in speaking of times, seasons, periods, &c. the latter with regard to occupations and pursuits; *conclusion* is used particularly in speaking of moral and intellectual operations. A reign, an entertainment, an age, a year, may have its *close;* a drawing, an exercise, a piece of work, may be *finished;* a discourse, a story, an affair, a negotiation may be *concluded.* The *close* of Alfred's reign was more peaceful than the commencement: those who are careful as to what they begin will be careful to *finish* what they have begun: some preachers seldom awaken attention in their hearers until they come to the *conclusion* of their discourse;

> Destruction hangs on every word we speak,
> On every thought, till the *concluding* stroke
> Determines all, and *closes* our design.
> ADDISON.

'The great work of which Justinian has the credit, although it comprehends the whole system of jurisprudence, was *finished,* we are told, in three years.'—SIR WM. JONES.

COMPLETE, PERFECT, FINISHED.

Complete, in French *complet,* Latin *completus,* participle of *compleo* to fill up, signifies the quality of being filled, or having all that is necessary; *perfect,* in Latin *perfectus,* participle of *perficio* to perform or do thoroughly, signifies the state of being done thoroughly; *finished* marks the state of being *finished* (*v. To close*).

That is *complete* which has no deficiency: that is *perfect* which has positive excellence; and that is *finished* which has no omission in it.

That to which any thing can be added is *incomplete;* when it can be improved it is *imperfect;* when more labour ought to be bestowed upon it it is *unfinished.* A thing is *complete* in all its parts; 'With us the reading of the Scripture is a part of our church liturgy, a special portion of the service which we do to God, and not an exercise to spend the time, when one doth wait for another coming, till the assembly of them that shall afterward worship him be *complete.*'—HOOKER. A thing is *perfect* as to the beauty and design of the construction; 'It has been observed of children, that they are longer before they can pronounce *perfect* sounds, because *perfect* sounds are not pronounced to them.'—HAWKESWORTH. We count those things *perfect* which want nothing requisite for the end, whereto they are instituted.'—HOOKER. A thing is *finished* as it comes from the hand of the workman, and answers his intention. A set of books is not *complete* when a volume is wanting: there is nothing in the proper sense *perfect* which is the work of man; but the term is used relatively for whatever makes the greatest approach to *perfection:* a *finished* performance evinces care and diligence on the part of the workman; 'I would make what bears your name as *finished* as my last work ought to be; that is more *finished* than the rest.'—POPE. A taste is said to be *perfect* to denote its intrinsick excellence, but it is said to be *finished* to denote its acquired excellence: 'It is necessary for a man who would form to himself a *finished* taste of good writing, to be well versed in the works of the best criticks, ancient and modern.'—ADDISON.

A thing may be *complete* or *finished* without being *perfect;* and it may be *perfect* without being either *complete* or *finished.* A sound is said to be *perfect,* but not *complete* or *finished.* The works of the ancients are, as they have been handed down to us, *incomplete,* and some probably *unfinished;* and yet the greater part are *perfect* in their way: the works of the moderns are mostly *complete* and *finished;* yet but a small part have any claims even to human *perfection.* The term *complete* may be applied in a bad as well as good sense: a *complete* knave implies one who is versed in every part of knavery;

> None better guard against a cheat,
> Than he who is a knave *complete.*—LEWIS.

TO COMPLETE, FINISH, TERMINATE.

Complete is to make complete; *finish* and *terminate* have been explained in the preceding article (*v. To end*).

We *complete** what is undertaken by continuing to labour at it; we *finish* what is begun in a state of forwardness by putting the last hand to it; we *terminate* what ought not to last by bringing it to a close. So that the characteristick idea of *completing* is the conducting of a thing to its final period; that of *finishing,* the arrival at that period; and that of *terminating,* the cessation of a thing.

Completing has properly relation to permanent works only, whether mechanical or intellectual, we desire a thing to be *completed* from a curiosity to see it in its entire state; 'It is perhaps kindly provided by nature, that as the feathers and strength of a bird grow together, and her wings are not *completed* till she is able to fly, so some proportion should be preserved in the human kind between judgement and courage.'—JOHNSON. To *finish* is employed for passing occupations; we wish a thing *finished* from an anxiety to proceed to something else, or a dislike to the thing in which we are engaged; 'The artificer, for the manufacture which he *finishes* in a day, receives a certain sum; but the wit frequently gains no advantage from a performance at which he has toiled many months.'—HAWKESWORTH. *Terminating* respects discussions, differences, and disputes. Light minds undertake many things without *completing* any. Children and unsteady people set about many things without *finishing* any. Litigious people *terminate* one dispute only to commence another.

CONSUMMATION, COMPLETION.

Consummation, Latin *consummatio,* compounded of *con* and *summa* the sum, signifies the summing or winding up of the whole—the putting a final period to any concern; *completion* signifies either the act of completing, or the state of being completed (*v. To complete*).

The arrival at a conclusion is comprehended in both these terms, but they differ principally in application; wishes are *consummated;* plans are *completed:* we often flatter ourselves that the *completion* of all our plans will be the *consummation* of all our wishes, and thus expose ourselves to grievous disappointments: the *consummation* of the nuptial ceremony is not always the *consummation* of hopes and joys: it is frequently the beginning of misery and disappointment; 'It is not to be doubted but it was a constant practice of all that is praiseworthy, which made her capable of beholding death, not as the dissolution but the *consummation* of life.'—STEELE. We often sacrifice much to the *completion* of a purpose which we afterward find not worth the labour of attaining; 'He makes it the utmost *completion* of an ill character to bear a malevolence to the best of men.'—POPE.

As epithets, *consummate* is employed only in a bad sense, and *complete* either in a good or bad sense those who are regarded as *complete* fools are not unfrequently *consummate* knaves: the theatre is not the only place for witnessing a farce; human life affords many of various descriptions; among the number of which we may reckon those as *complete* in their kind which are acted at elections, where *consummate* folly and *consummate* hypocrisy are practised by turns.

RIPE, MATURE.

Ripe is the English, *mature* the Latin word; the former has a universal application, both proper and improper; the latter has mostly an improper application. The idea of completion in growth is simply designated by the former term; the idea of moral perfection, as far at least as it is attainable, is marked by the latter: fruit is *ripe* when it requires no more sustenance from the parent stock; a judgement is *mature* which requires no more time and knowledge to render it perfect or fitted for exercise: in the same manner a project may be said to be *ripe* for execution, or a people *ripe* for revolt;

> So to his crowne, she him restor'd againe,
> In which he dyde, made *ripe* for death by eld
> SPENSER

On the contrary, reflection may be said to be *mature* to which sufficiency of time has been given, and age

* Vide Girard; "Achever, finir, terminer"

may be said to be *mature* which has attained the highest pitch of perfection;

> Th' Athenian sage, revolving in his mind
> This weakness, blindness, madness of mankind,
> Foretold that in *maturer* days, though late,
> When time should *ripen* the decrees of fate,
> Some god would light us.—JENYNS.

Ripeness is however not always a good quality; but *maturity* is always a perfection: the *ripeness* of some fruit diminishes the excellence of its flavour; there are some fruits which have no flavour until they come to *maturity*.

WHOLE, ENTIRE, COMPLETE, TOTAL, INTEGRAL.

Whole excludes subtraction; *entire* excludes division; *complete* excludes deficiency: a *whole* orange has had nothing taken from it; an *entire* orange is not yet cut; and a *complete* orange is grown to its full size. It is possible, therefore, for a thing to be *whole* and not *entire;* and to be both, and yet not *complete:* an orange cut into parts is *whole* while all the parts remain together, but it is not *entire*. Hence we speak of a *whole* house, an *entire* set, and a *complete* book. The *wholeness* or integrity of a thing is destroyed at one's pleasure; the *completeness* depends upon circumstances.

Total denotes the aggregate of the parts; *whole* the junction of all the parts: the former is, therefore, employed more in the moral sense to convey the idea of extent, and the latter mostly in the proper sense. Hence we speak of the *total* destruction of the *whole* city, or of some particular houses; the *total* amount of expenses; the *whole* expense of the war. *Whole* and *total* may in this manner be employed to denote things as well as qualities: in regard to material substances *wholes* are always opposed to the parts of which they are composed; the *total* is the collected sum of the parts: and the *integral* is the same as the *integral* number.

The first four may likewise be employed as adverbs; but *wholly* is a more familiar term than *totally* in expressing the idea of extent; *entirely* is the same as undividedly; *completely* is the same as perfectly, without any thing wanting. We are *wholly* or *totally* ignorant of the affair; we are *entirely* at the disposal or service of another; we are *completely* at variance in our accounts.

All these terms, except the last, are applied to moral objects with a similar distinction;

> And all so forming an harmonious *whole*.
> THOMSON.

'The *entire* conquest of the passions is so difficult a work, that they who despair of it should think of a less difficult task, and only attempt to regulate them.' —STEELE.

> And oft, when unobserv'd,
> Steal from the barn a straw, till soft and warm,
> Clean and *complete*, their habitation grows.
> THOMSON.

Nothing under a *total* thorough change in the convert will suffice.'—SOUTH.

GROSS, TOTAL.

Gross is connected with the word great: from the idea of size which enters into the original meaning of this term is derived that of quantity: *total*, from the Latin *totus*, signifies literally the whole. The *gross* implies that from which nothing has been taken: the *total* signifies that to which nothing need be added: the *gross* sum includes every thing without regard to what it may be: the *total* includes every thing which one wishes to include: we may, therefore, deduct from the *gross* that which does not immediately belong to it; but the *total* is that which admits of no deduction. The *gross* weight in trade is applicable to any article, the whole of which, good or bad, pure or dross, is included in opposition to the neat weight; the *total* amount supposes all to be included which ought to form a part, in opposition to any smaller amounts or subdivisions; when employed in the improper sense, they preserve the same distinction: things are said to be taken or considered in the *gross*, that is, in the large and comprehensive way, one with another. 'I have more than once found fault with those general reflections which strike at kingdoms or commonwealths in the *gross*.'—ADDISON. Things are said to undergo a *total* change; 'Nature is either collected into one *total*, or diffused and distributed.'—BACON.

TO ACCOMPLISH, EFFECT, EXECUTE, ACHIEVE.

Accomplish, in French *accomplir*, is compounded of the intensive syllable *ac* or *ad* and *complir*, in Latin *compleo* to complete, signifying to complete to the end: *effect*, in Latin *effectus*, participle of *efficio*, compounded of *ef* and *ex* out of or up, and *facio* to make, signifies to make up until nothing remains to be done: *execute*, in Latin *executus*, participle of *exequor*, compounded of *ex* and *equor* or *sequor* to follow, signifies to follow up or carry through to the end; *achieve*, in French *achever*, from *chef* a chief, signifies to perform as a chief, or perfectly.

We *accomplish* an object, *effect* a purpose, *execute* a project, *achieve* an enterprise. Perseverance is requisite for *accomplishing*, means for *effecting*, abilities for *executing*, and spirit for *achieving*. Some persons are always striving to attain an end without ever *accomplishing* what they propose; 'It is the first rule in oratory that a man must appear such as he would persuade others to be; and that can be *accomplished* only by the force of his life.'—SWIFT. It is the part of wisdom to suit the means to the end when we have any scheme to *effect;* 'Reason considers the motive, the means, and the end; and honours courage only when it is employed to *effect* the purpose of virtue.'—HAWKESWORTH. Those who are readiest in forming projects are not always the fittest for carrying them into *execution;* 'We are not to indulge our corporeal appetites with pleasures that impair our intellectual vigour, nor gratify our minds with schemes which we know our lives must fail in attempting to *execute*.'—JOHNSON. That ardour of character which impels to the *achievement* of arduous undertakings belongs but to very few; 'It is more than probable, that in case our freethinkers could once *achieve* their glorious design of sinking the credit of the Christian religion, and causing the revenues to be withdrawn which their wiser forefathers had appointed to the support and encouragement of its teachers, in a little time the Shaster would be as intelligible as the Greek Testament.'—BERKELEY.

We should never give up what we have the least chance of *accomplishing*, if it be worth the labour; nor pursue any plan which affords us no prospect of *effecting* what we wish; nor undertake what we do not feel ourselves competent to *execute*, particularly when there is any thing extraordinary to *achieve*. The friends of humanity exerted their utmost endeavours in behalf of the enslaved Africans, and after many years' noble struggle at length *accomplished* their wishes as far as respects Great Britain, by obtaining a legislative enactment against the slave trade; but they have not yet been able to *effect* the total abolition of this nefarious traffick: the vices of individuals still interfere with the due *execution* of the laws of their country: yet this triumph of humanity, as far as it has been successful, exceeds in greatness the boldest *achievements* of antiquity.

ACCOMPLISHED,* PERFECT.

These epithets express an assemblage of all the qualities suitable to the subject; and mark the qualification in the highest degree. *Accomplished* refers only to the artificial refinements of the mind; *perfect* is said of things in general, whether natural or artificial mental and corporeal.

An acquaintance with modern languages and the ornamental branches of the arts and sciences constitutes a person *accomplished;* 'For who expects that, under a tutor, a young gentleman should be an *accomplished* publick orator or logician.'—LOCKE. The highest possible degree of skill in any art constitutes a man a *perfect* artist;

* Vide Abbe Girard: "Accompli, parfait."

Within a ken our army lies,
Our men more *perfect* in the use of arms.
SHAKSPEARE.

An *accomplished* man needs no moral endowment to entitle him to the name; 'The English nation in the time of Shakspeare was yet struggling to emerge from barbarity; and to be able to read and write was an *accomplishment* still valued for its rarity.'—JOHNSON. A *perfect* man, if such a one there could be, must be free from every moral imperfection, and endowed with every virtue; 'A man endowed with great *perfections*, without good breeding, is like one who has his pocket full of gold, but always wants change for his ordinary occasions.'—STEELE. *Accomplished* is applied only to persons; *perfect* is applicable not only to persons but to works, and every thing else as occasion requires; it may likewise be employed in a bad sense to magnify any unfavourable quality.

QUALIFICATION, ACCOMPLISHMENT.

The *qualification* serves the purpose of utility; the *accomplishment* serves to adorn: by the first we are enabled to make ourselves useful; by the second we are enabled to make ourselves agreeable.

The *qualifications* of a man who has an office to perform must be considered: of a man who has only pleasure to pursue the *accomplishments* are to be considered. A readiness with one's pen, and a facility at accounts, are necessary *qualifications* either for a school or a counting-house; 'The companion of an evening, and the companion for life, require very different *qualifications*.'—JOHNSON. Drawing is one of the most agreeable and suitable *accomplishments* that can be given to a young person; 'Where nature bestows genius, education will give *accomplishments*.'—CUMBERLAND.

TO FULFIL, ACCOMPLISH, REALIZE.

To *fulfil* is literally to fill quite full, that is, to bring about *full* to the wishes of a person; *accomplish* (*v. To accomplish*) is to bring to perfection, but without reference to the wishes of any one; to *realize* is to make *real*, namely, whatever has been aimed at. The application of these terms is evident from their explications: the wishes, the expectations, the intentions, and promises of an individual, are appropriately said to be *fulfilled;* national projects, or undertakings, prophecies, and whatever is of general interest, are said to be *accomplished:* the fortune, or the prospects of an individual, or whatever results successfully from specifick efforts, is said to be *realized:* the *fulfilment* of wishes may be as much the effect of good fortune as of design; 'The palsied dotard looks round him, perceives himself to be alone; he has survived his friends, and he wishes to follow them; his wish is *fulfilled;* he drops torpid and insensible into that gulf which is deeper than the grave.'—HAWKESWORTH. The *accomplishment* of projects mostly results from extraordinary exertion, as the *accomplishment* of prophecies results from a miraculous exertion of power; 'God bless you, sweet boy! and *accomplish* the joyful hope I conceived of you.'—SIR PHILIP SIDNEY. The *realization* of hopes results more commonly from the slow process of moderate well-combined efforts than from any thing extraordinary; 'After my fancy had been busied in attempting to *realize* the scenes that Shakspeare drew, I regretted that the labour was ineffectual.' HAWKESWORTH.

TO KEEP, OBSERVE, FULFIL.

These terms are synonymous in the moral sense of abiding by, and carrying into execution, what is prescribed or set before one for his rule of conduct: to *keep* (*v. To keep*) is simply to have by one in such manner that it shall not depart; to *observe*, from the Latin *observo*, i. e. *ob* and *servo* to *keep* in one's view, is to *keep* with a steady attention; to *fulfil* (*v. To accomplish*) is to *keep* to the end or to the full intent. A day is either *kept* or *observed;* yet the former is not only a more familiar term, but it likewise implies a much less solemn act than the latter; one must add, therefore, the mode in which it is *kept*, by saying that it is *kept* holy, *kept* sacred or *kept* as a day of pleasure; the term *observe*, however, implies always that it is *kept* religiously: we may *keep*, but we do not *observe* a birth-day; we *keep* or *observe* the Sabbath.

To *keep* marks simply perseverance or continuance in a thing; a man *keeps* his word if he do not depart from it;

It is a great sin to swear unto a sin,
But greater sin to *keep* a sinful oath.—SHAKSPEARE

To *observe* marks fidelity and consideration; we *observe* a rule when we are careful to be guided by it; 'I doubt whether any of our authors have yet been able for twenty lines together, nicely to *observe* the true definition of easy poetry.'—JOHNSON. To *fulfil* marks the perfection and consummation of that which one has *kept;* we *fulfil* a promise by acting in strict conformity to it; 'You might have seen this poor child arrived at an age to *fulfil* all your hopes, and then you might have lost him.'—GRAY.

A person is said to *keep* the law when he does not commit any violent breach of it; he *observes* every minutia in the law, if he is anxious to show himself a good citizen; by this conduct he *fulfils* the intentions of the legislator: St. Paul recommends to Christians to *keep* the faith, which they can never do effectually, unless they *observe* all the precepts of our Saviour, and thereby *fulfil* the law: children may *keep* silence when they are desired; but it is seldom in their power to *observe* it as a rule, because they have not sufficient understanding.

TO EXECUTE, FULFIL, PERFORM.

To *execute* (*v. To accomplish*) is more than to *fulfil* and to *fulfil* than to *perform*, which signifies to form thoroughly or make complete. To *execute* is to bring about an end; it involves active measures, and is peculiarly applicable to that which is extraordinary, or that which requires particular spirit and talents; schemes of ambition are *executed*, and great designs are *executed;*

Why delays
His hand to *execute* what his decree
Fix'd on this day?—MILTON.

To *fulfil* is to satisfy a moral obligation; it is applicable to those duties in which rectitude and equity are involved; we *fulfil* the duties of citizens, but one may also *fulfil* purposes good or bad;

To whom the white-arm'd goddess thus replies
Enough thou know'st the tyrant of the skies,
Severely bent his purpose to *fulfil*,
Unmov'd his mind, and unrestrain'd his will.—POPE

To *perform* is to carry through by simple action or labour; it is more particularly applicable to the ordinary and regular business of life; we *perform* a work or an office:

When those who round the wasted fires remain,
Perform the last sad office to the slain.—DRYDEN.

One *executes* according to the intentions of others; the soldier *executes* the orders of his general; the merchant *executes* the commissions of his correspondent; 'He casts into the balance the promise of a reward to such as should *execute*, and of punishment to such as should neglect, their commission.'—SOUTH. One *fulfils* according to the wishes and expectations of others; it is the part of an honest man to enter into no engagements which he cannot *fulfil;* it is the part of a dutiful son, by diligence and assiduity, to endeavour to *fulfil* the expectations of an anxious parent;

If on my wounded breast thou drop'st a tear,
Think for whose sake my breast that wound did bear,
And faithfully my last desires *fulfil*,
As I perform my cruel father's will.

One *performs* according to circumstances, what suits one's own convenience and purposes; every good man is anxious to *perform* his part in life with credit and advantage to himself and others; 'He effectually *performed* his part with great integrity, learning, and acuteness; with the exactness of a scholar, and the judgement of a complete divine.'—WATERLAND.

TO EFFECT, PRODUCE, PERFORM.

The two latter are in reality included in the former; what is *effected* is both *produced* and *performed;* but what is *produced* or *performed* is not always *effected*; *effect* (*v. Accomplish*) signifies to make out any thing; *produce*, from the Latin *produco*, signifies literally to draw forth; *perform*, compounded of *per* and *form*, signifies to form thoroughly or carry through.

To *produce* signifies to bring something forth or into existence; to *perform*, to do something to the end: to *effect* is to *produce* by *performing*: whatever is *effected* is the consequence of a specifick design; it always requires therefore a conscious agent to effect; The united powers of hell are joined together for the destruction of mankind, which they *effected* in part.'—Addison. What is *produced* may follow incidentally, or arise from the action of an irrational agent or an inanimate object; 'Though prudence does in a great measure *produce* our good or ill fortune, there are many unforeseen occurrences which pervert the finest schemes that can be laid by human wisdom.'—Addison. What is *performed* is done by specifick efforts; it is therefore like what is *effected*, the consequence of design, and requires a rational agent; 'Where there is a power to *perform*, God does not accept the will.' —South.

Effect respects both the end and the means by which it is brought about; we speak of the object to be *effected*, and the way of *effecting* it: *produce* has a particular reference to the end or the thing *produced*; *perform* to the means or to the course pursued. No person ought to calculate on *effecting* a reformation in the morals of men, without the aid of religion. Small changes in society often *produce* great evils. The *performance* of a person's duty is estimated according as it is faithful or otherwise.

To *effect* is said of that which emanates from the mind of the agent himself; to *perform*, of that which is marked out by rule, or prescribed by another. We *effect* a purpose; we perform a part, a duty, or office. A true Christian is always happy when he can *effect* a reconciliation between parties who are at variance: it is a laudable ambition to strive to perform one's part creditably in society.

EFFECTIVE, EFFICIENT, EFFECTUAL, EFFICACIOUS.

Effective signifies capable of *effecting*; *efficient* signifies literally *effecting*; *effectual* and *efficacious* signify having the *effect*, or possessing the power to *effect*. The former two are used only in regard to physical objects, the latter two in regard to moral objects. An army or a military force is *effective*; 'I should suspend my congratulations on the new liberties of France, until I was informed how it had been combined with government, with the discipline of the armies, and the collection of an *effective* revenue.'—Burke. A cause is *efficient*; 'No searcher has yet found the *efficient* cause of sleep.'—Johnson. A remedy or cure is *effectual*; 'Nothing so *effectually* deadens the taste of the sublime, as that which is light and radiant.'—Burke. A medicine is *efficacious*, and in the moral sense motives or measures are termed *efficacious*.

The end or result is *effectual*, the means are *efficacious*. No *effectual* stop can be put to the vices of the lower orders, while they have a vicious example from their superiours; 'Sometimes the sight of the altar, and decent preparations for devotion, may compose and recover the wandering mind more *effectually* than a sermon.'—South. A seasonable exercise of severity on an offender is often very *efficacious* in quelling a spirit of insubordination. When a thing is not found *effectual*, it is requisite to have recourse to farther measures; that which has been proved to be *inefficacious* should never be adopted; 'He who labours to lessen the dignity of human nature, destroys many *efficacious* motives for practising worthy actions.'—Warton.

VAIN, INEFFECTUAL, FRUITLESS.

Vain, *v. Idle*; *ineffectual*, that is, not *effectual* (*v. Effective*); *fruitless*, that is, without *fruit*, signifies not producing the desired fruit of one's labour.

These epithets are all applied to our endeavours; but the term *vain* is the most general and indefinite; the other terms are particular and definite. What we aim at, as well as what we strive for, may be *vain*; but *ineffectual* and *fruitless* refer only to the termination of our labours. When the object aimed at is general in its import, it is common to term the endeavour *vain* when it cannot attain this object; it is *vain* to attempt to reform a person's character until he is convinced that he stands in need of reformation;

> *Vain* is the force of man
> To crush the pillars which the piles sustain.
> Dryden.
>
> Nature aloud calls out for balmy rest,
> But all in *vain*.—Gentleman.

When the means employed are inadequate for the attainment of the particular end, it is usual to call the endeavour *ineffectual*; cool arguments will be *ineffectual* in convincing any one inflamed with a particular passion;

> Thou thyself with scorn
> And anger would resent the offer'd wrong,
> Though *ineffectual* found.—Milton.

When labour is specifically employed for the attainment of a particular object, it is usual to term it *fruitless* if it fail: peace-makers will often find themselves in this condition, that their labours will be rendered *fruitless* by the violent passions of angry opponents; 'After many *fruitless* overtures, the Inca, despairing of any cordial union with a Spaniard, attacked him by surprise with a numerous body.'—Robertson.

EFFECT, CONSEQUENCE, RESULT, ISSUE, EVENT.

Effect signifies that which is effected or produced by an operating cause; *consequence*, in French *consequence*, Latin *consequentia*, from *consequor* to follow, signifies that which follows in connexion with something else; *result*, in French *resulte*, Latin *resulto* or *resultus* and *resilio* to rebound, signifies that which springs or bounds back from another thing; *event* has the same signification as given under the head of *Accident*; *issue* signifies that which issues or flows out of another thing.

Effect and *consequence* agree in expressing that which follows any thing, but the former marks what follows from a connexion between the two objects; the term *consequence* is not thus limited: an *effect* is that which necessarily flows out of the cause, between which the connexion is so intimate that we cannot think of the one without the other. In the nature of things, causes will have *effects*; and for every *effect* there will be a cause: a *consequence*, on the other hand, may be either casual or natural; it is that on which we cannot calculate. *Effect* applies either to physical or moral objects, *consequence* only to moral subjects.

There are many diseases which are the *effects* of mere intemperance: an imprudent step in one's first setting out in life is often attended with fatal *consequences*. A mild answer has the *effect* of turning away wrath; 'A passion for praise produces very good *effects*.'—Addison. The loss of character is the general *consequence* of an irregular life; 'Were it possible for any thing in the Christian faith to be erroneous, I can find no ill *consequences* in adhering to it.' —Addison.

Consequences flow of themselves from the nature of things; *results* are drawn. *Consequences* proceed from actions in general; *results* proceed from particular efforts and attempts. *Consequences* are good or bad; 'Jealousy often draws after it a fatal train of *consequences*.'—Addison. *Results* are successful or unsuccessful; 'The state of the world is continually changing, and none can tell the *result* of the next vicissitude.'—Johnson.

We endeavour to avert *consequences* which threaten to be bad; we endeavour to produce *results* that are according to our wishes. Not to foresee the *consequences* which are foreseen by others, evinces a more than ordinary share of indiscretion and infatuation. To calculate on a favourable *result* from an ill-judged and ill-executed enterprise, only proves a consistent blindness in the projector.

The term *event* respects great undertakings; *issue* particular efforts; *consequence* respects every thing which can produce a *consequence*. Hence we speak of the *event* of a war: the *issue* of a negotiation and the *consequences* of either. The measures of government are often unjustly praised or blamed according to the *event;* 'It has always been the practice of mankind to judge of actions by the *events.*'—JOHNSON. The fate of a nation sometimes hangs on the *issue* of a battle; 'A mild, unruffled, self-possessing mind is a blessing more important to real felicity than all that can be gained by the triumphant *issue* of some violent contest.'—BLAIR. The conquest of a nation is one of the *consequences* which follow the defeat of its armies; 'Henley in one of his advertisements had mentioned Pope's treatment of Savage; this was supposed by Pope to be the *consequence* of a complaint made by Savage to Henley, and was therefore mentioned by him with much resentment.'—JOHNSON. We must be prepared for *events*, which are frequently above our control: we must exert ourselves to bring about a favourable *issue:* address and activity will go far towards ensuring success: but if after all our efforts we still fail, it is our duty to submit with patient resignation to the *consequences.*

TO ARISE, PROCEED, ISSUE, SPRING, FLOW, EMANATE.

Arise in its original meaning signifies to go upwards (*v. To arise*), but is here taken in the sense of coming out from; *proceed*, in Latin *procedo*, that is *pro* and *cedo* to go, signifies to go forth; *issue*, in French *issue*, comes from the Latin *isse* or *ivisse*, infinite of *eo*, and the Hebrew יצא to go out; *spring*, in German *springen*, comes from *rinnen* to run like water, and is connected with the Greek *βρύειν* to pour out; *flow*, in Saxon *fleowan*, Low German *flogan*, High German *fliessen*, Latin *fluo*, &c., all from the Greek *βλύω* or *βλύζω*, which is an onomatopeïa expressing the murmur of waters; *emanate*, in Latin *emanatus*, participle of *emano*, compounded of *mano* to flow, from the Hebrew מים and Chaldee מין waters, expressing the motion of waters.

The idea of one object coming out of another is expressed by all these terms, but they differ in the circumstances of the action. What comes up out of a body and rises into existence is said to *arise*, as the mist which *rises* or *arises* out of the sea;

> From roots hard hazels, and from scions *rise*
> Tall ash, and taller oak that mates the skies.
> DRYDEN.

What comes forth as it were gradually into observation is said to *proceed;*

> Teach me the various labours of the moon,
> And whence *proceed* the eclipses of the sun.
> DRYDEN.

Thus the light *proceeds* from a certain quarter of the heavens, or from a certain part of a house: what comes out from a small aperture is said to *issue;* thus perspiration *issues* through the pores of the skin; water *issues* sometimes from the sides of rocks: what comes out in a sudden or quick manner, or comes from some remote source, is said to *spring;* thus blood *springs* from an artery which is pricked; water *springs* up out of the earth: what comes out in quantities or in a stream is said to *flow;* thus blood *flows* from a wound; to *emanate* is a species of *flowing* by a natural operation, when bodies send forth, or seem to send forth, particles of their own composition from themselves; thus light *emanates* from the sun.

This distinction in the signification of these terms is kept up in their moral acceptation, where the idea of one thing originating from another is common to them all; but in this case *arise* is a general term, which simply implies the coming into existence; but *proceed* conveys also the idea of a progressive movement into existence. Every object therefore may be said to *arise* out of whatever produces it; but it *proceeds* from it only when it is gradually produced: evils are continually *arising* in human society for which there is no specifick remedy; 'The greatest misfortunes men fall into *arise* from themselves.'—STEELE. In complicated disorders it is not always possible to say precisely from what the complaint of the patient *proceeds;*

> But whence *proceed* these hopes, or whence this dread,
> If nothing really can affect the dead?—JENYNS.

Issue is seldom used but in application to sensible objects; yet we may say, in conformity to the original meaning, that words *issue* from the mouth;

> As when some huntsman with a flying spear
> From the blind thicket wounds a stately deer,
> Down his cleft side while fresh the blood distils,
> He bounds aloft and scuds from hills to hills,
> Till life's warm vapour *issuing* through the wound
> Wild mountain wolves the fainting beast surround.
> POPE.

'Providence is the great sanctuary to the afflicted who maintain their integrity: and often there has *issued* from this sanctuary the most seasonable relief.'—BLAIR. The idea of the distant source or origin is kept up in the moral application of the term *spring*, when we say that actions *spring* from a generous or corrupt principle;

> All from utility this law approve,
> As every private bliss must *spring* from social love.
> JENYNS.

The idea of a quantity and a stream is preserved in the moral use of the terms *flow* and *emanate;* but the former may be said of that which is not inherent in the body: the latter respects that only which forms a component part of the body: God is the *spring* whence all our blessings *flow:* all authority *emanates* from God, who is the supreme source of all things: theologians, when speaking of God, say that the Son *emanates* from the Father, and the Holy Ghost from the Father and the Son, and that grace *flows* upon us incessantly from the inexhaustible treasures of Divine mercy; 'As light and heat *flow* from the sun as their centre, so bliss and joy *flow* from the Deity.'—BLAIR. 'As in the next world so in this, the only solid blessings are owing to the goodness of the mind, not the extent of the capacity; friendship here is an *emanation* from the same source as beatitude there.'—POPE.

TO RISE, ISSUE, EMERGE.

To *rise* (*v. To arise*) may either refer to open or enclosed spaces; *issue* (*v. To arise*) and *emerge*, in Latin *emergo* to rise out of, have both a reference to some confined body: a thing may either *rise* in a body, without a body, or out of a body; but they *issue* and *emerge* out of a body. A thing may either *rise* in a plain or a wood; it *issues* out of a wood: it may either *rise* in water or out of the water; it *emerges* from the water; that which *rises* out of a thing comes into view by becoming higher: in this manner an air balloon might *rise* out of a wood;

> Ye mists and exhalations that now *rise*,
> In honour to the world's great author rise.
> MILTON.

That which *issues* comes out in a line with the object; horsemen *issue* from a wood; that which *issues* comes from the very depths of it, and comes as it were out as a part of it; 'Does not the earth quit scores with all the elements in the noble fruits and productions that *issue* from it?'—SOUTH. That which *emerges* proceeds from the thing in which it has been, as it were, concealed;

> Let earth dissolve, yon ponderous orbs descend,
> And grind us into dust, the soul is safe,
> The man *emerges.*—YOUNG.

Hence in a moral or extended application, a person is said to *rise* in life without a reference to his former condition; but he *emerges* from obscurity: colour *rises* in the face; but words *issue* from the mouth

---

OFFSPRING, PROGENY, ISSUE.

Offspring is that which springs off or from: *progeny* that which is brought forth or out of; *issue* that which *issues* or proceeds from; and all in relation to the family or generation of the human species. *Offspring* is a familiar term applicable to one or many children, *progeny* is employed only as a collective noun for a number; *issue* is used in an indefinite manner without particular regard to number. When we speak of the children themselves, we denominate them the *offspring;* 'The same cause that has drawn the hatred of God and man upon the father of liars may justly entail it upon his *offspring* too.'—SOUTH. When we speak of the parents, we denominate the children their *progeny;*

> The base, degen'rate iron *offspring* ends,
> A golden *progeny* from Heav'n descends.
> DRYDEN.

A child is said to be the only *offspring* of his parents, or he is said to be the *offspring* of low parents; a man is said to have a numerous or a healthy *progeny*, or to leave his *progeny* in circumstances of honour and prosperity. The *issue* is said only in regard to a man that is deceased: he dies with male or female *issue;* with or without *issue;* his property descends to his male *issue* in a direct line;

> Next him King Leyr, in happy place long reigned,
> But had no *issue* male him to succeed.—SPENSER.

ORIGIN ORIGINAL, BEGINNING, RISE, SOURCE.

Origin or *original* both come from the Latin *orior* to rise: the former designating the abstract property of *rising;* the latter the thing that is *risen.* The *origin* is said only of things that *rise;* the *original* is said of those which give an *origin* to another: the *origin* serves to date the existence of a thing; the *original* serves to show the author of a thing, and is opposed to the copy. The *origin* of the world is described in the first chapter of Genesis; Adam was the *original* from whom all the human race has sprung;

> And had his better half, his bride,
> Carv'd from th' *original*, his side.—BUTLER.

The *origin* has respect to the cause; the *beginning* to the period of existence: every thing owes its existence to the *origin;* it dates its existence from the *beginning:* there cannot be an *origin* without a *beginning*; but there may be a *beginning* where we do not speak of an *origin.* We look to the *origin* of a thing in order to learn its nature; 'Christianity explains the *origin* of all the disorders which at present take place on earth.'—BLAIR. We look to the *beginning* in order to learn its duration or other circumstances;

> But wit and weaving had the same *beginning*,
> Pallas first taught in poetry and spinning.—SWIFT.

When we have discovered the *origin* of a quarrel, we are in a fair way of becoming acquainted with the aggressors; when we trace a quarrel to the *beginning*, we may easily ascertain how long it has lasted.

The *origin* and the *rise* are both employed for the primary state of existence; but the latter is a much more familiar term than the former: we speak of the *origin* of an empire, the *origin* of a family, the *origin* of a dispute, and the like; but we say that a river takes its *rise* from a certain mountain, that certain disorders take their *rise* from particular circumstances which happen in early life: it is moreover observable that the *origin* is confined solely to the first commencement of a thing's existence; but the *rise* comprehends its gradual progress in the first stages of its existence; 'The friendship which is to be practised or expected by common mortals must take its *rise* from mutual pleasure.'—JOHNSON. The *origin* of the noblest families is in the first instance sometimes ignoble; the largest rivers take their *rise* in small streams. We look to the *origin* as to the cause of existence: we look to the *rise* as to the situation in which the thing commences to exist, or the process by which it grows up into existence. It is in vain to attempt to search the *origin* of evil, unless as we find it explained in the word of God. Evil diseases take their *rise* in certain parts of the body, and after lying for some time dormant, break out in after-life.

The *origin* and *rise* are said of only one subject; the *source* is said of that which produces a succession of objects: the *origin* of evil in general has given *rise* to much speculation; the love of pleasure is the *source* of incalculable mischiefs to individuals, as well as to society at large;

> Famous Greece,
> That *source* of art and cultivated thought
> Which they to Rome, and Romans hither brought.
> WALLER

The *origin* exists but once; the *source* is lasting; 'One *source* of the sublime is infinity.'—BURKE. The *origin* of every family is to be traced to our first parent, Adam: we have a never-failing *source* of consolation in religion.

TO BEGIN, COMMENCE, ENTER UPON.

Begin, in German *beginnen*, is compounded of *b* and *ginnen*, probably a frequentative of *gehen* to go, signifying to go first to a thing; *commence*, in French *commencer*, is not improbably derived from the Latin *commendo*, signifying to betake one's self to a thing; *enter*, in Latin *intro* within, signifies, with the preposition *upon*, to go into a thing.

Begin and *commence* are so strictly allied in signification, that it is not easy to discover the difference in their application; although a minute difference does exist. To *begin* respects the order of time; 'When *beginning* to act your part, what can be of greater moment than to regulate your plan of conduct with the most serious attention?'—BLAIR. To *commence* implies the exertion of setting about a thing; 'By the destination of his Creator, and the necessities of his nature, man *commences* at once an active, not merely a contemplative, being.'—BLAIR. Whoever *begins* a dispute is termed the aggressor; no one should *commence* a dispute unless he can calculate the consequences, and as this is impracticable, it is better never to *commence* disputes, particularly such as are to be decided by law. *Begin* is opposed to end: *commence* to complete: a person *begins* a thing with a view of ending it; he *commences* a thing with a view of completing it.

To *begin* is either transitive or intransitive; to *commence* is mostly transitive: a speaker *begins* by apologizing; he *commences* his speech with an apology: happiness frequently ends where prosperity *begins;* whoever *commences* any undertaking, without estimating his own power, must not expect to succeed.

To *begin* is used either for things or persons; to *commence* for persons only: all things have their *beginning;* in order to effect any thing, we must make a *commencement:* a word *begins* with a particular letter, or a line *begins* with a particular word; a person *commences* his career. Lastly, *begin* is more colloquial than *commence:* thus we say, to *begin* the work; to *commence* the operation: to *begin* one's play; to *commence* the pursuit: to *begin* to write; to *commence* the letter.

To *commence* and *enter upon* are as closely allied in sense as the former words; they differ principally in application: to *commence* seems rather to denote the making an experiment;

> If wit so much from ign'rance undergo,
> Ah! let not learning too *commence* its foe!
> POPE.

To *enter upon*, that of first doing what has not been tried before: we *commence* an undertaking; 'If any man has a mind to *enter upon* such a voluntary abstinence, it might not be improper to give him the caution of Pythagoras, in particular: *Abstine a fabis*, that is, say the interpreters, "meddle not with elections."'—ADDISON. We *enter upon* an employment: speculating people are very ready to *commence* schemes; considerate people are always averse to *entering upon* any office, until they feel themselves fully adequate to discharge its duties.

TO MAKE, FORM, PRODUCE, CREATE.

The idea of giving birth to a thing is common to all these terms, which vary in the circumstances of the action: to *make* (*v. To make*) is the most general and unqualified term; to *form* signifies to give a *form* to a thing, that is, to *make* it after a given *form* (*v. Form*); to *produce* (*v. To effect*) is to bring forth into the light to call into existence; to *create* (*v. To cause*) is to bring into existence by an absolute exercise of power to *make* is the simplest action of all, and comprehend a simple combination by the smallest efforts; to *form* requires care and attention, and greater efforts; to *produce* requires time, and also labour: whatever is put together so as to become another thing, is *made:* a chair or a table is *made:* whatever is put into any distinct *form* is *formed;* the potter *forms* the clay into an earthen vessel: whatever emanates from a thing, so as to become a distinct object, is *produced;* fire is often *produced* by the violent friction of two pieces of wood with each other. The process of *making* is always performed by some conscious agent, who employs either mechanical means, or the simple exercise of power: a bird *makes* its nest; man *makes* various things, by the exercise of his understanding and his limbs; the Almighty Maker has *made* every thing by his word. The process of *forming* does not always require a conscious agent; things are likewise *formed* of themselves; or they are *formed* by the active operations of other bodies; melted lead, when thrown into water, will *form* itself into globules and masses of various shapes; hard substances are *formed* in the human body which give rise to the disease termed the gravel. What is *produced* is oftener *produced* by the process of nature, than by any express design; the earth *produces* all kinds of vegetables from seed; animals, by a similar process, *produce* their young. *Create*, in this natural sense of the term, is employed as the act of an intelligent being, and that of the Supreme Being only; it is the act of *making* by a simple effort of power, without the use of materials, and without any process.

They are all employed in the moral sense, and with a similar distinction: *make* is indefinite; we may *make* a thing that is difficult or easy, simple or complex; we may *make* a letter, or *make* a poem; we may *make* a word, or *make* a contract; 'In every treaty those concessions which he (Charles I.) thought he could not maintain, he never could by any motive or persuasion be induced to *make*.'—HUME. To *form* is the work either of intelligence, or of circumstances: education has much to do in *forming* the habits, but nature has more to do in *forming* the disposition and the mind altogether; sentiments are frequently *formed* by young people before they have sufficient maturity of thought and knowledge to justify them in coming to any decision; 'Homer's and Virgil's heroes do not *form* a resolution without the conduct and direction of some deity.'—ADDISON. To *produce* is the effect of great mental exertion; or it is the natural operation of things: no industry could ever *produce* a poem or a work of the imagination: but a history or a work of science may be *produced* by the force of mere labour. All things, both in the moral and intellectual world, are linked together upon the simple principle of cause and effect, by which one thing is the *producer*, and the other the thing *produced*: quarrels *produce* hatred, and kindness *produces* love; as heat *produces* inflammation and fever, or disease *produces* death; 'A supernatural effect is that which is above any natural power, that we know of, to *produce*.'—TILLOTSON. Since genius is a spark of the Divine power that acts by its own independent agency, the property of *creation* has been figuratively ascribed to it: the *creative* power of the human mind is a faint emblem of that power which brought every thing into existence out of nothing.

> A wondrous hieroglyphic robe she wore,
> In which all colours and all figures were,
> That nature or that fancy can *create*.—COWLEY.

FORM, FIGURE, CONFORMATION.

Form, in French *forme*, Latin *forma*, most probably from φόρημα and φορέω to bear, signifies properly the image borne or stamped; *figure* (*v. Figure*) signifies the image feigned or conceived; *conformation*, in French *conformation*, in Latin *conformatio*, from *conform*, signifies the image disposed or put together.

* *Form* is the generick term; *figure* and *conformation* are special terms. The *form* is the work either of nature or art; it results from the arrangement of the parts; the *figure* is the work of design: it includes the general contour or outline: the *conformation* includes such a disposition of the parts of a body as is adapted for performing certain functions. *Form* is the property of every substance; and the artificial *form* approaches nearest to perfection, as it is most natural;

> Matter, as wise logicians say,
> Cannot without a *form* subsist,
> And *form*, say I as well as they,
> Must fail if matter brings no grist.—SWIFT.

* Vide Girard: "Façon, figure, forme, conformation."

The *figure* is the fruit of the imagination; it is the representation of the actual *form* that belongs to things; it is more or less just as it approaches to the *form* of the thing itself; 'When Cæsar was one of the masters of the Roman mint, he placed the *figure* of an elephant upon the reverse of the publick money; the word Cæsar signifying an elephant in the Punick language.'—ADDISON. *Conformation* is said only with regard to animal bodies; nature renders it more or less suitable according to the accidental occurrence of physical causes; 'As the *conformation* of their organs are nearly the same in all men, so the manner of perceiving external objects is in all men the same.'—BURKE. The erect *form* of man is one of the distinguishing marks of his superiority over every other terrestrial being: the human *figure* when well painted is an object of admiration: the turn of the mind is doubtless influenced by the *conformation* of the bodily organs. A person's *form* is said to be handsome or ugly, common or uncommon; his *figure* to be correct or incorrect; a *conformation* to be good or bad. Heathens have worshipped the Deity under various *forms*: mathematical *figures* are the only true *figures* with which we are acquainted: the craniologist affects to judge of characters by the *conformation* of the skull.

Form and *figure* are used in a moral application, although *conformation* is not.

We speak of adopting a *form* of faith, a *form* of words, a *form* of godliness;

> O ceremony! show me but thy worth,
> Art thou aught else but place, degree, and *form*,
> Creating fear and awe in other men?
> SHAKSPEARE.

We speak of cutting a showy, a dismal, or ridiculous *figure*; 'Those who make the greatest *figure* in most arts and sciences are universally allowed to be of the British nation.'—ADDISON. *Form* may also sometimes be taken for the person who presents the *form*;

> Lo, in the deep recesses of the wood,
> Before my eyes a beauteous *form* appears;
> A virgin's dress, and modest looks, she wears.
> WYNNE.

The word *figure* is also used in a similar manner.

TO FORM, FASHION, MOULD, SHAPE.

To *form* is to put into a *form*, which is here as before (*v. Form*) the generick term: to *fashion* is to put into a particular or distinct *form*: to *mould* is to put into a set *form*: to *shape* is to *form* simply as it respects the exteriour. As every thing receives a *form* when it receives existence, to *form* conveys the idea of producing; 'Horace was intimate with a prince of the greatest goodness and humanity imaginable: and his court was *formed* after his example.'—STEELE. When we wish to represent a thing as *formed* in any distinct or remarkable way, we may speak of it as *fashioned*: 'By the best information that I could get of this matter, I am apt to think that this prodigious pile was *fashioned* into the *shape* it now bears by several tools and instruments, of which they have a wonderful variety in this country.'—ADDISON. God *formed* man out of the dust of the ground; he *fashioned* him after his own image. When we wish to represent a thing as *formed* according to a precise rule, we should say it was *moulded*; thus the habits of a man are *moulded* at the will of a superiour;

> How dare you, mother, endless date demand,
> For vessels *moulded* by a mortal hand?—DRYDEN.

When we wish to represent a thing as receiving the accidental qualities which distinguish it from others, we talk of *shaping* it: the potter *shapes* the clay; the milliner *shapes* the bonnet; a man *shapes* his actions to the humours of another; 'Those nature hath *shaped* with a great head, narrow breast, and shoulders sticking out, seem much inclined to a consumption.'—HARVEY.

Nature has *formed* all animated beings with an instinctive desire of self-preservation. Creatures *fashioned* like ourselves with flesh and blood cannot attain to the perfection of spiritual beings. It is supposed by some that the human mind may be *moulded* upon the principles of art at the will of the instructer, with the same ease that wax may be *shaped* into the figure of a bird, a beast, or a man, at the pleasure of the artist. This is however true only in part.

TO FORM, COMPOSE, CONSTITUTE.

Form (*v. Form, figure*) signifies to give a *form*; *compose* has the same signification as given under the head *To compose, settle;* and *constitute* that given under the head of *To constitute.*

Form is a generick and indefinite term. To *compose* and *constitute* are modes of forming. These words may be employed either to designate modes of action, or to characterize things. Things may be *formed* either by persons or things; they are *composed* and *constituted* only by conscious agents: thus persons *form* things, or things *form* one another: thus we *form* a circle, or the reflection of the light after rain *forms* a rainbow. Persons *compose* and *constitute*: thus a musician *composes* a piece of musick, or men *constitute* laws. *Form* in regard to persons is the act of the will and determination;

The liquid ore he drained
Into fit molds prepar'd; from which he *form'd*
First his own tools.—MILTON.

Compose is a work of the intellect; 'Words so pleasing to God as those which the Son of God himself hath *composed*, were not possible for men to frame.'—HOOKER. *Constitute* is an act of power, which men must submit to. We *form* a party; we *form* a plan; we *compose* a book; men *constitute* governments, offices, &c.

When employed to characterize things, *form* signifies simply to have a *form*, be it either simple or complex; *compose* and *constitute* are said only of those things which have complex *forms*: the former as respecting the material, the latter the essential parts of an object: thus we may say that an object *forms* a circle, or a semicircle, or the segment of a circle; 'All animals of the same kind which *form* a society are more knowing than others.'—ADDISON. A society is *composed* of individuals;

Nor did Israel 'scape
Th' infection, when their borrow'd gold *composed*
The calf in Oriel.—MILTON.

Law and order *constitute* the essence of society; 'To receive and to communicate assistance *constitutes* the happiness of human life.'—JOHNSON. So letters and syllables *compose* a word; but sense is essential to *constitute* a word.

FORMAL, CEREMONIOUS.

Formal and *ceremonious*, from *form* and *ceremony* (*v. Form, ceremony*), are either taken in an indifferent sense with respect to what contains *form* and *ceremony*, or in a bad sense, as expressing the excess of *form* and *ceremony*. A person expects to have a *formal* dismissal before he considers himself as dismissed; people of fashion pay each other *ceremonious* visits, by way of keeping up a distant intercourse. Whatever communications are made from one government to another must be made in a *formal* manner; 'As there are *formal* and written leagues, respective to certain enemies; so there is a natural and tacit confederation among all men against the common enemies of human society.'—BACON. It is the business of the church to regulate the *ceremonious* part of religion. 'Under a different economy of religion, God was more tender of the shell and *ceremonious* part of his worship.'—SOUTH.

Formal, in the bad sense, is opposed to easy: *ceremonious* to the cordial. A *formal* carriage prevents a person from indulging himself in the innocent familiarities of friendly intercourse;

Formal in apparel,
In gait and countenance surely like a father.
SHAKSPEARE.

A *ceremonious* carriage puts a stop to all hospitality and kindness. Princes, in their *formal* intercourse with each other, know nothing of the pleasures of society; *ceremonious* visitants give and receive entertainments, without tasting any of the enjoyments which flow from the reciprocity of kind offices; 'From the moment one sets up for an author, one must be treated as *ceremoniously*, that is, as unfaithfully, "as a king's favourite, or as a king."'—POPE.

TO CAUSE, OCCASION, CREATE.

To *cause*, from the substantive *cause*, naturally signifies to be the *cause* of; *occasion*, from the noun *occasion*, signifies to be the *occasion* of; *create*, in Latin *creatus*, participle of *creo*, comes from the Greek κρέω to command, and κεραίνω to perform.

What is *caused* seems to follow naturally; what is *occasioned* follows incidentally; what is *created* receives its existence arbitrarily. A wound *causes* pain; accidents *occasion* delay; busy-bodies *create* mischief. The misfortunes of the children *cause* great affliction to the parents;

Scarcely an ill to human life belongs,
But what our follies *cause*, or mutual wrongs.
JENYNS.

Business *occasions* a person's late attendance at a place; 'The good Psalmist condemns the foolish thoughts which a reflection on the prosperous state of his affairs had sometimes *occasioned* in him.'—ATTERBURY. Disputes and misunderstandings *create* animosity and ill-will; 'As long as the powers or abilities which are ascribed to others are exerted in a sphere of action remote from ours, and not brought into competition with talents of the same kind to which we have pretensions, they *create* no jealousy.'—BLAIR. The *cause* of a person's misfortunes may often be traced to his own misconduct: the improper behaviour of one person may *occasion* another to ask for an explanation: jealousies are *created* in the minds of relatives by an unnecessary reserve and distance.

TO MAKE, DO, ACT.

Make, in Dutch *maken*, Saxon *macan*, &c., comes from the Greek μηχανὴ art, signifying to put together with art; *do*, in German *thun*, comes probably from the Greek θεῖναι to put, signifying to put, or put in order, to bring to pass; *act*, in Latin *actus*, from *ago* to direct, signifies literally to put in motion.

We cannot *make* without *doing*, but we may *do* (*v. To act*) without *making*: to *do* is simply to move for a certain end; to *make* is to *do*, so as to bring something into being, which was not before: we *make* a thing what it was not before; we *do* a thing in the same manner as we *did* it before: what is *made* is either better or worse, or the same as another;

Empire! thou poor and despicable thing!
When such as these *make* and *unmake* a king.
DRYDEN

What is *done*, is *done* either wisely or unwisely;

What shall I *do* to be for ever known,
And *make* the age to come my own.—COWLEY.

We *act* whenever we *do* any thing, but we may *act* without *doing* any thing. The verb *act* is always intransitive; and *do* transitive; we *do* something, but not *act* something. The *act* approaches nearest to the idea of *move;* it is properly the exertion of power corporeal or mental: *do* is closely allied to *effect;* it is the producing an effect by such an exertion. They *act* very unwisely who attempt to *do* more than their abilities will enable them to complete: whatever we *do*, let us be careful to *act* considerately; 'We have made this a maxim, "That a man who is commonly called good-natured is hardly to be thanked for what he *does*, because half that is *acted* about him is *done* rather by his sufferance than approbation."'—STEELE

ACTION, ACT, DEED.

The words *action*, *act*, and *deed*, though derived from the preceding verbs, have an obvious distinction in their meaning.

* We mark the degrees of *action* which indicate energy; we mark the number of *acts* which may serve to designate a habit or character: we speak of a lively, vehement, or impetuous *action;* a man of *action*, in distinction from a mere talker or an idler; whatever rests without influence or movement has lost its *action:* we speak of many *acts* of a particular kind, we call him a fool who commits continued *acts* of folly; and him a niggard who commits nothing but *acts* of meanness.

Action is a continued exertion of power: *act* is a

* Roubaud: "Acte, action"

single exertion of power; the physical movement; the simple *acting*. Our *actions* are our works in the strict sense of the word; our *acts* are the operations of our faculties. The character of a man must be judged by his *actions*; the merit of *actions* depends on the motives that give rise to them: the *act* of speaking is peculiar to man; but the *acts* of walking, running, eating, &c. are common to all animals.

Actions may be considered either singly or collectively; *acts* are regarded only individually and specifically: we speak of all a man's *actions*, but not all his *acts*; we say a good *action*, a virtuous *action*, a charitable *action*; but an *act*, not an *action* of goodness, an *act* of virtue, an *act* of faith, an *act* of charity, and the like. It is a good *action* to conceal the faults of our neighbours; but a rare *act* of charity among men. Many noble *actions* are done in private, the consciousness of which is the only reward of the doer; the wisest of men may occasionally commit *acts* of folly which are not imputable to their general character; 'Many of those *actions* which are apt to procure fame are not in their nature conducive to our ultimate happiness.'—ADDISON. Nothing can be a greater *act* of imprudence than not to take an occasional review of our past *actions*; 'I desire that the same rule may be extended to the whole fraternity of heathen gods; it being my design to condemn every poem to the flames, in which Jupiter thunders or exercises any act of authority which does not belong to him.'—ADDISON.

*Action** is a term applied to whatever is done in general; *act* to that which is remarkable or that requires to be distinguished. The sentiments of the heart are easier to be discovered by one's *actions* than by one's words: it is an heroick *act* to forgive our enemy, when we are in a condition to be revenged on him. The good man is cautious in all his *actions* to avoid even the appearance of evil: a great prince is anxious to mark every year by some distinguished *act* of wisdom or virtue.

Act and *deed* are both employed for what is remarkable; but *act* denotes only one single thing done;

> Who forth from nothing call'd this comely frame,
> His will and *act*, his word and work the same.
> PRIOR.

Deed implies some complicated performance, something achieved: we display but one quality or power in performing an *act*; we display many, both physical and mental, in performing a *deed*. A prince distinguishes himself by *acts* of mercy; the commander of an army by martial *deeds*;

> I on the other side
> Us'd no ambition to commend my *deeds*;
> The *deeds* themselves, though mute, spoke loud the doer.—MILTON.

Acts of disobedience in youth frequently lead to the perpetration of the foulest *deeds* in more advanced life.

DEED, EXPLOIT, ACHIEVEMENT, FEAT.

Deed, from *do*, expresses the thing done; *exploit*, in French *exploit*, most probably changed from *explicatus*, signifies the thing unfolded or displayed; *achievement*, from *achieve*, signifies the thing *achieved*; *feat*, in French *fait*, Latin *factum*, from *facio*, signifies the thing done.

The first three words rise progressively on each other: *deeds*, compared with the others, is employed for that which is ordinary or extraordinary; *exploit* and *achievement* are used only for the extraordinary; the latter in a higher sense than the former.

Deeds must always be characterized as good or bad, magnanimous or atrocious, and the like, except in poetry, where the term becomes elevated;

> Great Pollio! thou for whom thy Rome prepares
> The ready triumph of thy finish'd wars;
> Is there in fate an hour reserv'd for me
> To sing thy *deeds* in numbers worthy thee?
> DRYDEN.

Exploit and *achievement* do not necessarily require any epithets; they are always taken in the proper sense for something great. *Exploit*, when compared with *achievement*, is a term used in plain prose; it designates not so much what is great as what is real; *achievement* is most adapted to poetry and romance; it soars above what the eye sees, and the ear hears, and affords scope for the imagination. Martial *deeds* are as interesting to the reader as to the performer: the pages of modern history will be crowded with the *exploits* of Englishmen both by sea and land, as those of ancient and fabulous history are with the *achievements* of their heroes and demi-gods. An *exploit* marks only personal bravery in action; an *achievement* denotes elevation of character in every respect, grandeur of design, promptitude in execution, and valour in action.

An *exploit* may be executed by the design and at the will of another; a common soldier or an army may perform *exploits*;

> High matter thou enjoin'st me, O prime of men!
> Sad task and hard; for how shall I relate
> To human sense th' invisible *exploits*
> Of warring spirits?—MILTON.

An *achievement* is designed and executed by the *achiever*; Hercules is distinguished for his *achievements*: and in the same manner we speak of the *achievements* of knights-errant or of great commanders;

> Great spoils and trophies gain'd by thee they bear,
> Then let thy own *achievements* be thy share.
> DRYDEN.

Feat approaches nearest to *exploit* in signification; the former marks skill, and the latter resolution. The *feats* of chivalry displayed in justs and tournaments were in former times as much esteemed as warlike *exploits*;

> Much I have heard
> Of thy prodigious might, and *feats* perform'd.
> MILTON.

Exploit and *feat* are often used in derision, to mark the absence of those qualities in the actions of individuals. The soldier who affects to be foremost in situations where there is no danger cannot be more properly derided than by terming his action an *exploit*: he who prides himself on the display of skill in the performance of a paltry trick may be laughed at for having performed a *feat*.

ACTION, GESTURE, GESTICULATION, POSTURE, ATTITUDE, POSITION.

Action is either the act of acting, or the manner of acting; *gesture*, in French *geste*, Latin *gestus*, participle of *gero* to carry one's self, signifies the manner of carrying one's body; *gesticulation*, in Latin *gesticulatio*, comes from *gesticulor* to make many *gestures*; *posture*, in French *posture*, Latin *positura* a position, comes from *positus*, participle of *pono*, signifying the manner of placing one's self; *attitude*, in French *attitude*, Italian *attitudine*, is changed from *aptitude*, signifying a propriety as to disposition.

All these terms are applied to the state of the body; the former three indicating a state of motion; the latter two a state of rest. *Action* respects the movements of the body in general; *gesture* is an action indicative of some particular state of mind; *gesticulation* is a species of artificial *gesture*. Raising the arm is an *action*; bowing is a *gesture*.

Actions may be ungraceful; *gestures* indecent A suitable *action* sometimes gives great force to the words that are uttered; 'Cicero concludes his celebrated book "de Oratore" with some precepts for pronunciation and *action*, without which part he affirms that the best orator in the world can never succeed.'—HUGHES. *Gestures* often supply the place of language between people of different nations; 'Our best actors are somewhat at a loss to support themselves with proper *gesture*, as they move from any considerable distance to the front of the stage.'—STEELE. *Actions* characterize a man as vulgar or well-bred; *gestures* mark the temper of the mind. There are many *actions* which it is the object of education to prevent from growing into habits: savages express the vehement passions of the mind, by vehement *gestures* on every occasion, even in their amusements. An extravagant or unnatural *gesture* is termed a *gesticulation*; a sycophant, who wishes to cringe into favour with

* Girard "Action, acte."

the great, deals largely in *gesticulation* to mark his devotion; a buffoon who attempts to imitate the *gestures* of another will use *gesticulation;* and the monkey who apes the *actions* of human beings does so by means of *gesticulations;* 'Neither the judges of our laws, nor the representatives of the people, would be much affected by laboured *gesticulation*, or believe any man the more, because he rolled his eyes, or puffed his cheeks.'—JOHNSON.

Posture * is a mode of placing the body more or less differing from the ordinary habits; *attitude* is the manner of keeping the body more or less suitable to the existing circumstances. A *posture*, however convenient, is never assumed without exertion; it is therefore willingly changed: an *attitude*, though not usual, is still according to the nature of things; it is therefore readily preserved. A *posture* is singular; it has something in it which departs from the ordinary carriage of the body, and makes it remarkable; 'Falsehood in a short time found by experience, that her superiority consisted only in the celerity of her course, and the change of her *posture*.'—JOHNSON. An *attitude* is striking; it is the natural expression of character or impression; 'Falsehood always endeavoured to copy the mien and *attitudes* of truth.'—JOHNSON. A brave man will put himself into a *posture* of defence, without assuming an *attitude* of defiance.

Strange and forced positions of the body are termed *postures;* noble, agreeable, and expressive forms of carriage, are called *attitudes:* mountebanks and clowns put themselves into ridiculous *postures* in order to excite laughter; actors assume graceful *attitudes* to represent their characters. *Postures* are to the body what grimaces are to the face; *attitudes* are to the body what air is to the figure: he who in attempting to walk assumes the *attitude* of a dancer, puts himself into a ridiculous *posture;* a graceful and elegant *attitude* in dancing becomes an affected and laughable *posture* in another case.

Postures are sometimes usefully employed in stage dancing; the *attitudes* are necessarily employed by painters, sculptors, dancing masters, and other artists. *Posture* is said of the whole body; the rest, of particular limbs or parts. *Attitude* and *posture* are figuratively applied to other objects besides the body: armies assume a menacing *attitude;* in a critical *posture* of affairs, extraordinary skill is required on the part of the government; 'Milton has presented this violent spirit (Moloch) as the first that rises in that assembly to give his opinion upon their present *posture* of affairs.'—ADDISON.

Position, when compared with *posture*, is taken only in regard to persons, in which case the *posture*, as observed above, is a species of *position*, namely, an artificial *position:* if a person stands tiptoe, in order to see to a greater distance, he may be said to put himself into that *position;* but if a dancer do the same, as a part of his performance, it becomes a *posture:* so, likewise, when one leans against the wall it is a leaning *position;* 'Every step, in the progression of existence, changes our *position* with respect to the things about us.'—JOHNSON. But when one theatrically bends his body backward or forward, it is a *posture:* one may, in the same manner, sit in an erect *position*, or in a reclining *posture;* 'When I entered his room, he was sitting in a contemplative *posture*, with his eyes fixed upon the ground; after he had continued in his reverie near a quarter of an hour, he rose up and seemed by his *gestures* to take leave of some invisible guest.'—HAWKESWORTH.

ACTION, AGENCY, OPERATION.

Action (*v. To act*) is the effect, *agency* the cause. *Action* is inherent in the subject;

> noble English, that could entertain
> With half their forces the full power of France,
> And let another half stand laughing by,
> All out of work, and cold for *action*.—SHAKSPEARE.

Agency is something exteriour; it is, in fact, putting a thing into *action:* in this manner, the whole world is in *action* through the *agency* of the Divine Being; 'A few advances there are in the following papers tending to assert the superintendence and *agency* of Providence in the natural world.'—WOODWARD. Sometimes the word *action* is taken in the sense of acting upon, when it approaches still nearer to *agency;* 'It is better therefore that the earth should move about its own centre, and make those useful vicissitudes of night and day, than expose always the same side to the *action* of the sun.'—BENTLEY. *Operation*, from the Latin *operatio*, and *opera* labour or *opus* need, signifying the work that is needful, is action for a specifick end, and according to a rule; as the *operation* of nature in the article of vegetation;

> The tree whose *operation* brings
> Knowledge of good and ill, shun thou to taste.
> MILTON.

ACTIVE, DILIGENT, INDUSTRIOUS, ASSIDUOUS, LABORIOUS.

Active, from the verb to *act*, implies a propensity to act, to be doing something without regard to the nature of the object; *diligent*, in French *diligent*, Latin *diligens*, participle of *diligo* to choose or like, implies an attachment to an object, and consequent attention to it; *industrious*, in French *industrieux*, Latin *industrius*, is probably formed from *intro* within and *struo* to build, make, or do, signifying an inward or thorough inclination to be engaged in some serious work; *assiduous*, in French *assidu*, in Latin *assiduus*, is compounded of *as* or *ad* and *siduus* from *sedeo* to sit, signifying to sit close to a thing; *laborious*, in French *laborieux*, Latin *laboriosus*, from *labour*, implies belonging to labour, or the inclination to labour.

We are *active* if we are only ready to exert our powers, whether to any end or not; 'Providence has made the human soul an *active* being.'—JOHNSON. We are *diligent* when we are active for some specifick end; 'A constant and unfailing obedience is above the reach of terrestrial *diligence*.'—JOHNSON. We are *industrious* when no time is left unemployed in some serious pursuit; 'It has been observed by writers of morality, that in order to quicken human *industry*, Providence has so contrived that our daily food is not to be procured without much pains and labour.'—ADDISON. We are *assiduous* if we do not leave a thing until it is finished; 'If ever a cure is performed on a patient, where quacks are concerned, they can claim no greater share in it than Virgil's Iapis in the curing of Æneas; he tried his skill, was very *assiduous* about the wound, and indeed was the only visible means that relieved the hero; but the poet assures us it was the particular assistance of a deity that speeded the operation.'—PEARCE. We are *laborious* when the bodily or mental powers are regularly employed in some hard labour; 'If we look into the brute creation, we find all its individuals engaged in a painful and *laborious* way of life to procure a necessary subsistence for themselves.'—ADDISON.

A man may be *active* without being *diligent*, since he may employ himself in what is of no importance; but he can scarcely be *diligent* without being *active*, since *diligence* supposes some degree of activity in one's application to a useful object. A man may be *diligent* without being *industrious*, for he may *diligently* employ himself about a particular favourite object without employing himself constantly in the same way; and he may be *industrious* without being *diligent*, since *diligence* implies a free exercise of the mental as well as corporeal powers, but *industry* applies principally to manual labour. *Activity* and *diligence* are therefore commonly the property of lively or strong minds, but *industry* may be associated with moderate talents. A man may be *diligent* without being *assiduous;* but he cannot be *assiduous* without being *diligent*, for *assiduity* is a sort of persevering *diligence*. A man may be *industrious*, without being *laborious*, but not *vice versâ;* for *laboriousness* is a severer kind of *industry*.

The *active* man is never easy without an employment; the *diligent* man is contented with the employment he has; the *industrious* man goes from one employment to the other; the *assiduous* man seeks to attain the end of his employment; the *laborious* man spares no pains or labour in following his employment.

Activity is of great importance for those who have the management of public concerns: *diligence* in business contributes greatly to success: *industry* is of great value in obtaining a livelihood: without *assiduity* no advances can be made in science or literature; and

* Roubaud. "Posture, attitude."

without *laborious* exertions, considerable attainments are not to be expected in many literary pursuits.

Active minds set on foot inquiries to which the *industrious*, by *assiduous* application, and *diligent* if not *laborious* research, often afford satisfactory answers.

ACTIVE, BRISK, AGILE, NIMBLE.

Active signifies the same as in the preceding article; *brisk* has a common origin with *fresh*, which is in Saxon *fersh*, Dutch *frisch* or *bersk*, Danish *frisk*, *fersk*, &c.; *agile*, in Latin *agilis*, comes from the same verb as active, signifying a fitness, a readiness to act or move; *nimble* is probably derived from the Saxon *nemen* to take, implying a fitness or capacity to take any thing by a celerity of movement.

Activity respects one's transactions; *briskness*, one's sports: men are *active* in carrying on business; children are *brisk* in their play. *Agility* refers to the light and easy carriage of the body in springing; *nimbleness* to its quick and gliding movements in running. A rope-dancer is *agile;* a female moves *nimbly*.

Activity results from ardour of mind; 'There is not a more painful action of the mind than invention; yet in dreams it works with that ease and *activity*, that we are not sensible when the faculty is employed.'—ADDISON. *Briskness* springs from vivacity of feeling; 'I made my next application to a widow, and attacked her so *briskly* that I thought myself within a fortnight of her.'—BUDGELL. *Agility* is produced by corporeal vigour, and habitual strong exertion; 'When the Prince touched his stirrup, and was going to speak, the officer, with an incredible *agility*, threw himself on the earth and kissed his feet.'—STEELE. *Nimbleness* results from an effort to move lightly;

> O friends, I hear the tread of *nimble* feet
> Hasting this way.—MILTON.

ACTIVE, BUSY, OFFICIOUS.

Active signifies the same as before; *busy*, in Saxon *gebisged*, from *bisgian*, in German *beschäfftigt*, from *beschäfftigen* to occupy, and *schaffen* to make or do, implies a propensity to be occupied; *officious*, in French *officieux*, Latin *officiosus*, from *officium* duty or service, signifies a propensity to perform some service or office.

Active respects the habit or disposition of the mind; *busy* and *officious*, either the disposition of the mind, or the employment of the moment: the former regards every species of employment; the latter only particular kinds of employment. An *active* person is ever ready to be employed; a person is *busy*, when he is actually employed in any object; he is *officious*, when he is employed for others.

Active is always taken in a good, or at least an indifferent sense; it is opposed to lazy; 'The pursuits of the *active* part of mankind are either in the paths of religion and virtue, or, on the other hand, in the roads to wealth, honour, or pleasures.'—ADDISON. *Busy*, as it respects occupation, is mostly in a good sense; 'We see multitudes *busy* in the pursuit of riches, at the expense of wisdom and virtue.'—JOHNSON. It is opposed to being at leisure; as it respects disposition, it is always in a bad sense; 'The air-pump, the barometer, the quadrant, and the like inventions, were thrown out to those *busy* spirits (politicians), as tubs and barrels are to a whale, that he may let the ship sail on without disturbance.'—ADDISON. *Officious* is never taken in a good sense; it implies being *busy* without discretion. To an *active* disposition, nothing is more irksome than inaction; but it is not concerned to inquire into the utility of the action. It is better for a person to be *busy* than quite unemployed; but a *busy* person will employ himself about the concerns of others, when he has none of his own sufficiently important to engage his attention: an *officious* person is as unfortunate as he is troublesome; when he strives to serve he has the misfortune to annoy; 'I was forced to quit my first lodgings by reason of an *officious* landlady, that would be asking me every morning how I had slept.'—ADDISON.

SEDULOUS, DILIGENT, ASSIDUOUS.

Sedulous, from the Latin *sedulus* and *sedeo*, signifies sitting close to a thing; *diligent*, *v. Active*, *diligent;* *assiduous*, *v. Active*, *diligent*.

The idea of application is expressed by these epithets, but *sedulous* is a particular, *diligent* is a general term: one is *sedulous* by habits; one is *diligent* either habitually or occasionally: a *sedulous* scholar pursues his studies with a regular and close application; a scholar may be *diligent* at a certain period, though not invariably so. *Sedulity* seems to mark the very essential property of application, that is, adhering closely to an object; but *diligence* expresses one's attachment to a thing, as evinced by an eager pursuit of it: the former, therefore, bespeaks the steadiness of the character; the latter merely the turn of one's inclination: one is *sedulous* from a conviction of the importance of the thing: one may be *diligent* by fits and starts, according to the humour of the moment.

Assiduous and *sedulous* both express the quality of sitting or sticking close to a thing, but the former may, like *diligent*, be employed on a partial occasion; the latter is always permanent: we may be *assiduous* in our attentions to a person; but we are *sedulous* in the important concerns of life. *Sedulous* peculiarly respects the quiet employments of life; a teacher may be entitled *sedulous;* 'One thing I would offer is that he would constantly and *sedulously* read Tully, which will insensibly work him into a good Latin style.'—LOCKE. *Diligent* respects the active employments; 'I would recommend a *diligent* attendance on the courts of justice (to a student for the bar).'—DUNNING. One is *diligent* at work: *assiduity* holds a middle rank; it may be employed equally for that which requires active exertion, or otherwise: we may be *assiduous* in the pursuits of literature, or we may be *assiduous* in our attendance upon a person, or the performance of any office;

> And thus the patient dam *assiduous* sits,
> Not to be tempted from her tender task.
> THOMSON.

READY, APT, PROMPT.

Ready, from the German *bereiten* to prepare, signifies prepared; *apt*, in Latin *aptus*, signifies literally fit; *prompt*, in Latin *promptus*, from *promo* to draw forth, signifies literally drawn to a point.

Ready is in general applied to that which has been intentionally prepared for a given purpose;

> The god himself with *ready* trident stands
> And opes the deep, and spreads the moving sands.
> DRYDEN.

Promptness and *aptness* are species of *readiness*, which lie in the personal endowments or disposition: hence we speak of things being *ready* for a journey; persons being *apt* to learn, or *prompt* to obey or to reply. *Ready*, when applied to persons, characterizes the talent; as a *ready* wit. *Apt* characterizes the habits; as *apt* to judge by appearance, or *apt* to decide hastily; and is also employed in the same sense figuratively; 'Poverty is *apt* to betray a man into envy, riches into arrogance.'—ADDISON. *Prompt* characterizes more commonly the particular action, and denotes the willingness of the agent, and the quickness with which he performs the action; as *prompt* in executing a command, or *prompt* to listen to what is said; so likewise when applied to things personal;

> Let not the fervent tongue,
> *Prompt* to deceive, with adulation smooth
> Gain on your purpos'd will.—THOMSON.

ALERTNESS, ALACRITY.

Alertness, from *ales* a wing, designates corporeal activity or readiness for action; *alacrity*, from *acer* sharp, brisk, designates mental activity.

We proceed with *alertness*, when the body is in its full vigour;

> The wings that waft our riches out of sight
> Grow on the gamester's elbows; and the *alert*
> And nimble motion of those restless joints
> That never tire, soon fans them all away.
> COWPER.

We proceed with *alacrity* when the mind is in full pursuit of an object; 'In dreams it is wonderful to observe with what sprightliness and *alacrity* the soul exerts herself.'—ADDISON.

ACTOR, AGENT.

These terms vary according to the different senses of the verb from which they are drawn; *actor* is used for one who does any thing or acts a part; 'Of all the patriarchal histories, that of Joseph and his brethren is the most remarkable, for the characters of the *actors*, and the instructive nature of the events.'—BLAIR. An *agent* is one who puts other things in action, particularly as distinguished from the patient or thing acted upon; 'They produced wonderful effects, by the proper application of *agents* to patients.'—TEMPLE. The *agent* is also an active being, or one possessing the faculty of action;

Heav'n made us *agents* free to good or ill,
And forc'd it not, tho' he foresaw the will.
DRYDEN.

An *agent* in a piece of fiction is the being who performs the actions narrated; 'I expect that no Pagan *agent* shall be introduced into the poem, or any fact related which a man cannot give credit to with a good conscience.'—ADDISON. Hence it is that the word *actor* is taken in the sense of a player, and an *agent* in the mercantile sense of a factor, or one who acts in another's stead.

ACTOR, PLAYER, PERFORMER.

The *actor* and *player* both perform on a stage; but the former is said in relation to the part that is acted, the latter to the profession that is followed. We may be *actors* occasionally without being *players* professionally, but we may be *players* without deserving the name of *actors*. Those who personate characters for their amusement are *actors* but not *players*: those who do the same for a livelihood are *players* as well as *actors*; hence we speak of a company of *players*, not *actors*. So likewise in the figurative sense, whoever acts a part, real or fictitious, that is, on the stage of life, or the stage of a theatre, is an *actor*; 'Our orators (says Cicero) are as it were the *actors* of truth itself; and the *players* the imitators of truth.'—HUGHES. But he only is a *player* who performs the fictitious part; hence the former is taken* in a bad or good sense, according to circumstances; 'Cicero is known to have been the intimate friend of Roscius the *actor*.'—HUGHES. *Player* is always taken in a less favourable sense, from the artificiality which attaches to his profession;

All the world 's a stage,
And all the men and women merely *players*.
SHAKSPEARE.

The term *performer* is now used in the sense of one who performs a part in a theatrical exhibition, and for the most part in application to the individual in estimating the merits of his performance, as a good or bad *performer*.

ACTUAL, REAL, POSITIVE.

Actual, in French *actuel*, Latin *actualis*, from *actio* a deed, signifies belonging to the thing done; *real*, in French *reel*, Latin *realis*, from *res*, signifies belonging to the thing as it is; *positive*, in French *positif*, Latin *positivus*, from *pono* to place or fix, signifies the state or quality of being fixed, established.

What is *actual* has proof of its existence within itself, and may be exposed to the eye; what is *real* may be satisfactorily proved to exist; and what is *positive* precludes the necessity of a proof. *Actual* is opposed to the supposititious, conceived or reported; *real* to the feigned, imaginary; *positive* to the uncertain, doubtful.

Whatever is the condition of a thing for the time being is the *actual* condition; sorrows are *real* which flow from a substantial cause; proofs are *positive* which leave the mind in no uncertainty. The *actual* state of a nation is not to be ascertained by individual instances of poverty, or the reverse; there are but few, if any, *real* objects of compassion among common beggars; many *positive* facts have been related of the deception which they have practised. By an *actual* survey of human life, we are alone enabled to form just opinions of mankind; 'The very notion of any duration being past implies that it was once present; for the idea of being once present is *actually* included in the idea of its being past.'—ADDISON. It is but too frequent for men to disguise their *real* sentiments, although it is not always possible to obtain *positive* evidence of their insincerity; 'We may and do converse with God in person *really*, and to all the purposes of giving and receiving, though not visibly.'—SOUTH. 'Dissimulation is taken for a man's *positive* professing himself to be what he is not.'—SOUTH

TO PERPETRATE, COMMIT.

The idea of doing something wrong is common to these terms; but *perpetrate*, from the Latin *perpetro*, compounded of *per* and *petro*, in Greek πράττω, signifying thoroughly to compass or bring about, is a much more determined proceeding than that of *committing* One may *commit* offences of various degree and magnitude; but one *perpetrates* crimes only, and those of the more heinous kind. A lawless banditti, who spend their lives in the *perpetration* of the most horrid crimes, are not to be restrained by the ordinary course of justice;

Then shows the forest which, in after-times,
Fierce Romulus, for *perpetrated* crimes,
A refuge made.'—DRYDEN.

He who *commits* any offence against the good order of society exposes himself to the censure of others, who may be his inferiours in certain respects; 'The miscarriages of the great designs of princes are of little use to the bulk of mankind, who seem very little interested in admonitions against errours which they cannot *commit*.'—JOHNSON.

INACTIVE, INERT, LAZY, SLOTHFUL, SLUGGISH.

A reluctance to bodily exertion is common to all these terms. *Inactive* is the most general and unqualified term of all; it expresses simply the want of a stimulus to exertion; *inert* is something more positive, from the Latin *iners* or *sine arte* without art or mind; it denotes a specifick deficiency either in body or mind; *lazy*, which has the same signification as given under the head of *Idle*; *slothful*, from *slow*, that is, full of slowness; and *sluggish* from *slug*, that is, like a *slug*, drowsy and heavy, all rise upon one another to denote an expressly defective temperament of the body which directly impedes action.

To be *inactive* is to be indisposed to action; that is, to the performance of any office, to the doing any specifick business: to be *inert* is somewhat more; it is to be indisposed to movement: to be *lazy* is to move with pain to one's self: to be *slothful* is never to move otherwise than slowly: to be *sluggish* is to move in a sleepy and heavy manner.

A person may be *inactive* from a variety of incidental causes, as timidity, ignorance, modesty, and the like, which combine to make him averse to enter upon any business, or take any serious step; a person may be *inert* from temporary indisposition; but *laziness*, *slothfulness*, and *sluggishness* are inherent physical defects: *laziness* is however not altogether independent of the mind or the will; but *slothfulness* and *sluggishness* are purely the offspring of nature, or, which is the same thing, habit superinduced upon nature. A man of a mild character is frequently *inactive*; he wants that ardour which impels perpetually to action; he wishes for nothing with sufficient warmth to make action agreeable; he is therefore *inactive* by a natural consequence;

Virtue conceal'd within our breast
Is *inactivity* at best.—SWIFT.

Hence the term *inactive* is properly applied to matter;

What laws are these? instruct us if you can;
There 's one design'd for brutes and one for man,
Another guides *inactive* matter's course.
JENYNS.

Some diseases, particularly of the melancholy kind, are accompanied with a strong degree of *inertness*; since they seem to deprive the frame of its ordinary powers to action, and to produce a certain degree of torpor. Hence the term is employed to express a

* Vide Girard: 'Acteur comedien.'

want of the power of action in the strongest possible degree, as displayed in the inanimate part of the creation,

> Informer of the planetary train,
> Without whose quickening glance their cumbrous orbs
> Were brute, unlovely mass, *inert* and dead.
> THOMSON.

Lazy people move as if their bodies were a burden to themselves; they are fond of rest, and particularly averse to be put in action; but they will sometimes move quickly, and perform much when once impelled to move; 'The first canto (in Thomson's Castle of Indolence) opens a scene of *lazy* luxury that fills the imagination.'—JOHNSON. *Slothful* people never vary their pace; they have a physical impediment in themselves to quick motion;

> Falsely luxurious, will not man awake,
> And, springing from the bed of *sloth*, enjoy
> The cool, the fragrant, and the silent hour?
> THOMSON.

Sluggish people are with difficulty brought into action; it is their nature to be in a state of stupor; 'Conversation would become dull and vapid, if negligence were not sometimes roused, and *sluggishness* quickened by due severity of reprehension.'—JOHNSON.

IDLE, LAZY, INDOLENT.

Idle is in German *eitel* vain; *lazy*, in German *lässig*, comes from the Latin *lassus* weary, because weariness naturally engenders *laziness; indolent*, in Latin *indolens*, signifies without feeling, having apathy or unconcern.

A propensity to inaction is the common idea by which these words are connected; they differ in the cause and degree of the quality: *idle* expresses less than *lazy*, and *lazy* less than *indolent:* one is termed *idle* who will do nothing useful; one is *lazy* who will do nothing at all without great reluctance; one is *indolent* who does not care to do any thing or set about any thing. There is no direct inaction in the *idler;* for a child is *idle* who will not learn his lesson, but he is active enough in that which pleases himself: there is an aversion to corporeal action in a *lazy* man, but not always to mental action; he is *lazy* at work, *lazy* in walking, or *lazy* in sitting; but he may not object to any employment, such as reading or thinking, which leaves his body entirely at rest: an *indolent* man, on the contrary, fails in activity from a defect both in the mind and the body; he will not only not move, but he will not even think, if it give him trouble; and trifling exertions of any kind are sufficient, even in prospect, to deter him from attempting to move.

Idleness is common to the young and the thoughtless, to such as have not steadiness of mind to set a value on any thing which may be acquired by exertion and regular employment; the *idle* man is opposed to one that is diligent; 'As pride is sometimes hid under humility, *idleness* is often covered by turbulence and hurry.'—JOHNSON. *Laziness* is frequent among those who are compelled to work for others; it is a habit of body superinduced upon one's condition; those who should labour are often the most unwilling to move at all, and since the spring of the mind which should impel them to action is wanting, and as they are continually under the necessity of moving at the will of another, they acquire an habitual reluctance to any motion, and find their comfort in entire inaction. hence *laziness* is almost confined to servants and the labouring classes: *laziness* is opposed to industry; 'Wicked condemned men will ever live like rogues, and not fall to work, but be *lazy* and spend victuals.'—BACON. *Lazy* may however be applied figuratively to other objects;

> The daw,
> The rook, and magpie, to the gray-grown oaks,
> That the calm village in their verdant arms
> Sheltering embrace, direct their *lazy* flight.
> THOMSON.

Indolence is a physical property of the mind, a want of motive or purpose to action: the *indolent* man is not so fond of his bodily ease as the *lazy* man, but he shrinks from every species of exertion still more than the latter; *indolence* is a disease most observable in the higher classes, and even in persons of the highest intellectual endowments, in whom there should be the most powerful motives to exertion; the *indolent* stands in direct opposition to nothing but the general term active; 'Nothing is so opposite to the true enjoyment of life as the relaxed and feeble state of an *indolent* mind.'—BLAIR.

The life of a common player is most apt to breed an habitual *idleness;* as they have no serious employment to occupy their hands or their heads, they grow averse to every thing which would require the exercise of either: the life of a common soldier is apt to breed *laziness:* he who can sit or lie for twelve hours out of the twenty-four, will soon acquire a disgust to any kind of labour, unless he be naturally of an active turn: the life of a rich man is most favourable to *indolence;* he who has every thing provided at his hand, not only for the necessities, but the comforts of life, may soon become averse to every thing that wears the face of exertion; he may become *indolent*, if he be not unfortunately so by nature.

IDLE, LEISURE, VACANT.

Idle signifies here emptiness or the absence of that which is solid; *leisure*, otherwise spelled *leasure*, comes from *lease*, as in the compound *release*, and the Latin *laxo* to make lax or loose, that is, loosed or set free; *vacant*, in Latin *vacans*, from *vaco* to free or be empty, signifies the same.

Idle is opposed here to busy; *at leisure* simply to employed: he therefore who is *idle*, instead of being busy, commits a fault; which is not always the case with him who is *at leisure* or free from his employment. *Idle* is therefore always taken in a sense more or less unfavourable; *leisure* in a sense perfectly indifferent: if a man says of himself that he has spent an *idle* hour in this or that place in amusement, company, and the like, he means to signify he would have spent it better if any thing had offered; on the other hand, he would say that he spends his *leisure* moments in a suitable relaxation: he who values his time will take care to have as few *idle* hours as possible; 'Life is sustained with so little labour, that the tediousness of *idle* time cannot otherwise be supported (than by artificial desires).'—JOHNSON. But since no one can always be employed in severe labour, he will occupy his *leisure* hours in that which best suits his taste;

> Here pause, my Gothick lyre, a little while:
> The *leisure* hour is all that thou canst claim.
> BEATTIE.

Idle and *leisure* are said in particular reference to the time that is employed; *vacant* is a more general term, that simply qualifies the thing: an *idle* hour is without any employment; a *vacant* hour is in general free from the employments with which it might be filled up; a person has *leisure* time according to his wishes; but he may have *vacant* time from necessity, that is, when he is in want of employment; '*Idleness* dictates expedients, by which life may be passed unprofitably, without the tediousness of many *vacant* hours'—JOHNSON.

IDLE, VAIN.

Idle, v. *Idle, lazy; vain*, in Latin *vanus*, is probably changed from *vacaneus*, signifying empty.

These epithets are both opposed to the solid or substantial; but *idle* has a more particular reference to what ought or ought not to engage the time or attention; *vain* seems to qualify the thing without any such reference. A pursuit may be termed either *idle* or *vain:* in the former case, it reflects immediately on the agent for not employing his time on something more serious; but in the latter case, it simply characterizes the pursuit as one that will be attended with no good consequences: when we consider ourselves as beings who have but a short time to live, and that every moment of that time ought to be thoroughly well spent, we shall be careful to avoid all *idle* concerns; when we consider ourselves as rational beings, who are responsible for the use of those powers with which we have been invested by our Almighty Maker, we shall be careful to reject all *vain* concerns: an *idle* effort is made by one who does not care to exert him self for any useful purpose, who works only to please himself; a *vain* effort may be made by one who is in a state of desperation. These terms preserve the same distinction when applied to other objects;

And let no spot of *idle* earth be found,
But cultivate the genius of the ground.—DRYDEN.

'Deluded by *vain* opinions, we look to the advantages of fortune as our ultimate goods.'—BLAIR.

HEAVY, DULL, DROWSY.

Heavy is allied to both *dull* and *drowsy*, but the latter have no close connexion with each other.

Heavy and *dull* are employed as epithets both for persons and things; *heavy* characterizes the corporeal state of a person; *dull* qualifies the spirits or the understanding of the subject. A person has a *heavy* look whose temperament seems composed of gross and weighty materials which weigh him down and impede his movements; he has a *dull* countenance in whom the ordinary brightness and vivacity of the mind is wanting: *heavy* is either a characteristick of the constitution, or only a particular state arising from external or internal causes;

Heavy with age, Entellus stands his ground,
But with his warping body wards the wound.
DRYDEN.

Dullness as it respects the frame of the spirits, is a partial state; as it respects the mental vigour, it is a characteristick of the individual;

O thou *dull* god! why liest thou with the vile
In loathsome beds: and leav'st the kingly couch,
A watch-case to a common larum bell?
SHAKSPEARE.

It is a misfortune frequently attached to those of a corpulent habit to be very *heavy:* there is no one who from the changes of the atmosphere may not be occasionally *heavy*. Those who have no resources in themselves are always *dull* in solitude: those who are not properly instructed, or have a deficiency of capacity, will appear *dull* in all matters of learning.

Heavy is either properly or improperly applied to things which are conceived to have an undue tendency to press or lean downwards: *dull* is in like manner employed for whatever fails in the necessary degree of brightness or vivacity; the weather is *heavy* when the air is full of thick and weighty materials; it may be *dull* from the intervention of clouds.

Heavy and *drowsy* are both employed in the sense of sleepy; but the former is only a particular state, the latter particular or general; all persons may be occasionally *heavy* or *drowsy;* some are habitually *drowsy* from disease; they likewise differ in degree; the latter being much the greater of the two; and occasionally they are applied to such things as produce sleepiness;

And *drowsy* tinklings lull the distant fold.—GRAY.

TO SLEEP, SLUMBER, DOZE, DROWSE, NAP.

Sleep, in Saxon *slæpan*, Low German *slap*, German *schlaf*, is supposed to come from the Low German *slap* or *slack* slack, because *sleep* denotes an entire relaxation of the physical frame; *slumber*, in Saxon *slumeran*, &c. is but an intensive verb of *schlummern*, which is a variation from the preceding *slæpan*, &c.; *doze*, in Low German *dusen*, is in all probability a variation from the French *dors*, and the Latin *dormio* to *sleep*, which was anciently *dermio*, and comes from the Greek δέρμα a skin, because people lay on skins when they *slept; drowse* is a variation of *doze; nap* is in all probability a variation of nob and nod.

Sleep is the general term, which designates in an indefinite manner that state of the body to which all animated beings are subject at certain seasons in the course of nature; to *slumber* is to *sleep* lightly and softly; to *doze* is to incline to *sleep*, or to begin *sleeping;* to *nap* is to *sleep* for a time: every one who is not indisposed *sleeps* during the night, those who are, accustomed to wake at a certain hour of the morning commonly *slumber* only after that time; there are many who, though they cannot *sleep* in a carriage will yet be obliged to *doze* if they travel in the night in hot climates the middle of the day is commonly chosen for a *nap*.

SLEEPY, DROWSY, LETHARGICK.

Sleepy (*v. To sleep*) expresses either a temporary or a permanent state: *drowsy*, which comes from the Low German *drusen*, and is a variation of *doze* (*v. To sleep*) expresses mostly a temporary state: *lethargick*, from *lethargy*, in Latin *lethargia*, Greek ληθαργία, compounded of λήθη forgetfulness, and ἀργός swift, signifying a proneness to forgetfulness or *sleep*, describes a permanent or habitual state.

Sleepy, as a temporary state, expresses also what is natural or seasonable; *drowsiness* expresses an inclination to *sleep* at unseasonable hours: it is natural to be *sleepy* at the hour when we are accustomed to retire to rest; it is common to be *drowsy* when sitting still after dinner. *Sleepiness*, as a permanent state, is an infirmity to which some persons are subject constitutionally; *lethargy* is a disease with which people, otherwise the most wakeful, may be occasionally attacked.

INDOLENT, SUPINE, LISTLESS, CARELESS.

Indolent, v. Idle, lazy; supine, in Latin *supinus*, from *super* above, signifies lying on one's back, or with one's face upward, which, as it is the action of a lazy or idle person, has been made to represent the qualities themselves; *listless*, without *list*, in German *lust* desire, signifies without desire; *careless* signifies without care or concern.

These terms represent a diseased or unnatural state of the mind, when its desires, which are the spring of action, are in a relaxed and torpid state, so as to prevent the necessary degree of exertion. *Indolence* has a more comprehensive meaning than *supineness*, and this signifies more than *listlessness* or *carelessness: indolence* is a general indisposition of a person to exert either his mind or his body; *supineness* is a similar indisposition that shows itself on particular occasions: there is a corporeal as well as a mental cause for *indolence;* but *supineness* lies principally in the mind: corpulent and large-made people are apt to be *indolent;* but timid and gentle dispositions are apt to be *supine*. An *indolent* person sets all labour, both corporeal and mental, at a distance from him; it is irksome to him;

Hence reasoners more refined but not more wise
Their whole existence fabulous suspect,
And truth and falsehood in a lump reject;
Too *indolent* to learn what may be known,
Or else too proud that ignorance to own.
JENYNS.

A *supine* person objects to undertake any thing which threatens to give him trouble;

With what unequal tempers are we fram'd!
One day the soul, *supine* with ease and fulness,
Revels secure. ROWE.

The *indolent* person is so for a permanency; he always seeks to be waited upon rather than wait on himself; and as far as it is possible he is glad for another to think for him, rather than to burden himself with thought; the *supine* person is so only in matters that require more than an ordinary portion of his exertion; he will defer such business, and sacrifice his interest to his ease. The *indolent* and *supine* are not, however, like the *listless*, expressly without desire: an *indolent* or *supine* man has desire enough to enjoy what is within his reach, although not always sufficient desire to surmount the aversion to labour in trying to obtain it; the *listless* man, on the contrary, is altogether without the desire, and is in fact in a state of moral torpor, which is however but a temporary or partial state arising from particular circumstances; after the mind has been wrought up to the highest pitch, it will sometimes sink into a state of relaxation in which it apparently ceases to have any active principle within itself. *Indolence* is a habit of both body and mind; *supineness* is sometimes only a mode of inaction flowing out of a particular frame of mind; *listlessness* is only a certain frame of mind: an active person may sometimes be *supine* in setting about a business which runs counter to his feelings; a *listless* person, on the other hand, if he be habitually so, will never be active in any thing, because he will have no impulse to action;

> Sullen, methinks, and slow the morning breaks,
> As if the sun were *listless* to appear.—DRYDEN.

Carelessness expresses less than any of the above; for though a man who is *indolent*, *supine*, and *listless*, is naturally *careless*, yet *carelessness* is properly applicable to such as have no such positive disease of mind or body. The *careless* person is neither averse to labour or thought, nor devoid of desire, but wants in reality that *care* or thought which is requisite for his state or condition. *Carelessness* is rather an errour of the understanding, or of the conduct, than the will; since the *careless* would *care*, be concerned for, or interested about things, if he could be brought to reflect on their importance, or if he did not for a time forget himself;

> Pert love with her by joint commission rules,
> Who by false arts and popular deceits,
> The *careless*, fond, unthinking mortal cheats.
> POMFRET.

TO STIR, MOVE.

Stir, in German *storen*, old German *stiren* or *steren*, Latin *turbo*, Greek *τύρβη* or *θόρυβος* trouble or tumult; *move*, *v. Motion.*

Stir is here a specifick, *move* a generick term; to *stir* is to *move* so as to disturb the rest and composure either of the body or mind;

> I've read that things inanimate have *mov'd*,
> And as with living souls have been inform'd,
> By magic numbers and persuasive sounds.
> CONGREVE.

> At first the groves are scarcely seen to *stir*.
> THOMSON.

Hence the term *stir* is employed to designate an improper or unauthorized motion; children are not allowed to *stir* from their seats in school hours; a soldier must not *stir* from the post which he has to defend. Atrocious criminals or persons raving mad are bound hand and foot, that they may not *stir*.

MOTION, MOVEMENT.

These are both abstract terms to denote the act of *moving*, but *motion* is taken generally and abstractedly from the thing that *moves*: *movement*, on the other hand, is taken in connexion with the agent or thing that *moves*; hence we speak of a state of *motion* as opposed to a state of rest, of perpetual *motion*, the laws of *motion*, and the like; on the other hand, to make a *movement* when speaking of an army, a general *movement* when speaking of an assembly.

When *motion* is qualified by the thing that *moves*, it denotes a continued *motion*; but *movement* implies only a particular *motion*: hence we say, the *motion* of the heavenly bodies, the *motion* of the earth; a person is in continual *motion*, or an army is in *motion*; but a person makes a *movement* who rises or sits down, or goes from one chair to another; the different *movements* of the springs and wheels of any instrument; 'It is not easy to a mind accustomed to the inroads of troublesome thoughts to expel them immediately by putting better images into *motion*.'—JOHNSON.

> Nature I thought perform'd too mean a part,
> Forming her *movements* to the rules of art.—PRIOR.

MOVING, AFFECTING, PATHETICK.

The *moving* is in general whatever moves the affections or the passions; the *affecting* and *pathetick* are what move the *affections* in different degrees. The good or bad feelings may be *moved*; the tender feelings only are *affected*. A field of battle is a *moving* spectacle; 'There is something so *moving* in the very image of weeping beauty.'—STEELE. The death of King Charles was an *affecting* spectacle; 'I do not remember to have seen any ancient or modern story more *affecting* than a letter of Anne of Boulogne.'—ADDISON. The *affecting* acts by means of the senses, as well as the understanding. The *pathetick* applies only to what is addressed to the heart; hence, a sight or a description is *affecting*: but an address is *pathetick*;

> What think you of the bard's enchanting art,
> Which whether he attempts to warm the heart
> With fabled scenes, or charm the ear with rhyme,
> Breathes all *pathetick*, lovely, and sublime?
> JENYNS.

TO COME, ARRIVE.

Come is general; *arrive* is particular.

Persons or things *come*; persons only, or what is personified, *arrive*.

To *come* specifies neither time nor manner; *arrival* is employed with regard to some particular period or circumstances. The *coming* of our Saviour was predicted by the prophets: the *arrival* of a messenger is expected at a certain hour. We know that evils must *come*, but we do wisely not to meet them by anticipation; the *arrival* of a vessel in the haven, after a long and dangerous voyage, is a circumstance of general interest in the neighbourhood where it happens;

> Hail, rev'rend priest! to Phœbus' awful dome,
> A suppliant I from great Atrides *come*.—POPE.

> Old men love novelties; the last *arriv'd*
> Still pleases best, the youngest steals their smiles.
> YOUNG.

TO ADVANCE, PROCEED.

To *advance* (*v. Advance*) is to go towards some point; to *proceed*, from the Latin *procedo*, is to go onward in a certain course. The same distinction is preserved between them in their figurative acceptation

A person *advances* in the world, who succeeds in his transactions and raises himself in society; he *proceeds* in his business, when he carries it on as he has done before; 'It is wonderful to observe by what a gradual progress the world of life *advances* through a prodigious variety of species, before a creature is formed that is complete in all its senses.'—ADDISON. 'If the scale of being rises by such a regular progress so high as man, we may by a parity of reason suppose that it still *proceeds* gradually through those beings which are of a superiour nature to him.'—ADDISON.

One *advances* by *proceeding*, and one *proceeds* in order to *advance*.

Some people pass their lives in the same situation without *advancing*. Some are always doing without *proceeding*.

Those who make considerable progress in learning stand the fairest chance of being *advanced* to dignity and honour.

PACE, STEP.

Pace, in French *pas*, Latin *passus*, comes from the Hebrew פּשע to pass, and signifies the act of passing, or the ground passed over; *step*, which comes through the medium of the northern languages, from the Greek ϛείβειν, signifies the act of *stepping*, or the ground *stepped* over.

As respects the act, *pace* expresses the general manner of passing on, or moving the body; *step* implies the manner of treading with the foot; the *pace* is distinguished by being either a walk or a run; and in regard to horses, a trot or a gallop; the *step* is distinguished by the right or the left, the forward or the backward. The same *pace* may be modified so as to be more or less easy, more or less quick; the *step* may vary as it is light or heavy, graceful or ungraceful, long or short. We may go a slow *pace* with long *steps*, or we may go a quick *pace* with short *steps*. A slow *pace* is best suited to the solemnity of a funeral; a long *step* must be taken by soldiers in a slow march.

As respects the space passed or *stepped* over, the *pace* is a measured distance, formed by a long *step*; the *step*, on the other hand, is indefinitely employed for any space *stepped* over, but particularly that ordinary space which one *steps* over without an effort. A thousand *paces* was the Roman measurement for a mile. A *step* or two designates almost the shortest possible distance;

> To-morrow, to-morrow, and to-morrow.
> Creeps in a stealing *pace* from day to day.
> SHAKSPEARE

> Grace was in all her *steps*, heaven in her eye,
> In every gesture dignity and love.—MILTON

ONWARD, FORWARD, PROGRESSIVE.

Onward is taken in the literal sense of going nearer to an object: *forward* is taken in the sense of going from an object, or going farther in the line before one: *progressive* has the sense of going gradually or step by step before one.

A person goes *onward* who does not stand still; he goes *forward* who does not recede; he goes *progressively* who goes *forward* at certain intervals.

Onward is taken only in the proper acceptation of travelling; the traveller who has lost his way feels it necessary to go *onward* with the hope of arriving at some point;

Remote, unfriended, melancholy, slow,
Or by the lazy Scheld, or wandering Po,
Or *onward* where the rude Carinthian boor
Against the houseless stranger shuts the door,
Where'er I roam, whatever realms to see,
My heart untravell'd fondly turns to thee.
GOLDSMITH.

Forward is employed in the improper as well as the proper application; a traveller goes *forward* in order to reach his point of destination as quickly as possible; a learner uses his utmost endeavours in order to get *forward* in his learning; 'Harbood the chairman was much blamed for his rashness; he said the duty of the chair was always to set things *forward*.'—BURNETT. *Progressively* is employed only in the improper application to what requires time and labour in order to bring it to a conclusion: every man goes on *progressively* in his art, until he arrives at the point of perfection attainable by him;

Reason *progressive*, instinct is complete.—YOUNG.

EXCURSION, RAMBLE, TOUR, TRIP, JAUNT.

Excursion signifies going out of one's course, from the Latin *ex* and *cursus* a course or prescribed path: a *ramble*, from *roam*, of which it is a frequentative, is a going without any course or regular path; *tour*, from the word turn or return, is a circuitous course: a *trip*, from the Latin *tripudio* to go on the toes like a dancer, is properly a pedestrian *excursion* or *tour*, or any short journey that might be made on foot: *jaunt*, is from the French *jante* the felly of a wheel, and *janter* to put the felly in motion.

To go abroad in a carriage is an idle *excursion*, or one taken for mere pleasure: travellers who are not contented with what is not to be seen from a high road make frequent *excursions* into the interiour of the country; 'I am now so rus-in-urbeish, I believe I shall stay here, except little *excursions* and vagaries, for a year to come.'—GRAY. Those who are fond of rural scenery, and pleased to follow the bent of their inclinations, make frequent *rambles*; 'I am going on a short *ramble* to my Lord Oxford's.'—POPE. Those who set out upon a sober scheme of enjoyment from travelling, are satisfied with making the *tour* of some one country or more; 'My last summer's *tour* was through Worcestershire, Gloucestershire, Monmouthshire, and Shropshire.'—GRAY. Those who have not much time for pleasure take *trips*; 'I hold the resolution I told you in my last of seeing you if you cannot take a *trip* hither before I go.'—POPE. Those who have no better means of spending their time make *jaunts*; 'If you are for a merry *jaunt*, I'll try for once who can foot it farthest.'—DRYDEN.

JOURNEY, TRAVEL, VOYAGE.

Journey, from the French *journée* a day's work, and Latin *diurnus* daily, signifies the course that is taken in the space of a day, or in general any comparatively short passage from one place to another: *travel*, from the French *travailler* to labour, signifies such a course or passage as requires labour, and causes fatigue; in general any long course: *voyage* is most probably changed from the Latin *via* a way, and originally signified any course or passage to a distance, but is now confined to passages by sea.

We take *journeys* in different parts of the same country; we make *voyages* by sea, and *travel* by land.

Journeys are taken in different parts of the same country for a specifick business·

To Paradise, the happy seat of man,
His *journey's* end, and our beginning wo.—MILTON.

Travels are made by land for amusement or information; 'In my *travels* I had been near their setting out in Thessaly, and at the place of their landing in Carniola.'—BROWN. *Voyages* are made by captains or merchants for purposes of commerce; 'Our ships went sundry *voyages* as well to the pillars of Hercules as to other parts in the Atlantick and Mediterranean seas.'—BACON.

We estimate *journeys* by the day, as one or two days' *journey*;

Scarce the sun
Hath finished half his *journey*.

We estimate *travels* and *voyages* by the months and years that are employed;

Cease mourners; cease complaint, and weep no more,
Your lost friends are not dead, but gone before,
Advanc'd a stage or two upon that road
Which you must *travel* in the steps they trode.
CUMBERLAND.

Calm and serene, he sees approaching death,
As the safe port, th' peaceful silent shore,
Where he may rest, life's tedious *voyage* o'er.
JENYNS.

The Israelites are said to have *journeyed* in the wilderness forty years, because they went but short distances at a time. It is a part of polite education for young men of fortune to *travel* into those countries of Europe which comprehend the 'grand tour' as it is termed. A *voyage* round the world, which was at first a formidable undertaking, is now become familiar to the mind by its frequency.

ARISE OR RISE, MOUNT, ASCEND, CLIMB, SCALE.

Arise, *v. To arise*; *mount*, from the Latin *mons* a mountain, signifies to go as it were up a mountain; *ascend*, in Latin *ascendo*, compounded of *ad* and *scando*, signifies to climb up towards a point; *climb*, in German *klimmen*, is probably connected with *klammer* a hook, signifying to rise by a hook; *scale*, in French *escalader*, Italian *scalare*, Latin *scala* a ladder, signifies to rise by a ladder.

The idea of going upwards is common to all these terms; *arise* is used only in the sense of simply getting up;

Th' inspected entrails could no fates foretell,
Nor, laid on altars, did pure flames *arise*.
DRYDEN.

But *rise* is employed to express a continued motion upward;

To contradict them, see all nature *rise!*
What object, what event the moon beneath,
But argues or endears an after-scene?—YOUNG.

A person *arises* from his seat or his bed; a bird *rises* in the air; the silver of the barometer *rises*: the first three of these terms convey a gradation in their sense; to *arise* or *rise* denotes a motion to a less elevated height than to *mount*, and to *mount* that which is less elevated than *ascend*: a person *rises* from his seat, *mounts* a hill, and *ascends* a mountain;

At length the fatal fabrick *mounts* the walls,
Big with destruction.—DRYDEN.

We view a *rising* land like distant clouds;
The mountain tops confirm the pleasing sight,
And curling smoke *ascending* from their height.
DRYDEN.

Arise and *rise* are intransitive only; the rest are likewise transitive; we *rise* from a point, we *mount* and *ascend* to a point, or we *mount* and *ascend* some thing: an air balloon *rises* when it first leaves the ground; it *mounts* higher and higher until it is out of sight; but if it *ascends* too high it endangers the life of the aërial adventurer.

Climb and *scale* express a species of *rising*: to *climb* is to *rise* step by step, by clinging to a certain body; to *scale* is to rise by an escalade, or species of ladder, employed in *mounting* the walls of fortified towns: trees and mountains are *climbed*; walls are *scaled*

While you (a.as, that I should find it so)
To shun my sight, your native soil forego,
And *climb* the frozen Alps, and tread the eternal snow.
DRYDEN.

But brave Messapus, Neptune's warlike son,
Broke down the pallisades, the trenches won,
And loud for ladders calls, to *scale* the town.
DRYDEN.

TO FALL, DROP, DROOP, SINK, TUMBLE.

Fall, v. Fall; drop and *droop*, in German *tropfen*, Low German, &c. *druppen*, is an onomatopeïa of the *falling* of a *drop; sink*, in German *sinken*, is an intensive of *siegen* to incline downward; *tumble*, in German *tummeln*, is an intensive of *taumeln* to reel backwards and forwards.

Fall is the generick, the rest specifick terms: to *drop* is to *fall* suddenly; to *droop* is to *drop* in part; to *sink* is to *fall* gradually; to *tumble* is to *fall* awkwardly or contrary to the usual mode. In cataracts the water *falls* perpetually and in a mass; in rain it *drops* partially; in ponds the water *sinks* low. The head *droops*, but the body may *fall* or *drop* from a height, it may *sink* down to the earth, it may *tumble* by accident;

Yet come it will, the day decreed by fates
(How my heart trembles, while my tongue relates!)
The day when thou, imperial Troy! must bend,
And see thy warriours *fall* and glories end.—POPE.

The wounded bird, ere yet she breathed her last,
With flagging wings alighted on the mast,
A moment hung, and spread her pinions there,
Then sudden *dropp'd* and left her life in air.—POPE.

Thrice Dido tried to raise her *drooping* head,
And fainting, thrice *fell* grov'ling on the bed.
DRYDEN.

Down *sunk* the priest; the purple hand of death
Clos'd his dim eye, and fate suppress'd his breath.
POPE.

Full on his ankle *dropp'd* the pond'rous stone,
Burst the strong nerves, and crush'd the solid bone,
Supine he *tumbles* on the crimson'd sands.—POPE.

Fall, drop, and *sink* are employed in a moral sense; *droop* in the physical sense. A person *falls* from a state of prosperity; words *drop* from the lips, and *sink* into the heart. Corn, or the price of corn, *falls;* a subject *drops;* a person *sinks* into poverty or in the estimation of the world.

TO SLIP, SLIDE, GLIDE.

Slip is in Low German *slipan*, from the Latin *labor* to slip, and *libo* to pour, which comes from the Greek λείβομαι to pour down as water does, and the Hebrew כלפ to turn aside; *slide* is a variation of *slip*, and *glide* of *slide*.

To *slip* is an involuntary, and *slide* a voluntary motion: those who go on the ice in fear will *slip;* 'A skilful dancer on the ropes *slips* willingly, and makes a seeming tumble that you may think him in great hazard, while he is only giving you a proof of dexterity.' --DRYDEN. Boys *slide* on the ice by way of amusement;

Thessander bold, and Sthenelus their guide,
And dire Ulysses down the cable *slide*.—DRYDEN.

To *slip* and *slide* are lateral movements of the feet; but to *glide* is the movement of the whole body, and just that easy motion which is made by *slipping, sliding*, flying, or swimming: a person *glides* along the surface of the ice when he *slides;* a vessel *glides* along through the water;

And softly let the running waters *glide*.—DRYDEN.

In the moral and figurative application, a person *slips* who commits unintentional errours, or the thoughts *slip* away contrary to our intention; 'Every one finds that many of the ideas which he desired to retain have irretrievably *slipped* away.'—JOHNSON. A person *slides* into a course of life, who wittingly, and yet without difficulty, falls into the practice and habits which are recommended; he *glides* through life if he pursues his course smoothly and without interruption.

TO STAGGER, REEL, TOTTER.

Stagger is in all probability a frequentative from the German *steigen*, and the Greek ϛοιχέω to go, signifying to go backward and forward; to *reel* signifies to go like a *reel* in a winding manner; *totter* most probably comes from the German *zittern* to tremble, because to *totter* is a tremulous action.

All these terms designate an involuntary and an unsteady motion; they vary both in the cause and the mode of the action; *staggering* and *reeling* are occasioned either by drunkenness or sickness;

Natheless it bore his foe not from his sell,
But made him *stagger* as he were not well.
SPENSER

The clouds, commix'd
With stars, swift gliding sweep along the sky:
All nature *reels*.—THOMSON.

Tottering is purely the effect of weakness, particularly the weakness of old age: a drunken man always *staggers* as he walks; one who is giddy *reels* from one part to another: to *stagger* is a much less degree of unsteadiness than to *reel;* for he who *staggers* is only thrown a little out of the straight path, but he who *reels* altogether loses his equilibrium; *reeling* is commonly succeeded by falling. To *stagger* and *reel* are said as to the carriage of the whole body; but *totter* has particular reference to the limbs; the knees and the legs *totter*, and consequently the footsteps become *tottering*. In an extended application, the mountains may be said to *stagger* and to *reel* in an earthquake: houses may *totter* from their very bases;

Troy nods from high, and *totters* to her fall.
DRYDEN.

In a figurative application, the faith or the resolution of a person *staggers* when its hold on the mind is shaken, and begins to give way: a nation or a government will *totter* when it is torn by intestine convulsions.

TO DRAW, DRAG, HAUL OR HALE, PULL PLUCK, TUG.

Draw comes from the Latin *traho* to draw, and the Greek δράσσω to lay hold of; *drag* through the medium of the German *tragen* to carry, comes also from *traho* to draw; *haul* or *hale* comes from the Greek ἕλκω to draw; *pull* is in all probability changed from *pello* to drive or thrust; *pluck* is in the German *plucken*, &c.; *tug* comes from the German *ziehen* to pull.

Draw expresses here the idea common to the first three terms, namely, of putting a body in motion from behind oneself or towards oneself; to *drag* is to *draw* a thing with violence, or to *draw* that which makes resistance; to *haul* is to *drag* it with still greater violence. A cart is *drawn;* a body is *dragged* along the ground; or a vessel is *hauled* to the shore;

Furious he said, and tow'rd the Grecian crew,
(Seiz'd by the crest) the unhappy warriour *drew;*
Struggling he follow'd, while th' embroider'd thong,
That ty'd his helmet, *dragg'd* the chief along.
POPE.

Some hoisting levers, some the wheels prepare,
And fasten to the horse's feet; the rest
With cables *haul* along the unwieldy beast.
DRYDEN.

To *pull* signifies only an effort to *draw* without the idea of motion: horses *pull* very long sometimes before they can *draw* a heavily laden cart up hill; 'Two magnets are placed, one of them in the roof and the other in the floor of Mahomet's burying-place at Mecca, and *pull* the impostor's iron coffin with such an equal attraction, that it hangs in the air between both of them.'—ADDISON. To *pluck* is to *pull* with a sudden twitch, in order to separate; thus feathers are *plucked* from animals;

Even children follow'd with endearing wile,
And *pluck'd* his gown, to share the good man's smile
GOLDSMITH.

To *tug* is to *pull* with violence; thus men *tug* at the oar;

Clear'd, as I thought, and fully fix'd at length
To learn the cause, I *tugg'd* with all my strength.
DRYDEN

In the moral application we may be *drawn* by any thing which can act on the mind to bring us near to an object; we are *dragged* only by means of force; we *pull* a thing towards us by a direct effort;

Hither we sail'd, a voluntary throng,
To avenge a private, not a publick wrong;
What else to Troy the assembled nations *draws*,
But thine, ungrateful! and thy brother's cause.
POPE.

'T is long since I for my celestial wife,
Loath'd by the gods have *dragg'd* a lingering life.
POPE.

Hear this, remember, and our fury dread,
Nor *pull* th' unwilling vengeance on thy head.
POPE.

To *haul*, *pluck*, and *tug* are seldom used but in the physical application.

TO CAST, THROW, HURL.

Cast probably comes from *casus*, participle of *cado* to fall, signifying to make or to let fall; *throw*, in Saxon *thrawan*, is most probably a variation of *thrust*, in Latin *trudo*, Chaldee *terad* to thrust repeatedly; *hurl*, like the word *whirl*, comes from the Saxon *hirfiven*, *hiveorfian*, German, &c. *wirbel*, Teutonic *wirvel*, Danish *hvirvel*, *hvirvler*, Latin *verto*, *gyro*, which are all derived from the Hebrew עגל round, signifying to turn round.

Cast conveys simply the idea of laying aside, or putting from one's self; *throw* and *hurl* designate more specifically the mode of the action: *cast* is an indifferent action, whether it respects ourselves or others; *throw* always marks a direct motive of dislike or contempt. What is not wanted is *cast* off; clothes which are no longer worn are *cast* off: what is worthless or hurtful is *thrown* away; the dross is separated from the wheat and *thrown* away; bad habits cannot be *thrown* off too soon.

Cast, as it respects others, is divested of all personalities; but nothing is *thrown* at any one without an intention of offending or hurting: a glance is *cast* at a person, or things are *cast* before him; but insinuations are *thrown* out against a person; things are *thrown* at him with the view of striking.

Cast requires no particular effort; it amounts in general to no more than let fall or go: *throw* is frequently accompanied with violence. Money is *cast* into a bag; stones are *thrown* from a great distance: animals *cast* their young at stated periods; a horse *throws* his rider; a lawless man *throws* off constraint;

As far as I could *cast* my eyes
Upon the sea, something methought did rise
Like bluish mists.—DRYDEN.

O war, thou son of hell!
Whom angry heavens do make their minister,
Throw in the frozen bosoms of our part
Hot coals of vengeance!—SHAKSPEARE.

Hurl is a violent species of *throwing* employed only on extraordinary occasions, expressive of an unusual degree of vehemence in the agent, and an excessive provocation on the part of the sufferer: the *hurler*, the thing *hurled*, and the cause of *hurling*, correspond in magnitude; a mighty potentate is *hurled* from his throne by some power superiour to his own; Milton represents the devils as *hurled* from Heaven by the word of the Almighty; the heathen poets have feigned a similar story of the giants who made war against Heaven, and were *hurled* by the thunderbolts of Jupiter down to the earth;

Wreath my head
With flaming meteors, load my arms with thunder,
Which as I nimbly cut my cloudy way
I'll *hurl* on this ungrateful earth.—TATE.

TO SPRING, START, STARTLE, SHRINK.

Spring, v *To spring*; *start* is in all probability an intensive of *stir*; *startle* is a frequentative of *start*; *shrink* is probably an intensive of *sink*, signifying to sink into itself.

The idea of a sudden motion is expressed by all these terms, but the circumstances and mode differ in all, *spring* (v *To arise*) is indefinite in these respects, and is therefore the most general term. To *spring* and *start* may be either voluntary or involuntary movements, but *spring* is mostly voluntary, and *start*, which is an intensive of *stir*, is mostly involuntary; a person *springs* out of a place, or one animal *springs* upon another;

Death wounds to cure; we fall, we rise, we reign,
Spring from our fetters, and fasten in the skies.
YOUNG.

A person or animal *starts* from a certain point to begin running, or *starts* with fright from one side to the other;

A shape within the wat'ry gleam appear'd,
Bending to look on me: I *started* back,
It *started* back.—MILTON.

To *startle* is always an involuntary action; a he *starts* by suddenly flying from the point on which he stands; but if he *startles* he seems to fly back on himself and stops his course;

'T is listening fear and dumb amazement,
When to the *startled* eye the sudden glance
Appears far south, eruptive through the cloud.
THOMSON.

To *spring* and *start* therefore always carry a person farther from a given point; but *startle* and *shrink* are movements within one's self; *startling* is a sudden convulsion of the frame which makes a person to stand in hesitation whether to proceed or not; *shrinking* is a contraction of the frame within itself; 'There is a horrour in the scene of a ravaged country which makes nature *shrink* back at the reflection.'—HERRING. Any sudden and unexpected sound makes a person *startle*: the approach of any frightful object makes him *shrink* back: *spring* and *start* are employed only in the proper sense of corporeal movements: *startle* and *shrink* are employed in regard to the movements of the mind as well as the body.

TO SHAKE, AGITATE, TOSS.

Shake, in German *schütten*, Latin *quatio*, Hebrew שדך to shed; *agitate*, in Latin *agito*, is a frequentative of *ago* to drive, that is, to drive different ways; *toss* is probably contracted from the Latin *torsi*, preterite of *torqueo* to twirl.

A motion more or less violent is signified by all these terms, which differ both in the manner and the cause of the motion. *Shake* is indefinite, it may differ in degree as to the violence; to *agitate* and *toss* rise in sense upon the word *shake*: a breeze *shakes* a leaf, a storm *agitates* the sea, and the waves *toss* a vessel to and fro: large and small bodies may be *shaken*; large bodies are *agitated*: a handkerchief may be *shaken*; the earth is *agitated* by an earthquake. What is *shaken* and *agitated* is not removed from its place; but what is *tossed* is thrown from place to place. A house may frequently be *shaken*, while the foundation remains good; 'An unwholesome blast of air, a cold, or a surfeit, may *shake* in pieces a man's hardy fabrick.'—SOUTH. The waters are most *agitated* while they remain within their bounds: 'We all must have observed that a speaker *agitated* with passion, or an actor, who is indeed strictly an imitator, are perpetually changing the tone and pitch of their voice as the sense of their words varies.'—SIR WM. JONES. A ball is *tossed* from hand to hand;

Toss'd all the day in rapid circles round,
Breathless I fell.—POPE.

To *shake* and *toss* are the acts either of persons or things; to *agitate* is the act of things, when taken in the active sense. A person *shakes* the hand of another, or the motion of a carriage *shakes* persons in general, and *agitates* those who are weak in frame; a child *tosses* his food about, or the violent motion of a vessel *tosses* every thing about which is in it. To *shake* arises from external or internal causes; we may be *shaken* by others, or *shake* ourselves from cold; to *agitate* and *toss* arise always from some external action, direct or indirect; the body may be *agitated* by violent concussion from without, or from the action of perturbed feelings: the body may be *tossed* by various circumstances, and the mind may be *tossed* to and fro by the violent action of the passions. Hence the propriety of using the terms in the moral application. The resolution is *shaken*, as the tree is by the wind:

Not my firm faith
Can by his fraud be *shaken* or seduc'd.—MILTON.

The mind is *agitated* like troubled waters; 'His mother could no longer bear the *agitations* of so many passions as thronged upon her.'—TATLER. A person is *tossed* to and fro in the ocean of life, as the vessel is *tossed* by the waves;

Your mind is *tossing* on the sea,
There where your argosies
Do overpeer the petty traffickers.—SHAKSPEARE.

SHOCK, CONCUSSION.

Shock denotes a violent *shake* or agitation; *concussion*, a shaking together. The *shock* is often instantaneous, but does not necessarily extend beyond the act of the moment; the *concussion* is permanent in its consequences, it tends to derange the system. Hence the different application of the terms: the *shock* may affect either the body or the mind; the *concussion* affects properly only the body, or corporeal objects; a violent and sudden blow produces a *shock* at the moment it is given; but it does not always produce a *concussion:* the violence of a fall will, however, sometimes produce a *concussion* in the brain, which may affect the intellects. Sudden news of an exceedingly painful nature will often produce a *shock* on the mind; but time mostly serves to wear away the effect which has been produced.

TO SHOOT, DART.

To *shoot* and *dart*, in the proper sense, are clearly distinguished from each other, as expressing different modes of sending bodies to a distance from a given point. From the circumstances of the actions arise their different application to other objects in the improper sense; as that which proceeds by *shooting* goes unexpectedly, and with great rapidity, forth from a body, so, in the figurative sense, a plant *shoots* up that comes so unexpectedly as not to be seen; a star is said to *shoot* in the sky, which seems to move in a *shooting* manner, from one place to another: a *dart*, on the other hand, or that which is *darted*, moves through the air visibly, and with less rapidity: hence the quick movements of persons or animals, are described by the word *dart;* a soldier *darts* forward to meet his antagonist; a hart *darts* past any one in order to make her escape.

TO REBOUND, REVERBERATE, RECOIL.

To *rebound* is to bound or spring back: a ball *rebounds*. To *reverberate* is to *verberate* or beat back: a sound *reverberates* when it echoes. To *recoil* is to *coil* or whirl back: a snake *recoils*. They preserve the same distinction in their figurative application; 'Honour is but the reflection of a man's own actions shining bright in the face of all about him, and from thence *rebounding* upon himself.'—SOUTH. 'You seemed to *reverberate* upon me with the beams of the sun.'—HOWEL.

Who in deep mines for hidden knowledge toils,
Like guns o'ercharg'd, breaks, misses, or *recoils*.
DENHAM.

TO SHAKE, TREMBLE, SHUDDER, QUIVER, QUAKE.

Shake, *shudder*, *quiver*, and *quake*, all come from the Latin *quatio* or *cutio* to shake, through the medium of the German *schutteln*, *schutten*, the Italian *scussere*, and the like; *tremble* comes from the Latin *tremo*.

To *shake* is a generick term, the rest are but modes of *shaking:* to *tremble* is to *shake* from an inward cause, or what appears to be so: in this manner a person *trembles* from fear, from cold, or weakness; and a leaf which is imperceptibly agitated by the air is also said to *tremble:* to *shudder* is to *tremble* violently: to *quiver* and *quake* are both to *tremble* quickly; but the former denotes rather a vibratory motion, as the point of a spear when thrown against wood; the latter a quick motion of the whole body, as in the case of bodies that have not sufficient consistency in themselves to remain still.

The rapid radiance instantaneous strikes
Th' illumin'd mountain, through the forest streams,
Shakes on the floods.—THOMSON.

The *trembling* pilot, from his rudder torn,
Was headlong hurl'd.—DRYDEN.

He said, and hurl'd against the mountain side
His *quivering* spear.—DRYDEN.

Thereto as cold and dreary as a snake,
That seem'd to *tremble* evermore and *quake*.
SPENSER.

TO PALPITATE, FLUTTER, PANT, GASP.

Palpitate, in Latin *palpitatus*, from *palpito*, is a frequentative of the Greek *πάλλω* to vibrate; *flutter* is a frequentative of fly, signifying to fly backward and forward in an agitated manner; *pant*, probably derived from *pent*, and the Latin *pendo* to hang in a state of suspense, so as not to be able to move backward or forward, as is the case with the breath when one *pants;* *gasp* is a variation of *gape*, which is the ordinary accompaniment in the action of *gasping*.

These terms agree in a particular manner, as they respect the irregular action of the heart or lungs: the two former are said of the heart; and the two latter of the lungs or breath; to *palpitate* expresses that which is strong; it is a strong beating of the blood against the vessels of the heart; 'No plays have oftener filled the eyes with tears, and the breast with *palpitation*, than those which are variegated with interludes of mirth.'—JOHNSON. To *flutter* expresses that which is rapid; it is a violent and alternate motion of the blood backward and forward;

She springs aloft, with elevated pride,
Above the tangling mass of low desires,
That bind the *fluttering* crowd.—THOMSON.

Fear and suspense produce commonly *palpitation*, but joy and hope produce a *fluttering: panting* is, with regard to the breath, what *palpitating* is with regard to the heart; *panting* is occasioned by the inflated state of the respiratory organs which renders this *palpitating* necessary:

All nature fades extinct, and she alone,
Heard, felt, and seen, possesses every thought,
Fills every sense, and *pants* in every vein.
THOMSON.

Gasping differs from the former, inasmuch as it denotes a direct stoppage of the breath; a cessation of action in the respiratory organs:

Had not the soul this outlet to the skies,
In this vast vessel of the universe,
How should we *gasp*, as in an empty void!
YOUNG.

ALARM, TERROUR, FRIGHT, CONSTERNATION.

Alarm, in French *alarmer*, is compounded of *al* or *ad* and *armes* arms, signifying a cry to arms, a signal of danger, a call to defence; *terrour*, in Latin *terror*, comes from *terreo* to produce fear; *fright*, from the German *furcht* fear, signifies a state of fear: *consternation*, in Latin *consternatus*, from *consterno* to lay low or prostrate, expresses the mixed emotion of *terrour* and amazement which confounds.

Alarm springs from any sudden signal that announces the approach of danger. *Terrour* springs from any event or phenomenon that may serve as a prognostic of some catastrophe. It supposes a less distinct view of danger than alarm, and affords room to the imagination, which commonly magnifies objects. *Alarm* therefore makes us run to our defence, and *terrour* disarms us;

None so renown'd
With breathing brass to kindle fierce *alarms*.
DRYDEN.

'I was once in a mixed assembly, that was full of noise and mirth, when on a sudden an old woman unluckily observed, there were thirteen of us in company. The remark struck a panick *terrour* into several of us.'—ADDISON.

Fright is a less vivid emotion than either, as it arises

from the simple appearance of danger. It is more personal than either *alarm* or *terrour;* for we may be *alarmed* or *terrified* for others, but we are mostly *frightened* for ourselves. *Consternation* is stronger than either *terrour* or *affright;* it springs from the view of some very serious evil; 'I have known a soldier that has entered a breach *affrighted* at his own shadow'.—ADDISON.

The son of Pelias ceased; the chiefs around
In silence wrapt, in *consternation* drown'd.—POPE.

Alarm affects the feelings, *terrour* the understanding, and *fright* the senses; *consternation* seizes the whole mind, and benumbs the faculties.

Cries *alarm;* horrid spectacles *terrify;* a tumult *frightens;* a sudden calamity fills with *consternation*. One is filled with *alarm*, seized with *terrour*, overwhelmed with *fright* or *consternation*.

We are *alarmed* for what we apprehend; we are *terrified* by what we imagine; we are *frightened* by what we see; *consternation* may be produced by what we learn.

TO DISMAY, DAUNT, APPAL.

Dismay is probably changed from the French *desmouvoir*, signifying to move or pull down the spirit; *daunt*, changed from the Latin *domitus* conquered, signifies to bring down the spirit; *appal*, compounded of the intensive *ap* or *ad* and *palleo* to grow pale, signifies to make pale with fear.

The effect of fear on the spirit is strongly expressed by all these terms; but *dismay* expresses less than *daunt*, and this than *appal*. We are *dismayed* by alarming circumstances; we are *daunted* by terrifying; we are *appalled* by horrid circumstances. A severe defeat will *dismay* so as to lessen the force of resistance;

So flies a herd of beeves, that hear, *dismay'd*,
The lions roaring through the midnight shade.
POPE.

The fiery glare from the eyes of a ferocious beast will *daunt* him who was venturing to approach;

Jove got such heroes as my sire, whose soul
No fear could *daunt*, nor earth, nor hell control.—POPE.

The sight of an apparition will *appal* the stoutest heart;

Now the last ruin the whole host *appals;*
Now Greece had trembled in her wooden walls,
But wise Ulysses call'd Tydides forth.—POPE.

BOLD, FEARLESS, INTREPID, UNDAUNTED.

Bold, v. Audacity; fearless signifies without fear (*v. To apprehend*); *intrepid*, compounded of *in* privative and *trepidus* trembling, marks the total absence of fear; *undaunted*, of *un* privative, and *daunted*, from the Latin *domitatus*, participle of *domitare* to impress with fear, signifies unimpressed or unmoved at the prospect of danger.

Boldness is positive; *fearlessness* is negative; we may therefore be *fearless* without being *bold*, or *fearless* through *boldness;*

Such unheard of prodigies hang o'er us,
As make the *boldest* tremble.—YOUNG.

Fearlessness is a temporary state: we may be *fearless* of danger at this, or at that time; *fearless* of loss, and the like;

The careful hen
Calls all her chirping family around,
Fed and defended by the *fearless* cock.—THOMSON.

Boldness is a characteristick; it is associated with constant *fearlessness;*

His party, press'd with numbers, soon grew faint,
And would have left their charge an easy prey;
While he alone, *undaunted* at the odds,
Though hopeless to escape, fought well and bravely.
ROWE.

Intrepidity and *undauntedness* denote a still higher degree of *fearlessness* than *boldness: boldness* is confident, it forgets the consequences; *intrepidity* is collected, it sees the danger, and faces it with composure; *undauntedness* is associated with unconquerable firmness and resolution; it is awed by nothing: the *bold* man proceeds on his enterprise with spirit and vivacity; the *intrepid* man calmly advances to the scene of death and destruction; 'I could not sufficiently wonder at the *intrepidity* of those diminutive mortals, who durst venture to walk upon my body, without trembling.'—SWIFT. The *undaunted* man keeps his countenance in the season of trial, in the midst of the most terrifying and overwhelming circumstances.

These good qualities may, without great care, degenerate into certain vices to which they are closely allied.

Of the three, *boldness* is the most questionable in its nature, unless justified by the absolute urgency of the case; in maintaining the cause of truth against the lawless and oppressive exercise of power, it is an essential quality, but it may easily degenerate into insolent defiance and contempt of superiours; it may lead to the provoking of resentment and courting of persecution. *Intrepidity* may become rashness if the contempt of danger lead to an unnecessary exposure of the life and person. *Undauntedness*, in the presence of a brutal tyrant, may serve to baffle all his malignant purposes of revenge: but the same spirit may be employed by the hardened villain to preserve himself from detection.

MANLY, MANFUL.

Manly, or like a man, is opposed to juvenile or puerile, and of course applied to those who are fitted to act the part of men; 'I love a *manly* freedom as much as any of the band of cashierers of kings.'—BURKE. *Manful*, or full of manhood, is opposed to effeminate, and is applicable to particular persons, or persons in particular cases; 'I opposed his whim *manfully*, which I think you will approve of.'—CUMBERLAND. A premature *manliness* in young persons is hardly less unseemly than a want of *manfulness* in one who is called upon to display his courage.

FEARFUL, DREADFUL, FRIGHTFUL, TREMENDOUS, TERRIBLE, TERRIFICK, HORRIBLE, HORRID.

Fearful here signifies full of that which causes fear (*v. Alarm*); *dreadful*, full of what causes *dread* (*v. Apprehension*); *frightful*, full of what causes *fright* (*v. Afraid*) or *apprehension; tremendous*, that which causes *trembling; terrible*, or *terrifick*, causing *terrour* (*v. Alarm*); *horrible*, or *horrid*, causing *horrour*. The application of these terms is easily to be discovered by these definitions: the first two affect the mind more than the senses; all the others affect the senses more than the mind: a contest is *fearful* when the issue is important, but the event doubtful;

She wept the terrours of the *fearful* wave,
Too oft, alas! the wandering lover's grave.
FALCONER.

The thought of death is *dreadful* to one who feels himself unprepared;

And dar'st thou threat to snatch my prize away,
Due to the deeds of many a *dreadful* day?—POPE.

The *frightful* is less than the *tremendous;* the *tremendous* than the *terrible;* the *terrible* than the *horrible:* shrieks may be *frightful;*

Frightful convulsions writh'd his tortur'd limbs
FENTON

The roaring of a lion is *terrible;*

Was this a face to be expos'd
In the most *terrible* and nimble stroke
Of quick, cross lightning?—SHAKSPEARE.

Thunder and lightning may be *tremendous*, or convulsions may be *tremendous:* the glare in the eye of a ferocious beast is *terrifick;* 'Out of the limb of the murdered monarchy has arisen a vast, *tremendous*, unformed spectre, in a far more *terrifick* guise than any which ever yet overpowered the imagination of man.'—BURKE. The actual spectacle of killing is *horrible* or *horrid;*

Deck'd in sad triumph for the mournful field
O'er her broad shoulders hangs his *horrid* shield
POPE.

In their general application, these terms are often employed promiscuously to characterize whatever produces very strong impressions: hence we may speak of a *frightful*, *dreadful*, *terrible*, or *horrid* dream; or *frightful*, *dreadful*, or *terrible* tempest: *dreadful*, *terrible*, or *horrid* consequences.

TO APPREHEND, FEAR, DREAD.

Apprehend, in French *appréhender*, Latin *apprehendo*, compounded of *ap* and *prehendo* to lay hold of, in a moral sense signifies to seize with the understanding; *fear* comes in all probability through the medium of the Latin *pavor* and *vereor*, from the Greek φρίσσω to feel a shuddering; *dread*, in Latin *territo*, comes from the Greek ταράσσω to trouble, signifying to fear with exceeding trouble.

These words rise progressively in their import; they mark a sentiment of pain at the prospect of evil: but the sentiment of *apprehension* is simply that of uneasiness; that of *fear* is anxiety; that of *dread* is wretchedness.

We *apprehend* an unpleasant occurrence; we *fear* a misfortune; we *dread* a calamity. What is possible is *apprehended;* 'Our natural sense of right and wrong produces an *apprehension* of merited punishment, when we have committed a crime.'—Blair. What is probable is *feared;* 'That which is *feared* may sometimes be avoided: but that which is regretted to-day may be regretted again to-morrow.'—Johnson. The symptom or prognostick of an evil is *dreaded* as if the evil itself were present;

> All men think all men mortal but themselves,
> Themselves, when some alarming shock of fate
> Strikes through their wounded hearts the sudden *dread*.—Young.

Apprehend respects things only; *fear* and *dread* relate to persons as well as things: we *fear* the person who has the power of inflicting pain or disgrace; we *dread* him who has no less the will than the power.

Fear is a salutary sentiment in society, it binds men together in their several relations and dependencies, and affords the fullest scope for the exercise of the benevolent feelings; it is the sentiment of a child towards its parent or instructer; of a creature to its Creator; it is the companion of love and respect towards men, of adoration in erring and sinful mortals towards their Maker. *Dread* is altogether an irksome sentiment; with regard to our fellow-creatures, it arises out of the abuse of power: we *dread* the tyrant who delights in punishing and tormenting, his image haunts the breast of the unhappy subject, his shadow awakens terrour as the approach of some direful misfortune: with regard to our Maker it springs from a consciousness of guilt, and the prospect of a severe and adequate punishment; the wrath of God may justly be *dreaded*.

AWE, REVERENCE, DREAD

Awe, probably from the German *achten*, conveys the idea of regarding; *reverence*, in French *reverence*, Latin *reverentia*, comes from *revereor* to fear strongly; *dread*, in Saxon *dread*, comes from the Latin *territo* to frighten, and Greek ταράσσω to trouble.

Awe and *reverence* both denote a strong sentiment of respect, mingled with some emotions of fear; but the former marks the much stronger sentiment of the two: *dread* is an unmingled sentiment of fear for one's personal security. *Awe* may be awakened by the help of the senses and understanding; *reverence* by that of the understanding only; and *dread* principally by that of the imagination.

Sublime, sacred, and solemn objects awaken *awe;* they cause the beholder to stop and consider whether he is worthy to approach them any nearer; they rivet his mind and body to a spot, and make him cautious, lest by his presence he should contaminate that which is hallowed; 'It were endless to enumerate all the passages, both in the sacred and profane writers, which establish the general sentiment of mankind concerning the inseparable union of a sacred and reverential *awe* with our ideas of the Divinity.'—Burke. Exalted and noble objects produce *reverence;* they lead to every outward mark of obeisance and humiliation which it is possible for a man to express; 'If the voice of universal nature, the experience of all ages, the light of reason, and the immediate evidence of my senses, cannot awake me to a dependence upon my God, a *reverence* for his religion, and an humble opinion of myself, what a lost creature am I.'—Cumberland. Terrifick objects excite *dread:* they cause a shuddering of the animal frame, and a revulsion of the mind which is attended with nothing but pain;

> To Phœbus next my trembling steps be led,
> Full of religious doubts and awful *dread*.
> Dryden.

When the creature places himself in the presence of the Creator; when he contemplates the immeasurable distance which separates himself, a frail and finite mortal, from his infinitely perfect Maker; he approaches with *awe:* even the sanctuary where he is accustomed thus to bow before the Almighty acquires the power of awakening the same emotions in his mind. Age, wisdom, and virtue, when combined in one person, are never approached without *reverence;* the possessor has a dignity in himself that checks the haughtiness of the arrogant, that silences the petulance of pride and self-conceit, that stills the noise and giddy mirth of the young, and communicates to all around a sobriety of mien and aspect. A grievous offender is seldom without *dread;* his guilty conscience pictures every thing as the instrument of vengeance, and every person as denouncing his merited sentence.

The solemn stillness of the tomb will inspire *awe*, even in the breast of him who has no *dread* of death. Children should be early taught to have a *reverence* for the Bible as a book, in distinction from all other books.

AFRAID, FEARFUL, TIMOROUS, TIMID.

Afraid is changed from *afeared*, signifying in a state of fear; *fearful*, as the words of which it is compounded imply, signifies full of fear; *timorous* and *timid* come from the Latin *timor* fear, *timidus* fearful, and *timeo* to fear.

The first denotes a temporary state, the three last a habit of the mind.

Afraid may be used either in a physical or moral application, either as it relates to ourselves only or to others; *fearful* and *timorous* are only applied physically and personally; *timid* is mostly used in a moral sense.

It is the character of the *fearful* or *timorous* person to be *afraid* of what he imagines would hurt himself; it is not necessary for the prospect of danger to exist in order to awaken fear in such a disposition; 'To be always *afraid* of losing life is, indeed, scarcely to enjoy a life that can deserve the care of preservation.'—Johnson. It is the characteristick of the *timid* person to be *afraid* of offending or meeting with some thing painful from others; such a disposition is prevented from following the dictates of its own mind; 'He who brings with him into a clamorous multitude the *timidity* of recluse speculation, will suffer himself to be driven by a burst of laughter from the fortresses of demonstration.'—Johnson.

Between *fearful* and *timorous* there is little distinction, either in sense or application, except that we say *fearful* of a thing, not *timorous* of a thing; 'By I know not what impatience of raillery, he is wonder fully *fearful* of being thought too great a believer' Steele.

> Then birds in airy space might safely move,
> And *tim'rous* hares on heaths securely rove.
> Dryden.

TO FRIGHTEN, INTIMIDATE.

Between *frighten* and *intimidate* there is the same difference as between *fright* (*v. Alarm*) and *fear* (*v. To apprehend*); the danger that is near or before the eyes *frightens;* that which is seen at a distance *intimidates*. hence females are oftener *frightened*, and men are oftener *intimidated:* noises will *frighten;* threats may *intimidate:* we may run away when we are *frightened;* we waver in our resolution when we are *intimidated:* we fear immediate bodily harm when we are *frightened;* we fear harm to our property as well as our persons when we are *intimidated:* *frighten*, therefore, is always applied to animals, but *intimidate* never;

> And perch, a horrour! on his sacred crown
> If that such profanation were permitted

Cf the bystanders, who with reverend care
Fright them away.—CUMBERLAND.

Cortes, unwilling to employ force, endeavoured alternately to sooth and *intimidate* Montezuma.'—ROBERTSON.

FORMIDABLE, DREADFUL, TERRIBLE, SHOCKING.

Formidable is applied to that which is apt to excite fear (*v. To apprehend*); *dreadful* (*v. To apprehend*), to what is calculated to excite dread; *terrible* (*v. Alarm*) to that which excites *terrour*; and *shocking* from to *shake* is applied to that which violently shakes or agitates (*v. To agitate*). The *formidable* acts neither suddenly nor violently; 'France continued not only powerful but *formidable* to the hour of the ruin of the monarchy.'—BURKE. The *dreadful* may act violently, but not suddenly: thus the appearance of an army may be *formidable*; that of a field of battle is *dreadful*;

Think, timely think, on the last *dreadful* day.
DRYDEN.

The *terrible* and *shocking* act both suddenly and violently; but the former acts both on the senses and the imagination, the latter on the moral feelings only: thus the glare of a tiger's eye is *terrible*; the unexpected news of a friend's death is *shocking*; 'When men are arrived at thinking of their very dissolution with pleasure, how few things are there that can be *terrible* to them.'—STEELE. 'Nothing could be more *shocking* to a generous nobility, than the intrusting to mercenary hands the defence of those territories which had been acquired or preserved by the blood of their ancestors.'—ROBERTSON.

TREMBLING, TREMOUR, TREPIDATION.

All these terms are derived from the very same source (*v. Agitation*), and designate a general state of agitation: *trembling* is not only the most familiar but also the most indefinite term of the three; *trepidation* and *tremour* are species of *trembling*. *Trembling* expresses any degree of involuntary shaking of the frame, from the affection either of the body or the mind; cold, nervous affections, fear, and the like, are the ordinary causes of *trembling*;

And with unmanly *tremblings* shook the car.
POPE

Tremour is a slight degree of *trembling*, which arises only from a mental affection; when the spirits are agitated, the mind is thrown into a *tremour* by any trifling incident; 'Laughter is a vent of any sudden joy that strikes upon the mind, which, being too volatile and strong, breaks out in this *tremour* of the voice.'—STEELE. *Trepidation* is more violent than either of the two, and springs from the defective state of the mind, it shows itself in the action, or the different movements of the body; those who have not the requisite composure of mind to command themselves on all occasions are apt to do what is required of them with *trepidation*; 'The ferocious insolence of Cromwell, the rugged brutality of Harrison, and the general *trepidation* of fear and wickedness (in the rebel parliament) would make a picture of unexampled variety.'—JOHNSON. *Trembling* is either an occasional or an habitual infirmity; there is no one who may not be sometimes seized with a *trembling*, and there are those who, from a lasting disease or from old age, are never rid of it; *tremour* is but occasional, and consequently depends rather on the nature of the occasion; no one who has a proper degree of modesty can make his first appearance in publick without feeling a *tremour*: *trepidation* may be either occasional or habitual, but oftener the latter, since it arises rather from the weakness of the mind than the strength of the cause.

Trembling and *tremulous* are applied as epithets, either to persons or things: a *trembling* voice evinces *trepidation* of mind, a *tremulous* voice evinces a *tremour* of mind: notes in musick are sometimes *trembling*; the motion of the leaves of trees is *tremulous*;

And rend the *trembling* unresisting prey.—POPE.

As thus th' effulgence *tremulous* I drank,
With cherish'd gaze.—THOMSON.

AGITATION, EMOTION, TREPIDATION, TREMOUR.

Agitation, in Latin *agitatio*, from *agito*, signifies the state of being *agitated*; *emotion*, in Latin *emotio*, from *emotus*, participle of *emoveo*, compounded of out of and *moveo* to move, signifies the state of being moved out of rest or put in motion; *trepidation*, in Latin *trepidatio*, from *trepido* to tremble, compounded of *tremo* and *pede* to tremble with the feet, signifies the condition of trembling in all one's limbs from head to foot; *tremour*, *v. Trembling*.

Agitation refers either to the body or mind, *emotion* to the mind only; *tremour* mostly, and *trepidation* only, to the body.

Agitation of mind is a vehement struggle between contending feelings; *emotion* is the awakening but one feeling; which in the latter case is not so vehement as in the former. Distressing circumstances produce *agitation*; 'The seventh book affects the imagination like the ocean in a calm, and fills the mind of the reader without producing in it any thing like tumult or *agitation*.'—ADDISON (*On Milton*). Affecting and interesting circumstances produce *emotions*; 'The description of Adam and Eve as they first appeared to Satan, is exquisitely drawn, and sufficient to make the fallen angel gaze upon them with all those *emotions* of envy in which he is represented.'—ADDISON (*On Milton*).

Agitations have but one character, namely, that of violence: *emotions* vary with the object that awakens them; they are *emotions* either of pain or pleasure, of tenderness or anger; they are either gentle or strong, faint or vivid.

With regard to the body, *agitation* is more than *trepidation*, and the latter more than *tremour*: the two former attract the notice of the bystander; the latter is scarcely visible.

Agitations of the mind sometimes give rise to distorted and extravagant *agitations* of the body; *emotions* of terrour or horrour will throw the body into a *trepidation*; or any publick misfortune may produce a *trepidation* among a number of persons; 'His first action of note was in the battle of Lepanto, where the success of that great day, in such *trepidation* of the state, made every man meritorious.'—WOTTON. *Emotions* of fear will cause a *tremour* to run through the whole frame; 'He fell into such a universal *tremour* of all his joints, that when going his legs trembled under him.'—HERVEY.

TO ACTUATE, IMPEL, INDUCE

Actuate, from the Latin *actum* an action, implies to call into action; *impel*, in Latin *impello*, is compounded of *in* towards and *pello* to drive, signifying to drive towards an object; *induce*, in Latin *induco*, is compounded of *in* and *duco*, signifying to lead towards an object.

One is *actuated* by motives, *impelled* by passions, and *induced* by reason or inclination.

Whatever *actuates* is the result of reflection: it is a steady and fixed principle: whatever *impels* is momentary and vehement, and often precludes reflection: whatever *induces* is not vehement, though often momentary.

We seldom repent of the thing to which we are *actuated*; as the principle, whether good or bad, is not liable to change; 'It is observed by Cicero, that men of the greatest and the most shining parts are most *actuated* by ambition.'—ADDISON. We may frequently be *impelled* to measures which cause serious repentance;

When youth *impell'd* him, and when love inspir'd,
The listening nymphs his Dorick lays admir'd.
SIR WM. JONES.

The thing to which we are *induced* is seldom of sufficient importance to call for repentance;

Induced by such examples, some have taught
That bees have portions of ethereal thought.
DRYDEN.

Revenge *actuates* men to commit the most horrid deeds; anger *impels* them to the most imprudent actions; phlegmatick people are not easily *induced* to take any one measure in preference to another

TO EXCITE, INCITE, PROVOKE.

Excite, v. *To awaken; incite*, v. *To encourage; provoke*, v. *To aggravate.*

To *excite* is said more particularly of the inward feelings; *incite* is said of the external actions; *provoke* is said of both.

A person's passions are *excited;* he is *incited* by any particular passion to a course of conduct; a particular feeling is *provoked*, or he is *provoked* by some feeling to a particular step. Wit and conversation *excite* mirth;

> Can then the sons of Greece (the sage rejoin'd)
> *Excite* compassion in Achilles' mind?—POPE.

Men are *incited* by a lust for gain to fraudulent practices;

> To her the god: Great Hector's soul *incite*
> To dare the boldest Greek to single fight,
> Till Greece *provok'd* from all her numbers show
> A warriour worthy to be Hector's foe.—POPE.

Men are *provoked* by the opposition of others to intemperate language and intemperate measures; 'Among the other torments which this passion produces, we may usually observe, that none are greater mourners than jealous men, when the person who *provoked* their jealousy is taken from them.'—ADDISON. To *excite* is very frequently used in a physical acceptation; *incite* always, and *provoke* mostly, in a moral application. We speak of *exciting* hunger, thirst, or perspiration; of *inciting* to noble actions; of *provoking* impertinence, *provoking* scorn or resentment.

When *excite* and *provoke* are applied to similar objects, the former designates a much stronger action than the latter. A thing may *excite* a smile, but it *provokes* laughter; it may *excite* displeasure, but it *provokes* anger; it may *excite* joy or sorrow, but it *provokes* to madness.

TO PRESS, SQUEEZE, PINCH, GRIPE.

Press, in Latin *pressus*, participle of *premo*, which probably comes from the Greek βάρημα; *squeeze*, in Saxon *quisan*, Latin *quasso*, Hebrew רשע to *press* together; *pinch* is but a variation from *pin*, *spine; gripe*, from the German *greifen*, signifies to seize, like the word grapple or grasp, the Latin *rapio*, the Greek γριπίζω to fish or catch, and the Hebrew גרם to catch.

The forcible action of one body on another is included in all these terms. In the word *press* this is the only idea; the rest differ in the circumstances. We may *press* with the foot, the hand, the whole body, or any particular limb; one *squeezes* commonly with the hand; one *pinches* either with the fingers, or an instrument constructed in a similar form; one *gripes* with teeth, claws, or any instrument that can gain a hold of the object. Inanimate as well as animate objects *press* or *pinch;* but to *squeeze* and *gripe* are more properly the actions of animate objects; the former is always said of persons, the latter of animals; stones *press* that on which they rest their weight; a door which shuts of itself may *pinch* the fingers; one *squeezes* the hand of a friend; lobsters and many other shell-fish *gripe* whatever comes within their claws.

In the figurative application they have a similar distinction; we *press* a person by importunity, or by some coercive measure; 'All these women (the thirty wives of Orodes) *pressed* hard upon the old king, each soliciting for a son of her own.'—PRIDEAUX. An extortioner *squeezes* in order to get that which is given with reluctance or difficulty; 'Ventidius, receiving great sums from Herod to promote his interest, and at the same time greater to hinder it, *squeezed* each of them to the utmost, and served neither.'—PRIDEAUX. A miser *pinches* himself by contracting his subsistence;

> Better dispos'd to clothe the tatter'd wretch,
> Who shrinks beneath the blast, to feed the poor
> *Pinch'd* with afflictive want.—SOMERVILLE.

A covetous person *gripes* all that comes within his possession; 'How can he be envied for his felicity who is conscious that a very short time will give him up to the *gripe* of poverty.'—JOHNSON.

TO RUB, CHAFE, FRET, GALL.

To *rub*, through the medium of the northern languages, comes from the Hebrew רזב. It is the generick term, expressing simply the act of moving bodies when in contact with each other; to *chafe*, from the French *chauffer*, and the Latin *calfacere* to make hot, signifies to *rub* a thing until it is heated; to *fret*, like the word *fritter*, comes from the Latin *frio* to crumble, signifying to wear away by *rubbing:* to *gall*, from the noun *gall*, signifies to make as bitter or painful as *gall*, that is, to wound by *rubbing*. Things are *rubbed* sometimes for purposes of convenience; but they are *chafed, fretted*, and *galled* injuriously: the skin is liable to *chafe* from any violence; leather will *fret* from the motion of a carriage; when the skin is once broken, animals will become *galled* by a continuance of the friction. These terms are likewise used in the moral or figurative sense to denote the actions of things on the mind, where the distinction is clearly kept up. We meet with *rubs* from the opposing sentiments of others; 'A boy educated at home meets with continual *rubs* and disappointments (when he comes into the world).'—BEATTIE. The angry humours are *chafed;*

> Accoutred as we were, we both plung'd in
> The troubled Tiber, *chafing* with the shores.
> SHAKSPEARE.

The mind is *fretted* and made sore by the frequent repetition of small troubles and vexations;

> And full of indignation *frets*,
> That women should be such coquettes.—SWIFT

The pride is *galled* by humiliation and severe degradations;

> Thus every poet in his kind
> Is bit by him that comes behind,
> Who, tho' too little to be seen,
> Can tease and *gall*, and give the spleen.—SWIFT.

EBULLITION, EFFERVESCENCE, FERMENTATION.

These technical terms have a strong resemblance in their signification, but they are not strictly synonymous; having strong characteristick differences.

Ebullition, from the Latin *ebullitio* and *ebullio*, compounded of *e* and *bullio* to boil forth, marks the * commotion of a liquid acted upon by fire, and in chymistry it is said of two substances, which by penetrating each other occasion bubbles to rise up; *effervescence*, from the Latin *effervescentia* and *effervesco* to grow hot, marks the commotion which is excited in liquors by a combination of substances; such as of acids, which are mixed and commonly produce heat; *fermentation*, from the Latin *fermentatio* and *fermentum* or *fervimentum*, from *ferveo* to grow hot, marks the internal movement which is excited in a liquid of itself, by which its components undergo such a change or decomposition, as to form a new body.

Ebullition is a more violent action than *effervescence; fermentation* is more gradual and permanent than either. Water is exposed to *ebullition* when acted upon by any powerful degree of external heat; iron in aqua fortis occasions an *effervescence;* beer and wine undergo a *fermentation* before they reach a state of perfection.

These words are all employed in a figurative sense, which is drawn from their physical application. The passions are exposed to *ebullitions*, in which they break forth with all the violence that is observable in water agitated by excessive heat; 'Milbourn, indeed, a clergyman, attacked it (Dryden's Virgil), but his outrages seem to be the *ebullitions* of a mind agitated by stronger resentment than bad poetry can excite.'—JOHNSON. The heart and affections are exposed to *effervescence* when powerfully awakened by particular objects, 'Dryden's was not one of the gentle bosoms: he hardly conceived love but in its turbulent *effervescence* with some other desires.'—JOHNSON. Minds are said to be in a *ferment* which are agitated by conflicting feelings; 'The tumult of the world raises that eager *fermentation* of spirit which will ever be sending

* Vide Beauzée: "Ebullition, effervescence, fermentation."

forth the dangerous fumes of folly.'—BLAIR. *Ebullition* and *effervescence* are applicable only to individuals; *fermentation* to one or many.

If the angry humours of an irascible temper be not restrained in early life, they but too frequently break forth in the most dreadful *ebullitions* in maturer years; religious zeal, when not constrained by the sober exercise of judgement, and corrected by sound knowledge, is an unhappy *effervescence* that injures the cause which it espouses, and often proves fatal to the individual by whom it is indulged: the *ferment* which was produced in the publick mind by the French revolution exceeded every thing that is recorded in history of popular commotions in past ages, and will, it is to be hoped, never have its parallel at any future period. There can be no *ebullition* or *fermentation* without *effervescence*; but there may be *effervescence* without either of the former.

INTOXICATION, DRUNKENNESS, INFATUATION.

Intoxication, from the Latin *toxicum* a poison, signifies imbued with a poison; *drunkenness* signifies the state of having drunk overmuch; *infatuation*, from *fatuus* foolish, signifies making foolish.

Intoxication and *drunkenness* are used either in the proper or the improper sense; *infatuation* in the improper sense only. *Intoxication* is a general state; *drunkenness* a particular state. *Intoxication* may be produced by various causes; *drunkenness* is produced only by an immoderate indulgence in some *intoxicating* liquor: a person may be *intoxicated* by the smell of strong liquors, or by vapours which produce a similar effect; he becomes *drunken* by the drinking of wine or other spirits. In the improper sense a deprivation of one's reasoning faculties is the common idea in the signification of all these terms. The *intoxication* and *drunkenness* spring from the intemperate state of the feelings; the *infatuation* springs from the ascendancy of the passions over the reasoning powers. A person is *intoxicated* with success, *drunk* with joy, and *infatuated* by an excess of vanity, or an impetuosity of character; 'This plan of empire was not taken up in the first *intoxication* of unexpected success.'—BURKE. 'Passion is the *drunkenness* of the mind.'—SOUTH. 'A sure destruction impends over those *infatuated* princes, who, in the conflict with this new and unheard of power, proceed as if they were engaged in a war that bore a resemblance to their former contests.'—BURKE.

A person who is naturally *intoxicated* reels and is giddy; he who is in the moral sense *intoxicated* is disorderly and unsteady in his conduct: a *drunken* man is deprived of the use of all his senses, and in the moral sense he is bewildered and unable to collect himself. An *infatuated* man is not merely foolish but wild: he carries his folly to the most extravagant pitch.

TO AWAKEN, EXCITE, PROVOKE, ROUSE, STIR UP.

To *awaken* is to make *awake* or alive; to *excite*, in Latin *excito*, compounded of the intensive syllables *ex* and *cito*, in Hebrew סת to move, signifies to move out of a state of rest; *provoke*, from the Latin *provoco* to call forth, signifies to call forth the feelings; to *rouse* is to cause them to rise; and to *stir*, from the German *stören*, and the Latin *turbo*, is to put in commotion.

To *excite* and *provoke* convey the idea of producing something; *rouse* and *stir up* that of only calling into action that which previously exists; to *awaken* is used in either sense.

To *awaken* is a gentler action than to *excite*, and this is gentler than to *provoke*. We *awaken* by a simple effort; we *excite* by repeated efforts or forcible means; we *provoke* by words, looks, or actions. The tender feelings are *awakened*; affections or the passions in general are *excited*; the angry passions are commonly *provoked*. Objects of distress *awaken* a sentiment of pity: competition among scholars *excites* a spirit of emulation; taunting words *provoke* anger.

Awaken is applied only to the individual and what passes within him; *excite* is applicable to the outward circumstances of one or many; *provoke* is applicable to the conduct or temper of one or many. The attention is *awakened* by interesting sounds that strike upon the ear; the conscience is *awakened* by the voice of the preacher, or by passing events; 'The soul has its curiosity more than ordinarily *awakened* when it turns its thoughts upon the conduct of such who have behaved themselves with an equal, a resigned, a cheerful, a generous, or heroic temper in the extremity of death.'—STEELE. A commotion, a tumult, or a rebellion is *excited* among the people by the active efforts of individuals; 'In our Saviour was no form of comeliness than men should desire, no artifice or trick to catch applause, or to *excite* surprise.'—CUMBERLAND. Laughter or contempt is *provoked* by preposterous conduct;

> See, Mercy! see with pure and loaded hands
> Before thy shrine my country's genius stands.
> When he whom e'en our joys *provoke*,
> The fiend of nature join'd his yoke,
> And rush'd in wrath to make our isles his prey;
> Thy form from out thy sweet abode,
> O'ertook him on the blasted road.—COLLINS.

To *awaken* is, in the moral, as in the physical sense, to call into consciousness from a state of unconsciousness; to *rouse* is forcibly to bring into action that which is in a state of inaction; and *stir up* is to bring into a state of agitation or commotion. We are *awakened* from an ordinary state by ordinary means; we are *roused* from an extraordinary state by extraordinary means; we are *stirred up* from an ordinary to an extraordinary state. The mind of a child is *awakened* by the action on its senses as soon as it is born;

> The spark of noble courage now awake (*awaken*)
> And strive your excellent self to excel.—SPENSER.

Some persons are not to be *roused* from their stupor by any thing but the most awful events;

> Go, study virtue, rugged ancient worth;
> *Rouse* up that flame our great forefathers felt.
> SHIRLEY.

The passions, particularly of anger, are in some persons *stirred up* by trifling circumstances; 'The use of the passions is to *stir up* the mind and put it upon action, to awake the understanding, and to enforce the will.'—ADDISON.

The conscience is sometimes *awakened* for a time, but the sinner is not *roused* to a sense of his danger, or to any exertions for his own safety, until an intemperate zeal is *stirred up* in him by means of enthusiastic preaching, in which case the vulgar proverb is verified, that the remedy is as bad as the disease. Death is a scene calculated to *awaken* some feeling in the most obdurate breast;

> The fair
> Repairs her smiles, *awakens* ev'ry grace,
> And calls forth all the wonders of her face.—POPE.

The tears and sighs of the afflicted *excite* a sentiment of commiseration; the most equitable administration of justice may *excite* murmurs among the discontented; the relation of worthy deeds may *excite* to honour and virtue; 'That kind of poetry which *excites* to virtue the greatest men, is of greatest use to human kind.'—DRYDEN. A harsh and unreasonable reproof will *provoke* a reply: or affronts *provoke* resentment;

> Such acts
> Of contumacy will *provoke* the Highest.—MILTON.

Continued provocations and affronts may *rouse* a sense of injuries in the meekest breast; 'The heat with which Luther treated his adversaries, though strained too far, was extremely well fitted by the providence of God to *rouse* up a people, the most phlegmatick of any in Christendom.'—ATTERBURY. Nothing is so calculated to *stir up* the rebellious spirits of men as the harangues of political demagogues; 'The turbulent and dangerous are for embroiling councils, *stirring up* seditions, and subverting constitutions, out of a mere restlessness of temper.'—STEELE.

TO ENCOURAGE, COUNTENANCE, SANCTION, SUPPORT.

Encourage has here the same general signification as in the preceding article; *countenance* signifies to keep in *countenance*; *sanction*, in French *sanction*,

Latin *sanctio* from *sanctus* sacred, signifies to ratify a decree or ordinance; in an extended sense to make any thing binding; *support*, in French *supporter*, Latin *supporto*, compounded of *sup* or *sub* and *porto* to bear, signifies to bear from underneath, to bear up.

These terms are allied in their application to persons or things personal; persons or things are *encouraged* and *supported; persons are *countenanced;* things are *sanctioned;* measures or persons are *encouraged* and *supported* by every means which may forward the object; persons are *countenanced* in their proceedings by the apparent approbation of others; measures are *sanctioned* by the consent or approbation of others.

To *encourage* is a general and indefinite term, we may *encourage* a person or his conduct by various ways: 'Every man *encourages* the practice of that vice which he commits in appearance, though he avoids it in fact.'—HAWKESWORTH. *Countenancing* is a direct mode of *encouragement*, it consists of some outward demonstration of regard or good will towards the person; 'A good man acts with a vigour and suffers with a patience more than human, when he believes himself *countenanced* by the Almighty.'—BLAIR. There is most of authority in *sanctioning;* it is the lending of a name, an authority, or an influence, in order to strengthen and confirm the thing; 'Men of the greatest sense are always diffident of their private judgement, until it receives a *sanction* from the publick.'—ADDISON. There is most of assistance and cooperation in *support;* it is the employment of means to an end; 'The apparent insufficiency of every individual to his own happiness or safety compels us to seek from one another assistance and *support*.'—JOHNSON. Persons in all conditions may *encourage* and *support:* superiours only can *countenance* or *sanction:* those who *countenance* evil doers give a *sanction* to their evil deeds; those who *support* either an individual or a cause ought to be satisfied that they are entitled to *support*.

TO ENCOURAGE, ANIMATE, INCITE, IMPEL, URGE, STIMULATE, INSTIGATE.

Encourage, compounded of *en* or *in* and *courage*, signifies to inspire with courage; *animate*, in Latin *animatus*, participle of *animo* and *anima* the soul, signifies in the proper sense to give life, and in the moral sense to give spirit; *incite*, from the Latin *cito*, and the Hebrew סת to stir up, signifies to put into motion towards an object; *impel* signifies the same as in the preceding article; *urge*, in Latin *urgeo*, comes from the Greek root ϵργέω to set to work; *stimulate*, from the Latin *stimulus* a spur or goad, and *instigate*, from the Latin *stigo*, and Greek ϛίξω, signify literally to goad.

The idea of actuating, or calling into action, is common to these terms, which vary in the circumstances of the action.

Encouragement acts as a persuasive, *animate* as an *impelling* or enlivening cause: those who are weak require to be *encouraged;* those who are strong become stronger by being *animated;* the former require to have their difficulties removed, their powers renovated, their doubts and fears dispelled; the latter may have their hopes increased, their prospects brightened, and their powers invigorated; we are *encouraged* not to give up or slacken in our exertions; we are *animated* to increase our efforts: the sinner is *encouraged* by offers of pardon, through the merits of a Redeemer, to turn from his sinful ways; 'He would have women follow the camp, to be spectators and *encouragers* of noble actions.'—BURTON. The Christian is *animated* by the prospect of a blissful eternity, to go on from perfection to perfection; 'He that prosecutes a lawful purpose, by lawful means, acts always with the approbation of his own reason: he is *animated* through the course of his endeavours by an expectation which he knows to be just.'—JOHNSON.

What *encourages* and *animates* acts by the finer feelings of our nature; what *incites* acts through the medium of our desires: we are *encouraged* by kindness; we are *animated* by the hope of reward; we are *incited* by the desire of distinction or the love of gain; 'While a rightful claim to pleasure or to affluence must be procured either by slow industry or uncertain hazard, there will always be multitudes whom cowardice or impatience *incite* to more safe and speedy methods of getting wealth.'—JOHNSON. What *impels urges, stimulates*, and *instigates*, acts forcibly, be the cause internal or external: we are *impelled* and *stimulated* mostly by what is internal; we are *urged* and *instigated* by both the internal and external, but particularly the latter: we are *impelled* by motives; we are *stimulated* by passions; we are *urged* and *instigated* by the representations of others: a benevolent man is *impelled* by motives of humanity to relieve the wretched;

> So Myrrha's mind, *impell'd* on either side,
> Takes ev'ry bent, but cannot long abide.
> DRYDEN.

An ardent mind is *stimulated* by ambition to great efforts; 'Some persons from the secret *stimulations* of vanity or envy, despise a valuable book, and throw contempt upon it by wholesale.'—WATTS. We are *urged* by entreaties to spare those who are in our power; one is *instigated* by malicious representations to take revenge on a supposed enemy.

We may be *impelled* and *urged* though not properly *stimulated* or *instigated* by circumstances; in this case the two former differ only in the degree of force in the *impelling* cause: less constraint is laid on the will when we are *impelled*, than when we are *urged*, which leaves no alternative or choice: a monarch is sometimes *impelled* by the state of the nation to make a peace less advantageous than he would otherwise do;

> Thus, while around the wave-subjected soil
> *Impels* the natives to repeated toil,
> Industrious habits in each bosom reign.
> GOLDSMITH.

A prince may be *urged* by his desperate condition to throw himself upon the mercy of the enemy;

> What I have done my safety *urg'd* me to.
> SHAKSPEARE.

A man is *impelled*, by the mere necessity of choosing, to take one road in preference to another; he is *urged* by his pecuniary embarrassments to raise money at a great loss.

We may be *impelled, urged*, and *stimulated* to that which is good or bad; we are never *instigated* to that which is good: we may be *impelled* by curiosity to pry into that which does not concern us; we may be *urged* by the entreaties of those we are connected with to take steps of which we afterward repent, or have afterward reason to approve; 'The magistrate cannot *urge* obedience upon such potent grounds as the minister.'—SOUTH. We may be *stimulated* by the desire of distinction or by necessity;

> For every want that *stimulates* the breast
> Becomes a source of pleasure when redres'd.
> GOLDSMITH.

Those who are not hardened in vice require the *instigation* of persons more abandoned than themselves, before they will commit any desperate act of wickedness; 'There are few *instigations* in this country to a breach of confidence.'—HAWKESWORTH.

The *encouragement* and *incitement* are the abstract nouns either for the act of *encouraging* or *inciting*, or the thing that *encourages* or *incites:* the *encouragement* of laudable undertakings is itself laudable; a single word or look may be an *encouragement;*

> For when he dies, farewell all honour, bounty,
> All generous *encouragement* of arts.—OTWAY.

The *incitement* of passion is at all times dangerous, but particularly in youth; money is said to be an *incitement* to evil; the prospect of glory is an *incitement* to great actions;

> Let his actions speak him, and this shield,
> Let down from heaven, that to his youth will yield
> Such copy of *incitement*.—B. JONSON.

Incentive, which is another derivative from *incite*, has a higher application for things that *incite*, being mostly applied to spiritual objects: a religious man wants no *incentives* to virtues; his own breast furnishes him with those of the noblest kind; 'Even the wisdom of God hath not suggested more pressing motives, more powerful *incentives* to charity, than these, that we shall be judged by it at the last dreadful day.'—ATTERBURY. *Impulse* is the derivative from *impel*, and denotes the act of *impelling* or the thing that *impels;*

stimulus, which is the root of the word *stimulate*, naturally designates the instrument, namely, the spur or goad with which one is *stimulated:* hence we speak of acting by a blind *impulse*, or of wanting a *stimulus* to exertion; 'If these little *impulses* set the great wheels of devotion on work, the largeness and height of that shall not at all be prejudiced by the smallness of the occasion.'—SOUTH.

TO ENCOURAGE, ADVANCE, PROMOTE, PREFER, FORWARD.

To *encourage* signifies the same as in the preceding article; *advance*, from the Latin *advenio* to come near, signifies here to cause to come near a point; *promote*, from the Latin *promoveo*, signifies to move forward; *prefer*, from the Latin *præfero*, or *fero* and *præ*, to set before, signifies to set up before others; to *forward* is to put forward.

The idea of exerting one's influence to the advantage of an object is included in the signification of all these terms, which differ in the circumstances and mode of the action: to *encourage*, *advance*, and *promote* are applicable to both persons and things; *prefer* to persons only; *forward* to things only.

First, as to persons, *encourage* is partial as to the end, and indefinite as to the means: we may *encourage* a person in any thing, however trivial, and by any means: thus we may *encourage* a child in his rudeness, by not checking him; or we may *encourage* an artist or a man of letters in some great national work; but to *advance*, *promote*, and *prefer* are more general in their end, and specifick in the means: a person may *advance* himself, or may be *advanced* by others; he is *promoted* and *preferred* only by others: a person's *advancement* may be the fruit of his industry, or result from the efforts of his friends; *promotion* and *preferment* are the work of one's friends; the former in regard to offices in general, the latter mostly in regard to ecclesiastical situations: it is the duty of every one to *encourage*, to the utmost of his power, those among the poor who strive to obtain an honest livelihood; 'Religion depends upon the *encouragement* of those that are to dispense and assert it.'—SOUTH. It is every man's duty to *advance* himself in life by every legitimate means; 'No man's lot is so unalterably fixed in this life, but that a thousand accidents may either forward or disappoint his *advancement*.'—HUGHES. It is the duty and the pleasure of every good man in the state to *promote* those who show themselves deserving of *promotion*; 'Your zeal in *promoting* my interest deserves my warmest acknowledgments.'—BEATTIE. It is the duty of a minister to accept of *preferment* when it offers, but it is not his duty to be solicitous for it; 'If I were now to accept *preferment* in the church, I should be apprehensive that I might strengthen the hands of the gainsayers.'—BEATTIE.

When taken in regard to things, *encourage* is used in an improper or figurative acceptation; the rest are applied properly: we *encourage* an undertaking by giving courage to the undertaker; 'The great *encouragement* which has been given to learning for some years last past, has made our own nation as glorious upon this account as for its late triumphs and conquests.'—ADDISON. But when we speak of *advancing* a cause, or *promoting* an interest, or *forwarding* a purpose, the terms properly convey the idea of keeping things alive, or in a motion towards some desired end: to *advance* is however generally used in relation to whatever admits of extension and aggrandizement; *promote* is applied to whatever admits of being brought to a point of maturity or perfection; 'I love to see a man zealous in a good matter, and especially when his zeal shows itself for *advancing* morality, and *promoting* the happiness of mankind.'—ADDISON. *Forward* is but a partial term, employed in the sense of *promote* in regard to particular objects; thus we *advance* religion or learning; we *promote* an art or an invention; we *forward* a plan; 'It behooves us not to be wanting to ourselves in *forwarding* the intention of nature by the culture of our minds.'—BERKELEY.

TO ENCOURAGE, EMBOLDEN.

To *encourage* is to give courage, and to *embolden* to make bold; the former impelling to action in general, the latter to that which is more difficult or dangerous: we are *encouraged* to persevere; the resolution is thereby confirmed: we are *emboldened* to begin; the spirit of enterprise is roused. Success *encourages;* the chance of escaping danger *emboldens*.

Outward circumstances, however trivial, serve to *encourage;*

> Intrepid through the midst of danger go,
> Their friends *encourage* and amaze the foe.
> DRYDEN.

The urgency of the occasion, or the importance of the subject, serves to *embolden;*

> *Embolden'd* then, nor hesitating more,
> Fast, fast they plunge amid the flashing wave.
> THOMSON.

A kind word or a gentle look *encourages* the suppliant to tender his petition; where the cause of truth and religion is at stake, the firm believer is *emboldened* to speak out with freedom: timid dispositions are not to be *encouraged* always by trivial circumstances, but sanguine dispositions are easily *emboldened;* the most flattering representations of friends are frequently necessary to *encourage* the display of talent; the confidence natural to youth is often sufficient of itself to *embolden* men to great undertakings.

TO DETER, DISCOURAGE, DISHEARTEN.

Deter, in Latin *deterreo*, compounded of *de* and *terreo*, signifies to frighten away from a thing; *discourage* and *dishearten*, by the privative *dis*, signify to deprive of courage or heart.

One is *deterred* from commencing any thing, one is *discouraged* or *disheartened* from proceeding. A variety of motives may *deter* any one from an undertaking; but a person is *discouraged* or *disheartened* mostly by the want of success or the hopelessness of the case. The wicked are sometimes *deterred* from committing enormities by the fear of punishment; projectors are *discouraged* from entering into fresh speculations by observing the failure of others; there are few persons who would not be *disheartened* from renewing their endeavours, who had experienced nothing but ill success. The prudent and the fearful are alike easily to be *deterred;*

> But thee or fear *deters*, or sloth detains,
> No drop of all thy father warms thy veins.
> POPE.

Impatient people are most apt to be *discouraged;* and proud people are the most apt to *discourage* the humble; 'The proud man *discourages* those from approaching him who are of a mean condition, and who must want his assistance.'—ADDISON. Faint-hearted people are easiest *disheartened;*

> Be not *disheartened* then, nor cloud those looks,
> That wont to be more cheerful and serene,
> Than when fair morning first smiles on the world.
> MILTON.

The fool-hardy and the obdurate are the least easily *deterred* from their object; the persevering will not suffer themselves to be *discouraged* by particular failures; the resolute and self-confident will not be *disheartened* by trifling difficulties.

TO EXHORT, PERSUADE.

Exhort, in Latin *exhortor*, is compounded of *ex* and *hortor*, from the Greek ὤρται, perfect passive of ὄρω to excite or impel; *persuade* has the same signification as given under the head of *Conviction*.

Exhortation has more of impelling in it; *persuasion* more of drawing: a superiour *exhorts;* his words carry authority with them, and rouse to action;

> Their pinions still
> In loose librations stretch'd, to trust the void
> Trembling refuse, till down before them fly
> The parent guides, and chide, *exhort*, command.
> THOMSON.

A friend or an equal *persuades;* he wins and draws by the agreeableness or kindness of his expressions; 'Gay's friends *persuaded* him to sell his share in the South Sea stock, but he dreamed of dignity and splendour.'—JOHNSON. *Exhortations* are employed only in matters of duty or necessity; *persuasions* are employed in matters of pleasure or convenience.

TO PERSUADE, ENTICE, PREVAIL UPON.

Persuade (*v. Conviction*) and entice (*v. To allure*) are employed to express different means to the same end · namely, that of drawing any one to a thing: one *persuades* a person by means of words; one *entices* him either by words or actions; one may *persuade* either to a good or bad thing; 'I beseech you let me have so much credit with you as to *persuade* you to communicate any doubt or scruple which occur to you, before you suffer them to make too deep an impression upon you.'—CLARENDON. One *entices* commonly to that which is bad;

> If gaming does an aged sire *entice*,
> Then my young master swiftly learns the vice.
> DRYDEN.

One uses arguments to *persuade*, and arts to *entice*.

Persuade and *entice* comprehend either the means or the end or both: *prevail upon* comprehends no more than the end: we may *persuade* without *prevailing upon*, and we may *prevail upon* without *persuading*. Many will turn a deaf ear to all our *persuasions*, and will not be *prevailed upon*, although *persuaded*: on the other hand, we may be *prevailed upon* by the force of remonstrance, authority, and the like; and in this case we are *prevailed upon* without being *persuaded*. We should never *persuade* another to do that which we are not willing to do ourselves; credulous or good-natured people are easily *prevailed upon* to do things which tend to their own injury; 'Herod, hearing of Agrippa's arrival in Upper Asia, went thither to him and *prevailed* with him to accept an invitation.'—PRIDEAUX.

DELIGHTFUL, CHARMING.

Delightful is applied either to material or spiritual objects; *charming* mostly to objects of sense.

When they both denote the pleasure of the sense, *delightful* is not so strong an expression as *charming*: a prospect may be *delightful* or *charming*; but the latter raises to a degree that carries the senses away captive.

Of musick we should rather say that it was *charming* than *delightful*, as it acts on the senses in so powerful a manner; 'Nothing can be more magnificent than the figure Jupiter makes in the first Iliad, nor more *charming* than that of Venus in the first Æneid.'—ADDISON. On the other hand, we should with more propriety speak of a *delightful* employment to relieve distress, or a *delightful* spectacle to see a family living together in love and harmony; 'Though there are several of those wild scenes that are more *delightful* than any artificial shows, yet we find the works of nature still more pleasant the more they resemble those of art.'—ADDISON.

BECOMING, COMELY, GRACEFUL.

Becoming, *v. Becoming*, *decent*; and *comely*, or *come like*, signifies coming or appearing as one would have it; *graceful* signifies full of *grace*.

These epithets are employed to mark in general what is agreeable to the eye. *Becoming* denotes less than *comely*, and this less than *graceful*: nothing can be *comely* or *graceful* which is *unbecoming*; although many things are *becoming* which are neither *comely* nor *graceful*.

Becoming respects the decorations of the person, and the exteriour deportment; *comely* respects natural embellishments; *graceful* natural or artificial accomplishments: manner is *becoming*; figure is *comely*; air, figure, or attitude is *graceful*.

Becoming is relative; it depends on taste and opinion; on accordance with the prevailing sentiments or particular circumstances of society; *comely* and *graceful* are absolute; they are qualities felt and acknowledged by all.

What is *becoming* is confined to no rank; the highest and the lowest have, alike, the opportunity of doing or being that which *becomes* their station; 'The care of doing nothing *unbecoming* has accompanied the greatest minds to their last moments. Thus Cæsar gathered his robe about him that he might not fall in a manner *unbecoming* of himself.'—SPECTATOR. What is *comely* is seldom associated with great refinement and culture; 'The *comeliness* of person, and the decency of behaviour, add infinite weight to what is pronounced by any one.'—SPECTATOR. What is *graceful* is rarely to be discovered apart from high rank, noble birth, or elevation of character; 'To make the acknowledgment of a fault in the highest manner *graceful*, it is lucky when the circumstances of the offender place him above any ill consequences from the resentment of the person offended.'—STEELE.

BEAUTIFUL, FINE, HANDSOME, PRETTY.

Beautiful, or full of *beauty*, in French *beauté*, comes from *beau*, *belle*, in Latin *bellus* fair, and *benus* or *bonus* good; *fine*, in French *fin*, German *fein*, &c. not improbably comes from the Greek φαινος bright, splendid, and φαίνω to appear, because what is *fine* is by distinction clear; *handsome*, from the word *hand*, denotes a species of *beauty* in the body, as *handy* denotes its agility and skill; *pretty*, in Saxon *praete* adorned, German *prächtig*, Swedish *präktig* splendid, is connected with our words parade and pride.

Of these epithets, which denote what is pleasing to the eye, *beautiful* conveys the strongest meaning; it marks the possession of that in its fullest extent, of which the other terms denote the possession in part only. *Fineness*, *handsomeness*, and *prettiness* are to *beauty* as parts to a whole.

When taken in relation to persons, a woman is *beautiful*, who in feature and complexion possesses a grand assemblage of graces; a woman is *fine*, who with a striking figure unites shape and symmetry; a women is *handsome* who has good features, and *pretty* if with symmetry of feature be united delicacy.

The *beautiful* is determined by fixed rules; it admits of no excess or defect; it comprehends regularity, proportion, and a due distribution of colour, and every particular which can engage the attention; the *fine* must be coupled with grandeur, majesty, and strength of figure; it is incompatible with that which is small; a little woman can never be *fine*; the *handsome* is a general assemblage of what is agreeable; it is marked by no particular characteristick, but the absence of all deformity.

Prettiness is always coupled with simplicity, it is incompatible with that which is large; a tall woman with masculine features cannot be *pretty*; '"Indeed, my dear," says she, "you make me mad sometimes, so you do, with the silly way you have of treating me like a *pretty* idiot."'—STEELE.

Beauty will always have its charms; they are, however, but attractions for the eye; they please and awaken ardent sentiments for a while; but the possessor must have something else to give her claims to lasting regard. This is, however, seldom the case. Providence has dealt out his gifts with a more even hand. Neither the *beautiful*, nor the *fine* woman have in general those durable attractions which belong either to the *handsome* or the *pretty*, who with a less inimitable tint of complexion, a less unerring proportion in the limbs, a less precise symmetry of feature, are frequently possessed of a sweetness of countenance; a vivacity in the eye, and a grace in the manner, that wins the beholder and inspires affection.

Beauty is peculiarly a female perfection; in the male sex it is rather a defect; a *beautiful* man will not be respected, because he cannot be respectable. The possession of *beauty* deprives him of his manly characteristicks; boldness and energy of mind; strength and robustness of limb. But though a man may not be *beautiful* or *pretty*, he may be *fine* or *handsome*; 'A *handsome* fellow immediately alarms jealous husbands, and every thing that looks young or gay turns their thoughts upon their wives.'—ADDISON. The same observation does not apply to the brute creation; 'It is observed among birds that nature has lavished all her ornaments upon the male, who very often appears in a most *beautiful* head-dress.'—ADDISON.

When relating to other objects, *beautiful*, *fine*, *pretty*, have a strong analogy.

With respect to the objects of nature, the *beautiful* is displayed in the works of creation, and wherever it appears it is marked by elegance, variety, harmony proportion; but above all by that softness, which is peculiar to female *beauty;* 'There is nothing that makes its way more directly to the soul than *beauty*, which immediately diffuses a secret satisfaction and complacency through the imagination.'—ADDISON.

The *fine* on the contrary is associated with the grand, and the *pretty* with the simple. The sky presents either a *beautiful* aspect, or a *fine* aspect; but not a *pretty* aspect.

A rural scene is *beautiful* when it unites richness and diversity of natural objects with superiour cultivation; it is *fine* when it presents the bolder and more impressive features of nature, consisting of rocks and mountains; it is *pretty*, when, divested of all that is extraordinary, it presents a smiling view of nature in the gay attire of shrubs, and many-coloured flowers, and verdant meadows, and luxuriant fields.

Beautiful sentiments have much in them to interest the affections, as well as the understanding; they make a vivid impression; *fine* sentiments mark an elevated mind and a loftiness of conception; they occupy the understanding, and afford scope for reflection; they make a strong impression; 'When in ordinary discourse, we say a man has a *fine* head, a long head, or a good head, we express ourselves metaphorically, and speak in relation to his understanding; whereas, when we say of a woman, she has a *fine*, a long, or a good head, we speak only in relation to her commode.' —ADDISON. *Pretty* ideas are but pleasing associations or combinations that only amuse for the time being, without producing any lasting impression. In the same manner expressions are termed *pretty;* 'An innocent creature, who would start at the name of strumpet, may think it *pretty* to be called a mistress.' —SPECTATOR.

We may speak of a *beautiful* poem, although not a *beautiful* tragedy; but a *fine* tragedy, and a *pretty* comedy.

Imagery may be *beautiful* and *fine*, but seldom *pretty*.

The celestial bodies, revolving with so much regularity in their orbits, and displaying so much brilliancy of light, are *beautiful* objects. The display of an army drawn up in battle array; the neatness of the men; the order, complexity, and variety of their movements, and the precision in their discipline, afford a *fine* spectacle. An assemblage of children imitating in their amusements the system and regularity of more serious employments, and preserving at the same time the playfulness of childhood, is a *pretty* sight.

Handsome is applied to some objects in the sense of ample or liberal, as a *handsome* fortune, or *handsome* treatment; 'A letter dated Sept. acquaints me that the writer, being resolved to try his fortune, had fasted all that day, and that he might be sure of dreaming upon something at night, procured a *handsome* slice of bride cake.'—SPECTATOR.

FINE, DELICATE, NICE.

It is remarkable of the word *fine* (*v. Beautiful*), that it is equally applicable to large and small objects; *delicate*, in Latin *delicatus*, from *deliciæ* delights, and *delicio* to allure, is applied only to small objects. *Fine* in the natural sense denotes smallness in general. *Delicate* denotes a degree of *fineness* that is agreeable to the taste. Thread is said to be *fine* as opposed to the coarse and thick; silk is said to be *delicate*, when to *fineness* of texture it adds softness. The texture of a spider's web is remarkable for its *fineness;* that of the ermine's fur is remarkable for its *delicacy*. In writing, all up-strokes must be *fine;* but in superiour writing they will be *delicately fine*. When applied to colours, the *fine* is coupled with the grand and the strong; *delicate* with what is minute, soft, and fair: blue and red may be *fine* colours; and white and pink *delicate* colours. The tulip is reckoned one of the *finest* flowers; the white moss-rose is a *delicate* flower. A *fine* painter delineates with boldness; but the artist who has a *delicate* taste, throws *delicate* touches into the grandest delineations.

In their moral application these terms admit of the same distinction; the *fine* approaches either to the strong or to the weak; 'Every thing that results from nature alone lies out of the province of instruction; and no rules that I know of will serve to give a *fine* form, a *fine* voice, or even those *fine* feelings, which are among the first properties of an actor.'—CUMBERLAND. The *delicate* is a high degree of the *fine*, as a *fine* thought, which may be lofty; or a *fine* feeling, which is acute and tender; and *delicate* feeling, which exceeds the former in *fineness;*

Chief, lovely Spring! in thee and thy soft scenes
The smiling God is seen; while water, earth,
And air attest his bounty, which exalts
The brute creation to this *finer* thought.—THOMSON

'Under this head of elegance I reckon those *delicate* and regular works of art, as elegant buildings or pieces of furniture.'—BURKE. The French use their word *fin* only in the latter sense, of acuteness, and apply it merely to the thoughts and designs of men, answering either to our word *subtle*, as *un homme fin*, or *neat*, as *une satire fine*.

Delicate is said of that which is agreeable to the sense and the taste; *nice* to what is agreeable to the appetite: the former is a term of refinement: the latter o. epicurism and sensual indulgence. The *delicate* affords pleasure only to those whose thoughts and desires are purified from what is gross; the *nice* affords pleasure to the young, ignorant, and the sensual: thus *delicate* food, *delicate* colours, *delicate* shapes and form, are always acceptable to the cultivated; a meal, a show, a colour, and the like, will be *nice* to a child, which suits its appetite, or meets its fancy.

When used in a moral application, *nice*, which is taken in a good sense, approaches nearer to the signification of *delicate*. A person may be said to have a *delicate* ear in music, whose ear is offended with the smallest discordance; he may be said to have a *nice* taste or judgement in music, who scientifically discriminates the beauties and defects of different pieces. A person is *delicate* in his choice, who is guided by taste and feeling; he is *nice* in his choice, who adheres to a strict rule.

A point in question may be either *delicate* or *nice;* it is *delicate*, as it is likely to touch the tender feelings of any party; it is *nice*, as it involves contrary interests, and becomes difficult of determination. There are *delicacies* of behaviour which are learned by good breeding, but which minds of a refined cast are naturally alive to, without any particular learning; 'The commerce in the conjugal state is so *delicate* that it is impossible to prescribe rules for it.'—STEELE. There are *niceties* in the law, which none but men of superiour intellect can properly enter into and discriminate; 'The highest point of good breeding, if any one can hit it, is to show a very *nice* regard to your own dignity, and, with that in your heart, to express your value for the man above you.'—STEELE.

DAINTY, DELICACY.

These terms, which are in vogue among epicures, have some shades of difference in their signification not altogether undeserving of notice.

Dainty, from *dain*, *deign*, and the Latin *dignus* worthy, signifies the thing that is of worth or value; it is of course applied only to such things as have a superiour value in the estimation of epicures; and consequently conveys a more positive meaning than *delicacy:* inasmuch as a *dainty* may be that which is extremely *delicate*, a *delicacy* is sometimes a species of *dainty;* but there are many *delicacies* which are altogether suited to the most *delicate* appetite, that are neither costly nor rare, two qualities which are almost inseparable from a *dainty:* those who indulge themselves freely in *dainties* and *delicacies* scarcely know what it is to eat with an appetite; but those who are temperate in their use of the enjoyments of life will be enabled to derive pleasure from ordinary objects;

My landlord's cellar stocked with beer and ale,
Instantly brings the choicest liquors out,
Whether we ask'd for home-brew'd or for stout,
For mead or cider; or with *dainties* fed,
Ring for a flask or two of white or red.—SWIFT.

She turns, on hospitable thoughts intent,
What choice to choose for *delicacy* best —MILTON.

GRACE, CHARM.

Grace is altogether corporeal; *charm* is either corporeal or mental; the *grace* qualifies the action of the body; 'Savage's method of life particularly qualified him for conversation, of which he knew how to practise all the *graces*.'—Johnson. The *charm* is an inherent quality in the body itself;

Music has *charms* to sooth the savage breast.
Congreve.

A lady moves, dances, and walks with *grace;* the *charms* of her person are equal to those of her mind.

GRACEFUL, COMELY, ELEGANT.

A *graceful* figure is rendered so by the deportment of the body. A *comely* figure has that in itself which pleases the eye. *Gracefulness* results from nature, improved by art; 'The first who approached her was a youth of *graceful* presence and courtly air, but dressed in a richer habit than had ever been seen in Arcadia.'—Steele. *Comeliness* is mostly the work of nature; 'Isidas the son of Phœbidas was at this time in the bloom of his youth, and very remarkable for the *comeliness* of his person.'—Addison. It is possible to acquire *gracefulness* by the aid of the dancing-master, but for a *comely* form we are indebted to nature aided by circumstances. *Grace* is a quality pleasing to the eye; but *elegance*, from the Latin *eligo*, *electus*, select and choice, is a quality of a higher nature, that inspires admiration; *elegant* is applicable, like *graceful*, to the motion of the body, or, like *comely*, to the person, and is extended in its meaning also to language and even to dress; 'The natural progress of the works of men is from rudeness to convenience, from convenience to *elegance*, and from *elegance* to nicety.'—Johnson. A person's step is *graceful;* his air or his movements are *elegant*.

Grace is in some degree a relative quality; the *gracefulness* of an action depends on its suitability to the occasion; *elegance* is a positive quality; it is, properly speaking, beauty in regard to the exteriour of the person; an *elegance* of air and manner is the consequence not only of superiour birth and station, but also of superiour natural endowments.

AWKWARD, CLUMSY.

Awkward, in Saxon *æwerd*, compounded of *æ* or *a* adversative and *ward*, from the Teutonic *währen* to see or look, that is, looking the opposite way, or being in an opposite direction, as *toward* signifies looking the same way, or being in the same direction; *clumsy*, from the same source as *clump* and *lump*, in German *lumpisch*, denotes the quality of heaviness and unseemliness.

These epithets denote what is contrary to rule and order, in form or manner. *Awkward* respects outward deportment; *clumsy* the shape and make of the object: a person has an *awkward* gait, or is *clumsy* in his whole person.

Awkwardness is the consequence of bad education; *clumsiness* is mostly a natural defect. Young recruits are *awkward* in marching, and *clumsy* in their manual labour.

They may be both employed figuratively in the same sense, and sometimes in relation to the same objects: when speaking of *awkward* contrivances, or *clumsy* contrivances, the latter expresses the idea more strongly than the former; 'Montaigne had many *awkward* imitators, who, under the notion of writing with the fire and freedom of this lively old Gascon, have fallen into confused rhapsodies and uninteresting egotisms.'—Warton. 'All the operations of the Greeks in sailing were *clumsy* and unskilful.'—Robertson.

AWKWARD CROSS, UNTOWARD, CROOKED, FROWARD, PERVERSE.

Awkward, *v. Awkward;* *cross*, from the noun *cross*, implies the quality of being like a *cross;* *untoward* signifies the reverse of *toward* (*v. Awkward*): *crooked* signifies the quality of resembling a *crook;* *froward*, that is, *from ward*, signifies running a contrary direction; *perverse*, Latin *perversus*, participle of *perverto*, compounded of *per* and *verto*, signifies turned aside.

Awkward, *cross*, *untoward*, and *crooked* are used as epithets in relation to the events of life or the disposition of the mind; *froward* and *perverse* respect only the disposition of the mind. *Awkward* circumstances are apt to embarrass: *cross* circumstances to pain; *crooked* and *untoward* circumstances to defeat. What is *crooked* springs from a *perverted* judgement; what is *untoward* is independent of human control. In our intercourse with the world there are always little *awkward* incidents arising, which a person's good sense and good nature will enable him to pass over without disturbing the harmony of society; 'It is an *awkward* thing for a man to print in defence of his own work against a chimera: you know not who or what you fight against.'—Pope. It is the lot of every one in his passage through life to meet with *cross* accidents that are calculated to ruffle the temper; but he proves himself to be the wisest whose serenity is not so easily dis turbed; 'Some are indeed stopped in their career by a sudden shock of calamity, or diverted to a different direction by the *cross* impulse of some violent passion.'—Johnson. A *crooked* policy obstructs the prosperity of individuals, as well as of states;

There are who can, by potent magic spells,
Bend to their *crooked* purpose nature's laws.
Milton.

Many men are destined to meet with severe trials in the frustration of their dearest hopes, by numberless *untoward* events which call for the exercise of patience; in this case the Christian can prove to himself and others the infinite value of his faith and doctrine;

The rabbins write when any Jew
Did make to God or man a vow,
Which afterward he found *untoward*,
Or stubborn to be kept, or too hard:
Any three other Jews o' th' nation
Might free him from the obligation.—Hudibras.

When used with regard to the disposition of the mind, *awkward* expresses less than *froward*, and *froward* less than *perverse*. *Awkwardness* is for the most part an habitual frailty of temper; it includes certain weaknesses and particularities, pertinaciously adhered to. Sometimes it is a temporary feeling that is taken up on a particular occasion;

A kind and constant riend
To all that regularly offend,
But was implacable and *awkward*,
To all that interlop'd and hawker'd.—Hudibras.

Crossness is a partial irritation resulting from the state of the humours, physical and mental. *Frowardness* and *perversity* lie in the will: a *froward* temper is capricious; it wills or wills not to please itself without regard to others· 'To fret and repine at every disappointment of our wishes is to discover the temper of *froward* children.'—Blair. *Perversity* lies deeper; taking root in the heart, it assumes the shape of malignity: a *perverse* temper is really wicked; it likes or dislikes by the rule of contradiction to another's will; 'Interference of interest, or *perversity* of disposition, may occasionally lead individuals to oppose, even to hate, the upright and the good.'—Blair. *Untowardness* lies in the principles; it runs counter to the wishes and counsels of another; 'Christ had to deal with a most *untoward* and stubborn generation.'—Blair.

An *awkward* temper is connected with self-sufficiency; it shelters itself under the sanction of what is apparently reasonable; it requires management and indulgence in dealing with it. *Crossness* and *frowardness* are peculiar to children; indiscriminate indulgence of the rising will engenders those diseases of the mind, which if fostered too long in the breast become incorrigible by any thing but a powerful sense of religion. *Perversity* is, however, but too commonly the result of a vicious habit, which imbitters the happiness of all who have the misfortune of coming in collision with it. *Untowardness* is also another fruit of these evil tempers. A *froward* child becomes an *untoward* youth, who turns a deaf ear to all the admonitions of an afflicted parent.

CAPTIOUS, CROSS, PEEVISH, PETULANT, FRETFUL.

Captious, in Latin *captiosus*, from *capio*, signifies taking or treating in an offensive manner; *cross*, after the noun *cross*, marks the temper which resembles a *cross;* *peevish*, probably changed from *beeish*, signifies easily provoked, and ready to sting like a bee; *fretful*, from the word *fret*, signifies full of *fretting; fret*, which is in Saxon *freotan*, comes from the Latin *fricatus*, participle of *frico* to wear away with rubbing;

petulant, in Latin *petulans*, from *peto* to seek, signifies seeking or catching up.

All these terms indicate an unamiable working and expression of temper. *Captious* marks a readiness to be offended: *cross* indicates a readiness to offend: *peevish* expresses a strong degree of *crossness*: *fretful* a complaining impatience: *petulant* a quick or sudden impatience. *Captiousness* is the consequence of misplaced pride; *crossness* of ill-humour; *peevishness* and *fretfulness* of a painful irritability; *petulance* is either the result of a naturally hasty temper or of a sudden irritability; adults are most prone to be *captious*; they have frequently a self-importance which is in perpetual danger of being offended; '*Captiousness* and jealousy are easily offended; and to him who studiously looks for an affront, every mode of behaviour will supply it.'—Johnson. An undisciplined temper, whether in young or old, will manifest itself on certain occasions by *cross* looks and words towards those with whom they come in connexion. Spoiled children are most apt to be *peevish*; they are seldom thwarted in any of their unreasonable desires, without venting their ill-humour by an irritating and offending action;

I was so good-humour'd, so cheerful and gay,
My heart was as light as a feather all day.
But now I so *cross* and so *peevish* am grown,
So strangely uneasy as never was known.—Byron.

'*Peevish* displeasure, and suspicions of mankind, are apt to persecute those who withdraw themselves altogether from the haunts of men.'—Blair. Sickly children are most liable to *fretfulness*; their unpleasant feelings vent themselves in a mixture of crying, complaints, and *crossness*; 'By indulging this *fretful* temper, you both aggravate the uneasiness of age, and you alienate those on whose affections much of your comfort depends.'—Blair. The young and ignorant are most apt to be *petulant* when contradicted; 'It was excellently said of that philosopher, that there was a wall or parapet of teeth set in our mouth, to restrain the *petulancy* of our words.'—B. Jonson.

BENT, CURVED, CROOKED, AWRY.

Bent, from *bend*, in Saxon *bendan*, is a variation of *wind*, in the sea phraseology *wend*, in German *winden*, &c. from the Hebrew ענך to wind or turn; *curved* is in Latin *curvus*, and in Greek *κυρτὸς*; *crooked*, *v. Awkward*; *awry* is a variation of writhed.

Bent is here the generick term, all the rest are but modes of the *bent*.

What is *bent* is opposed to that which is straight; things may therefore be *bent* to any degree, but when *curved* they are *bent* only to a small degree; when *crooked* they are *bent* to a great degree. A stick is *bent* any way; it is *curved* by being *bent* one specifick way; it is *crooked* by being *bent* different ways.

Things may be *bent* by accident or design;

And when too closely press'd, she quits the ground,
From her *bent* bow she sends a backward wound.
Dryden.

Things are *curved* by design, or according to some rule; 'Another thing observable in and from the spots is that they describe various paths or lines over the sun, sometimes straight, sometimes *curved* towards one pole of the sun.'—Derham. Things are *crooked*, by accident or in violation of some rule; 'It is the ennobling office of the understanding to correct the fallacious and mistaken reports of the senses, and to assure us that the staff in the water is straight, though our eye would tell us it is *crooked*.'—South. A stick is *bent* by the force of the hand; a line is *curved* so as to make a mathematical figure; it is *crooked* so as to lose all figure.

Awry marks a species of *crookedness*, but *crooked* is applied as an epithet, and *awry* is employed to characterize the action; hence we speak of a *crooked* thing and of sitting or standing *awry*;

Preventing fate directs the lance *awry*,
Which glancing only mark'd Achates' thigh.
Dryden.

BEND, BENT.

Both abstract nouns from the verb to *bend*: the one to express its proper, and the other its moral application: a stick has a *bend*; the mind has a *bent*;

His coward lips did from their colour fly,
And that same eye whose *bend* does awe the world,
Did lose its lustre.—Shakspeare.

'The soul does not always care to be in the same *bent*. The faculties relieve one another by turns, and receive an additional pleasure from the novelty of those objects about which they are conversant.'—Addison.

A *bend* in any thing that should be straight is a defect; a *bent* of the inclination that is not sanctioned by religion is detrimental to a person's moral character and peace of mind. For a vicious *bend* in a natural body there are various remedies; but nothing will cure a corrupt *bent* of the will except religion.

TURN, BENT.

These words are only compared here in the figurative application, as respects the state of a person's inclination: the *turn* is therefore, as before, indefinite as to the degree; it is the first rising inclination: *bent* is a positively strong *turn*, a confirmed inclination; a child may early discover a *turn* for musick or drawing; but the real *bent* of his genius is not known until he has made a proficiency in his education, and has had an opportunity of trying different things: it may be very well to indulge the *turn* of mind; it is of great importance to follow the *bent* of the mind as far as respects arts and sciences; 'I need not tell you how a man of Mr. Rowe's *turn* entertained me.'—Pope. 'I know the *bent* of your present attention is directed towards the eloquence of the bar.'—Melmouth (*Letters of Pliny*.)

TO TURN, WIND, WHIRL, TWIRL, WRITHE

To *turn* (*v. To turn*) is, as before, the generick term; the rest are but modes of *turning*;

How has this poison lost its wonted ways?
It should have burnt its passage, not have linger'd
In the blind labyrinths and crooked *turnings*
Of human composition.—Dryden.

To *wind* is to *turn* a thing round, or to move in a regular and circular manner;

The tracts of Providence like rivers *wind*,
Here run before us, there retreat behind.—Higgins.

To *whirl* is to *turn* a thing round in a violent manner;

Man is but man, inconstant still, and various
There 's no to-morrow in him like to-day;
Perhaps the atoms, *whirling* in his brain,
Make him think honestly this present hour;
The next, a swarm of base, ungrateful thoughts
May mount aloft.—Dryden.

To *twirl* is to *turn* a thing round in any irregular and unmeaning way; 'I had used my eye to such a quick succession of objects, that, in the most precipitate *twirl*, I could catch a sentence out of each author.'—Steele. To *writhe* is to *turn* round in convolutions within itself. A worm seldom moves in a straight line; it is, therefore, always *turning*: and sometimes it *writhes* in agony;

Dying, he bellowed out his dread remorse,
And *writh'd* with seeming anguish of the soul.
Shirley.

TO TURN, BEND, TWIST, DISTORT, WRING, WREST, WRENCH.

Turn, in French *tourner*, comes from the Greek *τορνέω* to turn, and *τόρνος* a turner's wheel; *bend*, *v. Bend*; *twist*, in Saxon *getwisan*, German *zeyen* to double, comes from *zwey* two; *distort*, in Latin *distortus*, participle of *distorqueo*, compounded of *dis* and *torqueo*, signifies to turn violently aside.

To *turn* signifies in general to put a thing out of its place in an uneven line;

Yet still they find a future task remain,
To *turn* the soil and break the clods again.
Dryden.

To *bend*, and the rest, are species of *turning:* we *turn* a thing by moving it from one point to another; thus we *turn* the earth over: to *bend* is simply to change its direction; thus a stick is *bent*, or a body may *bend* its direction to a particular point;

> Some to the house,
> The fold and dairy, hungry, *bend* their flight.
> THOMSON.

To *twist* is to *bend* many times, to make many *turns;*

> But let not on thy hook the tortur'd worm,
> Convulsive, *twist* in agonizing folds.—THOMSON.

To *distort* is to *turn* or *bend* out of the right course; thus the face is *distorted* in convulsions, or the looks may be *distorted* from passion or otherwise:

> We saw their stern, *distorted* looks from far.
> DRYDEN.

To *wring* is to *twist* with violence; thus linen which has been wetted is *wrung;* 'Our bodies are unhappily made the weapons of sin; therefore we must, by an austere course of duty, first *wring* these weapons out of its hands.'—SOUTH. To *wrest* or *wrench* is to separate from a body by means of *twisting;* thus a stick may be *wrested* out of the hand, or a hinge *wrenched* off the door;

> *Wresting* the text to the old giant's sense,
> That heaven once more must suffer violence.
> DENHAM.

> *Wrench* his sword from him.—SHAKSPEARE.

> She *wrench'd* the jav'lin with her dying hands.
> DRYDEN.

The same distinction holds good in the moral or extended application: a person is *turned* from his design; 'Strong passion dwells on that object which has seized and taken possession of the soul; it is too much occupied and filled by it to *turn* its view aside.'—BLAIR. The will of a person is *bent*, or the thoughts are *bent*, towards an object; 'Men will not *bend* their wits to examine whether things wherewith they have been accustomed be good or evil.'—HOOKER. The meaning of words is *twisted*, or by a stronger expression *distorted*, to serve a purpose; 'Something must be *distorted*, besides the intent of the divine Inditer.'—PEACHAM. A confession is *wrung*, or by a stronger expression *wrested*, from a person; 'To *wring* this sentence, to *wrest* thereby out of men's hands the knowledge of God's doctrines, is without all reason.'—ASCHAM.

TO EXACT, EXTORT.

Exact, in Latin *exactus*, participle of *exigo*, to drive out, signifies the exercise of simple force; but *extort*, from *extortus*, participle of *extorqueo* to wring out, marks the exercise of unusual force. In application, therefore, the term *exact* signifies to demand with force; it is commonly an act of injustice: to *extort* signifies to get with violence, it is an act of tyranny. The collector of the revenue *exacts* when he gets from the people more than he is authorized to take: an arbitrary prince *extorts* from his conquered subjects whatever he can grasp at. In the figurative sense, deference, obedience, applause, and admiration are *exacted;* 'While to the established church is given that protection and support which the interests of religion render proper and due, yet no rigid conformity is *exacted*.'—BLAIR. A confession, an acknowledgment, a discovery, and the like, are *extorted;* 'If I err in believing that the souls of men are immortal, not while I live would I wish to have this delightful errour *extorted* from me.'—STEELE.

TO CHARM, ENCHANT, FASCINATE, ENRAPTURE, CAPTIVATE.

Charm has the same signification as explained under the head of *Attractions; enchant* is compounded of *en* and *chant*, signifying to act upon as by the power of *chanting* or musick; *fascinate*, in Latin *fascino*, Greek *βασκαίνω*, signified originally among the ancients a species of witchcraft, performed by the eyes or the tongue; *enrapture*, compounded of *en* and *rapture*, signifies to put into a *rapture:* and *rapture*, from the Latin *rapio* to seize or carry away, signifies the state of being carried away; whence to *enrapture* signifies to put into that state; *captivate*, in Latin *captivatus*, participle of *captivo*, from *capio* to take, signifies to take as it were, prisoner.

The idea of an irresistible influence is common to these terms; *charm* expresses a less powerful effect than *enchant;* a *charm* is simply a magical verse used by magicians and sorcerers: *incantation* or *enchantment* is the use not only of verses but of any mysterious ceremonies, to produce a given effect.

To *charm* and *enchant* in this sense denote an operation by means of words or motions; to *fascinate* denotes an operation by means of the eyes or tongue: a person is *charmed* and *enchanted* voluntarily; he is *fascinated* involuntarily: the superstitious have always had recourse to *charms* and *enchantments*, for the purpose of allaying the passions of love or hatred; the Greeks believed that the malignant influence passed by *fascination* from the eyes or tongues of envious persons, which infected the ambient air, and through that medium penetrated and corrupted the bodies of animals and other things.

Charms and *enchantments* are performed by persons; *fascinations* are performed by animals: the former have always some supposed good in view; the latter have always a mischievous tendency: there are persons who pretend to *charm* away the tooth-ache, or other pains of the body: some serpents are said to have a *fascinating* power in their eyes, by which they can kill the animals on whom they have fixed them.

When these terms are taken in the improper sense, *charm, enchant*, and *fascinate* are employed to describe moral as well as natural operations: *enrapture* and *captivate* describe effects on the mind only: to *charm, enchant, fascinate*, and *enrapture* designate the effects produced by physical and moral objects; *captivate* designates those produced by physical objects only: we may be *charmed*, or *enchanted*, or *enraptured*, with what we see, hear, and learn; we may be *fascinated* with what we see or learn; we are *captivated* only with what we see: a fine voice, a fine prospect, or a fine sentiment, *charms, enchants*, or *enraptures;* a fine person *fascinates*, or the conversation of a person is *fascinating;* beauty, with all its accompaniments, *captivates*. When applied to the same objects, *charm, enchant*, and *enrapture* rise in sense: what *charms* produces sweet but not tumultuous emotions; in this sense musick in general *charms* a musical ear;

> So fair a landscape *charm'd* the wond'ring knight.
> GILBERT WEST.

What *enchants* rouses the feelings to a high pitch of tumultuous delight; in this manner the musician is *enchanted* with the finest compositions of Handel when performed by the best masters; or a lover of the country is *enchanted* with Swiss scenery;

> Trust not too much to that *enchanting* face:
> Beauty 's a *charm*, but soon the *charm* will pass.
> DRYDEN.

To *enrapture* is to absorb all the affections of the soul; it is of too violent a nature to be either lasting or frequent: it is a term applicable only to persons of an enthusiastick character, or to particularly powerful excitements;

> He play'd so sweetly, and so sweetly sung,
> That on each note th' *enraptur'd* audience hung.
> SIR WM. JONES.

What *charms, enchants*, and *enraptures* only affords pleasure for the time; what *fascinates* and *captivates* rivets the mind to the object: the former three convey the idea of a voluntary movement of the mind, as in the proper sense; the two latter imply a species of forcible action on the mind, which deprives a person of his free agency; the passions, as well as the affections, are called into play while the understanding is passive, which, with regard to *fascinate*, may be to the injury of the subject: a loose woman may have it in her power to *fascinate*, and a modest woman to *captivate;* 'One would think there was some kind of *fascination* in the eyes of a large circle of people when darting altogether upon one person.'—ADDISON.

> Her form the patriot's robe conceal'd,
> With studied blandishments she bow'd,
> And drew the *captivated* crowd.—MOORE.

TO ENSLAVE, CAPTIVATE.

To *enslave* is to bring into a state of *slavery;* to *captivate* is to make a *captive.*

There is as much difference between these terms as between *slavery* and *captivity:* he who is a *slave* is fettered both body and mind; he who is a *captive* is only constrained as to his body: hence to *enslave* is always taken in the bad sense; *captivate* mostly in the good sense: *enslave* is employed literally or figuratively; *captivate* only figuratively: we may be *enslaved* by persons, or by our gross passions; 'The will was then (before the fall) subordinate but not *enslaved* to the understanding.'—SOUTH. We are *captivated* by the charms or beauty of an object; 'Men should beware of being *captivated* by a kind of savage philosophy, women by a thoughtless gallantry.' —ADDISON.

ECSTASY, RAPTURE, TRANSPORT.

There is a strong resemblance in the meaning and application of these words. They all express an extraordinary elevation of the spirits, or an excessive tension of the mind; *ecstasy* marks a passive state, from the Greek ἔκϛασις and ἐξίϛημι to stand, or be out of oneself, out of one's mind. *Rapture*, from the Latin *rapio* to seize or carry away; and *transport*, from *trans* and *porto* to carry beyond oneself, rather designate an active state, a violent impulse with which the mind hurries itself forward. *Ecstasy* and *rapture* are always pleasurable, or arise from pleasurable causes: *transport* respects either pleasurable or painful feelings: joy occasions *ecstasies* or *raptures:* joy and anger have their *transports.*

An *ecstasy* benumbs the faculties; it will take away the power of speech and often of thought: it is commonly occasioned by sudden and unexpected events: *rapture*, on the other hand, often invigorates the powers, and calls them into action; it frequently arises from deep thought: the former is common to all persons of ardent feelings, but more particularly to children, ignorant people, or to such as have not their feelings under control;

> What followed was all *ecstasy* and trance:
> Immortal pleasures round my swimming eyes did dance.—DRYDEN.

Rapture, on the contrary, is applicable to persons of superiour minds, and to circumstances of peculiar importance;

> By swift degrees the love of nature works,
> And warms the bosom, till at last sublim'd
> To *rapture* and enthusiastick heat,
> We feel the present Deity.—THOMSON.

Transports are but sudden bursts of passion, which generally lead to intemperate actions, and are seldom indulged even on joyous occasions except by the volatile and passionate: a reprieve from the sentence of death will produce an *ecstasy* of delight in the pardoned criminal. Religious contemplation is calculated to produce holy *raptures* in a mind strongly imbued with pious zeal: in *transports* of rage men have committed enormities which have cost them bitter tears of repentance ever after. The word *transport* is however used in the higher style in a good sense;

> When all thy mercies, O my God!
> My rising soul surveys,
> *Transported* with the view, I'm lost
> In wonder, love, and praise.—ADDISON.

TO ATTRACT, ALLURE, INVITE, ENGAGE.

Attract, in Latin *attractum*, participle of *attraho*, compounded of *at* or *ad* and *traho*, signifies to draw towards; *allure*, *v. To allure; invite*, in French *inviter*, Latin *invito*, compounded of *in* privative and *vito* to avoid, signifies the contrary of avoiding, that is, to seek or ask; *engage*, compounded of *en* or *in* and the French *gage* a pledge, signifies to bind as by a pledge.

That is *attractive* which draws the thoughts towards itself; that is *alluring* which awakens desire; that is *inviting* which offers persuasion; that is *engaging* which takes possession of the mind. The attention is *attracted;* the senses are *allured;* the understanding is *invited;* the whole mind is *engaged.* A particular sound *attracts* the ear; the prospect of gratification *allures;* we are *invited* by advantages which offer; we are *engaged* by those which already accrue.

The person of a female is *attractive;* female beauty involuntarily draws all eyes towards itself; it awakens admiration; 'At this time of universal migration, when almost every one considerable enough to *attract* regard has retired into the country, I have often been tempted to inquire what happiness is to be gained by this stated secession.'—JOHNSON. The pleasures of society are *alluring;* they create in the receiver an eager desire for still farther enjoyment; but when too eagerly pursued they vanish in the pursuit, and leave the mind a prey to listless uneasiness: the weather is *inviting;* it seems to persuade the reluctant to partake of its refreshments; 'Seneca has attempted not only to pacify us in misfortune, but almost to *allure* us to it by representing it as necessary to the pleasures of the mind. He *invites* his pupil to calamity as the Syrens *allured* the passengers to their coasts, by promising that he shall return with increase of knowledge.'—JOHNSON. The manners of a person are *engaging;* they not only occupy the attention, but they lay hold of the affections; 'The present, whatever it be, seldom *engages* our attention so much as what is to come'—BLAIR.

ATTRACTIONS, ALLUREMENTS, CHARMS.

Attraction signifies the thing that attracts (*v. To attract*); *allurement* signifies the thing that *allures* (*v. To allure*); *charm*, from the Latin *carmen* a verse, signifies whatever acts by an irresistible influence, like poetry.

* Besides the synonymous signification which distinguishes these words, they are remarkable for the common property of being used only in the plural, when denoting the thing that *attracts*, *allures*, and *charms.* When applied to female endowments, or the influence of person on the heart: it seems that in *attractions* there is something natural; in *allurements* something artificial: in *charms* something moral and intellectual.

Attractions lead or draw; *allurements* win or entice: *charms* seduce or captivate. The human heart is always exposed to the power of female *attractions;* it is guarded with difficulty against the *allurements* of a coquette; it is incapable of resisting the united *charms* of body and mind.

Females are indebted for their *attractions* and *charms* to a happy conformation of features and figure, but they sometimes borrow their *allurements* from their toilet. *Attractions* consist of those ordinary graces which nature bestows on women with more or less liberality; they are the common property of the sex; 'This cestus was a fine party-coloured girdle, which, as Homer tells us, had all the *attractions* of the sex wrought into it.'—ADDISON. *Allurements* consist of those cultivated graces formed by the aid of a faithful looking-glass and the skilful hand of one anxious to please; 'How justly do I fall a sacrifice to sloth and luxury in the place where I first yielded to those *allurements* which seduced me to deviate from temperance and innocence.'—JOHNSON. *Charms* consist of those singular graces of nature which are granted as a rare and precious gift: they are the peculiar property of the individual possessor; 'Juno made a visit to Venus, the deity who presides over love, and begged of her as a particular favour, that she would lend her for a while those *charms* with which she subdued the hearts of gods and men.'—ADDISON.

Defects unexpectedly discovered tend to the diminution of *attractions; allurements* vanish when the artifice is discovered; *charms* lose their effect when time or habit have rendered them too familiar, so transitory is the influence of mere person. *Attractions* assail the heart and awaken the tender passion; *allurements* serve to complete the conquest, which will however be but of short duration if there be not more solid though less brilliant *charms* to substitute affection in the place of passion.

When applied as these terms may be to other objects besides the personal endowments of the female sex, *attractions* and *charms* express whatever is very amiable in themselves; *allurements* on the contrary whatever

* Vide Abbe Girard and Roubaud: "Attraits appas charmes."

is hateful and congenial to the baser propensities of human nature. A courtesan who was never possessed of *charms*, and has lost all personal *attractions*, may, by the *allurements* of dress and manners, aided by a thousand meretricious arts, still retain the wretched power of doing incalculable mischief.

An *attraction* springs from something remarkable and striking; it lies in the exteriour aspect, and awakens an interest towards itself: a *charm* acts by a secret, all-powerful, and irresistible impulse on the soul; it springs from an accordance of the object with the affections of the heart; it takes hold of the imagination, and awakens an enthusiasm peculiar to itself: an *allurement* acts on the senses; it flatters the passions; it enslaves the imagination. A musical society has *attractions* for one who is musically inclined; for musick has *charms* to soothe the troubled soul: fashionable society has too many *allurements* for youth, which are not easily withstood.

The musick, the eloquence of the preacher, or the crowds of hearers, are *attractions* for the occasional attendants at a place of worship: the society of cultivated persons, whose character and manners have been attempered by the benign influence of Christianity, possess peculiar *charms* for those who have a congeniality of disposition; the present lax and undisciplined age is however ill-fitted for the formation of such society, or the susceptibility of such *charms:* people are now more prone to yield to the *allurements* of pleasure and licentious gratification in their social intercourse. A military life has powerful *attractions* for adventurous minds; glory has irresistible *charms* for the ambitious: the *allurements* of wealth predominate in the minds of the great bulk of mankind.

TO ALLURE, TEMPT, SEDUCE, ENTICE, DECOY.

Allure is compounded of the intensive syllable *al* or *ad* and *lure*, in French *leurre*, in German *luder* a *lure* or bait, signifying to hold a bait in order to catch animals, and figuratively to present something to please the senses, or the understanding; *tempt*, in French *tenter*, Latin *tento* to try, comes from *tentus*, participle of *tendo* to stretch, signifying by efforts to impel to action; *seduce*, in French *seduire*, Latin *seduco*, is compounded of *se* apart and *duco* to lead, signifying to lead any one aside; *entice* is probably, *per metathesin*, changed from *incite; decoy* is compounded of the Latin *de* and *coy*, in Dutch *koy*, German, &c. *koi* a cage or enclosed place for birds, signifying to draw into any place for the purpose of getting them into one's power.

We are *allured* by the appearances of things; we are *tempted* by the words of persons as well as the appearances of things; we are *enticed* by persuasions: we are *seduced* or *decoyed* by the influence and false arts of others.

To *allure* and *tempt* are used either in a good or bad sense; *entice* sometimes in an indifferent, but mostly in a bad sense; *seduce* and *decoy* are always in a bad sense. The weather may *allure* us out of doors: the love of pleasures may *allure* us into indulgencies that afterward cause repentance; 'June 26, 1284, the rats and mice by which Hamelen was infested were *allured*, it is said, by a piper to a contiguous river, in which they were all drowned.'—Addison. We are sometimes *tempted* upon very fair grounds to undertake what turns out unfortunately in the end: our passions are our bitterest enemies; the devil uses them as instruments to *tempt* us to sin; 'In our time the poor are strongly *tempted* to assume the appearance of wealth.'—Johnson. When the wicked *entice* us to do evil, we should turn a deaf ear to their flattering representations: those who know what is right, and are determined to practice it, will not suffer themselves to be *enticed* into any irregularities; 'There was a particular grove which was called "the labyrinth of coquettes," where many were *enticed* to the chase, but few returned with purchase.'—Addison. Young men are frequently *seduced* by the company they keep; There is no kind of idleness by which we are so easily *seduced* as that which dignifies itself by the appearance of business.'—Johnson. Children are *decoyed* away by the evil-minded, who wish to get them into their possession; 'I have heard of barbarians, who, when tempests drive ships to their coasts, *decoy* them to the rocks that they may plunder their lading.' —Johnson.

The country has its *allurements* for the contemplative mind: the metropolis is full of *temptations*. Those who have any evil project to execute will omit no *enticement* in order to *seduce* the young and inexperienced from their duty. The practice of *decoying* children or ignorant people into places of confinement was formerly more frequent than at present.

Allure does not imply such a powerful influence as *tempt:* what *allures* draws by gentle means; it lies in the nature of the thing that affects: what *tempts* acts by direct and continued efforts: it presents motives to the mind in order to produce decision; it tries the power of resistance. *Entice* supposes such a decisive influence on the mind, as produces a determination to act; in which respect it differs from the two former terms. *Allure* and *tempt* produce actions on the mind, not necessarily followed by any result; for we may be *allured* or *tempted* to do a thing, without necessarily doing the thing; but we cannot be *enticed* unless we are led to take some step. *Seduce* and *decoy* have reference to the outward action, as well as the inward movements of the mind which give rise to them: they indicate a drawing aside of the person as well as the mind; it is a misleading by false representation. Prospects are *alluring*, offers are *tempting*, words are *enticing*, charms are *seductive*.

TRY, TEMPT.

To *try* (*v. To attempt*) is to call forth one's ordinary powers; to *tempt* is a particular species of trial; we *try* either ourselves or others; we *tempt* others: to *try* is for the most part an indifferent action, a person may be tried in order to ascertain his principles or his strength;

> League all your forces then, ye pow'rs above,
> Join all, and *try* the omnipotence of Jove.
>
> Pope.

To *tempt* is for the most part taken in a bad sense, men are *tempted* to depart from their duty;

> Still the old sting remain'd, and men began
> To *tempt* the serpent, as he *tempted* man.
>
> Denham.

It is necessary to *try* the fidelity of a servant before you place confidence in him; it is wicked to *tempt* any one to do that which we should think wrong to do ourselves: our strength is *tried* by frequent experience; we are *tempted* by the weakness of our principles, to give way to the violence of our passions.

EXPERIENCE, EXPERIMENT, TRIAL, PROOF, TEST.

Experience, *experiment*, from the Latin *experior*, compounded of *e* or *ex* and *perio* or *pario* to bring forth, signifies the thing brought to light, or the act of bringing to light; *trial* signifies the act of *trying*, from *try*, in Latin *tento*, Hebrew תר, to explore, examine, search; *proof* signifies either the act of *proving*, from the Latin *probo* to make good, or the thing made good, *proved* to be good; *test*, from the Latin *testis* a witness, is that which serves to attest or prove the reality of a thing.

By all the actions implied in these terms, we endeavour to arrive at a certainty respecting some unknown particular: the *experience* is that which has been tried; the *experiment* is the thing to be tried: the *experience* is certain, as it is a deduction from the past for the service of the present; the *experiment* is uncertain, and serves a future purpose: *experience* is an unerring guide, which no man can desert without falling into errour; *experiments* may fail, or be superseded by others more perfect.

Experience serves to lead us to moral truth, the *experiment* aids us in ascertaining speculative truth; we profit by *experience* to rectify practice; 'A man may, by *experience*, be persuaded that his will is free; that he can do this, or not do it.'—Tillotson. We make *experiments* in theoretical inquiries; 'Any one may easily make this *experiment*, and even plainly see that there is no bud in the corn which ants lay up.'—Addison. He, therefore, who makes *experiments* in matters of *experience* rejects a steady and definite mode of coming at the truth for one that is variable and uncertain, and that too in matters of the first moment: the consequences of such a mistake are obvious, and have been too fatally realized in the present age, in which *experience* has been set at nought by every wild speculator, who has recommended *experiments* to be made with all the forms of moral duty and civil society; 'It is good also not to try *experiments* in states, except the necessity be urgent, or the utility evident.'—BACON.

The *experiment*, *trial*, and *proof* have equally the character of uncertainty; but the *experiment* is employed only in matters of an intellectual nature; the *trial* is employed in matters of a personal nature, on physical as well as mental objects; the *proof* is employed in moral subjects: we make an *experiment* in order to know whether a thing be true or false; we make a *trial* in order to know whether it be capable or incapable, convenient or inconvenient, useful or the contrary; we put a thing to the *proof* in order to determine whether it be good or bad, real or unreal: *experiments* tend to confirm our opinions; they are the handmaids of science; the philosopher doubts every position which cannot be demonstrated by repeated *experiments;* 'That which showeth them to be wise, is the gathering of principles out of their own particular *experiments ;* and the framing of our particular *experiments*, according to the rule of their principles, shall make us such as they are.'—HOOKER. *Trials* are of absolute necessity in directing our conduct, our taste, and our choice; we judge of our strength or skill by *trials ;* we judge of the effect of colours by *trials*, and the like;

> But he himself betook another way,
> To make more *trial* of his hardiment,
> And seek adventures, as he with prince Arthur went.
> SPENSER.

The *proof* determines the judgement, as in common life, according to the vulgar proverb, 'The *proof* of the pudding is in the eating;' so in the knowledge of men and things, the *proof* of men's characters and merits is best made by observing their conduct;

> O goodly usage of those ancient tymes!
> In which the sword was servant unto right:
> When not for malice and contentious crymes,
> But all for praise and *proof* of manly might.
> SPENSER.

The *experiment* is a sort of trial; 'When we are searching out the nature or properties of any being by various methods of *trial*, this sort of observation is called *experiment*.'—WATTS. The *proof* results from the *trial ;* 'My paper gives a timorous writer an opportunity of putting his abilities to the *proof*.'—ADDISON. When the word *test* is taken in the sense of a *trial*, as in the phrases to stand the *test*, or to make a *test*, it derives its meaning from the chymical process of refining metals in a *test* or cupel, *testa* being in Italian the name of this vessel. The *test* is therefore a positive and powerful *trial ;*

> All thy vexations
> Were but my *trials* of thy love, and thou
> Hast strangely stood the *test*.—SHAKSPEARE.

When the *test* is taken for the means of trying or prov-.g, it bears a similar signification;

> Unerring nature, still divinely bright,
> One clear, unchang'd and universal light,
> Life, force, and beauty, must to all impart
> At once the source, and end, and *test* of every art.
> POPE.

Hence this word is used in the legal sense for the *proof* which a man is required to give of his religious creed.

ATTEMPT, TRIAL, ENDEAVOUR, ESSAY, EFFORT.

Attempt, in French *attenter*, Latin *attento*, from *at* or *ad* and *tento*, signifies to *try* at a thing; *trial* comes from *try* (*v. Experience*); *endeavour*, compounded of *en* and the French *devoir* to owe, signifies to try according to one's duty; *essay*, in French *essayer*, comes probably from the German *ersuchen*, compounded of *er* and *suchen* to seek, written in old German *suachen*, and is doubtless connected with *sehen* to see or look after, signifying to aspire after, to look up to; *effort*, in French *effort*, from the Latin *effert*, present tense of *effero*, compounded of *e* or *ex* and *fero*, signifies a bringing out or calling forth the strength.

To *attempt* is to set about a thing with a view of effecting it; to *try* is to set about a thing with a view of seeing the result. An *attempt* respects the action with its object; a *trial* is the exercise of power. We always act when we *attempt;* we use the senses and the understanding when we *try*. We *attempt* by *trying*, but we may *try* without *attempting ;* when a thief *attempts* to break into a house he first *tries* the locks and fastenings to see where he can most easily gain admittance.

Men *attempt* to remove evils; they *try* experiments. *Attempts* are perpetually made by quacks, whether in medicine, politicks, or religion, to recommend some scheme of their own to the notice of the publick; which are often nothing more than *trials* of skill to see who can most effectually impose on the credulity of mankind. Spirited people make *attempts ;* persevering people make *trials ;* players *attempt* to perform different parts; and *try* to gain applause.

An *endeavour* is a continued *attempt*. *Attempts* may be fruitless; *trials* may be vain; *endeavours*, though unavailing, may be well meant. Many *attempts* are made which exceed the abilities of the *attempter ; trials* are made in matters of speculation, the results of which are uncertain; *endeavours* are made in the moral concerns of life. People *attempt* to write books; they *try* various methods; and *endeavour* to obtain a livelihood.

An *essay* is used altogether in a figurative sense for an *attempt* or *endeavour ;* it is an intellectual exertion. A modest writer apologizes for his feeble *essay* to contribute to the general stock of knowledge and cultivation: hence short treatises which serve as *attempts* to illustrate any point in morals are termed *essays*, among which are the finest productions in our language from the pen of Addison, Steele, and their successors. An *effort* is to an *attempt* as a means to an end; it is the very act of calling forth those powers which are employed in an *attempt*. In *attempting* to make an escape, a person is sometimes obliged to make desperate *efforts*.

Attempts at imitation expose the imitator to ridicule when not executed with peculiar exactness; 'A natural and unconstrained behaviour has something in it so agreeable that it is no wonder to see people *endeavouring* after it; but at the same time it is so very hard to hit, when it is not born with us, that people often make themselves ridiculous in *attempting* it.'—ADDISON. *Trials* of strength are often foolhardy; in some cases attended with mischievous consequences to the *trier ;*

> To bring it to the *trial*, will you dare
> Our pipes, our skill, our voices to compare?
> DRYDEN.

Honest *endeavours* to please are to be distinguished from idle *attempts* to catch applause; 'Whether or no (said Socrates on the day of his execution) God will approve of my actions I know not; but this I am sure of, that I have at all times made it my *endeavour* to please him.'—ADDISON. The first *essays* of youth ought to meet with indulgence, in order to afford encouragement to rising talents; 'This treatise prides itself in no higher a title than that of an *essay*, or imperfect *attempt* at a subject.'—GLANVILLE. Great *attempts*, which require extraordinary *efforts* either of body or mind, always meet with an adequate share of publick applause; 'The man of sagacity bestirs himself to distress his enemy by methods probable and reducible to reason; so the same reason will fortify his enemy to elude these his regular *efforts :* but your fool projects with such notable inconsistency, that no course of thought can evade his machinations.'—STEELE.

ATTEMPT, UNDERTAKING, ENTERPRISE.

An *attempt* is the thing *attempted* (*v. To attempt*) ; an *undertaking*, from *undertake*, or take in hand, is the thing taken in hand; an *enterprise*, from the French *enterpris*, participle of *entreprendre* to undertake, has the same original sense.

The idea of something set about to be completed is common to all these terms. An *attempt* is less complicated than an *undertaking;* and that less arduous than an *enterprise. Attempts* are the common exertions of power for obtaining an object: an *undertaking* involves in it many parts and particulars which require thought and judgement: an *enterprise* has more that is hazardous and dangerous in it; it requires resolution. *Attempts* are frequently made on the lives and property of individuals; *undertakings* are formed for private purposes; *enterprises* are commenced for some great national object.

Nothing can be effected without making the *attempt; attempts* are therefore often idle and unsuccessful, when they are made by persons of little discretion, who are eager to do something without knowing how to direct their powers;

> Why wilt thou rush to certain death and rage,
> In rash *attempts* beyond thy tender age?—DRYDEN.

Undertakings are of a more serious nature, and involve a man's serious interests; if begun without adequate means of bringing them to a conclusion, they too frequently bring ruin by their failure on those who are concerned in them; 'When I hear a man complain of his being unfortunate in all his *undertakings*, I shrewdly suspect him for a very weak man in his affairs.'—ADDISON. *Enterprises* require personal sacrifices rather than those of interest; he who does not combine great resolution and perseverance with considerable bodily powers, will be ill-fitted to take part in grand *enterprises*.

The present age has been fruitful in *attempts* to bring premature genius into notice: literary *undertakings* have of late degenerated too much into mere commercial speculations: a state of war gives birth to naval and military *enterprises;* a state of peace is most favourable to those of a scientifick nature;

There would be few *enterprises* of great labour or hazard undertaken, if we had not the power of magnifying the advantages which we persuade ourselves to expect from them.'—JOHNSON.

FOOLHARDY, ADVENTUROUS, RASH.

Foolhardy signifies having the hardihood of a *fool; adventurous*, ready to *venture; rash*, in German *rasch*, which signifies swift, comes from the Arabick *raaschen* to go swiftly.

The *foolhardy* expresses more than the *adventurous;* and the *adventurous* than the *rash*.

The *foolhardy* man *ventures* in defiance of consequences: the *adventurous* man *ventures* from a love of the arduous and the bold; the *rash* man *ventures* for want of thought: courage and boldness become *foolhardihood* when they lead a person to run a fruitless risk; an *adventurous* spirit sometimes leads a man into unnecessary difficulties; but it is a necessary accompaniment of greatness. There is not so much design, but there is more violence and impetuosity in *rashness* than in *foolhardihood:* the former is the consequence of an ardent temper which will admit of correction by the influence of the judgement; but the latter comprehends the perversion of both the will and the judgement.

An infidel is *foolhardy*, who risks his future salvation for the mere gratification of his pride;

> If any yet be so *foolhardy*,
> T' expose themselves to vain jeopardy,
> If they come wounded off and lame,
> No honour 's got by such a maim.—BUTLER.

Alexander was an *adventurous* prince, who delighted in enterprises in proportion as they presented difficulties; he was likewise a *rash* prince, as was evinced by his jumping into the river Cydnus while he was hot, and by his leaping over the wall of Oxydrace and exposing himself singly to the attack of the enemy;

> 'Twas an old way of recreating,
> Which learned butchers called bearbaiting,
> A bold, *advent'rous* exercise.—BUTLER.

> Why wilt thou, then, renew the vain pursuit,
> And *rashly* catch at the forbidden fruit?
> PRIOR.

TO ENDEAVOUR, AIM, STRIVE, STRUGGLE.

To *endeavour* (*v. Attempt*) is general in its object; *aim* (*v. Aim*) is particular; we *endeavour* to do what ever we set about; we *aim* at doing something which we have set before ourselves as a desirable object. To *strive* (*v. Strife*) is to *endeavour* earnestly; to *struggle*, which is a frequentative of *strive*, is to *strive* earnestly.

An *endeavour* springs from a sense of duty; we *endeavour* to do that which is right, and avoid that which is wrong: *aiming* is the fruit of an aspiring temper; the object *aimed* at is always something superiour either in reality or imagination, and calls for particular exertion: *striving* is the consequence of an ardent desire; the thing *striven* for is always conceived to be of importance: *struggling* is the effect of necessity; it is proportioned to the difficulty of attainment, and the resistance which is opposed to it; the thing *struggled* for is indispensably necessary.

Those only who *endeavour* to discharge their duty to God and their fellow-creatures can expect real tranquillity of mind; ''T is no uncommon thing, my good Sancho, for one half of the world to use the other half like brutes, and then *endeavour* to make em so.'—STERNE. Whoever *aims* at the acquirement of great wealth or much power opens the door for much misery to himself;

> However men may *aim* at elevation,
> 'T is properly a female passion.—SHENSTONE.

As our passions are acknowledged to be our greatest enemies when they obtain the ascendancy, we should always *strive* to keep them under our control;

> All understand their great Creator's will,
> *Strive* to be happy, and in that fulfil,
> Mankind excepted, lord of all beside,
> But only slave to folly, vice, and pride.
> JENYNS.

There are some men who *struggle* through life to obtain a mere competence; and yet die without succeeding in their object;

> So the boat's brawny crew the current stem,
> And slow advancing *struggle* with the stream.
> DRYDEN.

We ought to *endeavour* to correct faults, to *aim* at attaining Christian perfection, to *strive* to conquer bad habits: these are the surest means of saving us from the necessity of *struggling* to repair an injured reputation.

ENDEAVOUR, EFFORT, EXERTION.

The idea of calling our powers into action is common to these terms: *endeavour* (*v. Attempt*) expresses little more than this common idea, being a term of general import: *effort*, from the Latin *effert*, from *effero* to bring forth, signifying the bringing out of power; and *exertion*, in Latin *exero*, signifying the putting forth power, are particular modes of *endeavour;* the former being a special strong *endeavour*, the latter a continued strong *endeavour*. The *endeavour* is called forth by ordinary circumstances; the *effort* and *exertion* by those which are extraordinary. The *endeavour* flows out of the condition of our being and constitution; as rational and responsible agents we must make daily *endeavours* to fit ourselves for an hereafter; as willing and necessitous agents, we use our *endeavours* to obtain such things as are agreeable or needful for us: when a particular emergency arises we make a great *effort;* and when a serious object is to be obtained we make suitable *exertions*.

The *endeavour* is indefinite both as to the end and the means: the end may be immediate or remote; the means may be either direct or indirect: but in the *effort* the end is immediate; the means are direct and personal: we may either make an *endeavour* to get into a room, or we may make an *endeavour* to obtain a situation in life, or act our part well in a particular situation; 'To walk with circumspection and steadiness in the right path ought to be the constant *endeavour* of every rational being.'—JOHNSON. We make *efforts* to speak, or we make *efforts* to get through a crowd, or we make *efforts* to overcome our feelings; 'The influence of custom is such, that to conquer it will require the utmost *efforts* of fortitude and virtue.'—JOHNSON The *endeavour* may call forth one or many powers; the *effort* calls forth but one power: the *endeavour* to please in society is laudable, if it do not lead to vicious compliances; it is a laudable *effort* of fortitude to suppress our complaints in the moment of suffering. The *exertion* is as comprehensive in its meaning as the *endeavour*, and as positive as the *effort;* but the *endeavour* is most commonly, and the *effort* always, applied to individuals only; whereas the *exertion* is applicable to nations as well as individuals. A tradesman uses his best *endeavours* to please his customers: a combatant makes desperate *efforts* to overcome his antagonist: a candidate for literary or parliamentary honours uses great *exertions* to surpass his rival; a nation uses great *exertions* to raise a navy or extend its commerce; 'The discomfitures which the republick of assassins has suffered have uniformly called forth new *exertions*.'—Burke.

TO EXERT, EXERCISE.

The employment of some power or qualification that belongs to oneself is the common idea conveyed by these terms; but *exert* (*v. Endeavour*) may be used for what is internal or external of oneself; *exercise*, in Latin *exerceo*, from *ex* and *arceo*, signifying to drive or force out, is employed only for that which forms an express part of oneself: hence we speak of *exerting* one's strength, or *exerting* one's voice, or *exerting* one's influence; of *exercising* one's limbs, *exercising* one's understanding, or *exercising* one's tongue; 'How has Milton represented the whole Godhead, *exerting* itself towards man in its full benevolence, under the threefold distinction of a Creator, a Redeemer, and Comforter.'—Addison. 'God made no faculty, but also provided it with a proper object upon which it might *exercise* itself.'—South.

Exert conveys simply the idea of calling forth into action; *exercise* always conveys the idea of repeated or continued *exertion* coupled with that of the purpose or end for which it is made: thus a person who calls to another *exerts* his voice; he who speaks aloud for any length of time *exercises* his lungs. When the will has *exerted* an act of command upon any faculty of the soul, or a member of the body, it has done all that the whole man, as a moral agent, can do for the actual *exercise* or employment of such a faculty or member.

TO EXERCISE, PRACTISE.

Exercise signifies the same as in the preceding article; *practise*, from the Greek πράσσω to do, signifies to perform a part.

These terms are equally applied to the actions and habits of men; but we *exercise* in that where the powers are called forth; we *practise* in that where frequency and habitude of action is requisite: we *exercise* an art; we *practise* a profession; 'The Roman tongue was the study of their youth; it was their own language they were instructed and *exercised* in.'—Locke. 'A woman that *practis'd* physick in man's clothes.'—Tatler. We may both *exercise* or *practise* a virtue; but the former is that which the particular occurrence calls forth, and which seems to demand a peculiar effort of the mind; the latter is that which is done daily and ordinarily: thus we in a peculiar manner are said to *exercise* patience, fortitude, or forbearance; to *practise* charity, kindness, benevolence, and the like: 'Every virtue requires time and place, a proper object, and a fit conjuncture of circumstances for the due *exercise* of it.'—Addison. 'All men are not equally qualified for getting money; but it is in the power of every one alike to *practise* this virtue (of thrift).'—Budgell.

A similar distinction characterizes these words as nouns: the former applying solely to the powers of the body or mind; the latter solely to the mechanical operations: the health of the body and the vigour of the mind are alike impaired by the want of *exercise*; 'Reading is to the mind what *exercise* is to the body.' —Addison. In every art *practice* is an indispensable requisite for acquiring perfection;

> Long *practice* has a sure improvement found,
> With kindled fires to burn the barren ground.
> Dryden.

The *exercise* of the memory is of the first importance in the education of children; constant *practice* in writing is almost the only means by which the art of penmanship is acquired.

CUSTOM, FASHION, MANNER, PRACTICE.

Customs, *fashions*, and *manners* are all employed for communities of men: *custom* (*v. Custom, habit*) respects established and general modes of action; *fashion*, in French *facon*, from *facio* to do or make, regards partial and transitory modes of making or doing things: *manner*, in the limited sense in which it is here taken, signifies the *manner* or mode of men's living or behaving in their social intercourse.

Custom is authoritative; it stands in the place of law, and regulates the conduct of men in the most important concerns of life: *fashion* is arbitrary and capricious, it decides in matters of trifling import: *manners* are rational; they are the expressions of moral feelings *Customs* are most prevalent in a barbarous state of society; *fashions* rule most where luxury has made the greatest progress; *manners* are most distinguishable in a civilized state of society.

Customs are in their nature as unchangeable as *fashions* are variable; *manners* depend on cultivation and collateral circumstances: *customs* die away or are abolished; *fashions* pass away, and new ones take their place; *manners* are altered either for the better or the worse: endeavours have been successfully employed in several parts of India to abolish the *custom* of infanticide, and that of women sacrificing themselves on the funeral piles of their husbands; 'The *custom* of representing the grief we have for the loss of the dead by our habits, certainly had its rise from the real sorrow of such as were too much distressed to take the care they ought of their dress.'—Steele. The votaries of *fashion* are not contented with giving the law for the cut of the coat, or the shape of the bonnet, but they wish to intrude upon the sphere of the scholar or the artist, by prescribing in matters of literature and taste;

> Of beasts, it is confess'd, the ape
> Comes nearest us in human shape:
> Like man, he imitates each *fashion*,
> And malice is his ruling passion.—Swift.

The influence of publick opinion on the *manners* of a people has never been so strikingly illustrated as in the instance of the French nation during and since the Revolution;

> Their arms, their arts, their *manners*, I disclose,
> And how they war, and whence the people rose.
> Dryden.

Practice, in Latin *practicus*, Greek πρακτικὸς, from πράσσω to do, signifies actual doing or the thing done, that is by distinction the regularly doing, or the thing regularly done, in which sense it is most analogous to *custom;* but *practice* simply conveys the idea of actual performance; *custom* includes also the accessory idea of repetition at stated periods: a *practice* must be defined as frequent or unfrequent, regular or irregular; but a *custom* does not require to be qualified by any such epithets: it may be the *practice* of a person to do acts of charity, as the occasion requires; but when he uniformly does a particular act of charity at any given period of the year, it is properly denominated his *custom;* 'Savage was so touched with the discovery of his real mother, that it was his frequent *practice* to walk in the dark evenings for several hours before her door, with hopes of seeing her as she might cross her apartments with a candle in her hand.'—Johnson.

Both *practice* and *custom* are general or particular, but the former is absolute, the latter relative; the *practice* may be adopted by a number of persons without reference to each other; but a *custom* is always followed either by imitation or prescription; the *practice* of gaming has always been followed by the vicious part of society; but it is to be hoped for the honour of man that it will never become a *custom*.

CUSTOM, HABIT.

Custom signifies the same as in the preceding article; *habit*, in Latin *habitudo*, from *habeo* to have, marks the state of having or holding.

Custom is a frequent repetition of the same act; 'It is the *custom* of the Mahometans, if they see any printed or written paper upon the ground, to take it up and lay it aside carefully, as not knowing but it may contain some piece of the Alcoran.'—ADDISON. *Habit* the effect of such repetition, 'If a loose and careless life has brought a man into *habits* of dissipation, and led him to neglect those religious duties which he owed to his Maker, let him return to the regular worship of God.'—BLAIR. The *custom* of rising early in the morning is conducive to the health, and may in a short time become such a *habit* as to render it no less agreeable than it is useful.

Custom applies to men collectively or individually; *habit* applies to the individual only. Every nation has *customs* peculiar to itself; 'I dare not shock my readers with the description of the *customs* and manners of these barbarians (the Hottentots).'—HUGHES. Every individual has habits peculiar to his age, station, and circumstances.

Custom, in regard to individuals, supposes an act of the will; *habit* implies an involuntary movement: a *custom* is followed; a *habit* is acquired: whoever follows the *custom* of imitating the look, tone, or gesture of another, is liable to get the *habit* of doing the same himself: as *habit* is said to be second nature, it is of importance to guard against all *customs* to which we do not wish to become *habituated:* the drunkard is formed by the *custom* of drinking intemperately, until he becomes *habituated* to the use of spirituous liquors: the profane swearer who *accustoms* himself in early life to utter the oaths which he hears, will find it difficult in advanced years to break himself of the *habit* of swearing; the love of imitation is so powerful in the human breast, that it leads the major part of mankind to follow *custom* even in ridiculous things: Solomon refers to the power of *habit* when he says, 'train up a child in the way in which he should go; and when he is old he will not depart from it;' a power which cannot be employed too early in the aid of virtue and religion. 'The force of education is so great, that we may mould the minds and manners of the young into what shape we please, and give the impressions of such *habits*, as shall ever afterward remain.'—ATTERBURY.

Customary and *habitual*, the epithets derived from these words, admit of a similar distinction: the *customary* action is that which is repeated after the manner of a *custom;* 'This *customary* superiority grew too delicate for truth, and Swift, with all his penetration, allowed himself to be delighted with low flattery.'—JOHNSON. The *habitual* action is that which is done by the force of *habit;* 'We have all reason to believe that, amid numberless infirmities which attend humanity, what the great Judge will chiefly regard is the *habitual* prevailing turn of our heart and life.'—BLAIR.

COMMON, VULGAR, ORDINARY, MEAN.

Common, in French *commun*, Latin *communis*, from *con* and *munus* the joint office or property of many, has regard to the multitude of objects; *vulgar*, in French *vulgaire*, Latin *vulgaris*, from *vulgus* the people, has regard to the number and quality of the persons; *ordinary*, in French *ordinaire*, Latin *ordinarius*, from *ordo* the order or regular practice, has regard to the repetition or disposition of things; *mean* expresses the same as *medium* or moderate, from which it is derived.

Familiar use renders things *common*, *vulgar*, and *ordinary;* but what is mean is so of itself; the *common*, *vulgar*, and *ordinary* are therefore frequently, though not always, *mean;* and on the contrary, what is *mean* is not always *common*, *vulgar*, or *ordinary;* consequently, in the primitive sense of these words, the first three are not strictly synonymous with the last; monsters are *common* in Africa; *vulgar* reports are little to be relied on; it is an *ordinary* practice for men to make light of their word.

Common is unlimited in its application; it includes both *vulgar* and *ordinary;* the latter are said in reference to persons only, *common* with regard to persons or things: an opinion is either *common* or *vulgar;* an employment is either *common* or *ordinary:* it was long a *vulgarly* received notion, that the sun turned round the earth: it is the *ordinary* pursuit of astronomers to observe the motions of the heavenly bodies: disputes on religion have rendered many facts *vulgar* or *common*, which were formerly known only to the learned; on that account it is now become an *ordinary* or a *common* practice for men to dispute about religion, and even to frame a new set of doctrines for them selves.

In the figurative sense, in which they convey the idea of low value, they are synonymous with *mean:* what is to be seen, heard, or enjoyed by every body is *common*, and naturally of little value, since the worth of objects frequently depends upon their scarcity and the difficulty of obtaining them: 'Men may change their climate, but they cannot their nature. A man that goes out a fool cannot ride or sail himself into *common* sense.'—ADDISON. What is peculiar to *common* people is *vulgar*, and consequently worse than *common;* it is supposed to belong to those who are ignorant and depraved in taste as well as in morals; 'The poet's thought of directing Satan to the sun, which in the *vulgar* opinion of mankind, is the most conspicuous part of the creation, and the placing in it an angel, is a circumstance very finely contrived.'—ADDISON. What is done and seen *ordinarily* may be done and seen easily; it requires no abilities or mental acquirements: it has nothing striking in it, it excites no interest; 'A very *ordinary* telescope shows us that a louse is itself a very lousy creature.'—ADDISON. What is *mean* is even below that which is *ordinary;* there is something defective in it;

> Under his forming hands a creature grew,
> Manlike, but diff'rent sex, so lovely fair,
> That what seem'd fair in all the world seem'd now
> *Mean*, or in her summ'd up.—MILTON.

Common is opposed to rare and refined; *vulgar* to polite and cultivated; *ordinary* to the distinguished; *mean* to the noble: a *common* mind busies itself with *common* objects; *vulgar* habits are easily contracted from a slight intercourse with *vulgar* people; an *ordinary* person is seldom associated with elevation of character; and a *mean* appearance is a certain mark of a degraded condition, if not of a degraded mind

COMMONLY, GENERALLY, FREQUENTLY, USUALLY.

Commonly, in the form of *common* (*v.* *Common*), *generally*, from *general*, and the Latin *genus* the kind, respects a whole body in distinction from an individual; *frequently*, from *frequent*, in French *frequent*, Latin *frequens*, from the old Latin *frago*, in Greek φράγω and φραγνύμι to go or turn about, signifies properly a crowding; *usually*, from *usual* and *use*, signifies according to *use* or custom.

What is *commonly* done is an action *common* to all: 'It is *commonly* observed among soldiers and seamen that though there is much kindness, there is little grief.'—JOHNSON. What is *generally* done is the action of the greatest part: 'It is *generally* not so much the desire of men, sunk into depravity, to deceive the world, as themselves.'—JOHNSON. What is *frequently* done is either the action of many, or an action many times repeated by the same person; 'It is too *frequently* the pride of students to despise those amusements and recreations which give to the rest of mankind strength of limbs and cheerfulness of heart.'—JOHNSON. What is *usually* done is done regularly by one or many; 'The inefficacy of advice is *usually* the fault of the counsellor.'—JOHNSON.

Commonly is opposed to rarely, *generally* and *frequently* to occasionally or seldom: *usually* to casually; men *commonly* judge of others by themselves; those who judge by the mere exteriour are *generally* deceived; but notwithstanding every precaution, one is *frequently* exposed to gross frauds; a man of business *usually* repairs to his counting-house every day at a certain hour.

GENERAL, UNIVERSAL.

The *general* is to the *universal* what the part is to the whole. What is *general* includes the greater part or number; what is *universal* includes every individual or part. The *general* rule admits of many exceptions; the *universal* rule admits of none. Human government has the *general* good for its object: the government of Providence is directed to *universal* good. *General* is opposed to particular, and *universal* to individual. A scientifick writer will not content himself with *general* remarks, when he has it in his power to enter into particulars; the *universal* complaint which we hear against men for their pride, shows that in every individual it exists to a greater or less degree. It is a *general* opinion that women are not qualified for scientifick pursuits; but Madame Dacier, Mrs. Carter, and many female writers, form exceptions, no less honourable to their whole sex, than to themselves in particular: it is a *universal* principle, that children ought to honour their parents; the intention of the Creator in this respect is manifested in such a variety of forms as to admit of no question. *General* philosophy considers the properties common to all bodies, and regards the distinct properties of particular bodies, only inasmuch as they confirm abstract *general* views. *Universal* philosophy depends on *universal* science or knowledge, which belongs only to the infinite mind of the Creator. *General* grammar embraces in it all principles that are supposed to be applicable to all languages: *universal* grammar is a thing scarcely attainable by the stretch of human power. What man can become so thoroughly acquainted with all existing languages, as to reduce all their particular idioms to any system?

USAGE, CUSTOM, PRESCRIPTION.

The *usage* is what one has been long used to do; *custom* (*v. Custom*) is what one generally does; *prescription* is what one is *prescribed* to do. The *usage* acquires force and sanction by dint of time; 'With the national assembly of France, possession is nothing, law and *usage* are nothing.'—BURKE. The *custom* acquires sanction by the frequency of its being done or the numbers doing it;

> For since the time of Saturn's holy reign,
> His hospitable *customs* we retain.—DRYDEN.

The *prescription* acquires force by the authority which *prescribes* it, namely, the universal consent of mankind; 'If in any case the shackles of *prescription* could be wholly shaken off, on what occasion should it be expected but in the selection of lawful pleasure?' —JOHNSON. Hence it arises that *customs* vary in every age, but that *usage* and *prescription* supply the place of written law.

POSSIBLE, PRACTICABLE, PRACTICAL.

Possible, from the Latin *possum* to be able, signifies properly to be able to be done: *practicable*, from *practice* (*v. To exercise*) signifies to be able to be put in *practice*: hence the difference between *possible* and *practicable* is the same as between doing once, or doing as a rule. There are many things *possible* which cannot be called *practicable*, but what is *practicable* must in its nature be *possible*. The *possible* depends solely on the power of the agent; 'How can we, without supposing ourselves under the constant care of a Supreme Being, give any *possible* account for that nice proportion which we find in every great city between the deaths and births of its inhabitants?'—ADDISON. The *practicable* depends on circumstances; 'He who would aim at *practicable* things should turn upon allaying our pain, rather than promoting our sorrow.'—STEELE. A child cannot say how much it is *possible* for him to learn until he has tried. Schemes have sometimes every thing to recommend them to notice, but that which is of the first importance, namely, their *practicability*.

The *practicable* is that which may or can be *practised*: the *practical* is that which is to be *practised*: the former therefore applies to that which men devise to carry into *practice*; the latter to that which they have to *practise*: projectors ought to consider what is *practicable*; divines and moralists have to consider what is *practical*. The *practicab e* is opposed to the *impracticable*; the *practical* to the theoretic or speculative; '*Practical* cunning shows itself in political matters.'—SOUTH.

MAY, CAN

May is in German *mögen* to wish, Greek μαίω to desire, from the connexion between wishing and complying with a wish; *can* denotes possibility, *may* liberty and probability: he who has sound limbs *can* walk; but he *may* not walk in [illegible]ces which are prohibited;

> For who *can* match Achilles? he who *can*
> Must yet be more than hero, more than man.
> POPE.

> Thou *canst* not call him from the Stygian shore,
> But thou, alas! *mayst* live to suffer more.—POPE.

AIM, OBJECT, END.

Aim is in all probability a variation of *home*, in old Germain *haim*. It is the *home* which the marksman wishes to reach; it is the thing aimed at; the particular point to which one's efforts are directed; which is had always in view, and to the attainment of which every thing is made to bend; *object*, from the Latin *objectus*, participle of *ob* and *jacio* to lie in the way, is more vague; it signifies the thing that lies before us; we pursue it by taking the necessary means to obtain it; it becomes the fruit of our labour; *end* in the improper sense of *end* is still more general, signifying the thing that ends one's wishes and endeavours; it is the result not only of action, but of combined action; it is the consummation of a scheme; we must take the proper measures to arrive at it.

It is the *aim* of every good Christian to live in peace; 'Cunning has only private, selfish *aims*, and sticks at nothing which may make them succeed.'—ADDISON. It is a mark of dulness or folly to act without an *object*; 'We should sufficiently weigh the *objects* of our hope, whether they be such as we may reasonably expect from them what we propose in their fruition.'—ADDISON. Every scheme is likely to fail, in which the means are not adequate to the *end*; 'Liberty and truth are not in themselves desirable, but only as they relate to a farther *end*.'—BERKELEY.

We have an *aim*; we propose to ourselves an *object*; we look to the *end*. An *aim* is attainable, an *object* worthy, an *end* important.

TO AIM, POINT, LEVEL.

Aim, signifying to take aim (*v. Aim*), is to direct one's view towards a point; *point*, from the noun *point*, signifies to direct the point to any thing; *level*, from the adjective *level*, signifies to put one thing on a level with another.

Aim expresses more than the other two words, inasmuch as it denotes a direction towards some minute point in an object, and the others imply direction towards the whole objects themselves. We *aim* at a bird; we *point* a cannon against a wall; we *level* a cannon at a wall. *Pointing* is of course used with most propriety in reference to instruments that have points; it is likewise a less decisive action than either *aiming* or *levelling*. A stick or a finger may be *pointed* at a person, merely out of derision; but a blow is *levelled* or *aimed* with an express intent of committing an act of violence;

> Their heads from *aiming* blows they bear afar,
> With clashing gauntlets then provoke the war.
> DRYDEN

> He calls on Bacchus, and propounds the prize:
> The groom his fellow-groom at buts defies,
> And bends his bow, and *levels* with his eyes.
> DRYDEN.

The same analogy is kept up in their figurative application.

The shafts of ridicule are but too often *aimed* with little effect against the follies of fashion; 'Another kind there is, which although we desire for itself, as health and virtue, and knowledge, nevertheless they are not the last mark whereat we *aim*, but have their further end whereunto they are referred.'—HOOKER. Remarks which seem merely to *point* at others, without being expressly addressed to them, have always a bad tendency;

> The story slily *points* at you.—CUMBERLAND.

It has hitherto been the fate of infidels to *level* their battery of sneers, declamation, and sophistry against the Christian religion only to strengthen the conviction of its sublime truths in the minds of mankind at large; 'In contemplation of which verity, St. Gregory Nazianzen, observing the declension from it, introduced in his times by the ambition of some prelates, did vent that famous exclamation, "O that there were not at all any presidency, or any preference in place and tyrannical enjoyment of prerogatives!" which earnest wish he surely did not mean to *level* against the ordinance of God, but against that which lately began to be intruded by men.'—BARROW.

TO AIM, ASPIRE.

Aim (*v. Aim*) includes efforts as well as views, in obtaining an object; *aspire*, from *as* or *ad* to or after and *spiro* to breathe, comprehends views, wishes, and hopes to obtain an object.

We *aim* at a certain proposed point, by endeavouring to gain it; 'Whether zeal or moderation be the point we *aim* at, let us keep fire out of the one, and frost out of the other.'—ADDISON. We *aspire* after that which we think ourselves entitled to, and flatter ourselves with gaining; 'The study of those who in the time of Shakspeare *aspired* to plebeian learning was laid upon adventures, giants, dragons, and enchantments.'—JOHNSON.

Many men *aim* at riches and honour;

> Lo, here the world is bliss; so here the end
> To which all men do *aim*, rich to be made,
> Such grace now to be happy is before thee laid.
> SPENSER.

It is the lot of but few to *aspire* to a throne;

> *Aspiring* to be gods, if angels fell,
> *Aspiring* to be angels, men rebel.—POPE.

We *aim* at what is attainable by ordinary efforts; we *aspire* after what is great and unusual. An emulous youth *aims* at acquiring the esteem of his teachers; he *aspires* to excel all his competitors in literary attainments.

TENDENCY, DRIFT, SCOPE, AIM.

Tendency, from to *tend*, denotes the property of tending towards a certain point, which is the characteristick of all these words, but this is applied only to things; and *drift*, from the verb to *drive*; *scope*, from the Greek σκέπτομαι to look; and *aim*, from the verb to *aim* (*v. Aim*); all characterize the thoughts of a person looking forward into futurity, and directing his actions to a certain point. Hence we speak of the *tendency* of certain principles or practices as being pernicious; the *drift* of a person's discourse; the *scope* which he gives himself either in treating of a subject, or in laying down a plan; or a person's *aim* to excel, or *aim* to supplant another, and the like. The *tendency* of most writings for the last-five-and twenty years has been to unhinge the minds of men; 'It is no wonder if a great deal of knowledge, which is not capable of making a man wise, has a natural *tendency* to make him vain and arrogant.'—ADDISON. Where a person wants the services of another, whom he dares not openly solicit, he will discover his wishes by the *drift* of his discourse;

> This said, the whole audience soon found out his *drift*,
> The convention was summoned in favour of Swift.
> SWIFT.

A man of a comprehensive mind will allow himself full *scope* in digesting his plans for every alteration which circumstances may require when they come to be developed; 'Merit in every rank has the freest *scope* (in England).'—BLAIR. Our desires will naturally give a cast to all our *aims*; and so long as they are but innocent, they are necessary to give a proper stimulus to exertion;

> Each nobler *aim*, repress'd by long control,
> Now sinks at last or feebly mans the soul.
> GOLDSMITH.

OBJECT, SUBJECT.

Object, in Latin *objectus*, participle of *objicio* to lie in the way, signifies the thing that lies in one's way; *subject*, in Latin *subjectus*, participle of *subjicio* to lie under, signifies the thing forming the groundwork.

The *object* puts itself forward; the *subject* is in the back-ground: we notice the *object*; we observe or reflect on the *subject*: *objects* are sensible; the *subject* is altogether intellectual; the eye, the ear, and all the senses, are occupied with the surrounding *objects*: the memory, the judgement, and the imagination are supplied with *subjects* suitable to the nature of the operations.

When *object* is taken for that which is intellectual, it retains a similar signification; it is the thing that presents itself to the mind; it is seen by the mind's eye: the *subject*, on the contrary, is that which must be sought for, and when found it engages the mental powers: hence we say an *object* of consideration, an *object* of delight, an *object* of concern; a *subject* of reflection, a *subject* of mature deliberation, the *subject* of a poem, the *subject* of grief, of lamentation, and the like. When the mind becomes distracted by too great a multiplicity of *objects*, it can fix itself on no one individual *object* with sufficient steadiness to take a survey of it; in like manner, if a child have too many *objects* set before it, for the exercise of its powers, it will acquire a familiarity with none;

> He whose sublime pursuit is God and truth,
> Burns like some absent and impatient youth,
> To join the *object* of his warm desires.—JENYNS.

Religion and politicks are interesting, but delicate *subjects* of discussion; 'The hymns and odes (of the inspired writers) excel those delivered down to us by the Greeks and Romans, in the poetry as much as in the *subject*.'—ADDISON.

MATTER, MATERIALS, SUBJECT.

Matter and *materials* are both derived from the same source, namely, the Latin *materia*, which comes in all probability from *mater*, because *matter*, from which every thing is made, acts in the production of bodies like a mother; *subject*, in Latin *subjectum*, participle of *subjicio* to lie, signifies the thing lying under and forming the foundation.

Matter in the physical application is taken for all that composes the sensible world in distinction from that which is spiritual, or discernible only by the thinking faculty; hence *matter* is always opposed to mind.

In regard to *materials* it is taken in an indivisible as well as a general sense; the whole universe is said to be composed of *matter*, though not of *materials*; 'It seems probable to me, that God in the beginning formed *matter* in solid, hard, impenetrable, moveable particles.'—NEWTON. On the other hand, *materials* consist of those particular parts of *matter* which serve for the artificial production of objects; 'The *materials* of that building very fortunately ranged themselves into that delicate order that it must be very great chance that parts them.'—TILLOTSON. *Matter* is said of those things which are the natural parts of the universe: a house, a table, and a chair consist of *materials*, because they are works of art; but a plant, a tree, an animal body, consist of *matter*, because they are the productions of nature.

The distinction of these terms in their moral application is very similar: the *matter* which composes a moral discourse is what emanates from the author. The *materials* are those with which one is furnished by others. The style of some writers is so indifferent that they disgrace the *matter* by the manner;

> Son of God, Saviour of men! thy name
> Shall be the copious *matter* of my song.—MILTON.

Periodical writers are furnished with *materials* for their productions out of the daily occurrences in the political and moral world; 'Simple ideas, the *materials* of all our knowledge, are suggested to the mind only by sensation and reflection.'—LOCKE. 'The principal *materials* of our comfort or uneasiness lie within ourselves.'—BLAIR. Writers of dictionaries endea vour to compress as much *matter* as possible into a small space; they draw their *materials* from other writers.

Matter seems to bear the same relation to *subject* as the whole does to any particular part, as it respects moral objects: the *subject* is the groundwork of the *matter*; the *matter* is that which flows out of the *subject*: the *matter* is that which we get by the force of invention; the *subject* is that which offers itself to notice: many persons may therefore have a *subject* who have no *matter*, that is, nothing in their own minds which they can offer by way of illustrating this *subject*; but it is not possible to have *matter* without a *subject*: hence the word *matter* is taken for the substance, and for that which is substantial; the *subject* is taken for that which engages the attention; we speak of a *subject* of conversation and *matter* for deliberation; a *subject* of inquiry, a *matter* of curiosity. Nations in a barbarous state afford but little *matter* worthy to be recorded in history;

Whence tumbled headlong from the height of life,
They furnish *matter* for the tragick muse.
THOMSON.

People who live a secluded life and in a contracted sphere have but few *subjects* to occupy their attention; 'Love hath such a strong virtual force that when it fasteneth on a pleasing *subject* it sets the imagination at a strange fit of working.'—HOWEL.

TO ALLUDE, REFER, HINT, SUGGEST.

Allude, in Latin *alludo*, is compounded of *al* or *ad* and *ludo* to sport, that is, to say any thing in a sportive or cursory manner; *refer*, in Latin *refero*, signifies to bring back, that is, to bring back a person's recollection to any subject by an indirect mention of it; *hint* may very probably be changed from *hind* or *behind*, in German *hinten*, signifying to convey from behind, or in an obscure manner; *suggest*, in Latin *suggestus*, participle of *suggero*, is compounded of *sub* and *gero* to bring under or near, and signifies to bring forward in an indirect or casual manner.

To *allude* is not so direct as to *refer*, but it is more clear and positive than either *hint* or *suggest*.

We *allude* to a circumstance by introducing something collaterally allied to it; we *refer* to an event by expressly introducing it into one's discourse; we *hint* at a person's intentions by darkly insinuating what may possibly happen; we *suggest* an idea by some poetical expressions relative to it.

There are frequent *allusions* in the Bible to the customs and manners of the East; 'I need not inform my reader that the author of Hudibras *alludes* to this strange quality in that cold climate, when, speaking of abstracted notions clothed in a visible shape, he adds that apt simile, "Like words congeal'd in northern air."'—ADDISON. It is necessary to *refer* to certain passages of a work when we do not expressly copy them; 'Those causes the divine historian *refers* us to, and not to any productions out of nothing.'—BURNET. It is mostly better in conversation to be entirely silent upon a subject, than to *hint* at what cannot be entirely explained; 'It is *hinted* that Augustus had in mind to restore the commonwealth.'—CUMBERLAND. Many improvements have owed their origin to some ideas casually *suggested* in the course of conversation; 'This image of misery, in the punishment of Tantalus, was perhaps originally *suggested* to some poet by the conduct of his patron.'—JOHNSON.

Allude and *refer* are always said with regard to things that have positively happened, and mostly such as are indifferent; *hint* and *suggest* have mostly a personal relation to things that are precarious. The whole drift of a discourse is sometimes unintelligible for want of knowing what is *alluded* to; although many persons and incidents are *referred* to with their proper names and dates. It is the part of the slanderer to *hint* at things discreditable to another, when he does not dare to speak openly; and to *suggest* doubts of his veracity which he cannot positively charge.

TO HINT, SUGGEST, INTIMATE, INSINUATE.

Hint, v. *To allude; suggest*, v. *To allude;* to *intimate* is to make one *intimate*, or specially acquainted with, to communicate one's most inward thoughts; *insinuate*, from the Latin *sinus* the bosom, is to introduce gently into the mind of another.

All these terms denote indirect expressions of what passes in one's own mind. We *hint* at a thing from fear and uncertainty; we *suggest* a thing from prudence and modesty; we *intimate* a thing from indecision; a thing is *insinuated* from artifice. A person who wants to get at the certain knowledge of any circumstance *hints* at it frequently in the presence of those who can give him the information; a man who will not offend others by an assumption of superiour wisdom, *suggests* his ideas on a subject instead of setting them forth with confidence; when a person's mind is not made up on any future action, he only *intimates* what may be done; he who has any thing offensive to communicate to another, will choose to *insinuate* it, rather than declare it in express terms. *Hints* are thrown out; they are frequently characterized as broken;

Willing to wound, and yet afraid to strike,
Just *hint* a fault, and hesitate dislike.—POPE.

Suggestions are offered; they are frequently termed idle or ill-grounded;

We must *suggest* to the people, in what hatred
He still hath held them.—SHAKSPEARE.

Intimations are given, and are either slight or broad;

'T is Heav'n itself that points out an hereafter,
And *intimates* eternity to man.—ADDISON.

Insinuations are thrown out; they are commonly designated as slanderous, malignant, and the like; 'Let it not be thought that what is here said *insinuates* any thing to the discredit of Greek and Latin criticism.'—WARBURTON.

To *hint* is taken either in a bad or an indifferent sense; it is commonly resorted to by tale-bearers, mischief-makers, and all who want to talk of more than they know: it is rarely necessary to have recourse to *hints* in lieu of positive inquiries and declarations, unless the term be used in regard to matters of science or morals, when it designates loose thoughts, casually offered, in distinction from those which are systematized and formally presented: upon this ground, a distinguished female writer of the present day modestly entitles her book, '*Hints* towards forming the Character of a Young Princess.' To *suggest* is oftener used in the good than the bad sense: while one *suggests* doubts, queries, difficulties, or improvements in matters of opinion, it is truly laudable, particularly for young persons; but to *suggest* any thing to the disadvantage of another is even worse than to speak ill of him openly, for it bespeaks cowardice as well as ill-nature. To *intimate* is taken either in a good or an indifferent sense; it commonly passes between relatives or persons closely connected, in the communication of their half-formed intentions or of doubtful intelligence; but to *insinuate* is always taken in a bad sense; it is the resource of an artful and malignant enemy to wound the reputation of another, whom he does not dare openly to accuse. A person is said to take a *hint*, to follow a *suggestion*, to receive an *intimation*, to disregard an *insinuation*.

TO REFER, RELATE, RESPECT, REGARD.

Refer, from the Latin *re* and *fero*, signifies literally to bring back; and *relate*, from the participle *relatus* of the same verb, signifies brought back: the former is, therefore, transitive, and the latter intransitive. One *refers* a person to a thing; one thing *refers*, that is, *refers* a person, to another thing: one thing *relates*, that is, *related*, to another. To *refer* is an arbitrary act, it depends upon the will of an individual; we may *refer* a person to any part of a volume, or to any work we please: to *relate* is a conditional act, it depends on the nature of things; nothing *relates* to another without some point of accordance between the two; orthography *relates* to grammar, that is, by being a part of the grammatical science. Hence it arises that *refer*, when employed for things, is commonly said of circumstances that carry the memory to events or circumstances; *relate* is said of things that have a natural connexion: the religious festivals and ceremonies of the Roman Catholicks have all a *reference* to some events that happened in the early periods of Christianity; 'Our Saviour's words (in his sermon on the mount) all *refer* to the Pharisees' way of speaking.'—SOUTH. The notes and observations at the end of a book *relate* to what has been inserted in the text; 'Homer artfully interweaves, in the several succeeding parts of his poem, an account of every thing material which *relates* to his princes.'—ADDISON.

Refer and *relate* carry us back to that which may be very distant; but *respect* and *regard* turn our views to that which is near. The object of the actions of *referring* and *relating* is indirectly acted upon, and consequently stands in the oblique case; we *refer* to an object; a thing *relates* to an object: but the object of the action *respect* and *regard* is directly acted upon, therefore it stands in the accusative or objective case: to *respect* or *regard* a thing, not to a thing. What *respects* comprehends in it more than what *relates*. To *relate* is to *respect;* but to *respect* is not always to *relate:* the former includes every species of affinity or accordance; the latter only that which flows out of the properties and circumstances of things: when a number of objects are brought together, which fitly associate, and properly *relate* the one to the other, they form a grand whole, as in the case of any scientifick work which is digested into a system; when all the incidental circumstances which *respect* either moral principles or moral conduct are properly weighed, they will enable one to form a just judgement.

Respect is said of objects in general; *regard* mostly of that which enters into the feelings: laws *respect* the general welfare of the community; 'Religion is a pleasure to the mind, as *respects* practice.'—SOUTH. The due administration of the laws *regards* the happiness of the individual; 'What I have said *regards* only the vain part of the sex.'—ADDISON.

TO REVERT, RETURN.

Revert is the Latin, and *return* the English word; the former is used however only in few cases, and the latter in general cases: they are allied to each other in the moral application; a speaker *reverts* to what has already passed on a preceding day; he *returns* after a digression to the thread of his discourse: we may always *revert* to something different, though more or less connected with that which we are discussing; we always *return* to that which we have left: we turn to something by *reverting* to it; we continue the same thing by *returning* to it;

> Whatever lies or legendary tales
> May taint my spotless deeds, the guilt, the shame,
> Will back *revert* on the inventor's head.
> SHIRLEY.

> One day, the soul supine with ease and fulness
> Revels secure, and fondly tells herself
> The hour of evil can *return* no more.—ROWE.

TO GLANCE AT, ALLUDE TO.

Glance, probably from the Teutonick *glaentzen* to shine, signifies to make a thing appear like a ray of light in an oblique direction: *allude* has the same general meaning as in the preceding article (*v. To allude*).

These terms are nearly allied in the sense of indirectly referring to any object, either in written or verbal discourse: but *glance* expresses a cursory and latent action; *allude*, simply an indirect but undisguised action: ill-natured satirists are perpetually *glancing* at the follies and infirmities of individuals; 'Entering upon his discourse, Socrates says, he does not believe any of the most comick genius can censure him for talking upon such a subject (the immortality of the soul) at such a time (that of death). This passage, I think, evidently *glances* upon Aristophanes, who writ a comedy on purpose to ridicule the discourses of that divine philosopher.'—ADDISON. The Scriptures are full of *allusions* to the manners and customs of the Easterns; 'The author, in the whole course of his poem, has infinite *allusions* to places of Scripture.'—ADDISON. He who attempts to write an epitome of universal history must take but a hasty *glance* at the most important events.

GLIMPSE, GLANCE.

The *glimpse* is the action of the object appearing to the eye; the *glance* is the action of the eye seeking the object: one catches a *glimpse* of an object; one casts a *glance* at an object: the latter therefore is properly the means for obtaining the former, which is the end: we get a *glimpse* by means of a *glance*. The *glimpse* is the hasty, imperfect, and sudden view which we get of an object: the *glance* is the hasty and imperfect view which we take of an object: the former may depend upon a variety of circumstances; the latter depends upon the will of the agent. We can seldom do more than get a *glimpse* of objects in a carriage that is going with rapidity; 'Of the state with which practice has not acquainted us, we snatch a *glimpse*, we discern a point, and regulate the rest by passion and by fancy.'—JOHNSON. When we do not wish to be observed to look, we take but a *glance* of an object;

> Here passion first I felt,
> Commotion strange! In all enjoyments else
> Superiour unmov'd; here only weak
> Against the charm of beauty's pow'rful *glance*.
> MILTON.

TO INSINUATE, INGRATIATE.

Insinuate (*v. To hint*) and *ingratiate*, from *gratus* grateful or acceptable, are employed to express the endeavour to gain favour; but they differ in the circumstances of the action. A person who *insinuates* adopts every art to steal into the good will of another; but he who *ingratiates* adopts unartificial means to conciliate good will. A person of insinuating manners wins upon another imperceptibly, even so as to convert dislike into attachment; a person with *ingratiating* manners procures good will by a permanent intercourse. *Insinuate* and *ingratiate* differ in the motive, as well as the mode, of the action: the motive is, in both cases, self-interest; but the former is unlawful, and the latter allowable. In proportion as the object to be attained by another's favour is base, so is it necessary to have recourse to *insinuation;* 'At the isle of Rhé he *insinuated* himself into the very good grace of the Duke of Buckingham.'—CLARENDON. While the object to be attained is that which may be avowed, *ingratiating* will serve the purpose; 'My resolution was now to *ingratiate* myself with men whose reputation was established.'—JOHNSON. Low persons *insinuate* themselves into the favour of their superiours, in order to obtain an influence over them: it is commendable in a young person to wish to *ingratiate* himself with those who are entitled to his esteem and respect.

Insinuate may be used in the improper sense for unconscious agents; ingratiate is always the act of a conscious agent. Water will *insinuate* itself into every body that is in the smallest degree porous; 'The same character of despotism *insinuated* itself into every court of Europe.'—BURKE. There are few persons of so much apathy, that it may not be possible, one way or another, to *ingratiate* one's self into their favour.

INSINUATION, REFLECTION.

These both imply personal remarks, or such remarks as are directed towards an individual; but the former is less direct and more covert than the latter. The *insinuation* always deals in half words; the *reflection* is commonly open. They are both levelled at the individual with no good intent: but the *insinuation* is general, and may be employed to convey any unfavourable sentiment; the *reflection* is particular, and commonly passes between intimates, and persons in close connexion.

The *insinuation* respects the honour, the moral character, or the intellectual worth, of the object; 'The prejudiced admirers of the ancients are very angry at the least *insinuation* that they had any idea of our barbarous tragi-comedy.'—TWINING. The *reflection* respects the particular conduct or feelings of an individual towards another; 'The ill-natured man gives utterance to *reflections* which a good-natured man stifles.'—ADDISON. Envious people throw out *insinuations* to the disparagement of others, whose merits they dare not openly question; when friends quarrel, they deal largely in *reflections* on the past.

PERTINENT, RELEVANT.

Pertinent, from the Latin *pertineo* to pertain or appertain, signifies belonging or relating to any subject in hand; *relevant*, from the Latin *relevo* to relieve or assist, signifies coming in aid or support of a subject. Remarks are *pertinent* when they bear on any question, and, on the other hand, they are *impertinent* when they have nothing to do with the question; 'Here I shall seem a little to digress, but you will by and-by find it *pertinent*.'—BACON. Matter in a discourse, and arguments are *relevant*, when they serve to strengthen a cause, and, on the other hand, they are *irrelevant* when they in no wise answer this end; 'Having showed you that we differ about the meaning of Scripture, and are like to do so, certainly there ought to be a rule or a judge between us, to determine our differences, or at least to make our probations and arguments *relevant*.'—K. CHARLES (*Letter to A. Henderson*). What is *relevant* is therefore, properly speaking, that which is *pertinent*, so as to aid a cause.

TO LABOUR, TAKE PAINS OR TROUBLE, USE ENDEAVOUR.

Labour, in Latin *labor*, comes, in all probability, from *labo* to falter or faint, because *labour* causes faintness; to *take pains* is to expose oneself to the *pains*; and to *take* the *trouble* is to impose the *trouble*; *endeavour*, *v. To endeavour.*

The first three terms suppose the necessity for a painful exertion: but to *labour* (*v. Work*) expresses more than to *take pains*, and this more than to *take trouble*; to *use endeavour* excludes every idea of pain or inconvenience: great difficulties must be conquered; great perfection or correctness requires *pains*: a concern to please will give *trouble*; but we *use endeavours* wherever any object is to be obtained, or any duty to be performed. To *labour* is either a corporeal or a mental action; to *take pains* is principally an effort of the mind or the attention; to *take trouble* is an effort either of the body or mind: a faithful minister of the Gospel *labours* to instil Christian principles into the minds of his audience, and to heal all the breaches which the angry passions make between them: when a child is properly sensible of the value of improvement, he will take the utmost *pains* to profit by the instruction of the master: he who is too indolent to *take* the *trouble* to make his wishes known to those who would comply with them, cannot expect others to *trouble* themselves with inquiring into their necessities: a good name is of such value to every man that he ought to *use* his best *endeavours* to preserve it unblemished; 'They (the Jews) were fain to *take pains* to rid themselves of their happiness; and it cost them *labour* and violence to become miserable.'—SOUTH. 'A good conscience hath always enough to reward itself, though the success fall not out according to the merit of the *endeavour*.'—HOWEL.

WORK, LABOUR, TOIL, DRUDGERY, TASK.

Work, in Saxon *weorc*, Greek ἔργον, comes doubtless from the Hebrew ארג to weave; *labour*, in Latin *labor*, signifies the same as in the preceding article (*v. To labour*); *toil* is probably connected with *to till*; *drudgery* is connected with *drag*, signifying painful *labour*.

Work is the general term, as including that which calls for the exertion of our strength: *labour* differs from it in the degree of exertion required; it is hard *work*: *toil* expresses a still higher degree of painful exertion: *drudgery* implies a mean and degrading *work*;

> The hireling thus,
> With *labour drudges* out the painful day.—ROWE.

Every member of society must *work* for his support, if he is not in independent circumstances: the poor are obliged to *labour* for their daily subsistence; some are compelled to *toil* incessantly for the pittance which they earn: *drudgery* falls to the lot of those who are the lowest in society. A man wishes to complete his *work*; he is desirous of resting from his *labour*; he seeks for a respite from his *toil*; he submits to *drudgery*.

Work is more or less voluntary, but *task*, in French *tasche*, and Italian *tassa*, is a *work* imposed by others;

> Relieves me from my *task* of servile *toil*,
> Daily in the common prison else enjoined me.
> MILTON.

In its improper application it may be taken in a good sense for a *work* which one has imposed on oneself;

> No happier *task* these faded eyes pursue,
> To read and weep is all they now can do.—POPE.

WORK, OPERATION.

Work, which is derived from the Hebrew, as in the preceding article, denotes either the act of *working*, or the result of that act: in both cases it is a simple exertion of power; as when speaking of the *works* of creation or of art and mechanical skill; as the *work* of the artist and artisan;

> O, fairest of creation! last and best
> Of all God's *works!* creature, in whom excels
> Whatever can to sight or thought be form'd,
> Holy, divine, good, amiable, or sweet,
> How art thou lost!—MILTON.
>
> Nor was the *work* impair'd by storms alone,
> But felt the approaches of too warm a sun.—POPE.

Operation (*v. Action*) denotes the act of *operating* and is a combined exertion, being the effect of method and skill; as in the case of the surgeon, who performs an *operation*; or a natural process, as the *operations* of thought, or the *operation* of vegetation; 'Speculative painting, without the assistance of manual *operation*, can never attain to perfection, but slothfully languishes; for it was not with his tongue that Apelles performed his noble *works*.—DRYDEN. 'There are in men *operations* natural, rational, supernatural, some politick, some finally ecclesiastick.'—HOOKER.

Between the verbs to *work* and *operate* there is even a nicer distinction, both being used in the sense of a process, physical, moral, or intellectual: but *work* always conveys the idea of the exertion of power, and *operate* that of a gradual course of action: so water *works* its way under ground; things *operate* on the mind by various ways;

> Some deadly draught, some enemy to life,
> Boils in my bowels, and *works* out my soul.
> DRYDEN.
>
> Sometimes a passion seems to *operate*,
> Almost in contradiction to itself.—SHIRLEY.

SERVANT, DOMESTICK, MENIAL, DRUDGE.

In the term *servant* is included the idea of the service performed; 'A *servant* dwells remote from all knowledge of his lord's purposes.'—SOUTH. In the term *domestick*, from *domus* a house, is included the idea of one belonging to the house or family; 'Montezuma was attended by his own *domesticks*, and served with his usual state.'—ROBERTSON. In the word *menial*, from *manus* the hand, is included the idea of labour; 'Some were his (King Charles') own *menial* servants, and ate bread at his table before they lifted up their heel against him.'—SOUTH. The term *drudge* includes *drudgery*; 'He who will be vastly rich must resolve to be a *drudge* all his days.'—SOUTH. We hire a *servant* at a certain rate, and for a particular service; we are attached to our *domesticks* according to their assiduity and attention to our wishes; we employ as a *menial* one who is unfit for a higher employment; and a *drudge* in any labour, however hard and disagreeable.

SERVITUDE, SLAVERY, BONDAGE.

Servitude expresses less than *slavery*, and this less than *bondage*.

Servitude, from *servio*, conveys simply the idea of performing a service, without specifying the principle upon which it is performed. Among the Romans *servus* signified a slave, because all who served were literally slaves, the power over the person being almost unlimited. The mild influence of Christianity has corrected men's notions with regard to their rights, as well as their duties, and established *servitude* on the just principle of a mutual compact, without any infraction on that most precious of all human gifts, personal liberty; 'It is fit and necessary that some persons in the world should be in love with a splendid *servitude*.'—SOUTH. *Slavery*, which marks a condition incompatible with the existence of this invaluable endowment, is a term odious to the Christian ear; it had its origin in the grossest state of society: the word being derived from the German *slave*, or *Sclavonians*, a fierce and intrepid people, who made a long stand against the Germans, and, being at last defeated, were made *slaves*. *Slavery*, therefore, includes not only *servitude*, but also the odious circumstance of the entire subjection of one individual to another; a condition which deprives him of every privilege belonging to a free agent, and a rational creature; and which forcibly bends the will and affections of the one to the humour of the other, and converts a thinking being into a mere senseless tool in the hands of its owner. *Slavery* unfortunately remains, though barbarism has ceased. Christianity has taught men their true end and destination; but it has not yet been able to extinguish that inordinate love of dominion, which is an innate propensity in the human breast. There are those who take the name of Christians, and yet cling to the practice of making their fellow-creatures an article of commerce. Some delude themselves with the idea that they can ameliorate the condition of those over whom they have usurped this unlicensed power; but they forget that he who begins to be a *slave* ceases to be a man; that *slavery* is the extinction of our nobler part; and the abuse even of that part in us which we have in common with the brutes; 'So different are the geniuses which are formed under Turkish *slavery* and Grecian liberty.'—ADDISON.

Bondage, from to *bind*, denotes the state of being *bound*, that is, *slavery* in its most aggravated form, in which, to the loss of personal liberty, is added cruel treatment; the term is seldom applied in its proper sense to any persons but the Israelites in Egypt. In a figurative sense, we speak of being a *slave* to our passions, and under the *bondage* of sin, in which cases the terms preserve precisely the same distinction;

Our cage
We make a choir, as doth the prison'd bird,
And sing our *bondage* freely.—SHAKSPEARE.

The same distinction exists between the epithets *servile* and *slavish*, which are employed only in the moral application. He who is *servile* has the mean character of a servant, but he is still a free agent; but he who is *slavish* is bound and fettered in every possible form;

That *servile* path thou nobly dost decline,
Of tracing word by word, and line by line.
Those are the labour'd births of *slavish* brains,
Not the effect of poetry but pains.—DENHAM.

PRODUCTION, PERFORMANCE, WORK.

When we speak of any thing as resulting from any specified operation, we term it a *production;* as the *production* of an author, signifying what he has *produced* by the effort of his mind: Homer's Iliad is esteemed as one of the finest *productions* of the imagination. When we speak of any thing as executed or *performed* by some person we term it a *performance*, as a drawing or a painting is denominated the *performance* of a particular artist. The term *production* cannot be employed without specifying or referring to the source from which it is *produced*, or the means by which it is *produced*,--as the *production* of art, the *production* of the inventive faculty, the *production* of the mind, &c.;

Nature, in her *productions* slow, aspires
By just degrees to reach perfection's height.
SOMERVILLE.

A *performance* cannot be spoken of without referring to the individual by whom it has been *performed;* hence we speak of this or that person's *performance;* 'The *performances* of Pope were burnt by those whom he had, perhaps, selected as most likely to publish them.'—JOHNSON. When we wish to specify any thing that results from *work* or labour, it is termed a *work:* in this manner we either speak of the *work* of one's hands, or a *work* of the imagination, a *work* of time, a *work* of magnitude; 'Yet there are some *works* which the author must consign unpublished to posterity.'—JOHNSON. The *production* results from a complicated operation; the *performance* consists of simple action; the *work* springs from active exertion: Shakspeare's plays are termed *productions*, as they respect the source from which they came, namely, his genius; they might be called his *performances*, as far as respected the *performance* or completion of some task or specifick undertaking; they would be called his *works*, as far as respected the labour which he bestowed upon them. The composition of a book is properly a *production*, when it is original matter; the sketching of a landscape, or drawing a plan, is a *performance;* the compilation of a history is a *work*.

ESSAY, TREATISE, TRACT, DISSERTATION.

All these words are employed by authors to characterize compositions varying in their form and contents *Essay*, which signifies a trial or attempt (*v. Attempt*) is here used to designate in a specifick manner an author's attempt to illustrate any point. It is most commonly applied to small detached pieces, which contain only the general thoughts of a writer on any given subject, and afford room for amplification into details; although by Locke in his "*Essay* on the Understanding," Beattie in his "*Essay* on Truth," and other authors, it is modestly used for their connected and finished endeavours to elucidate a doctrine: 'It is my frequent practice to visit places of resort in this town, to observe what reception my works meet with in the world; it being a privilege asserted by Monsieur Montaigne and others, of vain-glorious memory, that we writers of *essays* may talk of ourselves.'—STEELE.

A *treatise* is more systematick than an *essay;* it treats on the subject in a methodical form, and conveys the idea of something laboured, scientifick, and instructive; 'The very title of a moral *treatise* has something in it austere and shocking to the careless and inconsiderate.'—ADDISON. A *tract* is only a species of small *treatise*, drawn up upon particular occasions, and published in a separate form. They are both derived from the Latin *tractus*, participle of *traho* to draw, manage, or handle; 'I desire my reader to consider every particular paper or discourse as a distinct *tract* by itself.'—ADDISON. *Dissertation*, from *dissero* to argue, is with propriety applied to performances of an argumentative nature; 'A modern philosopher, quoted by Monsieur Bayle in his learned *dissertation* on the souls of brutes, says, Deus est anima brutorum, God himself is the soul of brutes.'—ADDISON.

Essays are either moral, political, philosophical, or literary: they are the crude attempts of the youth to digest his own thoughts; or they are the more mature attempts of the man to communicate his thoughts to others. Of the former description are the prize *essays* in schools; and of the latter are the *essays* innumerable which have been published on every subject, since the days of Bacon to the present day. *Treatises* are mostly written on ethical, political, or speculative subjects, such as Fenelon's, Milton's, or Locke's *treatise* on education; De Lolme's *treatise* on the constitution of England; Colquhoun's *treatise* on the police. *Dissertations* are employed on disputed points of literature, as Bentley's *dissertation* upon the epistles of Phalaris, De Pauw's *dissertations* on the Egyptians and Chinese. *Tracts* are ephemeral productions, mostly on political and religious subjects, which seldom survive the occasion which gave them birth. Of this description are the pamphlets which daily issue from the press, for or against the measures of government, or the public measures of any particular party.

The *essay* is the most popular mode of writing: it suits the writer who has not either talent or inclination to pursue his inquiries farther, and it suits the generality of readers who are amused with variety and superficiality: the *treatise* is adapted for the student; he will not be contented with the superficial *essay*, when more ample materials are within his reach; the *tract* is formed for the political partisan; it receives its interest from the occurrence of the motive; the *dissertation* interests the disputant.

PRODUCTION, PRODUCE, PRODUCT.

The term *production* expresses either the act of *producing* or the thing *produced; product* and *produce* express only the thing *produced:* the *production* of a tree from a seed, is one of the wonders of nature; the *produce* of a thing is said to be considerable or otherwise.

In the sense of the thing *produced*, *production* is applied to every individual thing that is *produced* by another: in this sense a tree is a *production; produce* and *product* are applied only to those *productions* which are to be turned to a purpose: the former in a collective sense, and in reference to some particular object; the latter in an abstract and general sense; the aggregate quantity of grain drawn from a field is termed the *produce* of the field; but corn, hay, vegetables and fruits in general, are termed *products* of the earth: the naturalist examines all the *productions* of nature; 'Nature also, as if desirous that so bright a *production* of her skill should be set in the fairest light, had bestowed on king Alfred every bodily accomplishment.'—HUME. The husbandman looks to the *produce* of his lands; 'A storm of hail, I am informed, has destroyed all the *produce* of my estate in Tuscany.'—MELMOUTH (*Letters of Cicero*). The topographer and traveller inquire about the *products* of different countries; 'Our British *products* are of such kinds and quantities as can turn the balance of trade to our advantage.'—ADDISON.

There is the same distinction between these terms in their improper, as in their proper, acceptation: a *production* is whatever results from an effort, physical or mental, as a *production* of genius, a *production* of art, and the like; 'What would become of the scrofulous consumptive *productions*, furnished by our men of wit and learning.'—SWIFT. The *produce* is the amount or aggregate result from physical or mental labour: thus, whatever the husbandman reaps from the cultivation of his land is termed the *produce* of his labour; whatever results from any publick subscription or collection is, in like manner, the *produce*; 'This tax has already been so often tried, that we know the exact *produce* of it.'—ADDISON. The *product* is seldom employed except in regard to the mental operation of figures, as the *product* from multiplication, but it may be used precisely in the sense of *production*; 'I cannot help thinking the Arabian tales the *product* of some woman's imagination.'—ATTERBURY.

TO BEAR, YIELD.

Bear, in Saxon *baran*, old German *beran*, Latin *pario*, and Hebrew ברא to create; *yield*, *v. To afford.*

Bear conveys the idea of creating within itself; *yield* that of giving from itself. Animals *bear* their young; inanimate objects *yield* their produce. An apple-tree *bears* apples; the earth *yields* fruits.

Bear marks properly the natural power of bringing forth something of its own kind; *yield* is said of the result or quantum brought forth: shrubs *bear* leaves, flowers, or berries, according to their natural properties;

> No keel shall cut the waves for foreign ware,
> For every soil shall ev'ry product *bear*.—DRYDEN.

Flowers *yield* seeds plentifully or otherwise as they are favoured by circumstances;

> Nor Bactria, nor the richer Indian fields,
> Nor all the gummy stores Arabia *yields*,
> Nor any foreign earth of greater name,
> Can with sweet Italy contend in fame.—DRYDEN.

TO BEAR, CARRY, CONVEY, TRANSPORT.

Bear, from the sense of generating (*v. To bear, yield*), has derived that of retaining; *carry*, in French *charier*, probably from the Latin *currus*, Greek καίρω or τρέχω to run, or κύρω, in Hebrew לרא to meet, signifies to move a thing from one place to another; *convey*, in Latin *conveho*, is compounded of *con* and *veho* to carry with one; *transport*, in French *transporter*, Latin *transporto*, compounded of *trans* over and *porto* to carry, signifies to carry to a distance.

To bear is simply to take the weight of any substance upon one's self; to *carry* is to remove that weight from the spot where it was: we always *bear* in *carrying*, but we do not always *carry* when we *bear*. Both may be applied to things as well as persons: whatever receives the weight of any thing *bears* it; whatever is caused to move with any thing *carries* it. That which cannot be easily *borne* must be burdensome to *carry*: in extremely hot weather it is sometimes irksome to *bear* the weight even of one's clothing; Virgil praises the pious Æneas for having *carried* his father on his shoulders in order to save him from the sacking of Troy. Weak people or weak things are not fit to *bear* heavy burdens: lazy people prefer to be *carried* rather than to *carry* any thing.

Since *bear* is confined to personal service it may be used in the sense of *carry*, when the latter implies the removal of any thing by means of any other body. The *bearer* of any letter or parcel is he who *carries* it in his hand;

> In hollow wood thy floating armies *bear*.—DRYDEN.

The *carrier* of parcels is he who employs a *conveyance*; 'A whale, besides those seas and oceans in the several vessels of his body which are filled with innumerable shoals of little animals, *carries* about him a whole world of inhabitants.'—ADDISON. Hence the word *bear* is often very appropriately substituted for *carry*, as Virgil praises Æneas for *bearing* his father on his shoulders.

Convey and *transport* are species of *carrying*. *Carry* in its particular sense is employed either for personal exertions or actions performed by the help of other means; *convey* and *transport* are employed for such actions as are performed not by immediate personal intervention or exertion: a porter *carries* goods on his knot; goods are *conveyed* in a wagon or a cart; they are *transported* in a vessel.

Convey expresses simply the mode of removing; *transport* annexes to this the idea of the place and the distance. Merchants get the goods *conveyed* into their warehouses, which they have had *transported* from distant countries. Pedestrians take no more with them than what they can conveniently *carry*: could armies do the same, one of the greatest obstacles to the indulgence of human ambition would be removed; for many an incursion into a peaceful country is defeated for the want of means to *convey* provisions sufficient for such numbers; and when mountains or deserts are to be traversed, another great difficulty presents itself in the *transportation* of artillery;

> Love cannot, like the wind, itself *convey*
> To fill two sails, though both are spread one way
> HOWARD.

It is customary at funerals for some to *bear* the pall and others to *carry* wands or staves; the body itself is *conveyed* in a hearse, unless it has to cross the ocean, in which case it is *transported* in a vessel; 'It is to navigation that men are indebted for the power of *transporting* the superfluous stock of one part of the earth to supply the wants of another.'—ROBERTSON.

TO BRING, FETCH, CARRY.

To *bring*, in German, &c. *bringen*, is supposed to be contracted from *beringen*, and *ringen* or *regen* to move; *fetch* is not improbably connected with the verb search, signifying to send for or go after; *carry* *v. To bear, carry.*

To *bring* is simply to take with one's self from the place where one is; to *fetch* is to go first to a place and then *bring* the thing away; to *fetch* therefore is a species of *bringing*; whatever is near at hand is *brought*; whatever is at a distance must be *fetched*. The porter at an inn *brings* a parcel, the servant *fetches* it.

Bring always respects motion towards the place in which the agent or speaker resides; 'What appeared to me wonderful was that none of the ants came home without *bringing* something.'—ADDISON. *Fetch* denotes a motion both to and from; 'I have said before that those ants which I did so particularly consider, *fetched* their corn out of a garret.'—ADDISON. *Carry* denotes always a motion directly from the place or at a distance from the place: 'How great is the hardship of a poor ant, when she *carries* a grain of corn to the second story, climbing up a wall with her head downwards.'—ADDISON. A servant *brings* the parcel home which his master has sent him to *fetch*; he *carries* a parcel from home. A *carrier carries* parcels to and from a place, but he only *brings* parcels to any place.

Bring is an action performed at the option of the agent; *fetch* and *carry* are mostly done at the command of another. Hence the old proverb, 'He who will *fetch* will *carry*,' to mark the character of the gossip and tale-bearer, who reports what he hears from two persons in order to please both parties.

TO AFFORD, YIELD, PRODUCE.

Afford is probably changed from *afferred*, and comes from the Latin *affero*, compounded of *af* or *ad* and *fero* signifying to bring to a person; *yield*, in Saxon *geldan*, German *gelten* to pay, restore, or give the value, is probably connected with the Hebrew ילד to breed, or bring forth; *produce*, in Latin *produco*, compounded of *pro* forth and *duco* to bring, signifies to bring out or into existence.

With *afford* is associated the idea of communicating a part or property of some substance, to a person: meat *affords* nourishment to those who make use of it; the sun *affords* light and heat to all living creatures; 'The generous man in the ordinary acceptation, without respect of the demands of his family, will soon find upon the foot of his account that he has sacrificed to fools, knaves, flatterers, or the deservedly unhappy, all the opportunities of *affording* any future assistance where it ought to be.'—STEELE.

Yielding is the natural operation of any substance to give up or impart the parts or properties inherent in it; it is the natural surrender which an object makes of itself; trees *yield* fruit; the seed *yields* grain; some sorts of grain do not *yield* much in particular soils;

> Their vines a shadow to their race shall *yield*,
> And the same hand that sowed shall reap the field.
> POPE.

Produce conveys the idea of one thing causing another to exist, or to spring out of it; it is a species of creation, the formation of a new substance: the earth *produces* a variety of fruits; confined air will *produce* an explosion;

> Their sharpen'd ends in earth their footing place,
> And the dry poles *produce* a living race.—DRYDEN.

In the moral application they are similarly distinguished: nothing *affords* so great a scope for ridicule as the follies of fashion; 'This is the consolation of all good men unto whom his ubiquity *affordeth* continual comfort and security.'—BROWN. Nothing *yields* so much satisfaction as religion. 'The mind of man desireth evermore to know the truth, according to the most infallible certainty which the nature of things can *yield*.'—HOOKER. Nothing *produces* so much mischief as the vice of drunkenness;

> Thou all this good of evil shalt *produce*.—MILTON.

The history of man does not *afford* an instance of any popular commotion that has ever *produced* such atrocities and atrocious characters as the French revolution.

Religion is the only thing that can *afford* true consolation and peace of mind in the season of affliction and the hour of death. The recollection of past incidents, particularly those which have passed in our infancy, *produces* the most pleasurable sensations in the mind.

BUSINESS, OCCUPATION, EMPLOYMENT, ENGAGEMENT, AVOCATION.

Business signifies what makes *busy* (*v. Active, busy*); *occupation*, from *occupy*, in French *occuper*, Latin *occupo*, that is, *ob* and *capio*, signifies that which serves or takes possession of a person or thing to the exclusion of other things; *employment*, from *employ*, in French *emploi*, Latin *implico*, Greek εμπλέκω, signifies that which engages or fixes a person; *engagement* also signifies what engages or binds a person; *avocation*, in Latin *avocatio*, from *a* and *voco*, signifies the thing that calls off from another thing.

Business occupies all a person's thoughts as well as his time and powers; *occupation* and *employment* *occupy* only his time and strength: the first is mostly regular, it is the object of our choice; the second is casual, it depends on the will of another. *Engagement* is a partial *employment*, *avocation* a particular *engagement*: an *engagement* prevents us from doing any thing else; an *avocation* calls off or prevents us from doing what we wish.

Every tradesman has a *business*, on the diligent prosecution of which depends his success in life; 'The materials are no sooner wrought into paper, but they are distributed among the presses, where they again set innumerable artists at work, and furnish *business* to another mystery.'—ADDISON. Every mechanick has his daily *occupation*, by which he maintains his family; 'How little must the ordinary *occupations* of men seem to one who is engaged in so noble a pursuit as the assimilation of himself to the Deity.'—BERKELEY. Every labourer has an *employment* which is fixed for him: 'Creatures who have the labours of the mind, as well as those of the body, to furnish them with *employments*.'—GUARDIAN.

Business and *occupation* always suppose a serious object. *Business* is something more urgent and important than *occupation*: a man of independent fortune has no occasion to pursue *business*, but as a rational agent he will not be contented to be without an *occupation*.

Employment, *engagement*, and *avocation* leave the object undefined. An *employment* may be a mere diversion of the thoughts, and a wasting of the hours in some idle pursuit; a child may have its *employment*, which may be its play in distinction from its *business*, 'I would recommend to every one of my readers the keeping a journal of their lives for one week, and setting down punctually their whole series of *employments* during that space of time.'—ADDISON. An *engagement* may have no higher object than that of pleasure; the idlest people have often the most *engagements*: the gratification of curiosity, and the love of social pleasure, supply them with an abundance of *engagements*; 'Mr. Baretti being a single man, and entirely clear from all *engagements*, takes the advantage of his independence.'—JOHNSON. *Avocations* have seldom a direct trifling object, although it may sometimes be of a subordinate nature, and generally irrelevant: numerous *avocations* are not desirable; every man should have a regular pursuit, the *business* of his life, to which the principal part of his time should be devoted: *avocations* therefore of a serious nature are apt to divide the time and attention to a hurtful degree; 'Sorrow ought not to be suffered to increase by indulgence, but must give way after a stated time to social duties and the common *avocations* of life.'—JOHNSON.

A person who is *busy* has much to attend to, and attends to it closely: a person who is *occupied* has a full share of *business* without any pressure; he is opposed to one who is idle: a person who is *employed* has the present moment filled up; he is not in a state of inaction: the person who is *engaged* is not at liberty to be otherwise *employed*; his time is not his own; he is opposed to one at leisure.

BUSINESS, TRADE, PROFESSION, ART.

These words are synonymous in the sense of a calling, for the purpose of a livelihood; *business* (*v. Business*) is general; *trade*, signifying that which employs the time by way of *trade*; *profession*, or that which one professes to do by way of employment; and *art* signifying that which is practised in the way of the *arts*, are particular; all *trade* is *business*, but all *business* is not *trade*.

Buying and selling of merchandise is inseparable from *trade*; but the exercise of one's knowledge and experience, for purposes of gain, constitutes a *business*; when learning or particular skill is required, it is a *profession*; and when there is a peculiar exercise of *art*, it is an *art*: every shopkeeper and retail dealer carries on a *trade*; 'Some persons, indeed, by the privilege of their birth and quality, are above a common *trade* and *profession*, but they are not hereby exempted from all *business*, and allowed to live unprofitably to others.'—TILLOTSON. Brokers, manufacturers, bankers, and others, carry on *business*; 'Those who are determined by choice to any particular kind of *business* are indeed more happy than those who are determined by necessity.'—ADDISON. Clergymen, medical, or military men, follow a *profession*; 'No one of the sons of Adam ought to think himself exempt from labour or industry; those to whom birth or fortune may seem to make such an application unnecessary, ought to find out some calling or *profession* that they may not lie as a burthen upon the species.'—ADDISON. Musicians and painters follow an *art*. 'The painter understands his *art*.'—SWIFT.

BUSINESS, OFFICE, DUTY.

Business is what one prescribes to one's self; *office*, in French *office*, Latin *officium*, from *officio*, or *ob* and *facio*, signifying to do for, or on account of any one, is prescribed by another; *duty*, from the Latin *debitum* and *debeo* to owe, signifying what is due, is prescribed or enjoined by a fixed rule of propriety: mercantile concerns are the *business* which a man take upon himself, the management of parish concerns is an *office* imposed upon a person often, much against his inclination; the maintenance of a family is a *duty* which a man's conscience enjoins upon him to perform.

Business and *duty* are publick or private; *office* is mostly of a publick nature: a minister of state, by virtue of his *office*, has always publick *business* to perform;

But now the feather'd youth their former bounds
Ardent disdain, and, weighing oft their wings,
Demand the free possession of the sky.
This one glad *office* more, and then dissolves
Parental love at once, now heedless grown.
THOMSON.

But men in general have only private *business* to transact; 'It is certain, from Suetonius, that the Romans thought the education of their children a *business* properly belonging to the parents themselves.'—BUDGELL. A minister of religion has publick *duties* to perform in his ministerial capacity; every other man has personal or relative *duties*, which he is called upon to discharge according to his station; 'Discretion is the perfection of reason, and a guide to us in all the *duties* of life.'—ADDISON.

AFFAIR, BUSINESS, CONCERN.

Affair, in French *affaire*, from *à* and *faire* to be done, signifies that which is to be done or is in hand; *business*, from *busy* (*v. Active*), signifies the thing that makes or interests a person, or with which he is busy or occupied; *concern*, in French *concerner*, Latin *concerno*, compounded of *con* and *cerno* to look, signifies the thing looked at, thought of, or taken part in.

An *affair* is what happens; a *business* is what is done; a *concern* is what is felt. An *affair* is general; it respects one, many, or all; every *business* and *concern* is an *affair*, though not *vice versâ*. *Business* and *concern* are personal; *business* is that which engages the attention: *concern* is that which interests the feelings, prospects, and condition, advantageously or otherwise. An *affair* is interesting; a *business* is serious; a *concern* momentous. The usurpation of power is an *affair* which interests a nation; 'I remember in Tully's epistle, in the recommendation of a man to an *affair* which had no manner of relation to money, it is said, you may trust him, for he is a frugal man.'—STEELE. The adjusting of a difference is a *business* most suited to the ministers of religion; 'We may indeed say that our part does not suit us, and that we could perform another better; but this, says Epictetus, is not our *business*.'—ADDISON. To make our peace with our Maker is the *concern* of every individual; 'The sense of other men ought to prevail over us in things of less consideration; but not in *concerns* where truth and honour are engaged.'—STEELE.

Affairs are administered; *business* is transacted; *concerns* are managed. The *affairs* of the world are administered by a Divine Providence. Those who are in the practice of the law require peculiar talents to fit them for transacting the complicated *business* which perpetually offers itself. Some men are so involved in the *affairs* of this world, as to forget the *concerns* of the next, which ought to be nearest and dearest to them.

TO AFFECT, CONCERN.

Affect, in French *affecter*, Latin *affectum*, participle of *afficio*, compounded of *ad* and *facio* to do or act, signifies to act upon; *concern*, *v. Affair*.

Things *affect* us which produce any change in our outward circumstances; they *concern* us if only connected with our circumstances in any shape.

Whatever *affects* must *concern*; but all that *concerns* does not *affect*. The price of corn *affects* the interest of the seller: and therefore it *concerns* him to keep it up, without regard to the publick good or injury.

Things *affect* either persons or things; but they *concern* persons only. Rain *affects* the hay or corn; and these matters *concern* every one more or less.

Affect and *concern* have an analogous meaning likewise, when taken for the influence on the mind. We are *affected* by things when our *affections* only are awakened by them; we are *concerned* when our understanding and wishes are engaged.

We may be *affected* either with joy or sorrow: 'We see that every different species of sensible creatures has its different notions of beauty, and that each of them is *affected* with the beauties of its own kind.'—ADDISON. We are *concerned* only in a painful manner:

Without *concern* he hears, but hears from far,
Of tumults, and descents, and distant war.
DRYDEN.

People of tender sensibility are easily *affected*: irritable people are *concerned* about trifles. It is natural for every one to be *affected* at the recital of misfortunes; but there are people of so cold and selfish a character as not to be *concerned* about any thing which does not immediately *affect* their persons or property.

INTEREST, CONCERN.

The *interest*, from the Latin *interesse* to be among, or have a part or a share in a thing, is more comprehensive than *concern* (*v. Affair*). We have an *interest* in whatever touches or comes near to our feelings or our external circumstances; we have a *concern* in that which respects our external circumstances. The *interest* is that which is agreeable; it consists of either profit, advantage, gain, or amusement; it binds us to an object, and makes us think of it: the *concern*, on the other hand, is something involuntary or painful. We have a *concern* in that which we are obliged to look to, which we are bound to from the fear of losing or of suffering. It is the *interest* of every man to cultivate a religious temper; it is the *concern* of all to be on their guard against temptation; 'O give us a serious comprehension of that one great *interest* of others as well as ourselves.'—HAMMOND.

And could the marble rocks but know,
They'd strive to find some secret way unknown,
Maugre the senseless nature of the stone,
Their pity and *concern* to show.—POMFRET

OFFICE, PLACE, CHARGE, FUNCTION.

Office, in Latin *officium*, from *officio*, or *efficio*, signifies either the duty performed or the situation in which the duty is performed. *Place* comprehends no idea of duty, for there may be sinecure *places* which are only nominal *offices*, and designate merely a relationship with the government: every *office* therefore of a publick nature is in reality a *place*, yet every *place* is not an *office*. The *place* of secretary of state is likewise an *office*, but that of ranger of a park is a *place* only and not an *office*. The *office* is held; the *place* is filled: the *office* is given or intrusted to a person; the *place* is granted or conferred: the *office* reposes a confidence, and imposes a responsibility; the *place* gives credit and influence: the *office* is bestowed on a man from his qualification; the *place* is granted to him by favour, or as a reward for past services: the *office* is more or less honourable;

You have contriv'd to take
From Rome all season'd *office*, and to wind
Yourself into a power tyrannical.—SHAKSPEARE.

The *place* is more or less profitable;

When rogues like these (a sparrow cries)
To honours and employment rise,
I court no favour, ask no *place*.—GAY.

In an extended application of the terms *office* and *place*, the latter has a much lower signification than that of the former, since the *office* is always connected with the State; but the *place* is a private concern; the *office* is a *place* of trust, but the *place* may be a *place* for menial labour; the *offices* are multiplied in time of war; the *places* for domestick service are more numerous in a state of peace and prosperity. The *office* is frequently taken not with any reference to the *place* occupied, but simply to the thing done; this brings it nearer in signification to the term *charge* (*v. Care*). An *office* imposes a task, or some performance;

'T is all men's *office* to speak patience
To those that wring under the load of sorrow.
SHAKSPEARE.

A *charge* imposes a responsibility; we have alway

something to do in *office*, always something to look after in a *charge*; 'Denham was made governour of Farnham Castle for the king, but he soon resigned that *charge* and retreated to Oxford.'—JOHNSON. The *office* is either publick or private, the *charge* is always of a private and personal nature: a person performs the *office* of a magistrate, or of a minister; he undertakes the *charge* of instructing youth, or of being a guardian, or of conveying a person's property from one place to another. The *office* is that which is assigned by another; *function* is properly the act of discharging or completing an *office* or business, from *fungor*, viz. *finem* and *ago* to put an end to or bring to a conclusion; it is extended in its acceptation to the *office* itself or the thing done, in which case the idea of duty predominates, as the *functions* of a minister of state or of a minister of the gospel; 'The ministry is not now bound to any one tribe; now none is secluded from that *function* of any degree, state, or calling.'—WHITGIFT. The *office* in its strict sense is performed only by conscious or intelligent agents, who act according to their instructions; the *function*, on the other hand, is sometimes an operation of unconscious objects according to the laws of nature. The *office* of a herald is to proclaim publick events or to communicate circumstances from one publick body to another: the *function* of the tongue is to speak; that of the ear, to hear: that of the eye, to see. The word *office* is sometimes employed in the same application by the personification of nature, which assigns an *office* to the ear, to the tongue, to the eye, and the like. When the frame becomes overpowered by a sudden shock, the tongue will frequently refuse to perform its *office*; 'The two *offices* of memory are collection and distribution.'—JOHNSON. When the animal *functions* are impeded for a length of time, the vital power ceases to exist;

Nature within me seems,
In all her *functions*, weary of herself.—MILTON.

PROCEEDING, PROCESS, PROGRESS.

The manner of performing actions for the attainment of a given end is the common idea comprehended in these terms. *Proceeding* is the most general, as it simply expresses the general idea of the manner of going on; the rest are specifick terms, denoting some particularity in the action, object, or circumstance. The *proceeding* is said commonly of such things as happen in the ordinary way of doing business; 'What could be more fair, than to lay open to an enemy all that you wished to obtain, and to desire him to imitate your ingenuous *proceeding*?'—BURKE. *Process* is said of such things as are done by rule: the former is considered in a moral point of view; the latter in a scientifick or technical point of view; the freemasons have bound themselves together by a law of secrecy not to reveal some part of their *proceedings*; the *process* by which paper is made has undergone considerable improvements since its first invention;

Saturnian Juno now, with double care,
Attends the fatal *process* of the war.—DRYDEN.

The *proceeding* and *progress* both refer to the moral actions of men; but the *proceeding* simply denotes the act of going on, or doing something; the *progress* denotes an approximation to the end: the *proceeding* may be only a partial action, comprehending both the beginning and the end; but the *progress* is applied to that which requires time, and a regular succession of action, to bring it to a completion; that is a *proceeding* in which every man is tried in a court of law; that is a *progress* which one makes in learning, by the addition to one's knowledge: hence we do not talk of the *proceeding* of life, but of the *progress* of life; 'Devotion bestows that enlargement of heart in the service of God, which is the greatest principle both of perseverance and *progress* in virtue.'—BLAIR.

PROCEEDING, TRANSACTION.

Proceeding signifies literally the thing that *proceeds*; and *transaction* the thing *transacted*: the former is, therefore, of something that is going forward; the latter of something that is already done: we are witnesses to the whole *proceeding*; we inquire into the whole *transaction*. The *proceeding* is said of every event or circumstance which goes forward through the agency of men; the *transaction* only comprehends those matters which have been deliberately *transacted* or brought to a conclusion: in this sense we use the word *proceeding* in application to an affray in the street; and the word *transaction* to some commercial negotiation that has been carried on between certain persons. The *proceeding* marks the manner of *proceeding*; as when we speak of the *proceedings* in a court of law; 'The *proceedings* of a council of old men in an American tribe, we are told, were no less formal and sagacious than those in a senate in more polished republicks.'—ROBERTSON. The *transaction* marks the business *transacted*; as the *transactions* on the Exchange; 'It was Bothwell's interest to cover, if possible, the whole *transaction* under the veil of darkness and silence.'—ROBERTSON. A *proceeding* may be characterized as disgraceful; a *transaction* as iniquitous.

TRADE, COMMERCE, TRAFFICK, DEALING.

Trade, in Italian *tratto*, Latin *tracto* to treat, signifies the transaction of business; *commerce*, *v. Intercourse*; *traffick*, in French *traffique*, Italian *traffico*, compounded of *tra* or *trans* and *facio*, signifies to make over from one to another; *dealing*, from the verb to *deal*, in German *theilen* to divide, signifies to put in parts according to a certain ratio, or at a given price.

The leading idea in *trade* is that of carrying on business for purposes of gain; the rest are but modes of *trade*: *commerce* is a mode of *trade* by exchange: *traffick* is a sort of personal *trade*, a sending from hand to hand; *dealing* is a bargaining or calculating kind of *trade*. *Trade* is either on a large or small scale; *commerce* is always on a large scale: we may *trade* retail or wholesale; we always carry on *commerce* by wholesale: *trade* is either within or without the country; *commerce* is always between different countries: there may be a *trade* between two towns; but there is a *commerce* between England and America, between France and Germany: hence it arises that the general term *trade* is of inferiour import when compared with *commerce*. The *commerce* of a country, in the abstract and general sense, conveys more to our mind, and is a more noble expression, than the *trade* of the country, as the merchant ranks higher than the *tradesman*, and a *commercial* house, than a *trading* concern;

Instructed ships shall sail to quick *commerce*,
By which remotest regions are ally'd;
Which makes one city of the universe,
Where some may gain, and all may be supply'd
DRYDEN.

Nevertheless the word *trade* may be used in the same general and enlarged sense; '*Trade*, without enlarging the British territories, has given us a kind of additional empire.'—ADDISON. *Trade* may be altogether domestick, and between neighbours; the *traffick* is that which goes forward between persons at a distance: in this manner there may be a great *traffick* between two towns or cities, as between London and the capitals of the different counties;

The line of Ninus this poor comfort brings,
We sell their dust, and *traffick* for their kings.
DRYDEN.

Trade may consist simply in buying and selling according to a stated valuation; *dealings* are carried on in matters that admit of a variation: hence we speak of *dealers* in wool, in corn, seeds, and the like, who buy up portions of these goods, more or less, according to the state of the market.

These terms will also admit of an extended application: hence we speak of the risk of *trade*, the narrowness of a *trading* spirit: the *commerce* of the world, a legal or illicit *commerce*; to make a *traffick* of honours, of principles, of places, and the like; plain *dealing* or underhand *dealing*.

INTERCOURSE, COMMUNICATION, CONNEXION, COMMERCE.

Intercourse, in Latin *intercursus*, signifies literally a running between; *communication*, the act of communicating or having some things in common; *connexion* is the state of being connected or linked together;

commerce, from *com* and *merx* a merchandise, signifies literally an exchange of merchandise and generally an interchange.

The *intercourse* and *commerce* subsist only between persons; the *communication* and *connexion* between persons and things. The *intercourse* with persons may be carried on in various forms; either by an interchange of civilities, which is a friendly *intercourse;* an exchange of commodities, which is a *commercial intercourse;* or an exchange of words, which is a verbal and partial *intercourse;* 'The world is maintained by *intercourse.*'—SOUTH. The *communication* in this sense, is a species of *intercourse;* namely, that which consists in the *communication* of one's thoughts to another; 'How happy is an intellectual being, who, by prayer and meditation, opens this *communication* between God and his own soul.'—ADDISON. The connexion consists of a permanent *intercourse*, since one who has a regular *intercourse* for purposes of trade with another is said to have a *connexion* with him, or to stand in *connexion* with him. There may, therefore, be a partial *intercourse* or *communication* where there is no *connexion*, nothing to bind or link the parties to each other; but there cannot be a *connexion* which is not kept up by continual *intercourse:* 'A very material part of our happiness or misery arises from the *connexions* we have with those around us.'—BLAIR.

The *commerce* is a species of general but close *intercourse;* it may consist either of frequent meeting and regular co-operation, or in cohabitation: in this sense we speak of the *commerce* of men one with another, or the *commerce* of man and wife, of parents and children, and the like; 'I should venture to call politeness benevolence in trifles, or the preference of others to ourselves, in little, daily, and hourly occurrences in the *commerce* of life.'—CHATHAM.

As it respects things, *communication* is said of places in the proper sense; *connexion* is used for things in the proper or improper sense: there is said to be a *communication* between two rooms when there is a passage open from one to the other; one house has a *connexion* with another when there is a common passage or thoroughfare to them: a *communication* is kept up between two countries by means of regular or irregular conveyances; a *connexion* subsists between two towns when the inhabitants trade with each other, intermarry, and the like.

INTERCHANGE, EXCHANGE, RECIPROCITY.

Interchange is a frequent and mutual *exchange* (*v. Change*); *exchange* consists of one act only; an *interchange* consists of many acts: an *interchange* is used only in the moral sense; *exchange* is used mostly in the proper sense; an *interchange* of civilities keeps alive good will; 'Kindness is preserved by a constant *interchange* of pleasures.'—JOHNSON. An *exchange* of commodities is a convenient mode of trade; 'The whole course of nature is a great *exchange.*'—SOUTH.

Interchange is an act; *reciprocity* is an abstract property: by an *interchange* of sentiment, friendships are engendered; the *reciprocity* of good services is what renders them doubly acceptable to those who do them, and to those who receive them; 'The services of the poor, and the protection of the rich, become *reciprocally* necessary.'—BLAIR.

MUTUAL, RECIPROCAL.

Mutual, in Latin *mutuus*, from *muto* to change, signifies exchanged so as to be equal or the same on both sides; *reciprocal*, in Latin *reciprocus*, from *recipio* to take back, signifies giving backward and forward by way of return. *Mutual* supposes a sameness in condition at the same time: *reciprocal* supposes an alternation or succession of returns. * Exchange is free and voluntary; we give in exchange, and this action is *mutual;* return is made either according to law or equity; it is obligatory, and when equally obligatory on each in return it is *reciprocal*. Voluntary disinterested services rendered to each other are *mutual:* imposed or merited services, returned from one to the other, are *reciprocal:* friends render one another *mutual* services; the services between servants and masters are *reciprocal*. The husband and wife pledge their faith to each other *mutually;* they are *reciprocally* bound to keep their vow of fidelity. The sentiment is *mutual*, the tie is *reciprocal*. *Mutual* applies mostly to matters of will and opinion, a *mutual* affection, a *mutual* inclination to oblige, a *mutual* interest for each other's comfort, a *mutual* concern to avoid that which will displease the other; these are the sentiments which render the marriage state happy; 'The soul and spirit that animates and keeps up society is *mutual* trust.'—SOUTH. *Reciprocal* ties, *reciprocal* bonds, *reciprocal* rights, *reciprocal* duties; these are what every one ought to bear in mind as a member of society, that he may expect of no man more than what in equity he is disposed to return; 'Life cannot subsist in society but by *reciprocal* concessions.'—JOHNSON. *Mutual* applies to nothing but what is personal; *reciprocal* is applied to things remote from the idea of personality, as *reciprocal* verbs, *reciprocal* terms, *reciprocal* relations, and the like.

* Vide Roubaud: "Mutual, reciproque."

TO CHANGE, EXCHANGE, BARTER, SUBSTITUTE.

Change, *v. To change, alter; exchange* is compounded of *e* or *ex* and *change*, signifying to *change* in the place of another; *barter* is supposed to come from the French *barater*, a sea term for indemnification, and also for circumvention; hence it has derived the meaning of a mercenary exchange; *substitute*, in French *substitut*, Latin *substitutus*, from *sub* and *statuo*, signifies to place one thing in the room of another.

The idea of putting one thing in the place of another is common to all these terms, which vary in the manner and the object. *Change* is the generick, the rest are specifick terms: whatever is *exchanged*, *bartered*, or *substituted*, is changed; but not *vice versâ*. *Change* is applied in general to things of the same kind, or of different kinds; *exchange* to articles of property or possession; *barter* to all articles of merchandise; *substitute* to all matters of service and office.

Things rather than persons are the proper objects for *changing* and *exchanging*, although whatever one has a control over may be *changed* or *exchanged;* a king may *change* his ministers; governments *exchange* prisoners of war. Things only are the proper objects for *barter;* but, to the shame of humanity, there are to be found people who will *barter* their countrymen, and even their relatives, for a paltry trinket.

Substituting may either have persons or things for an object; one man may be *substituted* for another, or one word *substituted* for another.

The act of *changing* or *substituting* requires but one person for an agent; that of *exchanging* and *bartering* requires two: a person *changes* his things or *substitutes* one for another; but one person *exchanges* or *barters* with another.

Change is used likewise intransitively, the others always transitively; things *change* of themselves, but persons always *exchange*, *barter*, or *substitute* things. *Changing* is not advisable, it is seldom advantageous; there is a greater chance of *changing* for the worse, than for the better; it is set on foot by caprice oftener than by prudence and necessity;

Those who beyond sea go will sadly find
They *change* their climate only, not their mind.
CREECH.

Exchanging is convenient; it is founded not so much on the intrinsic value of things, as their relative utility to the parties concerned; its end is mutual accommodation; 'Our English merchant converts the tin of his own country into gold, and *exchanges* its wool for rubies.'—ADDISON. *Bartering* is profitable; it proceeds upon a principle of mercantile calculation; the productiveness, and not the worth of the thing is considered; its main object is gain;

If the great end of being can be lost,
And thus perverted to the worst of crimes;
Let us shake off deprav'd humanity,
Exchange conditions with the savage brute,
And for his blameless instinct *barter* reason.
HAVARD

Substituting is a matter of necessity; it springs from the necessity of supplying a deficiency by some equivalent; it serves for the accommodation of the party whose place is filled up; 'Let never insulted beauty admit a second time into her presence the wretch who has once attempted to ridicule religion, and to *substitute* other aids to human frailty.'—HAWKESWORTH.

In the figurative application these terms bear the same analogy to each other. A person *changes* his opinions; but a proneness to such *changes* evinces a want of firmness in the character. The good king at his death *exchanges* a temporal for an eternal crown. The mercenary trader *barters* his conscience for paltry pelf. Men of dogmatical tempers *substitute* assertion for proof, and abuse for argument.

TO EXCHANGE, BARTER, TRUCK, COMMUTE.

To *exchange* (*v. To change*) is the general term signifying to take one for another, or put one thing in the place of another; the rest are but modes of *exchanging;* to *barter* (*v. To change*) is to *exchange* one article of trade for another; to *truck*, from the Greek τροχάω to wheel, signifying to bandy about, is a familiar term to express a familiar action for *exchanging* one article of private property for another; *commute*, from the Latin syllable *com* or *contra* and *muto* to change, signifies an *exchanging* one mode of punishment for another. We may *exchange* one book for another, or one moral object for another;

> Pleasure can be *exchanged* only for pleasure.
> HAWKESWORTH.

Traders *barter* trinkets for gold dust; so also in the figurative sense men *barter* their consciences for gold; 'Some men are willing to *barter* their blood for lucre.' —BURKE. Coachmen or stablemen *truck* a whip for a handkerchief;

> Shows all her secrets of house-keeping,
> For candles how she *trucks* her dripping.—SWIFT.

The government *commute* the punishment of death for that of banishment; 'Henry levied upon his vassals in Normandy a sum of money in lieu of their service, and this *commutation*, by reason of the great distance, was still more advantageous to his English vassals.'—HUME.

TO BUY, PURCHASE, BARGAIN, CHEAPEN.

Buy, in Saxon *byegean*, is in all probability connected with *bargain; purchase*, in French *pourchasser*, like the word pursue, *poursuivre*, comes from the Latin *persequor*, signifying to obtain by a particular effort; *bargain*, in Welch *bargen*, is most probably connected with the German *borgen* to borrow, and *bürge* a surety; *cheapen* is in Saxon *ceapan*, German *kaufen*, Dutch *koopen* to buy, &c.

Buy and *purchase* have a strong resemblance to each other, both in sense and application; but the latter is a term of more refinement than the former: *buy* may always be substituted for *purchase* without impropriety; but *purchase* would be sometimes ridiculous in the familiar application of *buy;* the necessaries of life are *bought;* luxuries are *purchased.*

The characteristick idea of *buying* is that of expending money according to a certain rule, and for a particular purpose; that of *purchasing* is the procuring the thing: the propensity of *buying* whatever comes in one's way is very injurious to the circumstances of some people; 'It gives me very great scandal to observe, wherever I go, how much skill, in *buying* all manner of things, there is necessary to defend yourself from being cheated.'—STEELE. What it is not convenient to procure for ourselves, we may commission another to *purchase* for us; so in the figurative acceptation we may *purchase* our pleasures at a dear rate;

> Pirates may make *cheap* pennyworths of their pillage
> And *purchase* friends.—SHAKSPEARE.

Buying implies simply the exchange of one's money for a commodity; *bargaining* and *cheapening* have likewise respect to the price: to *bargain* is to make a specifick agreement as to the price;

> So York must sit, and fret, and bite his tongue,
> While his own lands are *bargain'd* for, and sold.
> SHAKSPEARE.

To *cheapen* is not only to lower the price asked, but to deal in such things as are *cheap:* trade is supported by *buyers; bargainers* and *cheapeners* are not acceptable customers: mean people are prone to *bargaining*, poor people are obliged to *cheapen;* 'You may see many a smart rhetorician turning his hat in his hands, moulding it into several different cocks, examining sometimes the lining, and sometimes the button, during the whole course of his harangue. A deaf man would think he was *cheapening* a beaver, when perhaps he is talking of the fate of the British nation.'—ADDISON.

ARTICLE, CONDITION, TERM.

Article, in French *article*, Latin *articulus* a joint or a part of a member; *condition*, in French *condition*, Latin *conditio*, from *condo* to build or form, signifies properly the thing framed; *term*, in French *terme*, Latin *terminus* a boundary, signifies the point to which one is fixed.

These words agree in their application to matters of compact, or understanding between man and man. *Article* and *condition* are used in both numbers; *terms* only in the plural in this sense: the former may be used for any point individually; the latter for all the points collectively: *article* is employed for all matters which are drawn out in specifick *articles* or *points;* as the *articles* of an indenture, of a capitulation, or an agreement. *Condition* respects any point that is admitted as a ground of obligation or engagement: it is used for the general transactions of men, in which they reciprocally bind themselves to return certain equivalents. The word *terms* is employed in regard to mercantile transactions; as the *terms* of any bargain, the *terms* of any agreement, the *terms* on which any thing is bought or sold.

Articles are mostly voluntary; they are admitted by mutual agreement: *conditions* are frequently compulsory, sometimes hard; they are submitted to from policy or necessity: *terms* are dictated by interest or equity; they are fair, or unfair, according to the temper of the parties; they are submitted or agreed to. *Articles* are drawn up between parties who have to co-operate; 'In the mean time, they have ordered the preliminary treaty to be published, with observations on each *article*, in order to quiet the minds of the people.'—STEELE. Men undertake particular offices on *condition* of receiving a stipulated remuneration

> The Trojan by his word is bound to take
> The same *conditions* which himself did make.
> DRYDEN.

Men enter into dealings with each other on definite and precise *terms;*

> Those mountains fill'd with firs, that lower land
> If you consent, the Trojans shall command;
> Call'd into part of what is ours, and there,
> On *terms* agreed, the common country share.
> DRYDEN.

Clergymen subscribe to the *articles* of the established church before they are admitted to perform its sacred functions; in so doing they are presumed to be free agents; but they are not free to swerve from these *articles* while they remain in the church, and receive its emoluments: in all auctions there are certain *conditions* with which all must comply who wish to receive the benefits of the sale: in the time of war it is the business of the victor to prescribe *terms* to the vanquished; with the latter it is a matter of prudence whether they shall be accepted or rejected.

TRADER, MERCHANT, TRADESMAN.

Trader signifies in general any one who deals in goods, whether in a large or a small way, and is used therefore in the most extended sense;

> Now the victory 's won,
> We return to our lasses like fortunate *traders*,
> Triumphant with spoils.—DRYDEN.

Merchant signifies one dealing in foreign merchandise and, for the most part, in a large way;

> France hath flaw'd the league, and hath attach'd
> Our *merchants'* goods at Bourdeaux.—SHAKSPEARE

Hence these two terms may be used in contradistinction to each other; 'Many *traders* will necessitate *merchants* to trade for less profit, and consequently be more frugal.'—CHILD (*On Trade*). A *tradesman* is a retail dealer who commonly exposes his goods in a publick shop; 'From a plain *tradesman* in a shop, he is now grown a very rich country gentleman.'—ARBUTHNOT.

ARTIST, ARTISAN, ARTIFICER, MECHANICK.

Artist is a practiser of the fine arts; *artisan* is a practiser of the vulgar arts; *artificer*, from *ars* and *facio*, is one who does or makes according to art; *mechanick* is an *artisan* in the *mechanick* arts.

The *artist* ranks higher than the *artisan:* the former requires intellectual refinement in the exercise of his art; the latter requires nothing but to know the general rules of his art. The musician, painter, and sculptor are *artists;* 'If ever this country saw an age of *artists*, it is the present; her painters, sculptors, and engravers are now the only schools properly so called.'—CUMBERLAND. The carpenter, the sign-painter, and the blacksmith are *artisans;* 'The merchant, tradesman, and *artisan* will have their profit upon all the multiplied wants, comforts, and indulgences of civilized life.'—CUMBERLAND. The *artificer* is an intermediate term between the *artist* and the *artisan:* manufacturers are *artificers;* and South, in his sermons, calls the Author of the universe the great *Artificer;* 'Man must be in a certain degree the *artificer* of his own happiness; the tools and materials may be put into his hands by the bounty of Providence, but the workmanship must be his own.'—CUMBERLAND. The *mechanick* is that species of artisan who works at arts purely *mechanical*, in distinction from those which contribute to the completion and embellishment of any objects; on this ground a shoemaker is a *mechanick*, but a common painter is a simple *artisan;* 'The concurring assent of the world in preferring gentlemen to *mechanicks* seems founde in that preference which the rational part of our nature is entitled to above the animal.'—BARTLETT.

WRITER, PENMAN, SCRIBE.

Writer is an indefinite term; every one who *writes* is called a *writer;* but none are *penmen* but such as are expert at their pen. Many who profess to teach *writing* are themselves but sorry *writers:* the best *penmen* are not always the best teachers of *writing*. The *scribe* is one who *writes* for the purpose of copying: he is therefore an official *writer*.

WRITER, AUTHOR.

Writer refers us to the act of *writing; author* to the act of inventing. There are therefore many *writers*, who are not *authors;* but there is no *author* of books who may not be termed a *writer:* compilers and contributors to periodical works are *writers*, but not *authors*. Poets and historians are more properly termed *authors* than *writers*.

FARMER, HUSBANDMAN, AGRICULTURIST.

Farmer, from the Saxon *feorm* food, signifies one managing a *farm*, or cultivating the ground for a subsistence;

> To check this plague, the skilful *farmer* chaff
> And blazing straw before his orchard burns.
> THOMSON.

Husbandman is one following *husbandry*, that is, the tillage of land by manual labour; the *farmer*, therefore conducts the concern, and the *husbandman* labours under his direction;

> Old *husbandmen* I at Sabinum know,
> Who, for another year, dig, plough, and sow.
> DENHAM.

Agriculturist, from the Latin *ager* a field, and *colo* to till, signifies any one engaged in the art of cultivation. The *farmer* is always a practitioner; the *agriculturist* may be a mere theorist: the *farmer* follows husbandry solely as a means of living; the *agriculturist* follows it as a science: the former tills the land upon given admitted principles; the latter frames new principles, or alters those that are established. Between the *farmer* and the *agriculturist* there is the same difference as between practice and theory: the former may be assisted by the latter, so long as they can go hand in hand; but in the case of a collision, the *farmer* will be of more service to himself and his country than the *agriculturist: farming* brings immediate profit from personal service; *agriculture* may only promise future, and consequently contingent, advantages; 'An improved and improving *agriculture*, which implies a great augmentation of labour, has not yet found itself at a stand.'—BURKE.

RURAL, RUSTICK.

Although both these terms, from the Latin *rus* country, signify belonging to the country; yet the former is used in a good, and the latter in a bad or an indifferent sense. *Rural* applies to all country objects, except man; it is, therefore, always connected with the charms of nature: *rustick* applies only to persons, or what is personal, in the country, and is, therefore, always associated with the want of culture. *Rural* scenery is always interesting; but the *rustick* manners of the peasants have frequently too much that is uncultivated and rude in them to be agreeable: a *rural* habitation may be fitted for persons in a higher station;

> E'en now, methinks, as pondering here I stand,
> I see the *rural* virtues leave the land.
> GOLDSMITH

A *rustick* cottage is adapted only for the poorer inhabitants of the country; 'The freedom and laxity of a *rustick* life produces remarkable particularities of conduct.'—JOHNSON.

COUNTRYMAN, PEASANT, SWAIN, HIND, RUSTICK, CLOWN.

Countryman, that is, a man of the *country*, or one belonging to the *country*, is the general term applicable to all inhabiting the *country*, in distinction from a townsman; *peasant*, in French *paysan*, from *pays*, is employed in the same sense for any *countryman* among the inhabitants of the Continent, and is in consequence used in poetry or the grave style; *swain* in the Saxon signified a labourer, but it has acquired, from its use in poetry, the higher signification of a shepherd; *hind* may in all probability signify one who is in the back ground, an inferiour; *rustick*, from *rus* the country, signifies one born and bred in the country; *clown*, contracted from *colonus* a husbandman, signifies of course a menial in the *country*.

All these terms are employed as epithets to persons, and principally to such as live in the *country:* the term *countryman* is taken in an indifferent sense, and may comprehend persons of different descriptions; it designates nothing more than habitual residence in the *country;* 'Though considering my former condition, I may now be called a *countryman:* yet you cannot call me a *rustick* (as you would imply in your letter) as long as I live in so civil and noble a family.'—HOWELL. The other terms are employed for the lower orders of *countrymen*, but with collateral ideas favourable or unfavourable annexed to them. The *peasant* is a *countryman* who follows rural occupations for a livelihood. He is commonly considered as a labourer, and contracted in his education; 'If by the poor measures and proportions of a man we may take an estimate of this great action (our Saviour's coming in the flesh), we shall quickly find how irksome it is to flesh and blood "to have been happy," to descend some steps lower, to exchange the estate of a prince for that of a *peasant*.'—SOUTH. *Swain, hind*, both convey the idea of innocence in an humble station, and are therefore always employed in poetry in a good sense;

> As thus the snows arise, and foul and fierce
> All winter drives along the darken'd air,
> In his own loose revolving fields the *swain*
> Disastered stands.—THOMSON.

> The lab'ring *hind* his oxen shall disjoin.
> DRYDEN.

Rustick and *clown* both convey the idea of that uncouth rudeness and ignorance which is in reality found among the lowest orders of *countrymen;*

> In arguing too the parson own'd his skill,
> For ev'n tho' vanquish'd he could argue still.

While words of learned length and thundering sound
Amaz'd the gazing *rusticks* rang'd around.
GOLDSMITH.

Th' astonish'd mother finds a vacant nest,
By the hard hand of unrelenting *clowns*
Robb'd.—THOMSON.

CULTIVATION, TILLAGE, HUSBANDRY.

Cultivation has a much more comprehensive meaning than either *tillage* or *husbandry*;

O softly swelling hills
On which the power of *cultivation* lies,
And joys to see the wonders of his toil.
THOMSON.

Tillage is a mode of *cultivation* that extends no farther than the preparation of the ground for the reception of the seed; *cultivation* includes the whole process by which the produce of the earth is brought to maturity. We may *till* without *cultivating*, but we cannot *cultivate*, as far as respects the soil, without *tillage*; 'The south-east parts of Britain had already before the age of Cæsar made the first and most requisite step towards a civil settlement: and the Britons by *tillage* and *agriculture* had there increased to a great multitude.'—HUME. *Husbandry* is more extensive in its meaning than *tillage*, but not so extensive as *cultivation*; 'We find an image of the two states, the contemplative and the active, figured out in the persons of Abel and Cain, by the two primitive trades, that of the shepherd and that of the *husbandman*.'—BACON.

Tillage respects the act only of *tilling* the ground; *husbandry* is employed for the office of *cultivating* for domestick purposes. A *cultivator* is a general term, defined only by the object that is *cultivated*, as the *cultivator* of the grape, or the olive; a *tiller* is a labourer in the soil who performs that office for another; a *husbandman* is an humble species of *cultivator*, who himself performs the whole office of *cultivating* the ground for domestick purposes.

SEAMAN, WATERMAN, SAILOR, MARINER, BOATMAN, FERRYMAN.

All these words denote persons occupied in navigation; the *seaman*, as the word implies, follows his business on the *sea*; the *waterman* is one who gets his livelihood on fresh water; 'Many a lawyer who makes but an indifferent figure at the bar might have made a very elegant *waterman*.'—SOUTH. The *sailor* and the *mariner* are both specifick terms to designate the *seaman*; every *sailor* and *mariner* is a *seaman*; although every *seaman* is not a *sailor* or *mariner*; the former is one who is employed about the laborious part of the vessel; the latter is one who traverses the ocean to and fro, who is attached to the water and passes his life upon it.

Men of all ranks are denominated *seamen*, whether officers or men, whether in a merchantman or in a king's ship;

Thus the toss'd *seaman*, after boist'rous storms,
Lands on his country's breast.—LEE.

Sailor is only used for the common men, or, in the sea phrase, for those before the mast, particularly in vessels of war; hence our *sailors* and soldiers are spoken of as the defenders of our country;

Through storms and tempests so the *sailor* drives.
SHIRLEY.

A *mariner* is an independent kind of *seaman* who manages his own vessel and goes on an expedition on his own account; fishermen and those who trade along the coast are in a particular manner distinguished by the name of *mariners*;

Welcome to me, as to a sinking *mariner*
The lucky plank that bears him to the shore.
LEE.

Waterman, *boatman*, and *ferryman* are employed for persons who are engaged with boats; but the term *waterman* is specifically applied to such whose business it is to let out their boats and themselves for a given time; the *boatman* may use a boat only occasionally for the transfer of goods; a *ferryman* uses a boat only for the conveyance of persons or goods across a particular river or piece of water.

MARITIME, MARINE, NAVAL, NAUTICAL.

Maritime and *marine*, from the Latin *mare* a sea, signifies belonging to the sea; *naval*, from *navis* a ship, signifies belonging to a ship; and *nautical*, from *nauta* a sailor, signifies belonging to a sailor, or to navigation.

Countries and places are denominated *maritime* from their proximity to the sea, or their great intercourse by sea; hence England is called the most *maritime* nation in Europe; 'Octavianus reduced Lepidus to a necessity to beg his life, and be content to lead the remainder of it in a mean condition at Circeii, a small *maritime* town among the Latins.'—PRIDEAUX. *Marine* is a technical term, employed by persons in office, to denote that which is officially transacted with regard to the sea in distinction from what passes on land: hence we speak of the *marines* as a species of soldiers acting by sea, of the *marine* society, or *marine* stores; 'A man of a very grave aspect required notice to be given of his intention to set out on a certain day on a *submarine* voyage.'—JOHNSON.

Naval is another term of art as opposed to military, and used in regard to the arrangements of government or commerce: hence we speak of *naval* affairs, *naval* officers, *naval* tacticks, and the like; 'Sextus Pompey having together such a *naval* force as made up 350 vessels, seized Sicily.'—PRIDEAUX. *Nautical* is a scientifick term, connected with the science of navigation or the management of vessels; hence we talk of *nautical* instruction, of *nautical* calculations; 'He elegantly showed by whom he was drawn, which depainted the *nautical* compass with *aut magnes, aut magna*.'—CAMDEN. The *maritime* laws of England are essential for the preservation of the *naval* power which it has so justly acquired. The *marine* of England is one of its glories. The *naval* administration is one of the most important branches of our government in the time of war. *Nautical* tables, and *nautical* almanacks have been expressly formed for the benefit of all who apply themselves to *nautical* subjects.

MARTIAL, WARLIKE, MILITARY, SOLDIER-LIKE.

Martial, from *Mars*, the god of war, is the Latin term for belonging to war: *warlike* signifies literally like *war*, having the image of war. In sense these terms approach so near to each other, that they may be easily admitted to supply each other's place; but custom, the lawgiver of language, has assigned an office to each that makes it not altogether indifferent how they are used. *Martial* is both a technical and a more comprehensive term than *warlike*; on the other hand, *warlike* designates the temper of the individual more than *martial*: we speak of *martial* array, *martial* preparations, *martial* law, a court *martial*;

An active prince, and prone to *martial* deeds.
DRYDEN.

We speak of a *warlike* nation, meaning a nation who is fond of war; a *warlike* spirit or temper, also a *warlike* appearance, inasmuch as the temper is visible in the air and carriage of a man;

Last from the Volscians fair Camilla came,
And led her *warlike* troops, a warriour dame.
DRYDEN.

Military, from *miles* a soldier, signifies belonging to a soldier, and *soldier-like* like a soldier. *Military* in comparison with *martial* is a term of particular import; *martial* having always a reference to war in general, and *military* to the proceedings consequent upon that: hence we speak of *military* in distinction from naval, as *military* expeditions, *military* movements, and the like; 'The Tlascalans were, like all unpolished nations, strangers to *military* order and discipline.'—ROBERTSON. In characterizing the men, we should say that they had a *martial* appearance; but in speaking of a particular place, we should say it had a *military* appearance, if there were many soldiers in it.

Military, compared with *soldier-like*, is used for the

body, and the latter for the individual. The whole army is termed the *military*: the conduct of an individual is *soldier-like* or otherwise; 'The fears of the Spaniards led them to presumptuous and *unsoldier-like* discussions concerning the propriety of their general's measures.'—ROBERTSON.

TO PAINT, DEPICT, DELINEATE, SKETCH.

Paint and *depict* both come from the Latin *pingo*, to represent forms and figures: as a verb to *paint* is either literally to represent figures on paper, or to represent circumstances and events by means of words; to *depict* is used only in this latter sense, but the former word expresses a greater exercise of the imagination than the latter: it is the art of the poet to *paint* nature in lively colours: it is the art of the historian or narrator to *depict* a real scene of misery in strong colours. As nouns, *painting* rather describes the action or operation, and *picture* the result.

When we speak of a good *painting*, we think particularly of its execution as to drapery, disposition of colours, and the like;

> The *painting* is almost the natural man,
> He is but outside.—SHAKSPEARE.

When we speak of a fine *picture*, we refer immediately to the object represented, and the impression which it is capable of producing on the beholder; 'A *picture* is a poem without words.'—ADDISON. *Paintings* are confined either to oil *paintings* or *paintings* in colours: but every drawing, whether in pencil, in crayons, or in India ink, may produce a *picture*; and we have likewise *pictures* in embroidery, *pictures* in tapestry, and *pictures* in Mosaic.

Delineate, in Latin *delineatus* participle of *delineo*, signifies literally to draw the lines which include the contents; *sketch* is in the German *skizze*, Italian *schizzo*.

Both these terms are properly employed in the art of drawing, and figuratively applied to moral subjects to express a species of descriptions: a *delineation* expresses something more than a *sketch*; the former conveying not merely the general outlines or more prominent features, but also as much of the details as would serve to form a whole; the latter, however, seldom contains more than some broad touches, by which an imperfect idea of the subject is conveyed.

A *delineation* therefore may be characterized as accurate, and a *sketch* as hasty or imperfect: an attentive observer who has passed some years in a country may be enabled to give an accurate *delineation* of the laws, customs, manners, and character of its inhabitants: 'When the Spaniards first arrived in America expresses were sent to the emperor of Mexico in *painting*, and the news of his country *delineated* by the strokes of a pencil.'—ADDISON. A traveller who merely passes through a country can give only a hasty *sketch* from what passes before his eyes; '*Sketch* out a rough draught of my country, that I may be able to judge whether a return to it be really eligible.'—ATTERBURY.

SKETCH, OUTLINES.

A *sketch* may form a whole; *outlines* are but a part: the *sketch* may comprehend the *outlines* and some of the particulars; *outlines*, as the term bespeaks, comprehend only that which is on the exteriour surface: the *sketch* in drawing, may serve as a landscape, as it presents some of the features of a country; but the *outlines* serve only as bounding lines, within which the *sketch* may be formed. So in the moral application we speak of the *sketches* of countries, characters, manners, and the like, which serve as a description; but of the *outlines* of a plan, of a work, a project, and the like, which serve as a basis on which the subordinate parts are to be formed: barbarous nations present us with rude *sketches* of nature; an abridgment is little more than the *outlines* of a larger work;

> In few, to close the whole,
> The moral muse has shadow'd out a *sketch*
> Of most our weakness needs believe or do.
> YOUNG.

'This is the *outline* of the fable (King Lear).'—JOHNSON.

ASTRONOMY, ASTROLOGY.

Astronomy is compounded of the Greek ἀστὴρ and νόμος, signifying the laws of the stars, or a knowledge of their laws; *astrology*, from ἀστὴρ and λόγος, signifies a reasoning on the stars.

The * *astronomer* studies the course and movement of the stars; the *astrologer* reasons on their influence. The former observes the state of the heavens, marks the order of time, the eclipses and the revolutions which arise out of the established laws of motion in the immense universe: the latter predicts events, draws horoscopes, and announces all the vicissitudes of rain and snow, heat and cold, &c. The *astronomer* calculates and seldom errs, as his calculations are built on fixed rules and actual observations; the *astrologer* deals in conjectures, and his imagination often deceives him. The *astronomer* explains what he knows, and merits the esteem of the learned; the *astrologer* hazards what he thinks, and seeks to please.

A thirst for knowledge leads to the study of *astronomy*: an inquietude about the future has given rise to *astrology*. Many important results for the arts of navigation, agriculture, and of civil society in general, have been drawn from *astronomical* researches: many serious and mischievous effects have been produced on the minds of the ignorant, from their faith in the dreams of the *astrologer*.

FACTOR, AGENT.

Though both these terms, according to their origin, imply a maker or doer, yet, at present, they have a distinct signification: the word *factor* is used in a limited, and the word *agent* in a general sense: the *factor* only buys and sells on the account of others; 'Their devotion (that is of the puritanical rebels) served all along but as an instrument to their avarice, as a *factor* or under *agent* to their extortion.'—SOUTH. The *agent* transacts every sort of business in general; 'No expectations, indeed, were then formed from renewing a direct application to the French regicides through the *agent* general for the humiliation of sovereigns.'—BURKE. Merchants and manufacturers employ *factors* abroad to dispose of goods transmitted; lawyers are frequently employed as *agents* in the receipt and payment of money, the transfer of estates and various other pecuniary concerns.

FREIGHT, CARGO, LADING, LOAD, BURDEN.

Freight, through the northern languages in all probability comes from the Latin *fero* to bring, signifying the thing brought; *cargo*, in French *cargaison*, probably a variation from *carriage*, is employed for all the contents of a vessel, with the exception of the persons that it carries; *lading* and *load* (in German *laden* to *load*), comes most probably from the word *last* a *burden*, signifying the *burden* or weight imposed upon any carriage; *burden*, which through the medium of the northern languages, comes from the Greek φόρτος, and φέρω to carry, conveys the idea of weight which is borne by the vessel.

A captain speaks of the *freight* of his ship as that which is the object of his voyage, by which all who are interested in it are to make their profit; the value and nature of the *freight* are the first objects of consideration: he speaks of the *lading* as the thing which is to fill the ship; the quantity, and weight of the *lading*, are to be taken into the consideration: he speaks of the *cargo* as that which goes with the ship, and belongs as it were to the ship; the amount of the *cargo* is that which is first thought of: he speaks of the *burden* as that which his vessel will bear; it is the property of the ship which is to be estimated.

The ship-broker regulates the *freight*: the captain and the crew dispose the *lading*: the agent sees to the disposal of the *cargo*: the ship-builder determines the *burden*: the carrier looks to the *load* which he has to carry. The *freight* must consist of such merchandise as will pay for the transport and risk: the *lading* must consist of such things as can be most conveniently stowed: the value of a *cargo* depends not only on the nature of the commodity, but the market to which it is carried; the *burden* of a vessel is estimated by the number of tons which it can carry. *Freight* and

* Abbe Girard: "Astronomie, Astrologue."

burden may sometimes be used in a figurative application;

> Haste, my dear father ('t is no time to wait),
> And *load* my shoulders with a willing *freight*.
> DRYDEN.

> The surging air receives
> Its plumy *burden*.—THOMSON.

MERCANTILE, COMMERCIAL.

Mercantile, from *merchandise*, respects the actual transaction of business, or a transfer of *merchandise* by sale or purchase; *commercial* comprehends the theory and practice of *commerce:* hence we speak in a peculiar manner of a *mercantile* house, a *mercantile* town, a *mercantile* situation, and the like; 'Such is the happiness, the hope of which seduced me from the duties and pleasures of a *mercantile* life.'—JOHNSON. But of a *commercial* education, a *commercial* people, *commercial* speculations, and the like; 'The *commercial* world is very frequently put into confusion by the bankruptcy of merchants.'—JOHNSON.

VENAL, MERCENARY, HIRELING.

Venal, from the Latin *venalis*, signifies saleable or ready to be sold, which, applied as it commonly is to persons, is a much stronger term than *mercenary*. A *venal* man gives up all principle for interest; a *mercenary* man seeks his interest without regard to principle: *venal* writers are such as write in favour of the cause that can promote them to riches or honours; a servant is commonly a *mercenary* who gives his services according as he is paid: those who are loudest in their professions of political purity are the best subjects for a minister to make *venal:*

> The minister, well pleas'd at small expense
> To silence so much rude impertinence,
> With squeeze and whisper yields to his demands,
> And on the *venal* list enroll'd he stands.—JENYNS.

mercenary spirit is engendered in the minds of those ᴡho devote themselves exclusively to trade; 'For ᴛheir assistance they repair to the northern steel, and bring in an unnatural, *mercenary* crew.'—SOUTH.

Hireling from *hire*, and *mercenary* from *merx* wages, are applied to any one who follows a sordid employment; but *hireling* may sometimes be taken in its proper and less reproachful sense, for one who is *hired* as a servant to perform an allotted work; but in general they are both reproachful epithets: the former having particular reference to the meanness of the employment, and the latter to the sordid character of the person. *Hireling* prints are those which are in the pay of a party; 'It was not his carrying the bag which made Judas a thief and a *hireling*.'—SOUTH. A *mercenary* principle will sometimes actuate men in the highest station; 'These soldiers were not citizens, but *mercenary*, sordid deserters.'—BURKE.

COMMODITY, GOODS, MERCHANDISE, WARE.

These terms agree in expressing articles of trade under various circumstances.

Commodity, in Latin *commoditas*, signifies in its abstract sense *convenience*, and in an extended application the thing that is *convenient* or fit for use, which being also saleable, the word has been employed for the thing that is sold; *goods*, which denotes the thing that is good, has derived its use from the same analogy in its sense as in the former case; *merchandise*, in French *marchandise*, Latin *mercatura* or *merx*, Hebrew מכר to sell, signifies a saleable matter: *ware*, in Saxon *ware*, German, &c. *waare*, signifies properly any thing manufactured, and, by an extension of the sense, an article for sale.

Commodity is employed only for articles of the first necessity; it is the source of comfort and object of industry. *Goods* is applied to every thing belonging to tradesmen, for which there is a stipulated value: they are sold retail, and are the proper objects of trade. *Merchandise* applies to what belongs to merchants; it is the object of commerce. *Wares* are manufactured, and may be either *goods* or *merchandise*. A country has its *commodities;* a shopkeeper his *goods*; a merchant his *merchandise;* a manufacturer his *wares*.

The most important *commodities* in a country are what are denominated staple *commodities*, which constitute its main riches: yet, although England has fewer of such *commodities* than almost any other nation, it has been enabled, by the industry and energy of its inhabitants, the peculiar excellence of its government, and its happy insular situation, not only to obtain the *commodities* of other countries, but to increase their number, for the convenience of the whole world and its own aggrandizement: 'Men must have made some considerable progress towards civilization before they acquired the idea of property so as to be acquainted with the most simple of all contracts, that of exchanging by barter one rude *commodity* for another.'—ROBERTSON. It is the interest of every tradesman to provide himself with such *goods* as he can recommend to his customers; the proper choice of which depends on judgement and experience; 'It gives me very great scandal to observe, wherever I go, how much skill in buying all manner of *goods* there is necessary to defend yourself from being cheated.'—STEELE. The conveyance of *merchandise* into England is always attended with considerable risk, as they must be transported by water: on the continent it is very slow and expensive, as they are generally transported by land; 'If we consider this expensive voyage, which is undertaken in search of knowledge, and how few there are who take in any considerable *merchandise;* how hard is it, that the very small number who are distinguished with abilities to know how to vend their *wares*, should suffer being plundered by privateers under the very cannon that should protect them!'—ADDISON. All kinds of *wares* are not the most saleable commodities, but earthen *ware* claims a preference over every other.

GOODS, FURNITURE, CHATTELS, MOVEABLES, EFFECTS.

All these terms are applied to such things as belong to an individual; the first term is the most general both in sense and application; all the rest are species.

Furniture comprehends all household goods; wherefore in regard to an individual, supposing the house to contain all he has, the general is put for the specifick term, as when one speaks of a person's moving his *goods* for his *furniture:* but in the strict sense *goods* comprehends more than *furniture*, including not only that which is adapted for the domestick purposes of a family, but also every thing which is of value to a person: the chairs and tables are a part of *furniture;* papers, books, and money are included among his *goods;* it is obvious, therefore, that *goods*, even in its most limited sense, is of wider import than *furniture;* 'Now I give up my shop and dispose of all my poetical *goods* at once; I must therefore desire that the publick would please to take them in the gross, and that every body would turn over what he does not like.'—PRIOR. 'Considering that your houses, your place and *furniture*, are not suitable to your quality, I conceive that your expense ought to be reduced to two-thirds of your estate.'—WENTWORTH.

Chattels, which is probably changed from *cattle*, is a term not in ordinary use, but still sufficiently employed to deserve notice. It comprehends that species of *goods* which is in a special manner separated from one's person and house; a man's cattle, his implements of husbandry, the alienable rights which he has in land or buildings, are all comprehended under *chattels;* hence the propriety of the expression to seize a man's *goods* and *chattels*, as denoting the disposable property which he has about his person or at a distance. Sometimes this word is used in the singular number, and also in the figurative;

> Honour's a lease for lives to come,
> And cannot be extended from
> The legal tenant; 't is a *chattel*
> Not to be forfeited in battle.—HUDIBRAS

Moveables comprehends all the other terms in the limited application to property, as far as it admits of being removed from one place to the other; it is opposed either to fixtures, when speaking of *furniture*, or to land as contrasted to *goods* and *chattels;* 'There can be no doubt but that *moveables* of every kind become sooner appropriated than the permanent, substantial soil.'—BLACKSTONE.

Effects is a term of nearly as extensive a signification as *goods*, but not so extensive in application: whatever a man has that is of any supposed value, or convertible into money, is entitled his *goods;* whatever a man has that can effect, produce, or bring forth money by sale, is entitled his *effects: goods* therefore is applied only to that which a man has at his own disposal; *effects* more properly to that which is left at the disposal of others. A man makes a sale of his *goods* on his removal from any place; his creditors or executors take care of his *effects* either on his bankruptcy or decease: *goods*, in this case, is seldom employed but in the limited sense of what is removeable; but *effects* includes every thing personal, freehold, and copyhold; 'The laws of bankruptcy compel the bankrupt to give up all his *effects* to the use of the creditors without any concealment.'—BLACKSTONE.

GOODS, POSSESSIONS, PROPERTY.

All these terms are applicable to such things as are the means of enjoyment; but the former term respects the direct quality of producing enjoyment, the latter two have regard to the subject of the enjoyment: we consider *goods* as they are real or imaginary, adapted or not adapted for the producing of real happiness; those who abound in the *goods* of this world are not always the happiest; 'The worldling attaches himself wholly to what he reckons the only solid *goods*, the *possession* of riches and influence.'—BLAIR. *Possessions* must be regarded as they are lasting or temporary; he who is anxious for earthly *possessions* forgets that they are but transitory and dependent upon a thousand contingencies; 'While worldly men enlarge their *possessions*, and extend their connexions, they imagine they are strengthening themselves.'—BLAIR. *Property* is to be considered as it is legal or illegal, just or unjust; those who are anxious for great *property* are not always scrupulous about the means by which it is to be obtained.

> For numerous blessings yearly shower'd,
> And *property* with plenty crown'd,
> Accept our pious praise.—DRYDEN.

The purity of a man's Christian character is in danger from an overweaning attachment to earthly *goods;* no wise man will boast the multitude of his *possessions*, when he reflects that if they do not leave him, the time is not far distant when he must leave them; the validity of one's claim to *property* which comes by inheritance is better founded than any other.

RICHES, WEALTH, OPULENCE, AFFLUENCE.

Riches, in German *reichthum*, from *reiche* a kingdom, comes from the Latin *rego* to rule; because *riches* and power are intimately connected; *wealth*, from *well*, signifies well being; *opulence*, from the Latin *opes* riches, denotes the state of having riches; *affluence*, from the Latin *ad* and *fluo*, denotes either the act of riches flowing in to a person, or the state of having riches to flow in.

Riches is a general term denoting any considerable share of property, but without immediate reference to a possessor; *wealth* denotes the prosperous condition of the possessor; *opulence* characterizes the present possession of great *riches*; *affluence* denotes the increasing *wealth* of the individual. *Riches* is a condition opposed to poverty; the whole world is divided into *rich* and poor; '*Riches* are apt to betray a man into arrogance.'—ADDISON. *Wealth* is that positive and substantial share in the goods of fortune which distinguish an individual from his neighbours, by putting him in possession of all that is commonly desired and sought after by man;

> His best companions innocence and health,
> And his best *riches* ignorance of *wealth*.
> GOLDSMITH.

He who has much money has great *wealth;*

> Along the lawn where scatter'd hamlets rose,
> Unwieldy *wealth* and cumb'rous pomp repose.
> GOLDSMITH.

Opulence is likewise a positively great share of *riches*, but refers rather to the external possessions, than to the whole condition of the man. He who has much land, much cattle, many houses, and the like, is properly denominated *opulent;* 'Our Saviour did not choose for himself an easy and *opulent* condition.'—BLAIR. *Affluence* is a term peculiarly applicable to the fluctuating condition of things which flow in in quantities, or flow away in equally great quantities; 'Prosperity is often an equivocal word denoting merely *affluence* of possession.'—BLAIR. Hence we do not say that a man is *opulent*, but that he is *affluent* in his circumstances.

Wealth and *opulence* are applied to individuals, or communities: *affluence* is applicable only to an individual. The *wealth* of a nation must be procured by the industry of the inhabitants; the *opulence* of a town may arise from some local circumstance in its favour, as its favourable situation for trade and the like; he who lives in *affluence* is apt to forget the uncertain tenure by which he holds his *riches;* we speak of *riches* as to their effects upon men's minds and manners; it is not every one who knows how to use them We speak of *wealth* as it raises a man in the scale of society; the *wealthy* merchant is an important member of the community: we speak of *opulence* as it indicates the flourishing state of the individual: an *opulent* man shows unquestionable marks of his *opulence* around him: we speak of *affluence* to characterize the abundance of the individual, we show our *affluence* by the style of our living.

MONEY, CASH.

Money comes from the Latin *moneta*, which signified stamped coin, from *moneo* to advise, to inform of its value, by means of an inscription or stamp; *cash*, from the French *caisse* a chest, signifies that which is put in a chest.

* *Money* is applied to every thing which serves as a circulating medium: *cash* is, in a strict sense, put for coin only: bank notes are *money;* guineas and shillings are *cash:* all *cash* is therefore *money*, but all *money* is not *cash*. The only *money* the Chinese have are square bits of metal, with a hole through the centre, by which they are strung upon a string: travellers on the Continent must always be provided with letters of credit, which may be turned into *cash* as convenience requires.

TO HEAP, PILE, ACCUMULATE, AMASS.

To *heap* signifies to form into a *heap*, which through the medium of the northern languages is derivable from the Latin *copia* plenty. To *pile* is to form into a *pile*, which, being a variation of pole, signifies a high raised *heap*. To *accumulate*, from the Latin *cumulus* a *heap*, signifies to put *heap* upon *heap*. To *amass* is literally to form into a *mass*.

To *heap* is an indefinite action: it may be performed with or without order: to *pile* is a definite action done with design and order; thus we *heap* stones, or *pile* wood: to *heap* may be to make into large or small *heaps;*

> Within the circles arms and tripods lie,
> Ingots of gold and silver *heap'd* on high.
> DRYDEN.

To *pile* is always to make something considerable;

> This would I celebrate with annual games,
> With gifts on altars *pil'd*, and holy flames.
> DRYDEN.

Children may *heap* sticks together; men *pile* loads of wood together. To *heap* and *pile* are used mostly in the physical, *accumulate* and *amass* in the physical or moral acceptation; the former is a species of *heaping*, the latter of *piling:* we *accumulate* whatever is brought together in a loose manner; we *amass* that which can coalesce: thus a man *accumulates* guineas; he *amasses* wealth.

To *accumulate* and to *amass* are not always the acts of conscious agents: things may *accumulate* or *amass;* water or snow *accumulates* by the continual accession of fresh quantities; the ice *amasses* in rivers until it is frozen over: so in the moral acceptation, evils, abuses, and the like, *accumulate;* corruption *amasses*

* Vide Trusler: "Money, cash."

When overwhelmed with an *accumulation* of sorrows, the believer is never left comfortless; 'These odes are marked by glittering *accumulations* of ungraceful ornaments.'—JOHNSON. The industrious inquirer may collect a *mass* of intelligence; 'Sir Francis Bacon, by an extraordinary force of nature, compass of thought, and indefatigable study, had *amassed* to himself such stores of knowledge as we cannot look upon without amazement.'—HUGHES.

STOCK, STORE.

Stock, from *stick*, *stoke*, *stow*, and *stuff*, signifies any quantity laid up; *store*, in Welch *stor*, comes from the Hebrew סתר to hide.

The ideas of wealth and stability being naturally allied, it is not surprising that *stock*, which expresses the latter idea, should also be put for the former, particularly as the abundance here referred to serves as a foundation in the same manner as *stock* in the literal sense does to a tree

Store likewise implies a quantity; but agreeable to the derivation of the word, it implies an accumulated quantity. Any quantity of materials which is in hand may serve as a *stock* for a given purpose; thus a few shillings with some persons may be their *stock* in trade: any quantity of materials brought together for a given purpose may serve as a *store*; thus the industrious ant collects a *store* of grain for the winter: we judge of a man's substantial property by the *stock* of goods which he has on hand; we judge of a man's disposable property by the *store* which he has. The *stock* is that which must increase of itself; it is the source and foundation of industry: the *store* is that which we must add to occasionally; it is that from which we draw in time of need. By a *stock* we gain riches; by a *store* we guard against want: a *stock* requires skill and judgement to make the proper application; a *store* requires foresight and management to make it against the proper season. It is necessary for one who has a large trade to have a large *stock*; and for him who has no prospect of supply to have a large *store*.

The same distinction subsists between these words in their moral application; he who wishes to speak a foreign language must have a *stock* of familiar words; *stores* of learning are frequently lost to the world for want of means and opportunity to bring them forth to publick view; 'It will not suffice to rally all one's little utmost into one's discourse, which can constitute a divine. Any man would then quickly be drained; and his short *stock* would serve but for one meeting in ordinary converse; therefore there must be *store*, plenty, and a treasure, lest he turn broker in divinity.' —SOUTH.

As verbs, to *stock* and to *store* both signify to provide; but the former is a provision for the present use, and the latter for some future purpose: a tradesman *stocks* himself with such articles as are most saleable; a fortress or a ship is *stored*: a person *stocks* himself with patience, or *stores* his memory with knowledge.

TO TREASURE, HOARD.

The idea of laying up carefully is common to these verbs; but to *treasure* is to lay up for the sake of preserving; to *hoard*, to lay up for the sake of accumulating; we *treasure* up the gifts of a friend; the miser *hoards* up his money: we attach a real value to that which we *treasure*; a fictitious value to that which is *hoarded*. To *treasure* is used either in the proper or improper sense; to *hoard* only in the proper sense: we *treasure* a book on which we set particular value, or we *treasure* the words or actions of another in our recollection; 'Fancy can combine the ideas which memory has *treasured*.'—HAWKESWORTH. The miser *hoards* in his coffers whatever he can scrape together;

> *Hoards* ev'n beyond the miser's wish abound.
> GOLDSMITH.

PLENTIFUL, PLENTEOUS, ABUNDANT, COPIOUS, AMPLE.

Plentiful and *plenteous* signify the presence of *plenty*, *plenitude*, or *fulness*; *abundance*, in Latin *abundantia*, from *abundo* to overflow, compounded of the intensive *ab* and *unda* a wave, signifies flowing over in great quantities like the waves; *copious*, in Latin *copiosus*, from *copia*, or *con*, and *opes* a stock, signifies having a store; *ample*, in Latin *amplus*, from the Greek ἀνάπλεως, signifies over-full.

Plentiful and *plenteous* differ only in use; the former being most employed in the familiar, the latter in the grave style.

Plenty fills; *abundance* does more, it leaves a super fluity; as that, however, which fills suffices as much as that which flows over, the term *abundance* is often employed promiscuously with that of *plenty*: we can indifferently say a *plentiful* harvest, or an *abundant* harvest. *Plenty* is, however, more frequent in the literal sense for that which fills the body; *abundance*, for that which fills the mind, or the desire of the mind. A *plenty* of provisions is even more common than an *abundance*; a *plenty* of food; a *plenty* of corn, wine and oil;

> The resty knaves are overrun with ease,
> As *plenty* ever is the nurse of faction.—ROWE.

But an *abundance* of words; an *abundance* of riches, an *abundance* of wit and humour. In certain years fruit is *plentiful*, and at other times grain is *plentiful*: in all cases we have *abundant* cause for gratitude to the Giver of all good things;

> And God said, let the waters generate
> Reptile with spawn *abundant*, living soul.
> MILTON.

Copious and *ample* are modes either of *plenty* or *abundance*; the former is employed in regard to what is collected or brought into one point: the *ample* is employed only in regard to what may be narrowed or expanded. A *copious* stream of blood, or a *copious* flow of words, equally designate the quantity which is collected together;

> Smooth to the shelving brink a *copious* flood
> Rolls fair and placid.—THOMSON.

As an *ample* provision, an *ample* store, an *ample* share marks that which may at pleasure be increased or diminished;

> Peaceful beneath primeval trees, that cast
> Their *ample* shade o'er Niger's yellow stream,
> Leans the huge elephant, wisest of brutes.
> THOMSON.

FULNESS, PLENITUDE.

Although *plenitude* is no more than a derivative from the Latin for *fulness*, yet the latter is used either in the proper sense to express the state of objects that are *full*, or in the improper sense to express great quantity, which is the accompaniment of *fulness*; the former only in the higher style and in the improper sense: hence we say in the *fulness* of one's heart, in the *fulness* of one's joy, or the *fulness* of the Godhead bodily; but the *plenitude* of glory, the *plenitude* of power;

> All mankind
> Must have been lost, adjudg'd to death and hell,
> By doom severe, had not the Son of God,
> In whom the *fulness* dwells of love divine,
> His dearest meditation thus renew'd.—MILTON.

'The most beneficent Being is he who hath an absolute *fulness* of perfection in himself, who gave existence to the universe, and so cannot be supposed to want that which he communicated without diminishing from the *plenitude* of his own power and happiness.'—GROVE.

FERTILE, FRUITFUL, PROLIFICK.

Fertile, in Latin *fertilis*, from *fero* to bear, signifies capable of bearing or bringing to light; *fruitful* signifies full of *fruit*, or containing within itself much fruit; *prolifick* is compounded of *proles* and *facio* to make a progeny.

Fertile expresses in its proper sense the faculty of sending forth from itself that which is not of its own nature, and is peculiarly applicable to the ground which causes every thing within itself to grow up;

> Why should I mention those, whose oozy soil
> Is render'd *fertile* by the o'erflowing Nile.
> JENYNS.

Fruitful expresses a state containing or possessing

abundantly that which is of the same nature; it is, therefore, peculiarly applicable to trees, plants, vegetables, and whatever is said to bear fruit;

When first the soil receives the *fruitful* seed,
Make no delay, but cover it with speed.—DRYDEN.

Prolifick expresses the faculty of generating; it conveys therefore the idea of what is creative, and is peculiarly applicable to animals; 'All dogs are of one species they mingling together in generation, and the breed of such mixtures being *prolifick*.'—RAY. We may say that the ground is either *fertile* or *fruitful*, but not *prolifick*: we may speak of a female of any species being *fruitful* and *prolifick*, but not *fertile*; we may speak of nature as being *fruitful*, but neither *fertile* nor *prolifick*. A country is *fertile* as it respects the quality of the soil; it is *fruitful* as it respects the abundance of its produce: it is possible, therefore, for a country to be *fruitful* by the industry of its inhabitants, although not *fertile* by nature.

An animal is said to be *fruitful* as it respects the number of young which it has; it is said to be *prolifick* as it respects its generative power. Some women are more *fruitful* than others; but there are many animals more *prolifick* than human creatures. The lands in Egypt are rendered *fertile* by means of mud which they receive from the overflowing of the Nile: they consequently produce harvests more *fruitful* than in almost any other country. Among the Orientals barrenness was reckoned a disgrace, and every woman was ambitious to be *fruitful*: there are some insects, particularly among the noxious tribes, which are so *prolifick*, that they are not many hours in being before they begin to breed.

In the figurative application they admit of a similar distinction. A man is *fertile* in expedients who readily contrives upon the spur of the occasion; he is *fruitful* in resources who has them ready at his hand; his brain is *prolifick* if it generates an abundance of new conceptions. A mind is *fertile* which has powers that admit of cultivation and expansion; 'To every work Warburton brought a memory full fraught, together with a fancy *fertile* of combinations.'—JOHNSON. An imagination is *fruitful* that is rich in stores of imagery; a genius is *prolifick* that is rich in invention. Females are *fertile* in expedients and devices; ambition and avarice are the most *fruitful* sources of discord and misery in publick and private life; 'The philosophy received from the Greeks has been *fruitful* in controversies, but barren of works.'—BACON. Novel-writers are the most *prolifick* class of authors;

Parent of light! all-seeing sun,
Prolifick beam, whose rays dispense
The various gifts of Providence.—GAY.

LARGELY, COPIOUSLY, FULLY.

Largely (*v. Great*) is here taken in the moral sense, and, if the derivation given of it be true, in the most proper sense; *copiously* comes from the Latin *copia* plenty, signifying in a plentiful degree; *fully* signifies in a *full* degree; to the *full* extent, as far as it can reach.

Quantity is the idea expressed in common by all these terms; but *largely* has always a reference to the freedom of the will in the agent; *copiously* qualifies actions that are done by inanimate objects; *fully* qualifies the actions of a rational agent, but it denotes a degree or extent which cannot be surpassed.

A person deals *largely* in things, or he drinks *large* draughts; rivers are *copiously* supplied in rainy seasons; a person is *fully* satisfied, or *fully* prepared. A bountiful Providence has distributed his gifts *largely* among his creatures; 'There is one very faulty method of drawing up the laws, that is, when the case is *largely* set forth in the preamble.'—BACON. Blood flows *copiously* from a deep wound when it is first made;

The youths with wine the *copious* goblets crown'd,
And pleas'd dispense the flowing bowls around.
POPE.

When a man is not *fully* convinced of his own insufficiency, he is not prepared to listen to the counsel of others; 'Every word (in the Bible) is so weighty that ought to be carefully considered by all that desire *fully* to understand the sense.'—BEVERIDGE.

PROFUSION, PROFUSENESS.

Profusion, from the Latin *profundo* to pour forth, is taken in relation to unconscious objects, which pour forth in great plenty; *profuseness* is taken from the same, in relation to conscious agents, who likewise pour forth in great plenty. The term *profusion*, therefore, is put for plenty itself, and the term *profuseness* as a characteristick of persons in the sense of extravagance.

At the hospitable board of the rich there will naturally be a *profusion* of every thing which can gratify the appetite;

Ye glitt'ring towns with wealth and splendour crown'd,
Ye fields where summer spreads *profusion* round,
For me your tributary stores combine.—GOLDSMITH.

When men see an unusual degree of *profusion*, they are apt to indulge themselves in *profuseness*; 'I was convinced that the liberality of my young companions was only *profuseness*.'—JOHNSON.

EXTRAVAGANT, PRODIGAL, LAVISH, PROFUSE.

Extravagant, from *extra* and *vagans*, signifies in general wandering from the line; and *prodigal*, from the Latin *prodigus* and *prodigo* to launch forth, signifies in general to send forth, or give out in great quantities; *lavish* comes probably from the Latin *lavo* to wash, signifying to wash away in waste; *profuse*, from the Latin *profusus*, participle of *profundo* to pour forth, signifies pouring out freely.

The idea of using immoderately is implied in all these terms, but *extravagant* is the most general in its meaning and application. The *extravagant* man spends his money without reason; the *prodigal* man spends it in excesses; the former errs against plain sense, the latter violates the moral law: the *extravagant* man will ruin himself by his follies; the *prodigal* by his vices. One may be *extravagant* with a small sum where it exceeds one's means; one cannot be *prodigal* but with large sums.

Extravagance is practised by both sexes; *prodigality* is peculiarly the vice of the male sex. *Extravagance* is opposed to meanness; *prodigality* to avarice. Those who know the true value of money, as contributing to their own enjoyments, or those of others, will guard against *extravagance*. Those who lay a restraint on their passions, can never fall into *prodigality*.

Extravagant and *prodigal* serve to designate habitual as well as particular actions; *lavish* and *profuse* are employed only in particular: hence we say to be *lavish* of one's money, one's presents, and the like; to be *profuse* in one's entertainments, both of which may be modes of *extravagance*. An *extravagant* man, however, in the restricted sense, mostly spends upon himself to indulge his whims and idle fancies; but a man may be *lavish* and *profuse* upon others from a misguided generosity.

In a moral use of these terms, a man is *extravagant* in his praises who exceeds either in measure or application; 'No one is to admit into his petitions to his Maker, things superfluous and *extravagant*.'—SOUTH. He is *prodigal* of his strength who consumes it by an excessive use;

Here patriots live, who for their country's good,
In fighting fields were *prodigal* of blood.
DRYDEN.

He is *lavish* of his compliments who deals them out so largely and promiscuously as to render them of no service;

See where the winding vale its *lavish* stores
Irriguous spreads.—THOMSON.

He is *profuse* in his acknowledgments who repeats them oftener, or delivers them in more words, than are necessary; 'Cicero was most liberally *profuse* in commending the ancients and his contemporaries.'—ADDISON (*after Plutarch*).

Extravagant and *profuse* are said only of individuals; *prodigal* and *lavish* may be said of many in a general sense. A nation may be *prodigal* of its resources; a government may be *lavish* of the publick money, as an individual is *extravagant* with his own and *profuse* in what he gives another.

ENOUGH, SUFFICIENT.

Enough, in German *genug*, comes from *genügen*, to satisfy; *sufficient*, in Latin *sufficiens*, participle of *sufficio*, compounded of *sub* and *facio*, signifies made or suited to the purpose.

He has *enough* whose desires are satisfied; he has *sufficient* whose wants are supplied. We may therefore frequently have *sufficiency* when we have not *enough*. A greedy man is commonly in this case, he has never *enough*, although he has more than a *sufficiency*. *Enough* is said only of physical objects of desire; *sufficient* is employed in a moral application, for that which serves the purpose. Children and animals never have *enough* food, nor the miser *enough* money;

> My loss of honour 's great *enough*,
> Thou need'st not brand it with a scoff.
> BUTLER.

It is requisite to allow *sufficient* time for every thing that is to be done, if we wish it to be done well; 'The time present seldom affords *sufficient* employment for the mind of man.'—ADDISON.

EXCESS, SUPERFLUITY, REDUNDANCY.

Excess is that which exceeds any measure; *superfluity* from *super* and *fluo* to flow over; and *redundancy*, from *redundo* to stream back or over, signifies an *excess* of a good measure. We may have an *excess* of heat or cold, wet or dry, when we have more than the ordinary quantity; but we have a *superfluity* of provisions when we have more than we want. *Excess* is applicable to any object; but *superfluity* and *redundancy* are species of *excess*. *Superfluity* is applicable in a particular manner to that which is an object of our desire; and *redundancy* to matters of expression or feeling. We may have an *excess* of prosperity or adversity; 'It is wisely ordered in our present state that joy and fear, hope and grief, should act alternately as checks and balances upon each other, in order to prevent an *excess* in any of them.'—BLAIR. We may have a *superfluity* of good things; 'When by force or policy, by wisdom, or by fortune, property and superiority were introduced and established, then they whose possessions swelled above their wants naturally laid out their *superfluities* on pleasure.'—JOHNSON. There may be a *redundancy* of speech or words; 'The defect or *redundance* of a syllable might be easily covered in the recitation.'—TYRRWHIT.

EXCESSIVE, IMMODERATE, INTEMPERATE.

The *excessive* is beyond measure; the *immoderate*, from *modus* a mode or measure, is without measure; the *intemperate*, from *tempus* a time or term, is that which is not kept within bounds.

Excessive designates *excess* in general; *immoderate* and *intemperate* designate *excess* in moral agents. The *excessive* lies simply in the thing which exceeds any given point: the *immoderate* lies in the passions which range to a boundless extent: the *intemperate* lies in the will which is under no control. Hence we speak of an *excessive* thirst physically considered: an *immoderate* ambition or lust of power: an *intemperate* indulgence, an *intemperate* warmth. *Excessive* admits of degrees; what is *excessive* may exceed in a greater or less degree: *immoderate* and *intemperate* mark a positively great degree of *excess;* the former still higher than the latter: *immoderate* is in fact the highest conceivable degree of *excess*.

The *excessive* use of any thing will always be attended with some evil consequence; 'Who knows not the languor that attends every *excessive* indulgence in pleasure?'—BLAIR. The *immoderate* use of wine will rapidly tend to the ruin of him who is guilty of the *excess;* 'One of the first objects of wish to every one is to maintain a proper place and rank in society: this among the vain and ambitious is always the favourite aim. With them it arises to *immoderate* expectations founded on their supposed talents and imagined merits.'—BLAIR. The *intemperate* use of wine will proceed by a more gradual but not less sure process to his ruin; 'Let no wantonness of youthful spirits, no compliance with the *intemperate* mirth of others, ever betray you into profane sallies.'—BLAIR.

Excessive designates what is partial; *immoderate* is used oftener for what is partial than what is habitual; *intemperate* oftener for what is habitual than what is partial. A person is *excessively* displeased on particular occasions: he may be an *immoderate* eater at all times, or only *immoderate* in that which he likes: he is *intemperate* in his language when his anger is *intemperate;* or he leads an *intemperate* life. The *excesses* of youth do but too often settle into confirmed habits of *intemperance*.

EXUBERANT, LUXURIANT.

Exuberant, from the Latin *exuberans* or *ex* and *ubero*, signifies very fruitful or superabundant: *luxuriant*, in Latin *luxurians*, from *laxus*, signifies expanding with unrestrained freedom. These terms are both applied to vegetation in a flourishing state; but *exuberance* expresses the excess, and *luxuriance* the perfection: in a fertile soil where plants are left unrestrainedly to themselves there will be an *exuberance:*

> Another Flora there of bolder hues
> And richer sweets, beyond our garden's pride
> Plays o'er the fields, and showers with sudden hand
> *Exuberant* spring.—THOMSON.

Plants are to be seen in their *luxuriance* only in seasons that are favourable to them;

> On whose *luxurious* herbage, half conceal'd,
> Like a fall'n cedar, far diffus'd his train,
> Cas'd in green scales, the crocodile extends.
> THOMSON.

In the moral application, *exuberance* of intellect is often attended with a restless ambition that is incompatible both with the happiness and advancement of its possessor; 'His similes have been thought too *exuberant* and full of circumstances.'—POPE. *Luxuriance* of imagination is one of the greatest gifts which a poet can boast of; 'A fluent and *luxuriant* speech becomes youth well, but not age.'—BACON.

EMPTY, VACANT, VOID, DEVOID.

Empty, in Saxon *empti*, is not improbably derived from the Latin *inopis* poor or wanting; *vacant*, in Latin *vacans* or *vaco*, comes from the Hebrew בקק to draw out or exhaust; *void* and *devoid*, in Latin *viduus* and Greek ἴδιος, signifies solitary or bereft.

Empty is the term in most general use; *vacant*, *void*, and *devoid* are employed in particular cases: *empty* and *vacant* have either a proper or an improper application; *void* or *devoid* only a moral acceptation.

Empty, in the natural sense, marks an absence of that which is substantial, or adapted for filling; *vacant* designates or marks the absence of that which should occupy or make use of a thing. That which is hollow may be *empty;* that which respects any space may be *vacant*. A house is *empty* which has no inhabitants; a seat is *vacant* which is without an occupant: a room is *empty* which is without furniture; a space on paper is *vacant* which is free from writing.

In the figurative application *empty* and *vacant* have a similar analogy: a dream is said to be *empty*, or a title *empty*, &c.;

> To honour Thetis' son he bends his care,
> And plunge the Greeks in all the woes of war:
> Then bids an *empty* phantom rise to sight,
> And thus commands the vision of the night.
> POPE.

A stare is said to be *vacant*, or an hour *vacant;* 'An inquisitive man is a creature naturally very *vacant* of thought in itself, and therefore forced to apply itself to foreign assistance.'—STEELE. *Void* or *devoid* are used in the same sense as *vacant*, as qualifying epithets, but not prefixed as adjectives, and always followed by some object: thus we speak of a creature as *void* of reason; and of an individual as *devoid* of common sense;

> My next desire is, *void* of care and strife,
> To lead a soft, secure, inglorious life.—DRYDEN.

> We Tyrians are not so *devoid* of sense,
> Nor so remote from Phœbus' influence.—DRYDEN.

VACANCY, VACUITY, INANITY.

Vacancy and *vacuity* both denote the space unoccupied, or the abstract quality of being unoccupied. *Inanity*, from the Latin *inanis*, denotes the abstract quality of emptiness, or of not containing any thing: hence the former terms *vacancy* and *vacuity* are used in an indifferent or bad sense; *inanity* always in a bad sense: there may be a *vacancy* in the seat, or a *vacancy* in the mind, or a *vacancy* in life, which we may or may not fill up as we please;

How is 't
That thus you bend your eye on *vacancy*
And with th' incorporal air do hold discourse?
SHAKSPEARE.

Vacuities are supposed to be interspersed among the particles of matter, or, figuratively, they may be supposed to exist in the soul and in other objects; 'There are *vacuities* in the happiest life, which it is not in the power of the world to fill.'—BLAIR. *Inanity* of character denotes the want of the essentials that constitute a character; 'When I look up and behold the heavens, it makes me scorn the world and the pleasures thereof, considering the vanity of these and the *inanity* of the other.'—HOWELL.

HOLLOW, EMPTY.

Hollow, from *hole*, signifies being like a *hole; empty*, *v. Empty*.

Hollow respects the body itself; the absence of its own material produces hollowness: *empty* respects foreign bodies; their absence in another body constitutes *emptiness*. *Hollowness* is therefore a preparative to *emptiness*, and may exist independently of it; but *emptiness* presupposes the existence of *hollowness:* what is *empty* must be *hollow;* but what is *hollow* need not be *empty*. *Hollowness* is often the natural property of a body; *emptiness* is a contingent property: that which is *hollow* is destined by nature to contain; but that which is *empty* is deprived of its contents by a casualty: a nut is *hollow* for the purpose of receiving the fruit: it is *empty* if it contain no fruit.

They are both employed in a moral acceptation, and in a bad sense; the *hollow*, in this case, is applied to what ought to be solid or sound; and *empty* to what ought to be filled: a person is *hollow* whose goodness lies only at the surface, whose fair words are without meaning; a truce is *hollow* which is only an external cessation from hostilities;

He seem'd
For dignity compos'd, and high exploit;
But all was false and *hollow*.—MILTON.

A person is *empty* who is without the requisite portion of understanding and knowledge; an excuse is *empty* which is unsupported by fact and reason; a pleasure is *empty* which cannot afford satisfaction;

The creature man
Condemn'd to sacrifice his childish years
To babbling ignorance and *empty* fears.—PRIOR.

TO SPEND, EXHAUST, DRAIN.

Spend, contracted from *expend*, in Latin *expendo* to pay away, signifies to give from oneself; *exhaust*, from the Latin *exhaurio* to draw out, signifies to draw out all that there is; *drain*, a variation of draw, signifies to draw dry.

The idea of taking from the substance of any thing is common to these terms; but to *spend* is to deprive in a less degree than to *exhaust*, and that in a less degree than to *drain:* every one who exerts himself, in that degree *spends* his strength; if the exertions are violent he *exhausts* himself; a country which is *drained* of men is supposed to have no more left. To *spend* may be applied to that which is either external or inherent in a body;

Your tears for such a death in vain you *spend*,
Which straight in immortality shall end.
DENHAM.

Exhaust applies to that which is inherent or essential; *drain* to that which is external of the body in which it is contained; 'Teaching is not a flow of words nor the *draining* of an hour-glass.'—SOUTH. We may speak of *spending* our wealth, our resources, our time, and the like. The strength, the vigour, or the voice is *exhausted;* 'Many of our provisions for ease or happiness are *exhausted* by the present day.'—JOHNSON. *Draining* is applied in its proper application to a vessel which is *drained* of its liquid; or, in extended application, to a treasury which is *drained* of money. Hence arises this farther distinction, that to *spend* and to *exhaust* may tend, more or less, to the injury of a body; but to *drain* may be to its advantage. Inasmuch as what is *spent* or *exhausted* may be more or less essential to the soundness of a body, it cannot be parted with without diminishing its value, or even destroying its existence; as when a fortune is *spent* it is gone, or when a person's strength is *exhausted* he is no longer able to move: on the other hand, to *drain*, though a more complete evacuation, is not always injurious, but sometimes even useful to a body; as when the land is *drained* of a superabundance of water.

TO SPEND OR EXPEND, WASTE, DISSIPATE, SQUANDER.

Spend and *expend* are variations from the Latin *expendo;* but *spend* may be used in the sense of turning to some purpose, or making use of; to *expend* carries with it likewise the idea of exhausting; and *waste* moreover, comprehends the idea of exhausting to no good purpose: we *spend* money when we purchase any thing with it; we *expend* it when we lay it out in large quantities, so as essentially to diminish its quantity: individuals *spend* what they have; government *expends* vast sums in conducting the affairs of a nation; all persons *waste* their property who have not sufficient discretion to use it well: we *spend* our time, or our lives, in any employment;

Then having *spent* the last remains of light,
They give their bodies due repose at night.
DRYDEN.

We *expend* our strength and faculties upon some arduous undertaking; 'The king of England *wasted* the French king's country, and thereby caused him to *expend* such sums of money as exceeded the debt.'—HAYWARD. Men are apt to *waste* their time and talents in trifles;

What numbers, guiltless of their own disease,
Are snatch'd by sudden death, or *waste* by slow degrees!—JENYNS.

Dissipate, in Latin *dissipatus*, from *dissipo*, that is, *dis* and *sipo*, in Greek σίφω to scatter, signifies to scatter different ways, that is, to *waste* by throwing away in all directions: *squander*, which is a variation of *wander*, signifies to make to run wide apart. Both these terms, therefore, denote modes of *wasting;* but the former seems peculiarly applicable to that which is *wasted* in detail upon different objects, and by a distraction of the mind; the latter respects rather the act of *wasting* in the gross, in large quantities, by planless profusion: young men are apt to *dissipate* their property in pleasures;

He pitied man, and much he pitied those
Whom falsely smiling fate has curs'd with means
To *dissipate* their days in quest of joy.
ARMSTRONG.

The open, generous, and thoughtless are apt to *squander* their property; 'To how many temptations are all, but especially the young and gay, exposed to *squander* their whole time amid the circles of levity.'—BLAIR.

TO SPREAD, SCATTER, DISPERSE.

Spread (*v. To spread*) applies equally to divisible or indivisible bodies; we *spread* our money on the table, or we may *spread* a cloth on the table: but *scatter* which, like shatter, is a frequentative of shake, is applicable to divisible bodies only; we *scatter* corn on the ground. To *spread* may be an act of design or otherwise, but mostly the former; as when we *spread* books or papers before us: *scatter* is mostly an act without design; a child *scatters* the papers on the floor. When taken, however as an act of design, it is done without order; but *spread* is an act done in order: thus hay is *spread* out to dry, but corn is *scattered* over the land;

All in a row
Advancing broad, or wheeling round the field,
They *spread* their breathing harvest to the sun.
THOMSON.

Each leader now his *scatter'd* force conjoins.
POPE.

Things may *spread* in one direction, or at least without separation; but they *disperse* (*v. To dispel*) in many directions, so as to destroy the continuity of bodies: a leaf *spreads* as it opens in all its parts, and a tree also *spreads* as its branches increase; but a multitude *disperses*, an army *disperses*. Between *scatter* and *disperse* there is no other difference than that one is immethodical and involuntary, the other systematick and intentional: flowers are *scattered* along a path, which accidentally fall from the hand; a mob is *dispersed* by an act of authority: sheep are *scattered* along the hills; religious tracts are *dispersed* among the poor: the disciples were *scattered* as sheep without a shepherd, after the delivery of our Saviour into the hands of the Jews; they *dispersed* themselves, after his ascension, over every part of the world;

Straight to the tents the troops *dispersing* bend.
POPE.

TO SPREAD, EXPAND, DIFFUSE.

Spread, in Saxon *spredan*, Low German *spredan*, High German *spreiten*, is an intensive of *breit* broad, signifying to stretch wide; *expand*, in Latin *expando*, compounded of *ex* and *pando* to open, and the Greek φαίνω to show or make appear, signifies to open out wide; *diffuse*, *v. Diffuse*.

To *spread* is the general, the other two are particular terms. To *spread* may be said of any thing which occupies more space than it has done, whether by a direct separation of its parts, or by an accession to the substance; but to *expand* is to *spread* by means of separating or unfolding the parts: a mist *spreads* over the earth; a flower *expands* its leaves: a tree *spreads* by the growth of its branches; the opening bud *expands* when it feels the genial warmth of the sun.

Spread and *expand* are used likewise in a moral application; *diffuse* is seldom used in any other application: *spread* is here, as before, equally indefinite as to the mode of the action; every thing *spreads*, and it *spreads* in any way;

See where the winding vale its lavish'd stores
Irriguous *spreads*.—THOMSON.

Expansion is that gradual process by which an object opens or unfolds itself after the manner of a flower;

As from the face of heaven the shatter'd clouds
Tumultuous rove, th' interminable sky
Sublimer swells, and o'er the world *expands*
A purer azure.—THOMSON.

Diffusion is that process of *spreading* which consists literally in pouring out in different ways;

Th' uncurling floods *diffus'd*
In glassy breadth, seem, through delusive lapse,
Forgetful of their course.—THOMSON.

Evils *spread*, and reports *spread*; the mind *expands*, and prospects *expand*; knowledge *diffuses* itself, or cheerfulness is *diffused* throughout a company.

TO DILATE, EXPAND.

Dilate, in Latin *dilato*, from *di* apart and *latus*, wide, that is, to make very wide; *expand*, *v. To spread*, in the preceding article.

The idea of drawing any thing out so as to occupy a greater space is common to these terms in opposition to contracting. *Dilate* is an intransitive verb; *expand* is transitive or intransitive; the former marks the action of any body within itself; the latter an external action on any body. A bladder *dilates* on the admission of air, or the heart *dilates* with joy; knowledge *expands* the mind, or a person's views *expand* with circumstances. In the circulation of the blood through the body, the vessels are exposed to a perpetual *dilatation* and contraction: the gradual *expansion* of the mind by the regular modes of communicating knowledge to youth is unquestionably to be desired; but the sudden *expansion* of a man's thoughts from a comparative state of ignorance by any powerful action is very dangerous;

The conscious heart of charity would warm,
And her wide wish benevolence *dilate*.
THOMSON.

'The poet (Thomson) leads us through the appearances of things as they are successively varied by the vicissitudes of the year, and imparts to us so much of his own enthusiasm that our thoughts *expand* with his imagery.'—JOHNSON.

TO SPREAD, CIRCULATE, PROPAGATE, DISSEMINATE.

To *spread* (*v. To spread, expand*) is said of any object material or spiritual; the rest are mostly employed in the moral application. To *spread* is to extend to an indefinite width;

Love would between the rich and needy stand,
And *spread* heaven's bounty with an equal hand.
WALLER.

To *circulate* is to *spread* within a circle; thus news *spreads* through a country; but a story *circulates* in a village, or from house to house, or a report is *circulated* in a neighbourhood;

Our God, when heaven and earth he did create,
Form'd man, who should of both participate;
If our lives' motions theirs must imitate,
Our knowledge, like our blood, must *circulate*.
DENHAM.

Spread and *circulate* are the acts of persons or things; *propagate* and *disseminate* are the acts of persons only. A thing *spreads* and *circulates*, or it is *spread* and *circulated* by some one; it is always *propagated* and *disseminated* by some one. *Propagate*, from the Latin *propago* a breed, and *disseminate*, from *semen* a seed, are here figuratively employed as modes of *spreading*, according to the natural operations of increasing the quantity of any thing which is implied in the first two terms. What is *propagated* is supposed to generate new subjects; as when doctrines, either good or bad, are *propagated* among the people so as to make them converts;

He shall extend his *propagated* sway
Beyond the solar year, without the starry way.
DRYDEN.

What is *disseminated* is supposed to be sown in different parts; thus principles are *disseminated* among youth; 'Nature seems to have taken care to *disseminate* her blessings among the different regions of the world.'—ADDISON.

TO DISPEL, DISPERSE, DISSIPATE.

Dispel, from the Latin *pello* to drive, signifying to drive away, is a more forcible action than to *disperse*, which signifies merely to cause to come asunder: we destroy the existence of a thing by *dispelling* it; we merely destroy the junction or cohesion of a body by *dispersing* it: the sun *dispels* the clouds and darkness;

As when a western whirlwind, charg'd with storms,
Dispels the gathering clouds that Notus forms.
POPE.

The wind *disperses* the clouds, or a surgeon *disperses* a tumour; but the clouds and the tumour may both gather again:

The foe *dispers'd*, their bravest warriours kill'd,
Fierce as a whirlwind now I swept the field.
POPE.

Dispelling and *dispersing* are frequently natural and regular operations; *dissipating* is oftentimes a violent and disorderly proceeding. *Dissipate*, in Latin *dissipatum*, participle of *dissipo*, compounded of *dis* and the obsolete *sipo*, in Greek σίφω, was originally applied to fluids, whence the word *siphon* takes its rise. The word *dissipate* therefore denotes the act of scattering after the manner of fluids which are thus lost; whence that which is *dissipated* loses its existence as an aggregate body; 'The heat at length grows so great, that it again *dissipates* and bears off those corpuscles which it brought.'—WOODWARD. In the same manner wealth is said to be *dissipated* when it is lost to the owner by being spent. These terms admit of a similar distinction in the moral acceptation;

If the night
Have gather'd aught of evil, or conceal'd
Disperse it, as now light *dispels* the dark.—MILTON.

When the thoughts are *dissipated* the mind is as it were lost; 'I have begun two or three letters to you by snatches, and been prevented from finishing them by a thousand avocations and *dissipations*.'—SWIFT.

Dispel is used figuratively; *disperse* only in the natural sense: gloom, ignorance, and the like, are *dispelled;* books, people, papers, and the like, are *dispersed.*

TO POUR, SPILL, SHED.

Pour is probably connected with *pore*, and the Latin preposition *per* through, signifying to make to pass as it were through a channel; *spill* and splash, and the German *spillen* are probably onomatopeias; *shed* comes from the German *scheiden* to separate, signifying to cast from.

We *pour* with design; we *spill* by accident: we *pour* water over a plant or a bed; we *spill* it on the ground. To *pour* is an act of convenience; to *spill* and *shed* are acts more or less hurtful; the former is to cause to run in small quantities; the latter in large quantities: we *pour* wine out of a bottle into a glass; but the blood of a person is said to be *spilled* or *shed* when his life is violently taken away: what is *poured* is commonly no part of the body from whence it is *poured;* but what is shed is no other than a component part; hence trees are said to *shed* their leaves, animals their hair, or human beings to *shed* tears; 'Poesy is of so subtle a spirit, that in the *pouring* out of one language into another, it will evaporate.'—DENHAM.

O reputation! dearer far than life,
Thou precious balsam, lovely sweet of smell,
Whose cordial drops once *spill'd* by some rash hand,
Not all the owner's care, nor the repenting toil
Of the rude *spiller*, can collect.—SEWEL.

'Herod acted the part of a great mourner for the deceased Aristobulus, *shedding* abundance of tears.'—PRIDEAUX.

POVERTY, INDIGENCE, WANT, NEED, PENURY.

Poverty marks the condition of being *poor; indigence*, in Latin *indigentia*, comes from *indigeo* and the Greek δέομαι to *want*, signifying in the same manner as the word *want*, the abstract condition of *wanting; need, v. Necessity; penury*, in Latin *penuria*, comes in all probability from the Greek πένης poor.

Poverty is a general state of fortune opposed to that of riches; in which one is abridged of the conveniences of life: *indigence* is a particular state of *poverty*, which rises above it in such a degree, as to exclude the necessaries as well as the conveniences of life; *want* and *need* are both partial states, that refer only to individual things which are *wanting* to any one. *Poverty* and *indigence* comprehend all a man's external circumstances; but *want*, when taken by itself, denotes the *want* of food or clothing, and is opposed to abundance; *need*, when taken by itself, implies the want of money, or any other useful article; but they are both more commonly taken in connexion with the object which is *wanted*, and in this sense they are to the two former as species to the genus. *Poverty* and *indigence* are permanent states; *want* and *need* are temporary: *poverty* and *indigence* are the order of Providence, they do not depend upon the individual, and are, therefore, not reckoned as his fault; *want* and *need* arise more commonly from circumstances of one's own creation, and tend frequently to one's discredit. What man has not caused, man cannot so easily obviate; *poverty* and *indigence* cannot, therefore, be removed at one's will: but *want* and *need* are frequently removed by the aid of others. *Poverty* is that which one should learn to bear, so as to lessen its pains; 'That the *poverty* of the Highlanders is gradually diminished cannot be mentioned among the unpleasing consequences of subjection.'—JOHNSON *Indigence* is a calamity which the compassion of others may in some measure alleviate, if they cannot entirely remove it; 'If we can but raise him above *indigence*, a moderate share of good fortune and merit will be sufficient to open his way to whatever else we can wish him to obtain.'—MELMOTH (*Letters of Cicero*). *Want*, when it results from intemperance or extravagance, is not altogether entitled to any relief;

Want is a bitter and a hateful good,
Because its virtues are not understood;
Yet many things, impossible to thought,
Have been by *need* to full perfection brought.
DRYDEN.

But *need*, when it arises from casualties that are independent of our demerits, will always find friends.

It is a wise distribution of Providence which has made the rich and poor to be mutually dependent upon each other, and both to be essential to the happiness of the whole. Among all descriptions of *indigent* persons, none are more entitled to charitable attention than those who in addition to their wants suffer under any bodily infirmity. The old proverb says, "That waste makes *want*," which is daily realized among men without making them wiser by experience. "A friend in *need*," according to another vulgar proverb, "is a friend indeed," which, like all proverbial sayings, contains a striking truth; for nothing can be more acceptable than the assistance which we receive from a friend when we stand in *need* of it; 'God grant we never may have *need* of you.'—SHAKSPEARE. All these terms may be used, either in a general or in a particular sense, to denote a privation of things in general or a partial privation. *Penury* is used to denote a privation of things in general, but particularly of things most essential for existence; 'The *penury* of the ecclesiastical state.'—HOOKER.

Sometimes am I a king,
Then treason makes me with myself a beggar;
And so I am; then crushing *penury*
Persuades me, I was better when a king.
SHAKSPEARE.

NECESSITY, NEED.

Necessity (*v. Necessary*) respects the thing wanted; *need*, in German *noth*, probably from the Greek ἀνάγκη *necessity*, the person wanting. There would be no *necessity* for punishments, if there were not evil doers; he is peculiarly fortunate who finds a friend in time of *need*. *Necessity* is more pressing than *need:* the former places us in a positive state of compulsion to act: it is said to have no law, it prescribes the law for itself; the latter yields to circumstances, and leaves us in a state of deprivation. We are frequently under the *necessity* of going without that of which we stand most in *need;* 'Where *necessity* ends, curiosity begins.'—JOHNSON. 'One of the many advantages of friendship is, that one can say to one's friend the things that stand in *need* of pardon.'—POPE.

From these two nouns arise two epithets for each, which are worthy of observation, namely, *necessary* and *needful, necessitous* and *needy*. *Necessary* and *needful* are both applicable to the thing wanted; *necessitous* and *needy* to the person wanting *necessary* is applied to every object indiscriminately *needful* only to such objects as supply temporary or partial wants. Exercise is *necessary* to preserve the health of the body; restraint is *necessary* to preserve that of the mind; assistance is *needful* for one who has not sufficient resources in himself: it is *necessary* to go by water to the continent: money is *needful* for one who is travelling.

The dissemination of knowledge is *necessary* to dispel the ignorance which would otherwise prevail in the world;

It seems to me most strange that men should fear
Seeing that death, a *necessary* end,
Will come when it will come.—SHAKSPEARE

It is *needful* for a young person to attend to the instructions of his teacher, if he will improve;

Time, long expected, eas'd us of our load,
And brought the *needful* presence of a god.
DRYDEN.

Necessitous expresses more than *needy:* the former comprehends a general state of *necessity* or deficiency in the thing that is wanted or *needful*; *needy* expresses only a particular condition. The poor are in a *necessitous* condition who are in want of the first *necessaries*, or who have not wherewithal to supply the most pressing *necessities*; 'Steele's imprudence of generosity, or vanity of profusion, kept him always incurably *necessitous*.'—JOHNSON. Adventurers are said to be *needy*, when their vices make them in *need* of that which they might otherwise obtain; 'Charity is the work of heaven, which is always laying itself out on the *needy* and the impotent.'—SOUTH. It is charity to supply the wants of the *necessitous*, but those of the *needy* are sometimes not worthy of one's pity.

POOR, PAUPER.

Poor and *pauper* are both derived from the Latin *pauper*, which comes from the Greek παυρος small. *Poor* is the term of general use; *pauper* is a term of particular use: a *pauper* is a *poor* man who lives upon alms or the relief of the parish: the former is, therefore, indefinite in its meaning; the latter conveys a reproachful idea. The word *poor* is used as a substantive only in the plural number; *pauper* is a substantive both in the singular and plural: the *poor* of a parish are, in general, a heavy burden on the inhabitants; there are some persons who are not ashamed to live and die as *paupers*.

NECESSITIES, NECESSARIES.

Necessity, in Latin *necessitas*, and *necessary*, in Latin *necessarius*, from *necesse*, or *ne* and *cesso*, signify not to be yielded or given up. *Necessity* is the mode or state of circumstances, or the thing which circumstances render *necessary*; the *necessary* is that which is absolutely and unconditionally *necessary*.

Art has ever been busy in inventing things to supply the various *necessities* of our nature, and yet there are always numbers who want even the first *necessaries* of life. Habit and desire create *necessities*; nature only requires *necessaries*: a voluptuary has *necessities* which are unknown to a temperate man; the poor have in general little more than *necessaries*; 'Those whose condition has always restrained them to the contemplation of their own *necessities* will scarcely understand why nights and days should be spent in study.' —JOHNSON. 'To make a man happy, virtue must be accompanied with at least a moderate provision of all the *necessaries* of life, and not disturbed by bodily pains.'—BUDGELL.

TO WANT, NEED, LACK.

To be without is the common idea expressed by these terms: but to *want* is to be without that which contributes to our comfort, or is an object of our desire; to *need* is to be without that which is essential for our existence or our purposes. To *lack*, which is probably a variation from *leak*, and a term not in frequent use, expresses little more than the general idea of being without, unaccompanied by any collateral idea. From the close connexion which subsists between desiring and *want*, it is usual to consider what we *want* as artificial, and what we *need* as natural and indispensable. What one man *wants* is a superfluity to another; but that which is *needed* by one is in like circumstances *needed* by all: tender people *want* a fire when others would be glad not to have it; all persons *need* warm clothing and a warm house in the winter.

To *want* and *need* may extend indefinitely to many or all objects; to *lack*, or be deficient, is properly said of a single object: we may *want* or *need* every thing; we *lack* one thing, we *lack* this or that; a rich man may *lack* understanding, virtue, or religion. He who *wants* nothing is a happy man; 'To be rich is to have more than is desired, and more than is *wanted*.'—JOHNSON. He who *needs* nothing, may be happy if he *wants* no more than he has;

> The old from such affairs are only freed,
> Which vig'rous youth and strength of body *need*.
> DENHAM.

Contentment is often the only thing a man *lacks* to make him happy;

> See the mind of beastly man!
> That hath so soon forgot the excellence
> Of his creation, when he life began,
> That now he chooseth with vile difference
> To be a beast and *lacke* intelligence.—SPENSER

TO INCREASE, GROW.

Increase, from the Latin *in* and *cresco*, signifies to grow upon or grow to a thing, to become one with it; *grow*, in Saxon *growan*, very probably comes from, or is connected with, the Latin *crevi*, perfect of *cresco* to increase or grow.

The idea of becoming larger is common to both these terms: but the former expresses the idea in an unqualified manner: and the latter annexes to this general idea also that of the mode or process by which this is effected. To *increase* is either a gradual or an instantaneous act; to *grow* is a gradual process: a stream *increases* by the addition of other waters; it may come suddenly or in course of time, by means of gentle showers or the rushing in of other streams; but if we say that the river or stream *grows*, it is supposed to *grow* by some regular and continual process of receiving fresh water, as from the running in of different rivulets or smaller streams. To *increase* is either a natural or an artificial process; to *grow* is always natural: money *increases* but does not *grow*, because it *increases* by artificial means: corn may either *increase* or *grow*: in the former case we speak of it in the sense of becoming larger or *increasing* in bulk; in the latter case we consider the mode of its *increasing*, namely, by the natural process of vegetation. On this ground we say that a child *grows* when we wish to denote the natural process by which his body arrives at its proper size; but we may speak of his *increasing* in stature, in size, and the like;

> Then, as her strength with years *increas'd*, began
> To pierce aloft in air the soaring swan.—DRYDEN.

For this reason likewise *increase* is used in a transitive as well as intransitive sense; but *grow* always in an intransitive sense: we can *increase* a thing, though not properly *grow* a thing, because we can make it larger by whatever means we please; but when it *grows* it makes itself larger. 'Bones, after full *growth*, continue at a stay; as for nails, they *grow* continually.' —BACON.

In their improper acceptation these words preserve the same distinction: 'trade *increases*' bespeaks the simple fact of its becoming larger; but 'trade *grows*' implies that gradual *increase* which flows from the natural concurrence of circumstances. The affections which are awakened in infancy *grow* with one's growth; here is a natural and moral process combined;

> Children, like tender oziers, take the bow,
> And, as they first are fashion'd, always *grow*
> DRYDEN.

The fear of death sometimes *increases* as one *grows* old; the courage of a truly brave man *increases* with the sight of danger: here is a moral process which is both gradual and immediate, but in both cases produced by some foreign cause.

I have enlarged on these two words the more because they appear to have been involved in some considerable perplexity by the French writers Girard and Robaud, who have entered very diffusely into the distinction between the words *croitre* and *augmenter*, corresponding to *increas* and *grow*; but I trust that from the above explanation, the distinction is clearly to be observed.

INCREASE, ADDITION, ACCESSION, AUGMENTATION.

Increase is here as in the former article the generick term (*v. To increase*): there will always be *increase* where there is *augmentation*, *addition*, and *accession*, though not *vice versâ*.

Addition is to increase as the means to the end: the *addition* is the artificial mode of making two things into one; the *increase* is the result: when the value of one figure is added to another, the sum is *increased*: hence a man's treasures experience an *increase* by the *addition* of other parts to the main stock. *Addition* is an intentional mode of *increasing; accession* is an accidental mode: one thing is added to another, and thereby *increased;* but an *accession* takes place of itself; it is the coming or joining of one thing to another so as to *increase* the whole. A merchant *increases* his property by adding his gains in trade every year to the mass; but he receives an *accession* of property either by inheritance or any other contingency. In the same manner a monarch *increases* his dominions by *adding* one territory to another, or by various *accessions* of territory which fall to his lot.

When we speak of an *increase*, we think of the whole and its relative magnitude at different times;

> At will I crop the year's *increase*,
> My latter life is rest and peace.—DRYDEN.

When we speak of an *addition*, we think only of the part and the agency by which this part is joined; 'The ill state of health into which Tullia is fallen is a very severe *addition* to the many and great disquietudes that afflict my mind.'—MELMOTH (*Letters of Cicero*). When we speak of an *accession*, we think only of the circumstance by which one thing becomes thus joined to another; 'There is nothing in my opinion more pleasing in religion than to consider that the soul is to shine for ever with new *accessions* of glory.'—ADDISON. *Increase* of happiness does not depend upon *increase* of wealth; the miser makes daily *additions* to the latter without making any to the former: sudden *accessions* of wealth are seldom attended with any good consequences, as they turn the thoughts too violently out of their sober channel, and bend them too strongly on present possessions and good fortune.

Augmentation is another term for *increase*, which differs less in sense than in application: the latter is generally applied to all objects that admit such a change: but the former is applied only to objects of higher import or cases of a less familiar nature. We may say that a person experiences an *increase* or an *augmentation* in his family; or that he has had an *increase* or an *augmentation* of his salary, or that there is an *increase* or *augmentation* of the number: in all which cases the former term is most adapted to the colloquial, and the latter to the grave style.

TO ENLARGE, INCREASE, EXTEND.

Enlarge signifies literally to make large or wide, and is applied to dimension and extent; *increase*, from the Latin *incresco* to grow to a thing, is applicable to quantity, signifying to become greater in size by the junction of other matter; *extend*, in Latin *extendo*, or *ex* and *tendo*, signifies to stretch out, that is, to make greater in space. We speak of *enlarging* a house, a room, premises, or boundaries; of *increasing* the property, the army, the capital, expense, &c.; of *extending* the boundaries of an empire. We say the hole or cavity *enlarges*, the head or bulk *enlarges*, the number *increases*, the swelling, inflammation, and the like, *increase:* so likewise in the figurative sense, the views, the prospects, the powers, the ideas, and the mind, are *enlarged;*

> Great objects make
> Great minds, *enlarging* as their views *enlarge*,
> Those still more godlike, as these more divine.
> YOUNG.

Pain, pleasure, hope, fear, anger, or kindness, is *increased;* 'Good sense alone is a sedate and quiescent quality, which manages its possessions well, but does not *increase* them.'—JOHNSON. Views, prospects, connexions, and the like, are *extended;*

> The wise *extending* their inquiries wide,
> See how both states are by connexion tied;
> Fools view but part, and not the whole survey,
> So crowd existence all into a day.—JENYNS.

TO REACH, STRETCH, EXTEND.

Reach, through the medium of the northern languages, as also the Latin *regò* in the word *porrigo*, and the Greek ὀρέγω, comes from the Hebrew רקע to draw out, and ארח length; *stretch* is but an intensive of *reach; extend, v. To extend.*

The idea of drawing out in a line is common to these terms, but they differ in the mode and circumstances of the action. To *reach* and to *stretch* are employed only for drawing out in a straight line, that is, lengthwise; *extend* may be employed to express the drawing out in all directions. In this sense a wall is said to *reach* a certain number of yards; a neck of land is said to *stretch* into the sea; a wood *extends* many miles over a country. As the act of persons, in the proper sense, they differ still more widely; *reach* and *stretch* signify drawing to a given point, and for a given end: *extend* has no such collateral meaning. We *reach* in order to take hold of something; we *stretch* in order to surmount some object: a person *reaches* with his arm in order to get down a book; he *stretches* his neck in order to see over another person: in both cases we might be said simply to *extend* the arm or the neck, where the collateral circumstance is not to be expressed.

In the improper application, they have a similar distinction: to *reach* is applied to the movements which one makes to a certain end, and is equivalent to arriving at, or attaining. A traveller strives to *reach* his journey's end as quickly as possible; an ambitious man aims at *reaching* the summit of human power or honour; 'The whole power of cunning is privative; to say nothing, and to do nothing, is the utmost of its *reach*.'—JOHNSON. To *stretch* is applied to the direction which one gives to another object, so as to bring it to a certain point; a ruler *stretches* his power or authority to its utmost limits;

> Plains immense
> Lie *stretch'd* below interminable meads.
> THOMSON.

To *extend* retains its original unqualified meaning; as when we speak of extending the meaning or application of a word, of *extending* one's bounty or charity, *extending* one's sphere of action, and the like;

> Our life is short, but to *extend* that span
> To vast eternity is virtue's work.—SHAKSPEARE

SIZE, MAGNITUDE, GREATNESS, BULK.

Size, from the Latin *cisus* and *cædo* to cut, signifies that which is cut or framed according to a certain proportion; *magnitude*, from the Latin *magnitudo*, answers literally to the English word *greatness; bulk, v. Bulky.*

Size is a general term including all manner of dimension or measurement; *magnitude* is employed in science or in an abstract sense to denote some specifick measurement; *greatness* is an unscientifick term applied in the same sense to objects in general; *size* is indefinite, it never characterizes any thing either as large or small; but *magnitude* and *greatness* always suppose something *great;* and *bulk* denotes a considerable degree of *greatness:* things which are diminutive in *size* will often have an extraordinary degree of beauty, or some other adventitious perfection to compensate the deficiency;

> Soon grows the pigmy to gigantick *size*.—DRYDEN.

Astronomers have classed the stars according to their different *magnitudes;*

> Then form'd the moon,
> Globose, and every *magnitude* of stars.—MILTON.

Greatness is considered by Burke as one source of the sublime; 'Awe is the first sentiment that rises in the mind at the first view of God's *greatness*.'—BLAIR. *Bulk* is that species of *greatness* which destroys the symmetry, and consequently the beauty, of objects;

> His hugy *bulk* on seven high volumes roll'd.
> DRYDEN

BULKY, MASSIVE OR MASSY.

Bulky denotes having *bulk*, which is connected with our words, belly, body, bilge, bulge, &c., and the German *balg; massive*, in French *massif*, from *mass*, signifies having a mass or being like a mass, which, through the German *masse*, Latin *massa*, Greek μάζα dough, comes from μάσσω to knead, signifying made into a solid substance.

Whatever is *bulky* has a prominence of figure what is *massive* has compactness of matter. The *bulky*, therefore, though larger in size, is not so weighty as the *massive;* 'In Milton's time it was suspected that the whole creation languished, that neither trees nor animals had the height or *bulk* of their predecessors.'—JOHNSON.

His pond'rous shield,
Ethereal temper, *massy*, large, and round,
Behind him cast.—MILTON.

Hollow bodies commonly have a *bulk;* none but solid bodies can be *massive.*

A vessel is *bulky* in its form; lead, silver, and gold, *massive.*

LARGE, WIDE, BROAD.

Large (*v. Great*) is applied in a general way to express every dimension; it implies not only abundance in solid matter, but also freedom in the space, or extent of a plane superficies; *wide*, in German *weit*, is most probably connected with the French *wide*, and the Latin *viduus* empty, signifying properly an empty or open space unincumbered by any obstructions; *broad*, in German *breit*, probably comes from the noun *bret*, board; because it is the peculiar property of a board, that is to say, it is the *width* of what is particularly long. Many things are *large*, but not *wide;* as a *large* town, a *large* circle, a *large* ball, a *large* nut: other things are both *large* and *wide;* as a *large* field, or a *wide* field: a *large* house, or a *wide* house: but the field is said to be *large* from the quantity of ground it contains; it is said to be *wide* both from its figure, or the extent of its space in the cross directions; in like manner, a house is *large* from its extent in all directions; it is said to be *wide* from the extent which it runs in front: some things are said to be *wide* which are not denominated *large;* that is, either such things as have less bulk and quantity than extent of plane surface; as ell *wide* cloth, a *wide* opening, a *wide* entrance, and the like; or such as have an extent of space only one way; as a *wide* road, a *wide* path, a *wide* passage, and the like;

Wide was the wound,
But suddenly with flesh fill'd up and heal'd.
MILTON.

What is *broad* is in sense, and mostly in application, *wide*, but not *vice versâ:* a ribbon is *broad;* a ledge is *broad;* a ditch is *broad;* a plank is *broad;* the brim of a hat is *broad;* or the border of any thing is *broad:* on the other hand, a mouth is *wide*, but not *broad;* apertures in general are *wide*, but not *broad*. The *large* is opposed to the small; the *wide* to the close; the *broad* to the narrow. In the moral application, we speak of *largeness* in regard to liberality;

Shall grief contract the *largeness* of that heart,
In which nor fear nor anger has a part?
WALLER.

Wide and *broad* only in the figurative sense of space or size: as a *wide* difference; or a *broad* line of distinction; 'The *wider* a man's comforts extend, the *broader* is the mark which he spreads to the arrows of misfortune.'—BLAIR.

GREAT, LARGE, BIG.

Great, derived through the medium of the northern languages from the Latin *crassus* thick, and *cresco* to grow, is applied to all kinds of dimensions in which things can grow or increase; *large*, in Latin *largus* wide, is probably derived from the Greek λα and ῥέειν to flow plentifully; for *largior* signifies to give freely, and *large* has in English a similar sense; it is properly applied to space, extent, and quantity: *big*, from the German *bauch* belly, and the English *bulk*, denotes *great* as to expansion or capacity. A house, a room, a heap, a pile, an army, &c., is *great* or *large;* 'At one's first entrance into the Pantheon at Rome, how the imagination is filled with something *great* and amazing; and at the same time how little in proportion one is affected with the inside of a Gothick cathedral, although it be five times *larger* than the other.'—ADDISON. An animal or a mountain is *great* or *big;* a road, a city, a street, and the like, is termed rather *great* than *large;* 'An animal no *bigger* than a mite cannot appear perfect to the eye, because the sight takes it in at once.'—ADDISON. 'We are not a little pleased to find every green leaf swarm with millions of animals, that at their *largest* growth are not visible to the naked eye.'—ADDISON. *Great* is used generally in the improper sense; *large* and *big* are used only occasionally: a noise, a distance, a multitude, a number, a power, and the like, is termed *great*, but not *large;* we may, however, speak of a *large* portion, a *large* share, a *large* quantity; or of a mind *big* with conception, or of an event *big* with the fate of nations; 'Among all the figures of architecture, there are none that have a *greater* air than the concave and the convex.'—ADDISON.

Sure he that made us with such *large* discourse,
Looking before and after, gave us not,
That capability and godlike reason,
To rust in us unus'd.—SHAKSPEARE.

Amazing clouds on clouds continual heap'd,
Or whirl'd tempestuous by the gusty wind,
Or silent borne along heavy and slow,
With the *big* stores of streaming oceans charg'd.
THOMSON.

ENORMOUS, HUGE, IMMENSE, VAST.

Enormous, from *e* and *norma* a rule, signifies out of rule or order; *huge* is in all probability connected with high, which is *hoogh* in Dutch; *immense*, in Latin *immensus*, compounded of *in* privative and *mensus* measured, signifies not to be measured; *vast*, in French *vaste*, Latin *vastus*, from *vaco* to be vacant, open, or wide, signifies extended in space.

Enormous and *huge* are peculiarly applicable to magnitude; *immense* and *vast* to extent, quantity, and number. *Enormous* expresses more than *huge*, as *immense* expresses more than *vast:* what is *enormous* exceeds in a very great degree all ordinary bounds; what is *huge* is great only in the superlative degree. The *enormous* is always out of proportion; the *huge* is relatively extraordinary in its dimensions. Some animals may be made *enormously* fat by a particular mode of feeding: to one who has seen nothing but level ground common hills will appear to be *huge* mountains;

The Thracian Acamus his falchion found,
And hew'd the *enormous* giant to the ground.
POPE.

Great Areïthous, known from shore to shore,
By the *huge* knotted iron mace he bore,
No lance he shook, nor bent the twanging bow,
But broke with this the battle of the foe.
POPE.

The *immense* is that which exceeds all calculation. the *vast* comprehends only a very great or unusual excess. The distance between the earth and sun may be said to be *immense:* the distance between the poles is *vast;*

Well was the crime, and well the vengeance sparr'd,
E'en power *immense* had found such battle hard.
POPE.

Just on the brink they neigh and paw the ground,
And the turf trembles, and the skies resound;
Eager they view'd the prospect dark and deep,
Vast was the leap, and headlong hung the steep.
POPE.

Of all these terms *huge* is the only one confined to the proper application, and in the proper sense of size: the rest are employed with regard to moral objects. We speak only of a *huge* animal, a *huge* monster, a *huge* mass, a *huge* size, a *huge* bulk, and the like; but we speak of an *enormous* waste, an *immense* difference, and a *vast* number.

The epithets *enormous*, *immense*, and *vast* are applicable to the same objects, but with the same distinction in their sense. A sum is *enormous* which exceeds in magnitude not only every thing known, but every thing thought of or expected; a sum is *immense* that scarcely admits of calculation: a sum is *vast* which rises very high in calculation. The national debt of England has risen to an *enormous* amount: the revolutionary war has been attended with an *immense* loss of blood and treasure to the different nations of Europe: there are individuals who, while they are expending *vast* sums on their own gratifications, refuse to contribute any thing to the relief of the necessitous

ENORMOUS, PRODIGIOUS, MONSTROUS.

Enormous, v. Enormous; prodigious comes from *prodigy*, in Latin *prodigium*, which in all probability comes from *prodigo* to lavish forth, signifying literally breaking out in excess or extravagance; *monstrous*, from *monster*, in Latin *monstrum*, and *monstro* to show or make visible, signifies remarkable, or exciting notice.

The *enormous* contradicts our rules of estimating and calculating: the *prodigious* raises our minds beyond their ordinary standard of thinking: the *monstrous* contradicts nature and the course of things. What is *enormous* excites our surprise or amazement;

Jove's bird on sounding pinions beat the skies,
A bleeding serpent of *enormous* size,
His talons truss'd, alive and curling round,
He stung the bird whose throat receiv'd the wound.
POPE.

What is *prodigious* excites our astonishment; 'I dreamed that I was in a wood of so *prodigious* an extent, and cut into such a variety of walks and alleys, that all mankind were lost and bewildered in it.'—ADDISON. What is *monstrous* does violence to our senses and understanding;

Nothing so *monstrous* can be said or feign'd
But with belief and joy is entertain'd.—DRYDEN.

There is something *enormous* in the present scale upon which property, whether publick or private, is amassed and expended: the works of the ancients in general, but the Egyptian pyramids in particular, are objects of admiration, on account of the *prodigious* labour which was bestowed on them: ignorance and superstition have always been active in producing *monstrous* images for the worship of its blind votaries.

LITTLE, SMALL, DIMINUTIVE.

Little, in Low German *litje*, Dutch *lettel*, is, in all probability, connected with light, in Saxon *leoht*, old German *lihto*, Swedish *lätt*, &c.; *small* is, with some variations, to be found in most of the northern dialects, in which it signifies, as in English, a contracted space or quantity; *diminutive*, in Latin *diminutivus*, signifies made *small*.

Little is properly opposed to the great (*v. Great*), *small* to the large, and *diminutive* is a species of the *small*, which is made so contrary to the course of things: a child is said to be *little* as respects its age as well as its size; it is said to be *small* as respects its size only; it is said to be *diminutive* when it is exceedingly *small* considering its age: *little* children cannot be left with safety to themselves; *small* children are pleasanter to be nursed than large ones: if we look down from any very great height the largest men will look *diminutive*; 'The talent of turning men into ridicule, and exposing to laughter those one converses with. is the qualification of *little*, ungenerous tempers.' —ADDISON. 'He whose knowledge is at best but limited, and whose intellect proceeds by a *small, diminutive* light, cannot but receive an additional light by the conceptions of another man.'—SOUTH.

SPACE, ROOM.

Space, in Latin *spatium*, Greek ςάδιον, Æol. σπάδιον a race ground; *room*, in Saxon *rum*, &c. Hebrew *ramah* a wide place.

These are both abstract terms, expressive of that portion of the universe which is supposed not to be occupied by any solid body: *space* is a general term, which includes within itself that which infinitely surpasses our comprehension; *room* is a limited term, which comprehends those portions of *space* which are artificially formed: *space* is either extended or bounded; *room* is always a bounded *space*: the *space* between two objects is either natural, incidental, or designedly formed;

The man of wealth and pride
Takes up a *space* that many poor supplied.
GOLDSMITH.

The *room* is that which is the fruit of design, to suit the convenience of persons;

For the whole world, without a native home,
Is nothing but a prison of a larger *room*.—COWLEY.

There is a sufficient *space* between the heavenly bodies to admit of their moving without confusion; the value of a house essentially depends upon the quantity of *room* which it affords: in a row of trees there must always be vacant *spaces* between each tree; in a coach there will be only *room* for a given number of persons.

Space is only taken in the natural sense; *room* is also employed in the moral application: in every person there is ample *room* for amendment or improvement.

AMPLE, SPACIOUS, CAPACIOUS.

Ample, in French *ample*, Latin *amplus*, probably comes from the Greek ἀναπλέως full; *spacious*, in French *spacieux*, Latin *spaciosus*, comes from *spatium* a space, implying the quality of having *space*; *capacious*, in Latin *capax*, from *capio* to hold, signifies the quality of being able to hold.

These epithets convey the analogous ideas of extent in quantity, and extent in *space*. *Ample* is figuratively employed for whatever is extended in quantity; *spacious* is literally used for whatever is extended in *space*; *capacious* is literally and figuratively employed to express extension in both quantity and *space*. Stores are *ample*, room is *ample*, an allowance is *ample*: a room, a house, a garden is *spacious*: a vessel or hollow of any kind is *capacious*; the soul, the mind, and the heart are *capacious*.

Ample is opposed to scanty, *spacious* to narrow *capacious* to small. What is *ample* suffices and satisfies; it imposes no constraint; 'The pure consciousness of worthy actions, abstracted from the views of popular applause, is to a generous mind an *ample* re ward.'—HUGHES. What is *spacious* is free and open, it does not confine;

These mighty monarchies, that had o'erspread
The *spacious* earth, and stretch'd their conq'ring arms
From pole to pole by ensnaring charms
Were quite consumed.—MAY.

What is *capacious* readily receives and contains; it is *spacious*, liberal, and generous;

Down sunk, a hollow bottom broad and deep
Capacious bed of waters.—MILTON.

Although sciences, arts, philosophy, and languages afford to the mass of mankind *ample* scope for the exercise of their mental powers without recurring to mysterious or fanciful researches, yet this world is hardly *spacious* enough for the range of the intellectual faculties: the *capacious* minds of some are no less capable of containing than they are disposed for receiving whatever spiritual food is offered them.

DEPTH, PROFUNDITY.

Depth, from *deep*, *dip*, or *dive*, the Greek δύπτω, and the Hebrew טבצ to dive, signifies the point under water which is dived for; *profundity*, from *profound*, in Latin *profundus*, compounded of *pro* or *procul* far, and *fundus* the bottom, signifies remoteness from the surface of any thing.

These terms do not differ merely in their derivation; but *depth* is indefinite in its signification; and *profundity* is a positive and considerable degree of *depth*. Moreover, the word *depth* is applied to objects in general; 'By these two passions of hope and fear, we reach forward into futurity, and bring up to our present thoughts objects that lie in the remotest *depths* of time.'—ADDISON. *Profundity* is confined in its application to moral objects: thus we speak of the *depth* of the sea, or the *depth* of a person's learning; but his *profundity* of thought; 'The peruser of Swift will want very little previous knowledge: it will be sufficient that he is acquainted with common words and common things; he is neither required to mount elevations nor to explore *profundities*.'—JOHNSON.

OBLONG, OVAL.

Oblong, in Latin *oblongus*, from the intensive syllable *ob*, signifies very long, longer than broad: *oval*, from the Latin *ovum*, signifies egg-shaped.

The *oval* is a species of the *oblong*: what is *oval* is *oblong*; but what is *oblong* is not always *oval*. *Oblong* is peculiarly applied to figures formed by right lines, that is, all rectangular parallelograms, except squares, are *oblong:* but the *oval* is applied to curvilinear *oblong* figures, as ellipses, which are distinguished from the circle: tables are oftener *oblong* than *oval;* garden beds are as frequently *oval* as they are *oblong.*

ROUNDNESS, ROTUNDITY.

Roundness and *rotundity* both come from the Latin *rotundus* and *rota* a wheel, which is the most perfectly round body that is formed: the former term is however applied to all objects in general; the latter only to solid bodies which are round in all directions: one speaks of the *roundness* of a circle, the *roundness* of the moon, the *roundness* of a tree; but the *rotundity* of a man's body which projects in a *round* form in all directions, and the *rotundity* of a full cheek, or the *rotundity* of a turnip;

> Bracelets of pearls gave *roundness* to her arms.
> PRIOR.

'Angular bodies lose their points and asperities by frequent friction, and approach by degrees to uniform *rotundity.*'—JOHNSON.

OUTWARD, EXTERNAL, EXTERIOUR.

Outward, or inclined to the *out*, after the manner of the *out*, indefinitely describes the situation; *external*, from the Latin *externus* and *extra*, is more definite in its sense, since it is employed only in regard to such objects as are conceived to be independent of man as a thinking being: hence, we may speak of the *outward* part of a building, of a board, of a table, a box, and the like; but of *external* objects acting on the mind, or of an *external* agency; 'The controversy about the reality of *external* evils is now at an end.'—JOHNSON. *Exteriour* is still more definite than either, as it expresses a higher degree of the *outward* or *external;* the former being in the comparative, and the two latter in the positive degree: when we speak of any thing which has two coats, it is usual to designate the outermost by the name of the *exteriour;* when we speak simply of the surface, without reference to any thing behind, it is denominated *external:* as the *exteriour* coat of a walnut, or the *external* surface of things. In the moral application the *external* or *outward* is that which comes simply to the view; but the *exteriour* is that which is prominent, and which consequently may conceal something:

> But when a monarch sins, it should be secret,
> To keep *exteriour* show of sanctity,
> Maintain respect, and cover bad example.—DRYDEN.

A man may sometimes neglect the *outside*, who is altogether mindful of the in;

> And though my *outward* state misfortune hath
> Depress'd thus low, it cannot reach my faith.
> DENHAM.

A man with a pleasing *exteriour* will sometimes gain more friends than those who have more solid merit.

INSIDE, INTERIOUR.

The term *inside* may be applied to bodies of any magnitude, small or large; *interiour* is peculiarly appropriate to bodies of great magnitude. We may speak of the *inside* of a nut-shell, but not of its *interiour;* on the other hand, we speak of the *interiour* of St. Paul's, or the *interiour* of a palace; 'As for the *inside* of their nest, none but themselves were concerned in it, according to the inviolable laws established among those animals (the ants).'—ADDISON. 'The gates are drawn back, and the *interiour* of the fane is discovered.'—CUMBERLAND. This difference of application is not altogether arbitrary: for *inside* literally signifies the side that is inward; but *interiour* signifies the space which is more inward than the rest, which is enclosed in an enclosure: consequently cannot be applied to any thing but a large space that is enclosed.

THICK, DENSE.

Between *thick* and *dense* there is little other difference, than that the latter is employed to express that species of *thickness* which is philosophically considered as the property of the atmosphere in a certain condition; hence we speak of *thick* in regard to hard or soft bodies, as a *thick* board or *thick* cotton; solid or liquid, as a *thick* cheese or *thick* milk: but the term *dense* only in regard to the air in its various forms, as a *dense* air, a *dense* vapour, a *dense* cloud; 'I have discovered, by a long series of observations, that invention and elocution suffer great impediments from *dense* and impure vapours.'—JOHNSON.

THIN, SLENDER, SLIGHT, SLIM.

Thin, in Saxon *thinne*, German *dünn*, Latin *tener*, from *tendo*, in Greek *τείνω* to extend or draw out, and the Hebrew נטה; *slender*, *slight*, and *slim* are all variations from the German *schlank*, which are connected with the words *slime* and *sling*, as also with the German *schlingen* to wind or wreathe, and *schlange* a serpent, designating the property of length and smallness, which is adapted for bending or twisting.

Thin is the generick term, the rest are specifick: *thin* may be said of that which is small and short, as well as small and long; *slender* is always said of that which is small and long at the same time: a board is *thin* which wants solidity or substance; a poplar is *slender* because its tallness is disproportionate to its magnitude or the dimensions of its circumference. *Thinness* is sometimes a natural property; *slight* and *slim* are applied to that which is artificial: the leaves of trees are of a *thin* texture; a board may be made *slight* by continually planing; a paper box is very *slim.* *Thinness* is a good property sometimes; *thin* paper is frequently preferred to that which is thick: *slightness* and *slimness*, which is a greater degree of *slightness*, are always defects; that which is made *slight* is unfit to bear the stress that will be put upon it; that which is *slim* is altogether unfit for the purpose proposed; a carriage that is made *slight* is quickly broken, and always out of repair; paper is altogether too *slim* to serve the purpose of wood.

These terms admit of a similar distinction in the moral application; 'I have found dulness to quicken into sentiment in a *thin* ether.'—JOHNSON. 'Very *slender* differences will sometimes part those whom beneficence has united.'—JOHNSON. 'Friendship is often destroyed by a thousand secret and *slight* competitions.'—JOHNSON.

TO ABATE, LESSEN, DIMINISH, DECREASE.

Abate, from the French *abattre*, signified originally to beat down, in the active sense, and to come down, in the neuter sense; *diminish*, or, as it is sometimes written, *minish*, from the Latin *diminuo*, and *minuo* to lessen, and *minus* less, expresses, like the verb *lessen*, the sense of either making less or becoming less; *decrease* is compounded of the privative *de* and *crease*, in Latin *cresco* to grow, signifying to grow less.

The first three are used transitively or intransitively; the latter only intransitively.

Abate respects the vigour of action: a person's fever is *abated* or *abates;* the violence of the storm *abates;* pain and anger *abate;* 'My wonder *abated*, when upon looking around me, I saw most of them attentive to three Syrens clothed like goddesses, and distinguished by the names of Sloth, Ignorance, and Pleasure.'—ADDISON. *Lessen* and *diminish* are both applied to size, quantity, and number; but the former mostly in the proper and familiar sense, the latter in the figurative and higher acceptation; the size of a room or garden is *lessened;* the credit and respectability of a person is *diminished.*

Nothing is so calculated to *abate* the ardour of youth as grief and disappointment; 'Tully was the first who observed that friendship improves happiness and *abates* misery.'—ADDISON. An evil may be *lessened* when it cannot be removed by the application of remedies;

> He sought fresh fountains in a foreign soil;
> The pleasure *lessened* the attending toil.—ADDISON.

Nothing *diminishes* the lustre of great deeds more than cruelty; 'If Parthenissa can now possess her own mind, and think as little of her beauty, as she ought to have done when she had it, there will be no grea *diminution* of her charms.'—HUGHES.

The passion of an angry man ought to be allowed to *abate* before any appeal is made to his understanding; we may *lessen* the number of our evils by not dwelling upon them. Objects apparently *diminish* according to the distance from which they are observed.

To *decrease* is to *diminish* for a continuance: a retreating army will *decrease* rapidly when exposed to all the privations and hardships attendant on forced marches, it is compelled to fight for its safety: some things *decrease* so gradually that it is some time before they are observed to be *diminished;*

These leaks shall then *decrease;* the sails once more
Direct our course to some relieving shore.
FALCONER.

In the abstract sense the word *lessening* is mostly supplied by *diminution:* it will be no *abatement* of sorrow to a generous mind to know that the *diminution* of evil to itself has been produced by the abridgment of good to another.

TO OVERFLOW, INUNDATE, DELUGE.

What *overflows* simply *flows over;* what *inundates*, from *in* and *unda* a wave, *flows* into; what *deluges*, from *diluo*, washes away.

The *overflow* bespeaks abundance; whatever exceeds the measure of contents must *flow over*, because it is more than can be held: to *inundate* bespeaks not only abundance, but vehemence; when it *inundates* it *flows* in faster than is desired, it fills to an inconvenient height: to *deluge* bespeaks impetuosity; a *deluge* irresistibly carries away all before it. This explanation of these terms in their proper sense will illustrate their improper application: the heart is said to *overflow* with joy, with grief, with bitterness, and the like, in order to denote the superabundance of the thing; 'I am too full of you not to *overflow* upon those I converse with.'—POPE. A country is said to be *inundated* by swarms of inhabitants, when speaking of numbers who intrude themselves to the annoyance of the natives; 'There was such an *inundation* of speakers, young speakers in every sense of the word, that neither my Lord Germaine, nor myself, could find room for a single word.'—GIBBON. The town is said to be *deluged* with publications of different kinds, when they appear in such profusion and in such quick succession as to supersede others of more value;

At length corruption, like a general flood,
Shall *deluge* all.—POPE.

TO FLOW, STREAM, GUSH.

Flow, in Latin *fluo*, and Greek βλύω or φλύω, to be in a ferment, is in all probability connected with ῥέω, which signifies literally to *flow; stream*, in German *strömen*, from *riemen* a thong, signifies to run in a line; *gush* comes from the German *giessen*, &c. to pour out with force.

Flow is here the generick term: the two others are specifick terms expressing different modes: water may *flow* either in a large body or in a long but narrow course; the *stream* in a long, narrow course only: thus, waters *flow* in seas, rivers, rivulets, or in a small pond; they *stream* only out of spouts or small channels: they *flow* gently or otherwise; they *stream* gently; but they *gush* with violence: thus, the blood *flows* from a wound when it comes from it in any manner; it *streams* from a wound when it runs as it were in a channel; it *gushes* from a wound when it runs with impetuosity, and in as large quantities as the cavity admits;

Down his wan cheek a briny torrent *flows*.—POPE.

Fires *stream* in lightning from his sanguine eyes.
POPE.

Sunk in his sad companions' arms he lay,
And in short pantings sobb'd his soul away
(Like some vile worm extended on the ground),
While his life's torrent *gush'd* from out the wound.
POPE.

FLUID, LIQUID.

Fluid, from *fluo* to flow, signifies that which from its nature flows; *liquid*, from *liquesco* to melt, signifies that which is melted. These words may be employed as epithets to the same objects; but they have a distinct office which they derive from their original meaning: when we wish to represent a thing as capable of passing along in a stream or current, we should denominate it a *fluid;*

Or serve they as a flow'ry verge to bind
The *fluid* skirts of that same wat'ry cloud,
Lest it again dissolve, and show'r the earth.
MILTON.

When we wish to represent the body as passing from a congealed to a dissolved state, we should name it a *liquid;*

As when the fig's press'd juice, infus'd in cream,
To curds coagulates the *liquid* stream.—POPE.

Water and air are both represented as *fluids* from their general property of flowing through certain spaces; but ice when thawed becomes a *liquid* and melts; lead when melted is also a *liquid:* the humours of the animal body, and the juices of trees, are *fluids;* what we drink is a *liquid*, as opposed to what we eat which is solid.

LIQUID, LIQUOR, JUICE, HUMOUR.

Liquid (*v. Fluid*) is the generick term: *liquor*, which is but a variation from the same Latin verb, *liquesco*, whence *liquid* is derived, is a *liquid* which is made to be drunk: *juice*, in French *jus*, is a *liquid* that issues from bodies; and *humour*, in Latin *humor*, from *humeo*, and the Greek ὕω to rain, is a species of *liquid* which flows in bodies and forms a constituent part of them. All natural bodies consist of *liquids* or solids, or a combination of both;

How the bee
Sits on the bloom, extracting *liquid* sweet.
MILTON

Liquor serves to quench the thirst as food satisfies the hunger;

They who Minerva from Jove's head derive,
Might make old Homer's scull the muse's hive,
And from his brain that Helicon distill,
Whose racy *liquor* did his offspring fill.—DENHAM.

The *juices* of bodies are frequently their richest parts;

Give me to drain the cocoa's milky bowl,
And from the palm to draw its freshening wine,
More bounteous far than all the frantick *juice*
Which Bacchus pours.—THOMSON.

The *humours* are commonly the most important parts of any animal body; 'The perspicuity of the *humours* of the eye transmit the rays of light.'—STEELE. *Liquid* and *liquor* belong peculiarly to vegetable substances; *humour* to animal bodies; and *juice* to either; water is the simplest of all *liquids;* wine is the most inviting of all *liquors;* the orange produces the most agreeable *juice;* the *humours* of both men and brutes are most liable to corruption, whence the term is very frequently applied to *fluids* of the body when in a corrupt state: 'He denied himself nothing that he had a mind to eat or drink, which gave him a body full of *humours*, and made his fits of the gout frequent and violent.'—TEMPLE.

STREAM, CURRENT, TIDE.

A fluid body in a progressive motion is the object described in common by these terms; *stream* is the most general, the other two are but modes of the *stream; stream*, in Saxon *stream*, in German *strom*, is an onomatopeia which describes the prolongation of any body in a narrow line along the surface: a *current* from *curro* to run, is a running *stream;* and a *tide* from *tide*, in German *zeit* time, is a periodical *stream* or *current*. All rivers are *streams* which are more or less gentle according to the nature of the ground through which they pass; the force of the *current* is very much increased by the confinement of any water between rocks, or by means of artificial impediments. The *tide* is high or low, strong or weak, at different hours of the day; when the *tide* is high the *current* is strongest.

From knowing the proper application of the terms their figurative use becomes obvious; a *stream* of air, or a *stream* of light is a prolonged body of air or light; a *current* of air is a continued *stream* that has rapid motion; streets and passages which are open at each extremity are the channels of such *currents*. In the moral sense the *tide* is the ruling fashion or propensity of the day; it is in vain to stem the *tide* of folly; it is wiser to get out of its reach;

> When now the rapid *stream* of eloquence
> Bears all before it, passion, reason, sense,
> Can its dread thunder, or its lightning's force,
> Derive their essence from a mortal source.
> JENYNS.

> With secret course, which no loud storms annoy,
> Glides the smooth *current* of domestick joy.
> GOLDSMITH.

> There is a *tide* in the affairs of men,
> Which taken at the flood leads on to fortune.
> SHAKSPEARE.

SPRING, FOUNTAIN, SOURCE.

The *spring* denotes that which *springs*; the word, therefore, carries us back to the point from which the water issues. *Fountain*, in Latin *fons*, from *fundo* to pour out, signifies the *spring* which is visible on the the earth: and *source* (*v. Origin*) is said of that which is not only visible, but runs along the earth. *Springs* are to be found by digging a sufficient depth in all parts of the earth: in mountainous countries, and also in the East, we read of *fountains* which form themselves, and supply the surrounding parts with refreshing streams: the *sources* of rivers are always to be traced to some mountain.

These terms are all used in a figurative sense: in the Bible the gospel is depictured as a *spring* of living waters; the eye as a *fountain* of tears; 'The heart of the citizen is a perennial *spring* of energy to the state.' —BURKE.

> Eternal king! the author of all being.
> *Fountain* of light, thyself invisible.—MILTON.

In the general acceptation the *source* is taken for the channel through which any event comes to pass, the primary cause of its happening: a war is the *source* of many evils to a country; an imprudent step in the outset of life is oftentimes the *source* of ruin to a young person;

> These are thy blessings, industry! rough power!
> Yet the kind *source* of every gentle art.—THOMSON.

TO SPRINKLE, BEDEW.

To *sprinkle* is a frequentative of spring, and denotes either an act of nature or design: to *bedew* is to cover with *dew*, which is an operation of nature. By *sprinkling*, a liquid falls in sensible drops upon the earth; by *bedewing*, it covers by imperceptible drops: rain *besprinkles* the earth; dew *bedews* it. So likewise, figuratively, things are *sprinkled* with flour; the cheeks are *bedewed* with tears.

TO SPROUT, BUD.

Sprout, in Saxon *sprytan*, Low German *sprouyten*, is doubtless connected with the German *spritzen* to spurt, *spreiten* to spread, and the like; to *bud* is to put forth *buds*; the noun *bud* is a variation from button, which it resembles in form. To *sprout* is to come forth from the stem; to *bud*, to put forth in *buds*.

TO SPURT, SPOUT.

To *spurt* and *spout* are, like the German *spritzen*, variations of *spreiten* to spread (*v. To spread*), and *springen* to spring (*v. To arise*); they both express the idea of sending forth liquid in small quantities from a cavity; the former, however, does not always include the idea of the cavity, but simply that of springing up; the latter is however confined to the circumstance of issuing forth from some place; dirt may be *spurted* in the face by means of kicking it up; or blood may be *spurted* out of a vein when it is opened, water out of the mouth, and the like; but a liquid *spouts* out from a pipe. To *spurt* is a sudden action arising from a momentary impetus given to a liquid either intentionally or incidentally; the beer will *spurt* from a barrel when the vent peg is removed: to *spout* is a continued action produced by a perpetual impetus which the liquid receives equally from design or accident; the water *spouts* out from a pipe which is denominated a *spout*, or it will *spurt* out from any cavity in the earth, or in a rock which may resemble a *spout*;

> Far from the parent stream it boils again
> Fresh into day, and all the glittering hill
> Is bright with *spouting* rills.—THOMSON.

A person may likewise *spout* water in a stream from his mouth. Hence the figurative application of these terms; any sudden conceit which compels a person to an eccentrick action is a *spurt*, particularly if it springs from ill-humour or caprice; a female will sometimes take a *spurt* and treat her intimate friends very coldly, either from a fancied offence or a fancied superiority; to *spout*, on the other hand, is to send forth a stream of words in imitation of the stream of liquid, and is applied to those who affect to turn speakers, in whom there is commonly more sound than sense.

TO PLUNGE, DIVE.

Plunge is but a variation of pluck, pull, and the Latin *pello* to drive or force forward; *dive* is but a variation of *dip*, which is, under various forms, to be found in the northern languages.

One *plunges* sometimes in order to *dive*; but one may *plunge* without *diving*, and one may *dive* without *plunging*: to *plunge* is to dart head foremost into the water: to *dive* is to go to the bottom of the water, or towards it: it is a good practice for bathers to *plunge* into the water when they first go in, although it is not advisable for them to *dive*; ducks frequently *dive* into the water without ever *plunging*. Thus far they differ in their natural sense; but in the figurative application they diff[illegible] widely: to *plunge*, in this case is an act of rashness: to *dive* is an act of design: a young man hurried away by his passions will *plunge* into every extravagance when he comes into possession of his estate; 'The French *plunged* themselves into these calamities they suffer, to prevent themselves from settling into a British constitution.'—BURKE People of a prying temper seek to *dive* into the secret of others;

> How he did seem to *dive* into their hearts
> With humble and familiar courtesy.
> SHAKSPEARE.

WAVE, BILLOW, SURGE, BREAKER.

Wave, from the Saxon *waegan*, and German *wiegen* to weigh or rock, is applied to water in an undulating state; it is, therefore, the generick term, and the rest are specifick terms;

> The *wave* behind impels the *wave* before.—POPE.

Those *waves* which swell more than ordinarily are termed *billows*, which is derived from *bulge* or *bilge*, and German *balg*, the paunch or belly;

> I saw him beat the *billows* under him,
> And ride upon their backs.—SHAKSPEARE.

Those *waves* which rise higher than usual are termed *surges*, from the Latin *surgo* to rise;

> He flies aloft, and with impetuous roar
> Pursues the foaming *surges* to the shore.
> DRYDEN.

Those *waves* which dash against the shore, or against vessels with more than ordinary force, are termed *breakers*;

> Now on the mountain *wave* on high they ride,
> Then downward plunge beneath th' involving tide,
> Till one who seems in agony to strive
> The whirling *breakers* heave on shore alive.
> FALCONER.

BREEZE, GALE, BLAST, GUST, STORM, TEMPEST, HURRICANE.

All these words express the action of the wind, in different degrees and under different circumstances.

Breeze, in Italian *brezza*, is in all probability an onomatopeia for that kind of wind peculiar to southern climates; *gale* is probably connected with *call* and *yell*, denoting a sonorous wind; *blast*, in German *geblaset*, participle of *blasen*, signifies properly the act of blowing, but by distinction it is employed for any strong effort of blowing; *gust* is immediately of Ice andish origin, and expresses the phenomena which are characteristick of the northern climates; but in all probability it is a variation of *gush*, signifying a violent stream of wind; *storm*, in German *sturm*, from *stören* to put in commotion, like *gust*, describes the phenomenon of northern climates; *tempest*, in Latin *tempestus*, or *tempus* a time or season, describes that season or sort of weather which is most remarkable, but at the same time most frequent, in southern climates; *hurricane* has been introduced by the Spaniards into European languages from the Caribee islands; where it describes that species of *tempestuous* wind, most frequent in the tropical climates.

A *breeze* is gentle; a *gale* is brisk, but steady; we have *breezes* in a calm summer's day: the mariner has favourable *gales* which keep the sails on the stretch;

> Gradual sinks the *breeze*
> Into a perfect calm.—THOMSON.

> What happy *gale*
> Blows you to Padua here from old Verona?
> SHAKSPEARE.

A *blast* is impetuous; the exhalations of a trumpet, the breath of bellows, the sweep of a violent wind, are *blasts*. A *gust* is sudden and vehement; *gusts* of wind are sometimes so violent as to sweep every thing before them while they last;

> As when fierce northern *blasts* from th' Alps descend,
> From his firm roots with struggling *gusts* to rend
> An aged sturdy oak, the rustling sound
> Grows loud.—DENHAM.

Storm, *tempest*, and *hurricane* include other particulars besides wind.

A *storm* throws the whole atmosphere into commotion; it is a war of the elements, in which wind, rain, hail, and the like, conspire to disturb the heavens; *tempest* is a species of *storm*, which has also thunder and lightning to add to the confusion. *Hurricane* is a species of *storm*, which exceeds all the rest in violence and duration;

> Through *storms* and *tempests* so the sailor drives,
> While every element in combat strives;
> Loud roars the thunder, fierce the lightning flies,
> Winds wildly rage, and billows tear the skies.
> SHIRLEY.

> So where our wide Numidian wastes extend,
> Sudden th' impetuous *hurricanes* descend,
> Wheels through the air in circling eddies play,
> Tear up the sands, and sweep whole plains away.
> ADDISON.

Gust, *storm*, and *tempest*, which are applied figuratively, preserve their distinction in this sense. The passions are exposed to *gusts* and *storms*, to sudden bursts, or violent and continued agitations; the soul is exposed to *tempests* when agitated with violent and contending emotions;

> Stay these sudden *gusts* of passion,
> That hurry you away.—ROWE.

> I burn, I burn! The *storm* that 's in my mind
> Kindles my heart, like fires provok'd by wind.
> LANSDOWN.

> All deaths, all tortures, in one pang combin'd,
> Are gentle, to the *tempest* of my mind.—THOMSON.

TO HEAVE, SWELL.

Heave is used either transitively or intransitively, as a reflective or a neuter verb; *swell* is used only as a neuter verb. *Heave* implies raising, and *swell* implies distension: they differ therefore very widely in sense, but they sometimes agree in application. The bosom is said both to *heave* and to *swell*; because it happens that the bosom *swells* by *heaving*; the waves are likewise said to *heave* themselves or to *swell*, in which there is a similar correspondence between the actions: otherwise most things which *heave* do not *swell*, and those which *swell* do not *heave*;

> He *heaves* for breath, he staggers to and fro,
> And clouds of issuing smoke his nostrils loudly blow.
> DRYDEN.

> Meantime the mountain billows to the clouds,
> In dreadful tumult, *swell'd* surge above surge.
> THOMSON.

TO LIFT, HEAVE, HOIST.

Lift is in all probability contracted from *levatus* participle of *levo* to lift, which comes from *levis* light, because what is light is easily borne up; *heave*, in Saxon *heavian*, German *heben*, &c. comes from the absolute particle *ha*, signifying high, because to *heave* is to set upon high; *hoist*, in French *hausser*, Low German *hissen*, is a variation from the same source as *heave*.

The idea of making high is common to all these words, but they differ in the objects and the circumstances of the action; we *lift* with or without an effort: we *heave* and *hoist* always with an effort; we *lift* a child up to let him see any thing more distinctly; workmen *heave* the stones or beams which are used in a building; sailors *hoist* the long boat into the water. To *lift* and *hoist* are transitive verbs; they require an agent and an object: *heave* is intransitive, it may have an inanimate object for an agent: a person *lifts* his hand to his head; when whales are killed, they are *hoisted* into vessels: the bosom *heaves* when it is oppressed with sorrow, the waves of the sea *heave* when they are agitated by the wind;

> What god so daring in your aid to move,
> Or *lift* his hand against the force of Jove?—POPE.

> Murm'ring they move, as when old Ocean roars,
> And *heaves* huge surges to the trembling shores.
> POPE

> The reef enwrap'd, th' inserted knittles tied,
> To *hoist* the shorten'd sail again they tried.
> FALCONER.

TO LIFT, RAISE, ERECT, ELEVATE, EXALT.

Lift, *v. To lift; raise*, signifies to cause to *rise*; *erect*, in Latin *erectus*, participle of *erigo*, or *e* and *rego*, probably from the Greek ὀρέγω, signifies literally to extend or set forth in the height; *elevate* is a variation from the same source as *lift; exalt* comes from the Latin *altus* high, and the Hebrew *olah* to ascend, and signifies to cause to be high (*v. High*).

The idea of making one thing higher than another is common to these verbs, which differ in the circumstances of the action. To *lift* is to take off from the ground, or from any spot where it is supposed to be fixed; to *raise* and *erect* are to place in a higher position, while in contact with the ground: we *lift* up a stool; we *raise* a chair, by giving it longer legs; we *erect* a monument by heaping one stone on another:

> Now rosy morn ascends the court of Jove,
> *Lifts* up her light, and opens day above.—POPE.

> Such a huge bulk as not twelve bards could *raise*,
> Twelve starveling bards of these degenerate days.
> POPE

> From their assistance happier walls expect,
> Which, wand'ring long, at last thou shalt *erect*.
> DRYDEN

Whatever is to be carried is *lifted;* whatever is to be situated higher is to be *raised;* whatever is to be constructed above other objects is *erected*. A ladder is *lifted* upon the shoulders to be conveyed from one place to another; a standard ladder is *raised* against a building; a scaffolding is *erected*.

These terms are likewise employed in a moral acceptation; *exalt* and *elevate* are used in no other sense. *Lift* expresses figuratively the artificial action of setting aloft; as in the case of *lifting* a person into notice: to *raise* preserves the idea of making higher by the accession of wealth, honour, or power; as in the case of persons who are *raised* from beggary to a state of affluence: to *erect* retains its idea of artificially constructing, so as to produce a solid as well as lofty mass; as in the case of *erecting* a tribunal, *erecting* a system of spiritual dominion. A person cannot *lift* himself, but he may *raise* himself; individuals *lift* or *raise* up each other; but communities, or those only who are invested with power, have the opportunity of *erecting*.

To *lift* is seldom used in a good sense; to *raise* is used in a good or an indifferent sense; to *elevate* and *exalt* are always used in the best sense. A person is seldom *lifted* up for any good purpose, or from any merit in himself; it is commonly to suit the ends of party that people are *lifted* into notice, or *lifted* into office; on the same ground, if a person is *lifted* up in his own imagination, it is only his pride which gives him the *elevation;* 'Our successes have been great, and our hearts have been much *lifted* up by them, so that we have reason to humble ourselves.'—ATTERBURY. A person may be *raised* for his merits, or *raise* himself by his industry, in both which cases he is entitled to esteem; or he may with propriety be *raised* in the estimation of himself or others;

> *Rais'd* in his mind the Trojan hero stood,
> And long'd to break from out his ambient cloud.
> DRYDEN.

One is *elevated* by circumstances, but still more so by one's character and moral qualities; one is rarely *exalted* but by means of superiour endowments; 'Prudence operates on life in the same manner as rules on composition; it produces vigilance rather than *elevation*.'—JOHNSON.

> A creature of a more *exalted* kind
> Was wanting yet, and then was man design'd.
> DRYDEN.

To *elevate* may be the act of individuals for themselves; to *exalt* must be the act of others. There are some to whom *elevation* of rank is due, and others who require no adventitious circumstances to *elevate* them; the world have always agreed to *exalt* great power, great wisdom, and great genius.

HIGH, TALL, LOFTY.

High, in German *hoch*, &c. comes in all probability from the Hebrew אגג, the king of the Amalekites, so called on account of his size, and is connected with the Latin *gigas; tall*, in Welch *tal*, is derived by Davis from the Hebrew חלל to elevate; *lofty* is doubtless derived from *lift*, and that from the Latin *levatus* raised.

High is the term in most general use, which seems likewise in the most unqualified manner to express the idea of extension upwards, which is common to them all. Whatever is *tall* and *lofty* is *high*, but every thing is not *tall* or *lofty* which is *high*. *Tall* and *lofty* both designate a more than ordinary degree of *height;* but *tall* is peculiarly applicable to what shoots up or stands up in a perpendicular direction: while *lofty* is said of that which is extended in breadth as well as in *height;* that which is lifted up or raised by an accretion of matter or an expansion in the air. By this rule we say that a house is *high*, a chimney *tall*, a room *lofty*.

Trees are in general said to be *high* which exceed the ordinary standard of *height;* they are opposed to the low;

> *High* at their head he saw the chief appear,
> And bold Merion to excite their rear.—POPE.

A poplar is said to be *tall*, not only from its exceeding other trees in *height*, but from its perpendicular and spiral manner of growing is opposed to that which is bulky;

> Prostrate on earth their beauteous bodies lay,
> Like mountain firs, as *tall* and straight as they.
> POPE.

A man and a horse are likewise said to be *tall;* but a hedge, a desk, and other common objects, are *high*. A hill is *high*, but a mountain is *lofty;* churches are in general *high*, but the steeples or the domes of cathedrals are *lofty*, and their spires are *tall;*

> E'en now, O king! 't is giv'n thee to destroy
> The *lofty* tow'rs of wide-extended Troy.—POPE.

With the *high* is associated no idea of what is striking; but the *tall* is coupled with the aspiring or that which strives to out-top: the *lofty* is always coupled with the grand, and that which commands admiration.

High and *lofty* have a moral acceptation, but *tall* is taken in the natural sense only: *high* and *lofty* are applied to persons or what is personal, with the same difference in degree as before: a *lofty* title or *lofty* pretension conveys more than a *high* title or a *high* pretension. Men of *high* rank should have *high* ideas of virtue and personal dignity, and keep themselves clear from every thing low and mean;

> When you are tried in scandal's court,
> Stand *high* in honour, wealth, or wit,
> All others who inferiour sit
> Conceive themselves in conscience bound
> To join and drag you to the ground.—SWIFT.

A *lofty* ambition often soars too *high* to serve the purpose of its possessor, whose fall is the greater when he finds himself compelled to descend;

> Without thee, nothing *lofty* can I sing,
> Come, then, and with thyself thy genius bring.
> DRYDEN.

TO HEIGHTEN, RAISE, AGGRAVATE.

To *heighten* is to make *higher* (*v. Haughty*). To *raise* is to cause to *rise* (*v. To arise*). To *aggravate* (*v. To aggravate*) is to make *heavy*. *Heighten* refers more to the result of the action of making *higher;* *raise* to the mode: we *heighten* a house by *raising* the roof; as *raising* conveys the idea of setting up aloft, which is not included in the word *heighten;* 'Purity and virtue *heighten* all the powers of fruition.'—BLAIR. On the same ground a headdress may be said to be *heightened*, which is made *higher* than it was before; and a chair or a table is *raised* that is set upon something else: but in speaking of a wall, we may say, that it is either *heightened* or *raised*, because the operation and result must in both cases be the same; 'I would have our conceptions *raised* by the dignity of thought and sublimity of expression, rather than by a train of robes or a plume of feathers.'—ADDISON. In the improper sense of these terms they preserve a similar distinction: we *heighten* the value of a thing; we *raise* its price: we *heighten* the grandeur of an object; we *raise* a family.

Heighten and *aggravate* have connexion with each other only in application to offences: the enormity of an offence is *heightened*, the guilt of the offender is *aggravated* by particular circumstances. The horrours of a murder are *heightened* by being committed in the dead of the night; the guilt of the perpetrator is *aggravated* by the addition of ingratitude to murder; 'The counsels of pusillanimity are very rarely put off, while they are always sure to *aggravate* the evils from which they would fly.'—BURKE.

TO ANIMATE, INSPIRE, ENLIVEN, CHEER, EXHILARATE.

To *animate* is to give life (*v. To encourage*); *inspire*, in French *inspirer*, Latin *inspiro*, compounded of *in* and *spiro*, signifies to breathe life or spirit into any one; *enliven*, from *en* or *in* and *liven*, has the same sense; *cheer*, in French *chère*, Flemish *cière* the countenance, Greek χαρά joy, signifies the giving joy or spirit; *exhilarate*, in Latin *exhilaratus*, participle of *exhilaro*, from *hilaris*, Greek ἱλαρὸς joyful, Hebrew עלין to exult or leap for joy, signifies to make glad.

Animate and *inspire* imply the communication of the vital or mental spark; *enliven*, *cheer*, and *exhilarate* signify actions on the mind or body. To be *animated*, in its physical sense, is simply to receive the first spark of animal life in however small a degree; for there are *animated* beings in the world possessing the vital power in an infinite variety of degrees and forms;

> Through subterranean cells
> Where searching sunbeams scarce can find a way,
> Earth *animated* heaves.—THOMSON.

To be *animated* in the moral sense is to receive the smallest portion of the sentient or thinking faculty; which is equally varied in thinking beings: *animation* therefore never conveys the idea of receiving any strong degree of either physical or moral feeling; 'The more to *animate* the people, he stood on high, from whence he might best be heard, and cried unto them with a loud voice.'—KNOLLES. To *inspire*, on the contrary, expresses the communication of a strong moral sentiment or passion: hence to *animate* with courage is a less forcible expression than to *inspire* with courage: we likewise speak of *inspiring* with emulation or a thirst for knowledge; not of *animating* with emulation or a thirst for knowledge;

> Each gentle breast with kindly warmth she moves,
> *Inspires* new flames, revives extinguished loves.
> DRYDEN ON MAY

To *enliven* respects the mind; *cheer* relates to the heart; *exhilarate* regards the spirits, both animal and mental, they all denote an action on the frame by the communication of pleasurable emotions: the mind is *enlivened* by contemplating the scenes of nature; the imagination is *enlivened* by the reading of poetry;

> To grace each subject with *enlivening* wit.
> ADDISON.

The benevolent heart is *cheered* by witnessing the happiness of others; 'The creation is a perpetual feast to a good man; every thing he sees *cheers* and delights him.'—ADDISON. The spirits are *exhilarated* by the convivialities of social life;

> Nor rural sights alone, but rural sounds
> *Exhilarate* the spirit.—COWPER.

Conversation *enlivens* society; the conversation of a kind and considerate friend *cheers* the drooping spirits in the moments of trouble; unexpected good news is apt to *exhilarate* the spirits.

ANIMATION, LIFE, VIVACITY, SPIRIT.

Animation and *life* do not differ either in sense or application, but the latter is more in familiar use. They express either the particular or general state of the mind; *vivacity* and *spirit* express only the habitual nature and state of the feelings.

A person of no *animation* is divested of the distinguishing characteristick of his nature, which is mind: a person of no *vivacity* is a dull companion: a person of no *spirit* is unfit to associate with others. A person with *animation* takes an interest in every thing; a *vivacious* man catches at every thing that is pleasant and interesting: a *spirited* man enters into plans, makes great exertions, and disregards difficulties.

A speaker may address his audience with more or less *animation* according to the disposition in which he finds it; 'The British have a lively, *animated* aspect.'—STEELE. A painter may be said by his skill to throw *life* into his picture;

> The very dead creation from thy touch
> Assumes a mimick *life*.—THOMSON.

A man of a *vivacious* temper diffuses his *vivacity* into all his words and actions; 'His *vivacity* is seen in doing all the offices of life, with readiness of *spirit*, and propriety in the manner of doing them.'—STEELE. A man of *spirit* suits his measures to the exigency of his circumstances;

> Farewell the big war,
> The *spirit*-stirring drum, th' ear-piercing fife.
> SHAKSPEARE.

LIFELESS, DEAD, INANIMATE.

Lifeless and *dead* suppose the absence of life where it has once been; *inanimate* supposes its absence where it has never been; a person is said to be *lifeless* or *dead* from whom life has departed; the material world consists of objects which are by nature *inanimate*; 'We may in some sort be said to have a society even with the *inanimate* world.'—BURKE. *Lifeless* is negative; it signifies simply without life, or the vital spark: *dead* is positive; it denotes an actual and perfect change in the object. We may speak of a *lifeless* corpse, when speaking of a body which sinks from a state of *animation* into that of *inanimation*;

> Nor can his *lifeless* nostril please,
> With the once ravishing smell.—COWLEY.

We speak of *dead* bodies to designate such as have undergone an entire change; 'A brute and a man are another thing, when they are alive and when they are *dead*.'—HALES. A person, therefore, in whom *animation* is suspended, is, for the time being, *lifeless*, in appearance at least, although we should not say *dead*.

In the moral acceptation, *lifeless* and *inanimate* respect the spirits; *dead* respects the moral feeling. A person is said to be *lifeless* who has lost the spirits which he once had; he is said to be *inanimate* when he is naturally wanting in spirits: a person who is *lifeless* is unfitted for enjoyment; he who is *dead* to moral sentiment i[s t]otally bereft of the essential properties of his nat[ur]e. The epithet *dead* is sometimes applied in the sen[se] of having the stillness of death;

> How *dead* th[e ve]getable kingdom lies!—THOMSON

TO CHEE[R,] ENCOURAGE, COMFORT.

Cheer has the same signification as given under the head of *To animate*; *encourage*, compounded of *en* and *courage*, signifies to inspire with courage; *comfort*, compounded of *com* or *cum*, and *fortis* strong, signifies to invigorate or strengthen.

To *cheer* regards the spirits; to *encourage* the resolution: the sad require to be *cheered*; the timid to be *encouraged*. Mirthful company is suited to *cheer* those who labour under any depression; 'Every eye bestows the *cheering* look of approbation upon the humble man.'—CUMBERLAND. The prospect of success *encourages* those who have any object to obtain; 'Complaisance produces good nature and mutual benevolence, *encourages* the timorous, sooths the turbulent, humanizes the fierce, and distinguishes a society of civilized persons from savages.'—ADDISON.

To *cheer* and *comfort* have both regard to the spirits, but the latter differs in degree and manner: to *cheer* expresses more than to *comfort*; the former signifying to produce a lively sentiment, the latter to lessen or remove a painful one: we are *cheered* in the moments of despondency, whether from real or imaginary causes; we are *comforted* in the hour of distress;

> Sleep seldom visits sorrow,
> When it does, it is a *comforter*.—SHAKSPEARE.

Cheering is mostly effected by the discourse of others; *comforting* is effected by the actions, as well as the words, of others. Nothing tends more to *cheer* the drooping soul than endearing expressions of tenderness from those we love; the most effectual means of *comforting* the poor and afflicted, is by relieving their wants; 'There are writers of great distinction who have made it an argument for providence, that the whole earth is covered with green, rather than with any other colour, as being such a right mixture of light and shade, that *comforts* and strengthens the eye, instead of weakening or grieving it.'—ADDISON. The voice of the benevolent man is *cheering* to the aching heart; his looks *encourage* the sufferer to disclose his griefs; his hand is open to administer relief and *comfort*.

TO CONSOLE, SOLACE, COMFORT.

Console and *solace* are derived from the same source, in French *consoler*, Latin *consolor* and *solatium*, possibly from *solum* the ground, which nourishes all things; to *comfort* signifies to afford *comfort* (*v. To cheer*).

Console and *solace* denote the relieving of pain; *comfort* marks both the communication of positive pleasure and the relief of pain. We *console* others with words; we *console* or *solace* ourselves with reflections; we *comfort* by words or deeds. *Console* is used on more important occasions than *solace*. We *console* our friends when they meet with afflictions; we *solace* ourselves when we meet with disasters; we *comfort* those who stand in need of comfort.

The greatest *consolation* which we can enjoy on the death of our friends is derived from the hope that they have exchanged a state of imperfection and sorrow for one that is full of pure and unmixed felicity; 'In afflictions men generally draw their *consolation* out of books of morality, which indeed are of great use to fortify and strengthen the mind against the impressions of sorrow.'—ADDISON. It is no small *solace* to us in the midst of all our troubles, to consider that they are not so bad as that they might not have been worse; 'He that undergoes the fatigue of labour must *solace* his weariness with the contemplation of its reward.'—JOHNSON. The *comforts* which a person enjoys may be considerably enhanced by the comparison with what he has formerly suffered; 'If our afflictions are light, we shall be *comforted* by the comparison we make between ourselves and our fellow-sufferers.'—ADDISON.

COMFORT, PLEASURE.

Comfort (*v. To cheer*), that genuine English word, describes what England only affords: we may find *pleasure* in every country; but *comfort* is to be found in our own country only: the grand feature in *comfort* is substantiality; in that of *pleasure* is warmth. *Pleasure* is quickly succeeded by pain; it is the lot of humanity that to every *pleasure* there should be an alloy: *comfort* is that portion of *pleasure* which seems to lie exempt from this disadvantage; it is the most durable sort of *pleasure*.

Comfort must be sought for at home; *pleasure* is pursued abroad: *comfort* depends upon a thousand nameless trifles which daily arise; it is the relief of a pain, the heightening of a gratification, the supply of a want, or the removal of an inconvenience;

Thy growing virtues justified my cares,
And promis'd *comfort* to my silver hairs.—POPE.

Pleasure is the companion of luxury and abundance; it dwells in the palaces of the rich and the abodes of the voluptuary: but *comfort* is within the reach of the poorest, and the portion of those who know how to husband their means, and to adapt their enjoyments to their habits and circumstances in life. *Comfort* is less than *pleasure* in the detail; it is more than *pleasure* in the aggregate.

SYMPATHY, COMPASSION, COMMISERATION, CONDOLENCE.

Sympathy, from the Greek σὺμ or σὺν with, and πάθος feeling, has the literal meaning of fellow-feeling, that is, a kindred or like feeling, or feeling in company with another. *Compassion*, from *com* and *patior* to suffer; *commiseration*, from the Latin *com* and *miseria* misery; *condolence*, from the Latin *con* and *doleo* to grieve, signify a like suffering, or a suffering in company. Hence it is obvious, that according to the derivation of the words *sympathy* may be said either of pleasure or pain, the rest only of that which is painful. *Sympathy* preserves its original meaning in its application, for we laugh or cry by *sympathy;* this may, however, be only a merely physical affection; 'You are not young, no more am I; go to, then, there's *sympathy;* you are merry, so am I; ha! ha! then there's more *sympathy;* you love sack, and so do I; would you!'—SHAKSPEARE. Hence it is that the word *sympathy* may be taken for a secret alliance or kindred feeling between two minds or between the mind and other objects;

Or *sympathy* or some connatural force,
Powerful at greatest distance to unite,
With secret amity, things of like kind,
By secretest conveyance.—MILTON.

That mind and body often *sympathize*
Is plain; such is this union nature ties.—JENYNS.

But *sympathy* when taken in a sense the most closely allied to *compassion*, does not go beyond the feeling another's pleasures or pains; we may *sympathize* with others without essentially serving them; 'Their countrymen were particularly attentive to all their story, and *sympathized* with their heroes in all their adventures.'—ADDISON. *Compassion*, on the other hand, not only a moral, but an active feeling; if we feel *compassion*, we naturally turn our thoughts towards relieving the object;

'Mong those whom honest lives can recommend,
Our justice more *compassion* should extend.
DENHAM.

Compassion is awakened by any sort of suffering, but particularly those which are attributable to misfortune; 'The good-natured man is apt to be moved with *compassion* for those misfortunes and infirmities, which another would turn into ridicule.'—ADDISON. *Commiseration* is a stronger feeling awakened by deep distress, above all by the troubles which people bring on themselves; a criminal going to suffer the penalty of the law demands *commiseration;*

She indeed weeping; and her lovely plight
Immoveable, till peace obtain'd from fault
Acknowledg'd and deplor'd, in Adam wrought
Commiseration.—MILTON.

And the calamities of human life equally call for *commiseration;*

Then must we those who groan beneath the weight
Of age, disease, or want, *commiserate*?—DENHAM.

Compassion may be awakened in the minds of persons of very unequal condition; *commiseration* supposes a certain distance, at least in the external condition of the parties; he who *commiserates* being set above the chance of falling into the calamities of him who is commiserated: whence it is represented as the feeling which our wretchedness excites in the Supreme Being. *Condolence* supposes an entire equality; it excludes every thing but what flows out of the courtesy and good-will of one friend to another, and is called forth by events which the parties on either side are equally exposed to; we *condole* with a person on the death of a relative; 'Why should I think that all that devout multitude, which so lately cried Hosanna in the streets, did not also bear their part in these publick *condolings* (on the crucifixion of our Saviour).'—HALL.

Rather than all must suffer, some must die,
Yet nature must *condole* their misery.—DENHAM

GRACIOUS, MERCIFUL, KIND.

Gracious, when compared to *merciful*, is used only in the spiritual sense; the latter is applicable to the conduct of man as well as of the Deity.

Grace is exerted in doing good to an object that has merited the contrary; *mercy* is exerted in withholding the evil which has been merited. God is *gracious* to his creatures in affording them not only an opportunity to address him, but every encouragement to lay open their wants to him; their unworthiness and sinfulness are not made impediments of access to him. God is *merciful* to the vilest of sinners, and lends an ear to the smallest breath of repentance; in the moment of executing vengeance he stops his arm at the voice of supplication: he expects the same *mercy* to be extended by man towards his offending brother.

Grace, in the lofty sense in which it is here admitted, cannot with propriety be made the attribute of any human being, however elevated his rank: nothing short of infinite wisdom as well as goodness can be supposed capable of doing good to offenders without producing ultimate evil;

He heard my vows, and *graciously* decreed
My grounds to be restor'd, my former flocks to feed.
DRYDEN.

Were a king to attempt any display of *grace* by bestowing favours on criminals, his conduct would be highly injurious to the interests of society; but when we speak of the Almighty as dispensing his goods to sinners, and even courting them by every act of endearment to lay aside their sins, we clearly perceive that this difference arises from the infinite disparity between him and us; which makes that "his ways are not our ways, nor are his thoughts our thoughts." I am inclined therefore to think that in our language we have made a peculiarly just distinction between *grace* and *mercy*, by confining the former to the acts of the Almighty, and applying the latter indiscriminately to both; for it is obvious that *mercy* as far as it respects the suspension of punishment, lies altogether within the reach of human discretion;

He that's *merciful*
Unto the bad is cruel to the good.—RANDOLPH.

Gracious, when compared with *kind*, differs principally as to the station of the persons to whom it is applied. *Gracious* is altogether confined to superiours; *kind* is indiscriminately employed for superiours and equals: a king gives a *gracious* reception to the nobles who are presented to him; one friend gives a *kind* reception to another by whom he is visited. *Gracious* is a term in peculiar use at court, and among princes; it necessarily supposes a voluntary descent from a lofty station, to put oneself, for the time being, upon a level with those to whom one speaks: it comprehends, therefore, condescension in manner, affability in address; 'So *gracious* hath God been to us, that he hath made those things to be our duty which naturally tend to our felicity.'—TILLOTSON. *Kindness* is a domestick virtue; it is found mostly among those who have not so much ceremonial to dispense with; it is the display of our good-will not only in the manner, but in the action itself; it is not confined to the tone of the voice, the gesture of the body, or the mode of expression but extends to actual services in the closest relations of society; a master is *kind* to his servants in the time of their sickness; friends who are *kind* to one another have perpetual opportunities of displaying their *kindness* in various little offices;

Love! that would all men just and temp'rate make,
Kind to themselves and others for his sake.
WALLER.

PITY, COMPASSION.

The pain which one feels at the distresses of another is the idea that is common to the signification of both these terms, but they differ in the object that causes the distress. *Pity*, which is probably changed from *piety*, is excited principally by the weakness or degraded condition of the subject: *compassion* (*v. Sympathy*) by his uncontrollable and inevitable misfortunes. We *pity* a man of a weak understanding who exposes his weakness: we *compassionate* the man who is reduced to a state of beggary and want. *Pity* is kindly extended by those in higher condition to such as are humble in their outward circumstances; the poor are at all times deserving of *pity* when their poverty is not the positive fruit of vice;

Others extended naked on the floor,
Exil'd from human *pity* here they lie,
And know no end of mis'ry till they die.
POMFRET.

Compassion is a sentiment which extends to persons in all conditions; the good Samaritan had *compassion* on the traveller who fell among thieves;

His fate *compassion* in the victor bred;
Stern as he was, he yet rever'd the dead.—POPE.

Pity, though a tender sentiment, is so closely allied to contempt, that an ingenuous mind is always loath to be the subject of it, since it can never be awakened but by some circumstances of inferiority; it hurts the honest pride of a man to reflect that he can excite no interest but by provoking a comparison to his own disadvantage: on the other hand, such is the general infirmity of our natures, and such our exposure to the casualties of human life, that *compassion* is a pure and delightful sentiment, that is reciprocally bestowed and acknowledged by all with equal satisfaction.

PITY, MERCY.

The feelings we indulge, and the conduct we adopt, towards others who suffer for their demerits, is the common idea which renders these terms synonymous; but *pity* lays hold of those circumstances which do not affect the moral character, or which diminish the culpability of the individual: *mercy* lays hold of those external circumstances which may diminish punishment. *Pity* is often a sentiment unaccompanied with action; *mercy* is often a mode of action unaccompanied with sentiment: we have or take *pity* upon a person, but we show *mercy* to a person. *Pity* is bestowed by men in their domestic and private capacity; *mercy* is shown in the exercise of power: a master has *pity* upon his offending servant by passing over his offences, and affording him the opportunity of amendment, or an individual may feel a sentiment towards another whom he thinks in a degraded situation.

I *pity* from my soul unhappy men,
Compell'd by want to prostitute their pen.
ROSCOMMON.

The magistrate shows *mercy* to a criminal by abridging his punishment; 'Examples of justice must be made for terrour to some; examples of *mercy* for comfort to others; the one procures fear, and the other love.'—BACON. *Pity* lies in the breast of an individual, and may be bestowed at his discretion: *mercy* is restricted by the rules of civil society; it must not interfere with the administration of justice. Young offenders call for great *pity*, as their offences are often the fruit of inexperience and bad example, rather than of depravity: *mercy* is an imperative duty in those who have the power of inflicting punishment, particularly in cases where life and death are concerned.

Pity and *mercy* are likewise applied to the brute creation with a similar distinction: *pity* shows itself in relieving real misery, and in lightening burdens; *mercy* is displayed in the measure of pain which one inflicts. One takes *pity* on a poor ass to whom one gives fodder to relieve hunger; 'An ant dropped into the water; a wood-pigeon took *pity* on her, and threw her a little bough.'—L'ESTRANGE. One shows a brute *mercy* by abstaining to lay heavy stripes upon its back;

Cowards are cruel, but the brave
Love *mercy*, and delight to save.—GAY.

These terms are moreover applicable to the Deity, in regard to his creatures, particularly man. God takes *pity* on us as entire dependants upon him: he extends his *mercy* towards us as offenders against him: he shows his *pity* by relieving our wants; he shows his *mercy* by forgiving our sins.

PITIABLE, PITEOUS, PITIFUL.

These three epithets drawn from the same word have shades of difference in sense and application; *pitiable* signifies deserving of *pity*; *piteous*, moving *pity*; *pitiful*, full of that which awakens *pity*: a condition is *pitiable* which is so distressing as to call forth *pity*; a cry is *piteous* which indicates such distress as can excite *pity*; a conduct is *pitiful* which marks a character entitled to *pity*.

The first of these terms is taken in the best sense of the term *pity*; the last two in its unfavourable sense: what is *pitiable* in a person is independent of any thing in himself; circumstances have rendered him *pitiable*; 'Is it then impossible that a man may be found who without criminal ill intention, or *pitiable* absurdity, shall prefer a mixed government to either of the extremes?'—BURKE. What is *piteous* and *pitiful* in a man arises from the helplessness and imbecility or worthlessness of his character; the former respects that which is weak; the latter that which is worthless in him: when a poor creature makes *piteous* moans, it indicates his incapacity to help himself as he ought to do out of his troubles, or at least his impatience under suffering;

I have in view, calling to mind with heed
Part of our sentence, that thy seed shall bruise
The serpent's head; *piteous* amends, unless
Be meant, whom I conjecture, our grand foe.
MILTON.

When a man of rank has recourse to *pitiful* shifts to gain his ends, he betrays the innate meanness of his soul; 'Bacon wrote a *pitiful* letter to King James I not long before his death.'—HOWELL.

CLEMENCY, LENITY, MERCY.

Clemency is in Latin *clementia*, signifying mildness; *lenity*, in Latin *lenitas*, comes from *lenis* soft, or *lævis* smooth, and the Greek λεῖος mild; *mercy*, in Latin *misericordia*, compounded of *miseria* and *cordis*, i. e. affliction of the heart, signifies the pain produced by observing the pain of others.

Clemency and *lenity* are employed only towards offenders; *mercy* towards all who are in trouble, whether from their own fault, or any other cause.

Clemency lies in the disposition; *lenity* and *mercy* in the act; the former as respects superiours in general, the latter in regard to those who are invested with civil power: a monarch displays his *clemency* by showing *mercy*; a master shows *lenity* by not inflicting punishment where it is deserved.

Clemency is arbitrary on the part of the dispenser, flowing from his will independent of the object on whom it is bestowed;

We wretched Trojans, toss'd on ev'ry shore,
From sea to sea, thy *clemency* implore;
Forbid the fires our shipping to deface,
Receive th' unhappy fugitives to grace.—DRYDEN.

Lenity and *mercy* are discretionary, they always have regard to the object and the nature of the offence, or misfortunes; *lenity* therefore often serves the purposes of discipline, and *mercy* those of justice by forgiveness, instead of punishment; but *clemency* defeats its end by forbearing to punish where it is needful; 'The King (Charles II.) with *lenity* of which the world has had perhaps no other example, declined to be the judge or avenger of his own or his father' wrongs.'—JOHNSON.

The gods (if gods to goodness are inclin'd,
If acts of *mercy* touch their heav'nly mind),
And more than all the gods, your gen'rous heart,
Conscious of worth, requite its own desert.
DRYDEN.

A mild master who shows *clemency* to a faithless servant by not bringing him to justice, often throws a worthless wretch upon the public to commit more atrocious depredations. A well-timed *lenity* sometimes recalls an offender to himself, and brings him back to good order. Upon this principle, the English constitution has wisely left in the hands of the monarch the discretionary power of showing *mercy* in all cases that do not demand the utmost rigour of the law.

SOFT, MILD, GENTLE, MEEK.

Soft, in Saxon *soft*, German *sanft*, comes most probably from the Saxon *sib*, Gothick *sef*, Hebrew שבת rest; *mild*, in Saxon *milde*, German *milde*, &c. Latin *mollis*, Greek *μελινὸς*, comes from *μειλίσσω* to sooth with *soft* words, and *μέλι* honey; *gentle*, *v. Gentle; meek*, like the Latin *mitis*, may in all probability come from the Greek *μειόω* to make less, signifying to make one's self small, to be humble.

Soft and *mild* are employed both in the proper and the improper application; *meek* only in the moral application: *soft* is opposed to the hard; *mild* to the sharp or strong. All bodies are said to be *soft* which yield easily to the touch or pressure, as a *soft* bed, the *soft* earth, *soft* fruit;

Soft stillness, and the night,
Become the touches of sweet harmony.
SHAKSPEARE.

Some bodies are said to be *mild* which act weakly, but pleasantly, on the taste, as *mild* fruit, or a *mild* cheese; or on the feelings, as *mild* weather;

Sylvia 's like autumn ripe, yet *mild* as May,
More bright than noon, yet fresh as early day.
POPE.

Some things are said to be *gentle*, which in their nature might be boisterous as the winds;

As when the woods by *gentle* winds are stirr'd.
DRYDEN.

In the improper application, *soft*, *mild*, and *gentle* may be applied to that which acts weakly upon others, or is easily acted upon by others; *meek* is said of that only which is acted upon easily by others: in this sense they are all employed as epithets, to designate either the person, or that which is personal.

In the sense of acting weakly, but pleasantly, on others, *soft*, *mild*, and *gentle* are applied to the same objects, but with a slight distinction in the sense: the voice of a person is either *soft* or *mild*; it is naturally *soft*, it is purposely made *mild*; a *soft* voice strikes agreeably upon the ear; a *mild* voice, when assumed by those who have authority, dispels all fears in the minds of inferiours. A person moves either *softly* or *gently*, but in the first case he moves with but little noise, in the second he moves with a slow pace. It is necessary to go *softly* in the chamber of the sick, that they may not be disturbed; it is necessary for a sick person to move *gently*, when he first attempts to go abroad after his confinement, or at least his impatience under suffering;

Pray you tread *softly*, that the blind mole may not
Hear a foot fall.—SHAKSPEARE.

Close at mine ear one call'd me forth to walk,
With *gentle* voice.—MILTON.

To tread *softly* is an art which is acquired from the dancing-master; to go *gently* is a voluntary act: we may go a *gentle* or a quick pace at pleasure. Words are either *soft*, *mild*, or *gentle*: a *soft* word falls lightly upon the person to whom it is addressed; it does not excite any angry sentiment; the proverb says, "A *soft* answer turneth away wrath." A reproof is *mild* when it falls easily from the lips of one who has power to oppress and wound the feelings; a censure, an admonition, or a hint, is *gentle*, which bears indirectly on the offender, and does not expose the whole of his infirmity to view: a kind father always tries the efficacy of *mild* reproofs; a prudent friend will always try to correct our errours by *gentle* remonstrances.

In like manner we say that punishments are *mild* which inflict but a small portion of pain; they are opposed to those which are severe: those means of correction are *gentle*, which are opposed to those that are violent. It requires discretion to know how to inflict punishment with the due proportion of *mildness* and severity; it will be fruitless to adopt *gentle* means of correction, when there is not a power of resorting to those which are violent in case of necessity. Persons, or their manners, are termed *soft*, *mild*, and *gentle*, but still with similar distinctions: a *soft* address, a *soft* air, and the like, are becoming or not, according to the sex: in that which is denominated the *softer* sex, these qualities of *softness* are characteristick excellencies; but even in this sex they may degenerate, by their excess, into insipidity: and in the male sex they are compatible only in a small degree with manly firmness of carriage. *Mild* manners are peculiarly becoming in superiours, whereby they win the love and esteem of those who are in inferiour stations;

Nothing reserv'd or sullen was to see,
But sweet regards, and pleasing sanctity;
Mild was his accent, and his action free.
DRYDEN.

Gentle manners are becoming in all persons who take a part in social life: *gentleness* is, in fact, that due medium of *softness* which is alike suitable to both sexes, and which it is the object of polite education to produce; 'He had such a *gentle* method of reproving their faults, that they were not so much afraid as ashamed to repeat them.'—ATTERBURY.

In the sense of being acted on easily, the disposition is said to be not only *soft*, *mild*, and *gentle*, but also *meek*: *softness* of disposition and character is an infirmity both in the male and female, but particularly in the former; it is altogether incompatible with that steadiness and uniformity of conduct which is requisite for every man who has an independent part to act in life;

However *soft* within themselves they are,
To you they will be valiant by despair.
DRYDEN.

A man of a *soft* disposition often yields to the entreaties of others, and does that which his judgement condemns; *mildness* of disposition unfits a man altogether for command, and is to be clearly distinguished from that *mildness* of conduct which is founded on principle;

If that *mild* and *gentle* god thou be,
Who dost mankind below with pity see.
DRYDEN.

Gentleness, as a part of the character, is not so much to be recommended as *gentleness* from habit; human life contains so much in itself that is rough, that the *gentle* disposition is unable to make that resistance which is requisite for the purposes of self-defence:

Still she retains
Her maiden *gentleness*, and oft at eve
Visits the herds.—MILTON.

Meekness is a Christian virtue forcibly recommended to our practice by the example and precepts of our blessed Saviour; it consists not only in an unresisting, but a forgiving temper, a temper that is unruffled by injuries and provocations: it is, however, an infirmity, if it springs from a want of spirit, or an unconsciousness of what is due to ourselves: *meekness*, therefore, as a natural temper, sinks into meanness and servility; but when, as an acquired temper, built upon principle, and moulded into a habit of the mind, it is the grand distinctive characteristick of the religion we profess.

Gentle and *meek* are likewise applied to animals; the former to designate that easy flow of spirits which fits them for being guided in their movements, and the latter to mark that passive temper, that submits to every kind of treatment, however harsh, without an indication even of displeasure. A horse is *gentle*, as opposed to one that is spirited; the former is devoid of that impetus in himself to move, which renders the other ungovernable: the lamb is a pattern of *meekness*, and yields to the knife of the butcher without a struggle or a groan;

How *meek*, how patient, the *mild* creature lies,
What *softness* in its melancholy face,
What dumb-complaining innocence appears!
THOMSON.

GENTLE, TAME.

Gentleness lies rather in the natural disposition; *tameness* is the effect either of art or circumstances. Any unbroken horse may be *gentle*, but not *tame:* a horse that is broken in will be *tame*, but not always *gentle.*

Gentle (*v. Genteel*) signifies literally well-born, and is opposed either to the fierce or the rude; '*Gentleness* and gentility are the same thing, and, if they are not the same words, they come from one and the same original, from whence likewise is deduced the word *gentleman.*'—PEGGE. *Tame*, in German *zahm*, from *zaum* a bridle, signifies literally curbed or kept under, and is opposed either to the wild or the spirited.

Animals are in general said to be *gentle* which show a disposition to associate with man, and conform to his will: they are said to be *tame*, if either by compulsion or habit they are brought to mix with human society. Of the first description there are individuals in almost every species which are more or less entitled to the name of *gentle;* of the latter description are many species, as the dog, the sheep, the hen, and the like;

This said, the hoary king no longer staid,
But on his car the slaughter'd victims laid;
Then seiz'd the reins, his *gentle* steeds to guide,
And drove to Troy, Antenor at his side.—POPE.

For Orpheus' lute could soften steel and stone,
Make tigers *tame*, and huge leviathans.
SHAKSPEARE.

In the moral application *gentle* is always employed in the good, and *tame* in the bad sense: a *gentle* spirit needs no control; it amalgamates freely with the will of another: a *tame* spirit is without any will of its own; it is alive to nothing but submission; it is perfectly consistent with our natural liberty to have *gentleness*, but *tameness* is the accompaniment of slavery. The same distinction marks the use of these words when applied to the outward conduct or the language: *gentle* bespeaks something positively good; *tame* bespeaks the want of an essential good: the former is allied to the kind, the latter to the abject and mean qualities which naturally flow from the compression or destruction of energy and will in the agent. A *gentle* expression is devoid of all acrimony, and serves to turn away wrath: a *tame* expression is devoid of all force or energy, and ill calculated to inspire the mind with any feeling whatever. In giving counsel to an irritable and conceited temper, it is necessary to be *gentle: tame* expressions are nowhere such striking deformities as in a poem or an oration; '*Gentleness* stands opposed, not to the most determined regard to virtue and truth, but to harshness and severity, to pride and arrogance.'—BLAIR. 'Though all wanton provocations, and contemptuous insolence, are to be diligently avoided, there is no less danger in timid compliance and *tame* resignation.'—JOHNSON.

DOCILE, TRACTABLE, DUCTILE.

Docile, in Latin *docilis*, from *doceo* to teach, is the Latin term for ready to be taught; *tractable*, from the Latin *traho* to draw, signifies ready to be drawn; and *ductile*, from *duco* to lead, ready to be led.

The idea of submitting to the directions of another is comprehended in the signification of all these terms: *docility* marks the disposition to conform our actions in all particulars to the will of another, and lies altogether in the will; *tractability* and *ductility* are modes of *docility*, the former in regard to the conduct, the latter in regard to the principles and sentiments: *docility* is in general applied to the ordinary actions of the life, where simply the will is concerned; 'The Persians are not wholly void of martial spirit; and if they are not naturally brave, they are at least extremely *docile*, and might with proper discipline be made excellent soldiers.'—SIR WM. JONES. *Tractability* is applicable to points of conduct in which the judgement is concerned; *ductility* to matters in which the character is formed: a child ought to be *docile* with its parents at all times. A person ought to be *tractable* when acting under the direction of his superiour; 'The people, without being servile, must be *tractable.*'—BURKE. A young person ought to be *ductile* to imbibe good principles: the want of *docility* may spring from a defect in the disposition: the want of *tractableness* may spring either from a defect in the temper, or from self-conceit; the want of *ductility* lies altogether in a natural stubbornness of character: *docility*, being altogether independent of the judgement, is applicable to the brutes as well as to men;

Their reindeer form their riches; these their tents,
Their robes, their beds, and all their homely wealth,
Supply their wholesome fare, and cheerful cups;
Obsequious at their call, the *docile* tribe
Yield to the sledge their necks.—THOMSON.

Tractableness and *ductility* are applicable mostly to thinking and rational objects only, though sometimes extended to inanimate or moral objects: the ox is a *docile* animal; the humble are *tractable;* youth is *ductile;* 'The will was then (before the fall) *ductile* and pliant to all the motions of right reason.'—SOUTH

FLEXIBLE, PLIABLE, PLIANT, SUPPLE.

Flexible, in Latin *flexibilis*, from *flecto* to bend, signifies able to be bent; *pliable* signifies able to be *plied* or folded: *pliant*, *plying*, bending, or folding; *supple*, in French *souple*, from the intensive syllable *sub* and *ply*, signifies very *pliable.*

* *Flexible* is used in a natural or moral sense; *pliable* in the familiar and natural sense only; *pliant* in the higher and moral application only: what can be bent in any degree as a stick is *flexible;* what can be bent as wax, or folded like cloth, is *pliable. Supple*, whether in a proper or a figurative sense, is an excess of *pliability;* what can be bent backward and forward, like ozier twig, is *supple.*

In the moral application, *flexible* is indefinite both in degree and application; it may be greater or less in point of degree: whereas *pliant* supposes a great degree of *pliability;* and *suppleness*, a great degree of *pliancy* or *pliability:* it applies likewise to the outward actions, to the temper, the resolution, or the principles; but *pliancy* is applied to the principles, or the conduct dependent upon those principles; *suppleness* to the outward actions and behaviour only. A temper is *flexible* which yields to the entreaties of others; the person or character is *pliant* when it is formed or moulded easily at the will of another; a person is *supple* who makes his actions and his manners bend according to the varying humours of another: the first belongs to one in a superiour station who yields to the wishes of the applicant; the latter two belong to equals or inferiours who yield to the influence of others.

Flexibility may be either good or bad, according to circumstances; when it shortens the duration of resentments it produces a happy effect; but *flexibility* is not a respectable trait in a master or a judge, who ought to be guided by higher motives than what the momentary impulse of feeling suggests: *pliancy* is very commendable in youth, when it leads them to yield to the counsels of the aged and experienced; but it may sometimes make young men the more easy victims to the seductions of the artful and vicious: *suppleness* is in no case good, for it is *flexibility* either in indifferent matters, or such as are expressly bad. A good-natured man is *flexible;* a weak and thoughtless man is *pliant;* a parasite is *supple.*

Flexibility is frequently a weakness, but never a vice; it always consults the taste of others, sometimes to its own inconvenience, and often in opposition to its judgement; 'Forty-four is an age at which the mind begins less easily to admit new confidence, and the will to grow less *flexible.*'—JOHNSON. *Pliancy* is often both a weakness and a vice; it always yields for its own pleasure, though not always in opposition to its sense of right and wrong: 'As for the bending and forming the mind, we should doubtless do our utmost to render it *pliable*, and by no means stiff and refractory.'—BACON. 'The future is *pliant* and *ductile.*'—JOHNSON. *Suppleness* is always a vice, but never a weakness; it seeks its gratification to the injury of another by flattering his passions; 'Charles I. wanted *suppleness* and dexterity to give way to the encroachments of a popular assembly.'—HUME. *Flexibility* is opposed to firmness; *pliancy* to steadiness; *supplenes* to rigidity.

* Vide Roubaud: "Flexible, soupile, docile.

TO ALLAY, SOOTH, APPEASE, ASSUAGE, MITIGATE.

To *allay* is compounded of *al* or *ad*, and *lay* to lay to or by, signifying to lay a thing to rest, to abate it; *sooth* probably comes from *sweet*, which is in Swedish *söt*, Low German, &c. *söt*, and is doubtless connected with the Hebrew סות to allure, invite, compose; *appease*, in French *appaiser*, is compounded of *ap* or *ad* and *paix* peace, signifying to quiet; *assuage* is compounded of *as* or *ad* and *suage*, from the Latin *suasi*, perfect of *suadeo* to persuade, signifying to treat with gentleness, or to render easy; *mitigate*, from the Latin *mitis* gentle, signifies to make gentle or easy to be borne.

All these terms indicate a lessening of something painful. In a physical sense a pain is *allayed* by an immediate application; it is *soothed* by affording ease and comfort in other respects, and diverting the mind from the pain. Extreme heat or thirst is *allayed;* 'Without expecting the return of hunger, they eat for an appetite, and prepare dishes not to *allay*, but to excite it.'—Addison. Extreme hunger is *appeased;*

The rest
They cut in legs and fillets, for the feast,
Which drawn and served, their hunger they *appease*.
Dryden

A punishment or sentence is *mitigated;*

I undertook
Before thee, and, not repenting, this obtain
Of right, that I may *mitigate* their doom.
Milton.

In a moral sense one *allays* what is fervid and vehement;

If by your art you have
Put the wild waters in this war, *allay* them.
Shakspeare.

One *sooths* what is distressed; 'Nature has given all the little arts of *soothing* and blandishing to the female.'—Addison. One *appeases* what is tumultuous and boisterous; 'Charon is no sooner *appeased*, and the triple-headed dog laid asleep, but Æneas makes his entrance into the dominions of Pluto.'—Addison. One *assuages* grief or afflictions; 'If I can any way *assuage* private inflammations, or *allay* publick ferments, I shall apply myself to it with the utmost endeavours.'—Addison. One *mitigates* pains, or what is rigorous and severe; 'All it can do is, to devise how that which must be endured may be *mitigated*.'—Hooker. Nothing is so calculated to *allay* the fervour of a distempered imagination, as prayer and religious meditation: religion has every thing in it which can *sooth* a wounded conscience by presenting it with the hope of pardon, that can *appease* the angry passions by giving us a sense of our own sinfulness and need of God's pardon, and that can *assuage* the bitterest griefs by affording us the brightest prospect of future bliss.

TO ALLEVIATE, RELIEVE.

Alleviate, in Latin *alleviatus*, participle of *allevio*, is compounded of the intensive syllable *al* or *ad*, and *levo* to lighten, signifying to lighten by making less; *relieve*, from the Latin *relevo*, is *re* and *levo* to lift up, signifying to take away or remove.

A pain is *alleviated* by making it less burdensome; a necessity is *relieved* by supplying what is wanted. *Alleviate* respects our internal feelings only; *relieve* our external circumstances. That *alleviates* which affords ease and comfort; that *relieves* which removes the pain. It is no *alleviation* of sorrow to a feeling mind, to reflect that others undergo the same suffering; 'Half the misery of human life might be extinguished, would men *alleviate* the general curse they lie under, by mutual offices of compassion, benevolence, and humanity.'—Addison. A change of position is a considerable *relief* to an invalid, wearied with confinement;

Now sinking underneath a load of grief,
From death alone she seeks her last *relief*.
Dryden.

Condolence and sympathy tend greatly to *alleviate* the sufferings of our fellow-creatures; it is an essential part of the Christian's duty to *relieve* the wants of his indigent neighbour.

APPEASE, CALM, PACIFY, QUIET, STILL.

Appease, v. *To allay; calm*, in French *calmer*, from *almus* fair, signifies to make fair; *pacify*, in Latin *pacifico*, compounded of *pax* and *facio*, signifies to make peace or peaceable; *quiet*, in French *quiet*, Latin *quietus*, from *quies* rest, signifies to put to rest; *still*, signifies to make *still*.

To *appease* is to put an end to a violent motion; to *calm* is to produce a great tranquillity. * The wind is *appeased;* the sea is *calmed*. With regard to persons it is necessary to *appease* those who are in transports of passion, and to *calm* those who are in trouble, anxiety, or apprehension.

Appease respects matters of force or violence;

A lofty city by my hand is rais'd,
Pygmalion punish'd, and my lord *appeased*
Dryden.

Calm respects matters of inquietude and distress;

All-powerful harmony, that can assuage
And *calm* the sorrows of the phrensied wretch.
Marsh.

One is *appeased* by a submissive behaviour, and *calmed* by the removal of danger.

Pacify corresponds to *appease*, and *quiet* to *calm*. In sense they are the same, but in application they differ. *Appease* and *calm* are used only in reference to objects of importance; *pacify* and *quiet* may be applied to those of a more familiar nature. The uneasy humours of a child are *pacified*, or its groundless fears are *quieted*.

Still is a loftier expression than any of the former terms; serving mostly for the grave or poetick style. It is an onomatopeia for restraining or putting to silence that which is noisy and boisterous;

My breath can *still* the winds,
Uncloud the sun, charm down the swelling sea,
And stop the floods of heaven.—Beaumont

PEACE, QUIET, CALM, TRANQUILLITY.

Peace, in Latin *pax*, may either come from *pactio* an agreement or compact which produces *peace*, or it may be connected with *pausa*, and the Greek παύω to cease, because a cessation of all violent action and commotion enters into the idea of *peace; quiet*, in Latin *quietus*, probably from κεῖμαι to lie down, signifies a lying posture which best promotes *quiet; calm* signifies the state of being *calm; tranquillity*, in Latin *tranquillitas*, from *tranquillus*, that is, *trans*, the intensive syllable, and *quillus* or *quietus*, signifies altogether or exceedingly *quiet*.

Peace is a term of more general application, and more comprehensive meaning than the others; it respects either communities or individuals; but *quiet* respects only individuals or small communities. Nations are said to have *peace*, but not *quiet;* persons or families may have both *peace* and *quiet*. *Peace* implies an exemption from publick or private broils; *quiet* implies a freedom from noise or interruption. Every well-disposed family strives to be at peace with its neighbours, and every affectionate family will naturally act in such a manner as to promote *peace* among all its members; 'A false person ought to be looked upon as a publick enemy, and a disturber of the *peace* of mankind.'—South. The *quiet* of a neighbourhood is one of its first recommendations as a place of residence, 'A paltry tale-bearer will discompose the *quiet* of a whole family.'—South.

Peace and *quiet*, in regard to individuals, have likewise a reference to the internal state of the mind; but the former expresses the permanent condition of the mind, the latter its transitory condition. Serious matters only can disturb our *peace;* trivial matters may disturb our *quiet:* a good man enjoys the *peace* of a good conscience; 'Religion directs us rather to secure inward *peace* than outward ease, to be more careful to avoid everlasting torments than light affliction.'—Tillotson. The best of men may have unavoidable cares and anxieties which disturb his *quiet:*

* Vide Abbe Girard: "Appaiser, calmer."

Indulgent *quiet*, pow'r serene,
Mother of *peace*, and joy, and love.—HUGHES.

There can be no *peace* where a man's passions are perpetually engaged in a conflict with each other; there can be no *quiet* where a man is embarrassed in his pecuniary affairs.

Calm is a species of *quiet*, which respects objects in the natural or the moral world; it indicates the absence of violent motion, as well as violent noise; it is that state which more immediately succeeds a state of agitation. As storms at sea are frequently preceded as well as succeeded, by a dead *calm*, so political storms have likewise their *calms* which are their attendants, if not their precursors; 'Cheerfulness banishes all anxious care and discontent, sooths and composes the passions, and keeps the soul in a perpetual *calm*.'—ADDISON. *Peace*, *quiet*, and *calm* have all respect to the state contrary to their own; they are properly cessations either from strife, from disturbance, or from agitation and tumult. *Tranquillity*, on the other hand, is taken more absolutely: it expresses the situation as it exists in the present moment, independently of what goes before or after; it is sometimes applicable to society, sometimes to natural objects, and sometimes to the mind. The *tranquillity* of the state cannot be preserved unless the authority of the magistrates be upheld; the *tranquillity* of the air and of all the surrounding objects is one thing which gives the country its peculiar charms; the *tranquillity* of the mind in the season of devotion contributes essentially to produce a suitable degree of religious fervour; 'By a patient acquiescence under painful events for the present, we shall be sure to contract a *tranquillity* of temper.'—CUMBERLAND.

As epithets, these terms bear the same relation to each other: people are *peaceable* as they are disposed to promote *peace* in society at large, or in their private relations; they are *quiet*, inasmuch as they abstain from every loud expression, or are exempt from any commotion in themselves: they are *calm*, inasmuch as they are exempt from the commotion which at any given moment rages around them; they are *tranquil*, inasmuch as they enjoy an entire exemption from every thing which can discompose. A town is *peaceable* as respects the disposition of the inhabitants; it is *quiet*, as respects its external circumstances, or freedom from bustle and noise: an evening is *calm* when the air is lulled into a particular stillness, which is not interrupted by any loud sounds: a scene is *tranquil* which combines every thing calculated to sooth the spirits to rest.

PEACEABLE, PEACEFUL, PACIFICK.

Peaceable is used in the proper sense of the word *peace*, as it expresses an exemption from strife or contest (*v. Peace*); but *peaceful* is used in its improper sense, as it expresses an exemption from agitation or commotion. Persons or things are *peaceable;* things, particularly in the higher style, are *peaceful:* a family is designated as *peaceable*, in regard to its inhabitants; 'I know that my *peaceable* disposition already gives me a very ill figure here' (at Ratisbon).—LADY W. MONTAGUE. A house is designated as a *peaceful* abode, as it is remote from the bustle and hurry of a multitude;

Still as the *peaceful* walks of ancient night,
Silent as are the lamps that burn in tombs.
SHAKSPEARE.

Pacifick signifies either making *peace*, or disposed to make *peace*, and is applied mostly to what we do to others. We are *peaceable* when we do not engage in quarrels of our own; we are *pacifick* if we wish to keep *peace*, or make *peace*, between others. Hence the term *peaceable* is mostly employed for individual or private concerns, and *pacifick* most properly for national concerns: subjects ought to be *peaceable*, and monarchs *pacifick;* 'The most *peaceable* way for you, if you do take a thief, is to let him show himself, and steal out of your company.'—SHAKSPEARE. 'The tragical and untimely death of the French monarch put an end to all *pacifick* measures with regard to Scotland'.—ROBERTSON.

CALM, COMPOSED, COLLECTED.

Calm, v. To appease; composed, from the verb *compose*, marks the state of being *composed;* and *collected*, from *collect*, the state of being *collected.*

These terms agree in expressing a state; but *calm* respects the state of the feelings, *composed* the state of the thoughts and feelings, and *collected* the state of the thoughts more particularly.

Calmness is peculiarly requisite in seasons of distress, and amid scenes of horror; *composure*, in moments of trial, disorder, and tumult; *collectedness*, in moments of danger. *Calmness* is the companion of fortitude; no one whose spirits are easily disturbed can have strength to bear misfortune: *composure* is an attendant upon clearness of understanding; no one can express himself with perspicuity whose thoughts are any way deranged: *collectedness* is requisite for a determined promptitude of action; no one can be expected to act promptly who cannot think fixedly.

It would argue a want of all feeling to be *calm* on some occasions, when the best affections of our nature are put to a severe trial;

'T is godlike magnanimity to keep,
When most provok'd, our reason *calm* and clear.
THOMSON.

Composedness of mind associated with the detection of guilt, evinces a hardened conscience, and an insensibility to shame; 'A moping lover would grow a pleasant fellow by that time he had rid thrice about the island (Anticyra); and a hair-brained rake, after a short stay in the country, go home again a *composed* grave, worthy gentleman.'—STEELE. *Collectedness* of mind has contributed in no small degree to the preservation of some persons' lives, in moments of the most imminent peril;

Be *collected*,
No more amazement.—SHAKSPEARE

CALM, PLACID, SERENE.

Calm, v. To appease; placid, in Latin *placidus*, from *placeo* to please, signifies the state of being pleased, or free from uneasiness; *serene*, in Latin *serenus*, comes most probably from the Greek εἰρήνη peace, signifying a state of peace.

Calm and *serene* are applied to the elements; *placid* only to the mind. *Calmness* respects only the state of the winds, *serenity* that of the air and heavens: the weather is *calm* when it is free from agitation: it is *serene* when free from noise and vapour. *Calm* respects the total absence of all perturbation; *placid* the ease and contentment of the mind; *serene* clearness and composure of the mind.

As in the natural world a particular agitation of the wind is succeeded by a *calm*, so in the mind of man, when an unusual effervescence has been produced, it commonly subsides into a *calm;*

Preach patience to the sea, when jarring winds
Throw up the swelling billows to the sky'
And if your reasons mitigate her fury,
My soul will be as *calm*.—SMITH.

Placidity and *serenity* have more that is even and regular in them; they are positively what they are. *Calm* is a temporary state of the feelings; *placid* and *serene* are habits of the mind. We speak of a *calm* state; but a *placid* and *serene* temper. *Placidity* is more of a natural gift; *serenity* is acquired: people with not very ardent desires or warmth of feeling will evince *placidity;* they are pleased with all that passes inwardly or outwardly; '*Placid* and soothing is the remembrance of a life passed with quiet, innocence, and elegance.'—STEELE. Nothing contributes so much to *serenity* of mind as a pervading sense of God's good providence, which checks all impatience, softens down every asperity of humour, and gives a steady current to the feelings: 'Every one ought to fence against the temper of his climate or constitution, and frequently to indulge in himself those considerations which may give him a *serenity* of mind.'—ADDISON.

EASE, QUIET, REST, REPOSE.

Ease comes immediately from the French *aisé* glad and that from the Greek ἀιζηὸς young, fresh; *quiet*, in Latin *quietus*, comes probably from the Greek κεῖμαι to lie down, signifying a lying posture; *rest*, in German *rast*, comes from the Latin *resto* to stand still or make a halt; *repose* comes from the Latin *reposui*, perfect of *repono* to place back, signifying the state of placing one's self backward or downward.

The idea of a motionless state is common to all these terms: *ease* and *quiet* respect action on the body; *rest* and *repose* respect the action of the body: we are *easy* or *quiet* when freed from any external agency that is painful; we have *rest* or *repose* when the body is no longer in motion.

Ease denotes an exemption from any painful agency in general; *quiet* denotes an exemption from that in particular, which noise, disturbance, or the violence of others may cause; we are *easy* or at *ease*, when the body is in a posture agreeable to itself, or when no circumjacent object presses unequally upon it: we are *quiet* when there is an agreeable stillness around: our *ease* may be disturbed either by internal or external causes; our *quiet* is most commonly disturbed by external objects; we may have *ease* from pain, bodily or mental; we have *quiet* at the will of those around us: a sick person is often far from enjoying *ease*, although he may have the good fortune to enjoy the most perfect *quiet:* a man's mind is often *uneasy* from its own faulty constitution; it suffers frequent *disquietudes* from the vexatious tempers of others: let a man be in ever such *easy* circumstances, he may still expect to meet with *disquietudes* in his dealings with the world: wealth and contentment are the great promoters of *ease;*

> By this we plainly view the two imposthumes
> That choke a kingdom's welfare; *ease* and wantonness.—Beaumont and Fletcher.

Retirement is the most friendly to *quiet:*

> But *easy quiet*, a secure retreat,
> A harmless life that knows not how to cheat,
> With homebred plenty the rich owner bless,
> And rural pleasures crown his happiness.—Dryden.

Rest simply denotes the cessation of motion; *repose* is that species of *rest* which is agreeable after labour; we *rest* as circumstances require; in this sense, our Creator is said to have *rested* from the work of creation; 'Like the sun, it had light and agility; it knew no *rest* but in motion, no *quiet* but in activity.'—South. *Repose* is a circumstance of necessity; the weary seek *repose;* there is no human being to whom it is not sometimes indispensable;

> I all the livelong day
> Consume in meditation deep, recluse
> From human converse; nor at shut of eve
> Enjoy *repose*.—Phillips.

We may *rest* in a standing posture; we can *repose* only in a lying position; the dove which Noah first sent out could not find *rest* for the sole of its foot; soldiers who are hotly pursued by an enemy, have no time nor opportunity to take *repose:* the night is the time for *rest;* the pillow is the place for *repose*. *Rest* may be properly applied to things and persons;

> The peaceful peasant to the wars is press'd,
> The fields lie fallow in inglorious *rest*.—Dryden.

Repose may be employed figuratively in the same sense;

> Nor can the tortur'd wave here find *repose*,
> But raging still amid the shaggy rocks,
> Now flashes o'er the scatter'd fragments.
> Thomson.

EASE, EASINESS, FACILITY, LIGHTNESS.

Ease, (*v. Ease*) denotes either the abstract state of a person or quality of a thing; *easiness*, from *easy*, signifying having *ease*, denotes simply an abstract quality which serves to characterize the thing: a person enjoys *ease*, or he has an *easiness* of disposition: '*Ease* is the utmost that can be hoped from a sedentary and inactive habit.'—Johnson. 'His yielding unto them in one thing might happily put them in hope, that time would breed the like *easiness* of condescending further unto them.'—Hooker. *Ease* is said of that which is borne, or that which is done; *easiness* and *facility*, from the Latin *facilis* easy, most commonly of that which is to be done; the former in application to the thing as before, the latter either to the person or the thing: we speak of the *easiness* of the task, but of a person's *facility* in doing it: we judge of the *easiness* of a thing by comparing it with others more difficult; 'Nothing is more subject to mistake and disappointment than anticipated judgement, concerning the *easiness* or difficulty of any undertaking.'—Johnson. We judge of a person's *facility* by comparing him with others, who are less skilful; 'Every one must have remarked the *facility* with which the kindness of others is sometimes gained by those to whom he never could have imparted his own.'—Johnson.

Ease and *lightness* are both said of what is to be borne; the former in a general, the latter in a particular sense. Whatever presses in any form is not *easy;* that which presses by excess of weight is not *light:* a coat may be *easy* from its make; it can be *light* only from its texture. A work is *easy* which requires no great exertion either of body or mind; 'The service of God, in the solemn assembly of saints, is a work, though *easy*, yet withal very weighty, and of great respect.'—Hooker. A work is *light* which requires no effort of the body;

> Well pleas'd were all his friends, the task was *light*,
> The father, mother, daughter, they invite.
> Dryden.

The same distinction exists between their derivatives, to *ease*, *facilitate*, and *lighten;* to *ease* is to make *easy* or free from pain, as to *ease* a person of his labour; to *facilitate* is to render a thing more practicable or less difficult, as to *facilitate* a person's progress; to *lighten* is to take off an excessive weight, as to *lighten* a person's burdens.

EASY, READY.

Easy (*v. Ease*, *easiness*) signifies here a freedom from obstruction in ourselves; *ready*, in German *bereit*, Latin *paratus*, signifies prepared.

Easy marks the freedom of being done; *ready* the disposition or willingness to do; the former refers mostly to the thing or the manner, the latter to the person: the thing is *easy* to be done; the person is *ready* to do it: it is *easy* to make professions of friendship in the ardour of the moment; but every one is not *ready* to act up to them, when it interferes with his convenience or interest.

As epithets, both are opposed to difficult, but agreeably to the above explanation of the terms; the former denotes a freedom from such difficulties or obstacles as lie in the nature of the thing itself; the latter an exemption from such as lie in the temper and character of the person; hence we say a person is *easy* of access whose situation, rank, employments, or circumstances, do not prevent him from admitting others to his presence; he is *ready* to hear when he himself throws no obstacles in the way, when he lends a willing ear to what is said. So likewise a task is said to be *easy;* a person's wit, or a person's reply, to be *ready:* a young man who has birth and fortune, wit and accomplishments, will find an *easy* admittance into any circle; 'An *easy* manner of conversation is the most desirable quality a man can have.'—Steele. The very name of a favourite author will be a *ready* passport for the works to which it may be affixed;

> The scorpion, *ready* to receive thy laws,
> Yields half his region and contracts his claws.
> Dryden.

When used adverbially, they bear the same relation to each other. A man is said to comprehend *easily*, who from whatever cause finds the thing *easy* to be comprehended; he pardons *readily* who has a temper *ready* to pardon.

TO RECLINE, REPOSE.

To *recline* is to lean back; to *repose* is to place one's self back: he who *reclines reposes;* but we may *recline* without *reposing:* when we *recline* we put ourselves into a particular position;

> For consolation on his friend *reclin'd*.—Falconer.

When we *repose* we put ourselves into that position which will be most easy;

> I first awak'd, and found myself *repos'd*
> Under a shade, on flowers.—Milton

HARD, DIFFICULT, ARDUOUS.

Hard is here taken in the improper sense of trouble caused, and pains taken, in which sense it is a much stronger term than *difficult*, which, from the Latin *difficilis*, compounded of the privative *dis* and *facilis*, signifies merely not easy. *Hard* is therefore positive, and *difficult* negative. A *difficult* task cannot be got through without exertion, but a *hard* task requires great exertion. *Difficult* is applicable to all trivial matters which call for a more than usual portion either of labour or thought; 'As Swift's years increased, his fits of giddiness and deafness grew more frequent, and his deafness made conversation *difficult*.'—JOHNSON. *Hard* is applicable to those which are of the highest importance, and accompanied with circumstances that call for the utmost stretch of every power;

> Antigones, with kisses, often tried
> To beg this present in his beauty's pride,
> When youth and love are *hard* to be denied.
> DRYDEN.

It is a *difficult* matter to get admittance into some circles of society; it is a *hard* matter to find societies that are select: it is *difficult* to decide between two fine paintings which is the finest; it is a *hard* matter to come at any conclusion on metaphysical subjects. A child mostly finds it *difficult* to learn his letters: there are many passages in classical writers which are *hard* to be understood by the learned.

Arduous, in Latin *arduus* lofty, from *ardeo* to burn, because flame ascends upwards, denotes set on high or out of reach except by great efforts; *arduous* expresses a high degree of *difficulty*. What is *difficult* requires only the efforts of ordinary powers to surmount;

> Whatever melting metals can conspire,
> Or breathing bellows, or the forming fire,
> Is freely yours: your anxious fears remove,
> And think no task is *difficult* to love.—DRYDEN.

But what is *arduous* is set above the reach of common intellect, and demands the utmost stretch of power both physical and mental; 'The translation of Homer was an *arduous* undertaking, and the translator entered upon it with a candid confession that he was utterly incapable of doing justice to Homer.'—CUMBERLAND. A child may have a *difficult* exercise which he cannot perform without labour and attention: the man who strives to remove the *difficulties* of learners undertakes an *arduous* task. It is *difficult* to conquer our own passions: it is *arduous* to control the unruly and contending wills of others.

HARDLY, SCARCELY.

What is *hard* is not common, and in that respect *scarce*: hence the idea of unfrequency assimilates these terms both in signification and application. In many cases they may be used indifferently; but where the idea of practicability predominates, *hardly* seems most proper; and where the idea of frequency predominates, *scarcely* seems preferable. One can *hardly* judge of a person's features by a single and partial glance; 'I do not expect, as long as I stay in India, to be free from a bad digestion, the "morbus literatorum," for which there is *hardly* any remedy but abstinence from food, literary and culinary.'—SIR WM. JONES. We *scarcely* ever see men lay aside their vices from a thorough conviction of their enormity; 'In this assembly of princes and nobles [the Congress of the Hague], to which Europe has perhaps *scarcely* seen any thing equal, was formed the grand alliance against Lewis.'—JOHNSON. But in general sentences it may with equal propriety be said, *hardly* one in a thousand, or *scarcely* one in a thousand, would form such a conclusion.

TO HELP, ASSIST, AID, SUCCOUR, RELIEVE.

Help, in Saxon *helpan*, German *helfen*, probably comes from the Greek ὀφέλλω to do good to; *assist*, in Latin *assisto*, or *ad* and *sisto*, signifies to place one's self by another so as to give him our strength; *aid*, in Latin *adjuvo*, that is, the intensive syllable *ad* and *juvo*, signifies to profit towards a specifick end; *succour*, in Latin *succurro*, signifies to run to the help of any one; *relieve*, *v.* *To alleviate.*

The idea of communicating to the advantage of another is common to all these terms. *Help* is the generick term; the rest specifick: *help* may be substituted for the others, and in many cases where they would not be applicable. The first three are employed either to produce a positive good or to remove an evil, the two latter only to remove an evil. We *help* a person to prosecute his work, or *help* him out of a difficulty; we *assist* in order to forward a scheme, or we *assist* a person in the time of his embarrassment; we *aid* a good cause, or we *aid* a person to make his escape; we *succour* a person who is in danger; we *relieve* him in time of distress. To *help* and *assist* respect personal service, the former by corporeal, the latter by corporeal or mental labour: one servant *helps* another by taking a part in his employment; one author *assists* another in the composition of his work. We *help* up a person's load, we *assist* him to rise when he has fallen: we speak of a *helper* or a *helpmate* in mechanical employments, of an *assistant* to a professional man;

> Their strength united best may *help* to bear.—POPE.

> 'T is the first sanction nature gave to man,
> Each other to *assist* in what they can.—DENHAM.

To *assist* and *aid* are used for services directly or indirectly performed; but *assist* is said only of individuals, *aid* may be said of bodies as well as individuals. One friend *assists* another with his purse, with his counsel, his interest, and the like; 'She no sooner yielded to adultery, but she agreed to *assist* in the murder of her husband.'—BROWNE. One person *aids* another in carrying on a scheme; or one king, or nation, *aids* another with armies and subsidies;

> Your private right, should impious power invade,
> The peers of Ithaca would rise in *aid*.—POPE.

We come to the *assistance* of a person when he has met with an accident; we come to his *aid* when contending against numbers. *Assistance* is given, *aid* is sent.

To *succour* is a species of immediate *assistance*, which is given on the spur of the occasion; the good Samaritan went to the *succour* of the man who had fallen among thieves;

> Patroclus on the shore,
> Now pale and dead, shall *succour* Greece no more.
> POPE.

So in like manner we may *succour* one who calls us by his cries; or we may *succour* the poor whom we find in circumstances of distress;

> My father
> Flying for *succour* to his servant Banister,
> Being distress'd, was by that wretch betrayed.
> SHAKSPEARE.

The word *relieve* has nothing in common with *succour* except that they both express the removal of pain, but the latter does not necessarily imply any mode by which this is done, and therefore excludes the idea of personal interference.

All these terms, except *succour*, may be applied to things as well as persons; we may walk by the *help* of a stick; 'A man reads his prayers out of a book, as a means to *help* his understanding and direct his expressions.'—STILLINGFLEET. We read with the *assistance* of glasses; 'Acquaintance with method will *assist* one in ranging human affairs.'—WATTS. We learn a task quickly by the aid of a good memory;

> Wise, weighty counsels *aid* a state distress'd.—POPE

We obtain *relief* from medicine; 'An unbeliever feels the whole pressure of a present calamity, without being *relieved* by the memory of any thing that is past, or the prospect of any thing that is to come.'—ADDISON.

To *help* or *assist* is commonly an act of good nature; to *aid*, frequently an act of policy; to *succour* or *relieve*, an act of generosity or humanity. *Help* is necessary for one who has not sufficient strength to perform his task; *assistance* is necessary when a person's time or talent is too much occupied to perform the whole of his office; *aid* is useful when it serves to give strength and efficacy to our operations; *succour* is timely when it serves to ward off some danger; *relief* is salutary when it serves to lessen pain or want. When a person meets with an accident, he requires the *help* of the by-standers, the *assistance* of his friends, and the *aid* of a medical man; it is noble to *succour* an enemy; it is charitable to *relieve* the wretched

TO SECOND, SUPPORT.

To *second* is to give the assistance of a *second* person; to *support* is to bear up on one's own shoulders. To *second* does not express so much as to *support;* we *second* only by our presence, or our word; but we *support* by our influence, and all the means that are in our power: we *second* a motion by a simple declaration of our assent to it; we *support* a motion by the force of persuasion; so likewise we are said always to *second* a person's views when we give him openly our countenance by declaring our approbation of his measures;

The blasting vollied thunder made all speed,
And *seconded* thy else not dreaded spear.—MILTON.

And we are said to *support* him when we give the assistance of our purse, our influence, or any other thing essential for the attainment of an end;

Impeachments NO can best resist,
And AYE *support* the civil list.—GAY.

ABETTOR, ACCESSARY, ACCOMPLICE.

Abettor, or one that abets, gives aid and encouragement by counsel, promises, or rewards. An *accessary*, or one added and annexed, takes an active though subordinate part; an *accomplice*, from the word *accomplish*, implies the principal in any plot, who takes a leading part and brings it to perfection; *abettors* propose, *accessaries* assist, *accomplices* execute. The *abettor* and *accessary*, or the *abettor* and *accomplice*, may be one and the same person; but not so the *accessary* and *accomplice*.

In every grand scheme there must be *abettors* to set it on foot, *accessaries* to co-operate, and *accomplices* to put it into execution. In the gunpowder plot there were many secret *abettors*, some noblemen who were *accessaries*, and Guy Fawkes the principal *accomplice;* 'I speak this with an eye to those cruel treatments which men of all sides are apt to give the characters of those who do not agree with them. How many men of honour are exposed to publick obloquy and reproach? Those therefore who are either the instruments or *abettors* in such infernal dealings ought to be looked upon as persons who make use of religion to support their cause, not their cause to promote religion.'—ADDISON. 'Why are the French obliged to lend us a part of their tongue before we can know they are conquered? They must be made *accessaries* to their own disgrace, as the Britons were formerly so artificially wrought in the curtain of the Roman theatre, that they seemed to draw it up in order to give the spectators an opportunity of seeing their own defeat celebrated on the stage.'—ADDISON.

Either he picks a purse, or robs a house,
Or is *accomplice* with some knavish gang.
CUMBERLAND.

REDRESS, RELIEF.

Redress, like address (*v. Accost*) in all probability comes from the Latin *dirigo*, signifying to direct or bring back to the former point; *relief*, *v. To help*.

Redress is said only with regard to matters of right and justice; *relief* to those of kindness and humanity: by power we obtain *redress;* by active interference we obtain a *relief:* an injured person looks for *redress* to the government; an unfortunate person looks for *relief* to the compassionate and kind: what we suffer through the oppression or wickedness of others can only be *redressed* by those who have the power of dispensing justice; whenever we suffer, in the order of Providence, we may meet with some *relief* from those who are more favoured. *Redress* applies to publick as well as private grievances; 'Instead of *redressing* grievances, and improving the fabrick of their state, the French were made to take a very different course.'—BURKE. *Relief* applies only to private distresses;

This one
Relief the vanquish'd have, to hope for none.
DENHAM

Under a pretence of seeking *redress* of grievances, mobs are frequently assembled to the disturbance of the better disposed; under a pretence of soliciting charitable *relief*, thieves gain admittance into families

TO CURE, HEAL, REMEDY.

Cure, in Latin *curo*, signifies to take care of, that is by distinction, to take care of that which requires particular care, in order to remove an evil; *heal*, in German *heilen*, comes from *heil* whole, signifying to make whole that which is unsound; *remedy*, in Latin *re medium*, is compounded of *re* and *medeor* to *cure* or *heal*, which comes from the Greek *μηδόμαι* and *Μηδία Media*, the country which contained the greatest number of *healing* plants. The particle *re* is here but an intensive.

To *cure* is employed for what is out of order; to *heal* for that which is broken: diseases are *cured*, wounds are *healed;* the former is a complex, the latter is a simple process. Whatever requires to be *cured* is wrong in the system; it requires many and various applications internally and externally;

If the frail body feels disorder'd pangs,
Then drugs medicinal can give us ease;
The soul no Æsculapian medicine can *cure*
GENTLEMAN

Whatever requires to be *healed* is occasioned externally by violence, and requires external applications. In a state of refinement men have the greatest number of disorders to be *cured;* in a savage state there is more occasion for the *healing* art.

Cure is used as properly in the moral as the natural sense; *heal* in the moral sense is altogether figurative. The disorders of the mind are *cured* with greater difficulty than those of the body. The breaches which have been made in the affections of relatives towards each other can be *healed* by nothing but a Christian spirit of forbearance and forgiveness;

Scarcely an ill to human life belongs,
But what our follies cause, or mutual wrongs:
Or if some stripes from Providence we feel,
He strikes with pity, and but wounds to *heal*.
JENYNS.

To *remedy*, in the sense of applying *remedies*, has a moral application, in which it accords most with *cure*. Evils are either *cured* or *remedied*, but the former are of a much more serious nature than the latter. The evils in society require to be *cured;* an omission, a deficiency, or a mischief, requires to be *remedied*.

When bad habits become inveterate they are put out of the reach of *cure*. It is an exercise for the ingenuity of man to attempt to *remedy* the various troubles and inconveniences which are daily occurring; 'Every man has frequent grievances which only the solicitude of friendship will discover and *remedy*'—JOHNSON.

CURE, REMEDY.

Cure (*v. To cure*) denotes either the act of *curing*, or the thing that *cures*. *Remedy* is mostly employed for the thing that *remedies*. In the former sense the *remedy* is to the *cure* as the means to the end; a *cure* is performed by the application of a *remedy*. That is *incurable* for which no *remedy* can be found; but a *cure* is sometimes performed without the application of any specifick *remedy*. The *cure* is complete when the evil is entirely removed; the *remedy* is sure which by proper application never fails of effecting the *cure*. The *cure* of disorders depends upon the skill of the physician and the state of the patient; the efficacy of *remedies* depends upon their suitable choice and application; but a *cure* may be defeated or a *remedy* made of no avail by a variety of circumstances independent of either.

Cure is sometimes employed for the thing that *cures*, but only in the sense of what infallibly *cures*. Quacks always hold forth their nostrums as infallible *cures*, not for one but for every sort of disorder;

Why should he choose these miseries to endure
If death could grant an everlasting *cure?*
'T is plain there 's something whispers in his ear
(Tho' fain he 'd hide it) he has much to fear.
JENYNS

Experience has fatally proved that the *remedy* in most cases where quack medicines are applied is worse than the disease; 'The difference between poisons and *remedies* is easily known by their effects; and common reason soon distinguishes between virtue and vice.'—SWIFT.

HEALTHY, WHOLESOME, SALUBRIOUS, SALUTARY.

Healthy signifies not only having *health*, but also causing *health*, or keeping in *health; wholesome*, like the German *heilsam*, signifies making whole, keeping whole or sound; *salubrious* and *salutary*, from the Latin *salus* safety or *health*, signify likewise contributive to *health* or good in general.

These epithets are all applicable to such objects as have a kindly influence on the bodily constitution: *healthy* is the most general and indefinite; it is applied to exercise, to air, situation, climate, and most other things, but food, for which *wholesome* is commonly substituted: the life of a farmer is reckoned the most *healthy;* 'You are relaxing yourself with the *healthy* and manly exercise of the field.'—SIR WM. JONES. The simplest diet is reckoned the most *wholesome;*

> Here laid his scrip with *wholesome* viands fill'd;
> There, listening every noise, his watchful dog.
> THOMSON.

Healthy and *wholesome* are rather negative in their sense; *salubrious* and *salutary* are positive: that is *healthy* and *wholesome* which serves to keep one in *health;* that is *salubrious* which serves to improve the *health;* and that is *salutary* which serves to remove a disorder: climates are *healthy* or *unhealthy*, according to the constitution of the person; 'Gardening or husbandry, and working in wood, are fit and *healthy* recreations for a man of study or business.'—LOCKE. Water is a *wholesome* beverage for those who are not dropsical; bread is a *wholesome* diet for man; 'False decorations, fucuses, and pigments deserve the imperfections that constantly attend them, being neither commodious in application, nor *wholesome* in their use.'—BACON. The air and climate of southern France has been long famed for its *salubrity*, and has induced many invalids to repair thither for the benefit of their *health;* 'If that fountain (the heart) be once poisoned, you can never expect that *salubrious* streams will flow from it.'—BLAIR. The effects have not been equally *salutary* in all cases: it is the concern of government that the places destined for the publick education of youth should be in *healthy* situations; that their diet should be *wholesome* rather than delicate; and that in all their disorders care should be taken to administer the most *salutary* remedies.

Wholesome and *salutary* have likewise an extended and moral application; *healthy* and *salubrious* are employed only in the proper sense: *wholesome* in this case seems to convey the idea of making whole again what has been unsound; 'So the doctrine contained be but *wholesome* and edifying, a want of exactness in speaking may be overlooked.'—ATTERBURY. But *salutary* retains the idea of improving the condition of those who stand in need of improvement; 'A sense of the Divine presence exerts this *salutary* influence of promoting temperance and restraining the disorders incident to a prosperous state.'—BLAIR. Correction is *wholesome* which serves the purpose of amendment without doing any injury to the body; instruction or admonition is *salutary* when it serves the purpose of strengthening good principles and awakening a sense of guilt or impropriety: laws and punishments are *wholesome* to the body politick, as diet is to the physical body; restrictions are *salutary* in checking irregularities.

SAFE, SECURE.

Safe, in Latin *salvus*, comes from the Hebrew שלה to be tranquil; *secure*, *v. Certain.*

Safety implies exemption from harm, or the danger of harm; *secure*, the exemption from danger; a person may be *safe* or saved in the midst of a fire, if he be untouched by the fire; but he is, in such a case, the reverse of *secure*. In the sense of exemption from danger, *safety* expresses much less than *security:* we may be *safe* without using any particular measures; but none can reckon on any degree of *security* without great precaution: a person may be very *safe* on the top of a coach in the daytime; but if he wish to *secure* himself, at night, from falling off, he must be fastened; 'It cannot be *safe* for any man to walk upon a precipice, and to be always on the very border of destruction.'—SOUTH. 'No man can rationally account himself *secure* unless he could command all the chances of the world.'—SOUTH.

CERTAIN, SURE, SECURE.

Certain, in French *certain*, Latin *certus*, comes from *cerno* to perceive, because what we see or perceive is supposed to be put beyond doubt; *sure* and *secure* are variations of the same word, in French *sur*, German *sicher*, Low German *seker*, &c., Latin *securus*, this is compounded of *se* (*sine*) apart, and *cura*, signifying without care, requiring no care.

Certain respects matters of fact or belief; *sure* and *secure* the quality or condition of things. A fact is *certain*, a person's step is *sure*, a house is *secure*. *Certain* is opposed to dubious, *sure* to wavering, *secure* to dangerous. A person is *certain* who has no doubt remaining in his mind; 'It is very *certain* that a man of sound reason cannot forbear closing with religion upon an impartial examination of it.'—ADDISON. A person is *sure* whose conviction is steady and unchangeable; 'When these everlasting doors are thrown open, we may be *sure* that the pleasures and beauties of this place will infinitely transcend our present hopes and expectations, and that the glorious appearance of the throne of God will rise infinitely beyond whatever we are able to conceive of it.'—ADDISON. A person feels himself *secure* when the prospect of danger is removed;

> Weigh well the various terms of human fate,
> And seek by mercy to *secure* your state.
> DRYDEN.

When applied to things, *certain* is opposed to what is varying and irregular; *sure* to what is unerring; *secure* is used only in its natural sense. It is a defect in the English language, that there are at present no *certain* rules for its orthography or pronunciation; the learner, therefore, is at a loss for a *sure* guide. Amid opposing statements it is difficult to *ascertain* the real state of the case. No one can *ensure* his life for a moment, or *secure* his property from the contingencies to which all sublunary things are exposed.

SOUND, SANE, HEALTHY.

Sound and *sane*, in Latin *sanus*, come probably from *sanguis* the blood, because in that lies the seat of health or sickness; *healthy* signifies here the state of being in health.

Sound is extended in its application to all things that are in the state in which they ought to be, so as to preserve their vitality; thus, animals and vegetables are said to be *sound* when in the former there is nothing amiss in their limbs or vital parts, and in the latter in their root. By a figurative application, wood and other things may be said to be *sound* when they are entirely free from any symptom of decay, or mixture of corruption; in this sense the heart is said to be *sound;* 'He hath a heart as *sound* as a bell, and his tongue is the clapper, for what his heart thinks, his tongue speaks.'—SHAKSPEARE. *Sane* is applicable to human beings, in the same sense, but with reference to the mind; a *sane* person is opposed to one that is insane;

> How pregnant, sometimes, his replies are!
> A happiness that often madness hits on,
> Which *sanity* and reason could not be
> So prosperously delivered of.—SHAKSPEARE.

The mind is also said to be *sound* when it is in a state to form right opinions;

> But Capys, and the rest of *sounder* mind,
> The fatal present to the flames design'd.
> DRYDEN.

Healthy expresses more than either *sound* or *sane;* we are *healthy* in every part, but we are *sound* in that which is essential for life; he who is *sound* may live, but he who is *healthy* enjoys life; 'But the course of succession (to the crown) is the *healthy* habit of the British constitution.'—BURKE.

DISORDER, DISEASE, DISTEMPER, MALADY.

Disorder signifies the state of being out of order; *disease*, the state of being ill at ease; *distemper*, the state of being out of temper, or out of a due temperament; *malady*, from the Latin *malus* evil, signifies an ill.

All these terms agree in their application to the state of the animal body. *Disorder* is, as before (*v. To disorder*), the general term, and the others specifick. In this general sense *disorder* is altogether indefinite; but in its restricted sense it expresses less than all the rest: it is the mere commencement of a *disease*: *disease* is also more general than the other terms, for it comprehends every serious and permanent *disorder* in the animal economy, and is therefore of universal application. The *disorder* is slight, partial, and transitory: the *disease* is deep-rooted and permanent. The *disorder* may lie in the extremities: the *disease* lies in the humours and the vital parts. Occasional headaches, colds, or what is merely cutaneous, are termed *disorders*; fevers, dropsies, and the like, are *diseases*. *Distemper* is used for such particularly as throw the animal frame most completely out of its temper or course, and is consequently applied properly to virulent *disorders*, such as the small-pox. *Malady* has less of a technical sense than the other terms; it refers more to the suffering than to the state of the body. There may be many *maladies* where there is no *disease*; but *diseases* are themselves in general *maladies*. Our *maladies* are frequently born with us; but our *diseases* may come upon us at any time of life. Blindness is in itself a *malady*, and may be produced by a *disease* in the eye. Our *disorders* are frequently cured by abstaining from those things which caused them; the whole science of medicine consists in finding out suitable remedies for our *diseases*; our *maladies* may be lessened with patience, although they cannot always be alleviated or removed by art.

All these terms may be applied with a similar distinction to the mind as well as the body. The *disorders* are either of a temporary or a permanent nature; but unless specified to the contrary, are understood to be temporary; 'Strange *disorders* are bred in the mind of those men whose passions are not regulated by virtue.'—ADDISON. *Diseases* consist in vicious habits; 'The jealous man's *disease* is of so malignant a nature that it converts all it takes into its own nourishment.'—ADDISON. Our *distempers* arise from the violent operations of passion; 'A person that is crazed, though with pride or malice, is a sight very mortifying to human nature; but when the *distemper* arises from any indiscreet fervours of devotion, it deserves our compassion in a more particular manner.'—ADDISON. Our *maladies* lie in the injuries which the affections occasion; 'Phillips has been always praised without contradiction as a man modest, blameless, and pious, who bore narrowness of fortune without discontent, and tedious and painful *maladies* without impatience.'—JOHNSON. Any perturbation in the mind is a *disorder*: avarice is a *disease*: melancholy is a *distemper* as far as it throws the mind out of its bias; it is a *malady* as far as it occasions suffering.

SICK, SICKLY, DISEASED, MORBID.

Sick denotes a partial state; *sickly* a permanent state of the body, a proneness to be *sick*: he who is *sick* may be made well; but he who is *sickly* is seldom really well: all persons are liable to be *sick*, though few have the misfortune to be *sickly*: a person may be *sick* from the effect of cold, violent exercise, and the like; 'For aught I see, they are as *sick* that surfeit with too much, as they that starve with nothing.'—SHAKSPEARE. A person is *sickly* only from constitution; 'Both Homer and Virgil were of a very delicate and *sickly* constitution.'—WALSH.

Sickly expresses a permanent state of indisposition; but *diseased* expresses a violent state of derangement without specifying its duration; it may be for a time only, or for a permanency: the person, or his constitution, is *sickly*; the person, or his frame, or particular parts, as his lungs, his inside, his brain, and the like, may be *diseased*:

> We are all *diseased*,
> And with our surfeiting and wanton hours
> Have brought ourselves into a burning fever.
> SHAKSPEARE.

Sick, *sickly*, and *diseased* may all be used in a moral application; *morbid* is rarely used in any other except in a technical sense. *Sick* denotes a partial state, as before, namely, a state of disgust, and is always associated with the object of the *sickness*; we are *sick* of, turbulent enjoyments, and seek for tranquillity: *sickly* and *morbid* are applied to the habitual state of the feelings or character; a *sickly* sentimentality, a *morbid* sensibility; 'While the distempers of a relaxed fibre prognosticate all the *morbid* force of convulsion in the body of the state, the steadiness of the physician is overpowered by the very aspect of the *disease*.'—BURKE. *Diseased* is applied in general to individuals or communities, to persons or to things; a person's mind is in a *diseased* state when it is under the influence of corrupt passions of principles; society is in a *diseased* state when it is overgrown with wealth and luxury; 'For a mind *diseased* with vain longings after unattainable advantages, no medicine can be prescribed.'—JOHNSON.

SICKNESS, ILLNESS, INDISPOSITION.

Sickness denotes the state of being *sick* (*v. Sick*); *illness* that of being *ill* (*v. Evil*); *indisposition* that of being not well disposed. *Sickness* denotes the state generally or particularly: *illness* denotes it particularly: we speak of *sickness* as opposed to good health; in *sickness* or in health; but of the *illness* of a particular person: when *sickness* is said of the individual, it designates a protracted state; a person may be said to have much *sickness* in his family; '*Sickness* is a sort of early old age; it teaches us a diffidence in our earthly state.'—POPE. *Illness* denotes only a particular or partial *sickness*: a person is said to have had an *illness* at this or that time, in this or that place, for this or that period; 'This is the first letter that I have ventured upon, which will be written, I fear vacillantibus literis; as Tully says Tyro's Letters were after his recovery from an *illness*.'—ATTERBURY *Indisposition* is a slight *illness*, such a one as is capable of deranging a person either in his enjoyments or in his business; colds are the ordinary causes of *indisposition*; 'It is not, as you conceive, an *indisposition* of body, but the mind's disease.'—FORD.

INVALID, PATIENT.

Invalid, in Latin *invalidus*, signifies literally one not strong or in good health; *patient*, from the Latin *patiens* suffering, signifies one suffering under disease. *Invalid* is a general, and *patient* a particular term: a person may be an *invalid* without being a *patient*: he may be a *patient* without being an *invalid*. An *invalid* is so denominated from his wanting his ordinary share of health and strength; but the *patient* is one who is labouring under some bodily suffering. Old soldiers are called *invalids* who are no longer able to bear the fatigues of warfare: but they are not necessarily *patients*. He who is under the surgeon's hands for a broken limb is a *patient*, but not necessarily an *invalid*.

DEBILITY, INFIRMITY, IMBECILITY.

Debility, in Latin *debilitas*, from *debilis*, or *de* privative and *habilis*, signifies a deficiency, or not having; *infirmity*, in Latin *infirmitas*, from *infirmus*, or *in* privative and *firmus* strong, signifies the absence of strength; *imbecility*, in Latin *imbecilitas* from *imbecillis*, or *in* privative, and *becillis*, *bacillum*, or *baculus* a staff, signifies not having a staff or support.

All these terms denote a species of weakness, but the two former, particularly the first, respects that which is physical, and the latter that which is either physical or mental. *Debility* is constitutional, or otherwise; *imbecility* is always constitutional; *infirmity* is accidental, and results from sickness, or a decay of the frame. *Debility* may be either general or local; *infirmity* is always local; *imbecility* always general. *Debility* prevents the active performance of the ordinary functions of nature; it is a deficiency in the muscular power of the body: *infirmity* is a partial want of power, which interferes with, but does not necessarily destroy, the activity: *imbecility* lies in the whole frame, and renders it almost entirely powerless.

Young people are frequently troubled with *debilities* in their ankles or legs, of which they are never cured. 'As increasing years *debilitate* the body, so they weaken the force and diminish the warmth of the affections.'—BLAIR. Old age is most exposed to *infirmities;* but there is no age at which human beings are exempt from *infirmity* of some kind or another; 'This is weakness, not wisdom, I own, and on that account fitter to be trusted to the bosom of a friend, where I may safely lodge all my *infirmities.*'—ATTERBURY. The *imbecility* natural to youth, both in body and mind, would make them willing to rest on the strength of their elders, if they were not too often misled by a mischievous confidence in their own strength; 'It is seldom that we are otherwise than by affliction awakened to a sense of our *imbecility.*'—JOHNSON.

DECAY, DECLINE, CONSUMPTION.

Decay, French *dechoir*, from the Latin *decado*, signifies literally to fall off or away; *decline*, from the Latin *declino*, or *de* and *clino*, signifies to turn away or lean aside; the direction expressed by both these actions is very similar; it is a sideward movement, but *decay* expresses more than *decline*. What is *decayed* is fallen or gone; what *declines* leans towards a fall, or is going; when applied, therefore, to the same objects, a *decline* is properly the commencement of a *decay*. The health may experience a *decline* at any period of life from a variety of causes, but it naturally experiences a *decay* in old age; *consumption* (*v. To consume*) implies a rapid decay.

* By *decay* things lose their perfection, their greatness, and their consistency; by *decline* they lose their strength, their vigour, and their lustre; by *consumption* they lose their existence. *Decay* brings to ruin; *decline* leads to an end or expiration. There are some things to which *decay* is peculiar, and some things to which *decline* is peculiar, and other things to which both *decay* and *decline* belong. The corruption to which material substances are particularly exposed is termed *decay:* the close of life, when health and strength begin to fall away, is termed the *decline;* the *decay* of states in the moral world takes place by the same process as the *decay* of fabricks in the natural world; the *decline* of empires, from their state of elevation and splendour, is a natural figure drawn from the *decline* of the setting sun. *Consumption* is seldom applied to any thing but animal bodies;

> The seas shall waste, the skies in smoke *decay*,
> Rocks fall to dust, and mountains melt away;
> But fix'd his word, his saving power remains,
> Thy realm for ever lasts, thy own Messiah reigns.
> POPE.

After the death of Julius and Augustus Cæsar the Roman empire *declined* every day.'—SOUTH. 'By degrees the empire shrivelled and pined away; and from such a surfeit of immoderate prosperity passed at length into a final *consumption.*'—SOUTH.

WEAK, FEEBLE, INFIRM.

Weak, in Saxon *wace*, Dutch *wack*, German *schwach*, is in all probability an intensive of *weich* soft, which comes from *weichen* to yield, and this from *bewegen* to move; *feeble* is probably contracted from *failable; infirm*, *v. Debility.*

The Saxon term *weak* is here, as it usually is, the familiar and universal term; *feeble* is suited to a more polished style; *infirm* is only a species of the *weak:* we may be *weak* in body or mind; but we are commonly *feeble* and *infirm* only in the body: we may be *weak* from disease, or *weak* by nature, it equally conveys the gross idea of a defect; but the terms *feeble* and *infirm* are qualified expressions for *weakness:* a child is *feeble* from its infancy; an old man is *feeble* from age; the latter may likewise be *infirm* in consequence of sickness. We pity the *weak*, but their *weakness* often gives us pain;

> You, gallant Vernon! saw
> The miserable scene; you pitying saw
> To infant *weakness* sunk the warriour's arm.
> THOMSON.

We assist the *feeble* when they attempt to walk;

> Command th' assistance of a friend,
> But *feeble* are the succours I can send.—DRYDEN.

We support the *infirm* when they are unable to stand; 'At my age, and under my *infirmities*, I can have no relief but those with which religion furnishes me.'—ATTERBURY. The same distinction exists between *weak* and *feeble* in the moral use of the words: a *weak* attempt to excuse a person conveys a reproachful meaning; but the efforts which we make to defend an other may be praiseworthy, although *feeble*.

TO WEAKEN, ENFEEBLE, DEBILITATE, ENERVATE, INVALIDATE.

To *weaken* is to make *weak* (*v. Weak*), and is, as before, the generick term: to *enfeeble* is to make *feeble* (*v. Weak*); to *debilitate* is to cause *debility* (*v. Debility*); to *enervate* is to *unnerve;* and to *invalidate* is to make not valid or strong: all of which are but modes of *weakening* applicable to different objects. To *weaken* may be either a temporary or permanent act when applied to persons; *enfeeble* is permanent either as to the body or the mind: we may be *weakened* suddenly by severe pain; we are *enfeebled* in a gradual manner, either by the slow effects of disease or age. To *weaken* is either a particular or a complete act; to *enfeeble*, to *debilitate*, and *enervate* are properly partial acts: what *enfeebles* deprives of vital or essential power;

> So much hath hell debas'd, and pain
> *Enfeebled* me, to what I was in heav'n.—MILTON.

What *debilitates* may lessen power in one particular, though not in another; the severe exercise of any power, such as the memory or the attention, will tend to *debilitate* that faculty;

> Sometimes the body in full strength we find,
> While various ails *debilitate* the mind.—JENYNS

What *enervates* acts particularly on the nervous system; it relaxes the frame, and unfits the person for action either of body or mind; 'Elevated by success and *enervated* by luxury, the military, in the time of the emperors, soon became incapable of fatigue.'—GIBBON. To *weaken* is said of things as well as persons; to *invalidate* is said of things only: we *weaken* the force of an argument by an injudicious application; 'No article of faith can be true which *weakens* the practical part of religion.'—ADDISON. We *invalidate* the claim of another by proving its informality in law. 'Do they (the Jacobins) mean to *invalidate* that great body of our statute law, which passed under those whom they treat as usurpers?'—BURKE.

TO FLAG, DROOP, LANGUISH, PINE.

To *flag* is to hang down loose like a *flag; droop*, *v. To fall;* to *languish* is to become or continue languid (*v. Faint*); to *pine*, from the German *pein* pain, is to be or continue in pain.

In the proper application, nothing *flags* but that which can be distended and made to flutter by the wind, as the leaves of plants when they are in want of water or in a weakly condition; hence figuratively the spirits are said to *flag;* 'It is variety which keeps alive desire, which would otherwise *flag.*'—SOUTH. Things are said to *droop* when their heads *flag* or drop; the snowdrop *droops*, and flowers will generally *droop* from excess of drought or heat: the spirits in the same manner are said to *droop*, which expresses more than to *flag;* the human body also *droops* when the strength fails;

> Shrunk with dry famine, and with toils declin'd,
> The *drooping* body will desert the mind.—POPE.

Languish is a still stronger expression than *droop*, and is applicable principally to persons; some *languish* in sickness, some in prison, and some in a state of distress; 'How finely has the poet told us that the sick persons *languished* under lingering and incurable distempers.'—ADDISON. To *pine* is to be in a state of wearing pain which is mostly of a mental nature: a

* Vide Trusler: "Decay, decline, disease."

nild may *pine* when absent from all its friends, and opposing itself deserted;

From beds of raging fire to starve in ice
Their soft ethereal warmth, there to *pine*,
Immoveably infix'd.—MILTON.

FAINT, LANGUID.

Faint, from the French *faner* to fade, signifies that which is faded or withered, which has lost its spirit; *languid*, in Latin *languidus*, from *langueo* to languish, signifies languished.

Faint is less than *languid; faintness* is in fact in the physical application the commencement of *languor;* we may be *faint* for a short time, and if continued and extended through the limbs it becomes *languor;* thus we say to speak with a *faint* tone, and have a *languid* frame; and in the figurative application to make a *faint* resistance, to move with a *languid* air; to form a *faint* idea, to make a *languid* effort;

Low the woods
Bow their hoar head: and here the *languid* sun,
Faint from the west, emits his evening ray.
THOMSON.

PALE, PALLID, WAN.

Pale, in French *pale*, and *pallid*, in Latin *pallidus*, both come from *palleo* to turn *pale*, which probably comes from the Greek παλλύνω to make white, and that from πάλη flour; *wan* is connected with *want* and *wane*, signifying in general a deficiency or a losing colour.

Pallid rises upon *pale*, and *wan* upon *pallid:* the absence of colour in any degree, where colour is a requisite or usual quality, constitutes *paleness*, but *pallidness* is an excess of *paleness*, and *wan* is an unusual degree of *pallidness: paleness* in the countenance may be temporary; but *pallidness* and *wanness* are permanent; fear, or any sudden emotion, may produce *paleness:* but protracted sickness, hunger, and fatigue bring on *pallidness;* and when these calamities are combined and heightened by every aggravation, they may produce that which is peculiarly termed *wanness*.

Pale is an ordinary term for an ordinary quality, applicable to many very different objects, to persons, colours, lights, and luminaries. *Paleness* may be either a natural or an acquired deficiency: a person is said to be *pale*, a colour *pale*, a light pale, the sun *pale;* the deficiency may be desirable or otherwise; the *paleness* of the moon is agreeable, that of the complexion the contrary:

Now morn, her lamp *pale* glimmering on the sight,
Scatter'd before her sun reluctant night.
FALCONER.

Pallid is an ordinary term for an extraordinary quality: nothing is said to be *pallid* but the human face, and that not from the ordinary course of nature, but as the effect of disease; those who paint are most apt to look *pallid;*

Her spirits faint,
Her cheeks assume a *pallid* tint.—ADDISON.

Wan is an extraordinary term for an ordinary property, it is applicable only to ghostly objects, or such as are rendered monstrous by unusually powerful causes: the effects of death on the human visage are fully expressed by the term *wan*, when applied to an individual who is reduced, by severe abstinence or sickness, to a state bordering on the grave;

And with them comes a third with regal pomp,
But faded splendour *wan*.—MILTON.

FATIGUE, WEARINESS, LASSITUDE.

Fatigue, from the Latin *fatigo*, that is, *fatim* abundantly or powerfully, and *ago* to act, or *agito* to agitate, designates an effect from a powerful or stimulating cause; *weariness*, from *weary*, a frequentative of *wear*, marks an effect from a continued or repeated cause; *lassitude*, from the Latin *lassus*, changed from *laxus* relaxed, marks a state without specifying a cause.

Fatigue is an exhaustion of the animal or mental powers; *weariness* is a wearing out of the strength, or breaking the spirits; *lassitude* is a general relaxation of the animal frame. The labourer experiences *fatigue* from the toils of the day; the man of business, who is harassed by the multiplicity and complexity of his concerns, suffers *fatigue;* and the student, who labours to fit himself for a publick exhibition of his acquirements is in like manner exposed to *fatigue;* 'One of the amusements of idleness is reading without the *fatigue* of close attention.'—JOHNSON. *Weariness* attends the traveller who takes a long or pathless journey; *weariness* is the lot of the petitioner, who attends in the anti chamber of a great man; the critic is doomed to suffer *weariness*, who is obliged to drag through the shallow but voluminous writings of a dull author; and the en lightened hearer will suffer no less *weariness* in listening to the absurd effusions of an extemporaneous preacher; 'For want of a process of events, neither knowledge nor elegance preserves the reader from *weariness*.'—JOHNSON.

Lassitude is the consequence of a distempered system, sometimes brought on by an excess of *fatigue*, sometimes by sickness, and frequently by the action of the external air; 'The cattle in the fields show evident symptoms of *lassitude* and disgust in an unpleasant season.'—COWPER.

TO WEARY, TIRE, JADE, HARASS.

To *weary* is a frequentative of *wear*, that is, to *wear* out the strength; to *tire*, from the French *tirer*, and the Latin *traho* to draw, signifies to *draw* out the strength; to *jade* is the same as to *goad;* to *harass*, *v. Distress*.

Long exertion *wearies;* a little exertion will *tire* a child or a weak man; forced exertions *jade;* painful exertions, or exertions coupled with painful circumstances, *harass:* the horse is *jaded* which is forced on beyond his strength; the soldier is *harassed* who marches in perpetual fear of an attack from the enemy We are *wearied* with thinking when it gives us pain to think any longer; 'All pleasures that affect the body must needs *weary*.'—SOUTH. We are *tired* of our employment when it ceases to give us pleasure; 'Every meal is to a satisfied hunger is only a new labour to a *tired* digestion.'—SOUTH. We are *jaded* by incessant attention to business; 'I recall the time (and am glad it is over) when about this hour (six in the morning) I used to be going to bed surfeited with pleasure, or *jaded* with business.'—BOLINGBROKE. We are *harassed* by perpetual complaints which we cannot redress;

Bankrupt nobility, a factious, giddy, and
Divided Senate, *harass'd* commonalty,
Is all the strength of Venice.—OTWAY.

WEARISOME, TIRESOME, TEDIOUS.

Wearisome (*v. To weary*) is the general and indefinite term; *tiresome*, *v. To weary;* and *tedious*, causing *tedium*, a specifick form of *wearisomeness:* common things may cause *weariness;* that which acts painfully is either *tiresome* or *tedious;* but in different degrees the repetition of the same sounds will grow *tiresome;* long waiting in anxious suspense is *tedious:* there is more of that which is physical in the *tiresome*, and mental in the *tedious;* 'All weariness presupposes weakness, and consequently every long, importune, *wearisome* petition, is truly and properly a force upon him that is pursued with it.'—SOUTH.

Far happier were the meanest peasant's lot,
Than to be plac'd on high, in anxious pride,
The purple drudge and slave of *tiresome* state.
WEST

Happy the mortal man who now, at last,
Has through this doleful vale of mis ry pass'd,
Who to his destin'd stage has carried on
The *tedious* load, and laid his burden down.
PRIOR

WEIGHT, HEAVINESS, GRAVITY.

Weight, from to *weigh*, is that which a thing *weighs; heaviness*, from *heavy* and *heave*, signifies the abstract quality of the *heavy*, or difficult to heave·

gravity, from the Latin *gravis*, likewise denotes the same abstract qualities.

Weight is indefinite; whatever may be *weighed* has a *weight*, whether large or small: *heaviness* and *gravity* are the property of bodies having a great *weight*. *Weight* is only opposed to that which has or is supposed to have no *weight*, that is, what is incorporeal or immaterial: for we may speak of the *weight* of the lightest conceivable bodies, as the *weight* of a feather: *heaviness* is opposed to lightness; the *heaviness* of lead is opposed to the lightness of a feather.

Weight lies absolutely in the thing; *heaviness* is relatively considered with respect to the person: we estimate the *weight* of things according to a certain measure: we estimate the *heaviness* of things by our feelings.

Gravity is that species of *weight*, which is scientifically considered as inherent in certain bodies; the term is therefore properly scientifick.

WEIGHT, BURDEN, LOAD.

Weight, v. *Weight; burden*, from *bear*, signifies the thing borne; *load*, in German *laden*, is supposed by Adelung to admit of a derivation from different sources; but he does not suppose that which appears to me the most natural, namely, from *lay*, which becomes in our preterit *laid*, particularly since in Low German and Dutch *laden*, to *load*, is contracted into *laeyen*, and the literal meaning of *load* is to lay on or in any thing.

The term *weight* is here considered in common with the other terms, in the sense of a positive *weight*, as respects the persons or things by which it is allied to the word *burden:* the *weight* is said either of persons or things; the *burden* more commonly respects persons; the *load* may be said of either: a person may sink under the *weight* that rests upon him; a platform may break down from the *weight* upon it; a person sinks under his *burden* or *load;* a cart breaks down from the *load*. The *weight* is abstractedly taken for what is without reference to the cause of its being there; *burden* and *load* have respect to the person or thing by which they are produced; accident produces the *weight;* a person takes a *burden* upon himself, or has it imposed upon him; the *load* is always laid on; it is not proper to carry any *weight* that exceeds our strength; those who bear the *burden* expect to reap the fruit of their labour; he who carries *loads* must be contented to take such as are given him.

In the moral application, these terms mark the pain which is produced by a pressure; but the *weight* and *load* rather describe the positive severity of the pressure: the *burden* respects the temper and inclinations of the sufferer; the *load* is in this case a very great *weight:* a minister of state has a *weight* on his mind at all times, from the heavy responsibility which attaches to his station; 'With what oppressive *weight* will sickness, disappointment, or old age fall upon the spirits of that man who is a stranger to God!'—BLAIR. One who labours under strong apprehensions or dread of an evil has a *load* on his mind; 'How a man can have a quiet and cheerful mind under a *burden* and *load* of guilt, I know not, unless he be very ignorant.'—RAY. Any sort of employment is a *burden* to one who wishes to be idle; and time unemployed is a *burden* to him who wishes to be always in action;

I understood not that a grateful mind
By owing owes not, but still pays at once;
Indebted and discharg'd: what *burden* then?
MILTON.

HEAVY, BURDENSOME, WEIGHTY, PONDEROUS.

Heavy, from *heave*, signifies the causing to heave, or requiring to be lifted up with force; *burdensome*, having a *burden; weighty* and *ponderous*, from the Latin *pondus* a weight, both signify having a *weight*.

Heaviness is the natural property of some bodies: *burdensomeness* is incidental to others. In the vulgar sense, things are termed *heavy* which are found difficult to lift, in distinction from those which are light or easy to be lifted; but those things are *burdensome* which are too troublesome to be carried or borne: many things therefore are actually *heavy* that are never *burdensome;* and others are occasionally *burdensome* that are never *heavy:* that which is *heavy* is so whether lifted or not, but that which is *burdensome* must be *burdensome* to some one; 'Though philosophy teaches, that no element is *heavy* in its own place, yet experience shows that out of its own place it proves exceeding *burdensome*.'—SOUTH. Hard substances are mostly *heavy;* but to a weak person the softest substance may sometimes be *burdensome* if he is obliged to bear it. things are *heavy* according to the difficulty with which they are lifted; but they are *weighty* according as they *weigh* other things down. The *heavy* is therefore indefinite; but the *weighty* is definite, and something positively great: what is *heavy* to one may be light to another; but that which is *weighty* exceeds the ordinary weight of other things;

The sable troops along the narrow tracks
Scarce bear the *weighty* burden on their backs.
DRYDEN.

Ponderous expresses even more than *weighty*, for it includes also the idea of bulk; the *ponderous* therefore is that which is so *weighty* and large that it cannot easily be moved; 'The diligence of an idler is rapid and impetuous, as *ponderous* bodies forced into velocity move with violence proportionate to their weight.'—JOHNSON.

TO CLOG, LOAD, ENCUMBER.

Clog is probably changed from *clot* or *clod*, signifying to put a heavy lump in the way; *load*, from to *load*, in Saxon *laden*, Dutch, &c. *laden*, signifies to burden with a *load*, or lay any thing on so as to form a load; *encumber*, compounded of *en* or *in* and *cumber*, in German *kummer*, sorrow, signifies to burden with trouble.

Clog is figuratively employed for whatever impedes the motion or action of a thing, drawn from the familiar object which is used to impede the motion of animals: *load* is used for whatever occasions an excess of weight or materials. A wheel is *clogged*, or a machine is *clogged:* a fire may be *loaded* with coals, or a picture with colouring. The stomach and memory may be either *clogged* or *loaded:* in the former case by the introduction of improper food; and in the second case by the introduction of an improper quantity. A memory that is *clogged* becomes confused, and confounds one thing with another; that which is *loaded* loses the impression of one object by the introduction of another; 'Butler gives Hudibras that pedantick ostentation of knowledge, which has no relation to chivalry, and *loads* him with martial *encumbrances* that can add nothing to his civil dignity.'—JOHNSON.

Clog and *encumber* have the common signification of interrupting or troubling by means of something irrelevant. Whatever is *clogged* has scarcely the liberty of moving at all; whatever is *encumbered* moves and acts, but with difficulty. When the roots of plants are *clogged* with mould, or any improper substance, their growth is almost stopped: weeds and noxious plants are *encumbrances* in the ground where flowers should grow: the commands or prohibition of parents sometimes very fortunately *clog* those whose sanguine tempers would lead them into imprudence; 'Whatsoever was observed by the ancient philosophers, either irregular or defective in the workings of the mind, was all charged upon the body as its great *clog*.'—SOUTH. No one can expect to proceed with ease to himself in any transaction, who is *encumbered* with a variety of concerns at the same time; 'This minority is great and formidable. I do not know whether, if I aimed at the total overthrow of a kingdom. I should wish to be *encumbered* with a large body of partizans.'—BURKE.

TO POISE, BALANCE.

Poise, in French *peser*, probably comes from *pes* a foot, on which the body is as it were *poised; balance* in French *balancer*, comes from the Latin *bilanx*, or *bis* and *lanx*, a pair of scales.

The idea of bringing into an equilibrium is common to both terms; but *poise* is a particular, and *balance* a more general term: a thing is *poised* as respect itself; it is *balanced* as respects other things *poises* a plain stick in his hand when he wants it to lie even; he *balances* the stick if it has a particular weight at each end: a person may *poise* himself, but he *balances* others: when not on firm ground, it is necessary to *poise* oneself; when two persons are situated one at each end of a beam, they may *balance* one another. These terms preserve the same distinction in a figurative acceptation;

Some evil, terrible and unforeseen,
Must sure ensue, to *poise* the scale against
This vast profusion of exceeding pleasure.—Rowe.

This, O! this very moment let me die,
While hopes and fears in equal *balance* lie.
Dryden.

TO PERISH, DIE, DECAY.

Perish, in French *perir*, in Latin *pereo*, compounded of *per* and *eo*, signifies to go thoroughly away; *die*, *v.* *To die;* and *decay*, *v. To decay.*

To *perish* expresses more than to *die*, and is applicable to many objects; for the latter is properly applied only to express the extinction of animal life, and figuratively to express the extinction of life or spirit in vegetables or other bodies; but the former is applied to express the dissolution of substances, so that they lose their existence as aggregate bodies. What *perishes*, therefore, does not always *die*, although whatever *dies*, by that very act *perishes* to a certain extent. Hence we say that wood *perishes*, although it does not *die;* people are said either to *perish* or *die:* but as the term *perish* expresses even more than *dying*, it is possible for the same thing to *die* and not *perish;* thus a plant may be said to *die* when it loses its vegetative power; but it is said to *perish* if its substance crumbles into dust.

To *perish* expresses the end; to *decay*, the process by which this end is brought about: a thing may be long in *decaying*, but when it *perishes* it ceases at once to act or to exist: things may, therefore, *perish* without *decaying;* they may likewise *decay* without *perishing*. Things may *perish* by means of water, fire, lightning, and the like, which are altogether new, and have experienced no kind of *decay:* on the other hand, wood, iron, and other substances may begin to *decay*, but may be saved from immediately *perishing* by the application of preventives.

In a moral or extended application of the terms they preserve a similar distinction: to *die* signifies simply to fall away; thus, thoughts may *die* in one's breast which never return, or power may *die* with the possessor; 'Whatever pleasure any man may take in spreading whispers, he will find greater satisfaction in letting the secret *die* within his own breast.'—Spectator. With *perish* is always associated the manner and degree of the extinction, namely, that it is complete, and effected for the most part by violence;

Beauty and youth about to *perish* finds
Such noble pity in brave English minds.—Waller.

Decay is figuratively employed in the sense of gradually sinking into a state of non-existence;

The soul's dark cottage, batter'd and *decay'd*,
Lets in new light through chinks that time has made.
Waller.

TO DIE, EXPIRE.

Die, in Low German *doen*, Danish *doe*, from the Greek θύειν to kill, designates in general the extinction of being, which may be considered either as gradual or otherwise; 'She *died* every day she lived.'—Rowe. *Expire*, from the Latin *e* or *ex* and *spiro* to breathe out, designates the last action of life in certain objects, and is of course a momentary act; 'Pope *died* in the evening of the thirtieth day of May, 1744, so placidly, that the attendants did not discern the exact time of his *expiration*.'—Johnson.

* There are beings, such as trees and plants, which are said to live, although they have not breath; these *die*, but do not *expire:* there are other beings which absorb and emit air, but do not live; such as the flame of a lamp, which does not *die*, but it *expires*. By a natural metaphor, the time of being is put for the life of objects; and hence we speak of the date *expiring*, the term *expiring*, and the like; 'A parliament may *expire* by length of time.'—Blackstone. As life is applied figuratively to moral objects, so may *death* to objects not having physical life; 'A dissolution is the civil *death* of parliament.'—Blackstone. 'When Alexander the Great *died*, the Grecian monarchy *expired* with him.'—South.

* Vide Trusler: "Die, expire."

DEATH, DEPARTURE, DECEASE, DEMISE.

Death signifies the act of *dying;* *departure*, the act of *departing;* *decease*, from the Latin *decedo* to fall off, the act of falling away; *demise*, from *demitto* to lay down, signifies literally resigning possession.

Death is a general or a particular term; it marks in the abstract sense the extinction of life, and is applicable to men or animals; to one or many. *Departure*, *decease*, and *demise* are particular expressions suited only to the condition of human beings. * *Departure* is a Christian term, which carries with it an idea of a passage from one life to another; *decease* is a technical term in law, which is introduced into common language to designate one's falling off from the number of the living; *demise* is substituted for *decease* in speaking of princes, who by their *death* also put on their earthly power; 'So tender is the law of supposing even a possibility of the king's *death*, that his natural dissolution is generally called his *demise*'—Blackstone.

Death of itself has always something terrifick in it; but the Gospel has divested it of its terrours: the hour of *departure*, therefore, for a Christian is often the happiest period of his mortal existence; 'How quickly would the honours of illustrious men perish after *death*, if their souls performed nothing to preserve their fame.'—Hughes (*after Xenophon*). *Decease* presents only the idea of leaving life to the survivors. Of *death* it has been said, that nothing is more certain than that it will come, and nothing more uncertain than when it will come. Knowing that we have here no resting place of abode, it is the part of wisdom to look forward to our *departure;* 'The loss of our friends impresses upon us hourly the necessity of our own *departure*.' Johnson. Property is in perpetual occupancy; at the *decease* of one possessor, it passes into the hands of another; 'Though men see every day people go to their long home, they are not so apt to be alarmed at that, as at the *decease* of those who have lived longer in their sight.'—Steele.

The *death* of an individual is sometimes attended with circumstances peculiarly distressing to those who are nearly related. The tears which are shed at the *departure* of those we love are not always indications of our weakness, but rather testimonies of their worth.

As an epithet, *dead* is used collectively; *departed* is used with a noun only; *deceased* generally without a noun, to denote one or more according to the connexion.

There is a respect due to the *dead*, which cannot be violated without offence to the living;

The living and the *dead*, at his command,
Were coupled face to face, and hand to hand.
Dryden.

It is a pleasant reflection to conceive of *departed* spirits, as taking an interest in the concerns of those whom they have left: 'The sophistick tyrants of Paris are loud in their declamations against the *departed* regal tyrants, who in former ages have vexed the world.'—Burke. All the marks on the body of the *deceased* indicated that he had met with his *death* by some violence; 'It was enacted in the reign of Edward I., that the ordinary shall be bound to pay the debts of the intestate, in the same manner that executors were bound in case the *deceased* left a will.'—Blackstone.

DEADLY, MORTAL, FATAL.

Deadly or *deadlike* signifies like death itself in its effects; *mortal*, in Latin *mortalis*, signifies belonging to *death;* *fatal*, in Latin *fatalis*, i. e. according to *fate*.

Deadly is applied to what is productive of death;

* Vide Trusler: "Departure, death, decease."

On him amid the flying numbers found,
Eurypilus inflicts a *deadly* wound.—Pope.

Mortal to what terminates in or is liable to death; 'For my own part, I never could think that the soul, while in a *mortal* body, lives.'—Hughes (*after Xenophon*). *Fatal* applies not only to death, but every thing which may be of great mischief;

O *fatal* change! become in one sad day
A senseless corse! inanimated clay.—Pope.

A poison is *deadly;* a wound or a wounded part is *mortal;* a step in walking, or a step in one's conduct, may be *fatal.* Things only are *deadly,* creatures are *mortal.* Hatred is *deadly;* whatever has life is *mortal.* There may be remedies sometimes to counteract that which is *deadly;* but that which is *mortal* is past all cure; and that which is *fatal* cannot be retrieved.

NUMB, BENUMBED, TORPID.

Numb and *benumbed* come from the Hebrew *num* to sleep; the former denoting the quality, and the latter the state: there are but few things *numb* by nature; but there may be many things which may be *benumbed.* *Torpid,* in Latin *torpidus,* from *torpeo* to languish, is most commonly employed to express the permanent state of being *benumbed,* as in the case of some animals, which lie in a *torpid* state all the winter; or in the moral sense to depict the *benumbed* state of the thinking faculty; in this manner we speak of the *torpor* of persons who are *benumbed* by any strong affection, or by any strong external action; 'The night, with its silence and darkness, shows the winter, in which all the powers of vegetation are *benumbed.*'—Johnson. 'There must be a grand spectacle to rouse the imagination, grown *torpid* with the lazy enjoyment of sixty years' security.'—Burke.

EXIT, DEPARTURE.

Both these words are metaphorically employed for death, or a passage out of this life: the former is borrowed from the act of going off the stage; the latter from the act of setting off on a journey. The *exit* seems to convey the idea of volition; for we speak of making our *exit:* the *departure* designates simply the event; the hour of a man's *departure* is not made known to him. When we speak of the *exit,* we think only of the place left; when we speak of *departure,* we think not only of the object left, but of the place gone to. The unbeliever may talk of his *exit;* the Christian most commonly speaks of his *departure;* 'There are no ideas strike more forcibly upon our imaginations than those which are raised from reflections upon the *exits* of great and excellent men.'—Steele. 'Happy was their good prince in his timely *departure,* which barred him from the knowledge of his son's miseries.'—Sidney.

TO STRENGTHEN, FORTIFY, INVIGORATE.

Strengthen, from *strength,* and *fortify,* from *fortis* and *facio,* signify to make strong; *invigorate* signifies to put in vigour (*v.* *Energy*).

Whatever adds to the *strength,* be it in ever so small a degree, *strengthens;* exercise *strengthens* either body or mind; 'There is a certain bias towards knowledge, in every mind, which may be *strengthened* and improved.'—Budgell. Whatever gives *strength* for a particular emergence *fortifies;* religion *fortifies* the mind against adversity; 'This relation will not be wholly without its use, if those who languish under any part of its sufferings shall be enabled to *fortify* their patience by reflecting that they feel only those afflictions from which the abilities of Savage could not exempt him.'—Johnson. Whatever adds to the *strength,* so as to give a positive degree of *strength, invigorates;* morning exercise in fine weather *invigorates;*

For much the pack
(Rous'd from their dark alcoves) delight to stretch
And bask in his *invigorating* ray.—Somerville.

STRONG, FIRM, ROBUST, STURDY.

Strong is in all probability a variation of strict, which is in German *streng,* because strength is altogether derived from the close contexture of bodies *robust,* in Latin *robustus,* from *robur,* signifies literally having the strength of oak; *sturdy,* like the word stout, steady (*v.* *Firm*), comes in all probability from *stehen* to stand, signifying capable of standing.

Strong is here the generick term; the others are specifick, or specify strength under different circumstances; *robust* is a positive and high degree of strength arising from a peculiar bodily make; *sturdy* indicates not only strength of body but also of mind a man may be *strong* from the strength of his constitution, from the power which is inherent in his frame;

If thou hast *strength,* 't was Heaven that *strength* bestow'd.—Pope.

A *robust* man has strength both from the size and texture of his body, he has a bone and nerve which is endowed with great power. A little man may be *strong,* although not *robust;* a tall, stout man, in full health, may be termed *robust.*

A man may be *strong* in one part of his body and not in another; he may be *stronger* at one time, from particular circumstances, than he is at another: but a *robust* man is *strong* in his whole body; and as he is *robust* by nature, he will cease to be so only from disease;

The huntsman ever gay, *robust,* and bold,
Defies the noxious vapour.—Somerville.

Sturdiness lies both in the make of the body and the temper of the mind: a *sturdy* man is capable of making resistance, and ready to make it; he must be *naturally* strong, and not of slender make, but he need not be *robust:* a *sturdy* peasant presents us with the picture of a man who, both by nature and habit, is formed for withstanding the inroads of an enemy;

This must be done, and I would fain see
Mortal so *sturdy* as to gainsay.—Hudibras.

Sometimes this epithet is applied to those objects which cause a violent resistance;

Beneath their *sturdy* strokes the billows roar.
Dryden

Every object is termed *strong* which is the reverse of weak; persons only are termed *robust* who have every bodily requisite to make them more than ordinarily *strong;* persons only are *sturdy* whose habits of life qualify them both for action and for endurance.

SUBSTANTIAL, SOLID.

Substantial signifies having a substance: *solid* signifies having a firm substance. The *substantial* is opposed to that which is thin and has no consistency; the *solid* is opposed to the liquid, or that which is of loose consistency. All objects which admit of being handled are in their nature *substantial;* those which are of so hard a texture as to require to be cut are *solid.* *Substantial* food is that which has a consistency in itself, and is capable of giving fulness to the empty stomach: *solid* food is meat in distinction from drink.

In the moral application, an argument is said to be *substantial* which has weight in itself;

Trusting in its own native and *substantial* worth,
Scorns all meretricious ornaments.—Milton.

A reason is *solid* which has a high degree of *substantiality;*

As the swoln columns of ascending smoke,
So *solid* swells thy grandeur, pigmy man.
Young

ENERGY, FORCE, VIGOUR.

Energy, in French *energie,* Latin *energia,* Greek ἐνέργεια from ἐνεργέω to operate inwardly, signifies the power of producing positive effects; *force, v.* *To compel;* *vigour,* from the Latin *vigeo* to flourish, signifies unimpaired power, or that which belongs to a subject in a sound or flourishing state.

With *energy* is connected the idea of activity; with *force* that of capability; with *vigour* that of health. *Energy* lies only in the mind; *force* and *vigour* are the property of either body or mind. Knowledge and freedom combine to produce *energy* of character; 'Our powers owe much of their *energy* to our hopes, possunt quia posse videntur When success seems attainable, diligence is enforced.'—JOHNSON. *Force* is a gift of nature that may be increased by exercise;

On the passive main
Descends th' ethereal *force*, and with strong gust
Turns from its bottom the discolour'd deep.
THOMSON.

Vigour, both bodily and mental, is an ordinary accompaniment of youth, but is not always denied to old age; 'No man at the age and *vigour* of thirty is fond of sugar-plums and rattles.'—SOUTH.

HARD, FIRM, SOLID.

The close adherence of the component parts of a body constitutes *hardness*. The close adherence of different bodies to each other constitutes *firmness* (*v Fixed*). That is *hard* which will not yield to a closer compression; 'I see you labouring through all your inconveniences of the rough roads, the *hard* saddle, the trotting horse, and what not.'—POPE. That is *firm* which will not yield so as to produce a separation;

The loosen'd ice
Rustles no more; but to the sedgy bank
Fast grows, or gathers round the pointed stone,
A crystal pavement, by the breath of heaven
Cemented *firm*.—THOMSON.

Ice is *hard*, as far as it respects itself, when it resists every pressure; it is *firm*, with regard to the water which it covers, when it is so closely bound as to resist every weight without breaking.

Hard and *solid* respect the internal constitution of bodies, and the adherence of the component parts; but *hard* denotes a much closer degree of adherence than *solid*: the *hard* is opposed to the soft; the *solid* to the fluid; every *hard* body is by nature *solid*; although every *solid* body is not *hard*. Wood is always a *solid* body, but is sometimes *hard* and sometimes soft: water, when congealed, is a *solid* body, and admits of different degrees of *hardness*; 'A copious manner of expression gives strength and weight to our ideas, which frequently makes impression upon the mind, as iron does upon *solid* bodies, rather by repeated strokes than a single blow.'—MELMOTH (*Letters of Pliny*).

In the improper application, *hardness* is allied to insensibility; *firmness* to fixedness; *solidity* to substantiality; a *hard* man is not to be acted upon by any tender motives; a *firm* man is not to be turned from his purpose; a *solid* man holds no purposes that are not well founded. A man is *hardened* in that which is bad, by being made insensible to that which is good: a man is *confirmed* in any thing good or bad, by being rendered less disposed to lay it aside; his mind is *consolidated* by acquiring fresh motives for action.

HARD, CALLOUS, HARDENED, OBDURATE.

Hard is here, as in the former case (*v. Hard*), the general term, and the rest particular: *hard*, in its most extensive and physical sense, denotes the property of resisting the action of external force, so as not to undergo any change in its form, or motion in its parts: *callous* is that species of the *hard*, in application to the skin, which arises from its dryness, and the absence of all nervous susceptibility. *Hard* and *callous* are likewise applied in the moral sense: but *hard* denotes the absence of tender feeling, or the property of resisting any impression which tender objects are apt to produce;

Such woes
Not e'en the *hardest* of our foes could hear,
Nor stern Ulysses tell without a tear.—DRYDEN.

Callous denotes the property of not yielding to the force of objects acting on the senses of the mind; 'Licentiousness has so long passed for sharpness of wit, and greatness of mind, that the conscience is grown *callous*.'—L'ESTRANGE. A *hard* heart cannot be moved by the sight of misery, let it be presented in ever so affecting a form: a *callous* mind is not to be touched by any persuasions however powerful.

Hard does not designate any circumstance of its existence or origin: we may be *hard* from a variety of causes; but *callousness* arises from the indulgence of vices, passions, and the pursuit of vicious practices. When we speak of a person as *hard*, it simply determines what he is: if we speak of him as *callous*, it refers also to what he was, and from what he is become so; 'By degrees the sense grows *callous*, and loses that exquisite relish of trifles.'—BERKELEY.

Callous, *hardened*, and *obdurate* are all employed to designate a morally depraved character: but *callousness* belongs properly to the heart and affections; *hardened* to both the heart and the understanding; *obdurate* more particularly to the will. *Callousness* is the first stage of *hardness* in moral depravity; it may exist in the infant mind, on its first tasting the poisonous pleasures of vice, without being acquainted with its remote consequences; 'If they let go their hope of everlasting life with willingness, and entertain final perdition with exultation, ought they not to be esteemed destitute of common sense, and abandoned to a *callousness* and numbness of soul?'—BENTLEY. A *hardened* state is the work of time; it arises from a continued course of vice, which becomes as it were habitual, and wholly unfits a person for admitting of any other impressions;

His *harden'd* heart, nor prayers, nor threatenings move;
Fate and the gods had stopp'd his ears to love.
DRYDEN.

Obduracy is the last stage of moral *hardness*, which supposes the whole mind to be obstinately bent on vice;

Round he throws his baleful eyes,
That witness'd huge affliction and dismay,
Mix'd with *obdurate* pride and steadfast hate
MILTON.

A child discovers himself to be *callous*, when the tears and entreaties of a parent cannot awaken in him a single sentiment of contrition; a youth discovers himself to be *hardened* when he begins to take a pride and a pleasure in a vicious career; a man shows himself to be *obdurate* when he betrays a settled and confirmed purpose to pursue his abandoned course, without regard to consequences.

HARDHEARTED, CRUEL, UNMERCIFUL, MERCILESS.

Hardhearted is here, as the word *hard* (*v. Hard*) the strongest of these terms: in regard to *cruel*, it bespeaks a settled character; whereas that may be frequently a temporary disposition, or even extend no farther than the action. A *hardhearted* man must always be *cruel*; but it is possible to be *cruel*, and yet not *hardhearted*. A *hardhearted* parent is a monster who spurns from him the being that owes his existence to him, and depends upon him for support. A child is often *cruel* to animals from the mistaken conception that they are not liable to the same sufferings as himself.

The *unmerciful* and *merciless* are both modes or characteristicks of the *hardhearted*. An *unmerciful* man is *hardhearted*, inasmuch as he is unwilling to extend his compassion or mercy to one who is in his power; a *merciless* man, which is more than an *unmerciful* man, is *hardhearted*, inasmuch as he is restrained by no compunctious feelings from inflicting pain on those who are in his power. Avarice makes a man *hardhearted* even to those who are bound to him by the closest ties. *Avarice* will make a man *unmerciful* to those who are in his debt. There are many *merciless* tyrants in domestick life, who show their disposition by their *merciless* treatment of their poor brutes; 'Single men, though they be many times more charitable, on the other side, are more *cruel* and *hardhearted*, because their tenderness is not so oft called upon.'—BACON.

Relentless love the *cruel* mother led
The blood of her unhappy babes to shed.—DRYDEN.

'I saw how *unmerciful* you were to your eyes in your last letter to me.'—TILLOTSON.

To crush a *merciless* and *cruel* victor.—DRYDEN

CRUEL, INHUMAN, BARBAROUS, BRUTAL, SAVAGE.

Cruel, from the Latin *crudelis* and *crudus* raw rough, or untutored; *inhuman*, compounded of the privative *in* and *human*, signifies not human; *barbarous*, from the Greek βάρβαρος rude or unsettled, all mark a degree of bad feeling which is uncontrolled by culture or refinement; *brutal*, signifying like a *brute;* and *savage*, from the Latin *sævus* fierce, and the Hebrew זאב a wolf, marks a still stronger degree of this bad passion.

Cruel is the most familiar and the least powerful epithet of all these terms; it designates the ordinary propensity which is innate in man, and which if not overpowered by a better principle, will invariably show itself by the desire of inflicting positive pain on others, or abridging their comfort: *inhuman* and *barbarous* are higher degrees of *cruelty; brutal* and *savage* rise so much in degree above the rest, as almost to partake of another nature. A child gives early symptoms of his natural *cruelty* by his ill-treatment of animals; but we do not speak of his *inhumanity*, because this is a term confined to men, and more properly to their treatment of their own species, although extended in its sense to their treatment of the *brutes: barbarity* is but too common among children and persons of riper years. A person is *cruel* who neglects the creature he should protect and take care of;

> Now be thy rage, thy fatal rage resign'd,
> A *cruel* heart ill suits a manly mind.—Pope.

A person is *inhuman* if he withhold from him the common marks of tenderness or kindness which are to be expected from one *human* being to another;

> Love lent the sword, the mother struck the blow,
> *Inhuman* she, but more *inhuman* thou.—Dryden.

A person is *barbarous* if he find amusement in inflicting pain;

> I have found out a gift for my fair,
> I have found where the wood-pigeons breed,
> But let me that plunder forbear,
> She will say, 'twas a *barbarous* deed.
> Shenstone.

A person is *brutal* or *savage* according to the circumstances of aggravation which accompany the act of torturing; 'The play was acted at the other theatre, and the *brutal* petulance of Cibber was confuted, though perhaps not shamed, by general applause.'—Johnson.

> Brothers by brothers' impious hands are slain!
> Mistaken zeal, how *savage* is thy reign!
> Jenyns.

Cruel is applied either to the disposition or the conduct; *inhuman* and *barbarous* mostly to the outward conduct: *brutal* and *savage* mostly to the disposition. *Cruelties* and even *barbarities*, too horrid to relate, are daily practised by men upon dogs and horses, the usefullest and most unoffending of *brutes;* either for the indulgence of a naturally *brutal* temper, or from the impulse of a *savage* fury: we need not wonder to find the same men *inhuman* towards their children or their servants. Domitian was notorious for the *cruelty* of his disposition: the Romans indulged themselves in the *inhuman* practice of making their slaves and convicts fight with wild beasts; but the *barbarities* which have been practised on slaves in the colonies of European states, exceed every thing in atrocity that is reated of ancient times; proving that, in spite of all the refinement which the religion of our blessed Saviour has introduced into the world, the possession of uncontrolled power will inevitably *brutalize* the mind, and give a *savage* ferocity to the character.

FEROCIOUS, FIERCE, SAVAGE.

Ferocious and *fierce* are both derived from the Latin *ferox*, which comes from *fera* a wild beast: *savage*, v. *Cruel; ferocity* marks the untamed character of a cruel disposition: *fierceness* has a greater mixture of pride and anger in it, the word *fierté* in French being taken for haughtiness: *savageness* marks a more permanent, but not so violent, a sentiment of either cruelty or anger as the two former. *Ferocity* and *fierceness* are in common applied to the brutes, to designate their natural tempers: *savage* is mostly employed to designate the natural tempers of man, when uncontrolled by the force of reason and a sense of religion. *Ferocity* is the natural characteristick of wild beasts: it is a delight in blood that needs no outward stimulus to call it into action; but it displays itself most strikingly in the moment when the animal is going to grasp, or when in the act of devouring, its prey: *fierceness* may be provoked in many creatures, but it does not discover itself unless roused by some circumstances of aggravation; many animals become *fierce* by being shut up in cages, and exposed to the view of spectators: *savageness* is as natural a temper in the uncivilized man, as *ferocity* or *fierceness* in the brute; it does not wait for an enemy to attack, but is restless in search of some one whom it may make an enemy, and have an opportunity of destroying. It is an easy transition for the *savage* to become the *ferocious* cannibal, glutting himself in the blood of his enemies, or the *fierce* antagonist to one who sets himself up in opposition to him.

In an extended application of these terms, they bear the same relation to each other: the countenance may be either *ferocious, fierce*, or *savage*, according to circumstances. A robber who spends his life in the act of unlawfully shedding blood acquires a *ferocity* of countenance; 'The *ferocious* character of Moloch appears both in the battle and the council with exact consistency.'—Johnson. A soldier who follows a precatory and desultory mode of warfare betrays the licentiousness of his calling, and his undisciplined temper, in the *fierceness* of his countenance;

> The tempest falls,
> The weary winds sink, breathless. But who knows
> What *fiercer* tempest yet may shake this night?
> Thomson.

The wretch whose enjoyment consists in inflicting misery on his dependants or subjects, evinces the *savageness* of his temper by the *savage* joy with which he witnesses their groans and tortures;

> Nay, the dire monsters that infest the flood,
> By nature dreadful, and athirst for blood,
> His will can calm, their *savage* tempers bind,
> And turn to mild protectors of mankind.—Young

HARD, HARDY, INSENSIBLE, UNFEELING.

Hard (v. *Hard*) may either be applied to that which makes resistance to external impressions, or that which presses with a force upon other objects: *hardy*, which is only a variation of *hard*, is applicable only in the first case: thus, a person's skin may be *hard*, which is not easily acted upon; but the person is said to be *hardy* who can withstand the elements;

> Ocnus was next, who led his native train
> Of *hardy* warriours through the watery plain.
> Dryden.

On the other hand, *hard*, when employed as an active principle, is only applied to the moral character; hence, the difference between a *hardy* man who endures every thing, and a *hard* man who makes others endure. *Insensible* and *unfeeling* are but modes of the *hard;* that is, they designate the negative quality of *hardness*, or its incapacity to receive impression: *hard*, therefore, is always the strongest term of the three; and of the two, *unfeeling* is stronger than *insensible*. *Hard* and *insensible* are applied physically and morally; *unfeeling* is employed only as a moral characteristick. A horse's mouth is *hard*, inasmuch as it is insensible to the action of the bit; a man's heart is *hard* which is insensible to the miseries of others; a man is *unfeeling* who does not regard the feelings of others. The heart may be *hard* by nature, or rendered so by the influence of some passion; but the person is commonly *unfeeling* from circumstances. Shylock is depicted by Shakspeare as *hard*, from his strong antipathy to the Christians: people who enjoy an uninterrupted state of good health, are often *unfeeling* in cases of sickness.

As that which is *hard* mostly hurts or pains when it comes in contact with the soft, the term *hard* is peculiarly applicable to superiours, or such as have power to inflict pain: a creditor may be *hard* towards a debtor; 'To be inaccessible, contemptuous, and *hard* of heart, is to revolt against our own nature.'—Blair. As *insensible* signifies a want of sense, it may be sometimes necessary: a surgeon, when performing an operation, must be *insensible* to the present pain which he inflicts; but as a habit of the mind it is always bad;

It is both reproachful and criminal to have an *insensible* heart.'—BLAIR. As *unfeeling* signifies a want of feeling, it is always taken for a want of good *feeling* where the removal of pain is required: the surgeon shows himself to be *unfeeling* who does not do every thing in his power to lessen the pain of the sufferer;

> The father too a sordid man,
> Who love nor pity knew,
> Was all *unfeeling* as the rock
> From whence his riches grew.—MALLET.

INDIFFERENCE, INSENSIBILITY, APATHY.

Indifference signifies no *difference;* that is, having no *difference* of feeling for one thing more than another; *insensibility*, from *sense* and *able*, signifies incapable of feeling; *apathy*, from the Greek privative *a* and πάθος feeling, implies without feeling.

Indifference is a partial state of the mind; *apathy*, and *insensibility* are general states of the mind; he who has *indifference* is not to be awakened to feeling by some objects, though he may by others; but he who has not *sensibility* is incapable of feeling; and he who has *apathy* is without any feeling. *Indifference* is mostly a temporary state; *insensibility* is either a temporary or a permanent state; *apathy* is always a permanent state: *indifference* is either acquired or accidental; *insensibility* is either produced or natural; *apathy* is natural. A person may be in a state of *indifference* about a thing the value of which he is not aware of, or acquire an *indifference* for that which he knows to be of comparatively little value: he may be in a state of *insensibility* from some lethargick torpor which has seized his mind; or he may have an habitual *insensibility* arising either from the contractedness of his powers, or the physical bluntness of his understanding, and deadness of his passions; his *apathy* is born with him, and forms a prominent feature in the constitution of his mind.

Indifference is often the consequence of *insensibility;* for he who is not *sensible* or alive to any feeling must naturally be without choice or preference: but *indifference* is not always *insensibility*, since we may be *indifferent* to one thing because we have an equal liking to another; 'I could never prevail with myself to exchange joy and sorrow for a state of constant tasteless *indifference*.'—HOADLY. In like manner *insensibility* may spring from *apathy*, for he who has no feeling is naturally not to be awakened to feeling, that is, he is unfeeling or *insensible* by constitution; but since his *insensibility* may spring from other causes besides those that are natural, he may be *insensible* without having *apathy;* 'I look upon Iseus not only as the most eloquent but the most happy of men; as I shall esteem you the most *insensible* if you appear to slight his acquaintance.'—MELMOTH (*Letters of Pliny*). Moreover, it is observable that between *insensibility* and *apathy* there is this farther distinction, that the former refers only to our capacity for being moved by the outward objects that surround us; whereas *apathy* denotes an entire internal deadness of all the feelings: but we may be *insensible* to the present external objects from the total absorption of all the powers and feelings in one distant object; 'To remain *insensible* of such provocations, is not constancy, but *apathy*.'—SOUTH.

INDIFFERENT, UNCONCERNED, REGARDLESS.

Indifferent (*v. Indifference*) marks the want of inclination: *unconcerned*, that is, having no concern (*v. Care*); and *regardless*, that is, without regard (*v. Care*); mark the want of serious consideration.

Indifferent respects only the will, *unconcerned* either the will or the understanding, *regardless* the understanding only; we are *indifferent* about matters of minor consideration: we are *unconcerned* or *regardless* about serious matters that have remote consequences; an author will seldom be *indifferent* about the success of his work; he ought not to be *unconcerned* about the influence which his writings may have on the publick, or *regardless* of the estimation in which his own character as a man may be held. To be *indifferent* is sometimes an act of wisdom or virtue; to be *unconcerned* or *regardless* is mostly an act of folly or a breach of duty.

When the object is purely of a personal nature, it is but treating it as it deserves if we are *indifferent* about it; hence a wise man is *indifferent* about the applause of the multitude; 'As an author I am perfectly *indifferent* to the judgement of all except the few who are really judicious.'—COWPER. As religion should be the object of our concern, if we are *unconcerned* about any thing connected with it, the fault is in ourselves; a good parent will never be *unconcerned* about the religious education of his children;

> Not the most cruel of our conquering foes,
> So *unconcern'dly* can relate our woes.—DENHAM.

Whatever tends to increase our knowledge or to add to the comfort of others, ought to excite our regard; if therefore we are *regardless* of these things, we betray a culpable want of feeling; a good child will never be regardless of the admonition of a parent;

> *Regardless* of my words, he no reply
> Returns.—DRYDEN.

SENSIBLE, SENSITIVE, SENTIENT.

All these epithets, which are derived from the same source (*v. To feel*), have obviously a great sameness of meaning, though not of application. *Sensible* and *sensitive* both denote the capacity of being moved to feeling: *sentient* implies the very act of feeling. *Sensible* expresses either a habit of the body and mind, or only a particular state referring to some particular object; a person may be *sensible* of things in general, or *sensible* of cold, or *sensible* of injuries, or *sensible* of the kindnesses which he has received from an individual;

> And with affection wondrous *sensible*,
> He wrung Bassanio's hand, and so they parted
> SHAKSPEARE.

Sensitive signifies always an habitual or permanent quality; it is the characteristick of objects; a *sensitive* creature implies one whose sense is by distinction quickly to be acted upon: a *sensitive* plant is a peculiar species of plants, marked for the property of having *sense* or being *sensible* of the touch; 'Those creatures live more alone whose food, and therefore prey, is upon other *sensitive* creatures.'—TEMPLE.

Sensible and *sensitive* have always a reference to external objects; but *sentient* expresses simply the possession of feeling, or the power of feeling, and excludes the idea of the cause. Hence, the terms *sensible* and *sensitive* are applied only to persons or corporeal objects; but *sentient* is likewise applicable to spirits; *sentient* beings may include angels as well as men; 'This acting of the *sentient* phantasy is performed by the presence of sense, as the horse is under the sense of hunger, and that without any formal syllogism presseth him to eat.'—HALE.

SENSUALIST, VOLUPTUARY, EPICURE.

The *sensualist* lives for the indulgence of his senses, the *voluptuary*, from *voluptas* pleasure, is devoted to his pleasures, and as far as these pleasures are the pleasures of sense, the *voluptuary* is a *sensualist:* the *epicure*, from the philosopher *Epicurus*, who is charged with having been the votary of pleasure, is one who makes the pleasures of sense his god, and in this sense he is a *sensualist* and a *voluptuary*. In the application of these terms, however, the *sensualist* is one who is a slave to the grossest appetites; 'Let the *sensualist* satisfy himself as he is able; he will find that there is a certain living spark within which all the drink he can pour in will never be able to quench.'—SOUTH. The *voluptuary* is one who studies his pleasures so as to make them the most valuable to himself; 'To fill up the drawing of this personage, he conceived a *voluptuary*, who in his person should be bloated and blown up to the size of a Silenus; lazy, luxurious, in *sensuality;* in intemperance a bacchanalian.'—CUMBERLAND. The *epicure* is a species of *voluptuary* who practises more than ordinary refinement in the choice of his pleasures; 'What *epicure* can be always plying his palate?'—SOUTH.

SENTENTIOUS, SENTIMENTAL

Sententious signifies having or abounding in *sentences* or judgements: *sentimental*, having *sentiment* (*v. Opinion*). Books and authors are termed *sententious*; but travellers, society, intercourse, correspondence, and the like, are characterized as *sentimental*. Moralists like Dr. Johnson are termed *sententious*, whose works and conversation abound in moral *sentences*; 'His (Mr. Ferguson's) love of Montesquieu and Tacitus has led him into a manner of writing too short-winded and *sententious*.'—Gray. Novelists and romance writers, like Mrs. Radcliffe, are properly *sentimental*; 'In books, whether moral or amusing, there are no passages more captivating than those delicate strokes of *sentimental* morality which refer our actions to the determination of feeling.'—Mackenzie. *Sententious* books always serve for improvement; *sentimental* works, unless they are of a superiour order, are in general hurtful.

SENTIMENT, SENSATION, PERCEPTION.

Sentiment and *sensation* are obviously derived from the same source, namely, from the Greek συνετίζω to make intelligent, and συνίημι to understand; *perception*, from *perceive* (*v. To see*), expresses the act of *perceiving*, or the impressions produced by *perceiving*.

The impressions which objects make upon the person are designated by all these terms; but the *sentiment* has its seat in the heart, the *sensation* is confined to the senses, and the *perception* rests in the understanding. *Sentiments* are lively, *sensations* are grateful, *perceptions* are clear.

Gratitude is a *sentiment* the most pleasing to the human mind;

> Alike to council, or the assembly came,
> With equal souls and *sentiments* the same.—Pope.

The *sensation* produced by the action of electricity on the frame is generally unpleasant; 'Diversity of constitution, or other circumstances, vary the *sensations*, and to them Java pepper is cold.'—Glanville. A nice *perception* of objects is one of the first requisites for perfection in any art; 'Matter hath no life nor *perception*, and is not conscious of its own existence.'—Bentley * The *sentiment* extends to the manners and morals, and renders us alive to the happiness or misery of others as well as our own; 'I am framing every possible pretence to live hereafter according to my own taste and *sentiments*.'—Melmoth (*Letters of Cicero*). The *sensation* is purely physical; it makes us alive only to the effects of external objects on our physical organs; 'When we describe our *sensations* of another's sorrows in condolence, the customs of the world scarcely admit of rigid veracity.'—Johnson. *Perceptions* carry us into the district of science; they give us an interest in all the surrounding objects as intellectual observers;

> When first the trembling eye receives the day,
> External forms on young *perception* play.
> Langhorne.

A man of spirit or courage receives marks of honour, or affronts, with very different *sentiments* from the poltroon: he who bounds his happiness by the present fleeting existence must be careful to remove every painful *sensation*: we judge of objects as complex or simple, according to the number of *perceptions* which they produce in us.

TO FEEL, BE SENSIBLE, CONSCIOUS.

From the simple idea of a sense, the word *feel* has acquired the most extensive signification and application in our language, and may be employed indifferently for all the other terms, but not in all cases: to *feel* is said of the whole frame, inwardly and outwardly; it is the accompaniment of existence: to *be sensible*, from the Latin *sentio*, is said only of the senses. It is the property of all living creatures to *feel* pleasure and pain in a greater or a less degree: those creatures which have not the sense of hearing will not *be sensible* of sounds.

In the moral application, to *feel* is peculiarly the property or act of the heart; to *be sensible* is that of the understanding: an ingenuous mind *feels* pain when it is *sensible* of having committed an errour: one may, however, *feel* as well as *be sensible* by means of the understanding: a person *feels* the value of another's services, he is *sensible* of his kindness.

One *feels* or is *sensible* of what passes outwardly one is *conscious* only of what passes inwardly, fron *con* or *cum* and *scio* to know to oneself: we *feel* the force of another's remark; 'The devout man does not only believe, but *feels* there is a Deity.'—Addison We are *sensible* of the evil which must spring from the practice of vice; 'There is, doubtless, a faculty in spirits by which they apprehend one another, as our senses do material objects; and there is no question bu our souls, when they are disembodied, will, by this faculty, be always *sensible* of the Divine presence.'—Addison. We are *conscious* of having fallen short of our duty;

> A creature of a more exalted kind
> Was wanting yet, and then was man design'd;
> *Conscious* of thought, of more capacious breast,
> For empire form'd, and fit to rule the rest.—Dryden.

FEELING, SENSATION, SENSE.

Feeling and *sensation* express either the particular act, or the general property of *feeling*; *sense* expresses the general property, or the particular mode of *feeling*. *Feeling* is, as before (*v. To feel*), the general, *sensation* and *sense* are the special terms: the *feeling* is either physical or moral; the *sensation* is mostly physical; the *sense* physical in the general, and moral in the particular application.

We speak either of the *feeling* or *sensation* of cold. the *feeling* or *sense* of virtue: it is not easy to describe the *feelings* which are excited by the cutting of cork or the sharpening of a saw; 'I am sure the natural *feeling*, as I have just said, is a far more predominant ingredient in this war, than in that of any other that was ever waged by this kingdom.'—Burke. The *sensation* which pervades the frame after bathing is exceedingly grateful to one who is accustomed to the water; 'Those ideas to which any agreeable *sensation* is annexed are easily excited, as leaving behind them the most strong and permanent impressions.'—Somerville. The pleasures of *sense* are not comparable with those of intellect;

> In distances of things, their shapes, and size,
> Our reason judges better than our eyes;
> Declares not this the soul's pre-eminence,
> Superiour to, and quite distinct from *sense*?
> Jenyns.

The term *feeling* is most adapted to ordinary discourse; *sensation* is a term better suited to the grave or scientifick style: a child may talk of an unpleasant *feeling*; a professional man talks of the *sensation* of giddiness, a gnawing *sensation*, or of *sensations* from the rocking of a vessel, the motion of a carriage, and the like: it is our duty to command and curb our *feelings*; it is folly to watch every passing *sensation*.

The *feeling*, in a moral sense, has its seat in the heart; it is transitory and variable; 'Their king, out of a princely *feeling*, was sparing and compassionate towards his subjects.'—Bacon. *Sense* has its seat in the understanding; it is permanent and regular. We may have *feelings* of anger, ill-will, envy, and the like, which cannot be too quickly overpowered, and succeeded by thos of love, charity, and benevolence; although there is no *feeling*, however good, which does not require to be kept under control by a proper *sense* of religion; 'This Basilius having the quick *sense* of a lover took as though his mistress had given him a secret reprehension.'—Sidney.

FEELING, SENSIBILITY, SUSCEPTIBILITY.

Feeling, in the present case, is taken for a positive characteristick, namely, the property of *feeling* (*v. To feel*) in a strong degree; in this sense *feeling* expresses either a particular act, or an habitual property of the mind; *sensibility* is always taken in the sense of a habit. Traits of *feeling* in young people are happy omens in the estimation of the preceptor; 'Gentleness is native *feeling* improved by principle.'—Blair. An exquisite *sensibility* is not a desirable gift; it creates an infinite disproportion of pains; 'Modesty is a kind

* Abbe Girard: "Sentiment, sensation, perception."

of quick and delicate *feeling* in the soul; it is such an exquisite *sensibility*, as warns a woman to shun the first appearance of any thing hurtful.'—ADDISON. This term, like that of *feeling*, may sometimes be taken in a general sense, but still it expresses the idea more strongly; 'By long habit in carrying a burden we lose in great part our *sensibility* of its weight.'—JOHNSON. *Feeling* and *sensibility* are here taken as moral properties, which are awakened as much by the operations of the mind within itself as by external objects: *susceptibility*, from the Latin *suscipio* to take or receive, designates that property of the body or the mind which consists in being ready to take an affection from external objects; hence we speak of a person's *susceptibility* to take cold, or his *susceptibility* to be affected with grief, joy, or any other passion: if an excess of *sensibility* be an evil, an excess of *susceptibility* is a still greater evil; it makes us a slave to every circumstance, however trivial, which comes under our notice; 'It pleases me to think that it was from a principle of gratitude in me, that my mind was *susceptible* of such generous transport (in my dreams) when I thought myself repaying the kindness of my friend.'—BYRON.

HUMAN, HUMANE.

Though both derived from *homo* a man, they are thus far distinguished, that *human* is said of the genus, and *humane* of the species. The *human* race or *human* beings are opposed to the irrational part of the creation; a *humane* race or a *humane* individual is opposed to one that is cruel and fond of inflicting pain. He who is not *human* is divested of the first and distinguishing characteristicks of his kind; 'Christianity has rescued *human* nature from that ignominious yoke, under which in former times the one-half of mankind groaned.'—BLAIR. He who is not *humane*, is divested of the most important and elevated characteristick that belongs to his nature;

Life, fill'd with grief's distressful train,
For ever asks the tear *humane*.—LANGHORNE.

TO NOURISH, NURTURE, CHERISH.

To *nourish* and *nurture* are but variations from the same Latin verb *nutrio; cherish*, from the French *cher*, and the Latin *carus* dear, to treat as something dear to one.

The thing *nourishes*, the person *nurtures* and *cherishes*: to *nourish* is to afford bodily strength, to supply the physical necessities of the body; to *nurture* is to extend one's care to the supply of all its physical necessities, to preserve life, occasion growth, and increase vigour: the breast of the mother *nourishes;*

Air, and ye elements, the eldest birth
Of nature's womb, that in quaternion run
Perpetual circle, multiform; and mix
And *nourish* all things.—MILTON.

The fostering care and attention of the mother *nurtures;* 'They suppose mother earth to be a great animal, and to have *nurtured* up her young offspring with conscious tenderness.'—BENTLEY. To *nurture* is a physical act; to *cherish* is a mental as well as a physical act: a mother *nurtures* her infant while it is entirely dependent upon her; she *cherishes* her child in her bosom, and protects it from every misfortune, or affords consolation in the midst of all its troubles, when it is no longer an infant;

Of thy superfluous brood, she 'll *cherish* kind
The alien offspring.—SOMERVILLE.

TO FOSTER, CHERISH, HARBOUR, INDULGE.

To *foster* is probably connected with father, in the natural sense, to bring up with a parent's care; to *cherish*, from the Latin *carus* dear, is to feed with affection; to *harbour*, from a *harbour* or *haven*, is to provide with a shelter and protection; to *indulge*, from the Latin *dulcis* sweet, is to render sweet and agreeable. These terms are all employed here in the moral acceptation, to express the idea of giving nourishment to an object.

To *foster* in the mind is to keep with care and positive endeavours: as when one *fosters* prejudices by encouraging every thing which favours them; 'Th greater part of those who live but to infuse malignity and multiply enemies, have no hopes to *foster*, no designs to promote, nor any expectations of attaining power by insolence.'—JOHNSON. To *cherish* in the mind is to hold dear or set a value upon; as when one *cherishes* good sentiments, by dwelling upon them with inward satisfaction; 'As social inclinations are absolutely necessary to the well being of the world, it is the duty and interest of every individual to *cherish* and improve them to the benefit of mankind.'—BERKELEY To *harbour* is to allow room in the mind, and is generally taken in the worst sense, for giving admission to that which ought to be excluded; as when one *harbours* resentment by permitting it to have a resting place in the heart;

This is scorn,
Which the fair soul of gentle Athenais
Would ne'er have *harbour'd*.—LEE.

To *indulge* in the mind, is to give the whole mind to any thing, to make it the chief source of pleasure; as when one *indulges* an affection, by making the will and the outward conduct bend to its gratifications; 'The king (Charles I.) would *indulge* no refinements of casuistry, however plausible, in such delicate subjects, and was resolved, that what depredations soever fortune should commit upon him, she never should bereave him of his honour.'—HUME.

He who *fosters* pride in his breast lays up for himself a store of mortification in his intercourse with the world; it is the duty of a man to *cherish* sentiments of tenderness and kindness towards the woman whom he has made the object of his choice; nothing evinces the innate depravity of the human heart more forcibly than the spirit of malice, which some men *harbour* for years together; any affection of the mind, if *indulged* beyond the bounds of discretion, will become a hurtful passion, that may endanger the peace of society as much as that of the individual.

TO CARESS, FONDLE.

Both these terms mark a species of endearment; *caress*, like *cherish*, comes from the French *chérir*, and *cher*, Latin *carus* dear, signifying the expression of a tender sentiment; *fondle*, from *fond*, is a frequentative verb, signifying to become *fond* of, or express one's *fondness* for.

We *caress* by words or actions; we *fondle* by actions only: *caresses* are not always unsuitable; but *fondling*, which is the extreme of *caressing*, is not less unfit for the one who receives than for the one who gives: animals *caress* each other, as the natural mode of indicating their affection; *fondling*, which is for the most part the expression of perverted feeling, is peculiar to human beings, who alone abuse the faculties with which they are endowed.

TO CLASP, HUG, EMBRACE.

To *clasp*, from the noun *clasp*, signifies to lay hold of like a *clasp; hug*, in Saxon *hogan*, comes from the German *hägen*, which signifies to enclose with a hedge, and figuratively to cherish or take special care of; *embrace*, in French *embrasser*, is compounded of *en* or *im* and *bras* the arm, signifying to take or lock in the arms.

All these terms are employed to express the act of enclosing another in one's arms: *clasp* marks this action when it is performed with the warmth of true affection; *hug* is a ludicrous sort of *clasping*, which is the consequence of ignorance and extravagant feeling; *embrace* is simply a mode of ordinary salutation: a parent will *clasp* his long-lost child in his arms on their remeeting;

Thy suppliant,
I beg, and *clasp* thy knees.—MILTON.

A peasant in the excess of his raptures would throw his body, as well as his arms, over the object of his joy, and stifle with *hugging* him whom he meant to love;

Thyself a boy, assume a boy's dissembled face,
That when amid the fervour of the feast
The Tyrian *hugs* and fonds thee on her breast,
Thou mayest infuse thy venom in her veins.
DRYDEN

In the continental parts of Europe *embracing* between males, as well as females, is universal on meeting after a long absence, or on taking leave for a length of time; *embraces* are sometimes given in England between near relatives, but in no other case; 'The king at length having kindly reproached Helim for depriving him so long of such a brother, *embraced* Balsora with the greatest tenderness.'—ADDISON.

Clasp may also be employed in the same sense for other objects besides persons;

Some more aspiring catch the neighbouring shrub,
With *clasping* tendrils, and invest her branch.
COWPER.

Embrace may be employed figuratively in the sense of including (*v. Comprehend*).

INDULGENT, FOND.

Indulgent signifies disposed to indulge; *fond*, from to *find*, signifies trying to find, longing for.

Indulgence lies more in forbearing from the exercise of authority; *fondness* in the outward behaviour and endearments: they may both arise from an excess of kindness or love; but the former is of a less objectionable character than the latter. *Indulgence* may be sometimes wrong; but *fondness* is seldom right: an *indulgent* parent is seldom a prudent parent; but a *fond* parent does not rise above a fool: all who have the care of young people should occasionally relax from the strictness of the disciplinarian, and show an *indulgence* where a suitable opportunity offers; a *fond* mother takes away from the value of *indulgences* by an invariable compliance with the humours of her children: however, when applied generally or abstractedly, they are both taken in a good sense;

God then thro' all creation gives, we find,
Sufficient marks of an *indulgent* mind —JENYNS.

While, for a while his *fond* paternal care,
Feasts us with every joy our state can bear.—JENYNS.

AMOROUS, LOVING, FOND.

Amorous, from *amor* love, signifies full of love; *loving*, the act of *loving*, that is, of continually *loving*; *fond* has the same signification as given under the head of *Indulgent*, *fond*.

These epithets are all used to mark the excess or distortion of a tender sentiment. *Amorous* is taken in a criminal sense, *loving* and *fond* in a contemptuous sense: an indiscriminate and dishonourable attachment to the fair sex characterizes the *amorous* man; 'I shall range all old *amorous* dotards under the denomination of grinners.'—STEELE. An overweening and childish attachment to any object marks the *loving* and *fond* person.

Loving is less dishonourable than *fond*: men may be *loving*;

So *loving* to my mother
That he would not let ev'n the winds of heaven
Visit her face too roughly.—SHAKSPEARE.

Children, females, and brutes may be *fond*; 'I'm a foolish *fond* wife.'—ADDISON. Those who have not a well regulated affection for each other will be *loving* by fits and starts; children and animals who have no control over their appetites will be apt to be *fond* of those who indulge them. An *amorous* temper should be suppressed; a *loving* temper should be regulated; a *fond* temper should be checked. When *loving* and *fond* are applied generally, they may sometimes be taken in a good or indifferent sense;

This place may seem for shepherds' leisure made,
So *lovingly* these elms unite their shade.—PHILLIPS.

'My impatience for your return, my anxiety for your welfare, and my *fondness* for my dear Ulysses, were the only distempers that preyed upon my life.'—ADDISON.

AMIABLE, LOVELY, BELOVED.

Amiable, in Latin *amabilis*, from *amo* and *habilis*, signifies fit to be loved; *lovely*, compounded of *love* and *ly* or *like*, signifies like that which we love: *beloved*, having or receiving love.

The first two express the fitness of an object to awaken the sentiment of love; the latter expresses the state of being in actual possession of that love. The *amiable* designates that sentiment in its most spiritual form, as it is awakened by purely spiritual objects; the *lovely* applies to this sentiment as it is awakened by sensible objects.

One is *amiable* according to the qualities of the heart: one is *lovely* according to the external figure and manners; one is *beloved* according to the circumstances that bring him or her into connexion with others. Hence it is that things as well as persons may be *lovely* or *beloved*; but persons only, or that which is personal, is *amiable*;

Sweet Auburn, *loveliest* village of the plain.
GOLDSMITH.

Sorrow would be a rarity most *belov'd*,
If all could so become it.—SHAKSPEARE.

An *amiable* disposition, without a *lovely* person, will render a person *beloved*; 'Tully has a very beautiful gradation of thoughts to show how *amiable* virtue is. "We love a virtuous man," says he, "who lives in the remotest parts of the earth, although we are altogether out of the reach of his virtue, and can receive from it no manner of benefit."'—ADDISON. It is distressing to see any one who is *lovely* in person *unamiable* in character

AMICABLE, FRIENDLY.

Amicable, from *amicus* a friend, signifies able or fit for a friend; *friendly*, like a *friend*. The word *amicus* comes from *amo* to love, and *friend* in the northern languages from *fregan* to love. *Amicable* and *friendly* therefore both denote the tender sentiment of goodwill which all men ought to bear one to another; but *amicable* rather implies a negative sentiment, a freedom from discordance; and *friendly* a positive feeling of regard, the absence of indifference.

We make an *amicable* accommodation, and a *friendly* visit. It is a happy thing when people who have been at variance can *amicably* adjust all their disputes. Nothing adds more to the charms of society than a *friendly* correspondence.

Amicable is always said of persons who have been in connexion with each other; *friendly* may be applied to those who are perfect strangers. Neighbours must always endeavour to live *amicably* with each other; 'What first presents itself to be recommended is a disposition averse to offence, and desirous of cultivating harmony, and *amicable* intercourse in society.'—BLAIR. Travellers should always endeavour to keep up a *friendly* intercourse with the inhabitants, wherever they come;

Who slake his thirst; who spread the *friendly* board
To give the famish'd Belisarius food?—PHILLIPS.

The abstract terms of the preceding qualities admit of no variation but in the signification of *friendship*, which marks an individual feeling only; to live *amicably*, or in *amity* with all men, is a point of Christian duty, but we cannot live in *friendship* with all men; since *friendship* must be confined to a few;

Beasts of each kind their fellows spare;
Bear lives in *amity* with bear.—JOHNSON.

'Every man might, in the multitudes that swarm about him, find some kindred mind with which he could unite in confidence and *friendship*.'—JOHNSON.

AFFECTION, LOVE.

Affection denotes the state of being kindly *affected* towards a person; *love*, in Low German *leeve*, High German *liebe*, from the English *lief*, Low German *leef*, High German *lieb* dear or pleasing, the Latin *libet* it is pleasing, and by metathesis from the Greek φίλος dear, signifies the state of holding a person dear.

These words express two sentiments of the heart which do honour to human nature; they are the bonds by which mankind are knit to each other. Both imply good-will: but *affection* is a tender sentiment that dwells with pleasure on the object; *love* is a tender sentiment accompanied with longing for the object: we cannot have *love* without *affection*, but we may have *affection* without *love*.

Love is the natural sentiment between near relations: *affection* subsists between those who are less intimately connected, being the consequence either of relationship, friendship, or long intercourse; it is the sweetener of human society, which carries with it a thousand charms, in all the varied modes of kindness which it gives birth to; it is not so active as *love*, but it diffuses itself wider, and embraces a larger number of objects.

Love is powerful in its effects, awakening vivid sentiments of pleasure or pain; it is a passion exclusive, restless, and capricious. *Affection* is a chastened feeling under the control of the understanding; it promises no more pleasure than it gives, and has but few alloys. Marriage may begin with *love;* but it ought to terminate in *affection;*

> But thou, whose years are more to mine allied,
> No fate my vow'd *affection* shall divide
> From thee, heroic youth!—DRYDEN.

'The poets, the moralists, the painters, in all their descriptions, allegories, and pictures, have represented *love* as a soft torment, a bitter sweet, a pleasing pain, or an agreeable distress.'—ADDISON.

AFFECTIONATE, KIND, FOND.

Affectionate denotes the quality of having *affection* (*v. Affection*); *kind*, from the word *kind* kindred or family, denotes the quality or feeling engendered by the family tie; *fond*, from to *find*, denotes a vehement attachment to a thing.

Affectionate and *fond* characterize feelings, or the expression of those feelings; *kind* is an epithet applied to outward actions, as well as inward feelings; a disposition is *affectionate* or *fond;* a behaviour is *kind.*

Affection is a settled state of the mind; *kindness*, a temporary state of feeling, mostly discoverable by some outward sign: both are commendable and honourable, as to the nature of the feelings themselves, the objects of the feelings, and the manner in which they display themselves; the understanding always approves the *kindness* which *affection* dictates, or that which springs from a tender heart. *Fondness* is a less respectable feeling; it is sometimes the excess of *affection*, or an extravagant mode of expressing it, or an attachment to an inferiour object.

A person is *affectionate*, who has the object of his regard strongly in his mind, who participates in his pleasures and pains, and is pleased with his society. A person is *kind*, who expresses a tender sentiment, or does any service in a pleasant manner; 'Our salutations were very hearty on both sides, consisting of many *kind* shakes of the hand, and *affectionate* looks which we cast upon one another.'—ADDISON. A person is *fond*, who caresses an object, or makes it a source of pleasure to himself; 'Riches expose a man to pride and luxury, a foolish elation of heart, and too great *fondness* for the present world.'—ADDISON.

Relatives should be *affectionate* to each other: we should be *kind* to all who stand in need of our *kindness:* children are *fond* of whatever affords them pleasure, or of whoever gives them indulgences.

ATTACHMENT, AFFECTION, INCLINATION.

Attachment respects persons and things; *affection* (*v. Affection*) regards persons only; *inclination* has respect to things mostly, but it may be applied to objects generally.

Attachment, as it regards persons, is not so powerful or solid as *affection*. Children are *attached* to those who will minister to their gratifications: they have an *affection* for their nearest and dearest relatives.

Attachment is sometimes a tender sentiment between the persons of different sexes; *affection* is an affair of the heart without distinction of sex. The passing *attachments* of young people are seldom entitled to serious notice; although sometimes they may ripen by long intercourse into a laudable and steady *affection;* 'Though devoted to the study of philosophy, and a great master in the early science of the times, Solon mixed with cheerfulness in society, and did not hold back from those tender ties and *attachments* which connect a man to the world.'—CUMBERLAND. Nothing is so delightful as to see *affection* among brothers and sisters; 'When I was sent to school, the gayety of my look, and the liveliness of my loquacity, soon gained me admission to hearts not yet fortified against *affection* by artifice or interest.'—JOHNSON. *Attachment* is more powerful than *inclination;* the latter is a rising sentiment, the forerunner of *attachment*, which is positive and fixed; 'I am glad that he whom I must have loved from duty, whatever he had been, is such a one as I can love from *inclination*.'—STEELE.

As respects things generally, *attachment* and *inclination* are similarly distinguished. We strive to obtain that to which we are *attached;* but an *inclination* seldom leads to any effort for possession. Little minds are always betraying their *attachment* to trifles. It is the character of indifference not to show an *inclination* to any thing. *Attachments* are formed; *inclinations* arise of themselves.

Interest, similarity of character, or habit give rise to *attachment;* 'The Jews are remarkable for an *attachment* to their own country.'—ADDISON. A natural warmth of temper gives birth to various *inclinations;* 'A mere *inclination* to a thing is not properly a willing of that thing; and yet, in matters of duty, men frequently reckon it for such.'—SOUTH.

Suppress the first *inclination* to gaming, lest it grows into an *attachment.*

BENEVOLENCE, BENIGNITY, HUMANITY, KINDNESS, TENDERNESS.

Benevolence, from *bene* and *volo* to will, signifies wishing well; *benignity*, in Latin *benignitas*, from *bene* and *gigno*, signifies the quality or disposition for producing good; *humanity*, in French *humanité*, Latin *humanitas* from *humanus* and *homo*, signifies the quality of belonging to a man, or having what is common to man; *kindness* is the abstract quality of *kind* (*v. Affectionate*); *tenderness*, the abstract quality of *tender*, from the Latin *tener*, Greek τερὴν.

Benevolence and *benignity* lie in the will; *humanity* lies in the heart; *kindness* and *tenderness* in the affections: *benevolence* indicates a general good-will to all mankind; *benignity* a particular good-will, flowing out of certain relations; *humanity* is a general tone of feeling; *kindness* and *tenderness* are particular modes of feeling.

Benevolence consists in the wish or intention to do good; it is confined to no station or object: the *benevolent* man may be rich or poor, and his *benevolence* will be exerted wherever there is an opportunity of doing good: *benignity* is always associated with power, and accompanied with condescension.

Benevolence in its fullest sense is the sum of moral excellence, and comprehends every other virtue; when taken in this acceptation, *benignity*, *humanity*, *kindness*, and *tenderness* are but modes of *benevolence.*

Benevolence and *benignity* tend to the communicating of happiness; *humanity* is concerned in the removal of evil. *Benevolence* is common to the Creator and his creatures; it differs only in degree; the former has the knowledge and power as well as the will to do good; man often has the will to do good without having the power to carry it into effect; 'I have heard say, that Pope Clement XI. never passes through the people, who always kneel in crowds and ask his benediction, but the tears are seen to flow from his eyes. This must proceed from an imagination that he is the father of all these people, and that he is touched with so extensive a *benevolence*, that it breaks out into a passion of tears.'—STEELE. *Benignity* is ascribed to the stars, to heaven, or to princes; ignorant and superstitious people are apt to ascribe their good fortune to the *benign* influence of the stars rather than to the gracious dispensations of Providence; 'A constant *benignity* in commerce with the rest of the world, which ought to run through all a man's actions, has effects more useful to those whom you oblige, and is less ostentatious in yourself.'—STEELE. *Humanity* belongs to man only; it is his peculiar characteristick, and ought at all times to be his boast; when he throws off this his distinguishing badge, he loses every thing valuable in him; it is a virtue that is indispensable in his present suffering condition: *humanity* is as universal in its application as *benevolence;* wherever there is distress, *humanity* flies to its relief; 'The greatest wits I have conversed with are men eminent for their *humanity*.'—ADDISON. *Kindness* and *tenderness* are partial modes of affection, confined to those who know or are related to each other: we are *kind* to friends and acquaintances, *tender* towards those who are near and dear: *kindness* is a mode of affec tion most fitted for social beings; it is what every one can show, and every one is pleased to receive; '*Beneficence*, would the followers of Epicurus say, is all founded in weakness; and whatever be pretended, the *kindness* that passeth between men and men is by every man directed to himself. This it must be confessed is of a piece with that hopeful philosophy which, having patched man up out of the four elements, attributes his being to chance.'—GROVE. *Tenderness* is a state of feeling that is occasionally acceptable: the young and the weak demand *tenderness* from those who stand in the closest connexion with them, but this feeling may be carried to an excess so as to injure the object on which it is fixed; 'Dependence is a perpetual call upon *humanity*, and a greater incitement to *tenderness* and pity than any other motive whatsoever.'—ADDISON.

There are no circumstances or situation in life which preclude the exercise of *benevolence:* next to the pleasure of making others happy, the *benevolent* man rejoices in seeing them so; the *benign* influence of a *benevolent* monarch extends to the remotest corner of his dominions; *benignity* is a becoming attribute for a prince, when it does not lead him to sanction vice by its impunity; it is highly to be applauded in him as far as it renders him forgiving of minor offences, gracious to all who are deserving of his favours, and ready to afford a gratification to all whom it is in his power to serve: the multiplied misfortunes to which all men are exposed afford ample scope for the exercise of *humanity*, which, in consequence of the unequal distribution of wealth, power, and talent, is peculiar to no situation of life; even the profession of arms does not exclude *humanity* from the breasts of its followers: and when we observe men's habits of thinking in various situations, we may remark that the soldier, with arms by his side, is commonly more *humane* than the partisan with arms in his hands. *Kindness* is always an amiable feeling, and in a grateful mind always begets *kindness;* but it is sometimes ill bestowed upon selfish people who requite it by making fresh exactions; *tenderness* is frequently little better than an amiable weakness, when directed to a wrong end, and fixed on an improper object; the false *tenderness* of parents has often been the ruin of children.

LOVE, FRIENDSHIP.

Love (*v. Affection*) is a term of very extensive import; it may be either taken in the most general sense for every strong and passionate attachment, or only for such as subsist between the sexes; in either of which cases it has features by which it has been easily distinguished from *friendship*.

Love subsists between members of the same family; it springs out of their natural relationship, and is kept alive by their close intercourse and constant interchange of kindnesses: *friendship* excludes the idea of any tender and natural relationship; nor is it, like *love*, to be found in children, but is confined to maturer years; it is formed by time, by circumstances, by congruity of character, and sympathy of sentiment. *Love* always operates with ardour; *friendship* is remarkable for firmness and constancy. *Love* is peculiar to no station it is to be found equally among the high and the low, the learned and the unlearned: *friendship* is of nobler growth; it finds admittance only into minds of a loftier make; it cannot be felt by men of an ordinary stamp.

Both *love* and *friendship* are gratified by seeking the good of the object; but *love* is more selfish in its nature than *friendship;* in indulging another it seeks its own, and when this is not to be obtained, it will change into the contrary passion of hatred; *friendship*, on the other hand, is altogether disinterested, it makes sacrifices of every description, and knows no limits to its sacrifice. As *love* is a passion, it has all the errours attendant upon passion; but *friendship*, which is an affection tempered by reason, is exempt from every such exceptionable quality. *Love* is blind to the faults of the object of its devotion; it adores, it idolizes, it is fond, it is foolish: *friendship* sees faults, and strives to correct them; it aims to render the object more worthy of esteem and regard. *Love* is capricious, humoursome, and changeable; it will not bear contradiction, disappointment, nor any cross or untoward circumstance: *friendship* is stable; it withstands the rudest blasts, and is unchanged by the severest shocks of adversity; neither the smiles nor frowns of fortune can change its form, its serene and placid countenance is unruffled by the rude blasts of adversity; it rejoices and sympathizes in prosperity; it cheers, consoles, and assists in adversity. *Love* is exclusive in its nature; it insists upon a devotion to a single object; it is jealous of any intrusion from others: *friendship* is liberal and communicative; it is bounded by nothing but rules of prudence; it is not confined as to the number but as to the nature of the objects.

When *love* is not produced by any social relation, it has its groundwork in sexuality, and subsists only between persons of different sexes; in this case it has all the former faults with which it is chargeable to a still greater degree, and others peculiar to itself; it is even more selfish, more capricious, more changeable, and more exclusive, than when subsisting between persons of the same kindred. *Love* is in this case as unreasonable in its choice of an object, as it is extravagant in its regards of the object; it is formed without examination; it is the effect of a sudden glance, the work of a moment, in which the heart is taken by surprise, and the understanding is discarded: *friendship*, on the other hand, is the entire work of the understanding; it does not admit of the senses or the heart to have any undue influence in the choice. A fine eye, a fair hand, a graceful step, are the authors of *love;* talent, virtue, fine sentiment, a good heart, and a sound head, are the promoters of *friendship: love* wants no excitement from personal merit; *friendship* cannot be produced without merit. Time, which is the consolidator of *friendship*, is the destroyer of *love;* an object improvidently chosen is as carelessly thrown aside; and that which was not chosen for its merits, is seldom rejected for its demerits, the fault lying rather in the humour of *love*, which can abate of its ardour as the novelty of the thing ceases, and transfer itself to other objects: *friendship*, on the other hand, is slow and cautious in choosing, and still more gradual in the confirmation, as it rests on virtue and excellence; it grows only with the growth of one's acquaintance, and ripens with the maturity of esteem. *Love*, while it lasts, subsists even by those very means which may seem rather calculated to extinguish it; namely, caprice. disdain, cruelty, absence, jealousy, and the like;

> So every passion, but fond *love*,
> Unto its own redress does move.—WALLER.

Friendship is supported by nothing artificial; it depends upon reciprocity of esteem, which nothing but solid qualities can ensure or render durable;

> For natural affection soon doth cease,
> And quenched is with Cupid's greater flame,
> But faithful *friendship* doth them both suppress,
> And them with mastering discipline doth tame.
> SPENSER.

In the last place, *love* when misdirected is dangerous and mischievous; in ordinary cases it awakens flattering hopes and delusive dreams, which end in disappointment and mortification; and in some cases it is the origin of the most frightful evils; there is nothing more atrocious than what has owed its origin to slighted *love:* but *friendship*, even if mistaken, will awaken no other feeling than that of pity; when a friend proves faithless or wicked, he is lamented as one who has fallen from the high estate to which we thought him entitled.

LOVER, SUITOR, WOOER.

Lover signifies literally one who *loves*, and is applicable to any object; there are *lovers* of money, and *lovers* of wine, *lovers* of things individually, and things collectively, that is, *lovers* of particular women in the good sense, or *lovers* of women in the bad sense, but *lover*, taken absolutely, signifies one who feels or professes his love for a female: 'It is very natural for a young friend, and a young *lover*, to think the persons they *love* have nothing to do but to please them.'—POPE. The *suitor* is one who *sues* and strives after a thing; the term is equally undefined as to the object, but may be employed for such as *sue* for favours from their superiours, or *sue* for the affections and person of a female; 'What pleasure can it be to be thronged with petitioners, and those perhaps *suitors* for the same thing?'—SOUTH. The *wooer* is only a species of *lover*, who *woos* or solicits the kind regards of a female; 'I am glad this parcel of *wooers* are so reasonable, for there is not one of them but I dote on his very absence.'—SHAKSPEARE. When applied to the same object, namely, the female sex, the *lover* is employed or persons of all ranks, who are equally alive to the tender passion of *love*: *suitor* is a title adapted to that class of life where all the genuine affections of human nature are adulterated by a false refinement, or entirely lost in other passions of a guilty nature. *Wooer* is a tender and passionate title, which is adapted to that class of beings that live only in poetry and romance. There is most sincerity in the *lover*, he simply proffers his *love*; there is most ceremony in the *suitor*, he prefers his *suit*; there is most ardour in the *wooer*, he makes his vows.

GALLANT, BEAU, SPARK.

These words convey nothing respectful of the person to whom they are applied; but the first, as is evident from its derivation, has something in it to recommend it to attention above the others: as true valour is ever associated with a regard for the fair sex, a *gallant* man will always be a *gallant* when he can render the female any service; sometimes, however, his *gallantries* may be such as to do them harm rather than good;

> The god of wit, and light, and arts,
> With all acquir'd and natural parts,
> Was an unfortunate *gallant*.—SWIFT.

Insignificance and effeminacy characterize the *beau* or fine gentleman; he is the woman's man—the humble servant to supply the place of a lacquey;

> His pride began to interpose,
> Preferr'd before a crowd of *beaux*.—SWIFT.

The *spark* has but a *spark* of that fire which shows itself in impertinent puerilities; it is applicable to youth who are just broke loose from school or college, and eager to display their manhood;

> Oft it has been my lot to mark
> A proud, conceited, talking *spark*.—MERRICK.

MALEVOLENT, MALICIOUS, MALIGNANT.

These words have all their derivation from *malus* bad: that is, *malevolent*, wishing ill; *malicious* (*v. Malice*), having an evil disposition; and *malignant*, having an evil tendency.

Malevolence has a deep root in the heart, and is a settled part of the character; we denominate the person *malevolent*, to designate the ruling temper of his mind: *maliciousness* may be applied as an epithet to particular parts of a man's character or conduct; one may have a *malicious* joy or pleasure in seeing the distresses of another: *malignity* is not employed to characterize the person, but the thing; the *malignity* of a design is estimated by the degree of mischief which was intended to be done. Whenever *malevolence* has taken possession of the heart, all the sources of good-will are dried up; a stream of evil runs through the whole frame, and contaminates every moral feeling; the being who is under such an unhappy influence neither thinks nor does any thing but what is evil; 'I have often known very lasting *malevolence* excited by unlucky censures.'—JOHNSON. A *malicious* disposition is that branch of *malevolence* which is the next to it in the blackness of its character; it differs, however, in this, that *malice* will, in general, lie dormant, until it is provoked;

> Greatness, the earnest of *malicious* Fate
> For future wo, was never meant a good.
> SOUTHERN.

But *malevolence* is as active and unceasing in its operations for mischief, as its opposite, benevolence, is in wishing and doing good.

Malicious and *malignant* are both applied to things; but the former is applied to those which are of a personal nature, the latter to objects purely inanimate: a story or tale is termed *malicious*, which emanates from a *malicious* disposition; a star is termed *malignant*, which is supposed to have a bad or *malignant* influence;

> Still horrour reigns, a dreary twilight round,
> Of struggling night and day *malignant* mix'd
> THOMSON.

MALICE, RANCOUR, SPITE, GRUDGE, PIQUE.

Malice, in Latin *malitia*, from *malus* bad, signifies the very essence of badness lying in the heart; *rancour* (*v. Hatred*) is only continued *hatred*: the former requires no external cause to provoke it, it is inherent in the mind; the latter must be caused by some personal offence. *Malice* is properly the love of evil for evil's sake, and is, therefore, confined to no number or quality of objects, and limited by no circumstance; *rancour*, as it depends upon external objects for its existence, so it is confined to such objects only as are liable to cause displeasure or anger: *malice* will impel a man to do mischief to those who have not injured him, and are perhaps strangers to him;

> If any chance has hither brought the name
> Of Palamedes, not unknown to fame,
> Who suffer'd from the *malice* of the times.
> DRYDEN.

Rancour can subsist only between those who have had sufficient connexion to be at variance; 'Party spirit fills a nation with spleen and *rancour*.'—ADDISON.

Spite, from the Italian *dispetto* and the French *despit*, denotes a petty kind of *malice*, or disposition to offend another in trifling matters; it may be in the temper of the person, or it may have its source in some external provocation: children often show their *spite* to each other;

> Can heav'nly minds such high resentment show,
> Or exercise their *spite* in human wo?—DRYDEN.

Grudge, connected with *grumble* and *growl*, and *pique*, from *pike*, denoting the prick of a pointed instrument, are employed for that particular state of *rancorous* or *spiteful* feeling which is occasioned by personal offences: the *grudge* is that which has long existed;

> The god of wit, to show his *grudge*,
> Clapp'd asses' ears upon the judge.—SWIFT.

The *pique* is that which is of recent date; 'You may be sure the ladies are not wanting, on their side, in cherishing and improving these important *piques*, which divide the town almost into as many parties as there are families.'—LADY M. W. MONTAGUE. A person is said to owe another a *grudge* for having done him a disservice; or he is said to have a *pique* towards another, who has shown him an affront.

IMPLACABLE, UNRELENTING, RELENTLESS, INEXORABLE.

Implacable, unappeaseable, signifies not to be allayed nor softened; *unrelenting* or *relentless*, from the Latin *lenio* to soften, or to make pliant, signifies not rendered soft; *inexorable*, from *oro* to pray, signifies not to be turned by prayers.

Inflexibility is the idea expressed in common by these terms, but they differ in the causes and circumstance with which it is attended. Animosities are *implacable* when no misery which we occasion can diminish their force, and no concessions on the part of the offender can lessen the spirit of revenge; '*Implacable* as the enmity of the Mexicans was, they were so unacquainted with the science of war that they knew not how to take the proper measures for the destruction of the Spaniards.'—ROBERTSON. The mind or character of a man is *unrelenting*, when it is not to be turned from its purpose by a view of the pain which it inflicts;

> These are the realms of *unrelenting* fate.—DRYDEN.

A man is *inexorable* who turns a deaf ear to every solicitation or entreaty that is made to induce him to lessen the rigour of his sentence;

> You are more inhuman, more *inexorable*,
> Oh, ten times more, than tigers of Hyrcania!
> SHAKSPEARE.

A man's angry passions render him *implacable*; it is not the magnitude of the offence, but the temper of the offended that is here in question; by *implacability* he is rendered insensible to the misery he occasions, and to every satisfaction which the offender may offer him: fixedness of purpose renders a man *unrelenting* or *relentless*; an *unrelenting* temper is not less callous to the misery produced, than an *implacable* temper; but it is not grounded always on resentment for personal injuries, but sometimes on a certain principle of right and a sense of necessity: the *inexorable* man adheres to his rule, as the *unrelenting* man does to his purpose; the former is insensible to any workings of his heart which might shake his purpose, the latter turns a deaf ear to all the solicitations of others which would go to alter his decrees: savages are mostly *implacable* in their animosities; Titus Manlius Torquatus displayed an instance of *unrelenting* severity towards his son; Minos, Æacus, and Rhadamanthus were the *inexorable* judges of hell.

Implacable and *unrelenting* are said only of animate beings in whom is wanting an ordinary portion of the tender affections: *inexorable* may be improperly applied to inanimate objects; justice and death are both represented as *inexorable;*

> Acca, 't is past, he swims before my sight,
> *Inexorable* death, and claims his right.—Dryden.

HARSH, ROUGH, SEVERE, RIGOROUS.

These terms mark different modes of treating those that are in one's power, all of which are the reverse of the kind.

Harsh and *rough* borrow their moral signification from the physical properties of the bodies to which they belong. The *harsh* and the *rough* both act painfully upon the taste, but the former with much more violence than the latter. An excess of the sour mingled with other unpleasant properties constitutes *harshness:* an excess of astringency constitutes *roughness.* Cheese is said to be *harsh* when it is dry and biting: *roughness* is the peculiar quality of the damascene.

From this physical distinction between these terms we discover the ground of their moral application. *Harshness* in a person's conduct acts upon the feelings, and does violence to the affections: *roughness* acts only externally on the senses: we may be *rough* in the tone of the voice, in the mode of address, or in the manner of handling or touching an object: but we are *harsh* in the sentiment we convey, and according to the persons to whom it is conveyed: a stranger may be *rough* when he has it in his power to be so: a friend, or one in the tenderest relation, only can be *harsh.* An officer of justice deals *roughly* with the prisoner in his charge, to whom he denies every indulgence in a *rough* and forbidding tone;

> Know, gentle youth, in Lybian lands there are
> A people rude in peace, and *rough* in war.
> Dryden.

A parent deals *harshly* with a child who refuses every endearment, and only speaks to command or forbid; 'I would rather he was a man of a *rough* temper, who would treat me *harshly*, than of an effeminate nature.'—Addison. *Harsh* and *rough* are unamiable and always censurable qualities: they spring from the *harshness* and *roughness* of the humour; 'No complaint is more feelingly made than that of the *harsh* and *rugged* manners of persons with whom we have an intercourse.'—Blair. *Severe* and *rigorous* are not always to be condemned; they spring from principle, and are often resorted to by necessity. *Harshness* is always mingled with anger and personal feeling: *severity* or *rigour* characterizes the thing more than the temper of the person.

A *harsh* master renders every burden which he imposes doubly *severe*, by the grating manner in which he communicates his will: a *severe* master simply imposes the burden in a manner to enforce obedience. The one seems to indulge himself in inflicting pain: the other seems to act from a motive that is independent of the pain inflicted. A *harsh* man is therefore always *severe*, but with injustice: a *severe* man, however, is not always *harsh*. *Rigour* is a high degree of *severity*. One is *severe* in the punishment of offences: one is *rigorous* in exacting compliance and obedience. *Severity* is always more or less necessary in the army, or in a school, for the preservation of good order: *rigour* is essential in dealing with the stubborn will and unruly passions of men. A general must be *severe* while lying in quarters, to prevent drunkenness and theft: but he must be *rigorous* when invading a foreign country, to prevent the ill-treatment of the inhabitants; 'It is pride which fills the world with so much *harshness* and *severity*. We are *rigorous* to offences as if we had never offended.'—Blair.

A measure is *severe* that threatens heavy consequences to those who do not comply: a line of conduct is *rigorous* that binds men down with great exactitude to a particular mode of proceeding. A judge is *severe* who is ready to punish and unwilling to pardon.

AUSTERE, RIGID, SEVERE, RIGOROUS, STERN.

Austere, in Latin *austerus* sour or rough, from the Greek αὔω to dry, signifies rough or harsh, from drought; *rigid* and *rigorous*, from the Latin *rigeo* and the Greek ῥιγέω, signifies stiffness or unbendingness; *severe*, in Latin *severus*, comes from *sævus* cruel; *stern*, in Saxon *sterne*, German *streng* strong, has the sense of strictness.

Austere applies to ourselves as well as to others; *rigid* applies to ourselves only; *severe*, *rigorous*, *stern*, apply to others only. We are *austere* in our manner of living; *rigid* in our mode of thinking; *austere*, *severe*, *rigorous*, and *stern* in our mode of dealing with others. Effeminacy is opposed to *austerity*, pliability to *rigidity*.

The *austere* man mortifies himself; the *rigid* man binds himself to a rule: the *austerities* formerly practised among the Roman Catholicks were in many instances the consequence of *rigid* piety: the manners of a man are *austere* when he refuses to take part in any social enjoyments; his probity is *rigid*, that is, inaccessible to the allurements of gain, or the urgency of necessity: an *austere* life consists not only in the privation of every pleasure, but in the infliction of every pain: '*Austerity* is the proper antidote to indulgence, the diseases of the mind as well as body are cured by contraries.'—Johnson. *Rigid* justice is unbiassed, no less by the fear of loss than by the desire of gain: the present age affords no examples of *austerity*, but too many of its opposite extreme, effeminacy; and the *rigidity* of former times, in modes of thinking, has been succeeded by a culpable laxity; 'In things which are not immediately subject to religious or moral consideration, it is dangerous to be too long or too *rigidly* in the right.'—Johnson.

Austere, when taken with relation to others, is said of the behaviour; *severe* of the conduct: a parent is *austere* in his looks, his manners, and his words to his child; he is *severe* in the restraints he imposes, and the punishments he inflicts: an *austere* master speaks but to command, and commands so as to be obeyed; a *severe* master punishes every fault, and punishes in an undue measure: an *austere* temper is never softened; the countenance of such a one never relaxes into a smile, nor is he pleased to witness smiles: a *severe* temper is ready to catch at the imperfections of others, and to wound the offender: a judge should be a *rigid* administrator of justice between man and man, and *severe* in the punishment of offences as occasion requires; but nevere *austere* towards those who appear before him; *austerity* of manner would ill become him who sits as a protector of either the innocent or the injured.

Rigour is a species of great *severity*, namely, in the infliction of punishment; towards enormous offenders, or on particular occasions where an example is requisite, *rigour* may be adopted, but otherwise it mark a cruel temper. A man is *austere* in his manners, *severe* in his remarks, and *rigorous* in his discipline; 'If you are hard or contracted in your judgements, *severe* in your censures, and oppressive in your dealings; then conclude with certainty that what you had termed piety was but an empty name.'—Blair. 'It is not by *rigorous* discipline and unrelaxing *austerity* that the aged can maintain an ascendant over youthful minds.'—Blair.

Austerity, *rigidity*, and *severity* may be habitual; *rigour* and *sternness* are occasional. *Sternness* is a species of *severity* more in manner than in direct action; a commander may issue his commands *sternly*, or a despot may issue his *stern* decrees;

> A man *severe* he was, and *stern* to view,
> I knew him well, and every truant knew

Yet he was kind, or if *severe* in aught,
The love he bore to learning was in fault.
GOLDSMITH.

'It is *stern* criticism to say, that Mr. Pope's is not a translation of Homer.'—CUMBERLAND.

ACRIMONY, TARTNESS, ASPERITY, HARSHNESS.

These epithets are figuratively employed to denote sharpness of feeling corresponding to the quality in natural bodies.

Acrimony, in Latin *acrimonia*, from *acer* sharp, is the characteristick of garlick, mustard, and pepper, that is, a biting sharpness; *tartness*, from *tart*, is not improbably derived from *tartar*, the quality of which it in some degree resembles, expressing a high degree of acid peculiar to vinegar; *asperity*, in Latin *asperitas*, from *asper*, comes from the Greek ἄσπρος fallow, without culture and without fruit as applied to land that is too hard and rough to be tilled; *harshness*, from *harsh*, in German and Teutonick *herbe, herbisch*, Swedish *kerb*, Latin *acerbus*, denotes the sharp, rough taste of unripe fruit.

A quick sense produces *acrimony:* it is too frequent among disputants, who imbitter each other's feelings. An acute sensibility, coupled with quickness of intellect, produces *tartness:* it is too frequent among females. *Acrimony* is a transient feeling that discovers itself by the words; 'The genius even when he endeavours only to entertain or instruct, yet suffers persecution from innumerable criticks, whose *acrimony* is excited merely by the pain of seeing others pleased.'—JOHNSON. *Tartness* is an habitual irritability that mingles itself with the tone and looks; 'When his humours grew *tart*, as being now in the lees of favour, they brake forth into certain sudden excesses.'—WOTTON. An *acrimonious* reply frequently gives rise to much ill-will; a *tart* reply is often treated with indifference, as indicative of the natural temper, rather than of any unfriendly feeling.

Asperity and *harshness* respect one's conduct to inferiours; the latter expresses a strong degree of the former. *Asperity* is opposed to mildness and forbearance; *harshness* to kindness. A reproof is conveyed with *asperity*, when the words and looks convey strong displeasure; 'The charity of the one, like kindly exhalations, will descend in showers of blessings; but the rigour and *asperity* of the other, in a severe doom upon ourselves.'—GOVERNMENT OF THE TONGUE. A treatment is *harsh* when it wounds the feelings, and does violence to the affections:

Thy tender hefted nature shall not give
Thee o'er to *harshness:* her eyes are fierce, but
thine
Do comfort and not burn.—SHAKSPEARE.

Mistresses sometimes chide their servants with *asperity;* parents sometimes deal *harshly* with their children.

Harshness and *asperity* are also applied to other objects: the former to sounds or words, the latter figuratively to the atmosphere; 'Cowley seems to have possessed the power of writing easily beyond any other of our poets, yet his pursuit of remote thoughts led him often into *harshness* of expression.'—JOHNSON. 'The nakedness and *asperity* of the wintery world always fills the beholder with pensive and profound astonishment.'—JOHNSON.

TO SATISFY, PLEASE, GRATIFY.

To *satisfy* (*v. Contentment*) is rather to produce pleasure indirectly; to *please* (*v. Agreeable*) is to produce it directly: the former is negative, the latter positive, pleasure: as every desire is accompanied with more or less pain, *satisfaction* which is the removal of desire is itself to a certain extent pleasure; but what *satisfies* is not always calculated to *please;* nor is that which *pleases*, that which will always *satisfy:* plain food *satisfies* a hungry person, but does not *please* him when he is not hungry; social enjoyments *please*, but they are very far from *satisfying* those who do not restrict their indulgencies; 'He who has run over the whole circle of earthly *pleasures* will be forced to complain that either they were not *pleasures* or that *pleasure* was not *satisfaction*.'—SOUTH. To *gratify* is to *please* in a high degree, to produce a vivid *pleasure;* we may be *pleased* with trifles, but we are commonly *gratified* with such things as act strongly either on the senses or the affections: an epicure is *gratified* with those delicacies which suit his taste; an amateur in musick will be *gratified* with hearing a piece of Handel's composition finely performed; 'Did we consider that the mind of a man is the man himself, we should think it the most unnatural sort of self-murder to sacrifice the sentiment of the soul to *gratify* the appetites of the body.'—STEELE.

TO SATISFY, SATIATE, GLUT, CLOY.

To *satisfy* is to take enough; *satiate* is a frequentative formed from *satis* enough, signifying to have more than enough; *glut*, in Latin *glutio*, from *gula* the throat, signifies to take down the throat; *cloy* is a variation of *clog*.

Satisfaction brings pleasure; it is what nature demands; and nature therefore makes a suitable return *satiety* is attended with disgust; it is what appetite demands; but appetite is the corruption of nature and produces nothing but evil: *glutting* is an act of intemperance; it is what the inordinate appetite demands; it greatly exceeds the former in degree both of the cause and the consequence; *cloying* is the consequence of *glutting*. Every healthy person *satisfies* himself with a regular portion of food; children if unrestrained seek to *satiate* their appetites, and *cloy* themselves by their excesses; brutes, or men debased into brutes, *glut* themselves with that which is agreeable to their appetites.

The first three terms are employed in a moral application; the last may also be used figuratively; we *satisfy* desires in general, or any particular desire; 'The only thing that can give the mind any solid *satisfaction* is a certain complacency and repose in the good providence of God.'—HERRING. We *satiate* the appetite for pleasure or power;

'T was not enough,
By subtle fraud to snatch a single life;
Puny impiety! whole kingdoms fell,
To *sate* the lust of power.—PORTEUS.

One *gluts* the eyes or the ears by any thing that is horrid or extravagant; 'If the understanding be detained by occupations less pleasing, it returns again to study with greater alacrity than when it is *glutted* with ideal pleasures.'—JOHNSON. We may be *cloyed* by an uninterrupted round of pleasures; 'Religious pleasure is such a pleasure as can never *cloy* or over work the mind.'—SOUTH.

ENJOYMENT, FRUITION, GRATIFICATION.

Enjoyment, from *enjoy* to have the joy or pleasure, signifies either the act of *enjoying*, or the pleasure itself derived from that act; *fruition*, from *fruor* to *enjoy*, is employed only for the act of *enjoying*.

We speak either of the *enjoyment* of any pleasure, or of the *enjoyment* as a pleasure: we speak of those pleasures which are received from the *fruition*, in distinction from those which are only in expectation. The *enjoyment* is either corporeal or spiritual, as the *enjoyment* of musick, or the *enjoyment* of study; 'The *enjoyment* of fame brings but very little pleasure, though the loss or want of it be very sensible and afflicting.'—ADDISON. *Fruition* mostly relates to sensible, or at least to external objects; hope intervenes between the desire and the *fruition;* 'Fame is a good so wholly foreign to our natures that we have no faculty in the soul adapted to it, nor any organ in the body to relish it; an object of desire placed out of the possibility of *fruition*.'—ADDISON.

Gratification, from the verb to *gratify* make grateful or pleasant, signifies either the act of giving pleasure, or the pleasure received. *Enjoyment* springs from every object which is capable of yielding pleasure; by distinction however from moral and rationa objects; 'His hopes and expectations are bigger than his *enjoyments*.'—TILLOTSON. But the *gratification*, which is a species of *enjoyment*, is obtained through the medium of the senses; 'The man of pleasure little knows the perfect joy he loses for the disappointing *gratifications* which he pursues.'—ADDISON. The *enjoyment* is not so vivid as the *gratification:* the *gratification* is not so permanent as the *enjoyment.* Domestick life has its peculiar *enjoyments;* brilliant spectacles afford *gratification.* Our capacity for *enjoyments* depends upon our intellectual endowments; our *gratification* depends upon the tone of our feelings, and the nature of our desires.

CONTENTMENT, SATISFACTION.

Contentment, in French *contentment,* from *content,* in Latin *contentus,* participle of *contineo* to contain or hold, signifies the keeping one's self to a thing; *satisfaction,* in Latin *satisfacio,* compounded of *satis* and *facio,* signifies the making or having enough.

Contentment lies in ourselves: *satisfaction* is derived from external objects; one is *contented* when one wishes for no more: one is *satisfied* when one has obtained what one wishes; the *contented* man has always enough; the *satisfied* man receives enough.

The *contented* man will not be *dissatisfied;* but he who looks for *satisfaction* will never be *contented. Contentment* is the absence of pain; *satisfaction* is positive pleasure. *Contentment* is accompanied with the enjoyment of what one has; *satisfaction* is often quickly followed with the alloy of wanting more. A *contented* man can never be miserable; a *satisfied* man can scarcely be long happy. *Contentment* is a permanent and habitual state of mind; it is the restriction of all our thoughts, views, and desires within the compass of present possession and enjoyment;

True happiness is to no place confin'd,
But still is found in a *contented* mind.—ANONYMOUS.

Satisfaction is a partial and turbulent state of the feelings, which awakens rather than deadens desire; 'Women who have been married some time, not having it in their heads to draw after them a numerous train of followers, find their *satisfaction* in the possession of one man's heart.'—SPECTATOR. *Contentment* is suited to our present condition; it accommodates itself to the vicissitudes of human life: *satisfaction* belongs to no created being; one *satisfied* desire engenders another that demands *satisfaction. Contentment* is within the reach of the poor man, to whom it is a continual feast; but *satisfaction* has never been procured by wealth, however enormous, or ambition, however boundless and successful. We should therefore look for the *contented* man, where there are the fewest means of being *satisfied.* Our duty bids us be *contented;* our desires ask to be *satisfied;* but our duty is associated with our happiness; our desires are the sources of our misery.

PLAY, GAME, SPORT.

Play, from the French *plaire* to please, signifies in general what one does to please one's self; *game,* in Saxon *gaming,* very probably comes from the Greek γαμέω to marry, which is the season for *games;* the word γαμέω, itself, comes from γαίω to be buoyant or boasting, whence comes our word gay; *sport,* in German *spass* or *posse,* comes from the Greek παίζω to jest.

Play and *game* both include exercise, corporeal or mental, or both; but *play* is an unsystematick, *game* a systematick, exercise; children *play* when they merely run after each other, but this is no *game;* on the other hand, when they exercise with the ball according to any rule, this is a *game;* every *game* therefore is a *play,* but every *play* is not a *game:* trundling a hoop is a *play,* but not a *game:* cricket is both a *play* and a *game.* One person may have his *play* by himself, but there must be more than one to have a *game. Play* is adapted to infants; *games* to those who are more advanced. *Play* is the necessary unbending of the mind to give a free exercise to the body: *game* is the direction of the mind to the lighter objects of intellectual pursuit. An intemperate love of *play,* though prejudicial to the improvement of young people, is not always the worst indication which they can give; it is often coupled with qualities of a better kind; '*Play* is not unlawful merely as a contest.'—HAWKESWORTH. When *games* are pursued with too much ardour, particularly for the purposes of gain, they are altogether prejudicial to the understanding, and ruinous to the morals:

What arms to use, or nets to frame,
Wild beasts to combat or to tame,
With all the mysteries of that *game*.—WALLER.

Sport is a bodily exercise connected with the prosecution of some object; it is so far, therefore, distinct from either *play* or *game:* for *play* may be purely corporeal; *game,* principally intellectual; but *sport* is a mixture of both. The *game* comprehends the exercise of an art, and the perfection which is attained in that art is the end or source of pleasure; the *sport* is merely the prosecution of an object which may be, and mostly is, attainable by one's physical powers without any exercise of art: the *game,* therefore, is intellectual both in the end and the means; the *sport* only in the end. Draughts, backgammon, cards, and the like, are *games;* but hunting, shooting, racing, bowling, quoits, &c. are termed more properly *sports.* There are, however, many things which may be denominated either *game* or *sport* according as it has more or less of art in it. Wrestling, boxing, chariot-racing, and the like, were carried to such perfection by the ancients that they are always distinguished by the name of *games;* of which we have historical accounts under the different titles of the Olympick, the Pythian, the Nemean, and the Isthmian *games.* Similar exercises, when practised by the rusticks in England, have been commonly denominated rural *sports.* Upon this ground *game* is used abstractedly for the part of the *game* in which the whole art lies: 'There is no man of sense and honesty but must see and own, whether he understands the *game* or not, that it is an evident folly for any people, instead of prosecuting the old honest methods of industry and frugality, to sit down to a publick *gaming* table, and *play* off their money to one another.'—BERKELEY. *Sport* is used for the end of the *sport* or the pleasure produced by the attainment of that end: thus we say that the *game* is won or lost; to be clever or inexpert at a *game;* to have much *sport,* to enjoy the *sport,* or to spoil the *sport;*

Now for our mountain *sport* up to yon hill:
Your legs are young.—SHAKSPEARE.

Game is sometimes used figuratively for any scheme or course of conduct pursued;

War! that mad *game* the world so loves to play.
SWIFT.

Sport is sometimes used for the subject of *sport* to another;

Commit not thy prophetick mind
To flitting leaves, the *sport* of every wind,
Lest they disperse in air.—DRYDEN.

Why on that brow dwell sorrow and dismay,
Where loves were wont to *sport,* and smiles to play?
SWIFT.

The epithets *playful, gamesome,* and *sportive* bear a very similar distinction. *Playful* is taken in a general sense for a disposition to *play,* and applies peculiarly to children; 'He is scandalized at youth for being lively, and at childhood for being *playful.*'—ADDISON. *Gamesome* denotes a disposition to indulge in jest, but is seldom employed in a good sense;

Belial in like *gamesome* mood.—MILTON.

Sportive, which denotes a disposition to sporting or carrying on a *sport,* is a term of stronger import than *playful;*

I am not in a *sportive* humour now:
Tell me, and dally not, where is the money?
SHAKSPEARE.

FREAK, WHIM.

Freak most probably comes from the German *frech,* bold and petulant. *Whim,* from the Teutonick *wimmen* to whine or whimper: but they have at present somewhat deviated from their original meaning; for a *freak* has more of childishness and humour than boldness in it, a *whim* more of eccentricity than of childishness. Fancy and fortune are both said to have their *freaks,* as they both deviate most widely in their movements from all rule; but *whims* are at most but singular deviations of the mind from its ordinary and even course Females are most liable to be seized with *freaks,* which are in their nature sudden and not to be calculated upon: men are apt to indulge themselves in *whims* which are in their nature strange and often laughable. We should call it a *freak* for a female to put on the habit of a male, and so accoutred to sally forth into the streets;

But the long pomp, the midnight masquerade,
With all the *freaks* of wanton wealth array'd,
In these, ere trifles half their wish obtain,
The toiling pleasure sickens into pain.—GOLDSMITH.

We term it a *whim* in a man who takes a resolution never to shave himself any more;

'T is all bequeath'd to publick uses,
To publick uses! There's a *whim!*
What had the publick done for him?—SWIFT.

FANCIFUL, FANTASTICAL, WHIMSICAL, CAPRICIOUS.

Fanciful signifies full of *fancy* (*v. Conceit*); *fantastical* signifies belonging to the phantasy, which is the immediate derivative from the Greek; *whimsical* signifies either like a whim, or having a whim; *capricious* signifies having *caprice*.

Fanciful and *fantastical* are both employed for persons and things; *whimsical* and *capricious* are mostly employed for persons, or what is personal. *Fanciful*, in regard to persons, is said of that which is irregular in the taste or judgement; *fantastical* is said of that which violates all propriety, as well as regularity; the former may consist of a simple deviation from rule; the latter is something extravagant. A person may, therefore, sometimes be advantageously *fanciful*, although he can never be *fantastical* but to his discredit. Lively minds will be *fanciful* in the choice of their dress, furniture, or equipage; 'There is something very sublime, though very *fanciful*, in Plato's description of the Supreme Being, that "truth is his body, and light his shadow."'—ADDISON. The affectation of singularity frequently renders people *fantastical* in their manners as well as their dress;

Methinks heroick poesy, till now,
Like some *fantastick* fairy land did show.
COWLEY.

Fanciful is said mostly in regard to errours of opinion or taste; it springs from an aberration of the mind: *whimsical* is a species of the *fanciful* in regard to one's likes or dislikes: *capricious* respects errours of temper, or irregularities of feeling. The *fanciful* does not necessarily imply instability; but the *capricious* excludes the idea of fixedness. One is *fanciful* by attaching a reality to that which only passes in one's own mind; one is *whimsical* in the inventions of the *fancy*; one is *capricious* by acting and judging without rule or reason in that which admits of both. A person discovers himself to be *fanciful* who makes difficulties and objections which have no foundation in the external object, but in his own mind; 'The English are naturally *fanciful*.'—ADDISON. A person discovers himself to be *capricious* when he likes and dislikes the same thing in quick succession; 'Many of the pretended friendships of youth are founded on *capricious* liking.'—BLAIR. A person discovers himself to be *whimsical* who falls upon unaccountable modes, and imagines unaccountable things;

'T is this exalted power, whose business lies
In nonsense and impossibilities:
This made a *whimsical* philosopher
Before the spacious world a tub prefer.
ROCHESTER.

Sick persons are apt to be *fanciful* in their food; females, whose minds are not well disciplined, are apt to be *capricious*; the English have the character of being a *whimsical* nation. In application to things, the terms *fanciful* and *fantastical* preserve a similar distinction; what is *fanciful* may be the real and just combination of a well regulated *fancy*, or the unreal combination of a distempered *fancy*; the *fantastical* is not only the unreal, but the distorted combination of a disordered *fancy*. In sculpture or painting drapery may be *fancifully* disposed: the airiness and showiness which would not be becoming even in the dress of a young female, would be *fantastical* in that of an old woman

FASTIDIOUS, SQUEAMISH.

Fastidious, in Latin *fastidiosus*, from *fastus* pride signifies proudly, nice, not easily pleased: *squeamish*, changed from *qualmish* or weak-stomached, signifies, in the moral sense, foolishly sick, easily disgusted.

A female is *fastidious* when she criticises the dress or manners of her rival; 'The perception as well as the senses may be improved to our own disquiet; and we may by diligent cultivation of the powers of dislike raise in time an artificial *fastidiousness*.'—JOHNSON She is *squeamish* in the choice of her own dress, company, words, &c. Whoever examines his own imperfections will cease to be *fastidious*;

Were the fates more kind,
Our narrow luxuries would soon grow stale;
Were these exhaustless, nature would grow sick,
And, cloy'd with pleasure, *squeamishly* complain
That all is vanity, and life a dream.—ARMSTRONG.

Whoever restrains humour and caprice will cease to be *squeamish*.

PARTICULAR, SINGULAR, ODD, ECCENTRICK, STRANGE.

Particular, in French *particulier*, Latin *particularis*, from *particula* a particle, signifies belonging to a particle or a very small part; *singular*, in French *singulier*, Latin *singularis*, from *singulus* every one, which very probably comes from the Hebrew סגל *peculium*, or private property; *odd* is probably changed from *add*, signifying something arbitrarily added; *eccentrick*, from *ex* and *centre*, signifies out of the centre or direct line; *strange*, in French *étrange*, Latin *extra*, and Greek ἐξ out of, signifies out of some other part, or not belonging to this part.

All these terms are employed either as characteristicks of persons or things. What is *particular* belongs to some small *particle* or point to which it is confined: what is *singular* is *single*, or the only one of its kind; what is *odd* is without an equal or any thing with which it is fit to pair; what is *eccentrick* is not to be brought within any rule or estimate, it deviates to the right and the left; what is *strange* is different from that which one is accustomed to see, it does not admit of comparison or assimilation. A person is *particular* as it respects himself; he is *singular* as it respects others; he is *particular* in his habits or modes of action; he is *singular* in that which is about him; we may be *particular* or *singular* in our dress; in the former case we study the minute points of our dress to please ourselves; in the latter case we adopt a mode of dress that distinguishes us from all others.

One is *odd*, *eccentrick*, and *strange* more as it respects established modes, forms, and rules, than individual circumstances: a person is *odd* when his actions or his words bear no resemblance to that of others; he is *eccentrick* if he irregularly departs from the customary modes of proceeding; he is *strange* when that which he does makes him new or unknown to those who are about him. *Particularity* and *singularity* are not always taken in a bad sense; *oddness*, *eccentricity*, and *strangeness* are never taken in a good one. A person ought to be *particular* in the choice of his society, his amusements, his books, and the like; he ought to be *singular* in virtue, when vice is unfortunately prevalent: but *particularity* becomes ridiculous when it respects trifles; and *singularity* becomes culpable when it is not warranted by the most imperious necessity. As *oddness*, *eccentricity*, and *strangeness* consist in the violation of good order, of the decencies of human life, or the more important points of moral duty, they can never be justifiable, and often unpardonable. An *odd* man, whom no one can associate with, and who likes to associate with no one, is an outcast by nature, and a burden to the society which is troubled with his presence. An *eccentrick* character, who distinguishes himself by nothing but the breach of every established rule, is a being who deserves nothing but ridicule, or the more serious treatment of censure or rebuke. A *strange* person, who makes himself a *stranger* among those to whom he is bound by the closest ties, is a being as unfortunate as he is worthless. *Particularity*, in the bad sense, arises either from a naturally frivolous character, or the want of more serious objects to engage the mind; 'There is such a *particularity* for ever affected by great beauties, that they are encumbered with their charms in all they say or do.'—HUGHES. *Singularity*, which is much oftener taken in the bad than in the good sense, arises from a preposterous pride which thirsts after distinction even in folly; '*Singularity* is only vicious, as it makes men act contrary to reason.' —ADDISON. *Oddness* is mostly the effect of a distorted humour, attributable to an unhappy frame of mind;

So proud, I am no slave,
So impudent, I own myself no knave,
So *odd*, my country's ruin makes me grave.—POPE.

Eccentricity, which is the excess of *singularity*, arises commonly from the undisciplined state of strong powers; 'That acute, though *eccentrick* observer, Rousseau, had perceived that to strike and interest the publick, the marvellous must be produced.'—BURKE. *Strangeness*, which is a degree of *oddness*, has its source in the perverted state of the heart; 'A *strange*, proud return you may think I make you, madam, when I tell you, it is not from every body I would be thus obliged.'—SUCKLING. 'Artists, who propose only the imitation of such a *particular* person, without election of ideas, have been often reproached for that omission.'—DRYDEN.

So *singular* a madness
Must have a cause as *strange* as the effect.
DENHAM.

When applied to characterize inanimate objects they are mostly used in an indifferent sense, but sometimes in a bad sense: the *particular* serves to define or specify, it is opposed to the general or indefinite; a *particular* day or hour, a *particular* case, a *particular* person, are expressions which confine one's attention to one precise object in distinction from the rest; *singular*, like the word *particular*, marks but one object, and that which is clearly pointed out in distinction from the rest; but this term differs from the former, inasmuch as the *particular* is said only of that which one has arbitrarily made *particular*, but the *singular* is so from its own properties: thus a place is *particular* when we fix upon it, and mark it out in any manner so that it may be known from others; a place is *singular* if it have any thing in itself which distinguishes it from others. *Odd*, in an indifferent sense, is opposed to even, and applied to objects in general; an *odd* number, an *odd* person, an *odd* book, and the like: but it is also employed in a bad sense, to mark objects which are totally dissimilar to others, as an *odd* idea, an *odd* conceit, an *odd* whim, an *odd* way, an *odd* place; 'History is the great looking-glass, through which we may behold with ancestral eyes, not only the various actions of past ages, and the *odd* accidents that attend time, but also discern the different humours of men.'—HOWELL. *Eccentrick* is applied in its proper sense to mathematical lines or circles, which have not the same centre, and is never employed in regard to things in an improper sense: *strange*, in its proper sense, marks that which is unknown or unusual, as a *strange* face, a *strange* figure, a *strange* place; but in the moral application it is like the word *odd*, and conveys the unfavourable idea of that which is uncommon and not worth knowing; a *strange* noise designates not only that which has not been heard before, but that which it is not desirable to hear; a *strange* place may signify not only that which we have been unaccustomed to see, but that which has also much in it that is objectionable; 'Is it not *strange* that a rational man should worship an ox?'—SOUTH.

STRANGER, FOREIGNER, ALIEN.

Stranger, in French *étranger*, Latin *extraneus* or *extra*, in Greek ἐξ, signifies out of, that is, out of another country; *foreigner*, from *foris* abroad, and *alien*, from *alienus* another's, have obviously the same original meaning. They have, however, deviated in their acceptations. *Stranger* is a general term, and applies to one not known or not an inhabitant, whether of the same or another country; *foreigner* is applied only to *strangers* of another country; and *alien* is a technical term applied to *foreigners* as subjects or residents, in distinction from natural-born subjects. Ulysses after his return from the Trojan war, was a *stranger* in his own house. The French are *foreigners* in England, and the English in France. Neither can enjoy, as *aliens*, the same privileges in a foreign country as they do in their own. The laws of hospitality require us to treat *strangers* with more ceremony than we do members of the same family, or very intimate friends. The lower orders of the English are apt to treat *foreigners* with an undeserved contempt. Every *alien* is obliged in time of war to have a license for residing in England.

The term *stranger* is sometimes employed to denote one not acquainted with an object, or not having experienced its effects, as to be a *stranger* to sorrow, or to be a *stranger* to any work or subject; I was no *stranger* to the original; I had also studied Virgil's design, and his disposition of it. *Foreigner* is used only in the above-mentioned sense; but the epithet *foreign* sometimes signifies not belonging to an object;

All the distinctions of this little life
Are quite cutaneous, quite *foreign* to the man.
YOUNG.

Alien is sometimes employed by the poets in the sense of *foreigner;*

Like you an *alien* in a land unknown,
I learn to pity woes so like my own.—DRYDEN.

From *stranger* and *alien* come the verbs to *estrange* and *alienate*, which are extended in their meaning and application; the former signifying to make the understanding or mind of a person *strange* to an object, and the latter to make the heart or affections of one person *strange* to another. Thus we may say that the mind becomes *alienated* to one object, when it has fixed its affections on another; 'The manner of men's writing must not *alienate* our hearts from the truth.'—HOOKER. Or a person *estranges* himself from his family; 'Worldly and corrupt men *estrange* themselves from all that is divine.'—BLAIR.

FINICAL, SPRUCE, FOPPISH.

These epithets are applied to such as attempt at finery by improper means. The *finical* is insignificantly fine; the *spruce* is laboriously and artfully fine; the *foppish* is fantastically and affectedly fine. The *finical* is said mostly of manners and speech; the *spruce* is said of the dress; the *foppish* of dress and manners.

A *finical* gentleman clips his words and screws his body into as small a compass as possible to give himself the air of a delicate person; a *spruce* gentleman strives not to have a fold wrong in his frill or cravat, nor a hair of his head to lie amiss; a *foppish* gentleman seeks, by extravagance in the cut of his clothes, and by the tawdriness in their ornaments, to render himself distinguished for finery. A little mind, full of conceit of itself, will lead a man to be *finical;* 'I cannot hear a *finical* fop romancing how the king took him aside at such a time; what the queen said to him at another.'—L'ESTRANGE. A vacant mind that is anxious to be pleasing will not object to the employment of rendering the person *spruce;*

Methinks I see thee *spruce* and fine,
With coat embroider'd richly shine.—SWIFT.

A giddy, vain mind, eager after applause, impels a man to every kind of *foppery;*

The learned, full of inward pride,
The *fops* of outward show deride.—GAY.

Finical may also be applied in the same sense as an epithet for things; 'At the top of the building (Blenheim house) are several cupolas and little turrets that have but an ill effect, and make the building look at once *finical* and heavy.'—POPE.

HUMOUR, CAPRICE.

Humour (*v. Humour*) is general; *caprice* (*v. Fantastical*) is particular: *humour* may be good or bad, *caprice* is always taken in a bad sense. *Humour* is always independent of fixed principle; it is the feeling or impulse of the moment: *caprice* is always opposed to fixed principle, or rational motives of acting; it is the feeling of the individual setting at nought all rule, and defying all reason. The feeling only is perverted when the *humour* predominates;

You 'll ask me, why I rather choose to have
A weight of carrion flesh than to receive
Three thousand ducats; I 'll not answer that,
But say, it is my *humour*.—SHAKSPEARE.

The judgement and will are perverted by *caprice:* a child shows its *humour* in fretfulness and impatience; a man betrays his *caprice* in his intercourse with others, in the management of his concerns, in the choice of his amusements; 'Men will submit to any rule by which they may be exempted from the tyranny of *caprice* and chance.'—JOHNSON.

Indulgence renders children and subordinate persons *humorsome:* 'I am glad that though you are incredulous you are not *humorsome* too.'—GOODMAN. Prosperity or unlimited power is apt to render a man *capricious;* 'A subject ought to suppose that there are reasons, although he be not apprized of them, otherwise he must tax his prince of *capriciousness*, inconstancy, or ill design.'—SWIFT. A *humorsome* person commonly objects to be pleased, or is easily displeased; a *capricious* person likes and dislikes, approves and disapproves the same thing in quick succession. *Humour*, when applied to things, has the sense of wit; whence the distinction between *humorsome* and *humorous:* the former implying the existence of *humour* or perverted feeling in the person; the latter implying the existence of *humour* or wit in the person or thing;

Thy *humorous* vein, thy pleasing folly
Lies all neglected, all forgot,
And pensive, wayward, melancholy,
Thou dread'st and hop'st thou know'st not what.
PRIOR.

Caprice is improperly applied to things to designate their total irregularity and planlessness of proceeding; as, in speaking of fashion, we notice its *caprice*, when that which has been laid aside is again taken into use: diseases are termed *capricious* which act in direct opposition to all established rule; 'Does it imply that our language is in its nature irregular and *capricious?*' LOWTH.

HUMOUR, TEMPER, MOOD.

Humour literally signifies moisture or fluid, in which sense it is used for the fluids of the human body; and as far as these *humours* or their particular state is connected with, or has its influence on, the animal spirits and the moral feelings, so far is *humour* applicable to moral agents; *temper* (*v. Disposition*) is less specifick in its signification; it may with equal propriety, under the changed form of temperament, be applicable to the general state of the body or the mind; *mood*, which is but a change from *mode* or manner, has an original signification not less indefinite than the former; it is applied only to the mind.

As the *humours* of the body are the most variable parts of the animal frame, *humour* in regard to the mind denotes but a partial and transitory state when compared with the *temper*, which is a general and habitual state. The *humour* is so fluctuating that it varies in the same mind perpetually; but the *temper* is so far confined that it always shows itself to be the same whenever it shows itself at all: the *humour* makes a man different from himself; the *temper* makes him different from others. Hence we speak of the *humour* of the moment; of the *temper* of the youth or of old age: so likewise we say, to accommodate one's self to the *humour* of a person; to manage his *temper:* to put one into a certain *humour;* to correct or sour the *temper*. *Humour* is not less partial in its nature than in its duration; it fixes itself often on only one object, or respects only one particular direction of the feelings: *temper* extends to all the actions and opinions as well as feelings of a man; it gives a colouring to all he says, does, thinks, and feels: 'There are three or four single men who suit my *temper* to a hair.'—COWPER. We may be in a *humour* for writing, or reading; for what is gay or what is serious; for what is noisy or what is quiet: but our *temper* is discoverable in our daily conduct; we may be in a good or ill *humour* in company, but in domestic life and in our closet relations we show whether we are good or ill *tempered*. A man shows his *humour* in different or trifling actions; he shows his *temper* in the most important actions: it may be a man's *humour* to sit while others stand, or to go unshaven while others shave; but he shows his *temper* as a Christian or otherwise in forgiving injuries or harbouring resentments; in living peaceably, or indulging himself in contentions;

It is the curse of kings to be attended
By slaves, that take their *humours* for a warrant
To break into the bloodhouse of life.
SHAKSPEARE.

'This, I shall call it evangelical, *temper* is far from being natural to any corrupt son of Adam.'—HAMMOND.

The same distinction is kept up between the terms when applied to bodies of men. A nation may have its *humour* and its *temper* as much as an individual: the former discovers itself in the manners and fashion; the latter in its publick spirit towards its government or other nations. It has been the most unlucky *humour* of the present day to banish ceremony, and consequently decency, from all companies; 'True modesty is ashamed to do any thing that is opposite to the *humour* of the company.'—ADDISON. The *temper* of the times is somewhat more sober now than it was during the heat of the revolutionary mania; 'All irregular *tempers* in trade and business are but like irregular *tempers* in eating and drinking.'—LAW.

Humour and *mood* agree in denoting a particular and temporary state of feeling; but they differ in the cause. the former being attributable rather to the physical state of the body; and the latter to the moral frame of the mind: the former therefore is independent of all external circumstances, or at all events, of any that are reducible to system; the latter is guided entirely by events. *Humour* is therefore generally taken in a bad sense, unless actually qualified by some epithet to the contrary;

Their *humours* are not to be won
But when they are imposed upon.—HUDIBRAS

Mood is always taken in an indifferent sense; 'Strange as it may seem, the most ludicrous lines I ever wrote have been written in the saddest *mood*.'—COWPER. There is no calculating on the *humour* of a man; it depends upon his *mood* whether he performs ill or well: it is necessary to suppress *humour* in a child; we discover by the melancholy *mood* of a man that something distressing has happened to him.

DISPOSITION, TEMPER.

Disposition, from *dispose* (*v. To dispose*), signifies here the state of being *disposed;* *temper*, like *temperament*, from the Latin *temperamentum* and *tempero* to temper or manage, signifies the thing modelled or formed.

These terms are both applied to the mind and its bias; but *disposition* respects the whole frame and texture of the mind: *temper* respects only the bias or tone of the feelings.

Disposition is permanent and settled; 'My friend has his eye more upon the virtue and *disposition* of his children than their advancement or wealth.'—STEELE. *Temper* is transitory and fluctuating; 'The man who lives under an habitual sense of the Divine presence keeps up a perpetual cheerfulness of *temper*.'—ADDISON. The *disposition* comprehends the springs and motives of action; the *temper* influences the actions for the time being: it is possible and not unfrequent to have a good *disposition* with a bad *temper*, and *vice versâ*.

A good *disposition* makes a man a useful member of society, but not always a good companion; 'Akenside was a young man warm with every notion that by nature or accident had been connected with the sound of liberty, and by an eccentricity which such *dispositions* do not easily avoid, a lover of contradiction, and no friend to any thing established.'—JOHNSON. A good *temper* renders a man acceptable to all and peaceable with all, but essentially useful to none; 'In coffeehouses a man of my *temper* is in his element, for if he cannot talk he can be still more agreeable to his company as well as pleased in himself in being a hearer.'—STEELE. A good *disposition* will go far towards correcting the errours of *temper;* but where there is a bad *disposition* there are no hopes of amendment.

DISPOSITION, INCLINATION.

Disposition in the preceding section is taken for the general frame of the mind; in the present case for its particular frame; *inclination, v. Attachment.*

Disposition is more positive than *inclination.* We may always expect a man to do that which he is *disposed* to do: but we cannot always calculate upon his executing that to which he is merely *inclined.*

We indulge a *disposition;* we yield to an *inclination.* The *disposition* comprehends the whole state of the mind at the time; 'It is the duty of every man who would be true to himself, to obtain if possible a *disposition* to be pleased.'—STEELE. An *inclination* is particular, referring always to a particular object; 'There never was a time, believe me, when I wanted an *inclination* to cultivate your esteem, and promote your interest.'—MELMOTH'S (*Letters of Cicero*). After the performance of a serious duty, no one is expected to be in a *disposition* for laughter or merriment: it is becoming to suppress our *inclination* to laughter in the presence of those who wish to be serious; we should be careful not to enter into controversy with one who shows a *disposition* to be unfriendly. When a young person discovers any *inclination* to study, there are hopes of his improvement.

TEMPERAMENT, TEMPERATURE.

Temperament and *temperature* are both used to express that state which arises from the tempering of opposite or varying qualities; the *temperament* is said of animal bodies, and the *temperature* of the atmosphere Men of a sanguine *temperament* ought to be cautious in their diet; 'Without a proper *temperament* for the particular art which he studies, his utmost pains will be to no purpose.'—BUDGELL. All bodies are strongly affected by the *temperature* of the air; 'O happy England, where there is such a rare *temperature* of heat and cold.'—HOWELL.

FRAME, TEMPER, TEMPERAMENT, CONSTITUTION.

Frame in its natural sense is that which forms the exteriour edging of any thing, and consequently determines its form; it is applied to man physically or mentally, as denoting that constituent portion of him which seems to hold the rest together; which by an extension of the metaphor is likewise put for the whole contents, the whole body, or the whole mind; *temper* and *temperament,* in Latin *temperamentum,* from *tempero* to govern or dispose, signify the particular modes of being disposed or organized; *constitution,* from *constitute* to appoint, signifies the particular mode of being *constituted* or formed.

Frame, when applied to the body, is taken in its most universal sense; as when we speak of the *frame* being violently agitated, or the human *frame* being wonderfully constructed: when applied to the mind it will admit either of a general or restricted signification;

> The soul
> Contemplates what she is, and whence she came,
> And almost comprehends her own amazing *frame.*
> JENYNS.

Temper, which is applicable only to the mind, is taken for the general or particular state of the individual;

> 'T is he
> Sets superstition high on virtue's throne,
> Then thinks his Maker's *temper* like his own.
> JENYNS.

The *frame* comprehends either the whole body of mental powers, or the particular disposition of those powers in individuals; the *temper* comprehends the general or particular state of feeling as well as thinking in the individual. The mental *frame* which receives any violent concussion is liable to derangement;

> Your steady soul preserves her *frame,*
> In good and evil times the same.—SWIFT.

It is necessary for those who govern to be well acquainted with the *temper* of those whom they govern; 'The brain may devise laws for the blood, but a hot *temper* leaps o'er a cold decree.'—SHAKSPEARE. By reflection on the various attributes of the Divine Being, a man may easily bring his mind into a *frame* of devotion; 'There is a great tendency to cheerfulness in religion; and such a *frame* of mind is not only the most lovely, but the most commendable in a virtuous person.'—ADDISON. By the indulgence of a fretful, repining *temper,* a man destroys his own peace of mind, and offends his Maker; 'The sole strength of the sound from the shouting of multitudes so amazes and confounds the imagination, that the best established *tempers* can scarcely forbear being borne down.' —BURKE.

Temperament and *constitution* mark the general state of the individual; the former comprehends a mixture of the physical and mental; the latter has a purely physical application. A man with a warm *temperament* owes his warmth of character to the rapid impetus of the blood; a man with a delicate *constitution* is exposed to great fluctuations in his health; 'I have always more need of a laugh than a cry, being somewhat disposed to melancholy by my *temperament.*' —COWPER. 'How little our *constitution* is able to bear a remove into parts of this air, not much higher than that we commonly breathe in!'—LOCKE.

The whole *frame* of a new-born infant is peculiarly tender. Men of fierce *tempers* are to be found in all nations; men of sanguine *tempers* are more frequent in warm climates; the *constitutions* of females are more tender than those of the male, and their *frames* are altogether more susceptible.

TO QUALIFY, TEMPER, HUMOUR.

Qualify, compounded of the Latin *qualis* and *facio,* signifies to make a thing what it ought to be; to *temper,* from *tempero,* is to regulate the temperament; to *humour* is to suit to the *humour.*

Things are *qualified* according to circumstances: what is too harsh must be *qualified* by something that is soft and lenitive; things are *tempered* by nature so that things perfectly discordant should not be combined; things are *humoured* by contrivance: what is subject to many changes requires to be *humoured;* a polite person will *qualify* his refusal of a request by some expression of kindness; 'It is the excellency of friendship to rectifie or at least to *qualifie* the malignity of these surmises.'—SOUTH. Providence has *tempered* the seasons so as to mix something that is pleasant in them all: 'God in his mercy has so framed and *tempered* his word, that we have for the most part a reserve of mercy wrapped up in a curse.'—SOUTH. Nature itself is sometimes to be *humoured* when art is employed: but the *tempers* of men require still more to be *humoured;* 'Our British gardeners, instead of *humouring* nature, love to deviate from it as much as possible.'—ADDISON.

GOOD-NATURE, GOOD-HUMOUR.

Good-nature and *good-humour* both imply the disposition to please and be pleased: but the former is habitual and permanent, the latter is temporary and partial: the former lies in the nature and frame of the mind; the latter in the state of the humours or spirits. A *good-natured* man recommends himself at all times by his *good-nature;* a *good-humoured* man recommends himself particularly as a companion: *good-nature* displays itself by a readiness in doing kind offices; 'Affability, mildness, tenderness, and a word which I would fain bring back to its original signification of virtue, I mean *good-nature,* are of daily use.'—ADDISON. *Good-humour* is confined mostly to the ease and cheerfulness of one's outward deportment in social converse; 'There was but one who kept up his *good-humour* to the Land's End.'—ADDISON. *Good-nature* is apt to be guilty of weak compliances: *good-humour* is apt to be succeeded by fits of peevishness and depression. *Good-nature* is applicable only to the character of the individual; *good-humour* may be said of a whole company: it is a mark of *good-nature* in a man not to disturb the *good-humour* of the company he is in, by resenting the affront that is offered him by another.

Good-nature qualifies every thing we say or do, so as to render even reproof bearable; 'I concluded, however unaccountable the assertion might appear at first sight, that *good-nature* was an essential quality in a satirist.'—ADDISON. *Good-humour* takes off from the personality of every remark; 'When Virgil said "He that did not hate Bavius might love Mævius," he was in perfect *good-humour.*'—ADDISON.

JEALOUSY, ENVY, SUSPICION.

Jealousy, in French *jalousie*, Latin *zelotypia*, Greek ζηλοτυπία, compounded of ζῆλος and τύπτω to strike or fill, signifies properly filled with a burning desire; *envy*, in French *envie*, Latin *invidia*, from *invideo*, compounded of *in* privative and *video* to see, signifies not looking at, or looking at in a contrary direction.

We are *jealous* of what is our own, we are *envious* of what is another's. *Jealousy* fears to lose what it has; *envy* is pained at seeing another have. Princes are *jealous* of their authority; subjects are *jealous* of their rights: courtiers are *envious* of those in favour; women are *envious* of superior beauty.

The *jealous* man has an object of desire, something to get and something to retain: he does not look beyond the object that interferes with his enjoyment; a *jealous* husband may therefore be appeased by the declaration of his wife's animosity against the object of his *jealousy*. The *envious* man sickens at the sight of enjoyment; he is easy only in the misery of others: all endeavours, therefore, to satisfy an *envious* man are fruitless. *Jealousy* is a noble or an ignoble passion, according to the object; in the former case it is emulation sharpened by fear, in the latter case it is greediness stimulated by fear; 'Every man is more *jealous* of his natural than his moral qualities.'—HAWKESWORTH.

> 'T is doing wrong creates such doubts as these,
> Renders us *jealous*, and destroys our peace.
> WALLER.

Envy is always a base passion, having the worst passions in its train; 'The *envious* man is in pain upon all occasions which should give him pleasure.'—ADDISON.

Jealous is applicable to bodies of men as well as individuals; *envious* to individuals only. Nations are *jealous* of any interference on the part of any other power in their commerce, government, or territory; 'While the people are so *jealous* of the clergy's ambition, I do not see any other method left them to reform the world, than by using all honest arts to make themselves acceptable to the laity.'—SWIFT. Individuals are *envious* of the rank, wealth, and honours of each other; 'A woman does not *envy* a man for fighting courage, nor a man a woman for her beauty.'—COLLIER.

Jealousy and *suspicion* both imply a fear of another's will, intentions, or power, to dispossess one of some object of desire: but in *jealousy* there is none of the distrust which belongs to *suspicion*. The *jealous* man does not dispute the integrity or sincerity of his opponent; the suspicious man thinks ill of both. *Jealousy* exists properly between equals, or those who may without direct injustice make pretensions to the same thing; rival lovers are *jealous* of each other: *suspicion* fixes on the person who by fraud or circumvention is supposed to aim at getting what he has no right to; men *suspect* those who have once cheated them. *Jealousy* is most alive when the person's intentions are known; *suspicion* can only exist while the views of the party are concealed. According to this distinction Lord Clarendon has erroneously substituted the word *jealousy* for that of *suspicion* when he says, 'The obstinacy in Essex, in refusing to treat with the king, proceeded only from his *jealousy*, that when the king had got him into his hands, he would take revenge upon him.'—There can be no *jealousy* between a subject and a king, or between parties entering into a treaty; but there may be *suspicion* of the good faith of either side towards the other;

> Though wisdom wake, *suspicion* sleeps
> At wisdom's gate; and to simplicity
> Resigns her charge; while goodness thinks no ill
> Where no ill seems.

INVIDIOUS, ENVIOUS.

Invidious, in Latin *invidiosus*, from *invidia* and *invideo* not to look at, signifies looking at with an evil eye; *envious* is literally only a variation of *invidious*. *Invidious* in its common acceptation signifies causing ill will; *envious* signifies having ill will.

A task is *invidious* that puts one in the way of giving offence; a look is *envious* that is full of *envy*. *Invidious* qualifies the thing; *envious* qualifies the emper of the mind It is *invidious* for one author to be judge against another who has written on the same subject;

> For I must speak what wisdom would conceal,
> And truths *invidious* to the great reveal.—POPE.

A man is *envious* when the prospect of another's happiness gives him pain; 'They that desire to excel in too many matters out of levity and vainglory, are ever *envious*.'—BACON.

LIVELY, SPRIGHTLY, VIVACIOUS, SPORTIVE, MERRY, JOCUND.

Lively signifies having life, or the animal spirits which accompany the vital spark; *sprightly*, contracted from *sprightfully* or *spiritfully*, signifies full of spirits; *vivacious*, in Latin *vivax*, from *vivo* to live, has the same original meaning as *lively; sportive*, fond of or ready for sport; *merry*, *v. Cheerful; jocund*, in Latin *jocundus*, from *jucundus* and *juvo* to delight or please, signifies delighted or pleased.

The activity of the heart when it beats high with a sentiment of gayety is strongly depicted by all these terms: the *lively* is the most general and literal in its signification; *life*, as a moving or active principle, is supposed to be inherent in spiritual as well as material bodies; the feeling, as well as the body which has within a power of moving arbitrarily of itself, is said to have *life*, and in whatever object this is wanting, this object is said to be dead: in like manner, according to the degree or circumstances under which this moving principle displays itself, the object is denominated *lively*, *sprightly*, *vivacious*, and the like. *Liveliness* is the property of childhood, youth, or even maturer age: *sprightliness* is the peculiar property of youth; *vivacity* is a quality compatible with the sobriety of years: an infant shows itself to be *lively* or otherwise in a few months after its birth; a female, particularly in her early years, affords often a pleasing picture of *sprightliness;* a *vivacious* companion recommends himself wherever he goes. *Sportiveness* is an accompaniment of *liveliness* or *sprightliness:* a *sprightly* child will show its *sprightliness* by its *sportive* humour: *mirth* and *jocundity* are the forms of *liveliness* which display themselves in social life; the former is a familiar quality, more frequently to be discovered in vulgar than in polished society: *jocundity* is a form of *liveliness* which poets have ascribed to nymphs and goddesses, and other aërial creatures of the imagination.

The terms preserve the same sense when applied to the characteristicks or actions of persons as when applied to the persons themselves: imagination, wit, conception, representation, and the like, are *lively;* 'One study is inconsistent with a *lively* imagination, another with a solid judgement.'—JOHNSON. A person's air, manner, look, tune, dance, are *sprightly;*

> His *sportive* lambs,
> This way and that convolv'd, in friskful glee
> Their frolicks play. And now the *sprightly* race
> Invites them forth.—THOMSON.

A conversation, a turn of mind, a society, is *vivacious;* 'By every victory over appetite or passion, the mind gains new strength to refuse those solicitations by which the young and *vivacious* are hourly assaulted.'—JOHNSON. The muse, the pen, the imagination, is *sportive;* the meeting, the laugh, the song, the conceit, is *merry;*

> Warn'd by the streaming light and *merry* lark,
> Forth rush the jolly clans.—SOMERVILLE.

The train, the dance, is *jocund;*

> Thus *jocund* fleets with them the winter night.
> THOMSON.

CHEERFUL, MERRY, SPRIGHTLY, GAY.

Cheerful signifies full of *cheer*, or of that which *cheers* (*v. To animate*); *merry*, in Saxon *merig*, is probably connected with the word *mare*, and the Latin *meretrix* a strumpet; *sprightly* is contracted from spiritedly; *gay* is connected with joy and jocund, in Latin *jocundus*, from *juvo* to delight; *cheerful* marks an unruffled flow of spirits; with *mirth* there is more of tumult and noise; with *sprightliness* there is more buoyancy; *gayety* comprehends *mirth* and indulgence. A *cheerful* person smiles; the *merry* person laughs;

the *sprightly* person dances; the *gay* person takes his pleasure.

The *cheerful* countenance remains *cheerful;* it marks the contentment of the heart, and its freedom from pain: the *merry* face will often look sad; a trifle will turn *mirth* into sorrow: the *sprightliness* of youth is often succeeded by the listlessness of bodily infirmity, or the gloom of despondency: *gayety* is as transitory as the pleasures upon which it subsists; it is often followed by sullenness and discontent.

Cheerfulness is an habitual state of the mind; *mirth* is an occasional elevation of the spirits; *sprightliness* lies in the temperature and flow of the blood; *gayety* depends altogether on external circumstances. Religion is the best promoter of *cheerfulness:* it makes its possessor pleased with himself and all around him; 'I have always preferred *cheerfulness* to *mirth:* the latter I consider as an act, the former as a habit of the mind. *Mirth* is short and transient; *cheerfulness* fixed and permanent.'—Addison. Company and wine are but too often the only promoters of *mirth;* 'Mankind may be divided into the *merry* and the serious, who both of them make a very good figure in the species so long as they keep their respective humours from degenerating into the neighbouring extreme.'—Addison. Youth and health will naturally be attended with *sprightliness;*

> But Venus, anxious for her son's affairs,
> New counsels tries, and new designs prepares:
> That Cupid should assume the shape and face
> Of sweet Ascanius, and the *sprightly* grace.
> Dryden.

A succession of pleasures, an exemption from care, and the banishment of thought, will keep *gayety* alive.

Sprightly and *merry* are seldom employed but in the proper sense as respects persons: but *cheerful* and *gay* are extended to different objects; as a *cheerful* prospect, a *cheerful* room, *gay* attire, a *gay* scene, *gay* colours, &c.;

> To kinder skies, where gentler manners reign,
> I turn: and France displays her bright domain.
> *Gay, sprightly* land of *mirth* and social ease,
> Pleas'd with thyself, whom all the world can please.
> Goldsmith.

LIGHTNESS, LEVITY, FLIGHTINESS, VOLATILITY, GIDDINESS.

Lightness, from *light*, signifies the abstract quality; *levity*, in Latin *levitas*, from *levis* light, signifies the same; *volatility*, in Latin *volatilitas*, from *volo* to fly, signifies flitting, or ready to fly swiftly on; *flightiness*, from *flighty* and *fly*, signifies the readiness to fly; *giddiness*, from *giddy*, in Saxon *gidig*, is probably connected with the verb *gehen* to go, signifying a state of going unsteadily.

Lightness is taken either in the natural or metaphorical sense; the rest only in the moral sense: *lightness* is said of the outward carriage, or the inward temper; *levity* is said only of the outward carriage; a *light* minded man treats every thing *lightly*, be it ever so serious; the *lightness* of his mind is evident by the *lightness* of his motions. *Lightness* is common to both sexes; *levity* is peculiarly striking in females; and in respect to them, they are both exceptionable qualities in the highest degree: when a woman has *lightness* of mind, she verges very near towards direct vice; when there is *levity* in her conduct she exposes herself to the imputation of criminality; 'Innocence gives a *lightness* to the spirits, ill imitated and ill supplied by that forced *levity* of the vicious.'—Blair. *Volatility, flightiness*, and *giddiness* are degrees of *lightness*, which rise in signification one on another; *volatility* being more than *lightness*, and the others more than *volatility: lightness* and *volatility* are defects as they relate to age; those only who ought to be serious or grave are said to be *light* or *volatile*. When we treat that as *light* which is weighty, when we suffer nothing to sink into the mind, or make any impression, this is a defective *lightness* of character; when the spirits are of a buoyant nature, and the thoughts fly from one object to another, without resting on any for a moment, this *lightness* becomes *volatility;* 'If we see people dancing, even in wooden shoes, and a fiddle always at their heels, we are soon convinced of the *volatile* spirits of those merry slaves.'—Somerville. A *light* minded person sets care at a distance; a *volatile* person catches pleasure from every passing object. *Flightiness* and *giddiness* are the defects of youth; they bespeak that entire want of command over one's feelings and animal spirits which is inseparable from a state of childhood: a *flighty* child, however, only fails from a want of attention; but a *giddy* child, like one whose head is in the natural sense *giddy*, is unable to collect itself so as to have any consciousness of what passes: a *flighty* person commits improprieties; 'Remembering many *flightinesses* in her writing, I know not how to behave myself to her.'—Richardson. A *giddy* person commits extravagances;

> The *giddy* vulgar, as their fancies guide,
> With noise, say nothing, and in parts divide.
> Dryden.

FROLICK, GAMBOL, PRANK.

Frolick, in German, &c. *fröhlich* cheerful, comes from *froh* merry, and *freude* joy; *gambol* signifies literally leaping into the air, from the Italian *gamba*, in French *jamb* the leg; *prank* is changed from *prance*, which literally signifies to throw up the hind feet after the manner of a horse, and is most probably connected with the German *prangen* to make a parade or fuss, and the Hebrew פרע to set free, because the freedom indicated by the word *prank* is more or less discoverable in the sense of all these terms. The *frolick* is a merry, joyous entertainment; the *gambol* is a dancing, light entertainment; the *prank* is a freakish, wild entertainment. Laughing, singing, noise, and feasting constitute the *frolick* of the careless mind; it belongs to a company: conceit, levity, and trick, in movement, gesture, and contrivance, constitute the *gambol;* it belongs to the individual: adventure, eccentricity, and humour constitute the *prank;* it belongs to one or many. One has a *frolick;* one plays a *gambol*, or a *prank*. *Frolick* is the mirth rather of vulgar minds; servants have their *frolicks* in the kitchen while their masters have pleasures abroad; 'I have heard of some very merry fellows, among whom the *frolick* was started and passed by a great majority, that every man should immediately draw a tooth.'—Steele. *Gambols* are the diversions of youth; the Christmas season has given rise to a variety of *gambols* for the entertainment of both sexes. The term *gambol* may also be applied to the tricks of animals;

> The monsters of the flood
> *Gambol* around him in the wat'ry way,
> And heavy whales in awkward measures play
> Pope.

And in the same sense the term may be applied figuratively;

> What are those crested locks
> That make such wanton *gambols* with the wind?
> Shakspeare.

Pranks are the diversions of the undisciplined; the rude schoolboy broke loose from school spends his time in molesting a neighbourhood with his mischievous *pranks;* 'Some time afterward (1756), some young men of the college, whose chambers were near his (Gray's), diverted themselves by frequent and troublesome noises, and, as is said, by *pranks* yet more offensive and contemptuous.'—Johnson. *Frolick* is the diversion of human beings only; *gambol* and *prank* are likewise applicable to brutes; a kitten *gambols;* a horse, a monkey, and a squirrel will play *pranks*.

TO AMUSE, DIVERT, ENTERTAIN.

To *amuse* is to occupy the mind lightly, from the Latin *musa* a song, signifying to allure the attention by any thing as light and airy as a song; *divert*, in French *divertir*, Latin *diverto*, is compounded of *di* and *verto* to turn aside, signifying to turn the mind aside from an object; *entertain*, in French *entretenir*, compounded of *entre, inter*, and *tenir*, or the Latin *teneo* to keep, signifies to keep the mind fixed on a thing.

We *amuse* or *entertain* by engaging the attention on some present occupation; we *divert* by drawing the attention from a present object; all this proceeds by the means of that pleasure which the object produces, which in the first case is less vivid than in the second, and in the second case is less durable than in the third. Whatever *amuses* serves to kill time, to lull the faculties, and banish reflection; it may be solitary, sedentary, and lifeless, but also sociable or intellectual, according to the temper of the person; 'I yesterday passed a whole afternoon in the churchyard, the cloisters, and the church, *amusing* myself with the tombstones and inscriptions that I met with in those several regions of the dead.'—ADDISON. Whatever *diverts* causes mirth, and provokes laughter; it will be active, lively, and sometimes tumultuous; 'His *diversion* on this occasion was to see the cross-bows, mistaken signs, and wrong connivances that passed amid so many broken and refracted rays of sight.'—ADDISON. Whatever *entertains* acts on the senses, and awakens the understanding; it must be rational, and is mostly social; 'Will Honeycomb was very *entertaining*, the other night at the play, to a gentleman who sat on his right-hand, while I was at his left. The gentleman believed Will was talking to himself.'—ADDISON. The bare act of walking and changing place may *amuse;* the tricks of animals *divert;* conversation *entertains*. We sit down to a card-table to be *amused;* we go to a comedy or pantomime to be *diverted;* we go to a tragedy to be *entertained*. Children are *amused* with looking at pictures: ignorant people are *diverted* with shows; intelligent people are *entertained* with reading.

The dullest and most vacant, as well as the most intelligent, minds may be *amused;* the most volatile are *diverted;* the most reflective are *entertained:* the emperour Domitian *amused* himself with killing flies: the emperour Nero *diverted* himself with appearing before his subjects in the characters of gladiator and charioteer; Socrates *entertained* himself by discoursing on the day of his execution with his friends on the immortality of the soul.

TO AMUSE, BEGUILE.

Amuse signifies the same as in the preceding article; *beguile* is compounded of *be* and *guile* signifying to overreach with *guile*. As *amuse* denotes the occupation of the mind, so *beguile* expresses an effect or consequence of *amusement*.

When *amuse* and *beguile* express any species of deception, the former indicates what is effected by persons, and the latter that which is effected by things. To *amuse* is to practise a fraud upon the understanding; to *beguile* is to practise a fraud upon the memory and consciousness. We are *amused* by a false story; our misfortunes are *beguiled* by the charms of fine music or fine scenery. To suffer one's self to be *amused* is an act of weakness; to be *beguiled* is a relief and a privilege. Credulous people are easily *amused* by any idle tale, and thus prevented from penetrating the designs of the artful; 'In latter ages pious frauds were made use of to *amuse* mankind.'—ADDISON. Weary travellers *beguile* the tedium of the journey by lively conversation;

> With seeming innocence the crowd *beguil'd*,
> But made the desperate passes when he smil'd.
> DRYDEN.

AMUSEMENT, ENTERTAINMENT, DIVERSION, SPORT, RECREATION, PASTIME.

Amusement signifies here that which serves to *amuse* (*v. To amuse, divert*); *entertainment*, that which serves to *entertain* (*v. To amuse*); *diversion*, that which serves to *divert* (*v. To amuse, divert*); *sport*, that which serves to give *sport*; *recreation*, that which serves to *recreate*, from *recreatus*, participle of *recreo* or *re* and *creo* to create or make alive again; *pastime*, that which serves to *pass time*.

The first four of these terms are either applied to objects which specifically serve the purposes of pleasure, or to such as may accidentally serve this purpose; the last two terms are employed only in the latter sense.

The distinction between the first three terms are very similar in this as in the preceding case. *Amusement* is a general term, which comprehends little more than the common idea of pleasure, whether small or great;

> As Atlas groan'd
> The world beneath, we groan beneath an hour:
> We cry for mercy to the next *amusement*.
> The next *amusement* mortgages our fields.
> YOUNG.

Entertainment is a species of *amusement* which is always more or less of an intellectual nature; 'The stage might be made a perpetual source of the most noble and useful *entertainments*, were it under proper regulations.'—ADDISON. *Diversions* and *sports* are a species of *amusements* more adapted to the young and the active, particularly the latter: the theatre or the concert is an *entertainment:* fairs and publick exhibitions are *diversions;* 'When I was some years younger than I am at present, I used to employ myself in a more laborious *diversion*, which I learned from a Latin treatise of exercises that is written with great erudition; it is there called the σχιομαχια, or the fighting with a man's own shadow.'—ADDISON. Games of racing or cricket, hunting, shooting, and the like, are *sports;* 'With great respect to country *sports*, I may say this gentleman could pass his time agreeably, if there were not a fox or a hare in his county.'—STEELE.

Recreation and *pastime* are terms of relative import; the former is of use for those who labour; the latter for those who are idle. A *recreation* must partake more or less of the nature of an *amusement*, but it is an occupation which owes its pleasure to the relaxation of the mind from severe exertion: in this manner gardening may be a *recreation* to one who studies; 'Pleasure and *recreation* of one kind or other are absolutely necessary to relieve our minds and bodies from too constant attention and labour: where therefore publick *diversions* are tolerated, it behooves persons of distinction, with their power and example, to preside over them.'—STEELE. Company is a *recreation* to a man of business: the *pastime* is the *amusement* of the leisure hour; it may be alternately a *diversion*, a *sport*, or a simple *amusement*, as circumstances require; 'Your microscope brings to sight shoals of living creatures in a spoonful of vinegar; but we, who can distinguish them in their different magnitudes, see among them several huge Leviathans that terrify the little fry of animals about them, and take their *pastime* as in an ocean.'—ADDISON.

MIRTH, MERRIMENT, JOVIALITY, JOLLITY, HILARITY.

These terms all express that species of gayety or joy which belongs to company, or to men in their social intercourse.

Mirth refers to the feeling displayed in the outward conduct: *merriment*, and the other terms, refer rather to the external expressions of the feeling, or the causes of the feeling, than to the feeling itself: *mirth* shows itself in laughter, in dancing, singing, and noise; *merriment* consists of such things as are apt to excite *mirth:* the more we are disposed to laugh, the greater is our *mirth;* the more there is to create laughter, the greater is the *merriment:* the tricks of Punch and his wife, or the jokes of a clown, cause much *mirth* among the gaping crowd of rustics; the amusements with the swing, or the roundabout, afford much *merriment* to the visitants of a fair. *Mirth* is confined to no age or station; but *merriment* belongs more particularly to young people, or those of the lower station; *mirth* may be provoked wherever any number of persons is assembled; 'The highest gratification we receive here from company is *mirth*, which at the best is but a fluttering, unquiet motion.'—POPE. *Merriment* cannot go forward any where so properly as at fairs, or common and publick places; 'He who best knows our natures by such afflictions recalls our wandering thoughts from idle *merriment*.'—GRAY. *Joviality* or *jollity*, and *hilarity*, are species of *merriment* which belong to the convivial board, or to less refined indulgences: *joviality* or *jollity* is the unrefined, unlicensed indulgence in the pleasures of the table, or any social entertainments;

> Now swarms the village o'er the *jovial* mead.
> THOMSON

> With branches we the fanes adorn, and waste
> In *jollity* the day ordain'd to be the last.
> DRYDEN.

Hilarity is the same thing qualified by the cultivation

and good sense of the company: we may expect to find much *joviality* and *jollity* at a publick dinner of mechanicks, watermen, or labourers: we may expect to find *hilarity* at a publick dinner of noblemen: eating, drinking, and noise constitute the *joviality;* the conversation, the songs, the toasts, and the publick spirit of the company contribute to *hilarity;* 'He that contributes to the *hilarity* of the vacant hour will be welcomed with ardour.'—JOHNSON.

FESTIVITY, MIRTH.

There is commonly *mirth* with *festivity*, but there may be frequently *mirth* without *festivity*. The *festivity* lies in the outward circumstances: *mirth* in the temper of the mind. *Festivity* is rather the producer of *mirth* than the *mirth* itself. *Festivity* includes the social enjoyments of eating, drinking, dancing, cards, and other pleasures; 'Pisistratus, fearing that the *festivity* of his guests would be interrupted by the misconduct of Thrasippus, rose from his seat, and entreated him to stay.'—CUMBERLAND. *Mirth* includes in it the buoyancy of spirits which is engendered by a participation in such pleasures;

Low lies that house where nut-brown draughts inspir'd,
Where graybeard *mirth* and smiling toil retir'd.
GOLDSMITH.

GRAVE, SERIOUS, SOLEMN.

Grave, in Latin *gravis* heavy, denotes the weight which keeps the mind or person down, and prevents buoyancy; it is opposed to the light; *serious*, in Latin *serus* late or slow, marks the quality of slowness or considerateness, either in the mind, or that which occupies the mind: it is opposed to the jocose.

Grave expresses more than *serious;* it does not merely bespeak the absence of mirth, but that heaviness of mind which is displayed in all the movements of the body; *seriousness*, on the other hand, bespeaks no depression, but simply steadiness of action, and a refrainment from all that is jocular. A man may be *grave* in his walk, in his tone, in his gesture, in his looks, and all his exteriour; he is *serious* only in his general air, his countenance, and demeanour. *Gravity* is produced by some external circumstance; *seriousness* springs from the operation of the mind itself, or from circumstances. Misfortunes or age will produce *gravity: seriousness* is the fruit of reflection. *Gravity* is, in the proper sense, confined to the person, as a characteristick of his temper;

If then some *grave* and pious man appear,
They hush their noise, and lend a listening ear.
DRYDEN.

Serious, on the other hand, is a characteristick either of persons or things; 'In our retirements every thing disposes us to be *serious*.'—ADDISON. Hence we should speak of a *grave* assembly, not a *serious* assembly, of old men; *grave* senators, not *serious* senators; of a *grave* speaker, not a *serious* speaker: but a *serious*, not a *grave* sermon; a *serious*, not a *grave* writer; a *serious*, not a *grave* sentiment; a *serious*, not properly a *grave* objection: *grave* is, however, sometimes extended to things in the sense of weighty, as when we speak of *grave* matters of deliberation. *Gravity* is peculiarly ascribed to a judge, from the double cause, that much depends upon his deportment, in which there ought to be gravity, and that the weighty concerns which press on his mind are most apt to produce *gravity:* on the other hand, both *gravity* and *seriousness* may be applied to the preacher; the former only as it respects the manner of delivery; the latter as it respects especially the matter of his discourse: the person may be *grave* or *serious ;* the discourse only is *serious*.

Solemn expresses more than either *grave* or *serious*, from the Latin *solennis* yearly; as applied to the stated religious festivals of the Romans, it has acquired the collateral meaning of religious *gravity:* like *serious*, it is employed not so much to characterize the person as the thing: a judge pronounces the *solemn* sentence of condemnation in a *solemn* manner; a preacher delivers many *solemn* warnings to his hearers. *Gravity* may be the effect of corporeal habit, and *seriousness* of mental habit; but *solemnity* is something occasional and extraordinary; 'The necessary business of a man's calling, with some, will not afford much time for set and *solemn* prayer.'—WHOLE DUTY OF MAN. Some children discover a remarkable *gravity* as soon as they begin to observe; a regular attention to religious worship will induce a habit of *seriousness;* the admonitions of a parent on his death-bed will have peculiar *solemnity;* 'The stateliness and gravity of the Spaniards shows itself in the *solemnity* of their language.'—ADDISON. 'In most of our long words which are derived from the Latin, we contract the length of the syllables, that gives them a *grave* and *solemn* air in their own language.'—ADDISON.

EAGER, EARNEST, SERIOUS.

Eager signifies the same as in the preceding article; *earnest* most probably comes from the thing *earnest*, in Saxon *thornest* a pledge, or token of a person's real intentions, whence the word has been employed to qualify the state of any one's mind, as settled or fixed; *serious*, in Latin *serius* or *sine risu*, signifies without laughter.

Eager is used to qualify the desires or passions; *earnest* to qualify the wishes or sentiments: the former has either a physical or moral application, the latter altogether a moral application: a child is *eager* to get a plaything; a hungry person is *eager* to get food; a covetous man is *eager* to seize whatever comes within his grasp: a person is *earnest* in solicitation; *earnest* in exhortation; *earnest* in devotion.

Eagerness is mostly faulty; it cannot be too early restrained; we can seldom have any substantial reason to be *eager;*

With joy the ambitious youth his mother heard,
And, *eager* for the journey, soon prepar'd.
DRYDEN.

Whence this term is applied with particular propriety to brutes;

The panting steeds impatient fury breathe,
But snort and tremble at the gulf beneath;
Eager they view'd the prospect dark and deep,
Vast was the leap, and headlong hung the steep.
POPE.

Earnestness is always taken in a good sense; it denotes the inward conviction of the mind, and the warmth of the heart when awakened by important objects;

Then even superiour to ambition, we
With *earnest* eye anticipate those scenes
Of happiness and wonder.—THOMSON.

A person is said to be *earnest*, or in *earnest;* a person or thing is said to be *serious:* the former characterizes the temper of the mind, the latter characterizes the object itself. In regard to persons, in which alone they are to be compared, *earnest* expresses more than *serious;* the former is opposed to lukewarmness, the latter to unconcernedness: we are *earnest* as to our wishes, our prayers, or our persuasions; 'He which prayeth in due sort, is thereby made the more attentive to hear; and he which heareth, the more *earnest* to pray for the time which we bestow, as well in the one as the other.'—HOOKER. We are *serious* as to our intentions, or the temper of mind with which we set about things; 'It is hardly possible to sit down to the *serious* perusal of Virgil's works, but a man shall rise more disposed to virtue and goodness.'—WALSH. The *earnestness* with which we address another depends upon the force of our conviction; the *seriousness* with which we address them depends upon our sincerity, and the nature of the subject: the preacher *earnestly* exhorts his hearers to lay aside their sins; he *seriously* admonishes those who are guilty of irregularities.

SOBER, GRAVE.

Sober (*v. Abstinent*) expresses the absence of all exhilaration of spirits; *grave* (*v. Grave*) expresses a weight in the intellectual operations which makes them proceed slowly. *Sobriety* is therefore a more natural and ordinary state for the human mind than *gravity:* it behooves every man to be *sober* in all situations; but those who fill the most important stations in life must be *grave*. Even in our pleasures we may observe *sobriety*, which keeps us from every unseemly ebullition of mirth; but on particular occasions where the importance of the subject ought to weigh on the mind it becomes us to be *grave*. At a feast we have need of *sobriety*; at a funeral we have need of *gravity*: *sobriety* extends to many more objects than *gravity*; we must be *sober* in our thoughts and opinions, as well as in our outward conduct and behaviour; 'These confusions disposed men of any *sober* understanding to wish for peace.'—CLARENDON. We can be *grave*, properly speaking, only in our looks and our outward deportment;

> So spake the Cherub, and his *grave* rebuke,
> Severe in youthful beauty, added grace
> Invincible.—MILTON.

Sober is often poetically and figuratively applied;

> Now came still ev'ning on, and twilight gray
> Had in her *sober* liv'ry all things clad.—MILTON.

GLAD, PLEASED, JOYFUL, CHEERFUL.

Glad is obviously a variation of *glee* and *glow*; *pleased*, from to *please*, marks the state of being *pleased*; *joyful* bespeaks its own meaning, either as full of *joy* or productive of great *joy*; *cheerful*, v. *Cheerful*.

Glad denotes either a partial state, or a permanent and habitual sentiment: in the former sense it is most nearly allied to *pleased*; in the latter sense to *joyful* and merry.

Glad and *pleased* are both applied to the ordinary occurrence of the day; but the former denotes rather a lively and momentary sentiment, the latter a gentle but rather more lasting feeling; we are *glad* to see a friend who has been long absent; we are *glad* to have good intelligence from our friends and relatives; we are *glad* to get rid of a troublesome companion;

> O Sol, in whom my thoughts find all repose,
> My glory, my perfection! *glad* I see
> Thy face, and morn return'd.—MILTON.

We are *pleased* to have the approbation of those we esteem: we are *pleased* to hear our friends well spoken of; we are *pleased* with the company of an intelligent and communicative person; 'The soul has many different faculties, or, in other words, many different ways of acting, and can be intensely *pleased* or made happy by all these different faculties or ways of acting.' —ADDISON.

Glad, *joyful*, and *cheerful*, all express more or less lively sentiments; but *glad* is less vivid than *joyful*, and more so than *cheerful*. *Gladness* seems to rise as much from physical as mental causes; wine is said to make the heart *glad*: *joy* has its source in the mind, as it is influenced by external circumstances; instances of good fortune, either for ourselves, our friends, or our country, excite *joy*: *cheerfulness* is an even tenour of the mind, which it may preserve of itself independently of all external circumstances: religious contemplation produces habitual *cheerfulness*.

A comfortable meal to an indigent person *gladdens* his heart: a nation *rejoices* at the return of peace after a long protracted war: a traveller is *cheered* in a solitary desert by the sight of a human being, or the sound of a voice; or a sufferer is *cheered* by his trust in Divine Providence.

Glad is seldom employed as an epithet to qualify things, except in the scriptural or solemn style, as, *glad* tidings of great *joy*;

> Man superiour walks
> Amid the *glad* creation, musing praise.—THOMSON.

Joyful is seldomer used to qualify persons than things; hence we speak of *joyful* news, a *joyful* occurrence, *joyful* faces, *joyful* sounds, and the like;

> Thus *joyful* Troy maintain'd the watch of night,
> While fear, pale comrade of inglorious flight,
> And heaven-bred horrour, on the Grecian part,
> Sat on each face, and sadden'd every heart.—POPE.

Cheerful is employed either to designate the state of the mind or the property of the thing: we either speak of a *cheerful* disposition, a *cheerful* person, a *cheerful* society, or a *cheerful* face, a *cheerful* sound, a *cheerful* aspect, and the like;

> No sun e'er gilds the gloomy horrours there,
> No *cheerful* gales refresh the lazy air.—POPE.

When used to qualify a person's actions, they all bespeak the temper of the mind: *gladly* denotes a high degree of willingness as opposed to aversion; one who is suffering under excruciating pains *gladly* submits to any thing which promises relief;

> For his particular I'll receive him *gladly*,
> But not one follower.—SHAKSPEARE.

Joyfully denotes unqualified *pleasure*, unmixed with any alloy or restrictive consideration a convert to Christianity *joyfully* goes through all the initiatory ceremonies which entitle him to all its privileges, spiritual and temporal;

> Never did men more *joyfully* obey,
> Or sooner understood the sign to flie;
> With such alacrity they bore away,
> As if to praise them all the states stood by.
> DRYDEN

Cheerfully denotes the absence of unwillingness, it is opposed to reluctantly; the zealous Christian *cheerfully* submits to every hardship to which he is exposed in the course of his religious profession; 'Doctrine is that which must prepare men for discipline; and men never go on so *cheerfully*, as when they see where they go.'—SOUTH.

JOY, GLADNESS, MIRTH.

The happy condition of the soul is designated by all these terms (*v. Pleasure*); but *joy* and *gladness* lie more internally; *mirth*, or the feeling of being merry, (*v. Glad*) is the more immediate result of external circumstances. What creates *joy* and *gladness* is of a permanent nature; that which creates *mirth* is temporary: *joy* is the most vivid sensation in the soul; *gladness* is the same in quality, but inferiour in degree: *joy* is awakened in the mind by the most important events in life; *gladness* springs up in the mind on ordinary occasions: the return of the prodigal son awakened *joy* in the heart of his father; a man feels *gladness* at being relieved from some distress or trouble: publick events of a gratifying nature produce universal *joy*;

> His thoughts triumphant, heav'n alone employs,
> And hope anticipates his future *joys*.—JENYNS.

Relief from either sickness or want brings *gladness* to an oppressed heart; 'None of the poets have observed so well as Milton those secret overflowings of *gladness*, which diffuse themselves through the mind of the beholder upon surveying the gay scenes of nature.'—ADDISON. He who is absorbed in his private distresses is ill prepared to partake of the *mirth* with which he is surrounded at the festive board.

Joy is depicted on the countenance, or expresses itself by various demonstrations: *gladness* is a more tranquil feeling, which is enjoyed in secret, and seeks no outward expression: *mirth* displays itself in laughter, singing, and noise. 'Most of the appearing *mirth* in the world, is not *mirth*, but art. The wounded spirit is not seen, but walks under a disguise.'—SOUTH.

PLEASURE, JOY, DELIGHT, CHARM

Pleasure, from the Latin *placeo* to please or give content, is the generick term, involving in itself the common idea of the other terms; *joy*, *v. Glad*; *delight*, in Latin *deliciæ*, comes from *delicio* to allure, signify ing the thing that allures the mind.

Pleasure is a term of most extensive use; it embraces one grand class of our feelings or sensations, and is opposed to nothing but pain, which embraces the opposite class or division: *joy* and *delight* are but modes or modifications of *pleasure*, differing as to the degree, and as to the objects or sources. *Pleasure*, in its peculiar acceptation, is smaller in degree than either *joy* or *delight*, but in its universal acceptation it defines no degree: the term is indifferently employed for the highest as well as the lowest degree; whereas *joy* and *delight* can only be employed to express a positively high degree. *Pleasure* is produced by any or every object; every thing by which we are surrounded acts upon us more or less to produce it; we may have *pleasure* either from without or from within: *pleasure* from the gratification of our senses, from the exercise of our affections, or the exercise of our understand ings; *pleasures* from our own selves, or *pleasures* from others: but *joy* is derived from the exercise of the affections; and *delight* either from the affections or the understanding. In this manner we distinguish the *pleasures* of the table, social *pleasures*, or intellectual *pleasures;* the *joy* of meeting an old friend; or the *delight* of pursuing a favourite object.

Pleasures are either transitory or otherwise; they may arise from momentary circumstances, or be attached to some permanent condition: all earthly *pleasure* is in its nature fleeting; and heavenly *pleasure*, on the contrary, lasting; 'That every day has its pains and sorrows is universally experienced; but if we look impartially about us, we shall find that every day has likewise its *pleasures* and its *joys*.'—JOHNSON. *Joy* is in its nature commonly of short duration, it springs from particular events; it is *pleasure* at high tide, but it may come and go as suddenly as the events which caused it: one's *joy* may be awakened and damped in quick succession; earthly *joys* are peculiarly of this nature, and heavenly joys are not altogether divested of this characteristick; they are supposed to spring out of particular occurrences, when the spiritual and holy affections are peculiarly called into action;

While he who virtue's radiant course has run,
Descends like a serenely setting sun;
His thoughts triumphant heav'n alone employs,
And hope anticipates his future *joys*.—JENYNS.

Delight is not so fleeting as *joy*, but it may be less so than simple *pleasure; delight* arises from a state of outward circumstances which is naturally more durable than that of *joy;* but it is a state seldomer attainable, and not so much at one's command as *pleasure:* this last is very seldom denied in some form or another to every human being, but those only are susceptible of *delight* who have acquired a certain degree of mental refinement; we must have a strong capacity for enjoyment before we can find *delight* in the pursuits of literature, or the cultivation of the arts. *Pleasures* are often calm and moderate; they do not depend upon a man's rank or condition; they are within the reach of all, more or less, and more or less at one's command: *joys* are buoyant; they dilate the heart for a time, but they must and will subside; they depend likewise on casualties which are under no one's control: *delights* are ardent and excessive; they are within the reach of a few only, but depend less on external circumstances than on the temper of the receiver.

Pleasure may be had either by reflection on the past, or by anticipation of the future; *joy* and *delight* can be produced only by the present object: we have a *pleasure* in thinking on what we have once enjoyed, or what we may again enjoy; we experience *joy* on the receipt of particularly good news; one may experience *delight* from a musical entertainment. *Pleasure* and *delight* may be either individual or social; *joy* is rather of a social nature: we feel a *pleasure* in solitude when locked up only in our own contemplations; we experience *delight* in the prosecution of some great end; we feel *joy* in the presence of those whom we love, when we see them likewise happy. *Pleasures* are particularly divided into selfish or benevolent; *joys* and *delights* flow commonly from that which immediately interests ourselves, but very frequently spring from the higher source of interest in the happiness of others: the *pleasure* of serving a friend, or of relieving a distressed object, has always been esteemed by moralists as the purest of *pleasures;* we are told that in heaven there is more *joy* over one sinner that repenteth, than over the ninety and nine that need no repentance; the *delight* which a parent feels at seeing the improvement of his child is one of those enviable sorts of *pleasures* which all may desire to experience, but which many must be contented to forego.

Pleasure, *joy*, and *delight* are likewise employed for the things which give *pleasure*, *joy*, or *delight*.

Charm (*v. Attraction*) is used only in the sense of what *charms*, or gives a high degree of *pleasure;* but not a degree equal to that of *joy* or *delight*, though greater than of ordinary *pleasure: pleasure* intoxicates; the *joys* of heaven are objects of a Christian's pursuit; the *delights* of matrimony are lasting to those who are susceptible of true affection; 'Before the day of departure (from the country), a week is always appropriated for the payment and reception of ceremonial visits, at which nothing can be mentioned but the *delights* of London.'—JOHNSON. The *charms* of rural scenery never fail of their effect whenever they offer themselves to the eye;

When thus creation's *charms* around combine,
Amid the store should thankless pride repine?
GOLDSMITH

HAPPINESS, FELICITY, BLISS, BLESSEDNESS, BEATITUDE.

Happiness signifies the state of being *happy; felicity*, in Latin *felicitas*, from *felix* happy, most probably comes from the Greek ἧλιξ youth, which is the age of purest enjoyment; *bliss*, *blessedness*, signify the state or property of being *blessed; beatitude*, from the Latin *beatus*, signifies the property of being *happy* in a superiour degree.

Happiness comprehends that aggregate of pleasurable sensations which we derive from external objects; it is the ordinary term which is employed alike in the colloquial or the philosophical style: *felicity* is a higher expression, that comprehends inward enjoyment, or an aggregate of inward pleasure, without regard to the source whence they are derived: *bliss* is a still higher term, expressing more than either *happiness* or *felicity*, both as to the degree and nature of the enjoyment. *Happiness* is the thing adapted to our present condition, and to the nature of our being, as a compound of body and soul; it is impure in its nature, and variable in degree; it is sought for by various means and with great eagerness; but it often lies much more within our reach than we are apt to imagine: it is not to be found in the possession of great wealth, of great power, of great dominions, of great splendour, or the unbounded indulgence of any one appetite or desire; but it is to be found in moderate possessions, with a heart tempered by religion and virtue, for the enjoyment of that which God has bestowed upon us: it is, therefore, not so unequally distributed as some have been led to conclude.

Happiness admits of degrees, since every individual is placed in different circumstances, either of body or mind, which fit him to be more or less *happy;*

Ah! whither now are fled
Those dreams of greatness? those unsolid hopes
Of *happiness?*—THOMSON.

Felicity is not regarded in the same light; it is that which is positive and independent of all circumstances: domestick *felicity*, and conjugal *felicity*, are regarded as moral enjoyments, abstracted from every thing which can serve as an alloy; 'No greater *felicity* can genius attain than that of having purified intellectual pleasure, separated mirth from indecency, and wit from licentiousness.'—JOHNSON. *Bliss* is that which is purely spiritual; it has its source in the imagination, and rises above the ordinary level of human enjoyments: of earthly *bliss* little is known but in poetry; of heavenly *bliss* we form but an imperfect conception from the utmost stretch of our powers;

The fond soul,
Wrapp'd in gay visions of unreal *bliss*,
Still paints th' illusive form.—THOMSON.

'In the description of heaven and hell we are surely interested, as we are all to reside hereafter either in the regions of horrour or of *bliss*.'—JOHNSON. *Blessedness* is a term of spiritual import which refers to the happy condition of those who enjoy the Divine favour, and are permitted to have a foretaste of heavenly *bliss*, by the exaltation of their minds above earthly *happiness;* 'So solid a comfort to men, under all the troubles and afflictions of this world, is that firm assurance which the Christian religion gives us of a future *happiness*, as to bring even the greatest miseries which in this life we are liable to, in some sense, under the notion of *blessedness*.'—TILLOTSON. *Beatitude* denotes that quality or degree of *happiness* only which is most exalted; namely, heavenly *happiness;* 'As in the next world, so in this, the only solid blessings are owing to the goodness of the mind, not the extent of the capacity; friendship here is an emanation from the same source as *beatitude* there.'—POPE.

HAPPY, FORTUNATE.

Happy and *fortunate* are both applied to the external circumstances of a man; but the former conveys the idea of that which is abstractedly good, the latter implies rather what is agreeable to one's wishes. A man is *happy* in his marriage, in his children, in hi connexions, and the like: he is *fortunate* in his trading concerns. *Happy* excludes the idea of chance; *fortunate* excludes the idea of personal effort: a man is *happy* in the possession of what he gets; he is *fortunate* in getting it.

In the improper sense they bear a similar analogy. A *happy* thought, a *happy* expression, a *happy* turn, a *happy* event, and the like, denote a degree of positive excellence;

> O *happy*, if he knew his *happy* state,
> The swain, who, free from business and debate,
> Receives his easy food from nature's hand,
> And just returns of cultivated land.—Dryden.

A *fortunate* idea, a *fortunate* circumstance, a *fortunate* event, are all relatively considered, with regard to the wishes and views of the individual; 'Visit the gayest and most *fortunate* on earth only with sleepless nights, disorder any single organ of the senses, and you shall (will) presently see his gayety vanish.'—Blair.

TO FELICITATE, CONGRATULATE.

Felicitate, from the Latin *felix* happy, signifies to make happy, and is applicable only to ourselves; *congratulate*, from *gratus*, pleasant or agreeable, is to make agreeable, and is applicable either to ourselves or others: we *felicitate* ourselves on having escaped the danger; we *congratulate* others on their good fortune; 'The astronomers, indeed, expect her (night) with impatience, and *felicitate* themselves upon her arrival.'—Johnson. 'The fierce young hero who had overcome the Curiatii, instead of being *congratulated* by his sister for his victory, was upbraided by her for having slain her lover.'—Addison.

FORTUNATE, LUCKY, FORTUITOUS, PROSPEROUS, SUCCESSFUL.

Fortunate signifies having *fortune* (*v. Chance, fortune*); *lucky*, having *luck*, which is in German *gluck*, and in all probability comes from *gelingen* or *lingen* to succeed; *fortuitous*, after the manner of *fortune; prosperous*, having *prosperity; successful*, i. e. full of *success*, enabled to *succeed*.

The *fortunate* and *lucky* are both applied to that which happens without the control of man; but *lucky*, which is a collateral term, describes the capricious goddess *Fortune* in her most freakish humours, and *fortunate* represents her in her most sober mood: in other words, the *fortunate* is more according to the ordinary course of things; the *lucky* is something sudden, unaccountable, and singular: a circumstance is said to be *fortunate* which turns up suitably to our purpose; it is said to be *lucky* when it comes upon us unexpectedly at the moment that it is wanted;

> This *lucky* moment the sly traitor chose,
> Then starting from his ambush up he rose.
> Dryden.

Hence we speak of a man as *fortunate* in his business, and the ordinary concerns of life; 'Several of the Roman emperours, as is still to be seen upon their medals, among their other titles, gave themselves that of Felix or *fortunate*.'—Addison. A man is *lucky* in the lottery or in games of chance: a *fortunate* year will make up for the losses of the past year;

> O *fortunate* old man, whose farm remains
> For you sufficient, and requites your pains.
> Dryden.

A *lucky* hit may repair the ruined spendthrift's *fortune*, only to tempt him to still greater extravagances;

> Riches are oft by guilt or baseness earn'd,
> Or dealt by chance to shield a *lucky* knave.
> Armstrong.

Fortunate and *lucky* are applied to particular circumstances of *fortune* and *luck;* but *fortuitous* is employed only in matters of chance generally; 'A wonder it must be, that there should be any man found so stupid as to persuade himself that this most beautiful world could be produced by the *fortuitous* concourse of atoms.'—Ray.

Prosperous and *successful* seem to exclude the idea of what is *fortuitous*, although *prosperity* and *success* are both greatly aided by good *fortune*. *Fortunate* and *lucky* are applied as much to the removal of evil as to the attainment of good; *prosperous* and *successful* are concerned only in what is good, or esteemed as such: we may be *fortunate* in making our escape; we are *prosperous* in the acquirement of wealth. *Fortunate* is employed for single circumstances; *prosperous* only for a train of circumstances; a man may be *fortunate* in meeting with the approbation of a superiour; he is *prosperous* in his business; '*Prosperous* people (for happy there are none) are hurried away with a fond sense of their present condition, and thoughtless of the mutability of fortune.'—Steele *Prosperity* is extended to whatever is the object of our wishes in this world; *success* is that degree of *prosperity* which immediately attends our endeavours: wealth, honours, children, and all outward circumstances, constitute *prosperity;* whence the epithet *prosperous* may be applied to the winds as far as they favour our designs;

> Ye gods, presiding over lands and seas,
> And you who raging winds and waves appease,
> Breathe on our swelling sails a *prosp'rous* wind.
> Dryden.

The attainment of any object constitutes the *success;* 'The Count d'Olivares was disgraced at the court of Madrid, because it was alleged against him that he had never *success* in his undertakings.'—Addison. The *fortunate* and *lucky* man can lay no claim to merit, because they preclude the idea of exertion, *prosperous* and *successful* may claim a share of merit proportioned to the exertion.

TO FLOURISH, THRIVE, PROSPER.

Flourish, in French *fleurir, florissant*, Latin *floresco* or *floreo*, from *flos* a flower, signifies to have the vigour and health of a flower in bloom; *thrive* signifies properly to drive on; *prosper*, in Latin *prosper, prosperus*, compounded of *pro* and *spero* and *spes* hope, signifies to be agreeable to the hopes.

To *flourish* expresses the state of being that which is desirable; to *thrive*, the process of becoming so.

In the proper sense, *flourish* and *thrive* are applied to the vegetation: the former to that which is full grown; the latter to that which is in the act of growing: the oldest trees are said to *flourish*, which put forth their leaves and fruits in full vigour; young trees *thrive* when they increase rapidly towards their full growth.

Flourish and *thrive* are taken likewise in the moral sense; *prosper* is employed only in this sense: *flourish* is said either of individuals or communities of men; *thrive* and *prosper* only of individuals. To *flourish* is to be in full possession of one's powers, physical, intellectual, and incidental; an author *flourishes* at a certain period; an institution *flourishes;* literature or trade *flourishes;* a nation *flourishes*. To *thrive* is to carry on one's concerns to the advantage of one's circumstances; it is a term of familiar use for those who gain by positive labour: the industrious tradesman *thrives*. To *prosper* is to be already in advantageous circumstances: men *prosper* who accumulate wealth agreeably to their wishes, and beyond their expectations.

Flourish and *thrive* are always taken in the good sense: nothing *flourishes* but what ought to *flourish*, the word bespeaks the possession of that which ought to be possessed: when a poet *flourishes* he is the ornament of his country, the pride of human nature, the boast of literature: when a city *flourishes* it attains all the ends of civil association; it is advantageous not only to its own members, but to the world at large; 'There have been times in which no power has been brought so low as France. Few have ever *flourished* in greater glory.'—Burke. No one *thrives* without merit: what is gained by the *thriving* man is gained by those qualities which entitle him to all he has; 'Every *thriving* grazier can think himself but ill dealt with, if within his own country he is not courted.'—South To *prosper* admits of a different view: one may *prosper* by that which is bad, or *prosper* in that which is bad, or become bad by *prospering;* the attainment of one's ends, be they what they may, constitutes the *prosperity;* a man may *prosper* by means of fraud and injustice; he may *prosper* in the attainment of inordinate wealth or power; and he may become proud, unfeeling, and selfish, by his *prosperity:* so great an enemy has *prosperity* been considered to the virtue of man, that every good man has trembled to be in that condition; 'Betimes inure yourself to examine how your estate *prospers*.'—WENTWORTH.

WELL-BEING, WELFARE, PROSPERITY, HAPPINESS.

Well-being may be said of one or many, but more generally of a body; the *well-being* of society depends upon a due subordination of the different ranks of which it is composed; 'Have free-thinkers been authors of any inventions that conduce to the *well-being* of mankind?'—BERKELEY. *Welfare*, or *faring well*, from the German *fahren* to go, respects the good condition of an individual; a parent is naturally anxious for the *welfare* of his child;

For his own sake no duty he can ask,
The common *welfare* is our only task.—JENYNS.

Well-being and *welfare* consist of such things as more immediately affect our existence: *prosperity*, which comprehends both *well being* and *welfare*, includes likewise all that can add to the enjoyments of man. The *prosperity* of a state, or of an individual, therefore, consists in the increase of wealth, power, honours, and the like; 'Religion affords to good men peculiar security in the enjoyment of their *prosperity*.' —BLAIR. As outward circumstances more or less affect the *happiness* of man, *happiness* is, therefore, often substituted for *prosperity;* but it must never be forgotten that *happiness* properly lies only in the mind, and that consequently *prosperity* may exist without *happiness:* but *happiness*, at least as far as respects a body of men, cannot exist without some portion of *prosperity*.

TO ACQUIRE, OBTAIN, GAIN, WIN, EARN.

Acquire, in French *acquirer*, Latin *acquiro*, is compounded of *ac* or *ad* and *quæro* to seek, signifying to seek or get to one's self; *obtain*, in French *obtenir*, Latin *obtineo*, is compounded of *ob* and *teneo* to hold, signifying to lay hold or secure within one's reach; *gain* and *win* are derived from the same source; namely, the French *gagner*, German *gewinnen*, Saxon *winnen*, from the Latin *vinco*, Greek *καίνυμαι* or *νίκω* to conquer, signifying to get the mastery over, to get into one's possession; *earn* comes from the Saxon *tharnan*, German *erndten*, Frieslandish *arnan* to reap, which is connected with the Greek *ἄρνυμαι* to take or get.

The idea of getting is common to these terms, but the circumstances of the action vary. We *acquire* by our own efforts; we *obtain* by the efforts of others, as well as of ourselves; we *gain* or *win* by striving; we *earn* by labour. Talents and industry are requisite for *acquiring;* what we *acquire* comes gradually to us in consequence of the regular exercise of our abilities; in this manner, knowledge, honour, and reputation are *acquired;* 'It is Sallust's remark upon Cato, that the less he coveted glory, the more he *acquired* it.'—ADDISON. Things are *obtained* by all means, honest or dishonest; whatever comes into our possession agreeable to our wishes is *obtained:* favours and requests are always *obtained;* 'Were not this desire of fame very strong, the difficulty of *obtaining* it, and the danger of losing it when *obtained*, would be sufficient to deter a man from so vain a pursuit.'—ADDISON. Fortune assists in both *gaining* and *winning*, but particularly in the latter case: a subsistence, a superiority, a victory or battle, an advantage, or a pleasure, is *gained;* 'He whose mind is engaged by the *acquisition* or improvement of a fortune, not only escapes the insipidity of indifference and the tediousness of inactivity, but *gains* enjoyments wholly unknown to those who live lazily on the toils of others.'—JOHNSON. A game or a prize in the lottery is literally *won;*

An honest man may freely take his own;
The goat was mine, by singing fairly *won*.
DRYDEN.

But we may *win* many things, in the *gaining* of which fortune is more concerned than one's own exertions; 'Where the danger ends, the hero ceases: when he has *won* an empire, or *gained* his mistress, the rest of his story is not worth relating.'—STEELE. A good constitution and full employment are all that is necessary for *earning* a livelihood; 'They who have *earned* their fortune by a laborious and industrious life are naturally tenacious of what they have painfully *acquired*.'—BLAIR. Fortunes are *acquired* after a course of years; they are *obtained* by inheritance, or *gained* in trade; they are sometimes *won* at the gaming table, but seldom *earned*.

What is *acquired* is solid, and produces lasting benefit; what is *obtained* may often be injurious to one's health, one's interest, or one's morals; what is *gained* or *won* is often only a partial advantage, and transitory in its nature; it is *gained* or *won* only to be lost: what is *earned* serves only to supply the necessity of the moment; it is hardly got and quickly spent. Scholars *acquire* learning, *obtain* rewards, *gain* applause, and *win* prizes, which are often hardly *earned* by the loss of health.

TO ACQUIRE, TO ATTAIN

To *acquire* (*v. To acquire*) is a progressive and permanent action; to *attain*, from the Latin *attineo*, compounded of *ac* or *ad* and *teneo* to hold, signifying to rest at a thing, is a perfect and finished action; we always go on *acquiring;* but we stop when we have *attained*. What is *acquired* is something got into the possession; what is *attained* is the point arrived at. We *acquire* a language; we *attain* to a certain degree of perfection.

By abilities and perseverance we may *acquire* a considerable fluency in speaking several languages; but we can scarcely expect to *attain* to the perfection of a native in any foreign language. Ordinary powers, coupled with diligence, will enable a person to *acquire* whatever is useful; 'A genius is never to be *acquired* by art, but is the gift of nature.'—GAY. We cannot *attain* to superiority without extraordinary talents and determined perseverance; 'Inquiries after happiness, and rules for *attaining* it, are not so necessary and useful to mankind as the arts of consolation, and supporting one's self under affliction.'—SHEPHARD. *Acquirements* are always serviceable; *attainments* always creditable.

ACQUIREMENT, ACQUISITION,

Are two abstract nouns from the same verb, denoting the thing acquired.

Acquirement implies the thing acquired for and by ourselves; *acquisition* that which is acquired for another, or to the advantage of another.

People can expect to make but slender *acquirements* without a considerable share of industry; 'Men of the greatest application and *acquirements* can look back upon many vacant spaces and neglected parts of time.'—HUGHES. Men of slender *acquirements* will be no *acquisition* to the community to which they have attached themselves; 'To me, who have taken pains to look at beauty, abstracted from the consideration of its being an object of desire; at power only as it sits upon another, without any hopes of partaking any share of it; at wisdom and capacity without any pretension to rival or envy its *acquisitions;* the world is not only a mere scene, but a pleasant one.'—STEELE.

Acquirement respects rather the exertions employed; *acquisition*, the benefit or gain accruing. To learn a language is an *acquirement;* to gain a class or a degree, an *acquisition*. The *acquirements* of literature far exceed in value the *acquisitions* of fortune.

TO GET, GAIN, OBTAIN, PROCURE.

To *get* signifies simply to cause to have or possess, it is generick, and the rest specifick; to *gain* (*v. To acquire*) is to *get* the thing one wishes, or that is for one's advantage: to *obtain* is to *get* the thing aimed at or striven after: to *procure*, from *pro* and *curo* to care for, is to *get* the thing wanted or sought for.

Get is not only the most general in its sense, but in its application: it may be substituted in almost every case for the other terms, for we may say to *get* or *gain* a prize, to *get* or *obtain* a reward, to *get* or *procure* a book; and it is also employed in numberless familiar cases, where the other terms would be less suitable, for what this word gains in familiarity it loses in dignity: hence we may with propriety talk of a servant's getting some water, or a person getting a book off a shelf, or getting meat from the butcher, with numberless similar cases in which the other terms could not be employed without losing their dignity. Moreover, get is promiscuously used for whatever comes to the hand, whether good or bad, desirable or not desirable, sought for or not; 'The miser is more industrious than the saint: the pains of *getting*, the fears of losing, and the inability of enjoying his wealth, have been the mark of satire in all ages.'—SPECTATOR. *Gain*, *obtain*, and *procure* always include either the wishes, or the instrumentality of the agent, or both together. Thus a person is said to *get* a cold, or a fever, a good or an ill name, without specifying any of the circumstances of the action: but he is said to *gain* that approbation which is gratifying to his feelings; to *obtain* a recompense which is the object of his exertions; to *procure* a situation which is the end of his endeavours.

The word *gain* is peculiarly applicable to whatever comes to us fortuitously; what we *gain* constitutes our good fortune; we *gain* a victory, or we *gain* a cause; the result in both cases may be independent of our exertions; 'Neither Virgil nor Horace would have *gained* so great reputation in the world, had they not been the friends and admirers of each other.'—ADDISON. To *obtain* and *procure* exclude the idea of chance, and suppose exertions directed to a specifick end: but the former may include the exertions of others; the latter is particularly employed for one's own personal exertions. A person *obtains* a situation through the recommendation of a friend; he *procures* a situation by applying for it. *Obtain* is likewise employed only in that which requires particular efforts, that which is not immediately within our reach;

All things are blended, changeable, and vain!
No hope, no wish, we perfectly *obtain*.—JENYNS.

Procure is applicable to that which is to be got with ease, by the simple exertion of a walk, or of asking for; 'Ambition pushes the soul to such actions as are apt to *procure* honour and reputation to the actor'.—ADDISON.

GAIN, PROFIT, EMOLUMENT, LUCRE.

Gain signifies in general what is gained (*v. To acquire*); *profit*, in French *profit*, Latin *profectus*, participle of *proficio*, i. e. *pro* and *facio*, signifies that which makes for one's good; *emolument*, from *emolior*, signifies to work out or get by working; *lucre* is in Latin *lucrum* gain, which probably comes from *luo* to pay, signifying that which comes to a man's purse.

Gain is here a general term, the other terms are specifick: the *gain* is that which comes to a man: it is the fruit of his exertions, or agreeable to his wish: the *profit* is that which accrues from the thing. Thus when applied to riches that which increases a man's estate are his *gains*; 'The *gains* of ordinary trades and vocations are honest and furthered by two things, chiefly by diligence and by a good name.'—BACON. That which flows out of his trade are his *profits*; that is, they are his *gains* upon dealing; 'Why may not a whole estate, thrown into a kind of garden, turn as much to the *profit* as the pleasure of the owner?'—ADDISON. *Emolument* is a species of *gain* from labour, or a collateral *gain*; of this description are a man's *emoluments* from an office; 'Except the salary of the Laureate, to which King James added the office of Historiographer, perhaps with some additional *emoluments*, Dryden's whole revenue seems to have been casual.'—JOHNSON. A man estimates his *gains* by what he receives in the year; he estimates his *profits* by what he receives on every article; he estimates his *emoluments* according to the nature of the service which he has to perform: the merchant talks of his *gains*; the retail dealer of his *profits*; the place-man of his *emoluments*.

Gain and *profit* are also taken in an abstract sense; *lucre* is never used otherwise; but the latter always conveys a bad meaning; it is, strictly speaking, unhallowed *gain*; an immoderate thirst for *gain* is the vice of men who are always calculating *profit* and loss; a thirst for *lucre* deadens every generous feeling of the mind;

O sacred hunger of pernicious gold!
What bands of faith can impious *lucre* hold?
DRYDEN.

Gain and *profit* may be extended to other objects, and sometimes opposed to each other; for as that which we *gain* is what we wish only, it is often the reverse of *profitable*; hence the force of that important question in Scripture, What shall it *profit* a man if he gain the whole world and lose his own soul?

GOOD, GOODNESS.

Good, which under different forms runs through all the northern languages, and has a great affinity to the Greek ἀγαθὸς, is supposed by Adelung to be derived from the Latin *gaudeo*, Greek γηθέω, and Hebrew חדה, signifying to be joyful, joy or happiness being derived from that which is *good*.

Good and *goodness* are abstract terms, drawn from the same word; the former to denote the thing that is *good*, the latter the inherent *good* property of a thing. All *good* comes from God, whose *goodness* towards his creatures is unbounded.

The *good* we do is determined by the tendency of the action; but our *goodness* in doing it is determined by the motives of our actions. *Good* is of a two-fold nature, physical and moral, and is opposed to evil; *Goodness* is applicable either to the disposition of moral agents or the qualities of inanimate objects; it is opposed to badness. By the order of Providence the most horrible convulsions are made to bring about *good*;

Each form'd for all, promotes through private care
The publick good, and justly takes its share.
JENYNS.

The *goodness* or badness of any fruit depends upon its fitness to be enjoyed; 'The reigning errour of his life was, that Savage mistook the love for the practice of virtue, and was indeed not so much a *good* man as the friend of *goodness*.'—JOHNSON.

GOOD, BENEFIT, ADVANTAGE.

Good is an abstract universal term, which in its unlimited sense comprehends every thing that can be conceived of, as suited in all its parts to the end proposed. In this sense *benefit* and *advantage*, as well as utility, service, profit, &c. are all modifications of *good*; but the term *good* has likewise a limited application, which brings it to a just point of comparison with the other terms here chosen; the common idea which allies these words to each other is that of *good* as it respects a particular object. *Good* is here employed indefinitely; *benefit* and *advantage* are specified by some collateral circumstances. *Good* is done without regard to the person who does it, or him to whom it is done; but *benefit* has always respect to the relative condition of the giver and receiver, who must be both specified. Hence we say of a charitable man, that he does much *good*, or that he bestows *benefits* upon this or that individual. In like manner, when speaking of particular communities or society at large, we may say that it is for the *good* of society or for the *good* of mankind that every one submits to the sacrifice of some portion of his natural liberty; but it is intended for the *benefit* of the poorer orders that the charitably disposed employ so much time and money in giving them instruction.

Good is limited to no mode or manner, no condition of the person or the thing; it is applied indiscriminately;

Our present *good* the easy task is made,
To earn superiour bliss when this shall fade.
JENYNS.

Benefit is more particularly applicable to the external circumstances of a person, as to his health, his improvement, his pecuniary condition, and the like: it is likewise confined in its application to persons only; we may counsel another for his *good*, although we do not counsel him for his *benefit*; but we labour for the *benefit* of another when we set apart for him the fruits of our labour: exercise is always attended with some *good* to all persons; it is of particular *benefit* to those who are of a lethargick habit: an indiscreet zeal does more harm than *good* to the cause of religion; a patient cannot expect to derive *benefit* from a medicine when he counteracts its effects; 'Unless men were endowed by nature with some sense of duty or moral obligation, they could reap no *benefit* from revelation.' —BLAIR.

Good is mostly employed for some positive and direct *good; advantage* for an adventitious and indirect *good:* the *good* is that which would be *good* to all; the *advantage* is that which is partially *good*, or *good* only in particular cases: it is *good* for a man to exert his talents; it is an *advantage* to him if in addition to his own efforts he has the support of friends: it may however frequently happen that he who has the most *advantages* derives the least *good:* talents, person, voice, powerful interest, a pleasing address, are all *advantages;* but they may produce evil instead of *good* if they are not directed to the right purpose; 'The true art of memory is the art of attention. No man will read with much *advantage* who is not able at pleasure to evacuate his mind.'—JOHNSON.

ADVANTAGE, PROFIT.

Advantage, in French *avantage*, probably comes from the Latin *adventum*, participle of *advenio*, compounded of *ad* and *venio* to come to, signifying to come to any one according to his desire, or agreeable to his purpose; *profit*, in French *profite*, Latin *profectus*, participle of *proficio*, signifies that which makes for one's good.

The idea common to these terms is of some good received by a person. *Advantage* is general; it respects every thing which can contribute to the wishes, wants, and comforts of life: *profit* in its proper sense is specifick; it regards only pecuniary *advantage*. Situations have their *advantages;* trade has its *profits*.

Whatever we estimate as an *advantage* is so to the individual; but *profits* are something real; the former is a relative term, it depends on the sentiments of the person: what is an *advantage* to one may be a *disadvantage* to another;

> For he in all his am'rous battles
> N' *advantage* finds like goods and chattels.
> BUTLER.

The latter is an absolute term: *profit* is alike to all under all circumstances; 'He does the office of a counsellor, a judge, an executor, and a friend, to all his acquaintance, without the *profits* which attend such offices.'—STEELE.

ADVANTAGE, BENEFIT, UTILITY, SERVICE, AVAIL, USE.

Advantage has the same signification as in the preceding article; *benefit*, in French *bienfait*, Latin *benefactum*, compounded of *bene* well, and *factum* done, signifies done or made to one's wishes; *utility*, in French *utilité*, Latin *utilitas* and *utilis* useful, from *utor* to use, signifies the quality of being able to be used, which is also the meaning of *use; service*, in French *service*, Latin *servitium*, from *servio* to serve, signifies the quality of serving one's purpose; *avail* compounded of *a* or *ad* and *valeo* to be strong, signifies to be strong for a purpose.

Advantage respects external or extrinsick circumstances of profit, honour, and convenience; *benefit* respects the consequences of actions and events; *utility* and *service* respect the good which can be drawn from the use of any object. *Utility* implies the intrinsick good quality which renders a thing fit for use; *service* the actual state of a thing which may fit it for immediate use: a thing has its *utility* and is made of *service*.

A large house has its *advantages;* suitable exercise is attended with *benefit:* sun-dials have their *utility* in ascertaining the hour precisely by the sun; and may be made *serviceable* at times in lieu of watches. Things are sold to *advantage*, or *advantages* are derived from buying and selling: 'It is the great *advantage* of a trading nation, that there are very few in it so dull and heavy, who may not be placed in stations of life which may give them an opportunity of making their fortunes.'—ADDISON. Persons ride or walk for the *benefit* of their health; 'For the *benefit* of the gentle reader, I will show what to turn over unread, and what to peruse.'—STEELE. Things are purchased for their *utility;* 'If the gibbet does not produce virtue, it is yet of such incontestible *utility*, that I believe those gentlemen would be very unwilling that it should be removed, who are notwithstanding so zealous to steel every breast against damnation.'—HAWKESWORTH. Things are retained when they are found *serviceable;* 'His wisdom and knowledge are *serviceable* to all who think fit to make use of them.'—STEELE.

A good education has always its *advantages*, although every one cannot derive the same *benefit* from the cultivation of his talents, as all have not the happy art of employing their acquirements to the right objects: riches are of no *utility* unless rightly employed; and edge-tools are of no *service* which are not properly sharpened. It is of great *advantage* to young people to form good connexions on their entrance into life: it is no less *beneficial* to their morals to be under the guidance of the aged and experienced, from whom they may draw many *useful* directions for their future conduct, and many *serviceable* hints by way of admonition.

Utility, use, service, and *avail*, all express the idea of fitness to be employed to *advantage*. *Utility* is applied mostly in a general sense for that which may be used, and *use* for that which actually is used; thus things may be said to be of general *utility*, or of particular *use;* 'Those things which have long gone together are confederate; whereas new things piece not so well; but, though they help by their *utility*, yet they trouble by their inconformity.'—BACON. 'When will my friendship be of *use* to you?'—PHILLIPS *Use* comprehends in it whatever is derived from the *use* of a thing; *service* may imply that which *serves* for a particular purpose; *avail* implies that kind of *service* which may possibly be procured from any object, but which also may not be procured; it is therefore used in problematical cases, or in a negative sense. Prudence forbids us to destroy any thing that can be turned to a *use;* 'A man with great talents, but void of discretion, is like Polyphemus in the fable, strong and blind, endued with an irresistible force, which for want of sight is of no *use* to him.'—ADDISON. Economy enjoins that we should not throw aside a thing so long as it is fit for *service;* 'The Greeks in the heroick age seem to have been unacquainted with the *use* of iron, the most *serviceable* of all the metals.'—ROBERTSON. When entreaties are found to be of no *avail*, females sometimes try the force of tears; 'What does it *avail*, though Seneca had taught as good morality as Christ himself from the mount?'—CUMBERLAND.

The intercession of a friend may be *available* to avert the resentment of one who is offended: *useful* lessons of experience may be drawn from all the events of life: whatever is of the best quality will be found most *serviceable*.

TO EMPLOY, USE.

Employ, from the Latin *implico*, signifies to implicate, or apply for any special purpose; *use*, from the Latin *usus* and *utor*, signifies to enjoy or derive benefit from.

Employ expresses less than *use;* it is in fact a species of partial *using:* we always *employ* when we *use;* but we do not always *use* when we *employ*. We *employ* whatever we take into our service, or make subservient to our convenience for a time; we *use* whatever we entirely devote to our purpose. Whatever is *employed* by one person may, in its turn, be *employed* by another, or at different times be *employed* by the same person; but what is *used* is frequently consumed or rendered unfit for a similar *use*. What we *employ* may frequently belong to another; but what one *uses* is supposed to be his exclusive property. On this ground we may speak of *employing* persons as well as things; but we speak of *using* things only, and not persons, except in the most degrading sense. Persons, time, strength, and power are *employed;*

> Thou godlike Hector! all thy force *employ;*
> Assemble all th' united band of Troy.—POPE

Houses, furniture, and all materials, of which either necessities or conveniences are composed, are *used;*

> Straight the broad belt, with gay embroid'ry grac'd,
> He loos'd, the corslet from his breast unbrac'd,
> Then suck'd the blood, and sov'reign balm infus'd,
> Which Chiron gave, and Æsculapius *us'd*.—POPE.

It is a part of wisdom to *employ* well the short portion of time which is allotted to us in this sublunary state, and to *use* the things of this world so as not to abuse them. No one is exculpated from the guilt of an immoral action, by suffering himself to be *employed* as an instrument to serve the purposes of another: we ought to *use* our utmost endeavours to abstain from all connexion with such as wish to implicate us in their guilty practices.

INSTRUMENT, TOOL.

Instrument, in Latin *instrumentum*, from *instruo*, signifies the thing by which an effect is produced; *tool* comes probably from *toil*, signifying the thing with which one toils. These terms are both employed to express the means of producing an end; they differ principally in this, that the former is used in a good or an indifferent sense, the latter only in a bad sense, for persons. Individuals in high stations are often the *instruments* in bringing about great changes in nations; Devotion has often been found a powerful *instrument* in humanizing the manners of men.'—BLAIR. Spies and informers are the worthless *tools* of government;

Poor York! the harmless *tool* of others' hate,
He sues for pardon, and repents too late.—SWIFT.

TO ABUSE, MISUSE.

Abuse, in Latin *abusus*, participle of *abutor*, compounded of *ab* from and *utor* to use, signifies to use away or wear away with using; in distinction from *misuse*, which signifies to use amiss. Every thing is *abused* which receives any sort of injury; it is *misused*, if not used at all, or turned to a wrong use.

Young people are too prone to *abuse* books for want of setting a proper value on their contents; 'I know no evil so great as the *abuse* of the understanding, and yet there is no one vice more common.'—STEELE. People *misuse* books when they read for amusement only instead of improvement;

You *misuse* the reverence of your place,
As a false favourite doth his prince's name.
In deeds dishon'rable.—SHAKSPEARE.

Money is *abused* when it is clipped, or its value any way lessened; it is *misused* when it is spent in excess and debauchery.

TREATMENT, USAGE.

Treatment implies the act of treating, and *usage* that of using: *treatment* may be partial or temporary; but *usage* is properly employed for that which is permanent or continued: a passer-by may meet with ill *treatment*; but children or domesticks are liable to meet with ill *usage*. All persons may meet with *treatment* from others with whom they casually come in connexion: 'By promises of more indulgent *treatment*, if they would unite with him (Cortez) against their oppressors, he prevailed on the people to supply the Spanish camp with provisions.'—ROBERTSON. *Usage* is applied more properly to those who are more or less in the power of others: children may receive good or ill *usage* from those who have the charge of them, servants from their masters, or wives from their husbands; 'If we look further into the world, we shall find this *usage* (of our Saviour from his own) not so very strange; for kindred is not friendship.'—SOUTH.

TO PROVIDE, PROCURE, FURNISH, SUPPLY.

Provide, in Latin *provideo*, signifies literally to see before, but figuratively to get in readiness for some future purpose; *procure*, *v. To get*; *furnish*, in French *fournir*, may possibly be connected with the Latin *ferro* to bring; *supply*, in French *suppleer*, Latin *suppleo*, from *sub* and *pleo*, signifies to fill up a deficiency, or make up what is wanting.

Provide and *procure* are both actions that have a special reference to the future; *furnish* and *supply* are employed for that which is of immediate concern: one *provides* a dinner in the contemplation that some persons are coming to partake of it; one *procures* help in the contemplation that it may be wanted; one *furnishes* a room, as we find it necessary for the present purpose; one *supplies* a family with any article of domestick use. Calculation is necessary in *providing*; one does not wish to *provide* too much or too little; 'A rude hand may build walls, form roofs, and lay floors, and *provide* all that warmth and security require.'—JOHNSON. Labour and management are requisite in *procuring*; when the thing is not always at hand, or not easily come at, one must exercise one's strength or ingenuity to *procure* it; 'Such dress as may enable the body to endure the different seasons, the most unenlightened nations have been able to *procure*.'—JOHNSON. Judgement is requisite in *furnishing*; what one *furnishes* ought to be selected with due regard to the circumstances of the individual who *furnishes*, or for whom it is *furnished*; 'Auria having driven the Turks from Corone, both by sea and land, *furnished* the city with corn, wine, victual, and powder.'—KNOLLES. Care and attention are wanted in *supplying*; we must be careful to know what a person really wants, in order to *supply* him to his satisfaction;

Although I neither lend nor borrow,
Yet, to *supply* the ripe wants of my friend,
I 'll break a custom.—SHAKSPEARE.

One *provides* against all contingencies; one *procures* all necessaries; one *furnishes* all comforts; one *supplies* all deficiencies. *Provide* and *procure* are the acts of persons only; *furnish* and *supply* are the acts of unconscious agents. A person's garden and orchard may be said to *furnish* him with delicacies; the earth *supplies* us with food. So in the improper application: the daily occurrences of a great city *furnish* materials for a newspaper; a newspaper, to an Englishman, *supplies* almost every other want; 'Your ideas are new, and borrowed from a mountainous country, the only one that can *furnish* truly picturesque scenery.'—GRAY.

And clouds, dissolv'd, the thirsty ground *supply*.
DRYDEN

PROVIDENCE, PRUDENCE,

Providence and *prudence* are both derived from the verb to *provide*; but the former expresses the particular act of providing; the latter the habit of providing. The former is applied both to animals and men; the latter is employed only as a characteristick of men. We may admire the *providence* of the ant in laying up a store for the winter;

In Albion's isle, when glorious Edgar reign'd,
He, wisely *provident*, from her white cliffs
Launch'd half her forests.—SOMERVILLE.

The *prudence* of a parent is displayed in his concern for the future settlement of his child; '*Prudence* operates on life, in the same manner as rules on composition; it produces vigilance rather than elevation.'—JOHNSON. It is *provident* in a person to adopt measures of escape for himself, in certain situations of peculiar danger; it is *prudent* to be always prepared for all contingencies

PRUDENT, PRUDENTIAL.

Prudent (*v. Judgement*) characterizes the person or the thing; *prudential* characterizes only the thing *Prudent* signifies having *prudence*; *prudential*, according to the rules of *prudence*, or as respects *prudence*. The *prudent* is opposed to the *imprudent* and inconsiderate; the *providential* is opposed to the voluntary; the counsel is *prudent* which accords with the principles of *prudence*;

Ulysses first in publick care she found,
For *prudent* counsel like the gods renown'd.
POPE

The reason or motive is *prudential*, as flowing out of circumstances of *prudence* or necessity; 'Those who possess elevated understandings, are naturally apt to consider all *prudential* maxims as below their regard.—JOHNSON. Every one is called upon at certain times to adopt *prudent* measures; those who are obliged to consult their means in the management of their expenses, must act upon *prudential* motives

FORESIGHT, FORETHOUGHT, FORECAST, PREMEDITATION.

Foresight, from seeing before, and *forethought*, from thinking beforehand, denote the simple act of the mind in seeing a thing before it happens: *forecast*, from casting the thoughts onward, signifies coming at the knowledge of a thing beforehand by means of calculation: *premeditation* from *pre* before, and *meditate* signifies obtaining the same knowledge by force of meditating, or reflecting deeply on a thing beforehand. *Foresight* and *forethought* are general and indefinite terms; we employ them either on ordinary or extraordinary occasions; but *forethought* is of the two the most familiar term; *forecast* and *premeditation* mostly in the latter case: all business requires *foresight*; state concerns require *forecast*: *foresight* and *forecast* respect what is to happen; they are the operations of the mind in calculating futurity: *premeditation* respects what is to be said or done; it is a preparation of the thoughts and designs for action: by *foresight* and *forecast* we guard against evils and provide for contingencies; by *premeditation* we guard against errours of conduct. A man betrays his want of *foresight* who does not provide against losses in trade;

> The wary crane *foresees* it first, and sails
> Above the storm, and leaves the lowly vales.
> DRYDEN.

A person shows his want of *forecast* who does not provide against old age;

> Let him *forecast* his work with timely care,
> Which else is huddled, when the skies are fair.
> DRYDEN.

A man shows his want of *premeditation* who acts or speaks on the impulse of the moment; the man therefore who does a wicked act without *premeditation* lessens his guilt; 'The tongue may fail and falter in her sudden extemporal expressions, but the pen having a greater advantage of *premeditation* is not so subject to errour.'—HOWELL.

JUDGEMENT, DISCRETION, PRUDENCE.

These terms are all employed to express the various modes of practical wisdom, which serve to regulate the conduct of men in ordinary life. The *judgement* is that faculty which enables a person to distinguish right and wrong in general; *discretion* and *prudence* serve the same purpose in particular cases. The *judgement* is conclusive; it decides by positive inference; it enables a person to discover the truth: *discretion* is intuitive (*v. Discernment*); it discerns or perceives what is in all probability right. The *judgement* acts by a fixed rule; it admits of no question or variation: the *discretion* acts according to circumstances, and is its own rule. The *judgement* determines in the choice of what is good: the *discretion* sometimes only guards against errour or direct mistakes; it chooses what is nearest to the truth. The *judgement* requires knowledge and actual experience; the *discretion* requires reflection and consideration: a general exercises his *judgement* in the disposition of his army, and in the mode of attack; while he is following the rules of military art he exercises his *discretion* in the choice of officers for different posts, in the treatment of his men, in his negotiations with the enemy, and various other measures which depend upon contingencies; 'If a man have that penetration of *judgement* as he can discern what things are to be laid open, and what to be secreted, to him a habit of dissimulation is a hindrance and a poorness.'—BACON.

> Let your own
> *Discretion* be your tutor. Suit the action
> To the words.—SHAKSPEARE.

Discretion looks to the present; *prudence*, which is the same as providence or forethought calculates on the future: *discretion* takes a wide survey of the case that offers; it looks to the moral fitness of the thing, as well as the consequences which may follow from it; it determines according to the real propriety of the thing, as well as the ultimate advantages which it may produce; *prudence* looks only to the good or evil which may result from the thing; it is, therefore, but a mode or accompaniment of *discretion*; we must have *prudence* when we have *discretion*, but we may have *prudence* where there is no occasion for *discretion*. Those who have the conduct or direction of others require *discretion*; those who have the management of their own concerns require *prudence*. For want of *discretion* the master of a school, or the general of an army, may lose his authority: for want of *prudence* the merchant may involve himself in ruin; or the man of fortune may be brought to beggary; 'The ignorance in which we are left concerning good and evil, is not such as to supersede *prudence* in conduct.'—BLAIR.

As epithets, *judicious* is applied to things oftene than to persons; *discreet* is applied to persons rathe than to things; *prudent* is applied to both: a remark or a military movement is *judicious*; it displays the *judgement* of the individual from whom they emanate;

> So bold, yet so *judiciously* you dare,
> That your least praise is to be regular.—DRYDEN

A matron is *discreet*, who, by dint of years, experience, and long reflection, is enabled to determine on what is befitting the case;

> To elder years to be *discreet* and grave,
> Then to old age maturity she gave.—DENMAN.

A person is *prudent* who does not inconsiderately expose himself to danger; a measure is *prudent* that guards against the chances of evil;

> The monarch rose, preventing all reply,
> *Prudent* lest, from his resolution rais'd,
> Others among the chiefs might offer.—MILTON.

Counsels will be *injudicious* which are given by those who are ignorant of the subject: it is dangerous to entrust a secret to one who is *indiscreet*: the impetuosity of youth naturally impels them to be *imprudent*; an *imprudent* marriage is seldom followed by *prudent* conduct in the parties that have involved themselves in it.

WISDOM, PRUDENCE.

Wisdom (*v. Wit*) consists in speculative knowledge; *prudence* (*v. Prudent*) in that which is practical: the former knows what is past; the latter by foresight knows what is to come; many *wise* men are remarkable for their want of *prudence*; and those who are remarkable for *prudence* have frequently no other knowledge of which they can boast; 'Two things speak much the *wisdom* of a nation: good laws, and a *prudent* management of them.'—STILLINGFLEET.

FOLLY, FOOLERY.

Folly is the abstract of foolish, and characterizes the thing; *foolery* the abstract of fool, and characterizes the person: we may commit an act of *folly* without being chargeable with weakness or *folly*; but none are guilty of *fooleries* who are not themselves fools, either habitually or temporarily: young people are perpetually committing *follies* if not under proper control; 'This peculiar ill property has *folly*, that it enlarges men's desires while it lessens their capacities.'—SOUTH. Fashionable people only lay aside one *foolery* to take up another; 'If you are so much transported with the sight of beautiful persons, to what ecstasy would it raise you to behold the original beauty, not filled up with flesh and blood, or varnished with a fading mixture of colours, and the rest of mortal trifles and *fooleries*.'—WALSH.

FOOL, IDIOT, BUFFOON.

Fool is doubtless connected with our word *foul*, in German *faul*, which is either nasty or lazy, and the Greek φαῦλος which signifies worthless or good for nothing; *idiot* comes from the Greek ἰδιώτης, signifying either a private person or one that is rude and unskilled in the ways of the world; *buffoon*, in French *bouffon*, is in all probability connected with our word beef, buffalo, and bull, signifying a senseless fellow.

> The *fool* is either naturally or artificially a *fool*;
>
> Thought 's the slave of life, and life 's time's *fool*.
> SHAKSPEARE.

The *idiot* is a natural *fool*; '*Idiots* are still in request in most of the courts of Germany, where there is not a prince of any great magnificence who has not two or three dressed, distinguished, undisputed *fools* in his retinue.'—ADDISON. The *buffoon* is an artificial *fool*; 'Homer has described a Vulcan that is a *buffoon* among his gods, and a Thersites among his mortals.'—ADDISON. Whoever violates common sense in his actions is a *fool*; whoever is unable to act according to common sense is an *idiot*; whoever intentionally violates common sense is a *buffoon*.

SIMPLE, SILLY, FOOLISH.

Simple, v. *Simple; silly* is but a variation of *simple; foolish* signifies like a *fool* (v. *Fool*).

The *simple*, when applied to the understanding, implies such a contracted power as is incapable of combination; *silly* and *foolish* rise in sense upon the former, signifying either the perversion or the total deficiency of understanding; the behaviour of a person may be *silly*, who from any excess of feeling loses his sense of propriety; the conduct of a person will be *foolish* who has not judgement to direct himself. Country people may be *simple* owing to their want of knowledge;

And had the *simple* natives
Observ'd his sage advice,
Their wealth and fame some years ago
Had reach'd above the skies.—SWIFT.

Children will be *silly* in company if they have too much liberty given to them;

Two gods a *silly* woman have undone.—DRYDEN.

There are some persons who never acquire wisdom enough to prevent them from committing *foolish* errours; 'Virgil justly thought it a *foolish* figure for a grave man to be overtaken by death, while he was weighing the cadence of words and measuring verses.' —WALSH.

STUPID, DULL.

Stupid, in Latin *stupidus*, from *stupeo* to be amazed or bewildered, expresses an amazement which is equivalent to a deprivation of understanding; *dull*, through the medium of the German *toll*, and Swedish *stollig*, comes from the Latin *stultus* simple or foolish, and denotes a simple deficiency. *Stupidity* in its proper sense is natural to a man, although a particular circumstance may have a similar effect upon the understanding; he who is questioned in the presence of others may appear very *stupid* in that which is otherwise very familiar to him; 'A *stupid* butt is only fit for the conversation of ordinary people.'—ADDISON. *Dull* is an incidental quality, arising principally from the state of the animal spirits. A writer may sometimes be *dull* who is otherwise vivacious and pointed; a person may be *dull* in a large circle while he is very lively in private intercourse; 'It is the great advantage of a trading nation that there are very few in it so *dull* and heavy who may not be placed in stations of life which may give them an opportunity of making their fortunes.'—ADDISON.

YOUTHFUL, JUVENILE, PUERILE.

Youthful signifies full of *youth*, or in the complete state of *youth: juvenile*, from the Latin *juvenis*, signifies the same; but *pucrile*, from *puer* a boy, signifies literally *boyish*. Hence the first two terms are taken in an indifferent sense; but the latter in a bad sense, or at least always in the sense of what is suitable to a boy only: thus we speak of *youthful* vigour, *youthful* employments, *juvenile* performances, *juvenile* years, and the like: but *puerile* objections, *puerile* conduct, and the like. Sometimes *juvenile* is taken in the bad sense when speaking of *youth* in contrast with men, as *juvenile* tricks; but *puerile* is a much stronger term of reproach, and marks the absence of manhood in those who ought to be men. We expect nothing from a *youth* but what is *juvenile*; we are surprised and dissatisfied to see what is *puerile* in a man;

Chorœbus then, with *youthful* hopes beguil'd,
Swoln with success, and of a daring mind,
This new invention fatally design'd.—DRYDEN.

'Raw *juvenile* writers imagine that, by pouring forth figures often, they render their compositions warm and animated.'—BLAIR. 'After the common course of *puerile* studies, he was put an apprentice to a brewer.' —JOHNSON.

CHILDISH, INFANTINE.

Childish is in the manner of a *child; infantine* is in the manner of an *infant*.

What *children* do is frequently simple or foolish; what *infants* do is commonly pretty and engaging; therefore *childish* is taken in the bad, and *infantine* in the good or indifferent sense. *Childish* manners are very offensive in those who have ceased according to their years to be children; 'It may frequently be remarked of the studious and speculative, that they are proud of trifles, and that their amusements seem frivolous and *childish*.'—JOHNSON. The *infantine* actions of some children evince a simplicity of character; 'The sole comfort of his declining years, almost in *infantine* imbecility.'—BURKE.

PENETRATION, ACUTENESS, SAGACITY

As characteristicks of mind, these terms have much more in them in which they differ than in what they agree: *penetration* is a necessary property of mind; it exists to a greater or less degree in every rational being that has the due exercise of its rational powers: *acuteness* is an accidental property that belongs to the mind only, under certain circumstances. As *penetration* (v. *Discernment*) denotes the process of entering into substances physically or morally, so *acuteness* which is the same as sharpness, denotes the fitness of the thing that performs this process; and as the mind is in both cases the thing that is spoken of, the terms *penetration* and *acuteness* are in this particular closely allied. It is clear, however, that the mind may have *penetration* without having *acuteness*, although one cannot have *acuteness* without *penetration*. If by *penetration* we are commonly enabled to get at the truth which lies concealed, by *acuteness* we succeed in piercing the veil that hides it from our view; the former is, therefore, an ordinary, and the latter an extraordinary gift; 'Fairfax, having neither talents himself for cabal, nor *penetration* to discover the cabals of others, had given his entire confidence to Cromwell.'—HUME. 'Chillingworth was an *acute* disputant against the papists.'—HUME.

Sagacity, in Latin *sagacitas* and *sagio* to perceive quickly, comes in all probability from the Persian *sag* a dog, whence the term has been peculiarly applied to dogs, and from thence extended to all brutes which discover an intuitive wisdom, and also to children, or uneducated persons, in whom there is more *penetration* than may be expected from the narrow compass of their knowledge; hence, properly speaking, *sagacity* is natural or uncultivated *acuteness*; 'Activity to seize, not *sagacity* to discern, is the requisite which youth value.'—BLAIR.

SAGE, SAGACIOUS, SAPIENT.

Sage and *sagacious* are variations from the Latin *sagax* and *sagio* (v. *Penetration*); *sapient* is in Latin *sapiens*, from *sapio*, which comes probably from the Greek σοφὸς wise.

The first of these terms has a good sense, in application to men, to denote the faculty of discerning immediately, which is the fruit of experience, and very similar to that *sagacity* in brutes which instinctively perceives the truth of a thing without the deductions of reason;

So strange they will appear, but so it happen'd,
That these most *sage* academicians sate
In solemn consultation—on a cabbage.
CUMBERLAND.

Sagacious all to trace the smallest game,
And bold to seize the greatest.—YOUNG.

Sapient, which has very different meanings, in the original, is now employed only with regard to animals which are trained up to particular arts; its use is therefore mostly burlesque.

ACUTE, KEEN, SHREWD.

Acute, in French *acute*, Latin *acutus*, from *acus* a needle, signifies the quality of sharpness and pointedness peculiar to a needle; *keen*, in Saxon *cene*, probably comes from *snidan* to cut; signifying the quality of being able to cut; *shrewd*, probably from the Teutonick *beschreyen* to enchant, signifies inspired or endowed with a strong portion of intuitive intellect.

In the natural sense, a fitness to pierce is predominant in the word *acute;* and that of cutting, or a fitness for cutting, in the word *keen*. The same difference is observable in their figurative acceptation.

An *acute* understanding is quick at discovering truth in the midst of falsehood; it fixes itself on a single point with wonderful celerity; 'His *acuteness* was most eminently signalized at the masquerade, where he discovered his acquaintance through their disguises with such wonderful facility.'—JOHNSON. A *keen* understanding cuts or removes away the artificial veil under which the truth lies hidden from the view; 'The village songs and festivities of Bacchus gave a scope to the wildest extravagancies of mummery and grimace, mixed with coarse but *keen* raillery.'—CUMBERLAND. A *shrewd* understanding is rather quick at discovering new truths, than at distinguishing truth from falsehood;

> You statesmen are so *shrewd* in forming schemes!
> JEFFREY.

Acuteness is requisite in speculative and abstruse discussions; *keenness* in penetrating characters and springs of action; *shrewdness* in eliciting remarks and new ideas. The *acute* man detects errours, and the *keen* man falsehoods. The *shrewd* man exposes follies. Arguments may be *acute*, reproaches *keen*, and replies or retorts *shrewd*. A polemick, or a lawyer, must be *acute*, a satirist *keen*, and a wit *shrewd*.

SHARP, ACUTE, KEEN.

The general property expressed by these epithets is that of *sharpness* or an ability to cut. The term *sharp*, from the German *scharf* and *scheren* to cut, is generick and indefinite: the two others are modes of *sharpness* differing in the circumstance or the degree: the *acute* (*v. Acute*) is not only more than *sharp* in the common sense, but signifies also *sharp* pointed: a knife may be *sharp;* but a needle is properly *acute.* Things are *sharp* that have either a long or a pointed edge; but the *keen* is applicable only to the long edge; and that in the highest degree of *sharpness:* a common knife may be *sharp;* but a razor or a lancet are properly said to be *keen*. These terms preserve the same distinction in their figurative use. Every pain is *sharp* which may resemble that which is produced by cutting; 'Be sure you avoid as much as you can to inquire after those that have been *sharp* in their judgements towards me.'—EARL OF STRAFFORD. A pain is *acute* when it resembles that produced by piercing deep;

> Wisdom's eye
> *Acute* for what? To spy more miseries.—YOUNG.

Words are *keen* when they cut deep and wide;

> To this great end *keen* instinct stings him on.
> YOUNG.

TO PENETRATE, PIERCE, PERFORATE, BORE.

Penetrate, v. Discernment; pierce, in French *percer*, comes probably from the Hebrew פרק to break or rend; *perforate*, from the Latin *foris* a door, signifies to make a door through; *bore*, in Saxon *borian*, is probably changed from *fore* or *foris* a door, signifying to make a door or passage.

To *penetrate* is simply to make an entrance into any substance; to *pierce* is to go still deeper; to *perforate* and to *bore* are to go through, or at all events to make a considerable hollow. To *penetrate* is a natural and gradual process; in this manner rust *penetrates* iron, water *penetrates* wood: to *pierce* is a violent, and commonly artificial, process; thus an arrow or a bullet *pierces* through wood. The instrument by which the act of *penetration* is performed is in no case defined; but that of *piercing* commonly proceeds by some pointed instrument: we may *penetrate* the earth by means of a spade, a plough, a knife, or various other instruments; but one *pierces* the flesh by means of a needle, or one *pierces* the ground or a wall by means of a mattock.

To *perforate* and *bore* are modes of *piercing* that vary in the circumstances of the action, and the objects acted upon: to *pierce*, in its peculiar use, is a sudden action by which a hollow is produced in any substance; but to *perforate* and *bore* are commonly the effect of mechanical art. The body of an animal is *pierced* by a dart; but cannon is made by *perforating* or *boring* the iron: channels are formed under ground by *perforating* the earth; holes are made in the ear by *perforation;* 'Mountains were *perforated*, and bold arches thrown over the broadest and most rapid streams (by the Romans).'—GIBBON. Holes are made in leather, or in wood, by *boring;*

> But Capys, and the graver sort, thought fit,
> The Greeks' suspected present to commit
> To seas or flames, at least to search or *bore*
> The sides, and what that space contains t' explore.
> DENHAM.

These last two words do not differ in sense, but in application; the latter being a term of vulgar use.

To *penetrate* and *pierce* are likewise employed in an improper sense; to *perforate* and *bore* are employed only in the proper sense. The first two bear the same relation to each other as in the former: *penetrate* is, however, only employed as the act of persons; *pierce* is used in regard to things. There is a power in the mind to *penetrate* the looks and actions, so as justly to interpret their meaning;

> For if when dead we are but dust or clay,
> Why think of what posterity shall say?
> Their praise or censure cannot us concern,
> Nor ever *penetrate* the silent urn.—JENYNS.

The eye of the Almighty is said to *pierce* the thickest veil of darkness;

> Subtle as lightning, bright, and quick, and fierce,
> Gold through doors and walls did *pierce*.
> COWLEY.

Affairs are sometimes involved in such mystery, that the most enlightened mind is unable to *penetrate* either the end or the beginning; the shrieks of distress are sometimes so loud as to seem to *pierce* the ear.

ORIFICE, PERFORATION.

Orifice, in Latin *orificium* or *orifacium*, from *os* and *factum*, signifies a made mouth, that is, an opening made, as it were; *perforation*, in Latin *perforatio*, from *perforo*, signifies a piercing through.

These terms are both scientifically employed by medical men, to designate certain cavities in the human body; but the former respects that which is natural, the latter that which is artificial: all the vessels of the human body have their *orifices*, which are so constructed as to open or close of themselves. Surgeons are frequently obliged to make *perforations* into the bones. Sometimes the term *perforation* may describe what comes from a natural process, but it denotes a cavity made through a solid substance; but the *orifice* is particularly applicable to such openings as most resemble the mouth in form and use. In this manner the words may be extended in their application to other bodies besides animal substances, and in other sciences besides anatomy: hence we speak of the *orifice* of a tube, the *orifice* of any flower, and the like; or the *perforation* of a tree, by means of a cannon ball or an iron instrument.

OPENING, APERTURE, CAVITY.

Opening signifies in general any place left *open*, without defining any circumstances; the *aperture* is generally a specifick kind of *opening* which is considered scientifically: there are *openings* in a wood when the trees are partly cut away; *openings* in streets by the removal of houses; or *openings* in a fence that has been broken down;

> The scented dew
> Betrays her early labyrinth, and deep
> In scattered sullen *openings* far behind,
> With every breeze she hears the coming storm.
> THOMSON.

Anatomists speak of *apertures* in the skull or in the heart, and the naturalist describes the *apertures* in the nests of bees, ants, beavers, and the like; 'In less than a minute he had thrust his little person through the *aperture*, and again and again perches upon his neighbour's cage.'—COWPER. The *opening* or *aperture* is the commencement of an enclosure; the *cavity* is the whole enclosure: hence the first two are frequently as a part to the whole: many animals make a *cavity* in the earth for their nest with only a small *aperture* for their egress and ingress; 'In the centre of every floor, from top to bottom in the chief room, of no great extent, round which there are narrow *cavities* or recesses.'—JOHNSON.

GULF, ABYSS.

Gulf, in Greek κόλπος from κοῖλος hollow, is applied literally in the sense of a deep concave receptacle for water, as the *gulf* of Venice; *abyss*, in Greek ἄβυσσος, compounded of *a* privative and βυσσὸς a bottom, signifies literally a bottomless pit.

One is overwhelmed in a *gulf;* it carries with it the idea of liquidity and profundity, into which one inevitably sinks never to rise: one is lost in an *abyss;* it carries with it the idea of immense profundity, into which he who is cast never reaches a bottom, nor is able to return to the top: an insatiable voracity is the characteristick idea in the signification of this term.

A *gulf* is a capacious bosom, which holds within itself and burries all objects that suffer themselves to sink into it, without allowing them the possibility of escape; hell is represented as a fiery *gulf*, into which evil spirits are plunged, and remain perpetually overwhelmed: a guilty mind may be said, figuratively, to be plunged into a *gulf* of wo or despair, when filled with the horrid sense of its enormities;

> Sin and death amain
> Following his track, such was the will of heav'n,
> Pav'd after him a broad and beaten way
> Over the dark *abyss*, whose boiling *gulf*
> Tamely endur'd a bridge of wondrous length,
> From hell continued.—MILTON.

An *abyss* presents nothing but an interminable space, which has neither beginning nor end; he does wisely who does not venture in, or who retreats before he has plunged too deep to retrace his footsteps: as the ocean, in the natural sense, is a great *abyss*, so are metaphysicks an immense *abyss*, into which the human mind precipitates itself only to be bewildered;

> His broad wing'd vessel drinks the whelming tide,
> Hid in the bosom of the black *abyss*.—THOMSON.

LABYRINTH, MAZE.

Intricacy is common to both the objects expressed by these terms; but the term *labyrinth* has it to a much greater extent than *maze;* the *labyrinth*, from the Greek λαβύρινθος, was a work of antiquity which surpassed the *maze* in the same proportion as the ancients surpassed the moderns in all other works of art: it was constructed on so prodigious a scale, and with so many windings, that when a person was once entered, he could not find his way out without the assistance of a clue or thread. *Maze*, probably from the Saxon *mase* a gulf, is a modern term for a similar structure on a smaller scale, which is frequently made by way of ornament in large gardens. From the proper meaning of the two words we may easily see the ground of their metaphorical application: political and polemical discussions are compared to a *labyrinth;* because the mind that is once entangled in them is unable to extricate itself by any efforts of its own;

> From the slow mistress of this school, Experience,
> And her assistant, pausing, pale Distrust,
> Purchase a dear-bought clue to lead his youth
> Through serpentine obliquities of human life,
> And the dark *labyrinth* of human hearts.—YOUNG.

On the other hand, that perplexity and confusion into which the mind is thrown by unexpected or inexplicable events, is termed a *maze;* because, for the time, it is bereft of its power to pursue its ordinary functions of recollection and combination;

> To measur'd notes, while they advance,
> He in wild *maze* shall lead the dance.
> CUMBERLAND.

WONDER, ADMIRATION, SURPRISE, ASTONISHMENT, AMAZEMENT.

Wonder, in German *wunder*, is in all probability a variation of *wander*, because *wonder* throws the mind off its bias; *admiration*, from the Latin *miror*, and the Hebrew מראת vision, or looking at, signifies looking at attentively: *surprise*, compounded of *sur* and *prize*, or the Latin *prehendo*, signifies to take on a sudden; *astonish*, from the Latin *attonitus*, and *tonitru* thunder, signifies to strike, as it were, with the overpowering noise of thunder; *amaze* signifies to be in a *maze*, so as not to be able to collect one's self.

That particular feeling which any thing unusual produces on our minds is expressed by all these terms, but under various modifications. *Wonder* is the most indefinite in its signification or application, but it is still the least vivid sentiment of all; it amounts to little more than a pausing of the mind, a suspension of the thinking faculty, an incapacity to fix on a discernible point in an object that rouses our curiosity: it is that state which all must experience at times, but none so much as those who are ignorant; they *wonder* at every thing because they know nothing; 'The reader of the "Seasons" *wonders* that he never saw before what Thomson shows him.'—JOHNSON. *Admiration* is *wonder* mixed with esteem or veneration; the *admirer* suspends his thoughts, not from the vacancy but the fulness of his mind: he is riveted to an object which for a time absorbs his faculties: nothing but what is great and good excites *admiration*, and none but cultivated minds are susceptible of it; an ignorant person cannot *admire*, because he cannot appreciate the value of any thing;

> With eyes insatiate, and tumultuous joy,
> Beholds the presents, and *admires* the boy.
> DRYDEN.

Surprise and *astonishment* both arise from that which happens unexpectedly; they are a species of *wonder* differing in degree, and produced only by the events of life: the *surprise*, as its derivation implies, takes us unawares; we are *surprised* if that does not happen which we calculate upon, as the absence of a friend whom we looked for; or we are *surprised* if that happens which we did not calculate upon; thus we are *surprised* to see a friend returned whom we supposed was on his journey: *astonishment* may be awakened by similar events which are more unexpected and more unaccountable; thus we are *astonished* to find a friend at our house whom we had every reason to suppose was many hundred miles off; or we are *astonished* to hear that a person has got safely through a road which we conceived to be absolutely impassable; 'So little do we accustom ourselves to consider the effects of time, that things necessary and certain often *surprise* us like unexpected contingencies.'—JOHNSON. 'I have often been *astonished*, considering that the mutual intercourse between the two countries (France and England) has lately been very great, to find how little you seem to know of us.'—BURKE.

Surprise may for a moment startle; *astonishment* may stupify and cause an entire suspension of the faculties; but *amazement* has also a mixture of perturbation. We may be *surprised* and *astonished* at things in which we have no particular interest: we are mostly *amazed* at that which immediately concerns us. We may be *surprised* agreeably or otherwise; we may be *astonished* at that which is agreeable, although *astonishment* is not itself a pleasure; but we are *amazed* at that which happens contrary to our inclination. We are agreeably *surprised* to see our friends: we are *astonished* how we ever got through the difficulty: we are *amazed* at the sudden and unexpected events which have come upon us to our ruin. A man of experience will not have much to *wonder* at, for his observations will supply him with corresponding examples of whatever passes: a wise man will have but momentary *surprises;* as he has estimated the uncertainty of human life, few things of importance will happen contrary to his expectations: a generous mind will be *astonished* at gross instances of perfidy in others: there is no mind that may not sometimes be thrown into *amazement* at the awful dispensations of Providence;

> *Amazement* seizes all; the general cry
> Proclaims Laocoon justly doom'd to die.—DRYDEN.

WONDER, MIRACLE, MARVEL, PRODIGY MONSTER.

Wonder is that which causes *wonder* (*v. Wonder*); *miracle*, in Latin *miraculum*, from *mirror* to *wonder*, has the same signification, signifying that which strikes the sense; *marvel* is a variation of *miracle; prodigy* in Latin *prodigium*, from *prodigo*, or *procul* and *ago* to launch forth, signifies the thing launching forth; *monster*, in Latin *monstrum*, comes from *monstro* to point out, and *moneo* to advise or give notice; because among the Romans any unaccountable appearance was considered as an indication of some future event.

Wonders are natural; *miracles* are supernatural. The whole creation is full of *wonders*; the Bible contains an account of the *miracles* which happened in those days. Sometimes the term *miracle* or *miraculous* may be employed hyperbolically for what is exceedingly *wonderful*;

Murder, though it have no tongue, will speak
With most *mirac'lous* organ.—SHAKSPEARE.

Wonders are real; *marvels* are often fictitious; *prodigies* are extravagant and imaginary. Natural history is full of *wonders*;

His wisdom such as once it did appear
Three kingdoms *wonder*, and three kingdoms fear.
DENHAM.

Travels abound in *marvels* or in *marvellous* stories, which are the inventions either of the artful or the ignorant and credulous: ancient history contains numberless accounts of *prodigies*. *Wonders* are agreeable to the laws of nature; they are *wonderful* only as respects ourselves: *monsters* are violations of the laws of nature. The production of a tree from a grain of seed is a *wonder*; but the production of a calf with two heads is a *monster*;

Ill omens may the guilty tremble at,
Make every accident a *prodigy*,
And *monsters* frame where nature never err'd.—LEE.

DISADVANTAGE, INJURY, HURT, DETRIMENT, PREJUDICE.

Disadvantage implies the absence of an *advantage* (*v. Advantage*); *injury*, in Latin *injuria*, from *jus*, properly signifies what is contrary to right or justice, but extends in its sense to every loss or deficiency which is occasioned; *hurt* signifies in the northern languages beaten or wounded; *detriment*, in Latin *detrimentum*, from *detritum* and *deterrere* to wear away, signifies the effect of being worn out; *prejudice*, in the improper sense of the word (*v. Bias*), implies the ill which is supposed to result from *prejudice*.

The *disadvantage* is rather the absence of a good; the *injury* is a positive evil: the want of education may frequently be a disadvantage to a person by retarding his advancement; 'Even the greatest actions of a celebrated person labour under this *disadvantage*, that however surprising and extraordinary they may be, they are no more than what are expected from him.'—ADDISON. The ill word of another may be an *injury* by depriving us of friends; 'The places were acquired by just title of victory, and therefore in keeping of them no *injury* was offered.'—HAYWARD. The *disadvantage*, therefore, is applied to such things as are of an *adventitious* nature: the *injury* to that which is of essential importance. The *hurt*, *detriment*, and *prejudice* are all species of *injuries*. *Injury*, in general, implies whatever ill befalls an object by the external action of other objects, whether taken in relation to physical or moral evil to persons or to things; *hurt* is that species of *injury* which is produced by more direct violence; too close application to study is *injurious* to the health; reading by an improper light is *hurtful* to the eyes: so in a moral sense, the light reading which a circulating library supplies is often *injurious* to the morals of young people; 'Our repentance s not real, because we have not done what we can to undo our faults, or at least to hinder the *injurious* consequences of them from proceeding.'—TILLOTSON. All violent affections are hurtful to the mind; 'The number of those who by abstracted thoughts become useless is inconsiderable, in respect of them who are *hurtful* to mankind by an active and restless disposition.'—BARTLETT. The *detriment* and *prejudice* are species of *injury* which affect only the outward circumstances of a person; the former implying what may lessen the value of an object, the latter what may lower it in the esteem of others. Whatever affects the stability of a merchant's credit is highly *detrimental* to his interests; 'In many instances we clearly perceive that more or less knowledge dispensed to man would have proved *detrimental* to his state'—BLAIR. Whatever is *prejudicial* to the character of a man should not be made the subject of indiscriminate conversation: 'That the heathen have spoken things to the same sense of this saying of our Saviour is so far from being any *prejudice* to this saying, that it is a great commendation of it.'—TILLOTSON.

It is prudent to conceal that which will be to our *disadvantage* unless we are called upon to make the acknowledgment. There is nothing material that is not exposed to the *injuries* of time, if not to those of actual violence. Excesses of every kind carry their own punishment with them, for they are always *hurtful* to the body. The price of a book is often *detrimental* to its sale. The intemperate zeal, or the in consistent conduct of religious professors is highly *prejudicial* to the spread of religion.

TO LOSE, MISS.

Lose, in all probability, is but a variation of *loose*, because what gets *loose* or away from a person is *lost* to him; to *miss*, probably from the particle *mis*, implying a defect, signifies to *lose* by mistake.

What is *lost* is not at hand; what is *missing* is not to be seen; it does not depend upon ourselves to re cover what is *lost*; it is supposed to be irrevocably gone; what we *miss* at one time we may by diligence and care recover at another time. A person *loses* his health and strength by a decay of nature, and must submit patiently to the *loss* which cannot be repaired; 'Some ants are so unfortunate as to fall down with their load when they almost come home; when this happens they seldom *lose* their corn, but carry it up again.'—ADDISON. If a person *misses* the opportunity of improvement in his youth, he will never have another opportunity that is equally good;

For a time caught up to God, as once
Moses was in the mount, and *missing* long
MILTON

LOSS, DAMAGE, DETRIMENT.

Loss signifies the act of *losing* or the thing *lost*, *damage*, in French *dommage*, Latin *damnum*, from *demo* to take away, signifies the thing taken away. *detriment*, *v. Disadvantageous*.

Loss is here the generick term; *damage* and *detriment* are species or modes of *loss*. The person sustains the *loss*, the thing suffers the *damage* or *detriment*. Whatever is gone from us which we wish to retain is a *loss*; hence we may sustain a *loss* in our property, in our reputation, in our influence, in our intellect, and every other object of possession; 'What trader would purchase such airy satisfaction (as the charms of conversation) by the *loss* of solid gain.'—JOHNSON. Whatever renders an object less serviceable or valuable, by any external violence, is a *damage*; as a vessel suffers a *damage* in a storm; 'The ants were still troubled with the rain, and the next day they took a world of pains to repair the *damage*.'—ADDISON. Whatever is calculated to cross a man's purpose is a *detriment*; the bare want of a good name may be a *detriment* to a young tradesman; the want of prudence is always a great *detriment* to the prosperity of a family; 'The expenditure should be with the least possible *detriment* to the morals of those who expend.'—BURKE.

INJURY, DAMAGE, HURT, HARM, MISCHIEF.

The idea of making a thing otherwise than it ought is common to these terms. *Injury* (*v. Disadvantage*) is the most general term, simply implying what happens contrary to right; the rest are but modes of *injury*: *damage*, from the Latin *damnum* loss, is the *injury* which takes away from the value of a thing: *hurt* (*v. Disadvantage*) is the *injury* which destroys the soundness or wholeness of a thing: *harm* (*v. Evil*) is the *injury* which is attended with trouble and inconvenience: *mischief* is the *injury* which interrupts the order and consistency of things. The *injury* is applicable to all bodies physical and moral; *damage* is applicable only to physical bodies. Trade may suffer an *injury*; a building may suffer an *injury*: but a building, a vessel, a merchandise, suffers *damage*. When applied both to physical bodies, the *injury* comprehends every thing which makes an object otherwise than it ought to be: that is to say, all collateral circumstances which are connected with the end and purpose of things; but *damage* implies that actual *injury* which affects the structure and materials of the object: the situation of some buildings is an *injury* to them; the falling of a chimney, or the breaking of a roof, is a *damage:* the *injury* may not be easily removed; the *damage* may be easily repaired.

Injury and *hurt* are both applied to persons; but the *injury* may either affect their bodies, their circumstances, or their minds; the *hurt* in its proper sense affects only their bodies. We may receive an *injury* or a *hurt* by a fall; but the former is employed when the health or spirits of a person suffer, the latter when any fracture or wound is produced. A person sometimes sustains an *injury* from a fall, either by losing the use of a limb, or by the deprivation of his senses; 'Great *injuries* mice and rats do in a field.'—MORTIMER. A sprain, a cut, and a bruise are little *hurts* which are easily cured;

> No plough shall *hurt* the glebe, no pruning hook the vine.—DRYDEN.

The *hurt* is sometimes figuratively employed as it respects the circumstances of a man, where the idea of inflicting a wound or a pain is implied; as in *hurting* a man's good name, *hurting* his reputation, *hurting* his morals, and other such cases, in which the specifick term *hurt* may be substituted for the general term *injury;*

> In arms and science 't is the same,
> Our rival's *hurt* creates our fame.—PRIOR.

The *injury*, *harm*, and *mischief* are all employed for the circumstances of either things or men; but the *injury* comprehends cause and effect; the *harm* and *mischief* respect the evil as it is. If we say that the *injury* is done, we always think of either the agent by which it is done, or the object to which it is done, or both; 'Many times we do *injury* to a cause by dwelling upon trifling arguments.'—WATTS. When we speak of the *harm* and *mischief*, we only think of the nature and measure of the one or the other. It is an *injury* to society to let publick offenders go free; young people do not always consider the *harm* which there may be in some of their most imprudent actions; 'After their young are hatched, they brood them under their wings, lest the cold, and sometimes the heat, should *harm* them.'—RAY. The mischief of disseminating free principles among the young and the ignorant has now been found to exceed all the good which might result from the superiour cultivation of the human mind, and the more extended diffusion of knowledge;

> But furious Dido, with dark thoughts involv'd,
> Shook at the mighty *mischief* she resolv'd.—DRYDEN.

TO IMPAIR, INJURE.

Impair comes from the Latin *im* and *pejoro* or *pejor* worse, signifying to make worse; *injure*, from *in* and *jus* against right, signifies to make otherwise than it ought to be.

Impair seems to be in regard to *injure* as the species to the genus; what is *impaired* is *injured*, but what is *injured* is not necessarily *impaired*. To *impair* is a progressive mode of *injuring:* an *injury* may take place either by degrees, or by an instantaneous act: straining of the eyes *impairs* the sight, but a blow *injures* rather than *impairs* the eye. A man's health may be *impaired* or *injured* by his vices, but his limbs are *injured* rather than *impaired* by a fall. A person's circumstances are *impaired* by a succession of misfortunes; they are *injured* by a sudden turn of fortune. The same distinction is preserved in their figurative application; 'It is painful to consider that this sublime enjoyment of friendship may be *impaired* by innumerable causes.'—JOHNSON.

> Who lives to nature rarely can be poor.
> O what a patrimony this! a being
> Of such inherent strength and majesty,
> Not worlds possess'd can raise it; worlds destroy'd
> Can't *injure*.—YOUNG.

IMMINENT, IMPENDING, THREATENING.

Imminent, in Latin *imminens*, from *in* and *maneo* to remain, signifies resting or coming upon; *impending*, from the Latin *pendeo* to hang, signifies hanging, *threatening* is used in the sense of the verb to *threaten*.

All these terms are used in regard to some evil that is exceedingly near: *imminent* conveys no idea of duration; *impending* excludes the idea of what is momentary. A person may be in *imminent* danger of losing his life in one instant, and the danger may be over the next instant: but an *impending* danger is that which has been long in existence, and gradually approaching; 'There was an opinion, if we may believe the Spanish historians, almost universal among the Americans, that some dreadful calamity was *impending* over their heads.'—ROBERTSON. We can seldom escape *imminent* danger by any efforts of one's own; but we may be successfully warned to escape from an *impending* danger. *Imminent* and *impending* are said of dangers that are not discoverable; but a *threatening* evil gives intimations of its own approach; we perceive the *threatening* tempest in the blackness of the sky; we hear the *threatening* sounds of the enemy's clashing swords; 'The *threatening* voice and fierce gestures with which these words were uttered, struck Montezuma. He saw his own danger was *imminent*, the necessity unavoidable.'—ROBERTSON.

THREAT, MENACE.

Threat is of Saxon origin; *menace* is of Latin extraction. They do not differ in signification; but, as is frequently the case, the Saxon is the familiar term, and the Latin word is employed only in the higher style. We may be *threatened* with either small or great evils; but we are *menaced* only with great evils. One individual *threatens* to strike another: a general *menaces* the enemy with an attack. We are *threatened* by things as well as persons: we are *menaced* by persons only; a person is *threatened* with a look; he is *menaced* with a prosecution by his adversary;

> By turns put on the suppliant and the lord;
> *Threaten'd* this moment, and the next implor'd.
> PRIOR

> Of the sharp axe
> Regardless, that o'er his devoted head
> Hangs *menacing*.—SOMERVILLE.

EVIL OR ILL, MISFORTUNE, HARM, MISCHIEF.

Evil in its full sense comprehends every quality which is not good, and consequently the other terms express only modifications of *evil*.

The word is however more limited in its application than its meaning, and admits therefore of a just comparison with the other words here mentioned. They are all taken in the sense of *evils* produced by some external cause, or *evils* inherent in the object and arising out of it. The *evil*, or, in its contracted form, the *ill*, befalls a person; the *misfortune* comes upon him; the *harm* is taken, or he receives the *harm;* the *mischief* is done him. *Evil* in its limited application is taken for *evils* of the greatest magnitude; it is that which is *evil* without any mitigation or qualification of circumstances. The *misfortune* is a minor *evil;* it depends upon the opinion and circumstances of the individual; what is a *misfortune* in one respect may be the contrary in another respect. An untimely death, the fracture or loss of a limb, are denominated *evils;* the loss of a vessel, the overturning of a carriage, and the like, are *misfortunes*, inasmuch as they tend to the diminution of property; but as all the casualties of life may produce various consequences, it may sometimes happen that that which seems to have come upon us by our *ill* fortune turns out ultimately of the greatest benefit; in this respect, therefore, the *misfortune* is but a partial *evil:* of *evil* it is likewise observable, that it has no respect to the sufferer as a moral agent, but *misfortune* is used in regard to such things as are controllable or otherwise by human foresight;

> *Misfortune* stands with her bow ever bent
> Over the world; and he who wounds another,
> Directs the goddess by that part where he wounds
> There to strike deep her arrows in himself.
> YOUNG.

The *evil* which befalls a man is opposed only to th

good which he in general experiences; but the *misfortune* is opposed to the good fortune or the prudence of the individual. Sickness is an *evil*, let it be endured or caused by whatever circumstances it may; it is a *misfortune* for an individual to come in the way of having this *evil* brought on himself: his own relative condition in the scale of being is here referred to.

The *harm* and *mischief* are species of minor *evils;* the former of which is much less specifick than the latter, both in the nature and cause of the *evil*. A person takes *harm* from circumstances that are not known; the *mischief* is done to him from some positive and immediate circumstance. He who takes cold takes *harm;* the cause of which, however, may not be known or suspected: a fall from a horse is attended with *mischief*, if it occasion a fracture or any *evil* to the body. *Evil* and *misfortune* respect persons only as the objects; *harm* and *mischief* are said of inanimate things as the object. A tender plant takes *harm* from being exposed to the cold air: *mischief* is done to it when its branches are violently broken off or its roots are laid bare.

Misfortune is the incidental property of persons who are its involuntary subjects; but *evil*, *harm*, and *mischief* are the inherent and active properties of things that flow out of them as effects from their causes: *evil* is said either to lie in a thing or attend it as a companion or follower; 'A misery is not to be measured from the nature of the *evil*, but from the temper of the sufferer.'—ADDISON. *Harm* properly lies in the thing;

To me the labours of the field resign;
Me Paris injured: all the war be mine,
Fall he that must beneath his rival's arms,
And leave the rest secure of future *harms*.
POPE.

Mischief properly attends the thing as a consequence;

To mourn a *mischief* that is past and gone,
Is the next way to draw new *mischief* on.
SHAKSPEARE.

In political revolutions there is *evil* in the thing and *evil* from the thing; *evil* when it begins, *evil* when it ends, and *evil* long after it has ceased;

Yet think not thus, when freedom's *ills* I state,
I mean to flatter kings or court the great.
GOLDSMITH.

It is a dangerous question for any young person to put to himself—what *harm* is there in this or that indulgence? He who is disposed to put this question to himself will not hesitate to answer it according to his own wishes. The *mischiefs* which arise from the unskilfulness of those who undertake to be their own coachmen are of so serious a nature, that in course of time they will probably deter men from performing such unsuitable offices.

HURTFUL, PERNICIOUS, NOXIOUS, NOISOME.

Hurtful signifies full of *hurt*, or causing much *hurt;* *pernicious*, v. *Destructive;* *noxious* and *noisome*, from the Latin *noxius* and *noceo* to hurt, signifies the same originally as *hurtful*.

Between *hurtful* and *pernicious* there is the same distinction as between *hurting* and destroying: that which is *hurtful* may *hurt* in various ways;

The *hurtful* hazel in thy vineyard shun.
DRYDEN.

That which is *pernicious* necessarily tends to destruction: confinement is *hurtful* to the health: bad company is *pernicious* to the morals; or the doctrines of freethinkers are *pernicious* to the well-being of society;

Of strength, *pernicious* to myself, I boast,
The powers I have were given me to my cost.
LEWIS.

Noxious and *noisome* are species of the *hurtful:* things may be *hurtful* both to body and mind; *noxious* and *noisome* only to the body: that which is *noxious* inflicts a direct injury;

The serpent, subtlest beast of all the field,
Of huge extent sometimes, with brazen eyes,
And hairy mane, terrifick, though to thee
Not *noxious*, but obedient at thy call.
MILTON.

That which is *noisome* inflicts the injury indirectly: *noxious* insects are such as wound; *noisome* vapours are such as tend to create disorders;

The only prison that enslaves the soul
Is the dark habitation, where she dwells
As in a *noisome* dungeon.—BELLINGHAM.

Ireland is said to be free from every *noxious* weed or animal; where filth is brought together, there will always be *noisome* smells.

CALAMITY, DISASTER, MISFORTUNE MISCHANCE, MISHAP.

Calamity, in French *calamité*, Latin *calamitas*, from *calamus* a stalk; because hail or whatever injured the stalks of corn was termed a *calamity; disaster*, in French *désastre*, is compounded of the privative *des* or *dis* and *astre*, in Latin *astrum* a star, signifying what came from the adverse influence of the stars; *misfortune*, *mischance*, and *mishap* naturally express what comes amiss.

The idea of a painful event is common to all these terms, but they differ in the degree of importance.

A *calamity* is a great *disaster* or *misfortune;* a *misfortune* a great *mischance* or *mishap:* whatever is attended with destruction is a *calamity;* whatever occasions mischief to the person, defeats or interrupts plans, is a *disaster;* whatever is accompanied with a loss of property, or the deprivation of health, is a *misfortune;* whatever diminishes the beauty or utility of objects is a *mischance* or *mishap:* the devastation of a country by hurricanes or earthquakes, or the desolation of its inhabitants by famine or plague, are great *calamities;* the overturning of a carriage, and the fracture of a limb, are *disasters;* losses in trade are *misfortunes;* the spoiling of a book is, to a greater or less extent, a *mischance* or *mishap*.

A *calamity* seldom arises from the direct agency of man; the elements, or the natural course of things are mostly concerned in producing this source of misery to men; the rest may be ascribed to chance, as distinguished from design; 'They observed that several blessings had degenerated into *calamities*, and that several *calamities* had improved into blessings, according as they fell into the possession of wise or foolish men.'—ADDISON. *Disasters* mostly arise from some specifick known cause, either the carelessness of persons, or the unfitness of things for their use; as they generally serve to derange some preconcerted scheme or undertaking, they seem as if they were produced by some secret influence;

There in his noisy mansion, skill'd to rule,
The village master taught his little school:
A man severe he was, and stern to view,
I knew him well, and every truant knew.
Well had the boding tremblers learn'd to trace
The day's *disasters* in his morning face.
GOLDSMITH.

Misfortune is frequently assignable to no specifick cause, it is the bad fortune of an individual; a link in the chain of his destiny; an evil independent of himself, as distinguished from a fault; 'She daily exercises her benevolence by pitying every *misfortune* that happens to every family within her circle of notice.'—JOHNSON. *Mischance* and *mishap* are *misfortunes* of comparatively so trivial a nature, that it would not be worth while to inquire into their cause, or to dwell upon their consequences;

Permit thy daughter, gracious Jove, to tell,
How this *mischance* the Cyprian queen befell.
POPE.

For pity's sake tells undeserv'd *mishaps*,
And their applause to gain, recounts his claps.
CHURCHILL.

A *calamity* is dreadful; a *disaster* melancholy; a *misfortune* grievous or heavy; a *mischance* or *mishap* slight or trivial.

A *calamity* is either publick or private, but more frequently the former: a *disaster* is rather particular than private; it affects things rather than persons; journeys expeditions, and military movements are commonly attended with *disasters: misfortunes* are altogether personal; they immediately affect the interests of the individual: *mischances* and *mishaps* are altogether domestick. We speak of a *calamitous* period, a *disastrous* expedition, an *unfortunate* person, little *mischances* or *mishaps*.

ADVERSITY, DISTRESS.

Adversity, v. *Adverse; distress*, from the Latin *distringo*, compounded of *dis* twice, and *stringo* to bind, signifies that which binds very tight, or brings into a great strait.

Adversity respects external circumstances; *distress* regards either external circumstances or inward feelings. *Adversity* is opposed to prosperity; *distress* to ease.

Adversity is a general condition, *distress* a particular state. *Distress* is properly the highest degree of *adversity*. When a man's affairs go altogether *adverse* to his wishes and hopes, when accidents deprive him of his possessions or blast his prospects, he is said to be in *adversity*; 'The other extreme which these considerations should arm the heart of a man against, is utter despondency of mind in a time of pressing *adversity*.'—SOUTH. When a man is reduced to a state of want, deprived of friends and all prospect of relief, his situation is that of real *distress*; 'Most men, who are at length delivered from any great *distress*, indeed, find that they are so by ways they never thought of.'—SOUTH.

Adversity is trying, *distress* is overwhelming. Every man is liable to *adversity*, although few are reduced to *distress* but by their own fault.

DISTRESS, ANXIETY, ANGUISH, AGONY.

Distress, v. *Adversity; anxiety*, in French *anxieté*, and *anguish*, in French *angoisse*, both come from the Latin *ango*, *anxi* to strangle; *agony*, in French *agonie*, Latin *agonia*, Greek ἀγωνία, from ἀγωνίζω to contend or strive, signifies a severe struggle with pain and suffering.

Distress is the pain felt when in a strait from which we see no means of extricating ourselves; *anxiety* is that pain which one feels on the prospect of an evil. The *distress* always depends upon some outward cause; the *anxiety* often lies in the imagination. The *distress* is produced by the present, but not always immediate, evil;

> How many, rack'd with honest passions, droop
> In deep retir'd *distress!* How many stand
> Around the death-bed of their dearest friends,
> And point the parting *anguish*.—THOMSON.

The *anxiety* respects that which is future; 'If you have any affection for me, let not your *anxiety*, on my account, injure your health.'—MELMOTH (*Letters of Cicero*). *Anguish* arises from the reflection on the evil that is past; 'In the *anguish* of his heart, Adam expostulates with his Creator for having given him an unasked existence.'—ADDISON. *Agony* springs from witnessing that which is immediate or before the eye;

> These are the charming *agonies* of love,
> Whose misery delights. But through the heart
> Should jealousy its venom once diffuse,
> 'T is then delightful misery no more,
> But *agony* unmixed.—THOMSON.

Distress is not peculiar to any age, where there is a consciousness of good and evil, pain and pleasure; it will inevitably arise from some circumstance or another. *Anxiety*, *anguish*, and *agony* belong to riper years: infancy and childhood are deemed the happy periods of human existence; because they are exempt from the *anxieties* attendant on every one who has a station to fill, and duties to discharge. *Anguish* and *agony* are species of distress, of the severer kind, which spring altogether from the maturity of reflection, and the full consciousness of evil. A child is in *distress* when it loses its mother, and the mother is also in *distress* when she misses her child. The station of a parent is, indeed, that which is most productive, not only of *distress*, but *anxiety*, *anguish*, and *agony*: the mother has her peculiar *anxieties* for the child, while rearing it in its infant state; the father has his *anxiety* for its welfare on its entrance into the world: they both suffer the deepest *anguish* when the child disappoints their dearest hopes, by running a career of vice, and finishing its wicked course by an untimely, and sometimes ignominious, end: not unfrequently they are doomed to suffer the *agony* of seeing a child encircled in flames from which he cannot be snatched, or sinking into a watery grave from which he cannot be rescued.

TO DISTRESS, HARASS, PERPLEX.

Distress, v. *Distress; harass*, in French *harasser* probably from the Greek ἀράσσω to beat; *perplex*, in Latin *perplexus*, participle of *perplector*, compounded of *per* and *plector*, signifies to wind round and entangle.

A person is *distressed* either in his outward circumstances or his feelings; he is *harassed* mentally or corporeally; he is *perplexed* in his understanding, more than in his feelings: a deprivation *distresses*; provocations and hostile measures *harass*; stratagems and ambiguous measures *perplex*: a besieged town is *distressed* by the cutting off its resources of water and provisions;

> O friend! Ulysses' shouts invade my ear;
> *Distress'd* he seems, and no assistance near.
> POPE.

The besieged in a town are *harassed* by perpetual attacks; 'Persons who have been long *harassed* with business and care, sometimes imagine that when life declines, they cannot make their retirement from the world too complete.'—BLAIR. The besiegers of a town are sometimes *perplexed* in all their manœuvres and plans, by the counter-manœuvres and contrivances of their opponents; or a person is *perplexed* by the contradictory points of view in which an affair appears to him; a tale of wo *distresses*: continual alarms and incessant labour *harass*; unexpected obstacles and inextricable difficulties *perplex*;

> Would being end with our expiring breath,
> How soon misfortunes would be puff'd away!
> A trifling shock can shiver us to the dust,
> But th' existence of the immortal soul,
> Futurity's dark road *perplexes* still.—GENTLEMAN.

We are *distressed* and *perplexed* by circumstances; we are *harassed* altogether by persons, or the intentional efforts of others: we may relieve another in *distress*, or may remove a *perplexity*; but the *harassing* ceases only with the cause which gave rise to it.

PAIN, PANG, AGONY, ANGUISH.

Pain is to be traced, through the French and northern languages, to the Latin and Greek ποινὴ punishment, πόνος labour, and πένομαι to be poor or in trouble. *Pang* is but a variation of *pain*, contracted from the Teutonick *peinigen* to torment; *agony* comes from the Greek ἀγωνίζω to struggle or contend, signifying the labour or *pain* of a struggle; *anguish* comes from the Latin *ango*, contracted from *ante* and *ago*, to act against, or in direct opposition to, and signifies the *pain* arising from severe pressure.

Pain, which expresses the feeling that is most repugnant to the nature of all sensible beings, is here the generick, and the rest specifick terms: *pain* and *agony* are applied indiscriminately to what is physical and mental; *pang* and *anguish* mostly respect that which is mental: *pain* signifies either an individual feeling or a permanent state; *pang* is only a particular feeling; *agony* is sometimes employed for the individual feeling, but more commonly for the state; *anguish* is always employed for the state. *Pain* is indefinite with regard to the degree; it may rise to the highest, or sink to the lowest possible degree; the rest are positively high degrees of *pain*: the *pang* is a sharp *pain*; the *agony* is a severe and permanent *pain*; the *anguish* is an overwhelming *pain*.

The causes of *pain* are as various as the modes of *pain*, or as the circumstances of sensible beings; it attends disease, want, and sin, in an infinite variety of forms; 'We should pass on from crime to crime, heedless and remorseless, if misery did not stand in our way, and our own *pains* admonish us of our folly.'—JOHNSON. The *pangs* of conscience frequently trouble the man who is not yet hardened in guilt: the *pangs* of disappointed love are among the severest to be borne;

What *pangs* the tender breast of Dido tore!
DRYDEN.

Agony and *anguish* are produced by violent causes, and disease in its most terrible shape: wounds and torments naturally produce corporeal *agony*; a guilty conscience that is awakened to a sense of guilt will suffer mental *agony*;

Thou shalt behold him stretch'd in all the *agonies*
Of a tormenting and a shameful death.—OTWAY.

Anguish arises altogether from moral causes; the miseries and distresses of others, particularly of those who are nearly related, are most calculated to excite *anguish*; a mother suffers *anguish* when she sees her child labouring under severe *pain*, or in danger of losing its life, without having the power to relieve it;

Are these the parting *pangs* which nature feels,
When *anguish* rends the heart-strings?—ROWE.

TORMENT, TORTURE.

Torment (*v. To tease*) and *torture* both come from *torqueo* to twist, and express the agony which arises from a violent twisting or griping of any part; but the latter, which is more immediately derived from the verb, expresses much greater violence and consequent pain than the former. *Torture* is an excess of *torment.* We may be *tormented* by a variety of indirect means; but we are *tortured* only by the direct means of the rack, or similar instruments. *Torment* may be permanent: *torture* is only for a time, or on certain occasions. It is related in history that a person was once *tormented* to death, by a violent and incessant beating of drums in his prison: the Indians practise every species of *torture* upon their prisoners. A guilty conscience may *torment* a man all his life;

Yet in his empire o'er thy abject breast,
His flames and *torments* only are express'd.—PRIOR.

The horrours of an awakened conscience are a *torture* to one who is on his death-bed;

To a wild sonnet or a wanton air,
Offence and *torture* to a sober ear.—PRIOR.

TO AFFLICT, DISTRESS, TROUBLE.

Afflict, in Latin *afflictus*, participle of *affligo*, compounded of *af* or *ad* and *fligo*, in Greek θλίβω to press hard, signifies to bear upon any one; *distress*, *v. Adversity*; *trouble* signifies to cause a tumult, from the Latin *turba*, Greek τύρβη or θόρυβος a tumult.

When these terms relate to outward circumstances, the first expresses more than the second, and the second more than the third.

People are *afflicted* with grievous maladies;

A melancholy tear *afflicts* my eye,
And my heart labours with a sudden sigh.—PRIOR.

The mariner is *distressed* for want of water in the midst of the wide ocean, or an embarrassed tradesman is *distressed* for money to maintain his credit;

I often did beguile her of her tears,
When I did speak of some *distressful* stroke,
That my youth suffered.—SHAKSPEARE.

The mechanick is *troubled* for want of proper tools, or the head of a family for want of good domesticks;

The boy so *troubles* me,
'T is past enduring.—SHAKSPEARE.

When they respect the inward feelings, *afflict* conveys the idea of deep sorrow: *distress* that of sorrow mixed with anxiety; *trouble* that of pain in a smaller degree. The death of a parent *afflicts*; 'We last night received a piece of ill news at our club which very sensibly *afflicted* every one of us. I question not but my readers themselves will be *troubled* at the hearing of it. To keep them no longer in suspense, Sir Roger de Coverly is dead.'—ADDISON. The misfortunes of our family and friends *distress*; 'While the mind contemplates *distress*, it is acted upon and never acts, and by indulging in this contemplation it becomes more and more unfit for action.'—CRAIG. Crosses in trade and domestick inconveniences *trouble*.

In the season of *affliction* prayer affords the best consolation and surest supports. The assistance and sympathy of friends serve to relieve *distress*. We may often help ourselves out of our *troubles*, and remove the evil by patience and perseverance.

Afflictions may be turned to benefits if they lead a man to turn inwardly into himself, and examine the state of his heart and conscience in the sight of his Maker. The *distresses* of human life often serve only to enhance the value of our pleasures when we regain them. Among the *troubles* with which we are daily assailed, many of them are too trifling for us to be *troubled* by them.

AFFLICTION, GRIEF, SORROW.

Affliction, *v. To afflict*; *grief*, from *grieve*, in German *grämen*, Swedish *gramga*, &c.; *sorrow*, in German *sorge*, &c. signifies care, as well as sorrow.

All these words mark a state of suffering which differs either in the degree or the cause, or in both.

Affliction is much stronger than *grief*, it lies deeper in the soul, and arises from a more powerful cause; the loss of what is most dear, the continued sickness of our friends, or a reverse of fortune, will all cause *affliction*; 'Some virtues are only seen in *affliction*, and some in prosperity.'—ADDISON. The misfortunes of others, the failure of our favourite schemes, the troubles of our country, will occasion us *grief*; 'The melancholy silence that follows hereupon, and continues until he has recovered himself enough to reveal his mind to his friend, raises in the spectators a *grief* that is inexpressible.'—ADDISON.

Sorrow is less than *grief*; it arises from the untoward circumstances which perpetually arise in life. A disappointment, the loss of a game, our own mistake, or the negligences of others, cause *sorrow*. If more serious objects awaken *sorrow*, the feeling is less poignant than that of *grief*; 'The most agreeable objects recall the *sorrow* for her with whom he used to enjoy them.'—ADDISON.

Affliction lies too deep to be vehement; it discovers itself by no striking marks in the exteriour: it is lasting and does not cease when the external cause ceases to act; *grief* may be violent, and discover itself by loud and indecorous signs; it is transitory, and ceases even before the cause which gave birth to it; *sorrow* discovers itself by a simple expression; it is still more transient than *grief*, not existing beyond the moment in which it is produced.

A person of a tender mind is *afflicted* at the remembrance of his sins; he is *grieved* at the consciousness of his fallibility and proneness to errour; he is *sorry* for the faults which he has committed.

Affliction is allayed; *grief* subsides; *sorrow* is soothed.

TO GRIEVE, MOURN, LAMENT.

Grieve, *v. Affliction*; *mourn*, like *moan* and *murmur*, is probably but an imitation of the sound which is produced by pain.

To *grieve* is the general term; *mourn* the particular term. To *grieve*, in its limited sense, is an inward act; to *mourn* is an outward act: the *grief* lies altogether in the mind; the *mourning* displays itself by some outward mark. A man *grieves* for his sins; he *mourns* for the loss of his friends. One *grieves* for that which immediately concerns one's self;

Achates, the companion of his breast,
Goes *grieving* by his side, with equal cares oppress'd.
DRYDEN

One *mourns* for that which concerns others;

My brother's friends and daughters left behind,
False to them all, to Paris only kind;
For this I *mourn* till grief or dire disease
Shall waste the form whose crime it was to please.
POPE.

One *grieves* over the loss of property; one *mourns* the fate of a deceased relative.

Grieve is the act of an individual; *mourn* may be the common act of many; a nation *mourns*, though it does not *grieve*, for a publick calamity. To *grieve* is applicable to domestick troubles; *mourn* may refer to publick or private ills. Every good Frenchman has had occasion to *grieve* for the loss of that which is immediately dear to himself, and to *mourn* over the misfortunes which have overwhelmed his country.

Grieve and *mourn* are permanent sentiments; *lament* (*v. To bewail*) is a transitory feeling: the former produced by substantial causes, which come home to the feelings; the latter respects things of a more partial, oftentimes of a more remote and indifferent, nature. A real widow *mourns* all the remainder of her days for the loss of her husband; we *lament* a thing to-day which we may forget to-morrow. *Mourn* and *lament* are both expressed by some outward sign: but the former is composed and free from all noise; the latter displays itself either in cries or simple words;

So close in poplar shades, her children gone,
The mother nightingale *laments* alone.—DRYDEN.

In the moment of trouble, when the distress of the mind is at its height, it may break out into loud *lamentation*; but commonly *grieving* and *mourning* commence when *lamentation* ceases.

As epithets, *grievous*, *mournful*, and *lamentable* have a similar distinction. What presses hard on persons, their property, connexions, and circumstances, is *grievous*; what touches the tender feelings, and tears asunder the ties of kindred and friendship, is *mournful*; whatever excites a painful sensation in our minds is *lamentable*. Famine is a *grievous* calamity for a nation; the violent separation of friends by death is a *mournful* event at all times, but particularly so for those who are in the prime of life and the fulness of expectation; the ignorance which some persons discover even in the present cultivated state of society is truly *lamentable*. *Grievous* misfortunes come but seldom, although they sometimes fall thickly on an individual; a *mournful* tale excites our pity from the persuasion of its veracity; but *lamentable* stories are often fabricated for sinister purposes.

GRIEVANCE, HARDSHIP.

Grievance, from the Latin *gravis*, heavy or burdensome, implies that which lies heavy at heart; *hardship*, from the adjective *hard*, denotes that which presses or bears violently on the person.

Grievance is in general taken for that which is done by another to *grieve* or distress: *hardship* is a particular kind of *grievance*, that presses upon individuals. There are national *grievances*, though not national *hardships*.

An infraction of one's rights, an act of violence or oppression, are *grievances* to those who are exposed to them, whether as individuals or bodies of men: an unequal distribution of labour, a partial indulgence of one to the detriment of another, constitute the *hardship*. A weight of taxes levied by an unthinking government, will be esteemed a *grievance*; the partiality and caprice of tax-gatherers or subordinates in office in making it fall with unequal weight upon particular persons will be regarded as a peculiar *hardship*. Men seek a redress of their *grievances* from some higher power than that by which they are afflicted: they endure their *hardships* until an opportunity offers of getting them removed; 'It is better private men should have some injustice done them, than a publick *grievance* should not be redressed. This is usually pleaded in defence of all those *hardships* which fall on particular persons, in particular occasions which could not be foreseen when the law was made.'—SPECTATOR.

TO COMPLAIN, LAMENT, REGRET.

Complain, in French *complaindre* or *plaindre*, Latin *plango* to beat the breast as a sign of grief, in Greek πλήγω to beat; *lament*, *v. To bewail*; *regret*, compounded of *re* privative and *gratus* grateful, signifies to have a feeling the reverse of pleasant.

Complaint marks most of dissatisfaction; *lamentation* most of regret; *regret* most of pain. *Complaint* is expressed verbally; *lamentation* either by words or signs; *regret* may be felt without being expressed. *Complaint* is made of personal grievances; *lamentation* and *regret* may be made on account of others as well as ourselves. We *complain* of our ill health, of our inconveniences, or of troublesome circumstances; we *lament* our inability to serve another; we *regret* the absence of one whom we love. Selfish people have the most to *complain* of, as they demand the most of others, and are most liable to be disappointed; anxious people are the most liable to *lament*, as they feel every thing strongly; the best regulated mind may have occasion to *regret* some circumstances which give pain to the tender affections of the heart.

The folly of *complaint* has ever been the theme of moralists in all ages; it has always been regarded as the author and magnifier of evils; it dwells on little things until they become great; 'We all of us *complain* of the shortness of time, saith Seneca, and yet have much more than we know what to do with.'—ADDISON. *Lamentations* are not wiser though more excusable, especially if we *lament* over the misfortunes of others; 'Surely to dread the future is more reasonable than to *lament* the past.'—JOHNSON. *Regret* is frequently tender, and always moderate; hence it is allowable to mortals who are encompassed with troubles to indulge in *regret*; '*Regret* is useful and virtuous when it tends to the amendment of life.'—JOHNSON. We may *complain* without any cause, and *lament* beyond what the cause requires; but *regret* will always be founded on some real cause, and not exeeed the cause in degree. It would be idle for a man to *complain* of his want of education, or *lament* over the errours and misfortunes of his youth; but he can never look back upon mispent time without sincere *regret*.

TO COMPLAIN, MURMUR, REPINE.

Complain, *v. To complain*; *murmur*, in German *murmeln*, conveys both in sound and in sense the idea of dissatisfaction; *repine* is compounded of *re* and *pine*, from the English *pain*, Latin *pœna* punishment, and the Greek πεῖνα hunger, signifying to convert into pain.

The idea of expressing displeasure or dissatisfaction is common to these terms. *Complaint* is not so loud as *murmuring*, but more so than *repining*.

We *complain* or *murmur* by some audible method; we may *repine* secretly. *Complaints* are always addressed to some one; *murmurs* and *repinings* are often addressed only to one's self. *Complaints* are made of whatever creates uneasiness, without regard to the source from which they flow; *murmurings* are a species of *complaints* made only of that which is done by others for our inconvenience; when used in relation to persons, *complaint* is the act of a superiour; *murmuring* that of an inferiour; *repining* is always used in relation to the general disposition of things. When the conduct of another offends, it calls for *complaint*; when a superiour aggrieves by the imposition of what is burdensome, it occasions *murmuring* on the part of the aggrieved; when disappointments arrive, or ambition is thwarted, men *repine* at their destiny.

Complaints and *murmurs* may be made upon every trivial occasion; *repinings* only on matters of moment. *Complaints*, especially such as respect one's self, are at best but the offspring of an uneasy mind; they betray great weakness, and ought to be suppressed; *murmurs* are culpable; they violate the respect and obedience due to superiours; those who *murmur* have seldom substantial grounds for *murmuring*; *repinings* are sinful, they arraign the wisdom and the goodness of an infinitely wise and good Being. It will be difficult, by the aid of philosophy, to endure much pain without *complaining*; religion only can arm the soul against all the ills of life;

I'll not *complain*;
Children and cowards rail at their misfortunes.
TRAPP.

The rebellious Israelites were frequently guilty of *murmurings*, not only against Moses, but even against their Almighty Deliverer, notwithstanding the repeated manifestations of his goodness and power;

Yet, O my soul! thy rising murmurs stay,
Nor dare th' ALLWISE DISPOSER to arraign;
Or against his supreme decree,
With impious grief *complain*.—LYTTLETON.

A want of confidence in God is the only cause of *repinings*; he who sees the hand of God in all things cannot *repine*;

Would all the deities of Greece combine,
In vain the gloomy thunderer might *repine*;
Sole should he sit, with scarce a god to friend,
And see his Trojans to the shades descend.—POPE.

TO BEWAIL, BEMOAN, LAMENT, DEPLORE.

Bewail is compounded of *be* and *wail*, which is probably connected with the word *wo*, signifying to express sorrow; *bemoan*, compounded of *be* and *moan*, signifies to indicate grief with *moans; lament*, in French *lamenter*, Latin *lamentor* or *lamentum*, comes probably from the Greek *κλαῦμα* and *κλαίω* to cry out with grief; *deplore*, in Latin *deploro*, i. e. *de* and *ploro* or *plango*, signifies to give signs of distress with the face or mouth.

All these terms mark an expression of pain by some external sign. *Bewail* is not so strong as *bemoan*, but stronger than *lament; bewail* and *bemoan* are expressions of unrestrained grief or anguish: a wretched mother *bewails* the loss of her child; a person in deep distress *bemoans* his hard fate: *lamentation* may arise from simple sorrow or even imaginary grievances; a sensualist *laments* the disappointment of some expected gratification.

Bewail and *bemoan* are always indecorous, if not sinful, expressions of grief, which are inconsistent with the profession of a Christian; they are common among the uncultivated, who have not a proper principle to restrain the intemperance of their feelings. There is nothing temporal which is so dear to any one that he ought to *bewail* its loss: nor any condition of things so distressing or desperate as to make a man *bemoan* his lot. *Lamentations* are sometimes allowable; the miseries of others, or our own infirmities and sins, may justly be *lamented*.

Deplore is a much stronger expression than *lament;* the former calls forth tears from bitterness of the heart;

> The wounds they washed, their pious tears they shed,
> And laid along their oars *deplor'd* the dead.—POPE.

The latter excites a cry from the warmth of feeling;

> But let not chief the nightingale *lament*
> Her ruin'd care, too delicately fram'd
> To brook the harsh confinement of the cage.
> THOMSON.

The *deplorable* indicates despair; the *lamentable* marks only pain or distress.

Among the poor we have *deplorable* instances of poverty, ignorance, vice, and wretchedness combined. Among the higher classes we have often *lamentable* instances of people involving themselves in trouble by their own imprudence. A field of battle or a city overthrown by an earthquake is a spectacle truly *deplorable.* It is *lamentable* to see beggars putting on all the disguises of wretchedness in order to obtain what they might earn by honest industry. The condition of a dying man suffering under the agonies of an awakened conscience is *deplorable;* the situation of the relative or friend who witnesses the agony, without being able to afford consolation to the sufferer, is truly *lamentable.*

TO GROAN, MOAN.

Groan and *moan* are both an onomatopeïa, from the sounds which they express. *Groan* is a deep sound produced by hard breathing: *moan* is a plaintive, long-drawn sound produced by the organs of utterance. The *groan* proceeds involuntarily as an expression of severe pain, either of body or mind: the *moan* proceeds often from the desire of awakening attention or exciting compassion. Dying *groans* are uttered in the agonies of death: the *moans* of a wounded sufferer are sometimes the only resource he has left to make his destitute case known;

> The plain ox, whose toil,
> Patient and ever ready, clothes the land
> With all the pomp of harvest, shall he bleed,
> And struggling *groan* beneath the cruel hands
> E'en of the clown he feeds ?—THOMSON.

> The fair Alexis lov'd, but lov'd in vain,
> And underneath the beechen shade, alone,
> Thus to the woods and mountains made his *moan*
> DRYDEN.

MOURNFUL, SAD.

Mournful signifies full of what causes *mourning; sad* (*v. Dull*) signifies either a painful sentiment, or what causes this painful sentiment. The difference in the sentiment is what constitutes the difference between these epithets: the *mournful* awakens tender and sympathetick feelings: the *sad* oppresses the spirits and makes one heavy at heart; a *mournful* tale contains an account of others' distresses;

> Upon his tomb
> Shall be engrav'd the sack of Orleans;
> The treacherous manner of his *mournful* death.
> SHAKSPEARE.

A *sad* story contains an account of one's own distress;

> How *sad* a sight is human happiness
> To those whose thoughts can pierce beyond an hour
> YOUNG

A *mournful* event befalls our friends and relatives; a *sad* misfortune befalls ourselves. Selfish people find nothing *mournful*, but many things *sad:* tender-hearted people are always affected by what is *mournful*, and are less troubled about what is *sad.*

DULL, GLOOMY, SAD, DISMAL.

Dull may probably come from the Latin *dolor*, signifying generally that which takes off from the bright ness, vivacity, or perfection of any thing; *gloomy*, from the German *glumm* muddy, signifies the same as tarnished; *sad* is probably connected with shade, to imply obscurity, which is most suitable to sorrow; *dismal*, compounded of *dis* and *mal* or *malus*, signifies very evil.

When applied to natural objects they denote the want of necessary light: in this sense metals are more or less *dull* according as they are stained with dirt: the weather is either *dull* or *gloomy* in different degrees; that is, *dull* when the sun is obscured by clouds, and *gloomy* when the atmosphere is darkened by fogs or thick clouds. A room is *dull, gloomy*, or *dismal*, according to circumstances: it is *dull* if the usual quantity of light and sound be wanting; it is *gloomy* if the darkness and stillness be very considerable; it is *dismal* if it be deprived of every convenience that fits it for a habitation; in this sense a dungeon is a *dismal* abode; 'While man is a retainer to the elements and a sojourner in the body, it (the soul) must be content to submit its own quickness and spirituality to the *dulness* of its vehicle.'—SOUTH.

> Achilles' wrath, to Greece the direful spring
> Of woes unnumber'd, heav'nly goddess, sing!
> That wrath which hurl'd to Pluto's *gloomy* reign
> The souls of mighty chiefs untimely slain.—POPE.

> For nine long nights, through all the dusky air
> The pyres thick flaming shot a *dismal* glare.—POPE.

Sad is not applied so much to sensible as moral objects, in which sense the distressing events of human life, as the loss of a parent or a child, is justly denominated *sad;* 'Henry II. of France, by a splinter unhappily thrust into his eye at a solemn justing, was sent out of the world by a *sad* but very accidental death.'—SOUTH.

In regard to the frame of mind which is designated by these terms, it will be easily perceived from the above explanation. As slight circumstances produce *dulness*, any change, however small, in the usual flow of spirits may be termed *dull;*

> A man
> So *dull*, so dead in look, so wo-begone.
> SHAKSPEARE.

Gloom weighs heavy on the mind, and gives a turn to the reflections and the imagination: desponding thoughts of futurity will spread a *gloom* over every other object; 'Neglect spreads *gloominess* upon their humour, and makes them grow sullen and unconversable.'—COLLIER. The word *dismal* is seldom used except as an epithet to external objects. *Sadness* indicates a wounded state of the heart; feelings of unmixed pain;

> Six brave companions from each ship we lost;
> With sails outspread we fly the unequal strife,
> *Sad* for their loss, but joyful of our life.—POPE.

GLOOM, HEAVINESS.

Gloom has its source internally, and is often independent of outward circumstances; *heaviness* is a weight upon the spirits, produced by a foreign cause: the former belongs to the constitution; the latter is occasional. People of a melancholy habit have a particular *gloom* hanging over their minds which pervades all their thoughts; those who suffer under severe disappointments for the present, and have *gloomy* prospects for the future, may be expected to be *heavy* at heart; we may sometimes dispel the *gloom* of the mind by the force of reflection, particularly by the force of religious contemplation: *heaviness* of spirits is itself a temporary thing, and may be succeeded by vivacity or lightness of mind when the pressure of the moment has subsided; 'If we consider the frequent reliefs we receive from laughter, and how often it breaks the *gloom* which is apt to depress the mind, one would take care not to grow too wise for so great a pleasure of life.'—ADDISON. 'Worldly prosperity flattens as life descends. He who lately overflowed with cheerful spirits and high hopes, begins to look back with *heaviness* on the days of former years.'—BLAIR.

GLOOMY, SULLEN, MOROSE, SPLENETICK.

All these terms denote a temper of mind the reverse of easy or happy: *gloomy* lies either in the general constitution or the particular frame of the mind; *sullen* lies in the temper: a man of a *gloomy* disposition is an involuntary agent; it is his misfortune, and renders him in some measure pitiable: the *sullen* man yields to his evil humours; *sullenness* is his fault, and renders him offensive. The *gloomy* man distresses himself most; his pains are all his own: the *sullen* man has a great share of discontent in his composition; he charges his sufferings upon others, and makes them suffer in common with himself. A man may be rendered *gloomy* for a time by the influence of particular circumstances; but *sullenness* creates pains for itself when all external circumstances of a painful nature are wanting;

Th' unwilling heralds act their lord's commands,
Pensive they walk along the barren sands;
Arriv'd, the hero in his tent they find,
With *gloomy* aspect, on his arm reclin'd.—POPE.

At this they ceased; the stern debate expir'd:
The chiefs in *sullen* majesty retir'd.—POPE.

Sullenness and *moroseness* are both the inherent properties of the temper; but the former discovers itself in those who have to submit, and the latter in those who have to command: *sullenness* therefore betrays itself mostly in early life; *moroseness* is the peculiar characteristick of age; 'The *morose* philosopher is so much affected by these and some other authorities, that he becomes a convert to his friend, and desires he would take him with him when he went to his next ball.'—BUDGELL. The *sullen* person has many fancied hardships to endure from the control of others; the *morose* person causes others to endure many real hardships, by keeping them under too severe a control. *Sullenness* shows itself mostly by an unseemly reserve; *moroseness* shows itself by the hardness of the speech, and the roughness of the voice. *Sullenness* is altogether a sluggish principle, that leads more or less to inaction; *moroseness* is a harsh feeling, that is not contented with exacting obedience unless it inflicts pain.

Moroseness is a defect of the temper; but *spleen*, from *splen*, is a defect in the heart: the one betrays itself in behaviour, the other more in conduct. A *morose* man is an unpleasant companion; a *splenetick* man is a bad member of society: the former is ill-natured to those about him, the latter is ill-humoured with all the world. *Moroseness* vents itself in temporary expressions: *spleen* indulges itself in perpetual bitterness of expression: 'While in that *splenetick* mood, we amused ourselves in a sour critical speculation of which we ourselves were the objects, a few months effected a total change in our variable minds.'—BURKE.

PITEOUS, DOLEFUL, WOFUL, RUEFUL.

Piteous signifies moving *pity* (*v. Pity*); *doleful*, or full of *dole*, in Latin *dolor* pain, signifies indicative of much pain; *woful*, or full of *wo*, signifies likewise indicative of *wo*, which from the German *weh* implies pain; *rueful*, or full of *rue*, from the German *reuen* to repent, signifies indicative of much sorrow

The close alliance in sense of these words one to another is obvious from the above explanation; *piteous* is applicable to one's external expression of bodily or mental pain; a child makes *piteous* lamentations when it suffers for hunger, or has lost its way;

With pond'rous clubs
As weak against the mountain heaps they push
Their beating breast in vain and *piteous* bray,
He lays them quivering on th' ensanguin'd plain
THOMSON.

Doleful applies to those sounds which convey the idea of pain; there is something *doleful* in the tolling of a funeral bell, or in the sound of a muffled drum;

Entreat, pray, beg, and raise a *doleful* cry.—DRYDEN.

Woful applies to the circumstances and situations of men; a scene is *woful* in which we witness a large family of young children suffering under the complicated horrours of sickness and want; 'A brutish temptation made Samson, from a judge of Israel, a *woful* judgement upon it.'—SOUTH. *Rueful* applies to the outward indications of inward sorrow depicted in the looks or countenance. The term is commonly applied to the sorrows which spring from a gloomy or distorted imagination, and has therefore acquired a somewhat ludicrous acceptation; hence we find in Don Quixote, the knight of the *rueful* countenance introduced. The term is however used in poetry in a serious sense;

Cocytus nam'd, of lamentation loud,
Heard on the *rueful* stream.—MILTON.

MEAN, PITIFUL, SORDID.

The moral application of these terms to the characters of men, in their transactions with each other, is what constitutes their common signification. Whatever a man does in common with those below him is *mean;* it evinces a temper that is prone to sink rather than to rise in the scale of society: whatever makes him an object of pity, and consequently of contempt for his sunken character, makes him *pitiful:* whatever makes him grovel and crawl in the dust, licking up the dross and filth of the earth, is *sordid*, from the Latin *sordeo* to be filthy and nasty. *Meanness* is in many cases only relatively bad as it respects the disposal of our property: for instance, what is *meanness* in one, might be generosity or prudence in another: the due estimate of circumstances is allowable in all, but it is *meanness* for any one to attempt to save, at the expense of others, that which he can conveniently afford either to give or pay: hence an undue spirit of seeking gain or advantage for one's self to the detriment of others, is denominated a *mean* temper: of this temper the world affords such abundant examples, that it may almost seem unnecessary to specify any particulars, or else I would say it is *mean* in those who keep servants, to want to deprive them of any fair sources of emolument: it is *mean* for ladies in their carriages, and attended by their livery servants, to take up the time of a tradesman by bartering with him about sixpences or shillings in the price of his articles. it is *mean* for a gentleman to do that for himself which, according to his circumstances, he might get another to do for him;

Can you imagine I so *mean* could prove,
To save my life by changing of my love?
DRYDEN.

Pitifulness goes farther than *meanness:* it is not merely that which degrades, but unmans the person; it is that which is bad as well as low: when the fear of evil or the love of gain prompts a man to sacrifice his character and forfeit his veracity he becomes truly *pitiful:* Blifield in Tom Jones is the character whom all pronounce to be *pitiful;* 'The Jews tell us of a two-fold Messiah, a vile and most *pitiful* fetch, invented only to evade what they cannot answer '—PRIDEAUX. *Sordidness* is peculiarly applicable to one's love of gain: although of a more corrupt, yet it is not of so degrading a nature as the two former: the *sordid* man does not deal in trifles like the *mean* man; and has nothing so low and vicious in him as the *pitiful* man. A continual habit of getting money will engender a *sordid* love of it in the human mind; but nothing short of a radically contemptible character leads a man to be *pitiful.* A *mean* man is thought lightly of: a *pitiful* man is held in profound contempt: a *sordid* man is hated. *Meanness* descends to that which is insignificant and worthless;

> Nature, I thought, perform'd too *mean* a part,
> Forming her movements to the rules of art.
> SWIFT.

Pitifulness sinks into that which is despicable; 'Those men who give themselves airs of bravery on reflecting upon the last scenes of others, may behave the most *pitifully* in their own.'—RICHARDSON. *Sordidness* contaminates the mind with what is foul; 'It is strange, since the priest's office heretofore was always splendid, that it is now looked upon as a piece of religion, and to make it low and *sordid*.'—SOUTH.

> This my assertion proves, he may be old,
> And yet not *sordid*, who refuses gold.
> DENHAM.

SORRY, GRIEVED, HURT.

Sorry and *grieved* are epithets somewhat differing from their primitives *sorrow* and *grief* (*v. Affliction*), inasmuch as they are applied to ordinary subjects. We speak of being *sorry* for any thing, however trivial, which concerns ourselves;

> The ass, approaching next, confess'd
> That in his heart he lov'd a jest;
> One fault he hath, is *sorry* for 't,
> His ears are half a foot too short.—SWIFT.

We are commonly *grieved* for that which concerns others;

> The mimick ape began to chatter,
> How evil tongues his name bespatter;
> He saw, and he was *griev'd* to see 't,
> His zeal was sometimes indiscreet.—SWIFT.

I am *sorry* that I was not at home when a person called upon me; I am *grieved* that it is not in my power to serve a friend who stands in need. Both these terms respect only that which we do ourselves: *hurt* (*v. To displease* and *To injure*) respects that which is done to us, denoting a painful feeling from *hurt* or wounded feelings; we are *hurt* at being treated with disrespect; 'No man is *hurt*, at least few are so, by hearing his neighbour esteemed a worthy man.'—BLAIR.

UNHAPPY, MISERABLE, WRETCHED.

Unhappy is literally not to be happy; this is the negative condition of many who might be happy if they pleased. *Miserable*, from *misereor* to pity, signifies to deserve pity, which is to be positively and extremely *unhappy*: this is the lot only of a comparatively few. *Wretched*, from our word *wreck*, the Saxon *wrecca* an exile, and the like, signifies cast away or abandoned; that is, particularly *miserable*, which is the lot of still fewer. As happiness lies properly in the mind, *unhappy* is taken in the proper sense, with regard to the state of the feelings, but is figuratively extended to the outward circumstances which occasion the painful feelings; we lead an *unhappy* life, or are in an *unhappy* condition: as that which excites the compassion of others must be external, and the state of abandonment must of itself be an outward state, *miserable* and *wretched* are properly applied to the outward circumstances which cause the pain, and improperly to the pain which is occasioned. We can measure the force of these words, that is to say, the degree of *unhappiness* which they express, only by the circumstance which causes the *unhappiness*. *Unhappy* is an indefinite term; as we may be *unhappy* from slight circumstances, or from those which are important; a child may be said to be *unhappy* at the loss of a plaything; a man is *unhappy* who leads a vicious life: *miserable* and *wretched* are more limited in their application; a child cannot be either *miserable* or *wretched*; and he who is so, has some serious cause either in his own mind or in his circumstances to make him so: a man is *miserable* who is tormented by his conscience; a mother will be *wretched* who sees her child violently torn from her.

The same distinction holds good when taken to designate the outward circumstances themselves; he is an *unhappy* man whom nobody likes, and who likes nobody; every criminal suffering the punishment of his offences is an *unhappy* man;

> Such is the fate *unhappy* women find,
> And such the curse entail'd upon our kind.
> ROWE.

The condition of the poor is particularly *miserable* in countries which are not blessed with the abundance that England enjoys;

> These *miseries* are more than may be borne.
> SHAKSPEARE.

Philoctetes, abandoned by the Greeks in the island of Lemnos, a prey to the most poignant grief and the horrours of indigence and solitude, was a *wretched* man;

> 'T is murmur, discontent, distrust,
> That makes you *wretched*.—GAY.

Unhappy is only applicable to that which respects the happiness of man; but *miserable* and *wretched* may be said of that which is mean and worthless in its nature; a writer may be either *miserable* or *wretched* according to the lowness of the measure at which he is rated; so likewise any performance may be *miserable* or *wretched*, a house may be *miserable* or *wretched*, and the like.

TO EMBARRASS, PERPLEX, ENTANGLE

Embarrass (*v. Difficult*) respects a person's manners or circumstances; *perplex* (*v. To distress*) his views and conduct; *entangle* (*v. To disengage*) is said of particular circumstances. *Embarrassments* depend altogether on ourselves; the want of prudence and presence of mind are the common causes: *perplexities* depend on extraneous circumstances as well as ourselves; extensive dealings with others are mostly attended with *perplexities; entanglements* arise mostly from the evil designs of others.

That *embarrasses* which interrupts the even course or progress of one's actions; 'Cervantes had so much kindness for Don Quixote, that however he *embarrasses* him with absurd distresses, he gives him so much sense and virtue as may preserve our esteem.'—JOHNSON. That *perplexes* which interferes with one's opinions; 'It is scarcely possible, in the regularity and composure of the present time, to image the tumult of absurdity and clamour of contradiction which *perplexed* doctrine, disordered practice, and disturbed both publick and private quiet in the time of the rebellion.'—JOHNSON. That *entangles* which binds a person in his decisions; 'I presume you do not *entangle* yourself in the particular controversies between the Romanists and us.'—CLARENDON. Pecuniary difficulties *embarrass*, or contending feelings produce *embarrassment*: contrary counsels or interests *perplex*: law-suits *entangle*. Steadiness of mind prevents *embarrassment* in the outward behaviour. Firmness of character is requisite in the midst of *perplexities*: caution must be employed to guard against *entanglements*.

TO TROUBLE, DISTURB, MOLEST.

Whatever uneasiness or painful sentiment is produced in the mind by outward circumstances is effected either by *trouble* (*v. Affliction*), by *disturbance* (*v. Commotion*), or by *molestation* (*v. To inconvenience*) *Trouble* is the most general in its application; we may be *troubled* by the want of a thing, or *troubled* by that which is unsuitable; we are *disturbed* and *molested* only by that which actively *troubles*. Pecuniary wants are the greatest *troubles* in life; the perverseness of servants, the indisposition or ill behaviour of children, are domestick *troubles*; 'Ulysses was exceedingly *troubled* at the sight of his mother (in the Elysian fields).'—ADDISON. The noise of children is a *disturbance*, and the prospect of want *disturbs* the mind. *Trouble* may be permanent; *disturbance* and *molestation* are temporary, and both refer to the peace which is destroyed: a *disturbance* ruffles or throws out of a tranquil state; a *molestation* burdens or bears hard either on the body or the mind: noise is always a *disturbance* to one who wishes to think or to remain in quiet;

> No buzzing sounds *disturb* their golden sleep.
> DRYDEN.

Talking, or any noise, is a *molestation* to one who is in an irritable frame of body or mind;

> Both are doom'd to death;
> And the dead wake not to *molest* the living.
> ROWE.

TROUBLESOME, IRKSOME, VEXATIOUS.

These epithets are applied to the objects which create *trouble* or *vexation*.

Irksome is compounded of *irk* and *some*, from the German *arger* vexation, which probably comes from the Greek ἀργὸς; *troublesome* (*v. To afflict*) is here, as before, the generick term; *irksome* and *vexatious* are species of the *troublesome*: what is *troublesome* creates either bodily or mental pain; what is *irksome* creates a mixture of bodily and mental pain; and what is *vexatious* creates purely mental pain. What requires great exertion, or a too long continued exertion or exertions, coupled with difficulties, is *troublesome*; in this sense the laying in stores for the winter is a *troublesome* work for the ants, and compiling a dictionary is a *troublesome* labour to some writers; 'The incursions of *troublesome* thoughts are often violent and importunate.'—JOHNSON. What requires any exertion which we are unwilling to make, or interrupts the quiet which we particularly long for, is *irksome*; in this sense giving and receiving of visits is *irksome* to some persons; travelling is *irksome* to others;

> For not to *irksome* toil, but to delight he made us.
> MILTON.

What comes across our particular wishes, or disappoints us in a particular manner, is *vexatious*; in this sense the loss of a prize which we had hoped to gain may be *vexatious*;

> The pensive goddess has already taught
> How vain is hope, and how *vexatious* thought.
> PRIOR.

DIFFICULTIES, EMBARRASSMENTS, TROUBLES.

These terms are all applicable to a person's concerns in life; but *difficulties* relate to the *difficulty* (*v. Difficulty*) of conducting a business; *embarrassments* relate to the confusion attending a state of debt; and *trouble* to the pain which is the natural consequence of not fulfilling engagements or answering demands. Of the three, *difficulties* expresses the least, and *troubles* the most. A young man on his entrance into the world will unavoidably experience *difficulties*, if not provided with ample means in the outset; 'Young Cunningham was recalled to Dublin, where he continued for four or five years, and of course experienced all the *difficulties* that attend distressed situations.'—JOHNSON. Let a man's means be ever so ample, if he have not prudence and talents fitted for business, he will hardly keep himself free from *embarrassments*; 'Few men would have had resolution to write books with such *embarrassments* (as Milton laboured under).'—JOHNSON. There are no *troubles* so great as those which are produced by pecuniary *difficulties*, which are the greatest *troubles* that can arise to disturb the peace of a man's mind; 'Virgil's sickliness, studies, and the *troubles* he met with, turned his hair gray before the usual time'—WALSH.

DEJECTION, DEPRESSION, MELANCHOLY.

Dejection, from *dejicio* to cast down, and *depression*, from *deprimo* to press or sink down, have both regard to the state of the animal spirits; *melancholy*, from the Greek μελαγχολία black bile, regards the state of the humours in general, or of the particular humour called the bile.

Dejection and *depression* are occasional, and depend on outward circumstances; *melancholy* is permanent, and lies in the constitution. *Depression* is but a degree of *dejection*: slight circumstances may occasion a *depression*; distressing events occasion a *dejection*: the death of a near and dear relative may be expected to produce *dejection* in persons of the greatest equanimity;

> So bursting frequent from Atrides' breast,
> Sighs following sighs his inward fears confess'd;
> Now o'er the fields *dejected* he surveys,
> From thousand Trojan fires the mountain blaze.
> POPE.

Lively tempers are most liable to *depressions*; 'I will only desire you to allow me that Hector was in an absolute certainty of death, and *depressed* over and above with the conscience of being in an ill cause.'—POPE. *Melancholy* is a disease which nothing but clear views of religion can possibly correct; 'I have read somewhere in the history of ancient Greece, that the women of the country were seized with an unaccountable *melancholy*, which disposed several of them to make away with themselves.'—ADDISON.

DESPAIR, DESPERATION, DESPONDENCY.

Despair and *desperation*, from the French *desespoir*, compounded of the privative *de* and the Latin *spes* hope, signifies the absence or the annihilation of all hope; *despondency*, from *despond*, in Latin *despondeo*, compounded of the privative *de* and *spondeo* to promise, signifies literally to deprive in a solemn manner, or cut off from every gleam of hope.

Despair is a state of mind produced by the view of external circumstances; *desperation* and *despondency* may be the fruit of the imagination; the former therefore always rests on some ground, the latter are sometimes ideal: *despair* lies mostly in reflection; *desperation* and *despondency* in the feelings; the former marks a state of vehement and impatient feeling, the latter that of fallen and mournful feeling. *Despair* is often the forerunner of *desperation* and *despondency*, but it is not necessarily accompanied with effects so powerful: the strongest mind may have occasion to *despair* when circumstances warrant the sentiment; men of an impetuous character are apt to run into a state of *desperation*; a weak mind full of morbid sensibility is most liable to fall into *despondency*.

Despair interrupts or checks exertion

> *Despair* and grief distract my lab'ring mind;
> Gods! what a crime my impious heart design'd.
> POPE

Desperation impels to greater exertions; 'It may be generally remarked of those who squander what they know their fortune is not sufficient to allow, that in their most jovial moments there always breaks out some proof of discontent and impatience; they either scatter with a wild *desperation*, or pay their money with a peevish anxiety.'—JOHNSON. *Despondency* unfits for exertion; 'Thomson submitting his productions to some who thought themselves qualified to criticise, he heard of nothing but faults; but finding other judges more favourable, he did not suffer himself to sink into *despondence*.'—JOHNSON. When a physician *despairs* of making a cure, he lays aside the application of remedies; when a soldier sees nothing but death or disgrace before him, he is driven to *desperation*, and redoubles his efforts; when a tradesman sees before him nothing but failure for the present, and want for the future, he may sink into *despondency*. *despair* is justifiable as far as it is a rational calculation into futurity from the present appearances: *desperation* may arise from extraordinary circumstances or the action of strong passions; in the former case it is unavoidable, and may serve to rescue from great distress; in the latter case it is mostly attended with fatal consequences: *despondency* is a disease of the mind, which nothing but a firm trust in the goodness of Providence can obviate.

DESPERATE, HOPELESS.

Desperate (*v. Despair*) is applicable to persons or things; *hopeless* to things only: a person makes a *desperate* effort; he undertakes a *hopeless* task.

Desperate, when applied to things, expresses more than *hopeless*; the latter marks the absence of hope as to the attainment of good, the former marks the absence of hope as to the removal of an evil: a person who is in a *desperate* condition is overwhelmed with actual trouble for the present, and the prospect of its continuance for the future; he whose case is *hopeless* is without the prospect of effecting the end he has in view: gamesters are frequently brought into *desperate* situations when bereft of every thing that might possibly serve to lighten the burdens of their misfortunes;

Before the ships a *desperate* stand they made,
And fir'd the troops, and call'd the gods to aid.
POPE.

It is a *hopeless* undertaking to endeavour to reclaim men who have plunged themselves deep into the labyrinths of vice;

Th' Eneans wish in vain their wanted chief,
Hopeless of flight, more *hopeless* of relief.
DRYDEN.

HOPE, EXPECTATION, TRUST, CONFIDENCE.

Anticipation of futurity is the common idea expressed by all these words. *Hope*, in German *hoffen*, probably from the Greek ὀπιπεύω to look at with pleasure, is welcome; *expectation* (*v. To await*) is either welcome or unwelcome: we *hope* only for that which is good; we *expect* the bad as well as the good. In bad weather we *hope* it will soon be better; but in a bad season we *expect* a bad harvest, and in a good season a good harvest. *Hope* is simply a presentiment; it may vary in degree, more according to the temper of the mind than the nature of the circumstances; some *hope* where there is no ground for *hope*, and others despair where they might *hope: expectation* is a conviction that excludes doubt;* we *expect* in proportion as that conviction is positive: we *hope* that which may be or can possibly be; we *expect* that which must be or which ought to be. The young man *hopes* to live many years; the old man *expects* to die in a few years. *Hope* is a precious gift to man; it is denied to no one under any circumstances; it is a solace in affliction, and a support under adversity; it throws a ray of light over the darkest scene: *expectation* is an evil rather than a good; whether we *expect* the thing that is agreeable or otherwise, it is seldom attended with any thing but pain. *Hope* is justified by the nature of our condition; since every thing is changing, we have also reason to *hope* that a present evil, however great, may be succeeded by something less severe;

Regions of sorrow, doleful shades, where peace
And rest can never dwell; *hope* never comes,
That comes to all.—MILTON.

Expectation is often an act of presumption, in which the mind outsteps its own powers, and estimates the future as if it were present; since every thing future is uncertain, but death, there is but that one legitimate subject of *expectation;*

All these within the dungeon's depth remain,
Despairing pardon, and *expecting* pain.—DRYDEN.

Hope may be deferred, but never dies; it is a pleasure as lasting as it is great: *expectation* is swallowed up in certainty; it seldom leaves any thing but disappointment.

Trust (*v. Belief*) and *confidence* (*v. To confide*) agree with *hope* in regard to the objects anticipated; they agree with *expectation* in regard to the certainty of the anticipation: *expectation*, *trust*, and *confidence*, when applied to some future good, differ principally in the grounds on which this certainty or positive conviction rests. *Expectation* springs either from the character of the individual or the nature of the event which is the subject of anticipation: in the former it is a decision; in the latter a rational conclusion: *trust* springs altogether from a view of the circumstances connected with the event, and is an inference or conclusion of the mind drawn from the whole;

Our country's gods, in whom our *trust* we place.
DRYDEN.

Confidence arises more from the temper of the mind, than from the nature of the object; it is rather an instantaneous decision than a rational conclusion;

His pride
Humbled by such rebuke, so far beneath
His *confidence* to equal God in pow'r.—MILTON.

* See Eberhardt: "Hoffnung, Erwartung, Vertrauen, Zuversicht.

Expectation and *confidence* therefore are often erroneous, and mostly unwarrantable; the latter still more frequently than the former: *trust*, like *hope*, is always warrantable, even though it may sometimes be deceived.

If we *expect* our friends to assist us in time of need, it may be a reasonable *expectation* founded upon their tried regard for us and promises of assistance; or it may be an extravagant *expectation* founded upon our self-love and selfishness: if we *trust* that an eminent physician will cure us, it is founded upon our knowledge of his skill, and of the nature of our case; if we indulge a *confident expectation* that our performances will meet with universal approbation, it is founded upon our vanity and ignorance of ourselves. The most modest man is permitted to *hope* that his endeavours to please will not fail of success; and to *trust* so far in his own powers as to be encouraged to proceed: a prudent man will never think himself authorized to *expect* success, and still less to be *confident* of it, when a thousand contingencies may intervene to defeat the proposed end.

TO CONFIDE, TRUST.

Both these verbs express a reliance on the fidelity of another, but *confide*, in Latin *confido*, compounded of *con* and *fido*, signifying to place a trust in a person, is to *trust* (*v. Belief*) as the species to the genus; we always *trust* when we *confide*, but not *vice versâ*. We *confide* to a person that which is of the greatest importance to ourselves; we *trust* to him whenever we rest on his word for any thing. We need rely only on a person's integrity when we *trust* to him, but we rely also on his abilities and mental qualifications when we place *confidence*; it is an extraordinary *trust*, founded on a powerful conviction in a person's favour.

Confidence frequently supposes something secret as well as personal; *trust* respects only the personal interest. A king *confides* in his ministers and generals for the due execution of his plans, and the administration of the laws; one friend *confides* in another when he discloses to him all his private concerns: a merchant *trusts* to his clerks when he employs them in his business; individuals *trust* each other with portions of their property;

Men live and prosper but in mutual *trust*,
A *confidence* of one another's truth.—SOUTHERN

Hence, credit
And publick *trust* 'twixt man and man are broken.
ROWE.

A breach of *trust* evinces a want of that common principle which keeps human society together; but a breach of *confidence* betrays a more than ordinary share of baseness and depravity.

CONFIDENT, DOGMATICAL, POSITIVE.

Confident, from *confide* (*v. To confide*), marks the temper of *confiding* in one's self; *dogmatical*, from *dogma* a maxim or assertion, signifies the temper of dealing in unqualified assertions; *positive*, in Latin *positivus*, from *positus*, signifies fixed to a point.

The first two of these words denote an habitual or permanent state of mind; the latter either a partial or an habitual temper. There is much of *confidence* in *dogmatism* and *positivity*, but it expresses more than either. *Confidence* implies a general reliance on one's abilities in whatever we undertake; *dogmatism* implies a reliance on the truth of our opinions; *positivity* a reliance on the truth of our assertions. A *confident* man is always ready to act, as he is sure of succeeding, a *dogmatical* man is always ready to speak, as he is sure of being heard; a *positive* man is determined to maintain what he has asserted, as he is convinced that he has made no mistake.

Confidence is opposed to diffidence; *dogmatism* to skepticism; *positivity* to hesitation. A *confident* man mostly fails for want of using the necessary means to ensure success; 'People forget how little it is that they know and how much less it is that they can do, when they grow *confident* upon any present state of things.'—SOUTH. A *dogmatical* man is mostly in errour, because he substitutes his own partial opinions for such as are established; 'If you are neither *dogmatical*, nor show either by your words or your actions that you are full of yourself, all will the more heartily rejoice at your victory.'—BUDGELL. A *positive* man is mostly deceived, because he trusts more to his own senses and memory than he ought; '*Positive* as you now are in your opinions, and *confident* in your assertions, be assured that the time approaches when both men and things will appear to you in a different light.' —BLAIR. Self-knowledge is the most effectual cure for *self-confidence;* an acquaintance with men and things tends to lessen *dogmatism.* The experience of having been deceived one's self, and the observation that others are perpetually liable to be deceived, ought to check the folly of being *positive* as to any event or circumstance that is past.

ASSURANCE, CONFIDENCE.

Assurance implies either the act of making another sure (*v. To affirm*), or of being sure one's self; *confidence* implies simply the act of the mind in *confiding*, which is equivalent to a feeling.

Assurance, as an action, is to *confidence* as the means to the end. We *give* a person an *assurance* in order to inspire him with *confidence.*

Assurance and *confidence*, as a sentiment in ourselves, may respect either that which is external of us, or that which belongs to ourselves; in the first case they are both taken in an indifferent sense: but the feeling of *assurance* is much stronger than that of *confidence*, and applies to objects that interest the feelings; 'I appeal to posterity, says Æschylus; to posterity I consecrated my works, in the *assurance* that they will meet that reward from time which the partiality of my contemporaries refuses to bestow.'—CUMBERLAND. *Confidence*, on the other hand, applies only to such objects as exercise the understanding; 'All the arguments upon which a man, who is telling the private affairs of another, may ground his *confidence* of security, he must, upon reflection, know to be uncertain, because he finds them without effect upon himself.'—JOHNSON. Thus we have an *assurance* of a life to come; an *assurance* of a blessed immortality: we have a *confidence* in a person's integrity. As respects ourselves exclusively, *assurance* is employed to designate either an occasional feeling, or a habit of the mind; *confidence* is for the most part an occasional feeling: *assurance*, therefore, in this sense, may be used indifferently, but in general it has a bad acceptation; but *confidence* has an indifferent or a good sense.

Assurance is a self-possession of the mind, arising from the conviction that all in ourselves is right; 'I never sit silent in company when secret history is talking, but I am reproached for want of *assurance.*'—JOHNSON. *Confidence* is self-possession only in particular cases, grounded on the reliance we have in our abilities or our character; 'The hope of fame is necessarily connected with such considerations as must abate the ardour of *confidence*, and repress the vigour of pursuit.'—JOHNSON.

The man of *assurance* never loses himself under any circumstances, however trying; he is calm and easy when another is abashed and confounded: the man who has *confidence* will generally have it in cases that warrant him to trust to himself.

A liar utters his falsehoods with an air of *assurance*, in order the more effectually to gain belief; conscious innocence enables a person to speak with *confidence* when interrogated.

Assurance shows itself in the behaviour, *confidence* in the conduct. Young people are apt to assert every thing with a tone of *assurance;* 'Modesty, the daughter of Knowledge, and *Assurance*, the offspring of Ignorance, met accidentally upon the road; and as both had a long way to go, and had experienced from former hardships that they were alike unqualified to pursue their journey alone, they agreed, for their mutual advantage, to travel together.'—MOORE. No man should undertake any thing without a certain degree of *confidence* in himself; 'I must observe that there is a vicious modesty which justly deserves to be ridiculed, and which those very persons often discover, who value themselves most upon a well-bred *confidence.* This happens when a man is ashamed to act up to his reason, and would not, upon any consideration, be surprised in the practice of those duties for the performance of which he was sent into the world' —ADDISON.

ASSURANCE, IMPUDENCE.

Assurance (*v. Assurance*), and *impudence*, which literally implies shamelessness, are so closely allied to each other, that *assurance* is distinguished from *impudence* more in the manner than the spirit; for *impudence* has a grossness attached to it which does not belong to *assurance.*

Vulgar people are *impudent* because they have *assurance* to break through all the forms of society; but those who are more cultivated will have their *assurance* controlled by its decencies and refinements; 'A man of *assurance*, though at first it only denoted a person of a free and open carriage, is now very usually applied to a profligate wretch, who can break through all the rules of decency and morality without a blush. I shall endeavour, therefore, in this essay, to restore these words to their true meaning, to prevent the idea of modesty from being confounded with that of sheepishness, and to hinder *impudence* from passing for *assurance.*'—BUDGELL.

TO AWAIT, WAIT FOR, LOOK FOR, EXPECT.

Await and *wait*, in German *warten*, comes from *wahren* to see or look after; *expect*, in Latin *expecto* or *exspecto*, compounded of *ex* and *specto*, signifies to look out after.

All these terms have a reference to futurity, and our actions with regard to it.

Await, *wait for*, and *look for* mark a calculation of consequences and a preparation for them; and *expect* simply a calculation; we often *expect* without *awaiting*, *waiting*, or *looking for*, but never the reverse.

Await is said of serious things; *wait* and *look for* are terms in familiar use; *expect* is employed either seriously or otherwise.

A person *expects* to die, or *awaits* the hour of his dissolution; he *expects* a letter, *waits for* its coming, and *looks for* it when the post is arrived.

Await indicates the disposition of the mind; *wait for* the regulation of the outward conduct as well as that of the mind; *look for* is a species of *waiting* drawn from the physical action of the eye, and may be figuratively applied to the mind's eye, in which latter sense it is the same as *expect.*

It is our duty, as well as our interest, to *await* the severest trials without a murmur;

> This said, he sat, and *expectation* held
> His looks suspense, *awaiting* who appeared
> To second, or oppose, or undertake
> The perilous attempt.—MILTON.
>
> Not less resolv'd, Antenor's valiant heir
> Confronts Achilles, and *awaits* the war.—POPE.

Prudence requires us to *wait* patiently for a suitable opportunity, rather than be premature in our attempts to obtain any objects; '*Wait* till thy being shall be unfolded.'—BLAIR. When children are too much indulged and caressed, they are apt to *look for* a repetition of caresses at inconvenient seasons; 'If you *look for* a friend, in whose temper there is not to be found the least inequality, you *look for* a pleasing phantom.'—BLAIR. It is in vain to *look for* or *expect* happiness from the conjugal state, which is not founded on a cordial and mutual regard; 'We are not to *expect*, from our intercourse with others, all that satisfaction which we fondly wish.'—BLAIR.

TO CONSIGN, COMMIT, INTRUST.

Consign, in French *consigner*, Latin *consigno*, compounded of *con* and *signo*, signifies to seal for a specifick purpose, also to deposite; *commit*, in French *commettre*, Latin *committo*, compounded of *com* and *mitto* to put together, signifies to put into a person's hands; *intrust*, compounded of *in* and *trust*, signifies to put in trust.

The idea of transferring from one's self to the care of another is common to these terms. What is *consigned* is either given absolutely away from one's self, or only conditionally for one's own purpose:

And oft I wish, amid the scene, to find
Some spot to real happiness *consign'd.*—GOLDSMITH.

What is *committed* or *intrusted* is given conditionally. A person *consigns* his property over to another by a deed in law; a merchant *consigns* his goods to another, to dispose of them for his advantage; he *commits* the management of his business to his clerks, and *intrusts* them with the care of his property.

Consign expresses a more positive measure than *commit*, but *intrusting* is more or less positive or important, according to the nature of the thing *intrusted.* When a child is *consigned* to the care of another, it is an unconditional surrender of one's trust into the hands of another;

Atrides, parting for the Trojan war,
Consign'd the youthful consort to his care.—POPE.

Any person may be *committed* to the care of another with various limitations; 'In a very short time Lady Macclesfield removed her son from her sight, by *committing* him to the care of a poor woman.'—JOHNSON (*Life of Savage*). When a person is *intrusted* to the care of another, it is both a partial and temporary matter, referring mostly to his personal safety, and that only for a limited time. A parent does most wisely to *consign* the whole management of his child's education to one individual, in whom he can confide; if he *commit* it in part only to any one's care, the deficiency in the charge is likely to remain unsupplied; in infancy children must be more or less *intrusted* to the care of servants, but prudent parents will diminish the frequency of these occasions as much as possible.

In this sense the word *intrust* may be applied to other minor objects. In an extended application of the terms, papers are said to be *consigned* to an editor of a work for his selection and arrangement. The inspection of any publick work is *committed* to proper officers. A person is *intrusted* with a secret, but he may also be *intrusted* with the lives of others, and every thing else which they hold; on the same ground power is *intrusted* by the Almighty to kings, or, according to republican phraseology, it is *intrusted* by the commonwealth to the magistrate; 'Supposing both equal in their natural integrity, I ought in common prudence to fear foul play from an indigent person rather than from one whose circumstances seem to have placed him above the base temptation of money. This reason makes the commonwealth regard her richest subjects as the fittest to be *intrusted* with her highest employments.'—ADDISON.

Consign and *commit* are used in the figurative sense. A thing is *consigned* to destruction, or *committed* to the flames. Death *consigns* many to an untimely grave: a writer *commits* his thoughts to the press; 'At the day of general account, good men are then to be *consigned* over to another state, a state of everlasting love and charity.'—ATTERBURY.

Is my muse controll'd
By servile awe? Born free, and not be bold!
At least I 'll dig a hole within the ground,
And to the trusty earth *commit* the sound.—DRYDEN.

DEPENDENCE, RELIANCE.

Dependence, from the Latin *dependo*, *de* and *pendo* to hang from, signifies literally to rest one's weight by hanging from that which is held; *rely*, compounded of *re* and *ly* or *lie*, signifies likewise to rest one's weight by lying or hanging back from the object held.

Dependence is the general term; *reliance* is a species of *dependence:* we *depend* either on persons or things; we *rely* on persons only: *dependence* serves for that which is immediate or remote; *reliance* serves for the future only. We *depend* upon a person for that which we are obliged to receive or led to expect from him: we *rely* upon a person for that which he has given us reason to expect from him.

Dependence is an outward condition, or the state of external circumstances; *reliance* is a state of the feelings with regard to others. We *depend* upon God for all that we have or shall have; 'A man who uses his best endeavours to live according to the dictates of virtue and right reason has two perpetual sources of cheerfulness, in the consideration of his own nature, and of that Being on whom he has a *dependence.*'—ADDISON. We *rely* upon the word of man for that which he has promised to perform; 'They afforded a sufficient conviction of this truth, and a firm *reliance* on the promises contained in it.'—ROGERS. We may *depend* upon a person's coming from a variety of causes; but we *rely* upon it only in reference to his avowed intention. This latter term may also denote the act of things in the same sense;

The tender twig shoots upward to the skies,
And on the faith of the new sun *relies.*—DRYDEN

FAITHFUL, TRUSTY.

Faithful signifies full of *faith* or *fidelity* (*v. Faith. fidelity*); *trusty* signifies fit or worthy to be *trusted* (*v. Belief*).

Faithful respects the principle altogether; it is suited to all relations and stations, publick and private: *trusty* includes not only the principle, but the mental qualifications in general; it applies to those in whom particular *trust* is to be placed. It is the part of a Christian to be *faithful* to all his engagements; it is a particular excellence in a servant to be *trusty;*

The steeds they left their *trusty* servants hold.
POPE.

Faithful is applied in the improper sense to an unconscious agent; *trusty* may be applied with equal propriety to things as to persons. We may speak of a *faithful* saying, or a *faithful* picture; a *trusty* sword, or a *trusty* weapon;

What we hear
With weaker passion will affect the heart,
Than when the *faithful* eye beholds the part.
FRANCIS

He took the quiver from the *trusty* bow
Achates used to bear.—DRYDEN.

FAITH, FIDELITY.

Though derived from the same source (*v. Belief*), they differ widely in meaning: *faith* here denotes a mode of action, namely, an acting true to the *faith* which others repose in us; *fidelity*, a disposition of the mind to adhere to that *faith* which others repose in us. We keep our *faith*, we show our *fidelity*.

Faith is a publick concern, it depends on promises: *fidelity* is a private or personal concern, it depends upon relationships and connexions. A breach of *faith* is a crime that brings a stain on a nation; for *faith* ought to be kept even with an enemy. A breach of *fidelity* attaches disgrace to the individual; for *fidelity* is due from a subject to a prince, or from a servant to his master, or from married people one to another. No treaty can be made with him who will keep no *faith;* no confidence can be placed in him who discovers no *fidelity*. The Danes kept no *faith* with the English;

The pit resounds with shrieks, a war succeeds,
For breach of publick *faith* and unexampled deeds.
DRYDEN.

Fashionable husbands and wives in the present day seem to think there is no *fidelity* due to each other; 'When one hears of negroes who upon the death of their masters hang themselves upon the next tree, who can forbear admiring their *fidelity*, though it expresses itself in so dreadful a manner?'—ADDISON.

DISTRUSTFUL, SUSPICIOUS, DIFFIDENT.

Distrustful signifies full of *distrust*, or not putting *trust* in (*v. Belief*); *suspicious* signifies having *suspicion*, from the Latin *suspicio*, or *sub* and *specio* to look at askance, or with a wry mind; *diffident*, from the Latin *diffido* or *disfido*, signifies having no faith.

Distrustful is said either of ourselves or others; *suspicious* is said only of others; *diffident* only of ourselves: to be *distrustful* of a person, is to impute no good to him; to be *suspicious* of a person, is to impute positive evil to him: he who is *distrustful* of another's honour or prudence, will abstain from giving him his confidence; he who is *suspicious* of another's honesty, will be cautious to have no dealings with him. *Distrustful* is a particular state of feeling; *suspicious* an habitual state of feeling: a person is *distrustful* of another, owing to particular circumstances; he may be *suspicious* from his natural temper

As applied to himself, a person is *distrustful* of his own powers to execute an office assigned, or he is generally of a *diffident* disposition: it is faulty to *distrust* that in which we ought to trust; there is nothing more criminal than a *distrust* in Providence, and nothing better than a *distrust* in our own powers to withstand temptation; 'Before strangers, Pitt had something of the scholar's timidity and *distrust*.'—JOHNSON. *Suspicion* is justified more or less according to circumstances; but a too great proneness to *suspicion* is liable to lead us into many acts of injustice towards others; 'Nature itself, after it has done an injury, will for ever be *suspicious*, and no man can love the person he *suspects*.'—SOUTH. *Diffidence* is becoming in youth, so long as it does not check their laudable exertions; 'As an actor, Mr. Cunningham obtained little reputation, for his *diffidence* was too great to be overcome.'—JOHNSON.

TO DISTURB, INTERRUPT.

Disturb, *v. Commotion; interrupt*, from the Latin *inter* and *rumpo*, signifies to break in between so as to stop the progress.

We may be disturbed either inwardly or outwardly; we are *interrupted* only outwardly; our minds may be *disturbed* by disquieting reflections, or we may be *disturbed* in our rest or in our business by unseemly noises; but we can be *interrupted* only in our business or pursuits; the *disturbance* therefore depends upon the character of the person; what *disturbs* one man will not *disturb* another: an *interruption* is however something positive; what *interrupts* one person will *interrupt* another: the smallest noises may *disturb* one who is in bad health; illness or the visits of friends will *interrupt* a person in any of his business.

The same distinction exists between these words when applied to things as to persons: whatever is put out of its order or proper condition is *disturbed;* thus water which is put into motion from a state of rest is *disturbed;*

> If aught *disturb* the tenour of his breast,
> 'T is but the wish to strike before the rest.—POPE.

Whatever is stopped in the evenness or regular'ty of its course is *interrupted;* thus water which is turned out of its ordinary channel is *interrupted;* 'The foresight of the hour of death would continually *interrupt* the course of human affairs.'—BLAIR.

COMMOTION, DISTURBANCE.

Commotion, compounded of *com* or *cum* and *motion*, expresses naturally a *motion* of several together; *disturbance* signifies the state of *disturbing* or being *disturbed* (*v. To trouble*).

There is mostly a *commotion* where there is a *disturbance;* but there is frequently no *disturbance* where there is a *commotion; commotion* respects the physical movement; *disturbance* the mental agitation. *Commotion* is said only of large bodies of men, and is occasioned only by something extraordinary; *disturbance* may be said of a few, or even of a single individual: whatever occasions a bustle, awakens general inquiry, and sets people or things in motion, excites a *commotion;*

> Ocean, unequally press'd, with broken tide
> And blind *commotion* heaves.—THOMSON.

Whatever interrupts the peace and quiet of one or many produces a *disturbance;* 'A species of men to whom a state of order would become a sentence of obscurity, are nourished into a dangerous magnitude by the heat of intestine *disturbances*.'—BURKE. Any wonderful phenomenon, or unusually interesting intelligence, may throw the publick into a *commotion;* 'Nothing can be more absurd than that perpetual contest for wealth which keeps the world in *commotion*.'—JOHNSON. Drunkenness is a common cause of *disturbances* in the streets or in families: civil *commotions* are above all others the most to be dreaded; they are attended with *disturbances* general and partial.

TO INCONVENIENCE, ANNOY, MOLEST.

To *inconvenience* is to make not *convenient;* to *annoy*, from the Latin *noceo* to hurt, is to do some hurt to; to *molest*, from the Latin *moles* a mass o. weight, signifies to press with a weight.

We *inconvenience* in small matters, or by omitting such things as might be *convenient;* we *annoy* or *molest* by doing that which is positively painful; we are *inconvenienced* by a person's absence; we are *annoyed* by his presence if he renders himself offensive: we are *inconvenienced* by what is temporary; we are *annoyed* by that which is either temporary or durable; we are *molested* by that which is weighty and oppressive: we are *inconvenienced* simply in regard to our circumstances; we are *annoyed* mostly in regard to our corporeal feelings; we are *molested* mostly in regard to our minds: the removal of a seat or a book may *inconvenience* one who is engaged in business; 'I have often been tempted to inquire what happiness is to be gained, or what *inconvenience* to be avoided, by this stated recession from the town in the summer season.'—JOHNSON. The buzzing of a fly, or the stinging of a gnat may *annoy;*

> Against the Capitol I met a lion,
> Who glar'd upon me and went surly by,
> Without *annoying* me.—SHAKSPEARE.

The impertinent freedom, or the rude insults of ill-disposed persons may *molest;*

> See all with skill acquire their daily food,
> Produce their tender progeny and feed,
> With care parental, while that care they need,
> In these lov'd offices completely blest,
> No hopes beyond them, nor vain fears *molest*.
> JENYNS.

COMMODIOUS, CONVENIENT, SUITABLE

Commodious, from the Latin *commodus*, or *con* and *modus*, according to the measure and degree required, *convenient*, from the Latin *conveniens*, participle of *con* and *venio* to come together, signifies that which comes together with something else as it ought.

Both these terms convey the idea of what is calculated for the pleasure of a person. *Commodious* regards the physical condition, and *convenience* the circumstances or mental feelings;

> Within an ancient forest's ample verge,
> There stands a lonely but a healthful dwelling,
> Built for *convenience* and the use of life.—ROWE.

That is *commodious* which suits one's bodily ease; that is *convenient* which suits one's purpose. A house or a chair is *commodious;* 'Such a place cannot be *commodious* to live in; for being so near the moon, it had been too near the sun.'—RALEIGH. A time, an opportunity, a season, or the arrival of any person, is *convenient*. A noise *incommodes;* the staying or going of a person may *inconvenience*. A person wishes to sit *commodiously*, and to be *conveniently* situated for witnessing any spectacle.

Convenient regards the circumstances of the individual; *suitable* (*v. Conformable*) respects the established opinions of mankind, and is closely connected with moral propriety: nothing is *convenient* which does not favour one's purpose; nothing is *suitable* which does not suit the person, place, and thing: whoever has any thing to ask of another must take a *convenient* opportunity in order to ensure success; 'If any man think it *convenient* to seem good, let him be so indeed, and then his goodness will appear to every body's satisfaction.'—TILLOTSON. The address of a suitor on such an occasion would be very *unsuitable*, if he affected to claim as a right what he ought to solicit as a favour; 'Pleasure in general is the consequent apprehension of a *suitable* object, *suitably* applied to a rightly disposed faculty.'—SOUTH.

NECESSARY, EXPEDIENT, ESSENTIAL, REQUISITE.

Necessary, (*v. Necessity*), from the Latin *necesse* and *ne cedo*, signifies not to be departed from; *expedient* signifies belonging to, or forming a part of, expedition; *essential*, containing that essence or property which cannot be omitted; *requisite*, i. e. literally required (*v. To demand*).

Necessary is a general and indefinite term; things may be *necessary* in the course of nature; it is *necessary* for all men once to die; they may be *necessary* according to the circumstances of the case, or our views of *necessity;* in this manner we conceive it *necessary* to call upon a persor

Expedient, *essential*, and *requisite* are modes of relative *necessity;* the *expedience* of a thing is a matter of discretion and calculation, and, therefore, not so self-evidently *necessary* as many things which we so denominate; 'One tells me he thinks it absolutely *necessary* for women to have true notions of right and equity.'—ADDISON. It may be *expedient* for a person to consult another, or it may not, according as circumstances may present themselves; 'It is highly *expedient* that men should, by some settled scheme of duties, be rescued from the tyranny of caprice.'—JOHNSON. The *requisite* and the *essential* are more obviously *necessary* than the *expedient;* but the former is less so than the latter: what is *requisite* may be *requisite* only in part or entirely; it may be *requisite* to complete a thing when begun, but not to begin it; the *essential*, on the contrary, is that which constitutes the *essence*, and without which a thing cannot exist. It is *requisite* for one who will have a good library to select only the best authors; exercise is *essential* for the preservation of good health. In all matters of dispute it is *expedient* to be guided by some impartial judge; it is *requisite* for every member of the community to contribute his share to the publick expenditure as far as he is able; 'It is not enough to say that faith and piety, joined with active virtue, constitute the *requisite* preparation for heaven; they in truth begin the enjoyment of heaven.'—BLAIR. It is *essential* to a teacher, particularly a spiritual teacher, to know more than those he teaches; 'The English do not consider their church establishment as convenient, but as *essential* to their state.'—BURKE.

EXPEDIENT, FIT.

Expedient, from the Latin *expedio* to get in readiness for a given occasion, supposes a certain degree of necessity from circumstances; *fit* (*v. Fit*), i. e. made for the purpose, signifies simply an agreement with, or suitability to, the circumstances; what is *expedient* must be *fit*, because it is called for; what is *fit* need be *expedient*, for it may not be required. The *expediency* of a thing depends altogether upon the outward circumstances; the *fitness* is determined by a moral rule: it is imprudent not to do that which is *expedient;* it is disgraceful to do that which is *unfit;* it is *expedient* for him who wishes to prepare for death, occasionally to take an account of his life; 'To far the greater number it is highly *expedient* that they should by some settled scheme of duties be rescued from the tyranny of caprice.'—JOHNSON. It is not *fit* for him who is about to die to dwell with anxiety on the things of this life;

> Salt earth and bitter are not *fit* to sow,
> Nor will be tam'd and mended by the plough.
> DRYDEN.

OCCASION, OPPORTUNITY.

Occasion, in Latin *occasio*, from *oc* or *ob* and *cado* to fall, signifies that which falls in the way so as to produce some change; *opportunity*, in Latin *opportunitas*, from *opportunis* fit, signifies the thing that happens fit for the purpose.

These terms are applied to the events of life; but the *occasion* is that which determines our conduct, and leaves us no choice; it amounts to a degree of necessity: the *opportunity* is that which invites to action; it tempts us to embrace the moment for taking the step. We do things, therefore, as the *occasion* requires, or as the *opportunity* offers. There are many *occasions* on which a man is called upon to uphold his opinions. There are but few *opportunities* for men in general to distinguish themselves. The *occasion* obtrudes upon us; the *opportunity* is what we seek or desire. On particular *occasions* it is necessary for a commander to be severe; 'Waller preserved and won his life from those who were most resolved to take it, and in an *occasion* in which he ought to have been ambitious to have lost it (to lose it).'—CLARENDON. A man of a humane disposition will profit by every *opportunity* to show his lenity to offenders; 'Every man is obliged by the Supreme Maker of the universe to improve all the *opportunities* of good which are afforded him.'—JOHNSON.

OCCASION, NECESSITY.

Occasion (*v. Occasion*) includes, *necessity* (*v. Necessity*) excludes, the idea of choice or alternative. We are regulated by the *occasion*, and can exercise our own discretion; we yield or submit to the *necessity*, without even the exercise of the will. On the death of a relative we have *occasion* to go into mourning, if we will not offer an affront to the family, but there is no express *necessity;*

> A merrier man
> Within the limit of becoming mirth,
> I never spent an hour's talk withal;
> His eye begets *occasion* for his wit.
> SHAKSPEARE.

In case of an attack on our persons, there is a *necessity* of self-defence for the preservation of life; 'Where *necessity* ends curiosity begins.'—JOHNSON.

OCCASIONAL, CASUAL.

These are both opposed to what is fixed or stated; but *occasional* carries with it more the idea of unfrequency, and *casual* that of unfixedness, or the absence of all design.

A minister is termed an *occasional* preacher, who preaches only on certain *occasions:* his preaching at a particular place, or a certain day may be *casual*. Our acts of charity may be *occasional;* but they ought not to be *casual;* 'The beneficence of the Roman emperours and consuls was merely *occasional*.'—JOHNSON.

> What wonder if so near
> Looks intervene, and smiles, or object new,
> *Casual* discourse draws on.—MILTON.

TO ADD, JOIN, UNITE, COALESCE.

Add, in Latin *addo*, compounded of *ad* and *do*, signifies to put to an object; *join*, in French *joindre*, Latin *jungo*, comes from *jugum* a yoke, and the Greek *ζεύγω* to yoke, signifying to bring into close contact; *unite*, in Latin *unitus*, participle of *unio*, from *unus* one, implies to make into one: *coalesce*, in Latin *coalesco*, compounded of *co* or *con*, and *alesco* for *cresco*, signifies to grow or form one's self together.

We *add* by affixing a part of one thing to another so as to make one whole; we *join* by attaching one whole to another, so that they may adhere in part; we *unite* by putting one thing to another, so that all their parts may adhere to each other; things *coalesce* by coming into an entire cohesion of all their parts.

Adding is either a corporeal or spiritual action; *joining* is mostly said of corporeal objects; *uniting* and *coalescing* of spiritual objects. We *add* a wing to a house by a mechanical process, or we *add* quantities together by calculation,

> Now, best of kings, since you propose to send
> Such bounteous presents to your Trojan friend,
> *Add* yet a greater at our *joint* request,
> One which he values more than all the rest;
> Give him the fair Lavinia for his bride.—DRYDEN.

We *join* two houses together, or two armies, by placing them on the same spot; 'The several great bodies which compose the solar system are kept from *joining* together at the common centre of gravity by the rectilinear motions the Author of nature has impressed on each of them.'—BERKELEY. People are *united* who are bound to each other by similarity of opinion, sentiment, condition, or circumstances; 'Two Englishmen meeting at Rome or Constantinople soon run into familiarity. And in China or Japan, Europeans would think their being so a sufficient reason for their *uniting* in particular converse.'—BERKELEY. Parties *coalesce* when they agree to lay aside their leading distinctions of opinion so as to co-operate; 'The Danes had been established during a longer period in England than in France; and though the similarity of their original language to that of the Saxons invited them to a more early *coalition* with the natives, they had found as yet so little example of civilized manners among the English, that they retained all their ancient ferocity.'—HUME.

Nothing can be *added* without some agent to perform the act of *adding;* but things may be *joined* by casually coming in contact; and things will *unite* of themselves which have an aptitude to accordance, *coalition* is that species of union which arises mostly from external agency. The *addition* of quantities produces vast sums; the *junction* of streams forms great rivers; the *union* of families or states constitutes their principal strength; by the *coalition* of sounds, dipthongs are formed. Bodies are enlarged by the *addition* of other bodies; people are sometimes *joined* in matrimony who are not *united* in affection; no two things can *coalesce*, between which there is an essential difference, or the slightest discordance.

Addition is opposed to subtraction; *junction* and *union*, to division; *coalition*, to distinction.

TO CONNECT, COMBINE, UNITE.

The idea of being put together is common to these terms, but with different degrees of proximity. To *connect*, from the Latin *connecto*, compounded of *con* and *necto*, signifying to knit together, is more remote than to *combine* (*v. Association*), and this than to *unite* (*v. To add*).

What is *connected* and *combined* remains distinct, but what is *united* loses all individuality.

Things the most dissimilar may be *connected* or *combined;* things of the same kind only can be *united.*

Things or persons are *connected* more or less remotely by some common property or circumstance that serves as a tie; 'A right opinion is that which *connects* distant truths by the shortest train of intermediate propositions.'—JOHNSON. Things or persons are *combined* by a species of juncture; 'Fancy can *combine* the ideas which memory has treasured.'—HAWKESWORTH. Things or persons are *united* by a coalition; 'A friend is he with whom our interest is *united.*'—HAWKESWORTH. Houses are *connected* by means of a common passage: the armies of two nations are *combined;* two armies of the same nation are *united.*

Trade, marriage, and general intercourse create a *connexion* between individuals; co-operation and similarity of tendency are grounds for *combination:* entire accordance leads to a *union.* It is dangerous to be *connected* with the wicked in any way; our reputation, if not our morals, must be the sufferers thereby. The most obnoxious members of society are those in whom wealth, talents, influence, and a lawless ambition are *combined. United* is an epithet that should apply equally to nations and families; the same obedience to laws should regulate every man who lives under the same government; the same heart should animate every breast; the same spirit should dictate every action of every member in the community, who has a common interest in the preservation of the whole.

CONNECTED, RELATED.

Connected, v. To connect; related, from *relate,* in Latin *relatus,* participle of *refero* to bring back, signifies brought back to the same point.

These terms are employed in the moral sense, to express an affinity between subjects or matters of thought.

Connexion marks affinity in an indefinite manner; 'It is odd to consider the *connexion* between despotism and barbarity, and how the making one person more than man, makes the rest less.'—ADDISON. *Relation* denotes affinity in a specifick manner: 'All mankind are so *related,* that care is to be taken, in things to which all are liable, you do not mention what concerns one in terms which shall disgust another.'—STEELE. A *connexion* may be either close or remote; a *relation* direct or indirect. What is *connected* has some common principle on which it depends: what is *related* has some likeness with the object to which it is *related:* it is a part of some whole.

TO AFFIX, SUBJOIN, ATTACH, ANNEX.

Affix, in Latin *affixus,* participle of *affigo,* compounded of *af* or *ad* and *figo* to fix, signifies to fix to a thing; *subjoin* is compounded of *sub* and *join,* signifying to join to the lower or farther extremity of a body; *attach, v. To adhere; annex,* in Latin *annexus,* participle of *annecto,* compounded of *an* or *ad* and *necto* to knit, signifies to knit or tie to a thing.

To *affix* is to put any thing as an essential to any whole; to *subjoin* is to put any thing as a subordinate part to a whole: in the former case the part to which it is put is not specified; in the latter the syllable *sub* specifies the extremity as the part: to *attach* is to make one thing *adhere* to another as an accompaniment; to *annex* is to bring things into a general connexion with each other.

A title is *affixed* to a book; a few lines are *subjoined* to a letter by way of postscript; we *attach* blame to a person; a certain territory is *annexed* to a kingdom.

Letters are *affixed* to words in order to modify their sense, or names are *affixed* to ideas; 'He that has settled in his mind determined ideas, with names *affixed* to them, will be able to discern their differences one from another.'—LOCKE. It is necessary to *subjoin* remarks to what requires illustration; 'In justice to the opinion which I would wish to impress of the amiable character of Pisistratus, I *subjoin* to this paper some explanation of the word tyrant.'—CUMBERLAND. We are apt from prejudice or particular circumstances to *attach* disgrace to certain professions, which are not only useful but important; 'As our nature is at present constituted, *attached* by so many strong connexions to the world of sense, and enjoying a communication so feeble and distant with the world of spirits, we need fear no danger from cultivating intercourse with the latter as much as possible.'—BLAIR. Papers are *annexed* by way of appendix to some important transaction.

It is improper to *affix* opprobrious epithets to any community of persons on account of their calling in life. Men are not always scrupulous about the means of *attaching* others to their interest, when their ambitious views are to be forwarded. Every station in life, above that of extreme indigence, has certain privileges *annexed* to it, but none greater than those which are enjoyed by the middling classes; 'The evils inseparably *annexed* to the present condition are numerous and afflictive.'—JOHNSON.

TO STICK, CLEAVE, ADHERE.

Stick, in Saxon *stican,* Low German *steken,* is connected with the Latin *stigo,* Greek *ςίγω* to prick; *cleave,* in Saxon *cleofen,* Low German *kliven,* Danish *klaeve,* is connected with our words glue and lime, in Latin *gluten,* Greek *κόλλα* lime; *adhere, v. To attach.*

To *stick* expresses more than to *cleave,* and *cleave* than *adhere:* things are made to *stick* either by incision into the substance, or through the intervention of some glutinous matter; they are made to *cleave* and *adhere* by the intervention of some foreign body; what *sticks,* therefore, becomes so fast joined as to render the bodies inseparable; what *cleaves* and *adheres* is less tightly bound, and more easily separable.

Two pieces of clay will *stick* together by the incorporation of the substance in the two parts; paper is made to *stick* to paper by means of glue: the tongue in a certain state will *cleave* to the roof of the mouth: paste, or even occasional moisture, will make soft substances *adhere* to each other, or to hard bodies. Animals *stick* to bodies by means of their claws; persons in the moral sense *cleave* to each other by never parting company: and they *adhere* to each other by uniting their interests.

Stick is employed for the most part on familiar subjects, but is sometimes applied to moral objects

> Adieu, then, O my soul's far better part,
> Thy image *sticks* so close
> That the blood follows from my rending heart.
> DRYDEN.

Cleave and *adhere* are peculiarly proper in the moral acceptation;

> Gold and his gains no more employ his mind,
> But, driving o'er the billows with the wind,
> *Cleaves* to one faithful plank, and leaves the rest behind.—ROWE.

> That there's a God from nature's voice is clear;
> And yet, what errours to this truth *adhere?*
> JENYNS

FOLLOWER, ADHERENT, PARTISAN.

A *follower* is one who *follows* a person generally; an *adherent* is one who *adheres* to his cause; a *partisan* is the follower of a party: the *follower* follows either the person, the interests, or the principles of any one; thus, the retinue of a nobleman, or the friends of a statesman, or the friends of any man's opinions may be styled his *followers;*

The mournful *followers*, with assistant care,
The groaning hero to his chariot bear.—POPE.

The *adherent* is that kind of *follower* who espouses the interests of another, as the *adherents* of Charles I.; 'With Addison, the wits, his *adherents* and *followers*, were certain to concur.'—JOHNSON. A *follower* follows near or at a distance; but the *adherent* is always near at hand; the *partisan* hangs on or keeps at a certain distance: the *follower* follows from various motives; the *adherent* adheres from a personal motive; the *partisan*, from a partial motive; 'They (the Jacobins) then proceed in argument, as if all those who disapprove of their new abuses must of course be *partisans* of the old.'—BURKE. Charles I. had as many *adherents* as he had *followers;* the rebels had as many *partisans* as they had *adherents*.

TO ADDUCE, ALLEGE, ASSIGN, ADVANCE.

Adduce, in Latin *adduco*, compounded of *ad* and *duco* to lead, signifies to bring forwards, or for a thing; *allege*, in French *alleguer*, in Latin *allego*, compounded of *al* or *ad* and *lego*, in Greek λέγω to speak, signifies to speak for a thing; *assign*, in French *assigner*, Latin *assigno*, compounded of *as* or *ad* and *signo* to sign or mark out, signifies to set apart for a purpose; *advance* comes from the Latin *advenio*, compounded of *ad* and *venio* to come, or cause to come, signifying to bring forward a thing.

An argument is *adduced;* a fact or a charge is *alleged;* a reason is *assigned;* a position or an opinion is *advanced*. What is *adduced* tends to corroborate or invalidate; 'I have said that Celsus *adduces* neither oral nor written authority against Christ's miracles.'—CUMBERLAND. What is *alleged* tends to criminate or exculpate; 'The criminal *alleged* in his defence, that what he had done was to raise mirth, and to avoid ceremony.'—ADDISON. What is *assigned* tends to justify; 'If we consider what providential reasons may be *assigned* for these three particulars, we shall find that the numbers of the Jews, their dispersion and adherence to their religion, have furnished every age, and every nation of the world, with the strongest arguments for the Christian faith.'—ADDISON. What is *advanced* tends to explain and illustrate; 'I have heard of one that, having *advanced* some erroneous doctrines of philosophy, refused to see the experiments by which they were confuted.'—JOHNSON. Whoever discusses disputed points must have arguments to *adduce* in favour of his principles: censures should not be passed where nothing improper can be *alleged:* a conduct is absurd for which no reason can be *assigned:* those who *advance* what they cannot maintain expose their ignorance as much as their folly.

The reasoner *adduces* facts in proof of what he has *advanced*. The accuser *alleges* circumstances in support of his charge. The philosophical investigator *assigns* causes for particular phenomena.

We may controvert what is *adduced* or *advanced;* we may deny what is *alleged*, and question what is *assigned*.

TO ADHERE, ATTACH.

Adhere, from the French *adherer*, Latin *adhæreo*, is compounded of *ad* and *hæreo* to stick close to; *attach*, in French *attacher*, is compounded of *at* or *ad* and *tach* or *touch*, both which come from the Latin *tango* to touch, signifying to come so near as to touch.

A thing is *adherent* by the union which nature produces; it is *attached* by arbitrary ties which keep it close to another thing. Glutinous bodies are apt to *adhere* to every thing they touch: a smaller building is sometimes *attached* to a larger by a passage, or some other mode of communication.

What *adheres* to a thing is closely joined to its outward surface; but what is *attached* may be fastened to it by the intervention of a third body. There is a universal *adhesion* in all the particles of matter one to another: the sails of a vessel are *attached* to a mast by means of ropes; 'The play which this pathetick prologue was *attached* to, was a comedy, in which Laberius took the character of a slave.'—CUMBERLAND.

In a figurative sense, the analogy is kept up in the use of these two words. *Adherence* is a mode of conduct; *attachment* a state of feeling. We *adhere* to opinions which we are determined not to renounce; 'The firm *adherence* of the Jews to their religion is no less remarkable than their numbers and dispersion.'—ADDISON. We are *attached* to opinions for which our feelings are strongly prepossessed. It is the character of obstinacy to *adhere* to a line of conduct after it is proved to be injurious; some persons are not to be *attached* by the ordinary ties of relationship or friendship; 'The conqueror seems to have been fully apprized of the strength which the new government might derive from a clergy more closely *attached* to himself.'—TYRWHITT.

ADHESION, ADHERENCE.

These terms are both derived from the verb *adhere*, one expressing the proper or figurative sense, and the other the moral sense or acceptation.

There is a power of *adhesion* in all glutinous bodies; 'We suffer equal pain from the pertinacious *adhesion* of unwelcome images, as from the evanescence of those which are pleasing and useful.'—JOHNSON. There is a disposition for *adherence* in steady minds 'Shakspeare's *adherence* to general nature has exposed him to the censure of criticks, who form their judgements upon narrower principles.'—JOHNSON.

ADJACENT, ADJOINING, CONTIGUOUS

Adjacent, in Latin *adjacens*, participle of *adjaceo*, is compounded of *ad* and *jaceo* to lie near; *adjoining*, as the words imply, signifies being joined together; *contiguous*, in French *contigu*, Latin *contiguus*, comes from *contingo* or *con* and *tango*, signifying to touch close.

What is *adjacent* may be separated altogether by the intervention of some third object; 'They have been beating up for volunteers at York, and the towns *adjacent;* but nobody will list.'—GRANVILLE. What is *adjoining* must touch in some part; 'As he happens to have no estate *adjoining* equal to his own, his oppressions are often borne without resistance.'—JOHNSON. What is *contiguous* must be fitted to touch entirely on one side; 'We arrived at the utmost boundaries of a wood which lay *contiguous* to a plain.'—STEELE. Lands are *adjacent* to a house or a town; fields are *adjoining* to each other; houses *contiguous* to each other.

EPITHET, ADJECTIVE.

Epithet is the technical term of the rhetorician; *adjective* that of the grammarian. The same word is an *epithet* as it qualifies the sense; it is an *adjective* as it is a part of speech: thus in the phrase 'Alexander the Great,' great is an *epithet*, inasmuch as it designates Alexander in distinction from all other persons: it is an *adjective* as it expresses a quality in distinction from the noun Alexander, which denotes a thing. The *epithet* ἐπίθετον is the word added by way of ornament to the diction; the *adjective*, from *adjectivum*, is the word added to the noun as its appendage, and made subservient to it in all its inflections. When we are estimating the merits of any one's style or composition, we should speak of the *epithets* he uses; when we are talking of words, their dependencies, and relations, we should speak of *adjectives:* an *epithet* is either gentle or harsh, an *adjective* is either a noun or a pronoun *adjective*.

All *adjectives* are *epithets*, but all *epithets* are not *adjectives;* thus in Virgil's *Pater Æneas*, the *pater* is an *epithet*, but not an *adjective*.

TO ABSTRACT, SEPARATE, DISTINGUISH

Abstract, *v. Absent; separate*, in Latin *separatus* participle of *separo*, is compounded of *se* and *paro* to dispose apart, signifying to put things asunder, or at a distance from each other; *distinguish*, in French *distinguer*, Latin *distinguo*, is compounded of the separative preposition *dis* and *tingo* to tinge or colour, signifying to give different marks by which they may be known from each other.

Abstract is used in the moral sense only; *separate* mostly in a physical sense; *distinguish* either in a moral or physical sense: we *abstract* what we wish to regard particularly and individually; we *separate* what we wish not to be united; we *distinguish* what we wish not to confound. The mind performs the office of *abstraction* for itself; *separating* and *distinguishing* are exerted on external objects.* Arrangement, place, time, and circumstances serve to *separate;* the ideas formed of things, the outward marks attached to them, the qualities attributed to them, serve to *distinguish.*

By the operation of *abstraction* the mind creates for itself a multitude of new ideas: in the act of *separation* bodies are removed from each other by distance of place: in the act of *distinguishing* objects are discovered to be similar or dissimilar. Qualities are *abstracted* from the subjects in which they are inherent: countries are *separated* by mountains or seas: their inhabitants are *distinguished* by their dress, language, or manners. The mind is never less *abstracted* from one's friends than when *separated* from them by immense oceans: it requires a keen eye to *distinguish* objects that bear a great resemblance to each other. Volatile persons easily *abstract* their minds from the most solemn scenes to fix them on trifling objects that pass before them; 'We ought to *abstract* our minds from the observation of an excellence in those we converse with, till we have received some good information of the disposition of their minds.'—STEELE. An unsocial temper leads some men to *separate* themselves from all their companions; 'It is an eminent instance of Newton's superiority to the rest of mankind that he was able to *separate* knowledge from those weaknesses by which knowledge is generally disgraced.'—JOHNSON. An absurd ambition leads others to *distinguish* themselves by their eccentricities; 'Fontenelle, in his panegyrick on Sir Isaac Newton, closes a long enumeration of that philosopher's virtues and attainments with an observation that he was not *distinguished* from other men by any singularity either natural or affected.'—JOHNSON.

TO DEDUCT, SUBTRACT.

Deduct, from the Latin *deductus* participle of *deduco*, and *subtract*, from *subtractum* participle of *subtraho*, have both the sense of taking from, but the former is used in a general, and the latter in a technical sense. He who makes an estimate is obliged to *deduct;* he who makes a calculation is obliged to *subtract.*

The tradesman *deducts* what has been paid from what remains due; 'The popish clergy took to themselves the whole residue of the intestate's estate, after the two-thirds of the wife and children were *deducted.*' —BLACKSTONE. The accountant *subtracts* small sums from the gross amount; 'A codicil is a supplement to a will, being for its explanation or alteration, or to make some addition to or else some *subtraction* from the former dispositions of the testator.'—BLACKSTONE.

TO SEPARATE, SEVER, DISJOIN, DETACH.

Whatever is united or joined in any way may be *separated* (*v. To subtract*), be the junction natural or artificial; 'Can a body be inflammable from which it would puzzle a chymist to *separate* an inflammable ingredient?'—BOYLE. To *sever*, which is but a variation of the verb to *separate*, is a mode of *separating* natural bodies, or bodies naturally joined: 'To mention only that species of shell-fish that grow to the surface of several rocks, and immediately die upon their being *severed* from the place where they grow.'—ADDISON. We may *separate* in part or entirely; we *sever* entirely: we *separate* with or without violence; we *sever* with violence only: we may *separate* papers which have been pasted together, or fruits which have grown together; but the head is *severed* from the body, or a branch from the trunk. There is the same distinction between these terms in their moral application; 'They (the French republicans) never have abandoned, and never will abandon, their old steady maxim of *separating* the people from their government.—BURKE.

> Better I were distract;
> So should my thoughts be *sever'd* from my griefs.
> SHAKSPEARE.

To *separate* may be said of things which are only remotely connected; *disjoin*, which signifies to destroy a junction, is said of things which are so intimately connected that they might be joined; 'In times and regions, so *disjoined* from each other that there can scarcely be imagined any communication of sentiments, has prevailed a general and uniform expectation of propitiating God by corporeal austerities.'—JOHNSON. We *separate* as convenience requires; we may *separate* in a right or a wrong manner: we mostly *disjoin* things which ought to remain joined: we *separate* syllables in order to distinguish them, but they are sometimes *disjoined* in writing by an accidental erasure. To *detach*, which signifies to destroy a con tract, has an intermediate sense between *separate* and *disjoin*, applying to bodies which are neither so loosely connected as the former, nor so closely as the latter: we *separate* things that directly meet in no point; we *disjoin* those which meet in every point; we *detach* those things which meet in one point only; 'The several parts of it are *detached* one from the other, and yet join again, one cannot tell how.'—POPE. Sometimes the word *detach* has a moral application, as to *detach* persons, that is, the minds of persons, from their party; so likewise *detached*, in distinction from a connected piece of composition; 'As for the *detached* rhapsodies which Lycurgus in more early times brought with him out of Asia, they must have been exceedingly imper fect.'—CUMBERLAND.

TO DISJOINT, DISMEMBER.

Disjoint signifies to separate at the joint; *dismember* signifies to separate the members.

The terms here spoken of derive their distinct meaning and application from the signification of the words *joint* and *member*. A limb of the body may be *disjointed* if it be so put out of the *joint* that it cannot act; but the body itself is *dismembered* when the different limbs or parts are separated from each other. So in the metaphorical sense our ideas are said to be *disjointed* when they are so thrown out of their order that they do not fall in with one another; and king doms are said to be *dismembered* where any part or parts are separated from the rest;

> Along the woods, along the moorish fens,
> Sighs the sad genius of the coming storm,
> And up among the loose *disjointed* cliffs.
> THOMSON.

> Where shall I find his corpse! What earth sustains
> His trunk *dismembered* and his cold remains?
> DRYDEN.

> And yet, deluded man,
> A scene of crude *disjointed* visions past,
> And broken slumbers, rises still resolv'd
> With new flush'd hopes to run the giddy round.
> THOMSON.

'The kingdom of East Saxony was *dismembered* from that of Kent.'—HUME.

TO ADDICT, DEVOTE, APPLY.

Addict, in Latin *addictus*, participle of *addico*, com pounded of *ad* and *dico*, signifies to speak or declare in favour of a thing, to exert one's self in its favour, *devote*, in Latin *devotus*, participle of *devoveo*, signi fies to vow or make resolutions for a thing; *apply*, in French *appliquer*, Latin *applico*, is compounded of *ap* or *ad* and *plico*, signifying to knit or join one's self to a thing.

To *addict* is to indulge one's self in any particular practice; to *devote* is to direct one's powers and means to any particular pursuit; to *apply* is to employ one's time or attention about any object. Men are *addicted* to vices: they *devote* their talents to the acquirement of any art or science: they *apply* their minds to the investigation of a subject.

Children begin early to *addict* themselves to lying when they have any thing to conceal. People who are *devoted* to their appetites are burdensome to them-

* Vide Abbe Girard: "Distinguer, separer."

selves, and to all with whom they are connected. Whoever *applies* his mind to the contemplation of nature, and the works of creation, will feel himself impressed with sublime and reverential ideas of the Creator.

We are *addicted* to a thing from an irresistible passion or propensity; 'As the pleasures of luxury are very expensive, they put those who are *addicted* to them upon raising fresh supplies of money by all the methods of rapaciousness and corruption.'—ADDISON. We are *devoted* to a thing from a strong but settled attachment to it; 'Persons who have *devoted* themselves to God are venerable to all who fear him.'—BERKELEY. We *apply* to a thing from a sense of its utility; 'Tully has observed that a lamb no sooner falls from its mother, but immediately, and of its own accord, it *applies* itself to the teat.'—ADDISON. We *addict* ourselves to study by yielding to our passion for it: we *devote* ourselves to the service of our king and country by employing all our powers to their benefit: we *apply* to business by giving it all the time and attention that it requires.

Addict is seldomer used in a good than in a bad sense; *devote* is mostly employed in a good sense; *apply* in an indifferent sense.

TO ADDRESS, APPLY.

Address is compounded of *ad* and *dress*, in Spanish *derecar*, Latin *direxi*, preterit of *dirigo* to direct, signifying to direct one's self to an object; *apply*, *v. To addict.*

An *address* is immediately directed from one party to another, either personally or by writing; an *application* may be made through the medium of a third person. An *address* may be made for an indifferent purpose or without any express object; but an *application* is always occasioned by some serious circumstance.

We *address* those to whom we speak or write; 'Many are the inconveniences which happen from the improper manner of *address*, in common speech, between persons of the same or different quality.'—STEELE. We *apply* to those to whom we wish to communicate some object of personal interest; 'Thus all the words of lordship, honour, and grace, are only repetitions to a man that the king has ordered him to be called so, but no evidences that there is any thing in himself that would give the man, who *applies* to him, those ideas without the creation of his master.'—STEELE. An *address* therefore may be made without an *application;* and an *application* may be made by means of an *address*.

It is a privilege of the British Constitution, that the subject may *address* the monarch, and *apply* for a redress of grievances. We cannot pass through the streets of the metropolis without being continually *addressed* by beggars, who *apply* for the relief of artificial more than for real wants. Men in power are always exposed to be publickly *addressed* by persons who wish to obtrude their opinions upon them, and to have perpetual *applications* from those who solicit favours.

An *address* may be rude or civil, an *application* may be frequent or urgent. It is impertinent to *address* any one with whom we are not acquainted, unless we have any reason for making an *application* to them.

TO ATTEND TO, MIND, REGARD, HEED, NOTICE.

Attend, in French *attendre*, Latin *attendo*, compounded of *at* or *ad* and *tendo* to stretch, signifies to stretch or bend the mind to a thing; *mind*, from the noun *mind*, signifies to have in the mind; *regard*, in French *regarder*, compounded of *re* and *garder*, comes from the German *wahren* to see or look at, signifying to look upon again or with attention; *heed*, in German *hüthen*, in all probability comes from *vito*, and the Latin *video* to see or pay attention to; *notice*, from the Latin *notitia* knowledge, signifies to get the knowledge of or have in one's mind.

The idea of fixing the mind on an object is common to all these terms. As this is the characteristick of *attention*, *attend* is the generick, the rest are specifick terms. We *attend* in *minding*, *regarding*, *heeding*, and *noticing*, and also in many cases in which these words are not employed. To *mind* is to *attend to* a thing, so that it may not be forgotten; to *regard* is to look on a thing as of importance; to *heed* is to *attend to* a thing from a principle of caution; to *notice* is to think on that which strikes the senses.

We *attend to* a speaker when we hear and understand his words; 'Conversation will naturally furnish us with hints which we did not *attend to*, and make us enjoy other men's parts and reflections as well as our own.'—ADDISON. We *mind* what is said when we bear it in mind;

> Cease to request me, let us *mind* our way,
> Another song requires another day.—DRYDEN.

We *regard* what is said by dwelling and reflecting on it; 'The voice of reason is more to be *regarded* than the bent of any present inclination.'—ADDISON. *Heed* is given to whatever awakens a sense of danger;

> Ah! why was ruin so attractive made,
> Or why fond man so easily betray'd?
> Why *heed* we not, while mad we haste along,
> The gentle voice of peace or pleasure's song?
> COLLINS.

Notice is taken of what passes outwardly; 'I believe that the knowledge of Dryden was gleaned from accidental intelligence and various conversation, by vigilance that permitted nothing to pass without *notice*.'—JOHNSON. Children should always *attend* when spoken to, and *mind* what is said to them; they should *regard* the counsels of their parents, so as to make them the rule of their conduct, and *heed* their warnings so as to avoid the evil; they should *notice* what passes before them so as to apply it to some useful purpose. It is a part of politeness to *attend to* every minute circumstance which affects the comfort and convenience of those with whom we associate: men who are actuated by any passion seldom pay any *regard* to the dictates of conscience; nor *heed* the unfavourable impressions which their conduct makes on others; for in fact they seldom think what is said of them to be worth their *notice*.

TO ATTEND, HEARKEN, LISTEN.

Attend, *v. To attend to; hearken*, in German *horchen*, is an intensive of *hören* to hear; *listen* probably comes from the German *lüsten* to lust after, because *listening* springs from an eager desire to hear.

Attend is a mental action; *hearken* both corporeal and mental; *listen* simply corporeal. To *attend* is to have the mind engaged on what we hear; to *hearken* and *listen* are to strive to hear. People *attend* when they are addressed;

> Hush'd winds the topmost branches scarcely bend,
> As if thy tuneful song they did *attend*.—DRYDEN

They *hearken* to what is said by others; 'What a deluge of lust, and fraud, and violence would in a little time overflow the whole nation, if these wise advocates for morality (the freethinkers) were universally *hearkened* to.'—BERKELEY. Men *listen* to what passes between others;

> While Chaos hush'd stands *listening* to the noise,
> And wonders at confusion not his own.—DENNIS.

It is always proper to *attend*, and mostly of importance to *hearken*, but frequently improper to *listen*. The mind that is occupied with another object cannot *attend:* we are not disposed to *hearken* when the thing does not appear interesting: curiosity often impels to *listening* to what does not concern the *listener*.

Listen is sometimes used figuratively for *hearing*, so as to *attend:* it is necessary at all times to *listen* to the dictates of reason. It is of great importance for a learner to *attend* to the rules that are laid down: it is essential for young people in general to *hearken* to the counsels of their elders, and to *listen* to the admonitions of conscience.

TO HEAR, HEARKEN, OVERHEAR.

To *hear* is properly the act of the ear; it is sometimes totally abstracted from the mind, when we *hear* and do not understand;

> I look'd, I listen'd, dreadful sounds I *hear*,
> And the dire forms of hostile gods appear.
> DRYDEN.

To *hearken* is an act of the ear, and the mind in conjunction; it implies an effort to *hear*, a tendency of the ear;

But aged Nereus *hearkens* to his love.—Dryden.

To *overhear* is to *hear* clandestinely, or unknown to the person who is heard, whether designedly or not;

If he fail of that
He will have other means to cut you off;
I *overheard* him and his practices.—Shakspeare.

We *hear* sounds: we *hearken* for the sense; we *overhear* the words: a quick ear *hears* the smallest sound; a willing mind *hearkens* to what is said: a prying curiosity leads to *overhearing*.

ATTENTION, APPLICATION, STUDY.

These terms indicate a direction of the thoughts to an object, but differing in the degree of steadiness and force.

Attention (*v. To attend to*) marks the simple bending of the mind; *application* (*v. To address*) marks an envelopment or engagement of the powers; a bringing them into a state of close contact; *study*, from the Latin *studeo* to desire eagerly, marks a degree of *application* that arises from a strong desire of attaining the object.

Attention is the first requisite for making a progress in the acquirement of knowledge; it may be given in various degrees, and it rewards according to the proportion in which it is given; a divided attention is however more hurtful than otherwise; it retards the progress of the learner while it injures his mind by improper exercise; 'Those whom sorrow incapacitates to enjoy the pleasures of contemplation, may properly *apply* to such diversions, provided they are innocent, as lay strong hold on the *attention*.'—Johnson. *Application* is requisite for the attainment of perfection in any pursuit; it cannot be partial or variable, like *attention;* it must be the constant exercise of power or the regular and uniform use of means for the attainment of an end: youth is the period for *application*, when the powers of body and mind are in full vigour; no degree of it in after-life will supply its deficiency in younger years; 'I could heartily wish there was the same *application* and endeavours to cultivate and improve our church musick as have been lately bestowed upon that of the stage.'—Addison. *Study* is that species of *application* which is most purely intellectual in its nature; it is the exercise of the mind for itself and in itself, its native effort to arrive at maturity; it embraces both *attention* and *application*. The student *attends* to all he hears and sees; *applies* what he has learned to the acquirement of what he wishes to learn, and digests the whole by the exercise of reflection: as nothing is thoroughly understood or properly reduced to practice without *study*, the professional man must choose this road in order to reach the summit of excellence; 'Other things may be seized with might, or purchased with money, but knowledge is to be gained only with *study*.'—Johnson.

TO DISREGARD, NEGLECT, SLIGHT.

To *disregard* signifies properly not to *regard; neglect*, in Latin *neglectus*, participle of *negligo*, compounded of *nec* and *lego*, signifies not to choose; *slight*, from *light*, signifies to make light of or set light by.

We *disregard* the warnings, the words, or opinions of another; we *neglect* their injunctions or their precepts. To *disregard* results from the settled purpose of the mind; to *neglect* from a temporary forgetfulness or oversight. What is *disregarded* is seen and passed over; what is *neglected* is generally not thought of at the time required. What is *disregarded* does not strike the mind at all; what is *neglected* enters the mind only when it is before the eye: the former is an action employed on present objects; the latter on that which is past: what we *disregard* is not esteemed; 'The new notion that has prevailed of late years that the Christian religion is little more than a good system of morality, must in course draw on a *disregard* to spiritual exercise.'—Gibson. What we *neglect* is often esteemed, but not sufficiently to be remembered or practised;

Beauty 's a charm, but soon the charm will pass;
As lilies lie *neglected* on the plain,
While dusky hyacinths for use remain.—Dryden.

A child *disregards* the prudent counsels of a parent; he *neglects* to use the remedies which have been prescribed to him.

Disregard and *neglect* are frequently not personal acts; they respect the thing more than the person; *slight* is altogether an intentional act towards an individual. We *disregard* or *neglect* things often from a heedlessness of temper; the consequence either of youth or habit: we *slight* a person from feelings of dislike or contempt. Young people should *disregard* nothing that is said to them by their superiours; nor *neglect* any thing which they are enjoined to do; nor *slight* any one to whom they owe personal attention; 'You cannot expect your son should have any regard for one whom he sees you *slight*.'—Locke. *Slight* is also sometimes applied to moral objects in the same sense; 'When once devotion fancies herself under the influence of a divine impulse, it is no wonder she *slights* human ordinances.'—Addison.

INADVERTENCY, INATTENTION, OVERSIGHT.

Inadvertency, from *advert* to turn the mind to, is allied to *inattention* (*v. Attentive*), when the act of the mind is signified in general terms; and to *oversight* when any particular instance of *inadvertency* occurs. *Inadvertency* never designates a habit, but *inattention* does; the former term, therefore, is unqualified by the reproachful sense which attaches to the latter: any one may be guilty of *inadvertencies*, since the mind that is occupied with many subjects equally serious may be turned so steadily towards some that others may escape notice; 'Ignorance or *inadvertency* will admit of some extenuation.'—South. *Inattention*, which designates a direct want of *attention*, is always a fault, and belongs only to the young, or such as are thoughtless, either by nature or circumstances; 'The expense of attending (the Scottish Parliament), the *inattention* of the age to any legal or regular system of government, but above all, the exorbitant authority of the nobles, made this privilege of so little value as to be almost neglected.'—Robertson. Since *inadvertency* is an occasional act, it must not be too often repeated, or it becomes *inattention* An *oversight* is properly a species of *inadvertency* which arises from looking over, or passing by, a thing *Inadvertency* seems to refer rather to the cause of the mistake, namely, the particular abstraction of the mind from the object; the term *oversight* seems to refer to the mistake itself, namely, the missing something which ought to have been taken: it is an *inadvertency* in a person to omit speaking to one of the company; it is an *oversight* in a tradesman who omits to include certain articles in his reckoning: we pardon an *inadvertency* in another, since the consequences are never serious; we must be guarded against *oversights* in business, as their consequences may be serious; 'The ancient criticks discover beauties which escape the observation of the vulgar, and very often find reasons for palliating such little slips and *oversights* in the writings of eminent authors.'—Addison.

TO NEGLECT, OMIT.

Neglect, *v. To disregard; omit*, in Latin *omitto*, or *ob* and *mitto*, signifies to put aside.

The idea of letting pass or slip, or of not using, is comprehended in the signification of both these terms; the former is, however, a culpable, the latter an indifferent, action. What we *neglect* ought not to be *neglected;*

Heaven,
Where honour due and reverence none *neglect*.
Milton.

What we *omit* may be *omitted* or otherwise, as convenience requires; 'These personal comparisons I *omit*, because I would say nothing that may savour of a spirit of flattery.'—Bacon. In indifferent matters they may sometimes be applied indifferently; 'It is the great excellence of learning, that it borrows very little from time or place; but this quality which constitutes much of its value is one occasion of *neglect* Wha may be done at all times with equal propriety is deferred from day to day, till the mind is gradually reconciled to the *omission*.'—JOHNSON. These terms differ, however, in the objects to which they are applied: that is *neglected* which is practicable or serves for action; that is *omitted* which serves for intellectual purposes: we *neglect* an opportunity, we *neglect* the means, the time, the use, and the like; we *omit* a word, a sentence, a figure, a stroke, a circumstance, and the like.

NEGLIGENT, REMISS, CARELESS, THOUGHTLESS, HEEDLESS, INATTENTIVE.

Negligent (*v. To disregard*) and *remiss* respect the outward action: *careless*, *heedless*, *thoughtless*, and *inattentive* respect the state of the mind.

Negligence and *remissness* consist in not doing what ought to be done; *carelessness* and the other mental defects may show themselves in doing wrong, as well as in not doing at all; *negligence* and *remissness* are therefore, to *carelessness* and the others, as the effect to the cause; for no one is so apt to be *negligent* and *remiss* as he who is *careless*, although at the same time *negligence* and *remissness* arise from other causes, and *carelessness*, *thoughtlessness*, &c. produce likewise other effects. *Negligent* is a stronger term than *remiss*: one is *negligent* in *neglecting* the thing that is expressly before one's eyes; one is *remiss* in forgetting that which was enjoined some time previously: the want of will renders a person *negligent*; the want of interest renders a person *remiss*: one is *negligent* in regard to business, and the performance of bodily labour; one is *remiss* in duty, or in such things as respect mental exertion. Servants are commonly *negligent* in what concerns their master's interest; teachers are *remiss* in not correcting the faults of their pupils. *Negligence* is therefore the fault of persons of all descriptions, but particularly those in low condition; 'The two classes most apt to be *negligent* of this duty (religious retirement) are the men of pleasure, and the men of business.'—BLAIR. *Remissness* is a fault peculiar to those in a more elevated station;

My gen'rous brother is of gentle kind,
He seems *remiss*, but bears a valiant mind.—POPE.

A clerk in an office is *negligent* in not making proper memorandums; a magistrate, or the head of an institution, is *remiss* in the exercise of his authority by not checking irregularities.

Careless denotes the want of care (*v. Care*) in the manner of doing things; *thoughtless* denotes the want of thought or reflection about things; *heedless* denotes the want of heeding (*v. To attend*) or regarding things; *inattentive* denotes the want of attention to things (*v. To attend to*).

One is *careless* only in trivial matters of behaviour; one is *thoughtless* in matters of greater moment, in what respects the conduct. *Carelessness* leads children to make mistakes in their exercises, or in whatever they commit to memory or to paper; *thoughtlessness* leads many who are not children into serious errours of conduct, when they do not think of or bear in mind the consequences of their actions. *Carelessness* is occasional, *thoughtlessness* is permanent; the former is inseparable from a state of childhood, the latter is a constitutional defect, and sometimes attends a man to his grave. *Carelessness* as well as *thoughtlessness* betrays itself not only in the thing that immediately employs the mind, but *thoughtlessness* respects that which is past, and *carelessness* lies in that which regards futurity; 'If the parts of time were not variously coloured, we should never discern their departure and succession, but should live *thoughtless* of the past, and *careless* of the future.'—JOHNSON. We may not only be *careless* in not doing the thing well that we are about, but we may be *careless* in *neglecting* to do it at all, or *careless* about the event, or *careless* about our future interest; it still differs, however, from *thoughtless* in this, that it bespeaks a want of interest or desire for the thing; but *thoughtless* bespeaks the want of thinking or reflecting upon it: the *careless* person abstains from using the means, because he does not care about the end; the *thoughtless* person cannot act, because he does not think: the *careless* person sees the thing, but does not try to obtain it; the *thoughtless* person has not the thought of it in his mind.

Careless is applied to such things as require permanent care; *thoughtless* to such as require permanent thought; *heedless* and *inattentive* are applied to passing objects that engage the senses or the thoughts of the moment. One is *careless* in business, *thoughtless* in conduct, *heedless* in walking or running, *inattentive* in listening: *careless* and *thoughtless* persons neglect the necessary use of their powers; the *heedless* and *inattentive* neglect the use of their senses. *Careless* people are unfit to be employed in the management of any concerns; *thoughtless* people are unfit to have the management of themselves; *heedless* children are unfit to go by themselves; *inattentive* children are unfit to be led by others. One is *careless* and *inattentive* in providing for his good; one is *thoughtless* and *heedless* in not guarding against evil: a *careless* person does not trouble himself about advancement; an *inattentive* person does not concern himself about improvement; a *thoughtless* person brings himself into distress; a *heedless* person exposes himself to accidents.

Heedless and *inattentive* are, for the most part, applied to particular circumstances, and in that case they are not taken in a bad sense. We may be *heedless* of a thing of which it is not needful to take any heed;

There in the ruin, *heedless* of the dead,
The shelter-seeking peasant builds his shed.
GOLDSMITH

Or *inattentive* if the thing does not demand attention; 'In the midst of his glory the Almighty is not *inattentive* to the meanest of his subjects.'—BLAIR.

THOUGHTFUL, CONSIDERATE, DELIBERATE.

Thoughtful, or full of *thinking* (*v. To think, reflect*), *considerate*, or ready to *consider* (*v. To consider, reflect*), and *deliberate*, ready to *deliberate* (*v. To consult*), rise upon each other in their signification: he who is *thoughtful* does not forget his duty; he who is *considerate* pauses, and *considers* properly what is his duty; he who *deliberates considers deliberately*. It is a recommendation to a subordinate person to be *thoughtful* in doing what is wished of him; 'Men's minds are in general inclined to levity, much more than to *thoughtful* melancholy.'—BLAIR. It is the recommendation of a confidential person to be *considerate*, as he has often to judge according to his own discretion; 'Some things will not bear much zeal; and the more earnest we are about them, the less we recommend ourselves to the approbation of sober and *considerate* men.'—TILLOTSON. It is the recommendation of a person who is acting for himself in critical matters to be *deliberate*; 'There is a vast difference between sins of infirmity and those of presumption, as vast as between inadvertency and *deliberation*.'—SOUTH. There is this farther distinction in the word *deliberate*, that it may be used in the bad sense to mark a settled intention to do evil; young people may sometimes plead in extenuation of their guilt, that their misdeeds do not arise from *deliberate* malice.

ATTENTIVE, CAREFUL.

Attentive marks a readiness to attend (*v. To attend to*); *careful* signifies full of care (*v. Care, solicitude*).

These epithets denote a fixedness of mind: we are *attentive* in order to understand and improve; we are *careful* to avoid mistakes. An *attentive* scholar profits by what is told him in learning his task; a *careful* scholar performs his exercise correctly.

Attention respects matters of judgement; *care* relates to mechanical or ordinary actions: we listen *attentively*; we read or write *carefully*. A servant must be *attentive* to the orders that are given him, and *careful* not to injure his master's property. A translator must be *attentive*; a transcriber *careful*. A tradesman ought to be *attentive* to the wishes of his customers, and *careful* in keeping his accounts. In an extended and moral application of these terms they preserve a similar distinction; 'The use of the passions is to stir up the soul, to awaken the understanding, and to make the whole man more vigorous and *attentive* in the prosecution of his designs.'—ADDISON. 'We should be as *careful* of our words as our actions, and as far from speaking as doing ill.'—STEELE.

CARE, SOLICITUDE, ANXIETY.

Care, in Latin *cura*, comes probably from the Greek κῦρος power, because whoever has power has a weight of *care; solicitude*, in French *solicitude*, Latin *sollicitudo* from *sollicito* to disquiet, compounded of *solum* and *cito* to put altogether in commotion, signifies a complete state of restless commotion; *anxiety*, in French *anxieté*, Latin *anxietas*, from *anxius* and *ango*, Greek ἄγχω, Hebrew חנק to hang, suffocate, torment, signifies a state of extreme suffering.

These terms express mental pain in different degrees; *care* less than *solicitude*, and this less than *anxiety*. *Care* consists of thought and feeling; *solicitude* and *anxiety* of feeling only. *Care* respects the past, present, and future; *solicitude* and *anxiety* regard the present and future. *Care* is directed towards the present and absent, near or at a distance; *solicitude* and *anxiety* are employed about that which is absent and at a certain distance.

We are *careful* about the means; *solicitous* and *anxious* about the end; we are *solicitous* to obtain a good; we are *anxious* to avoid an evil. The *cares* of a parent exceed every other in their weight. He has an unceasing *solicitude* for the welfare of his children, and experiences many an *anxious* thought lest all his *care* should be lost upon them.

Care, though in some respects an infirmity of our nature, is a consequence of our limited knowledge, which we cannot altogether remove; as it respects the present, it is a bounden duty; but when it extends to futurity, it must be kept within the limits of pious resignation;

But his face
Deep scars of thunder had intrench'd, and *care*
Sat on his faded cheek.—MILTON.

Solicitude and *anxiety*, as habits of the mind, are irreconcilable with the faith of a Christian, which teaches him to take no thought for the morrow; 'Can your *solicitude* alter the course, or unravel the intricacy, of human events?'—BLAIR. 'The story of a man who grew gray in the space of one night's *anxiety* is very famous.'—SPECTATOR.

CARE, CONCERN, REGARD.

Care, in Latin *cura*, comes probably from the Greek κῦρος authority, because the weight of *care* rests with those in authority; *concern*, from the Latin *concerno*, compounded of *con* and *cerno*, signifies the looking thoroughly into a thing; *regard*, in French *regarder*, compounded of *re* and *garder* to look, signifies looking back upon a thing.

Care and *concern* consist both of thought and feeling, but the latter has less of thought than feeling: *regard* consists of thought only. We *care* for a thing which is the object of our exertions and wishes;

His trust was equal with the Deity to be deem'd,
Equal in strength, and rather than be less
Car'd not to be at all.—MILTON.

We *concern* ourselves about a thing when it engages our attention;

Our country's welfare is our first *concern*.—HAVARD.

We have *regard* for a thing on which we set some value and bestow some reflection;

Slander meets no *regard* from noble minds:
Only the base believe what the base only utter.
BELLER.

Care is altogether an active principle: the *careful* man leaves no means untried in the pursuit of his object; *care* actuates him to personal endeavours; it is opposed to negligence. *Concern* is not so active in its nature: the person who is *concerned* will be contented to see exertions made by others; it is opposed to indifference. *Regard* is only a sentiment of the mind; it may lead to action, but of itself extends no farther than reflection.

The business of life is the subject of *care;*

Well, on my terms thou wilt not be my heir:
If thou *car'st* little, less shall be my *care*.—DRYDEN.

Religion is the grand object of *concern*. 'The more the authority of any station in society is extended, the more it *concerns* publick happiness that it be committed to men fearing God.'—ROGERS. The esteem of others is an object of *regard;* 'He has rendered himself worthy of their most favourable *regards*.'—SMITH.

No one ought to expect to be exempt from *care*: the provision of a family, and the education of children, are objects for which we ought to take some *care*, or at least have some *concern*, inasmuch as we have a *regard* for our own welfare, and the well-being of society.

CARE, CHARGE, MANAGEMENT.

Care, *v. Care, solicitude; charge*, in French *charge* a burden, in Armorick and Bretan *carg*, which is probably connected with cargo and carry, is figuratively employed in the sense of a burden; a *management*, in French *ménagement*, from *ménager* and *méner* to lead, and the Latin *manus* a hand, signifies direction.

Care (*v. Care, concern*) includes generally both *charge* and *management;* but in the strict senso, it comprehends personal labour: *charge* involves responsibility: *management* (*v. To conduct*) includes regulation and order.

A gardener has the *care* of a garden; a nurse has the *charge* of children; a steward has the *management* of a farm: we must always act in order to take *care;* we must look in order to take *charge;* we must always think in order to *manage*.

Care is employed in the ordinary affairs of life, *charge* in matters of trust and confidence; *management* in matters of business and experience: the female has the *care* of the house, and the man that of providing for his family;

Care 's a father's right—a pleasing right,
In which he labours with a home-felt joy.—SHIRLEY

An instructer has the *charge* of youth; 'I can never believe that the repugnance with which Tiberius took the *charge* of the government upon him was wholly feigned.'—CUMBERLAND. A clerk has the *management* of a business; 'The woman, to whom her husband left the whole *management* of her lodgings, and who persisted in her purpose, soon found an opportunity to put it into execution.'—HAWKESWORTH.

CAREFUL, CAUTIOUS, PROVIDENT.

Careful signifies full of *care* (*v. Care, solicitude*); *cautious* is in Latin *cautus*, participle of *caveo*, which comes from *cavus* hollow, or a cave, which was originally a place of security; hence the epithet *cautious* in the sense of seeking security; *provident*, in Latin *providens*, signifies foreseeing or looking to beforehand, from *pro* and *video*.

We are *careful* to avoid mistakes; *cautious* to avoid danger; *provident* to avoid straits and difficulties: *care* is exercised in saving and retaining what we have; *caution* must be used in guarding against the evils that may be; *providence* must be employed in supplying the good, or guarding against the contingent evils of the future. *Providence* is a determinate and extended kind of *caution*.

Care consists in the use of means, in the exercise of the faculties for the attainment of an end; a *careful* person omits nothing;

To cure their mad ambition they were sent
To rule a distant province, each alone;
What could a *careful* father have done more?
DRYDEN.

Caution consists rather in abstaining from action; a *cautious* person will not act where he ought not;

Flush'd by the spirit of the genial year,
Be greatly *cautious* of your sliding hearts.
THOMSON.

Providence respects the use of things; it is both *care* and *caution* in the *management* of property; a *provident* person acts for the future by abstaining for the present;

Blest above men if he perceives and feels
The blessings he is heir to: he! to whom
His *provident* forefathers have bequeathed
In this fair district of their native isle
A free inheritance.—CUMBERLAND.

CAUTIOUS, WARY, CIRCUMSPECT.

Cautious, *v. Careful; wary*, from the same as *aware* (*v. To be aware of*), signifies ready to look out: *cir-*

cumspect, in Latin *circumspectus*, participle of *circumspicio* to look about, signifies ready to look on all sides.

These epithets denote a peculiar care to avoid evil; but *cautious* expresses less than the other two; it is necessary to be *cautious* at all times; to be *wary* in cases of peculiar danger; to be *circumspect* in matters of peculiar delicacy and difficulty.

Caution is the effect of fear; *wariness* of danger; *circumspection* of experience and reflection. The *cautious* man reckons on contingencies; he guards against the evils that may be, by pausing before he acts;

> The strong report of Arthur's death has worse
> Effect on them, than on the common sort;
> The vulgar only shake their *cautious* heads,
> Or whisper in the ear wisely suspicious.—Cibber.

The *wary* man looks for the danger which he suspects to be impending, and seeks to avoid it; 'Let not that *wary* caution, which is the fruit of experience, degenerate into craft.'—Blair. The *circumspect* man weighs and deliberates; he looks around and calculates on possibilities and probabilities; he seeks to attain his end by the safest means; 'No pious man can be so *circumspect* in the care of his conscience, as the covetous man is in that of his pocket.'—Steele. A tradesman must be *cautious* in his dealings with all men; he must be *wary* in his intercourse with designing men; he must be *circumspect* when transacting business of particular importance and intricacy. The traveller must be *cautious* when going a road not familiar to him; he must be *wary* when passing over slippery and dangerous places; he must be *circumspect* when going through obscure, uncertain, and winding passages.

A person ought to be *cautious* not to give offence; he ought to be *wary* not to entangle himself in ruinous litigations; he ought to be *circumspect* not to engage in what is above his abilities to complete. It is necessary to be *cautious* not to disclose our sentiments too freely before strangers; to be *wary* in one's speech before busy bodies and calumniators; to be *circumspect* whenever we speak on publick matters, respecting either politicks or religion.

MINDFUL, REGARDFUL, OBSERVANT.

Mindful, signifies full of minding, or thinking on that which is past; it mostly regards matters of prudence, or the counsel we receive from others;

> Be *mindful*, when thou hast entomb'd the shoot,
> With store of earth around to feed the root.—Dryden.

Regardful respects that which in itself demands *regard* or serious thought;

> No, there is none; no ruler of the stars
> *Regardful* of my miseries.—Hill.

Observant respects that which has been imposed upon us, or become a matter of obligation;

> *Observant* of the right, religious of his word.
> Dryden.

A child should always be *mindful* of its parents' instructions; they should never be forgotten: every one should be *regardful* of his several duties and obligations; they never ought to be neglected: one ought to be *observant* of the religious duties which one's profession enjoins upon him; they cannot with propriety be passed over. By being *mindful* of what one hears from the wise and good, one learns to be wise and good; by being *regardful* of what is due to one's self, and to society at large, one learns to pass through the world with satisfaction to one's own mind and esteem from others; by being *observant* of all rule and order, we afford to others a salutary example for their imitation.

AWARE, ON ONE'S GUARD, APPRIZED, CONSCIOUS.

Aware, compounded of *a* or *on* and *ware*, signifies to be on the look out, from the Saxon *waer*, German, &c. *wahren*, Greek ὁράω to see; *guard*, in French *garder*, is connected with *ward*, in Saxon *waerd*, German, &c. *gewahrt*, participle of *wahren*; *apprized*, in French *appris*, from *apprendre* to apprehend, learn, or understand; *conscious*, in Latin *conscius*, of *con* and *scius* knowing, signifies knowing within one's self.

The idea of having the expectation or knowledge of a thing is common to all these terms. We are *aware* of a thing when we calculate upon it; 'The first steps in the breach of a man's integrity are more important than men are *aware* of.'—Steele. We are *on our guard* against an evil when we are prepared for it 'What establishment of religion more friendly to publick happiness could be desired or framed (than our own). How zealous ought we to be for its preservation; how much *on our guard* against every danger which threatens to trouble it.'—Blair. We are *apprized* of that of which we have had an intimation, or have been informed of; 'In play the chance of loss and gain ought always to be equal, at least each party should be *apprized* of the force employed against him.'—Steele. We are *conscious* of that in which we have ourselves been concerned; 'I know nothing so hard for a generous mind to get over as calumny and reproach, and cannot find any method of quieting the soul under them, besides this single one, of our being *conscious* to ourselves that we do not deserve them.'—Addison.

To be aware, and *on one's guard*, respect the future; to be *apprized*, either the past or present; to be *conscious*, only the past. Experience enables a man to be *aware* of consequences; prudence and caution dictate to him the necessity of being *on his guard* against evils. Whoever is fully *aware* of the precarious tenure by which he holds all his goods in this world, will be *on his guard* to prevent any calamities, as far as the use of means in his control.

We are *apprized* of events, or what passes outwardly, through the medium of external circumstances; we are *conscious* only through the medium of ourselves, of what passes within. We are *apprized* of what has happened from indications that attract our notice; we are *conscious* of our guilt from the recollection of what we have done. A commander who is not *aware* of all the contingencies that influence the fate of a battle, who is not *on his guard* against the stratagems of the enemy, who is not fully *apprized* of their intentions, and *conscious* of his own strength to frustrate them, has no grounds to expect a victory; the chances of defeat are greatly against him.

HEED, CARE, ATTENTION

Heed, which through the medium of the German *hüthen* probably comes from the Latin *vito* to avoid, and *video* to see, applies to matters of importance to one's moral conduct; *care* (*v. Care, concern*) applies to matters of minor import: a man is required to take *heed*; a child is required to take *care*: the former exercises his understanding in taking *heed*; the latter exercises his thoughts and his senses in taking *care*: the former looks to the remote and probable consequences of his actions, and endeavours to prevent the evil that may happen; the latter sees principally to the thing that is immediately before him. When a young man enters the world, he must take *heed* lest he be not ensnared by his companions into vicious practices;

> Next you, my servants, *heed* my strict command,
> Without the walls a ruin'd temple stands.
> Dryden.

In a slippery path we must take *care* that we do not fall 'I believe the hiatus should be avoided with more *care* in poetry than in oratory.'—Pope.

Heed has moreover the sense of thinking on what is proposed to our notice, in which it agrees with *attention*, which from the Latin *attendo*, or *at* and *tendo* to stretch, signifies a tension or stretching the mind towards an object; hence we speak of giving *heed* and paying *attention*: but the former is applied only to that which is conveyed to us by another, in the shape of a direction, a caution, or an instruction; but the latter is said of every thing which we are set to perform. A good child gives *heed* to his parents when they caution him against any dangerous or false step; he pays *attention* to the lesson which is set him to learn. He who gives no *heed* to the counsels of others is made to repent his folly by bitter experience; 'It is a way of calling a man a fool, when no *heed* is given to what he says.'—L'Estrange. He who fails in paying *attention* to the instruction of others cannot expect to grow wiser; 'He perceived nothing but silence, and signs of *attention* to what he would further say.' —BACON.

All were *attentive* to the godlike man.—DRYDEN.

ESTEEM, RESPECT, REGARD.

Esteem, from the Latin *æstimo*, signifies literally to set a value upon; *respect*, from the Latin *respicio*, signifies to look back upon, to look upon with attention; *regard*, *v. To attend to.*

A favourable sentiment towards particular objects is included in the meaning of all these terms.

Esteem and *respect* flow from the understanding; *regard* springs from the heart, as well as the head: *esteem* is produced by intrinsick worth; *respect* by extrinsick qualities; *regard* is affection blended with *esteem:* it is in the power of every man, independently of all collateral circumstances, to acquire the *esteem* of others; but *respect* and *regard* are within the reach of a limited number only: the high and the low, the rich and the poor, the equal and the unequal, are each, in their turn, the objects of *esteem;* 'How great honour and *esteem* will men declare for one whom perhaps they never saw before.'—TILLOTSON. Those only are objects of *respect* who have some mark of distinction, or superiority either of birth, talent, acquirements, or the like;

Then for what common good my thoughts inspire,
Attend, and in the son *respect* the sire.—POPE.

Regard subsists only between friends, or those who stand in close connexion with each other; industry and sobriety excite our *esteem* for one man, charity and benevolence our *esteem* for another; superiour learning or abilities excite our *respect* for another; a long acquaintance, or a reciprocity of kind offices, excite a mutual *regard;* 'He has rendered himself worthy of their most favourable *regards*.'—SMITH. This latter term is also used figuratively, and in a moral application; 'Cheerfulness bears the same friendly *regard* to the mind as to the body.'—ADDISON.

TO HONOUR, REVERENCE, RESPECT.

These terms agree in expressing the act of an inferiour towards his superiour; but *honour* (*v. Glory*) expresses less than *reverence* (*v. To adore*), and more than *respect* (*v. To esteem*).

To *honour*, as applied to persons, is mostly an outward act; to *reverence* is either an act of the mind, or the outward expression of a sentiment; to *respect* is only an act of the mind. We *honour* God by adoration and worship, as well as by the performance of his will; we *honour* our parents by obeying them and giving them our personal service: we *reverence* our Maker by cherishing in our minds a dread of offending him, and making a fearful use of his holy name and word; we *reverence* our parents by holding a similar sentiment in a less degree; 'This is a duty in the fifth commandment required towards our prince and our parent, a *respect* which in the notion of it implies a mixture of love and fear, and in the object equally supposes goodness and power.'—ROGERS. 'The foundation of every proper disposition towards God must be laid in *reverence*, that is, admiration mixed with awe.'—BLAIR. We *respect* the wise and good; 'Establish your character on the *respect* of the wise, not on the flattery of dependants.'—BLAIR.

To *honour* and *respect* are extended to other objects besides our Maker and our parents; but *reverence* is confined to objects of a religious description; "We *honour* the king and all that are put in authority under him," by rendering to them the tribute that is due to their station; we *respect* all who possess superiour qualities: the former is an act of duty, it flows out of the constitution of civil society; the latter is a voluntary act flowing out of the temper of the mind towards others. To *respect*, as I have before observed, signifies merely to feel *respect;* but to show *respect*, or a mark of *respect*, supposes an outward action which brings it still nearer to *honour*. It is a mark of *honour* in subjects to keep the birth-day of their sovereign; it is a mark of *respect* to any individual to give him the upper seat in a room or at a table. Divine *honours* were formerly paid by the Romans to some of their emperours· *respect* is always paid to age in all Christian countries; among the heathens it differed according to the temper of the people.

To *honour* when applied to things is also used in the sense of holding in *honour*, in which case it expresses a stronger sentiment than *respect*, which solely implies regard to; 'Of learning, as of virtue, it may be affirmed that it is at once *honoured* and neglected.'—JOHNSON

The bless'd gods do not love
Ungodly actions; but *respect* the right
And in the works of pious men delight.—CHAPMAN

HONESTY, HONOUR.

These terms both respect the principle which actuates men in the adjustment of their rights with each other. The words are both derived from the same source, namely, the Hebrew הון substance or wealth (*v. Honesty*), which, being the primitive source of esteem among men, became at length put for the measure or standard of esteem, namely, what is good. Hence *honesty* and *honour* are both founded upon what is estimable; with this difference, that *honesty* is confined to the first principles or laws upon which civil society is founded, and *honour* is an independent principle that extends to every thing which by usage has been admitted as estimable or entitled to esteem; '*Honesty*, in the language of the Romans, as well as in French, rather signifies a composition of those qualities which generally acquire *honour* and esteem to those who possess them.'—TEMPLE. 'If by *honour* be meant any thing distinct from conscience, 't is no more than a regard to the censure and esteem of the world.'—ROGERS. An *honest* action, therefore, can never reflect so much credit on the agent as an *honourable* action; since in the performance of the one he may be guided by motives comparatively low, whereas in the other case he is actuated solely by a fair regard for the *honour* or the esteem of others. To a breach of *honesty* is attached punishment and personal inconvenience in various forms; but to a breach of *honour* is annexed only disgrace or the ill opinion of others: he, therefore, who sets more value or interest on the gratification of his passions, than on the esteem of the world, may gain his petty purpose with the sacrifice of his *honour;* but he who strives to be *dishonest* is thwarted in his purpose by the intervention of the laws, which deprive him of his unworthy gains: consequently, men are compelled to be *honest* whether they will or not, but they are entirely free in the choice of being *honourable*.

On the other hand, since *honesty* is founded on the very first principles of human society, and *honour* on the incidental principles which have been annexed to them in the progress of time and culture; the former is positive and definite, and he who is actuated by this principle can never err; but the latter is indefinite and variable, and as it depends upon opinion it will easily mislead. We cannot have a false *honesty*, but we may have false *honour*. *Honesty* always keeps a man within the line of his duty; but a mistaken notion of what is *honourable* may carry a man very far from what is right, and may even lead him to run counter to common *honesty*.

HONESTY UPRIGHTNESS, INTEGRITY, PROBITY.

Honesty, *v. Fair; uprightness*, from *upright*, in German *aufrichtig* or *aufgerichtet*, from *aufrichten* to set up, signifies in a straight direction, not deviating nor turning aside.

Honest is the most familiar and universal term, it is applied alike to actions and principles, to a mode of conduct or a temper of mind: *upright* is applied to the conduct, but always with reference to the moving principle. As it respects the conduct, *honesty* is a much more homely virtue than *uprightness:* a man is said to be *honest* who in his dealings with others does not violate the laws; thus a servant is *honest* who does not take any of the property of his master, or suffer it to be taken; a tradesman is *honest* who does not sell bad articles; and people in general are denominated *honest* who pay what they owe, and do not adopt any methods of defrauding others: *honesty* in this sense, therefore, consists in negatives; but *up·*

rightness is positive, and extends to all matters which are above the reach of the law, and comprehends not only every thing which is known to be hurtful, but also whatever may chance to be hurtful. To be *honest* requires nothing but a knowledge of the first principles of civil society; it is learned, and may be practised, by the youngest and most ignorant: but to be *upright* supposes a superiority of understanding or information, which qualifies a person to discriminate between that which may or may not injure another. An *honest* man is contented with not overcharging another for that which he sells to him; but an *upright* man seeks to provide him with that which shall fully answer his purpose: a man will not think himself *dishonest* who leaves another to find out defects which it is possible may escape his notice; but an *upright* man will rather suffer a loss himself than expose another to an errour which may be detrimental to his interests. From this difference between *honesty* and *uprightness* arises another, namely, that the *honest* man may be *honest* only for his own convenience, out of regard to his character, or a fear of the laws; but the *upright* man is always *upright*, from his sense of what is right, and his concern for others.

Honest, in its extended sense, as it is applied to principles, or to the general character of a man, is of a higher cast than the common kind of *honesty* above mentioned; *uprightness*, however, in this case, still preserves its superiority. An *honest* principle is the first and most universally applicable principle, which the mind forms of what is right and wrong; and the *honest* man, who is so denominated on account of his having this principle, is looked upon with respect, inasmuch as he possesses the foundation of all moral virtue in his dealings with others. *Honest* is here the generick, and *uprightness* the specifick term; the former does not exclude the latter, but the latter includes the former. There may be many *honest* men and *honest* minds; but there are not so many *upright* men nor *upright* minds. The *honest* man is rather contrasted with the rogue, and an *honest* principle is opposed to the selfish or artful principle; but the *upright* man or the *upright* mind can be compared or contrasted with nothing but itself. An *honest* man will do no harm if he know it; but an *upright* man is careful not to do to another what he would not have another do to him.

Honesty is a feeling that actuates and directs by a spontaneous impulse; *uprightness* is a principle that regulates or puts every thing into an even course. *Honesty* can be dispensed with in no case; but *uprightness* is called into exercise only in certain cases. We characterize a servant or the lowest person as *honest:* but we do not entitle any one in so low a capacity as *upright*, since *uprightness* is exercised in matters of higher moment, and rests upon the evidence of a man's own mind; a judge, however, may with propriety be denominated *upright*, who scrupulously adheres to the dictates of an unbiassed conscience in the administration of justice.

Uprightness is applicable only to principles and actions; *integrity* (from the Latin *integer* whole) is applicable to the whole man or his character; and *probity* (from *probus* or *prohibus* restraining, that is, restraining from evil) is in like manner used only in the comprehensive sense. *Uprightness* is the straightness of rule by which actions and conduct in certain cases is measured; *integrity* is the wholeness or unbrokenness of a man's character throughout life in his various transactions; *probity* is the excellence and purity of a man's character in his various relations. When we call a man *upright*, we consider him in the detail; we bear in mind the uniformity and fixedness of the principle by which he is actuated: when we call him a man of *integrity*, we view him in the gross, not in this nor that circumstance of life, but in every circumstance in which the rights and interests of others are concerned. *Uprightness* may therefore be looked upon in some measure as a part of *integrity;* with this difference, that the acting principle is in the one case only kept in view, whereas in the other case the conduct and principle are both included. The distinction between these terms is farther evident by observing their different application. We do not talk of a man's *uprightness* being shaken, or of his preserving his *uprightness;* but of his *integrity* being shaken, and his preserving his *integrity*. We may however, ascribe the particular conduct of any individual as properly to the *integrity* of his principles or mind, as to the *uprightness* of his principles. A man's *uprightness* displays itself in his dealings, be they ever so trifling; but the *integrity* of his character is seen in the most important concerns of life. A judge shows his *uprightness* in his daily administration of justice, when he remains uninfluenced by any partial motive; he shows his *integrity* when he resists the most powerful motives of personal interest and advantage out of respect to right and justice.

Integrity and *probity* are both general and abstract terms; but the former is relative, the latter is positive: *integrity* refers to the external injuries by which it may be assailed or destroyed; it is goodness tried and preserved: *probity* is goodness existing of itself, without reference to any thing else. There is no *integrity* where private interest is not in question; there is no *probity* wherever the interests of others are injured: *integrity* therefore includes *probity*, but *probity* does not necessarily suppose *integrity*. *Probity* is a free principle, that acts without any force; *integrity* is a defensive principle, that is obliged to maintain itself against external force. *Probity* excludes all injustice; *integrity* excludes in a particular manner that injustice which would favour one's self. *Probity* respects the rights of every man, and seeks to render to every one what is his due; it does not wait to be asked, it does not require any compulsion; it voluntarily enters into all the circumstances and conditions of men, and measures out to each his portion: *probity* therefore forbids a man being malignant, hard, cruel, ungenerous, unfair, or any thing else which may press unequally and unjustly on his neighbour: *integrity* is disinterested; it sacrifices every personal consideration to the maintenance of what is right: a man of *integrity* will not be contented to abstain from selling himself for gold; he will keep himself aloof from all private partialities or resentments, all party cabals or intrigue, which are apt to violate the *integrity* of his mind. We look for *honesty* and *uprightness* in citizens; it sets every question at rest between man and man: we look for *integrity* and *probity* in statesmen, or such as have to adjust the rights of many; they contribute to the publick as often as to the private good.

Were I to take an estimate of the comparative value of these four terms, I should denominate *honesty* a current coin which must be in every man's hands; he cannot dispense with it for his daily use: *uprightness* is fine silver: *probity* fine gold without any alloy: and *integrity* gold tried and purified: all which are in the hands of but comparatively few, yet carry a value with them independently of the use which is made of them.

RECTITUDE, UPRIGHTNESS.

Rectitude is properly rightness, which is expressed in a stronger manner by *uprightness:* we speak of the *rectitude* of the judgement; but of the *uprightness* of the mind, or of the moral character, which must be something more than straight, for it must be elevated above every thing mean or devious; 'We are told by Cumberland that *rectitude* is merely metaphorical, and that as a right line describes the shortest passage from point to point, so a right action effects a good design by the fewest means.'—JOHNSON.

> Who to the fraudulent impostor foul,
> In his *uprightness*, answer thus return'd.
> MILTON.

FAIR, HONEST, EQUITABLE, REASONABLE.

Fair, in Saxon *fagar*, comes probably from the Latin *pulcher* beautiful; *honest*, in Latin *honestus*, comes from *honos* honour; *equitable* signifies having *equity*, or according to *equity; reasonable*, having *reason*, or according to *reason*.

Fair is said of persons or things; *honest* mostly characterizes the person, either as to his conduct or his principle. When *fair* and *honest* are both applied to the external conduct, the former expresses more than the latter: a man may be *honest* without being *fair;* he cannot be *fair* without being *honest*. *Fairness* enters into every minute circumstance connected with the interests of the parties, and weighs them alike for both; *honesty* is contented with a literal conformity to the law, it consults the interest of one party: the *fair* dealer looks to his neighbour as well as himself, he wishes only for an equal share of advantage; a man may be an *honest* dealer while he looks to no one's advantage but his own: the *fair* man always acts from a principle of right; the *honest* man may be so from a motive of fear.

When these epithets are employed to characterize the man generally, *fairness* expresses less than *honesty*. *Fairness* is employed only in regard to commercial transactions or minor personal concerns; 'If the worldling prefer those means which are the *fairest*, it is not because they are *fair*, but because they seem to him most likely to prove successful.'—BLAIR. *Honesty* ranks among the first moral virtues, and elevates a man high above his fellow-creatures;

> An *honest* man's the noblest work of God.—POPE.

> Should he at length, so truly good and great,
> Prevail, and rule with *honest* views the state,
> Then must he toil for an ungrateful race,
> Submit to clamour, libels, and disgrace.
> JENYNS.

A man is *fair* who is ready to allow his competitor the same advantages as he enjoys himself in every matter however trivial; or he is *honest* in all his looks, words, and actions: neither his tongue nor his countenance ever belie his heart. A *fair* man makes himself acceptable.

When *fair* is employed as an epithet to qualify things, or to designate their nature, it approaches very near in signification to *equitable* and *reasonable;* they are all opposed to what is unjust: *fair* and *equitable* suppose two objects put in collision; *reasonable* is employed abstractedly; what is *fair* and *equitable* is so in relation to all circumstances; what is *reasonable* is so of itself. An estimate is *fair* in which profit and loss, merit and demerit, with every collateral circumstance, is duly weighed; a judgement is *equitable* which decides suitably and advantageously for both parties; a price is *reasonable* which does not exceed the limits of reason or propriety. A decision may be either *fair* or *equitable;* but the former is said mostly in regard to trifling matters, even in our games and amusements, and the latter in regard to the important rights of mankind. It is the business of the umpire to decide *fairly* between the combatants or the competitors for a prize; it is the business of the judge to decide *equitably* between men whose property is at issue; 'A man is very unlikely to judge *equitably* when his passions are agitated by a sense of wrong.'—JOHNSON.

A demand, a charge, a proposition, or an offer may be said to be either *fair* or *reasonable:* but the former term always bears a relation to what is right between man and man; the latter to what is right in itself, according to circumstances; 'The *reasonableness* of a test is not hard to be proved.'—JOHNSON.

HONOUR, DIGNITY.

Honour (*v. Honour*) may be taken either for that which intrinsically belongs to a person, or for that which is conferred on him; *dignity*, from the Latin *dignus* worthy, signifying worthiness, may be equally applied to what is intrinsick or extrinsick of a man.

In the first case *honour* has a reference to what is esteemed by others; *dignity* to that which is esteemed by ourselves: a sense of *honour* impels a man to do that which is esteemed *honourable* among men; a sense of *dignity* to do that which is consistent with the worth and greatness of his nature: the former strives to elevate himself as an individual; the latter to raise himself to the standard of his species: the former may lead a person astray; but the latter is an unerring guide. It is *honour* which sometimes makes a man first insult his friend, then draw his sword upon him whom he has insulted: it is *dignity* which makes him despise every paltry affront from others, and apologize for every apparent affront on his own part. This distinction between the terms is kept up in their application to what is extraneous of a man: the *honour* is that which is conferred on him by others; 'When a proud aspiring man meets with *honours* and preferments, these are the things which are ready to lay hold of his heart and affections.'—SOUTH. The *dignity* is the worth or value which is added to his condition;

> Him Tullus next in *dignity* succeeds.—DRYDEN.

Hence we always speak of *honours* as conferred or received; but *dignities* as possessed or maintained. *Honours* may sometimes be casual; but *dignities* are always permanent an act of condescension from the sovereign is an *honour;* but the *dignity* lies in the elevation of the office. Hence it is that *honours* are mostly civil or political; *dignities* ecclesiastical.

GLORY, HONOUR.

Glory is something dazzling and widely diffused. The Latin word *gloria*, anciently written *glosia*, is in all probability connected with our words *gloss*, *glaze*, *glitter*, *glow*, through the medium of the northern words *gleissen*, *glotzen*, *glänzen*, *glühen*, all which come from the Hebrew גחל a live coal. That the moral idea of *glory* is best represented by light is evident from the *glory* which is painted round the head of our Saviour; *honour* is something less splendid, but more solid (*v. Honour*).

Glory impels to extraordinary efforts and to great undertakings;

> Hence is our love of fame; a love so strong,
> We think no dangers great nor labours long,
> By which we hope our beings to extend,
> And to remotest times in *glory* to descend.
> JENYNS

Honour induces to a discharge of one's duty; 'As virtue is the most reasonable and genuine source of *honour*, we generally find in titles an intimation of some particular merit that should recommend men to the high stations which they possess.'—ADDISON. Excellence in the attainment, and success in the exploit, bring *glory;* a faithful exercise of one's talents reflects *honour*. *Glory* is connected with every thing which has a peculiar publick interest; *honour* is more properly obtained within a private circle. *Glory* is not confined to the nation or life of the individual by whom it is sought; it spreads over all the earth, and descends to the latest posterity: *honour* is limited to those who are connected with the subject of it, and eye-witnesses to his actions. *Glory* is attainable but by few, and may be an object of indifference to any one; *honour* is more or less within the reach of all, and must be disregarded by no one. A general at the head of an army goes in pursuit of *glory;* the humble citizen who acts his part in society so as to obtain the approbation of his fellow-citizens is in the road for *honour*. A nation acquires *glory* by the splendour of its victories, and its superiority in arts as well as arms; it obtains *honour* by its strict adherence to equity and good faith in all its dealings with other nations. Our own nation has acquired *glory* by the help of its brave warriours; it has gained *honour* by the justice and generosity of its government. The military career of Alexander was *glorious;* his humane treatment of the Persian princesses who were his prisoners was an *honourable* trait in his character. The abolition of the slave trade by the English government was a *glorious* triumph of Christianity over the worst principles of human nature; the national conduct of England during the revolutionary period reflects *honour* on the English name.

Glory is a sentiment, selfish in its nature, but salutary or pernicious in its effect, according as it is directed;

> If *glory* cannot move a mind so mean,
> Nor future praise from fading pleasures wean,
> Yet why should he defraud his son of fame,
> And grudge the Romans their immortal name?
> DRYDEN

Honour is a principle disinterested in its nature, and beneficial in its operations; 'Sir Francis Bacon, for greatness of genius and compass of knowledge, did *honour* to his age and country.'—ADDISON. A thirst for *glory* is seldom indulged but at the expense of others, as it is not attainable in the plain path of duty; there are but few opportunities of acquiring it by elevated acts of goodness, and still fewer who have the virtue to embrace the opportunities that offer: a love of *honour* can never be indulged but to the advantage of others; it is restricted by fixed laws; it requires a sacrifice of every selfish consideration, and a due regard to the rights of others; it is associated with nothing but virtue.

DISHONEST, KNAVISH.

Dishonest marks the contrary to *honest; knavish* marks the likeness to a *knave*.

Dishonest characterizes simply the mode of action; *knavish* characterizes the agent as well as the action: what is *dishonest* violates the established laws of man; what is *knavish* supposes peculiar art and design in the accomplishment. It is *dishonest* to take any thing from another which does not belong to one; it is *knavish* to get it by fraud or artifice, or by imposing on the confidence of another. We may prevent *dishonest* practices by ordinary means of security; but we must not trust ourselves in the company of *knavish* people if we do not wish to be overreached; 'Gaming is too unreasonable and *dishonest* for a gentleman to addict himself to it.'—Lord Lyttleton. 'Not to laugh when nature prompts is but a *knavish*, hypocritical way of making a mask of one's face.'—Pope.

RIGHT, JUST, PROPER.

Right, in German *recht*, Latin *rectus*, signifies upright, not leaning to one side or the other, standing as it ought; *just*, in Latin *justus*, from *jus* law, signifies according to a rule of *right; fit, v. Fit; proper*, in Latin *proprius*, signifies belonging to a given rule.

Right is here the general term; the others express modes of *right*. The *right* and wrong are defined by the written will of God, or are written in our hearts according to the original constitutions of our nature; the *just* and *unjust* are determined by the written laws of men; the *fit* and *proper* are determined by the established principles of civil society.

Between the *right* and the wrong there are no gradations: a thing cannot be more *right* or more wrong; whatever is *right* is not wrong, and whatever is wrong is not *right:* the *just* and *unjust, proper* and *improper, fit* and *unfit*, on the contrary, have various shades and degrees that are not so easily definable by any forms of speech or written rules.

The *right* and wrong depend upon no circumstance; what is once *right* or wrong is always *right* or wrong: but the *just* or *unjust, proper* or *improper*, are relatively so according to the circumstances of the case: it is a *just* rule for every man to have that which is his own; but what is *just* to the individual may be unjust to society. It is *proper* for every man to take charge of his own concerns; but it would be improper for a man in an unsound state of mind to undertake such a charge.

The *right* and the wrong are often beyond the reach of our faculties to discern; but the *just, fit*, and *proper* are always to be distinguished sufficiently to be observed. *Right* is applicable to all matters, important or otherwise; *just* is employed only in matters of essential interest; *proper* is rather applicable to the minor concerns of life. Every thing that is done may be characterized as *right* or wrong: every thing done to others may be measured by the rule of *just* or *unjust:* in our social intercourse, as well as in our private transactions, *fitness* and *propriety* must always be consulted. As Christians, we desire to do that which is *right* in the sight of God and man; as members of civil society, we wish to be *just* in our dealings; as rational and intelligent beings, we wish to do what is *fit* and *proper* in every action, however trivial;

> Hear then my argument—confess we must
> A God there is supremely wise and *just*.
> If so, however things affect our sight,
> As sings our bard, whatever is is *right*.
> Jenyns.

'There is a great difference between good pleading and *just* composition.'—Melmoth (*Letters of Pliny*). 'Visiters are no *proper* companions in the chamber of sickness.'—Johnson.

STRAIGHT, RIGHT, DIRECT.

Straight, from the Latin *strictus*, participle of *stringo* to tighten or bind, signifies confined, that is, turning neither to the *right* nor left. *Straight* is applied, therefore, in its proper sense, to corporeal objects; a path which is *straight* is kept within a shorter space than if it were curved; 'Truth is the shortest and nearest way to our end, carrying us thither in a *straight* line.'—Tillotson. *Right* and *direct*, from the Latin *rectus*, regulated or made as it ought, are said of that which is made by the force of the understanding, or by an actual effort, what one wishes it to be: hence, the mathematician speaks of a *right* line, as the line which lies most justly between two points and has been made the basis of mathematical figures and the moralist speaks of the *right* opinion, as that which has been formed by the best rule of the understanding;

> Then from pole to pole
> He views in breadth, and without longer pause,
> Down *right* into the world's first region throws
> His flight precipitant.—Milton.

On the same ground, we speak of a *direct* answer, as that which has been framed so as to bring soonest and easiest to the point desired; 'There be, that are in nature faithful and sincere, and plain and *direct*, not crafty and involved.'—Bacon.

CANDID, OPEN, SINCERE.

Candid, in French *candide*, Latin *candidus*, from *candeo* to shine, signifies to be pure as truth itself; *open* is in Saxon *open*, French *ouvert*, German *offen*, from the preposition *up*, German *auf*, Dutch *op*, &c., because erectness is a characteristick of truth and *openness; sincere*, French *sincère*, Latin *sincerus*, probably from the Greek σὺν and κῆρ the heart, signifying dictated by or going with the heart.

Candour arises from a conscious purity of intention; *openness* from a warmth of feeling and love of communication; *sincerity* from a love of truth.

Candour obliges us to acknowledge whatever may make against ourselves; it is disinterested;

> Self-conviction is the path to virtue,
> An honourable *candour* thus adorns
> Ingenuous minds.—C. Johnson.

Openness impels us to utter whatever passes in the mind; it is unguarded; 'The fondest and firmest friendships are dissolved by such *openness* and *sincerity* as interrupt our enjoyment of our own approbation.'—Johnson. *Sincerity* prevents us from speaking what we do not think; it is positive;

> His words are bonds, his oaths are oracles,
> His love *sincere*, his thoughts immaculate.
> Shakspeare.

A *candid* man will have no reserve when *openness* is necessary: an *open* man cannot maintain a reserve at any time; a *sincere* man will maintain a reserve only as far as it is consistent with truth.

Candour wins much upon those who come in connexion with it; it removes misunderstandings and obviates differences; the want of it occasions suspicion and discontent. *Openness* gains as many enemies as friends; it requires to be well regulated not to be offensive; there is no mind so pure and disciplined that all the thoughts and feelings which it gives birth to, may or ought to be made publick. *Sincerity* is an indispensable virtue; the want of it is always mischievous and frequently fatal.

SINCERE, HONEST, TRUE, PLAIN.

Sincere (*v. Candid*) is here the most comprehensive term; *honest* (*v. Honesty*), *true*, and *plain* (*v. Even*) are but modes of *sincerity*.

Sincerity is a fundamental characteristick of the person; a man is *sincere* from the conviction of his mind: *honesty* is the expression of the feeling; it is the dictate of the heart: we look for a *sincere* friend, and an *honest* companion;

> Rustick mirth goes round,
> The simple joke that takes the shepherd's heart,
> Easily pleas'd, the long, loud laugh *sincere*.
> Thomson.

'This book of the Sybils was afterward interpolated by some Christian, who was more zealous than either *honest* or wise therein.'—Prideaux. *Truth* is a characteristick of *sincerity; for a sincere* friend is a *true* friend: but *sincerity* is a permanent quality in the character; and *truth* may be an occasional one: we cannot be *sincere* without being *true*, but we may be *true* without being *sincere;* 'Poetical ornaments destroy that character of *truth* and *plainness* which ought to characterize history.'—REYNOLDS.

> Fear not my *truth;* the moral of my wit
> is *plain* and *true.*—SHAKSPEARE.

In like manner a *sincere* man must be *plain:* since *plainness* consists in an unvarnished style, the *sincere* man will always adopt that mode of speech which expresses his sentiments most forcibly; but it is possible for a person to be occasionally *plain* who does not act from any principle of *sincerity.*

It is *plain*, therefore, that *sincerity* is the habitual principle of communicating our real sentiments; and that the *honest, true*, and *plain* are only the modes which it adopts in making the communication; *sincerity* is therefore altogether a personal quality, but the other terms are applied also to the acts, as an *honest* confession, a *true* acknowledgment, and a *plain* speech.

FRANK, CANDID, INGENUOUS, FREE, OPEN, PLAIN.

Frank, in French *franc*, German, &c. *frank*, is connected with the word *frech* bold, and *frei* free; *candid* and *open, v. Candid; ingenuous* comes from the Latin *ingenuus*, which signifies literally free-born, as distinguished from the *liberti*, who were afterward made *free:* hence the term has been employed by a figure of speech to denote nobleness of birth or character. According to Girard, *ingenu* in French is taken in a bad sense; and Dr. Trusler, in translating his article *Sincerité, franchise, naïveté, ingénuité*, has erroneously assigned the same office to our word *ingenuous;* but this, however, in its use has kept true to the original, by being always an epithet of commendation; *free* is to be found in most of the northern languages under different forms, and is supposed by Adelung to be connected with the preposition *from*, which denotes a separation or enlargement; *plain, v. Apparent*, also *Evident.*

All these terms convey the idea of a readiness to communicate and be communicated with; they are all opposed to concealment, but under different circumstances. The *frank* man is under no restraint; his thoughts and feelings are both set at ease, and his lips are ever ready to give utterance to the dictates of his heart; he has no reserve: the *candid* man has nothing to conceal; he speaks without regard to self-interest or any partial motive; he speaks nothing but the truth: the *ingenuous* man throws off all disguise; he scorns all artifice, and brings every thing to light; he speaks the whole truth. *Frankness* is acceptable in the general transactions of society; it inspires confidence, and invites communication: *candour* is of peculiar use in matters of dispute; it serves the purposes of equity, and invites to conciliation: *ingenuousness* is most wanted when there is most to conceal; it courts favour and kindness by an acknowledgment of that which is against itself.

Frankness is associated with unpolished manners, and frequently appears in men of no rank or education; sailors have commonly a deal of *frankness* about them: *candour* is the companion of uprightness; it must be accompanied with some refinement, as it acts in cases where nice discriminations are made: *ingenuousness* is the companion of a noble and elevated spirit; it exists most frequently in the unsophisticated period of youth.

Frankness displays itself in the outward behaviour; we speak of a *frank* air and *frank* manner: *candour* displays itself in the language which we adopt, and the sentiments we express: we speak of a *candid* statement, a *candid* reply: *ingenuousness* shows itself in all the words, looks, or actions: we speak of an *ingenuous* countenance, an *ingenuous* acknowledgment, an *ingenuous* answer *Frankness* and *candour* may be either habitual or occasional; *ingenuousness* is a permanent character: a disposition may be *frank*, or an air of *frankness* and *candour* may be assumed for the time; but an *ingenuous* character remains one and the same

Frankness is a voluntary effusion of the mind between equals; a man *frankly* confesses to his friend the state of his affections or circumstances; 'My own private opinion with regard to such recreations (as poetry and musick) I have given with all the *frankness* imaginable.'—STEELE. *Candour* is a debt paid to justice from one independent being to another; he who is *candid* is so from the necessity of the case; when a *candid* man feels himself to have been in an errour which affects another, he is impelled to make the only reparation in his power by acknowledging it; 'If you have made any better remarks of your own, communicate them with *candour;* if not, make use of those I present you with.'—ADDISON. *Ingenuousness* is the offering of an uncorrupted mind at the shrine of truth; it presupposes an inferiority in outward circumstances, and a motive, if not a direct necessity, for communication; the lad who does not wish to screen himself from punishment by a lie will *ingenuously* confess his offence; he who does not wish to obtain false applause will *ingenuously* disclaim his share in the performance which has obtained the applause; 'We see an *ingenuous* kind of behaviour not only make up for faults committed, but in a manner expiate them in the very commission.'—STEELE.

Free, open, and *plain* have not so high an office as the first three: *free* and *open* may be taken either in a good, bad, or indifferent sense; but seldomer in the first than in the two last senses.

The *frank, free*, and *open* man all speak without constraint; but the *frank* man is not impertinent like the *free* man, nor indiscreet like the *open* man. The *frank* man speaks only of what concerns himself; the *free* man speaks of what concerns others: a *frank* man may confess his own faults or inadvertencies; the *free* man corrects those which he sees in another: the *frank* man opens his heart from the warmth of his nature; the *free* man opens his mind from the conceit of his temper; and the *open* man says all he knows and thinks, from the inconsiderate levity of his temper.

A *frank* man is not *frank* to all, nor on all occasions; he is *frank* to his friends, or he is *frank* in his dealings with others: but the *open* man lets himself out like a running stream to all who choose to listen, and communicates trivial or important matters with equal eagerness: on the other hand, it is sometimes becoming in one to be *free* where counsel can be given with advantage and pleasure to the receiver; and it is pleasant to see an *open* behaviour, particularly in young persons, when contrasted with the odious trait of cunning and reserve;

> We cheer the youth to make his own defence,
> And *freely* tell us what he was and whence.
> DRYDEN.

'If I have abused your goodness by too much *freedom*, I hope you will attribute it to the *openness* of my temper.'—POPE.

Plainness, the last quality to be here noticed, is a virtue which, though of the humbler order, is not to be despised: it is sometimes employed like *freedom* in the task of giving counsel; but it does not convey the idea of any thing unauthorized either in matter or manner. A *free* counsellor is more ready to display his own superiority, than to direct the wanderer in his way; he rather aggravates faults, than instructs how to amend them; he seems more like a supercilious enemy than a friendly monitor: the *plain* man is free from these faults: he speaks *plainly* but truly; he gives no false colouring to his speech; it is not calculated to offend, and it may serve for improvement: it is the part of a true friend to be *plain* with another whom he sees in imminent danger. A *free* speaker is in danger of being hated; a *plain* dealer must at least be respected; 'Pope hardly drank tea without a stratagem. if at the house of his friends he wanted any accommodation, he was not willing to ask for it in *plain* terms, but would mention it remotely as something convenient.'—JOHNSON.

HEARTY, WARM, SINCERE, CORDIAL.

Hearty, which signifies having the heart in a thing, and *warm* (*v. Fire*), express a stronger feeling than *sincere; cordial*, from *cor*, signifying according to the heart, is a mixture of the *warm* and *sincere.* There are cases in which it may be peculiarly proper to be *hearty*, as when we are supporting the cause of religion and virtue; there are other cases in which it is peculiarly proper to be *warm*, as when the affections ought to be roused in favour of our friends; in all cases we ought to be *sincere*, when we express either a sentiment or a feeling; and it is peculiarly happy to be on terms of *cordial* regard with those who stand in any close relation to us. The man himself should be *hearty;* the heart should be *warm;* the professions *sincere;* and the reception *cordial.* It is also possible to speak of a *hearty* reception, but this conveys the idea of less refinement than *cordial;*

> Yet should some neighbour feel a pain
> Just in the parts where I complain,
> How many a message would he send,
> What *hearty* prayers that I should mend.—SWIFT.

'Youth is the season of *warm* and generous emotions.' —BLAIR.

> I have not since we parted been at peace,
> Nor known one joy *sincere.*—ROWE.

'With a gratitude the most *cordial*, a good man looks up to that Almighty Benefactor, who aims at no end but the happiness of those whom he blesses.'—BLAIR.

INGENUOUS, INGENIOUS.

It would not have been necessary to point out the distinction between these two words, if they had not been confounded in writing, as well as in speaking. *Ingenuous*, in Latin *ingenuus*, and *ingenious*, in Latin *ingeniosus*, are, either immediately or remotely, both derived from *ingigno* to be inborn; but the former respects the freedom of the station, and consequent nobleness of the character which is inborn; the latter respects the genius or mental powers which are inborn. Truth is coupled with freedom or nobility of birth; the *ingenuous*, therefore, bespeaks the inborn freedom, by asserting the noblest right, and following the noblest impulse, of human nature, namely, that of speaking the truth: *genius* is altogether a natural endowment, that is born with us, independent of external circumstances; the *ingenious* man, therefore, displays his powers as occasion may offer. We love the *ingenuous* character, on account of the qualities of his heart; we admire the *ingenious* man on account of the endowments of his mind. One is *ingenuous* as a man; or *ingenious* as an author: a man confesses an action *ingenuously;* he defends it *ingeniously;* 'Compare the *ingenuous* pliableness to virtuous counsels which is in youth, to the confirmed obstinacy in an old sinner.' —SOUTH.

> *Ingenious* to their ruin, every age
> Improves the arts and instruments of rage.
> WALLER.

TO APPRAISE, OR APPRECIATE, ESTIMATE, ESTEEM.

Appraise, *appreciate*, from *apprecio* and *appreciatus*, participle of *apprecio*, compounded of *ap* or *ad* and *pretium* a price, signify to set a price or value on a thing; *estimate* comes from *estimatus*, participle of *estimo* to value; to *esteem* is a variation of *estimate.*

Appraise and *appreciate* are used in precisely the same sense for setting a value on any thing according to relative circumstances; but the one is used in the proper, and the other in the figurative sense: a sworn *appraiser appraises* goods according to the condition of the article and its saleable property; the characters of men are *appreciated* by others when their good and bad qualities are justly put in a balance; 'To the finishing of his course, let every one direct his eye; and let him now *appreciate* life according to the value it will be found to have when summed up at the close.' —BLAIR. To *estimate* a thing is to get the sum of its value by calculation; to *esteem* any thing is to judge its actual and intrinsick value.

Estimate is used either in a proper or a figurative acceptation; *esteem* only in a moral sense: the expense of an undertaking, losses by fire, gains by trade, are *estimated* at a certain sum; the *estimate* may be too high or too low; 'The extent of the trade of the Greeks, how highly soever it may have been *estimated* in ancient times, was in proportion to the low condition of their marine.'—ROBERTSON The moral worth of men is often *estimated* above or below the reality according to the particular bias of the *estimator;* but there are individuals of such an unquestionable worth that they need only be known in order to be *esteemed;* 'If a lawyer were to be *esteemed* only as he uses his parts in contending for justice, and were immediately despicable when he appeared in a cause which he could not but know was an unjust one, how honourable would his character be.'—STEELE.

TO ESTIMATE, COMPUTE, RATE.

Estimate has the same signification as in the preceding article; *compute*, in Latin *computo*, or *con* and *puto* to think, signifies to put together in one's mind, *rate*, in Latin *ratus*, participle of *reor* to think, signifies to weigh in the mind.

All these terms mark the mental operation by which the sum, amount, or value of things is obtained: to *estimate* is to obtain the aggregate sum in one's mind, either by an immediate or a progressive act; to *compute* is to obtain the sum by the gradual process of putting together items; to *rate* is to fix the relative value in one's mind by deduction and comparison: a builder *estimates* the expense of building a house on a given plan; a proprietor of houses *computes* the probable diminution in the value of his property in consequence of wear and tear; the surveyor *rates* the present value of lands or houses.

In the moral acceptation they bear the same analogy to each other: some men are apt to *estimate* the adventitious privileges of birth or rank too high; 'To those who have skill to *estimate* the excellence and difficulty of this great work (Pope's translation of Homer) it must be very desirable to know how it was performed.'—JOHNSON. It would be a useful occupation for men to *compute* the loss they sustain by the idle waste of time on the one hand, and its necessarily unprofitable consumption on the other; 'From the age of sixteen the life of Pope, as an author, may be *computed.*'—JOHNSON. He who *rates* his abilities too high is in danger of despising the means which are essential to secure success; and he who *rates* them too low is apt to neglect the means, from despair of success;

> Sooner we learn and seldomer forget
> What criticks scorn, than what they highly *rate.*
> HUGHES

TO CALCULATE, COMPUTE, RECKON, COUNT, OR ACCOUNT, NUMBER.

Calculate, in Latin *calculatus*, participle of *calculo* comes from *calculus*, Greek χάλιξ a pebble; because the Greeks gave their votes, and the Romans made out their accounts, by little stones; hence it denotes the action itself of *reckoning; compute* signifies the same as in the preceding article; *reckon*, in Saxon *reccan*, Dutch *rekenen*, German *rechnen*, is not improbably derived from *row*, in Dutch *reck*, because stringing of things in a row was formerly, as it is now sometimes, the ordinary mode of *reckoning; count*, in French *compter*, is but a contraction of *computer*, but signifies a forming into an *account*, or setting down in an *account;* to *number* signifies literally to put into a *number.*

These words indicate the means by which we arrive at a certain result in regard to quantity.

To *calculate* is the generick term, the rest are specifick:* *computation* and *reckoning* are branches of *calculation*, or an application of those operations to the objects of which a result is sought: to *calculate* comprehends arithmetical operations in general, or particular applications of the science of numbers, in order to obtain a certain point of knowledge: to *compute* is to combine certain given numbers in order to learn the grand result: to *reckon* is to enumerate and set down things in the detail: to *count* is to add up the individual items contained in many different parts, in order to determine the quantity.

Calculation particularly respects the operation itself, *compute* respects the gross sum; *reckon* and *count* refer to the details. To *calculate* denotes any numerical operation in general, but in its limited sense; it is the

* Vide Roubaud: "Calculer, supputer, compter"

abstract science of figures used by mathematicians and philosophers; *computation* is a numerical estimate, a simple species of *calculation* used by historians, chronologists, and financial speculators, in drawing great results from complex sources: *reckon* and *count* are still simpler species of *calculation*, applicable to the ordinary business of life, and employed by tradesmen, mechanicks, and people in general; *reckoning* and *counting* were the first efforts made by men in acquiring a knowledge of number, quantity, or degree.

The astronomer *calculates* the return of the stars; the geometrician makes algebraick *calculations*. The Banians, Indian merchants, make prodigious *calculations* in an instant upon their thumb nails, doubtless after the manner of algebra, by signs, which the *calculator* employs as he pleases. The chronologist *computes* the times of particular events, by comparing them with those of other known events. Many persons have attempted from the prophecies to make a *computation* as to the probable time of the millennium: financiers *compute* the produce of a tax according to the measure and circumstances of its imposition. At every new consulate the Romans used to drive a nail into the wall of the Capitol, by which they *reckoned* the length of time that their state had been erected: tradesmen *reckon* their profits and losses. Children begin by *counting* on their fingers, one, two, three.

An almanack is made by *calculation*, *computation*, and *reckoning*. The rising and setting of the heavenly bodies are *calculated;* from given astronomical tables is *computed* the moment on which any celestial phenomenon may return; and by *reckoning* are determined the days on which holydays, or other periodical events fall.

Buffon, in his moral arithmetick, has *calculated* tables as guides to direct our judgements in different situations, where we have only vague probability, on which to draw our conclusions. By this we have only to *compute* what the fairest gain may cost us; how much we must lose in advance from the most favourable lottery; how much our hopes impose upon us, our cupidity cheats us, and our habits injure us.

Calculate and *reckon* are employed in a figurative sense; *compute* and *count* in an extended application of the same sense.

Calculate, *reckon*, and *count* respect mostly the future; *compute* the past.

Calculate is rather a conjectural deduction from what is, as to what may be; *computation* is a rational estimate of what has been, from what is; *reckoning* is a conclusive conviction, a complacent assurance that a thing will happen; *counting* indicates an expectation. We *calculate* on a gain; *compute* any loss sustained, or the amount of any mischief done; we *reckon* on a promised pleasure; we *count* the hours and minutes until the time of enjoyment arrives.

A spirit of *calculation* arises from the cupidity engendered by trade; it narrows the mind to the mere prospect of accumulation and self-interest; 'In this bank of fame, by an exact *calculation*, and the rules of political arithmetick, I have allotted ten hundred thousand shares; five hundred thousand of which is the due of the general; two hundred thousand I assign to the general officers; and two hundred thousand more to all the commissioned officers, from the colonels to ensigns; the remaining hundred thousand must be distributed among the non-commissioned officers and private men: according to which *computation*, I find sergeant Hall is to have one share and a fraction of two-fifths.'—Steele. *Computations* are inaccurate that are not founded upon exact numerical *calculations;* 'The time we live ought not to be *computed* by the number of years, but by the use that has been made of it.'—Addison. Inconsiderate people are apt to *reckon* on things that are very uncertain, and then lay up to themselves a store of disappointments; 'Men *reckon* themselves possessed of what their genius inclines them to, and so bend all their ambition to excel in what is out of their reach.'—Spectator. Children who are uneasy at school *count* the hours, minutes, and moments for their return home;

> The vicious *count* their years, virtuous their acts.
> Jonson.

Those who have experienced the instability of human affairs, will never *calculate* on an hour's enjoyment beyond the moment of existence. It is difficult to *compute* the loss which an army sustains upon being defeated, especially if it be obliged to make a long retreat. Those who know the human heart will never *reckon* on the assistance of professed friends in the hour of adversity. A mind that is ill at ease seeks a resource and amusement in *counting* the moments as they fly; but this is often an unhappy delusion that only adds to the bitterness of sorrow.

To *reckon*, *count* or *account*, and *number* are very nearly allied to each other in the sense of esteeming or giving to any object a place in one's account or *reckoning;* they differ mostly in the application, *reckoning* being applied to more familiar objects than the others, which are only employed in the grave style; '*Reckoning* themselves absolved by Mary's attachment to Bothwell from the engagements which they had come under when she yielded herself a prisoner, they carried her next evening, under a strong guard, to the castle of Lochleven.'—Robertson. 'Applause and admiration are by no means to be *counted* among the necessaries of life.'—Johnson. 'There is no bishop of the Church of England but *accounts* it his interest, as well as his duty, to comply with this precept of the Apostle Paul to Titus, "These things teach and exhort."'—South. 'He whose mind never pauses from the remembrance of his own sufferings, may justly be *numbered* among the most miserable of human beings.'—Johnson.

ACCOUNT, RECKONING, BILL.

Account, compounded of *ac* or *ad* and *count*, signifies to count to a person, or for a thing; an *account* is the thing so counted: *reckoning*, from the verb to *reckon*, signifies the thing reckoned up: *bill*, in Saxon *bill*, in all probability comes from the Swedish *byla*, to build, signifying a written contract for building vessels, which in German is still called a *beilbrief;* hence it has been employed to express various kinds of written documents. These words, which are very similar in signification, may frequently be substituted for one another.

Account is the generick, the others the specifick terms: a *reckoning* and *bill* is an *account*, though not always *vice versâ: account* expresses the details, with the sum of them counted up; *reckoning* implies the register and rotation of the things to be reckoned up: *bill* denotes the details, with their particular charges. An *account* should be correct, containing neither more nor less than is proper; a *reckoning* should be explicit, leaving nothing unnoticed as to dates and names; a *bill* should be fair.

We speak of keeping an *account*, of coming to a *reckoning*, of sending in a *bill*. Customers have an *account* with their tradespeople; masters have a *reckoning* with their workpeople; tradesmen send in their *bills* at stated periods.

Account, from the extensive use of the term, is applicable to every thing that is noted down; the particulars of which are considered worthy of notice individually or collectively: merchants keep their *accounts;* an *account* is taken at the Custom House of all that goes in and out of the kingdom; an *account* is taken of all transactions, of the weather, of natural phenomena, and whatever is remarkable;

> At many times I brought in my *accounts*,
> Laid them before you; you would throw them off,
> And say you found them in my honesty.
> Shakspeare.

Reckoning, as a particular term, is more partial in its use: it is mostly confined to the dealings of men with one another; in which sense it is superseded by the preceding term, and now serves to express only an explanatory enumeration, which may be either verbal or written; 'Merchant with some rudeness demanded a room, and was told that there was a good fire in the next parlour, which the company were about to leave, being then paying their *reckoning*.'—Johnson. *Bill*, as implying something charged or engaged, is used not only in a mercantile but a legal sense: hence we speak of a *bill* of lading; a *bill* of parcels; a *bill* of exchange; a *bill* of indictment, or a *bill* in parliament; 'Ordinary expense ought to be limited by a man's estate, and ordered to the best, that the *bills* may be less than the estimation abroad.'—Bacon.

CALENDAR, ALMANACK, EPHEMERIS.

Calendar comes from *calendæ*, the Roman name for the first days of every month; *almanack*, that is *al* and *mana*, signifies properly the reckoning or thing reckoned, from the Arabick *mana* and Hebrew מנה to reckon; *ephemeris*, in Greek ἐφημερὶς, from ἐπι and ημερα the day, implies that which happens by the day.

These terms denote a date-book: but the *calendar* is a book which registers events under every month; the *almanack* is a book which registers times, or the divisions of the year; and an *ephemeris* is a book which registers the planetary movements every day. An *almanack* may be a *calendar*, and an *ephemeris* may be both an *almanack* and a *calendar;* but every *almanack* is not a *calendar*, nor every *calendar* an *almanack*. The Gardener's *calendar* is not an *almanack*, and sheet *almanacks* are seldom *calendars:* likewise the nautical *ephemeris* may serve as an *almanack*, although not as a *calendar;* 'He was sitting upon the ground upon a little straw, in the farthest corner of his dungeon, which was alternately his chair and bed: a little *calendar* of small sticks were laid at the head, notched all over with the dismal nights and days he had passed there.'—STERNE. 'When the reformers were purging the *calendar* of legions of visionary saints, they took due care to defend the niches of real martyrs from profanation. They preserved the holy festivals which had been consecrated for many ages to the great luminaries of the church, and at once paid proper observance to the memory of the good, and fell in with the proper humour of the vulgar, which loves to rejoice and mourn at the discretion of the *almanack*.'—WALPOLE. 'That two or three suns or moons appear in any man's life or reign, it is not worth the wonder; but that the same should fall out at a remarkable time or point of some decisive action, that those two should make but one line in the book of fate, and stand together in the great *ephemerides* of God, besides the philosophical assignment of the cause, it may admit a Christian apprehension in the signality.'—BROWN'S VULGAR ERRORS.

COUPLE, BRACE, PAIR.

Couple, in French *couple*, comes from the Latin *copulo* to join or tie together, *copula*, in Hebrew כבל a rope or a shackle, signifying things tied together; and as two things are with most convenience bound together, it has by custom been confined to this number: *brace*, from the French *bras* arm, signifies things locked together after the manner of the folded arms, which on that account are confined to the number of two: *pair*, in French *paire*, Latin *par* equal, signifies things that are equal, which can with propriety be said only of two things with regard to each other.

From the above illustration of these terms, it is clear that the number of two, which is included in all them, is, with regard to the first, entirely arbitrary; of that with regard to the second, it arises from the nature of the junction; and with regard to the third, it arises altogether from the nature of the objects: *couples* and *braces* are made by *coupling* and *bracing;* *pairs* are either so of themselves, or are made so by others: *couples* and *braces* always require a junction in order to make them complete; *pairs* require similarity only to make them what they are: *couples* are joined by a foreign tie; *braces* are produced by a peculiar mode of junction with the objects themselves.

Couple and *pair* are said of persons or things; *brace* in particular cases only of animals or things, except in the burlesque style, where it may be applied to persons. When used for persons, the word *couple* has relation to the marriage tie; the word *pair* to the association or the moral union: the former term is therefore more appropriate when speaking of those who are soon to be married, or have just entered that state; the latter when speaking of those who are already fixed in that state: most *couples* that are joined together are equally happy in prospect, but not so in the completion of their wishes: it is the lot of comparatively very few to claim the title of the happy *pair;* 'Scarce any *couple* comes together, but their nuptials are declared in the newspaper with encomiums on each party'—JOHNSON.

> Your fortune, happy *pair*, already made,
> Leaves you no farther wish.—DRYDEN.

The term *pair* may be used in the burlesque style for any two persons allied to each other by similarity of sentiment or otherwise;

> Dear Sheridan! a gentle *pair*
> Of Gaulstown lads (for such they are),
> Besides a *brace* of grave divines,
> Adore the smoothness of your lines.—SWIFT

When used for things, *couple* is promiscuously employed in familiar discourse for any two things put together; 'In the midst of these sorrows which I had in my heart, methought there passed by me a *couple* of coaches with purple liveries.'—ADDISON. *Brace* is used by sportsmen for birds which are shot, and supposed to be locked together; by sailors for a part of their tackling, which is folded crosswise; as also in common life for an article of convenience crossed in a singular way, which serves to keep the dress of men in its proper place;

> First hunter then, pursu'd a gentle *brace*,
> Goodliest of all the forest, hart and hind.—MILTON.

Pair is of course restricted in its application to such objects only as are really *paired;*

> Six wings he wore, to shade
> His lineaments divine; the *pair* that clad
> Each shoulder broad came mantling o'er his breast
> With regal ornament.—MILTON.

RATE, PROPORTION, RATIO.

Rate signifies the thing rated, or the measure at which it is rated; *ratio* has the same original meaning as *rate; proportion*, v. *Proportionate.*

Rate and *ratio* are in sense species of *proportion;* that is, they are supposed or estimated *proportions*, in distinction from *proportions* that lie in the nature of things. The first term, *rate*, is employed in ordinary concerns; a person receives a certain sum weekly at the *rate* of a certain sum yearly; 'At Ephesus and Athens, Anthony lived at his usual *rate* in all manner of luxury.'—PRIDEAUX. *Ratio* is applied only to numbers and calculations; as two is to four, so is four to eight, and eight to sixteen; the *ratio* in this case being double; 'The rate of interest (to lenders) is generally in a compound *ratio* formed out of the inconvenience and the hazard.'—BLACKSTONE. *Proportion* is employed in matters of science, and in all cases where the two more specifick terms are not admissible; the beauty of an edifice depends upon observing the doctrine of *proportions;* in the disposing of soldiers a certain regard must be had to *proportion* in the height and size of the men; 'Repentance cannot be effectual but as it bears some *proportion* to sin.'—SOUTH.

PROPORTIONATE, COMMENSURATE, ADEQUATE.

Proportionate, from the Latin *proportio*, compounded of *pro* and *portio*, signifies having a *portion* suitable to, or in agreement with, some other object; *commensurate*, from the Latin *commensus* or *commetior* signifies measuring in accordance with some other thing, being suitable in measure to something else; *adequate*, in Latin *adæquatus*, participle of *adæquo*, signifies made level with some other body.

Proportionate is here a term of general use; the others are particular terms, employed in a similar sense, in regard to particular objects: that is *proportionate* which rises as a thing rises, and falls as a thing falls; that is *commensurate* which is made to rise to the same measure or degree; that is *adequate* which is made to come up to the height of another thing. *Proportionate* is employed either in the proper or improper sense; in all recipes and prescriptions of every kind, *proportionate* quantities must always be taken; when the task increases in difficulty and complication, a *proportionate* degree of labour and talent must be employed upon it; 'All envy is *proportionate* to desire.'—JOHNSON. *Commensurate* and *adequate* are employed only in the moral sense; the former in regard to matters of distribution, the latter in regard to the equalizing of powers: a person's recompense should in some measure be *commensurate* with his labour and deserts; 'Where the matter is not *commensurate* to the words, all speaking is but tautology.'—SOUTH. A person's resources should be *adequate* to the work he is engaged in; 'Outward actions are not *adequate* expressions of our virtues.'—ADDISON.

DISPARITY, INEQUALITY.

Disparity, from *dis* and *par*, in Greek παρά with or by, signifies an unfitness of objects to be by one another; *inequality*, from the Latin *æquus* even, signifies having no regularity.

Disparity applies to two or more objects which should meet or stand in coalition with each other; *inequality* is applicable to objects that are compared with each other: the *disparity* of age, situation, and circumstances, is to be considered with regard to persons entering into a matrimonial connexion; the *inequality* in the portion of labour which is to be performed by two persons, is a ground for the *inequality* of their recompense: there is a great *inequality* in the chance of success, where there is a *disparity* of acquirements in rival candidates: the *disparity* between David and Goliah was such as to render the success of the former more strikingly miraculous; 'Between Elihu and the rest of Job's familiars, the greatest *disparity* was but in years.'—HOOKER. The *inequality* in the conditions of men is not attended with a corresponding *inequality* in their happiness; '*Inequality* of behaviour, either in prosperity or adversity, are alike ungraceful in man that is born to die.'—STEELE.

SYMMETRY, PROPORTION.

Symmetry, in Latin *symmetria*, Greek συμμετρία, from σὺν and μέτρον, signifies a measure that accords; *proportion*, in Latin *proportio*, compounded of *pro* and *portio*, signifies every portion or part according with the other, or with the whole.

The signification of these terms is obviously the same, namely, a due admeasurement of the parts to each other and to the whole: but *symmetry* seems to convey the idea of a beautiful adaptation; and *proportion* is applied in general to every thing which admits of dimensions and an adaptation of the parts: hence we speak of *symmetry* of feature, or *symmetry* abstractedly;

She by whose lines *proportion* should be
Examin'd, measure of all *symmetry*;
Whom had that ancient seen, who thought souls made
Of harmony, he would at next have said
That harmony was she.—DONNE.

But we say *proportion* of limbs, the *proportion* of the head to the body; 'The inventors of stuffed hips had a better eye for due *proportion* than to add to a redundancy, because in some cases it was convenient to fill up a vacuum.'—CUMBERLAND.

EQUAL, EVEN, EQUABLE, LIKE, OR ALIKE, UNIFORM.

Equal, in Latin *æqualis*, comes from *æquus*, and probably the Greek εἰκὸς, *similis*, like; *even* is in Saxon *efen*, German *eben*, Sweden *efwen*, *jafn*, or *aem*, Greek οἷος like; *equable*, in Latin *equabilis*, signifies susceptible of *equality*; *like*, in Dutch *lik*, Saxon *gelig*, German *gleich*, Gothick *tholick*, Latin *talis*, Greek τηλίκος such as; *uniform*, compounded of *unus* one and *forma* form, bespeaks its own meaning.

All these epithets are opposed to difference. *Equal* is said of degree, quantity, number, and dimensions, as *equal* in years, of an *equal* age, an *equal* height: *even* is said of the surface and position of bodies; a board is made *even* with another board; the floor or the ground is *even*: *like* is said of accidental qualities in things, as *alike* in colour or in feature: *uniform* is said of things only as to their fitness to correspond; those which are *unlike* in colour, shape, or make, or not *uniform*, cannot be made to match as pairs: *equable* is used only in the moral acceptation, in which all the others are likewise employed.

As moral qualities admit of degree, they admit of *equality*; justice is dealt out in *equal* portions to the rich and the poor; God looks with an *equal* eye on all mankind. Some men are *equal* to others in external circumstances; '*Equality* is the life of conversation, and he is as much out who assumes to himself any part above another, as he who considers himself below the rest of society.'—STEELE. As the natural path is rendered *uneven* by high and low ground, so the *evenness* of the temper, in the figurative sense, is destroyed by changes of humour, by elevations and depressions of the spirits; 'Good-nature is insufficient (in the marriage state) unless it be steady and *uniform*, and accompanied with an *evenness* of temper.'—SPECTATOR. The *equability* of the mind is hurt by the vicissitudes of life, from prosperous to adverse; 'There is also moderation in toleration of fortune which of Tully is called *equabilitie*.'—SIR T. ELYOT. This term may also be applied to motion, as the *equable* motion of the planets; and figuratively to the style; 'In Swift's works is found an *equable* tenour of easy language, which rather trickles than flows.'—JOHNSON. *Even* and *equable* are applied to the same mind in relation to itself; *like* or *alike* is used to the minds of two or more: hence we say they are *alike* in disposition, in sentiment, in wishes, &c.;

E'en now as familiar as in life he came;
Alas! how diff'rent, yet how *like* the same.—POPE.

Uniform is applied to the temper, habits, character, or conduct; hence a man is said to preserve a *uniformity* of behaviour towards those whom he commands. The term may also be applied to the modes which may be adopted by men in society; 'The only doubt is about the manner of their unity, how far churches are bound to be *uniform* in their ceremonies, and what way they ought to take for that purpose.'—HOOKER. Friendship requires that the parties be *equal* in station, *alike* in mind, and *uniform* in their conduct: wisdom points out to us an *even* tenour of life, from which we cannot depart either to the right or to the left, without disturbing our peace; it is one of her maxims that we should not lose the *equability* of our temper under the most trying circumstances.

FLAT, LEVEL.

Flat, in German *flach*, is connected with *platt* broad, and that with the Latin *latus*, and Greek πλατὺς; *level*, in all probability from *libella* and *libra* a balance, signifies the evenness of a balance.

Flat is said of a thing with regard to itself; it is opposed to the round or protuberant; *level* as it respects another; the former is opposed to the uneven: a country is *flat* which has no elevation; a wall is *level* with the roof of a house when it rises to the height of the roof; 'A *flat* can hardly look well on paper.'—COUNTESS OF HERTFORD.

At that black hour, which gen'ral horrour sheds
On the low *level* of the inglorious throng.—YOUNG

EVEN, SMOOTH, LEVEL, PLAIN.

Even (*v. Equal*) and *smooth*, which is in all probability connected with smear, are both opposed to roughness: but that which is *even* is free only from great roughnesses or irregularities; that which is *smooth* is free from every degree of roughness, however small: a board is *even* which has no knots or holes; it is not *smooth* unless its surface be an entire plane: the ground is said to be *even*, but not *smooth*; the sky is *smooth*, but not *even*; 'When we look at a naked wall, from the *evenness* of the object the eye runs along its whole space, and arrives quickly at its termination.'—BURKE. 'The effects of a rugged and broken surface seem stronger than where it is *smooth* and polished.'—BURKE.

Even is to *level* (*v. Flat*), when applied to the ground, what *smooth* is to *even*: the *even* is free from protuberances and depressions on its exteriour surface; the *level* is free from rises or falls: a path is said to be *even*; a meadow is *level*: ice may be *level*, though it is not *even*; a walk up the side of a hill may be *even*, although the hill itself is the reverse of a *level*: the *even* is said of that which unites and forms one uninterrupted surface; but the *level* is said of things which are at a distance from each other, and are discovered by the eye to be in a parallel line: hence the floor of a room is *even* with regard to itself; it is *level* with that of another room;

The top is *level*, an offensive seat
Of war.—DRYDEN

'A blind man would never be able to imagine how the several prominences and depressions of a human body could be shown on a *plain* piece of canvass that has on it no *unevenness*.'—ADDISON.

Evenness respects the surface of bodies; *plainness* respects the direction of bodies and their freedom from external obstructions: a path is *even* which has no indentures or footmarks; a path is *plain* which is not stopped up or interrupted by wood, water, or any other thing intervening.

When applied figuratively, these words preserve their analogy: an *even* temper is secured from all violent changes of humour; a *smooth* speech is divested of every thing which can ruffle the temper of others: but the former is always taken in a good sense; and the latter mostly in a bad sense, as evincing an illicit design or a purpose to deceive; 'A man who lives in a state of vice and impenitence can have no title to that *evenness* and tranquillity of mind which is the health of the soul.'—ADDISON.

> This *smooth* discourse and mild behaviour oft
> Conceal a traitor.—ADDISON.

A *plain* speech, on the other hand, is divested of every thing obscure or figurative, and is consequently a speech free from disguise and easy to be understood;

> Express thyself in *plain*, not doubtful, words,
> That ground for quarrels or disputes affords.
> DENHAM.

Even and *level* are applied to conduct or condition; the former as regards ourselves; the latter as regards others: he who adopts an *even* course of conduct is in no danger of putting himself upon a *level* with those who are otherwise his inferiours; 'Falsehood turns all above us into tyranny and barbarity; and all of the same *level* with us into discord.'—SOUTH.

ODD, UNEVEN.

Odd, probably a variation from *add*, seems to be a mode of the *uneven*; both are opposed to the even, but *odd* is only said of that which has no fellow; the *uneven* is said of that which does not square or come to an even point: of numbers we say that they are either *odd* or *uneven*; but of gloves, shoes, and every thing which is made to correspond, we say that they are *odd*, when they are single; but that they are *uneven* when they are not exactly alike: in like manner a plank is *uneven* which has an unequal surface, or disproportionate dimensions; but a piece of wood is *odd* which will not match nor suit with any other piece.

VALUE, WORTH, RATE, PRICE.

Value, from the Latin *valeo* to be strong, respects those essential qualities of a thing which constitute its strength; *worth*, in German *werth*, from *währen* to perceive, signifies that good which is experienced or felt to exist in a thing; *rate* signifies the same as under the article *Rate, proportion*; *price*, in Latin *pretium*, from the Greek πράσσω to sell, signifies what a thing is sold for.

Value is a general and indefinite term applied to whatever is really good or conceived as such in a thing: the *worth* is that good only which is conceived or known as such. The *value* therefore of a thing is as variable as the humours and circumstances of men; it may be nothing or something very great in the same object at the same time in the eyes of different men;

> Life has no *value* as an end, but means:
> An end deplorable! A means divine.—YOUNG.

The *worth* is however that *value* which is acknowledged; it is therefore something more fixed and permanent: we speak of the *value* of external objects which are determined by taste; but the *worth* of things as determined by rule. The *value* of a book that is out of print is fluctuating and uncertain; but its real *worth* may not be more than what it would fetch for waste paper;

> Pay
> No moment, but in purchase of its *worth*;
> And what its *worth* ask death-beds.—YOUNG.

The *rate* and *price* are the measures of that *value* or *worth*; the former in a general, the latter in a particular application to mercantile transactions. Whatever we give in exchange for another thing, whether according to a definite or an indefinite estimation, that is said to be done at a certain *rate*; thus we purchase pleasure at a dear *rate*, when it is at the expense of our health, 'If you will take my humour as it runs, you shall have hearty thanks into the bargain, for taking it off at such a *rate*.'—EARL OF SHAFTESBURY. *Price* is the *rate* of exchange estimated by coin or any other medium; hence *price* is a fixed *rate*, and may be figuratively applied in that sense to moral objects; as when health is expressly sacrificed to pleasure, it may be termed the *price* of pleasure;

> The soul's high *price*
> Is writ in all the conduct of the skies.—YOUNG.

TO VALUE, PRIZE, ESTEEM.

To *value* is in the literal sense to fix the real *value* of a thing; to *prize*, signifying to fix a *price*, and *esteem* (*v. Esteem*), are both modes of *valuing*. In the extended sense, to *value* may mean to ascertain the relative or supposed *value* of a thing: in this sense men *value* gold above silver, or an appraiser *values* goods. To *value* may either be applied to material or spiritual subjects, to corporeal or mental actions: *prize* and *esteem* are taken only as mental actions; the former in reference to sensible or moral objects, the latter only to moral objects: we may *value* books according to their market price, or we may *value* them according to their contents; we *prize* books only for their contents, in which sense *prize* is a much stronger term than *value*; we also *prize* men for their usefulness to society;

> The *prize*, the beauteous *prize*, I will resign,
> So dearly *valu'd*, and so justly mine.—POPE.

We *esteem* men for their moral characters; 'Nothing makes women *esteemed* by the opposite sex more than chastity; whether it be that we always *prize* those most who are hardest to come at, or that nothing besides chastity, with its collateral attendants, fidelity and constancy, gives a man a property in the person he loves.'—ADDISON.

COST, EXPENSE, PRICE, CHARGE.

Cost, in German *kost* or *kosten*, from the Latin *gustare* to taste, signifies originally support, and by an extended sense what is given for support; *expense* is compounded of *ex* and *pense*, in Latin *pensus* participle of *pendo* to pay, signifying the thing paid or given out; *price*, from the Latin *pretium*, and the Greek πράσσω to sell, signifies the thing given for what is bought; *charge*, from to *charge*, signifies the thing laid on as a *charge*.

The *cost* is what a thing *costs* or occasions to be laid out; the *expense* is that which is actually laid out; the *price* is that which a thing may fetch or cause to be laid out; the *charge* is that which is required to be laid out. As a *cost* commonly comprehends an *expense*, the terms are on various occasions used indifferently for each other: we speak of counting the *cost* or counting the *expense* of doing any thing; at a great *cost* or at a great *expense*: on the other hand, of venturing to do a thing to one's *cost*, of growing wise at other people's *expense*.

The *cost* and the *price* have respect to the thing and its supposed value; the *expense* and the *charge* depend on the option of the persons. The *cost* of a thing must precede the *price*, and the *expense* must succeed the *charge*; we can never set a *price* on any thing until we have ascertained what it has *cost* us; nor can we know or defray the *expense* until the *charge* be made. There may, however, frequently be a *price* where there is no *cost*, and *vice versâ*; there may also be an *expense* where there is no *charge*; but there cannot be a *charge* without an *expense*; 'Would a man build for eternity, that is, in other words, would he be saved, let him consider with himself what *charges* he is willing to be at that he may be so.'—SOUTH. *Costs* in suit often exceed in value and amount the thing contended for: the *price* of things depends on their relative value in the eyes of others: what *costs* nothing sometimes fetches a high *price*; and other things cannot obtain a *price* equal to the first *cost*. *Expenses* vary with modes of living and men's desires; whoever wants much, or wants that which is not easily obtained, will have many *expenses* to defray; when the *charges* are exorbitant the *expenses* must necessarily bear a proportion.

Between the epithets *costly* and *expensive* there is the same distinction. Whatever is *costly* is naturally *expensive*, but not *vice versâ*. Articles of furniture, of luxury, or indulgence, are *costly*, either from their variety or their intrinsick value; every thing is *expensive* which is attended with much *expense*, whether of little or great value. Jewels are *costly;* travelling is *expensive*. The *costly* treasures of the East are imported into Europe for the gratification of those who cannot be contented with the produce of their native soil: those who indulge themselves in *expensive* pleasures often lay up in store for themselves much sorrow and repentance in the time to come.

In the moral acceptation, the attainment of an object is said to *cost* much pains;

> The real patriot bears his private wrongs,
> Rather than right them at the publick *cost*,
>
> BELLER.

A thing is persisted in at the *expense* of health, of honour, or of life; 'If ease and politeness be only attainable at the *expense* of sincerity in the men, and chastity in the women, I flatter myself there are few of my readers who would not think the purchase made at too high a *price*.'—ABERCROMBY.

UNWORTHY, WORTHLESS.

Unworthy is a term of less reproach than *worthless*, for the former signifies not to be *worthy* of praise or honour; the latter signifies to be without any worth, and consequently in the fullest sense bad. It may be a mark of modesty or humility to say that I am an *unworthy* partaker of your kindness; but it would be folly and extravagance to say, that I am a *worthless* partaker of your kindness. There are many *unworthy* members in every religious community; but every society that is conducted upon proper principles will take care to exclude *worthless* members. In regard to one another we are often *unworthy* of the distinctions or privileges we enjoy; in regard to our Maker we are all *unworthy* of his goodness, for we are all *worthless* in his eyes;

> Since in dark sorrow I my days did spend,
> Till now disdaining his *unworthy* end.
>
> DENHAM.

'The school of Socrates was at one time deserted by every body, except Æschines the parasite of the tyrant Dionysius, and the most *worthless* man living.'—CUMBERLAND.

VALUABLE, PRECIOUS, COSTLY.

Valuable signifies fit to be *valued; precious*, having a high price; *costly*, *costing* much money. *Valuable* expresses directly the idea of *value; precious* and *costly* express the same idea indirectly: on the other hand, that which is *valuable* is only said to be fit or deserving of *value;* but *precious* and *costly* denote that which is highly *valuable*, according to the ordinary measure of *valuing* objects, that is, by the *price* they bear: hence, the two latter express the idea much more strongly than the former. A book is *valuable* according to its contents, or according to the estimate which men set upon it, either individually or collectively; 'What an absurd thing it is to pass over all the *valuable* parts of a man, and fix our attention on his infirmities.'—ADDISON. The Bible is the only *precious* book in the world that has intrinsick *value*, that is, set above all *price;* 'It is no improper comparison that a thankful heart is like a box of *precious* ointment.'—HOWELL. There are many *costly* things, which are only *valuable* to the individuals who are disposed to expend money upon them; 'Christ is sometimes pleased to make the profession of himself *costly*.'—SOUTH.

INTRINSICK, REAL, GENUINE, NATIVE.

Intrinsick, in Latin *intrinsecus*, signifies on the inside, that is, lying in the thing itself; *real*, from the Latin *res*, signifies belonging to the very thing: *genuine*, in Latin *genuinus* from *geno* or *gigno* to bring forth, signifies actually brought forth, or springing out of a thing; *native*, in Latin *nativus* and *natus* born, signifies actually born, or arising from a thing.

The value of a thing is either *intrinsick* or *real:* but the *intrinsick* value is said in regard to its extrinsick value; the *real* value in regard to the artificial: the *intrinsick* value of a book is that which it will fetch when sold in a regular way, in opposition to the extrinsick value, as being the gift of a friend, a particular edition, or a particular type: the *real* value of a book [illegible] proper sense, lies in the fineness of the paper, [illegible] costliness of its binding; and, in the improper sense, it lies in the excellence of its contents, in opposition to the artificial value which it acquires in the minds of bibliomaniacks from being a scarce edition; 'Men, however distinguished by external accidents or *intrinsick* qualities, have all the same wants, the same pains, and, as far as the senses are consulted, the same pleasures.'—JOHNSON. 'You have settled, by an economy as perverted as the policy, two establishments of government, one *real*, the other fictitious.'—BURKE.

The worth of a man is either *genuine* or *native:* the *genuine* worth of a man lies in the excellence of his moral character, as opposed to his adventitious worth, which he acquires from the possession of wealth, power, and dignity; his *native* worth is that which is inborn in him, and natural, in opposition to the meretricious and borrowed worth which he may derive from his situation, his talent, or his efforts to please;

> His *genuine* and less guilty wealth t' explore.
> Search not his bottom, but survey his shore.
>
> DENHAM.

'How lovely does the human mind appear in its *native* purity.'—EARL OF CHATHAM.

An accurate observer will always discriminate between the *intrinsick* and extrinsick value of every thing; a wise man will always appreciate things according to their *real* value; the most depraved man will sometimes be sensible of *genuine* worth when it displays itself; it is always pleasant to meet with those unsophisticated characters whose *native* excellence shines forth in all their words, looks, and actions.

EXTRANEOUS, EXTRINSICK, FOREIGN.

Extraneous, compounded of *exterraneus*, or *ex* and *terra*, signifies out of the land, not belonging to it; *extrinsick*, in Latin *extrinsecus*, compounded of *extra* and *secus*, signifies outward, external; *foreign*, from the Latin *foris* out of doors, signifies not belonging to the family, tribe, or people.

The *extraneous* is that which forms no necessary or natural part of any thing: the *extrinsick* is that which forms a part or has a connexion, but only in an indirect form; it is not an inherent or component part: the *foreign* is that which forms no part whatever, and has no kind of connexion. A work is said to contain *extraneous* matter, which contains much matter not necessarily belonging to, or illustrative of the subject. a work is said to have *extrinsick* merit when it borrows its value from local circumstances, in distinction from the intrinsick merit, or that which lies in the contents.

Extraneous and *extrinsick* have a general and abstract sense; but *foreign* has a particular signification; they always pass over to some object either expressed or understood. hence we say *extraneous* ideas, or *extrinsick* worth; but that a particular mode of acting is *foreign* to the general plan pursued. Anecdotes of private individuals would be *extraneous* matter in a general history; 'That which makes me believe is something *extraneous* to the thing that I believe.'—LOCKE. The respect and credit which men gain from their fellow-citizens by an adherence to rectitude is the *extrinsick* advantage of virtue, in distinction from the peace of a good conscience and the favour of God, which are its intrinsick advantages; 'Affluence and power are advantages *extrinsick* and adventitious.'—JOHNSON. It is *foreign* to the purpose of one who is making an abridgment of a work, to enter into details in any particular part;

> For loveliness
> Needs not the aid of *foreign* ornaments;
> But is when unadorn'd adorn'd the most.
>
> THOMSON.

DESERT, MERIT, WORTH.

Desert, from *deserve*, in Latin *deservio*, signifies to do service or be serviceable; *merit*, in Latin *meritus*, participle of *mereor*, comes from the Greek μείρω to distribute, because *merit* serves as a rule for distributing or apportioning; *worth*, in German *werth*, is connected with *würde* dignity, and *bürde* a burden, because one bears *worth* as a thing attached to the person.

Desert is taken for that which is good or bad; *merit* for that which is good only. We *deserve* praise or blame: we *merit* a reward. The *desert* consists in the action, work, or service performed; the *merit* has regard to the character of the agent or the nature of the action. The person does not *deserve* the recompense until he has performed the service; he does not *merit* approbation if he has not done his part well.

Deserve is a term of ordinary import; *merit* applies to objects of greater moment: the former includes matters of personal and physical gratification; the latter those altogether of an intellectual nature. Children are always acting so as to *deserve* either reproof or commendation, reward or punishment;

The beauteous champion views with marks of fear,
Smit with a conscious sense, retires behind,
And shuns the fate he well *deserv'd* to find.—POPE.

Candidates for publick applause or honours conceive they have frequent occasion to complain that they are not treated according to their *merits;*

Praise from a friend or censure from a foe
Are lost on hearers that our *merits* know.—POPE.

Criminals cannot always be punished according to their *deserts;* a noble mind is not contented with barely obtaining, it seeks to *merit* what it obtains.

The idea of value, which is prominent in the signification of the term *merit*, renders it closely allied to that of *worth*. The man of *merit* looks to the advantages which shall accrue to himself; the man of *worth* contented with the consciousness of what he possesses in himself: *merit* respects the attainments or qualifications of a man; *worth* respects his moral qualities only. It is possible therefore for a man to have great *merit* and little or no *worth*. He who has great powers, and uses them for the advantage of himself or others, is a man of *merit;*

She valued nothing less
Than titles, figures, shape, and dress;
That *merit* should be chiefly plac'd
In judgement, knowledge, wit, and taste.—SWIFT.

He only who does good from a good motive is a man of *worth;*

To birth or office no respect be paid,
Let *worth* determine here.—POPE.

We look for *merit* among men in the discharge of their several offices or duties; we look for *worth* in their social capacities.

From these words are derived the epithets *deserved* and *merited*, in relation to what we receive from others; and *deserving*, *meritorious*, *worthy*, and *worth*, in regard to what we possess in ourselves: a treatment is *deserved* or *undeserved;* reproofs are *merited* or *unmerited:* the harsh treatment of a master is easier to be borne when it is *undeserved* than when it is *deserved;* the reproaches of a friend are very severe when *unmerited*.

A person is *deserving* on account of his industry or perseverance; 'A man has frequent opportunities of mitigating the fierceness of a party; or doing justice to the character of a *deserving* man.'—ADDISON. An artist is *meritorious* on account of his professional abilities, or a statesman in the discharge of his duties; 'He carried himself *meritoriously* in foreign employments in time of the interdict, which held up his credit among the patriots.'—WALTON. But for the most part actions, services, &c. are said to be *meritorious;* 'Pilgrimages to Rome were represented as the most *meritorious* acts of devotion.'—HUME. A citizen is *worthy* on account of his benevolence and uprightness;

Then the last *worthies* of declining Greece,
Fate call'd to glory, in unequal times,
Pensive appear.—THOMSON.

One person *deserves* to be well paid and encouraged; another *merits* the applause which is bestowed on him; a third is *worthy* of confidence and esteem from all men. Between *worthy* and *worth* there is this difference, that the former is said of the intrinsick and moral qualities, the latter of extrinsick qualities: a *worthy* man possesses that which calls for the esteem of others, but a man is *worth* the property which he can call his own: so in like manner a subject may be *worthy* the attention of a writer, or a thing may not be *worth* the while to consider.

COMPENSATION, SATISFACTION, AMENDS, REMUNERATION, RECOMPENSE, REQUITAL, REWARD.

The first three of these terms are employed to express a return for some evil; *remuneration*, *recompense*, and *requital*, a return for some good; *reward*, a return for either good or evil.

Compensation, Latin *compensatio*, compounded of *com* and *pensatio*, *pensus* and *pendo* to pay, signifies the paying what has become due; *satisfaction*, from *satisfy*, signifies the thing that satisfies, or makes up in return; *amends*, from the word to *amend*, signifies the thing that makes good what has been bad; *remuneration*, from *remunerate*, Latin *remuneratus* or *remunero*, compounded of *re* and *munus* an office or service, signifies what is given in return for a service; *recompense*, compounded of *re* and *compense*, signifies the thing paid back as an equivalent; *requital*, compounded of *re* and *quital*, or *quittal*, from *quit*, signifies the making one's self clear by a return; *reward* is probably connected with regard, implying to take cognizance of the deserts of any one.

A *compensation* is something real; it is made for some positive injury sustained; justice requires that it should be equal in value, if not like in kind, to that which is lost or injured;

All other debts may *compensation* find,
But love is strict, and will be paid in kind.
DRYDEN.

A *satisfaction* may be imaginary, both as to the injury and the return; it is given for personal injuries, and depends on the disposition of the person to be *satisfied:* *amends* is real, but not always made so much for injuries done to others, as for offences committed by ourselves. Sufferers ought to have a *compensation* for the injuries they have sustained through our means, but there are injuries, particularly those which wound the feelings, for which there can be no *compensation:* tenacious and quarrelsome people demand *satisfaction;* their offended pride is not *satisfied* without the humiliation of their adversary: an *amends* is honourable which serves to repair a fault; the best *amends* which an offending person can make is to acknowledge his errour, and avoid a repetition: Christianity enjoins upon its followers to do good, even to its enemies; but there is a thing called honour, which impels some men after they have insulted their friends to give them the *satisfaction* of shedding their blood; this is termed an honourable *amends;* but will the survivors find any *compensation* in such an *amends* for the loss of a husband, a father, or a brother? Not to offer any *compensation* to the utmost of our power, for any injury done to another, evinces a gross meanness of character, and selfishness of disposition: *satisfaction* can seldom be demanded with any propriety for any personal affront; although the true Christian will refuse no *satisfaction* which is not inconsistent with the laws of God and man. As respects the offence of man towards his Maker, nothing but the atonement of our Saviour could be a *satisfaction;*

Die he or justice must; unless for him
Some other able, and as willing, pay
The rigid *satisfaction*, death for death.—MILTON.

Compensation often denotes a return for services done, in which sense it approaches still nearer to *remuneration*, *recompense*, and *requital:* but the first two are obligatory; the latter are gratuitous. *Compensation* is an act of justice; the service performed involves a debt; the omission of paying it becomes an injury to the performer: the labourer is worthy of his hire; the time and strength of a poor man ought not to be employed without his receiving a *compensation*. *Remuneration* is a higher species of *compensation;* it is a matter of equity dependent upon a principle of honour in those who make it; it differs from the ordinary *compensation*, both in the nature of the service, and of the return. *Compensation* is made for bodily labour and menial offices; *remuneration* for mental exertions, for literary, civil, or political offices: *compensation* is made to inferiours, or subordinate persons; *remuneration* to equals, and even superiours in education and birth, though not in wealth: a *compensation* is prescribed by a certain ratio; *remuneration* depends on collateral circumstances; '*Remuneratory* honours are proportioned at once to the usefulness and difficulty of performances.'—JOHNSON. A *recompense* is voluntary, both as to the service and the return; it is an act of generosity; it is not founded on the value of the service so much as on the intention of the server; it is not received as a matter of right, but of courtesy: there are a thousand acts of civility performed by others which are entitled to some *recompense*, though not to any specifick *compensation*;

Patriots have toiled, and in their country's cause
Bled nobly, and their deeds, as they deserve,
Receive proud *recompense*.—COWPER.

Requital is a return for a kindness: the making it is an act of gratitude; the omission of it wounds the feelings: it sometimes happens that the only *requital* which our kind action obtains, is the animosity of the person served; 'As the world is unjust in its judgements, so it is ungrateful in its *requitals*.'—BLAIR.

It belongs to the wealthy to make *compensation* for the trouble they give: it is scarcely possible to estimate too high what is done for ourselves, nor too low what we do for others. It is a hardship not to obtain the *remuneration* which we expect, but it is folly to expect that which we do not deserve. He who will not serve another, until he is sure of a *recompense*, is not worthy of a *recompense*. Those who befriend the wicked must expect to be ill *requited*.

Reward conveys no idea of obligation; whoever *rewards* acts altogether optionally; the conduct of the agent produces the *reward*. In this sense, it is comparable with *compensation*, *amends*, and *recompense*; but not with *satisfaction*, *remuneration*, or *requital*: things, as well as persons, may *compensate*, make *amends*, *recompense*, and *reward*; but persons only can give *satisfaction*, *remuneration*, and *requital*.

Reward respects the merit of the action; but *compensate* and the other words simply refer to the connexion between the actions and their results: what accrues to a man as the just consequence of his conduct, be it good or bad, is the *reward*. *Rewards* and punishments do always presuppose something willingly done, well or ill; without which respect, though we may sometimes receive good, yet then it is only a benefit and not a *reward*. *Compensation* and *amends* serve to supply the loss or absence of any thing; *recompense* and *reward* follow from particular exertions. It is but a poor *compensation* for the loss of peace and health to have one's coffers filled with gold;

Now goes the nightly thief prowling abroad
For plunder, much solicitous how best
He may *compensate* for a day of sloth,
By works of darkness and nocturnal wrongs.
COWPER.

A social intercourse by letter will make *amends* for the absence of those who are dear; 'Nature has obscurely fitted the mole with eyes. But for *amends*, what she is capable of for her defence, and warning of danger, she has very eminently conferred upon her, for she is very quick of hearing.'—ADDISON. It is a mark of folly to do any thing, however trifling, without the prospect of a *recompense*, and yet we see this daily realized in persons who give themselves much trouble to no purpose;

Thou 'rt so far before,
That swiftest wing of *recompense* is slow
To overtake thee.—SHAKSPEARE.

The *reward* of industry is ease and content: when a deceiver is caught in his own snare, he meets with the *reward* which should always attend deceit; 'There are no honorary *rewards* among us which are more esteemed by the person who receives them, and are cheaper to the prince, than the giving of medals.'—ADDISON.

What can *compensate* for the loss of honour? What can make *amends* to a frivolous mind for the want of company? What *recompenses* so sweet as the consciousness of having served a friend? When *reward* equals the *reward* of a good conscience?

RESTORATION RESTITUTION, REPARATION, AMENDS.

Restoration is employed in the ordinary application of the verb *restore*: *restitution*, from the same verb, is employed simply in the sense of making good that which has been unjustly taken. *Restoration* of property may be made by any one, whether the person taking it or not: *restitution* is supposed to be made by him who has been guilty of the injustice. The dethronement of a king may be the work of one set of men, and his *restoration* that of another; 'All men (during the usurpation) longed for the *restoration* of the liberties and laws.'—HUME. But it is the bounden duty of every individual who has committed any sort of injustice to another to make *restitution* to the utmost of his power; 'The justices may, if they think it reasonable, direct *restitution* of a ratable share of the money given with an apprentice (upon his discharge).'—BLACKSTONE.

Restitution and *reparation* are both employed in the sense of undoing that which has been done to the injury of another; but the former respects only injuries that affect the property, and *reparation* those which affect a person in various ways. He who is guilty of theft, or fraud, must make *restitution* by either *restoring* the stolen article or its full value: he who robs another of his good name, or does any injury to his person, has it not in his power so easily to make *reparation*; 'Justice requires that all injuries should be *repaired*.'—JOHNSON.

Reparation and *amends* (*v. Compensation*) are both employed in cases where some mischief or loss is sustained; but the *reparation* comprehends the idea of the act of *repairing*, as well as the thing by which we *repair*; *amends* is employed only for the thing that will *amend* or make better: hence we speak of the *reparation* of an injury; but of the *amends* by itself The *reparation* comprehends all kinds of injuries, particularly those of a serious nature; the *amends* is applied only to matters of inferiour importance.

It is impossible to make *reparation* for taking away the life of another; 'The king should be able, when he had cleared himself, to make him *reparation*.'—BACON. It is easy to make *amends* to any one for the loss of a day's pleasure; 'We went to the cabin of the French, who, to make *amends* for their three weeks' silence, were talking and disputing with greater rapidity and confusion than I ever heard in an assembly even of that nation.'—MANDEVILLE.

RESTORE, RETURN, REPAY.

Restore, in Latin *restauro*, from the Greek σαυρὸς a pale, signifies properly to new pale, that is, to repair by a new paling, and, in an extended application, to make good what has been injured or lost; *return* signifies properly to turn again, or to send back; and *repay* to pay back.

The common idea of all these terms is that of giving back. What we *restore* to another may or may not be the same as what we have taken; justice requires that it should be an equivalent in value, so as to prevent the individual from being in any degree a sufferer: what we *return* and *repay* must be precisely the same as we have received; the former in application to general objects, the latter in application only to pecuniary matters. We *restore* upon a principle of equity; we *return* upon a principle of justice and honour; we *repay* upon a principle of undeniable right. We cannot always claim that which ought to be *restored*; but we can not only claim but enforce the claim in regard to what is to be *returned* or *repaid*: an honest man will be scrupulous not to take any thing from another without *restoring* to him its full value. Whatever we have borrowed we ought to *return*; and when it is money which we have obtained, we ought to *repay* it with punctuality. We *restore* to many as well as to one, to communities as well as to individuals: we *restore* a king to his crown; or one nation *restores* a territory to another;

When both the chiefs are sunder'd from the fight,
Then to the lawful king *restore* his right.
DRYDEN.

We *return* and *repay* not only individually, but personally and particularly: we *return* a book to its owner;

The swain
Receives his easy food from Nature's hand,
And just *returns* of cultivated land.—DRYDEN.

We *repay* a sum of money to him from whom it was borrowed.

Restore and *return* may be employed in their improper application, as respects the moral state of persons and things; as a king *restores* a courtier to his favour, or a physician *restores* his patient to health: we *return* a favour; we *return* an answer or a compliment;

When answer none *return'd*, I set me down.
MILTON.

Repay may be figuratively employed in regard to moral objects, as an ungrateful person *repays* kindnesses with reproaches;

Cæsar, whom, fraught with eastern spoils,
Our heav'n, the just reward of human toils,
Securely shall *repay* with rights divine.—DRYDEN.

RETALIATION, REPRISAL.

Retaliation, from *retaliate*, in Latin *retaliatum*, participle of *retalio*, compounded of *re* and *talis* such, signifies such again, or like for like; *reprisal*, in French *reprisal*, from *repris* and *reprendre*, in Latin *reprehendo* to take again, signifies to take in return for what has been taken. The idea of making another suffer in return for the suffering he has occasioned is common to these terms; but the former is employed in ordinary cases; the latter mostly in regard to a state of warfare, or to active hostilities. A trick practised upon another in return for a trick is a *retaliation*; but a *reprisal* always extends to the capture of something from another, in return for what has been taken. When neighbours fall out, the incivilities and spite of the one are too often *retaliated* by like acts of incivility and spite on the part of the other: when one nation commences hostilities against another by taking any thing away violently, it produces *reprisals* on the part of the other. *Retaliation* is very frequently employed in the good sense for what passes innocently between friends: *reprisal* has always an unfavourable sense. Goldsmith's poem, entitled the *Retaliation*, was written for the purpose of *retaliating* on his friends the humour they had practised upon him; 'Therefore, I pray, let me enjoy your friendship in that fair proportion, that I desire to return unto you by way of correspondence and *retaliation*.'—HOWELL. When the quarrels of individuals break through the restraints of the law, and lead to acts of violence on each other's property, *reprisals* are made alternately by both parties;

Go publish o'er the plain,
How mighty a proselyte you gain!
How noble a *reprisal* on the great!—SWIFT.

RETRIBUTION, REQUITAL.

Retribution, from *tribuo* to bestow, signifies a bestowing back or giving in return; *requital*, *v. Reward.*

Retribution is a particular term; *requital* is general: the *retribution* comes from Providence; *requital* is the act of man: *retribution* is by way of punishment; 'Christ substituted his own body in our room, to receive the whole stroke of that dreadful *retribution* inflicted by the hand of an angry Omnipotence.'—SOUTH. *Requital* is mostly by way of reward; 'Leander was indeed a conquest to boast of, for he had long and obstinately defended his heart, and for a time made as many *requitals* upon the tender passions of her sex as she had raised contributions upon his.'—CUMBERLAND. *Retribution* is not always dealt out to every man according to his deeds; it is a poor *requital* for one who has done a kindness, to be abused.

TO RECOVER, RETRIEVE, REPAIR, RECRUIT.

Recover is to get again under one's cover or protection; *retrieve*, from the French *trouver* to find, is to get again that which has been lost: *repair*, in French *réparer*, Latin *reparo*, from *paro* to get, signifies likewise to get again, or make good as it was before; *recruit*, in French *recru*, from *cru*, and the Latin *cresco* to grow, signifies to grow again, or come fresh again.

Recover is the most general term, and applies to objects in general; *retrieve*, *repair*, and the others, are only partial applications: we *recover* things either by our own means or by casualties; we *retrieve* and *repair* by our own efforts only: we *recover* that which has been taken, or that which has been any way lost; we *retrieve* that which we have lost; we *repair* that which has been injured; we *recruit* that which has been diminished: we *recover* property from those who wish to deprive us of it; or we *recover* our principles, &c.; 'The serious and impartial retrospect of our conduct is indisputably necessary to the confirmation or *recovery* of our virtue.'—JOHNSON. We *retrieve* our misfortunes, or our lost reputation;

Why may not the soul receive
New organs, since ev'n art can these *retrieve?*
JENYNS.

We *repair* the mischief which has been done to our property;

Your men shall be received, your fleet *repaired.*
DRYDEN.

We *recruit* the strength which has been exhausted;

With greens and flowers *recruit* their empty hives.
DRYDEN.

We do not seek after that which we think *irrecoverable;* we give that up which is *irretrievable;* we lament over that which is *irreparable;* our power of *recruiting* depends upon circumstances; he who makes a moderate use of his resources may in general easily *recruit* himself when they are gone.

RECOVERY, RESTORATION.

Recovery is one's own act; *restoration* is the act of another; we *recover* the thing we have lost, when it comes again into our possession; but it is *restored* to us by another; 'Let us study to improve the assistance which this revelation affords for the *restoration* of our nature, and the *recovery* of our felicity.'—BLAIR. A king *recovers* his crown by force of arms from the hands of a usurper; his crown is *restored* to him by the will of his people: the *recovery* of property is good fortune; the *restoration* of property an act of justice.

Both are employed likewise in regard to one's health; but the former simply designates the regaining of health; the latter refers to the instrument by which it is brought about: the *recovery* of one's health is an object of the first importance to every man; the *restoration* of one s health seldomer depends upon the efficacy of medicine, than the benignant operations of nature.

TO REDEEM, RANSOM.

Redeem, in Latin *redimo*, is compounded of *re* and *emo* to buy off, or back to one's self; *ransom* is in all probability a variation of *redeem.*

Redeem is a term of general application; *ransom* is employed only on particular occasions: we *redeem* persons as well as things; we *ransom* persons only: we may *redeem* by labour, or any thing which supplies as an equivalent to money; we *ransom* properly with money only: we *redeem* a watch, or whatever has been given in pawn; we *ransom* a captive: *redeem* is employed in the improper application; *ransom* only in the proper sense: we may *redeem* our character, *redeem* our life, or *redeem* our honour; and in this sense our Saviour *redeems* repentant sinners;

Thus in her crime her *confidence* she plac'd,
And with new treasons would *redeem* the past.
DRYDEN.

But those who are *ransomed* only recover their bodily liberty; 'A third tax was paid by vassals to the king, to *ransom* him if he should happen to be taken prisoner.'—ROBERTSON.

GRATUITY, RECOMPENSE.

The distinction between these terms is very similar to the terms *Gratuitous, Voluntary.* They both imply a gift, and a gift by way of return for some supposed service: but the *gratuity* is independent of all expectation as well as right; the *recompense* is founded upon some admissible claim. Those who wish to confer a favour in a delicate manner, will sometimes do it under the shape of a *gratuity;* 'If there be one or two scholars more, that will be no great addition to his trouble, considering that, perhaps, their parents may *recompense* him by their *gratuities*.'—MOLYNEUX. Those who overrate their services will in all probability be disappointed in the *recompense* they receive;

What could be less than to afford him praise,
The easiest *recompense*.—MILTON.

GRATUITOUS, VOLUNTARY.

Gratuitous is opposed to that which is obligatory; *voluntary* is opposed to that which is compulsory, or involuntary. A gift is *gratuitous* which flows entirely from the free will of the giver, independent of right: an offer is *voluntary* which flows from the free will, independent of all external constraint. *Gratuitous* is therefore to *voluntary* as a species to the genus. What is *gratuitous* is *voluntary*, although what is *voluntary* is not always *gratuitous*. The *gratuitous* is properly the *voluntary* in regard to the disposal of one's property; 'The heroick band of cashierers of monarchs were in haste to make a generous diffusion of the knowledge which they had thus *gratuitously* received.' —BURKE. The *voluntary* is applicable to subjects in general; 'Their privileges relative to contribution were *voluntarily* surrendered.'—BURKE.

THANKFULNESS, GRATITUDE.

Thankfulness or a *fulness* of thanks, is the outward expression of a *grateful* feeling; *gratitude*, from the Latin *gratitudo*, is the feeling itself. Our *thankfulness* is measured by the number of our words; our *gratitude* is measured by the nature of our actions. A person appears very *thankful* at the time, who afterward proves very *ungrateful*. *Thankfulness* is the beginning of *gratitude: gratitude* is the completion of *thankfulness*.

TO AFFIRM, ASSEVERATE, ASSURE, VOUCH, AVER, PROTEST.

Affirm, in French *affermer*, Latin *affirmo*, compounded of *af* or *ad* and *firmo* to strengthen, signifies to give strength to what has been said; *asseverate*, in Latin *asseveratus*, participle of *assevero*, compounded of *as* or *ad* and *severus*, signifies to make strong and positive; *assure*, in French *assurer*, is compounded of the intensive syllable *as* or *ad* and *sure*, signifying to make sure; *vouch* is probably changed from *vow; aver*, in French *averer*, is compounded of the intensive syllable *a* or *ad* and *verus* true, signifying to bear testimony to the truth; *protest*, in French *protester*, Latin *protesto*, is compounded of *pro* and *testor* to call to witness, signifying to call others to witness as to what we think about a thing.

All these terms indicate an expression of a person's conviction.

In one sense, to *affirm* is to declare that a thing is in opposition to denying or declaring that it is not; in the sense here chosen, it signifies to declare a thing as a fact on our credit. To *asseverate* is to declare it with confidence. To *vouch* is to rest the truth of another's declaration on our own responsibility. To *aver* is to express the truth of a declaration unequivocally. To *protest* is to declare a thing solemnly, and with strong marks of sincerity.

Affirmations are made of the past and present; a person *affirms* what he has seen and what he sees;

An infidel, and fear!
Fear what? a dream? a fable?—How thy dread,
Unwilling evidence, and therefore strong,
Affords my cause an undesigned support!
How disbelief *affirms* what it denies!—YOUNG.

Asseverations are strong *affirmations*, made in cases of doubt to remove every impression disadvantageous to one's sincerity; 'I judge in this case as Charles the Second victualled his navy, with the bread which one of his dogs chose of several pieces thrown before him, rather than trust to the *asseverations* of the victuallers.'—STEELE. *Assurances* are made of the past, present, and future; they mark the conviction of the speaker as to what has been, or is, and his intentions as to what shall be; they are appeals to the estimation which another has in one's word; 'My learned friend *assured* me that the earth had lately received a shock from a comet that crossed its vortex.'—STEELE. *Vouching* is an act for another; it is the supporting of another's *assurance* by our own; 'All the great writers of the Augustan age, for whom singly we have so great an esteem, stand up together as *vouchers* for one another's reputation.'—ADDISON. *Averring* is employed in matters of fact; we *aver* as to the accuracy of details; we *aver* on positive knowledge that sets aside all question; 'Among ladies, he positively *averred* that nonsense was the most prevailing part of eloquence, and had so little complaisance as to say, "a woman is never taken by her reason but always by her passion."'—STEELE. *Protestations* are stronger than either *asseverations* or *assurances;* they are accompanied with every act, look, or gesture that can tend to impress conviction on another; 'I have long loved her, and I *protest* to you, bestowed much on her, followed her with a doting observance.'—SHAKSPEARE.

Affirmations are employed in giving evidence, whether accompanied with an oath or not; liars deal much in *asseverations* and *protestations*. People *asseverate* in order to produce a conviction of their veracity; they *protest* in order to obtain a belief of their innocence; they *aver* where they expect to be believed. *Assurances* are altogether personal; they are always made to satisfy some one of what they wish to know and believe. We ought to be sparing of our *assurances* of regard for another, as we ought to be suspicious of such *assurances* when made to ourselves. Whenever we *affirm* any thing on the authority of another, we ought to be particularly cautious not to *vouch* for its veracity, if it be not unquestionable.

TO AFFIRM, ASSERT.

Affirm, v. To affirm, asseverate; assert, in Latin *assertus*, participle of *assero*, compounded of *as* or *ad* and *sero* to connect, signifies to connect words into a proposition.

To *affirm* is said of facts; to *assert*, of opinions: we *affirm* what we know; we *assert* what we believe: whoever *affirms* what he does not know to be true is guilty of falsehood; 'That this man, wise and virtuous as he was, passed always unentangled through the snares of life, it would be prejudice and temerity to *affirm*.'—JOHNSON (*Life of Collins*). Whoever *asserts* what he cannot prove to be true is guilty of folly; 'It is *asserted* by a tragick poet, that "est miser nemo nisi comparatus,"—"no man is miserable, but as he is compared with others happier than himself." This position is not strictly and philosophically true.'—JOHNSON. We contradict an *affirmation;* we confute an *assertion*.

TO ASSERT, MAINTAIN, VINDICATE

To *assert, v. To affirm, assert; maintain*, in French *maintenir*, from the Latin *manus* and *teneo*, signifies to hold by the hand, that is, closely and firmly; *vindicate*, in Latin *vindicatus*, participle of *vindico*, compounded of *vim* and *dico*, signifies to pronounce a violent or positive sentence.

To *assert* is to declare a thing as our own; to *maintain* is to abide by what we have so declared; to *vindicate* is to stand up for that which concerns ourselves or others. We *assert* any thing to be true; 'Sophocles also, in a fragment of one of his tragedies, *asserts* the unity of the Supreme Being.'—CUMBERLAND. We *maintain* an opinion by adducing proofs, facts, or arguments; 'I am willing to believe that Dryden wanted rather skill to discover the right, than virtue to *maintain* it.'—JOHNSON. We *vindicate* our own conduct or that of another when it is called in question; 'This is no *vindication* of her conduct. She still acts a mean part, and through fear becomes an accomplice in endeavouring to betray the Greeks.' —BROOME. We *assert* boldly or impudently; we *maintain* steadily or obstinately; we *vindicate* resolutely or insolently. A right or claim is *asserted* which is avowed to belong to any one;

When the great soul buoys up to this high point,
Leaving gross Nature's sediments below,
Then, and then only, Adam's offspring quits
The sage and hero of the fields and woods,
Asserts his rank, and rises into man.—YOUNG.

A right is *maintained* when attempts are made to prove its justice, or regain its possession; the cause of the *assertor* or *maintainer* is *vindicated* by another;

'T is just that I should *vindicate* alone,
The broken truce, or for the breach atone.
DRYDEN.

Innocence is *asserted* by a positive declaration; it is *maintained* by repeated *assertions* and the support of testimony; it is *vindicated* through the interference of another.

The most guilty persons do not hesitate to *assert* their innocence with the hope of inspiring credit; and some will persist in *maintaining* it, even after their guilt has been pronounced; but the really innocent man will never want a friend to *vindicate* him when his honour or his reputation is at stake. *Assertions* which are made hastily and inconsiderately are seldom long *maintained* without exposing a person to ridicule; those who attempt to *vindicate* a bad cause expose themselves to as much reproach as if the cause were their own.

TO ACKNOWLEDGE, OWN, CONFESS, AVOW.

Acknowledge, compounded of *ac* or *ad* and *knowledge*, implies to bring to knowledge, to make known; *own* is a familiar figure, signifying to take to one's self, to make one's own: it is a common substitute for *confess; confess*, in French *confesser*, Latin *confessus*, participle of *confiteor*, compounded of *con* and *fateor*, signifies to impart to any one; *avow*, in French *avouer*, Latin *advoveo*, signifies to vow, or protest to any one.

Acknowledging is a simple declaration; *confessing* or *owning* is a specifick private communication; *avowal* is a publick declaration. We *acknowledge* facts; *confess* our *own* faults; *avow* motives, opinions, &c.

We *acknowledge* in consequence of a question; we *confess* in consequence of an accusation; we *own* in consequence of a charge; we *avow* voluntarily. We *acknowledge* having been concerned in a transaction; we *confess* our guilt; we *own* that a thing is wrong; but we are ashamed to *avow* our motives. Candour leads to an *acknowledgment;* repentance produces a *confession;* the desire of forgiveness leads to *owning;* generosity or pride occasions an *avowal*.

An *acknowledgment* of what is not demanded may be either politick or impolitick, according to circumstances; 'I must *acknowledge*, for my own part, that I take greater pleasure in considering the works of the creation in their immensity, than in their minuteness.'—ADDISON. A *confession* dictated merely by fear is of avail only in the sight of man;

Spite of herself e'en Envy must *confess*,
That I the friendship of the great possess.
FRANCIS.

Those who are most ready to *own* themselves in an errour are not always the first to amend; 'And now, my dear, cried she to me, I will fairly *own*, that it was I that instructed my girls to encourage our landlord's addresses.'—GOLDSMITH. An *avowal* of the principles which actuate the conduct is often the greatest aggravation of guilt; 'Whether by their settled and *avowed* scorn of thoughtless talkers, the Persians were able to diffuse to any great extent the virtue of taciturnity, we are hindered by the distance of those times from being able to discover.'—JOHNSON.

RECOGNISE, ACKNOWLEDGE.

Recognise, in Latin *recognoscere*, is to take the knowledge of, or bring to one's own knowledge; *acknowledge*, *v. To acknowledge*.

To *recognise* is to take *cognizance* of that which comes again before our notice; to *acknowledge* is to admit to one's *knowledge* whatever comes fresh under our notice. We *recognise* a person whom we have known before; we *recognise* him either in his former character or in some newly assumed character; we *acknowledge* either former favours, or those which have been just received. Princes *recognise* certain principles which have been admitted by previous consent; they *acknowledge* the justice of claims which are preferred before them; 'When conscience threatens punishment to secret crimes, it manifestly *recognises* a Supreme Governour from whom nothing is hidden.'—BLAIR. 'I call it atheism by establishment, when any state, as such, shall not *acknowledge* the existence of God, as the moral governour of the world.'—BURKE.

TO PROFESS, DECLARE.

Profess, in Latin *professus*, participle of *profiteor*, compounded of *pro* and *fateor* to speak, signifies to set forth, or present to publick view; *declare*, *v. To declare*.

An exposure of one's thoughts or opinions is the common idea in the signification of these terms; but they differ in the manner of the action, as well as the object: one *professes* by words or by actions; one *declares* only by words: a man *professes* to believe that on which he acts; but he *declares* his belief of it either with his lips or in his writings. The *profession* may be general and partial; it may amount to little more than an intimation: the *declaration* is positive and explicit; it leaves no one in doubt: a *profession* may, therefore, sometimes be hypocritical; he who *professes* may wish to imply that which is not real; 'A naked *profession* may have credit, where no other evidence can be given.'—SWIFT. A *declaration* must be either directly true or false; he who *declares* expressly commits himself upon his veracity; 'We are a considerable body, who, upon a proper occasion, would not fail to *declare* ourselves.'—ADDISON. One *professes* either as respects single actions, or a regular course of conduct; one *declares* either passing thoughts or settled principles. A person *professes* to have walked to a certain distance; to have taken a certain route, and the like: a Christian *professes* to follow the doctrine and precepts of Christianity; a person *declares* that the thing is true or false, or he *declares* his firm belief in a thing.

To *profess* is employed only for what concerns one's self; to *declare* is likewise employed for what concerns others: one *professes* the motives and principles by which one is guided; one *declares* facts and circumstances with which one is acquainted: one *professes* nothing but what one thinks may be creditable and fit to be known, or what may be convenient for one's purpose;

Pretending first
Wise to fly pain, *professing* next the spy,
Argues no leader.—MILTON.

One *declares* whatever may have fallen under one's notice, or passed through one's mind, as the case requires; 'It is too common to find the aged at *declared* enmity with the whole system of present customs and manners.'—BLAIR. There is always a particular and private motive for *profession;* there are frequently publick grounds for making a *declaration*. A general *profession* of Christianity, according to established forms, is the bounden duty of every one born in the Christian persuasion; but a particular *profession*, according to a singular and extraordinary form, is seldom adopted by any who do not deceive themselves, or wish to deceive others: no one should be ashamed of making a *declaration* of his opinions, when the cause of truth is thereby supported; every one should be ready to *declare* what he knows, when the purposes of justice are forwarded by the *declaration;* 'There are no where so plain and full *declarations* of mercy and love to the sons of men, as are made in the Gospel'.—TILLOTSON.

TO DECLARE, PUBLISH, PROCLAIM.

The idea of making known is common to all these terms: this is simply the signification of *declare* (*v. To profess*); but *publish* (*v. To announce*) and *proclaim*, in Latin *proclamo*, compounded of *pro* and *clamo*, signifying to cry before or in the ears of others, include accessory ideas.

The word *declare* does not express any particular mode or circumstance of making known, as is implied by the others: we may *declare* publickly or privately; we *publish* and *proclaim* only in a publick manner we may *declare* by word of mouth, or by writing; we *publish* or *proclaim* by any means that will render the thing most generally known.

In *declaring*, the leading idea is that of speaking out that which passes in the mind; in *publishing*, the leading idea is that of making publick or common; in *proclaiming*, the leading idea is that of crying aloud: we may therefore often *declare* by *publishing* and *proclaiming*: a *declaration* is a personal act; it concerns the person *declaring*, or him to whom it is *declared*; its truth or falsehood depends upon the veracity of the speaker: a *publication* is of general interest; the truth or falsehood of it does not always rest with the *publisher*: a *proclamation* is altogether a publick act, in which no one's veracity is implicated. Facts and opinions and feelings are *declared*;

> The Greeks in shouts their joint assent *declare*,
> The priest to rev'rence and release the fair.
> POPE.

Events and circumstances are *published*; 'I am surprised that none of the fortune-tellers, or, as the French call them, the *Diseurs de bonne avanture*, who *publish* their bills in every quarter of the town, have not turned our lotteries to their advantage.'—ADDISON. The measures of government are *proclaimed*;

> Nine sacred heralds now, *proclaiming* loud
> The monarch's will, suspend the list'ning crowd.
> POPE.

It is folly for a man to *declare* any thing to be true, which he is not certain to be so, and wickedness in him to *declare* that to be true which he knows to be false: whoever *publishes* all he hears will be in great danger of *publishing* many falsehoods; whatever is *proclaimed* is supposed to be of sufficient importance to deserve the notice of all who may hear or read.

In cases of war or peace, princes are expected to *declare* themselves on one side or the other; in the political world intelligence is quickly *published* through the medium of the publick papers; in private life domestick occurrences are *published* with equal celerity through the medium of tale-bearers; a *proclamation* is the ordinary mode by which a prince makes known his wishes, and issues his commands to his subjects; it is an act of indiscretion very common to young and ardent inquirers to *declare* their opinions before they are properly matured; the *publication* of domestick circumstances is oftentimes the source of much disquiet and ill-will in families; ministers of the Gospel are styled messengers, who should *proclaim* its glad tidings to all people, and in all tongues.

DECREE, EDICT, PROCLAMATION.

Decree, in French *decret*, Latin *decretus*, from *decerno* to give judgement or pass sentence, signifies the sentence or resolution that is passed; *edict*, in Latin *edictus*, from *edico* to say out, signifies the thing spoken out or sent forth; *proclamation*, *v. To declare*.

A *decree* is a more solemn and deliberative act than an *edict*; on the other hand an *edict* is more authoritative than a *decree*. A *decree* is the decision of one or many; an *edict* speaks the will of an individual: councils and senates, as well as princes, make *decrees*; despotick rulers issue *edicts*.

Decrees are passed for the regulation of publick and private matters; they are made known as occasion requires, but are not always publick;

> If you deny me, fie upon your law!
> There is no force in the *decrees* of Venice.
> SHAKSPEARE.

Edicts and *proclamations* contain the commands of the sovereign authority, and are directly addressed by the prince to his people. An *edict* is peculiar to a despotick government; 'This statute or act of parliament is placed among the records of the kingdom, there needing no formal promulgation to give it the force of a law, as was necessary by the civil law with regard to the emperour's *edicts*.'—BLACKSTONE. A *proclamation* is common to a monarchical and aristocratick form of government; 'From the same original of the king's being the fountain of justice, we may also deduce the prerogative of issuing *proclamations*, which is vested in the king alone.'—BLACKSTONE. The ukase in Russia is a species of *edict*, by which the emperour makes known his will to his people; the king of England communicates to his subjects the determinations of himself and his council by means of a *proclamation*.

TO ANNOUNCE, PROCLAIM, PUBLISH, ADVERTISE.

Announce, in Latin *annuncio*, is compounded of *an* or *ad* and *nuncio* to tell to any one in a formal manner; *proclaim*, in Latin *proclamo*, is compounded of *pro* and *clamo* to cry before, or cry aloud; *publish*, in Latin *publico*, from *publicus* and *populus*, signifies to make *publick* or known to the people at large; *advertise*, from the Latin *adverto*, or *ad* and *verto*, signifies to turn the attention to a thing.

The characteristick sense of these words is the making of a thing known to several individuals: a thing is *announced* to an individual or small community; it is *proclaimed* to a neighbourhood, and *published* to the world. An event that is of particular interest is *announced*; 'We might with as much reason doubt whether the sun was intended to enlighten the earth, as whether he who has framed the human mind intended to *announce* righteousness to mankind as a law.'—BLAIR. An event is *proclaimed* that requires to be known by all the parties interested;

> But witness, heralds! and *proclaim* my vow,
> Witness to gods above, and men below.—POPE.

That is *published* which is supposed likely to interest all who know it; 'It very often happens that none are more industrious in *publishing* the blemishes of an extraordinary reputation, than such as lie open to the same censures in their own character.'—ADDISON.

Announcements are made verbally, or by some well known signal; *proclamations* are made verbally, and accompanied by some appointed signal; *publications* are ordinarily made through the press, or by oral communication from one individual to another. The arrival of a distinguished person is *announced* by the ringing of the bells; the *proclamation* of peace by a herald is accompanied with certain ceremonies calculated to excite notice; the *publication* of news is the office of the journalist.

Advertise denotes the means, and *publish* the end. To *advertise* is to direct the publick attention to any event or circumstance; 'Every man that *advertises* his own excellence should write with some consciousness of a character which dares to call the attention of the publick.'—JOHNSON. To *publish* is to make known either by an oral or printed communication; 'The criticisms which I have hitherto *published*, have been made with an intention rather to discover beauties and excellences in the writers of my own time, than to *publish* any of their faults and imperfections.'—ADDISON.

We *publish* by *advertising*, but we do not always *advertise* when we *publish*. Mercantile and civil transactions are conducted by means of *advertisements*. Extraordinary circumstances are speedily *published* in a neighbourhood by circulating from mouth to mouth.

TO PUBLISH, PROMULGATE, DIVULGE, REVEAL, DISCLOSE.

To *publish* signifies the same as in the preceding article; *promulgate*, in Latin *promulgatus*, participle of *promulgo*, for *provulgo*, signifies to make vulgar; *divulge*, in Latin *divulgo*, that is, in *diversos vulgo*, signifies to make vulgar in different parts; *reveal*, in Latin *revelo*, from *velo* to veil, signifies to take off the veil or cover; *disclose* signifies to make the reverse of *close*.

To *publish* is the most general of these terms, conveying in its extended sense the idea of making known; 'By the execution of several of his benefactors, Maximin *published* in characters of blood the indelible history of his baseness and ingratitude.'—GIBBON. *Publishing* is an indefinite act, whereby we may make known to many or few; but to *promulgate* is always to make known to many. We may *publish* that which is a domestick or a national concern, we *promulgate* properly only that which is of general interest: the affairs of a family or of a nation are *published* in the newspapers; doctrines, principles, precepts, and the like, are *promulgated;* 'An absurd theory on one side of a question forms no justification for alleging a false fact or *promulgating* mischievous maxims on the other.'—BURKE. We may *publish* things to be known, or things not to be known; we *divulge* things mostly not to be known; we may *publish* our own shame, or the shame of another, and we may *publish* that which is advantageous to another; but we commonly *divulge* the secrets or the crimes of another;

Tremble, thou wretch,
That hast within thee *undivulged* crimes.
SHAKSPEARE.

To *publish* is said of that which was never before known, or never before existed; to *reveal* and *disclose* are said of that which has been only concealed or lay hidden: we *publish* the events of the day; we *reveal* the secret or the mystery of a transaction; 'In confession, the *revealing* is not for worldly use, but for the ease of a man's heart.'—BACON. We *disclose* the whole of an affair from beginning to end, which has never been properly known or accounted for;

Then earth and ocean various forms *disclose.*
DRYDEN.

TO UNCOVER, DISCOVER, DISCLOSE.

To *uncover*, like *discover*, implies to take off the covering; but the former refers to an artificial material and occasional covering; the latter to a moral, natural, or permanent covering: plants are *uncovered* that they may receive the benefit of the air; they are *discovered* to gratify the researches of the botanist. To *discover* and *disclose* both signify to lay open, but they differ in the object and manner of the action: that is *discovered* which is supposed to be covered; and that is *disclosed* which is supposed to be shut out from the view: a country is *discovered*, a scene is *disclosed;*

Go draw aside the curtains, and *discover*
The several caskets to this noble prince.
SHAKSPEARE.

'The shells being broken, struck off, and gone, the stone included in them is thereby *disclosed* and set at liberty.'—WOODWARD. A plot is *discovered* when it becomes known to one's self; a secret is *disclosed* when it is made known to another; 'He shall never, by any alteration in me, *discover* my knowledge of his mistake.'—POPE.

If I *disclose* my passion,
Our friendship's at an end; if I conceal it,
The world will call me false.—ADDISON.

TO DISCOVER, MANIFEST, DECLARE.

The idea of making known is conveyed by all these terms; but *discover*, which signifies simply the taking off the covering from any thing, expresses less than *manifest*, and that than *declare:* we *discover* by indirect means or signs more or less doubtful; we *manifest* by unquestionable marks; we *declare* by express words: talents and dispositions *discover* themselves; particular feelings and sentiments *manifest* themselves; facts, opinions, and sentiments are *declared:* children early *discover* a turn for some particular art or science; 'Several brute creatures *discover* in their actions something like a faint glimmering of reason.'—ADDISON. A person *manifests* his regard for another by unequivocal proofs of kindness; 'At no time perhaps did the legislature *manifest* a more tender regard to that fundamental principle of British constitutional policy, hereditary monarchy, than at the time of the revolution.'—BURKE. A person of an open disposition is apt to *declare* his sentiments without disguise; 'Langhorne, Boyer, and Powel, presbyterian officers who commanded bodies of troops in Wales, were the first that *declared* themselves against the parliament.'—HUME.

Things are said to *discover*, persons only *manifest* or *declare* in the proper sense; but they may be used figuratively: it is the nature of every thing sublunary to *discover* symptoms of decay more or less early; it is particularly painful when any one *manifests* an unfriendly disposition from whom we had reason to expect the contrary.

TO PROVE, DEMONSTRATE, EVINCE, MANIFEST.

Prove, in Latin *probo*, signifies to make good · *demonstrate*, from the Latin *demonstro*, signifies, by virtue of the intensive syllable *de*, to show in a specifick manner; *evince, v. To argue; manifest* signifies to make *manifest.*

Prove is here the general and indefinite term, the rest imply different modes of *proving;* to *demonstrate* is to prove specifically: we may *prove* any thing by simple assertion; but we must *demonstrate* by intellectual efforts: we may *prove* that we were in a certain place; but we *demonstrate* some point in science: we may *prove* by personal influence; but we can *demonstrate* only by the force of evidence: we *prove* our own merit by our actions; we *demonstrate* the existence of a Deity by all that surrounds us;

Why on those shores are they with joy survey'd,
Admir'd as heroes, and as gods obey'd,
Unless great acts superiour merit *prove?*—POPE.

'By the very setting apart and consecrating places for the service of God, we *demonstrate* our acknowledgment of his power and sovereignty over us.'—BEVERIDGE.

To *prove, evince*, and *manifest* are the acts either of persons or things; to *demonstrate*, that of persons only: in regard to persons, we *prove* either the facts which we know, or the mental endowments which we possess: we *evince* and *manifest* a disposition or a state of mind: we *evince* our sincerity by our actions; it is a work of time; 'We must *evince* the sincerity of our faith by good works.'—BLAIR. We *manifest* a friendly or a hostile disposition by a word or a single action, it is the act of the moment; 'In the life of a man of sense, a short life is sufficient to *manifest* himself a man of honour and virtue.'—STEELE. All these terms are applied to things, inasmuch as they may tend either to produce conviction, or simply to make a thing known: to *prove* and *evince* are employed in the first case; to *manifest* in the latter case: the beauty and order in the creation *prove* the wisdom of the Creator; a persistance in a particular course of conduct may either *evince* great virtue or great folly; the miracles wrought in Egypt *manifested* the Divine power.

PROOF, EVIDENCE, TESTIMONY.

The *proof* is that which simply *proves;* the *evidence* is that which makes *evident*, which rises in sense upon the *proof;* the *testimony* is a species of *evidence* by means of witnesses, from *testis* a witness.

In the legal acceptation of the terms, *proofs* are commonly denominated *evidence*, because no *proof* can be admitted as such which does not tend to make *evident;* but as the word *proof* is sometimes taken for the act of *proving* as well as the thing *proved*, the terms are not always indifferently used; 'Positive *proof* is always required, where, from the nature of the case, it appears it might possibly have been had. But next to positive *proof*, circumstantial *evidence*, or the doctrine of presumptions, must take place.'—BLACKSTONE. '*Evidence* is either written or parol.'—BLACKSTONE. *Testimony* is properly parol *evidence;* but the term is only used in relation to the person giving the *evidence;* 'Our law considers that there are many transactions to which only one person is privy, and therefore does not always demand the *testimony* of two.'—BLACKSTONE.

In an extended application of the words they are taken in the sense of a sign or mark, by which a thing is known to exist; and, with a similar distinction, the *proof* is the sign which *proves;* 'Of the fallaciousness of hope, and the uncertainty of schemes, every day gives some new *proof.*'—JOHNSON. The *evidence* is the sign which makes *evident;* hence we speak of the *evidences* of the senses; 'Cato Major, who had borne all the great offices, has left us an *evidence*, under his own hand, how much he was versed in country affairs.'—LOCKE. The *testimony* is that which is offered or given by persons or things personified in *proof* of any thing; '*Evidence* is said to arise from *testimony*, when we depend upon the credit and relation of others for the truth or falsehood of any thing.'—WILKINS. Hence a person makes another a present, or performs any other act of kindness, as a *testimony* of his regard: and persons or things personified bear *testimony* in favour of persons; 'I must bear this *testimony* to Otway's memory, that the passions are truly touched in his Venice Preserved.'—DRYDEN.

> Ye Trojan flames, your *testimony* bear
> What I perform'd, and what I suffer'd there.
> DRYDEN.

The *proof* is employed mostly for facts or physical objects; the *evidence* is applied to that which is moral or intellectual. All that our Saviour did and said were *evidences* of his divine character, which might have produced faith in the minds of many, even if they had not such numerous and miraculous *proofs* of his power. The *evidence* may be internal, or lie in the thing itself; 'Of Swift's general habits of thinking, if his letters can be supposed to afford any *evidence*, he was not a man to be either loved or envied.'—JOHNSON. The *proof* is always external: 'Men ought not to expect either sensible *proof* or demonstration for such matters as are not capable of such *proofs*, supposing them to be true.'—WILKINS. The internal *evidences* of the truth of Divine Revelation are even more numerous than those which are external: our Saviour's reappearance among his disciples did not satisfy the unbelieving Thomas of his identity, until he had the farther *proofs* of feeling the holes in his hands and his side.

DEPONENT, EVIDENCE, WITNESS.

Deponent, from the Latin *depono*, is the one laying down or open what he has heard or seen; *evidence*, from *evident*, is the one producing *evidence* or making *evident*; *witness*, from the Saxon *witan*, Teutonick *weissen*, Greek εἰδέω, and Hebrew ידע to know, is one who knows or makes known.

The *deponent* always declares upon oath; he serves to give information: the *evidence* is likewise generally bound by an oath; he serves to acquit or condemn: the *witness* is employed upon oath or otherwise he serves to confirm or invalidate;

> The pleader having spoke his best,
> And *witness* ready to attest;
> Who fairly could on oath depose,
> When questions on the fact arose,
> That ev'ry article was true.
> Nor further these *deponents* knew.—SWIFT.

A *deponent* declares either in writing or by word of mouth; the *deposition* is preparatory to the trial: an *evidence* may give *evidence* either by words or action; whatever serves to clear up the thing, whether a person or an animal, is used as an *evidence*; the *evidence* always comes forward on the trial; 'Of the *evidence* which appeared against him (Savage) the character of the man was not unexceptionable; that of the woman notoriously infamous.'—JOHNSON. A *witness* is always a person in the proper sense, but may be applied figuratively to inanimate objects; he declares by word of mouth what he personally knows. Every *witness* is an *evidence* at the moment of trial, but every *evidence* is not a *witness*. When a dog is employed as an *evidence* he cannot be called a *witness*; 'In case a woman be forcibly taken away and married, she may be a *witness* against her husband in order to convict him of felony.'—BLACKSTONE. 'In every man's heart and conscience, religion has many *witnesses* to its importance and reality.'—BLAIR.

Evidence on the other hand is confined mostly to judicial matters; and *witness* extends to all the ordinary concerns of life. One person appears as an *evidence* against another on a criminal charge: a *witness* appears for or against; he corroborates the word of another, and is a security in all dealings or matters of question between man and man.

TO CONVICT, DETECT, DISCOVER.

Convict, from the Latin *convictus*, participle of *convinco* to make manifest, signifies to make clear; *detect*, from the Latin *detectus*, participle of *detego*, compounded of the privative *de* and *tego* to cover, signifies to uncover or lay open. To *detect* and *discover* serve to denote the laying open of crimes or errours. A person is convicted by means of evidence; he is *detected* by means of ocular demonstration. One is *convicted* of having been the perpetrator of some evil deed; 'Advice is offensive, not because it lays us open to unexpected regret, or *convicts* us of any fault which had escaped our notice, but because it shows us that we are known to others as well as ourselves.'—JOHNSON. One is *detected* in the very act of committing the deed. One is *convicted* of crimes in a court of judicature, one is *detected* in various misdemeanours by different casualties; 'Every member of society feels and acknowledges the necessity of *detecting* crimes.'—JOHNSON. Punishment necessarily follows the *conviction*; but in the case of *detection*, it rests in the breast of the individual against whom the offence is committed.

Detect is always taken in a bad sense: *discover* (v. *Uncover*) in an indifferent sense. A person is *detected* in what he wishes to conceal; a person or a thing is *discovered* that has unintentionally lain concealed. Thieves are *detected* in picking pockets; a lost child is *discovered* in a wood, or in some place of security. *Detection* is the act of the moment; it is effected by the aid of the senses: a *discovery* is the consequence of efforts, and is brought about by circuitous means, and the aid of the understanding. A plot is *detected* by any one who communicates what he has seen and heard; many murders have been *discovered* after a lapse of years by ways the most extraordinary. Nothing is *detected* but what is actually passing; many things are *discovered* which have long passed. Wicked men go on in their career of vice with the hope of escaping *detection*; the *discovery* of one villany often leads to that of many more; 'Cunning when it is once *detected* loses its force.'—ADDISON. 'We are told that the Spartans, though they punished theft in the young men when it was *discovered*, looked upon it as honourable if it succeeded.'—ADDISON.

TO FIND, FIND OUT, DISCOVER, ESPY, DESCRY.

Find, in German *finden*, &c. is most probably connected with the Latin *venio*, signifying to come in the way *discover*, v. *To uncover*; *espy*, in French *espier*, comes from the Latin *espicio*, signifying to see a thing out; *descry*, from the Latin *discerno*, signifies to distinguish a thing from others.

To *find* signifies simply to come within sight of a thing, which is the general idea attached to all these terms: they vary, however, either in the mode of the action or in the object. What we *find* may become visible to us by accident, but what we *find out* is the result of an effort. We may *find* any thing as we pass along in the streets; but we *find out* mistakes in an account by carefully going over it, or we *find out* the difficulties which we meet with in learning, by redoubling our diligence; 'Socrates, who was a great admirer of Cretan institutions, set his excellent wit to *find out* some good cause and use of this evil inclination (the love of boys).'—WALSH. What is *found* may have been lost to ourselves, but visible to others;

> He *finds* the fraud, and with a smile demands,
> On what design the boy had bound his hands.
> DRYDEN.

What is *discovered* is always remote and unknown, and when *discovered* is something new; 'Cunning is a kind of short-sightedness that *discovers* the minutest objects which are near at hand, but is not able to discern things at a distance.'—ADDISON. A piece of money may be *found* lying on the ground; but a mine is *discovered* under ground. When Captain Cook *discovered* the islands in the South Sea, many plants and animals were *found*. What is not *discoverable* may be presumed not to exist; but that which is *found* may be only what has been lost. What has once been *discovered* cannot be *discovered* again; but what is *found* may be many times *found*. *Find out* and *discover* differ principally in the application; the former being applied to familiar, and the latter to scientifick objects: scholars *find out* what they have to learn; men of research *discover* what escapes the notice of others.

To *espy* is a species of *finding out*, namely, to *find out* what is very secluded or retired;

> There Agamemnon, Priam here he *spies*,
> And fierce Achilles, who both kings defies.
> DRYDEN.

Descry is a species of *discovering*, or observing at a distance, or among a number of objects;

> Through this we pass, and mount the tower from whence,
> With unavailing arms, the Trojans make defence;
> From this the trembling king had oft *descried*,
> The Grecian camp, and saw their navy ride.
> DRYDEN.

An astronomer *discovers* fresh stars or planets; he *finds* those on particular occasions which have been already *discovered*. A person *finds out* by continued inquiry any place to which he had been wrong directed: he *espies* an object which lies concealed in a corner or secret place: he *descries* a horseman coming down a hill.

Find and *discover* may be employed with regard to objects, either of a corporeal or intellectual kind; *espy* and *descry* only with regard to sensible objects of corporeal vision: *find*, either for those that are external or internal; *discover*, only for those that are external. The distinction between them is the same as before; we *find* by simple inquiry; we *discover* by reflection and study: we *find* or *find out* the motives which influence a person's conduct; we *discover* the reasons or causes of things: the *finding* serves the particular purpose of the *finder;* the *discovery* serves the purpose of science, by adding to the stock of general knowledge.

When *find* is used as a purely intellectual operation, it admits of a new view, in relation both to *discover* and to *invent*, as may be seen in the following article.

TO FIND, FIND OUT, DISCOVER, INVENT.

To *find* or *find out* (*v. To find*) is said of things which do not exist in the forms in which a person *finds* them: to *discover* (*v. To uncover*) is said of that which exists in an entire state: *invent*, in Latin *inventum*, from *invenio*, signifying to come at or light upon, is said of that which is new made or modelled. The merit of *finding* or *inventing* consists in newly applying or modifying the materials which exist separately; the merit of *discovering* consists in removing the obstacles which prevent us from knowing the real nature of the thing: imagination and industry are requisite for *finding* or *inventing;* acuteness and penetration for *discovering*. A person *finds* reasons for justifying himself: he *discovers* traits of a bad disposition in another. Cultivated minds *find* sources of amusement within themselves, or a prisoner *finds* means of escape. Many traces of a universal deluge have been *discovered:* the physician *discovers* the nature of a particular disorder.

Find is applicable to the operative arts;

> Long practice has a sure improvement *found*,
> With kindled fires to burn the barren ground.
> DRYDEN.

Discover is applied to speculative objects; 'Since the harmonick principles were *discovered*, musick has been a great independent science.'—SEWARD. *Invent* is applied to the mechanical arts;

> The sire of gods and men, with hard decrees,
> Forbids our plenty to be bought with ease;
> Himself *invented* first the shining share,
> And whetted human industry by care.—DRYDEN.

We speak of *finding* modes for performing actions, and effecting purposes; of *inventing* machines, instruments, and various matters of use or elegance; of *discovering* the operations and laws of nature. Many fruitless attempts have been made to *find* the longitude: men have not been so unsuccessful in *finding out* various arts for communicating their thoughts, commemorating the exploits of their nations, and supplying themselves with luxuries; nor have they failed in every species of machine or instrument which can aid their purpose. Harvey *discovered* the circulation of the blood: Torricelli *discovered* the gravity of the air: by geometry the properties of figures are *discovered;* by chymistry the properties of compound substances: but the geometrician *finds* by reasoning the solution of any problem; or by investigating, he *finds out* a clearer method of solving the same problems; or he *invents* an instrument by which the proof can be deduced from ocular demonstration. Thus the astronomer *discovers* the motions of the heavenly bodies, by means of the telescope which has been *invented*.

EMISSARY, SPY.

Emissary, in Latin *emissarius*, from *emitto* to send forth, signifies one sent out; *spy*, in French *espion*, from the Latin *specio* to look into or look about, signifies one narrowly searched.

Both these words designate a person sent out by a body on some publick concern among their enemies; but they differ in their office according to the etymology of the words.

The *emissary* is by distinction sent forth, he is sent so as to mix with the people to whom he goes, to be in all places, and to associate with every one individually as may serve his purpose; the *spy*, on the other hand, takes his station wherever he can best perceive what is passing; he keeps himself at a distance from all but such as may particularly aid him in the object of his search.

The object of an *emissary* is by direct communication with the enemy to sow the seeds of dissension, to spread false alarms, and to disseminate false principles; the object of a *spy* is to get information of an enemy's plans and movements.

Although the office of *emissary* and *spy* are neither of them honourable, yet that of the former is more disgraceful than that of the latter. The *emissary* is generally employed by those who have some illegitimate object to pursue; 'The Jesuits send over *emissaries* with instructions to personate themselves members of the several sects among us.'—SWIFT. *Spies* on the other hand are employed by all regular governments in a time of warfare; 'He (Henry I.) began with the Earl of Shrewsbury, who was watched for some time by *spies* and then indicted upon a charge of forty-five articles.'—HUME.

In the time of the Revolution, the French sent their *emissaries* into every country, civilized or uncivilized, to fan the flame of rebellion against established governments. At Sparta, the trade of a *spy* was not so vile as it has been generally esteemed; it was considered as a self-devotion for the publick good, and formed a part of their education.

These terms are both applied in an extended application with a similar distinction; 'What generally makes pain itself, if I may so say, more painful, is that it is considered as the *emissary* of the king of terrours.'—BURKE.

> These wretched *spies* of wit must soon confess,
> They take more pains to please themselves the less.
> DRYDEN.

MARK, PRINT, IMPRESSION, STAMP.

Mark is the same in the northern languages, and in the Persian *marz;* *print* and *impression*, both from the Latin *premo* to press, signify the visible effect produced by *printing* or pressing; *stamp* signifies the effect produced by *stamping*.

The word *mark* is the most general in sense: whatever alters the external face of an object is a *mark;* the *print* is some specifick *mark*, or a figure drawn upon the surface of an object; the *impression* is the *mark* pressed either upon or into a body; the *stamp* is the *mark* that is *stamped* in or upon the body. The *mark* is confined to no size, shape, or form; the *print* is a *mark* that represents an object: the *mark* may consist of a spot, a line, a stain, or a smear; but a *print* describes a given object, as a house, a man, &c. A *mark* is either a protuberance or a depression; an *impression* is always a sinking in of the object: a hillock or a hole are both *marks;* but the latter is properly the *impression:* the *stamp* mostly resembles the *impression*, unless in the case of a seal, which is *stamped* upon paper, and occasions an elevation with the wax.

The *mark* is occasioned by every sort of action, gentle or violent, artificial or natural; by the voluntary act of a person, or the unconscious act of inanimate bodies; by means of compression or friction; by a touch or a blow, and the like: all the others are occasioned by one or more of these modes; 'De la Chambre asserts positively that from the *marks* on the body, the configuration of the planets at a nativity may be gathered.'—WALSH. The *print* is occasioned by artificial means of compression, as when the *print* of letters or pictures is made on paper; or by accidental and natural compression, as when the *print* of the hand is made on the wall, or the *print* of the foot is made on the ground;

> From hence Astrea took her flight, and here
> The *prints* of her departing steps appear.
> DRYDEN.

The *impression* is made by means more or less violent, as when an *impression* is made upon wood by the axe or hammer; or by means gradual and natural, as by the dripping of water on stone. The *stamp* is made by means of direct pressure with an artificial instrument.

Mark is of such universal application that it is confined to no objects whatever, either in the natural or moral world; *print* is mostly applied to material objects, the face of which undergoes a lasting change, as the *printing* made on paper or wood; *impression* is more commonly applied to such natural objects as are particularly solid; *stamp* is generally applied to paper, or still softer and more yielding bodies. *Impression* and *stamp* have both a moral application: events or speeches make an *impression* on the mind: things bear a certain *stamp* which bespeaks their origin. Where the passions have obtained an ascendancy, the occasional good *impressions* which are produced by religious observances but too frequently die away; 'No man can offer at the change of the government established, without first gaining new authority, and in some degree debasing the old by appearance and *impressions* of contrary qualities in those who before enjoyed it.'—TEMPLE. The Christian religion carries with itself the *stamp* of truth;

> Adult'rate metals to the sterling *stamp*
> Appear not meaner than mere human lines
> Compar'd with those whose inspiration shines.
> ROSCOMMON.

MARK, SIGN, NOTE, SYMPTOM, TOKEN, INDICATION.

Mark, v. *Mark*, *impression; sign*, in Latin *signum*, Greek ςίγμα from ςίζω to punctuate, signifies the thing that points out; *symptom*, in Latin *symptoma*, Greek σύμπτωμα from συμπίπτω to fall out in accordance with any thing, signifies what presents itself to confirm one's opinion; *token*, through the medium of the northern languages, comes from the Greek τεκμήριον; *indication*, in Latin *indicatio* from *indico*, and the Greek ἐνδείκω to point out, signifies the thing which points out.

The idea of an external object which serves to direct the observer, is common to all these terms; the difference consists in the objects that are employed. Any thing may serve as a *mark*, a stroke, a dot, a stick set up, and the like; it serves simply to guide the senses: the *sign* is something more complex; it consists of a figure or representation of some object, as the twelve *signs* of the zodiack, or the *signs* which are affixed to houses of entertainment, or to shops. *Marks* are arbitrary; every one chooses his *mark* at pleasure: *signs* have commonly a connexion with the object that is to be observed: a house, a tree, a letter, or any external object may be chosen as a *mark;* but a tobacconist chooses the *sign* of a black man; the innkeeper chooses the head of the reigning prince. *Marks* serve in general simply to aid the memory in distinguishing the situation of objects, or the particular circumstances of persons or things, as the *marks* which are set up in the garden to distinguish the ground that is occupied; they may, therefore, be private, and known only to the individual or individuals that make them, as the private *marks* by which a tradesman distinguishes the prices; they may likewise be changeable and fluctuating, according to the humour and convenience of the maker, as the private *marks* which are employed by the military on guard. *Signs*, on the contrary, serve to direct the understanding: they have either a natural or an artificial resemblance to the object to be represented; they are consequently chosen, not by the will of one, but by the universal consent of a body; they are not chosen for the moment, but for a permanency, as in the case of language, either oral or written, in the case of the zodiacal *signs*, or the *sign* of the cross, the algebraical *signs*, and the like. It is clear, therefore, that many objects may be both a *mark* and a *sign*, according to the above illustration: the cross which is employed in books, by way of reference to notes, is a *mark* only, because it serves merely to guide the eye, or assist the memory; but the figure of the cross, when employed in reference to the cross of our Saviour, is a *sign*, inasmuch as it conveys a distinct idea of something else to the mind; so likewise, little strokes over letters, or even letters themselves, may merely be *marks*, while they only point out a difference between this or that letter, this or that object; but this same stroke becomes a *sign*, if, as in the first declension of Latin nouns, it points out the ablative case, it is the *sign* of the ablative case; and a single letter affixed to different parcels is merely a *mark* so long as it simply serves this purpose; but the same letter, suppose it were a word, is a *sign* when it is used as a *sign*. It is, moreover, clear from the above, that there are many objects which serve as *marks*, which are never *signs;* and on the other hand, although *signs* are mostly composed, yet there are two sorts of *signs* which have nothing to do with the *mark;* namely, those which we obtain by any other sense than that of sight; or those which are only figures in the mind. When words are spoken, and not written, they are *signs* and not *marks;* and in like manner the *sign* of the cross, when made on the forehead of children in baptism, is a *sign*, but not a *mark*. This illustration of these two words in their strict and proper sense, will serve to explain them in their extended and metaphorical sense. A *mark* stands for nothing but what is visible; the *sign* stands for that only which is real. A star on the breast of an officer or nobleman is a *mark* of distinction or honour, because it distinguishes one person from another, and in a way that is apt to reflect honour; but it is not a *sign* of honour, because it is not the indubitable test of a man's honourable feelings, since it may be conferred by favour or by mistake, or from some partial circumstance.

The *mark* and *sign* may both stand for the appearance of things, and in that case the former shows the cause by the effect, the latter the consequent by the antecedent. When a thing is said to bear the *marks* of violence, the cause of the *mark* is judged of by the *mark* itself; but when we say that a lowering sky is a *sign* of rain, the future or consequent event is judged of by the present appearance;

> So plain the *signs*, such prophets are the skies.
> DRYDEN.

So likewise we judge by the *marks* of a person's foot that some one has been walking in a given place: when mariners meet with birds at sea, they consider them a *sign* that land is near at hand.

It is here worthy of observation, however, that *mark* is only used for that which may be seen, but that the *sign* may serve to direct our conclusions, even in that which affects the hearing, feeling, smell, or taste; thus hoarseness is a *sign* that the person has a cold; the effects which it produces on the patient are to himself sensible *signs* that he labours under such an affection. The smell of fire is a *sign* that some place is on fire; one of the two travellers, in La Mothe's fable, considered the taste of the wine as a *sign* that there must be leather in the bottle, and the other that there must be iron; and it proved that they were both right, for a little key with a bit of leather tied to it was found at the bottom.

In this sense of the words they are applied to moral objects with precisely the same distinction: the *mark* illustrates the spring of the action; the *sign* shows the state of the mind or sentiments: it is a *mark* of folly or weakness in a man to yield himself implicitly to the guidance of an interested friend; 'The ceremonial laws of Moses were the *marks* to distinguish the people of God from the Gentiles.'—BACON. Tears are not always a sign of repentance; 'The sacring of the kings of France (as Loysel says) is the *sign* of their sovereign priesthood.'—TEMPLE.

A *note* is rather a *sign* than a *mark;* but it is properly the *sign* which consists of *marks*, as a *note* of admiration (!), and likewise a *note* which consists of many letters and words.

Symptom is rather a *mark* than a *sign;* it explains the cause or origin of complaints, by the appearances they assume, and is employed as a technical term only in the science of medicine: as a foaming at the mouth, and an abhorrence of drink, are *symptoms* of canine madness; motion and respiration are *signs* of life. *Symptom* may likewise be used figuratively in application to moral objects; 'This fall of the French monarchy was far from being preceded by any exteriour *symptoms* of decline.'—BURKE.

Token is a species of *mark* in the moral sense, *indication* a species of *sign*; the *mark* shows what is, the *token* serves to keep in mind what has been: a gift to a friend is a *mark* of one's affection and esteem; if it be permanent in its nature it becomes a *token*: friends who are in close intercourse have perpetual opportunities of showing each other *marks* of their regard by reciprocal acts of courtesy and kindness; when they separate for any length of time, they commonly leave some *token* of their tender sentiments in each other's hands, as a pledge of what shall be, as well as an evidence of what has been; 'The famous bull-feasts are an evident *token* of the Quixotism and romantick taste of the Spaniards.'—SOMERVILLE.

Sign, as it respects an *indication*, is said in abstract and general propositions: *indication* itself is only employed for some particular individual referred to; it bespeaks the act of the persons: but the *sign* is only the face or appearance of the thing. When a man does not live consistently with the profession which he holds, it is a *sign* that his religion is built on a wrong foundation; parents are gratified when they observe the slightest *indications* of genius or goodness in their children; 'It is certain Virgil's parents gave him a good education, to which they were inclined by the early *indications* he gave of a sweet disposition and excellent wit.'—WALSH.

MARK, TRACE, VESTIGE, FOOTSTEP, TRACK.

The word *mark* has already been considered at large in the preceding article, but it will admit of farther illustration when taken in the sense of that which is visible, and serves to show the existing state of things; *mark* is here, as before, the most general and unqualified term; the other terms varying in the circumstances or manner of the *mark*; *trace*, in Italian *treccia*, Greek τρέχειν to run, and Hebrew דרך way, signifies any continued *mark*; *vestige*, in Latin *vestigium*, not improbably contracted from *pedis* and *stigium* or *stigma*, from ςίζω to imprint, signifies a print of the foot; *footstep* is taken for the place in which the foot has stepped, or the *mark* made by that step; *track*, derived from the same source as trace, signifies the way run, or the *mark* produced by that running.

The *mark* is said of a fresh and uninterrupted line; the *trace* is said of that which is broken by time: a carriage, in driving along the sand leaves *marks* of the wheels, but in a short time all *traces* of its having been there will be lost: the *mark* is produced by the action of bodies on one another in every possible form; the spilling of a liquid may leave a *mark* on the floor; the blow of a stick leaves a *mark* on the body;

> I have served him
> In this old body; yet the *marks* remain
> Of many wounds.—OTWAY.

The *trace* is a *mark* produced only by bodies making a progress or proceeding in a continued course: the ship that cuts the waves, and the bird that cuts the air, leaves no *traces* of their course behind; so men pass their lives, and after death they leave no *traces* that they ever were; 'The greatest favours to an ungrateful man are but like the motion of a ship upon the waves: they leave no *trace*, no sign behind them.'—SOUTH. These words are both applied to moral objects, but the *mark* is produced by objects of inferiour importance; it excites a momentary observation, but does not carry us back to the past; its cause is either too obvious or too minute to awaken attention; a *trace* is generally a *mark* of something which we may wish to see. *Marks* of haste and imbecility in a common writer excite no surprise, and call forth no observation;

> These are the monuments of Helen's love,
> The shame I bear below, the *marks* I bore above.
> DRYDEN.

In a writer of long standing celebrity, we look for *traces* of his former genius.

The *vestige* is a species of the *mark* caused literally by the foot of man, and consequently applied to such places as have been inhabited, where the active industry of man has left visible *marks*; it is a species of *trace*, inasmuch as it carries us back to that which was, but is not at present. We discover by *marks* that things have been; we discover by *traces* and *vestiges* what they have been: a hostile army always leaves sufficiently evident *marks* of its having passed through a country; there are *traces* of the Roman roads still visible in London and different parts of England: Rome contains many *vestiges* of its former greatness; 'Both Britain and Ireland had temples for the worship of the gods, the *vestiges* of which are now remaining.'—PARSONS.

Mineralogists assert that there are many *marks* of a universal deluge discoverable in the fossils and strata of the earth; philological inquirers imagine that there are *traces* in the existing languages of the world sufficient to ascertain the progress by which the earth became populated after the deluge; the pyramids are *vestiges* of antiquity which raise our ideas of human greatness beyond any thing which the modern state of the arts can present. *Vestige*, like the two former, may be applied to moral as well as natural objects with the same line of distinction. A person betrays *marks* of levity in his conduct. Wherever we discover *traces* of the same customs or practices in one country which are prevalent in another, we suppose those countries to have had an intercourse or connexion of some kind with one another at a certain remote period.

Footstep and *track* are sometimes employed as a *mark*, but oftener as a road or course: when we talk of following the *footsteps* of another, it may signify either to follow the *marks* of his *footsteps* as a guide for the course we should take, or to walk in the very same steps as he has done: the former is the act of one who is in pursuit of another; the latter is the act of him who follows in a train. *Footsteps* is employed only for the *steps* of an individual; the *track* is made by the *steps* of many; it is the line which has been beaten out or made by stamping: the term *footstep* can only be employed for men or brutes; but *track* is applied to inanimate objects, as the wheel of a carriage. When Cacus took away the oxen of Hercules, he dragged them backward that they might not be *traced* by their *footsteps*: a *track* of blood from the body of a murdered man may sometimes lead to the detection of the murderer.

In the metaphorical application they do not signify a *mark*, but a course of conduct; the former respects one's moral feelings or mode of dealing; the latter one's mechanical and habitual manner of acting: the former is the consequence of having the same principles; the latter proceeds from imitation or constant repetition.

A good son will walk in the *footsteps* of a good father. In the management of business it is rarely wise in a young man to leave the *track* which has been *marked* out for him by his superiours in age and experience;

> Virtue alone ennobles humankind,
> And power should on her glorious *footsteps* wait.
> WYNNE.

> Though all seems lost, 't is impious to despair,
> The *tracks* of Providence like rivers wind.
> HIGGONS

MARK, BADGE, STIGMA.

Mark (*v. Mark*, *print*) is still the general, and the two other specifick terms; they are employed for whatever externally serves to characterize persons, or betoken any part either of his character or his circumstances: *mark* is employed either in a good, bad, or indifferent sense; *badge* in an indifferent; *stigma* in a bad sense: a thing may either be a *mark* of honour, of disgrace, or of simple distinction: a *badge* is a *mark* simply of distinction; the *stigma* is a *mark* of disgrace. The *mark* is conferred upon a person for his merits, as medals, stars, and ribands are bestowed by princes upon meritorious officers and soldiers; or the *mark* attaches to a person, or is affixed to him, in consequence of his demerits; as a low situation in his class is a *mark* of disgrace to a scholar; or a fool's cap is a *mark* of ignominy affixed to idlers and dunces; or a brand in the forehead is a *mark* of ignominy for criminals; 'In these revolutionary meetings, every counsel, in proportion as it is daring and violent and perfidious, is taken for the *mark* of superiour genius.'—BURKE. The *badge* is voluntarily assumed by one's self according to established custom; it consists of dress by which the office, station, and even religion of a particular community is distinguished: as the gown and wig is the *badge* of gentlemen in the law; the gown and surplice that of clerical men; the uniform of charity children is the *badge* of their condition; the peculiar habit of the Quakers and Methodists is the *badge* of their religion; 'The people of England look upon hereditary succession as a security for their liberty, not as a *badge* of servitude.'—BURKE.

The *stigma* consists not so much in what is openly imposed upon a person as what falls upon him in the judgement of others; it is the black *mark* which is set upon a person by the publick, and is consequently the strongest of all *marks*, which every one most dreads, and every good man seeks least to deserve. A simple *mark* may sometimes be such only in our own imagination; as when one fancies that dress is a *mark* of superiority, or the contrary; that the courtesies which we receive from a superiour are *marks* of his personal esteem and regard: but the *stigma* is not what an individual imagines for himself, but what is conceived towards him by others; the office of a spy and informer is so odious, that every man of honest feeling holds the very name to be a *stigma:* although a *stigma* is in general the consequence of a man's real unworthiness, yet it is possible for particular prejudices and ruling passions to make that a *stigma* which is not so deservedly; as in the case of men's religious profession, inasmuch as it is not accompanied with any moral depravity; it is mostly unjust to attach a *stigma* to a whole body of men for their speculative views; 'The cross, which our Saviour's enemies thought was to *stigmatize* him with infamy, became the ensign of his renown.'—BLAIR.

MARK, BUTT.

After all that has been said upon the word *mark* (*v. Mark, print*), it has this additional meaning in common with the word *butt*, that it implies an object aimed at: the *mark* is however literally a *mark* that is said to be shot at by the *marksman* with a gun or a bow;

A fluttering dove upon the top they tie,
The living *mark* at which their arrows fly.
DRYDEN.

Or it is metaphorically employed for the man who by his peculiar characteristicks makes himself the object of notice; he is the *mark* at which every one's looks and thoughts are directed;

He made the *mark*
For all the people's hate, the prince's curses.
DENHAM.

The *butt*, from the French *but* the end, is a species of *mark* in this metaphorical sense; but the former only calls forth general observation, the latter provokes the laughter and jokes of every one. Whoever renders himself conspicuous by his eccentricities either in his opinions or his actions, must not complain if he becomes a *mark* for the derision of the publick; it is a man's misfortune rather than his fault if he become the *butt* of a company who are rude and unfeeling enough to draw their pleasures from another's pain; 'I mean those honest gentlemen that are pelted by men, women, and children, by friends and foes, and in a word stand as *butts* in conversation.'—ADDISON.

TO DERIVE, TRACE, DEDUCE.

Derive, from the Latin *de* and *rivus* a river, signifies to drain after the manner of water from its source; *trace*, in Italian *tracciare*, Greek τρέχω to run, Hebrew דרך to go, signifies to go by a line drawn out, to follow the line; *deduce*, in Latin *deduco*, signifies to bring from.

The idea of drawing one thing from another is included in all the actions designated by these terms. The act of *deriving* is immediate and direct; that of *tracing* a gradual process; that of *deducing* by a ratiocinative process.

We discover causes and sources by *derivation;* we discover the course, progress, and commencement of things by *tracing;* we discover the grounds and reasons of things by *deduction*. A person *derives* his name from a given source; he *traces* his family up to a given period; principles or powers are *deduced* from circumstances or observations. The Trojans *derived* the name of their city from Tros, a king of Phrygia; they *traced* the line of their kings up to Dardanus; 'The kings among the heathens ever *derived* them selves or their ancestors from some good.'—TEMPLE

Let Newton, pure intelligence! whom God
To mortals lent to *trace* his boundless works,
From laws sublimely simple speak thy fame.
THOMSON.

Copernicus *deduced* the principle of the earth's turning round from several simple observations, particularly from the apparent and contrary motion of bodies that are really at rest. The English tongue is of such mixed origin that there is scarcely any known language from which some one of its words is not *derivable;* it is an interesting employment to *trace* the progress of science and civilization in countries which have been involved in ignorance and barbarism; from the writings of Locke and other philosophers of an equally loose stamp, have been *deduced* principles both in morals and politicks that are destructive to the happiness of men in civil society; 'From the discovery of some natural authority may perhaps be *deduced* a truer original of all governments among men than from any contracts.'—TEMPLE.

TO IMPLANT, INGRAFT, INCULCATE, INSTIL, INFUSE.

To *plant* is properly to fix plants in the ground, to *implant* is, in the improper sense, to fix principles in the mind. *Graft* is to make one plant grow on the stock of another; to *ingraft* is to make particular principles flourish in the mind, and form a part of the character. *Calco* is in Latin to tread; and *inculcate* to stamp into the mind. *Stillo*, in Latin, is literally to fall dropwise; *instillo*, to *instil*, is, in the improper sense, to make sentiments as it were drop into the mind *Fundo*, in Latin, is literally to pour in a stream; *infundo*, to *infuse*, is, in the improper sense, to pour principles or feelings into the mind.

To *implant*, *ingraft*, and *inculcate* are said of abstract opinions, or rules of right and wrong; *instil* and *infuse* of such principles as influence the heart, the affections, and the passions. It is the business of the parent in early life to *implant* sentiments of virtue in his child;

With various seeds of art deep in the mind
Implanted.—THOMSON.

It is the business of the teacher to *ingraft* them; 'The reciprocal attraction in the minds of men is a principle *ingrafted* in the very first formation of the soul, by the Author of our nature.'—BERKELEY. The belief of a Deity, and all the truths of Divine Revelation, ought to be *implanted* in the mind of the child as soon as it can understand any thing: if it have not enjoyed this privilege in its earliest infancy, the task of *ingrafting* these principles afterward into the mind is attended with considerable difficulty and uncertainty of success. To *inculcate* is a more immediate act than either to *implant* or *ingraft*. It is the business of the preacher to *inculcate* the doctrines of Christianity from the pulpit; 'To preach practical sermons, as they are called, that is, sermons upon virtues and vices, without *inculcating* the great Scripture truths of redemption, grace, &c. which alone can enable and incite us to forsake sin and follow after righteousness; what is it, but to put together the wheels and set the hands of a watch, forgetting the spring which is to make them all go?'—BISHOP HORNE. *Instilling* is a corresponding act with *implanting;* we *implant* belief; we *instil* the feeling which is connected with this belief. It is not enough to have an abstract belief of a God *implanted* into the mind: we must likewise have a love and a fear of him, and reverence for his holy name and Word, *instilled* into the mind.

To *instil* is a gradual process which is the natural work of education; to *infuse* is a more arbitrary and immediate act. Sentiments are *instilled* into the mind, not altogether by the personal efforts of any individual, but likewise by collateral endeavours; they are however *infused* at the express will, and with the express endeavour of some person. By the reading of the Scriptures, an attendance on publick worship, and the influence of example, combined with the instructions of a parent, religious sentiments are *instilled* into the mind; 'The apostle often makes mention of sound doctrine in opposition to the extravagant and corrupt opinions which false teachers, even in those days, *instilled* into the minds of their ignorant and unwary disciples.'—BEVERIDGE. By the counsel and conversation of an intimate friend, an even current of the feeling becomes *infused* into the mind;

> No sooner grows
> The soft *infusion* prevalent and wide,
> Than, all alive, at once their joy o'erflows
> In musick unconfin'd.—THOMSON.

Instil is applicable only to permanent sentiments; *infuse* may be said of any partial feeling: hence we speak of *infusing* a poison into the mind by means of insidious and mischievous publications, or *infusing* a jealousy by means of crafty insinuations, or *infusing* an ardour into the minds of soldiers by means of spirited addresses coupled with military successes.

TO IMPRINT, IMPRESS, ENGRAVE.

Print and *press* are both derived from *pressus*, participle of *premo*, signifying in the literal sense to press, or to make a mark by pressing; to *impress* and *imprint* are morally enployed in the same sense. Things are *impressed* on the mind so as to produce a conviction: they are *imprinted* on it so as to produce recollection. If the truths of Christianity be *impressed* on the mind, they will show themselves in a corresponding conduct: whatever is *imprinted* on the mind in early life, or by any particular circumstance, is not readily forgotten;

> Whence this disdain of life in ev'ry breast,
> But from a notion on their minds *impress'd*
> That all who for their country die are bless'd!
> JENYNS.

'Such a strange, sacred, and inviolable majesty has God *imprinted* upon this faculty (the conscience), that it can never be deposed.'—SOUTH. *Engrave*, from *grave* and the German *graben* to dig, expresses more in the proper sense than either, and the same in its moral application; for we may truly say that if the truths of Christianity be *engraven* in the minds of youth, they can never be eradicated;

> Deep on his front *engraven*,
> Deliberation sat, and publick care.—MILTON.

SEAL, STAMP.

Seal is a specifick, *stamp* a general, term: there cannot be a *seal* without a *stamp*; but there may be many *stamps* where there is no *seal*. *Seal*, in Latin *sigillum*, signifies a signet or little sign, consisting of any one's coat of arms, or any other device; the *stamp* is, in general, any impression whatever which has been made by *stamping*, that is, any impression which is not easily to be effaced. In the improper sense, the *seal* is the authority; thus to set one's *seal* is the same as to authorize, and the *seal* of truth is any outward mark which characterizes it;

> Therefore, not long in force this charter stood,
> Wanting that *seal*, it must be *seal'd* in blood.
> DENHAM.

In the *stamp* is the impression by which we distinguish the thing; thus a thing is said to bear the *stamp* of truth, of sincerity, of veracity, and the like;

> Wisdom for parts is madness for the whole,
> This *stamps* the paradox, and gives us leave
> To call the wisest weak.—YOUNG.

PICTURE, PRINT, ENGRAVING.

Picture (*v. Painting*) is any likeness taken by the hand of the artist; the *print* is the copy of the *painting* in a *printed* state; and the *engraving* is that which is produced by an *engraver*: every *engraving* is a *print*; but every *print* is not an *engraving*; for the *picture* may be *printed* off from something besides an *engraving*, as in the case of wood cuts. The *picture* is sometimes taken for any representation of a likeness without regard to the mode by which it is formed: in this case it is employed mostly for the representations of the common kind that are found in books; but the *print* and *engraving* are said of the higher specimens of the art. On certain occasions the word *engraving* is most appropriate, as to take an *engraving* of a particular object; on other occasions the word *print*, as a handsome *print* or a large *print*;

> The *pictures* plac'd for ornament and use,
> The twelve good rules, the royal game of goose.
> GOLDSMITH

> Tim, with surprise and pleasure staring,
> Ran to the glass, and then comparing
> His own sweet figure with the *print*,
> Distinguish'd every feature in 't.—SWIFT.

'Since the publick has of late begun to express a relish for *engravings*, drawings, copyings, and for the original paintings of the chief Italian school, I doubt not that in very few years we shall make an equal progress in this other science.'—EARL OF SHAFTESBURY.

TO MARK, NOTE, NOTICE.

Mark is here taken in the intellectual sense, fixing as it were a *mark* (*v. Mark*) upon a thing so as to keep it in mind, which is in fact to fix one's attention upon it in such a manner as to be able to distinguish it by its characteristick qualities; to *mark* is therefore altogether an intellectual act: to *note* has the same end as that of *marking*, namely, to aid the memory; but one *notes* a thing by making a written *note* of it; this is therefore a mechanical act: to *notice*, on the other hand, is a sensible operation, from *notitia* knowledge signifying to bring to one's knowledge, perception, or understanding by the use of our senses. We *mark* and *note* that which particularly interests us. *Marking* serves a present purpose. *Noting* is applied to that which may be of use in future. The impatient lover *marks* the hours until the time arrives for meeting his mistress; 'Many who *mark* with such accuracy the course of time appear to have little sensibility of the decline of life.'—JOHNSON. Travellers *note* whatever strikes them of importance to be remembered when they return home;

> O treach'rous conscience! while she seems to sleep,
> *Unnoted*, *notes* each moment misapply'd.—YOUNG.

To *notice* may serve either for the present or the future: we may *notice* things merely by way of amusement, as a child will *notice* the actions of animals; or we may *notice* a thing for the sake of bearing it in mind, as a person *notices* a particular road when he wishes to return; 'An Englishman's *notice* of the weather is the natural consequence of changeable skies and uncertain seasons.'—JOHNSON.

TO NOTICE, REMARK, OBSERVE.

To *notice* (*v. To attend to*) is either to take or to give *notice*: to *remark*, compounded of *re* and *mark* (*v. Mark*), signifies to reflect or bring back any mark to our own mind, or communicate the same to another: to mark is to mark a thing once, but to *remark* is to mark it again; *observe* (*v. Looker-on*) signifies either to keep a thing present before one's own view, or to communicate our view to another.

In the first sense of these words, as the action respects ourselves, to *notice* and *remark* require simple attention, to *observe* requires examination. To *notice* is a more cursory action than to *remark*: we may *notice* a thing by a single glance, or on merely turning one's head; but to *remark* supposes a reaction of the mind on an object: we *notice* that a person passes our door on a certain day and at a certain hour; but we *remark* to others that he goes past every day at the same hour: we *notice* that the sun sets this evening under a cloud, and we *remark* that it has done so for several evenings successively: we *notice* the state of a person's health or his manners in company, we *remark* his habits and peculiarities in domestick life. What is *noticed* and *remarked* strikes on the senses, and awakens the mind; what is *observed* is looked after and sought for. *Noticing* and *remarking* are often involuntary acts; we see, hear, and think, because the objects obtrude themselves uncalled for: but *observing* is intentional as well as voluntary; we see, hear, and think on that which we have watched. We *remark* things as matters of fact; we *observe* them in order to judge of, or draw conclusions from, them: we *remark* that the wind lies for a long time in a certain quarter; we *observe* that whenever it lies in a certain quarter it brings rain with it. A general *notices* any thing particular in the appearance of his army; he *remarks* that the men have not for a length of time worn contented faces; he consequently *observes* their actions, when they think they are not seen, in order to discover the cause of their dissatisfaction: people who have no curiosity are sometimes attracted to *notice* the stars or planets, when they are particularly bright; those who look frequently will *remark* that the same star does not rise exactly in the same place for two successive nights; but the astronomer goes farther, and *observes* all the motions of the heavenly bodies, in order to discover the scheme of the universe; 'The depravity of mankind is so easily discoverable, that nothing but the desert or cell can exclude it from *notice*.'—JOHNSON. 'The glass that magnifies its objects contracts the sight to a point, and the mind must be fixed upon a single character, to *remark* its minute peculiarities.'—JOHNSON. 'The course of time is so visibly marked, that it is *observed* even by the birds of passage.'—JOHNSON.

In the latter sense of these verbs, as respects the communications to others of what passes in our own minds, to *notice* is to make known our sentiments by various ways; to *remark* and *observe* are to make them known only by means of words: to *notice* is a personal act towards an individual, in which we direct our attention to him, as may happen either by a bow, a nod, a word, or even a look; 'As some do perceive, yea, and like it well, they should be so *noticed*.'—HOWARD. To *remark* and *observe* are said only of the thoughts which pass in our own minds, and are expressed to others: friends *notice* each other when they meet; they *remark* to others the impression which passing objects make upon their minds; 'He cannot distinguish difficult and noble speculations from trifling and vulgar *remarks*.'—COLLIER. The *observations* which intelligent people make are always entitled to *notice* from young persons; 'Wherever I have found her notes to be wholly another's, which is the case in some hundreds, I have barely quoted the true proprietor, without *observing* upon it.'—POPE.

OBSERVATION, OBSERVANCE.

These terms derive their use from the different significations of the verb; *observation* is the act of observing objects with the view to examine them (*v. To notice*); *observance* is the act of observing a thing in the sense of keeping or holding it sacred (*v. To keep*). From a minute *observation* of the human body, anatomists have discovered the circulation of the blood, and the source of all the humours; 'The pride which, under the check of publick *observation* would have been only vented among domesticks, becomes, in a country baronet, the torment of a province.'—JOHNSON. By a strict *observance* of truth and justice, a man acquires the title of an upright man; 'You must not fail to behave yourself towards my Lady Clare, your grandmother, with all duty and *observance*.'—EARL STAFFORD.

EXTRAORDINARY, REMARKABLE,

Are epithets both opposed to the ordinary; and in that sense the *extraordinary* is that which in its own nature is *remarkable*; but things, however, may be *extraordinary* which are not *remarkable*, and the contrary. The *extraordinary* is that which is out of the ordinary course; but it does not always excite remark, and is not therefore *remarkable*; as when we speak of an *extraordinary* loan, an *extraordinary* measure of government: on the other hand, when *extraordinary* conveys the idea of what deserves notice, it expresses much more than *remarkable*. There are but few *extraordinary* things; many things are *remarkable*: the *remarkable* is eminent; the *extraordinary* is supereminent: the *extraordinary* excites our astonishment; the *remarkable* only awakens our interest and attention. The *extraordinary* is unexpected; the *remarkable* is sometimes looked for: every instance of sagacity and fidelity in a dog is *remarkable*, and some *extraordinary* instances have been related, which would almost stagger our belief; 'The love of praise is a passion deep in the mind of every *extraordinary* person.'—HUGHES 'The heroes of literary history have been no less *remarkable* for what they have suffered than for what they have achieved.'—JOHNSON.

REMARK, OBSERVATION, COMMENT, NOTE, ANNOTATION, COMMENTARY.

Remark and *observation*, *v. To notice*; *comment*, in Latin *commentum*, from *comminiscor* to call to mind, are either spoken or written; *note*, *annotation*, *v. Note*; and *commentary*, a variation of *comment*, are always written. *Remark* and *observation*, admitting of the same distinction in both cases, have been sufficiently explained in the article referred to; 'Spence, in his *remarks* on Pope's Odyssey, produces what he thinks an unconquerable quotation from Dryden's preface to the Æneid, in favour of translating an epick poem into blank verse.'—JOHNSON. 'If the critick has published nothing but rules and *observations* on criticism, I then consider whether there be a propriety and elegance in his thoughts and words.'—ADDISON. *Comment* is a species of *remark* which often loses in good-nature what it gains in seriousness; it is mostly applied to particular persons or cases, and more commonly employed as a vehicle of censure than of commendation; publick speakers and publick performers are exposed to all the *comments* which the vanity, the envy, and ill-nature of self-constituted criticks can suggest; but when not employed in personal cases, it serves for explanation;

> Sublime or low, unbended or intense,
> The sound is still a *comment* to the sense.
> ROSCOMMON

The other terms are used in this sense only, but with certain modifications: the *note* is most general, and serves to call the attention to, as well as illustrate, particular passages in the text; 'The history of the *notes* (to Pope's Homer) has never been traced.'—JOHNSON. *Annotations* and *commentaries* are more minute; the former being that which is added by way of appendage, the latter being employed in a general form; as the *annotations* of the Greek scholiasts, and the *commentaries* on the sacred writings; 'I love a critick who mixes the rules of life with *annotations* upon writers.'—STEELE. 'Memoirs or memorials are of two kinds whereof the one may be termed *commentaries*, the other registers.'—BACON.

TO MENTION, NOTICE.

These terms are synonymous only inasmuch as they imply the act of calling things to another person's mind. *Mention*, from *mens* mind, signifies here to bring to mind. We *mention* a thing in direct terms. To *notice* (*v. To mark*), signifies to take *notice* of a thing indirectly or in a casual manner: we *mention* that which may serve as information; we *notice* that which may be merely of a personal or incidental nature. One friend *mentions* to another what has passed at a particular meeting: in the course of conversation he *notices* or calls to the *notice* of his companion the badness of the road, the wideness of the street, or the like; 'The great critick I have before *mentioned*, though a heathen, has taken *notice* of the sublime manner in which the lawgiver of the Jews has described the creation.'—ADDISON.

TO SHOW, POINT OUT, MARK, INDICATE

Show, in German *schauen*, &c. Greek θεάομαι, comes from the Hebrew שעה to look upon; to *point out* is to fix a *point* upon a thing.

Show is here the general term, and the others specifick: the common idea included in the signification of them all is that of making a thing visible to another. To *show* is an indefinite term; one *shows* by simply setting a thing before the eyes of another: to *point out* is specifick; it is to *show* some particular *point* by a direct and immediate application to it: we *show* a person a book, when we put it into his hands; but we *point out* the beauties of its contents by making a *point* upon them, or accompanying the action with some particular movement which shall direct the attention of the observer in a specifick manner. Many things, therefore, may be *shown* which cannot be *pointed out:* a person *shows* himself but he does not *point* himself *out;* towns, houses, gardens, and the like, are *shown;* but single things of any description are *pointed out.*

To *show* and *point out* are personal acts, which are addressed from one individual to another; but to *mark* (*v. Mark, impression*) is an indirect means of making a thing visible or observable: a person may *mark* something in the absence of others, by which he intends to distinguish it from all others: thus a tradesman *marks* the prices and names of the articles which he sets forth in his shop. We *show* by holding in one's hand; we *point out* with the finger; we *mark* with a pen or pencil. To *show* and *mark* are the acts either of a conscious or an unconscious agent; to *point out* is the act of a conscious agent only, unless taken figuratively;

> His faculties unfolded, *pointed out*
> Where lavish nature the directing hand
> Of art demanded.—Thomson.

To *indicate* (*v. Mark, sign*) that of an unconscious agent only: persons or things *show*, persons only *point out*, and things only *indicate.*

As applied to things, *show* is a more positive term than *mark* or *indicate;* that which *shows* serves as a proof;

> The glow-worm *shows* the matin to be near,
> And 'gins to pale his ineffectual fire.—Shakspeare.

That which *marks* serves as a rule or guide for distinguishing; 'For our quiet possession of things useful, they are naturally *marked* where there is need.'—Grew. Nothing *shows* us the fallacy of forming schemes for the future, more than the daily evidences which we have of the uncertainty of our existence; nothing *marks* the character of a man more strongly than the manner in which he bestows or receives favours. To *mark* is commonly applied to that which is habitual and permanent; to *indicate* to that which is temporary or partial. A single act or expression sometimes *marks* the ruling temper of the mind; a look may *indicate* what is passing in the mind at the time. A man's abstaining to give relief to great distress when it is in his power, *marks* an unfeeling character; when a person gives another a cold reception, it *indicates* at least that there is no cordiality between them; 'Amid this wreck of human nature, traces still remain which *indicate* its author.'—Blair.

TO SHOW, EXHIBIT, DISPLAY.

To *show* is here, as before, the generick term; to *exhibit* (*v. To give*), and *display*, in French *deployer*, in all probability changed from the Latin *plico*, signifying to unfold or set forth to view, are specifick: they may all designate the acts of either persons or things: the first, however, does this either in the proper or the improper sense; the two latter rather in the improper sense. To *show* is an indefinite action applied to every object: we may *show* that which belongs to others, as well as ourselves; we commonly *exhibit* that which belongs to ourselves: we *show* corporeal or mental objects; we *exhibit* that which is mental or the work of the mind: one *shows* what is worth seeing in a house or grounds; he *exhibits* his skill on a stage. To *show* is an indifferent action: we may *show* accidentally or designedly, to please others, or to please ourselves;

> If I do feign
> O let me in my present wildness die,
> And never live to *show* the incredulous world
> The noble change that I have purposed.
> Shakspeare.

We *exhibit* and *display* with an express intention, and that mostly to please ourselves; we may *show* in a private or a publick manner before one or many; we commonly *exhibit* and *display* in a publick manner, or at least in such a manner as will enable us best to be seen. *Exhibit* and *display* have this farther distinction, that the former is mostly taken in a good or an indifferent sense, the latter in a bad sense: we may *exhibit* our powers from a laudable ambition to be esteemed; but we seldom make a *display* of any quality that is in itself praiseworthy, or from any motive but vanity: what we *exhibit* is, therefore, intrinsically good; what we *display* may often be only an imaginary or fictitious excellence. A musician *exhibits* his skill on any particular instrument; a fop *displays* his gold seals, or an ostentatious man *displays* his plate or his fine furniture; 'The *exhibitors* of that *show* politickly had placed whifflers armed and linked through the hall.'—Guyton. 'They are all couched in a pit, with obscured lights, which at the very instant of our meeting they will at once *display* to the night.'—Shakspeare.

Exhibit, when taken as the involuntary act of persons, may be applied to unfavourable objects in the sense of setting forth to the view of others; 'One of an unfortunate constitution is perpetually *exhibiting* a miserable example of the weakness of mind and body.'—Pope. *Display*, on the other hand, is applied in a favourable sense; but it expresses the setting forth to view more strikingly than the word *exhibit;*

> Thou heav'ns alternate beauty canst *display*
> The blush of morning and the milky way.
> Dryden.

When said of things, they differ principally in the manner and degree of clearness with which the thing appears to present itself to view: to *show* is, as before, altogether indefinite, and implies simply to bring to view; *exhibit* implies to bring inherent properties to light, that is, apparently by a process; to *display* is to set forth so as to strike the eye: the windows on a frosty morning will *show* the state of the weather;

> Then let us fall, but fall amid our foes;
> Despair of life the means of living *shows.*
> Dryden.

Experiments with the air-pump *exhibit* the many wonderful and interesting properties of air; 'The world has ever been a great theatre, *exhibiting* the same repeated scene of the follies of men.'—Blair. The beauties of the creation are peculiarly *displayed* in the spring season;

> Which interwoven Britons seem to raise,
> And *show* the triumph that their shame *displays.*
> Dryden.

SHOW, EXHIBITION, REPRESENTATION, SIGHT, SPECTACLE.

Show signifies the thing shown (*v. To show*): *exhibition* signifies the thing exhibited (*v. To show*); *representation*, the thing represented: *sight*, the thing to be seen; and *spectacle*, from the Latin *specto*, stands for the thing to be beheld.

Show is here, as in the former article, the most general term. Every thing set forth to view is *shown;* and if set forth for the amusement of others, it is a *show.* This is the common idea included in the terms *exhibition* and *representation:* but *show* is a term of vulgar meaning and application; the others have a higher use and signification. The *show* consists of that which merely pleases the eye; it is not a matter either of taste or action, but merely of curiosity;

> Charm'd with the wonders of the *show*,
> On ev'ry side, above, below,
> She now of this or that inquires,
> What least was understood admires.—Gay.

Exhibition, on the contrary, presents some effort of talent or some work of genius; 'Copley's picture of Lord Chatham's death is an *exhibition* of itself.'—Beattie. *Representation* sets forth the image or imitation of some thing by the power of art; 'There are many virtues which in their own nature are incapable of any outward *representation.*'—Addison. Hence we speak of a *show* of wild beasts; an *exhibition* of paintings; and a theatrical *representation.* The conjurer makes a *show* of his tricks at a fair to the wonder of the gazing multitude; the artist makes an *exhibition* of his works; *representations* of men and manners are given on the stage: *shows* are necessary to keep the populace in good humour; *exhibitions* are necessary for the encouragement of genius; *representations* are proper for the amusement of the cultivated, and the refinement of society. The *show, exhibition* and *representation* are presented by some one to the view of others; the *sight* and *spectacle* present themselves to view. *Sight*, like *show*, is a vulgar term; and *spectacle* the nobler term. Whatever is to be seen to excite notice is a *sight*, in which general sense it would comprehend every *show*, but in its particular sense it includes only that which casually offers itself to view: a *spectacle*, on the contrary, is that species of *sight* which has something in it to interest either the heart or the head of the observer: processions, reviews, sports, and the like, are *sights*; but battles, bull-fights, or publick games of any description are *spectacles*, which interest but shock the feelings;

Their various arms afford a pleasing *sight*.
DRYDEN.

The weary Britons, whose warrable youth
Was by Maximilian lately ledd away,
Were to those pagans made an open prey,
And daily *spectacle* of sad decay.—SPENSER.

SHOW, OUTSIDE, APPEARANCE, SEMBLANCE.

Where there is *show* (*v. To show*) there must be *outside* and *appearance;* but there may be the last without the former. The term *show* always denotes an action, and refers to some person as agent; but the *outside* may be merely the passive quality of something. We speak, therefore, of a thing as mere *show*, to signify that what is shown is all that exists; and in this sense it may be termed mere *outside*, as consisting only of what is on the *outside;*

You 'll find the friendship of the world is *show*,
Mere outward *show*.—SAVAGE.

The greater part of men behold nothing more than the rotation of human affairs. This is only the *outside* of things.'—BLAIR. In describing a house, however, we speak of its *outside*, and not of its *show;* as also of the *outside* of a book, and not of the *show*. *Appearance* denotes an action as well as *show;* but the former is the act of an unconscious agent, the latter of one that is conscious and voluntary: the *appearance* presents itself to the view; the *show* is purposely presented to view. A person makes a *show* so as to be seen by others; his *appearance* is that which *shows* itself in him. To look only to *show*, or be concerned for *show* only, signifies to be concerned for that only which will attract notice; to look only to the *outside* signifies to be concerned only for that which may be seen in a thing, to the disregard of that which is not seen: to look only to *appearances* signifies the same as the former, except that *outside* is said in the proper sense of that which literally strikes the eye; but *appearances* extend to the conduct, and whatever may affect the reputation; 'Every accusation against persons of rank was heard with pleasure (by James I. of Scotland). Every *appearance* of guilt was examined with rigour.'—ROBERTSON.

Semblance or *seeming* (*v. To seem*) always conveys the idea of an unreal *appearance*, or at least is contrasted with that which is real; he who only wears the *semblance* of friendship would be ill deserving the confidence of a friend;

But man, the wildest beast of prey,
Wears friendship's *semblance* to betray.—MOORE.

SHOW, PARADE, OSTENTATION.

These terms are synonymous when they imply abstract actions: *show* is here, as in the preceding article, taken in the vulgar sense; *ostentation* and *parade* include the idea of something particular: a man makes a *show* of his equipage, furniture, and the like, by which he strikes the eye of the vulgar, and seeks to impress them with an idea of his wealth and superiour rank; this is often the paltry refuge of weak minds to conceal their nothingness: a man makes a *parade* with his wealth, his knowledge, his charities, and the like, by which he endeavours to give weight and dignity to himself, proportioned to the solemnity of his proceedings: the *show* is, therefore, but a simple setting forth to view;

Great in themselves
They smile superiour of external *show*.
SOMERVILLE.

The *parade* requires art, it is a forced effort to attract notice by the number and extent of the ceremonies: 'It was not in the mere *parade* of royalty that the Mexican potentates exhibited their power.'—ROBERTSON. The *show* and *parade* are confined to the act of *showing*, or the means which are employed to *show;* but the *ostentation* necessarily includes the purpose for which the display is made; he who does a thing so as to be seen and applauded by others, does it from *ostentation*, particularly in application to acts of charity, or of publick subscription, in which a man strives to impress others with the extent of his wealth by the liberality of his gift; 'We are dazzled with the splendour of titles, the *ostentation* of learning, and the noise of victories.'—SPECTATOR.

SHOWY, GAUDY, GAY.

Showy, having or being full of *show* (*v. Show, outside*), is mostly an epithet of dispraise; that which is *showy* has seldom any thing to deserve notice beyond that which catches the eye; *gaudy*, from the Latin *gaudeo* to rejoice, signifies literally full of joy: and is applied figuratively to the exteriour of objects, but with the annexed bad idea of being striking to an excess: *gay*, on the contrary, which is only a contraction of *gaudy*, is used in the same sense as an epithet of praise. Some things may be *showy*, and in their nature properly so; thus the tail of a peacock is *showy:* artificial objects may likewise be *showy*, but they will not be preferred by persons of taste; 'Men of warm imaginations neglect solid and substantial happiness for what is *showy* and superficial.'—ADDISON. That which is *gaudy* is always artificial, and is always chosen by the vain, the vulgar, and the ignorant; a maid-servant will bedizen herself with *gaudy* coloured ribbons;

The *gaudy*, babbling, and remorseful day
Is crept into the bosom of the sea.—SHAKSPEARE.

That which is *gay* is either nature iself, or nature imitated in the best manner: spring is a *gay* season, and flowers are its *gayest* accompaniments;

Jocund day
Upon the mountain tops sits *gayly* dress'd.
SHAKSPEARE.

MAGNIFICENCE, SPLENDOUR, POMP.

Magnificence, from *magnus* and *facio*, signifies doing largely, or on a large scale; *splendour*, in Latin *splendor*, from *splendeo* to shine, signifies brightness in the external; *pomp*, in Latin *pompa*, in Greek πομπὴ a procession, from πέμπω to send, signifies in general formality and ceremony.

Magnificence lies not only in the number and extent of the objects presented, but in their degree of richness as to their colouring and quality; *splendour* is but a characteristick of *magnificence*, attached to such objects as dazzle the eye by the quantity of light, or the beauty and strength of colouring: the entertainments of the eastern monarchs and princes are remarkable for their *magnificence*, from the immense number of their attendants, the crowd of equipages, the size of their palaces, the multitude of costly utensils, and the profusion of viands which constitute the arrangements for the banquet;

Not Babylon,
Nor great Alcairo, such *magnificence*
Equall'd in all their glories.—MILTON.

The entertainments of Europeans present much *splendour*, from the richness, the variety, and the brilliancy of dress, of furniture, and all the apparatus of a feast, which the refinements of art have brought to perfection;

Vain transitory *splendours* could not all
Reprieve the tottering mansion from its fall.
GOLDSMITH.

Magnificence is seldomer unaccompanied with *splendour* than *splendour* with *magnificence;* since quantity, as well as quality, is essential to the one; but quality, more than quantity, is an essential to the other: a large army drawn up in battle array is a *magnificent* spectacle, from the immensity of their numbers, and the order of their disposition; it will in all probability be a *splendid* scene if there be much richness in the dresses; the *pomp* will here consist in such large bodies of men acting by one impulse, and directed by one will. hence military *pomp;* it is the appendage of power, when displayed to publick view: on particular occasions, a monarch seated on his throne, surrounded by his courtiers, and attended by his guards, is said to appear with *pomp;*

Was all that *pomp* of wo for this prepar'd?
These fires, this fun'ral pile, these altars rear'd?
DRYDEN.

MAGISTERIAL, MAJESTICK, STATELY, POMPOUS, AUGUST, DIGNIFIED.

Magisterial, from *magister* a master, and *majestick*, from *majestas*, are both derived from *magis* more or *major* greater, that is, more or greater than others: but they differ in this respect, that the *magisterial* is something assumed, and is therefore often false; the *majestick* is natural, and consequently always real: an upstart, or an intruder into any high station or office, may put on a *magisterial* air, in order to impose on the multitude; but it will not be in his power to be *majestick*, which never shows itself in a borrowed shape; none but those who have a superiority of character, of birth, or outward station, can be *majestick:* a petty magistrate in the county may be *magisterial;* 'Government being the noblest and most mysterious of all arts, is very unfit for those to talk *magisterially* of who never bore any share in it.'—SOUTH. A king or queen cannot uphold their station without a *majestick* deportment;

Then Aristides lifts his honest front,
In pure *majestick* poverty rever'd.—THOMSON.

The *stately* and *pompous* are most nearly allied to the *magisterial;* the *august* and *dignified* to the *majestick:* the former being merely extrinsick and assnmed; the latter intrinsick and inherent. *Magisterial* respects the authority which is assumed; *stately* regards the splendour and rank; 'There is for the most part as much real enjoyment under the meanest cottage, as within the walls of the *stateliest* palace.'—SOUTH. *Pompous* regards the personal importance, with all the appendages of greatness and power;

Such seems thy gentle height, made only proud
To be the basis of that *pompous* load.—DENHAM.

A person is *magisterial* in the exercise of his office, and the distribution of his commands; he is *stately* in his ordinary intercourse with his inferiours and equals; he is *pompous* on particular occasions of appearing in publick: a person demands silence in a *magisterial* tone; he marches forward with a *stately* air; he comes forward in a *pompous* manner, so as to strike others with a sense of his importance.

Majestick is an epithet that characterizes the exteriour of an object;

A royal robe he wore with graceful pride,
Embroider'd sandals glitter'd as he trod,
And forth he mov'd, *majestick* as a god.
POPE.

August is that which marks an essential characteristick in the object;

How poor, how rich, how abject, how *august*,
How complicate, how wonderful, is man!
YOUNG.

Dignified serves to characterize the action, or the station;

Nor can I think that God, Creator wise,
Though threat'ning, will in earnest so destroy
Us, his prime creatures, *dignified* so high.
MILTON.

The form of a female is termed *majestick* which has something imposing in it, suited to the condition of majesty, or the most elevated station in society; a monarch is entitled *august* in order to describe the extent of his empire; an assembly is denominated *august* to bespeak its high character, and its weighty influence in the scale of society; a reply is termed *dignified* when it upholds the individual and personal character of a man, as well as his relative character in the community to which he belongs: the two former of these terms are associated only with grandeur of outward circumstances; the last is applicable to men of all stations, who have each in his sphere a *dignity* to maintain which belongs to a man as an independent moral agent.

GRANDEUR, MAGNIFICENCE.

Grandeur, from *grand*, in French *grande*, Latin *grandis*, probably from γεραιὸς ancient, because the term in Latin is applied mostly to great age, and afterward extended in its application to greatness in general, but particularly that greatness which is taken in the good sense; *magnificence*, in Latin *magnificentia*, from *magnus* and *facio*, signifies made on a large scale.

An extensive assemblage of striking qualities in the exteriour constitutes the common signification of these terms, of which *grandeur* is the genus, and *magnificence* the species. *Magnificence* cannot exist without *grandeur*, but *grandeur* exists without *magnificence:* the former is distinguished from the latter both in degree and in application. When applied to the same objects they differ in degree; *magnificence* being the highest degree of *grandeur*. As it respects the style of living, *grandeur* is within the reach of subjects; *magnificence* is mostly confined to princes. A person is said to live in a style of *grandeur*, who rises above the common level, as to the number of his servants, the quality of his equipage, and the size of his establishment. No one is said to live in a style of *magnificence* who does not surpass the *grandeur* of his contemporaries. Wealth, such as falls to the lot of many, may enable them to display *grandeur;* but nothing short of a princely fortune gives either a title or a capacity to aim at *magnificence*. *Grandeur* admits of degrees and modifications; it may display itself in various ways, according to the taste of the individual; but *magnificence* is that which has already reached the highest degree of superiority in every particular.

Those who are ambitious for earthly *grandeur* are rarely in a temper of mind to take a just view of themselves and of all things that surround them; they forget that there is any thing above this, in comparison with which it sinks into insignificance and meanness; 'There is a kind of *grandeur* and respect, which the meanest and most insignificant part of mankind endeavour to procure in the little circle of their friends and acquaintance.'—ADDISON. The *grandeur* of European courts is lost in a comparison with the *magnificence* of eastern princes; 'The wall of China is one of those eastern pieces of *magnificence* which makes a figure even in the map of the world, although an account of it would have been thought fabulous, were not the wall itself extant.'—ADDISON.

Grandeur is applicable to the works of nature as well as art, of mind as well as matter; *magnificence* is altogether the creature of art. A structure, a spectacle, an entertainment, and the like, may be *grand* or *magnificent;* but a scene, a prospect, a conception, and the like, are *grand*, but not *magnificent*.

NOBLE, GRAND.

Noble, in Latin *nobilis*, from *nosco* to know, signifies knowable, or worth knowing; *grand*, v. *Grandeur*.

Noble is a term of general import; it simply implies the quality by which a thing is distinguished for excellence above other things: the *grand* is, properly speaking, one of those qualities by which an object acquires the name of *noble;* but there are many *noble* objects which are not denominated *grand*. A building may be denominated *noble* for its beauty as well as its size; but a *grand* building is rather so called for the expense which is displayed upon it: *nobleness* of acting or thinking comprehends all moral excellence that rises to a high pitch; but *grandeur* of mind is peculiarly applicable to such actions or traits as denote an elevation of character, rising above all that is common. A family may be either *noble* or *grand;* but it is *noble* by birth; it is *grand* by wealth, and an expensive style of living;

What then worlds
In a far thinner element sustain'd,
And acting the same part with greater skill,
More rapid movement, and for *noblest* ends?
YOUNG.

More obvious ends to pass, are not these stars,
The seats majestick, proud imperial thrones,
On which angelick delegates of heav'n
Discharge high trusts of vengeance or of love,
To clothe in outward *grandeur grand* designs?
YOUNG.

GREAT, GRAND, SUBLIME.

These terms are synonymous only in the moral application. *Great* simply designates extent; *grand* includes likewise the idea of excellence and superiority. A *great* undertaking characterizes only the extent of the undertaking; a *grand* undertaking bespeaks its superiour excellence: *great* objects are seen with facility; *grand* objects are viewed with admiration. It is a *great* point to make a person sensible of his faults; it should be the *grand* aim of all to aspire after moral and religious improvement; 'There is nothing in this whole art of architecture which pleases the imagination, but as it is *great*, uncommon, or beautiful.'—ADDISON. 'There is generally in nature something more *grand* and august than what we meet with in the curiosities of art.'—ADDISON.

Grand and *sublime* are both superiour to *great*; but the former marks the dimension of *greatness*; the latter, from the Latin *sublimis*, designates that of height. A scene may be either *grand* or *sublime*; it is *grand* as it fills the imagination with its immensity; it is *sublime* as it elevates the imagination beyond the surrounding and less important objects. There is something *grand* in the sight of a vast army moving forward, as it were, by one impulse; there is something peculiarly *sublime* in the sight of huge mountains and craggy cliffs of ice, shaped into various fantastick forms. *Grand* may be said either of the works of art or nature: *sublime* is applicable only to the works of nature. The Egyptian pyramids, or the ocean, are both *grand* objects; a tempestuous ocean is a *sublime* object. *Grand* is sometimes applied to the mind; *sublime* is applied both to the thoughts and the expressions; 'Homer fills his readers with *sublime* ideas.'—ADDISON. There is a *grandeur* of conception in the writings of Milton; there is a *sublimity* in the inspired writings, which far surpasses all human productions.

TO EXPRESS, DECLARE, SIGNIFY, TESTIFY, UTTER.

To *express*, from the Latin *exprimo* to press out, is said of whatever passes in the mind; to *declare* (*v. To declare*) is said only of sentiments and opinions. A man *expresses* anger, joy, sorrow, and all the affections in their turn; he *declares* his opinion for or against any particular measure.

To *express* is the simple act of communication, resulting from our circumstances as social agents; to *declare* is a specifick and positive act that is called for by the occasion: the former may be done in private, the latter is always more or less publick. An *expression* of one's feelings and sentiments to those whom we esteem is the supreme delight of social beings; the *declaration* of our opinions may be prudent or imprudent, according to circumstances. Words, looks, gestures, or movements, serve to *express*;

Thus Roman youth, deriv'd from ruin'd Troy,
In rude Saturnian rhymes *express* their joy.
DRYDEN.

Actions, as well as words, may sometimes *declare*;

Th' unerring sun by certain signs *declares*,
What the late ev'n or early morn prepares.
DRYDEN.

Sometimes we cannot *express* our contempt in so strong a manner as by preserving a perfect silence when we are required to speak; an act of hostility, on the part of a nation, is as much a *declaration* of war as if it were *expressed* in positive terms; 'As the Supreme Being has *expressed*, and as it were printed his ideas in the creation, men *express* their ideas in books.'—ADDISON.

On him confer the Poet's sacred name,
Whose lofty voice *declares* the heavenly flame.
ADDISON.

To *express* and *signify* are both said of words; but *express* has always regard to the agent, and the use which he makes of the words. *Signify*, from *signum* a sign, and *facio* to make, has respect to the things of which the words are made the usual signs: hence it is that a word may be made to *express* one thing while it *signifies* another; and hence it is that many words, according to their ordinary *signification*, will not *express* what the speaker has in his mind, and wishes to communicate: the monosyllable no *signifies* simple negation: but according to the temper of the speaker and the circumstances under which it is spoken, it may *express* ill-nature, anger, or any other bad passion; 'If there be no cause *expressed*, the jailer is not bound to detain the prisoner. For the law judges in this respect, saith sir Edward Coke, like Festus the Roman governour, that it is unreasonable to send a prisoner, and not to *signify* withal the crimes alleged against him.'—BLACKSTONE.

To *signify* and *testify*, like the word *express*, are employed in general for any act of communication otherwise than by words; but *express* is used in a stronger sense than either of the former. The passions and strongest movements of the soul are *expressed*; the simple intentions or transitory feelings of the mind are *signified* or *testified*. A person *expresses* his joy by the sparkling of his eye, and the vivacity of his countenance; he *signifies* his wishes by a nod; he *testifies* his approbation by a smile. People of vivid sensibility must take care not to *express* all their feelings; those who expect a ready obedience from their inferiours must not adopt a haughty mode of *signifying* their will; nothing is more gratifying to an ingenuous mind than to *testify* its regard for merit wherever it may discover itself.

Express may be said of all sentient beings, and, by a figure of speech, even of those which have no sense; *signify* is said of rational agents only. The dog has the most *expressive* mode of showing his attachment and fidelity to his master;

And four fair queens, whose hands sustain a flow'r,
Th' *expressive* emblem of their softer pow'r.—POPE.

A *significant* look or smile may sometimes give rise to suspicion, and lead to the detection of guilt; 'Common life is full of this kind of *significant* expressions, by knocking, beckoning, frowning, and pouting; and dumb persons are sagacious in the use of them.'—HOLDER. To *signify* and *testify*, though closely allied in sense and application, have this difference, that to *signify* is simply to give a sign of what passes inwardly, to *testify* is to give that sign in the presence of others. A person *signifies* by letter his intention of being at a certain place at a given time; he *testifies* his sense of favours conferred by every mark of gratitude and respect: 'What consolation can be had, Dryden has afforded, by living to repent, and to *testify* his repentance (for his immoral writings).'—JOHNSON.

Utter, from the preposition *out*, signifying to bring out, differs from *express* in this, that the latter respects the thing which is communicated, and the former the means of communication. We *express* from the heart; we *utter* with the lips: to *express* an uncharitable sentiment is a violation of Christian duty; to *utter* an unseemly word is a violation of good manners: those who say what they do not mean, *utter*, but not *express*; those who show by their looks what is passing in their hearts, *express* but do not *utter*;

The multitude of angels, with a shout
Loud as from numbers without number, sweet
As from blessed voices, *uttering* joy.—MILTON

SIGN, SIGNAL.

Sign and *signal* are both derived from the same source (*v. Mark, sign*), and the latter is but a species of the former;* the *sign* enables us to recognise an object; it is therefore sometimes natural: *signal* serves to give warning; it is always arbitrary.

The movements which are visible in the countenance are commonly the *signs* of what passes in the heart;

The nod that ratifies the Will Divine,
The faithful, fix'd, irrevocable *sign*,
This seals thy suit.—POPE.

The beat of the drum is the *signal* for soldiers to repair to their post;

Then first the trembling earth the *signal* gave,
And flashing fires enlighten all the cave.—DRYDEN.

We converse with those who are present by *signs*; we make ourselves understood by those who are at a distance by means of *signals*.

* Vide Girard: "Signe, signal"

SIGNIFICANT, EXPRESSIVE.

The *significant* is that which serves as a sign; the *expressive* is that which speaks out or declares: the latter is therefore a stronger term than the former: a look is *significant* when it is made to *express* an idea that passes in the mind; but it is *expressive* when it is made to *express* a feeling of the heart: looks are but occasionally *significant*, but the countenance may be habitually *expressive*. *Significant* is applied in an indifferent sense, according to the nature of the thing signified; but *expressive* is always applied to that which is good: a *significant* look may convey a very bad idea; 'I could not help giving my friend the merchant a *significant* look upon this occasion.'—CUMBERLAND. An *expressive* countenance always *expresses* good feeling; 'The English, Madam, particularly what we call the plain English, is a very copious and *expressive* language.'—RICHARDSON.

The distinction between these words is the same when applied to things as to persons: a word is *significant* of whatever it is made to signify; but a word is *expressive* according to the force with which it conveys an idea. The term *significant*, in this case, simply explains the nature; but the epithet *expressive* characterizes it as something good: technical terms are *significant* only of the precise ideas which belong to the art; most languages have some terms which are peculiarly *expressive*, and consequently adapted for poetry.

SIGNIFICATION, MEANING, IMPORT, SENSE.

The *signification* (*v. To express*) is that of which the word is made the sign; the *meaning* is that which the person attaches to it; the *import* is that which is *imported* or carried into the understanding; the *sense* is that which is comprehended by the sense or the understanding.

The *signification* of a word includes either the whole or the part of what is understood by it; 'A lie consists in this, that it is a false *signification* knowingly and voluntarily used.'—SOUTH. The *meaning* is that which the person wishes to convey who makes use of a word. This may be correct or incorrect according to the information of the person explaining himself; 'When beyond her expectation I hit upon her *meaning*, I can perceive a sudden cloud of disappointment spread over her face.'—JOHNSON. The *import* of a word includes its whole force and value; 'To draw near to God is an expression of awful and mysterious *import*.'—BLAIR. The *sense* of a word is applicable mostly to a part of its *signification*; 'There are two *senses* in which we may be said to draw near, in such a degree as mortality admits, to God.'—BLAIR. The *signification* of a word is fixed by the standard of custom; it is not therefore to be changed by any individual: the *import* of a term is estimated by the various acceptations in which it is employed: a *sense* is sometimes arbitrarily attached to a word which is widely different from that in which it is commonly acknowledged.

It is necessary to get the true *signification* of every word, or the particular meaning attached to it, to weigh the *import* of every term, and to comprehend the exact *sense* in which it is taken. Every word expressing either a simple or a complex idea, is said to have a *signification*, though not an *import*. Technical and moral terms have an *import* and different *senses*. A child learns the *significations* of simple terms as he hears them used; a writer must be acquainted with the full *import* of every term which he has occasion to make use of. The different *senses* which words admit of is a great source of ambiguity and confusion with illiterate people.

Signification and *import* are said mostly of single words only; *sense* is said of words either in connexion with each other, or as belonging to some class: thus we speak of the *signification* of the word house, of the *import* of the term love; but the *sense* of the sentence, the *sense* of the author, the employment of words in a technical, moral, or physical *sense*.

TO DENOTE, SIGNIFY, IMPLY.

Denote, in Latin *denoto* or *noto*, from *notum*, participle of *nosco*, signifies to cause to know; *signify*, from the Latin *signum* a sign and *fio* to become, is to become or be made a sign, or guide for the understanding; *imply*, from the Latin *implico* to fold in, signifies to fold or involve an idea in an object.

Denote is employed with regard to things and their characters; *signify* with regard to the thoughts or movements. A letter or character may be made to *denote* any number, as words are made to *signify* the intentions and wishes of the person. Among the ancient Egyptians hieroglyphicks were very much employed to *denote* certain moral qualities; in many cases looks or actions will *signify* more than words. Devices and emblems of different descriptions drawn either from fabulous history or the natural world are likewise now employed to *denote* particular circumstances or qualities: the cornucopia *denotes* plenty; the beehive *denotes* industry; the dove *denotes* meekness; and the lamb gentleness: he who will not take the trouble to *signify* his wishes otherwise than by nods or signs must expect to be frequently misunderstood; 'Another may do the same thing, and yet the action want that air and beauty which distinguish it from others, like that inimitable sunshine Titian is said to have diffused over his landscapes, which *denotes* them his.'—SPECTATOR. 'Simple abstract words are used to *signify* some one simple idea, without much adverting to others which may chance to attend it.'—BURKE.

To *signify* and *imply* may be employed either as respects actions or words. In the first case *signify* is the act of the person making known by means of a *sign*, as we *signify* our approbation by a look: *imply* marks the value or force of the action; our assent is *implied* in our silence. When applied to words or marks, *signify* denotes the positive and established act of the thing; *imply* is its relative act: a word *signifies* whatever it is made literally to stand for; it *implies* that which it stands for figuratively or morally. The term house *signifies* that which is constructed for a dwelling; the term residence *implies* something superiour to a house. A cross, thus, + *signifies* addition in arithmetick or algebra; a long stroke, thus, ——, with a break in the text of a work, *implies* that the whole sentence is not completed. It frequently happens that words which *signify* nothing particular in themselves, may be made to *imply* a great deal by the tone, the manner, and the connexion; 'Words *signify* not immediately and primarily things themselves, but the conceptions of the mind concerning things.'—SOUTH. 'Pleasure *implies* a proportion and agreement to the respective states and conditions of men.'—SOUTH.

SIGNIFICATION, AVAIL, IMPORTANCE, CONSEQUENCE, WEIGHT, MOMENT.

Signify (*v. To signify*) is here employed with regard to events of life, and their relative importance; *avail* (*v. To avail*) is never used otherwise. That which a thing *signifies* is what it contains; if it *signifies* nothing, it contains nothing, and is worth nothing; if it *signifies* much, it contains much, or is worth much. That which *avails* produces: if it *avails* nothing it produces nothing, is of no use; if it *avails* much, it produces or is worth much.

We consider the end as to its *signification*, and the means as to their *avail*. Although it is of little or no *signification* to a man what becomes of his remains, yet no one can be reconciled to the idea of leaving them to be exposed to contempt; words are but too often of little *avail* to curb the unruly wills of children, 'As for wonders, what *signifieth* telling us of them?' —CUMBERLAND. 'What *avail* a parcel of statutes against gaming, when they who make them conspire together for the infraction of them.'—CUMBERLAND.

Importance, from *porto* to carry, signifies the carrying or bearing with, or in itself; *consequence*, from *consequor* to follow, or result, signifies the following or resulting from a thing.

Weight signifies the *quantum* that the thing weighs; *moment*, from *momentum*, signifies the force that puts in motion.

Importance is what things have in themselves; they may be of more or less *importance*, according to the value which is set upon them: this may be real or unreal; it may be estimated by the experience of their past utility, or from the presumption of their utility for the future: the idea of *importance*, therefore, enters into the meaning of the other terms more or less. He that considers how soon he must close his life, will find nothing of so much *importance* as to close it well.' —JOHNSON. *Consequence* is the *importance* of a thing from its *consequence*. This term therefore is peculiarly applicable to such things, the *consequences* of which may be more immediately discerned either from the neglect or the attention: it is of *consequence* for a letter to go off on a certain day, for the affairs of an individual may be more or less affected by it; an hour's delay sometimes in the departure of a military expedition may be of such *consequence* as to determine the fate of a battle; 'The corruption of our taste is not of equal *consequence* with the depravation of our virtue.' —WARTON. The term *weight* implies a positively great degree of *importance*: it is that *importance* which a thing has intrinsically in itself, and which makes it *weigh* in the mind: it is applied therefore to such things as offer themselves to deliberation; hence the counsels of a nation are always *weighty*, because they involve the interests of so many; 'The finest works of invention are of very little *weight*, when put in the balance with what refines and exalts the rational mind.' —SPECTATOR. *Moment* is that *importance* which a thing has from the power in itself to produce effects, or to determine interests: it is applicable, therefore, only to such things as are connected with our prosperity or happiness: when used without any adjunct, it implies a great degree of *importance*, but may be modified in various ways; as a thing of no *moment*, or small *moment*, or great *moment*; but we cannot say with the same propriety, a thing of small *weight*, and still less a thing of great *weight*: it is a matter of no small *moment* for every one to choose that course of conduct which will stand the test of a death-bed reflection; 'Whoever shall review his life, will find that the whole tenour of his conduct has been determined by some accident of no apparent *moment*.'—JOHNSON.

UNIMPORTANT, INSIGNIFICANT, IMMATERIAL, INCONSIDERABLE.

The want of *importance*, of *consideration*, of *signification*, and of matter or substance, is expressed by these terms. They differ therefore principally according to the meaning of the primitives; but they are so closely allied that they may be employed sometimes indifferently. *Unimportant* regards the consequences of our actions: it is *unimportant* whether we use this or that word in certain cases; 'Nigno and Guerra made no discoveries of any *importance*.'—ROBERTSON. *Inconsiderable* and *insignificant* respect those things which may attract notice: the former is more adapted to the grave style, to designate the comparative low value of things; the latter is a familiar term which seems to convey a contemptuous meaning: in a description we may say that the number, the size, the quantity, &c. is *inconsiderable*; in speaking of persons we may say they are *insignificant* in stature, look, talent, station, and the like; or speaking of things, an *insignificant* production, or an *insignificant* word; 'That the soul cannot be proved mortal by any principle of natural reason is, I think, no *inconsiderable* point gained.'—SOUTH. 'As I am *insignificant* to the company in publick places, I gratify the vanity of all who pretend to make an appearance.'—ADDISON. *Immaterial* is a species of the *unimportant*, which is applied only to familiar subjects; it is *immaterial* whether we go to-day or to-morrow; it is *immaterial* whether we have a few or many; 'If in the judgement of impartial persons the arguments be strong enough to convince an unbiassed mind, it is not *material* whether every wrangling atheist will sit down contented with them.'—STILLINGFLEET.

TRIFLING, TRIVIAL, PETTY, FRIVOLOUS, FUTILE.

Trifling, *trivial*, both come from *trivium*, a common place of resort where three roads meet, and signify common; *petty* is in French *petit* little, in Latin *putus* a boy or minion, and the Hebrew פתי foolish; *frivolous*, in Latin *frivolus*, comes in all probability from *frio* to crumble into dust, signifying reduced to nothing; *futile*, in Latin *futilis*, from *futio* to pour out, signifies cast away as worthless.

All these epithets characterize an object as of little or no value: *trifling* and *trivial* differ only in degree; the latter denoting a still lower degree of value than the former. What is *trifling* or *trivial* is that which does not require any consideration, and may be easily passed over as forgotten: *trifling* objections can never weigh against solid reason; *trivial* remarks only expose the shallowness of the remarker; 'We exceed the ancients in doggerel humour, burlesque, and all the *trivial* arts of ridicule.'—ADDISON. What is *petty* is beneath our consideration, it ought to be disregarded and held cheap; it would be a *petty* consideration for a minister of state to look to the small savings of a private family; 'There is scarcely any man without some favourite *trifle* which he values above greater attainments; some desire of *petty* praise which he cannot patiently suffer to be frustrated.'—JOHNSON. What is *frivolous* and *futile* is disgraceful for any one to consider; the former in relation to all the objects of our pursuit or attachment, the latter only in regard to matters of reasoning: dress is a *frivolous* occupation when it forms the chief business of a rational being; 'It is an endless and *frivolous* pursuit to act by any other rule than the care of satisfying our own minds.'—STEELE. The objections of freethinkers against revealed religion are as *futile* as they are mischievous; 'Out of a multiplicity of criticisms by various hands many are sure to be *futile*.'—COWPER.

SUPERFICIAL, SHALLOW, FLIMSY.

The *superficial* is that which lies only at the surface: it is therefore by implication the same as the *shallow*, which has nothing underneath: *shallow* being a variation of hollow or empty. Hence a person may be called either *superficial* or *shallow*, to indicate that he has not a profundity of knowledge; but otherwise, *superficiality* is applied to the exercise of the thinking faculty, and *shallowness* to its extent. Men of free sentiments are *superficial* thinkers, although they may not have understandings more *shallow* than others. *Superficial* and *shallow* are applicable to things as well as persons: *flimsy* is applicable to things only. *Flimsy* most probably comes from flame, that is, flamy, showy, easily seen through. In the proper sense, we may speak of giving a *superficial* covering of paint or colour to a body; of a river or piece of water being *shallow*; of cotton or cloth being *flimsy*. In the improper sense, a survey or a glance may be *superficial* which does not extend beyond the *superficies* of things; 'By much labour we acquire a *superficial* acquaintance with a few sensible objects.'—BLAIR. A conversation or a discourse may be *shallow*, which does not contain a body of sentiment;

> I know thee to thy bottom; from within
> Thy *shallow* centre to the utmost skin.—DRYDEN.

A work or performance may be *flimsy* which has nothing solid in it to engage the attention;

> Proud of a vast extent of *flimsy* lines.—POPE

SURFACE, SUPERFICIES.

Surface, compounded of *sur* for *super* and *face*, is a variation of the Latin term *superficies*; and yet they have acquired this distinction, that the former is the vulgar, and the latter the scientifick term: of course the former has a more indefinite and general application than the latter. A *surface* is either even or uneven, smooth or rough; but the mathematician always conceives of a plane *superficies* on which he founds his operations. They are employed in a figurative sense with a similar distinction;

> Errours like straws upon the *surface* flow;
> He who would search for pearls must dive below.
> DRYDEN.

'Those who have undertaken the task of reconciling mankind to their present state frequently remind us that we view only the *superficies* of life.'—JOHNSON.

TO EXPLAIN, EXPOUND, INTERPRET.

To *explain* is to make *plain*; *expound*, from the Latin *expono*, compounded of *ex* and *pono*, signifies to set forth in detail; *interpret*, in Latin *interpreto* and *interpretes*, compounded of *inter* and *partes*, that in, *linguas* tongues, signifies literally to get the sense of one language by means of another.

To *explain* is the generick term, the rest are specifick: to *expound* and *interpret* are each modes of *explaining*. Single words or sentences are *explained;* a whole work, or considerable parts of it, are *expounded;* the sense of any writing or symbolical sign is *interpreted*. It is the business of the philologist to *explain* the meaning of words by a suitable definition; 'It is a serious thing to have connexion with a people, who live only under positive, arbitrary, and changeable institutions; and these not perfected, nor supplied, nor *explained*, by any common acknowledged rule of moral science.'—BURKE. It is the business of the divine to *expound* Scripture; One meets now and then with persons who are extremely learned and knotty in *expounding* clear cases.' —STEELE. It is the business of the antiquarian to *interpret* the meaning of old inscriptions on stones, or of hieroglyphicks on buildings; 'It does not appear that among the Romans any man grew eminent by *interpreting* another; and perhaps it was more frequent to translate for exercise or amusement than for fame.' —JOHNSON.

An *explanation* serves to assist the understanding, to supply a deficiency, and remove obscurity; an *exposition* is an ample *explanation*, in which minute particulars are detailed, and the connexion of events in the narrative is kept up; it serves to assist the memory and awaken the attention: both the *explanation* and *exposition* are employed in clearing up the sense of things as they are, but the *interpretation* is more arbitrary; it often consists of affixing or giving a sense to things which they have not previously had: hence it is that the same passages in authors admit of different *interpretations*, according to the character or views of the commentator.

There are many practical truths in the Bible which are so plain and positive, that they need no literal *explanation:* but its doctrines, when faithfully *expounded*, may be brought home to the hearts and consciences of men; although the partial *interpretations* of illiterate and enthusiastick men are more apt to disgrace than to advance the cause of religion.

To *explain* and *interpret* are not confined to what is written or said, they are employed likewise with regard to the actions of men; *exposition* is, however, used only with regard to writings. The major part of the misunderstandings and animosities which arise among men, might easily be obviated by a timely *explanation;* it is the characteristick of good-nature to *interpret* the looks and actions of men as favourably as possible. The *explanation* may sometimes flow out of circumstances; the *interpretation* is always the act of a voluntary and rational agent. The discovery of a plot or secret scheme will serve to *explain* the mysterious and strange conduct of such as were previously acquainted with it. According to an old proverb, "Silence gives consent;" for thus at least they are pleased to *interpret* it, who are interested in the decision.

TO MISCONSTRUE, MISINTERPRET.

Misconstrue and *misinterpret* signify to explain in a wrong way; but the former respects the sense of one's words or the implication of one's actions: those who indulge themselves in a light mode of speech towards children are liable to be *misconstrued;* a too great tenderness to the criminal may be easily *misinterpreted* into favour of the crime.

These words may likewise be employed in speaking of language in general; but the former respects the literal transmission of foreign ideas into our native language; the latter respects the general sense which one affixes to any set of words, either in a native or foreign language: the learners of a language will unavoidably *misconstrue* it at times; in all languages there are ambiguous expressions, which are liable to *misinterpretation*. *Misconstruing* is the consequence of ignorance;

In ev'ry act and turn of life he feels
Publick calamities or household ills:
The judge corrupt, the long-depending cause,
And doubtful issue of *misconstrued* laws.—PRIOR.

Misinterpretation of particular words are oftener the consequence of prejudice and voluntary blindness, particularly in the explanation of the law of the Scriptures; 'Some purposely misrepresent or put a wrong *interpretation* on the virtues of others.'—ADDISON.

DEFINITE, POSITIVE.

Definite, in Latin *definitum*, participle of *definio*, compounded of *de* and *finis*, signifies that which is bounded by a line or limit; *positive*, in Latin *positivus*, from *pono* to place, signifies that which is placed or fixed.

The understanding and reasoning powers are connected with what is *definite;* the will with what is *positive*. A *definite* answer leaves nothing to be explained; a *positive* answer leaves no room for hesitation or question. It is necessary to be *definite* in giving instructions, and to be *positive* in giving commands. A person who is *definite* in his proceedings with another, puts a stop to all unreasonable expectations; 'We are not able to judge of the degree of conviction which operated at any particular time upon our own thoughts, but as it is recorded by some certain and *definite* effect.'—JOHNSON. It is necessary for those who have to exercise authority to be *positive*, in order to enforce obedience from the self-willed and contumacious; 'The Earl Rivers being now in his own opinion on his death-bed, thought it his duty to provide for Savage among his other natural children, and therefore demanded a *positive* account of him.'—JOHNSON.

DEFINITION, EXPLANATION.

A *definition* is properly a species of *explanation*. The former is used scientifically, the latter on ordinary occasions; the former is confined to words, the latter is employed for words or things.

A *definition* is correct or precise; an *explanation* is general or ample.

The *definition* of a word defines or limits the extent of its signification; it is the rule for the scholar in the use of any word; 'As to politeness, many have attempted *definitions* of it. I believe it is best to be known by description, *definition* not being able to comprise it.'—LORD CHATHAM. The *explanation* of a word may include both *definition* and illustration: the former admits of no more words than will include the leading features in the meaning of any term; the latter admits of an unlimited scope for diffuseness on the part of the explainer; 'If you are forced to desire further information or *explanation* upon a point, do it with proper apologies for the trouble you give.'—LORD CHATHAM.

TO EXPLAIN, ILLUSTRATE, ELUCIDATE.

Explain, *v. To explain, expound; illustrate*, in Latin *illustratus*, participle of *illustro*, compounded of the intensive syllable *in* and *lustro*, signifies to make a thing bright, or easy to be surveyed and examined; *elucidate*, in Latin *elucidatus*, participle of *elucido*, from *lux* light, signifies to bring forth into the light.

To *explain* is simply to render intelligible; to *illustrate* and *elucidate* are to give additional clearness: every thing requires to be *explained* to one who is ignorant of it; but the best informed will require to have abstruse subjects *illustrated*, and obscure subjects *elucidated*. We always *explain* when we *illustrate* or *elucidate*, and we always *elucidate* when we *illustrate*, but not *vice versâ*.

We *explain* by reducing compounds to simples, and generals to particulars; 'I know I meant just what you *explain;* but I did not *explain* my own meaning so well as you.'—POPE. We *illustrate* by means of examples, similes, and allegorical figures; 'It is indeed the same system as mine, but *illustrated* with a ray of your own.'—POPE. We *elucidate* by commentaries, or the statement of facts; 'If our religious tenets should ever want a farther *elucidation*, we shall not call on atheism to *explain* them.'—BURKE. Words are the common subject of *explanation;* moral truths require *illustration;* poetical allusions and dark passages in writers require *elucidation*. All *explanations* given to children should consist of as few words as possible, so long as they are sufficiently explicit.

EXPLANATORY, EXPLICIT, EXPRESS.

Explanatory signifies containing or belonging to *explanation* (*v. To explain*); *explicit*, in Latin *explicatus*, from *explico* to unfold, signifies unfolded or laid open; *express*, in Latin *expressus*, signifies the same as expressed or delivered in specifick terms.

The *explanatory* is that which is superadded to clear up difficulties or obscurities. A letter is *explanatory* which contains an *explanation* of something preceding, in lieu of any thing new; 'An *explanatory* law stops the current of a precedent statute, nor does either of them admit extension afterwards.'—BACON. The *explicit* is that which of itself obviates every difficulty; an *explicit* letter, therefore, will leave nothing that requires *explanation*; 'Since the revolution the bounds of prerogative and liberty have been better defined, the principles of government more thoroughly examined and understood, and the rights of the subject more *explicitly* guarded by legal provisions, than in any other period of the English history.'—BLACKSTONE. The *explicit* admits of a free use of words; the *express* requires them to be unambiguous. A person ought to be *explicit* when he enters into an engagement; he ought to be *express* when he gives commands, or conveys his wishes; 'I have destroyed the letter I received from you by the hands of Lucius Aruntius, though it was much too innocent to deserve so severe a treatment; however, it was your *express* desire I should destroy it, and I have complied accordingly.'—MELMOTH (*Letters of Cicero*).

TO EXPOSTULATE, REMONSTRATE.

Expostulate, from *postulo* to demand, signifies to demand reasons for a thing; *remonstrate*, from *monstro* to show, signifies to show reasons against a thing.

We *expostulate* in a tone of authority; we *remonstrate* in a tone of complaint. He who *expostulates* passes a censure, and claims to be heard; he who *remonstrates* presents his case, and requests to be heard. *Expostulation* may often be the precursor of violence; *remonstrance* mostly rests on the force of reason and representation: he who admits of *expostulation* from an inferiour undermines his own authority; he who is deaf to the *remonstrances* of his friends is far gone in folly: the *expostulation* is mostly on matters of personal interest; the *remonstrance* may as often be made on matters of propriety. The Scythian ambassadors *expostulated* with Alexander against his invasion of their country; King Richard *expostulated* with Wat Tyler on the subject of his insurrection; 'With the hypocrite it is not my business at present to *expostulate*.'—JOHNSON. Artabanes *remonstrated* with Xerxes on the folly of his projected invasion; 'I have been but a little time conversant with the world, yet I have had already frequent opportunities of observing the little efficacy of *remonstrance* and complaint.'—JOHNSON.

TO UTTER, SPEAK, ARTICULATE, PRONOUNCE.

Utter, from *out*, signifies to put out; that is, to send forth a sound: this therefore is a more general term than *speak*, which is to *utter* an intelligible sound. We may *utter* a groan; we *speak* words only, or that which is intended to serve as words. To *speak* therefore is only a species of *utterance*; a dumb man has *utterance*, but not *speech*;

> At each word that my destruction *utter'd*
> My heart recoiled.—OTWAY.

> What you keep by you, you may change and mend,
> But words once *spoke*, can never be recall'd.
> WALLER.

Articulate and *pronounce* are modes of *speaking*; to *articulate*, from *articulum* a joint, is to *pronounce* distinctly the letters or syllables of words; which is the first effort of a child beginning to *speak*. It is of great importance to make a child *articulate* every letter when he first begins to *speak* or read. To *pronounce*, from the Latin *pronuncio* to speak out loud, is a formal mode of *speaking*.

A child must first *articulate* the letters and the syllables, then he *pronounces* or sets forth the whole word; this is necessary before he can *speak* to be understood; 'The torments of disease can sometimes only be signified by groans or sobs, or *inarticulate* ejaculations.'—JOHNSON. '*Speak* the speech, I pray you, as I *pronounced* it to you.'—SHAKSPEARE.

TO SPEAK, TALK, CONVERSE, DISCOURSE.

Speak, in Saxon *specan*, is probably connected with the German *sprechen* to speak, and *brechen* to break, the Latin *precor* to pray, and the Hebrew ברך; *talk* is but a variation of *tell*; *converse*, *v. Conversation*; *discourse*, in Latin *discursus*, expresses properly an examining or deliberating upon

The idea of communicating with, or communicating to, another, by means of signs, is common in the signification of all these terms: to *speak* is an indefinite term, specifying no circumstance of the action; we may *speak* only one word or many; but we *talk* for a continuance: we *speak* from various motives; we *talk* for pleasure; we *converse* for improvement or intellectual gratification: we *speak* with or to a person, we *talk* commonly to others; we *converse* with others. *Speaking* a language is quite distinct from writing; publick *speaking* has at all times been cultivated with great care, but particularly under popular governments; 'Falsehood is a *speaking* against our thoughts.'—SOUTH. *Talking* is mostly the pastime of the idle and the empty; those who think least *talk* most; '*Talkers* are commonly vain, and credulous withal; for he that *talketh* what he knoweth, will also *talk* what he knoweth not.'—BACON. *Conversation* is the rational employment of social beings, who seek by an interchange of sentiment to purify the affections, and improve the understanding;

> Go, therefore, half this day, as friend with friend,
> *Converse* with Adam.—MILTON.

Conversation is the act of many together; *talk* and *discourse* may be the act of one addressing himself to others: *conversation* loses its value when it ceases to be general; *talk* has seldom any value but what the *talker* attaches to it; the *discourse* derives its value from the nature of the subject as well as the character of the *speaker*: *conversation* is adapted for mixed companies; children *talk* to their parents, or to their companions; parents and teachers *discourse* with young people on moral duties;

> Let thy *discourse* be such, that thou mayst give
> Profit to others, or from them receive.—DENHAM.

TO BABBLE, CHATTER, CHAT, PRATTLE, PRATE.

Babble, in French *babiller*, probably receives its origin from the tower of *Babel*, when the confusion of tongues took place, and men talked unintelligibly to each other; *chatter*, *chat*, is in French *caquet*, Low German *tatern*, High German *schnattern*, Latin *blatero*, Hebrew *bata*; *prattle*, *prate*, in Low German *praten*, is probably connected with the Greek φραζω to speak.

All these terms mark a superfluous or improper use of speech: *babble* and *chatter* are onomatopeias drawn from the noise or action of speaking; *babbling* denotes rapidity of speech which renders it unintelligible; hence the term is applied to all who make use of many words to no purpose; 'To stand up and *babble* to a crowd in an ale-house, till silence is commanded by the stroke of a hammer, is as low an ambition as can taint the human mind.'—HAWKESWORTH. *Chatter* is an imitation of the noise of speech properly applied to magpies or parrots, and figuratively to a corresponding vicious mode of speech in human beings;

> Some birds there are who, prone to noise,
> Are hir'd to silence wisdom's voice;
> And, skill'd to *chatter* out the hour,
> Rise by their emptiness to power.—MOORE.

The vice of *babbling* is most commonly attached to men, that of *chattering* to women; the *babbler* talks much to impress others with his self-importance; the *chatterer* is actuated by self-conceit, and a desire to display her volubility: the former cares not whether he is understood; the latter cares not if she be but heard.

Chattering is harmless, if not respectable: the winter's fireside invites neighbours to assemble and *chat* away many an hour which might otherwise hang heavy on hand, or be spent less inoffensively;

> Sometimes I dress, with women sit,
> And *chat* away the gloomy fit.—GREEN.

Chatting is the practice of adults; *prattling* and *prating* that of children; the one innocently, the other impertinently: the *prattling* of babes has an interest for every feeling mind, but for parents it is one of their highest enjoyments;

> Now blows the surly north, and chills throughout
> The stiff'ning regions; while by stronger charms
> Than Circe e'er or fell Medea brew'd,
> Each brook that wont to *prattle* to its banks
> Lies all bestill'd.—ARMSTRONG.

Prating is the consequence of ignorance and childish assumption: a *prattler* has all the unaffected gayety of an uncontaminated mind; a *prater* is forward, obtrusive, and ridiculous;

> My prudent counsels prop the state;
> Magpies were never known to *prate*.—MOORE.

TALKATIVE, LOQUACIOUS, GARRULOUS.

Talkative implies ready or prone to *talk* (*v. To speak*); *loquacious*, from *loquor* to speak or talk, has the same original meaning; *garrulous*, in Latin *garrulus*, from *garrio* to blab, signifies prone to tell or make known.

These reproachful epithets differ principally in the degree. To *talk* is allowable and consequently it is not altogether so unbecoming to be occasionally *talkative*: but *loquacity*, which implies always an immoderate propensity to *talk*, is always bad, whether springing from affectation or an idle temper: and *garrulity*, which arises from the excessive desire of communicating, is a failing that is pardonable only in the aged, who have generally much to tell; 'Every absurdity has a champion to defend it; for errour is always *talkative*.'—GOLDSMITH.

> Thersites only clamour'd in the throng,
> *Loquacious*, loud, and turbulent of tongue.—POPE.

> Pleas'd with that social, sweet *garrulity*,
> The poor disbanded vet'ran's sole delight.
> SOMERVILLE.

UNSPEAKABLE, INEFFABLE, UNUTTERABLE, INEXPRESSIBLE.

Unspeakable and *ineffable*, from the Latin *for* to speak, have precisely the same meaning; but *unspeakable* is said of objects in general, particularly of that which is above human conception, and surpasses the power of language to describe; as the *unspeakable* goodness of God; 'The vast difference of God's nature from ours makes the difference between them so *unspeakably* great.'—SOUTH. *Ineffable* is said of such objects as cannot be painted in words with adequate force, as the *ineffable* sweetness of a person's look; 'The influences of the Divine nature enliven the mind with *ineffable* joy.'—SOUTH. *Unutterable* and *inexpressible* are extended in their signification to that which is incommunicable by signs from one being to another; thus grief is *unutterable* which it is not in the power of the sufferer by any sounds to bring home to the feelings of another; grief is *inexpressible* which is not to be expressed by looks, or words, or any signs. *Unutterable* is therefore applied only to the individual who wishes to give *utterance*; *inexpressible* may be said of that which is to be expressed concerning others: our own pains are *unutterable*; the sweetness of a person's countenance is *inexpressible*;

> Nature breeds,
> Perverse, all monstrous, all prodigious things,
> Abominable, *unutterable*.—MILTON.

The evil which lies lurking under a temptation is intolerable and *inexpressible*.'—SOUTH.

CONVERSATION, DIALOGUE, CONFERENCE, COLLOQUY.

Conversation denotes the act of holding *converse*; *dialogue*, in French *dialogue*, Latin *dialogus*, Greek διάλογος, compounded of διὰ and λόγος, signifies a speech between two; *conference*, from the Latin *con* and *fero* to put together, signifies consulting together on subjects; *colloquy*, in Latin *colloquium*, from *col* or *con* and *loquor* to speak, signifies the act of talking together.

A *conversation* is always something actually held between two or more persons; a *dialogue* is mostly fictitious, and written as if spoken: any number of persons may take part in a *conversation*; but a *dialogue* always refers to the two persons who are expressly engaged: a *conversation* may be desultory, in which each takes his part at pleasure; a *dialogue* is formal, in which there will always be reply and rejoinder: a *conversation* may be carried on by any signs besides words, which are addressed personally to the individual present; a *dialogue* must always consist of express words: a prince holds frequent *conversations* with his ministers on affairs of state; 'I find so much Arabick and Persian to read, that all my leisure in a morning is hardly sufficient for a thousandth part of the reading that would be agreeable and useful, as I wish to be a match in *conversation* with the learned natives whom I happen to meet.'—SIR WM. JONES. Cicero wrote *dialogues* on the nature of the gods, and many later writers have adopted the *dialogue* form as a vehicle for conveying their sentiments; 'Aurengzebe is written in rhyme, and has the appearance of being the most elaborate of all Dryden's plays. The personages are imperial, but the *dialogue* is often domestick, and therefore susceptible of sentiments accommodated to familiar incidents.'—JOHNSON. A *conference* is a species of *conversation*; a *colloquy* is a species of *dialogue*: a *conversation* is indefinite as to the subject, or the parties engaged in it; a *conference* is confined to particular subjects and descriptions of persons: a *conversation* is mostly occasional; a *conference* is always specifically appointed: a *conversation* is mostly on indifferent matters; a *conference* is mostly on national or publick concerns. Men hold a *conversation* as friends; they hold a *conference* as ministers of state; 'The *conference* between Gabriel and Satan abounds with sentiments proper for the occasion, and suitable to the persons of the two speakers.'—ADDISON.

The *dialogue* naturally limits the number to two; the *colloquy* is indefinite as to number: there may be *dialogues* therefore which are not *colloquies*; but every *colloquy* may be denominated a *dialogue*; 'The close of this divine *colloquy* (between the Father and the Son) with the hymn of Angels that follow, are wonderfully beautiful and poetical.'—ADDISON.

ANSWER, REPLY, REJOINDER, RESPONSE.

Answer, in Saxon *andswaren* and *varan*, Goth. *award andward*, German *antwort*, compounded of *ant* or *anti* against, and *wort* a word, signifies a word used against or in return for another; *reply* comes from the French *repliquer*, Latin *replico* to unfold, signifying to unfold or enlarge upon by way of explanation; *rejoin* is compounded of *re* and *join*, signifying to join or add in return; *response*, in Latin *responsus*, participle of *respondeo*, compounded of *re* and *spondeo*, signifies to declare or give a sanction to in return.

Under all these terms is included the idea of using words in return for other words. An *answer* is given to a question; a *reply* is made to an assertion; a *rejoinder* is made to a *reply*; a *response* is made in accordance with the words of another.

One *answers* either for the purpose of affirmation assent, information, or contradiction;

> The blackbird whistles from the thorny brake,
> The mellow bulfinch *answers* from the grove.
> THOMSON.

We always *reply*, or *rejoin*, in order to explain or confute; 'He again took sometime to consider, and civilly *replied*, "I do."—"If you do agree with me," *rejoined* I, "in acknowledging the complaint, tell me if you will concur in promoting the cure."'—CUMBERLAND. *Responses* are made by way of assent or confirmation, and sometimes in the case of oracular *answers* by way of information; 'Lacedæmon, always disposed to control the growing consequence of her neighbours, and sensible of the bad policy of her late measures, had opened her eyes to the folly of expelling Hippias on the forged *responses* of the Pythia.'—CUMBERLAND. It is impolite not to *answer* when we are addressed: arguments are maintained by the alternate *replies* and *rejoinders* of two parties; but such arguments seldom tend to the pleasure and improvement of society: the *responses* in the liturgy are peculiarly calculated to keep alive the attention of those who take a part in the devotion.

An *answer* may be either spoken or written; *reply* and *rejoinder* are used in personal discourse only; a *response* may be said or sung.

RETORT, REPARTEE.

Retort, from *re* and *torqueo* to twist or turn back, to recoil, is an ill-natured reply: *repartee*, from the word *part*, signifies a smart reply, a ready taking one's own part. The *retort* is always in answer to a censure, objection, or argument against a thing, for which one returns a like censure; 'Those who have so vehemently urged the dangers of an active life, have made use of arguments that may be *retorted* upon themselves.'—Johnson. The *repartee* is commonly in answer to the wit of another, where one returns wit for wit; 'Henry IV. of France would never be transported beyond himself with choler, but he would pass by any thing with some *repartee*.'—Howell. In the acrimony of disputes it is common to hear *retort* upon *retort* to an endless extent; the vivacity of discourse is sometimes greatly enhanced by the quick *repartee* of those who take a part in it. There is nothing wanting in order to make a *retort*, but the disposition to aggravate one with whom we are offended; the talent for *repartee* is altogether a natural endowment which does not depend in any degree upon the will of the individual.

FACETIOUS, CONVERSABLE, PLEASANT, JOCULAR, JOCOSE.

All these epithets designate that companionable quality which consists in liveliness of speech. *Facetious*, in Latin *facetus*, may probably come from *for* to speak, denoting the versatility with which a person makes use of his words; *conversable* is literally able to hold a conversation; *pleasant* (*v. Agreeable*) signifies making ourselves *pleasant* with others, or them pleased with us; *jocular*, after the manner of a *joke; jocose*, using or having *jokes*.

Facetious may be employed either for writing or conversation; the rest only in conversation: the *facetious* man deals in that kind of discourse which may excite laughter; 'I have written nothing since I published, except a certain *facetious* history of John Gilpin.'—Cowper. A *conversable* man may instruct as well as amuse;

But here my lady will object,
Your intervals of time to spend,
With so *conversable* a friend,
It would not signify a pin
Whatever climate you were in.—Swift.

The *pleasant* man says every thing in a *pleasant* manner; his *pleasantry* even on the most delicate subject is without offence; 'Aristophanes wrote to please the multitude; his *pleasantries* are coarse and impolite.'—Warton. The person speaking is *jocose;* the thing said, or the manner of saying it, is *jocular:* it is not for one to be always *jocose*, although sometimes one may assume a *jocular* air when we are not at liberty to be serious;

Thus Venus sports,
When, cruelly *jocose*,
She ties the fatal noose,
And binds unequals to the brazen yokes.—Creech.

'Pope sometimes condescended to be *jocular* with servants or inferiours.'—Johnson. A man is *facetious* from humour; he is *conversable* by means of information; he indulges himself in occasional *pleasantry*, or allows himself to be *jocose*, in order to enliven conversation; a useful hint is sometimes conveyed in *jocular* terms.

ADDRESS, SPEECH, HARANGUE, ORATION.

Address, v. To address; speech, from *speak*, signifies the thing spoken; *harangue* probably comes from *ara* an altar, where *harangues* used to be delivered; *oration*, from the Latin *oro* to beg or entreat, signifies that which is said by way of entreaty.

All these terms denote a set form of words directed or supposed to be directed to some person: an *address* in this sense is always written, but the rest are really spoken or supposed to be so; 'When Louis of France had lost the battle of Fontenoy, the *addresses* to him at that time were full of his fortitude.'—Hughes. A *speech* is in general that which is *addressed* in a formal manner to one person or more; 'Every circumstance in their *speeches* and actions is with justice and delicacy adapted to the persons who speak and act.'—Addison *on Milton*. An *harangue* is a noisy, tumultuous *speech addressed* to many; 'There is scarcely a city in Great Britain but has one of this tribe who takes it into his protection, and on the market days *harangues* the good people of the place with aphorisms and recipes.'—Pearce *on Quacks*. An *oration* is a solemn *speech* for any purpose; 'How cold and unaffecting the best *oration* in the world would be without the proper ornaments of voice and gesture, there are two remarkable instances in the case of Ligarius and that of Milo.'—Swift.

Addresses are frequently sent up to the throne by publick bodies. *Speeches* in Parliament, like *harangues* at elections, are often little better than the crude effusions of party spirit. The *orations* of Demosthenes and Cicero, which have been so justly admired, received a polish from the correcting hand of their authors, before they were communicated to the publick.

Addresses of thanks are occasionally presented to persons in high stations by those who are anxious to express a sense of their merits. It is customary for the King to deliver *speeches* to both houses of Parliament at their opening. In all popular governments there is a set of persons who have a trick of making *harangues* to the populace, in order to render them dissatisfied with the men in power. Funeral *orations* are commonly spoken over the grave.

TO ACCOST, SALUTE, ADDRESS.

Accost, in French *accoster*, is compounded of *ac* or *ad*, and the Latin *costa* a rib or side, signifying to come by the side of a person; *salute*, in Latin *saluto*, from *salus* health, signifies to bid good speed; *address*, in French *addresser*, is compounded of *ad* and *dresser*, from the Latin *direxi*, preterit of *dirigo* to direct or apply, signifying to direct one's discourse to a person.

We *accost* a stranger whom we casually meet by the way; we *salute* our friends on meeting them; we *address* indifferent persons in company. Curiosity or convenience prompt men to *accost;* 'When Æneas is sent by Virgil to the shades, he meets Dido, the Queen of Carthage, whom his perfidy had hurried to the grave; he *accosts* her with tenderness and excuses, but the lady turns away like Ajax in mute disdain.'—Johnson. Good-will or intimacy prompt men to *salute* others; business or social communication lead men to *address* each other. Rude people *accost* every one whom they meet; familiar people *salute* those with whom they are barely acquainted; impertinent people *address* those with whom they have no business; 'I was harassed by the multitude of eager *salutations*, and returned the common civilities with hesitation and impropriety.'—Johnson. 'I still continued to stand in the way, having scarcely strength to walk farther, when another soon *addressed* me in the same manner.'—Johnson.

We must *accost* by speaking; but we may *salute* by signs as well as words; and *address* by writing as well as by speaking.

SALUTE, SALUTATION, GREETING.

Salute and *salutation*, from the Latin *salus*, signifies literally wishing health to a person; *greeting* comes from the German *grüssen* to kiss or salute.

Salute respects the thing, and *salutation* the person giving the *salute;* a *salute* may consist either of a word or an action; 'Strabo tells us he saw the statue of Memnon, which, according to the poets, *saluted* the morning sun, every day, at its first rising, with an harmonious sound.'—Prideaux. *Salutations* pass from one friend to another; 'Josephus makes mention of a Manaken who had the spirit of prophecy, and one time meeting with Herod among his school-fellows *greeted* him with this *salutation*, "Hail, King of the Jews."'—PRIDEAUX. The *salute* may be either direct or indirect; the *salutation* is always direct and personal: guns are fired by way of a *salute;* bows are given in the way of a *salutation;* *greeting* is a familiar kind of *salutation*, which may be given vocally or in writing;

> Not only those I nam'd I there shall *greet*,
> But my own gallant, virtuous Cato meet.
> DENHAM.

ELOCUTION, ELOQUENCE, ORATORY, RHETORICK.

Elocution and *eloquence* are derived from the same Latin verb *eloquor* to speak out; *oratory*, from *oro* to implore, signifies the art of making a set speech.

Elocution consists in the manner of delivery; *eloquence* in the matter that is delivered. We employ *elocution* in repeating the words of another; we employ *eloquence* to express our own thoughts and feelings. *Elocution* is requisite for an actor; *eloquence* for a speaker,

> Soft *elocution* does thy style renown,
> And the sweet accents of the peaceful gown,
> Gentle or sharp, according to thy choice,
> To laugh at follies or to lash at vice.—DRYDEN.

> Athens or free Rome, where *eloquence*
> Flourish'd, since mute.—MILTON.

Eloquence lies in the person; it is a natural gift: *oratory* lies in the mode of expression; it is an acquired art; 'As harsh and irregular sounds are not harmony, so neither is banging a cushion *oratory*.'—SWIFT. *Rhetorick*, from ῥέω to speak, is properly the theory of that art of which *oratory* is the practice. But the term *rhetorick* may be sometimes employed in an improper sense for the display of *oratory* or scientifick speaking. *Eloquence* speaks one's own feelings; it comes from the heart, and speaks to the heart: *oratory* is an imitative art; it describes what is felt by another. *Rhetorick* is the affectation of *oratory;* 'Be but a person in credit with the multitude, he shall be able to make popular rambling stuff pass for high *rhetorick* and moving preaching.'—SOUTH.

An afflicted parent, who pleads for the restoration of her child that has been torn from her, will exert her *eloquence;* a counsellor at the bar, who pleads the cause of his client, will employ *oratory;* vulgar partisans are full of *rhetorick*.

Eloquence often consists in a look or an action; *oratory* must always be accompanied with language. There is a dumb *eloquence* which is not denied even to the brutes, and which speaks more than all the studied graces of speech and action employed by the orator;

> His infant softness pleads a milder doom,
> And speaks with all the *eloquence* of tears.—HEIGH.

Between *eloquence* and *oratory* there is the same distinction as between nature and art: the former can never be perverted to any base purposes; it always speaks truth: the latter will as easily serve the purposes of falsehood as of truth. The political partisan, who paints the miseries of the poor in glowing language and artful periods, may often have *oratory* enough to excite dissatisfaction against the government, without having *eloquence* to describe what he really feels.

EFFUSION, EJACULATION.

Effusion signifies the thing poured out, and *ejaculation* the thing ejaculated or thrown out, both indicating a species of verbal expression; the former either by utterance or in writing, the latter only by utterance. The *effusion* is not so vehement or sudden as the *ejaculation;* the *ejaculation* is not so ample or diffuse as the *effusion;* *effusion* is seldom taken in a good sense; *ejaculation* rarely otherwise. An *effusion* commonly flows from a heated imagination uncorrected by the judgement; it is therefore in general not only incoherent, but extravagant and senseless: an *ejaculation* is produced by the warmth of the moment, but never without reference to some particular circumstance. Enthusiasts are full of extravagant *effusions;* contrite sinners will often express their penitence in pious *ejaculations;* 'Brain-sick opiniators please themselves in nothing but the ostentation of their own extemporary *effusions*.'—SOUTH. 'All which prayers of our Saviour's and others of like brevity are properly such as we call *ejaculations*.'—SOUTH.

WORD, TERM, EXPRESSION.

* *Word* is here the generick term; the other two are specifick. Every *term* and *expression* is a *word;* but every *word* is not denominated a *term* or *expression*. Language consists of *words;* they are the connected sounds which serve for the communication of thought. *Term*, from *terminus* a boundary, signifies any *word* that has a specifick or limited meaning; *expression* (*v. To express*) signifies any *word* which conveys a forcible meaning. Usage determines *words;* science fixes *terms;* sentiment provides *expressions*. The purity of a style depends on the choice of *words;* the precision of a writer depends upon the choice of his *terms;* the force of a writer depends upon the aptitude of his *expressions*.

The grammarian treats on the nature of *words;* the philosopher weighs the value of scientifick *terms;* the rhetorician estimates the force of *expressions*. The French have coined many new *words* since the revolution; *terms* of art admit of no change after the signification is fully defined; *expressions* vary according to the connexion in which they are introduced;

> As all *words* in few letters live,
> Thou to few *words* all sense dost give.—COWLEY.

'The use of the *word* minister is brought down to the literal signification of it, a servant; for now, to serve and to minister, servile and ministerial, are *terms* equivalent.'—SOUTH. 'A maxim, or moral saying, naturally receives this form of the antithesis, because it is designed to be engraven on the memory, which recalls it more easily by the help of such contrasted *expressions*.'—BLAIR.

VERBAL, VOCAL, ORAL.

Verbal, from *verbum* a word, signifies after the manner of a spoken word; *oral*, from *os* the mouth, signifies by word of mouth; and *vocal*, from *vox* the voice, signifies by the voice: the two former of these words are used to distinguish speaking from writing; the latter to distinguish the sounds of the voice from any other sounds, particularly in singing: a *verbal* message is distinguished from one written on a paper, or in a note; 'Among all the northern nations, shaking of hands was held necessary to bind the bargain, a custom which we still retain in many *verbal* contracts.'—BLACKSTONE. *Oral* tradition is distinguished from that which is handed down to posterity by means of books; 'In the first ages of the world instruction was commonly *oral*.'—JOHNSON. *Vocal* musick is distinguished from instrumental; *vocal* sounds are more harmonious than those which proceed from any other bodies;

> Forth came the human pair,
> And join'd their *vocal* worship to the choir
> Of creatures wanting voice.—MILTON.

VOTE, SUFFRAGE, VOICE.

Vote, in Latin *votum*, from *voveo* to vow, is very probably derived from *vox* a voice, signifying the *voice* that is raised in supplication to heaven; *suffrage*, in Latin *suffragium*, is in all probability compounded of *sub* and *frango* to break out or declare for a thing; *voice* is here figuratively taken for the *voice* that is raised in favour of a thing.

The *vote* is the wish itself, whether expressed or not; a person has a *vote*, that is, the power of wishing: but the *suffrage* and the *voice* are the wish that is expressed; a person gives his *suffrage* or his *voice*.

The *vote* is the settled and fixed wish; it is that by which the most important concerns in life are determined;

> The popular *vote*
> Inclines here to continue.—MILTON.

The *suffrage* is a *vote* given only in particular cases; 'Reputation is commonly lost, because it never was

* Girard: "Terme, expression

deserved; and was conferred at first, not by the *suffrage* of criticism, but by the fondness of friendship.'—JOHNSON. The *voice* is a partial or occasional wish, expressed only in matters of minor importance;

> I 've no words.
> My *voice* is in my sword! Thou bloodier villain
> Than terms can give thee out.—SHAKSPEARE.

But sometimes it may be employed to denote the publick opinion;

> That something 's ours when we from life depart,
> This all conceive, all feel it at the heart;
> The wise of learn'd antiquity proclaim
> This truth; the publick *voice* declares the same.
> JENYNS.

The *vote* and *voice* are given either for or against a person or thing; the *suffrage* is commonly given in favour of a person: in all publick assemblies the majority of *votes* decides the question; members of Parliament are chosen by the *suffrages* of the people; in the execution of a will every executor has a *voice* in all that is transacted.

LANGUAGE, TONGUE, SPEECH, IDIOM, DIALECT.

Language, from the Latin *lingua* a *tongue*, signifies, like the word *tongue*, that which is spoken by the *tongue*; *speech* is the act or power of speaking, or the thing spoken; *idiom*, in Latin *idioma*, Greek ἰδίωμα, from ἴδιος *proprius* proper or peculiar, signifies a peculiar mode of speaking; *dialect*, in Latin *dialectus*, Greek διάλεκτικος, from διαλέγομαι to speak in a distinct manner, signifies a distinct mode of speech.

All these terms mark the manner of expressing our thoughts, but under different circumstances. *Language* is the most general term in its meaning and application; it conveys the general idea without any modification, and is applied to other modes of expression, besides that of words, and to other objects besides persons: the *language* of the eyes frequently supplies the place of that of the *tongue*; the deaf and dumb use the *language* of signs; birds and beasts are supposed to have their peculiar *language*;

> Nor do they trust their tongue alone,
> But speak a *language* of their own.—SWIFT.

On the other hand, *tongue*, *speech*, and the others, are applicable only to human beings. *Language* is either written or spoken; but a *tongue* is conceived of mostly as a something to be spoken; and *speech* is, in the strict sense, that only which is spoken or uttered. A *tongue* is a totality, or an entire assemblage, of all that is necessary for the expressions; it comprehends not only words, but modifications of meaning, changes of termination, modes and forms of words, with the whole scheme of syntactical rules; a *tongue* therefore comprehended, in the first instance, only those *languages* which were originally formed: the Hebrew, Greek, and Latin are in the proper sense *tongues*; but those which are spoken by Europeans, and owe their origin to the former, commonly bear the general denomination of *languages*; 'What if we could discourse with people of all the nations upon the earth in their own mother *tongue*? Unless we know Jesus Christ, also, we should be lost for ever.'—BEVERIDGE.

Speech is an abstract term, implying either the power of uttering articulate sounds, as when we speak of the gift of *speech*, which is denied to those who are dumb; or the words themselves which are spoken, as when we speak of the parts of *speech*; or the particular mode of expressing one's self, as when we say that a man is known by his *speech*; 'When *speech* is employed only as the vehicle of falsehood, every man must disunite himself from others.'—JOHNSON. *Idiom* and *dialect* are not properly a *language*, but the properties of *language*: the *idiom* is the peculiar construction and turn of a *language*, which distinguishes it altogether from others; it is that which enters into the composition of the *language*, and cannot be separated from it; 'The *language* of this great poet is sometimes obscured by old words, transpositions, and foreign *idioms*.'—ADDISON. The *dialect* is that which is engrafted on a *language* by the inhabitants of particular parts of a country, and admitted by its writers and learned men to form an incidental part of the *language*; as the *dialects* which originated with the Ionians, the Athenians, the Æolians, and were afterward amalgamated into the Greek tongue; as also the *dialects* of the High and Low German which are distinguished by similar peculiarities; 'Every art has its *dialect*, uncouth and ungrateful to all whom custom has not reconciled to its sound.'—JOHNSON.

Languages simply serve to convey the thoughts: *tongues* consist of words written or spoken: *speech* consists of words spoken: *idioms* are the expression of national manners, customs, and turns of sentiment, which are the most difficult to be transferred from one language to another: *dialects* do not vary so much in the words themselves, as in the forms of words; they are prejudicial to the perspicuity of a *language*, but add to its harmony.

DICTION, STYLE, PHRASE, PHRASEOLOGY.

Diction, from the Latin *dictio*, saying, is put for the mode of expressing ourselves; *style* comes from the Latin *stylus* the bodkin with which the Romans both wrote and corrected what they had written on their waxen tablets: whence the word has been used for the manner of writing in general; *phrase*, in Greek φράσις, from φράζω to speak; and *phraseology* from φράσις and λόγος, both signify the manner of speaking.

Diction expresses much less than *style*: the former is applicable to the first efforts of learners in composition; the latter only to the original productions of a matured mind. Errours in grammar, false construction, a confused disposition of words, or an improper application of them, constitutes bad *diction*; but the niceties, the elegancies, the peculiarities, and the beauties of composition, which mark the genius and talent of the writer, are what is comprehended under the name of *style*. *Diction* is a general term, applicable alike to a single sentence or a connected composition; *style* is used in regard to a regular piece of composition.

As *diction* is a term of inferiour import, it is of course mostly confined to ordinary subjects, and *style* to the productions of authors. We should speak of a person's *diction* in his private correspondence, but of his *style* in his literary works. *Diction* requires only to be pure and clear; 'Prior's *diction* is more his own than that of any among the successors of Dryden.'—JOHNSON. *Style* may likewise be terse, polished, elegant, florid, poetick, sober, and the like; 'I think we may say with justice, that when mortals converse with their Creator, they cannot do it in so proper a style as in that of the Holy Scriptures.'—ADDISON.

Diction is said mostly in regard to what is written; *phrase* and *phraseology* are said as often of what is spoken as what is written; as that a person has adopted a strange *phrase* or *phraseology*. The former respects single words; the latter comprehends a succession of *phrases*;

> Rude am I in speech,
> And little blest with the soft *phrase* of speech.
> SHAKSPEARE.

'I was no longer able to accommodate myself to the accidental current of my conversation; my notions grew particular and paradoxical, and my *phraseology* formal and unfashionable.'—JOHNSON.

DICTIONARY, ENCYCLOPÆDIA.

Dictionary, from the Latin *dictum* a saying or word, is a register of words; *encyclopædia*, from the Greek ἐνκυκλοπαιδεία or ἐν in κύκλος and παιδεία learning, signifies a register of things.

The definition of words, with their various changes, modifications, uses, acceptations, and applications, are the proper subjects of a *dictionary*; 'If a man that lived an age or two ago should return into the world again, he would really want a *dictionary* to help him to understand his own language.'—TILLOTSON. The nature and property of things, with their construction, uses, powers, &c. are the proper subjects of an *encyclopædia*; 'Every science borrows from all the rest, and we cannot attain any single one without the *encyclopædia*.'—GLANVILLE. A general acquaintance with all arts and sciences as far as respects the use of technical terms, and a perfect acquaintance with the classical writers in the language, are essential for the composition of a *dictionary*; an entire acquaintance with all the minutiæ of every art and science is requisite for the composition of an *encyclopædia*. A single individual may qualify himself for the task of writing a *dictionary;* but the universality and diversity of knowledge contained in an *encyclopædia* render it necessarily the work of many.

A *dictionary* has been extended in its application to any work alphabetically arranged, as biographical, medical, botanical *dictionaries*, and the like, but still preserving this distinction, that the *dictionary* always contains only a general or partial illustration of the subject proposed, while the *encyclopædia* embraces the whole circle of science.

DICTIONARY, LEXICON, VOCABULARY, GLOSSARY, NOMENCLATURE.

Dictionary (*v. Dictionary*) is a general term. *Lexicon* from λέγω to say, *vocabulary* from *vox* a word, *glossary* from *gloss* to explain, and *nomenclature* from *nomen*, are all species of the *dictionary*.

Lexicon is a species of *dictionary* appropriately applied to the dead languages. A Greek or Hebrew *lexicon* is distinguished from a *dictionary* of the French or English. A *vocabulary* is a partial kind of *dictionary* which may comprehend a simple list of words, with or without explanation, arranged in order or otherwise. A *glossary* is an explanatory *vocabulary*, which commonly serves to explain the obsolete terms employed in any old author. A *nomenclature* is literally a list of names, and in particular reference to proper names.

TURGID, TUMID, BOMBASTICK.

Turgid and *tumid* both signify swollen, but they differ in their application: *turgid* belongs to diction, as a *turgid* style; *tumid* is applicable to the water and other objects, as the *tumid* waves. *Bombastick*, from *bombyx* a kind of cotton, signifies puffed up like cotton, and is, like *turgid*, applicable to words; but the *bombastick* includes the sentiments expressed: *turgidity* is confined mostly to the mode of expression. A writer is *turgid* who expresses a simple thought in a lofty language: a person is *bombastick* who deals in large words and introduces high sentiments in common discourse.

DIFFUSE, PROLIX.

Both mark defects of style opposed to brevity. *Diffuse*, in Latin *diffusus*, participle of *diffundo* to pour out or spread wide, marks the quality of being extended in space; *prolix*, in French *prolixe*, changed from *prolaxus*, signifies to let loose in a wide space.

The *diffuse* is properly opposed to the precise; the *prolix* to the concise or laconick. A *diffuse* writer is fond of amplification, he abounds in epithets, tropes, figures, and illustrations; the *prolix* writer is fond of circumlocution, minute details, and trifling particulars. *Diffuseness* is a fault only in degree, and according to circumstances; *prolixity* is a positive fault at all times. The former leads to the use of words unnecessarily; the latter to the use of phrases as well as words that are altogether useless: the *diffuse* style has too much of repetition; the *prolix* style abounds in tautology. *Diffuseness* often arises from an exuberance of imagination; *prolixity* from the want of imagination; on the other hand the former may be coupled with great superficiality, and the latter with great solidity.

Gibbon and other modern writers have fallen into the error of *diffuseness*. Lord Clarendon and many English writers preceding him are chargeable with *prolixity;* 'Few authors are more clear and perspicuous on the whole than Archbishop Tillotson and Sir William Temple, yet neither of them are remarkable for precision; they are loose and *diffuse*.'—Blair. 'I look upon a tedious talker, or what is generally known by the name of a story-teller, to be much more insufferable than a *prolix* writer.'—Steele.

SENTENCE, PROPOSITION, PERIOD, PHRASE.

Sentence, in Latin *sententia*, is but a variation of *sentiment* (*v. Opinion*); *proposition*, *v. Proposal;* *period*, in Latin *periodus*, Greek περίοδος, from περὶ about and ὁδὸς way, signifies the circuit or round of words, which renders the sense complete; *phrase*, from the Greek φράζω to speak, signifies the words uttered

The *sentence* consists of any words which convey sentiment; the *proposition* consists of the thing set before the mind, that is, either before our own minds or the minds of others; hence the term *sentence* has more especial regard to the form of words, and the *proposition* to the matter contained; 'Some expect in letters pointed *sentences* and forcible *periods*.'—Johnson. 'In 1417, it required all the eloquence and authority of the famous Gershon to prevail upon the council of Constance to condemn this *proposition*, that there are some cases in which assassination is a virtue more meritorious in a knight than a squire.'—Robertson. *Sentence* and *proposition* are both used technically or otherwise: the former in grammar and rhetorick, the latter in logick. The *sentence* is simple and complex; the *proposition* is universal or particular. *Period* and *phrase*, like *sentence*, are forms of words, but they are solely so, whereas the *sentence* depends on the connexion of ideas by which it is formed; we speak of *sentences* either as to their structure or their sentiment; hence the *sentence* is either grammatical or moral; 'A *sentence* may be defined, a moral instruction couched in a few words.'—Broome. The *period* regards only the structure; it is either well or ill-turned, long or short, it is in fact a complete *sentence* from one full stop to another; '*Periods* are beautiful when they are not too long.'—Ben Jonson. The term *phrase* denotes the character of the words;

> Disastrous words can best disasters show,
> In angry *phrase* the angry passions glow.
>
> Elphinstone.

Hence it is either vulgar or polite, idiomatick or general: the sentence must consist of at least two words to make sense; the *phrase* may be a single word or otherwise

SILENCE, TACITURNITY.

* The Latins have the two verbs *sileo* and *taceo*, the former of which is interpreted by some to signify to cease to speak; and the latter not to begin to speak: others maintain the direct contrary. According to the present use of the words, *silence* expresses less than *taciturnity:* the silent man does not speak; the *taciturn* man will not speak at all. The Latins designated the most profound *silence* by the epithet of *taciturna silentia*.

Silence is either occasional or habitual; it may arise from circumstances or character: *taciturnity* is mostly habitual, and springs from disposition. A loquacious man may be *silent* if he has no one to speak to him, and a prudent man will always be *silent* where he finds that speaking would be dangerous: a *taciturn* man, on the other hand, may occasionally make an effort to speak, but he never speaks without an effort When *silence* is habitual, it does not spring from an unamiable character: but *taciturnity* has always its source in a vicious temper of the mind. A *silent* man may frequently contract a habit of *silence* from thoughtfulness, modesty, or the fear of offending: a man is *taciturn* only from the sullenness and gloominess of his temper Habits of retirement render men *silent;* savages seldom break their *silence:* company will not correct *taciturnity*, but rather increase it. The observer is necessarily *silent;* if he speaks, it is only in order to observe: the melancholy man is naturally *taciturn;* if he speaks, it is with pain to himself. Seneca says, talk little with others and much with yourself; the *silent* man observes this precept; the *taciturn* man exceeds it;

> *Silence* is the perfectest herald of joy:
> I were but little happy, if I could say how much.
>
> Shakspeare.

'Pythagoras enjoined his scholars in absolute *silence* for a long noviciate. I am far from approving such a *taciturnity;* but I highly approve the end and intent of Pythagoras' injunction.'—Chatham

SILENT, DUMB, MUTE, SPEECHLESS.

Not speaking is the common idea included in the signification of these terms, which differ either in the cause or the circumstance: *silent* (*v. Silent*) is altogether an indefinite and general term, expressing little more than the common idea. We may be *silent*

* Vide Abbe Roubaud: "Silencieux, taciturne."

because we will not speak, or we may be *silent* because we cannot speak; but in distinction from the other terms it is always employed in the former case. Sometimes it is also used figuratively to denote sending forth no sound;

And just before the confines of the wood,
The gliding Lethe leads her *silent* flood.
DRYDEN.

Dumb, from the German *dumm* stupid or idiotick, denotes a physical incapacity to speak: hence persons are said to be born *dumb;* they may likewise be *dumb* from temporary physical causes, as from grief, shame, and the like; or a person may be struck *dumb;* 'The truth of it is, half the great talkers in the nation would be struck *dumb* were this fountain of discourse (party lies) dried up.'—ADDISON.

'T is listening fear and *dumb* amazement all.
THOMSON.

Mute, in Latin *mutus*, Greek μυττὸς from μύω to shut, signifies having a shut mouth, or a temporary disability to speak from arbitrary and incidental causes: hence the office of *mutes*, or of persons who engage not to speak for a certain time; and, in like manner, persons are said to be *mute* who dare not give utterance to their thoughts;

Mute was his tongue, and upright stood his hair.
DRYDEN.

Long *mute* he stood, and leaning on his staff,
His wonder witness'd with an idiot laugh.
DRYDEN.

Speechless, or void of speech, denotes a physical incapacity to speak from incidental causes; as when a person falls down *speechless* in an apoplectick fit, or in consequence of a violent contusion;

But who can paint the lover as he stood,
Pierc'd by severe amazement, hating life,
Speechless, and fix'd in all the death of wo.
THOMSON.

TO SPEAK, SAY, TELL.

Speak, v. To speak; say, in Saxon *seegan*, German *sagen*, Latin *seco* or *sequor*, changed into *dico*, and Hebrew שוע to vociferate; *tell*, in Saxon *taellan*, Low German *tellan*, &c., is probably an onomatopeia in language.

To *speak* may simply consist in uttering an articulate sound; but to *say* is to communicate some idea by means of words: a child begins to *speak* the moment it opens its lips to utter any acknowledged sound; but it will be some time before it can *say* any thing: a person is said to *speak* high or low, distinctly or indistinctly; but he *says* that which is true or false, right or wrong: a dumb man cannot *speak;* a fool cannot *say* any thing that is worth hearing: we *speak* languages, we *speak* sense or nonsense, we *speak* intelligibly or unintelligibly; but we *say* what we think at the time. In an extended sense, *speak* may refer as much to sense as to sound; but then it applies only to general cases, and *say* to particular and passing circumstances of life: it is a great abuse of the gift of speech not to *speak* the truth; it is very culpable in a person to *say* that he will do a thing and not to do it.

To *say* and *tell* are both the ordinary actions of men in their daily intercourse; but *say* is very partial, it may comprehend single, unconnected sentences, or even single words: we may *say* yes or no; but we *tell* that which is connected, and which forms more or less of a narrative. To *say* is to communicate that which passes in our own minds, to express our ideas and feelings as they rise; to *tell* is to communicate events or circumstances respecting ourselves or others: it is not good to let children *say* foolish things for the sake of talking; it is still worse for them to be encouraged in *telling* every thing they hear: when every one is allowed to *say* what he likes and what he thinks, there will commonly be more *speakers* than hearers; those who accustom themselves to *tell* long stories impose a tax upon others, which is not repaid by the pleasure of their company.

Men's reputations depend upon what others *say* of them; reports are spread by means of one man *telling* another; 'He that questioneth much shall learn much, and content much for he shall give occasion to those whom he asketh to please themselves in *speaking*.'—BACON.

Say, Yorke (for sure, if any, thou canst *tell*),
What virtue is, who practise it so well.
JENYNS.

NEWS, TIDINGS.

News implies any thing *new* that is related or circulated; but *tidings*, from *tide*, signifies that which flows in periodically like the *tide*, and comes in at the moment the thing happens. *News* is unexpected; it serves to gratify idle curiosity; 'I wonder that in the present situation of affairs you can take pleasure in writing any thing but *news*.'—SPECTATOR. *Tidings* are expected; they serve to allay anxiety;

Too soon some demon to my father bore
The *tidings* that his heart with anguish tore.
FALCONER.

In time of war the publick are eager after *news;* and they who have relatives in the army are anxious to have *tidings* of them.

TO REPEAT, RECITE, REHEARSE, RECAPITULATE.

The idea of going over any words, or actions, is common to all these terms. *Repeat*, from the Latin *repeto* to seek, or go over again, is the general term including only the common idea. To *recite, rehearse* and *recapitulate*, are modes of *repetition*, conveying each some accessory idea. To *recite* is to *repeat* in a formal manner; to *rehearse* is to *repeat* or *recite* by way of preparation; to *recapitulate* is to *repeat* in a minute and specifick manner. We *repeat* both actions and words; we *recite* only words: we *repeat* single words, or even sounds; we *recite* always a form of words: we *repeat* our own words, or the words of another; we *recite* only the words of another: we *repeat* a name; we *recite* an ode, or a set of verses: we *repeat* for purposes of general convenience; we *recite* for the convenience or amusement of others; we *rehearse* for some specifick purpose, either for the amusement or instruction of others: we *recapitulate* for the instruction of others. One *repeats* that which he wishes to be heard;

I could not half those horrid crimes *repeat*,
Nor half the punishments those crimes have met.
DRYDEN

A piece of poetry is *recited* before a company 'Whenever the practice of *recitation* was disused, the works, whether poetical or historical, perished with the authors.'—JOHNSON. A piece is *rehearsed* in private, which is intended to be *recited* in publick;

Now take your turns, ye muses, to *rehearse*
His friend's complaints, and mighty magick verse.
DRYDEN

One *recapitulates* the general heads of that which we have already spoken in detail; 'The parts of a judge are to direct the evidence to moderate length, repetition, or impertinency of speech, to *recapitulate*, select, and collate the material points of that which has been said.'—BACON. A master must always *repeat* to his scholars the instruction which he wishes them to remember; Homer is said to have *recited* his verses in different parts; players *rehearse* their different parts before they perform in publick; ministers *recapitulate* the leading points in their discourse.

To *repeat* is commonly to use the same words; to *recite*, to *rehearse*, and to *recapitulate*, do not necessarily require any verbal sameness. We *repeat* literally what we hear spoken by another; but we *recite* and *rehearse* events; and we *recapitulate* in a concise manner what has been uttered in a particular manner. An echo *repeats* with the greatest possible precision; Homer *recites* the names of all the Grecian and Trojan leaders, together with the names and account of their countries, and the number of the forces which they commanded; Virgil makes Æneas to *rehearse* before Dido and her courtiers the story of the capture of Troy, and his own adventures; a judge *recapitulates* evidence to a jury.

To *repeat, recite*, and *recapitulate* are employed in writing, as well as in speaking; *rehearse* is only a mode of speaking. It is sometimes a beauty in style to *repeat* particular words on certain occasions; an historian finds it necessary to *recapitulate* the principal events of any particular period.

REPETITION, TAUTOLOGY.

Repetition is to *tautology* as the genus to the species: the latter being a species of vicious *repetition*. There may be frequent *repetitions* which are warranted by necessity or convenience; but *tautology* is that which nowise adds to either the sense or the sound. A *repetition* may, or may not, consist of literally the same words; but *tautology*, from the Greek ταυτὸ the same, and λόγος a word, supposes such a sameness in expression, as renders the signification the same. In the liturgy of the church of England there are some *repetitions*, which add to the solemnity of the worship; in most extemporary prayers there is much *tautology*, that destroys the religious effect of the whole; 'That is truly and really *tautology*, where the same thing is repeated, though under never so much variety of expression.'—SOUTH.

TO RELATE, RECOUNT, DESCRIBE.

Relate, in Latin *relatus*, participle of *referro*, signifies to bring that to the notice of others which has before been brought to our own notice; *recount* is properly to *count* again, or *count* over again; *describe*, from the Latin *scribo* to write, is literally to write down.

The idea of giving an account of events or circumstances is common to all these terms, which differ in the object and circumstances of the action. *Relate* is said generally of all events, both of those which concern others as well as ourselves;

> O Muse! the causes and the crimes *relate*,
> What goddess was provok'd, and whence her hate.
> DRYDEN.

Recount is said particularly of those which concern ourselves, or in which we are interested;

> To *recount* Almighty works
> What words or tongue of seraph can suffice?
> MILTON.

Those who *relate* all they hear often *relate* that which never happened; it is a gratification to an old soldier to *recount* all the transactions in which he bore a part during the military career of his early youth. Events are *related* that have happened at any period of time immediate or remote; one *recounts* mostly those things which have been long passed: in *recounting*, the memory reverts to past scenes, and *counts* over all that has deeply interested the mind. Travellers are pleased to *relate* to their friends whatever they have seen remarkable in other countries; the *recounting* of our adventures in distant regions of the globe has a peculiar interest for all who hear them. We may *relate* either by writing or by word of mouth; we *recount* only by word of mouth: writers of travels sometimes give themselves a latitude in *relating* more than they have either heard or seen; he who *recounts* the exploits of heroism, which he has either witnessed or performed, will always meet with a delighted audience.

Relate and *recount* are said of that only which passes; *describe* is said of that which exists: we *relate* the particulars of our journey; and we *describe* the country we pass through. Personal adventure is always the subject of a *relation;* the quality and condition of things are those of the *description*. We *relate* what happened on meeting a friend; we *describe* the dress of the parties, or the ceremonies which are usual on particular occasions; 'In *describing* a rough torrent or deluge, the numbers should run easy and flowing.'—POPE.

RELATION, RECITAL, NARRATION.

Relation, from the verb *relate*, denotes the act of *relating; recital*, from *recite*, denotes the act of *reciting; narrative*, from *narrate*, denotes the thing *narrated*. *Relation* is here, as in the former paragraph (*v. To relate*), the general, and the others particular terms. *Relation* applies to every object which is related, whether of a publick or private, a national or an individual nature; history is the *relation* of national events; biography is the *relation* of particular lives; 'Those *relations* are commonly of most value in which the writer tells his own story.'—JOHNSON. *Recital* is the *relation* or repetition of actual or existing circumstances; we listen to the *recital* of misfortunes, distresses, and the like; 'Old men fall easily into *recitals* of past transactions.'—JOHNSON. The *relation* may concern matters of indifference; the *recital* is always of something that affects the interests of some individual: the pages of the journalist are filled with the *relation* of daily occurrences which simply amuse in the reading; but the *recital* of another's woes often draws tears from the audience to whom it is made.

Relation and *recital* are seldom employed but in connexion with the object *related* or *recited; narrative* is mostly used by itself: hence we say the *relation* of any particular circumstance; the *recital* of any one's calamities; but an affecting *narrative*, or a simple *narrative;* 'Cynthia was much taken with my *narrative*.'—TATLER.

ANECDOTES, MEMOIRS, CHRONICLES, ANNALS.

Anecdote, from the Greek ἀνέκδοτος, signifies what is communicated in a private way; *memoirs*, in French *memoires*, from the word *memory*, signifies what serves to help the memory; *chronicle*, in French *chronicle*, from the Greek χρόνος time, signifies an account of the times; *annals*, from the French *annales*, the Latin *annus* a year, signifies a detail of what passes in the year.

All these terms mark a species of narrative more or less connected, that may serve as materials for a regular history.

Anecdotes consist of personal or detached circumstances of a publick or private nature, involving one subject or more. *Anecdotes* may be either moral or political, literary or biographical; they may serve as characteristicks of any individual, or of any particular nation or age; 'I allude to those papers in which I treat of the literature of the Greeks, carrying down my history in a chain of *anecdotes* from the earliest poets to the death of Menander.'—CUMBERLAND.

Memoirs may include *anecdotes*, as far as they are connected with the leading subject on which they treat; *memoirs* are rather connected than complete; they are a partial narrative respecting an individual, and comprehending matter of a publick or private nature; they serve as *memorials* of what ought not to be forgotten, and lay the foundation either for a history or a life; 'Cæsar gives us nothing but *memoirs* of his own times.'—CULLEN.

Chronicles and *annals* are altogether of a publick nature; and approach the nearest to the regular and genuine history. *Chronicles* register the events as they pass; *annals* digest them into order, as they occur in the course of the year. *Chronicles* are minute as to the exact point of time; *annals* only preserve a general order within the period of a year.

Chronicles detail the events of small as well as large communities, as of particular districts and cities; *annals* detail only the events of nations. *Chronicles* include domestick incidents or such things as concern individuals. The word *annals*, in its proper sense, relates only to such things as affect the great body of the publick, but it is frequently employed in an improper sense. *Chronicles* may be confined to simple matter of fact; *annals* may enter into the causes and consequences of events; 'His eye was so piercing that, as ancient *chronicles* report, he could blunt the weapons of his enemies only by looking at them' JOHNSON.

> Could you with patience hear, or I relate,
> O nymph! the tedious *annals* of our fate,
> Through such a train of woes if I should run
> The day would sooner than the tale be done.
> DRYDEN.

Anecdotes require point and vivacity, as they seem rather to amuse than instruct; the grave historian will always use them with caution; *memoirs* require authenticity; *chronicles* require accuracy; *annals* require clearness of narration, method in the disposition, impartiality in the representation, with almost every requisite that constitutes the true historian.

Anecdotes and *memoirs* are of more modern use: *chronicles* and *annals* were frequent in former ages; they were the first historick monuments which were stamped with the impression of the simple, frank, and rude manners of early times. The *chronicles* of our present times are principally to be found in newspapers and magazines; the *annals* in *annual* registers or retrospects.

ACCOUNT, NARRATIVE, DESCRIPTION.

Account, v. Account, reckoning; narrative, from *narrate*, is in Latin *narratus*, participle of *narro* or *gnarro*, signifies that which is made known; *description*, from *describe*, in Latin *describo*, or *de* and *scribo*, signifies that which is written down.

Account is the most general of these terms; whatever is noted as worthy of remark is an *account; narrative* is an account narrated; *description* an account described.

Account has no reference to the person giving the account; a *narrative* must have a narrator; a *description* must have a describer. An *account* may come from one or several quarters, or no specified quarter; but a *narrative* and *description* bespeak themselves as the production of some individual.

An *account* may be the statement of a single fact only; a *narrative* must always consist of several connected incidents; a *description* of several unconnected particulars respecting some common object.

An *account* and a *description* may be communicated either verbally or in writing; a *narrative* is mostly written.

An *account* may be given of political events, natural phenomena, and domestick occurrences; as the signing of a treaty, the march of an army, the death and funeral of an individual; 'A man of business, in good company, who gives an *account* of his abilities and despatches, is hardly more insupportable than her they call a notable woman.'—STEELE. A *narrative* is mostly personal, respecting the adventures, the travels, the dangers, and the escapes of some particular person; 'Few *narratives* will, either to men or women, appear more incredible than the histories of the Amazons.'—JOHNSON. A *description* does not so much embrace occurrences, as characters, appearances, beauties, defects, and attributes in general; 'Most readers, I believe, are more charmed with Milton's *description* of paradise than of hell.'—ADDISON.

Accounts from the armies are anxiously looked for in time of war. Whenever a *narrative* is interesting, it is a species of reading eagerly sought after. The *descriptions* which are given of the eruptions of volcanoes are calculated to awaken a strong degree of curiosity. An *account* may be false or true; a *narrative* clear or confused; a *description* lively or dull.

FABLE, TALE, NOVEL, ROMANCE.

Fable, in Latin *fabula*, from *for* to speak or tell, and *tale*, from to *tell*, both designate a species of narration; *novel*, in Italian *novella*, is an extended *tale* that has *novelty; romance*, from the Italian *romanzo*, is a wonderful *tale*, or a *tale* of wonders, such as was most in vogue in the dark ages of European literature.

Different species of composition are expressed by the above words. The *fable* is allegorical; its actions are natural, but its agents are mostly imaginary; 'When I travelled, I took a particular delight in hearing the songs and *fables* that are come from father to son, and are most in vogue among the common people.'—ADDISON. The *tale* is fictitious, but not imaginary; both the agents and actions are drawn from the passing scenes of life;

> Of Jason, Theseus, and such worthies old,
> Light seem the *tales* antiquity has told.—WALLER.

Gods and goddesses, animals and men, trees, vegetables, and inanimate objects in general, may be made the agents of a *fable*: but of a *tale*, properly speaking, only men or supernatural spirits can be the agents: of the former description are the celebrated *fables* of Æsop; and of the latter the *tales* of Marmontel, the *tales* of the Genii, the Chinese *tales*, &c. *Fables* are written for instruction; *tales* principally for amusement: *fables* consist mostly of only one incident or action, from which a moral may be drawn; *tales* always of many, which excite an interest for an individual.

The *tale* when compared with the *novel* is a simple kind of fiction, it consists of but few persons in the drama; while the *novel* on the contrary admits of every possible variety in characters: the *tale* is told without much art or contrivance to keep the reader in suspense, without any depth of plot or importance in the catastrophe; the *novel* affords the greatest scope for exciting an interest by the rapid succession of events, the involvements of interests, and the unravelling of its plots; 'A *novel* conducted upon one uniform plan, containing a series of events in familiar life, is in effect a protracted comedy not divided into acts.'—CUMBERLAND. If the *novel* awakens the attention, the *romance* rivets the whole mind and engages the affections; it presents nothing but what is extraordinary and calculated to fill the imagination: of the former description, Cervantes, La Sage, and Fielding have given us the best specimens; and of the latter we have the best modern specimens from the pen of Mrs. Radcliffe; 'In the *romances* formerly written, every transaction and sentiment was so remote from all that passes among men, that the reader was in little danger of making any application to himself.'—JOHNSON.

ANECDOTE, STORY, TALE.

Anecdote, v. Anecdotes; story, like history, comes from the Greek ἱστορέω to relate.

An *anecdote* (*v. Anecdotes*) has but little incident, and no plot: a *story* may have many incidents, and an important catastrophe annexed to it, the word *story* being a contraction of history: there are many *anecdotes* related of Dr. Johnson, some of which are of a trifling nature, and others characteristick; *stories* are generally told to young people of ghosts and visions, which are calculated to act on their fears.

An *anecdote* is pleasing and pretty; a *story* is frightful or melancholy: an *anecdote* always consists of some matter of fact; a *story* is founded on that which is real. *Anecdotes* are related of some distinguished persons, displaying their characters or the circumstances of their lives; 'How admirably Rapin, the most popular among the French criticks, was qualified to sit in judgement upon Homer and Thucydides, Demosthenes and Plato, may be gathered from an *anecdote* preserved by Menage, who affirms upon his own knowledge that Le Fevre and Saumur furnished this assuming critick with the Greek passages which he had to cite, Rapin himself being totally ignorant of that language.'—WARTON. *Stories* from life, however striking and wonderful, will seldom impress so powerfully as those which are drawn from the world of spirits; 'This *story* I once intended to omit, as it appears with no great evidence; nor have I met with any confirmation but in a letter of Farquhar, and he only relates that the funeral of Dryden was tumultuary and confused.'—JOHNSON. *Anecdotes* serve to amuse men, *stories* to amuse children.

The *story* is either an actual fact, or something feigned; the *tale* is always feigned: *stories* are circulated respecting the accidents and occurrences which happen to persons in the same place; *tales* of distress are told by many merely to excite compassion. When both are taken for that which is fictitious, the *story* is either an untruth, or falsifying of some fact, or it is altogether an invention; the *tale* is always an invention. As an untruth, the *story* is commonly told by children; and as a fiction, the *story* is commonly made for children;

> Meantime the village rouses up the fire,
> While well attested, and as well believed,
> Heard solemn, goes the goblin *story* round.
> THOMSON.

The *tale* is of deeper invention, and serves for a more serious end, good or bad;

> He makes that pow'r to trembling nations known,
> But rarely this, not for each vulgar end,
> As superstitious idle *tales* pretend.—JENYNS.

CAST, TURN, DESCRIPTION, CHARACTER.

Cast, from the verb to *cast* (*v. To cast*), signifies that which is *cast*, and here, by an extension of the sense, the form in which it is *cast; turn*, from the verb to *turn*, signifies also the act of *turning*, or the manner of *turning*; *description* signifies the act of *describing*, or the thing which is to be *described*; *character* is that by which the *character* is known or determined (*v.* *Character*).

What is *cast* is artificial; what *turns* is natural: the former is the act of some foreign agent; the latter is the act of the subject itself: hence the *cast*, as applicable to persons, respects that which they are made by circumstances; the *turn*, that which they are by themselves: thus there are religious *casts* in India, that is, men *cast* in a certain form of religion; and men of a particular moral *cast*, that is, such as are *cast* in a particular mould as respects their thinking and acting; so in like manner men of a particular *turn*, that is, as respects their inclinations and tastes; 'My mind is of such a particular *cast*, that the falling of a shower of rain, or the whistling of the wind at such a time (the night season) is apt to fill my thoughts with something awful and solemn.'—Addison. 'There is a very odd *turn* of thought required for this sort of writing (the fairy way of writing, as Dryden calls it); and it is impossible for a poet to succeed in it, who has not a particular *cast* of fancy.'—Addison. *Description* is a term less definite than either of the two former; it respects all that may be said of a person, but particularly that which distinguishes a man from others, either in his mode of thinking or acting, in his habits, in his manners, in his language, or his taste; 'Christian statesmen think that those do not believe Christianity who do not care it should be preached to the poor. But as they know that charity is not confined to any *description*, they are not deprived of a due and anxious sensation of pity to the distresses of the miserable great.'—Burke. The *character* in this sense is a species of *description*, namely, the *description* of the prominent features by which an object is distinguished;

> Each drew fair *characters*, yet none
> Of those they feign'd excels their own.
> Denham.

The *cast* is that which marks a man to others; the *turn* is that which may be known only to a man's self; the *description* or *character* is that by which he is *described* or made known to others.

The *cast* is that which is fixed and unchangeable; the *turn* is that which may be again *turned*; and the *description* or *character* is that which varies with the circumstances.

LIST, ROLL, CATALOGUE, REGISTER.

List, in French *liste*, and German *liste*, comes from the German *leiste* a last, signifying in general any long and narrow body; *roll* signifies in general any thing *rolled* up, particularly paper with its written contents; *catalogue*, in Latin *catalogus*, Greek *κατάλογος*, from *καταλέγω* to write down, signifies a written enumeration; *register* comes from the Latin verb *regero* (*v.* *To enrol*).

A collection of objects brought into some kind of order is the common idea included in the signification of these terms. The contents and disposition of a *list* is the most simple; it consists of little more than names arranged under one another in a long narrow line, as a *list* of words, a *list* of plants and flowers, a *list* of voters, a *list* of visits, a *list* of deaths, of births, of marriages; 'After I had read over the *list* of the persons elected into the Tiers Etat, nothing which they afterward did could appear astonishing.'—Burke. *Roll*, which is figuratively put for the contents of a *roll*, is a *list rolled* up for convenience, as a long *roll* of saints; 'It appears from the ancient *rolls* of parliament, and from the manner of choosing the lords of articles, that the proceedings of that high court must have been in a great measure under their direction.'—Robertson. *Catalogue* involves more details than a simple *list*; it specifies not only names, but dates, qualities, and circumstances. A *list* of books contains their titles; a *catalogue* of books contains an enumeration of their size, price, number of volumes, edition, &c.; a *roll* of saints simply specifies their names; a *catalogue* of saints enters into particulars of their ages, deaths, &c.;

> Ay! in the *catalogue* ye go for men,
> As hounds, and greyhounds, mongrels, spaniels, curs,
> All by the name of dogs.—Shakspeare.

A *register* contains more than either; for it contains events, with dates, actors, &c. in all matters of publick interest; I am credibly informed by an antiquary who has searched the *registers*, that the maids of honour, in Queen Elizabeth's time, were allowed three rumps of beef for their breakfast.'—Addison.

TO ENROL, ENLIST OR LIST, REGISTER, RECORD.

Enrol, compounded of *en* or *in* and *roll*, signifies to place in a roll, that is, in a roll of paper or a book; *enlist*, compounded of *in* and *list*, signifies to put down in a list; *register* is in Latin *registrum*, from *regestum*, participle of *regero*, signifying to put down in writing; *record*, in Latin *recordor*, compounded of *re* back or again, and *cor* the heart, signifies to bring back to the heart, or call to mind by a memorandum.

Enrol and *enlist* respect persons only: *register* respects persons and things; *record* respects things only *Enrol* is generally applied to the act of inserting names in an orderly manner into any book; 'Anciently no man was suffered to abide in England above forty days, unless he were *enrolled* in some tithing or decennary.'—Blackstone. *Enlist* is a species of *enrolling* applicable only to the military, or persons intended for military purposes; 'The lords would, by *listing* their own servants, persuade the gentlemen of the town to do the like.'—Clarendon. The *enrolment* is an act of authority; the *enlisting* is the voluntary act of an individual. Among the Romans it was the office of the censor to *enrol* the names of all the citizens in order to ascertain their number, and estimate their property In modern times soldiers are mostly raised by means of *enlisting*.

In the moral application of the terms, to *enrol* is to assign a certain place or rank: to *enlist* is to put one's self under a leader, or attach one's self to a party. Hercules was *enrolled* among the gods; 'We find ourselves *enrolled* in this heavenly family as servants and as sons.'—Sprat. The common people are always ready to *enlist* on the side of anarchy and rebellion; 'The time never was when I would have *enlisted* under the banners of any faction, though I might have carried a pair of colours, if I had not spurned them, in either legion.'—Sir Wm. Jones.

To *enrol* and *register* both imply writing down in a book; but the former is a less formal act than the latter The insertion of the bare name or designation in a certain order is enough to constitute an *enrolment*. *Registering* comprehends the birth, family, and other collateral circumstances of the individual. The object of *registering* likewise differs from that of *enrolling* What is *registered* serves for future purposes and is of permanent utility to society in general; but what is *enrolled* often serves only a particular or temporary end Thus in numbering the people it is necessary simply to *enrol* their names; but when in addition to this it was necessary, as among the Romans, to ascertain their rank in the state, every thing connected with their property, their family, and their connexions required to be *registered*. So in like manner in more modern times, it has been found necessary for the good government of the state to *register* the births, marriages, and deaths of every citizen. It is manifest, therefore, that what is *registered*, as far as respects persons, may be said to be *enrolled*; but what is *enrolled* is not always *registered*; 'I hope you take care to keep an exact journal, and to *register* all occurrences and observations, for your friends here expect such a book of travels as has not often been seen.'—Johnson.

Register, in regard to *record*, has a no less obvious distinction: the former is used for domestick and civil transactions, the latter for publick and political events What is *registered* serves for the daily purposes of the community collectively and individually; what is *recorded* is treasured up in a special manner for particular reference and remembrance at a distant period. The number or names of streets, houses, carriages, and the like, are *registered* in different offices; the deeds and documents which regard grants, charters, privileges, and the like, either of individuals or particular towns, are *recorded* in the archives of nations. To *record* is, therefore, a formal species of *registering*: we *register* when we *record*, but we do not always *record* when we *register*; 'The medals of the Romans were their current money; when an action deserved to be *recorded* in coin, it was stamped perhaps upon a hundred thousand pieces of money, like our shillings or half-pence.'—ADDISON.

In an extended and figurative application things may be said to be *registered* in the memory, or events *recorded* in history. We have a right to believe that the actions of good men are *registered* in heaven, and that their names are *enrolled* among the saints and angels; the particular sayings and actions of princes are *recorded* in history, and handed down to the latest posterity.

RECORD, REGISTER, ARCHIVE.

Record is taken for the thing *recorded; register*, either for the thing *registered*, or the place in which it is *registered; archive*, mostly for the place, and sometimes for the thing. The *records* are either historical details, or short notices; the *registers* are but short notices of particular and local circumstances; the *archives* are always connected with the state. Every place of antiquity has its *records* of the different circumstances which have been connected with its rise and progress, and the various changes which it has experienced. In publick *registers* we find accounts of families, and of their various connexions and fluctuations; in publick *archives* we find all legal deeds and instruments, which involve the interests of the nation, both in its internal and external economy.

TO CALL, BID, SUMMON, INVITE.

Call, in its abstract and original sense, signifies simply to give an expression of the voice, in which it agrees with the German *schall*, Swedish *skalla* a sound, Greek καλέω to call, Hebrew קול the voice; *bid* and *invite* have the same derivation as explained in the preceding article; *summon*, in French *sommer*, changed from *summoner*, Latin *submoneo*, signifies to give private notice.

The idea of signifying one's wish to another to do any thing is included in all these terms.

To *call* is not confined to any particular sound; we may *call* by simply raising the voice: to *invite* is not even confined to sounds; we may *invite* by looks, or signs, or even by writing: to *bid* and *summon* require the express use of words. The actions of *calling* and *inviting* are common to animals as well as men: the sheep *call* their young when they bleat, and the oxen their companions when they low; cats and other females among the brutes *invite* their young to come out from their bed when it is proper for them to begin to walk; to *bid* and *summon* are altogether confined to human beings.

Call and *bid* are direct addresses: to *invite* and *summon* may pass through the medium of a second person. I *call* or *bid* the person whom I wish to come, but I send him a *summons* or *invitation.*

Calling of itself expresses no more than the simple desire; but according to circumstances it may be made to express a command or entreaty. When equals *call* each other, or inferiours *call* their superiours, it amounts simply to a wish; 'Ladronius, that famous captain, was *called* up and told by his servants that the general was fled.'—KNOWLES. When the dam *calls* her young it amounts to supplicating entreaty; but when a father *calls* his son, or a master his servant, it is equivalent to a command; 'Why came not the slave back when I *called* him?'—SHAKSPEARE. To *bid* expresses either a command or an entreaty: when superiours *bid* it is a positive command;

Saint Withold footed thrice the wold;
He met the night-mare and her ninefold,
Bid her alight and her troth plight.—SHAKSPEARE.

When equals *bid* it is an act of civility, particularly in the phrases to *bid* welcome, to *bid* God speed, to *bid* farewell, and the like, which, though they may be used by superiours, are nevertheless terms of kindness and equality;

I am *bid* forth to supper, Jessica;
There are my keys.—SHAKSPEARE.

To *summon* is always imperative; to *invite* always in the spirit of kindness and courtesy. Persons in all tations of life have occasion to *call* each other; but t is an action most befitting the superiour; to *bid* and *invite* are alike the actions of superiours and equals, to *summon* is the act of a superiour only.

Calling is mostly for the purpose of drawing the object to or from a person or another object, whence the phrases to *call* up, or to *call* off, &c. *Bidding*, as a command, may be employed for what we wish to be done; but *bidding* in the sense of an *invitation* is employed for drawing the object to our place of residence. *Inviting* is employed for either purpose. *Summoning* is an act of authority, by which a person is obliged to make his appearance at a given place.

These terms preserve the same distinction in their extended and figurative acceptation;

In a deep vale, or near some ruin'd wall,
He would the ghosts of slaughter'd soldiers *call*.
DRYDEN.

'Be not amazed, *call* all your senses to you, defend my reputation, or bid farewell to your good life for ever.'—SHAKSPEARE. 'The soul makes use of her memory to *call* to mind what she is to treat of.'—DUPPA.

The star that *bids* the shepherd fold,
Now the top of heaven doth hold.—MILTON.

This minute may be mine, the next another's;
But still all mortals ought to wait the *summons*.
SMITH.

Still follow where auspicious fates *invite*,
Caress the happy, and the wretched slight.—LEWIS.

TO CITE, SUMMON.

Cite, v. *To cite, quote; summon*, in French *sommer*, Latin *summoneo* or *submoneo*, compounded of *sub* and *moneo*, signifies to give a private intimation.

The idea of calling a person authoritatively to appear is common to these terms. *Cite* is used in a general sense, *summon* in a particular and technical sense: a person may be *cited* to appear before his superiour; he is *summoned* to appear before a court: the station of the individual gives authority to the act of *citing;* the law itself gives authority to that of *summoning*.

When *cite* is used in a legal sense, it is mostly employed for witnesses, and *summon* for every occasion: a person is *cited* to give evidence, he is *summoned* to answer a charge. *Cite* is seldomer used in the legal sense than in that of calling by name, in which general acceptation it is employed with regard to authors, as specified in the succeeding article: it may, however, be sometimes used in a general sense;

E'en social friendship duns his ear,
And *cites* him to the publick sphere.—SHENSTONE.

The legal is the ordinary sense of *summon;* it may, however, be extended in its application to any call for which there may be occasion; as when we speak of the *summons* which is given to attend the death-bed of a friend, or, figuratively, death is said to *summon* mortals from this world;

The sly enchantress *summon'd* all her train,
Alluring Venus, queen of vagrant love,
The boon companion Bacchus, loud and vain,
And tricking Hermes, god of fraudful gain.—WEST

TO CITE, QUOTE.

Cite and *quote* are both derived from the same Latin verb *cito* to move, and the Hebrew סות to stir up, signifying to put in action.

To *cite* is employed for persons or things; to *quote* for things only: authors are *cited;* passages from their works are *quoted:* we *cite* only by authority; we *quote* for general purposes of convenience. Historians ought to *cite* their authority in order to strengthen their evidence and inspire confidence; 'The great work of which Justinian has the credit, consists of texts collected from law books of approved authority; and those texts are adjusted according to a scientifical analysis; the names of the original authors and the titles of their several books being constantly *cited*.'—SIR WM. JONES. Controversialists must *quote* the objectionable passages in those works which they wish to confute: it is prudent to *cite* no one whose authority is questionable; it is superfluous to *quote* any thing that can be easily perused in the original; 'Let us consider what is truly glorious according to the author I have to-day *quoted* in the front of my paper.'—STEELE.

NOISE, CRY, OUTCRY, CLAMOUR.

Noise is any loud sound; *cry*, *outcry*, and *clamour* are particular kinds of noises, differing either in the cause or the nature of the sounds. A *noise* proceeds either from animate or inanimate objects; the *cry* proceeds only from animate objects. The report of a cannon, or the loud sounds occasioned by a high wind, are *noises*, but not *cries*;

> Nor was his ear less peal'd
> With *noises* loud and ruinous.—MILTON.

Cries issue from birds, beasts, and men;

> From either host, the mingled shouts and *cries*
> Of Trojans and Rutilians rend the skies.—DRYDEN.

A *noise* is produced often by accident; a *cry* is always occasioned by some particular circumstance: when many horses and carriages are going together, they make a great *noise*; hunger and pain cause *cries* to proceed both from animals and human beings.

Noise, when compared with *cry*, is sometimes only an audible sound; the *cry* is a very loud *noise*; whatever disturbs silence, as the falling of a pin in a perfectly still assembly, is denominated a *noise*; but a *cry* is that which may often drown other *noises*, as the *cries* of people selling things about the streets. A *cry* is in general a regular sound, but *outcry* and *clamour* are irregular sounds; the former may proceed from one or many, the latter from many in conjunction. A *cry* after a thief becomes an *outcry* when set up by many at a time; it becomes a *clamour*, if accompanied with shouting, bawling, and *noises* of a mixed and tumultuous nature;

> And now great deeds
> Had been achiev'd, whereof all hell had rung,
> Had not the snaky sorceress that sat
> Fast by hell gate, and kept the fatal key,
> Ris'n, and with hideous *outcry* rush'd between.
> MILTON.

> Their darts with *clamour* at a distance drive,
> And only keep the languish'd war alive.—DRYDEN.

These terms may all be taken in an improper as well as a proper sense. Whatever is obtruded upon the publick notice so as to become the universal subject of conversation and writing, is said to make a *noise*; in this manner a new and good performer at the theatre makes a *noise* on his first appearance; 'What *noise* have we had about transplantation of diseases, and transfusion of blood.'—BAKER. 'Socrates lived in Athens during the great plague, which has made so much *noise* through all ages, and never caught the infection.'—ADDISON. *Noise* and *clamour* may be for or against an object; *cry* and *outcry* are always against the object, varying in the degree and manner in which they display themselves: the *cry* is less than the *outcry*, and this is less than the *clamour*. When the publick voice is raised in an audible manner against any particular matter, it is a *cry*; if it be mingled with intemperate language it is an *outcry*; if it be vehement, and exceedingly *noisy*, it is a *clamour*. Partisans raise a *cry* in order to form a body in their favour;

> Amazement seizes all; the general *cry*
> Proclaims Laocoon justly doom'd to die.—DRYDEN.

The discontented are ever ready to set up an *outcry* against men in power; 'These *outcries* the magistrates there shun, since they are hearkened unto here.'—SPENSER (*on Ireland*). A *clamour* for peace in the time of war is easily raised by those who wish to thwart the government; 'The people grew then exorbitant in their *clamours* for justice.'—CLARENDON.

TO CRY, WEEP.

Cry comes from the Greek *κραζέω*, and the Hebrew קרא to *cry* or call; *weep*, in Low German *wapen*, is a variation of whine, in German *weinen*, which is an onomatopeia. An outward indication of pain is expressed by both these terms, but the former comprehends an audible expression accompanied or not with tears; the latter simply indicates the shedding of tears.

Crying arises from an impatience in suffering corporeal pains; children and weak people commonly *cry*: *weeping* is occasioned by mental grief; the wisest and best of men will not disdain sometimes to *weep*.

Crying is as selfish as it is weak; it serves to relieve the pain of the individual to the annoyance of the hearer;

> The babe clung *crying* to his nurse's breast,
> Scared at the dazzling helm and nodding crest
> POPE

Weeping, when called forth by others' sorrows, is an infirmity which no man would wish to be without; as an expression of generous sympathy it affords essential relief to the sufferer;

> Thy Hector, wrapt in everlasting sleep,
> Shall neither hear thee sigh, nor see thee *weep*
> POPE.

TO CRY, SCREAM, SHRIEK.

Cry, *v. To cry, weep; scream* and *shriek* are variations of *cry*.

To *cry* indicates the utterance of an articulate or an inarticulate sound; *scream* is a species of *crying* in the first sense of the word; *shriek* is a species of *crying* in its latter sense.

Crying is an ordinary mode of loud utterance resorted to on common occasions; one *cries* in order to be heard: *screaming* is an intemperate mode of *crying*, resorted to from an impatient desire to be heard, or from a vehemence of feeling. People *scream* to deaf people from the mistaken idea of making themselves heard; whereas a distinct articulation will always be more efficacious. It is frequently necessary to *cry* when we cannot render ourselves audible by any other means; but it is never necessary or proper to *scream*. *Shriek* may be compared with *cry* and *scream*, as expressions of pain; in this case to *shriek* is more than to *cry*, and less than to *scream*. They both signify to *cry* with a violent effort. We may *cry* from the slight est pain or inconvenience; but one *shrieks* or *screams* only on occasions of great agony, either corporeal or mental. A child cries when it has hurt its finger; it *shrieks* in the moment of terrour at the sight of a frightful object; or *screams* until some one comes to its assistance.

To *cry* is an action peculiar to no age or sex; to *scream* and to *shriek* are the common actions of women and children. Men *cry*, and children *scream*, for assistance; excess of pain will sometimes compel a man to *cry* out; a violent alarm commonly makes females *shriek*;

> Like a thin smoke he sees the spirit fly,
> And hears a feeble, lamentable *cry*.—POPE.

> Rapacious at the mother's throat they fly,
> And tear the *screaming* infant from her breast.
> THOMSON.

> The house is fill'd with loud laments and *cries*,
> And *shrieks* of women rend the vaulted throne.
> DRYDEN

TO CRY, EXCLAIM, CALL.

All these terms express a loud mode of speaking, which is all that is implied in the sense of the word *cry*, while in that of the two latter are comprehended accessory ideas.

To *exclaim*, from the Latin *exclamo* or *ex* and *clamo*, to *cry* out or aloud, signifies to *cry* with an effort; *call* comes from the Greek *καλέω*.

We *cry* from the simple desire of being heard at a distance: we *exclaim* from a sudden emotion or agitation of mind. As a *cry* bespeaks distress and trouble, an *exclamation* bespeaks surprise, grief, or joy. We *cry* commonly in a large assembly or an open space, but we may *exclaim* in conversation with an individual.

To *cry* is louder and more urgent than to *call*. A man who is in danger of being drowned *cries* for help, he who wants to raise a load *calls* for assistance: a *cry* is a general or indirect address; a *call* is a particular and immediate address. We *cry* to all or any who may be within hearing; we *call* to an individual by name with a direct reference to him;

> There while you groan beneath the load of life,
> They *cry*, behold the mighty Hector's wife!—POPE

> The dreadful day
> No pause of words admits, no dull delay;
> Fierce Discord storms, Apollo loud *exclaims*,
> Fame *calls*, Mars thunders, and the field 's in flames
> POPE

LOUD, NOISY, HIGHSOUNDING, CLAMOROUS.

Loud is doubtless connected, through the medium of the German *laut* a sound, and *lauschen* to listen, with the Greek κλύω to hear, because sounds are the object of hearing: *noisy*, having a *noise*, like *noisome* and *noxious*, comes from the Latin *noceo* to hurt, signifying in general offensive, that is, to the sense of hearing, of smelling, and the like: *highsounding* signifies the same as pitched upon an elevated key, so as to make a great noise, to be heard at a distance: *clamorous*, from the Latin *clamo* to cry, signifies crying with a loud voice.

Loud is here the generick term, since it signifies a great sound, which is the idea common to them all. As an epithet for persons, *loud* is mostly taken in an indifferent sense; all the others are taken for being *loud* beyond measure: *noisy* is to be intemperately *loud; highsounding* is only to be *loud* from the bigness of one's words; *clamorous* is to be disagreeably and painfully *loud.* We must speak *loudly* to a deaf person in order to make ourselves heard;

> The clowns, a boist'rous, rude, ungovern'd crew,
> With furious haste to the *loud* summons flew.
> DRYDEN.

Children will be *noisy* at all times if not kept under control;

> O leave the *noisy* town.—DRYDEN.

Flatterers are always *highsounding* in their eulogiums of those by whom they expect to be served; 'I am touched with sorrow at the conduct of some few men, who have lent the authority of their *highsounding* names to the designs of men with whom they could not be acquainted.'—BURKE. Children will be *clamorous* for what they want, if they expect to get it by dint of *noise;* they will be turbulent in case of refusal, if not under proper discipline;

> *Clam'rous* around the royal hawk they fly.
> DRYDEN.

In the improper application, *loud* is taken in as bad a sense as the rest: the *loudest* praises are the least to be regarded: the applause of a mob is always *noisy: highsounding* titles serve only to excite contempt where there is not some corresponding sense: it is the business of an opposition party to be *clamorous*, which serves the purpose of exciting turbulence among the ignorant.

TO NOMINATE, NAME.

Nominate comes immediately from the Latin *nominatus*, participle of *nomino: name* comes from the Teutonick, &c. *name*, and both from the Latin *nomen*, &c. (*v. To name*).

To *nominate* and to *name* are both to mention by *name:* but the former is to mention for a specifick purpose; the latter is to mention for general purposes: persons only are *nominated;* things as well as persons are *named:* one *nominates* a person in order to propose him, or appoint him, to an office; 'Elizabeth *nominated* her commissioners to hear both parties.'—ROBERTSON. One *names* a person casually, in the course of conversation, or one *names* him in order to make some inquiry respecting him;

> Then Calchas (by Ulysses first inspir'd)
> Was urg'd to *name* whom th' angry gods requir'd.
> DENHAM.

To be *nominated* is a publick act; to be *named* is generally private: one is *nominated* before an assembly; one is *named* in any place: to be *nominated* is always an honour; to be *named* is either honourable, or the contrary, according to the circumstances under which it is mentioned: a person is *nominated* as member of Parliament; he is *named* in terms of respect or otherwise whenever he is spoken of.

TO NAME, CALL.

Name is properly to pronounce some word, from the Latin *nomen*, Greek ὄνομα, Hebrew נאם; *call, v. To call.*

Both these words imply the direction of the sound to an object: but *naming* is confined to the use of some distinct and significant sound, *calling* is said of any sound whatever: we may *call* without *naming*, but we cannot *name* without *calling.* A person is *named* by his name, whether proper, patronymick, or whatever is usual; he is *called* according to the characteristicks by which he is distinguished. The emperour Tiberius was *named* Tiberius; he was *called* a monster. William the First of England is *named* William; he is *called* the Conqueror. Helen went three times round the wooden horse in order to discover the snare, and, with the hope of taking the Greeks by surprise, *called* their principal captains, *naming* them by their *names*, and counterfeiting the voices of their wives. Many ancient nations in *naming* any one *called* him the son of some one, as Richardson the son of Richard, and Robertson the son of Robert;

> Some haughty Greek who lives thy tears to see,
> Imbitters all thy woes by *naming* me.—POPE.

> I lay the deep foundations of a wall,
> And Ænos, *nam'd* from me, the city *call.*—DRYDEN.

NAME, APPELLATION, TITLE, DENOMINATION.

Name, v. To name; appellation, in French *appellation*, Latin *appellatio*, from *appello* to call, signifies that by which a person or thing is called; *title*, in French *titre*, Latin *titulus*, from the Greek τίω to honour, signifies that appellation which is assigned to any one for the purpose of honour; *denomination* signifies that which *denominates* or distinguishes.

Name is a generick term, the rest are specifick. Whatever word is employed to distinguish one thing from another is a *name;* therefore an *appellation* and a *title* is a *name*, but not *vice versâ;*

> Then on your *name* shall wretched mortals call,
> And offer'd victims at your altars fall.—DRYDEN.

A *name* is either common or proper; an *appellation* is generally a common *name* given for some specifick purpose as characteristick. Several kings of France had the *names* of Charles, Louis, Philip, but one was distinguished with the *appellation* of Stammerer, another by that of the Simple, and a third by that of the Hardy, arising from particular characters or circumstances; 'The *names* derived from the profession of the ministry in the language of the present age, are made but the *appellatives* of scorn.'—SOUTH. A *title* is a species of *appellation*, not drawn from any thing personal, but conferred as a ground of political distinction. An *appellation* may be often a term of reproach; but a *title* is always a mark of honour. An *appellation* is given to all objects, animate or inanimate; a *title* is given mostly to persons, sometimes to things. A particular house may have the *appellation* of 'the Cottage,' or 'the Hall;' as a particular person may have the *title* of Duke, Lord, or Marquis; 'We generally find in *titles* an intimation of some particular merit that should recommend men to the high stations which they possess.'—ADDISON.

Denomination is to particular bodies, what *appellation* is to an individual; namely, a term of distinction, drawn from their peculiar character and circumstances. The Christian world is split into a number of different bodies or communities, under the *denominations* of Catholicks, Protestants, Calvinists, Presbyterians, &c. which have their origin in the peculiar form of faith and discipline adopted by these bodies; 'It has cost me much care and thought to marshal and fix the people under their proper *denominations.*'—ADDISON

TO NAME, DENOMINATE, STYLE, ENTITLE, DESIGNATE, CHARACTERIZE.

To *name* (*v. To name, call*) signifies simply to give a *name* to, or to address or specify by the given *name;* 'I could *name* some of our acquaintance who have been obliged to travel as far as Alexandria in pursuit of money.'—MELMOTH (*Letters of Cicero*). To *denominate* is to give a specifick *name* upon some specifick ground, or to distinguish by the *name;* 'A fable in tragick or epick poetry is *denominated* simple when the events it contains follow each in an unbroken tenour.'—WARTON. To *style*, from the noun *style* or manner (*v. Diction, style*), signifies to address by a specifick *name;*

Happy those times,
When lords were *styled* fathers of families.
SHAKSPEARE.

To *entitle* is to give a specifick or appropriate *name;* 'Besides the Scripture, the books which they call ecclesiastical were thought not unworthy to be brought into publick audience, and with that *name* they *entitled* the books which we term Apocryphal.'—HOOKER. Adam *named* every thing; we *denominate* the man who drinks excessively 'a drunkard;' subjects *style* their monarch 'His Majesty;' books are *entitled* according to the judgement of the author.

To *name, denominate, style,* and *entitle* are the acts of conscious agents only. To *designate,* signifying to mark out, and *characterize,* signifying to form a *characteristick,* are said only of things, and agree with the former only inasmuch as words may either *designate* or *characterize:* thus the word 'capacity' is said to *designate* the power of holding; and 'finesse' *characterizes* the people by whom it was adopted; 'This is a plain *designation* of the Duke of Marlborough; one kind of stuff used to fatten land is called marle, and every one knows that borough is the *name* of town.'—SWIFT. 'There are faces not only individual, but gentilitious and national. European, Asiatick, Chinese, African, and Grecian faces are *characterized.*'—ARBUTHNOT.

NAME, REPUTATION, REPUTE, CREDIT.

Name is here taken in the improper sense for a *name* acquired in publick by any peculiarity or quality in an object; *reputation* and *repute,* from *reputo* or *re* and *puto* to think back, or in reference to some immediate object, signifies the state of being thought of by the publick, or held in publick estimation; *credit* (*v. Credit*) signifies the state of being believed or trusted in general.

Name implies something more specifick than *reputation;* and *reputation* something more substantial than *name:* a *name* may be acquired by some casualty or by some quality that has more show than worth; *reputation* is acquired only by time, and built only on merit: a *name* may be arbitrarily given, simply by way of distinction; *reputation* is not given, but acquired, or follows as a consequence of one's honourable exertions. A physician sometimes gets a *name* by a single instance of professional skill, which by a combination of favourable circumstances he may convert to his own advantage in forming an extensive practice; but unless he have a commensurate degree of talent, this *name* will never ripen into a solid *reputation;*

Who fears not to do ill, yet fears the *name,*
And, free from conscience, is a slave to fame.
DENHAM.

'Splendour of *reputation* is not to be counted among the necessaries of life.'—JOHNSON.

Inanimate objects get a *name,* but *reputation* is applied only to persons or that which is personal. Fashion is liberal in giving a *name* to certain shops, certain streets, certain commodities, as well as to certain tradespeople, and the like. Universities, academies, and publick institutions, acquire a *reputation* for their learning, their skill, their encouragement and promotion of the arts or sciences: *name* and *reputation* are of a more extended nature than *repute* and *credit.* Strangers and distant countries hear of the *name* and the *reputation* of any thing; but only neighbours and those who have the means of personal observation can take a part in its *repute* and *credit.* It is possible, therefore, to have a *name* and *reputation* without having *repute* and *credit,* and *vice versâ,* for the objects which constitute the former are sometimes different from those which produce the latter. A manufacturer has a *name* for the excellence of a particular article of his own manufacture; a book has a *name* among witlings and pretenders to literature: a good writer, however, seeks to establish his *reputation* for genius, learning, industry, or some praiseworthy characteristick: a preacher is in high *repute* among those who attend him: a master gains great *credit* from the good performances of his scholars; 'Mutton has likewise been in great *repute* among our valiant countrymen.'—ADDISON.

Would you true happiness attain,
Let honesty your passions rein,
So live in *credit* and esteem,
And the good *name* you lost, redeem —GAY.

Name and *repute* are taken either in a good or bad sense; *reputation* and *credit* are taken in the good sense only: a person or thing may get a good or an ill *name;* a person or thing may be in good or ill *repute; reputation* may rise to different degrees of height, or it may sink again to nothing, but it never sinks into that which is bad; *credit* may likewise be high or low, but when it becomes bad it is *discredit.* Families get an ill *name* for their meanness; houses of entertainment get a good *name* for their accommodation; houses fall into bad *repute* when said to be haunted; a landlord comes into high *repute* among his tenants, if he be considerate and indulgent towards them.

CHARACTER, REPUTATION.

From the natural sense of a stamp or mark (*v. Character, letter*), this word is figuratively employed for the moral mark which distinguishes one man from another; *reputation,* from the French *reputer,* Latin *reputo* to think, signifies what is thought of a person: *character* lies in the man; it is the mark of what he is; it shows itself on all occasions: *reputation* depends upon others; it is what they think of him.

A *character* is given particularly: a *reputation* is formed generally. Individuals give a *character* of another from personal knowledge: publick opinion constitute the *reputation. Character* has always some foundation; it is a positive description of something: *reputation* has more of conjecture in it; its source is hearsay.

It is possible for a man to have a fair *reputation* who has not in reality a good *character;* although men of really good *character* are not likely to have a bad *reputation;* 'Let a man think what multitudes of those among whom he dwells are totally ignorant of his name and *character;* how many imagine themselves too much occupied with their own wants and pursuits to pay him the least attention; and where his *reputation* is in any degree spread, how often it has been attacked, and how many rivals are daily rising to abate it.'—BLAIR.

FAME, REPUTATION, RENOWN.

Fame, from the Greek φημὶ to say, is the most noisy and uncertain; it rests upon report: *reputation* (*v. Character, reputation*) is silent and solid; it lies more in the thoughts, and is derived from observation: *renown,* in French *renommée,* from *nom* a name, signifies the reverberation of a name; it is as loud as *fame,* but more substantial and better founded: hence we say that a person's *fame* has gone abroad; his *reputation* is established; and he has got *renown.*

Fame may be applied to any object, good, bad, or indifferent;

Europe with Afric in his *fame* shall join,
But neither shore his conquests shall confine.
DRYDEN.

Reputation is applied only to real eminence in some department; 'Pope doubtless approached Addison, when the *reputation* of their wit first brought them together, with the respect due to a man whose abilities were acknowledged.'—JOHNSON. *Renown* is employed only for extraordinary men and brilliant exploits; 'Well constituted governments have always made the profession of a physician both honourable and advantageous. Homer's Machaon and Virgil's Iapis were men of *renown,* heroes in war.'—JOHNSON. The *fame* of a quack may be spread among the ignorant multitude by means of a lucky cure, or the *fame* of an author may be spread by means of a popular work; 'The artist finds greater returns in profit, as the author in *fame.*'—ADDISON. The *reputation* of a physician rests upon his tried skill and known experience; the *renown* of a general is proportioned to the magnitude of his achievements;

How doth it please and fill the memory,
With deeds of brave *renown,* while on each hand
Historick urns and breathing statues rise,
And speaking busts.—DYER.

FAME, REPORT, RUMOUR, HEARSAY.

Fame (*v. Fame*) has a reference to the thing which gives birth to it; it goes about of itself without any apparent instrumentality. The *report*, from *re* and *porto*, to carry back, or away from an object, has always a reference to the *reporter*. *Rumour*, in Latin *rumor*, from *ruo* to rush or to flow, has a reference to the flying nature of words that are carried; it is therefore properly a flying *report*. *Hearsay* refers to the receiver of that which is said; it is limited therefore to a small number of speakers or reporters. The *fame* serves to form or establish a character either of a person or a thing; it will be good or bad according to circumstances; the *fame* of our Saviour's miracles went abroad through the land;

> Space may produce new worlds, whereof so rife
> There went a *fame* in heav'n, that he ere long
> Intended to create.—MILTON.

The *report* serves to communicate information of events; it may be more or less correct according to the veracity or authenticity of the *reporter; reports* of victories mostly precede the official confirmation; 'What liberties any man may take in imputing words to me which I never spoke, and what credit Cæsar may give to such *reports*, these are points for which it is by no means in my power to be answerable.'—MELMOTH (*Letters of Cicero*). The *rumour* serves the purposes of fiction; it is more or less vague, according to the temper of the times and the nature of the events; every battle gives rise to a thousand *rumours*;

> For which of you will stop
> The vent of hearing, when loud *rumour*
> Speaks?—SHAKSPEARE.

The *hearsay* serves for information or instruction, and is seldom so incorrect as it is familiar; 'What influence can a mother have over a daughter, from whose example the daughter can only have *hearsay* benefits?'—RICHARDSON.

FAMOUS, CELEBRATED, RENOWNED, ILLUSTRIOUS.

Famous signifies literally having *fame* or being the cause of *fame;* it is applicable to that which causes a noise or sensation; to that which is talked of, written upon, discussed, and thought of; to that which is reported of far and near; to that which is circulated among all ranks and orders of men: *celebrated* signifies literally kept in the memory by a *celebration* or memorial, and is applicable to that which is praised and honoured with solemnity: *renowned* signifies literally possessed of a name, and is applicable to whatever extends the name, or causes the name to be often repeated: *illustrious* signifies literally what has or gives a lustre; it is applicable to whatever confers dignity.

Famous is a term of indefinite import; it conveys of itself frequently neither honour nor dishonour, since it is employed indifferently as an epithet for things praiseworthy or otherwise; it is the only one of these terms which may be used in a bad sense. The others rise in a gradually good sense; 'I thought it an agreeable change to have my thoughts diverted from the greatest among the dead and fabulous heroes, to the most *famous* among the real and living.'—ADDISON.

* The *celebrated* is founded upon merit and the display of talent in the arts and sciences; it gains the subject respect; 'While I was in this learned body, I applied myself with so much diligence to my studies, that there are very few *celebrated* books either in the learned or modern tongues which I am not acquainted with.'—ADDISON. The *renowned* is founded upon the possession of rare or extraordinary qualities, upon successful exertions and an accordance with publick opinion; it brings great honour or glory to the subject;

> Castor and Pollux first in martial force,
> One bold on foot, and one *renown'd* for horse.
> POPE.

The *illustrious* is founded upon those solid qualities which not only render one known but distinguished; it ensures regard and veneration; 'The reliefs of the envious man are those little blemishes that discover themselves in an *illustrious* character.'—ADDISON.

A person may be *famous* for his eccentricities; *celebrated* as an artist, a writer, or a player; *renowned* as a warriour or a statesman; *illustrious* as a prince, a statesman, or a senator.

The maid of Orleans, who was decried by the English, and idolized by the French, is equally *famous* in both nations. There are *celebrated* authors whom to censure even in that which is censurable, would endanger one's reputation. The *renowned* heroes of antiquity have, by the perusal of their exploits, given birth to a race of modern heroes not inferiour to themselves. Princes may shine in their lifetime, but they cannot render themselves *illustrious* to posterity except by the monuments of goodness and wisdom which they leave after them.

* Vide Abbe Girard; Fameux, illustre, celebre, renommé."

NOTED, NOTORIOUS.

Noted (v. *Distinguished*) may be employed either in a good or a bad sense; *notorious* is never used but in a bad sense: men may be *noted* for their talents, or their eccentricities; they are *notorious* only for their vices: *noted* characters excite many and diverse remarks from their friends and their enemies; *notorious* characters are universally shunned;

> An engineer of *noted* skill,
> Engag'd to stop the growing ill.—GAY.

'What principles of ordinary prudence can warrant a man to trust a *notorious* cheat?'—SOUTH.

DISTINGUISHED, CONSPICUOUS, NOTED, EMINENT, ILLUSTRIOUS.

Distinguished signifies having a mark of distinction by which a thing is to be *distinguished; conspicuous*, in Latin *conspicuus*, from *conspicio*, signifies easily to be seen; *noted*, from *notus* known, signifies well known; *eminent*, in Latin *eminens*, from *emineo* or *e* and *maneo*, signifies remaining or standing out above the rest; *illustrious*, in Latin *illustris*, from *lustro* to shine, signifies shone upon.

The idea of an object having something attached to it to excite notice is common to all these terms.

Distinguished in its general sense expresses little more than this idea; the rest are but modes of the *distinguished*. A thing is *distinguished* in proportion as it is distinct or separate from others; it is *conspicuous* in proportion as it is easily seen; it is *noted* in proportion as it is widely known. In this sense a rank is *distinguished;* a situation is *conspicuous;* a place is *noted*. Persons are *distinguished* by external marks or by characteristick qualities; persons or things are *conspicuous* mostly from some external mark; persons or things are *noted* mostly by collateral circumstances.

A man may be *distinguished* by his decorations, or he may be *distinguished* by his manly air, or by his abilities; 'It has been observed by some writers that man is more *distinguished* from the animal world by devotion than by reason.'—ADDISON. A person is *conspicuous* by the gaudiness of his dress; a house is *conspicuous* that stands on a hill;

> Before the gate stood Pyrrhus, threat'ning loud,
> With glitt'ring arms, *conspicuous* in the crowd.
> DRYDEN.

A person is *noted* for having performed a wonderful cure; a place is *noted* for its fine waters; 'Upon my calling in lately at one of the most *noted* Temple coffeehouses, I found the whole room, which was full of young students, divided into several parties, each of which was deeply engaged in some controversy.'—BUDGELL.

We may be *distinguished* for things, good, bad, or indifferent: we may be *conspicuous* for our singularities or that which only attracts vulgar notice: we may be *noted* for that which is bad, and mostly for that which is the subject of vulgar discourse: we can be *eminent* and *illustrious* only for that which is really good and praiseworthy; the former applies however mostly to those things which set a man high in the circle of his acquaintance; the latter to that which makes him shine before the world. A man of *distinguished* talent will be apt to excite envy if he be not also *distinguished* for his private virtue: affectation is never better pleased than when it can place itself in such a *conspicuous* situation as to draw all eyes upon itself: lovers of fame are sometimes contented to render themselves *noted* for their vices or absurdities nothing is more gratifying to a man than to render himself *eminent* for his professional skill; 'Of Prior, *eminent* as he was both by his abilities and station, very few memorials have been left by his contemporaries.'—JOHNSON. It is the lot of but few to be *illustrious*, and those few are very seldom to be envied;

Hail, sweet Saturnian soil! of fruitful grain
Great parent, greater of *illustrious* men.
DRYDEN.

In an extended and moral application, these terms may be employed to heighten the character of an object; a favour may be said to be *distinguished*, piety *eminent*, and a name *illustrious;* 'Amid the agitations of popular government, occasions will sometimes be afforded for *eminent* abilities to break forth with peculiar lustre. But while publick agitations allow a few individuals to be uncommonly *distinguished*, the general condition of the publick remains calamitous and wretched.'—BLAIR.

Next add our cities of *illustrious* name,
Their costly labour and stupendous frame
DRYDEN.

SIGNAL, MEMORABLE.

Signal signifies serving as a sign; *memorable* signifies worthy to be remembered.

They both express the idea of extraordinary, or being distinguished from ordinary, or being distinguished from every thing else: whatever is *signal* deserves to be stamped on the mind, and to serve as a *sign* of some property or characteristick; whatever is *memorable* impresses upon the memory, and refuses to be forgotten: the former applies to the moral character; the latter to events and times: the Scriptures furnish us with many *signal* instances of God's vengeance against impenitent sinners, as also of his favour towards those who obey his will; 'We find, in the Acts of the Apostles, not only no opposition to Christianity from the Pharisees, but several *signal* occasions in which they assisted its first teachers.'—WOTTON. The Reformation is a *memorable* event in the annals of ecclesiastical history; 'That such deliverances are actually afforded, those three *memorable* examples of Abimelech, Esau, and Balaam sufficiently demonstrate.'—SOUTH.

TO SIGNALIZE, DISTINGUISH.

To *signalize*, or make one's self a sign of any thing, is a much stronger term than simply to *distinguish;* it is in the power of many to do the latter, but few only have the power of effecting the former; the English have always *signalized* themselves for their unconquerable valour in battle; 'The knight of La Mancha gravely recounts to his companion the adventure by which he is to *signalize* himself.'—JOHNSON. There is no nation that has not *distinguished* itself, at some period or another, in war;

The valued file
Distinguishes the swift, the slow, the subtle.
SHAKSPEARE.

OF FASHION, OF QUALITY, OF DISTINCTION.

These epithets are employed promiscuously in colloquial discourse; but not with strict propriety;* by men *of fashion* are understood such men as live in the *fashionable* world, and keep the best company; 'The free manner in which people *of fashion* are discoursed on at such meetings (of tradespeople), is but a just reproach of their failures in this kind (in payment).'—STEELE. By men of *quality* are understood men of rank or title; 'The single dress of a lady of *quality* is often the product of a hundred climes.'—ADDISON. By men *of distinction* are understood men of honourable superiority, whether by wealth, office, or preeminence in society; 'It behooves men *of distinction*, with their power and example, to preside over the publick diversions in such a manner as to check any thing that tends to the corruption of manners.'—STEELE.

Gentry and merchants, though not men *of quality*, may, by their mode of living, be men *of fashion;* and by the office they hold in the state, they may likewise be men *of distinction*.

PROMINENT, CONSPICUOUS.

Prominent signifies hanging over; *conspicuous* (*v Distinguished*) signifies easy to be beheld: the former is, therefore, to the latter, in some measure, as the species to the genus: what is *prominent* is, in general, on that very account *conspicuous;* but many things may be *conspicuous* besides those which are *prominent*. The terms *prominent* and *conspicuous* have, however an application suited to their peculiar meaning: nothing is *prominent* but what projects beyond a certain line every thing is *conspicuous* which may be seen by many the nose on a man's face is a *prominent* feature, owing to its projecting situation; and it is sometimes *conspicuous*, according to the position of the person: a figure in a painting is said to be *prominent*, if it appears to stand forward or before the others; but it is not properly *conspicuous*, unless there be something in it which attracts the general notice, and distinguishes it from all other things: on the contrary, it is *conspicuous*, but not expressly *prominent*, when the colours are vivid; 'Lady Macbeth's walking in her sleep is an incident so full of tragick horrour, that it stands out as a *prominent* feature in the most sublime drama in the world.'—CUMBERLAND. 'That innocent mirth which had been so *conspicuous* in Sir Thomas More's life, did not forsake him to the last.'—ADDISON.

BRIGHTNESS, LUSTRE, SPLENDOUR, BRILLIANCY.

Brightness, from the English *bright*, Saxon *breorht*, probably comes, like the German *pracht* splendour, from the Hebrew ברק to shine or glitter; *lustre*, in French *lustre*, Latin *lustrum* a purgation or cleansing, that is, to make clean or pure; *splendour*, in French *splendeur*, Latin *splendor*, from *splendeo* to shine, comes either from the Greek σπληδὸς embers, or σπινθὴρ a spark; *brilliancy*, from *brilliant* and *briller* to shine, comes from the German *brille* spectacles, and the middle Latin *beryllus* a crystal.

Brightness is the generick, the rest are specifick terms: there cannot be *lustre*, *splendour*, and *brilliancy*, without *brightness;* but there may be *brightness* where these do not exist. These terms rise in sense; *lustre* rises on *brightness*, *splendour* on *lustre*, and *brilliancy* on *splendour*.

Brightness and *lustre* are applied properly to natural lights; *splendour* and *brilliancy* have been more commonly applied to that which is artificial: there is always more or less *brightness* in the sun or moon; there is an occasional *lustre* in all the heavenly bodies when they shine in their unclouded *brightness;* there is *splendour* in the eruptions of flame from a volcano or an immense conflagration; there is *brilliancy* in a collection of diamonds. There may be both *splendour* and *brilliancy* in an illumination: *splendour* arises from the mass and richness of light; *brilliancy* from the variety and *brightness* of the lights and colours. *Brightness* may be obscured, *lustre* may be tarnished, *splendour* and *brilliancy* diminished.

The analogy is closely preserved in the figurative application. *Brightness* attaches to the moral character of men in ordinary cases; 'Earthly honours are both short-lived in their continuance, and, while they last, tarnished with spots and stains. On some quarter or other their *brightness* is obscured. But the honour which proceeds from God and virtue is unmixed and pure. It is a *lustre* which is derived from heaven.'—BLAIR. *Lustre* attaches to extraordinary instances of virtue and greatness; *splendour* and *brilliancy* attach to the achievements of men; 'Thomson's diction is in the highest degree florid and luxuriant, such as may be said to be to his images and thoughts "both their *lustre* and their shade;" such as invest them with *splendour* through which they are not easily discernible.'—JOHNSON. 'There is an appearance of *brilliancy* in the pleasures of high life which naturally dazzles the young.'—CRAIG.

Our Saviour is strikingly represented to us as the *brightness* of his Father's glory, and the express image of his person. The humanity of the English in the

* Vide Trusler: "Of fashion, of quality, of distinction."

ɀour of conquest adds a *lustre* to their victories which are either *splendid* or *brilliant*, according to the number and nature of the circumstances which render them remarkable.

FIRE, HEAT, WARMTH, GLOW.

In the proper sense these words are easily distinguished, but not so easily in the improper sense; and as the latter depends principally upon the former, it is not altogether useless to enter into some explanation of their physical meaning.

Fire is with regard to *heat* as the cause to the effect: it is itself an inherent property in some material bodies, and when in action communicates *heat;** *fire* is perceptible to us by the eye, as well as the touch; *heat* is perceptible only by the touch: we distinguish *fire* by means of the flame it sends forth, or by the changes which it produces upon other bodies; but we discover *heat* only by the sensations which it produces in ourselves.

Fire has within itself the power of communicating *heat* to other bodies at a distance from it; but *heat*, when it lies in bodies without *fire*, is not communicable or even perceptible, except by coming in contact with the body. *Fire* is producible in some bodies at pleasure, and when in action will communicate itself without any external influence; but *heat* is always to be produced and kept in being by some external agency: *fire* spreads; but *heat* dies away. *Fire* is producible only in certain bodies; but *heat* may be produced in many more bodies; *fire* may be elicited from a flint, or from wood, steel, and some few other materials; but *heat* is producible, or exists to a greater or less degree, in all material substances.

Heat and *warmth* differ principally in degree; the latter being a gentle degree of the former. The term *heat* is, however, in its most extensive sense applicable to that universal principle which pervades all nature, animate and inanimate, and seems to vivify the whole; it is this principle which appears either under the form of *fire*, or under the more commonly conceived form of *heat*, as it is generally understood, and as I have here considered it. *Heat* in this limited sense is less active than *fire*, and more active than *warmth;* the former is produced in bodies, either by the violent action of *fire*, as in the boiling of water, the melting of lead, or the violent friction of two hard bodies; the latter is produced by the simple expulsion of the cold, as in the case of feathers, wool, and other substances, which produce and retain *warmth*.

Heat may be the greatest possible remove, but *warmth* may be the smallest possible remove, from cold; the latter is opposed to the cool, which borders on the cold. *Heat* is that which to our feelings is painful; but *warmth* is that which is always grateful. In animate bodies *fire* cannot long exist, as it is in its nature consuming and destructive; it is incompatible with animal life: *heat* will not exist, unless when the body is in a diseased or disordered state: but *warmth* is that portion of *heat* which exists in every healthy subject; by this the hen hatches and rears her young, by this the operation of gestation is carried on in the female. *Glow* is a partial *heat* or *warmth* which exists or is known to exist, mostly in the human frame; it is commonly produced in the body when it is in its most vigorous state, and its nerves are firmly braced by the cold.

From the above analysis the figurative application of these terms, and the grounds upon which they are so employed, will be easily discerned. As *fire* is the strongest and most active principle in nature, which seizes every thing within its reach with the greatest possible rapidity, genius is said to be possessed of *fire* which flies with rapidity through all the regions of thought, and forms the most lively images and combinations;

> That modern love is no such thing,
> As what those ancient poets sing,
> A *fire* celestial, chaste, refined.—SWIFT.

But when *fire* is applied to the eye or the looks, it borrows its meaning from the external property of flame, which is very aptly depicted in the eye or the looks of lively people. As *heat* is always excessive and mostly violent, those commotions and fermentations of the mind which flow from the agitation of the passions, particularly of the angry passions, is termed *heat*. As *warmth* is a gentle and grateful property, it has with most propriety been ascribed to the affections. As *glow* is a partial but vivid feeling of the body, so is friendship a strong but particular affection of the mind: hence the propriety of ascribing a *glow* to friendship

Age damps the *fire* of the poet. Disputants in the *heat* of the contest are apt to forget all the forms of good-breeding; 'The *heat* of Milton's mind might be said to sublimate his learning.'—JOHNSON. A man of tender moral feelings speaks with *warmth* of a noble action, or takes a *warm* interest in the concerns of the innocent and the distressed; 'I fear I have pressed you farther upon this occasion than was necessary: however, I know you will excuse my *warmth* in the cause of a friend.'—MELMOUTH (*Letters of Cicero to Cæsar*). A youth in the full *glow* of friendship feels himself prepared to make any sacrifice in supporting the cause of his friend;

> The frost-concocted glebe
> Draws in abundant vegetable soul,
> And gathers vigour for the coming year:
> A stronger *glow* sits on the lively cheek
> Of ruddy fire.—THOMSON.

* Vide Eberhardt: "Hitze, feuer, wärme."

FERVOUR, ARDOUR.

Fervour, from *ferveo* to boil, is not so violent a heat as *ardour*, from *ardeo* to burn. The affections are properly *fervent;* the passions are *ardent:* we are *fervent* in feeling, and *ardent* in acting: the *fervour* of devotion may be rational; but the *ardour* of zeal is mostly intemperate. The first martyr, Stephen, was filled with a holy *fervour;* St. Peter, in the *ardour* of his zeal, promised his master to do more than he was able to perform; 'The joy of the Lord is not to be understood of high raptures and transports of religious *fervour*.'—BLAIR. 'Do men hasten to their devotions with that *ardour* that they would to a lewd play?'—SOUTH.

HOT, FIERY, BURNING, ARDENT.

Hot, in German *heiss*, Latin *æstus*, comes from the Hebrew אש fire; *fiery* signifies having fire; *burning*, the actual state of *burning; ardent*, the having ardour (*v. Fervour*).

These terms characterize either the presence of *heat* or the cause of *heat; hot* is the general term which marks simply the presence of *heat: fiery* goes farther, it denotes the presence of *fire* which is the cause of *heat; burning* denotes the action of *fire*, and consequently is more expressive than the two; *ardent*, which is literally the same in signification, is employed either in poetry or in application to moral objects: a room is *hot;* a furnace or the tail of a comet *fiery;* a coal *burning;* the sun *ardent;*

> Let loose the raging elements. Breath'd *hot*
> From all the boundless furnace of the sky,
> And the wide, glittering waste of *burning* sand
> A suffocating wind the pilgrim smites
> With instant death.—THOMSON.

> E'en the camel feels,
> Shot through his wither'd heart, the *fiery* blast.
> THOMSON.

> The royal eagle draws his vigorous young,
> Strong pounc'd, and *ardent* with paternal fire.
> THOMSON.

In the figurative application, a temper is said to be *hot* or *fiery;* rage is *burning;* the mind is *ardent* in pursuit of an object. Zeal may be *hot, fiery, burning*, and *ardent;* but in the first three cases, it denotes the intemperance of the mind when *heated* by religion or politicks; the latter is admissible so long as it is confined to a good object.

RADIANCE, BRILLIANCY

Both these terms express the circumstance of a great light in a body: but *radiance*, from *radius* a ray, denotes the emission of rays, and is, therefore, peculiarly applicable to bodies naturally luminous, like the heavenly bodies; and *brilliancy* (*v. Bright*) denotes the whole body of light emitted and may, therefore be applied equally to natural and artificial light. The *radiancy* of the sun, moon, and stars constitutes a part of their beauty; the *brilliancy* of a diamond is frequently compared with that of a star.

TO SHINE, GLITTER, GLARE, SPARKLE, RADIATE.

Shine, in Saxon *schinean*, German *scheinen*, is in all probability connected with the words *show*, *see*, &c.; *glitter* and *glare* are variations from the German *gleissen*, *glänzen*, &c. which have a similar meaning; to *sparkle* signifies to produce *sparks*; and *spark* is in Saxon *spearce*, Low German and Dutch *spark*; to *radiate* is to produce rays, from the Latin *radius* a ray.

The emission of light is the common idea conveyed by these terms. To *shine* expresses simply this general idea; *glitter* and the other verbs include some collateral ideas in their signification.

To *shine* is a steady emission of light; to *glitter* is an unsteady emission of light, occasioned by the reflection on transparent or bright bodies: the sun and moon *shine* whenever they make their appearance; but a set of diamonds *glitter* by the irregular reflection of the light on them; or the brazen spire of a steeple *glitters* when the sun in the morning *shines* upon it. In a moral application, what *shines* appears with a true light;

> Yet something *shines* more glorious in his word,
> His mercy this.—WALLER.

What *glitters* appears with a false or borrowed light; 'The happiness of success *glittering* before him withdraws his attention from the atrociousness of the guilt.'—JOHNSON.

Shine specifies no degree of light; it may be barely sufficient to render itself visible, or it may be a very strong degree of light: *glare* on the contrary denotes the highest possible degree of light: the sun frequently *glares*, when it *shines* only at intervals; 'This glorious morning star was not the transitory light of a comet which *shines* and *glares* for a while, and then presently vanishes into nothing.'—SOUTH. All naked light, the strength of which is diminished by any shade, will produce a *glare*, as the *glare* of the eye when fixed full upon an object;

> Against the Capitol I met a lion,
> Who *glar'd* upon me, and went surly by
> Without annoying me.—SHAKSPEARE.

To *shine* is to emit light in a full stream; but to *sparkle* is to emit it in small portions; and to *radiate* is to emit it in long lines. The fire *sparkles* in the burning of wood; or the light of the sun *sparkles* when it strikes on knobs or small points: the sun *radiates* when it seems to emit its light in rays;

> His eyes so *sparkled* with a lively flame.
> DRYDEN.

> Now had the sun withdrawn his *radiant* light.
> DRYDEN.

FLAME, BLAZE, FLASH, FLARE, GLARE.

Flame, in Latin *flamma*, from the Greek φλέγω to burn, signifies the luminous exhalation emitted from fire; *blaze*, from the German *blasen* to blow, signifies a *flame* blown up, that is, an extended *flame*; *flash* and *flare*, which are but variations of *flame*, denote different species of *flame*; the former a sudden *flame*, the latter a dazzling, unsteady *flame*. *Glare*, which is a variation of glow, denotes a glowing, that is a strong *flame*, that emits a strong light: a candle burns only by *flame*, paper commonly by a *blaze*, gunpowder by a *flash*, a torch by a *flare*, and a conflagration by a *glare*;

> His lightning your rebellion shall confound,
> And hurl ye headlong *flaming* to the ground.
> POPE.

> Swift as a flood of fire when storms arise
> Floats the wide field, and *blazes* to the skies.
> POPE.

> Have we not seen round Britain's peopled shore,
> Her useful sons exchang'd for useless ore,
> Seen all her triumphs but destruction haste,
> Like *flaring* tapers brightening as they waste.
> GOLDSMITH.

> Ev'n in the height of noon oppress'd, the sun
> Sheds weak and blunt, his wide refracted ray,
> Whence *glaring* oft, with many a broaden'd orb
> He frights the nations.—THOMSON.

GLARING, BAREFACED.

Glaring is here used in the figurative sense, drawn from its natural signification of broad light, which strikes powerfully upon the senses; *barefaced* signifies literally having a *bare* or *uncovered face*, which denotes the absence of all disguise or all shame.

Glaring designates the thing; *barefaced* characterizes the person: a *glaring* falsehood is that which strikes the observer in an instant to be falsehood; a *barefaced* lie or falsehood betrays the effrontery of him who utters it. A *glaring* absurdity will be seen instantly without the aid of reflection; 'The *glaring* side is that of enmity.'—BURKE. A *barefaced* piece of impudence characterizes the agent as more than ordinarily lost to all sense of decorum; 'The animosities increased, and the parties appeared *barefaced* against each other.'—CLARENDON.

GLEAM, GLIMMER, RAY, BEAM.

Gleam is in Saxon *gleomen*, German *glimmen*, &c. *Glimmer* is a variation of the same verb; *ray* is connected with the word row; *beam* comes from the German *baum* a tree.

Certain portions of light are designated by all these terms: but *gleam* and *glimmer* are indefinite; *ray* and *beam* are definite. A *gleam* is properly the commencement of light, or that portion of opening light which interrupts the darkness; a *glimmer* is an unsteady *gleam*;

> A dreadful *gleam* from his bright armour came,
> And from his eye-balls flash'd the living flame.
> POPE.

'The *glimmering* light which shot into the chaos from the utmost verge of the creation, is wonderfully beautiful and poetick.'—ADDISON. *Ray* and *beam* are portions of light which emanate from some luminous body; the former from all luminous bodies in general, the latter more particularly from the sun: the former is, as its derivation denotes, a row or line of light issuing in a greater or less degree from any body; the latter is a great line of light, like a pole issuing from a body;

> A sudden *ray* shot beaming o'er the plain,
> And show'd the shores, the navy, and the main
> POPE

> The stars shine smarter; and the moon adorns,
> As with unborrow'd *beams*, her horns.
> DRYDEN.

There may be a *gleam* of light visible on the wall of a dark room, or a *glimmer* if it be moveable; there may be *rays* of light visible at night on the back of a glow-worm, or *rays* of light may break through the shutters of a closed room;

> The stars emit a shiver'd *ray*.—THOMSON.

The sun in the height of its splendour sends forth its *beams*; and in the same manner the human countenance or eyes may be said to send forth *beams*;

> The modest virtues mingle in her eyes,
> Still on the ground dejected, darting all
> Their humid *beams* into the blooming flowers.
> THOMSON.

Gleam and *ray* may be applied figuratively; *beam* only in the natural sense: a *gleam* of light may break in on the benighted understanding; but a *glimmer* of light rather confuses; *rays* of light may dart into the mind of the most ignorant savage who is taught the principles of Christianity by the pure practice of its professors.

CLEAR, LUCID, BRIGHT, VIVID.

Clear, v. *To absolve*; *lucid*, in Latin *lucidus*, from *luceo* to shine, and *lux* light, signifies having light bright, v. *Brightness; vivid*, Latin *vividus* from *vivo* to live, signifies being in a state of life.

These epithets mark a gradation in their sense: the idea of light is common to them; but *clear* expresses less than *lucid*, *lucid* than *bright*, and *bright* less than *vivid*: a mere freedom from stain or dulness constitutes *clearness*;

> Some choose the *clearest* light,
> And boldly challenge the most piercing eye.
> ROSCOMMON.

The return of light, and consequent removal of darkness, constitutes *lucidity*;

> Nor is the stream
> Of purest crystal, nor the *lucid* air,
> Though one transparent vacancy it seems,
> Void of their unseen people.—THOMSON.

Brightness supposes a certain strength of light;

> This place, the *brightest* mansion of the sky,
> I 'll call the palace of the Deity.—DRYDEN.

Vividness indicates freshness combined with strength, and even a degree of brilliancy;

> From the moist meadow to the wither'd hill,
> Led by the breeze, the *vivid* verdure runs,
> And swells, and deepens to the cherish'd eye.
> THOMSON.

A sky is *clear* that is divested of clouds; the atmosphere is *lucid* in the day, but not in the night; the sun shines *bright* when it is unobstructed by any thing the atmosphere; lightning sometimes presents a *vivid* redness, and sometimes a *vivid* paleness: the light of the stars may be *clear*, and sometimes *bright*, but never *vivid*; the light of the sun is rather *bright* than *clear* or *vivid*; the light of the moon is either *clear*, *bright*, or *vivid*.

These epithets may with equal propriety be applied to colour, as well as to light: a *clear* colour is unmixed with any other; a *bright* colour has something striking and strong in it; a *vivid* colour something lively and fresh in it.

In their moral application these epithets preserve a similar distinction: a conscience is said to be *clear* when it is free from every stain or spot; 'I look upon a sound imagination as the greatest blessing of life, next to a *clear* judgement, and a good conscience.'—ADDISON. A deranged understanding may have *lucid* intervals; 'I believe were Rousseau alive, and in one of his *lucid* intervals, he would be shocked at the practical phrensy of his scholars.'—BURKE. A *bright* intellect throws light on every thing around it;

> But in a body which doth freely yield
> His parts to reason's rule obedient,
> There Alma, like a virgin queen most *bright*,
> Doth flourish in all beauty excellent.—SPENSER.

A *vivid* imagination glows with every image that nature presents;

> There let the classick page thy fancy lead
> Through rural scenes, such as the Mantuan swain
> Paints in the matchless harmony of song,
> Or catch thyself the landscape, glided swift
> Athwart imagination's *vivid* eye.—THOMSON.

PELLUCID, TRANSPARENT.

Pellucid, in Latin *pellucidus* changed from *perlucidus*, signifies very shining; *transparent*, in Latin *transparens*, from *trans* through or beyond, and *pareo* to appear, signifies visible throughout.

Pellucid is said of that which is pervious to the light, or that into which the eye can penetrate; *transparent* is said of that which is throughout bright: a stream is *pellucid*; it admits of the light so as to reflect objects, but it is not *transparent* for the eye.

CLEARLY, DISTINCTLY.

That is seen *clearly* of which one has a general view; that is seen *distinctly* which is seen so as to distinguish the several parts.

We see the moon *clearly* whenever it shines; but we cannot see the spots in the moon *distinctly* without the help of glasses.

What we see *distinctly* must be seen *clearly*, but a thing may be seen *clearly* without being seen *distinctly*.

A want of light, or the intervention of other objects, prevents us from seeing *clearly*; distance, or a defect in the sight, prevents us from seeing *distinctly*.

* Old men often see *clearly* but not *distinctly*; they perceive large or luminous objects at a distance, but they cannot distinguish such small objects as the characters of a book without the help of convex glasses; short-sighted persons, on the contrary, see near objects *distinctly*, but they have no *clear* vision of distant ones, unless they are viewed through concave glasses; 'The custom of arguing on any side, even against our persuasion, dims the understanding, and makes it by degrees lose the faculty of discerning *clearly* between truth and falsehood.'—LOCKE. 'Whether we are able to comprehend all the operations of nature, and the manners of them, it matters not to inquire; but this is certain, that we can comprehend no more of them than we can *distinctly* conceive.'—LOCKE.

CLEARNESS, PERSPICUITY.

Clearness, from *clear* (*v. Clear, lucid*), is here used figuratively, to mark the degree of light by which one sees things distinctly; *perspicuity*, in French *perspicuité*, Latin *perspicuitas* from *perspicuus* and *perspicio* to look through, signifies the quality of being able to be seen through.

These epithets denote qualities equally requisite to render a discourse intelligible, but each has its peculiar character. † *Clearness* respects our ideas, and springs from the distinction of the things themselves that are discussed: *perspicuity* respects the mode of expressing the ideas, and springs from the good qualities of style. It requires a *clear* head to be able to see a subject in all its bearings and relations; to distinguish all the niceties and shades of difference between things that bear a strong resemblance, and to separate it from all irrelevant objects that intermingle themselves with it. But whatever may be our *clearness* of conception, it is requisite, if we would communicate our conceptions to others, that we should observe a purity in our mode of diction, that we should be particular in the choice of our terms, careful in the disposition of them, and accurate in the construction of our sentences; that is *perspicuity*, which, as it is the first, so, according to Quintilian, it is the most important part of composition.

Clearness of intellect is a natural gift; *perspicuity* is an acquired art: although intimately connected with each other, yet it is possible to have *clearness* without *perspicuity*, and *perspicuity* without *clearness*. People of quick capacities will have *clear* ideas on the subjects that offer themselves to their notice, but for want of education they may often use improper or ambiguous phrases; or by errours of construction render their phraseology the reverse of *perspicuous*: on the other hand, it is in the power of some to express themselves *perspicuously* on subjects far above their comprehension, from a certain facility which they acquire of catching up suitable modes of expression.

The study of the classicks and mathematicks are most fitted for the improvement of *clearness*; the study of grammar, and the observance of good models, will serve most effectually for the acquirement of *perspicuity*; 'Whenever men think *clearly* and are thoroughly interested, they express themselves with *perspicuity* and force.'—ROBERTSON. 'No modern orator can dare to enter the lists with Demosthenes and Tully. We have discourses, indeed, that may be admired for their *perspicuity*, purity, and elegance; but can produce none that abound in a sublimity which whirls away the auditor like a mighty torrent.'—WARTON.

FAIR, CLEAR.

Fair, in Saxon *fagar*, probably from the Latin *pulcher* beautiful; *fair* (*v. Clear*) is used in a positive sense; *clear* in a negative sense: there must be some brightness in what is *fair*; there must be no spots in what is *clear*. The weather is said to be *fair*, which is not only free from what is disagreeable, but somewhat enlivened by the sun; it is *clear* when it is free from clouds or mists. A *fair* skin approaches t white; a *clear* skin is without spots or irregularities;

* Vide Trusler: " Clearly, distinctly."
† Vide Abbe Girard: " Clarté, perspicuité "

His *fair* large front, and eyes sublime, declar'd
Absolute rule.—MILTON.

I thither went
With unexperienced thought, and laid me down
On the green bank, to look into the *clear*
Smooth lake —MILTON.

In the moral application, a *fair* fame speaks much in praise of a man; a *clear* reputation is free from faults. A *fair* statement contains every thing that can be said *pro* and *con;* a *clear* statement is free from ambiguity or obscurity. *Fairness* is something desirable and inviting; *clearness* is an absolute requisite, it cannot be dispensed with.

APPARENT, VISIBLE, CLEAR, PLAIN, OBVIOUS, EVIDENT, MANIFEST.

Apparent, in Latin *apparens*, participle of *appareo* to appear, signifies the quality of appearing; *visible*, in Latin *visibilis*, from *visus*, participle of *video* to see, signifies capable of being seen; *clear*, *v. Clear, lucid; plain*, in Latin *planus* even, signifies what is so smooth and unencumbered that it can be seen; *obvious*, in Latin *obvius*, compounded of *ob* and *via*, signifies the quality of lying in one's way, or before one's eyes; *evident*, in French *evident*, Latin *evidens*, from *video*, Greek εἴδω, Hebrew ידע to know, signifies as good as certain or known; *manifest*, in French *manifeste*, Latin *manifestus*, compounded of *manus* the hand, and *festus*, participle of the old verb *fendo* to fall in, signifies the quality of falling in or coming so near that it can be laid hold of by the hand.

These words agree in expressing various degrees in the capability of seeing; but *visible* is the only one used purely in a physical sense; *apparent*, *clear*, *plain*, and *obvious* are used physically and morally; *evident* and *manifest* solely in a moral acceptation. That which is simply an object of sight is *visible;*

The *visible* and present are for brutes:
A slender portion, and a narrow bound.—YOUNG.

That of which we see only the surface is *apparent;* 'The perception intellective often corrects the report of phantasy, as in the *apparent* bigness of the sun, and the *apparent* crookedness of the staff in air and water.' —HALE. The stars themselves are *visible* to us; but their size is merely *apparent:* the rest of these terms denote not only what is to be seen, but what is easily to be seen: they are all applied as epithets to objects of mental discernment.

What is *apparent* appears but imperfectly to view; it is opposed to that which is real: what is *clear* is to be seen in all its bearings; it is opposed to that which is obscure: what is *plain* is seen by a plain understanding; it requires no deep reflection nor severe study; it is opposed to what is intricate: what is *obvious* presents itself readily to the mind of every one; it is seen at the first glance, and is opposed to that which is abstruse: what is *evident* is seen forcibly, and leaves no hesitation on the mind; it is opposed to that which is dubious: *manifest* is a greater degree of the *evident;* it strikes on the understanding and forces conviction; it is opposed to that which is dark.

A contradiction may be *apparent;* on closer observation it may be found not to be one. Men's virtues or religion may be only *apparent;* 'The outward and *apparent* sanctity of actions should flow from purity of heart.'—ROGERS. A case is *clear;* it is decided on immediately; 'We pretend to give a *clear* account how thunder and lightning are produced.'—TEMPLE. A truth is *plain;* it is involved in no perplexity; it is not multifarious in its bearings: a falsehood is *plain;* it admits of no question; 'It is *plain* that our skill in literature is owing to the knowledge of Greek and Latin, which that they are still preserved among us, can be ascribed only to a religious regard.'—BERKELEY. A reason is *obvious;* it flows out of the nature of the case; 'It is *obvious* to remark that we follow nothing heartily unless carried to it by inclination.'—GROVE. A proof is *evident;* it requires no discussion, there is nothing in it that clashes or contradicts; the guilt or innocence of a person is *evident* when every thing serves to strengthen the conclusion; 'It is *evident* that fame, considered merely as the immortality of a name, is not less likely to be the reward of bad actions than of good.'—JOHNSON. A contradiction or absurdity is *manifest*, which is felt by all as soon as it is perceived, 'Among the many inconsistencies which folly produces in the human mind, there has often been observed a *manifest* and striking contrariety between the life of an author and his writings.'—JOHNSON.

APPEARANCE, AIR, ASPECT.

Appearance, which signifies the thing that *appears*, is the generick: *air*, *v. Air, manner;* and *aspect*, in Latin *aspectus*, from *aspicio* to look upon, signifying the thing that is looked upon or seen, are specifick terms. The whole external form, figure, or colours, whatever is visible to the eye, is its *appearance;* 'The hero answers with the respect due to the beautiful *appearance* she made.'—STEELE. *Air* is a particular *appearance* of any object as far as it is indicative of its quality, condition, or temper; an *air* of wretchedness or of assumption; 'Some who had the most assuming *air* went directly of themselves to errour without expecting a conductor.'—PARNELL. *Aspect* is the partial *appearance* of a body as it presents one of its sides to view; a gloomy or cheerful *aspect;* 'Her motions were steady and composed, and her *aspect* serious but cheerful; her name was Patience.'—ADDISON.

It is not safe to judge of any person or thing altogether by *appearances;* the *appearance* and reality are often at variance: the *appearance* of the sun is that of a moving body, but modern astronomers are of opinion that it has no motion round the earth; there are particular towns, habitations, or rooms, which have always an *air* of comfort, or the contrary; this is a sort of *appearance* the most to be relied on. Politicians of a certain stamp are always busy in judging of the future from the *aspect* of affairs; but their predictions, like those of astrologers, who judge from the *aspect* of the heavens, turn out to the discredit of the prophet.

HIDEOUS, GHASTLY, GRIM, GRISLY.

Hideous, in French *hideux*, comes probably from *hide*, signifying fit only to be hidden from the view; *ghastly* signifies like a ghost; *grim*, in German *grimm*, signifies fierce; *grisly*, from *grizzle*, signifies *grizzled*, or motley-coloured.

An unseemly exteriour is characterized by these terms; but the *hideous* respects natural objects, and the *ghastly* more properly that which is supernatural or what resembles it. A mask with monstrous grinning features looks *hideous;*

From the broad margin to the centre grew
Shelves, rocks, and whirlpools, *hideous* to the view.
FALCONER.

A human form with a visage of deathlike paleness is *ghastly;*

And death
Grinn'd horribly a *ghastly* smile.—MILTON.

The *grim* is applicable only to the countenances; dogs or wild beasts may look very *grim;*

Even hell's *grim* king Alcides' pow'r confess'd.—POPE.

Grisly refers to the whole form, but particularly to the colour; as blackness or darkness has always something terrifick in it, a *grisly* figure, having a monstrous assemblage of dark colour, is particularly calculated to strike terrour;

All parts resound with tumults, plaints, and fears,
And *grisly* death in sundry shapes appears.—POPE.

Hideous is applicable to objects of hearing also, as a *hideous* roar; but the rest to objects of sight only.

FACE, FRONT,

Figuratively designate the particular parts of bodies which bear some sort of resemblance to the human *face* or forehead.

The *face* is applied to that part of bodies which serves as an index or rule, and contains certain marks to direct the observer; the *front* is employed for that part which is most prominent or foremost: hence we speak of the *face* of a wheel or clock, the *face* of a painting, or the *face* of nature; but the *front* of a house or building, and the *front* of a stage: hence likewise, the propriety of the expressions, to put a good *face* on a thing, to show a bold *front;* 'A common soldier, a child, a girl, the door of an inn, have changed the *face* of fortune, and almost of nature.'—BURKE.

Where the deep trench in length extended lay,
Compacted troops stand wedged in firm array,
A dreadful *front.*—POPE.

FACE, COUNTENANCE, VISAGE.

Face, in Latin *facies*, from *facio* to make, signifies the whole form or make; *countenance*, in French *contenance*, from the Latin *contineo*, signifies the contents, or what is contained in the *face; visage*, from *visuo* and *video* to see, signifies the particular form of the *face* as it presents itself to view; properly speaking a kind of *countenance.*

The *face* consists of a certain set of features; the *countenance* consists of the general aggregate of looks produced by these features; the *visage* consists of such looks in particular cases: the *face* is the work of nature; the *countenance* and *visage* are the work of the mind: the *face* remains the same, but the *countenance* and *visage* are changeable. The *face* belongs to brutes as well as men; the *countenance* is the peculiar property of man; *visage* is a term peculiarly applicable to superiour beings; it is employed only in the grave or lofty style; 'No part of the body besides the *face* is capable of as many changes as there are different emotions in the mind, and of expressing them all by those changes.'—HUGHES. 'As the *countenance* admits of so great variety it requires also great judgement to govern it.'—HUGHES.

A sudden trembling seized on all his limbs
His eyes distorted grew, his *visage* pale;
His speech forsook him.—OTWAY.

TO GAPE, STARE, GAZE.

To *gape*, in German *gaffen*, Saxon *geopnian* to make open or wide, is to look with an open or wide mouth; *stare*, from the German *starr* fixed, signifies to look with a fixed eye; *gaze* comes very probably from the Greek ἀγάζομαι to admire, because it signifies to look steadily from a sentiment of admiration.

Gape and *stare* are taken in the bad sense; the former indicating the astonishment of gross ignorance; the latter not only ignorance but impertinence: *gaze* is taken always in a good sense, as indicating a laudable feeling of astonishment, pleasure, or curiosity. A clown *gapes* at the pictures of wild beasts which he sees at a fair; 'It was now a miserable spectacle to see us nodding and *gaping* at one another, every man talking, and no man heard.'—SIR JOHN MANDEVILLE. An impertinent fellow *stares* at every woman he looks at, and *stares* a modest woman out of countenance;

Astonish'd Aunus just arrives by chance
To see his fall, nor farther dares advance;
But, fixing on the maid his horrid eye,
He *stares* and shakes, and finds it vain to fly.
DRYDEN.

A lover of the fine arts will *gaze* with admiration and delight at the productions of Raphael or Titian;

For while expecting there the queen, he rais'd
His wond'ring eyes, and round the temple *gaz'd*,
Admir'd the fortune of the rising town,
The striving artists, and their art's renown.
DRYDEN.

When a person is stupified by affright, he gives a vacant *stare.* Those who are filled with transport *gaze* on the object of their ecstasy.

VIEW, SURVEY, PROSPECT.

View, v. *To look*, and *survey*, compounded of *vey* or *view* and *sur* over, mark the act of the person, namely, the looking at a thing with more or less attention: *prospect*, from the Latin *prospectus* and *prospicio* to see before, designates the thing seen. We take a *view* or *survey;* the *prospect* presents itself: the *view* is of an indefinite extent; the *survey* is always comprehensive in its nature. Ignorant people take but narrow *views* of things; men take more or less enlarged *views*, according to their cultivation: the capacious mind of a genius takes a *survey* of all nature;

Fools *view* but part, and not the whole *survey*,
So crowd existence all into a day.—JENYNS.

The *view* depends altogether on the train of a person's thoughts; the *prospect* is set before him, it depends upon the nature of the thing; our *views* of advancement are sometimes very fallacious; our *prospects* are very delusive; both occasion disappointment; the former is the keener, as we have to charge the miscalculation upon ourselves. Sometimes our *prospects* depend upon our *views*, at least in matters of religion; he who forms erroneous *views* of a future state has but a wretched *prospect* beyond the grave;

No land so rude but looks beyond the tomb
For future *prospects* in a world to come.—JENYNS

VIEW, PROSPECT, LANDSCAPE.

View and *prospect* (v. *View, prospect*), though applied here to external objects of sense, have a similar distinction as in the preceding article. The *view* is not only that which may be seen, but that which is actually seen; the *prospect* is that which may be seen: that ceases, therefore, to be a *view*, which has not an immediate agent to *view;* although a *prospect* exists continually, whether seen or not: hence we speak with more propriety of our *view* being intercepted, than our *prospect* intercepted; a confined and bounded *view*, but a lively or dreary *prospect.* The terms, however, are are sometimes indifferently applied:

Thus was this place
A happy rural seat of various *views.*—MILTON.

Now skies and seas their *prospect* only bound.
DRYDEN.

View is an indefinite term; it may be said either of a number of objects, or of a single object, of a whole or of a part; *prospect* is said only of an aggregate number of objects: we may have a *view* of a town, of a number of scattered houses, of a single house, or of the spire of a steeple; but a *prospect* comprehends all that comes within the range of the eye. *View* may be said of that which is seen directly or indirectly; *prospect* only of that which directly presents itself to the eye; hence a drawing of an object may be termed a *view*, although not a *prospect. View* is confined to no particular objects; *prospect* mostly respects rural objects; and *landscape* respects no others. *Landscape, landskip*, or *landshape* denotes any portion of country which is in a particular form: hence the *landscape* is a species of *prospect.* A *prospect* may be wide, and comprehend an assemblage of objects both of nature and art; but a *landscape* is narrow, and lies within the compass of the naked eye: hence it is also that *landscape* may be taken also for the drawing of a *landscape*, and consequently for a species of *view:* the taking of *views* or *landscapes* is the last exercise of the learner in drawing;

So lovely seem'd
That *landscape*, and of pure now purer air
Meets his approach.—MILTON.

VISION, APPARITION, PHANTOM, SPECTRE, GHOST.

Vision, from the Latin *visus* seeing or seen, signifies either the act of seeing or the thing seen; *apparition*, from *appear*, signifies the thing that appears. As the thing seen is only the improper signification, the term *vision* is never employed but in regard to some agent: the *vision* depends upon the state of the *visual* organ; the *vision* of a person whose sight is defective will frequently be fallacious; he will see some things double which are single, long which are short, and the like. In like manner, if the sight be miraculously impressed his *vision* will enable him to see that which is supernatural; hence it is that *vision* is either true or false, according to the circumstances of the individual; and a *vision*, signifying a thing seen, is taken for a supernatural exertion of the *vision: apparition*, on the contrary, refers us to the object seen; this may be true or false according to the manner in which it presents itself.

Joseph was warned by a *vision* to fly into Egypt with his family; *Mary Magdalen was informed of the resurrection of our Saviour by an *apparition*;

* Vide Trusler: "Vision, apparition"

feverish people often think they see *visions;* timid and credulous people sometimes take trees and posts for *apparitions;*

> *Visions* and inspirations some expect
> Their course here to direct.—Cowley.

> Full fast he flies, and dares not look behind him,
> Till out of breath he overtakes his fellows,
> Who gather round and wonder at the tale
> Of horrid *apparition*.—Blair.

Phantom, from the Greek φαίνω to *appear*, is used for a false *apparition*, or the *appearance* of a thing otherwise than what it is; thus the *ignis fatuus*, vulgarly called Jack-o'-Lantern, is a *phantom;* besides which there are many *phantoms* of a moral kind which haunt the imagination; 'The *phantoms* which haunt a desert are want, and misery, and danger.'—Johnson.

Spectre, from *specio* to behold, and *ghost*, from *geist* a spirit, are the *apparitions* of immaterial substances. The *spectre* is taken for any spiritual being that appears; but the *ghost* is taken only for the spirits of departed men who appear to their fellow-creatures: a *spectre* is sometimes made to appear on the stage; *ghosts* exist mostly in the imagination of the young and the ignorant;

> Rous'd from their slumbers,
> In grim array the grisly *spectres* rise.—Blair.

> The lonely tower
> Is also shunn'd, whose mournful chambers hold,
> So night-struck fancy dreams, the yelling *ghost*.
> Thomson.

RETROSPECT, REVIEW, SURVEY.

Retrospect is literally looking back, from *retro* behind, and *spicio* to behold or cast an eye upon; a *review* is a view repeated; and a *survey* is a looking over at once, from the French *sur* over, and *voir* to see.

A *retrospect* is always taken of that which is past and distant; a *review* may be taken of that which is present and before us; every *retrospect* is a species of *review*, but every *review* is not a *retrospect*. We take a *retrospect* of our past life in order to draw salutary reflections from all that we have done and suffered; we take a *review* of any particular circumstance which is passing before us, in order to regulate our present conduct. The *retrospect* goes further by virtue of the mind's power to reflect on itself, and to recall all past images to itself; the *review* may go forward by the exercise of the senses on external objects. The historian takes a *retrospect* of all the events which have happened within a given period; the journalist takes a *review* of all the events that are passing within the time in which he is living; 'Believe me, my lord, I look upon you as a spirit entered into another life, where you ought to despise all little views and mean *retrospects*.'—Pope (*Letters to Atterbury*). 'The *retrospect* of life is seldom wholly unattended by uneasiness and shame. It too much resembles the *review* which a traveller takes from some eminence of a barren country.'—Blair.

The *review* may be said of the past as well as the present; it is a *view* not only of what is, but what has been: the *survey* is entirely confined to the present; it is a *view* only of that which is; 'Every man accustomed to take a *survey* of his own notions, will, by a slight *retrospection*, be able to discover that his mind has undergone many revolutions.'—Johnson.

We take a *review* of what we have already *viewed*, in order to get a more correct insight into it; we take a *survey* of a thing in all its parts in order to get a comprehensive *view* of it, in order to examine it in all its bearings. A general occasionally takes a *review* of all his army; he takes a *survey* of the fortress which he is going to besiege or attack.

REVISAL, REVISION, REVIEW.

Revisal, *revision*, and *review*, all come from the Latin *video* to see, and signify looking back upon a thing or looking at it again: the terms *revisal* and *revision* are however mostly employed in regard to what is written; *review* is used for things in general. The *revisal* of a book is the work of the author, for the purposes of correction; 'There is in your persons a difference and a peculiarity of character preserved through the whole of your actions, that I could never imagine but that this proceeded from a long and careful *revisal* of your work.'—Loftus. The *review* of a book is the work of the critick, for the purpose of estimating its value; 'A commonplace book accustoms the mind to discharge itself of its reading on paper, instead of relying on its natural powers of retention aided by frequent *revisions* of its ideas.'—Earl of Chatham. *Revisal* and *revision* differ neither in sense nor application, unless that the former is more frequently employed abstractedly from the object *revised*, and *revision* mostly in conjunction: whoever wishes his work to be correct, will not spare a *revisal*; the *revision* of classical books ought to be intrusted only to men of profound erudition. The term *revision* may also sometimes be applied to other objects besides those of literature; 'How enchanting must such a *review* (of their memorandum books) prove to those who make a figure in the polite world.'—Hawkesworth.

TO ECLIPSE, OBSCURE.

Eclipse, in Greek ἔκλειψις, comes from ἐκλείπω to fail, signifying to cause a failure of light; *obscure*, from the adjective *obscure* (*v. Dark*), signifies to cause the intervention of a shadow.

In the natural as well as the moral application, *eclipse* is taken in a particular and relative signification; *obscure* is used in a general sense. Heavenly bodies are *eclipsed* by the intervention of other bodies between them and the beholder; things are in general *obscured* which are in any way rendered less striking or visible. To *eclipse* is therefore a species of *obscuring:* that is always *obscured* which is *eclipsed;* but every thing is not *eclipsed* which is *obscured*.

So figuratively real merit is *eclipsed* by the intervention of that which is superiour;

> Sarcasms may *eclipse* thine own,
> But cannot blur my lost renown.—Butler.

Merit is often *obscured* by an ungracious exteriour in the possessor, or by the unfortunate circumstances of his life; 'Among those who are the most richly endowed by nature and accomplished by their own industry, how few are there whose virtues are not *obscured* by the ignorance, prejudice, or envy of their beholders.'—Addison.

DARK, OBSCURE, DIM, MYSTERIOUS.

Dark, in Saxon *deore*, is doubtless connected with the German *dunkel* dark and *dunst* a vapour, which is a cause of *darkness;* *obscure*, in Latin *obscurus*, compounded of *ob* and *scurus*, Greek σκιερὸς and σκία a shadow, signifies literally interrupted by a shadow; *dim* is but a variation of *dark*, *dunkel*, &c.

Darkness expresses more than *obscurity:* the former denotes the total privation of light; the latter only the diminution of light.

Dark is opposed to light; *obscure* to bright: what is *dark* is altogether hidden; what is *obscure* is not to be seen distinctly, or without an effort.

Darkness may be used either in the natural or moral sense; *obscurity* only in the moral sense; in this case the former conveys a more unfavourable idea than the latter: *darkness* serves to cover that which ought not to be hidden; *obscurity* intercepts our view of that which we would wish to see: the former is the consequence of design; the latter of neglect or accident: the letter sent by the conspirator in the gunpowder plot to his friend was *dark;*

> Why are thy speeches *dark* and troubled,
> As Cretan seas when vex'd by warring winds?
> Smith.

All passages in ancient writers which allude to circumstances no longer known, must necessarily be *obscure;* 'He that reads and grows no wiser seldom suspects his own deficiency, but complains of hard words and *obscure* sentences.'—Johnson. A corner may be said to be *dark* or *obscure;* but the former is used literally and the latter figuratively: the owl is obliged, from the weakness of its visual organs, to seek the *darkest* corners in the daytime; men of distorted minds often seek *obscure* corners, only from disappointed ambition.

Dim expresses a degree of *darkness*, but it is em

ployed more in relation to the person seeing than to the object seen. The eyes are said to grow *dim*, or the sight *dim*. The light is said to be *dim*, by which things are but *dimly* seen;

> The stars shall fade away, the sun himself
> Grow *dim* with age, and nature sink in years,
> But thou shalt flourish in immortal youth.
> ADDISON.

Mysterious denotes a species of the *dark*, in relation to the actions of men: where a veil is intentionally thrown over any object so as to render it as incomprehensible as that which is sacred. *Dark* is an epithet taken always in the bad sense, but *mysterious* is always in an indifferent sense. We are told in the Sacred Writings, that men love *darkness* rather than light, because their deeds are evil. Whatever, therefore, is *dark* in the ways of men, is naturally presumed to be evil; but things may be *mysterious* in the events of human life, without the express intention of an individual to render them so. The speeches of an assassin and conspirator will be *dark;* 'Randolph, an agent extremely proper for conducting any *dark* intrigue, was despatched into Scotland, and, residing secretly among the lords of the congregation, observed and quickened their motions.'—ROBERTSON. Any intricate affair which involves the characters and conduct of men may be *mysterious;* 'The affection which Mary in her letter expresses for Bothwell, fully accounts for every subsequent part of her conduct, which, without admitting this circumstance, appears altogether *mysterious* and inconsistent.'—ROBERTSON.

The same distinction exists between these terms when applied to the ways of Providence, which are said to be sometimes *dark*, inasmuch as they present a cloudy aspect; and mostly *mysterious*, inasmuch as they are past finding out.

UNSEARCHABLE, INSCRUTABLE.

These terms are both applied to the Almighty, but not altogether indifferently; for that which is *unsearchable* is not set at so great a distance from us as that which is *inscrutable:* for that which is *searched* is in common concerns easier to be found than that which requires a *scrutiny*. The ways of God are all, to us finite creatures, more or less *unsearchable;*

> Things else by me *unsearchable*, now heard
> With wonder.—MILTON.

The mysterious plans of Providence as frequently evinced in the affairs of men are altogether *inscrutable;* 'To expect that the intricacies of science will be pierced by a careless glance, is to expect a particular privilege; but to suppose that the maze is *inscrutable* to diligence, is to enchain the mind in voluntary shackles.'—JOHNSON

OPAQUE, DARK.

Opaque, in Latin *opacus*, comes from *ops* the earth, because the earth is the *darkest* of all bodies; the word *opaque* is to *dark* as the species to the genus, for it expresses that species of *darkness* which is inherent in solid bodies, in distinction from those which emit light from themselves, or admit of light into themselves; it is therefore employed scientifically for the more vulgar and familiar term *dark*. On this ground, the earth is termed an *opaque* body in distinction from the sun, moon, or other luminous bodies: any solid substance, as a tree or a stone, is an *opaque* body, in distinction from glass, which is a clear or transparent body.

> But all sunshine, as when his beams at noon,
> Culminate from th' equator as they now
> Shot upward still, whence no way round
> Shadow from body *opaque* can fall.—MILTON.

SHADE, SHADOW.

Shade and *shadow*, in German *schatten*, are in all probability connected with the word *shine*, *show*, (*v. To show*, &c.)

Both these terms express that darkness which is occasioned by the sun's rays being intercepted by any body; but *shade* simply expresses the absence of the light, and *shadow* signifies also the figure of the body which thus intercepts the light. Trees naturally produce a *shade*, by means of their branches and leaves; and wherever the image of the tree is reflected on the earth, that forms its *shadow*. It is agreeable in the heat of summer to sit in the *shade;*

> Welcome, ye *shades!* ye bowery thickets, hail!
> THOMSON.

The constancy with which the *shadow* follows the man has been proverbially adopted as a simile for one who clings close to another;

> At every step,
> Solemn and slow, the *shadows* blacker fall,
> And all is awful listening gloom around.
> THOMSON.

The distinction between these terms, in the moral sense, is precisely the same: a person is said to be in the *shade*, if he lives in obscurity, or unnoticed; "the law (says St. Paul) is a *shadow* of things to come."

TO DISAPPEAR, VANISH.

To *disappear* signifies not to *appear* (*v. Air*); *vanish*, in French *evanir*, Latin *evaneō* or *evanesco*, compounded of *e* and *vaneo*, in Greek φαίνω to *appear*, signifies to go out of sight.

To *disappear* comprehends no particular mode of action; to *vanish* includes in it the idea of a rapid motion. A thing *disappears* either gradually or suddenly; it *vanishes* on a sudden: it *disappears* in the ordinary course of things; it *vanishes* by an unusual effort, a supernatural or a magick power. Any object that recedes or moves away will soon *disappear;*

> Red meteors ran across th' ethereal space,
> Stars *disappear'd*, and comets took their place
> DRYDEN.

In fairy tales things are made to *vanish* the instant they are beheld; 'While I was lamenting this sudden desolation that had been made before me, the whole scene *vanished*.'—ADDISON. To *disappear* is often a temporary action; to *vanish* generally conveys the idea of being permanently lost to the sight. The stars *appear* and *disappear* in the firmament; lightning *vanishes* with a rapidity that is unequalled.

TO LOOK, APPEAR.

Look is here taken in the neuter and improper sense, signifying the act of things figuratively striving to be seen; *appear*, from the Latin *appareo* or *pareo*, Greek πάρειμι, signifies to be present or at hand, within sight.

The *look* of a thing respects the impressions which it makes on the senses, that is, the manner in which it *looks;* its *appearance* implies the simple act of its coming into sight: the *look* of any thing is therefore characterized as good or bad, mean or handsome, ugly or beautiful; the *appearance* is characterized as early or late, sudden or unexpected: there is something very unseemly in the *look* of a clergyman affecting the airs of a fine gentleman; the *appearance* of the stars in an evening presents an interesting view even to the ordinary beholder. As what *appears* must *appear* in some form, the signification of the term has been extended to the manner of the *appearance*, and brought still nearer to *look* in its application; in this case, the term *look* is rather more familiar than that of *appearance:* we may speak either of regarding the *look* or the *appearance* of a thing, as far as it may impress others; but the latter is less colloquial than the former: a man's conduct is said to *look* rather than to *appear* ill; but on the other hand, we say a thing assumes an *appearance*, or has a certain *appearance*.

Look is always employed for what is real; what a thing *looks* is that which it really is: *appear*, however, sometimes refers not only to what is external, but to what is superficial. If we say a person *looks* ill, it supposes some positive and unequivocal evidence of illness: if we say he *appears* to be ill, it is a less positive assertion than the former; it leaves room for doubt, and allows the possibility of a mistake. We are at liberty to judge of things by their *looks*, without being chargeable with want of judgement; but as *appearances* are said to be deceitful, it becomes necessary to admit them with caution as the rule of our judgement. *Look* is employed mostly in regard to objects of sense; *appearance* respects natural and moral ob jects indifferently: the sky *looks* lowering; an object *appears* through a microscope greater than it really is;

Distressful nature pants;
The very streams *look* languid from afar.
THOMSON.

A person's conduct *appears* in a more culpable light when seen through the representation of an enemy; 'Never does liberty *appear* more amiable than under the government of a pious and good prince.'—ADDISON.

LOOK, GLANCE.

Look (*v. Air*) is the generick, and *glance* (*v. To glance at*) the specifick term; that is to say, a casual or momentary *look*: a *look* may be characterized as severe or mild, fierce or gentle, angry or kind; a *glance* as hasty or sudden, imperfect or slight: so likewise we speak of taking a *look*, or catching a *glance*;

Here the soft flocks, with the same harmless *look*
They wore alive.—THOMSON.

The tiger, darting fierce
Impetuous on his prey, the *glance* has doom'd.
THOMSON.

TO LOOK, SEE, BEHOLD, VIEW, EYE.

Look, in Saxon *locan*, Upper German *lugen*, comes from *lux* light, and the Greek λάω to see; *see*, in German *sehen*, probably a variation from the Latin *video* to see; *behold*, compounded of the intensive *be* and *hold*, signifies to *hold* or fix the eye on an object; *view*, from the French *voir*, and the Latin *video*, signifies simply to *see*; to *eye*, from the noun *eye*, naturally signifies to fathom with the *eye*.

We *look* voluntarily; we *see* involuntarily: the *eye sees*; the person *looks*: absent people often *see* things before they are fully conscious that they are at hand: we may *look* without *seeing*, and we may *see* without *looking*: near-sighted people often *look* at that which is too distant to strike the visual organ. To *behold* is to *look* at for a continuance; to *view* is to *look* at in all directions; to *eye* is to *look* at earnestly, and by side glances: that which is *seen* may disappear in an instant; it may strike the *eye* and be gone: but what is *looked* at must make some stay; consequently, lightning, and things equally fugitive and rapid in their flight, may be *seen*, but cannot be *looked* at.

To *look* at is the familiar, as well as the general term, in regard to the others; we *look* at things in general, which we wish to *see*, that is, to *see* them clearly, fully, and in all their parts; but we *behold* that which excites a moral or intellectual interest; 'The most unpardonable malefactor in the world going to his death, and bearing it with composure, would win the pity of those who should *behold* him.'—STEELE. We *view* that which demands intellectual attention;

They climb the next ascent, and, *looking* down,
Now at a nearer distance *view* the town;
The prince with wonder *sees* the stately tow'rs
(Which late were huts and shepherds' bow'rs).
DRYDEN.

We *eye* that which gratifies any particular passion;

Half afraid, he first
Against the window beats, then brisk alights
On the warm hearth; then, hopping o'er the floor,
Eyes all the smiling family askance.—THOMSON.

An inquisitive child *looks* at things which are new to it, but does not *behold* them; we *look* at plants, or finery, or whatever gratifies the senses, but we do not *behold* them: on the other hand, we *behold* any spectacle which excites our admiration, our astonishment, our pity, or our love: we *look* at objects in order to observe their external properties; but we *view* them in order to find out their component parts, their internal properties, their powers of motion and action, &c.: we *look* at things to gratify the curiosity of the moment, or for mere amusement; but the jealous man *eyes* his rival, in order to mark his movements, his designs, and his successes; the envious man *eyes* him who is in prosperity, with a malignant desire to *see* him humbled.

To *look* is an indifferent, to *behold* and *view* are good and honourable actions; to *eye*, as the act of persons, is commonly a mean, and even base action.

LOOKER-ON, SPECTATOR, BEHOLDER, OBSERVER.

The *looker-on* and the *spectator* are both opposed to the agents or actors in any scene; but the former is still more abstracted from the objects he sees than the latter.

A *looker-on* (*v. To look*) is careless; he has no part and takes no part in what he sees; he *looks on*, because the thing is before him, and he has nothing else to do: a *spectator* may likewise be unconcerned, but in general he derives amusement, if nothing else, from what he sees. A clown may be a *looker-on*, who with open mouth gapes at all that is before him, without understanding any part of it; but he who *looks on* to draw a moral lesson from the whole is in the moral sense not an uninterested *spectator*; '*Lookers-on* many times see more than gamesters.'—BACON.

But high in heaven they sit, and gaze from far,
The tame *spectators* of his deeds of war.—POPE.

The *beholder* has a nearer interest than the *spectator*; and the *observer* has an interest not less near than that of the *beholder*, but somewhat different the *beholder* has his affections roused by what he sees; 'Objects imperfectly discerned take forms from the hope or fear of the *beholder*.'—JOHNSON. The *observer* has his understanding employed in that which passes before him; 'Swift was an exact *observer* of life.'—JOHNSON. The *beholder* indulges himself in contemplation; the *observer* is busy in making it subservient to some proposed object; every *beholder* of our Saviour's sufferings and patience was struck with the conviction of his Divine character, not excepting even some of those who were his most prejudiced adversaries; every calm *observer* of our Saviour's words and actions was convinced of his Divine mission

TO SEE, PERCEIVE, OBSERVE.

See, in the German *sehen*, Greek θεάομαι, Hebrew זנה, is a general term; it may be either a voluntary or involuntary action; *perceive*, from the Latin *percipio* or *per* and *capio* to take into the mind, is always a voluntary action; and *observe* (*v. To notice*) is an intentional action. The eye *sees* when the mind is absent; the mind and the eye *perceive* in conjunction: hence, we may say that a person *sees*, but does not *perceive*: we *observe*, not merely by a simple act of the mind, but by its positive and fixed exertion. We *see* a thing without knowing what it is; we *perceive* a thing, and know what it is, but the impression passes away; we *observe* a thing, and afterward retrace the image of it in our mind. We *see* a star when the eye is directed towards it; we *perceive* it move if we look at it attentively; we *observe* its position in different parts of the heavens. The blind cannot *see*, the absent cannot *perceive*, the dull cannot *observe*.

Seeing, as a corporeal action, is the act only of the eye; *perceiving* and *observing* are actions in which all the senses are concerned. We *see* colours, we *perceive* the state of the atmosphere, and *observe* its changes. *Seeing* is sometimes extended to the mind's operations, in which it has an indefinite meaning; but *perceive* and *observe* have both a definite sense: we may *see* a thing distinctly and clearly, or otherwise; we *perceive* it always with a certain degree of distinctness; and *observe* it with a positive degree of minuteness: we *see* the truth of a remark; we *perceive* the force of an objection; we *observe* the reluctance of a person. It is farther to be *observed*, however, that when *see* expresses a mental operation, it expresses what is purely mental; *perceive* and *observe* are applied to such objects as are seen by the senses as well as the mind.

See is either employed as a corporeal or incorporeal action; *perceive* and *observe* are obviously a junction of the corporeal and incorporeal We *see* the light with our eyes, or we *see* the truth of a proposition with our mind's eye;

There plant eyes, all mist from thence
Purge and disperse, that I may *see* and tell
Of things invisible to mortal sight.—MILTON.

We *perceive* the difference of climate, or we *perceive* the difference in the comfort of our situation;

Sated at length, ere long I might *perceive*
Strange alteration in me.—MILTON.

We *observe* the motions of the heavenly bodies; 'Every part of your last letter glowed with that warmth of friendship, which, though it was by no means new to me, I could not but *observe* with peculiar satisfaction.'
MELMOTH (*Letters of Cicero*).

TO SEEM, APPEAR.

The idea of coming to the view is expressed by both these terms; but the word *seem* rises upon that of *appear*. *Seem*, from the Latin *similis* like, signifies literally to *appear* like, and is therefore a species of *appearance*, which is from the Latin *appareo* or *pareo*, and the Greek παρεἰμι to be present, signifies to be present, or before the eye. Every object may *appear*; but nothing *seems*, except that which the mind admits to *appear* in any given form. To *seem* requires some reflection and comparison of objects in the mind one with another; this term is, therefore, peculiarly applicable to matters that may be different from what they *appear*, or of an indeterminate kind: that the sun *seems* to move, is a conclusion which we draw from the exercise of our senses, and by comparing this case with others of a similar nature; it is only by a farther research into the operations of nature that we discover this to be no conclusive proof of its motion. To *appear*, on the contrary, is the express act of the things themselves on us; it is, therefore, peculiarly applicable to such objects as make an impression on us: to *appear* is the same as to present itself; the stars *appear* in the firmament, but we do not say that they *seem* there; the sun *appears* dark through the clouds.

They are equally applicable to moral as well as natural objects with the above-mentioned distinction. *Seem* is said of that which is dubious, contingent, or future; *appear* of that which is actual, positive, and past. A thing *seems* strange which we are led to conclude as strange from what we see of it; a thing *appears* clear when we have a clear conception of it; a plan *seems* practicable or impracticable; an author *appears* to understand his subject, or the contrary. It *seems* as if all efforts to reform the bulk of mankind will be found inefficient; it *appears* from the long catalogue of vices which are still very prevalent, that little progress has hitherto been made in the work of reformation;

> Lash'd into foam, the fierce conflicting brine
> *Seems* o'er a thousand raging waves to burn.
> THOMSON.

> O heavenly poet! such thy verse *appears*,
> So sweet, so charming to my ravish'd ears.—DRYDEN.

TO PERCEIVE, DISCERN, DISTINGUISH.

Perceive, in Latin *percipio*, or *per* and *capio*, signifies to take hold of thoroughly; *discern*, *v. Discernment.*

To *perceive* (*v. To see*) is a positive, to *discern* a relative, action: we *perceive* things by themselves; we *discern* them amid many others: we *perceive* that which is obvious; we *discern* that which is remote, or which requires much attention to get an idea of it. We *perceive* by a person's looks and words what he intends; we *discern* the drift of his actions. We may *perceive* sensible or spiritual objects; we commonly *discern* only that which is spiritual; we *perceive* light, darkness, colours, or the truth or falsehood of any thing;

> And lastly, turning inwardly her eyes,
> *Perceives* how all her own ideas rise.—JENYNS.

We *discern* characters, motives, the tendency and consequences of actions, &c.; 'One who is actuated by party spirit, is almost under an incapacity of *discerning* either real blemishes or beauties.'—ADDISON. It is the act of a child to *perceive* according to the quickness of its senses; it is the act of a man to *discern* according to the measure of his knowledge and understanding.

To *discern* and *distinguish* (*v. Difference*) approach the nearest in sense to each other; but the former signifies to see only one thing, the latter to see two or more in quick succession. We *discern* what lie in things; we *distinguish* things according to their outward marks; we *discern* things in order to understand their essences; we *distinguish* in order not to confound them together. Experienced and discreet people

may *discern* the signs of the times; it is just to *distinguish* between an action done from inadvertence, and that which is done from design. The conduct of people is sometimes so veiled by art, that it is not easy to *discern* their object; 'The custom of arguing on any side, even against our persuasions, dims the understanding, and makes it by degrees lose the faculty of *discerning* between truth and falsehood.'—LOCKE. It is necessary to *distinguish* between practice and profession; 'Mr. Boyle observes, that though the mole be not totally blind (as is generally thought), she has not sight enough to *distinguish* objects.'—ADDISON

TO OBSERVE, WATCH.

These terms agree in expressing the act of looking at an object; but to *observe* (*v. To notice*) is not to look after so strictly as is implied by to *watch* (*v. To watch*); a general *observes* the motions of an enemy when they are in no particular state of activity; he *watches* the motions of an enemy when they are in a state of commotion: we *observe* a thing in order to draw an inference from it; we *watch* any thing in order to discover what may happen: we *observe* with coolness; we *watch* with eagerness: we *observe* carefully; we *watch* narrowly: the conduct of mankind in general is *observed;*

> Nor must the ploughman less *observe* the skies.
> DRYDEN

The conduct of suspicious individuals is *watched;*

> For thou know'st
> What hath been warn'd us, what malicious foe
> *Watches*, no doubt, with greedy hope to find,
> His wish and best advantage, us asunder.—MILTON

WAKEFUL, WATCHFUL, VIGILANT.

We may be *wakeful* without being *watchful;* but we cannot be *watchful* without being *wakeful.*

Wakefulness is an affair of the body, and depends upon the temperament; *watchfulness* is an affair of the will, and depends upon the determination. Some persons are more *wakeful* than they wish to be;

> Musick shall wake her, that hath power to charm
> Pale sickness, and avert the stings of pain;
> Can raise or quell our passions, and becalm
> In sweet oblivion the too *wakeful* sense.—FENTON.

Few persons are as *watchful* as they ought to be; 'He who remembers what has fallen out will be *watchful* against what may happen.'—SOUTH. *Vigilance*, from the Latin *vigil*, and the Greek ἀγαλλιάω to be on the alert, expresses a high degree of *watchfulness:* a sentinel is *watchful* who on ordinary occasions keeps good *watch;* but it is necessary for him, on extraordinary occasions, to be *vigilant*, in order to detect whatever may pass.

We are *watchful* mostly in the proper sense of *watching;* but we may be *vigilant* in detecting moral as well as natural evils; 'Let a man strictly observe the first hints and whispers of good and evil that pass in his heart: this will keep conscience quick and *vigilant.*'—SOUTH.

TO ABSTRACT, SEPARATE, DISTINGUISH.

To *abstract*, from the Latin *abstractum*, participle of *abstraho* to draw from, signifies to draw one thing from another; *separate*, in Latin *separatus*, participle of *separo*, is compounded of *se* and *paro* to dispose apart, signifying to put things asunder, or at a distance from each other; *distinguish*, in French *distinguer*, Latin *distinguo*, is compounded of the separative preposition *dis* and *tingo* to tinge or colour, signifying to give different marks by which things may be known from each other.

Abstract is used for the most part in the moral or spiritual sense; *separate* mostly in a physical sense; *distinguish* either in a moral or physical sense: we *abstract* what we wish to regard particularly and individually; we *separate* what we wish not to be united; we *distinguish* what we wish not to confound. The mind performs the office of *abstraction* for itself; *separating* and *distinguishing* are exerted on external objects.* Arrangement, place, time, and circum-

* Vide Abbe Girard: "Distinguer, separer.

stances serve to *separate:* the ideas formed of things, the outward marks attached to them, the qualities attributed to them serve to *distinguish.*

By the operation of *abstraction* the mind creates for itself a multitude of new ideas: in the act of *separation* bodies are removed from each other by distance of place: in the act of *distinguishing* objects are discovered to be similar or dissimilar. Qualities are *abstracted* from the subjects in which they are inherent: countries are *separated* by mountains or seas: their inhabitants are *distinguished* by their dress, language, or manners. The mind is never less *abstracted* from one's friends than when *separated* from them by immense oceans: it requires a keen eye to *distinguish* objects that bear a great resemblance to each other. Volatile persons easily *abstract* their minds from the most solemn scenes to fix them on trifling objects that pass before them; 'We ought to *abstract* our minds from the observation of an excellence in those we converse with, till we have received some good information of the disposition of their minds.'—STEELE. An unsocial temper leads some men to *separate* themselves from all their companions; 'It is an eminent instance of Newton's superiority to the rest of mankind that he was able to *separate* knowledge from those weaknesses by which knowledge is generally disgraced.'—JOHNSON. An absurd ambition leads others to *distinguish* themselves by their eccentricities; 'Fontenelle, in his panegyrick on Sir Isaac Newton, closes a long enumeration of that philosopher's virtues and attainments with an observation that he was not *distinguished* from other men by any singularity either natural or affected.'—JOHNSON.

ABSENT, ABSTRACTED, DIVERTED, DISTRACTED.

Absent, in French *absent,* Latin *absens,* comes from *ab* and *sum* to be from, signifying away or at a distance from all objects; *abstracted,* in French *abstrait,* Latin *abstractus,* participle of *abstraho,* or *ab* and *traho* to draw from, signifies drawn or separated from all objects; *diverted,* in French *divertir,* Latin *diverto,* compounded of *di* or *dis* asunder and *verto* to turn, signifies to turn aside from the object that is present; *distracted* of course implies drawn asunder by different objects.

A want of attention is implied in all these terms, but in different degrees and under different circumstances.

Absent and *abstracted* denote a total exclusion of present objects; *diverted* and *distracted* a misapplied attention to surrounding objects, an attention to such things as are not the immediate object of concern.

Absent and *abstracted* differ less in sense than in application: the former is an epithet expressive either of a habit or a state, and precedes the noun; the latter expresses a state only, and is never adjoined to the noun: we say, a man is *absent* or an *absent* man; he is *abstracted,* but not an *abstracted* man, although when applied to other objects it may be applied to denote a temporary state;

> A voice, than human more, th' *abstracted* ear
> Of fancy strikes, "Be not afraid of us,
> Poor kindred man."—THOMSON.

We are *absent* or *abstracted* when not thinking on what passes before us; we are *diverted* when we listen to any other discourse than that which is addressed to us; we are *distracted* when we listen to the discourse of two persons at the same time.

The *absent* man has his mind and person never in the same place: he is *abstracted* from all the surrounding scenes; his senses are locked up from all the objects that seek for admittance; he is often at Rome while walking the streets of London, or solving a problem of Euclid in a social party; 'Theophrastus called one who barely rehearsed his speech, with his eyes fixed, an "*absent* actor."'—HUGHES. The man who is *diverted* seeks to be present at every thing; he is struck with every thing, and ceases to be attentive to one thing in order to direct his regards to another; he turns from the right to the left, but does not stop to think on any one point; 'The mind is refrigerated by interruption; the thoughts are *diverted* from the principal subject; the reader is weary, he knows not why.'—JOHNSON (*Preface to Shakspeare*). The *distracted* man can be present at nothing, as all objects strike him with equal force; his thoughts are in a state of vacillation and confusion; 'He used to rave for his Marianne, and call upon her in his *distracted* fits'—ADDISON.

A habit of profound study sometimes causes *absence;* it is well for such a mind to be sometimes *diverted:* the ardent contemplation of any one subject occasions frequent *abstractions;* if they are too frequent, or ill-timed, they are reprehensible: the juvenile and versatile mind is most prone to be *diverted;* it follows the bias of the senses, which are caught by the outward surface of things; it is impelled by curiosity to look rather than to think: a well-regulated mind is rarely exposed to *distractions,* which result from contrariety of feeling, as well as thinking, peculiar to persons of strong susceptibility or dull comprehension.

The *absent* man neither derives pleasure from society, nor imparts any to it; his resources are in himself. The man who is easily *diverted* is easily pleased; but he may run the risk of displeasing others by the *distractions* of his mind. The *distracted* man is a burden to himself and others.

TO DISTINGUISH, DISCRIMINATE.

To *distinguish* (*v. To abstract*) is the general, to *discriminate* (*v. Discernment*) is the particular, term the former is an indefinite, the latter a definite, action To *discriminate* is in fact to *distinguish* specifically hence we speak of a *distinction* as true or false, but of a *discrimination* as nice.

We *distinguish* things as to their divisibility or unity; we *discriminate* them as to their inherent properties: we *distinguish* things that are alike or unlike to separate or collect them; we *discriminate* those that are different, for the purpose of separating one from the other: we *distinguish* by means of the senses as well as the understanding; we *discriminate* by the understanding only: we *distinguish* things by their colour, or we *distinguish* moral objects by their truth or falsehood;

> 'T is easy to *distinguish* by the sight
> The colour of the soil, and black from white
> DRYDEN

We *discriminate* the characters of men, or we *discriminate* their merits according to circumstances, 'A satire should expose nothing but what is corrigible, and make a due *discrimination* between those who are and those who are not the proper objects of it.'—ADDISON.

TO DIVIDE, SEPARATE, PART.

To *divide* signifies the same as in the preceding; to *separate,* in Latin *separatus,* participle of *separo,* or *se* apart and *paro* to dispose, signifies to put things asunder, or at a distance from each other; to *part* signifies to make into *parts.*

That is said to be *divided* which has been, or is conceived to be, a whole; that is *separated* which might be joined: a river *divides* a town by running through it;

> Nor cease your sowing till mid-winter ends,
> For this, through twelve bright signs Apollo guides
> The year, and earth in several climes *divides.*
> DRYDEN.

Mountains or seas *separate* countries; 'Can a body be inflammable from which it would puzzle a chymist to *separate* an inflammable ingredient?'—BOYLE. To *divide* does not necessarily include a *separation;* although a *separation* supposes a *division:* an army may be *divided* into larger or smaller portions, and yet remain united; but during a march, or an engagement, these companies are frequently *separated.*

Opinions, hearts, minds, &c. may be *divided;* corporeal bodies only are *separated:* the minds of men are often most *divided,* when in person they are least *separated;* and those, on the contrary, who are *separated* at the greatest distance from each other may be the least *divided;* 'Where there is the greatest and most honourable love, it is sometimes better to be joined in death, than *separated* in life.'—STEELE.

To *part* approaches nearer to *separate* than to *divide:* the latter is applied to things only; the two former to persons, as well as things: a thing becomes smaller by being *divided;* 'If we *divide* the life of most men into twenty parts, we shall find at least nineteen of them filled with gaps and chasms, which are neither filled up with pleasure or business.'—ADDISON. One thing loses its junction with, or cohesion to, another, by being *parted:* a loaf of bread is *divided* by being cut into two; two loaves are *parted* which have been baked together.

Sometimes *part*, as well as *divide*, is used in the application of that which is given to several, in which case they bear the same analogy as before: several things are *parted*, one thing is *divided:* a man's personal effects may be *parted*, by common consent, among his children; but his estate, or the value of it, must be *divided:* whatever can be disjoined without losing its integrity is *parted*, otherwise it is *divided:* in this sense our Saviour's garments are said to have been *parted*, because they were distinct things; but the vesture which was without seam must have been *divided* if they had not cast lots for it.

As disjunction is the common idea attached to both *separate* and *part*, they are frequently used in relation to the same objects: houses may be both *separated* and *parted;* they are *parted* by that which does not keep them at so great a distance, as when they are said to be *separated:* two houses are *parted* by a small opening between them; they are *separated* by an intervening garden: fields are with more propriety said to be *separated;* rooms are said more properly to be *parted.*

With regard to persons, *part* designates the actual leaving of the person; *separate* is used in general for that which lessens the society: the former is often casual, temporary, or partial; the latter is positive and serious: the *parting* is momentary;

The prince pursu'd the *parting* deity
With words like these, "Ah, whither do you fly?
Unkind and cruel to deceive your son."—DRYDEN.

The *separation* may be longer or shorter; 'I pray let me retain some room, though never so little, in your thoughts, during the time of this our *separation.*'—HOWELL. Two friends *part* in the streets after a casual meeting; two persons *separate* on the road who had set out to travel together: men and their wives often *part* without coming to a positive *separation:* some couples are *separated* from each other in every respect but that of being directly *parted:* the moment of *parting* between friends is often more painful than the *separation* which afterward ensues.

TO DIVIDE, DISTRIBUTE, SHARE.

To *divide*, in Latin *divido*, from *di* or *dis* and *vido*, in the Etruscan *iduo* to part, which comes from the Greek εἰς δύω into two, signifies literally to make into two; *distribute*, in Latin *distributus*, from *distribuo*, or *dis* and *tribuo*, signifies to bestow apart; *share*, from the word *shear*, and the German *scheeren*, signifies simply to cut.

The act of *dividing* does not extend beyond the thing *divided;* that of *distributing* and *sharing* comprehends also the purpose of the action: we *divide* the thing; we *distribute* to the person: we may *divide* therefore without *distributing;* or we may *divide* in order to *distribute:* thus we *divide* our land into distinct fields for our private convenience; or we *divide* a sum of money into so many parts, in order to *distribute* it among a given number of persons;

Let old Timotheus yield the prize,
Or both *divide* the crown;
He rais'd a mortal to the skies,
She drew an angel down.—DRYDEN.

Two urns by Jove's high throne have ever stood
The source of evil one, and one of good;
From thence the cup of mortal man he fills,
Blessings to these, to those *distributes* ill.—POPE.

On the other hand, we may *distribute* without *dividing;* for guineas, books, apples, and many other things may be *distributed*, which require no *division.*

To *share* is to make into parts the same as *divide*, and it is to give those parts to some persons, the same as *distribute:* but the person who *shares* takes a part himself;

Why grieves my son? Thy anguish let me *share*,
Reveal the cause, and trust a parent's care.—POPE.

He who *distributes* gives it always to others; 'Providence has made an equal *distribution* of natural gifts whereof each creature severally has a *share.*'—L'ESTRANGE. A loaf is *divided* in order to be eaten; bread is *distributed* in loaves among the poor; the loaf is *shared* by a poor man with his poorer neighbour, or the profits of a business are *shared* by the partners.

To *share* may imply either to give or receive; to *distribute* implies giving only: we *share* our own with another, or another *shares* what we have; but we *distribute* our own to others; 'They will be so much the more careful to determine properly as they shall (will) be obliged to *share* the expenses of maintaining the masters.'—MELMOTH (*Letters of Pliny*).

TO DISPENSE, DISTRIBUTE.

Dispense, from the Latin *pendo* to pay or bestow, signifies to bestow in different directions; and *distribute*, from the Latin *tribuo* to bestow, signifies the same thing.

Dispense is an indiscriminate action; *distribute* is a particularizing action: we *dispense* to all; we *distribute* to each individually: nature *dispenses* her gifts bountifully to all the inhabitants of the earth;

Though Nature weigh our talents, and *dispense*
To every man his modicum of sense;
Yet much depends, as in the tiller's toil,
On culture, and the sowing of the soil.
COWPER.

A parent *distributes* among his children different tokens of his parental tenderness; 'Pray be no niggard in *distributing* my love plentifully among our friends at the inns of court.'—HOWELL.

Dispense is an indirect action that has no immediate reference to the receiver; *distribute* is a direct and personal action communicated by the giver to the receiver: Providence *dispenses* his favours to those who put a sincere trust in him; 'Those to whom Christ has committed the *dispensing* of his Gospel.'—DECAY OF PIETY. A prince *distributes* marks of his favour and preference among his courtiers; 'The king sent over a great store of gentlemen and warlike people, among whom he *distributed* the land.'—SPENSER *on Ireland.*

PART, DIVISION, PORTION, SHARE.

Part, in Latin *pars*, comes from the Hebrew פרש to divide, signifying the thing divided or parted from another; *division* signifies the same as *portion; portion*, in Latin *portio*, is supposed to be changed from *partio*, which comes from *partior* to distribute, and originally from the Hebrew, as the word *part; share*, in Saxon *scyran* to divide, comes in all probability from the Hebrew שרד to remain, that is, what remains after a *division.*

Part is a term not only of more general use, but of more comprehensive meaning than *division;* it is always employed for the thing *divided*, but *division* may be either employed for the act of *dividing*, or the thing that is *divided:* but in all cases the word *division* has always a reference to some action, and the agent by whom it has been performed; whereas *part*, which is perfectly abstract, has altogether lost this idea. We always speak of a *part* as opposed to the whole, but of a *division* as it has been made of the whole.

A *part* is formed of itself by accident, or made by design; a *division* is always the effect of design: a *part* is indefinite as to its quantity or nature, it may be large or small, round or square, of any dimension, of any form, of any size, or of any character; but a *division* is always regulated by some certain principles, it depends upon the circumstances of the *divisor* and thing to be *divided.* A page, a line, or a word is the *part* of any book; but the books, chapters, sections, and paragraphs are the *divisions* of the book. Stones, wood, water, air, and the like, are *parts* of the world; fire, air, earth, and water are physical *divisions* of the globe; continents, seas, rivers, mountains, and the like, are geographical *divisions*, under which are likewise included its political *divisions* into countries, kingdoms, &c.;

Shall little haughty Ignorance pronounce
His works unwise, of which the smallest *part*
Exceeds the narrow vision of her mind?—THOMSON

'A *division* (in a discourse) should be natural and simple.'—BLAIR.

A *part* may be detached from the whole; a *division* is always conceived of in connexion with the whole; *portion* and *share* are particular species of *divisions*, which are said of such matters as are assignable to individuals; *portion* respects individuals without any distinction;

> The jars of gen'rous wine, Acestes' gift,
> He set abroach, and for the feast prepar'd,
> In equal *portions* with the ven'son *shar'd*.
> DRYDEN.

Share respects individuals specially referred to;

> The monarch, on whom fertile Nile bestows
> All which that grateful earth can bear,
> Deceives himself if he suppose
> That more than this falls to his *share*.—COWLEY.

The *portion* of happiness which falls to every man's lot is more equal than is generally supposed; the *share* which partners have in the profits of any undertaking depends upon the sum which each has contributed towards its completion. The *portion* is that which simply comes to any one; but the *share* is that which belongs to him by a certain right. According to the ancient customs of Normandy, the daughters could have no more than a third *part* of the property for their *share*, which was *divided* in equal *portions* between them.

PART, PIECE, PATCH.

Part signifies the same as in the preceding article; *piece*, in French *piece*, comes from the Hebrew פס to diminish; whence also comes *patch*, signifying the thing in its diminished form, that which is less than a whole. The *part* in its strict sense is taken in connexion with the whole; the *piece* is the *part* detached from the whole; the *patch* is that *piece* which is distinguished from others. Things may be divided into *parts* without any express separation; but when divided into *pieces* they are actually cut asunder. Hence we may speak of a loaf as divided into twelve *parts* when it is conceived only to be so; and divided into twelve *pieces*, when it is really so. On this ground, we talk of the *parts* of a country, but not of the *pieces;* and of a *piece* of land, not a *part* of land: so likewise letters are said to be the component *parts* of a word, but the half or the quarter of any given letter is called a *piece*. The chapters, the pages, the lines, &c. are the various *parts* of a book; certain passages or quantities drawn from the book are called *pieces:* the *parts* of matter may be infinitely decomposed; various bodies may be formed out of so ductile a *piece* of matter as clay. The *piece* is that which may sometimes serve as a whole; but the *patch* is that which is always broken and disjointed,—something imperfect: many things may be formed out of a *piece;* but the *patch* only serves to fill up a chasm.

TO PARTAKE, PARTICIPATE, SHARE.

Partake and *participate*, the one English, and the other Latin, signify literally to take a *part* in a thing. The former is employed in the proper or improper sense; and the latter in the improper sense only: we may *partake* of a feast, or we may *partake* of pleasure; but we *participate* only in pleasure or pain, &c.

To *partake* is a selfish action; to *participate* is either a selfish or a benevolent action: we *partake* of that which pleases ourselves;

> All else of nature's common gift *partake*,
> Unhappy Dido was alone awake.—DRYDEN.

We *participate* in that which pleases another;

> Our God, when heav'n and earth he did create,
> Form'd man, who should of both *participate*
> DENHAM.

We *partake* of a meal with a friend; we *participate* in the gifts of Providence, or in the enjoyments which another feels.

To *partake* is the act of taking the thing, or getting the thing to one's self; to *share* is the act of having a title to a *share*, or being in the habits of receiving a *share:* we may, therefore, *partake* of a thing without *sharing* it, and *share* it without *partaking*. We *partake* of things mostly through the medium of the senses whatever, therefore, we take *part* in, whether gratuitously or casually, that we may be said to *partake* of: in this manner we *partake* of an entertainment without *sharing* it; or we *partake* in a design, &c.;

> By-and-by, thy bosom shall *partake*
> The secrets of my heart.—SHAKSPEARE.

On the other hand, we *share* things that promise to be of advantage or profit, and what we *share* is what we claim; in this manner we *share* a sum of money which has been left to us in common with others;

> Avoiding love, I had not found despair,
> But *shar'd* with savage beasts the common air.
> DRYDEN.

DEAL, QUANTITY, PORTION.

Deal, in Saxon *dæl*, Dutch *deel*, and German *theil*, from *dælen*, *theilen*, &c. to divide, signifies literally the thing divided or taken off; *quantity*, in Latin *quantitas*, comes from *quantum*, signifying how much; *portion*, through the Latin *pars* and *portio*, comes from the Hebrew פרש to divide, signifying, like the word *deal*, the thing taken off.

Deal always denotes something great, and cannot be coupled with any epithet that does not express much: *quantity* is a term of relative import; it either marks indefinitely the how, or so much of a thing, or may be defined by some epithet to express much or little: *portion* is of itself altogether indefinite, and admits of being qualified by any epithet to express much or little: *deal* is a term confined to familiar use, and sometimes substituted for *quantity*, and sometimes for *portion*. It is common to speak of a *deal* or a *quantity* of paper, a great *deal* or a great *quantity* of money; likewise of a great *deal* or a great *portion* of pleasure, a great *deal* or a great *portion* of wealth: and in some cases *deal* is more usual than either *quantity* or *portion*, as a *deal* of heat, a *deal* of rain, a *deal* of frost, a *deal* of noise, and the like; but it is altogether inadmissible in the higher style of writing; 'This, my inquisitive temper, or rather impertinent humour, of prying into all sorts of writing, with my natural aversion to loquacity, gives me a good *deal* of employment when I enter any house in the country.'—ADDISON. 'There is never room in the world for more than a certain *quantity* or measure of renown.'—JOHNSON.

Portion is employed only for that which is detached from the whole; *quantity* may sometimes be employed for a number of wholes. We may speak of a large or a small *quantity* of books; a large or a small *quantity* of plants or herbs; but a large or a small *portion* of food, a large or small *portion* of colour. *Quantity* is used only in the natural sense: *portion* also in the moral application, and mostly in the sense of a stated *quantity*. Material substances, as wood, stone, metals, and liquids, are necessarily considered with regard to *quantity;* the qualities of the mind and the circumstances of human life are divided into *portions*. A builder estimates the *quantity* of materials which he will want for the completion of a house; the work man estimates the *portion* of labour which the work will require;

> In battles won, fortune a part did claim,
> And soldiers have their *portion* in the fame.
> WALLER

TO COMMUNICATE, IMPART.

Communicate, in Latin *communicatus*, participle of *communico*, contracted from *communifico*, signifies to make common property with another; *impart*, compounded of *in* and *part*, signifies to give in part to another.

Imparting is a species of *communicating;* one always *communicates* in *imparting*, but not *vice versâ*.

Whatever can be enjoyed in common with others is *communicated;* whatever can be shared by another is *imparted:* what one knows or thinks is *communicated*, or made commonly known; what one feels is *imparted* and participated in: intelligence or information is *communicated;* 'A man who publishes his works in a volume has an infinite advantage over one who *communicates* his writings to the world in loose tracts'—ADDISON. Secrets or sorrows are *imparted;*

Yet hear what an unskilful friend may say,
As if a blind man should direct your way:
So I myself, though wanting to be taught,
May yet *impart* a hint that 's worth your thought.
GOLDING.

Those who always *communicate* all they hear, sometimes *communicate* more than they really know; it is the characteristick of friendship to allow her votaries to *impart* their joys and sorrows to each other.

A person may *communicate* what belongs to another, as well as that which is his own; but he *imparts* that only which concerns or belongs to himself: an openness of temper leads some men to *communicate* their intentions as soon as they are formed; loquacity impels others to *communicate* whatever is told them: a generosity of temper leads some men to *impart* their substance for the relief of their fellow-creatures; a desire for sympathy leads others to *impart* their sentiments. There is a great pleasure in *communicating* good intelligence and in *imparting* good advice.

COMMUNICATIVE, FREE,

Are epithets that convey no respectful sentiment of the object to which they are applied: a person is *communicative*, who is ready to tell all he knows; he is *free*, when he is ready to say all he thinks: the *communicative* person has no regard for himself; the *free* person has no regard for others.

A *communicative* temper leads to the breach of all confidence; a *free* temper leads to violation of all decency: *communicativeness* of disposition produces much mischief; *freedom* of speech and behaviour occasions much offence. *Communicativeness* is the excess of sincerity; it offends by revealing what it ought to conceal: *freedom* is the abuse of sincerity; it offends by speaking what it ought not to think.

These terms are sometimes taken in a good sense; when a person is *communicative* for the instruction or amusement of others, and is *free* in imparting to others whatever he can of his enjoyments; 'The most miserable of all beings is the most envious; as on the other hand the most *communicative* is the happiest.'—GROVE. 'Aristophanes was in private life of a *free*, open, and companionable temper.'—CUMBERLAND.

COMMUNION, CONVERSE.

Communion, from *commune* and *common*, signifies the act of making common (*v. Common*); *converse*, from the Latin *converto* to *convert* or translate, signifies a transferring.

Both these terms imply a communication between minds; but the former may take place without corporeal agency, the latter never does; spirits hold *communion* with each other, or men may hold spiritual *communion* with God; 'Where a long course of piety and close *communion* with God has purged the heart and rectified the will, knowledge will break in upon such a soul.'—SOUTH. People hold *converse* together;

In varied *converse* softening every theme,
You frequent pausing turn; and from her eyes,
Where meeken'd sense, and amiable grace,
And lively sweetness dwell, enraptured drink
That nameless spirit of ethereal joy.—THOMSON.

For the same reason a man may hold *communion* with himself; he holds *converse* always with another.

COMMUNITY, SOCIETY.

Both these terms are employed for a body of rational beings; *community*, from *communitas* and *communis* common (*v. Common*), signifies abstractedly the state of being *common*, and in an extended sense those who are in a state of common possession; *society*, in Latin *societas*, from *socius* a companion, signifies the state of being companions, or those who are in that state.

Community in any thing constitutes a *community*; a common interest, a common language, a common government, is the basis of that *community* which is formed by any number of individuals; *communities* are therefore divisible into large or small; the former may be states, the latter families; 'Was there ever any *community* so corrupt as not to include within it individuals of real worth?'—BLAIR. The coming together of many constitutes a *society*; *societies* are either private or publick, according to the purpose for which they meet together; friends form *societies* for the purpose of pleasure; indifferent persons form *societies* for the purposes of business; 'The great *community* of mankind is necessarily broken into smaller independent *societies*.'—JOHNSON.

Community has always a restrictive and relative sense; *society* has a general and unlimited import: the most dangerous members of the *community* are those who attempt to poison the minds of youth with contempt for religion and disaffection to the state; the morals of *society* are thus corrupted as it were at the fountain-head.

Community refers to spiritual as well as corporeal agents; *society* mostly to human beings only: the angels, the saints, and the spirits of just men made perfect, constitute a *community*; with them there is more communion than association.

CONVIVIAL, SOCIAL, SOCIABLE.

Convivial, in Latin *convivialis*, from *convivo* to live together, signifies being entertained together; *social*, from *socius* a companion, signifies pertaining to company.

The prominent idea in *convivial* is that of sensual indulgence; the prominent idea in *social* is that of enjoyment from an intercourse with society. The *convivial* is a species of the *social*; it is the *social* in matters of festivity. What is *convivial* is *social*, but what is *social* is something more; the former is excelled by the latter as much as the body is excelled by the mind. We speak of *convivial* meetings, *convivial* enjoyments, or the *convivial* board; but *social* intercourse, *social* pleasure, *social* amusements, and the like; 'It is related by Carte, of the Duke of Ormond, that he used often to pass a night with Dryden, and those with whom Dryden consorted; who they were Carte has not told, but certainly the *convivial* table at which Ormond sat was not surrounded with a plebeian society.'—JOHNSON. 'Plato and Socrates shared many *social* hours with Aristophanes.'—CUMBERLAND.

Social signifies belonging or allied to a companion, having the disposition of a companion; *sociable*, from the same root, signifies able or fit to be a companion; the former is an active, the latter a passive quality: *social* people seek others; *sociable* people are sought for by others. It is possible for a man to be *social* and not *sociable*; to be *sociable* and not *social*: he who draws his pleasures from society without communicating his share to the common stock of entertainments is *social* but not *sociable*; men of a taciturn disposition are often in this case; they receive more than they give: he, on the contrary, who has talents to please company, but not the inclination to go into company, may be *sociable*, but is seldom *social*; of this description are [illegible] who go into company to gratify their pri[illegible] away to indulge their humour. *Social* [illegible] likewise applicable to things, with a[illegible]tion; *social* intercourse is that intercou[illegible] have together for the purposes of society[illegible]sures are what they enjoy by associating toge[illegible]

Social friends,
Attun'd to happy unison of soul.—THOMSON.

A path or a carriage is denominated *sociable* which encourages the association of many; 'Sciences are of a *sociable* disposition, and flourish best in the neighbourhood of each other.'—BLACKSTONE.

SOCIETY, COMPANY.

Society (*v. Association*) and *company* (*v. Association*) here express either the persons associating or the act of associating.

In either case, *society* is a general, and *company* a particular, term; as respects persons associating, *society* comprehends either all the associated part of mankind, as when we speak of the laws of *society*, the well-being of *society*; or it is said only of a particular number of individuals associated: in which latter case it comes nearest to *company*, and differs from it only as to the purpose of the association. A *society* is always formed for some solid purpose, as the Humane *Society*; and the *company* is always brought together for pleasure or profit, as has already been observed.

Good sense teaches us the necessity of conforming to the rules of the *society* to which we belong; good breeding prescribes to us to render ourselves agreeable to the *company* of which we form a part.

When expressing the abstract action of associating, *society* is even more general and indefinite than before; it expresses that which is common to mankind; and *company* that which is peculiar to individuals. The love of *society* is inherent in our nature; it is weakened or destroyed only by the vice of our constitution or the derangement of our system;

> Solitude sometimes is best *society*,
> And short retirement urges sweet return.—MILTON.

Every one naturally likes the *company* of his own friends and connexions in preference to that of strangers. *Society* is a permanent and habitual act; *company* is only a particular act suited to the occasion; it behooves us to shun the *society* of those from whom we can learn no good, although we may sometimes be obliged to be in their *company*. The *society* of intelligent men is desirable for those who are entering life: the *company* of facetious men is agreeable in travelling; '*Company*, though it may reprieve a man from his melancholy, cannot secure him from his conscience.'—SOUTH.

ASSOCIATE, COMPANION.

Associate, in Latin *associatus*, participle of *associo*, compounded of *as* or *ad* and *socio* to ally, signifies one united with a person; *companion*, from company, signifies one that bears company (*v. To accompany*).

Associates are habitually together; *companions* are only occasionally in each other's company: as our habits are formed from our *associates*, we ought to be particular in our choice of them; as our *companions* contribute much to our enjoyments, we ought to choose such as are suitable to ourselves; 'We see many struggling single about the world, unhappy for want of an *associate*, and pining with the necessity of confining their sentiments to their own bosoms.'—JOHNSON. Many men may be admitted as *companions*, who would not altogether be fit as *associates*; 'There is a degree of want by which the freedom of agency is almost destroyed, and long association with fortuitous *companions* will at last relax the strictness of truth, and abate the fervour of sincerity.'—JOHNSON.

An *associate* may take part with us in some business, and share with us in the labour; 'Addison contributed more than a fourth part (of the last volume of the Spectator), and the other contributors are by no means unworthy of appearing as his *associates*.'—JOHNSON. A *companion* takes part with us in some concern, and shares with us in the pleasure or the pain;

> Thus while the cordage stretch'd [illegible] guide
> Our brave *companions* through the swe[illegible]de;
> This floating lumber shall sustain them o[illegible]
> The rocky shelves, in safety to the shore.—[illegible]CONER.

ASSOCIATION, SOCIETY, COMPANY, PARTNERSHIP.

All these terms denote a union of several persons into one body.

Association (*v. To associate*) is general, the rest specifick. Whenever we habitually or frequently meet together for some common object, it is an *association*. *Associations* are therefore political, religious, commercial, and literary; a *society* is an *association* for some specifick purpose, moral or religious, civil or political; a *company* is, in this application of the term, an *association* of many for the purpose of trade; a *partnership* is an *association* of a few for the same object.

Whenever *association* is used in distinction from the others, it denotes that which is partial in its object and temporary in its duration. It is founded on unity of sentiment as well as unity of object; but it is mostly unorganized, and kept together only by the spirit which gives rise to it. It is not, however, the less dangerous on this account; and when politicks are the subject, it commonly breathes a spirit hostile to the established order of things; as the last thirty years have evinced to us by woful experience; 'For my own part, I could wish that all honest men would enter into an *association* for the support of one another against the endeavours of those whom they ought to look upon as their common enemies, whatever side they may belong to.'—ADDISON.

A *society* requires nothing but unity of object, which is permanent in its nature; it is well organized, and commonly set on foot to promote the cause of humanity, literature, or religion. No country can boast such numerous and excellent *societies*, whether of a charitable, a religious, or a literary description, as England; 'What I humbly propose to the publick is, that there may be a *society* erected in London to consist of the most skilful persons of both sexes, for the inspection of modes and fashions.'—BUDGELL.

Companies are brought together for the purposes of interest, and are dissolved when that object ceases to exist; their duration depends on the contingencies of profit and loss. The South Sea *Company*, which was founded on an idle speculation, was formed for the ruin of many, and dispersed almost as soon as it was formed. The East India *Company*, on the other hand, which is one of the grandest that ever was raised, promises as much permanency as is commonly allotted to human transactions; 'The nation is a *company* of players.' ADDISON.

Partnerships are altogether of an individual and private nature. As they are without organization and system, they are more precarious than any other *association*. Their duration depends not only on the chances of trade, but the compatibility of individuals to co-operate in a close point of union. They are often begun rashly and end ruinously; 'Gay was the general favourite of the whole *association* of wits; but they regarded him as a playfellow rather than a *partner*, and treated him with more fondness than respect.' —JOHNSON. The term *partnership* is sometimes used figuratively, in reference to other objects; '*Society* is a *partnership* in all science; a *partnership* in every virtue and in all perfection.'—BURKE

ASSOCIATION, COMBINATION.

Association, *v. Associate*; *combination*, from the Latin *combino*, or *con* and *binus*, signifies tying two into one.

An *association* is something less binding than a *combination*; *associations* are formed for purposes of convenience; *combinations* are formed to serve either the interests or passions of men. The word *association* is therefore always taken in a good or an indifferent sense; *combination* in an indifferent or bad sense. An *association* is publick; it embraces all classes of men: a *combination* is often private, and includes only a particular description of persons. *Associations* are formed for some general purpose; 'In my yesterday's paper I proposed that the honest men of all parties should enter into a kind of *association* for the defence of one another.'—ADDISON. *Combinations* are frequently formed for particular purposes, which respect the interest of the few, to the injury of many; 'The cry of the people in cities and towns, though unfortunately (from a fear of their multitude and *combination*) the most regarded, ought in fact to be the least regarded, on the subject of monopoly.'—BURKE. *Associations* are formed by good citizens; *combinations* by discontented mechanicks, or low persons in general. The latter term may, however, be used in a good sense when taken for the general act of *combining*, in which case it expresses a closer union than *association*; 'There is no doubt but all the safety, happiness, and convenience that men enjoy in this life, is from the *combination* of particular persons into societies or corporations. —SOUTH.

When used for things, *association* is a natural action; *combination* an arbitrary action. Things *associate* of themselves, but *combinations* are formed either by design or accident. Nothing will *associate* but what harmonizes: things the most opposite in their nature are *combined* together. We *associate* persons with places, or events with names; discordant properties are *combined* in the same body. With the name of one's birthplace are *associated* pleasurable recollections; virtue and vice are often so *combined* in the same character as to form a contrast. The *association* of ideas is a remarkable phenomenon of the human mind, but it can never be admitted as solving any difficulty respecting the structure and composition of the soul; 'Meekness and courtesy will always recommend the first address, but soon pall and nauseate unless they are *associated* with more sprightly qualities.'—JOHNSON. The *combination* of letters forms syllables, and that of syllables forms words; 'Before the time of Dryden, those happy *combinations* of words which distinguish poetry from prose had been rarely attempted.'—JOHNSON.

COMBINATION, CABAL, PLOT, CONSPIRACY.

Combination, v. *Association*, *combination; cabal*, in French *cabale*, comes from the Hebrew *kabala*, signifying a secret science, pretended to by the Jewish Rabbi, whence it is applied to any association that has a pretended secret; *plot*, in French *complot*, is derived, like the word *complicate*, from the Latin *plico* to entangle, signifying any intricate or dark concern; *conspiracy*, in French *conspiration*, from *con* and *spiro* to breathe together, signifies the having one spirit.

An association for a bad purpose is the idea common to all these terms, and peculiar to *combination*. A *combination* may be either secret or open, but secrecy forms a necessary part in the signification of the other terms; a *cabal* is secret as to its end; a *plot* and *conspiracy* are secret both as to the means and the end.

Combination is the close adherence of many for their mutual defence in obtaining their demands, or resisting the claims of others. A *cabal* is the intrigue of a party or faction, formed by cunning practices in order to give a turn to the course of things to its own advantage: the natural and ruling idea of *cabal* is that of assembling a number, and manœuvring secretly with address. A *plot* is a clandestine union of some persons for the purpose of mischief: the ruling idea in a *plot* is that of a complicated enterprise formed in secret, by two or more persons. A *conspiracy* is a general intelligence among persons united to effect some serious change: the ruling and natural idea in this word is that of unanimity and concert in the prosecution of a plan.

A *combination* is seldom of so serious a nature as a *cabal* or a *plot*, though always objectionable; a *combination* may have many or few. A *cabal* requires a number of persons sufficient to form a party, it gains strength by numbers; a *plot* is generally confined to a few, it diminishes its security by numbers; a *conspiracy* mostly requires many for the fulfilment of its purposes, although it is thereby the more exposed to discovery.

Selfishness, insubordination, and laxity of morals give rise to *combinations;* they are peculiar to mechanicks, and the lower orders of society; 'The protector, dreading *combinations* between the parliament and the malecontents in the army, resolved to allow no leisure for forming *conspiracies* against him.'—HUME. Restless, jealous, ambitious, and little minds are ever forming *cabals;* they are peculiar to courtiers;

I see you court the crowd,
When with the shouts of the rebellious rabble,
I see you borne on shoulders to *cabals*.—DRYDEN.

Malignity, revenge, and every foul passion is concerned in forming *plots;*

Oh! think what anxious moments pass between
The birth of *plots*, and their last fatal periods.
ADDISON.

Disaffected subjects and bad citizens form *conspiracies*, which are frequently set on foot by disappointed ambition;

O *Conspiracy!*
Sham'st thou to show thy dangerous brow by night,
When evils are most free.—SHAKSPEARE.

The object of a *combination*, although not less formidable than the others, is not always so criminal; it rests on a question of claims which it proposes to decide by force; the end is commonly as unjustifiable as the means: to this description are the *combinations* formed by journeymen against their masters, which are expressly contrary to law. The object of a *cabal* is always petty, and mostly contemptible; its end is to gain favour, credit, and influence; to be the distributor of places, honours, emoluments, reputation, and all such contingencies as are eagerly sought for by the great mass of mankind: at court it makes and unmakes ministers, generals, and officers; in the republick of letters it destroys the reputation of authors, and blasts the success of their works; in publick societies it stops the course of equity, and nips merit in the bud; in the world at large it is the never-ending source of vexation, broils, and animosities. A *plot* has always the object of committing some atrocity, whether of a private or publick nature, as the murder or plunder of individuals, the traitorous surrender of a town, or the destruction of something very valuable. Astarba in Telemachus is represented as having formed a *plot* for the poisoning of Pygmalion: the annihilation of the English government was the object of that *plot* which received the name of gunpowder treason. The object of a *conspiracy* is oftener to bring about some evil change in publick than in private concerns; it is commonly directed against the governour, in order to overturn the government: in a republick, *conspiracies* are justified and hailed as glorious events when sanctioned by success: the *conspiracy* of Brutus against Cæsar is always represented by the favourers of a republick as a magnanimous exploit. Where every man can rule, there will always be usurpers and tyrants, and where every man has an equal right to set himself up against his ruler, there will never be wanting *conspiracies* to crush the usurpers; hence usurpations and *conspiracies* succeed each other as properly and naturally in republicks as cause and effect; the right of the strongest, the most daring, or the most unprincipled, is the only right which can be acknowledged upon the principles of republican equality: on the contrary, in a monarchy, where the person of the sovereign and his authority are alike sacred, every *conspirator* to his country, and every *conspiracy*, does no less violence to the laws of God, than to those of man.

* Vide Roubaud: "Cabale, complot, conspiration, conjuration."

FELLOWSHIP, SOCIETY.

Both these terms are employed to denote a close intercourse; but *fellowship* is said of men as individuals, *society* of them collectively: we should be careful not to hold *fellowship* with any one of bad character, or to join the *society* of those who profess bad principles;

Ill becomes it me
To wear at once thy garter and thy chains;
Though by my former dignity I swear,
That were I reinstated in my throne,
Thus to be join'd in *fellowship* with thee
Would be the first ambition of my soul.
GILBERT WEST

Unhappy he! who from the first of joys,
Society, cut off, is left alone,
Amid this world of death.—THOMSON.

ASSEMBLE, MUSTER, COLLECT.

Assemble, in French *assembler*, Latin *adsimulare* or *assimulare*, from *similis* like and *simul* together, signifies to make alike or bring together; *muster*, in German *mustern* to set out for inspection, comes from the Latin *monstror* to show or display; *collect*, in Latin *collectus*, participle of *colligo*, compounded of *col* or *con* and *lego* to bind, signifies to bring together, or into one point.

Assemble is said of persons only; *muster* and *collect* of persons or things. To *assemble* is to bring together by a call or invitation; to *muster* is to bring together by an act of authority, into one point of view, at one time, and from one quarter; to *collect* is to bring together at different times, and from different quarters: the parliament is *assembled:* soldiers are *mustered* every day in order to ascertain their numbers;

Assemble all their choirs, and with their notes,
Salute and welcome up the rising sun.—OTWAY.

An army is *collected* in preparation for war: a king *assembles* his council in order to consult with them or publick measures; a general *musters* his forces before he undertakes an expedition, and *collects* more troops if he finds himself too weak.

Collect is used for every thing which can be brought together in numbers; *muster* is used figuratively for bringing together, for an immediate purpose, whatever is in one's possession: books, coins, curiosities, and the like, are *collected;* a person's resources, his strength, courage, resolution, &c., are *mustered:* some persons have a pleasure in *collecting* all the pieces of antiquity which fall in their way;

Each leader now his scatter'd force conjoins
In close array, and forms the deep'ning lines;
Not with more ease the skilful shepherd swain
Collects his flock, from thousands on the plain.
POPE.

On a trying occasion it is necessary to *muster* all the fortitude of which we are master;

Oh! thou hast set my busy brain at work!
And now she *musters* up a train of images.
ROWE

TO ASSEMBLE, CONVENE, CONVOKE.

Assemble, *v. To assemble, muster; convene*, in Latin *convenio*, signifies to come or bring together; *convoke*, in Latin *convoco*, signifies to call together.

The idea of collecting many persons into one place, for a specifick purpose, is common to all these terms. *Assemble* conveys this sense without any addition; *convene* and *convoke* include likewise some collateral idea: people are *assembled*, whenever they are *convened* or *convoked*, but not *vice versâ*. *Assembling* is mostly by the wish of one; *convening* by that of several: a crowd is *assembled* by an individual in the streets; a meeting is *convened* at the desire of a certain number of persons: people are *assembled* either on publick or private business; they are always *convened* on a publick occasion. A king *assembles* his parliament; a particular individual *assembles* his friends;

He ceas'd; the *assembled* warriours all assent,
All but Atrides.—CUMBERLAND.

The inhabitants of a district are *convened:*

They form one social shade, as if *conven'd*
By magick summons of the Orphean lyre.
COWPER.

Animals also as well as men may be said to be *assembled* or *convened;*

Where on the mingling boughs they sit embowered
All the hot noon, till cooler hours arrive,
Faint underneath, the household fowls *convene.*
THOMSON.

There is nothing imperative on the part of those that *assemble* or *convene*, and nothing binding on those *assembled* or *convened:* one *assembles* or *convenes* by invitation or request; one attends to the notice or not at pleasure. To *convoke*, on the other hand, is an act of authority: it is the call of one who has the authority to give the call; it is heeded by those who feel themselves bound to attend. *Assembling* and *convening* are always for domestick or civil purposes: *convoking* is always employed in civil or spiritual matters: a dying man *assembles* his friends round his death-bed; a meeting is *convened* in order to present an address; the dignitaries in the church are *convoked* by the supreme authority, or a king *convokes* his council;

Here cease thy fury, and the chiefs and kings,
Convoke to council, weigh the sum of things.
POPE.

ASSEMBLY, ASSEMBLAGE, GROUP, COLLECTION.

Assembly, *assemblage*, are collective terms derived from the verb *assemble; group* comes from the Italian *gruppo*, which among painters signifies an *assemblage* of figures in one place; *collection* expresses the act of *collecting*, or the body *collected* (*v. To assemble, muster*).

Assembly respects persons only; *assemblage*, things only; *group* and *collection*, persons or things: an *assembly* is any number either brought together, or come together of themselves; an *assemblage* is any number standing together: a *group* is come together by accident, or put together by design; a *collection* is mostly put or brought together by design.

A general alarm will cause an *assembly* to disperse; Love and marriage are the natural effects of these anniversary *assemblies.*'—BUDGELL. An agreeable *assemblage* of rural objects, whether in nature or in representation, constitutes a landscape;

O Hertford! fitted or to shine in courts
With unaffected grace, or walk the plain
With innocence and meditation join'd
In soft *assemblage*, listen to my song.
THOMSON.

A painting will sometimes consist only of a *group* of figures, but if they be well chosen it will sometimes produce a wonderful effect: a *collection* of evil-minded persons ought to be immediately dispersed by the authority of the magistrate. In a large *assembly* you may sometimes observe a singular *assemblage* of characters, countenances, and figures; when people come together in great numbers on any occasion, they will often form themselves into distinct *groups;*

A lifeless *group* the blasted cattle lie.
THOMSON

The *collection* of scarce books and curious editions has become a passion, which is justly ridiculed under the title of bibliomania; 'There is a manuscript at Oxford containing the lives of a hundred and thirty-five of the finest Persian poets, most of whom left very ample *collections* of their poems behind them.'—SIR W. JONES

ASSEMBLY, COMPANY, MEETING, CONGREGATION, PARLIAMENT, DIET, CONGRESS, CONVENTION, SYNOD, CONVOCATION, COUNCIL.

An *assembly* (*v. To assemble, muster*) is simply the *assembling* together of any number of persons, or the persons so *assembled:* this idea is common to all the rest of these terms, which differ in the object, mode, and other collateral circumstances of the action; *company*, a body linked together (*v. To accompany*), is an *assembly* for purposes of amusement; *meeting*, a body met together, is an *assembly* for general purposes of business; *congregation*, a body flocked or gathered together, from the Latin *grex* a flock, is an *assembly* brought together from congeniality of sentiment, and community of purpose; *parliament*, in French *parlement*, from *parler* to speak, signifies an *assembly* for speaking or debating on important matters; *diet*, from the Greek διαιτάω to govern, is an *assembly* for governing or regulating affairs of state; *congress*, from the Latin *congredior* to march in a body, is an *assembly* coming together in a formal manner from distant parts for the special purposes; *convention*, from the Latin *convenio* to come together, is an *assembly* coming together in an unformal and promiscuous manner from a neighbouring quarter; *synod*, in Greek σύνοδος, compounded of σὺν and ὁδὸς, signifies literally going the same road, and has been employed to signify an *assembly* for consultation on matters of religion; *convocation* is an *assembly convoked* for an especial purpose; *council* is an *assembly* for consultation either on civil or ecclesiastical affairs.

An *assembly* is, in its restricted sense, publick, and under certain regulations; 'Lucan was so exasperated with the repulse, that he muttered something to himself, and was heard to say, "that since he could not have a seat among them himself, he would bring in one who alone had more merit than their whole *assembly;*" upon which he went to the door and brought in Cato of Utica.'—ADDISON. A *company* is private and confined to friends and acquaintances; 'As I am insignificant to the *company* in publick places, and as it is visible I do not come thither as most do to show myself, I gratify the vanity of all who pretend to make an appearance.'—STEELE. A *meeting* is either publick or private: a *congregation* is always publick *Meetings* are held by all who have any common business to arrange or pleasure to enjoy; 'It is very natural for a man who is not turned for mirthful *meetings* of men, or *assemblies* of the fair sex, to delight in that sort of conversation which we meet with in coffee-houses.'—STEELE. A *congregation* in its limited sense consists of those who follow the same form of doctrine and discipline; 'As all innocent means are to be used for the propagation of truth, I would not deter those who are employed in preaching to common *congregations* from any practice which they may find persuasive.'—JOHNSON. But the term may be extended to bodies either of men or brutes *congregated* for some common purpose;

> Their tribes adjusted, clean'd their vig'rous wings,
> And many a circle, many a short essay,
> Wheel'd round and round: in *congregation* full
> The figur'd flight ascends.—THOMSON.

All these different kinds of *assemblies* are formed by individuals in their private capacity; the other terms designate *assemblies* that come together for national purposes, with the exception of the word *convention*, which may be either domestick or political.

A *parliament* and *diet* are popular *assemblies* under a monarchical form of government; *congress* and *convention* are *assemblies* under a republican government: of the first description are the *parliaments* of England and France, the *diets* of Germany and Poland, which consisted of subjects *assembled* by the monarch, to deliberate on the affairs of the nation; 'The word *parliament* was first applied to general *assemblies* of the states under Louis VII. in France, about the middle of the twelfth century.'—BLACKSTONE. 'What further provoked their indignation was that instead of twenty-five pistoles formerly allowed to each member for their charge in coming to the *diet*, he had presented them with six only.'—STEELE. Of the latter description are the *congress* of the United Provinces of Holland, and that of the United States of America, and the late national *convention* of France: but there is this difference observable between a *congress* and a *convention*, that the former consists of deputies or delegates from higher authorities, that is, from independent governments already established; but a *convention* is a self-constituted *assembly*, which has no power but what it assumes to itself; 'Prior had not, however, much reason to complain; for he came to London, and obtained such notice, that (in 1691) he was sent to the *congress* at the Hague, as secretary to the embassy.'—JOHNSON. 'The office of conservators of the peace was newly erected in Scotland; and these, instigated by the clergy, were resolved, since they could not obtain the king's consent, to summon in his name, but by their own authority, a *convention* of states.'—HUME.

A *synod* and *convocation* are in religious matters what a *diet* and *convention* are in civil matters: the former exist only under an episcopal form of government; the latter may exist under any form of church discipline, even where the authority lies in the whole body of the ministry; 'A *synod* of the celestials was convened, in which it was resolved that patronage should descend to the assistance of the sciences.'—JOHNSON. 'The *convocation* is the miniature of a *parliament*, wherein the archbishop presides with regal state.'—BLACKSTONE.

A *council* is more important than all other species of *assembly;* it consists of persons invested with the highest authority, who, in their consultations, do not so much transact ordinary concerns, as arrange the forms and fashions of things. Religious *councils* used to determine matters of faith and discipline; political *councils* frame laws and determine the fate of empires;

> Inspir'd by Juno, Thetis' godlike son
> Conven'd to *council* all the Grecian train.
> POPE.

GUEST, VISITER, OR VISITANT.

Guest, from the northern languages, signifies one who is entertained; *visiter* is the one who pays the visit. The *guest* is to the *visiter* as a species to the genus: every *guest* is a *visiter*, but every *visiter* is not a *guest*. The *visiter* simply comes to see the person, and enjoy social intercourse; but the *guest* also partakes of hospitality. We are *visiters* at the tea-table, at the card-table, and round the fire: we are *guests* at the festive board;

> Some great behest from heav'n
> To us perhaps he brings, and will vouchsafe
> This day to be our *guest*.—MILTON.

> No palace with a lofty gate he wants,
> T' admit the tides of early *visitants*.—DRYDEN.

COLLEAGUE, PARTNER, COADJUTOR, ASSISTANT.

Colleague, in French *collègue*, Latin *collega*, compounded of *col* or *con* and *legatus* sent, signifies sent or employed upon the same business; *partner*, from the word *part*, signifies one having a part or share.

Colleague is more noble than *partner:* men in the highest offices are *colleagues;* tradesmen, mechanicks, and subordinate persons are *partners:* every Roman consul had a *colleague;* every workman has commonly a *partner*.

Colleague is used only with regard to community of office; *partner* is most generally used with regard to community of interest: whenever two persons are employed to act together on the same business they stand in the relation of *colleagues* to each other; whenever two persons unite their endeavours either in trade or in games they are denominated *partners:* ministers, judges, commissioners, and plenipotentiaries are *colleagues;*

> But from this day's decision, from the choice
> Of his first *colleagues*, shall succeeding times
> Of Edward judge, and on his frame pronounce.
> WEST.

Bankers, merchants, chess-players, card-players, and the like, have *partners;*

> And lo! sad *partner* of the general care,
> Weary and faint I drive my [illegible] ar.
> WARTON

Coadjutor, compounded of *co* or *con* and *adjutor* a helper, signifying a fellow-labourer, is more noble than *assistant*, which signifies properly one that *assists* or takes a part; the latter being mostly in a subordinate station, but the former is an equal.

The *assistant* performs menial offices in the minor concerns of life, and a subordinate part at all times; the *coadjutor* labours conjointly in some concern of common interest and great importance. An *assistant* is engaged for a compensation; a *coadjutor* is a voluntary fellow-labourer. In every publick concern where the purposes of charity or religion are to be promoted, *coadjutors* often effect more than the original promoters; 'Advices from Vienna import that the Archbishop of Saltzburg is dead, who is succeeded by Count Harrach, formerly bishop of Vienna, and for these last three years *coadjutor* to the said Archbishop.'—STEELE. In the medical and scholastick professions *assistants* are indispensable to relieve the pressure of business; 'As for you, gentlemen and ladies, my *assistants* and grand juries, I have made choice of you on my right-hand, because I know you to be very jealous of your honour; and you on my left, because I know you are very much concerned for the reputation of others.'—ADDISON. *Coadjutors* ought to be zealous and unanimous; *assistants* ought to be assiduous and faithful.

ALLY, CONFEDERATE, ACCOMPLICE.

Although the terms *ally* and *confederate* are derived from the words *alliance* and *confederacy* (*v. Alliance*), they are used only in part of their acceptations.

An *ally* is one who forms an *alliance* in the political sense; a *confederate* is one who forms *confederacies* in general, but more particularly when such *confederacies* are unauthorized.

The Portuguese and English are *allies;* 'We could hinder the accession of Holland to France, either as subjects with great immunities for the encouragement of trade, or as an inferiour and dependent *ally* under their protection.'—TEMPLE. William Tell had some few particular friends who were his *confederates;* 'Having learned by experience that they must expect a vigorous resistance from this warlike prince, they entered into an *alliance* with the Britons of Cornwall, and landing two years after in that country made an inroad with their *confederates* into the county of Devon.'—HUME. This latter term is however used with more propriety in its worst sense, for an associate in a rebellious faction, as in speaking of Cromwell and his *confederates* who were concerned in the death of the king.

Confederate and *accomplice* both imply a partner in some proceeding, but they differ as to the nature of the proceeding: in the former case it may be lawful or unlawful; in the latter unlawful only. In this latter sense a *confederate* is a partner in a plot or secret association: an *accomplice* is a partner in some active violation of the laws. Guy Fawkes retained his resolution till the last extremity, not to reveal the names of his *confederates:* it is the common refuge of all robbers and desperate characters to betray their *accomplices* in order to screen themselves from punishment;

Now march the bold *confed'rates* through the plain,
Well hors'd, well clad, a rich and shining train.
DRYDEN.

It is not improbable that the Lady Mason (the grandmother of Savage) might persuade or compel his mother to desist, or perhaps she could not easily find *accomplices* wicked enough to concur in so cruel an action, as that of banishing him to the American plantations.'—JOHNSON.

ALLIANCE, LEAGUE, CONFEDERACY.

Alliance, in French *alliance*, from the Latin *alligo* to knit or tie together, signifies the moral state of being tied; *league*, in French *ligue*, comes from the same verb *ligo* to bind; *confederacy* or confederation, in Latin *confederatio*, from *con* and *fœdus* an agreement, or *fides* faith, signifies a joining together under a certain pledge.

* Relationship, friendship, the advantage of a good understanding, the prospect of aid in case of necessity, are the ordinary motives for forming *alliances*. A *league* is a union of plan, and a junction of force, for the purpose of effectuating some common enterprise, or obtaining some common object. A *confederacy* is a union of interest and support on particular occasions, for the purpose of obtaining a redress of supposed wrong, or of defending right against usurpation and oppression.

Treaties of *alliance* are formed between sovereigns; it is a union of friendship and convenience concluded upon precise terms, and maintained by honour or good faith. *Leagues* are mostly formed between parties or small communities; as they are occasioned by circumstances of an imperative nature, they are in this manner rendered binding on each party. *Confederacies* are formed between individuals or communities; they continue while the impelling cause that set them in motion remains; and every individual is bound more by a common feeling of safety, than by any express contract.

History mentions frequent *alliances* which have been formed between the courts of England and Portugal;

Who but a fool would wars with Juno choose,
And such *alliances* and such gifts refuse?
DRYDEN.

The cantons of Switzerland were bound to each other by a famous *league*, which was denominated the Helvetic *league*, and which took its rise in a *confederacy* formed against the Austrian government by William Tell and his companions;

Rather in *leagues* of endless peace unite,
And celebrate the hymenial rite.—ADDISON.

The history of mankind informs us that a single power is very seldom broken by a *confederacy*.'—JOHNSON.

Confederacy is always taken in a civil or political sense: *alliance* and *league* are sometimes employed in a moral sense; the former being applied to marriage, the latter to plots or factions. *Alliance* is taken only in a good acceptation; *league* and *confederacy* frequently in relation to that which is bad. *Alliances* are formed for the mutual advantage of the parties concerned; 'Though domestick misery must follow an *alliance* with a gamester, matches of this sort are made every day.'—CUMBERLAND. *Leagues* may have plunder for their object, and *confederacies* may be treasonable;

Tiger with tiger, bear with bear, you'll find
In *leagues* offensive and defensive join'd.
TATE.

When Babel was confounded, and the great
Confederacy of projectors wild and vain
Was split into diversity of tongues,
Then, as a shepherd separates his flock,
These to the upland, to the valley those,
God drave asunder.—COWPER.

* Vide Girard and Roubaud: "Alliance, ligue, confederation."

ALLIANCE, AFFINITY.

Alliance, v. *Alliance, league; affinity*, in Latin *affinitas*, from *af* or *ad* and *finis* a border, signifies a contiguity of borders.

Alliance is artificial: *affinity* is natural; an *alliance* is formed either by persons or by circumstances; an *affinity* exists of itself: an *alliance* subsists between persons only in the proper sense, and between things figuratively; 'Religion (in England) has maintained a proper *alliance* with the state.'—BLAIR. An *affinity* exists between things as well as persons; 'It cannot be doubted but that signs were invented originally to express the several occupations of their owners; and to bear some *affinity*, in their external designations, with the wares to be disposed of.'—BATHURST. The *alliance* between families is matrimonial;

O horrour! horrour! after this *alliance*
Let tigers match with hinds, and wolves with sheep,
And every creature couple with its foe.—DRYDEN.

The *affinity* arises from consanguinity

BAND, COMPANY, CREW, GANG.

Band, in French *bande*, in German, &c. *band*, from *binden* to bind, signifies the thing bound; *company*, v. *To accompany; crew*, from the French *cru*, participle of *croitre*, and the Latin *cresco* to grow or gather, signifies the thing grown or formed into a mass; *gang*, in Saxon, German, &c. *gang* a walk, from *gehen* to go, signifies a body going the same way.

All these terms denote a small association for a particular object: a *band* is an association where men are bound together by some strong obligation, whether taken in a good or bad sense, as a *band* of soldiers, a *band* of robbers;

Behold a ghastly *band*
Each a torch in his hand!
These are Grecian ghosts that in battle were slain,
And unbury'd remain,
Inglorious in the plain.—DRYDEN.

A *company* marks an association for convenience without any particular obligation, as a *company* of travellers, a *company* of strolling players; 'Chaucer supposes in his prologue to his tales that a *company* of pilgrims going to Canterbury assemble at an Inn in Southwark, and agree that for their common amusement on the road each of them shall tell at least one tale in going to Canterbury, and another in coming back from thence.'—TYRWHIT.

Crew marks an association collected together by some external power, or by coincidence of plan and motive: in the former case it is used for a ship's *crew;* in the latter and bad sense of the word it is employed for any number of evil-minded persons met together from different quarters, and co-operating for some bad purpose;

The clowns, a boist'rous, rude, ungovern'd *crew*,
With furious haste to the loud summons flew.
DRYDEN.

Gang is mostly used in a bad sense for an association of thieves, murderers, and depredators in general; for such an association is rather a casual meeting from the similarity of pursuits, than an organized body under any leader: it is more in common use than *band:* the robbers in Germany used to form themselves into *bands* that set the government of the country at defiance; housebreakers and pickpockets commonly associate now in *gangs;*

Others again who form a *gang*,
Yet take due measures not to hang;
In magazines their forces join,
By legal methods to purloin.—MALLET.

TROOP, COMPANY.

In a military sense a *troop* is among the horse what a *company* is among the foot; but this is only a partial acceptation of the terms. *Troop*, in French *troupe*

Spanish *tropa*, Latin *turba*, signifies an indiscriminate multitude; *company* (*v. To accompany*) is any number joined together, and bearing each other *company*: hence we speak of a *troop* of hunters, a *company* of players; a *troop* of horsemen, a *company* of travellers.

ACCOMPANIMENT, COMPANION, CONCOMITANT.

Accompaniment is properly a collective term to express what goes in company, and is applied only to things; *companion*, which also signifies what is in the company, is applied either to persons or to things; *concomitant*, from the intensive syllable *con* and *comes* a companion, implies what is attached to an object, or goes in its train, and is applied only to things.

When said in relation to things, *accompaniment* implies a necessary connexion; *companion* an incidental connexion: the former is as a part to a whole, the latter is as one whole to another: the *accompaniment* belongs to the thing accompanied, inasmuch as it serves to render it more or less complete; the *companion* belongs to the thing accompanied, inasmuch as they correspond: in this manner singing is an *accompaniment* in instrumental musick; subordinate ceremonies are the *accompaniments* in any solemn service; 'We may well believe that the ancient heathen bards, who were chiefly Asiatick Greeks, performed religious rites and ceremonies in metre with *accompaniments* of musick, to which they were devoted in the extreme.'—CUMBERLAND. A picture may be the *companion* of another picture from their fitness to stand together; 'Alas, my soul! thou pleasing *companion* of this body, thou fleeting thing that art now deserting it, whither art thou flying?'—STEELE.

The *concomitant* is as much of an appendage as the *accompaniment*, but it is applied only to moral objects: th[illegible]orality is a *concomitant* to religion; 'As the b[illegible] of the body *accompanies* the health of it, so certainly is decency *concomitant* to virtue.'—HUGHES.

TO ACCOMPANY, ATTEND, ESCORT, WAIT ON.

Accompany, in French *accompagner*, is compounded of *ac* or *ad* and *compagner*, in Latin *compagino* to put or join together, signifying to give one's company and presence to any object, to join one's self to its company; *attend*, in French *attendre*, compounded of *at* or *ad* and *tendo* to tend or incline towards, signifies to direct one's notice or care towards any object; *escort*, in French *escorter*, from the Latin *cohors* a cohort or band of soldiers that attended a magistrate on his going into a province, signifies to accompany by way of safeguard.

We *accompany** those with whom we wish to go; we *attend* those whom we wish to serve; we *escort* those whom we are called upon to protect or guard. We *accompany* our equals, we *attend* our superiours, and *escort* superiours or inferiours. The desire of pleasing or being pleased actuates in the first case; the desire of serving or being served, in the second case; he fear of danger or the desire of security, in the last lace.

One is said to have a numerous *company*, a crowd of *attendants*, and a strong *escort*; but otherwise one erson only may *accompany* or *attend*, though several are wanting for an *escort*. Friends *accompany* each other in their excursions; 'This account in some measure excited our curiosity, and at the entreaty of the ladies I was prevailed upon to *accompany* them to he playhouse, which was no other than a barn.'—GOLDSMITH. Princes are *attended* with a considerable retinue whenever they appear in publick, and with a strong *escort* when they travel through unfrequented and dangerous roads, 'When the Marquis of Wharton was appointed Lord-Lieutenant of Ireland, Addison attended him as his secretary.'—JOHNSON. Creüsa the wife of Æneas *accompanied* her husband on his eaving Troy; Socrates was *attended* by a number of his illustrious pupils, whom he instructed by his example and his doctrines; St. Paul was *escorted* as a prisoner by a band of three hundred men; 'He very prudently called up four or five of the hostlers that belonged to the yard, and engaged them to enlist under his command as an *escort* to the coach.'—HAWKESWORTH.

Accompany and *attend* may likewise be said of persons as well as things. In this case the former is applied to what goes with an object so as to form a part of it; the latter to that which follows an object as a dependant upon it; 'The old English plainness and sincerity, that generous integrity of nature and honesty of disposition, which always argues true greatness of mind, and is usually *accompanied* with undaunted courage and resolution, is in a great measure lost among us.'—TILLOTSON. 'Humility lodged in a worthy mind is always *attended* with a certain homage, which no haughty soul, with all the arts imaginable, can purchase.'—HUGHES. Pride is often *accompanied* with meanness, and *attended* with much inconvenience to the possessor; 'The practice of religion will not only be *attended* with that pleasure which naturally *accompanies* those actions to which we are habituated, but with those supernumerary joys that rise from the consciousness of such a pleasure.'—ADDISON.

Attend (*v. To attend to*) is here employed in the improper sense for the devotion of the person to an object. To *wait on* is the same as to wait for or expect the wishes of another.

Attendance is an act of obligation; *waiting on* that of choice. A physician *attends* his patient; a member *attends* in parliament; one gentleman *waits on* another. We *attend* a person at the time and place appointed; we *wait on* those with whom we wish to speak. Those who dance *attendance* on the great must expect every mortification; it is wiser, therefore, only to *wait on* those by whom we can be received upon terms of equality.

Attend and *wait on* are likewise used for being about the person of any one; to *attend* is to bear company or be in readiness to serve; to *wait on* is actually to perform some service. A nurse *attends* a patient in order to afford him assistance as occasion requires; the servant *waits on* him to perform the menial duties. *Attendants* about the great are always near the person; but men and women in *waiting* are always at call. People of rank and fashion have a crowd of *attendants*,

> At length, her lord descends upon the plain
> In pomp, *attended* with a num'rous train.—DRYDEN.

Those of the middle classes have only those who *wait on* them; 'One of Pope's constant demands was of coffee in the night; and to the woman that *waited on* him in his chamber he was very burdensome; but he was careful to recompense her want of sleep.'—JOHNSON.

PROCESSION, TRAIN, RETINUE.

Procession, from the verb *proceed*, signifies the act of going forward or before, that is, in the present instance, of going before others, or one before another; *train* in all probability comes from the Latin *traho* to draw, signifying the thing drawn after another, and in the present instance the persons who are led after, or follow, any object; *retinue*, from the verb to *retain*, signifies those who are retained as attendants.

All these terms are said of any number of persons who follow in a certain order; but this, which is the leading idea in the word *procession*, is but collateral in the terms *train* and *retinue*: on the other hand, the *procession* may consist of persons of all ranks and stations; but the *train* and *retinue* apply only to such as follow some person or thing in a subordinate capacity: the former in regard to such as make up the concluding part of some *procession*; the latter only in regard to the servants or attendants on the great. At funerals there is frequently a long *train* of coaches belonging to the friends of the deceased, which close the *procession*; princes and nobles never go out on state or publick occasions, without a numerous *retinue*.

The beauty of every *procession* consists in the order with which every one keeps his place, and the regularity with which the whole goes forward;

> And now the priests, Potitius at their head,
> In skins of beasts involv'd, the long *procession* led.
> DRYDEN.

The length of the *train* is what renders it most worthy of notice;

* Vide Girard: "Accompagner, escorter."

My *train* are men of choice and rarest parts,
That in the most exact regard support
The worships of their names.—SHAKSPEARE.

Train is also applied to other objects besides persons;

The moon, and all the starry *train*,
Hung the vast vault of heav'n.—GAY.

The number of the *retinue* in Eastern nations is one criterion by which the wealth of the individual is estimated;

Him and his sleeping slaves, he slew; then spies
Where Remus with his rich *retinue* lies.—DRYDEN.

MULTITUDE, CROWD, THRONG, SWARM.

The idea of many is common to all these terms, and peculiar to that of *multitude*, from the Latin *multus; crowd*, from the verb to *crowd*, signifies the many that crowd together; *throng*, from the German *drängen* to press, signifies the many that press together; and *swarm*, from the German *schwärmen* to fly about, signifies running together in numbers.

These terms vary, either in regard to the object, or the circumstance: *multitude* is applicable to any object; *crowd, throng*, and *swarm* are in the proper sense applicable only to animate objects: the first two in regard to persons; the latter to animals in general, but particularly brutes. A *multitude* may be either in a stagnant or a moving state; all the rest denote a *multitude* in a moving state;

A *multitude* is incapable of framing orders.
TEMPLE.

A *crowd* is always pressing, generally eager and tumultuous;

The *crowd* shall Cæsar's Indian war behold.
DRYDEN.

A *throng* may be busy and active, but not always pressing or incommodious. This term is best adapted to poetry to express a *multitude* of agreeable objects;

I shone amid the heavenly *throng*.—MASON.

It is always inconvenient, sometimes dangerous, to go into a *crowd;* it is amusing to see the *throng* that is perpetually passing in the streets of the city: the *swarm* is more active than either of the two others; it is commonly applied to bees which fly together in numbers, but sometimes to human beings, to denote their very great numbers when scattered about; thus the children of the poor in low neighbourhoods *swarm* in the streets;

Numberless nations, stretching far and wide,
Shall (I foresee it) soon with Gothick *swarms* come forth,
From ignorance's universal North.—SWIFT.

MEETING, INTERVIEW.

Meeting, from to meet, is the act of meeting or coming into company; *interview* compounded of *inter* between, and *view* to view, is a personal view of each other. The *meeting* is an ordinary concern, and its purpose familiar; *meetings* are daily taking place between friends;

I have not joy'd an hour since you departed,
For publick miseries and private fears;
But this bless'd *meeting* has o'erpaid them all.
DRYDEN.

The interview is extraordinary and formal; its object is commonly business; an *interview* sometimes takes place between princes or commanders of armies;

His fears were, that the *interview* between
England and France might through their amities
Breed him some prejudice.—SHAKSPEARE.

TO FREQUENT, RESORT TO, HAUNT.

Frequent comes from *frequent*, in Latin *frequens* crowded, signifying to come in numbers, or come often to the same place; *resort*, in French *resortir*, compounded of *re* and *sortir*, signifies to go backward and forward; *haunt* comes from the French *hanter*, which is of uncertain original.

Frequent is more commonly used for an individual who does often to a place *resort* and *haunt* for a number of individuals. A man is said to *frequent* a publick place; but several persons may *resort to* a private place: men who are not fond of home *frequent* taverns; in the first ages of Christianity, while persecution raged, the disciples used to *resort to* private places for purposes of worship.

Frequent and *resort* are indifferent actions; but *haunt* is always used in a bad sense. A man may *frequent* a theatre, a club, or any other social meeting, innocent or otherwise; 'For my own part I have ever regarded our inns of court as nurseries of statesmen and lawgivers, which makes me often *frequent* that part of the town.'—BUDGELL. People from different quarters may *resort to* a fair, a church, or any other place where they wish to meet for a common purpose;

Home is the *resort*
Of love, of joy, of peace, and plenty, where,
Supporting and supported, polish'd friends
And dear relations mingle into bliss.—THOMSON.

Those who *haunt* any place go to it in privacy for some bad or selfish purpose;

But harden'd by affronts, and still the same,
Lost to all sense of honour and of fame,
Thou yet canst love to *haunt* the great man's board,
And think no supper good but with a lord.—LEWIS.

Our Saviour *frequented* the synagogues: the followers of the prophet Mahomet *resort to* his tomb at Mecca; thieves *haunt* the darkest and most retired parts of the city in order to concert their measures for obtaining plunder.

PEOPLE, NATION.

People, in Latin *populus*, comes from the Greek λαὸς people, πληθὺς a multitude, and πολὺς many. Hence the simple idea of numbers is expressed by the word *people;* but the term *nation*, from *natus*, marks the connexion of numbers by birth: *people* is, therefore, the generick, and *nation* the specifick term. A *nation* is a *people* connected by birth; there cannot, therefore, strictly speaking, be a *nation* without a *people;* but there may be a *people* where there is not a *nation*. *The Jews are distinguished as a *people* or a *nation*, according to the different aspects under which they are viewed: when considered as an assemblage, under the special direction of the Almighty, they are termed the *people* of God; but when considered in regard to their common origin, they are denominated the Jewish *nation*. The Americans, when spoken of in relation to Britain, are a distinct *people*, because they have each a distinct government; but they are not a distinct *nation*, because they have a common descent. On this ground the Romans are not called the Roman *nation*, because their origin was so various, but the Roman *people*, that is, an assemblage living under one form of government.

In a still closer application *people* is taken for a part of the state, namely, that part of a state which consists of a multitude, in distinction from its government; whence arises a distinction in the use of the terms; for we may speak of the British *people*, the French or the Dutch *people*, when we wish merely to talk of the mass, but we speak of the British *nation*, the French *nation*, and the Dutch *nation*, when publick measures are in question, which emanate from the government, or the whole *people*. The English *people* have ever been remarkable for their attachment to liberty; 'It is too flagrant a demonstration how much vice is the darling of any *people*, when many among them are preferred for those practices for which in other places they can scarce be pardoned.'—SOUTH. The abolition of the slave trade is one of the most glorious acts of publick justice, which was ever performed by the British *nation;* 'When we read the history of *nations*, what do we read but the crimes and follies of men?'—BLAIR. The impetuosity and volatility of the French *people* render them peculiarly unfit to legislate for themselves; the military exploits of the French *nation* have rendered them a highly distinguished *people* in the annals of history. Upon the same ground republican states are distinguished by the name of *people;* but kingdoms are commonly spoken of in history as *nations*. Hence we say, the Spartan *people*,

* Vide Roubaud: "Nation, people."

the Athenian *people*, the *people* of Genoa, the *people* of Venice; but the *nations* of Europe, the African *nations*, the English, French, German, and Italian *nations*.

PEOPLE, POPULACE, MOB, MOBILITY.

People and *populace* are evidently changes of the same word to express a number. The signification of these terms is that of a number gathered together. *People* is said of any body *supposed* to be assembled, as well as really assembled;

> The *people* like a headlong torrent go,
> And every dam they break or overflow.
> SHAKSPEARE.

Populace is said of a body only, when actually assembled;

> The pliant *populace*,
> Those dupes of novelty, will bend before us.
> MALLET.

The voice of the *people* cannot always be disregarded; the *populace* of England are fond of dragging their favourites in carriages.

Mob and *mobility* are from the Latin *mobilis*, signifying moveableness, which is the characteristick of the multitude; hence Virgil's *mobile vulgus*. These terms, therefore, designate not only what is low, but tumultuous. A *mob* is at all times an object of terrour: the *mobility*, whether high or low, are a fluttering order that mostly run from bad to worse; 'By the senseless and insignificant clink of misapplied words, some restless demagogues had inflamed the mind of the sottish *mobile* to a strange, unaccountable abhorrence of the best of men.'—SOUTH.

PEOPLE, PERSONS, FOLKS.

The term *people* has already been considered in two acceptations (*v. People, nation; People, populace*), under the general idea of an assembly; but in the present case it is employed to express a small number of individuals: the word *people*, however, is always considered as one undivided body, and the word *person* may be distinctly used either in the singular or plural; as we cannot say one, two, three, or four *people*; but we may say one, two, three, or four *persons*: yet on the other hand, we may indifferently say, such *people* or *persons*; many *people* or *persons*; some *people* or *persons*, and the like.

With regard to the use of these terms, which is altogether colloquial, *people* is employed in general propositions; and *persons* in those which are specifick or referring directly to some particular individuals: *people* are generally of that opinion; some *people* think so; some *people* attended;

> Performance is even the duller for
> His act; and, but in the plainer and simple
> Kind of the *people*, the deed is quite out of
> Use.—SHAKSPEARE.

There were but few *persons* present at the entertainment; the whole company consisted of six *persons*; 'You may observe many honest, inoffensive *persons* strangely run down by an ugly word.'—SOUTH.

As the term *people* is employed to designate a promiscuous multitude, it has acquired a certain meanness of acceptation which makes it less suitable than the word *persons*, when *people* of respectability are referred to: were I to say, of any individuals, I do not know who those *people* are, it would not be so respectful as to say, I do not know who those *persons* are: in like manner, one says, from *people* of that stamp better is not to be expected; *persons* of their appearance do not frequent such places.

Folks, through the medium of the northern languages, comes from the Latin *vulgus*, the common *people*: it is not unusual to say good *people*, or good *folks*; and in speaking jocularly to one's friends, the latter term is likewise admissible: but in the serious style it is never employed except in a disrespectful manner: such *folks* (speaking of gamesters) are often put to sorry shifts; 'I paid some compliments to great *folks*, who like to be complimented.'—HERRING.

GENTILE, HEATHEN, PAGAN.

*The Jews comprehended all strangers under the name of גוים nations or *gentiles*: among the Greeks and Romans they were designated by the name of barbarians. By the name *Gentile* was understood especially those who were not of the Jewish religion, including, in the end, even the Christians; for, as Fleury remarks, there were some among these uncircumcised *Gentiles*, who worshipped the true God, and were permitted to dwell in the holy land, provided they observed the law of nature and abstinence; 'There might be several among the *Gentiles* in the same condition that Cornelius was before he became a Christian.'—TILLOTSON.

Some learned men pretend that the *Gentiles* were so named from their having only a natural law, and such as they imposed on themselves, in opposition to the Jews and Christians, who have a positive revealed law to which they are obliged to submit.

Frisch and others derive the word *heathen* from the Greek ἔθνος, a nation, which derivation is corroborated by the translation in the Anglo-saxon law of the word *haethne* by the Greek ἔθνος. Adelung, however, thinks it to be more probably derived from the word *heide* a field, for the same reason as *pagan* is derived from *pagus* a village, because when Constantine banished idolaters from the towns they repaired to the villages, and secretly adhered to their religious worship, whence they were termed by the Christians of the fourth century *Pagani*, which, as he supposes, was translated literally into the German *heidener* a villager or worshipper in the field. Be this as it may, it is evident that the word *Heathen* is in our language more applicable than *Pagan*, to the Greeks, the Romans, and the cultivated nations who practised idolatry; and, on the other hand, *Pagan* is more properly employed for any rude and uncivilized people who worship false gods.

The *Gentile* does not expressly believe in a Divine Revelation; but he either admits of the truth in part, or is ready to receive it: the *Heathen* adopts a positively false system that is opposed to the true faith: the *Pagan* is the species of *Heathen* who obstinately persists in a worship which is merely the fruit of his own imagination. The *Heathens* or *Pagans* are *Gentiles*; but the *Gentiles* are not all either *Heathens* or *Pagans*. Confucius and Socrates, who rejected the plurality of gods, and the followers of Mahomet, who adore the true God, are, properly speaking, *Gentiles*. The worshippers of Jupiter, Juno, Minerva, and all the deities of the ancients, are termed *Heathens*. The worshippers of Fo, Brama, Xaca, and all the deities of savage nations, are termed *Pagans*.

The *Gentiles* were called to the true faith, and obeyed the call: many of the illustrious *Heathens* would have doubtless done the same, had they enjoyed the same privilege; 'Not that I believe that all the virtues of the *Heathens* were counterfeit, and destitute of an inward principle of goodness. God forbid we should pass so hard a judgement upon those excellent men, Socrates, and Epictetus, and Antoninus.'—TILLOTSON.

There are many *Pagans* to this day who reject this advantage, to pursue their own blind imaginations:

> And nations laid in blood; dread sacrifice
> To Christian pride! which had with horror shock
> The darkest *Pagans*, offered to their gods.—YOUNG

FAMILY, HOUSE, LINEAGE, RACE.

Divisions of men, according to some rule of relationship or connexion, is the common idea in these terms.

Family, from the Latin *familia* a family, and *famulus* a servant, in Greek ὁμιλία an assembly, and the Hebrew עמל to labour, is the most general term, being applicable to those who are bound together upon the principle of dependence; *house* figuratively denotes those who live in the same *house*, and is commonly extended in its signification to all that passes under the same roof: hence we rather say that a woman manages her *family*; that a man rules his *house*.

The *family* is considered as to its relationships, the number, union, condition, and quality of its mem-

* Vide Roubaud: "Gentils, païens"

bers: the *house* is considered more as to what is transacted within its walls. We speak of a numerous *family*, a united or affectionate *family*, a mercantile *house;* the *house* (meaning the members of the *house* of parliament). If a man cannot find happiness in the bosom of his *family*, he will seek for it in vain elsewhere; 'To live in a *family* where there is but one heart and as many good strong heads as persons, and to have a place in that enlarged single heart, is such a state of happiness as I cannot hear of without feeling the utmost pleasure.'—FIELDING. The credit of a *house* is to be kept up only by prompt payments; or, in a general sense of the term, the business of the *house* is performed by the domesticks; 'They two together rule the *house*. The *house* I call here the man, the woman, their children, their servants.'—SMITH.

In an extended application of these words they are made to designate the quality of the individual, in which case *family* bears the same familiar and indiscriminate sense as before: *house* is employed as a term of grandeur.

* When we consider the *family* in its domestick relations; in its habits, manners, connexions, and circumstances; we speak of a genteel *family*, a respectable *family*, the royal *family;* 'An empty man of a great *family* is a creature that is scarce conversible.'—ADDISON. When we consider the *family* with regard to its political and civil distinctions, its titles, and its power, then we denominate it a *house*, as an illustrious *house;* the *house* of Bourbon, of Brunswick, or of Hanover; the imperial *house* of Austria. Any subject may belong to an ancient or noble *family*. Princes are said to be descended from ancient *houses;* 'The princes of the *house* of Tudor, partly by the vigour of their administration, partly by the concurrence of favourable circumstances, had been able to establish a more regular system of government.'—HUME. A man is said to be of a *family* or of no *family:* we may say likewise that he is of a certain *house;* but to say that he is of no *house* would be superfluous.† In republicks there are *families* but not *houses*, because there is no nobility; in China likewise, where the private virtues only distinguish the individual or his *family*, the term *house* is altogether inapplicable.

Family includes in it every circumstance of connexion and relationship; *lineage* respects only consanguinity: *family* is employed mostly for those who are coeval; *lineage* is generally used for those who have gone before. When the Athenian general Iphicrates, son of a shoemaker, was reproached by Hermodius with his birth, he said, I had rather be the first than the last of my *family*. David was of the *lineage* of Abraham, and our Saviour was of the *lineage* of David;

> We want not cities, nor Sicilian coasts,
> Where king Acestes Trojan *lineage* boasts.
> DRYDEN.

Race, from the Latin *radix* a root, denotes the origin or that which constitutes their original point of resemblance. A *family* supposes the closest alliance; a *race* supposes no closer connexion than what a common property creates. *Family* is confined to a comparatively small number; 'A nation properly signifies a great number of *families* derived from the same blood, born in the same country, and living under the same government and civil constitutions.'—TEMPLE. *Race* is a term of extensive import, including all mankind, as the human *race;* or particular nations, as the *race* of South Sea islanders; or a particular *family*, as the *race* of the Heraclides: from Hercules sprung a *race* of heroes;

> Nor knows our youth of noblest *race*,
> To mount the manag'd steed or urge the chase;
> More skill'd in the mean arts of vice,
> The whirling troque or law-forbidden dice.
> FRANCIS.

NATAL, NATIVE, INDIGENOUS.

Natal, in Latin *natalis*, from *natus*, signifies belonging to one's birth, or the act of one's being born; but *native*, in Latin *nativus*, likewise from *natus*, signifies having the origin or beginning; *indigenous*, in Latin *indigena*, from *inde* and *genitus*, signifies sprung from a particular place.

* Vide Abbe Girard: "Famille, maison."

† Abbe Roubaud: "Race lineage, famille, maison."

The epithet *natal* is applied only to the circumstance of a man's birth, as his *natal* day; his *natal* hour a *natal* song; a *natal* star;

> Safe in the hand of one disposing pow'r,
> Or in the *natal* or the mortal hour.—POPE.

Native has a more extensive meaning, as it comprehends the idea of one's relationship by origin to an object; as one's *native* country, one's *native* soil, *native* village, or *native* place, *native* language, and the like;

> Nor can the grov'ling mind
> In the dark dungeon of the limbs confin'd,
> Assert the *native* skies or own its heav'nly kind.
> DRYDEN.

Indigenous is the same with regard to plants, as *native* in regard to human beings or animals; but it is sometimes applied to people when taken in a collective sense, 'Negroes were all transported from Africa, and are not *indigenous* or proper natives of America'

NATIVE, NATURAL.

Native (v. *Natal*) is to *natural* as a species to the genus: every thing *native* is according to its strict signification *natural;* but many things are *natural* which are not *native*. Of a person we may say that his worth is *native*, to designate that it is some valuable property which is born with him, not foreign to him, or ingrafted upon his character: but we say of his disposition, that it is *natural*, as opposed to that which is acquired by habit. *Native* is always employed in a good sense, in opposition to what is artful, assumed, and unreal; 'In heaven we shall pass from the darkness of our *native* ignorance into the broad light of everlasting day.'—SOUTH. *Natural* is used in an indifferent sense, as opposed to whatever is the effect of habit or circumstances; 'Scripture ought to be understood according to the familiar, *natural* way of construction.'—SOUTH. When children display them selves with all their *native* simplicity, they are interesting objects of notice: when they display their *natural* turn of mind, it is not always that which tends to raise human nature in our esteem.

RELATION, RELATIVE, KINSMAN, KINDRED.

Relation is here taken to express the person *related*, and is the general term both in sense and application; *relative* is employed only as respects the particular individual to whom one is *related; kinsman* designates the particular kind of *relation;* and *kindred* is a collective term to comprehend all one's *relations*, or those who are akin to one. In abstract propositions we speak of *relations;* a man who is without *relations* feels himself an outcast in society; 'You are not to imagine that I think myself discharged from the duties of gratitude, only because my *relations* do not adjust their looks to my expectation.'—JOHNSON. In designating one's close and intimate connexion with persons we use the term *relative;* our near and dear *relatives* are the first objects of our regard; 'It is an evil undutifulness in friends and *relatives*, to suffer one to perish without reproof.'—TAYLOR. In designating one's *relationship* and connexion with persons, *kinsman* is preferable; when a man has not any children he frequently adopts one of his *kinsmen* as his heir: when the ties of *relationship* are to be specified in the persons of any particular family, they are denominated *kindred;* a man cannot abstract himself from his *kindred* while he retains any spark of human feeling; 'Herod put all to death whom he found in Trechoritis of the families and *kindred* of any of those at Repta'—PRIDEAUX

KIND, SPECIES, SORT.

Kind comes most probably from the Teutonick *kind* a child, signifying related, or of the same family; *species*, in Latin *species*, from *specio* to behold, signifies literally the form or appearance, and in an extended sense that which comes under a particular form; *sort*, in Latin *sors* a lot, signifies that which constitutes a particular lot or parcel.

Kind and *species* are both employed in their proper sense; *sort* has been diverted from its original meaning by colloquial use: *kind* is properly employed for animate objects, particularly for mankind, and improperly for moral objects; *species* is a term used by philosophers, classing things according to their external or internal properties. *Kind*, as a term in vulgar use, has a less definite meaning than *species*, which serves to form the groundwork of science: we discriminate things in a loose or general manner by saying that they are of the animal or vegetable *kind*, of the canine or feline *kind*; but we discriminate them precisely if we say that they are a *species* of the arbutus, of the pomegranate, of the dog, the horse, and the like. By the same rule we may speak of a *species* of madness, a *species* of fever, and the like; 'If the French should succeed in what they propose, and establish a democracy in a country circumstanced like France, they will establish a very bad government, a very bad *species* of tyranny.'—BURKE. Because diseases have been brought under a systematick arrangement: but, on the other hand, we should speak of a *kind* of language, a *kind* of feeling, a *kind* of influence; and in similar cases where a general resemblance is to be expressed; 'An ungrateful person is a *kind* of thoroughfare or common shore for the good things of the world to pass into.'—SOUTH.

Sort may be used for either *kind* or *species*; it does not necessarily imply any affinity, or common property in the objects, but simple assemblage, produced as it were by *sors*, chance: hence we speak of such *sort* of folks or people; such *sort* of practices; different *sorts* of grain; the various *sorts* of merchandises: and in similar cases where things are *sorted* or brought together, rather at the option of the person, than according to the nature of the thing; 'The French made and recorded a *sort* of institute and digest of anarchy, called the rights of man.'—BURKE.

KINDRED, RELATIONSHIP, AFFINITY, CONSANGUINITY.

The idea of a state in which persons are placed with regard to each other is common to all these terms, which differ principally in the nature of this state. *Kindred* signifies that of being of the same *kind* (*v. Kind*): *relationship* signifies that of holding a nearer *relation* than others (*v. To connect*); *affinity* (*v. Alliance*) signifies that of being affined or coming close to each other's boundaries; *consanguinity*, from *sanguis* the blood, signifies that of having the same blood.

The *kindred* is the most general state here expressed: it may embrace all mankind, or refer to particular families or communities; it depends upon possessing the common property of humanity, or of being united by some family tie;

> Like her, of equal *kindred* to the throne,
> You keep her conquests, and extend your own.
> DRYDEN.

The philanthropist claims *kindred* with all who are unfortunate, when it is in his power to relieve them. The term *kindred* is likewise distinguished from the rest, as it expresses not only a state, but the persons collectively who are in that state; 'Though separated from my *kindred* by little more than half a century of miles, I know as little of their concerns as if oceans and continents were between us.'—COWPER.

Relationship is a state less general than *kindred*, but more extended than either *affinity* or *consanguinity*; i applies to particular families only, but it applies to all of the same family, whether remotely or distantly related; 'Herein there is no objection to the succession of a relation of the half-blood, that is, where the *relationship* proceeds not from the same couple of ancestors (which constitutes a kinsman of the whole blood), but from a single ancestor only.'—BLACKSTONE. The term *relationship* is likewise extended to other subjects besides that of families. Men stand in different relations to each other in society; 'The only general private relation now remaining to be discussed is that of guardian and ward.—In examining this species of *relationship* I shall first consider the different kind of guardians.'—BLACKSTONE.

Affinity denotes a close *relationship*, whether of an artificial or a natural kind. there is an *affinity* between the husband and the wife in consequence of the marriage tie; and there is an *affinity* between those who descend from the same parents or relations in a direct line. *Consanguinity* is, strictly speaking, this latter species of descent; and the term is mostly employed in all questions of law respecting descent and inheritance; '*Consanguinity* or *relation* by blood, and *affinity* or *relation* by marriage, are canonical disabilities (to contract a marriage).'—BLACKSTONE.

RACE, GENERATION, BREED.

Race, *v. Family*; *generation*, in Latin *generatio* from *genero*, and the Greek γεννάω, to engender or beget, signifies the thing begotten; *breed* signifies that which is *bred* (*v. To breed.*)

These terms are all employed in regard to a number of animate objects which have the same origin; the former is said only of human beings, the latter only of brutes: the term is employed in regard to the dead as well as the living; *generation* is employed only in regard to the living: hence we speak of the *race* of the Heraclidæ, the *race* of the Bourbons, the *race* of the Stuarts, and the like; but the present *generation*, the whole *generation*, a worthless *generation*, and the like; 'Where *races* are thus numerous and thus combined, none but the chief of a clan is thus addressed by his name.'—JOHNSON.

> Like leaves on trees the *race* of man is found,
> Now green in youth, now with'ring on the ground,
> So *generations* in their course decay,
> So flourish these when those are pass'd away.
> POPE.

Breed is said of those animals which are brought forth, and brought up in the same manner. Hence we denominate some domestick animals as of a good *breed*, where particular care is taken not only as to the animals from which they come, but also of those which are brought forth;

> Nor last forget thy faithful dogs, but feed
> With fatt'ning whey the mastiff's gen'rous *breed*.
> DRYDEN

TO BREED, ENGENDER.

Breed, in Saxon *breetan*, is probably connected with *braten* to roast, being an operation principally performed by fire or heat; *engender*, compounded of *en* and *gender*, from *genitus* participle of *gigno*, signifies to lay or communicate the seeds for production.

These terms are figuratively employed for the act of procreation.

To *breed* is to bring into existence by a slow operation: to *engender* is to be the author or prime cause of existence. So, in the metaphorical sense, frequent quarrels are apt to *breed* hatred and animosity: the levelling and inconsistent conduct of the higher classes in the present age serves to *engender* a spirit of insubordination and assumption in the inferiour order.

Whatever *breeds* acts gradually; whatever *engenders* produces immediately, as cause and effect. Uncleanliness *breeds* diseases of the body; want of occupation *breeds* those of the mind; 'The strong desire of fame *breeds* several vicious habits in the mind.'—ADDISON. Playing at chance games *engenders* a love of money; 'Eve's dream is full of those high conceits *engendering* pride, which, we are told, the Devil endeavoured to instil into her.'—ADDISON.

LAND, COUNTRY.

Land, in German *land*, &c. from *lean* and *line*, signifies an open, even space, and refers strictly to the earth; *country*, in French *contrée*, from *con* and *terra*, signifies *lands* adjoining so as to form one portion. The term *land*, therefore, properly excludes the idea of habitation; the term *country* excludes that of the earth, or the parts of which it is composed. hence we speak of the *land*, as rich or poor, according to what it yields; of a *country*, as rich or poor, according to what its inhabitants possess: so, in like manner, we say, the *land* is ploughed or prepared for receiving the grain; but the *country* is cultivated; the *country* is under a good government; or, a man's *country* is dear to him In an extended application, however, these words may be put for one another: the word *land* may sometimes be put for any portion of *land* that is under a government, as the *land* of liberty; 'You are still in the *land* of the living, and have all the means that can be desired, whereby to prevent your falling into condemnation.'—BEVERIDGE. *Country* may be put for the soil, as a rich *country;* 'We love our *country* as the seat of religion, liberty, and laws.'—BLAIR.

NEIGHBOURHOOD, VICINITY.

Neighbourhood, from *nigh*, signifies the place which is nigh, that is, nigh to one's habitation; *vicinity*, from *vicus* a village, signifies the place which does not exceed in distance the extent of a village.

Neighbourhood, which is of Saxon origin, and first admitted into our language, is employed in reference to the inhabitants, or in regard to inhabited places; that is, it signifies either a community of neighbours, or the place they occupy: but *vicinity*, which in Latin bears the same acceptation as *neighbourhood*, is employed in English for the place in general, that is, near to the person speaking, whether inhabited or otherwise: hence the propriety of saying, a populous *neighbourhood*, a quiet *neighbourhood*, a respectable *neighbourhood*, and a pleasant *neighbourhood*, either as it respects the people or the country; to live in the *vicinity* of a manufactory, to be in the *vicinity* of the metropolis or of the sea; 'Though the soul be not actually debauched, yet it is something to be in the *neighbourhood* of destruction.'—SOUTH. 'The Dutch, by the *vicinity* of their settlements to the coast of Caraccas, gradually engrossed the greatest part of the cocoa trade.'—ROBERTSON.

DISTRICT, REGION, TRACT, QUARTER.

District, in Latin *districtus*, from *distringo* to bind separately, signifies a certain part marked off specifically; *region*, in Latin *regio* from *rego* to rule, signifies a portion that is within rule; *tract*, in Latin *tractus*, from *traho* to draw, signifies a part drawn out; *quarter* signifies literally a fourth part.

These terms are all applied to country: the former two comprehending divisions marked out on political grounds; the latter a geographical or an indefinite division: *district* is smaller than a *region;* the former refers only to part of a country, the latter frequently applies to a whole country: a *quarter* is indefinite, and may be applied either to a *quarter* of the world or a particular neighbourhood: a *tract* is the smallest portion of all, and comprehends frequently no more than what may fall within the compass of the eye. We consider a *district* only with relation to government; every magistrate acts within a certain *district;* 'The very inequality of representation, which is so foolishly complained of, is perhaps the very thing which prevents us from thinking or acting as members for *districts*.'—BURKE. We speak of a *region* when considering the circumstances of climate, or the natural properties which distinguish different parts of the earth, as the *regions* of heat and cold;

> Between those *regions* and our upper light
> Deep forests and impenetrable night
> Possess the middle space.—DRYDEN.

We speak of a *tract* to designate the land that runs on in a line, as a mountainous *tract;* so likewise figuratively to pursue a *tract* or a line of thinking;

> My timorous muse
> Unambitious *tracts* pursues.—COWLEY.

We speak of the *quarter* simply to designate a point of the compass; as a person lives in a certain *quarter* of the town that is north, or south-east, or west, &c. and so also in an extended application, we say, to meet with opposition in an unexpected *quarter;* 'There is no man in any rank who is always at liberty to act as he would incline. In some *quarter* or other he is limited by circumstances.'—BLAIR.

TO FOUND, GROUND, REST, BUILD.

Found, in French *fonder*, Latin *fundo*, comes from *fundus* the *ground*, and, like the verb *ground*, properly signifies to make firm in the *ground*, to make the *ground* the support.

To *found* implies the exercise of art and contrivance in making a support; to *ground* signifies to lay a thing so deep that it may not totter; it is merely in the moral sense that they are here considered, as the verb *to ground* with this signification is never used otherwise. *Found* is applied to outward circumstances; *ground* to what passes inwardly: a man *founds* his charge against another upon certain facts that are come to his knowledge; he *grounds* his belief upon the most substantial evidence: a man should be cautious not to make any accusations which are not well *founded;* nor to indulge any expectations which are not well *grounded:* monarchs commonly *found* their claims to a throne upon the right of primogeniture; 'The only sure principles we can lay down for regulating our conduct must be *founded* on the Christian religion.'—BLAIR. Christians *ground* their hopes of immortality on the word of God; 'I know there are persons who look upon these wonders of art (in ancient history) as fabulous; but I cannot find any *ground* for such a suspicion.'—ADDISON.

To *found* and *ground* are said of things which demand the full exercise of the mental powers; to *rest* is an action of less importance: whatever is *founded* requires and has the utmost support; whatever is *rested* is more by the will of the individual: a man *founds* his reasoning upon some unequivocal fact; he *rests* his assertion upon mere hearsay; 'Our distinction must *rest* upon a steady adherence to rational religion, when the multitude are deviating into licentious and criminal conduct.'—BLAIR. The words *found*, *ground*, and *rest* have always an immediate reference to the thing that supports; to *build* has an especial reference to that which is supported, to the superstructure that is raised: we should not say that a person *founds* an hypothesis, without adding something, as observations, experiments, and the like, upon which it was *founded;* but we may speak of his simply *building* systems, supposing them to be the mere fruit of his distempered imagination; or we may say that a system of astronomy has been *built* upon the discovery of Copernicus respecting the motion of the earth; 'They who from a mistaken zeal for the honour of Divine revelation, either deny the existence, or vilify the authority, of natural religion, are not aware, that by disallowing the sense of obligation, they undermine the foundation on which revelation *builds* its power of commanding the heart.'—BLAIR.

FOUNDATION, GROUND, BASIS.

Foundation and *ground* derive their meaning and application from the preceding article: a report is said to be without any *foundation*, which has taken its rise in mere conjecture, or in some arbitrary cause independent of all fact; 'If the *foundation* of a high name be virtue and service, all that is offered against it is but rumour, which is too short-lived to stand up in competition with *glory*, which is everlasting.'—STEELE. A man's suspicion is said to be without *ground*, which is not supported by the shadow of external evidence: *unfounded* clamours are frequently raised against the measures of government; *groundless* jealousies frequently arise between families, to disturb the harmony of their intercourse; 'Every subject of the British government has good *grounds* for loving and respecting his country.'—BLAIR.

Foundation and *basis* may be compared with each other, either in the proper or the improper signification: both *foundation* and *basis* are the lowest parts of any structure; but the former lies under *ground*, the latter stands above: the *foundation* supports some large and artificially erected pile; the *basis* supports a simple pillar: hence we speak of the *foundation* of St. Paul's, and the *base* or *basis* of the monument: this distinction is likewise preserved in the moral application of the terms: disputes have too often their *foundation* in frivolous circumstances; treaties have commonly their *basis* in acknowledged general principle; with governments that are at war pacifick negotiations may be commenced on the *basis* of the *uti possidetis;* 'It is certain that the *basis* of all lasting reputation is laid in moral worth.'—BLAIR.

TO BUILD, ERECT, CONSTRUCT.

Build, in Saxon *bytlian*, French *batir*, German *bauen*, Gothick *boa*, *bua*, *bygga*, to erect houses, from the Hebrew בית a habitation; *erect*, in French *eriger*,

Latin *erectus*, participle of *erigo*, compounded of *e* and *rego*, comes from the Greek ὀρέχω to stretch or extend, signifies literally to carry upward; *construct*, in Latin *constructus*, participle of *construo*, compounded of *con* together, and *struo* to put, in Greek στρωννύμι to strow, in Hebrew ערך to dispose or put in order, signifies to form together into a mass

The word *build* by distinction expresses the purpose of the action; *erect* indicates the mode of the action; *construct* indicates contrivance in the action.

What is *built* is employed for the purpose of receiving, retaining, or confining; what is *erected* is placed in an elevated situation; what is *constructed* is put together with ingenuity.

All that is *built* may be said to be *erected* or *constructed;* but all that is *erected* or *constructed* is not said to be *built;* likewise what is *erected* is mostly *constructed*, though not *vice versâ*. We *build* from necessity; we *erect* for ornament; we *construct* for utility and convenience. Houses are *built*, monuments *erected*, machines are *constructed;* 'Montesquieu wittily observes, that by *building* professed madhouses, men tacitly insinuate that all who are out of their senses are to be found only in those places.'—WARTON. 'It is as rational to live in caves till our own hands have *erected* a palace, as to reject all knowledge of architecture which our understandings will not supply.' —JOHNSON. 'From the raft or canoe, which first served to carry a savage over the river, to the *construction* of a vessel capable of conveying a numerous crew with safety to a distant coast, the progress in improvement is immense. —ROBERTSON.

ARCHITECT, BUILDER.

Architect, from *architecture*, in Latin *architectus*, from *architectura*, Greek ἀρχιτεκτονική, compounded of ἀρχὸς the chief, and τεχνὴ art or contrivance, signifies the chief of contrivers; *builder*, from the verb to *build*, denotes the person concerned in buildings, who causes the structure of houses, either by his money or his personal service.

An *architect* is an artist employed only to form the plans for large buildings; 'Rome will bear witness that the English artists are as superiour in talents as they are in numbers to those of all nations besides. I reserve the mention of her *architects* as a separate class.'—CUMBERLAND. A *builder* is a simple tradesman, or even workman, who *builds* common dwelling-houses; 'With his ready money, the *builder*, mason, and carpenter are enabled to make their market of gentlemen in his neighbourhood who inconsiderately employ them.'—STEELE.

EDIFICE, STRUCTURE, FABRICK.

Edifice, in Latin *ædificium*, from *ædifico* or *ædes* and *facio*, to make a house, signifies properly the house made; *structure*, from the Latin *structura* and *struo* to raise, signifies the raising a thing, or the thing raised; *fabrick*, from the Latin *fabrico*, signifies the *fabricating* or the thing *fabricated*.

Edifice in its proper sense is always applied to a building; *structure* and *fabrick* are either employed as abstract actions, or the results and fruits of actions: in the former case they are applied to many objects besides buildings; *structure* referring to the act of raising or setting up together; *fabrick* to that of framing or contriving.

As the *edifice* bespeaks the thing itself, it requires no modification, since it conveys of itself the idea of something superiour; 'The levellers only pervert the natural order of things; they load the *edifice* of society, by setting up in the air what the solidity of the *structure* requires to be on the ground.'—BURKE. The word *structure* must always be qualified; it is employed only to designate the mode of action; 'In the whole *structure* and constitution of things, God hath shown himself to be favourable to virtue, and inimical to vice and guilt.'—BLAIR. The *fabrick* is itself a species of epithet; it designates the object as something contrived by the power of art or by design;

> By destiny compell'd, and in despair,
> The Greeks grew weary of the tedious war,
> And, by Minerva's aid, a *fabrick* rear'd.
> DRYDEN.

The *edifices* dedicated to the service of religion have in all ages been held sacred: it is the business of the architect to estimate the merits or demerits of the *structure:* when we take a survey of the vast *fabrick* of the universe, the mind becomes bewildered with contemplating the infinite power of its Divine Author.

When employed in the abstract sense of actions, *structure* is limited to objects of magnitude, or such as consist of complicated parts; *fabrick* is extended to every thing in which art or contrivance is requisite; hence we may speak of the *structure* of vessels, and the *fabrick* of cloth, iron ware, and the like.

CORNER, ANGLE.

Corner answers to the French *coin*, and Greek γωνία, which signifies either a *corner* or a hidden place; *angle*, in Latin *angulus*, comes in all probability from ἀγκὼν the elbow.

The vulgar use of *corner* in the ordinary concerns of life, and the technical use of *angle* in the science of mathematicks, is not the only distinction between these terms.

Corner properly implies the outer extreme point of any solid body; *angle*, on the contrary, the inner extremity produced by the meeting of two right lines. When speaking therefore of solid bodies, *corner* and *angle* may be both employed; but in regard to simple right lines, the word *angle* only is applicable: in the former case a *corner* is produced by the meeting of the different parts of a body whether inwardly or outwardly; but an *angle* is produced by the meeting of two bodies: one house has many *corners;* two houses or two walls, at least, are requisite to make an *angle;* 'Jewellers grind their diamonds with many sides and *angles*, that their lustre may appear many ways.'—DERHAM.

We likewise speak of making an *angle* by the direction that is taken in going either by land or sea, because such a course is equivalent to a right line; in that case the word *corner* could not be substituted: on the other hand, the word *corner* is often used for a place of secrecy or obscurity, agreeably to the derivation of the term; 'Some men, like pictures, are fitter for a *corner* than for a full light.'—POPE

PILLAR, COLUMN.

Pillar, in French *pilier*, in all probability comes from *pile*, signifying any thing piled up in an artificial manner. *Column*, in Latin *columna*, comes from *columen* a prop or support. In their original meaning, therefore, it is obvious that these words differ essentially, although in their present use they refer to the same object. The *pillar* mostly serves as a *column* or support, and the *column* is always a *pillar;* but sometimes a *pillar* does not serve as a prop, and then it is called by its own name; but when it supplies the place of a prop, then it is more properly denominated a *column;*

> Whate'er adorns
> The princely dome, the *column*, and the arch,
> The breathing marbles, and the sculptur'd gold,
> Beyond the proud possessor's narrow claim,
> His tuneful breast enjoys.—AKENSIDE.

Hence the monument is a *pillar*, and not a *column;* but the *pillars* on which the roofs of churches are made to rest, may with more propriety be termed *columns*. *Pillar* is more frequently employed in a moral application than *column*, and in that case it always implies a prop; 'Withdraw religion, and you shake all the *pillars* of morality.'—BLAIR. Government is the *pillar* on which all social order rests.

LODGINGS, APARTMENTS.

A *lodging*, or a place to *lodge* or dwell in, comprehends single rooms, or many rooms, or in fact any place which can be made to serve the purpose; *apartments* respect only suits of rooms: *apartments*, therefore, are, in the strict sense, *lodgings;* but all *lodgings* are not *apartments:* on the other hand, the word *lodgings* is mostly used for rooms that are let out to hire, or that serve a temporary purpose; but the word *apartments* may be applied to the suits of rooms in any large house: hence the word *lodging* becomes on one ground restricted in its use, and *apartments* on the other: all *apartments* to let out for hire are *lodgings;* but *apartments* not to let out for hire are not *lodgings.*

MONUMENT, MEMORIAL, REMEMBRANCER.

Monument, in Latin *monumentum* or *monimentum*, from *moneo* to advise or remind, signifies that which puts us in mind of something; *memorial*, from *memory*, signifies the thing that helps the memory; and *remembrancer*, from *remember* (*v. Memory*), the thing that causes to *remember*.

From the above it is clear that these terms have, in their original derivation, precisely the same signification, and differ only in their collateral acceptations: *monument* is applied to that which is purposely set up to keep a thing in mind; *memorials* and *remembrancers* are any things which are calculated to call a thing to mind. a *monument* is used to preserve a publick object of notice from being forgotten; a *memorial* serves to keep an individual in mind: the *monument* is commonly understood to be a species of building; as a tomb which preserves the *memory* of the dead, or a pillar which preserves the *memory* of some publick event: the *memorial* always consists of something which was the property, or in the possession, of another; as his picture, his handwriting, his hair, and the like. The *Monument* at London was built to commemorate the dreadful fire of the city in the year 1666: friends who are at a distance are happy to have some token of each other's regard, which they likewise keep as a *memorial* of their former intercourse.

The *monument*, in its proper sense, is always made of wood or stone for some specifick purpose; but, in the improper sense, any thing may be termed a *monument* when it serves the purpose of reminding the publick of any circumstance: thus, the pyramids are *monuments* of antiquity; the actions of a good prince are more lasting *monuments* than either brass or marble; 'If (in the Isle of Sky) the remembrance of papal superstition is obliterated, the *monuments* of papal piety are likewise effaced.'—JOHNSON.

Memorials are always of a private nature, and at the same time such as remind us naturally of the object to which they have belonged; this object is generally some person, but it may likewise refer to some thing, if it be of a personal nature: our Saviour instituted the Sacrament of the Lord's Supper as a *memorial* of his death; 'Any *memorial* of your good-nature and friendship is most welcome to me.'—POPE.

A *memorial* respects some object external of ourselves; the *remembrancer* is said of that which directly concerns ourselves and our particular duty; a man leaves *memorials* of himself to whomsoever he leaves his property; but the *remembrancer* is that which we acquire for ourselves: the *memorial* carries us back to another; the *remembrancer* brings us back to ourselves: the *memorial* revives in our minds what we owe to another; the *remembrancer* puts us in mind of what we owe to ourselves; it is that which recalls us to a sense of our duty: a gift is the best *memorial* we can give of ourselves to another: a sermon is often a good *remembrancer* of the duties which we have neglected to perform; 'When God is forgotten, his judgements are his *remembrancers*.'—COWPER.

GRAVE, TOMB, SEPULCHRE.

All these terms denote the place where bodies are deposited. *Grave*, from the German *graben* to dig, has a reference to the hollow made in the earth; *tomb*, from *tumulus* and *tumeo* to swell, has a reference to the rising that is made above it; *sepulchre*, from *sepelio* to bury, has a reference to the use for which it is employed. From this explanation it is evident, that these terms have a certain propriety of application; 'to sink into the *grave*' is an expression that carries the thoughts where the body must rest in death;

> The path of glory leads but to the *grave*.—GRAY.

To inscribe on the *tomb*, or to encircle the *tomb* with flowers, carries our thoughts to the external of that place in which the body is interred;

> Nor you, ye proud, impute to these the fault,
> If mem'ry o'er their *tombs* no trophies raise.—GRAY.

To inter in a *sepulchre*, or to visit or enter a *sepulchre*, reminds us of a place in which bodies are deposited; 'The Lay itself is either lost or buried, perhaps for ever, in one of those *sepulchres* of MSS. which by courtesy are called libraries.'—TYRWHITT

TO ADORN, DECORATE, EMBELLISH.

Adorn, in Latin *adorno*, is compounded of the intensive syllable *ad* and *orno*, in Greek *ὡραίω* to make beautiful, signifying to dispose for the purpose of ornament; *decorate*, in Latin *decoratus*, participle of *decoro*, from *decorus* becoming, signifies to make becoming; *embellish*, in French *embellir*, is compounded of the intensive syllable *em* or *in* and *bellir* or *bel*, in Latin *bellus* handsome, signifying to make handsome.

One *adorns* by giving the best external appearance to a thing:

> As vines the trees, as grapes the vines *adorn*.
> DRYDEN.

One *decorates* by annexing something to improve its appearance; 'A few years afterward (1751), by the death of his father, Lord Lyttleton inherited a baronet's title, with a large estate, which, though perhaps he did not augment, he was careful to *adorn* by a house of great elegance, and by much attention to the *decoration* of his park.'—JOHNSON. One *embellishes* by giving a finishing stroke to a thing that is well executed; 'I shall here present my reader with a letter from a projector, concerning a new office which he thinks may very much contribute to the *embellishment* of the city.'—ADDISON. Females *adorn* their persons by the choice and disposal of their dress: a headdress is *decorated* with flowers, or a room with paintings: fine writing is *embellished* by suitable flourishes.

Adorn and *embellish* are figuratively employed; *decorate* only in the proper sense. The mind is *adorned* by particular virtues which are implanted in it; a narrative is *embellished* by the introduction of some striking incidents.

OBLONG, OVAL.

Oblong, in Latin *oblongus*, from the intensive syllable *ob*, signifies very long, longer than it is broad; *oval* from the Latin *ovum* an egg, signifies egg shaped.

The *oval* is a species of the *oblong:* what is *oval* is *oblong;* but what is *oblong* is not always *oval*. *Oblong* is peculiarly applied to figures formed by right lines, that is, all rectangular parallelograms, except squares, are *oblong;* but the *oval* is applied to curvilinear *oblong* figures, as ellipses, which are distinguished from the circle: tables are oftener *oblong* than *oval;* garden beds are as frequently *oval* as they are *oblong*.

GLOBE, BALL.

Globe, in Latin *globus*, comes probably from the Greek *γήλοφος* a hillock of earth; *ball*, in Teutonick *ball*, is doubtless connected with the words *bowl*, *bow*, *bend*, and the like, signifying that which is turned or rounded.

Globe is to *ball* as the species to the genus; a *globe* is a *ball*, but every *ball* is not a *globe*. The *globe* does not in its strict sense require to be of an equal rotundity in all its parts; it is properly an irregularly round body; 'It is said by modern philosophers, that not only the great *globes* of matter are thinly scattered through the universe, but the hardest bodies are so porous, that if all matter were compressed to perfect solidity, it might be contained in a cube of a few feet.'—JOHNSON. A *ball* on the other hand is generally any round body, but particularly one that is entirely regularly round. the earth itself is therefore properly denominated a *globe*, from its unequal rotundity; and for the same reason the mechanical body which is made to represent the earth is also denominated a *globe;* but in the higher style of writing the earth is frequently denominated a *ball*, and in familiar discourse every solid body which assumes a circular form is entitled a *ball*:

> What though in solemn silence all
> Move round the dark terraqueous *ball*,
> In reason's ear they all rejoice,
> And utter forth a glorious voice.—ADDISON.

TO EMIT, EXHALE, EVAPORATE.

Emit, from the Latin *emitto*, expresses properly the act of sending out. *exhale*, from *halitus* the breath, and *evaporate*, from *vapor* vapour or steam, are both modes of *emitting*.

Emit is used to express a more positive effort to send out; *exhale* and *evaporate* designate the natural and progressive process of things: volcanoes *emit* fire and flames;

Full in the blazing sun great Hector shin'd
Like Mars commission'd to confound mankind;
His nodding helm *emits* a streamy ray,
His piercing eyes through all the battle stray.—POPE.

The earth *exhales* the damps, or flowers *exhale* perfumes;

Here paus'd a moment, while the gentle gale
Convey'd that freshness the cool seas *exhale*.
POPE.

Liquids *evaporate*; 'After allowing the first fumes and heat of their zeal to *evaporate*, she (Elizabeth) called into her presence a certain number of each house.'—ROBERTSON.

Animals may *emit* by an act of volition; things *exhale* or *evaporate* by an external action upon them: they *exhale* that which is foreign to them; they *evaporate* that which constitutes a part of their substance.

The pole-cat is reported to *emit* such a stench from itself when pursued, as to keep its pursuers at a distance from itself: bogs and fens *exhale* their moisture when acted upon by the heat: water *evaporates* by means of steam when put into a state of ebullition.

ERUPTION, EXPLOSION.

The *eruption*, from *e* and *rumpo*, signifies the breaking forth, that is, the coming into view by a sudden bursting; *explosion*, from *ex* and *plaudo*, signifies bursting out with a noise: hence of flames there will be properly an *eruption*, but of gunpowder an *explosion*; volcanoes have their *eruptions* at certain intervals, which are sometimes attended with *explosions*: on this account the term *eruption* is applied to the human body, for whatever comes out as the effects of humour, and may be applied in the same manner to any indications of humour in the mind; the term *explosion* is also applied to the agitations of the mind which burst out; 'Sin may truly reign where it does not actually rage and pour itself forth in continual *eruptions*.'—SOUTH. 'A burst of fury, an exclamation seconded by a blow, is the first natural *explosion* of a soul so stung by scorpions as Macbeth's.'—CUMBERLAND.

BREACH, BREAK, GAP, CHASM.

Breach and *break* are both derived from the same verb *break* (*v. To break*), to denote what arises from being broken, in the figurative sense of the verb itself; *gap*, from the English *gape*, signifies the thing that gapes or stands open; *chasm*, in Greek χάσμα from χαίνω, and the Hebrew גוח to be open, signifies the thing that has opened itself.

The idea of an opening is common to these terms, but they differ in the nature of the opening. A *breach* and a *gap* are the consequence of a violent removal which destroys the connexion; a *break* and a *chasm* may arise from the absence of that which would form a connexion. A *breach* in a wall is made by means of cannon;

A mighty *breach* is made; the rooms conceal'd
Appear, and all the palace is reveal'd.—DRYDEN.

Gaps in fences are commonly the effects of some violent effort to pass through;

Or if the order of the world below
Will not the *gap* of one whole day allow,
Give me that minute when she made her vow.
DRYDEN.

A *break* is made in a page of printing by leaving off in the middle of a line; 'Considering probably, how much Homer had been disfigured by the arbitrary compilers of his works, Virgil, by his will, obliged Tucca and Varius to add nothing, nor so much as fill up the *breaks* he had left in his poem.'—WALSH. A *chasm* is left in writing when any words in the sentence are omitted; 'The whole *chasm* in nature, from a plant to a man, is filled up with diverse kinds of creatures.'—ADDISON.

A *breach* and a *chasm* always imply a larger opening than a *break* or *gap*. A *gap* may be made in a knife; a *breach* is always made in the walls of a building or fortification: the clouds sometimes separate so as to leave small *breaks*; the ground is sometimes so convulsed by earthquakes as to leave frightful *chasms*

Breach and *chasm* are used morally; *break* and *gap* seldom otherwise than in application to natural objects. Trifling circumstances occasion wide *breaches* in families;

When *breach* of faith join'd hearts does disengage,
The calmest temper turns to wildest rage.—LEE.

The death of relatives often produces a sad *chasm* in the enjoyments of individuals;

Some lazy ages, lost in ease,
No action leave to busy chronicles;
Such, whose supine felicity but makes
In story *chasms*, in epochas mistakes.—DRYDEN

TO BREAK, RACK, REND, TEAR.

Break, in Saxon *brecan*, Danish and Low German *breken*, High German *brechen*, Latin *frango*, Greek βρηγνύμι, βρηχνύω, Chaldee פרק to separate; *rack* comes from the same source as *break*; it is properly the root of this word, and an onomatopeïa, conveying a sound correspondent with what is made by *breaking*; *rak* in Swedish, and *racco* in Icelandish, signifies a *breaking* of the ice; *rend* is in Saxon *hrendan*, *hreddan*, Low German *ritan*, High German *reissen* to split, Greek ῥήσσω, Hebrew רעץ to break in pieces; *tear*, in Saxon *taeran*, Low German *tiren*, High German *zerren*, is an intensive verb from *ziehen* to pull, Greek τρώω, τείρω to bruise, Hebrew תור to split, divide, or cleave.

The forcible division of any substance is the common characteristick of these terms.

Break is the generick term, the rest specifick: every thing *racked*, *rent*, or *torn* is broken, but not *vice versâ*. *Break* has however a specifick meaning, in which it is comparable with the others. *Breaking* requires less violence than either of the others: brittle things may be *broken* with the slightest touch, but nothing can be *racked* without intentional violence of an extraordinary kind. Glass is quickly *broken*; a table is *racked*. Hard substances only are *broken* or *racked*; but every thing of a soft texture and composition may be *rent* or *torn*.

Breaking is performed by means of a blow; *racking* by that of a violent concussion; but *rending* and *tearing* are the consequences of a pull. Any thing of wood or stone is *broken*; any thing of a complicated structure, with hinges and joints, is *racked*; cloth is *rent*, paper is *torn*. *Rend* is sometimes used for what is done by design; a *tear* is always faulty. Cloth is sometimes *rent* rather than cut when it is wanted to be divided; but when it is *torn* it is injured. These terms are similarly distinguished in their figurative application;

But out affection!
All bond and privilege of nature *break*.
SHAKSPEARE.

Long has this secret struggl'd in my breast;
Long has it *rack'd* and *rent* my tortur'd bosom.
SMITH

The people *rend* the skies with loud applause,
And heaven can hear no other name but yours.
DRYDEN.

She sigh'd, she sobb'd, and, furious with despair,
She *rent* her garments, and she *tore* her hair.
DRYDEN.

Who would not bleed with transport for his country
Tear every tender passion from his heart?
THOMSON.

TO BREAK, BRUISE, SQUEEZE, POUND, CRUSH.

Break, *v. To break*, *rack*; *bruise*, in French *briser* Saxon *brysed*, not improbably from the same source as press: *squeeze*, in Saxon *cwysin*, Low German *quietsen*, *quoesen*, Swedish *quæsa*, Latin *quatio* to shake, or produce a concussion; *pound*, in Saxon *punian*, is not improbably derived by a change of letters from the Latin *tundo* to bruise; *crush*, in French *ecraser*, is most probably only a variation of the word *squeeze*, like *crash*, or *squash*.

Break always implies the separation of the component parts of a body; *bruise* denotes simply the destroying the continuity of the parts. Hard, brittle substances, as glass, are *broken;*

Dash my devoted bark! ye surges, *break* it!
'T is for my ruin that the tempest rises.—ROWE.

Soft, pulpy substances, as flesh or fruits, are *bruised;*

Yet lab'ring well his little spot of ground,
Some scatt'ring potherbs here and there he found;
Which, cultivated with his daily care,
And, *bruis'd* with vervain, were his daily fare.
DRYDEN.

The operation of *bruising* is performed either by a violent blow or by pressure; that of *squeezing* by compression only. Metals, particularly lead and silver, may be *bruised;* fruits may be either *bruised* or *squeezed*. In this latter sense *bruise* applies to the harder substances, or indicates a violent compression; *squeeze* is used for soft substances or a gentle compression. The kernels of nuts are *bruised;* oranges or apples are *squeezed;*

He therefore first among the swains was found,
To reap the produce of his labour'd ground,
And *squeeze* the combs with golden liquor crown'd.
DRYDEN.

To *pound* is properly to *bruise* in a mortar so as to produce a separation of parts;

And where the rafters on the columns meet,
We push them headlong with our arms and feet:
Down goes the top at once; the Greeks beneath
Are piecemeal torn, or *pounded* into death.
DRYDEN.

To *crush* is the most violent and destructive of all operations, which amounts to the total dispersion of all the parts of a body; 'Such were the sufferings of our Lord, so great and so grievous as none of us are in any degree able to undergo. That weight under which he crouched, would *crush* us.'—TILLOTSON.

What is *broken* may be made whole again; what is *bruised* or *squeezed* may be restored to its former tone and consistency; what is *pounded* is only reduced to smaller parts for convenience; but what is *crushed* is destroyed. When the wheel of a carriage passes over any body that yields to its weight, it *crushes* it to powder; thus in the figurative sense this term marks a total annihilation: if a conspiracy be not *crushed* in the bud, it will prove fatal to the power which has suffered it to grow;

To *crush* rebellion every way is just.—DARCY.

TO BREAK, BURST, CRACK, SPLIT.

Break, v. To break, rack; burst, in Saxon *beorstan, bersten, byrsten*, Low German *baisten, basten*, High German *bersten*, Old German *bresten*, Swedish *brysta*, is but a variation of *break; crack* is in Saxon *cearcian*, French *cracquer*, High German *krachen*, Low German *kraken*, Danish *krakke*, Greek *κρέκειν*, which are in all probability but variations of *break*, &c.; *split*, in Dutch *split*, Danish *splitter*, Low German *splieten*, High German *spalten*, Old German *spilten*, Swedish *splita*, which are all connected with the German *platzen* to *burst*, from the Greek *σπαλύσσομαι* to tear or *split*, and the Hebrew *pelah* to separate, *palect* or *palety* to cut in pieces.

Break denotes a forcible separation of the constituent parts of a body. *Burst* and *crack* are onomatopeias or imitations of the sound which are made in *bursting* and *cracking*. *Splitting* is a species of *cracking* that takes place in some bodies in a similar manner without being accompanied with the noise.

Breaking is generally the consequence of some external violence: every thing that is exposed to violence may without distinction be *broken;*

Ambitious thence the manly river *breaks*,
And gathering many a flood, and copious fed
With all the mellowed treasures of the sky,
Winds in progressive majesty along.—THOMSON.

Bursting arises mostly from an extreme tension: hol low bodies, when over-filled, *burst;*

Off, traitors! Off! or my distracted soul
Will *burst* indignant from this jail of nature.
THOMSON.

Cracking is caused by the application of excessive heat, or the defective texture of the substance: glass *cracks;* the earth *cracks;* leather *cracks;*

And let the weighty roller run the round,
To smooth the surface of th' unequal ground;
Lest *crack'd* with summer heats the flooring flies,
Or sinks, and through the crannies weeds arise.
DRYDEN.

Splitting may arise from a combination of external and internal causes: wood in particular is liable to *split;*

Is 't meet that he
Should leave the helm, and like a fearful lad,
With tearful eyes, add water to the sea?
While in his mean, the ship *splits* on the rock,
Which industry and courage might have saved.
SHAKSPEARE.

A thing may be *broken* in any shape, form, and degree. *Bursting* leaves a wide gap; *cracking* and *splitting* leave a long aperture; the latter of which is commonly wider than that of the former.

RUPTURE, FRACTURE, FRACTION.

Rupture, from *rumpo* to break or burst, and *fracture* or *fraction*, from *frango* to break, denote different kinds of breaking, according to the objects to which the action is applied. Soft substances may suffer a *rupture;* as the *rupture* of a blood-vessel: hard substances a *fracture;* as the *fracture* of a bone. *Rupture* and *fraction*, though not *fracture*, are used in an improper application; as the *rupture* of a treaty, or the *fraction* of a unit into parts; 'To be an enemy, and once to have been a friend, does it not imbitter the *rupture?*'—SOUTH.

And o'er the high-pil'd hills of *fractur'd* earth,
Wide dash'd the waves.—THOMSON.

FRAGILE, FRAIL, BRITTLE.

Fragile and *frail*, in French *frêle*, both come from the Latin *fragilis*, signifying breakable; but the former is used in the proper sense only, and the latter more generally in the improper sense: man, corporeally considered, is a *fragile* creature, his frame is composed of *fragile* materials; mentally considered, he is a *frail* creature, for he is liable to every sort of *frailty;*

What joys, alas! could this *frail* being give,
That I have been so covetous to live.—DRYDEN.

Brittle comes from the Saxon *brittan* to break, and by the termination *le* or *lis*, denotes likewise a capacity to break, that is, properly breakable; but it conveys a stronger idea of this quality than *fragile:* the latter applies to whatever will break from the effects of time; *brittle* to that which will not bear a temporary violence: in this sense all the works of men are *fragile*, and in fact all sublunary things; 'An appearance of delicacy, and even of *fragility*, is almost essential to beauty.'—BURKE. But glass, stone, and ice are peculiarly denominated *brittle;* and friendships are sometimes termed *brittle;* 'The *brittle* chain of this world's friendships is as effectually broken when one is "oblitus meorum," as when one is "obliviscendus et illis."'—CROFT.

SAP, UNDERMINE.

Sap signifies the juice which springs from the root of a tree; hence to *sap* signifies to come at the root of any thing by digging: to *undermine* signifies to form a mine under the ground, or under whatever is upon the ground: we may *sap*, therefore, without *undermining;* and *undermine* without *sapping:* we may *sap* the foundation of a house without making any mine underneath; and in fortifications we may *undermine* either a mound, a ditch, or a wall, without striking immediately at the foundation: hence, in the moral application, to *sap* is a more direct and decisive mode of destruction; *undermine* is a gradual, and may be a partial, action. Infidelity *saps* the morals of a nation;

With morning drams,
A filthy custom which he caught from thee,
Clean from his former practice, now he *saps*
His youthful vigour.—CUMBERLAND.

Courtiers *undermine* one another's interests at court; 'To be a man of business is, in other words, to be a plague and spy, a treacherous supplanter and *underminer* of the peace of families.'—SOUTH.

TO ERADICATE, EXTIRPATE, EXTERMINATE.

To *eradicate*, from *radix* the root, is to get out by the root; *extirpate*, from *ex* and *stirps* the stem, is to get out the stock, to destroy it thoroughly. In the natural sense we may *eradicate* noxious weeds whenever we pull them from the ground; but we can never *extirpate* all noxious weeds, as they always disseminate their seeds and spring up afresh. These words are seldomer used in the physical than in the moral sense; where the former is applied to such objects as are conceived to be plucked up by the roots, as habits, vices, abuses, evils; and the latter to whatever is united or supposed to be united into a race or family, and is destroyed root and branch. Youth is the season when vicious habits may be thoroughly *eradicated;* 'It must be every man's care to begin by *eradicating* those corruptions which, at different times, have tempted him to violate conscience.'—BLAIR. By the universal deluge the whole human race was *extirpated*, with the exception of Noah and his family;

Go thou, inglorious, from th' embattled plain;
Ships thou hast store, and nearest to the main·
A nobler care the Grecians shall employ,
To combat, conquer, and *extirpate* Troy.—POPE.

Exterminate, in Latin *exterminatus*, participle of *extermino*, from *ex* or *extra*, and *terminus*, signifies to expel beyond a boundary (of life), that is, out of existence. It is used only in regard to such things as have life, and designates a violent and immediate action; *extirpate*, on the other hand, may designate a progressive action: the former may be said of individuals, but the latter is employed in the collective sense only. Plague, pestilence, famine, *extirpate:* the sword *exterminates;* 'So violent and black were Haman's passions, that he resolved to *exterminate* the whole nation to which Mordecai belonged.'—BLAIR.

TO DEFACE, DISFIGURE, DEFORM.

Deface, *disfigure*, and *deform* signify literally to spoil the *face*, *figure*, and *form*.

Deface expresses more than either *deform* or *disfigure*. To *deface* is an act of destruction; it is the actual destruction of that which has before existed: to *disfigure* is either an act of destruction or an erroneous execution, which takes away the figure: to *deform* is altogether an imperfect execution, which renders the *form* what it should not be. A thing is *defaced* by design; it is *disfigured* either by design or accident; it is *deformed* either by an errour or by the nature of the thing.

Persons only *deface;* persons or things *disfigure;* things are most commonly *deformed* of themselves. That may be *defaced*, the face or external surface of which may be injured or destroyed;

Yet she had heard an ancient rumour fly
(Long cited by the people of the sky),
That times to come should see the Trojan race
Her Carthage ruin, and her tow'rs deface.—DRYDEN.

That may be *disfigured* or *deformed*, the figure or form of which is imperfect or may be rendered imperfect; 'It is but too obvious that errours are committed in this part of religion (devotion). These frequently *disfigure* its appearance before the world, and subject it to unjust reproach.'—BLAIR.

A beauteous maid above; but magick art
With barking dogs *deform'd* her nether part.
DRYDEN.

A fine painting or piece of writing is *defaced* which is torn or besmeared with dirt: a fine building is *disfigured* by any want of symmetry in its parts: a building is *deformed* that is made contrary to all form. A statue may be *defaced*, *disfigured*, and *deformed*. It is *defaced* when any violence is done to the face or any outward part of the body; it is *disfigured* by the loss of a limb; it is *deformed* if made contrary to the perfect form of a person or thing to be represented.

Inanimate objects are mostly *defaced* or *disfigured*, but seldom *deformed;* animate objects are either *disfigured* or *deformed*, but not *defaced*. A person may *disfigure* himself by his dress; he is *deformed* by the hand of nature.

BANE, PEST, RUIN.

Bane, in its proper sense, is the name of a poisonous plant; *pest*, in French *peste*, Latin *pestis* a plague, from *pastum*, participle of *pasco* to feed upon or consume; *ruin*, in French *ruine*, Latin *ruina*, from *ruo* to rush, signifies the falling into a *ruin*, or the cause of *ruin*.

These terms borrow their figurative signification from three of the greatest evils in the world; namely, poison, plague, and destruction. *Bane* is said of things only; *pest* of persons only: whatever produces a deadly corruption is the *bane;* whoever is as obnoxious as the plague is a *pest:* luxury is the *bane* of civil society; gaming is the *bane* of all youth; sycophants are the *pests* of society;

First dire Chimæra's conquest was enjoined;
This *pest* he slaughter'd (for he read the skies),
And trusted heaven's informing prodigies.—POPE.

Be this, O mother! your religious care;
I go to rouse soft Paris to the war.
Oh! would kind earth the hateful wretch embrace,
That *pest* of Troy, that ruin of our race.
Deep to the dark abyss might he descend,
Troy yet should flourish, and my sorrows end.
POPE.

Bane when compared with *ruin* does not convey so strong a meaning; the former in its positive sense is that which tends to mischief;

Pierc'd through the dauntless heart then tumbles slain,
And from his fatal courage finds his *bane*.—POPE.

Ruin is that which actually causes *ruin:* a love of pleasure is the *bane* of all young men whose fortune depends on the exercise of their talents: drinking is the *ruin* of all who indulge themselves in it to excess

POISON, VENOM.

Poison, in French *poison*, comes from the Latin *potia* a potion or drink; *venom*, in French *venin*, Latin *venenum*, comes probably from *venæ* the veins, because it circulates rapidly through the veins, and infects the blood in a deadly manner.

Poison is a general term; in its original meaning it signifies any potion which acts destructively upon the system; *venom* is a species of deadly or malignant *poison:* a *poison* may be either slow or quick; a *venom* is always most active in its nature: a *poison* must be administered inwardly to have its effect; a *venom* will act by an external application: the juice of the hellebore is a *poison;* the tongue of the adder and the tooth of the viper contain *venom:* many plants are unfit to be eaten on account of the *poisonous* quality which is in them; the Indians are in the habit of dipping the tips of their arrows in a *venomous* juice, which renders the slightest wound mortal.

The moral application of these terms is clearly drawn from their proper acceptation: the *poison* must be infused or injected into the subject; the *venom* acts upon him externally: bad principles are justly compared to a *poison*, which some are so unhappy as to suck in with their mothers' milk; 'The Devil can convey the *poison* of his suggestions quicker than the agitation of thought or the strictures of fancy.'—SOUTH. The shafts of envy are peculiarly *venomous* when directed against those in elevated situations;

As the *venom* spread
Frightful convulsions writh'd his tortur'd limbs.
FENTON.

TO OVERTURN, OVERTHROW, SUBVERT, INVERT, REVERSE.

To *overturn* is simply to turn over, which may be more or less gradual: but to *overthrow* is to throw over, which will be more or less violent. To *overturn* is to turn a thing either with its side or its bottom upward; but to *subvert* is to turn that under which should be upward: to *reverse* is to turn that before which should be behind; and to *invert* is to place that on its head which should rest on its feet. These terms differ accordingly in their application and circumstances: things are *overturned* by contrivance and gradual means; infidels attempt to *overturn* Christianity by the arts of ridicule and falsehood;

An age is rip'ning in revolving fate,
When Troy shall *overturn* the Grecian state.
DRYDEN.

The French revolutionists *overthrew* their lawful government by every act of violence;

Thus prudes, by characters *o'erthrown*,
Imagine that they raise their own.—GAY.

To *overturn* is said of small matters; to *subvert* only of national or large concerns: domestick economy may be *overturned;* religious or political establishments may be *subverted;* 'Others, from publick spirit, laboured to prevent a civil war, which, whatever party should prevail, must shake, and perhaps *subvert*, the Spanish power.'—ROBERTSON. That may be *overturned* which is simply set up; that is *subverted* which has been established: an assertion may be *overturned;* the best sanctioned principles may by artifice be *subverted.*

To *overturn*, *overthrow*, and *subvert* generally involve the destruction of the thing so *overturned*, *overthrown*, or *subverted*, or at least render it for the time useless, and are, therefore, mostly unallowed acts; but *reverse* and *invert*, which have a more particular application, have a less specifick character of propriety: we may *reverse* a proposition by taking the negative instead of the affirmative; a decree may be *reversed* so as to render it nugatory; but both of these acts may be right or wrong, according to circumstances; 'Our ancestors affected a certain pomp of style, and this affectation, I suspect, was the true cause of their so frequently *inverting* the natural order of their words, especially in poetry.'—TYRRWHITT. The order of particular things may be *inverted* to suit the convenience of parties; but the order of society cannot be *inverted* without *subverting* all the principles on which civil society is built; 'He who walks not uprightly has neither from the presumption of God's mercy *reversing* the decree of his justice, nor from his own purposes of a future repentance, any sure ground to set his foot upon.'—SOUTH.

TO OVERWHELM, CRUSH.

To *overwhelm* (*v. To overbear*) is to cover with a heavy body, so that one should sink under it: to *crush* is to destroy the consistency of a thing by violent pressure. A thing may be *crushed* by being *overwhelmed*, but it may be *overwhelmed* without being *crushed;* and it may be *crushed* without being *overwhelmed.* The girl Tarpeia, who betrayed the Capitoline hill to the Sabines, is said to have been *overwhelmed* with their arms, by which she was *crushed* to death. When many persons fall on one, he may be *overwhelmed*, but not necessarily *crushed;* when a wagon goes over a body, it may be *crushed*, but not *overwhelmed;* 'Let not the political metaphysicks of Jacobins break prison, to burst like a Levanter, to sweep the earth with their hurricane, and to break up the fountains of the great deep to *overwhelm* us.'—BURKE.

Melt his cold heart, and wake dead nature in him,
Crush him in thy arms.—OTWAY.

TO ROT, PUTREFY, CORRUPT.

The dissolution of bodies by an internal process is implied by all these terms: but the first two are applied to natural bodies only; the last to all bodies natural and moral. *Rot* is the strongest of all these terms; it denotes the last stage in the progress of dissolution: *putrefy* expresses the progress towards rottenness; and *corruption* the commencement. After fruit has arrived at its maturity or proper state of ripeness, it *rots;*

Debate destroys despatch, as fruits we see
Rot when they hang too long upon the tree.
DENHAM.

Meat which is kept too long *putrefies;*

And draws the copious stream from swampy fens,
Where *putrefaction* into life ferments.—THOMSON.

There is a tendency in all bodies to *corruption;* iron and wood *corrupt* with time; whatever is made, or done, or wished by men, is equally liable to be *corrupt* or to grow *corrupt;*

After that they again returned beene,
That in that gardin planted be agayne
And grow afresh, as they had never seene
Fleshly *corruption* nor mortal payne.—SPENSER

DESTRUCTION, RUIN.

Destruction, from *destroy*, and the Latin *destruo*, signifies literally to unbuild that which is raised up; *ruin*, from the Latin *ruo* to fall, signifies to fall into pieces: *destruction* is an act of immediate violence; *ruin* is a gradual process: a thing is *destroyed* by some external action upon it; a thing falls to *ruin* of itself. We witness *destruction* wherever war or the adverse elements rage; we witness *ruin* whenever the works of man are exposed to the effects of time. Nevertheless, if *destruction* be more forcible and rapid, *ruin* is on the other hand more sure and complete. What is *destroyed* may be rebuilt or replaced; but what is *ruined* is lost for ever; it is past recovery.

When houses or towns are *destroyed*, fresh ones rise up in their place; but when commerce is *ruined*, it seldom returns to its old course.

Destruction admits of various degrees: *ruin* is something positive and general. The property of a man may be *destroyed* to a greater or less extent without necessarily involving his *ruin;*

Destruction hangs o'er yon devoted wall,
And nodding Ilion waits th' impending fall.—POPE.

The *ruin* of a whole family is oftentimes the consequence of *destruction* by fire;

The day shall come, that great avenging day,
Which Troy's proud glories in the dust shall lay;
When Priam's pow'rs, and Priam's self, shall fall,
And one prodigious *ruin* swallow all.—POPE.

The health is *destroyed* by violent exercise or some other active cause; it is *ruined* by a course of imprudent conduct.

The happiness of a family is *destroyed* by broils and discord; the morals of a young man are *ruined* by a continued intercourse with vicious companions.

Destruction may be used either in the proper, or the improper sense; *ruin* has mostly a moral application. The *destruction* of both body and soul is the consequence of sin; the *ruin* of a man, whether in his temporal or spiritual concerns, is inevitable, if he follow the dictates of misguided passion.

DESTRUCTIVE, RUINOUS, PERNICIOUS.

Destructive signifies producing *destruction* (*v. Destruction*); *ruinous*, either having or causing *ruin* (*v. Destruction*); *pernicious*, from the Latin *pernicies* or *per* and *neco* to kill violently, signifies causing violent and total dissolution.

Destructive and *ruinous*, as the epithets of the preceding terms, have a similar distinction in their sense and application: fire and sword are *destructive* things; a poison is *destructive;* consequences are *ruinous;* a condition or state is *ruinous;* intestine commotions are *ruinous* to the prosperity of a state;

'T is yours to save us if you cease to fear;
Flight, more than shameful, is *destructive* here.
POPE.

'There have been found in history few conquests more *ruinous* than that of the Saxons.'—HUME.

Pernicious approaches nearer to *destructive* than to *ruinous;* both the former imply tendency to dissolution, which may be more or less gradual; but the latter refers us to the result itself, to the dissolution as already having taken place: hence we speak of the instrument or cause as being *destructive* or *pernicious*, and the action or event as *ruinous;* *destructive* is applied in the most extended sense to every object which has been created or supposed to be so; *pernicious* is applicable only to such objects as act only in a limited way; sin is equally *destructive* to both body and soul; certain food is *pernicious* to the body; certain books are *pernicious* to the mind; 'The effects of divisions (in a state) are *pernicious* to the last degree, not only with regard to those advantages which they give the common enemy; but to those private evils which they produce in the heart of almost every particular person.'—ADDISON.

TO CONSUME, DESTROY, WASTE.

Consume, in French *consumer*, Latin *consumo*, compounded of *con* and *sumo*, signifies to take away altogether; *destroy*, in Latin *destruo*, compounded of *de* privative and *struo* to build, signifies to undo or scatter that which has been raised; *waste*, from the adjective *waste* or *desert*, signifies to make waste or naked.

The idea of bringing that to nothing which has been something is common to all these terms.

What is *consumed* is lost for any future purpose; what is *destroyed* is rendered unfit for any purpose whatever: *consume* may therefore be to *destroy* as the means to the end; things are often *destroyed* by being *consumed:* when food is *consumed* it serves the intended purpose; but when it is *destroyed* it serves no purpose, and is likewise unfit for any.

When iron is *consumed* by rust, or the body by disease, or a house by the flames, the things in these cases are literally *destroyed* by *consumption:* on the other hand, when life or health is taken away, and when things are either worn or torn so as to be useless, they are *destroyed;*

Let not a fierce unruly joy
The settled quiet of the mind *destroy*.—ADDISON.

In the figurative signification *consume* is synonymous with *waste:* the former implies a reducing to nothing; the latter conveys also the idea of misuse: to *waste* is to *consume* uselessly; much time is *consumed* in complaining, which might be employed in remedying the evils complained of; 'Mr. Boyle, speaking of a certain mineral, tells us that a man may *consume* his whole life in the study, without arriving at the knowledge of its qualities.'—ADDISON. Idlers *waste* their time because they do not properly estimate its value: those who *consume* their strength and their resources in fruitless endeavours to effect what is impracticable, are unfitted for doing what might be beneficial to themselves: it is an idle *waste* of one's powers to employ them in building up new systems, and making men dissatisfied with those already established;

For this I mourn, till grief or dire disease,
Shall *waste* the form whose crime it was to please.
POPE.

TO DEMOLISH, RAZE, DISMANTLE, DESTROY.

The throwing down what has been built up is the common idea included in all these terms.

Demolish, from the Latin *demolior*, and *moles* a mass, signifies to decompound what has been in a mass; *raze* like *erase* (*v. To blot out*) signifies the making smooth or even with the ground; *dismantle*, in French *demanteler*, signifies to deprive of the mantle or guard; *destroy*, from the Latin *destruo*, compounded of the privative *de* and *struo* to build, signifies properly to pull down.

A fabrick is *demolished* by scattering all its component parts; it is mostly an unlicensed act of caprice; it is * *razed* by way of punishment, that it may be left as a monument of publick vengeance; a fortress is *dismantled* from motives of prudence, in order to render it defenceless; places are *destroyed* by various means and from various motives, that they may not exist any longer.

Individuals may *demolish;* justice causes a *razure;* a general orders towers to be *dismantled* and fortifications to be *destroyed;*

From the *demolish'd* tow'rs the Trojans throw
Huge heaps of stones, that falling crush the foe.
DRYDEN.

Great Diomede has compass'd round with walls
The city which Argyripa he calls,
From his own Argos nam'd; we touch'd with joy
The royal hand that *raz'd* unhappy Troy.—DRYDEN.

* Vide Abbe Girard: "Demolir, raser, demanteler, detruire"

O'er the drear spot see desolation spread,
And the *dismantled* walls in ruin lie.—MOORE.

We, for myself I speak, and all the name
Of Grecians who to Troy's *destruction* came,
Not one but suffered and too dearly bought
The prize of honour which in arms he sought.
DRYDEN

TO BEREAVE, DEPRIVE, STRIP.

Bereave, in Saxon *bereafian*, German *berauben*, &c is compounded of *be* and *reave* or *rob*, Saxon *reafian*, German *rauben*, Low German *roofen*, &c. Latin *rapina* and *rapio* to catch or seize, signifying to take away contrary to one's wishes; *deprive*, compounded of *de* and *prive*, French *priver*, Latin *privo*, from *privus* private, signifies to make that one's own which was another's; *strip* is in German *streifen*, Low German *streipen*, *stroepen*, Swedish *ströfva*, probably changed from the Latin *surripio* to snatch by stealth.

To *bereave* expresses more than *deprive*, but less than *strip*, which in this sense is figurative, and denotes a total *bereavement;* one is *bereaved* of children, *deprived* of pleasures, and *stripped* of property: we are *bereaved* of that on which we set most value; the act of *bereaving* does violence to our inclination: we are *deprived* of the ordinary comforts and conveniences of life; they cease to be ours: we are *stripped* of the things which we most want; we are thereby rendered as it were naked. *Deprivations* are preparatory to *bereavements;* if we cannot bear the one patiently, we may expect to sink under the other; common prudence should teach us to look with unconcern on our *deprivations:* Christian faith should enable us to consider every *bereavement* as a step to perfection; that when *stripped* of all worldly goods we may be invested with those more exalted and lasting honours which await the faithful disciple of Christ.

We are *bereaved* of our dearest hopes and enjoyments by the dispensations of Providence;

O first-created Being, and thou great Word,
Let there be light, and light was over all;
Why am I thus *bereav'd* thy prime decree?
MILTON.

Casualties *deprive* us of many little advantages or gratifications which fall in our way;

Too daring bard! whose unsuccessful pride
Th' immortal muses in their art defied;
Th' avenging muses of the light of day
Depriv'd his eyes, and snatch'd his voice away.
POPE.

Men are active in *stripping* each other of their just rights and privileges; 'From the uncertainty of life, moralists have endeavoured to sink the estimation of its pleasures, and if they could not *strip* the seductions of vice of their present enjoyment, at least to load them with the fear of their end.'—MACKENZIE.

DEPREDATION, ROBBERY.

Depredation, in Latin *deprædatio*, from *præda* a prey, signifies the act of spoiling or laying waste, as well as taking away; *robbery*, on the other hand, signifies simply the removal or taking away from another by violence. Every *depredation*, therefore, includes a *robbery*, but not *vice versâ*. A *depredation* is always attended with mischief to some one, though not always with advantage to the *depredator;* but the *robber* always calculates on getting something for himself. *Depredations* are often committed for the indulgence of private animosity; *robbery* is always committed from a thirst for gain.

Depredation is either the publick act of a community, or the private act of individuals; *robbery* mostly the private act of individuals. *Depredations* are committed wherever the occasion offers; in open or covert places: *robberies* are committed either on the persons or houses of individuals. In former times neighbouring states used to commit frequent *depredations* on each other, even when not in a state of open hostility; *robberies* were, however, then less frequent than at present; 'As the delay of making war may sometimes be detrimental to individuals, who have suffered by *depredations* from foreign potentates, our laws have in some respects, armed the subject with powers to impel the prerogative, by directing the ministers to issue letters of marque.'—BLACKSTONE. 'From all this, what is my inference? That this new system of *robbery* in France cannot be rendered safe by any art.' —BURKE

Depredation is used in the proper and bad sense, for animals as well as for men; *robbery* may be employed figuratively and in the indifferent sense. Birds are great *depredators* in the cornfields; bees may be said to plunder or *rob* the flowers of their sweets.

TO DEPRIVE, DEBAR, ABRIDGE.

Deprive (*v. To bereave*) conveys the idea of either taking away that which one has, or withholding that which one may have; *debar*, from *de* and *bar*, signifying to prevent by means of a bar, conveys the idea only of withholding; *abridge* (*v. To abridge*) conveys that also of taking away. *Depriving* is a coercive measure; *debar* and *abridge* are merely acts of authority. We are *deprived* of that which is of the first necessity; we are *debarred* of privileges, enjoyments, opportunities, &c.; we are *abridged* of comforts, pleasures, conveniences, &c. Criminals are *deprived* of their liberty; their friends are in extraordinary cases *debarred* the privilege of seeing them; thus men are often *abridged* of their comforts in consequence of their own faults.

Deprivation and *debarring* sometimes arise from things as well as persons; *abridging* is always the voluntary act of conscious agents. Misfortunes sometimes *deprive* a person of the means of living; the poor are often *debarred*, by their poverty, of the opportunity to learn their duty; it may sometimes be necessary to *abridge* young people of their pleasures when they do not know how to make a good use of them. Religion teaches men to be resigned under the severest *deprivations*; it is painful to be *debarred* the society of those we love, or to *abridge* others of any advantage which they have been in the habit of enjoying.

When used as reflective verbs they preserve the same analogy in their signification. An extravagant person *deprives* himself of the power of doing good; 'Of what small moment to your real happiness are many of those injuries which draw forth your resentment? Can they *deprive* you of peace of conscience, of the satisfaction of having acted a right part?'—BLAIR. A person may *debar* himself of any pleasure from particular motives of prudence; 'Active and masculine spirits, in the vigour of youth, neither can nor ought to remain at rest. If they *debar* themselves from aiming at a noble object, their desires will move downward.'—HUGHES. A miser *abridges* himself of every enjoyment in order to gratify his ruling passion; 'The personal liberty of individuals in this kingdom cannot ever be *abridged* at the mere discretion of the magistrate.'—BLACKSTONE.

CAPTURE, SEIZURE, PRIZE.

Capture, in French *capture*, Latin *captura*, from *captus*, participle of *capio* to take, signifies either the act of taking, or the thing taken, but mostly the former; *seizure*, from *seize*, in French *saisir*, signifies only the act of *seizing*; *prize*, in French *prise*, from *pris*, participle of *prendre* to take, signifies only the thing taken.

Capture and *seizure* differ in the mode: a *capture* is made by force of arms; a *seizure* by direct and personal violence. The *capture* of a town or an island requires an army; the *seizure* of property is effected by the exertions of an individual. A *seizure* always requires some force, which a *capture* does not. A *capture* may be made on an unresisting object; it is merely the taking into possession: a *seizure* supposes much eagerness for possession on the one hand, and reluctance to yield on the other. Merchant vessels are *captured* which are not in a state to make resistance; contraband goods are *seized* by the police officers.

A *capture* has always something legitimate in it; it is a publick measure flowing from authority, or in the course of lawful warfare; 'The late Mr. Robert Wood, in his essay on the original genius and writings of Homer, inclines to think the Iliad and Odyssey were finished about half a century after the *capture* of Troy.—CUMBERLAND. A *seizure* is a private measure, frequently as unlawful and unjust as it is violent; it depends on the will of the individual; 'Many of the dangers imputed of old to exorbitant wealth are now at an end. The rich are neither waylaid by robbers, nor watched by informers; there is nothing to be dreaded from proscriptions or *seizures*.'—JOHNSON. A *capture* is general, it respects the act of taking: a *prize* is particular, it regards the object taken, and its value to the *captor*: many *captures* are made by sea which never become *prizes*; 'Sensible of their own force, and allured by the prospect of so rich a *prize*, the northern barbarians, in the reign of Arcadius and Honorius, assailed at once all the frontiers of the Roman empire.'—HUME.

BOOTY, SPOIL, PREY.

These words mark a species of capture.

Booty, in French *butin*, Danish *bytte*, Dutch *buyt*, Teutonick *beute*, probably comes from the Teutonick *bat* a useful thing, denoting the thing taken for its use; *spoil*, in French *depouillé*, Latin *spolium*, in Greek σκῦλον, signifies the things stripped off from the dead, from συλάω, Hebrew סלל to spoil; *prey*, in French *proie*, Latin *præda*, is not improbably changed from *prændo*, *prendo*, or *prehendo* to lay hold of, signifying the thing seized.

The first two are used as military terms or in attacks on an enemy, the latter in cases of particular violence. The soldier gets his *booty*; the combatant his *spoils*; the carnivorous animal his *prey*. *Booty* respects what is of personal service to the captor; *spoils* whatever serves to designate his triumph; *prey* includes whatever gratifies the appetite and is to be consumed. When a town is taken, soldiers are too busy in the work of destruction and mischief to carry away much *booty*; in every battle the arms and personal property of the slain enemy are the lawful *spoils* of the victor; the hawk pounces on his *prey*, and carries him up to his nest;

> 'T was in the dead of night, when sleep repairs
> Our bodies worn with toils, our minds with cares,
> When Hector's ghost before my sight appears:
> A bloody shroud he seem'd, and bath'd in tears,
> Unlike that Hector who return'd from toils
> Of war, triumphant in Æacian *spoils*.—DRYDEN.

Greediness stimulates to take *booty*; ambition produces an eagerness for *spoils*; a ferocious appetite impels to a search for *prey*. Among the ancients the prisoners of war who were made slaves constituted a part of their *booty*; and even in later periods such a capture was good *booty*, when ransom was paid for those who could liberate themselves. Among some savages the head or limb of an enemy constituted part of their *spoils*. Among cannibals the prisoners of war are the *prey* of the conquerors.

Booty and *prey* are often used in an extended and figurative sense. Plunderers obtain a rich *booty*; the diligent bee returns loaded with its *booty*;* 'When they (the French National Assembly) had finally determined on a state resource from church *booty*, they came on the 14th of April, 1790, to a solemn resolution on the subject.'—BURKE. It is necessary that animals should become a *prey* to man, in order that man may not become a *prey* to them; every thing in nature becomes a *prey* to another thing, which in its turn falls a *prey* to something else. All is change but order. Man is a *prey* to the diseases of his body or his mind, and after death to the worms;

> The wolf, who from the nightly ford
> Forth drags the bleating *prey*, ne'er drank her milk,
> Nor wore her warming fleece.—THOMSON.

RAVAGE, DESOLATION, DEVASTATION.

Ravage comes from the Latin *rapio*, and the Greek ἁρπάζω, signifying a seizing or tearing away; *desolation*, from *solus* alone, signifies made solitary or reduced to solitude; *devastation*, in Latin *devastatio*, from *devasto* to lay waste, signifies reducing to a waste or desert.

* Vide Roubaud: "Proie, butin"

Ravage expresses less than either *desolation* or *devastation:* a breaking, tearing, or destroying is implied in the word *ravage;* but the *desolation* goes to the entire unpeopling a land, and the *devastation* to the entire clearing away of every vestige of cultivation. Torrents, flames, tempests, and wild beasts *ravage;*

> Beasts of prey retire, that all night long,
> Urg'd by necessity, had rang'd the dark,
> As if their conscious *ravage* shunn'd the light,
> Asham'd.—THOMSON.

War, plague, and famine *desolate;*

> Amid thy bow'rs the tyrant's hand is seen,
> And *desolation* saddens all thy green.
> GOLDSMITH.

Armies of barbarians, who inundate a country, carry *devastation* with them wherever they go; 'How much the strength of the Roman republick is impaired, and what dreadful *devastation* has gone forth into all its provinces!'—MELMOTH (*Letters of Cicero*). * Nothing resists *ravages*, they are rapid and terrible; nothing arrests *desolation*, it is cruel and unpitying; *devastation* spares nothing, it is ferocious and indefatigable. *Ravages* spread alarm and terrour; *desolation*, grief and despair; *devastation*, dread and horrour.

Ravage is employed likewise in the moral application; *desolation* and *devastation* only in the proper application to countries. Disease makes its *ravages* on beauty; death makes its *ravages* among men in a more terrible degree at one time than at another;

> Would one think 't were possible for love
> To make such *ravage* in a noble soul?—ADDISON.

OVERSPREAD, OVERRUN, RAVAGE.

To *overspread* signifies simply to cover the whole surface of a body; but to *overrun* is a mode of spreading, namely, by running: things in general, therefore, are said to *overspread* which admit of extension; nothing can be said to *overrun* but what literally or figuratively runs: the face is *overspread* with spots; the ground is *overrun* with weeds. To *overrun* and to *ravage* are both employed to imply the active and extended destruction of an enemy; but the former expresses more than the latter; a small body may *ravage* in particular parts; but immense numbers are said to *overrun*, as they run into every part: the Barbarians *overran* all Europe, and settled in different countries; detachments are sent out to *ravage* the country or neighbourhood; 'The storm of hail and fire, with the darkness that *overspread* the land for three days, are described with great strength.'—ADDISON. 'Most despotick governments are naturally *overrun* with ignorance and barbarity.'—ADDISON. 'While Herod was absent, the thieves of Trachonites *ravaged* with their depredations all the parts of Judea and Cœlo-Syria that lay within their reach.'—PRIDEAUX.

RAPINE, PLUNDER, PILLAGE.

The idea of property taken from another contrary to his consent is included in all these terms: but the term *rapine* includes most violence; *plunder* includes most removal or carrying away; *pillage* most search and scrutiny after. A soldier, who makes a sudden incursion into an enemy's country, and carries away whatever comes within his reach, is guilty of *rapine;*

> Upon the banks
> Of Tweed, slow winding thro' the vale, the seat
> Of war and *rapine* once.—SOMERVILLE.

Robbers frequently carry away much *plunder* when they break into houses; 'Ship-money was pitched upon as fit to be formed by excise and taxes, and the burden of the subjects took off by *plunderings* and sequestrations.'—SOUTH. When an army sack a town they strip it of every thing that is to be found, and go away loaded with *pillage;* 'Although the Eretrians for a time stood resolutely to the defence of their city, it was given up by treachery on the seventh day, and *pillaged* and destroyed in a most barbarous manner by the Persians.'—CUMBERLAND. Mischief and bloodshed attend *rapine;* loss attends *plunder;* distress and ruin follow wherever there has been *pillage.*

RAPACIOUS, RAVENOUS, VORACIOUS.

Rapacious, in Latin *rapax*, from *rapio* to seize, signifies seizing or grasping a thing with an eager desire to have; *ravenous*, from the Latin *rabies* a fury, and *rapio* to seize, signifies the same as *rapacious; voracious*, from *voro* to devour, signifies an eagerness to devour.

The idea of greediness, which forms the leading features in the signification of all these terms, is varied in the subject and the object: *rapacious* is the quality peculiar to beasts of prey, or of men who are actuated by a similar spirit of plunder; 'A display of our wealth before robbers is not the way to restrain their boldness, or to lessen their *rapacity.*'—BURKE. *Ravenous* and *voracious* are common to all animals, when impelled by hunger. The beasts of the forest are *rapacious* at all times; all animals are more or less *ravenous* or *voracious*, as circumstances may make them: the *rapacious* applies to the seizing of other animals as food; the *ravenous* applies to the seizing of any thing which one takes for one's food;

> Again the holy fires on altars burn,
> And once again the *rav'nous* birds return.
> DRYDEN.

A lion is *rapacious* when it seizes on its prey; it is *ravenous* in the act of consuming it. The word *ravenous* respects the haste with which one eats; the word *voracious* respects the quantity which one consumes;

> Ere you remark another's sin,
> Bid thy own conscience look within;
> Control thy more *voracious* bill,
> Nor for a breakfast nations kill.—GAY.

A *ravenous* person is loath to wait for the dressing of his food; he consumes it without any preparation: a *voracious* person not only eats in haste, but he consumes great quantities, and continues to do so for a long time. Abstinence from food, for an unusual length, will make any healthy creature *ravenous;* habitual intemperance in eating, or a diseased appetite, will produce *voracity.*

As the leading idea in the term *rapacious* is that of plunder, it may be extended to things figuratively. 'Any of these, without regarding the pains of churchmen, grudge them those small remains of ancient piety, which the *rapacity* of some ages has scarce left to the church.'—SPRAT.

SANGUINARY, BLOODY, BLOOD-THIRSTY.

Sanguinary, from *sanguis*, is employed both in the sense of *bloody* or having *blood; blood-thirsty*, or the thirsting after *blood: sanguinary*, in the first case, relates only to *blood* shed, as a *sanguinary* engagement, or a *sanguinary* conflict; 'They have seen the French rebel against a mild and lawful monarch with more fury than ever any people has been known to rise against the most illegal usurper or the most *sanguinary* tyrant.'—BURKE. *Bloody* is used in the familiar application, to denote the simple presence of *blood*, as a *bloody* coat, or a *bloody* sword;

> And from the wound,
> Black *bloody* drops distill'd upon the ground.
> DRYDEN.

In the second case, *sanguinary* is employed to characterize the tempers of persons only; *blood-thirsty* to characterize the tempers of persons or animals: the French revolution has given us many specimens how *sanguinary* men may become who are abandoned to their own furious passions; tigers are by nature the most *blood-thirsty* of all creatures; 'The Peruvians fought not like the Mexicans, to glut *blood-thirsty* divinities with human sacrifices.'—ROBERTSON.

TO ENCROACH, INTRENCH, INTRUDE, INVADE, INFRINGE.

Encroach, in French *encrocher*, is compounded of *en* or *in* and *crouch* cringe or creep, signifying to creep into any thing; *intrench*, compounded of *in* and *trench*, sig

* Vide Roubaud: "Ravager, desoler, devaster, saccager."

nifies to *trench* or dig beyond one's own into another's ground, *intrude*, from the Latin *intrudo*, signifies literally to thrust upon; and *invade*, from *invado*, signifies to march in upon; *infringe*, from the Latin *infringo*, compounded of *in* and *frango*, signifies to break in upon.

All these terms denote an unauthorized procedure; but the two former designate gentle or silent actions, the latter violent if not noisy actions.

Encroach is often an imperceptible action, performed with such art as to elude observation; it is, according to its derivation, an insensible creeping into: *intrench* is in fact a species of *encroachment*, namely, that perceptible species which consists in exceeding the boundaries in marking out the ground or space: it should be one of the first objects of a parent to check the first indications of an *encroaching* disposition in their children; according to the building laws, it is made actionable for any one to *intrench* upon the street or publick road with their houses or gardens.

In an extended application of these terms we may speak of *encroaching* on a person's time, or *intrenching* on the sphere, &c. of another: *intrude* and *invade* designate an unauthorized entry; the former in violation of right, equity, or good manners; the latter in violation of publick law: the former is more commonly applied to individuals; the latter to nations or large communities: unbidden guests *intrude* themselves sometimes into families to their no small annoyance; an army never *invades* a country without doing some mischief: nothing evinces a greater ignorance and impertinence than to *intrude* one's self into any company where we may of course expect to be unwelcome; in the feudal times, when civil power was invested in the hands of the nobility and petty princes, they were incessantly *invading* each other's territories; 'It is observed by one of the fathers that he who restrains himself in the use of things lawful will never *encroach* upon things forbidden.'—JOHNSON. 'Religion *intrenches* upon none of our privileges, *invades* none of our pleasures.'—SOUTH. 'One of the chief characteristicks of the golden age, of the age in which neither care nor danger had *intruded* on mankind, is the community of possessions.'—JOHNSON.

Invade has likewise an improper as well as a proper acceptation; in the former case it bears a close analogy to *infringe*: we speak of *invading* rights, or *infringing* rights; but the former is an act of greater violence than the latter: by an authorized exercise of power the rights of a people may be *invaded*; by gradual steps and imperceptible means their liberties may be *infringed*: *invade* is used only for publick privileges; *infringe* is applied also to those which belong to individuals.

King John of England *invaded* the rights of the Barons in so senseless a manner as to give them a colour for their resistance; it is of importance to the peace and well-being of society that men should, in their different relations, stations, and duties, guard against any *infringement* on the sphere or department of such as come into the closest connexion with them;

> No sooner were his eyes in slumber bound,
> When from above a more than mortal sound
> *Invades* his ears.—DRYDEN.

'The King's partisans maintained that, while the prince commands no military force, he will in vain by violence attempt an *infringement* of laws so clearly defined by means of late disputes.'—HUME.

TO INFRINGE, VIOLATE, TRANSGRESS.

Infringe, *v.* *To encroach*; *violate*, from the Latin *vis* force, signifies to use force towards; *transgress*, *v.* *Offence*.

Civil and moral laws are *infringed* by those who act in opposition to them; 'I hold friendship to be a very holy league, and no less than a piacle to *infringe* it.'—HOWELL. Treaties and engagements are *violated* by those who do not hold them sacred;

> No *violated* leagues with sharp remorse
> Shall sting the conscious victor.—SOMERVILLE.

The bounds which are prescribed by the moral law are *transgressed* by those who are guilty of any excess;

> Why hast thou, Satan, broke the bounds prescrib'd
> To thy *transgressions*?—MILTON.

It is the business of government to see that the rights and privileges of individuals or particular bodies be not *infringed*: policy but too frequently runs counter to equity; where the particular interests of princes are more regarded than the dictates of conscience, treaties and compacts are first *violated* and then justified: the passions, when not kept under proper control, will ever hurry men on to *transgress* the limits of right reason.

INFRINGEMENT, INFRACTION.

Infringement and *infraction*, which are both derived from the Latin verb *infringo* or *frango* (*v.* *To infringe*), are employed according to the different senses of the verb *infringe*: the former being applied to the rights of individuals, either in their domestick or publick capacity; and the latter rather to national transactions. Politeness, which teaches us what is due to every man in the smallest concerns, considers any unasked-for interference in the private affairs of another as an *infringement*; 'We see with Orestes (or rather with Sophocles), that "it is fit that such gross *infringements* of the moral law (as parricide) should be punished with death."'—MACKENZIE. Equity, which enjoins on nations as well as individuals, an attentive consideration to the interests of the whole, forbids the *infraction* of a treaty in any case; 'No people can, without the *infraction* of the universal league of social beings, incite those practices in an other dominion which they would themselves punish in their own.'—JOHNSON.

INVASION, INCURSION, IRRUPTION, INROAD.

The idea of making a forcible entrance into a foreign territory is common to all these. *Invasion*, from *vado* to go, expresses merely this general idea, without any particular qualification; *incursion*, from *curro* to run, signifies a hasty and sudden *invasion*; *irruption*, from *rumpo* to break, signifies a particularly violent *invasion*; *inroad*, from *in* and *road*, signifies a making a road or way for one's self, which includes *invasion* and occupation. *Invasion* is said of that which passes in distant lands; Alexander *invaded* India; Hannibal crossed the Alps, and made an *invasion* into Italy;

> The nations of the Ausonian shore
> Shall hear the dreadful rumour, from afar,
> Of arm'd *invasion*, and embrace the war.
> DRYDEN

Incursion is said of neighbouring states; the borderers on each side the Tweed used to make frequent *incursions* into England or Scotland; 'Britain by its situation was removed from the fury of these barbarous *incursions*.'—HUME. *Invasion* is the act of a regular army; it is a systematick military movement: *irruption* is the irregular and impetuous movement of undisciplined troops. The *invasion* of France by the allies was one of the grandest military movements that the world ever witnessed; the *irruption* of the Goths and Vandals into Europe has been acted over again by the late revolutionary armies of France; 'The study of ancient literature was interrupted in Europe, by the *irruption* of the northern nations.'—JOHNSON.

An *invasion* may be partial and temporary; one *invades* from various causes, but not always from hostility to the inhabitants: an *inroad* is made by a conqueror who determines to dispossess the existing occupier of the land: *invasion* is therefore to *inroad* only as a means to an end. He who *invades* a country, and gets possession of its strong places so as to have an entire command of the land, is said to make *inroads* into that country; but since it is possible to get forcible possession of a country by other means besides that of a military entry, there may be an *inroad* where there is no express *invasion*; 'From Scotland we have had in former times some alarms, and *inroads* into the northern parts of this kingdom.'—BACON. Alexander made such *inroads* into Persia, as to become master of the whole country; but the French republick, and all its usurped authorities, made *inroads* into different countries by means of spies and revolutionary incen liaries, who effected more than the sword in subjecting them to the power of France.

These terms bear a similar distinction in the improper sense. In this case *invasion* is figuratively employed to express a violent seizure, in general of what belongs to individuals, particularly that which he enjoys by civil compact, namely, his rights and privileges. The term may also be extended to other objects, as when we speak of *invading* a person's province, &c.; 'Encouraged with success, he *invades* the province of philosophy.'—DRYDEN. Things may likewise be said to *invade;*

Far off we hear the waves, which surly sound,
Invade the rocks; the rocks their groans rebound.
DRYDEN.

In like manner we speak of the *inroads* which disease makes on the constitution; of the *incursion* or *irruption* of unpleasant thoughts in the mind; 'Rest and labour equally perceive their reign of short duration and uncertain tenure, and their empire liable to *inroads* from those who are alike enemies to both.'—JOHNSON.

I refrain, too suddenly,
To utter what will come at last too soon:
Lest evil tidings, with too rude *irruption*,
Hitting thy aged ear should pierce too deep.
MILTON.

Sins of daily *incursion*, and such as human frailty is unavoidably liable to.'—SOUTH.

INTRUDER, INTERLOPER.

An *intruder* (v. *To intrude*) thrusts himself in; an *interloper*, from *laufen*, runs in between and takes his station. The *intruder* may be so only for a short space of time, in an unimportant degree; or may *intrude* only in unimportant matters; the *interloper* abridges another of his essential rights and for a permanency. A man is an *intruder* who is an unbidden guest at the table of another;

Will you, a bold *intruder*, never learn
To know your basket and your bread discern?
DRYDEN.

A man is an *interloper* when he joins any society in such manner as to obtain its privileges, without sharing its burdens; 'Some proposed to vest the trade to America in exclusive companies, which interest would render the most vigilant guardians of the Spanish commerce, against the encroachments of *interlopers*.'—ROBERTSON. The term *intruder* may, however, be applied to any who takes violent or unauthorized possession of what belongs to another; 'I would not have you to offer it to the doctor, as eminent physicians do not love *intruders*.'—JOHNSON. 'They were but *intruders* upon the possession during the minority of the heir; they knew those lands were the rightful inheritance of that young lady.'—DAVIES.

TO INTRUDE, OBTRUDE.

To *intrude* is to thrust one's self into a place; to *obtrude* is to thrust one's self in the way. It is *intrusion* to go into any society unasked and undesired; it is *obtruding* to join any company and take a part in the conversation without invitation or consent. We violate the rights of another when we *intrude;* we set up ourselves by *obtruding:* one *intrudes* with one's person in the place which does not belong to one's self; one *obtrudes* with one's person, remarks, &c., upon another: a person *intrudes* out of curiosity or any other personal gratification; he *obtrudes* out of vanity.

Politeness denominates it *intrusion* to pass the threshold of another, without having first ascertained that we are perfectly welcome; modesty denominates it *obtruding* to offer an opinion in the presence of another, unless we are expressly invited or authorized by our relationship and situation. There is no thinking man who does not feel the value of having some place of retirement, which is free from the *intrusion* of all impertinent visitants; it is the fault of young persons, who have formed any opinions for themselves, to *obtrude* them upon every one who will give them a hearing

In the moral acceptation they preserve the same distinction. In moments of devotion the serious man endeavours to prevent the *intrusion* of improper ideas in his mind: 'The *intrusion* of scruples, and the recollection of better notions, will not suffer some to live contented with their own conduct.'—JOHNSON. The stings of conscience *obtrude* themselves upon the guilty even in the season of their greatest merriment; 'Artists are sometimes ready to talk to an incidental inquirer as they do to one another, and to make their knowledge ridiculous by injudicious *obtrusion*.'—JOHNSON.

TO ABSORB, SWALLOW UP, INGULF, ENGROSS.

Absorb, in French *absorber*, Latin *absorbeo*, is compounded of *ab* and *sorbeo* to sup up, in distinction from *swallow up;* the former denoting a gradual consumption; the latter a sudden envelopement of the whole object. The excessive heat of the sun *absorbs* all the nutritious fluids of bodies animal and vegetable. The gaming table is a vortex in which the principle of every man is *swallowed up* with his estate; 'Surely the bare remembrance that a man was formerly rich or great cannot make him at all happier there, where an infinite happiness or an infinite misery shall equally *swallow up* the sense of these poor felicities.'—SOUTH *Ingulf*, compounded of *in* and *gulf*, signifies to be enclosed in a great gulf, which is a strong figurative representation for being *swallowed up*. As it applies to grand and sublime objects, it is used only in the higher style;

Ingulf'd, all helps of art we vainly try
To weather leeward shores, alas! too nigh.
FALCONER.

Engross, which is compounded of the French words *en gros* in whole, signifies to purchase wholesale, so as to *swallow up* the profits of others. In the moral application, therefore, it is very analogous to *absorb*.

The mind is *absorbed* in the contemplation of any subject, when all its powers are so bent upon it as not to admit distraction;

Absorbed in that immensity I see,
I shrink abased, and yet aspire to thee.—COWPER

The mind is *engrossed* by any subject when the thoughts of it force themselves upon its contemplation to the exclusion of others which should engage the attention. 'Those two great things that so *engross* the desires and designs of both the nobler and ignobler sort of mankind, are to be found in religion, namely, wisdom and pleasure.'—SOUTH. The term *engross* may also convey the idea of taking from another, as well as taking to ourselves, which it is still more distinguished from the other terms; 'This inconvenience the politician must expect from others, as well as they have felt from him, unless he thinks that he can *engross* this principle to himself, and that others cannot be as false and atheistical as himself.'—SOUTH.

TO MUTILATE, MAIM, MANGLE.

Mutilate, in Latin *mutilatus*, from *mutilo* and *mutilus*, Greek μύτιλος or μίτυλος without horns, signifies to take off any necessary part; *maim* and *mangle* are in all probability derived from the Latin *mancus*, which comes from *manus*, signifying to deprive of a hand, or to wound in general.

Mutilate has the most extended meaning; it implies the abridging of any limb: *mangle* is applied to irregular wounds in any part of the body: *maim* is confined to wounds in the hands. Men are exposed to be *mutilated* by means of cannon balls; they are in danger of being *mangled* when attacked promiscuously with the sword; they frequently get *maimed* when boarding vessels or storming places. One is *mutilated* and *mangled* by active means; one becomes *maimed* by natural infirmity.

They are similarly distinguished in the moral application, but *maiming* is the effect of a direct effort whereby an object loses its value; 'I have shown the evil of *maiming* and splitting religion.'—BLAIR. *Mangling* is a much stronger term than *mutilating*, the latter signifies to lop off an essential part; to *mangle* is to *mutilate* a thing to such a degree as to render it useless or worthless. Every sect of Christians is fond of *mutilating* the Bible by setting aside such parts as do not favour their own ideas, so that among them the sacred Scriptures have been literally *mangled*, and stripped of all their most important doctrines; 'How

Hales would have borne the *mutilations* which his *Plea of the Crown* has suffered from the editor, they who know his character will easily conceive.'—JOHNSON. 'What have they (the French nobility) done that they should be hunted about, *mangled*, and tortured?'—BURKE.

TO KILL, MURDER, ASSASSINATE, SLAY OR SLAUGHTER.

Kill, which is in Saxon *cyelan*, and Dutch *kelan*, is of uncertain origin; *murder*, in German *mord*, &c. is connected with the Latin *mors* death; *assassinate* signifies to *kill* after the manner of an *assassin;* which word probably comes from the *Levant*, where a prince of the Arsacides or *assassins*, who was called the old man of the mountains, lived in a castle between Antioch and Damascus, and brought up young men to lie in wait for passengers; *slay* or *slaughter*, in German *schlagen*, &c. is probably connected with *liegen* to lie, signifying to lay low.

To *kill* is the general and indefinite term, signifying simply to take away life; to *murder* is to *kill* with open violence and injustice; to *assassinate* is to *murder* by surprise, or by means of lying in wait; to *slay* is to *kill* in battle: to *kill* is applicable to men, animals, and also vegetables; to *murder* and *assassinate* to men only; to *slay* mostly to men, but sometimes to animals; to *slaughter* only to animals in the proper sense, but it may be applied to men in the improper sense, when they are *killed* like brutes, either as to the numbers or to the manner of *killing* them; 'The fierce young hero who had overcome the Curiatii, being upbraided by his sister for having *slain* her lover, in the height of his resentment *kills* her.'—ADDISON. '*Murders* and executions are always transacted behind the scenes in the French theatre.'—ADDISON. 'The women interposed with so many prayers and entreaties, that they prevented the mutual *slaughter* which threatened the Romans and the Sabines.'—ADDISON.

On this vain hope, adulterers, thieves rely,
And to this altar vile *assassins* fly.—JENYNS.

CARNAGE, SLAUGHTER, MASSACRE, BUTCHERY.

Carnage, from the Latin *caro carnis* flesh, implies properly a collection of dead flesh, that is, the reducing to the state of dead flesh; *slaughter*, from *slay*, is the act of taking away life; *massacre*, in French *massacre*, comes from the Latin *mactare*, to kill for sacrifice; *butchery*, from to *butcher*, signifies the act of *butchering;* in French *boucherie*, from *bouche* the mouth, signifies the killing for food.

Carnage respects the number of dead bodies made; it may be said either of men or animals, but more commonly of the former; *slaughter* respects the act of taking away life, and the circumstances of the agent; *massacre* and *butchery* respect the circumstances of the objects who are the sufferers of the action: the three latter are said of human beings only.

Carnage is the consequence of any impetuous attack from a powerful enemy. Soldiers who get into a besieged town, or a wolf who breaks into a sheepfold, commonly make a dreadful *carnage;*

The *carnage* Juno from the skies survey'd,
And, touch'd with grief, bespoke the blue-ey'd maid.
POPE.

Slaughter is the consequence of warfare. In battles the *slaughter* will be very considerable where both parties defend themselves pertinaciously;

Yet, yet a little, and destructive *slaughter*
Shall rage around and mar this beauteous prospect.
ROWE.

A *massacre* is the consequence of secret and personal resentment between bodies of people. It is always a stain upon the nation by whom it is practised, as it cannot be effected without a violent breach of confidence, and a direct act of treachery; of this description was the *massacre* of the Danes by the original Britons, and the *massacre* of the Hugenots in France;

Our groaning country bled at every vein;
When murders, rapes, and *massacres* prevail'd.
ROWE.

Butchery is the general accompaniment of a *massacre*, defenceless women and children are commonly *butchered* by the savage furies who are most active in this work of blood;

Let us be sacrificers, but not *butchers*.—SHAKSPEARE.

BODY, CORPSE, CARCASS.

Body is here taken in the improper sense for a dead *body;* *corpse*, from the Latin *corpus* a body, has also been turned from its derivation to signify a dead body; *carcass*, in French *carcasse*, is compounded of *caro* and *cassa vita*, signifying flesh without life.

Body is applicable to either men or brutes, *corpse* to men only, and *carcass* to brutes only, unless when taken in a contemptuous sense. When speaking of any particular person who is deceased we should use the simple term *body;* the *body* was suffered to lie too long unburied: when designating its condition as lifeless, the term *corpse* is preferable; he was taken up as a *corpse:* when designating the body as a lifeless lump separated from the soul, it may be characterized (though contemptuously) as a *carcass;* the fowls devour the *carcass;*

A groan, as of a troubled ghost, renew'd
My fright, and then these dreadful words ensued.
Why dost thou thus my buried *body* rend,
Oh! spare the *corpse* of thy unhappy friend.
DRYDEN.

On the bleak shore now lies th' abandon'd king,
A headless *carcass*, and a nameless thing.
DRYDEN.

EMBRYO, FŒTUS.

Embryo, in French *embrion*, Greek ἔμβρυον, from βρύω to germinate, signifies the thing germinated; *fœtus*, in French *fetus*, Latin *fœtus*, from *foveo* to cherish, signifies the thing cherished, both words referring to what is formed in the womb of the mother; but *embryo* properly implies the first fruit of conception, and the *fœtus* that which is arrived to a maturity of formation. Anatomists tell us that the *embryo* in the human subject assumes the character of the *fœtus* about the forty-second day after conception.

Fœtus is applicable only in its proper sense to animals: *embryo* has a figurative application to plants and fruits when they remain in a confused and imperfect state, and also a moral application to plans, or whatever is roughly conceived in the mind.

CORPORAL, CORPOREAL, BODILY.

Corporal, *corporeal*, and *bodily*, as their origin bespeaks, have all relation to the same object, the *body;* but the two former are employed to signify relating or appertaining to the *body;* the latter to denote containing or forming part of the *body*. Hence we say, *corporal* punishment, *bodily* vigour or strength, *corporeal* substances; the Godhead *bodily*, the *corporeal* frame, *bodily* exertion; 'Bettesworth was so little satisfied with this account, that he publickly professed his resolution of a violent and *corporal* revenge, but the inhabitants of St. Patrick's district imbodied themselves in the Dean's (Swift's) defence.'—JOHNSON.

Corporal is only employed for the animal frame in its proper sense; *corporeal* is used for animal substance in an extended sense; hence we speak of *corporal* sufferance and *corporeal* agents; 'When the soul is freed from all *corporeal* alliance then it truly exists.'—HUGHES. *Corporeal* is distinguished from spiritual; *bodily* from mental. It is impossible to represent spiritual beings any other way than under a *corporeal* form; *bodily* pains, however severe, are frequently overpowered by mental pleasures; 'The soul is beset with a numerous train of temptations to evil, which arise from *bodily* appetites.'—BLAIR.

CORPOREAL, MATERIAL.

Corporeal is properly a species of *material;* whatever is *corporeal* is *material*, but not *vice versâ*. *Corporeal* respects animate bodies; *material* is used for every thing which can act on the senses, animate or inanimate. The world contains *corporeal* beings and consists of *material* substances;

Grant that *corporeal* is the human mind,
It must have parts in infinitum join'd;
And each of these must will, perceive, design,
And draw confus'dly in a diff'rent line.—JENYNS.

'In the present *material* system in which we live, and where the objects that surround us are continually exposed to the examination of our senses, how many things occur that are mysterious and unaccountable.'—BLAIR.

CORPULENT, STOUT, LUSTY.

Corpulent from *corpus* the body, signifies having fulness of body; *stout*, in Dutch *stott*, is no doubt a variation of the German *stätig* steady, signifying able to stand, solid, firm; *lusty*, in German, &c. *lustig* merry, cheerful, implies here a vigorous state of body.

Corpulent respects the fleshy state of the body; *stout* respects also the state of the muscles and bones: *corpulence* is therefore an incidental property; *stoutness* is a natural property; *corpulence* may come upon a person according to circumstances; 'Mallet's stature was diminutive, but he was regularly formed; his appearance, till he grew *corpulent*, was agreeable, and he suffered it to want no recommendation that dress could give it.'—JOHNSON. *Stoutness* is the natural make of the body which is born with us;

Hence rose the Marsian and Sabellian race,
Strong limb'd and *stout*, and to the wars inclin'd.
DRYDEN.

Corpulence and *lustiness* are both occasioned by the state of the health; but the former may arise from disease; the latter is always the consequence of good health: *corpulence* consists of an undue proportion of fat; *lustiness* consists of a due and full proportion of all the solids in the body;

Though I look old, yet I am strong and *lusty*,
For in my youth I never did apply
Hot and rebellious liquors to my blood.
SHAKSPEARE.

LEAN, MEAGRE.

Lean is in all probability connected with line, lank, and long, signifying that which is simply long without any other dimension; *meagre*, in Latin *macer*, Greek μικρος small.

Lean denotes want of fat; *meagre* want of flesh: what is *lean* is not always *meagre*; but nothing can be *meagre* without being *lean*. Brutes as well as men are *lean*, but men only are said to be *meagre*: *leanness* is frequently connected with the temperament; *meagreness* is the consequence of starvation and disease. There are some animals by nature inclined to be *lean*; a *meagre* pale visage is to be seen perpetually in the haunts of vice and poverty;

Who ambles time withal
With a priest that lacks Latin,
And with a rich man that hath not the gout,
The one lacking the burthen of *lean* and
Wasteful learning; the other knowing nor
Burthen of heavy tedious penury.—SHAKSPEARE.

So thin, so ghastly *meagre*, and so wan,
So bare of flesh, he scarce resembled man.
DRYDEN.

MEMBER, LIMB.

Member, in Latin *membrum*, probably from the Greek μέρος a part, because a *member* is properly a part; *limb* is connected with the word *lame*.

Member is a general term applied either to the animal body or to other bodies, as a *member* of a family, or a *member* of a community: *limb* is applicable to animal bodies: *limb* is therefore a species of *member*; for every *limb* is a *member*, but every *member* is not a *limb*.

The *members* of the body comprehend every part which is capable of performing a distinct office: but the *limbs* are those jointed *members* that are distinguished from the head and the body: the nose and the eyes are *members* but not *limbs*; the arms and legs are properly denominated *limbs*; 'A man's *limbs* (by which for the present we only understand those *members* the loss of which only amounts to mayhem by the common law) are the gifts of the wise Creator to enable him to protect himself from external injuries.'—BLACKSTONE.

ANIMAL, BRUTE, BEAST.

Animal, in French *animal*, Latin *animal*, from *anima* life, signifies the thing having life; *brute* is in French *brute*, Latin *brutus* dull, Greek βαρύτης, Chaldee ברות foolishness; *beast*, in French *bête*, Latin *bestia*, changed from *bostema*, Greek βοσκήμα a beast of burden, and βόσκω to feed, signifies properly the thing that feeds.

Animal is the generick, *brute* and *beast* are the specifick terms. The *animal* is the thing that lives and moves. If *animal* be considered as thinking, willing, reflecting, and acting, it is confined in its signification to the human species; if it be regarded as limited in all the functions which mark intelligence and will, if it be divested of speech and reason, it belongs to the *brute*; if *animal* be considered, moreover, as to its appetites, independent of reason, of its destination, and consequent dependence on its mental powers; it descends to the *beast*.

Man and *brute* are opposed. To man an immortal soul is assigned; but we are not authorized by Scripture to extend this dignity to the *brutes*. "The *brutes* that perish" is the ordinary mode of distinguishing that part of the *animal* creation from the superiour order of terrestrial beings who are destined to exist in a future world. Men cannot be exposed to a greater degradation than to be divested of their particular characteristicks, and classed under the general name of *animal*, unless we except that which assigns to them the epithet of *brute* or *beast*, which, as designating peculiar atrocity of conduct, does not always carry with it a reproach equal to the infamy of a thing; the perversion of the rational faculty is at all times more shocking and disgraceful than the absence of it by nature; 'Some would be apt to say, he is a conjurer; for he has found that a republick is not made up of every body of *animals*, but is composed of men only and not of horses.'—STEELE. 'As nature has framed the several species of beings as it were in a chain; so man seems to be placed as the middle link between angels and *brutes*.'—ADDISON.

Whom e'en the savage *beasts* had spar'd they kill'
And strew'd his mangled limbs about the field.
DRYDEN.

SOUND, TONE.

Sound, in Latin *sonus*, and *tone*, in Latin *tonus* may probably both come from the Greek τείνω to stretch or exert, signifying simply an exertion of the voice; but I should rather derive *sound* from the Hebrew שוע.

Sound is that which issues from any body, so as to become audible; *tone* is a species of *sound*, which is produced from particular bodies: the *sound* may be accidental; we may hear the *sounds* of waters or leaves, of animals or men: *tones* are those particular *sounds* which are made either to express a particular feeling, or to produce harmony; a sheep will cry for its lost young in a *tone* of distress; an organ is so formed as to send forth the most solemn *tones*; 'The *sounds* of the voice, according to the various touches which raise them, form themselves into an acute or grave, quick or slow, loud or soft, *tone*.'—HUGHES.

SMELL, SCENT, ODOUR, PERFUME, FRAGRANCE.

Smell and melt are in all probability connected together, because *smells* arise from the evaporation of bodies; *scent*, changed from *sent*, comes from the Latin *sentio*, to perceive or feel; *odour*, in Latin *odor*, comes from *oleo*, in Greek ὄζω to smell; *perfume*, compounded of *per* or *pro* and *fumo* or *fumus* a smoke or vapour, that is, the vapour that issues forth; *fragrance*, in Latin *fragrantia*, comes from *fragro*, anciently *frago*, that is, to *perfume* or *smell* like the *fraga* or strawberry.

Smell and *scent* are said either of that which receives, or that which gives the *smell*; the *odour*, the *perfume*, and *fragrance* of that which communicates the *smell*. In the first case, *smell* is said generally of all living things without distinction; *scent* is said only of such animals as have this peculiar faculty of tracing objects by their *smell:* some persons have a much quicker *smell* than others, and some have an acuter *smell* of particular objects than they have of things in general: dogs are remarkable for their quickness of *scent*, by which they can trace their masters and other objects at an immense distance: other animals are gifted with this faculty to a surprising degree, which serves them as a means of defence against their enemies;

> Then curses his conspiring feet, whose *scent*
> Betrays that safety which their swiftness lent.
> DENHAM.

In the second case, *smell* is compared with *odour*, *perfume*, and *fragrance*, either as respects the objects communicating the *smell*, or the nature of the *smell* which is communicated. *Smell* is indefinite in its sense, and universal in its application; *odour*, *perfume*, and *fragrance* are species of *smells:* every object is said to *smell* which acts on the olfactory nerves; flowers, fruits, woods, earth, water, and the like, have a *smell;* but *odour* is said of that which is artificial; the *perfume* and *fragrance* of that which is natural: the burning of things produces an *odour;*

> So flowers are gathered to adorn a grave,
> To lose their freshness among bones and rottenness,
> And have their *odours* stifled in the dust.—ROWE.

The *perfume* and *fragrance* arise from flowers or sweet *smelling* herbs, spices, and the like. The terms *smell* and *odour* do not specify the exact nature of that which issues from bodies; they may both be either pleasant or unpleasant; but *smell*, if taken in certain connexions, signifies a bad *smell*, and *odour* signifies that which is sweet: meat which is kept too long will have a *smell*, that is, of course, a bad *smell;* the *odours* from a sacrifice are acceptable, that is, the sweet *odours* ascend to heaven. *Perfume* is properly a wide-spreading *smell*, and when taken without any epithet signifies a pleasant *smell;*

> At last a soft and solemn breathing sound
> Rose like a steam of rich distill'd *perfumes*.
> MILTON.

Fragrance never signifies any thing but what is good; it is the sweetest and most powerful *perfume:* the *perfume* from flowers and shrubs is as grateful to one's sense as their colours and conformation are to the other; the *fragrance* from groves of myrtle and orange trees surpasses the beauty of their fruits or foliage;

> Soft vernal *fragrance* clothe the flow'ring earth.
> MASON.

TO SOAK, DRENCH, STEEP.

Soak is a variation of *suck;* *drench* is a variation of *drink;* *steep*, in Saxon *steapan*, &c. from the Hebrew *satep*, signifies to overflow or overwhelm.

The idea of communicating or receiving a liquid is common to these terms. We *soak* things in water when we wish to soften them; animals are *drenched* with liquid as a medicinal operation. A person's clothes are *soaked* in rain when the water has penetrated every thread; he himself is *drenched* in the rain when it has penetrated as it were his very body; *drench* therefore in this case only expresses the idea of *soak* in a stronger manner. To *steep* is a species of *soaking* employed as an artificial process; to *soak* is however a permanent action by which hard things are rendered soft; to *steep* is a temporary action by which soft bodies become penetrated with a liquid: thus salt meat requires to be *soaked;* fruits are sometimes *steeped* in brandy;

> Drill'd through the sandy stratum, every way
> The waters with the sandy stratum rise,
> And clear and sweeten as they *soak* along.
> THOMSON.

> And deck with fruitful trees the fields around,
> And with refreshing waters *drench* the ground.
> DRYDEN.

> O sleep, O gentle sleep,
> Nature's soft nurse! How have I frighted thee,
> That thou no more wilt weigh my eyelids down,
> And *steep* my senses in forgetfulness?
> SHAKSPEARE

TASTE, FLAVOUR, RELISH, SAVOUR.

Taste comes from the Teutonick *tasten* to touch lightly, and signifies either the organ which is easily affected, or the act of discriminating by a light touch of the organ, or the quality of the object which affects the organ; in this latter sense it is closely allied to the other terms; *flavour* most probably comes from the Latin *flo* to breathe, signifying the rarefied essence of bodies which affect the organ of *taste;* *relish* is derived by Minshew from *relécher* to lick again, signifying that which pleases the palate so as to tempt to a renewal of the act of *tasting;* *savour*, in Latin *sapor* and *sapio* to smell, taste, or be sensible, most probably comes from the Hebrew שפה the mouth or palate, which is the organ of taste.

Taste is the most general and indefinite of all these; it is applicable to every object that can be applied to the organ of *taste*, and to every degree and manner in which the organ can be affected: some things are *tasteless*, other things have a strong *taste*, and others a mixed *taste;*

> Ten thousand thousand precious gifts
> My daily thanks employ!
> Nor is the least a cheerful heart,
> That *tastes* those gifts with joy.—ADDISON.

The *flavour* is the predominating *taste*, and consequently is applied to such objects as may have a different kind or degree of *taste;* an apple may not only have the general *taste* of apple, but also a *flavour* peculiar to itself: the *flavour* is commonly said of that which is good, as a fine *flavour*, a delicious *flavour;* but it may designate that which is not always agreeable, as the *flavour* of fish, which is unpleasant in things that do not admit of such a *taste;* 'The Philippick islands give a *flavour* to our European bowls.' —ADDISON. The *relish* is also a particular *taste;* but it is that which is artificial, in distinction from the *flavour*, which may be the natural property. We find the *flavour* such as it is; we give the *relish* such as it should be, or we wish it to be: milk and butter receive a *flavour* from the nature of the food with which the cow is supplied; sauces are used in order to give a *relish* to the food that is dressed;

> I love the people,
> But do not like to stage me to their eyes,
> Though it do well, I do not *relish* well
> Their loud applause.—SHAKSPEARE.

Savour is a term in less frequent use than the others, but, agreeable to the Latin derivation, it is employed to designate that which smells as well as *tastes*, a sweet smelling *savour;*

> The pleasant *savoury* smell
> So quicken'd appetite, that I methought
> Could not but *taste*.—MILTON.

So likewise, in the moral application, a man's actions or expressions may be said to *savour* of vanity. *Taste* and *relish* may be moreover compared as the act of persons: we *taste* whatever affects our *taste;* but we *relish* that only which pleases our *taste;* we *taste* fruits in order to determine whether they are good or bad; we *relish* fruits as a dessert, or at certain seasons of the day. So likewise, in the moral application, we have a *relish* for books, for learning, for society, and the like.

PALATE, TASTE.

Palate, in Latin *palatum*, comes either from the Greek πάω to eat, or, which is more probable, from the Etruscan word *farlantum*, signifying the roof or arch of Heaven, or, by an extended application, the roof of the mouth; *taste* comes from the German *tasten* to touch lightly, because the sense of *taste* requires but the slightest touch to excite it.

Palate is, in an improper sense, employed for *taste*, because it is the seat of *taste;* but *taste* is never employed for *palate:* a person is said to have a nice *palate* when he is nice in what he eats or drinks; but his *taste* extends to all matters of sense, as well as those which are intellectual;

> No fruit our *palate* courts, or flow'r our smell
> JENYNS

A man of *taste*, or of a nice *taste*, conveys much more as a characteristick, than a man of a nice *palate:* the former is said only in a good sense; but the latter is particularly applicable to the epicure;

In more exalted joys to fix our *taste*,
And wean us from delights that cannot last.
JENYNS.

INSIPID, DULL, FLAT.

A want of spirit in the moral sense is designated by these epithets, which borrow their figurative meaning from different properties in nature: the taste is referred to in the word *insipid*, from the Latin *sapio* to taste; the properties of colours are considered under the word *dull* (*v. Dull*); the property of surface is referred to by the word *flat* (*v. Flat*). As the want of flavour in any meat constitutes it *insipid*, and renders it worthless, so does the want of mind or character in a man render him equally *insipid*, and devoid of the distinguishing characteristick of his nature: as the beauty and perfection of colours consist in their brightness, and the absence of this essential property, which constitutes *dulness*, renders them uninteresting objects to the eye, so the want of spirit in a moral composition, which constitutes its *dulness*, deprives it at the same time of that ingredient which should awaken attention: as in the natural world objects are either elevated or *flat*, so in the moral world the spirits are either raised or depressed, and such moral representations as are calculated to raise the spirits are termed spirited, while those which fail in this object are termed *flat*. An *insipid* writer is without sentiment of any kind or degree; a *dull* writer fails in vivacity and vigour of sentiment; a *flat* performance is wanting in the property of provoking mirth, which should be its peculiar ingredient; 'To a covetous man all other things but wealth are *insipid*.'—SOUTH.

But yet beware of councils when too full,
Number makes long disputes and graveness *dull*.
DENHAM.

The senses are disgusted with their old entertainments, and existence turns *flat* and *insipid*.'—GROVE.

FEAST, BANQUET, CAROUSAL, ENTERTAINMENT, TREAT.

As *feasts*, in the religious sense, from *festus*, are always days of leisure, and frequently of publick rejoicing, this word has been applied to any social meal for the purposes of pleasure: this is the idea common to the signification of all these words, of which *feast* seems to be the most general; and for all of which it may frequently be substituted, although they have each a distinct application: *feast* conveys the idea merely of enjoyment: *banquet* is a splendid *feast*, attended with pomp and state; it is a term of noble use, particularly adapted to poetry and the high style: *carousal*, in French *carouse*, in German *geräusch*, or *rausch* intoxication, from *rauschen* to intoxicate, is a drunken *feast: entertainment* and *treat* convey the idea of hospitality.

A *feast* may be given by princes or their subjects, by nobility or commonalty;

New purple hangings clothe the palace walls,
And sumptuous *feasts* are made in splendid halls.
DRYDEN.

The *banquet* is confined to men of high estate; and more commonly spoken of in former times, when ranks and distinctions were less blended than they are at present: the dinner which the Lord Mayor of London annually gives is properly denominated a *feast;* the mode in which Cardinal Wolsey received the French ambassadors might entitle every meal he gave to be denominated a *banquet;*

With hymns divine the joyous *banquet* ends,
The pæans lengthen'd till the sun descends.—POPE.

A *feast* supposes indulgence of the appetite, both in eating and drinking, but not intemperately; a *carousal* is confined mostly to drinking, and that for the most part to an excess;

This game, these *carousals*, Ascanius taught,
And, building Alba, to the Latins brought.
DRYDEN.

A *feast*, therefore, is always a good thing, unless it ends in a *carousal:* a *feast* may be given by one or many, at private or publick expense; but an *entertainment* and a *treat* are altogether personal acts, and the terms are never used but in relation to the agents: every *entertainment* is a *feast* as far as respects enjoyment at a social board; but no *feast* is an *entertainment* unless there be some individual who specifically provides for the *entertainment* of others: we may all be partakers of a *feast*, but we are guests at an *entertainment:* the Lord Mayor's *feast* is not strictly an *entertainment*, although that of Cardinal Wolsey was properly so: an *entertainment* is given between friends and equals, to keep alive the social affections; a *treat* is given by way of favour to those whom one wishes to oblige: a nobleman provides an *entertainment* for a particular party whom he has invited; 'I could not but smile at the account that was yesterday given me of a modest young gentleman, who, being invited to an *entertainment*, though he was not used to drink, had not the confidence to refuse his glass in his turn.'—ADDISON. A nobleman may give a *treat* to his servants, his tenants, his tradespeople, or the poor of his neighbourhood; 'I do not insist that you spread your table with so unbounded a profusion as to furnish out a splendid *treat* with the remains.'—MELMOTH (*Letters of Cicero*).

Feast, *entertainment*, and *treat* are taken in a more extended sense, to express other pleasures besides those of the table: *feast* retains its signification of a vivid pleasure, such as voluptuaries derive from delicious viands; *entertainment* and *treat* retain the idea of being granted by way of courtesy: we speak of a thing as being a *feast* or high delight; 'Beattie is the only author I know, whose critical and philosophical researches are diversified and embellished by a poetical imagination, that makes even the driest subject and the leanest a *feast* for an epicure in books.'—COWPER. And of a person contributing to one's *entertainment*, or giving one a *treat;* 'Let us consider to whom we are indebted for all these *entertainments* of sense.'—ADDISON.

Sing my praise in strain sublime.
Treat not me with dogg'rel rhyme.—SWIFT

To an envious man the sight of wretchedness, in a once prosperous rival, is a *feast;* to a benevolent mind the spectacle of an afflicted man relieved and comforted is a *feast;* to a mind ardent in the pursuit of knowledge, an easy access to a well-stocked library is a continual *feast:* men of a happy temper give and receive *entertainment* with equal facility; they afford *entertainment* to their guests by the easy cheerfulness which they impart to every thing around them; they in like manner derive *entertainment* from every thing they see, or hear, or observe: a *treat* is given or received only on particular occasions; it depends on the relative circumstances and tastes of the giver and receiver; to one of a musical turn one may give a *treat* by inviting him to a musical party; and to one of an intelligent turn it will be equally a *treat* to be of the party which consists of the enlightened and conversible.

FARE, PROVISION.

Fare, from the German *fahren* to go or be, signifies in general the condition or thing that comes to one: *provision*, from *provide*, signifies the thing provided for one.

These terms are alike employed for the ordinary concerns of life, and may either be used in the limited sense for the food one procures, or in general for what ever is necessary or convenient to be procured: to the term *fare* is annexed the idea of accident; *provision* includes that of design: a traveller on the continent must frequently be contented with humble *fare*, unless he has the precaution of carrying his *provisions* with him;

This night at least with me forget your care,
Chesnuts, and curds, and cream shall be your *fare*.
DRYDEN.

The winged nation wanders through the skies,
And o'er the plains and shady forest flies;
They breed, they brood, instruct, and educate,
And make *provision* for the future state.—DRYDEN.

FOOD, DIET, REGIMEN.

Food signifies the thing which one feeds upon, in Saxon *fode*, Low German *fôde* or *fôder*, Greek *βόσκειν*; *diet* comes from *διαιτάω* to live medicinally, signifying any particular mode of living; *regimen*, in Latin *regimen*, from *rego* to regulate, signifies a system or practice by rule.

All these terms refer to our living, or that by which we live: *food* is here the general term; the others are specifick. *Food* specifies no circumstance: whatever is taken to maintain life is *food*; *diet* is properly a prescribed or regular *food*. It is the hard lot of some among the poor to obtain with difficulty *food* and clothing for themselves and their families; an attention to the *diet* of children is an important branch of their early education; their *diet* can scarcely be too simple: no one can be expected to enjoy his *food* who is not in a good state of health; we cannot expect to find a healthy population where there is a spare and unwholesome *diet*, attended with hard labour.

Food is a term applicable to all living creatures, and also used figuratively for what serves to nourish; 'The poison of other states (that is, bankruptcy) is the *food* of the new republick.'—BURKE. *Diet* is employed only with regard to human beings who make choice of their *food*: corn is as much the natural *food* of some animals as of men; the *diet* of the peasantry consists mostly of bread, milk, and vegetables; 'The *diet* of men in a state of nature must have been confined almost wholly to the vegetable kind.'—BURKE.

Diet and *regimen* are both particular modes of living; but the former respects the quality of *food*; the latter the quantity as well as quality: *diet* is confined to modes of taking nourishment; *regimen* often respects the abstinence from *food*, bodily exercise, and whatever may conduce to health: *diet* is generally the consequence of an immediate prescription from a physician, and during the period of sickness; *regimen* commonly forms a regular part of a man's system of living: *diet* is in certain cases of such importance for the restoration of a patient that a single deviation may defeat the best medicine; it is the misfortune of some people to be troubled with diseases, from which they cannot get any exemption but by observing a strict *regimen*; 'Prolongation of life is rather to be expected from stated *diets* than from any common *regimen*.'—BACON. 'I shall always be able to entertain a friend of a philosophical *regimen*.'—SHENSTONE.

FEMALE, FEMININE, EFFEMINATE.

Female is said of the sex itself, and *feminine* of the characteristicks of the sex. *Female* is opposed to male, *feminine* to masculine.

In the *female* character we expect to find that which is *feminine*. The *female* dress, manners, and habits have engaged the attention of all essayists, from the time of Addison to the present period;

> Once more her haughty soul the tyrant bends,
> To prayers and mean submissions she descends;
> No *female* arts or aids she left untried,
> Nor counsels unexplor'd, before she died.
>
> DRYDEN.

The *feminine* is natural to the *female*; the *effeminate* is unnatural to the male. A *feminine* air and voice, which is truly grateful to the observer in the one sex, is an odious mark of *effeminacy* in the other. Beauty and delicacy are *feminine* properties;

> Her heav'nly form
> Angelick: but more soft and *feminine*
> Her graceful innocence.—MILTON.

Robustness and vigour are masculine properties; the former therefore when discovered in a man entitle him to the epithet of *effeminate*; 'Our martial ancestors, like some of their modern successors, had no other amusement (but hunting) to entertain their vacant hours; despising all arts as *effeminate*.'—BLACKSTONE.

GENDER, SEX.

Gender, in Latin *genus*, signifies properly a *genus* or kind; *sex*, in French *sexe*, Latin *sexus*, comes from the Greek *ἕξις* signifying the habit or nature. The *gender* is that distinction in words which marks the distinction of *sex* in things; there are therefore three *genders*, but only two *sexes*. By the inflections of words are denoted whether things are of this or that *sex*, or of no *sex*. The *genders*, therefore, are divided in grammar into *masculine*, *feminine*, and *neuter*; and animals are divided into male and female *sex*.

GOLD, GOLDEN.

These terms are both employed as epithets, but *gold* is the substantive used in composition, and *golden* the adjective, in ordinary use. The former is strictly applied to the metal of which the thing is made, as a *gold* cup, or a *gold* coin; but the latter to whatever appertains to *gold*, whether properly or figuratively: as the *golden* lion, the *golden* crown, the *golden* age, or a *golden* harvest.

COOL, COLD, FRIGID.

In the natural sense, *cool* is simply the absence of warmth; *cold* and *frigid* are positively contrary to warmth; the former in regard to objects in general, the latter to moral objects: in the physical sense the analogy is strictly preserved. *Cool* is used as it respects the passions and the affections; *cold* only with regard to the affections; *frigid* only in regard to the inclinations.

With regard to the passions, *cool* designates a freedom from agitation, which is a desirable quality *Coolness* in a time of danger, and *coolness* in an argument, are alike commendable.

As *cool* and *cold* respect the affections, the *cool* is opposed to the friendly, the *cold* to the warm-hearted, the *frigid* to the animated; the former is but a degree of the latter. A reception is said to be *cool*; an embrace to be *cold*; a sentiment *frigid*. *Coolness* is an enemy to social enjoyments; *coldness* is an enemy to every moral virtue; *frigidity* destroys all force of character. *Coolness* is engendered by circumstances; it supposes the previous existence of warmth; *coldness* lies often in the temperament, or is engendered by habit; it is always something vicious; *frigidity* is occasional, and is always a defect. Trifling differences produce *coolness* sometimes between the best friends; 'The jealous man's disease is of so malignant a nature, that it converts all it takes into its own nourishment. A *cool* behaviour is interpreted as an instance of aversion: a fond one raises his suspicions.'—ADDISON. Trade sometimes engenders a *cold* calculating temper in some minds; 'It is wondrous that a man can get over the natural existence and possession of his own mind, so far as to take delight either in paying or receiving *cold* and repeated civilities.'—STEELE. Those who are remarkable for apathy will often express themselves with *frigid* indifference on the most important subjects; 'The religion of the moderns abounds in topicks so incomparably noble and exalted, as might kindle the flames of genuine oratory in the most *frigid* and barren genius.'—WHARTON.

CHILL, COLD.

Chill and *cold* are but variations of the same word, in German *kalt*, &c.

Chill expresses less than *cold*, that is to say, it expresses a degree of *cold*. The weather is often *chilly* in summer; but it is *cold* in winter.

We speak of taking the *chill* off water when the *cold* is in part removed; and of a *chill* running through the frame when the *cold* begins to penetrate the frame that is in a state of warmth;

> When men once reach their autumn, fickle joys
> Fall off apace, as yellow leaves from trees;
> Till left quite naked of their happiness,
> In the *chill* blasts of winter they expire.
>
> YOUNG.

'Thus ease after torment is pleasure for a time, and we are very agreeably recruited when the body, *chilled* with the weather, is gradually recovering its natural tepidity; but the joy ceases when we have forgot the *cold*.'—JOHNSON.

TO STAIN, SOIL, SULLY, TARNISH.

Stain, v. *Blemish*; *soil* and *sully*, from *soil* dirt, signify to smear with dirt; *tarnish* in French *ternir* comes probably from the Latin *tero* to bruise

All these terms imply the act of diminishing the brightness of an object; but the term *stain* denotes something grosser than the other terms, and is applied to inferiour objects: things which are not remarkable for purity or brightness may be *stained*, as hands when *stained* with blood, or a wall *stained* with chalk;

> Thou, rather than thy justice should be *stained*,
> Didst *stain* the cross.—YOUNG.

Nothing is *sullied* or *tarnished*, but what has some intrinsick value; a fine picture or piece of writing may be easily *soiled* by a touch of the finger; 'I cannot endure to be mistaken, or suffer my purer affections to be *soiled* with the odious attributes of covetousness and ambitious falsehood.'—LORD WENTWORTH. The finest glass is the soonest *tarnished*: hence, in the moral application, a man's life may be *stained* by the commission of some gross immorality: his honour may be *sullied*, or his glory *tarnished*;

> Oaths would debase the dignity of virtue,
> Else I could swear by him, the power who clothed
> The sun with light, and gave yon starry host
> Their chaste, *unsullied* lustre.—FRANCIS.

'I am not now what I once was; for since I parted from thee fate has *tarnished* my glories.'—TRAPP.

TO SMEAR, DAUB.

To *smear* is literally to do over with *smear*, in Saxon *smer*, German *schmeer*, in Greek μύρος a salve. To *daub*, from *do* and *ub* *über* over, signifies literally to do over with any thing unseemly, or in an unsightly manner.

To *smear* in the literal sense is applied to such substances as may be rubbed like grease over a body; if said of grease itself it may be proper, as coachmen *smear* the coach wheels with tar or grease; but if said of any thing else it is an improper action, and tends to disfigure, as children *smear* their hands with ink, or *smear* their clothes with dirt. To *smear* and *daub* are both actions which tend to disfigure; but we *smear* by means of rubbing over; we *daub* by rubbing, throwing, or any way covering over: thus a child *smears* the window with his finger, or he *daubs* the wall with dirt. By a figurative application, *smear* is applied to bad writing, and *daub* to bad painting: indifferent writers who wish to excel are fond of retouching their letters until they make their performance a sad *smear*; bad artists, who are injudicious in the use of their pencil, load their paintings with colour, and convert them into *daubs*.

MOISTURE, HUMIDITY, DAMPNESS.

Moisture, from the French *moite* moist, is probably contracted from the Latin *humidus*, from which *humidity* is immediately derived; *dampness* comes from the German *dampf* a vapour.

Moisture is used in general to express any small degree of infusion of a liquid into a body; *humidity* is employed scientifically to describe the state of having any portion of such liquid: hence we speak of the *moisture* of a table, the *moisture* of paper, or the *moisture* of a floor that has been wetted; but of the *humidity* of the air, or of a wall that has contracted *moisture* of itself. *Dampness* is that species of *moisture* that arises from the gradual contraction of a liquid in bodies capable of retaining it; in this manner a cellar is *damp*, or linen that has lain long by may become *damp*;

> The plumy people streak their wings with oil,
> To throw the lucid *moisture* trickling off.
> THOMSON.

> Now from the town
> Buried in smoke, and sleep, and noisome *damps*,
> Oft let me wander.—THOMSON.

NASTY, FILTHY, FOUL.

Nasty is connected with *nauseous*, and the German *nass* wet; *filthy* and *foul* are variations from the Greek φαῦλος.

The idea of dirtiness is common to these terms, but in different degrees, and with different modifications. Whatever dirt is offensive to any of the senses, renders that thing *nasty* which is soiled with it: the *filthy* exceeds the *nasty*, not only in the quantity but in the offensive quality of the dirt; and the *foul* exceeds the *filthy* in the same proportion;

> We look behind, then view his shaggy beard,
> His clothes were tagg'd with thorns, and *filth* his
> limbs besmear'd.—DRYDEN.

> Only our foe
> Tempting affronts us with his *foul* esteem.
> MILTON.

DREGS, SEDIMENT, DROSS, SCUM, REFUSE.

Dregs, from the German *dreck* dirt, signifies the dirty part which separates from a liquor; *sediment*, from *sedeo* to sit, signifies that which settles at the bottom; *dross* is probably but a variation of *dregs*; *scum*, from the German *schaum*, signifies the same as foam or froth, or that which rises on the surface of any liquor; *refuse* signifies literally that which is refused or thrown away.

All these terms designate the worthless part of any body; but *dregs* is taken in a worse sense than *sediment*: for the *dregs* are that which is altogether of no value; but the *sediment* may sometimes form a necessary part of the body. The *dregs* are mostly a *sediment* in liquors, but many things are a *sediment* which are not *dregs*. After the *dregs* are taken away, there will frequently remain a *sediment*; the *dregs* are commonly the corrupt part which separates from compound liquids, as wine or beer; the *sediment* consists of the heavy particles which belong to all simple liquids, not excepting water itself. The *dregs* and *sediment* separate of themselves, but the *scum* and *dross* are forced out by a process; the former from liquids, and the latter from solid bodies rendered liquid or otherwise.

Refuse, as its derivation implies, is always said of that which is intentionally separated to be thrown away, and agrees with the former terms only inasmuch as they express what is worthless.

Of these terms, *dregs*, *scum*, and *refuse* admit likewise of a figurative application. The *dregs* and *scum* of the people are the corruptest part of any society; and the *refuse* is that which is most worthless and unfit for a respectable community; 'Epitomes of history are the corruptions and moths that have fretted and corroded many sound and excellent bodies of history and reduced them to base and unprofitable *dregs*.'—BACON. 'For it is not bare agitation, but the *sediment* at the bottom that troubles and defiles the water.'—SOUTH. 'For the composition too, I admit the Algerine community resemble that of France, being formed out of the very *scum*, scandal, disgrace, and pest of the Turkish Asia.'—BURKE.

> Now cast your eyes around, while I dissolve
> The mist and film that mortal eyes involve:
> Purge from your sight the *dross*, and make you see
> The shape of each avenging deity.—DRYDEN.

> Next of his men and ships he makes review,
> Draws out the best and ablest of the crew;
> Down with the falling stream the *refuse* run
> To raise with joyful news his drooping son.
> DRYDEN.

TO GLOSS, VARNISH, PALLIATE.

Gloss and *varnish* are figurative terms, which borrow their signification from the act of rendering the outer surface of any physical object shining. To *gloss*, which is connected with to glaze, is to give a *gloss* or brightness to any thing by means of friction, as in the case of japan or mahogany: to *varnish* is to give an artificial *gloss*, by means of applying a foreign substance. Hence, in the figurative use of the terms, to *gloss* is to put the best face upon a thing by various little distortions and artifices; but to *varnish* is to do the same thing by means of direct falsehood; to *palliate*, which likewise signifies to give the best possible outside to a thing (*v. To extenuate*), requires still less artifice than either. One *glosses* over that which is bad, by giving it a soft name; as when a man's vices are *glossed* over with the name of indiscretion, or a man's mistress is termed his good friend; 'If a jealous man once finds a false *gloss* put upon any single action he quickly suspects all the rest.'—ADDISON. One *varnishes* a bad character by ascribing good motives to his bad actions, by withholding many facts that are to his discredit, and fabricating other circumstances in his favour an *unvarnished* tale contains nothing but th simple truth; the *varnished* tale on the other hand contains a great mixture of falsehood; the French accounts of their victories in the time of the revolution were mostly *varnished;*

The waiting tears stood ready for command,
And now they flow to *varnish* the false tale.
ROWE.

To *palliate* is to diminish the magnitude of an offence, by making an excuse in favour of the offender; as when an act of theft is *palliated* by considering the starving condition of the thief; 'A man's bodily defects should give him occasion to exert a noble spirit, and to *palliate* those imperfections which are not in his power, by those perfections which are.'—ADDISON.

CLOAK, MASK, BLIND, VEIL.

These are figurative terms, expressive of different modes of intentionally keeping something from the view of others. They are borrowed from those familiar objects which serve similar purposes in common life. *Cloak* and *mask* express figuratively and properly more than *blind* or *veil*. The two former keep the whole object out of sight; the two latter only partially intercept the view. In this figurative sense they are all employed for a bad purpose.

The *cloak*, the *mask*, and the *blind* serve to deceive others; the *veil* serves to deceive one's self.

The whole or any part of a character may be concealed by a *blind;* a part, though not the whole, may be concealed by a *mask*. A *blind* is not only employed to conceal the character but the conduct or proceedings. We carry a *cloak* and a *mask* about with us; but a *blind* is something external.

The *cloak*, as the external garment, is the most convenient of all coverings for entirely keeping concealed what we do not wish to be seen; a good outward deportment serves as a *cloak* to conceal a bad character; 'When this severity of manners is hypocritical, and assumed as a *cloak* to secret indulgence, it is one of the worst prostitutions of religion.'—BLAIR. A *mask* only hides the face; a *mask* therefore serves to conceal only as much as words and looks can effect;

Thou art no ruffian, who, beneath the *mask*
Of social commerce, com'st to rob their wealth.
THOMSON.

A *blind* is intended to shut out the light and prevent observation; whatever, therefore, conceals the real truth, and prevents suspicion by a false exteriour, is a *blind;* 'Those who are bountiful to crimes will be rigid to merit, and penurious to service. Their penury is even held out as a *blind* and cover to their prodigality.'—BURKE. A *veil* prevents a person from seeing as well as being seen; whatever, therefore, obscures the mental sight acts as a *veil* to the mind's eye; 'As soon as that mysterious *veil* which covers futurity was lifted up, all the gayety of life would disappear; its flattering hopes, its pleasing illusions would vanish, and nothing but vanity and sadness remain.'—BLAIR.

Religion may unfortunately serve to *cloak* the worst of purposes and the worst of characters: its importance, in the eyes of all men, makes it the most effectual passport to their countenance and sanction; and its external observances render it the most convenient mode of presenting a false profession to the eyes of the world: those, therefore, who set an undue value on the ceremonial part of religion, do but encourage this most heinous of all sins, by suffering themselves to be imposed upon by a *cloak* of religious hypocrisy. False friends always wear a *mask;* they cover a malignant heart under the smiles and endearments of friendship. Illicit traders mostly make use of some *blind* to facilitate the carrying on their nefarious practices. Among the various arts resorted to in the metropolis by the needy and profligate, none is so bad as that which is made to be a *blind* for the practice of debauchery. Prejudice and passion are the ordinary *veils* which obscure the judgement, and prevent it from distinguishing the truth.

TO COLOUR, DYE, TINGE, STAIN.

Colour, in Latin *color*, comes probably from *colo* to adorn; *dye*, in Saxon *deagen*, is a variation of *tinge;* *tinge* is in Latin *tingo*, from the Greek *τέγγω* to sprinkle; *stain*, like the French *desteindre* is but variation of *tinge*.

To *colour* is to put *colour* on; to *dye* is to dip in any *colour;* to *tinge* is to touch lightly with a *colour;* to *stain* is to put on a bad *colour* or in a bad manner: we *colour* a drawing, we *dye* clothes of any *colour*, we *tinge* a painting with blue by way of intermixture, we *stain* a painting when we put blue instead of red; 'That childish *colouring* of her cheeks is now as ungraceful as that shape would have been when her face wore its real countenance.'—STEELE.

Now deeper blushes *ting'd* the glowing sky,
And evening rais'd her silver lamp on high.
SIR WM. JONES.

'We had the fortune to see what may be supposed to be the occasion of that opinion which Lucian relates concerning this river (Adonis), that is, that this stream at certain seasons of the year is of a bloody *colour;* something like this we actually saw come to pass, for the water was *stained* with redness.'—MAUNDRELL.

They are taken in a moral acceptation with a similar distinction: we *colour* a description by the introduction of strong figures, strong facts, and strong expressions; 'All these amazing incidents to the inspired historians relate nakedly and plainly, without any of the *colourings* and heightenings of rhetorick.'—WEST. Hence the term is employed to denote the giving a false or exaggerated representation; 'He *colours* the falsehood of Æneas by an express command from Jupiter to forsake the queen.'—DRYDEN. A person is represented as *dying* his hands in blood, who is so engaged in the shedding of blood as that he may change the *colour* of his skin, or the soil may be *dyed* in blood;

With mutual blood the Ausonian soil is *dyed*,
While on its borders each their claim decide.
DRYDEN.

A person's mind is *tinged* with melancholy or enthusiasm; 'Sir Roger is something of a humorist, and his virtues as well as imperfections are *tinged* by a certain extravagance, which makes them particularly his.'—ADDISON. A man'sch aracter may be said to be *stained* with crimes;

Of honour void, of innocence, of faith, of purity,
Our wonted ornaments, now soil'd and *stain'd*.
MILTON.

COLOUR, HUE, TINT.

Colour (*v. To colour*) is here the generick term: *hue*, which is probably connected with *eye* and *view*, and *tint*, from *tinge*, are but modes of *colour;* the former of which expresses a faint or blended *colour;* the latter a shade of *colour*. Between the *colours* of black and brown, as of all other leading *colours*, there are various *hues* and *tints*, by the due intermixture of which, natural objects are rendered beautiful;

Her *colour* chang'd, her face was not the same,
And hollow groans from her deep spirit came.
DRYDEN.

Infinite numbers, delicacies, smells,
With *hues* on *hues*, expression cannot paint
The breath of nature, and her endless bloom.
THOMSON.

Among them shells of many a *tint* appear,
The heart of Venus and her pearly ear.
SIR WM. JONES.

COLOURABLE, SPECIOUS, OSTENSIBLE, PLAUSIBLE, FEASIBLE.

Colourable, from to *colour* or *tinge*, expresses the quality of being able to give a fair appearance; *specious*, from the Latin *specio* to see, signifies the quality of looking as it ought; *ostensible*, from the Latin *ostendo* to show, signifies the quality of being able or fit to be shown or seen; *plausible*, from *plaudo* to clap or make a noise, signifies the quality of sounding as it ought; *feasible*, from the French *faire*, and Latin *facio* to do, signifies literally *doable;* but here it denotes seemingly practicable.

The first three of these are figures of speech drawn from what naturally pleases the eye; *plausible* is drawn from what pleases the ear: *feasible* takes its signification from what meets the judgement or conviction.

What is *colourable* has an aspect or face upon it that lulls suspicion and affords satisfaction; what is *specious* has a fair outside when contrasted with that which it may possibly conceal; what is *ostensible* is that which presents such an appearance as may serve for an indication of something real; what is *plausible* is that which meets the understanding merely through he ear; that which is *feasible* recommends itself from its intrinsick value rather than from any representation given of it.

A pretence is *colourable* when it has the *colour* of truth impressed upon it; it is *specious* when its fallacy s easily discernible through the thin guise it wears; a motive is *ostensible* which is the one soonest to be discovered; an excuse is *plausible* when the well-connected narrative of the maker impresses a belief of its justice; an account is *feasible* which contains nothing improbable or singular.

It is necessary, in order to avoid suspicion, to have some *colourable* grounds for one's conduct when it is marked by eccentricity or directed to any bad object; All his (James I. of Scotland's) acquisitions, however fatal to the body of the nobles, had been gained by attacks upon individuals; and being founded on circumstances peculiar to the persons who suffered, might excite murmurs and apprehensions, but afforded no *colourable* pretext for a general rebellion.'—ROBERTSON. Sophists are obliged to deal in *specious* arguments for want of more substantial ones in support of their erroneous opinions; 'The guardian directs one of his pupils to think with the wise, but speak with the vulgar. This is a precept *specious* enough, but not always practicable.'—JOHNSON. Men who have no *ostensible* way of supporting themselves, naturally excite the suspicion that they have some illicit source of gain; 'What is truly astonishing, the partisans of those two opposite systems were at once prevalent and at once employed, the one *ostensibly*, the other secretly, during the latter part of the reign of Louis XV.'—BURKE. Liars may sometimes be successful in inventing a *plausible* tale, but they must not scruple to support one lie by a hundred more as occasion requires; In this superficial way indeed the mind is capable of more variety of *plausible* talk, but is not enlarged as it should be in its knowledge.'—LOCKE. If what an accused person has to say in justification of himself be no more than *feasible*, it will always subject him to unpleasant imputations; 'It is some years since I thought the matter *feasible*, that if I could by an exact time-keeper find in any part of the world what o'clock it is at Dover, and at the same time where the ship is, the problem is solved.'—ARBUTHNOT.

TO COVER, HIDE.

Cover, in French *couvrir*, is contracted from *contra* and *ouvrir*, signifying to do the contrary of open, to put out of view: *hide, v. To conceal.*

Cover is to *hide* as the means to the end: we commonly *hide* by *covering*; but we may easily *cover* without *hiding*, as also *hide* without *covering*. The ruling idea in the word *cover* is that of throwing or putting something over a body; in the word *hide* is that of keeping carefully from observation

To *cover* is an indifferent action, springing from a variety of motives, of convenience, or comfort; to *hide* is an action that springs from one specifick intent, from care and concern for the thing, and the fear of foreign intrusion. In most civilized countries it is common to *cover* the head: in the eastern countries females commonly wear veils to *hide* the face. There are many things which decency as well as health require to be *covered*; and others which from their very nature must always be *hidden*. Houses must be *covered* with roofs, and bodies with clothing; the earth contains many treasures, which in all probability will always be *hidden*;

Or lead me to some solitary place
And *cover* my retreat from human race.—DRYDEN.

Hide me from the face
Of God, whom to behold was then my height
Of happiness.—MILTON.

In a moral application, *cover* may be used in the good sense of sheltering;

Thou mayst repent,
And one bad deed with many deeds well done
Mayst *cover*.—MILTON.

And also in the bad sense of *hiding* by means of falsehood;

Specious names are lent to *cover* vice.—SPECTATOR.

COVER, SHELTER, SCREEN.

Cover properly denotes what serves as a *cover*, and in the literal sense of the verb from which it is derived (*v. To cover*); *shelter*, like the word shield, comes from the German *schild*, old German *schelen*, to *cover*; *screen*, from the Latin *secerno*, signifies to keep off or apart.

Cover is literally applied to many particular things which are employed in *covering*; but in the general sense which makes it analogous to the other terms, it includes the idea of concealing: *shelter* comprehends that of protecting from some immediate or impending evil: *screen* includes that of warding off some trouble. A *cover* always supposes something which can extend over the whole surface of a body; a *shelter* or a *screen* may merely interpose to a sufficient extent to serve the intended purpose. Military operations are sometimes carried on under *cover* of the night; a bay is a convenient *shelter* for vessels against the violence of the winds; a chair may be used as a *screen* to prevent the violent action of the heat, or the external air.

In the moral sense, a *cover* may be employed allowably to diminish an imperfection or deformity; 'There are persons who *cover* their own rudeness by calling their conduct honest bluntness.'—RICHARDSON. But is for the most part taken in the bad sense of an endeavour to conceal the truth: a fair reputation is sometimes made the *cover* for the commission of gross irregularities in secret; 'The truth and reason of things may be artificially and effectually insinuated under the *cover* either of a real fact, or of a supposed one.'—L'ESTRANGE. When a person feels himself unable to withstand the attacks of his enemies, he seeks a *shelter* under the sanction and authority of a great name;

When on a bed of straw we sink together,
And the bleak winds shall whistle round our heads,
Wilt thou then talk to me thus?
Thus hush my cares, and *shelter* me with love?
OTWAY.

Bad men sometimes use wealth and power to *screen* them from the punishment which is due to their offences; 'It is frequent for men to adjudge that in an art impossible, which they find that art does not effect; by which means they *screen* indolence and ignorance from the reproach they merit.'—BACON.

TO HARBOUR, SHELTER, LODGE.

The idea of giving a resting place is common to these terms: but *harbour* (*v. To foster*) is used mostly in a bad sense, at least in its ordinary use: *shelter* (*v. Asylum*) in an indefinite sense; *lodge*, in French *loge*, from the German *liegen* to lie, in an indifferent sense. One *harbours* that which ought not or cannot find room any where; 'My lady bids me tell you, that though she *harbours* you as her uncle, she is nothing allied to your disorders.'—SHAKSPEARE. As the word *harbour* does not, in its original sense, mean any thing more than affording entertainment, or receiving into one's house for a time, it may be employed in a good sense to imply an act of hospitality; 'We owe this old house the same kind of gratitude that we do to an old friend, who *harbours* us in his declining condition, nay, even in his last extremities.'—POPE. One *shelters* that which cannot find security elsewhere. It is for the most part an act of charity, obligation, or natural feeling; 'The hen *shelters* her first brood of chickens with all the prudence that she ever attains —JOHNSON. One *lodges* that which wants a resting place; it is an act of discretion. Thieves, traitors, or conspirators are *harboured* by those who have an interest in securing them from detection: either the wicked or the unfortunate may be *sheltered* from the evil with which they are threatened: travellers are *lodged* as occasion may require.

In the moral sense, a man *harbours* resentment, ill will, evil thoughts, and the like;

She *harbours* in her breast a furious hate
(And thou shalt find the dire effects too late),
Fix'd on revenge, and obstinate to die.—DRYDEN.

A man *shelters* himself from a charge by retorting it upon his adversary;

In vain I strove to check my growing flame,
Or *shelter* passion under friendship's name;
You saw my heart.—PRIOR.

A person *lodges* a complaint or information against any one with the magistrate, or a particular passion may be *lodged* in the breast, or ideas *lodged* in the mind; 'In viewing again the ideas that are *lodged* in the memory, the mind is more than passive.'—LOCKE.

They too are tempered high,
With hunger stung, and wild necessity,
Nor *lodges* pity in their shaggy breast.—THOMSON.

All these terms may be employed also as the acts of unconscious agents. Beds and bed-furniture *harbour* vermin; trees, as well as houses, *shelter* from a storm: a ball from a gun *lodges* in the human body, or any other solid substance.

HARBOUR, HAVEN, PORT.

The idea of a resting place for vessels is common to these terms, of which *harbour* is general, and the two others specifick in their signification.

Harbour, from the Teutonick *herbenger* to shelter, carries with it little more than the common idea of affording a resting or anchoring place; *haven*, from the Teutonick *haben* to have or hold, conveys the idea of security; *port*, from the Latin *portus* and *porta* a gate, conveys the idea of an enclosure. A *haven* is a natural *harbour;* a *port* is an artificial *harbour*. We characterize a *harbour* as commodious; a *haven* as snug and secure; a *port* as safe and easy of access. A commercial country profits by the excellence and number of its *harbours;* it values itself on the security of its *havens*, and increases the number of its *ports* accordingly. A vessel goes into a *harbour* only for a season; it remains in a *haven* for a permanency; it seeks a *port* as the destination of its voyage. Merchantmen are perpetually going in and out of a *harbour;*

But here she comes,
In the calm *harbour* of whose gentle breast,
My tempest-beaten soul may safely rest.—DRYDEN.

A distressed vessel, at a distance from home, seeks some *haven* in which it may winter;

Safe through the war her course the vessel steers,
The *haven* gain'd, the pilot drops his fears.
SHIRLEY.

The weary mariner looks to the *port* not as the termination of his labour but as the commencement of all his enjoyments; 'What though our passage through this world be never so stormy and tempestuous, we shall arrive at a safe *port*.'—TILLOTSON.

ASYLUM, REFUGE, SHELTER, RETREAT.

Asylum, in Latin *asylum*, in Greek *ασυλιν*, compounded of *a* privative and *συλή* plunder, signified a place exempt from plunder, and exactions of every kind, and also a privileged place where accused persons were permitted to reside without molestation: *refuge*, in Latin *refugium*, from *refugio* to fly away, signifies the place which one may fly away to: *shelter* comes from *shell*, in High German *schalen*, Saxon *sceala*, &c. from the Hebrew כלא to hide, signifying a cover or hiding-place: *retreat*, in French *retraite*, Latin *retractus*, from *retraho* or *re* and *traho* to draw back, signifies the place that is situated behind or in the back ground.

Asylum, *refuge*, and *shelter* all denote a place of safety; but the former is fixed, the two latter are occasional: the *retreat* is a place of tranquillity rather than of safety. An *asylum* is chosen by him who has no home, a *refuge* by him who is apprehensive of danger: the French emigrants found a *refuge* in England, but very few will make it an *asylum*. The inclemencies of the weather make us seek a *shelter*. The fatigues and toils of life make us seek a *retreat*.

It is the part of a Christian to afford an *asylum* to the helpless orphan and widow. The terrified passenger takes *refuge* in the first house he comes to, when assailed by an evil-disposed mob. The vessel shattered in a storm takes *shelter* in the nearest haven. The man of business, wearied with the anxieties and cares of the world, disengages himself from the whole, and seeks a *retreat* suited to his circumstances. In a moral or extended application they are distinguished in the same manner; 'The adventurer knows he has not far to go before he will meet with some fortress that has been raised by sophistry for the *asylum* of errour.'—HAWKESWORTH. 'Superstition, now retiring from Rome, may yet find *refuge* in the mountains of Tibet.'—CUMBERLAND.

In rueful gaze
The cattle stand, and on the scowling heavens
Cast a deploring eye, by man forsook;
Who to the crowded cottage hies him fast,
Or seeks the *shelter* of the downward cave.
THOMSON.

TEGUMENT, COVERING.

Tegument, in Latin *tegumentum*, from *tego* to cover, is properly but another word to express *covering*, yet it is now employed in cases where the latter term is inadmissible. *Covering* signifies mostly that which is artificial; but *tegument* is employed for that which is natural: clothing is the *covering* for the body; the skin of vegetable substances, as seeds, is called the *tegument*. The *covering* is said of that which covers the outer surface: the *tegument* is said of that which covers the inner surface; the pods of some seeds are lined with a soft *tegument*.

SKIN, HIDE, PEEL, RIND.

Skin, which is in German *schin*, Swedish *skinn*, Danish *skind*, probably comes from the Greek *σκῆνος* a tent or covering; *hide*, in Saxon *hyd*, German *haut*, Low German *huth*, Latin *cutis*, comes from the Greek *κεύθειν* to *hide*, cover; *peel*, in German *fell*, &c. Latin *pellis* a skin, in Greek *φελλὸς* or *φλοιὸς* bark, comes from *φλαω* to burst or crack, because the bark is easily broken; *rind* is in all probability changed from round, signifying that which goes round and envelopes.

Skin is the term in most general use, it is applicable both to human creatures and to animals; *hide* is used only for the *skins* of large animals: we speak of the *skins* of birds or insects; but of the *hides* of oxen or horses, and other animals, which are to be separated from the body and converted into leather. *Skin* is equally applied to the inanimate and the animate world; but *peel* and *rind* belong only to inanimate objects; the *skin* is generally said of that which is interiour, in distinction from the exteriour, which is the *peel:* an orange has both its *peel* and its thin *skin* underneath; an apple, a pear, and the like, has a *peel*. The *peel* is a soft substance on the outside; the *rind* is generally interiour, and of a harder substance: in regard to a stick, we speak of its *peel* and the inner *skin;* in regard to a tree, we speak of its bark and its *rind;* hence, likewise, the term *rind* is applied to cheese, and other incrusted substances that envelope bodies.

TO PEEL, PARE.

Peel, from the Latin *pellis* a skin, is the same as to skin or to take off the skin: to *pare*, from the Latin *paro* to trim or make in order, signifies to smooth. The former of these terms denotes a natural, the latter an artificial process: the former excludes the idea of a forcible separation; the latter includes the idea of separation by means of a knife or sharp instrument: potatoes and apples are *peeled* after they are boiled; they are *pared* before they are boiled: an orange and a walnut are always *peeled*, but not *pared:* a cucumber must be *pared* and not *peeled:* in like manner the skin may sometimes be *peeled* from the flesh, and the nails are *pared*.

GUISE, HABIT.

Guise and wise are both derived from the northern languages, and denote the manner; but the former is employed for a particular or distinguished manner of dress; *habit*, from the Latin *habitus* a habit, fashion or form, is taken for a settled or permanent mode of dress.

The *guise* is that which is unusual, and often only occasional; the *habit* is that which is usual among particular classes: a person sometimes assumes the *guise* of a peasant, in order the better to conceal himself; he who devotes himself to the clerical profession puts on the *habit* of a clergyman;

Anubis, Sphinx,
Idols of antique *guise*, and horned Pan,
Terrifick, monstrous shapes!—DYER.

For 't is the mind that makes the body rich,
And as the sun breaks through the darkest cloud,
So honour appeareth in the meanest *habit*.
SHAKSPEARE.

TO CONCEAL, HIDE, SECRETE.

Conceal, *v. To conceal; hide*, from the German *hüthen* to guard against, and the Old German *hedan* to *conceal*, and the Greek κεύθω to cover or put out of sight; *secrete*, in Latin *secretus*, participle of *secerno*, or *se* and *cerno*, to see or know by one's self, signifies to put in a place known only to one's self.

Concealing conveys simply the idea of not letting come to observation; *hiding* that of putting under cover; *secreting* that of setting at a distance or in unfrequented places: whatever is not seen is *concealed*, but whatever is *hidden* or *secreted* is intentionally put out of sight: a person *conceals* himself behind a hedge; he *hides* his treasures in the earth; he *secretes* what he has stolen under his cloak.

Conceal is more general than either *hide* or *secrete*; all things are *concealed* which are *hidden* or *secreted*, but they are not always *hidden* or *secreted* when they are *concealed*: both mental and corporeal objects are *concealed*; corporeal objects mostly and sometimes mental ones are *hidden*; corporeal objects only are *secreted*; we *conceal* in the mind whatever we do not make known: that is *hidden* which may not be discovered or cannot be discerned; that is *secreted* which may not be seen. Facts are *concealed*, truths are *hidden*, goods are *secreted*.

Children should never attempt to *conceal* from their parents or teachers any errour they have committed, when called upon for an acknowledgment;

Be secret and discreet; Love's fairy favours
Are lost when not *conceal'd*.—DRYDEN.

We are told in Scripture for our consolation that nothing is *hidden* which shall not be revealed;

Yet to be secret makes not sin the less,
'T is only *hidden* from the vulgar view.—DRYDEN.

People seldom wish to *secrete* any thing but with the intention of *concealing* it from those who have a right to demand it back; 'The whole thing is too manifest to admit of any doubt in any man how long this thing has been working; how many tricks have been played with the Dean's (Swift's) papers; how they were *secreted* from time to time.'—POPE.

CONCEALMENT, SECRECY.

Concealment (*v. To conceal*) is itself an action; *secrecy*, from *secret*, is the quality of an action: *concealment* may respect the state of things; *secrecy* the conduct of persons: things may be *concealed* so as to be known to no one; but *secrecy* supposes some person to whom the thing *concealed* is known.

Concealment has to do with what concerns others; *secrecy* with that which concerns ourselves: what is *concealed* is kept from the observation of others; what is *secret* is known only to ourselves: there may frequently be *concealment* without *secrecy*, although there cannot be *secrecy* without *concealment*: *concealment* is frequently practised to the detriment of others; *secrecy* is always adopted for our own advantage or gratification: *concealment* aids in the commission of crimes; *secrecy* in the execution of schemes: many crimes are committed with impunity when the perpetrators are protected by *concealment*; 'There is but one way of conversing safely with all men, that is, not by *concealing* what we say or do, but by saying or doing nothing that deserves to be *concealed*.'—POPE. The best concerted plans are often frustrated for want of observing *secrecy*;

That 's not suddenly to be perform'd
But with advice and silent *secrecy*.—SHAKSPEARE.

Secrecy is, however, in our dealings with others, frequently not less impolitick than it is improper. An open and straight forward conduct is as a rule the only proper conduct in our commerce with the world,

Shun *secrecy*, and talk in open sight;
So shall you soon repair your present evil plight.
SPENSER.

When *concealment* is taken as the act of the Divine Being, or as the state of things, it is used in the best sense; 'One instance of Divine Wisdom is so illustrious that I cannot pass it over without notice; that is, the *concealment* under which Providence has placed the future events of our life on earth.'—BLAIR. When *secrecy* respects a man's own concerns with himself or his Maker, it is also proper; 'It is not with publick as with private prayer; in this, rather *secrecy* is commanded than outward show.'—HOOKER.

TO CONCEAL, DISSEMBLE, DISGUISE.

Conceal, compounded of *con* and *ceal*, in French *celer*, Latin *celo*, Hebrew כלא to have privately; *dissemble*, in French *dissimuler*, compounded of *dis* and *simulo* or *similis*, signifies to make a thing appear unlike what it is; *disguise*, in French *disguiser*, compounded of the privative *dis* or *de* and *guise*, in German *weise* a manner or fashion, signifies to take a form opposite to the reality.

To *conceal* is simply to abstain from making known what we wish to keep secret; to *dissemble* and *disguise* signify to *conceal*, by assuming some false appearance: we *conceal* facts; we *dissemble* feelings, we *disguise* sentiments.

* Caution only is requisite in *concealing*; it may be effected by simple silence: art and address must be employed in *dissembling*; it mingles falsehood with all its proceedings: labour and cunning are requisite in *disguising*; it has nothing but falsehood in all its movements.

The *concealer* watches over himself that he may not be betrayed into any indiscreet communication; the *dissembler* has an eye to others so as to prevent them from discovering the state of his heart; *disguise* assumes altogether a different face from the reality, and rests secure under this shelter: it is sufficient to *conceal* from those who either cannot or will not see; it is necessary to *dissemble* with those who can see without being shown; but it is necessary to *disguise* from those who are anxious to discover and use every means to penetrate the veil that intercepts their sight.

Concealment is a matter of prudence often advisable, mostly innocent; when we have not resolution to shake off our vices, it is wisdom at least to *conceal* them from the knowledge of others; 'Ulysses himself adds, he was the most eloquent, and the most silent of men; he knew that a word spoke never wrought so much good as a word *concealed*.'—BROOME. 'Ridicule is never more strong than when it is *concealed* in gravity.'—SPECTATOR.

According to Girard, it was a maxim with Louis XI., that in order to know how to govern, it was necessary to know how to *dissemble*; this, he adds, is true in all cases even in domestick government; but if the word conveys as much the idea of falsehood in French as in English, then is this a French and not an English maxim; there are, however, many cases in which it is prudent to *dissemble* our resentments, if by allowing them time to die away we keep them from the knowledge of others. *Disguise* is altogether opposed to candour: an ingenuous mind revolts at it; an honest man will never find it necessary, unless the Abbe Girard be right, in saying that "when the necessity of circumstances and the nature of affairs call for *disguise* it is politick." Yet what train of circumstances can we conceive to exist which will justify policy founded upon the violation of truth? Intriguers, conspirators, and all who have dishonest purposes to answer, must practise *disguise* as the only means of success; but true policy is as remote from *disguise* as cunning is from wisdom;

* Vide Abbe Girard: "Cacher, dissimuler déguiser"

Let school-taught pride *dissemble* all it can,
These little things are great to little man.
GOLDSMITH.

'Good-breeding has made the tongue falsify the heart, and act a part of continual restraint, while nature has preserved the eyes to herself, that she may not be *disguised* or misrepresented.'—STEELE.

HYPOCRITE, DISSEMBLER.

Hypocrite, in Greek ὑποκριτής, from ὑπὸ and κρίνομαι, signifies one appearing under a mask; *dissembler*, from *dissemble*, in Latin *dissimulo* or *dis* and *similis*, signifies one who makes himself appear unlike what he really is.

The *hypocrite* feigns to be what he is not; 'In regard to others, *hypocrisy* is not so pernicious as barefaced irreligion.'—ADDISON. The *dissembler* conceals what he is: the former takes to himself the credit of virtues which he has not; the latter conceals the vices that he has;

So spake the false *dissembler* unperceived.
MILTON.

Every *hypocrite* is a *dissembler;* but every *dissembler* is not a *hypocrite;* the *hypocrite* makes truth serve the purpose of falsehood; the *dissembler* is content with making falsehood serve his own particular purpose.

SIMULATION, DISSIMULATION.

Simulation, from *similis*, is the making one's self like what one is not; and *dissimulation*, from *dissimilis* unlike, is the making one's self appear unlike what one really is. The hypocrite puts on the semblance of virtue to recommend himself to the virtuous. The dissembler conceals his vices when he wants to gain the simple or ignorant to his side; 'The learned make a difference between *simulation* and *dissimulation*. *Simulation* is a pretence of what is not; and *dissimulation* is a concealment of what is.'—TATLER.

SECRET, HIDDEN, LATENT, OCCULT, MYSTERIOUS.

Secret (*v. Clandestine*) signifies known to one's self only; *hidden*, *v. To conceal; latent*, in Latin *latens*, from *lateo* to lie hid, signifies the same as hidden; *occult*, in Latin *occultus*, participle of *occulo*, compounded of *oc* or *ob* and *culo* or *colo* to cover over by tilling or ploughing, that is, to cover over with the earth; *mysterious*, *v. Dark.*

What is *secret* is known to some one; what is *hidden* may be known to no one: it rests in the breast of an individual to keep a thing *secret;* it depends on the course of things if any thing remains *hidden:* every man has more or less of that which he wishes to keep *secret;* the talent of many lies *hidden* for want of opportunity to bring it into exercise; as many treasures lie *hidden* in the earth for want of being discovered and brought to light. A *secret* concerns only the individual or individuals who hold it; but that which is *hidden* may concern all the world; sometimes the success of a transaction depends upon its being kept *secret;* the stores of knowledge which yet remain *hidden* may be much greater than those which have been laid open;

Ye boys, who pluck the flow'rs and spoil the spring,
Beware the *secret* snake that shoots a sting.
DRYDEN.

The blind, laborious mole
In winding mazes works her *hidden* hole.
DRYDEN.

The *latent* is the *secret* or concealed, in cases where it ought to be open: a *latent* motive is that which a person intentionally, though not justifiably, keeps to himself; the *latent* cause for any proceeding is that which is not revealed;

Mem'ry confus'd, and interrupted thought,
Death's harbingers, lie *latent* in the draught.
PRIOR.

Occult and *mysterious* are species of the *hidden:* the former respects that which has a veil naturally thrown over it; the latter respects that mostly which is covered with a supernatural veil: an *occult* science is one that is *hidden* from the view of persons in general, which is attainable but by few; *occult* causes or qualities are those which lie too remote to be discovered by the inquirer: the operations of Providence are said to be *mysterious*, as they are altogether past our finding out; many points of doctrine in our religion are equally *mysterious*, as connected with and dependent upon the attributes of the Deity; 'Some men have an *occult* power of stealing on the affections'—JOHNSON.

From his void embrace,
Mysterious heaven! That moment to the ground,
A blackened corse, was struck the beauteous maid.
THOMSON.

Mysterious is sometimes applied to human transactions in the sense of throwing a veil intentionally over any thing, in which sense it is nearly allied to the word *secret*, with this distinction, that what is *secret* is often not known to be *secret;* but that which is *mysterious* is so only in the eyes of others. Things are sometimes conducted with such *secrecy* that no one suspects what is passing until it is seen by its effects; an air of *mystery* is sometimes thrown over that which is in reality nothing when seen: hence *secrecy* is always taken in a good sense, since it is so great an essential in the transactions of men; but *mystery* is often employed in a bad sense; either for the affected concealment of that which is insignificant, or the purposed concealment of that which is bad: an expedition is said to be *secret*, but not *mysterious;* on the other hand, the disappearance of a person may be *mysterious*, but is not said to be *secret.*

MYSTERIOUS, MYSTICK.

Mysterious (*v. Dark*) and *mystick* are but variations of the same original; the former however is more commonly applied to that which is supernatural, or veiled in an impenetrable obscurity; the latter to that which is natural, but in part concealed from the view; hence we speak of the *mysterious* plans of Providence: *mystick* schemes of theology or *mystick* principles; 'As soon as that *mysterious* veil, which now covers futurity, was lifted up, all the gayety of life would disappear.'—BLAIR.

And ye five other wand'ring fires that move
In *mystick* dance not without song,
Resound his praise.—MILTON.

TO ABSCOND, STEAL AWAY, SECRETE ONE'S SELF.

Abscond, in Latin *abscondo*, is compounded of *abs* and *condo*, signifying to hide from the view, which is the original meaning of the other words; to *abscond* is to remove one's self for the sake of not being discovered by those with whom we are acquainted; to *steal away* is to get away so as to elude observation; to *secrete one's self* is to get into a place of secrecy without being perceived.

Dishonest men *abscond*, thieves *steal away* when they dread detection, and fugitives *secrete themselves.* Those who *abscond* will have frequent occasion to *steal away*, and still more frequent occasion to *secrete themselves.*

CLANDESTINE, SECRET.

Clandestine, in Latin *clandestinus*, comes from *clam* secretly; *secret*, in French *secret*, Latin *secretus*, participle of *secerno* to separate, signifies remote from observation.

Clandestine expresses more than *secret.* To do a thing *clandestinely* is to elude observation; to do a thing *secretly* is to do it without the knowledge of any one: what is *clandestine* is unallowed, which is not necessarily the case with what is *secret.*

With the *clandestine* must be a mixture of art; with *secrecy*, caution and management are requisite: a *clandestine* marriage is effected by a studied plan to escape notice; a *secret* marriage is conducted by the forbearance of all communication: conspirators have many *clandestine* proceedings and *secret* meetings: an unfaithful servant *clandestinely* conveys his master's property from the premises of his master; 'I went to this *clandestine* lodging, and found to my amazement all the ornaments of a fine gentleman, which he has taken upon credit.'—JOHNSON. A person makes a *secret* communication of his intentions to another; 'Some may place their chief satisfaction in giving *secretly* what is to be distributed; others in being the open and avowed instruments of making such distributions.'—ATTERBURY.

POLITICAL, POLITICK.

Political has the proper meaning of the word *polity*, which, from the Greek πολιτεία and πόλις a city, signifies the government either of a city or a country; *politick*, like the word policy, has the improper meaning of the word polity, namely, that of clever management, because the affairs of states are sometimes managed with considerable art and finesse: hence we speak of *political* government as opposed to that which is ecclesiastick; and of *politick* conduct as opposed to that which is unwise and without foresight: in *political* questions, it is not *politick* for individuals to set themselves up in opposition to those who are in power; the study of *politicks*, as a science, may make a man a clever statesman; but it may not always enable him to discern true *policy* in his private concerns; 'Machiavel laid down this for a master rule, in his *political* scheme, that the show of religion was helpful to the politician.'—SOUTH. 'A *politick* caution, a guarded circumspection, were among the ruling principles of our forefathers.'—BURKE.

ART, CUNNING, DECEIT.

Art, in Latin *ars*, probably comes from the Greek ἄρω to fit or dispose, Hebrew חרש to contrive, in which action the mental exercises of *art* principally consists; *cunning* is in Saxon *cuning*, German *kennend* knowing, in which sense the English word was formerly used; *deceit*, from the Latin *deceptum*, participle of *decipio* or *de* and *capio*, signifies taking by surprise or unawares.

Art implies a disposition of the mind, to use circumvention or artificial means to attain an end: *cunning* marks the disposition to practise disguise in the prosecution of a plan: *deceit* leads to the practice of dissimulation and gross falsehood, for the sake of gratifying a desire. *Art* is the property of a lively mind; *cunning* of a thoughtful and knowing mind; *deceit* of an ignorant, low, and weak mind.

Art is practised often in self-defence; as a practice therefore it is even sometimes justifiable, although not as a disposition: *cunning* has always self in view; the *cunning* man seeks his gratification without regard to others; *deceit* is often practised to the express injury of another: the *deceitful* man adopts base means for base ends. Animals practise *art* when opposed to their superiours in strength; but they are not *artful*, as they have not that versatility of power which they can habitually exercise to their own advantage like human beings; 'It has been a sort of maxim that the greatest *art* is to conceal *art*; but I know not how, among some people we meet with, their greatest *cunning* is to appear *cunning*.'—STEELE. Animals may be *cunning*, inasmuch as they can by contrivance and concealment seek to obtain the object of their desire; '*Cunning* can in no circumstance imaginable be a quality worthy a man, except in his own defence, and merely to conceal himself from such as are so, and in such cases it is wisdom.'—STEELE. No animal is *deceitful* except man: the wickedest and the stupidest of men have the power and the will of *deceiving* and practising falsehood upon others, which is unknown to the brutes; 'Though the living man can wear a mask and carry on *deceit*, the dying Christian cannot counterfeit.'—CUMBERLAND.

ARTFUL, ARTIFICIAL, FICTITIOUS.

Artful, compounded of *art* and *ful*, marks the quality of being full of *art* (*v. Art*); *artificial*, in Latin *artificialis*, from *ars* and *facio* to do, signifies done with *art*; *fictitious*, in Latin *fictitious*, from *fingo* to feign, signifies the quality of being *feigned*.

Artful respects what is done with art or design; *artificial* what is done by the exercise of workmanship; *fictitious* what is made out of the mind. *Artful* and *artificial* are used either for natural or moral objects; *fictitious* always for those that are moral: *artful* is opposed to what is *artless*, *artificial* to what is natural, *fictitious* to what is real: the ringlets of a lady's hair are disposed in an *artful* manner; the hair itself may be *artificial*: a tale is *artful* which is told in a way to gain credit; manners are *artificial* which do not seem to suit the person adopting them; a story is *fictitious* which has no foundation whatever in truth, and is the invention of the narrator.

Children sometimes tell their stories so *artfully* as to impose on the most penetrating and experienced; 'I was much surprised to see the ants' nest which I had destroyed, very *artfully* repaired.'—ADDISON. Those who have no character of their own are induced to take an *artificial* character in order to put themselves on a level with their associates; 'If we compare two nations in an equal state of civilization, we may remark that where the greater freedom obtains, there the greater variety of *artificial* wants will obtain also.'—CUMBERLAND. Beggars deal in *fictitious* tales of distress in order to excite compassion; 'Among the numerous stratagems by which pride endeavours to recommend folly to regard, there is scarcely one that meets with less success than affectation, or a perpetual disguise of the real character by *fictitious* appearances.'—JOHNSON.

ARTIFICE, TRICK, FINESSE, STRATAGEM

Artifice, in French *artifice*, Latin *artifex* an artificer, from *artem facio* to execute an art, signifies the performance of an art; *trick*, in French *tricher*, comes from the German *triegen* to deceive; *finesse*, a word directly imported from France with all the meaning attached to it, which is characteristick of the nation itself, means properly fineness; the word *fin* fine, signifying in French, as well as in the northern languages from which it is taken, subtlety or mental acumen; *stratagem*, in French *stratagème*, from the Greek στρατήγημα and στρατηγέω to lead an army, signifies by distinction any military scheme, or any scheme conducted for some military purpose.

All these terms denote the exercise of an art calculated to mislead others. *Artifice* is the generick term; the rest specifick: the former has likewise a particular use and acceptation distinct from the others: it expresses a ready display of art for the purpose of extricating one's self from a difficulty, or securing to one's self an advantage. *Trick* includes in it more of design to gain something for one's self, or to act secretly to the inconvenience of others:* it is rather a cheat on the senses than the understanding. *Finesse* is a species of *artifice* in which art and cunning are combined in the management of a cause: it is a mixture of invention, falsehood, and concealment. *Stratagem* is a display of art in plotting and contriving, a disguised mode of obtaining an end.

Females who are not guarded by fixed principles of virtue and uprightness are apt to practise *artifices* upon their husbands. Men without honour, or an honourable means of living, are apt to practise various *tricks* to impose upon others to their own advantage: every trade therefore is said to have its *tricks*; and professions are not entirely clear from this stigma, which has been brought upon them by unworthy members. Diplomatick persons have most frequent recourse to *finesse*, in which no people are more skilful practitioners than those who have coined the word. Military operations are sometimes considerably forwarded by well-concerted and well-timed *stratagems* to surprise the enemy.

An *artifice* may be perfectly innocent when it serves to afford a friend an unexpected pleasure; 'Among the several *artifices* which are put in practice by the poets, to fill the minds of an audience with terrour, the first place is due to thunder and lightning.'—ADDISON. A *trick* is childish which only serves to deceive or amuse children; 'Where men practise falsehood and show *tricks* with one another, there will be perpetual suspicions, evil surmisings, doubts, and jealousies.'—SOUTH. *Stratagems* are allowable not in war only; the writer of a novel or a play may sometimes adopt a successful *stratagem* to cause the reader a surprise;

* Trusler: "Cunning, finesse, device, artifice, trick stratagem."

On others practise thy Ligurian arts;
The *stratagems* and *tricks* of little hearts
Are lost on me.—DRYDEN.

One of the most successful *stratagems*, whereby Mahomet became formidable, was the assurance that impostor gave his votaries, that whoever was slain in battle should be immediately conveyed to that luxurious paradise his wanton fancy had invented.'—STEELE. *Finesse* is never justifiable; it carries with it too much of concealment and disingenuousness to be practised but for selfish and unworthy purposes;

Another can't forgive the paltry arts
By which he makes his way to shallow hearts,
Mere pieces of *finesse*, traps for applause.
CHURCHILL.

CUNNING, CRAFTY, SUBTLE, SLY, WILY.

Cunning, v. *Art*; *crafty* signifies having *craft*, that is, according to the original meaning of the word, having a knowledge of some trade or art; hence figuratively applied to the character; *subtle*, in French *subtil*, and Latin *subtilis* thin, from *sub* and *tela* a thread drawn to be fine; hence in the figurative sense in which it is here taken, fine or acute in thought; *sly* is in all probability connected with slow and sleek, or smooth; deliberation and smoothness entering very much into the sense of *sly*; *wily* signifies disposed to *wiles* or stratagems.

All these epithets agree in expressing an aptitude to employ peculiar and secret means to the attainment of an end; they differ principally in the secrecy of the means, or the degree of circumvention that is employed. The *cunning* man shows his dexterity simply in concealing; this requires little more than reservedness and taciturnity; 'There is still another secret that can never fail if you can once get it believed, and which is often practised by women of greater *cunning* than virtue. This is to change sides for awhile with the jealous man, and to turn his own passion upon himself.'—ADDISON. The *crafty* man goes farther; he shapes his words and actions so as to lull suspicion: hence it is that a child may be *cunning*, but an old man will be *crafty*; '*Cunning* is often to be met with in brutes themselves, and in persons who are but the fewest removes from them.'—ADDISON. 'You will find the examples to be few and rare of wicked, unprincipled men attaining fully the accomplishment of their *crafty* designs.'—BLAIR. A *subtle* man has more acuteness of invention than either, and all his schemes are hidden by a veil that is impenetrable by common observation; the *cunning* man looks only to the concealment of an immediate object; the *crafty* and *subtle* man has a remote object to conceal: thus men are *cunning* in their ordinary concerns; politicians are *crafty* or *subtle*; but the former is more so as to the end, and the latter as to the means. A man is *cunning* and *crafty* by deeds; he is *subtle* mostly by means of words alone, or words and actions combined; 'The part of Ulysses, in Homer's Odyssey, is very much admired by Aristotle, as perplexing that fable with very agreeable plots and intricacies, not only by the many adventures in his voyage and the *subtlety* of his behaviour, but by the various concealments and discoveries of his person in several parts of his poem.' —ADDISON. *Slyness* is a vulgar kind of *cunning*; the *sly* man goes cautiously and silently to work; 'If you or your correspondent had consulted me in your discourse upon the eye, I could have told you that the eye of Leonora is *slyly* watchful while it looks negligent.' —STEELE. *Wiliness* is a species of *cunning* or *craft*, applicable only to cases of attack or defence;

Implore his aid; for Proteus only knows
The secret cause, and cure of all thy woes;
But first the *wily* wizard must be caught,
For, unconstrain'd, he nothing tells for nought.
DRYDEN.

TO DECEIVE, DELUDE, IMPOSE UPON.

Deceive, in French *décevoir*, Latin *decipio*, compounded of *de* privative, and *capio* to take, signifies to take wrong; *delude*, in Latin *deludo*, compounded of *de* and *ludo*, signifies to play upon or to mislead by a trick; *impose*, in Latin *imposui*, perfect of *impono*, signifies literally to lay or put upon.

Falsehood is the leading feature in all these terms they vary however in the circumstances of the action To *deceive* is the most general of the three; it signifies simply to produce a false conviction; the other terms are properly species of *deceiving*, including accessory ideas. *Deception* may be practised in various degrees; *deluding* is always something positive, and considerable in degree. Every false impression produced by external objects, whether in trifles or important matters, is a *deception*: *delusion* is confined to errours in matters of opinion. We may be *deceived* in the colour or the distance of an object; we are *deluded* in what regards our principles or moral conduct; 'I would have all my readers take care how they mistake themselves for uncommon geniuses and men above rule, since it is very easy for them to be *deceived* in this particular.'—BUDGELL. '*Deluded* by a seeming excellence.'—ROSCOMMON.

A *deception* does not always suppose a fault on the part of the person *deceived*, but a *delusion* does. A person is sometimes *deceived* in cases where *deception* is unavoidable;

I now believ'd
The happy day approach'd, nor are my hopes *deceiv'd.*
DRYDEN.

A person is *deluded* through a voluntary blindness of the understanding;

Who therefore seeks in these
True wisdom, finds her not, or by *delusion*
Far worse, her false resemblance only meets.
PRIOR.

Artful people are sometimes capable of *deceiving* so as not even to excite suspicion; their plausible tales justify the credit that is given to them: when the ignorant enter into nice questions of politicks or religion, it is their ordinary fate to be *deluded*.

Deception is practised by an individual on himself or others;

Wanton women in their eyes
Men's *deceivings* do comprise.—GREENE.

A *delusion* is commonly practised on one's self;

I, waking, view'd with grief the rising sun,
And fondly mourn'd the dear *delusion* gone.
PRIOR.

An *imposition* is always practised on another; 'As there seems to be in this manuscript some anachronisms and deviations from the ancient orthography, I am not satisfied myself that it is authentick, and not rather the production of one of those Grecian sophisters who have *imposed upon* the world several spurious works of this nature.'—ADDISON. Men deceive others from a variety of motives; they always *impose upon* them for purposes of gain, or the gratification of ambition. Men *deceive* themselves with false pretexts and false confidence; they *delude* themselves with vain hopes and wishes.

Professors in religion often *deceive* themselves as much as they do others: the grossest and most dangerous *delusion* into which they are liable to fall is that of substituting faith for practice, and an extravagant regard to the outward observances of religion in lieu of the mild and humble temper of Jesus: no *imposition* was ever so successfully practised upon mankind as that of Mahomet.

DECEIVER, IMPOSTOR.

Deceiver and *impostor*, the derivatives from *deceive* and *impose*, have a farther distinction worthy of notice *Deceiver* is a generick term; *impostor* specifick: every *impostor* is a species of *deceiver*: the words have however a distinct use. The *deceiver* practises *deception* on individuals; the *impostor* only on the publick at large. The false friend and the faithless lover are *deceivers*; the assumed nobleman who practises frauds under his disguise, and the pretended prince who lays claim to a crown to which he was never born, are *impostors*.

Deceivers are the most dangerous members of society; they trifle with the best affections of our nature, and violate the most sacred obligations; 'That tradition of the Jews that Christ was stolen out of the grave is ancient; it was the invention of the Jews, and denies the integrity of the witnesses of his resurrection, making them *deceivers.'*—TILLOTSON. *Impostors* are seldom so culpable as those who give them credit; 'Our Saviour wrought his miracles frequently, and for a long time together: a time sufficient to have detected any *impostor* in.'—TILLOTSON. It would require no small share of credulity to be *deceived* by any of the *impositions* which have been hitherto practised upon the inconsiderate part of mankind.

DECEIT, DECEPTION.

Deceit (*v. To deceive*) marks the propensity to *deceive*, or the practice of *deceiving; deception* the act of *deceiving* (*v. To deceive*).

A *deceiver* is full of *deceit:* but a *deception* may be occasionally practised by one who has not this habit of *deceiving*. *Deceit* is a characteristick of so base a nature, that those who have it practise every species of *deception* in order to hide their characters from the observation of the world.

The practice of *deceit* springs altogether from a design, and that of the worst kind; but a *deception* may be practised from indifferent, if not innocent, motives, or may be occasioned even by inanimate objects;

I mean to plunge the boy in pleasing sleep,
And ravish'd in Idalian bow'rs to keep,
Or high Cythera, that the sweet *deceit*
May pass unseen, and none prevent the cheat.
DRYDEN.

'All the joy or sorrow for the happiness or calamities of others is produced by an act of the imagination that realizes the event however fictitious, so that we feel, while the *deception* lasts, whatever emotions would be excited by the same good or evil happening to ourselves.'—JOHNSON.

A person or a conduct is *deceitful;* an appearance is *deceptive*. A *deceitful* person has always guile in his heart and on his tongue: jugglers practise various *deceptions* in the performance of their tricks for the entertainment of the populace. Parasites and sycophants are obliged to have recourse to *deceit*, in order to inveigle themselves into the favour of their patrons: there is no sense on which a *deception* can be practised with greater facility than on that of sight; sometimes it is an agreeable *deception*, as in the case of a panoramick exhibition.

DECEIT, DUPLICITY, DOUBLE-DEALING.

Deceit, v. Deceit, deception; duplicity signifies *doubleness* in dealing, the same as *double-dealing*

The former two may be applied either to habitual or particular actions, the latter only to particular actions. There may be much *deceit* or *duplicity* in a person's character or in his proceedings; there is *double-dealing* only where dealing goes forward. The *deceit* may be more or less veiled; the *duplicity* lies very deep, and is always studied whenever it is put into practice. *Duplicity* in reference to actions is mostly employed for a course of conduct: *double-dealing* is but another term for *duplicity* on particular occasions. Children of reserved characters are frequently prone to *deceit*, which grows into consummate *duplicity* in riper years: the wealthy are often exposed to much *duplicity* when they choose their favourites among the low and ignorant; 'The arts of *deceit* do continually grow weaker and less serviceable to them that use them.'—TILLOTSON. 'Necessity drove Dryden into a *duplicity* of character that is painful to reflect upon.'—CUMBERLAND. Nothing gives rise to more *double-dealing* than the fabrication of wills; 'Maskwell (in the *Double-Dealer*) discloses by soliloquy, that his motive for *double-dealing* was founded in his passion for Cynthia.'—CUMBERLAND.

DECEIT, FRAUD, GUILE.

Deceit (*v. Deceit, deception*) is allied to *fraud* in reference to actions; to *guile* in reference to the character.

Deceit is here, as in the preceding article, indeterminate when compared with *fraud*, which is a specifick mode of deceiving: *deceit* is practised only in private transactions· *fraud* is practised towards bodies as well as individuals, in publick as well as private: a child practises *deceit* towards its parents;

With such *deceits* he gain'd their easy hearts,
Too prone to credit his perfidious arts.—DRYDEN.

Frauds are practised upon government, on the publick at large, or on tradesmen; 'The story of the three books of the Sybils sold to Tarquin was all a *fraud* devised for the convenience of state.'—PRIDEAUX. *Deceit* involves the violation of moral law, *fraud* that of the civil law. A servant may *deceive* his master as to the time of his coming or going, but he *defrauds* him of his property if he obtains it by any false means. *Deceit* as a characteristick is indefinite in magnitude; *guile* marks a strong degree of moral turpitude in the individual;

Was it for force or *guile*,
Or some religious end you rais'd this pile?
DRYDEN.

The former is displayed in petty concerns: the latter, which contaminates the whole character, displays itself in inextricable windings and turnings that are suggested in a peculiar manner by the author of all evil. *Deceitful* is an epithet commonly and lightly applied to persons in general; but *guileless* is applied to characters which are the most diametrically opposed to and at the greatest possible distance from, that which is false.

FALLACIOUS, DECEITFUL, FRAUDULENT.

Fallacious comes from the Latin *fallax* and *fallo* to deceive, signifying the property of misleading; *deceitful, v. To deceive; fraudulent* signifies after the manner of a *fraud*.

The *fallacious* has respect to falsehood in opinion; *deceitful* to that which is externally false; our hopes are often *fallacious;* the appearances of things are often *deceitful*. *Fallacious*, as characteristick of the mind, excludes the idea of design;

But when Ulysses, with *fallacious* arts,
Had made impression on the people's hearts,
And forg'd a treason in my patron's name,
My kinsman fell.—DRYDEN.

Deceitful excludes the idea of mistake; *fraudulent* is a gross species of the *deceitful;* 'Such is the power which the sophistry of self-love exercises over us, that almost every one may be assured he measures himself by a *deceitful* scale.'—BLAIR. It is a *fallacious* idea for any one to imagine that the faults of others can serve as any extenuation of his own; it is a *deceitful* mode of acting for any one to advise another to do that which he would not do himself; it is *fraudulent* to attempt to get money by means of a falsehood;

Ill-fated Paris! slave to womankind,
As smooth of face as *fraudulent* of mind.—POPE.

FALLACY, DELUSION, ILLUSION.

Fallacy, in Latin *fallacia*, from *fallo*, has commonly a reference to the act of some conscious agent, whose intention is to deceive; the *delusion* (*v. To deceive*) and *illusion* may be the work of inanimate objects. We endeavour to detect the *fallacy* which lies concealed in a proposition; 'There is indeed no transaction which offers stronger temptations to *fallacy* and sophistication than epistolary intercourse.'—JOHNSON. One endeavours to remove the *delusion* to which the judgement has been exposed;

As when a wandering fire,
Hovering and blazing with *delusive* light,
Misleads th' amaz'd night-wanderer from his way.
MILTON.

It is sometimes difficult to dissipate the *illusion* to which the senses or the fancy are liable; 'Fame, glory, wealth, honour, have in the prospect pleasing *illusions*.'—STEELE.

In all the reasonings of freethnkers, there are *fallacies* against which a man cannot always be on his guard. The ignorant are perpetually exposed to *delusions* when they attempt to speculate on matters of opinion; among the most serious of these *delusions* we may reckon that of substituting their own feelings for the operations of Divine grace. The ideas of ghosts and apparitions are mostly attributable to the *illusions* of the senses and the imagination.

FAITHLESS, PERFIDIOUS, TREACHEROUS.

Faithless (*v. Faithless*) is the generick term, the rest are specifick terms; a breach of good *faith* is expressed by them all, but *faithless* expresses no more; the others include accessory ideas in their signification: *perfidious*, in Latin *perfidiosus*, signifies literally breaking through faith in a great degree, and now implies the addition of hostility to the breach of *faith; treacherous*, most probably changed from *traitorous*, comes from the Latin *trado* to betray, and signifies one species of active hostile breach of *faith*.

A *faithless* man is *faithless* only for his own interest; a *perfidious* man is expressly so to the injury of another. A friend is *faithless* who consults his own safety in the time of need; he is *perfidious* if he profits by the confidence reposed in him to plot mischief against the one to whom he has made vows of friendship. *Faithlessness* does not suppose any particular efforts to deceive; it consists of merely violating that *faith* which the relation produces; *perfidy* is never so complete as when it has most effectually assumed the mask of sincerity. Whoever deserts his friend in need is guilty of *faithlessness;* but he is guilty of *perfidy* who draws from him every secret in order to effect his ruin;

Old Priam, fearful of the war's event,
This hapless Polydore to Thracia sent,
From noise and tumults, and destructive war,
Committed to the *faithless* tyrant's care.—DRYDEN.

'When a friend is turned into an enemy the world is just enough to accuse the *perfidiousness* of the friend, rather than the indiscretion of the person who confided in him.'—ADDISON.

Incle was not only a *faithless* but a *perfidious* lover. *Faithlessness*, though a serious offence, is unhappily not unfrequent: there are too many men who are unmindful of their most important engagements; but we may hope for the honour of humanity that there are not many instances of *perfidy*, which exceeds every other vice in atrocity, as it makes virtue itself subservient to its own base purposes.

Perfidy may lie in the will to do; *treachery* lies altogether in the thing done: one may therefore be *perfidious* without being *treacherous*. A friend is *perfidious* whenever he evinces his *perfidy;* but he is said to be *treacherous* only in the particular instance in which he betrays the confidence and interests of another. I detect a man's *perfidy*, or his *perfidious* aims, by the manner in which he attempts to draw my secrets from me; I am made acquainted with his *treachery* not before I discover that my confidence is betrayed and my secrets are divulged. On the other hand we may be *treacherous* without being *perfidious*. *Perfidy* is an offence mostly between individuals; it is rather a breach of fidelity (*v. Faith, fidelity*) than of faith: *treachery* on the other hand includes breaches of private or publick faith. A servant may be both *perfidious* and *treacherous* to his master; a citizen may be *treacherous*, but not *perfidious* towards his country;

Shall then the Grecians fly, oh dire disgrace!
And leave unpunish'd this *perfidious* race?—POPE.

And had not Heav'n the fall of Troy design'd,
Enough was said and done t' inspire a better mind:
Then had our lances pierc'd the *treach'rous* wood,
And Ilian's towers and Priam's empire stood.
DRYDEN.

It is said that in the South Sea islands, when a chief wants a human victim, their officers will sometimes invite their friends or relations to come to them, when they take the opportunity of suddenly falling upon them and despatching them: here is *perfidy* in the individual who acts this false part; and *treachery* in the act of betraying him who is murdered. When the schoolmaster of Falerii delivered his scholars to Camillus, he was guilty of *treachery* in the act, and of *perfidy* towards those who had reposed confidence in him When Romulus ordered the Sabine women to be seized, it was an act of *treachery* but not of *perfidy;* so in like manner when the daughter of Tarpeius opened the gates of the Roman citadel to the enemy.

FAITHLESS, UNFAITHFUL.

Faithless is mostly employed to denote a breach of faith; and *unfaithful* to mark the want of fidelity (*v. Faith, fidelity*). The former is positive; the latter is rather negative, implying a deficiency. A prince, a government, a people, or an individual is said to be *faithless;*

So spake the seraph Abdiel, faithful found;
Among the *faithless*, faithful only he.—MILTON.

A husband, a wife, a servant, or any individual is said to be *unfaithful*. Meffus Tuffetius, the Alban Dicta tor, was *faithless* to the Roman people when he with held his assistance in the battle, and strove to go over to the enemy;

The sire of men and monarch of the sky
Th' advice approv'd, and bade Minerva fly,
Dissolve the league, and all her arts employ
To make the breach the *faithless* act of Troy.
POPE.

At length, ripe vengeance o'er their head impends,
But Jove himself the *faithless* race defends.—POPE.

A man is *unfaithful* to his employer who sees him injured by others without doing his utmost to prevent it; 'If you break one jot of your promise, I will think you the most atheistical break-promise, and the most unworthy that may be chosen out of the gross band of the *unfaithful*.'—SHAKSPEARE. A woman is *faithless* to her husband who breaks the marriage vow; she is *unfaithful* to him when she does not discharge the duties of a wife to the best of her abilities.

The term *unfaithful* may also be applied figuratively to things;

If e'er with life I quit the Trojan plain,
If e'er I see my sire and spouse again,
This bow, *unfaithful* to my glorious aims,
Broke by my hands shall feed the blazing flames.
POPE.

TREACHEROUS, TRAITOROUS, TREASONABLE.

These epithets are all applied to one who betrays his trust; but *treacherous* (*v. Faithless*) respects a man's private relations; *traitorous*, his publick relation to his prince and his country: he is a *treacherous* friend, and a *traitorous* subject. We may be *treacherous* to our enemies as well as our friends, for nothing can lessen the obligation to preserve the fidelity of promise; 'This very charge of folly should make men cautious how they listen to the *treacherous* proposals which come from his own bosom.'—SOUTH. We may be *traitorous* to our country by abstaining to lend that aid which is in our power, for nothing but death can do away the obligation which we owe to it by the law of nature; 'All the evils of war must unavoidably be endured, as the necessary means to give success to the *traitorous* designs of the rebel.'—SOUTH. *Traitorous* and *treasonable* are both applicable to subjects: but the former is extended to all publick acts; the latter only to those which affect the supreme power: a soldier is *traitorous* who goes over to the side of the enemy against his country; a man is guilty of *treasonable* practices who meditates the life of the king, or aims at subverting his government: a man may be a *traitor* under all forms of government; but he can be guilty of *treason* only in a monarchical state; 'Herod trumped up a sham plot against Hyrcanus, as if he held correspondence with Malchus King of Arabia, for accomplishing *treasonable* designs against him.'—PRIDEAUX

INSIDIOUS, TREACHEROUS.

Insidious, in Latin *insidiosus*, from *insidiæ* stratagem or ambush, from *insideo* to lie in wait or ambush, signifies after the manner of a stratagem, or prone to adopt stratagems; *treacherous* is changed from *traitorous*, and derived from *trado* to betray, signifying in general the disposition to betray.

The *insidious* man is not so bad as the *treacherous* man; for the former only lies in wait to ensnare us, when we are off our guard; but the latter throws us off our guard, by lulling us into a state of security, in order the more effectually to get us into his power: an enemy is, therefore, denominated *insidious*, but a friend is *treacherous*. The *insidious* man has recourse to various little artifices, by which he wishes to effect his purpose, and gain an advantage over his opponent; the *treacherous* man pursues a system of direct falsehood, in order to ruin his friend: the *insidious* man objects to a fair and open contest; but the *treacherous* man assails in the dark him whom he should support. The opponents to Christianity are fond of *insidious* attacks upon its sublime truths, because they have not always courage to proclaim their own shame; 'Since men mark all our steps, and watch our haltings, let a sense of their *insidious* vigilance excite us so to behave ourselves, that they may find a conviction of the mighty power of Christianity towards regulating the passions.' —ATTERBURY. The *treachery* of some men depends for its success on the credulity of others; as in the case of the Trojans, who listened to the tale of Simon, the Grecian spy;

> The world must think him in the wrong,
> Would say he made a *treach'rous* use
> Of wit, to flatter and seduce.—SWIFT.

TO CHEAT, DEFRAUD, TRICK.

Cheat, in Saxon *cettu*, in all probability comes from *captum* and *capio*, as deceit comes from *decipio; defraud*, compounded of *de* and *fraud*, signifies to practise fraud, or to obtain by fraud; *trick*, in French *tricher*, German *trügen*, signifies simply to deceive, or get the better of any one.

The idea of deception which is common to these terms varies in degree and circumstance.

One *cheats* by a gross falsehood; one *defrauds* by a settled plan; one *tricks* by a sudden invention: *cheating* is as low in its ends, as it is base in its means; *cheats* are contented to gain by any means: *defrauding* is a serious measure; its consequences are serious, both to the perpetrator and the sufferer. A person *cheats* at play; he *defrauds* those who place confidence in him.

Cheating is not punishable by laws; it involves no other consequence than the loss of character: *frauds* are punished in every form, even with death, when the occasion requires; they strike at the root of all confidence, and affect the publick security: *tricking* is a species of dexterous *cheating;* the means and the end are alike trifling. Dishonest people *cheat;* villains *defraud;* cunning people *trick*. These terms preserve the same distinction in their extended application;

> If e'er ambition did my fancy *cheat*
> With any wish so mean as to be great;
> Continue, Heav'n, still from me to remove
> The humble blessings of that life I love.
> COWLEY.

> Thou, varlet, dost thy master's gains devour,
> Thou milk'st his ewes, and often twice an hour;
> Of grass and fodder thou *defraud'st* the dams,
> And of the mother's dugs the starving lambs.
> DRYDEN.

'He who has the character of a crafty, *tricking* man is entirely deprived of a principal instrument of business, trust, whence he will find nothing succeed to his wish.' —BACON.

COQUET, JILT.

There are many *jilts* who become so from *coquets*, but one may be a *coquet* without being a *jilt*. *Coquetry* is contented with employing little arts to excite notice; *jilting* extends to the violation of truth and honour, in order to awaken a passion which it afterward disappoints. Vanity is the main spring by which *coquets* and *jilts* are impelled to action; but the former indulges her propensity mostly at her own expense only, while the latter does no less injury to the peace of others than she does to her own reputation. The *coquet* makes a traffick of her own charms by seeking a multitude of admirers; the *jilt* sports with the sacred passion of love, and barters it for the gratification of any selfish propensity. *Coquetry* is a fault which should be guarded against by every female as a snare to her own happiness; *jilting* is a vice which cannot be practised without some depravity of the heart; 'The *coquet* is indeed one degree towards the *jilt;* but the heart of the former is bent upon admiring herself, and giving false hopes to her lovers; but the latter is not contented to be extremely amiable, but she must add to that advantage a certain delight in being a torment to others.'—STEELE.

TO INSNARE, ENTRAP, ENTANGLE, INVEIGLE.

The idea of getting any object artfully into one's power is common to all these terms; to *insnare* is to take in or by means of a *snare;* to *entrap* is to take in a *trap* or by means of a *trap;* to *entangle* is to take in a *tangle*, or by means of *tangled* thread; to *inveigle* is to take by means of making blind, from the French *aveugle* blind.

Insnare and *entangle* are used either in the natural or moral sense; *entrap* mostly in the natural, *inveigle* only in the moral sense. In the natural sense birds are *ensnared* by means of birdlime, nooses, or whatever else may deprive them of their liberty: men and beasts are *entrapped* in whatever serves as a *trap* or enclosure; they may be *entrapped* by being lured into a house or any place of confinement: all creatures are *entangled* by nets, or that which confines the limbs and prevents them from moving forward.

In the moral sense men are said to be *ensnared* by their own passions and the allurements of pleasure into a course of vice which deprives them of the use of their faculties, and makes them virtually captives; 'This lion (the literary lion) has a particular way of imitating the sound of the creature he would *ensnare* —ADDISON. Men may be *entrapped* by promises or delusive hopes into measures which they afterward repent of;

> Though the new-dawning year in its advance
> With hope's gay promise may *entrap* the mind,
> Let memory give one retrospective glance.
> CUMBERLAND.

Men are *entangled* by their errours and imprudencies in difficulties which interfere with their moral freedom, and prevent them from acting uprightly; 'Some men weave their sophistry till their own reason is *entangled*.'—JOHNSON. Men are *inveigled* by the artifices of others, when the consequences of their own actions are shut out from their view, and they are made to walk like blind men; 'Why the *inveigling* of a woman before she is come to years of discretion should not be as criminal as the seducing her before she is ten years old, I am at a loss to comprehend.'—ADDISON Insidious freethinkers make no scruple of *insnaring* the immature understanding by the proposal of such doubts and difficulties as shall shake their faith When a man is *entangled* in the evil courses of a wicked woman, the more he plunges to get his liberty, the faster she binds him in her toils. The practice of *inveigling* young persons of either sex into houses of ill fame is not so frequent at present as it was in former times.

TO COAX, WHEEDLE, CAJOLE, FAWN

Coax probably comes from *coke* a simpleton, signifying to treat as a simpleton; *wheedle* is a frequentative of *wheel*, signifying to come round a person with smooth art; *cajole* is in French *cajoler;* to *fawn*, from the noun *fawn*, signifies to act or move like a *fawn*.

The idea of using mean arts to turn people to one's selfish purposes is common to all these terms: *coax* has something childish in it; *wheedle* and *cajole* that which is knavish; *fawn* that which is servile.

The act of *coaxing* consists of urgent entreaty and whining supplication; the act of *wheedling* consists of smooth and winning entreaty; *cajoling* consists mostly of trickery and stratagem, disguised under a soft address and insinuating manners; the act of *fawning* consists of supplicant grimace and anticks, such as characterize the little animal from which it derives its name; children *coax* their parents in order to obtain their wishes; 'The nurse had changed her note, she was nuzzling and *coaxing* the child; "that's a good dear," says she.'—L'ESTRANGE. The greedy and covetous *wheedle* those of an easy temper; 'Regulus gave his son his freedom in order to entitle him to the estate left him by his mother, and when he got into possession of it endeavoured (as the character of the man made it generally believed) to *wheedle* him out of it by the most indecent complaisance.'—MELMOTH (*Letters of Pliny*). Knaves *cajole* the simple and unsuspecting; 'I must grant it a just judgement upon poets, that they whose chief pretence is wit, should be treated as they themselves treat fools, that is, be *cajoled* with praises.'—POPE. Parasites *fawn* upon those who have the power to contribute to their gratification;

Unhappy he,
Who, scornful of the flatterer's *fawning* art,
Dreads ev'n to pour his gratitude of heart.
ARMSTRONG.

Coaxing is mostly resorted to by inferiours towards those on whom they are dependent; *wheedling* and *cajoling* are low practices confined to the baser sort of men with each other; *fawning*, though not less mean and disgraceful than the above-mentioned vices, is commonly practised only in the higher walks of life, where men of base character, though not mean education, come in connexion with the great.

TO ADULATE, FLATTER, COMPLIMENT.

Adulate, in Latin *adulatus*, participle of *adulor*, is changed from *adoleo* to offer incense; *flatter*, in French *flatter*, comes from the Latin *flatus* wind or air, signifying to say what is airy and unsubstantial; *compliment* comes from *comply*, and the Latin *complaceo*, to please greatly.

We *adulate* by discovering in our actions an entire subserviency; we *flatter* simply by words expressive of an unusual admiration; we *compliment* by fair language or respectful civilities. An *adulatory* address is couched in terms of feigned devotion to the object; a *flattering* address is filled with the fictitious perfections of the object; a *complimentary* address is suited to the station of the individual and the occasion which gives rise to it; it is full of respect and deference. Courtiers are guilty of *adulation*; lovers are addicted to *flattery*; people of fashion indulge themselves in a profusion of *compliments*.

Adulation can never be practised without falsehood; its means are hypocrisy and lying, its end private interest; 'The servile and excessive *adulation* of the senate soon convinced Tiberius that the Roman spirit had suffered a total change under Augustus.'—CUMBERLAND. *Flattery* always exceeds the truth; it is extravagant praise dictated by an overweening partiality, or, what is more frequent, by a disingenuous temper; 'You may be sure a woman loves a man when she uses his expressions, tells his stories, or imitates his manner. This gives a secret delight; for imitation is a kind of artless *flattery*, and mightily favours the principle of self-love.'—SPECTATOR. *Compliments* are not incompatible with sincerity, unless they are dictated from a mere compliance to the prescribed rules of politeness or the momentary desire of pleasing; 'I have known a hero *complimented* upon the decent majesty and state he assumed after victory.'—POPE. *Adulation* may be fulsome, *flattery* gross, *compliments* unmeaning. *Adulation* inspires a person with an immoderate conceit of his own importance; *flattery* makes him in love with himself; *compliments* make him in good-humour with himself.

FLATTERER, SYCOPHANT, PARASITE.

Flatterer, v. *To adulate*; *sycophant*, in Greek συκοφάντης, signified originally an informer on the matter of figs, but has now acquired the meaning of an obsequious and servile person; *parasite*, in Greek παράσιτος, from παρὰ and σῖτος corn or meat, originally referred to the priests who attended feasts, but it is now applied to a hanger-on at the tables of the great.

The *flatterer* is one who *flatters* by words; the *sycophant* and *parasite* is therefore always a *flatterer*, and something more, for the *sycophant* adopts every mean artifice by which he can ingratiate himself, and the *parasite* submits to every degradation and servile compliance by which he can obtain his base purpose. These terms differ more in the object than in the means: the former having general purposes of favour; and the latter particular and still lower purposes to answer. Courtiers may be *sycophants* in order to be well with their prince and obtain preferment, but they are seldom *parasites*, for the latter are generally poor and in want of a meal; '*Flatterers* are the bosom enemies of princes.'—SOUTH. 'By a revolution in the state, the fawning *sycophant* of yesterday is converted into the austere critick of the present hour.'—BURKE.

The first of pleasures
Were to be rich myself; but next to this
I hold it best to be a *parasite*,
And feed upon the rich.—CUMBERLAND.

TO GLORY, BOAST, VAUNT.

To *glory* is to hold as one's *glory*; to *boast* is to set forth to one's advantage; to *vaunt* is to *boast* loudly. The first two terms denote the value which the individual sets upon that which belongs to himself; the last term may be applied to that which respects others as well as ourselves.

To *glory* is more particularly the act of the mind, the indulgence of the internal sentiment: to *boast* and *vaunt* denote rather the expression of the sentiment. To *glory* is applied only to matters of moment; *boast* is rather suitable to trifling points; *vaunt* is a term of less familiar use than either, being suited rather to poetry or romance. A Christian martyr *glories* in the cross of Christ; 'All the laymen who have exerted a more than ordinary genius in their writings, and were the *glory* of their times, were men whose hopes were filled with immortality.'—ADDISON. A soldier *boasts* of his courage and his feats in battle; 'If a man looks upon himself in an abstracted light, he has not much to *boast* of.'—ADDISON.

Not that great champion
Whom famous poets' verse so much doth *vaunt*,
And hath for twelve huge labours high extoll'd
So many furies and sharp hits did haunt.
SPENSER

Glory is but seldom used in a bad sense, and *boast* still seldomer in a good sense. A royalist *glories* in the idea of supporting his prince and the legitimate rights of a sovereign; but there are republicans and traitors who *glory* in their shame, and *boast* of the converts they make to their lawless cause. It is an unbecoming action for an individual to *boast* of any thing in himself; but a nation, in its collective capacity, may *boast* of its superiority without doing violence to decorum. An Englishman *glories* in the reflection of belonging to such a distinguished nation, although he would do very idly to *boast* of it as a personal quality; no nation can *boast* of so many publick institutions for the relief of distress as England.

TO EVÂDE, EQUIVOCATE, PREVARICATE

Evade, v. *To escape*; *equivocate*, v. *Ambiguity*; *prevaricate*, in Latin *prævaricatus*, participle of *præ* and *varicor* to go loosely, signifies to shift from side to side.

These words designate an artful mode of escaping the scrutiny of an inquirer; we *evade* by artfully turning the subject or calling off the attention of the inquirer; we *equivocate* by the use of *equivocal* expressions; we *prevaricate* by the use of loose and indefinite expressions: we avoid giving satisfaction by *evading*; we give a false satisfaction by *equivocating*; we give dissatisfaction by *prevaricating*. *Evading* is not so mean a practice as *equivocating*: it may be sometimes needful to *evade* a question which we do not wish to answer; 'Whenever a trader has endeavoured to *evade* the just demands of his creditors, this hath been declared by the legislature to be an act of bankruptcy.'—BLACKSTONE. *Equivocations* are employed for the purposes of falsehood and interest; 'When Satan told Eve "Thou shalt not surely die," it was in his *equivocation*, "Thou shalt not incur present death."'—BROWN (*Vulgar Errours*). *Prevarications* are still meaner; and are resorted to mostly by criminals in order to escape detection; 'There is no *prevaricating* with God when we are on the very threshold of his presence.'—CUMBERLAND.

EVASION, SHIFT, SUBTERFUGE.

Evasion (v. *To evade*) is here taken only in the bad sense; *shift* and *subterfuge* are modes of *evasion*: the *shift* signifies that gross kind of *evasion* by which one attempts to *shift* off an obligation from one's self; the *subterfuge*, from *subter* under and *fugio* to fly, is a mode of *evasion* in which one has recourse to some screen or shelter.

The *evasion*, in distinction from the others, is resorted to for the gratification of pride or obstinacy: whoever wishes to maintain a bad cause must have recourse to *evasions;* candid minds despise all *evasions;* 'The question of a future state was hung up in doubt, or banded between conflicting disputants through all the quirks and *evasions* of sophistry and logick.'—CUMBERLAND. The *shift* is the trick of a knave; it always serves a paltry, low purpose; he who has not courage to turn open thief, will use any *shifts* rather than not get money dishonestly; 'When such little *shifts* come once to be laid open, how poorly and wretchedly must that man needs sneak, who finds himself both guilty and baffled too.'—SOUTH. The *subterfuge* is the refuge of one's fears; it is not resorted to from the hope of gain, but from the fear of a loss; not for purposes of interest, but for those of character; he who wants to justify himself in a bad cause, has recourse to *subterfuges;*

What farther *subterfuge* can Turnus find?
DRYDEN.

TO ESCAPE, ELUDE, EVADE.

Escape, in French *echapper*, comes in all probability from the Latin *excipio* to take out of, to get off; *elude*, v. *To avoid; evade*, from the Latin *evado*, compounded of *e* and *vado*, signifies to go or get out of a hing.

The idea of being disengaged from that which is not agreeable is comprehended in the sense of all these terms; but *escape* designates no means by which this is effected; *elude* and *evade* define the means, namely, the efforts which are used by one's self: we are simply disengaged when we *escape;* but we disengage ourselves when we *elude* and *evade:* we *escape* from danger; we *elude* the search: our *escapes* are often providential, and often narrow; our success in *eluding* depends on our skill: there are many bad men who *escape* hanging by the mistake of a word; there are many who *escape* detection by the art with which they *elude* observation and inquiry;

Vice oft is hid in virtue's fair disguise,
And in her borrow'd form *escapes* inquiring eyes.
SPECTATOR.

It is a vain attempt
To bind the ambitious and unjust by treaties;
These they *elude* a thousand specious ways.
THOMSON

'The earl Rivers had frequently inquired for his son (Savage), and had always been amused with *evasive* answers.'—JOHNSON.

Elude and *evade* both imply the practice of art; but the former consists mostly of actions, the latter of words as well as actions: a thief *eludes* those who are in pursuit of him by dexterous modes of concealment; he *evades* the interrogatories of the judge by equivocating replies. One is said to *elude* a punishment, and to *evade* a law.

AMBIGUOUS, EQUIVOCAL.

Ambiguous, in Latin *ambiguus*, from *ambigo*, compounded of *ambo* and *ago*, signifies acting both ways; *equivocal*, in French *equivoque*, Latin *æquivocus*, composed of *æquus* and *vox*, signifies that which may be applied equally to two or more objects.

An *ambiguity* arises from a too general form of expression, which leaves the sense of the author indeterminate; an *equivocation* lies in the power of particular terms used, which admit of a double interpretation: the *ambiguity* leaves us in entire incertitude as to what is meant; the *equivocation* misleads us by the use of a term in the sense which we do not suspect.

The *ambiguity* may be unintentional, arising from the nature both of the words and the things; or it may be employed to withhold information respecting our views; the *equivocation* is always intentional, and may be employed for purposes of fraud; 'An honest man will never employ an *equivocal* expression; a confused man may often utter *ambiguous* ones without any design.'—BLAIR. The histories of heathen nations are full of confusion and *ambiguity:* the heathen oracles are mostly veiled by some *equivocation;* of this we have a remarkable instance in the oracle of the Persian mule, by which Crœsus was misled; 'We make use of an *equivocation* to deceive; of an *ambiguity* to keep in the dark.'—TRUSLER. *Ambiguous* may sometimes be applied to other objects besides words;

Th' *ambiguous* god, who rul'd her lab'ring breast,
In these mysterious words his mind express'd,
Some truths reveal'd, in terms involv'd the rest.
DRYDEN.

'The parliament of England is without comparison the most voluminous author in the world, and there is such a happy *ambiguity* in its works, that its students have as much to say on the wrong side of every question as upon the right.'—CUMBERLAND. The term *equivocal* may sometimes be employed in an indifferent sense; 'Give a man all that is in the power of the world to bestow, but leave him at the same time under some secret oppression or heaviness of heart. You bestow indeed the materials of enjoyment, but you deprive him of the ability to extract it. Hence prosperity is so often an *equivocal* word, denoting merely affluence of possession, but unjustly applied to the possessor.'—BLAIR.

TO AVOID, ESCHEW, SHUN, ELUDE.

Avoid, in French *eviter*, Latin *evito*, compounded of *e* and *vito*, probably from *viduus* void, signifies to make one's self void or free from a thing; *eschew* and *shun* both come from the German *scheuen*, Swedish *sky*, &c. when it signifies to fly; *elude*, in French *eluder*, Latin *eludo*, compounded of *e* and *ludo*, signifies to get one's self out of a thing by a trick.

Avoid is both generick and specifick; we *avoid* in *eschewing* or *shunning*, or we *avoid* without *eschewing* or *shunning*. Various contrivances are requisite for *avoiding; eschewing* and *shunning* consist only of going out of the way, of not coming in contact; *eluding*, as its derivation denotes, has more of artifice in it than any of the former. We *avoid* a troublesome visiter under real or feigned pretences of ill health, prior engagement, and the like; we *eschew* evil company by not going into any but what we know to be good; we *shun* the sight of an offensive object by turning into another road; we *elude* a punishment by getting out of the way of those who have the power of inflicting it.

Prudence enables us to *avoid* many of the evils to which we are daily exposed; 'Having thoroughly considered the nature of this passion, I have made it my study how to *avoid* the envy that may accrue to me from these my speculations.'—STEELE. Nothing but a fixed principle of religion can enable a man to *eschew* the temptations to evil which lie in his path. This term is particularly applicable to poetry and the grave style;

Thus Brute this realm into his rule subdued,
And reigned long in great felicity,
Lov'd of his friends, and of his foes *eschewed*.
SPENSER.

Fear will lead one to *shun* a madman, whom it is not in one's power to bind;

Of many things, some few I shall explain;
Teach thee to *shun* the dangers of the main,
And how at length the promised shore to gain.
DRYDEN.

A want of all principle leads a man to *elude* his creditors, whom he wishes to defraud;

The wary Trojan, bending from the blow,
Eludes the death, and disappoints his foe.—POPE.

The best means of *avoiding* quarrels is to *avoid* giving offence. The surest preservative of our innocence is to *eschew* evil company, and the surest preservative of our health is to *shun* every intemperate practice. Those who have no evil design in view will have no occasion to *elude* the vigilance of the law.

We speak of *avoiding* a danger, and *shunning* a danger: but to *avoid* it is in general not to fall into it; to *shun* it is with care to keep out of the way of it.

TO INVENT, FEIGN, FRAME, FABRICATE, FORGE.

Invent, v. To contrive; feign, v. To feign; frame signifies to make according to a *frame, fabricate,* in Latin *fabricatus,* from *faber* a workman, is changed from *facio,* signifying to make according to art; *forge,* from the noun *forge,* signifies to make in a *forge.*

All these terms are employed to express the production of something out of the mind, by means of its own efforts. To *invent* (*v. To contrive*) is the general term; the other terms imply modes of *invention* under different circumstances. To *invent,* as distinguished from the rest, is busied in creating new forms, either by means of the imagination or the reflective powers; it forms combinations either purely spiritual, or those which are mechanical and physical: the poet *invents* imagery; the philosopher *invents* mathematical problems or mechanical instruments; 'Pythagoras *invented* the forty-seventh proposition of the first book of Euclid.'—Bartelet.

Invent is used for the production of new forms to real objects, or for the creation of unreal objects; to *feign* (*v. To feign*) is used for the creation of unreal objects, or such as have no existence but in the mind: a play or story is *invented* from what passes in the world; Mahomet's religion consists of nothing but *inventions:* the heathen poets *feigned* all the tales and fables which constitute the mythology, or history of their deities;

Their savage eyes turned to a modest gaze
By the sweet power of musick; therefore, the poet
Did *feign* that Orpheus drew trees, stones, and floods.
Shakspeare.

To *frame,* or make according to a *frame,* is a species of *invention* which consists in the disposition as well as the combination of objects. Thespis was the *inventor* of tragedy: Psalmanazar *framed* an entire new language, which he pretended to be spoken on the island of Formosa; Solon *framed* a new set of laws for the city of Athens;

Nature hath *fram'd* strange fellows in her time.
Shakspeare.

To *invent, feign,* and *frame* are all occasionally employed in the ordinary concerns of life, and in a bad sense; *fabricate* and *forge* are never used any otherwise. *Invent* is employed as to that which is the fruit of one's own mind; to *feign* is employed as to that which is unreal; to *frame* is employed as to that which requires deliberation and arrangement; to *fabricate,* from *faber* a workman, signifying to make in a workmanlike manner, and to *forge,* signifying to make as in a *forge,* are employed as to that which is absolutely false, and requiring more or less exercise of the *inventive* power. A person *invents* a lie, and *feigns* sorrow; *invents* an excuse, and *feigns* an attachment. A story is *invented* inasmuch as it is new, and not before conceived by others, or occasioned by the suggestions of others; it is *framed* inasmuch as it required to be duly disposed in all its parts, so as to be consistent; it is *fabricated* inasmuch as it runs in direct opposition to the actual circumstances, and therefore has required the skill and labour of a workman; it is *forged* inasmuch as it seems by its utter falsehood and extravagance to have caused as much severe action in the brain, as what is produced by the fire in a furnace or *forge;* 'The very idea of the *fabrication* of a new government is enough to fill us with horrour.'—Burke.

As chymists gold from brass by fire would draw,
Pretexts are into treason *forg'd* by law.—Denham.

FICTION, FABRICATION, FALSEHOOD.

Fiction is opposed to what is real; *fabrication,* as it is here understood, and *falsehood* are opposed to what is true. *Fiction* relates what may be, though not what is: *fabrication* and *falsehood* relate what is not as what is, and *vice versâ. Fiction* serves for amusement and instruction; *fabrication* and *falsehood* serve to mislead and deceive. *Fiction* and *fabrication* both require invention: *falsehood* consists of simple assertions of what is not true. The fables of Æsop are *fictions* of the simplest kind, but yet such as required a peculiarly lively fancy and inventive genius to produce: the *fabrication* of a play as the production of Shakspeare's pen, was once executed with sufficient skill to impose for a time upon the publick credulity: a good memory is all that is necessary in order to avoid uttering *falsehoods* that can be easily contradicted and confuted. In an extended sense of the word *fiction,* it approaches still nearer to the sense of *fabricate,* when said of the *fictions* of the ancients, which were delivered as truth, although admitted now to be false: the motive of the narrator is what here constitutes the difference; namely, that in the former case he believes, or is supposed to believe, what he relates to be true, in the latter he knows it to be false. The heathen mythology consists principally of the *fictions* of the poets: newspapers commonly abound in *fabrication;* 'All that the Jews tell us of their two-fold Messiah is a mere *fiction,* framed without as much as a pretence to any foundation in Scripture for it.'—Prideaux. 'The translator or *fabricator* of Ossian's poems.'—Mason. Sometimes, however, the term *fabricate* may be applied to any effort of genius, without regard to the veracity of the *fabricator;* 'With reason has Shakspeare's superiority been asserted in the *fabrication* of his preternatural machines.'—Cumberland.

As epithets *fictitious* and *false* are very closely allied; for what is *fictitious* is *false,* though all that is *false* is not *fictitious:* the *fictitious* is that which has been feigned, or *falsely* made by some one; the *false* is simply that which is *false* by the nature of the thing the *fictitious* account is therefore the invention of an individual, whose veracity is thereby impeached; but there may be many *false* accounts unintentionally circulated.

UNTRUTH, FALSEHOOD, FALSITY, LIE.

An *untruth* is an *untrue* saying; a *falsehood* and a *lie* are false sayings: *untruth* of itself reflects no disgrace on the agent; it may be unintentional or not: a *falsehood* and a *lie* are intentional *false* sayings, differing only in degree as the guilt of the offender: a *falsehood* is not always spoken for the express intention of deceiving, but a *lie* is uttered only for the worst of purposes. Some persons have a habit of telling *falsehoods* from the mere love of talking: those who are guilty of bad actions endeavour to conceal them by *lies.* Children are apt to speak *untruths* for want of understanding the value of words; 'Above all things tell no *untruth,* no, not even in trifles.'—Sir Henry Sydney. Travellers from a love of exaggeration are apt to introduce *falsehoods* into their narrations; 'Many temptations to *falsehood* will occur in the disguise of passions too specious to fear much resistance.'—Johnson. It is the nature of a *lie* to increase itself to a tenfold degree: one *lie* must be backed by many more; 'The nature of a *lie* consists in this, that it is a *false* signification knowingly and voluntarily used.'—South.

Falsehood is also used in the abstract sense for what is *false. Falsity* is never used but in the abstract sense, for the property of the *false.* The former is general, the latter particular in the application: the truth or *falsehood* of an assertion is not always to be distinctly proved; 'When speech is employed only as the vehicle of *falsehood,* every man must disunite himself from others.'—Johnson. The *falsity* of any particular person's assertion may be proved by the evidence of others;

Can you on him such *falsities* obtrude?
And as a mortal the Most Wise delude?
Sandys.

TRUTH, VERACITY.

Truth belongs to the thing; *veracity* to the person: the *truth* of the story is admitted upon the *veracity* of the narrator; 'I shall think myself obliged for the future to speak always in *truth* and sincerity of heart.' —Addison. 'Many relations of travellers have been slighted as fabulous, till more frequent voyages have confirmed their *veracity.*'—Johnson.

TO FEIGN, PRETEND.

Feign, in Latin *fingo* or *figo,* from the Greek πηγω to fix or stamp; *pretend,* in Latin *prætendo,* signifies properly to stretch before, that is, to put on the outside

These words may be used either for doing or saying; they are both opposed to what is true, but they differ from the motive of the agent. To *feign* is taken either in a bad or an indifferent sense; to *pretend* always in a bad sense. One *feigns* in order to gain some future end; a person *feigns* sickness in order to be excused from paying a disagreeable visit; one *pretends* in order to serve a present purpose; a child *pretends* to have lost his book who wishes to excuse himself for his idleness.

To *feign* consists often of a line of conduct; to *pretend* consists always of words. Ulysses *feigned* madness in order to escape from going to the Trojan war. According to Virgil, the Grecian Sinon *pretended* to be a deserter come over to the Trojan camp. In matters of speculation, to *feign* is to invent by force of the imagination; to *pretend* is to set up by force of self-conceit. It is *feigned* by the poets that Orpheus went down into hell and brought back Euridice his wife;

> To win me from his tender arms,
> Unnumber'd suitors came,
> Who prais'd me for imputed charms,
> And felt or *feign'd* a flame.—GOLDSMITH.

Infidel philosophers *pretend* to account for the most mysterious things in nature upon natural, or, as they please to term it, rational principles; 'An affected delicacy is the common improvement in those who *pretend* to be refined above others.'—STEELE.

SPURIOUS, SUPPOSITIOUS, COUNTERFEIT.

Spurious, in Latin *spurius*, from σπορὰ, because the ancients called the female *spurium*; hence, one who is of uncertain origin on the father's side is termed *spurious*; *suppositious*, from *suppose*, signifies to be supposed or conjectured, in distinction from being positively known; *counterfeit*, *v. To imitate*.

All these terms are modes of the false; the two former indirectly, the latter directly: whatever is uncertain that might be certain, and whatever is conjectural that might be conclusive, are by implication false; that which is made in imitation of another thing, so as to pass for it as the true one, is positively false. Hence, the distinction between these terms, and the ground of their applications. An illegitimate offspring is said to be *spurious* in the literal sense of the word, the father in this case being always uncertain; and any offspring which is termed *spurious* falls necessarily under the imputation of not being the offspring of the person whose name they bear. In the same manner an edition of a work is termed *spurious* which comes out under a false name, or a name different from that in the titlepage; 'Being to take leave of England, I thought it very handsome to take my leave also of you, and my dearly honoured mother, Oxford; otherwise both of you may have just grounds to cry me up, you for a forgetful friend, she for an ungrateful son, if not some *spurious* issue.'—HOWELL. *Suppositious* expresses more or less of falsehood, according to the nature of the thing. A *suppositious* parent implies little less than a directly false parent; but in speaking of the origin of any thing in remote periods of antiquity, it may be merely *suppositious* or conjectural from the want of information; 'The fabulous tales of early British history, *suppositious* treaties and charters, are the proofs on which Edward founded his title to the sovereignty of Scotland.'—ROBERTSON. *Counterfeit* respects rather works of art which are exposed to imitation: coin is *counterfeit* which bears a false stamp, and every invention which comes out under the sanction of the inventor's name is likewise a *counterfeit* if not made by himself or by his consent;

> Words may be *counterfeit*,
> False coin'd, and current only from the tongue,
> Without the mind.—SOUTHERN.

TO IMITATE, COPY, COUNTERFEIT.

The idea of taking a likeness of some object is common to all these terms; but *imitate* (*v. To follow*) is the generick, *copy* (*v. To copy*) and *counterfeit* (*v. Spurious*) the specifick: to *imitate* is to take a general likeness; to *copy*, to take an exact likeness; to *counterfeit*, to take a false likeness: to *imitate* is, therefore, almost always used in a good or an indifferent sense; to *copy* mostly, and to *counterfeit* always, in a bad sense: to *imitate* an author's style is at all times allowable for one who cannot form a style for himself; but to *copy* an author's style would be a too slavish adherence even for the dullest writer. To *imitate* is applicable to every object, for every external object is susceptible of *imitation*; and in man the *imitative* faculty displays itself alike in the highest and the lowest matters, in works of art and in moral conduct, 'Poetry and musick have the power of *imitating* the manners of men.'—SIR WM. JONES. To *copy* is applicable only to certain objects which will admit of a minute likeness being taken; thus, an artist may be said to *copy* from nature, which is almost the only circumstance in which *copying* is justifiable, except when it is a mere manual act; to *copy* any thing in others, whether it be their voice, their manners, their language, or their works, is inconsistent with the independence which belongs to every rational agent; 'Some imagine, that whatsoever they find in the picture of a master, who has acquired reputation, must of necessity be excellent; and never fail when they *copy*, to follow the bad as well as the good things.'—DRYDEN. In a general application, however, the term *copy* may be used in an indifferent sense;

> The mind, impressible and soft, with ease
> Imbibes and *copies* what she hears and sees.
> COWPER.

To *counterfeit* is applicable but to few objects, and happily practicable but in few cases; we may *counterfeit* the coin, or we may *counterfeit* the person, or the character, or the voice, or the handwriting of any one for whom we would wish to pass; but if the likeness be not very exact, the falsehood is easily detected;

> I can *counterfeit* the deep tragedian,
> Speak and look big, and pry on every side.
> SHAKSPEARE

TO IMITATE, MIMICK, MOCK, APE.

Imitate, *v. To follow*; *mimick*, from the Greek μιμος, has the same origin as *imitate*; *mock*, in French *mocquer*, Greek μωκαω to laugh at; to *ape* signifies to *imitate* like an *ape*.

To *imitate* is here the general term: to *mimick* and to *ape* are both species of vicious *imitation*.

One *imitates* that which is deserving of *imitation*, or the contrary: one *mimicks* either that which is not an authorized subject of *imitation*, or which is *imitated* so as to excite laughter. A person wishes to make that his own which he *imitates*, but he *mimicks* for the entertainment of others;

> Because we sometimes walk on two.
> I hate the *imitating* crew.—GAY.

The force of example is illustrated by the readiness with which people *imitate* each other's actions when they are in close intercourse: the trick of *mimickry* is sometimes carried to such an extravagant pitch that no man, however sacred his character, or exalted his virtue, can screen himself from being the object of this species of buffoonery: to *ape* is a serious though an absurd act of *imitation*;

> A courtier any *ape* surpasses;
> Behold him humbly cringing wait
> Upon the minister of state.
> View him soon after to inferiours
> *Aping* the conduct of superiours.—SWIFT

To *mimick* is a jocose act of *imitation*;

> Nor will it less delight th' attentive sage
> T' observe that instinct which unerring guides
> The brutal race which *mimicks* reason's love.
> SOMERVILLE

To *mock* is an ill-natured, or at least an unmeaning, act of *imitation*;

> What though no friends in sable weeds appear,
> Grieve for an hour, perhaps, then mourn a year,
> And bear about the *mockery* of wo
> To midnight dances.—POPE.

The *ape imitates* to please himself, but the *mimick imitates* to please others. The *ape* seriously tries to come as near the original as he can; the *mimick* tries to render the *imitation* as ridiculous as possible: the former *apes* out of deference to the person *aped*; the latter *mimicks* out of contempt or disregard.

Mimickry belongs to the merry-andrew or buffoon; *aping* to the weakling who has no originality in himself. Show-people display their talents in *mimicking* the cries of birds or beasts, for the entertainment of the gaping crowd; weak and vain people, who wish to be admired for that which they have not in themselves, *ape* the dress, the manners, the voice, the mode of speech, and the like, of some one who is above them. *Mimickry* excites laughter from that which is burlesque in it; *aping* excites laughter from that which is absurd and unsuitable in it; *mockery* excites laughter from the malicious temper of those who enjoy it.

TO FOLLOW, IMITATE.

Follow, *v. To follow, succeed; imitate*, in Latin *imitatus*, participle of *imitor*, from the Greek μιμέω to mimick and ὅμοιος alike, signifies to do or make alike.

Both these terms denote the regulating our actions by something that offers itself to us, or is set before us; but we *follow* that which is either internal or external; we *imitate* that only which is external: we either *follow* the dictates of our own minds or the suggestions of others: but we *imitate* the conduct of others; in regard to external objects we *follow* either a rule or an example; but we *imitate* an example only: we *follow* the footsteps of our forefathers; we *imitate* their virtues and their perfections: it is advisable for young persons to *follow* as closely as possible the good example of those who are older and wiser than themselves;

And I with the same greediness did seek,
As water when I thirst, to swallow Greek;
Which I did only learn that I might know
Those great examples which I *follow* now.
DENHAM.

It is the bounden duty of every Christian to *imitate* the example of our blessed Saviour to the utmost of his power; 'The *imitators* of Milton seem to place all the excellency of that sort of writing in the use of uncouth or antique words.'—JOHNSON.

To *follow* and *imitate* may both be applied to that which is good or bad: the former to any action; but the latter only to the behaviour or the external manners: we may *follow* a person in his career of virtue or vice; we *imitate* his gestures, tone of voice, and the like. Parents should be guarded in all their words and actions; for whatever may be their example, whether virtuous or vicious, it will in all probability be *followed* by their children: those who have the charge of young people should be particularly careful to avoid all bad habits of gesture, voice, or speech; as there is a much greater propensity to *imitate* what is ridiculous than what is becoming.

TO COPY, TRANSCRIBE.

Copy is probably changed from the Latin *capio* to take, because we take that from an object which we *copy; transcribe*, in Latin *transcribo*, that is, *trans* over and *scribo*, signifies literally to write over from something else, to make to pass over in writing from one body to another.

To *copy* respects the matter; to *transcribe* respects simply the act of writing. What is *copied* must be taken immediately from the original, with which it must exactly correspond; what is *transcribed* may be taken from the *copy*, but not necessarily in an entire state. Things are *copied* for the sake of getting the contents: they are often *transcribed* for the sake of clearness and fair writing. A *copier* should be very exact; a *transcriber* should be a good writer. Lawyers *copy* deeds, and have them afterward frequently *transcribed* as occasion requires. *Transcribe* is sometimes used to signify a literal *copy* in a figurative application; 'Aristotle tells us that the world is a *copy* or *transcript* of those ideas which are in the mind of the First Being, and that those ideas which are in the mind of man are a *transcript* of the world. To this we may add that words are the *transcript* of those ideas which are in the mind of man, and that writing or printing are the *transcript* of words.'—ADDISON.

COPY, MODEL, PATTERN, SPECIMEN.

Copy, from the verb to *copy* (*v. To copy*), marks either the thing from which we *copy* or the thing *copied; model*, in French *modèle*, Latin *modulus* a little mode or measure, signifies the thing that serves as a measure, or that is made after a measure; *pattern*, which is a variation of *patron*, from the French *patron*, Latin *patronus*, signifies the thing that directs; *specimen*, in Latin *specimen*, from *specio* to behold, signifies what is looked at for the purpose of forming our judgement by it.

* A *copy* and a *model* may be both employed either as an original work or as a work formed after an original. In the former sense, *copy* is used in relation to impressions, manuscripts, or writings, which are made to be *copied* by the printer, the writer, or the engraver: *model* is used in every other case, whether in morality or the arts: the proof will seldom be faulty when the *copy* is clear and correct. There can be no good writing formed after a bad *copy*, or in an extended application of the terms, the poet or the artist may *copy* after nature; 'Longinus has observed that the description of love in Sappho is an exact *copy* of nature, and that all the circumstances which follow one another in such a hurry of sentiments, notwithstanding they appear repugnant to each other, are really such as happen in the phrensies of love.'—ADDISON. No human being has ever presented us with a perfect *model* of virtue; the classick writers of antiquity ought to be carefully perused by all who wish to acquire a pure style, of which they contain unquestionably the best *models*; 'Socrates recommends to Alcibiades, as the *model* of his devotions, a short prayer which a Greek poet composed for the use of his friends.'—ADDISON.

Respecting these words, however, it is here farther to be observed, that a *copy* requires the closest imitation possible in every particular, but a *model* ought only to serve as a general rule: the former must be literally retraced by a mechanical process in all its lines and figures; it leaves nothing to be supplied by the judgement or will of the executor. A *model* often consists of little more than the outlines and proportions, while the dimensions and decorations are left to the choice of the workman. One who is anxious to acquire a fine hand will in the first instance rather imitate the errours of his *copy* than attempt any improvement of his own. A man of genius will not suffer himself to be cramped by a slavish adherence to any *model* however perfect.

In the second sense *copy* is used for painting, and *model* for relief. A *copy* ought to be faithful, a *model* ought to be just; the former should delineate exactly what is delineated by the original; the latter should adhere to the precise rules of proportion observed in the original. The pictures of Raphael do not lose their attractions even in bad *copies:* the simple *models* of antiquity often equal in value originals of modern conception.

Pattern and *specimen* approach nearest to *model* in signification: the idea of guidance or direction is prominent in them. The *model* always serves to guide in the execution of a work; the *pattern* serves either to regulate the work, or simply to determine the choice; the *specimen* helps only to form the opinion. The architect builds according to a certain *model;* 'A fault it would be if some king should build his mansion-house by the *model* of Solomon's palace.'—HOOKER. The mechanick makes any thing according to a *pattern*, or a person fixes on having a thing according to the *pattern* offered to him; 'A gentleman sends to my shop for a *pattern* of stuff; if he like it, he compares the *pattern* with the whole piece, and probably we bargain.'—SWIFT. The nature and value of things are estimated by the *specimen* shown of them; 'Several persons have exhibited *specimens* of this art before multitudes of beholders.'—ADDISON. A *model* is always some whole complete in itself; a *pattern* may be either a whole or the part of a whole; a *specimen* is always a part. *Models* of ships, bridges, or other pieces of mechanism are sometimes constructed for the purpose of explaining most effectually the nature and design of the invention: whenever the make, colour, or materials of any article, either of convenience or luxury, is an object of consideration, it can not be so rightly determined by any means as by producing a similar article to serve as a *pattern:* a single sentence in a book may be a sufficient *specimen* of the whole performance.

In the moral sense *pattern* respects the whole conduct or behaviour; *specimen* only individual actions The female who devotes her time and attention to the

* Vide Girard: "Copie, modèle."

management of her family and the education of her offspring is a *pattern* to those of her sex who depute the whole concern to the care of others. A person gives but an unfortunate *specimen* of his boasted sincerity, who is found guilty of an evasion; 'Xenophon, in the life of his imaginary prince, whom he describes as a *pattern* for real ones, is always celebrating the philanthropy or good-nature of his hero.'—ADDISON. 'We know nothing of the scanty jargon of our barbarous ancestors; but we have *specimens* of our language when it began to be adapted to civil and religious purposes, and find it such as might naturally be expected, artless and simple.'—JOHNSON.

EXAMPLE, PATTERN, ENSAMPLE.

Example, in Latin *exemplum*, very probably changed from *exsimulum* and *exsimulo* or *simulo*, signifies the thing framed according to a likeness; *pattern, v. Copy; ensample* signifies that which is done according to a *sample* or *example*.

All these words are taken for that which ought to be followed: but the *example* must be followed generally; the *pattern* must be followed particularly, not only as to what, but how a thing is to be done: the former serves as a guide to the judgement; the latter to guide the actions. The *example* comprehends what is either to be followed or avoided; the *pattern* only that which is to be followed or copied; the *ensample* is a species of *example*, the word being employed only in the solemn style. The *example* may be presented either in the object itself, or the description of it; the *pattern* displays itself most completely in the object itself; the *ensample* exists only in the description. Those who know what is right should set the *example* of practising it; and those who persist in doing wrong, must be made an *example* to deter others from doing the same;

The king of men his hardy host inspires
With loud command, with great *examples* fires.
POPE.

Every one, let his age and station be what they may, may afford a *pattern* of Christian virtue; the child may be a *pattern* to his playmates of diligence and dutifulness; the citizen may be a *pattern* to his fellow-citizens of sobriety and conformity to the laws; the soldier may be a *pattern* of obedience to his comrades; 'The fairy way of writing, as Mr. Dryden calls it, is more difficult than any other that depends upon the poet's fancy, because he has no *pattern* to follow in it.'—ADDISON. Our Saviour has left us an *example* of Christian perfection, which we ought to imitate, although we cannot copy it: the Scripture characters are drawn as *ensamples* for our learning;

Sir Knight, that doest that voyage rashly take,
By this forbidden way in my despight,
Doest by other's death *ensample* take.—SPENSER.

EXAMPLE, PRECEDENT.

Example, v. Example; precedent, from the Latin *precedens* preceding, signifies by distinction that preceding which is entitled to notice.

Both these terms apply to that which may be followed or made a rule; but the *example* is commonly present or before our eyes; the *precedent* is properly something past: the *example* may derive its authority from the individual; the *precedent* acquires its sanction from time and common consent: we are led by the *example*, or we copy the *example*; we are guided or governed by the *precedent*. The former is a private and often a partial affair; the latter is a publick and often a national concern: we quote *examples* in literature, and *precedents* in law;

Thames! the most lov'd of all the ocean's sons,
O could I flow like thee! and make thy stream
My great *example*, as it is my theme.—DENHAM.

At the revolution they threw a politick veil over every circumstance which might furnish a *precedent* for any future departure from what they had then settled for ever.'—BURKE.

EXAMPLE, INSTANCE.

Example (*v. Example, pattern*) refers in this case to the thing; *instance*, from the Latin *insto*, signifies that which stands or serves as a resting point.

The *example* is set forth by way of illustration or instruction; the *instance* is adduced by way of evidence or proof. Every *instance* may serve as an *example*, but every *example* is not an *instance*. The *example* consists of moral or intellectual objects; the *instance* consists of actions only. Rules are illustrated by *examples*;

Let me, my son, an ancient fact unfold,
A great *example* drawn from times of old.—POPE.

Characters are illustrated by *instances*; 'Many *instances* may be produced, from good authorities, that children actually suck in the several passions and depraved inclinations of their nurses.'—STEELE. The best mode of instructing children is by furnishing them with *examples* for every rule that is laid down; the Roman history furnishes us with many extraordinary *instances* of self-devotion for their country.

FIGURE, METAPHOR, ALLEGORY, EMBLEM SYMBOL, TYPE.

Figure, in Latin *figura*, from *fingo* to feign, signifies any thing painted or feigned by the mind; *metaphor*, in Greek μεταφορὰ, from μεταφέρω to transfer, signifies a transfer of one object to another; *allegory*, in Greek ἀλληγορία, from ἄλλος another thing, and ἀγορεύω to relate, signifies the relation of something under a borrowed form; *emblem*, in Greek ἔμβλημα, from ἐμβάλλω to impress, signifies the thing stamped on as a mark; *symbol*, from the Greek συμβάλλω to consider attentively, signifies the thing cast or conceived in the mind, from its analogy to represent something else; *type*, in Greek τύπος, from τύπτω to strike or stamp, signifies an image of something that is stamped on something else.

Likeness between two objects by which one is made to represent the other, is the common idea in the signification of these terms. *Figure* is the most general of these terms, comprehending every thing which is *figured* by means of the imagination; the rest are but modes of the *figure*. The *figure* consists either in words or in things generally: we may have a *figure* in expression, a *figure* on paper, a *figure* on wood or stone, and the like. It is the business of the imagination to draw figures out of any thing; 'The spring bears the same *figure* among the seasons of the year, that the morning does among the divisions of the day, or youth among the stages of life.'—ADDISON. The *metaphor* and *allegory* consist of a representation by means of words only: the *figure*, in this case, is any representation which the mind makes to itself of a resemblance between objects, which is properly a *figure* of thought, which when clothed in words is a *figure* of speech: the *metaphor* is a *figure* of speech of the simplest kind, by which a word acquires other meanings besides that which is originally affixed to it; as when the term head, which properly signifies a part of the body, is applied to the leader of an army; 'No man had a happier manner of expressing the affections of one sense by *metaphors* taken from another than Milton.'—BURKE. The *allegory* is a continued *metaphor* when attributes, modes and actions are applied to the objects thus *figured*, as in the *allegory* of sin and death in Milton; 'Virgil has cast the whole system of Platonick philosophy, so far as regards the soul of man, into beautiful *allegories*.'—ADDISON.

The *emblem* is that sort of *figure* of thought by which we make corporeal objects to stand for moral properties: thus the dove is represented as the *emblem* of meekness, or the bee-hive is conceived to be the *emblem* of industry; 'The stork's the *emblem* of true piety.'—BEAUMONT. The *symbol* is that species of *emblem* which is converted into a constituted sign among men; thus the olive and laurel are the *symbols* of peace, and have been recognised as such among barbarous as well as enlightened nations; 'I need not mention the justness of thought which is observed in the generation of these *symbolical* persons (in Milton's *allegory* of sin and death).'—ADDISON. The *type* is that species of *emblem* by which one object is made to represent another mystically; it is, therefore, only employed in religious matters, particularly in relation to the coming, the office, and the death of our Saviour; in this manner the offering of Isaac is considered as a *type* of our Saviour's offering himself as an atoning sacrifice

All the remarkable events under the law were *types* of Christ.'—BLAIR.

PARABLE, ALLEGORY.

Parable, in French *parabole*, Greek παραβολή from παραβάλλω signifies what is thrown out or set before one, in lieu of something which it resembles, *allegory*, *v. Figure*.

* Both these terms imply a veiled mode of speech, which serves more or less to conceal the main object of the discourse by presenting it under the appearance of something else, which accords with it in most of the particulars: the *parable* is mostly employed for moral purposes; the *allegory* in describing historical events.

The *parable* substitutes some other subject or agent, who is represented under a character that is suitable to the one referred to. In the *allegory* are introduced strange and arbitrary persons in the place of the real personages, or imaginary characteristicks and circumstances are ascribed to real persons.

The *parable* is principally employed in the sacred writings; the *allegory* forms a grand feature in the productions of the eastern nations.

SIMILE, SIMILITUDE, COMPARISON.

Simile and *similitude* are both drawn from the Latin *similis* like: the former signifying the thing that is like; the latter either the thing that is like, or the quality of being like: in the former sense only it is to be compared with *simile*, when employed as a figure of speech or thought; every thing is a *simile* which associates objects together on account of any real or supposed likeness between them; but a *similitude* signifies a prolonged or continued *simile*. The latter may be expressed in a few words, as when we say the god-like Achilles; but the former enters into minute circumstances of *comparison*, as when Homer *compares* any of his heroes fighting and defending themselves against multitudes to lions who are attacked by dogs and men. Every *simile* is more or less a *comparison*, but every *comparison* is not a *simile*: the latter *compares* things only as far as they are alike; but the former extends to those things which are different. in this manner, there may be a *comparison* between large things and small, although there can be no good *simile*; 'There are also several noble *similes* and all[illegible] in the first book of Paradise Lost.'—ADDISON. '[illegible]ch as have a natural bent to solitude (to carry on the former *similitude*) are like waters which may be forced into fountains.'—POPE. 'Your image of worshipping once a year in a certain place, in imitation of the Jews, is but a *comparison*, and *simile* non est idem.'—JOHNSON.

LIKENESS, RESEMBLANCE, SIMILARITY, OR SIMILITUDE.

Likeness denotes the quality of being *alike* (*v. Equal*); *resemblance*, from *resemble*, compounded of *re* and *semble*, in French *sembler*, Latin *simulo*, signifies putting on the form of another thing; *similarity*, in Latin *similaritas*, from *similis*, in Greek ὁμαγὸς like, from the Hebrew סמל an image, denotes the abstract property of *likeness*.

Likeness is the most general, and at the same time the most familiar, term of the three; it respects either external or internal properties: *resemblance* respects only the external properties; *similarity* only the internal properties: we speak of a *likeness* between two persons; of a *resemblance* in the cast of the eye, a *resemblance* in the form or figure; of a *similarity* in age and disposition.

Likeness is said only of that which is actual; *resemblance* may be said of that which is apparent: the *likeness* consists of something specifick; the *resemblance* may be only partial and contingent. A thing is said to be, but not to appear, *like* another; it may, however, have the shadow of a *resemblance*: whatever things are *alike* are *alike* in their essential properties; but they may *resemble* in a partial degree, or in certain particulars, but are otherwise essentially different. We are most like the Divine Being in the act of doing good; there is nothing existing in nature which has not certain points of resemblance with something else.

* Vide Abbe Girard: "Parable, allegorie."

Similarity, or *similitude*, which is a higher term, is in the moral application, in regard to *likeness*, what *resemblance* is in the physical sense: what is *alike* has the same nature; what is *similar* has certain features of *similarity*: in this sense feelings are *alike*, sentiments are *alike*, persons are *alike*; but cases are *similar*, circumstances are *similar*, conditions are *similar*. *Likeness* excludes the idea of difference; *similarity* includes only the idea of casual *likeness*;

With friendly hand I hold the glass
To all promisc'ous as they pass;
Should folly there her *likeness* view,
I fret not that the mirror 's true.—MOORE.

So, faint *resemblance*! on the marble tomb
The well-dissembled lover stooping stands,
For ever silent and for ever sad.—THOMSON.

'Rochefoucault frequently makes use of the antithesis, a mode of speaking the most tiresome of any, by the *similarity* of the periods.'—WARTON. 'As it addeth deformity to an ape to be so like a man, so the *similitude* of superstition to religion makes it the more deformed.'—BACON.

LIKENESS, PICTURE, IMAGE, EFFIGY.

In the former article *likeness* is considered as an abstract term, but in connexion with the words *picture* and *image* it signifies the representation of *likeness*; *picture*, in Latin *pictura*, from *pingo* to paint, signifies the thing painted; *image*, in Latin *imago*, contracted from *imitago*, comes from *imitor* to imitate, signifying an imitation; *effigy*, in Latin *effigies*, from *effingo*, signifies that which was formed after another thing.

Likeness is a general and indefinite term; *picture* and *image* express something positively *like*. A *likeness* is the work of nature or art; if it be the work of man, it is sketched by the pencil, and is more or less real;

God, Moses first, then David, did inspire,
To compose anthems for his heav'nly choir;
To th' one the style of friend he did impart,
On th' other stamp'd the *likeness* of his heart.
DENHAM.

A *picture* is either the work of design or accident; it may be drawn by the pencil or the pen, or it may be found in the incidental resemblances of things; it is more or less exact;

Or else the comick muse
Holds to the world a *picture* of itself.—THOMSON.

The *image* lies in the nature of things, and is more or less striking; 'The mind of man is an *image*, not only of God's spirituality, but of his infinity.'—SOUTH. It is the peculiar excellence of the painter to produce a *likeness*; the withering and falling off of the leaves from the trees in autumn is a *picture* of human nature in its decline; children are frequently the very *image* of their parents.

A *likeness* is that which is to represent the actual *likeness*; but an *effigy* is an artificial or arbitrary *likeness*; 'I have read somewhere that one of the popes refused to accept an edition of a saint's works, which were presented to him, because the saint in his *effigies* before the book, was drawn without a beard.'—ADDISON. It may be represented on wood or stone, or in the figure of a person, or in the copy of the figure. Artists produce *likenesses* in different manners. they carve *effigies*, or take impressions from those that are carved. Hence any thing dressed up in the figure of a man to represent a particular person is termed his *effigy*.

TO CONTRIVE, DEVISE, INVENT.

Contrive, in French *controuver*, compounded of *con* and *trouver*, signifies to find out by putting together; *devise*, compounded of *de* and *vise*, in Latin *visus* seen, signifies to show or present to the mind; *invent*, in Latin *inventus*, participle of *invenio*, compounded of *in* and *venio*, signifies to come or bring into the mind.

To *contrive* and *devise* do not express so much as to *invent*: we *contrive* and *devise* in small matters; we *invent* in those of greater moment. *Contriving* and *devising* respect the manner of doing things; *inventing* comprehends the action and the thing itself; the former are but the new fashioning of things that already exist; the latter is, as it were, the creation of something new: to *contrive* and *devise* are intentional actions, the result of a specifick effort; *invention* naturally arises from the exertion of an inherent power: we require thought and combination to *contrive* or *devise*; ingenuity is the faculty which is exerted in *inventing*;

My sentence is for open war; of wiles
More unexpert I boast not; them let those
Contrive who need, or when they need, not now.
MILTON.

The briskest nectar
Shall be his drink, and all th' ambrosial cates
Art can *devise* for wanton appetite,
Furnish his banquet.—NABB.

'Architecture, painting, and statuary, were *invented* with the design to lift up human nature.'—ADDISON.

Contriving requires even less exercise of the thoughts than *devising*: we *contrive* on familiar and common occasions; we *devise* in seasons of difficulty and trial. A *contrivance* is simple and obvious to a plain understanding: a *device* is complex and far-fetched; it requires a ready conception and a degree of art.

Contrivances serve to supply a deficiency, or increase a convenience; *devices* are employed to extricate from danger, to remove an evil, or forward a scheme: the history of Robinson Crusoe derives considerable interest from the relation of the various *contrivances*, by which he provided himself with the first articles of necessity and comfort; the history of robbers and adventurers is full of the various *devices* by which they endeavour to carry on their projects of plunder, or elude the vigilance of their pursuers; the history of civilized society contains an account of the various *inventions* which have contributed to the enjoyment or improvement of mankind.

DEVICE, CONTRIVANCE.

These nouns, derived from the preceding verbs, have also a similar distinction.

There is an exercise of art displayed in both these actions; but the former has most of ingenuity, trick, or cunning; the latter more of deduction and plain judgement in it. A *device* always consists of some invention or something newly made; a *contrivance* mostly respects the mode, arrangement, or disposition of things. Artists are employed in conceiving *devices*; men in general use *contrivances* for the ordinary concerns.

A *device* is often employed for bad and fraudulent purposes; *contrivances* mostly serve for innocent purposes of domestick life. Beggars have various *devices* for giving themselves the appearance of wretchedness and exciting the compassion of the spectator. Those who are reduced to the necessity of supplying their wants commonly succeed by forming *contrivances* of which they had not before any conception. *Devices* are the work of the human understanding only; *contrivances* are likewise formed by animals.

Men employ *devices* with an intention either to deceive or to please others; 'As I have long lived in Kent, and there often heard how the Kentish men evaded the conqueror by carrying green boughs over their heads; it put me in mind of practising this *device* against Mr. Simper.'—STEELE. Animals have their *contrivances* either to supply some want or to remove some evil; 'All the temples as well as houses of the Athenians were the effects of Nestor's (the architect) study and labour, insomuch that it was said, "Sure Nestor will now be famous; for the habitations of gods, as well as men, are built by his *contrivance*."'—STEELE.

TO CONCERT, CONTRIVE, MANAGE.

Concert is either a variation of *consort* a companion, or from the Latin *concerto* to debate together; *contrive*, from *contrivi*, perfect of *contero* to bruise together, signifies to pound or put together in the mind so as to form a composition; *manage*, in French *menager*, compounded of the Latin *manus* and *ago*, signifies to lead by the hand.

There is a secret understanding in *concerting*; invention in *contriving*; execution in *managing*. There is mostly *contrivance* and *management* in *concerting*; but there is not always *concerting* in *contrivance* or *management*. Measures are *concerted*; schemes are *contrived*; affairs are *managed*.

Two parties at least are requisite in *concerting*, one is sufficient for *contriving* and *managing*. *Concerting* is always employed in all secret transactions; *contrivance* and *management* are used indifferently.

Robbers who have determined on any scheme of plunder *concert* together the means of carrying their project into execution; 'Modern statesmen are *concerting* schemes and engaged in the depth of politicks, at the time when their forefathers were laid down quietly to rest, and had nothing in their heads but dreams.'—STEELE. Thieves *contrive* various devices to elude the vigilance of the police; 'When Cæsar was one of the masters of the mint, he placed the figure of an elephant upon the reverse of the publick money: the word Cæsar signifying an elephant in the Punick language. This was artfully *contrived* by Cæsar; because it was not lawful for a private man to stamp his own figure upon the coin of the commonwealth.'—ADDISON. Those who have any thing bad to do *manage* their concerns in the dark; 'It is the great act and secret of Christianity, if I may use that phrase, to *manage* our actions to the best advantage.'—ADDISON.

Those who are debarred the opportunity of seeing each other unrestrainedly, *concert* measures for meeting privately. The ingenuity of a person is frequently displayed in the *contrivances* by which he strives to help himself out of his troubles. Whenever there are many parties interested in a concern, it is never so well *managed* as when it is in the hands of one individual suitably qualified.

DESIGN, PURPOSE, INTEND, MEAN.

Design, from the Latin *designare*, signifies to mark out as with a pen or pencil; *purpose*, like *propose* comes from the Latin *proposui*, perfect of *propono* signifying to set before one's mind as an object of pursuit; *intend*, in Latin *intendo* to bend towards, signifies the bending of the mind towards an object; *mean*, in Saxon *maenen*, German, &c. *meinen*, is probably connected with the word mind, signifying to have in the mind.

Design and *purpose* are terms of higher import than *intend* and *mean*, which are in familiar use; the latter still more so than the former. The *design* embraces many objects; the *purpose* consists of only one:* the former supposes something studied and methodical, it requires reflection; the latter supposes something fixed and determinate, it requires resolution. A *design* is attainable; a *purpose* is steady. We speak of the *design* as it regards the thing conceived; we speak of the *purpose* as it regards the temper of the person. Men of a sanguine or aspiring character are apt to form *designs* which cannot be carried into execution; whoever wishes to keep true to his *purpose* must not listen to many counsellors;

Jove honours me and favours my *designs*,
His pleasure guides me, and his will confines.
POPE.

Proud as he is, that iron heart retains
His stubborn *purpose*, and his friends disdains.
POPE.

The *purpose* is the thing proposed or set before the mind; the *intention* is the thing to which the mind bends or inclines: *purpose* and *intend* differ therefore both in the nature of the action and the object; we *purpose* seriously; we *intend* vaguely: we set about that which we *purpose*; we may delay that which we have only *intended*: the execution of one's *purpose* rests mostly with one's self; the fulfilment of an *intention* depends upon circumstances: a man of a resolute temper is not to be diverted from his *purpose* by trifling objects; we may be disappointed in our *intentions* by a variety of unforeseen but uncontrollable events.

* Vide Trusler: "Intention, design."

Mean, which is a term altogether of colloquial use, differs but little from *intend*, except that it is used for more familiar objects: to *mean* is simply to have in the mind; to *intend* is to lean with the mind towards any thing.

Purpose is always applied to some proximate or definite object;

And I persuade me God hath not permitted
His strength again to grow, were not his *purpose*
To use him further yet.

Intend and *mean* to that which is general or remote; 'The gods would not have delivered a soul into the body, which hath arms and legs, instruments of doing, but that it were *intended* the mind should employ them.'—SIDNEY.

And life more perfect have attain'd than fate
Meant me, by venturing higher than my lot.
MILTON.

We *purpose* to set out at a certain time or go a certain route; we *mean* to set out as soon as we can, and go the way that shall be found most agreeable; the moralist *designs* by his writings to effect a reformation in the manners of men: a writer *purposes* to treat on a given subject in some particular manner; it is ridiculous to lay down rules which are not *intended* to be kept; an honest man always *means* to satisfy his creditors.

Design and *purpose* are taken sometimes in the abstract sense; *intend* and *mean* always in connexion with the agent who *intends* or *means*: we see a *design* in the whole creation, which leads us to reflect on the wisdom and goodness of the Creator; whenever we see any thing done we are led to inquire the *purpose* for which it is done; or are desirous of knowing the *intention* of the person for so doing: things are said to be done with a *design*, in opposition to that which happens by chance; they are said to be done for a *purpose*, in reference to the immediate *purpose* which is expected to result from them. *Design*, when not expressly qualified by a contrary epithet, is used in a bad sense in connexion with a particular agent; *purpose*, *intention*, and *meaning* in an indifferent sense: a *designing* person is full of latent and interested *designs*;

His deep *design* unknown, the hosts approve
Atrides' speech.—POPE.

There is nothing so good that it may not be made to serve the *purposes* of those who are bad;

Change this *purpose*,
Which, being so horrible, so bloody, must
Lead on to some foul issue.

The *intentions* of a man must always be taken into the account when we are forming an estimate of his actions; 'I wish others the same *intention* and greater successes.'—TEMPLE. Ignorant people frequently *mean* much better than they do.

Nothing can evince greater depravity of mind than *designedly* to rob another of his good name; when a person wishes to get any information he *purposely* directs his discourse to the subject upon which he desires to be informed; if we *unintentionally* incur the displeasure of another, it is to be reckoned our misfortune rather than our fault; it is not enough for our endeavours to be well *meant*, if they be not also well directed;

Then first Polydamus the silence broke,
Long weigh'd the signal, and to Hector spoke:
How oft, my brother! thy reproach I bear,
For words well *meant* and sentiments sincere.
POPE.

DESIGN, PLAN, SCHEME, PROJECT.

Design, *v. To design*; *plan*, in French *plan*, comes from *plane* or *plain*, in Latin *planus*, smooth or even, signifying in general any *plane* place, or in particular the even surface on which a building is raised; and by an extended application the sketch of the *plane* surface of any building or object; *scheme*, in Latin *schema*, Greek *σχῆμα* the form or figure, signifies the thing drawn out in the mind; *project*, in Latin *projectus*, from *projicio*, compounded of *pro* and *jacio*, signifies to cast or put forth, that is, the thing proposed.

Arrangement is the idea common to these terms: the *design* includes the thing that is to be brought about; the *plan* includes the means by which it is to be brought about: a *design* was formed in the time of James I. for overturning the government of the country; the *plan* by which this was to have been realized, consisted in placing gunpowder under the parliament-house and blowing up the assembly; 'Is he a prudent man, as to his temporal estate, that lays *designs* only for a day without any prospect to the remaining part of his life?'—TILLOTSON. 'It was at Marseilles that Virgil formed the *plan*, and collected the materials, of all those excellent pieces which he afterward finished.'—WALSH.

A *design* is to be estimated according to its intrinsick worth; a *plan* is to be estimated according to its relative value, or fitness for the *design*: a *design* is noble or wicked; a *plan* is practicable: every founder of a charitable institution may be supposed to have a good *design*; but he may adopt an erroneous *plan* for obtaining the end proposed.

Scheme and *project* respect both the end and the means, which makes them analogous to *design* and *plan*: the *design* stimulates to action; the *plan* determines the mode of action: the *scheme* and *project* consist most in speculation: the *design* and *plan* are equally practical, and suited to the ordinary and immediate circumstances of life: the *scheme* and *project* are contrived or conceived for extraordinary or rare occasions: no man takes any step without a *design*; a general forms the *plan* of his campaign; adventurous men are always forming *schemes* for gaining money; ambitious monarchs are full of *projects* for increasing their dominions;

The happy people in their waxen cells
Sat tending publick cares, and planning *schemes*
Of temperance for winter poor.—THOMSON.

'Manhood is led on from hope to hope, and from *project* to *project*.'—JOHNSON.

Scheme and *project* differ principally in the magnitude of the objects to which they are applied; the former being much less vast and extensive than the latter: a *scheme* may be formed by an individual for attaining any trifling advantage; *projects* are mostly conceived in matters of state, or of publick interest; the metropolis abounds with persons whose inventive faculties are busy in devising *schemes*, either of a commercial, a literary, a philosophical, or political description, by which they propose great advantages to the publick, but still greater to themselves; the *project* of universal conquest which entered into the wild speculations of Alexander the Great, did not, unfortunately for the world, perish at his death.

TO PURPOSE, PROPOSE.

We *purpose* (*v. To design*) that which is near at hand, or immediately to be set about; we *propose* that which is more distant: the former requires the setting before one's mind, the latter requires deliberation and plan. We *purpose* many things which we never think worth while doing: but we ought not to *propose* any thing to ourselves, which is not of too much importance to be lightly adopted or rejected. We *purpose* to go to town on a certain day;

When listening Philomela deigns
To let them joy, and *purposes* in thought
Elate to make her night excel their day.
THOMSON.

We *propose* to spend our time in a particular study 'There are but two plans on which any man can *propose* to conduct himself through the dangers and distresses of human life.'—BLAIR.

INTENT, INTENSE.

Intent and *intense* are both derived from the verb to *intend*, signifying to stretch towards a point, or to a great degree: the former is said only of the person or mind; the latter qualifies things in general: a person is *intent* when his mind is on the stretch towards an object; his application is *intense* when his mind is for a continuance closely fixed on certain objects: cold is *intense* when it seems to be wound up to its highest pitch; 'There is an evil spirit continually active and *intent* to seduce.'—SOUTH. 'Mutual favours naturally beget an *intense* affection in generous minds.'—SPECTATOR.

SAKE, ACCOUNT, REASON, PURPOSE, END.

These terms, all employed adverbially, modify or connect propositions: hence, one says, for his *sake*, on his *account*, for this *reason*, for this *purpose*, and to this *end*.

Sake, which comes from the word to seek, is mostly said of persons; what is done for a person's *sake* is the same as because of his seeking or at his desire; one may, however, say in regard to things, for the *sake* of good order, implying what good order requires: *account* is indifferently employed for persons or things; what is done on a person's *account* is done in his behalf, and for his interest; what is done on *account* of indisposition is done in consequence of it, the indisposition being the cause: *reason, purpose*, and *end* are applied to things only: we speak of the *reason* as the thing that justifies; we explain why we do a thing when we say we do it for this or that *reason:* we speak of the *purpose* and the *end* by way of explaining the nature of the thing: the propriety of measures cannot be known unless we know the *purpose* for which they were done; nor will a prudent person be satisfied to follow any course, unless he knows to what *end* it will lead.

EXPEDIENT, RESOURCE.

The *expedient* is an artificial means; the *resource* is a natural means: a cunning man is fruitful in *expedients;* a fortunate man abounds in *resources:* Robinson Crusoe adopted every *expedient* in order to prolong his existence, at a time when his *resources* were at the lowest ebb; 'When there happens to be any thing ridiculous in a visage, the best *expedient* is for the owner to be pleasant upon himself.'—STEELE. 'Since the accomplishment of the revolution, France has destroyed every *resource* of the state which depends upon opinion.'—BURKE.

THE END.

Stiles's Austria in 1848 and 1849. Being a History of the late Political Movements in Vienna, Milan, Venice, and Prague; with Details of the Campaigns of Lombardy and Novara; a full Account of the Rise, Progress, and Conclusion of the Revolution in Hungary; and Historical Sketches of the Austrian Government and the Provinces of the Empire. With Portraits of the Emperor, Metternich, Radetzky, Jellacic, and Kossuth. 2 vols. 8vo, Muslin, $3 50.

Brodhead's History of the State of New York. 2 vols. 8vo.

Creasy's Fifteen Decisive Battles of the World; from Marathon to Waterloo. 12mo, Muslin, $1 00.

Rule and Misrule of the English in America. By the Author of "Sam Slick the Clock-maker," "Attaché," "The Letter Bag," "Old Judge," etc. 12mo, Muslin, 75 cents.

Dickens's Child's History of England. 2 vols. 16mo, Muslin.

Lamartine's History of the Restoration of Monarchy in France. Being a Sequel to the "History of the Girondists." Portrait. Vols. I. and II., 12mo, Muslin, 75 cents each.

Lamartine's History of the Girondists; or, Personal Memoirs of the Patriots of the French Revolution. From Unpublished Sources. 3 vols. 12mo, Muslin, $2 10.

Lamartine's Past, Present, and Future of the Republic. 12mo, Paper, 37½ cents; Muslin, 50 cents.

Carlyle's History of the French Revolution. Newly Revised by the Author, with Index, &c. 2 vols. 12mo, Muslin, $2 00.

Mrs. Markham's History of France, from the Conquest of Gaul by Julius Cæsar to the Reign of Louis Philippe. With Conversations at the End of each Chapter. For the Use of Young Persons. Edited by Jacob Abbott. 12mo, Muslin, $1 00.

Stephen's Lectures on the History of France. 8vo, Muslin, $1 75.

Lord Holland's Foreign Reminiscences. Edited by his Son, Henry Edward Lord Holland. 12mo, Paper, 60 cents; Muslin, 75 cents.

Layard's Popular Account of the Discoveries at Nineveh. Abridged by him from his larger Work. With numerous Wood Engravings. 12mo, 75 cents.

Mills's Literature aud Literary Men of Great Britain and Ireland. 2 vols. 8vo, Muslin, $3 50; half Calf, $4 00.

Monette's Valley of the Mississippi. A History of the Discovery and Settlement of the Valley of the Mississippi, by the three great European Powers, Spain, France, and Great Britain; and the Subsequent Occupation, Settlement, and Extension of Civil Government by the United States, until the Year 1846. Maps. 2 vols. 8vo, Muslin, $5 00; Sheep, $5 50.

Miss Pardoe's Louis XIV., and the Court of France in the Seventeenth Century. With Engravings, Portraits, &c. 2 vols. 12mo, Muslin, $3 50.

Rollin's Ancient History. The Ancient History of the Egyptians, Carthaginians, Assyrians, Babylonians, Medes and Persians, Grecians, and Macedonians; including a History of the Arts and Sciences of the Ancients. With a Life of the Author, by James Bell. The only complete American Edition. Numerous Maps and Engravings. 8vo, Sheep extra. In 2 vols., $2 75; 1 vol., $2 50.

Sismondi's Historical View of the Literature of the South of Europe. Translated, with Notes, by Thomas Roscoe. 2 vols. 12mo, Muslin, $1 80.

Sismondi's History of the Italian Republics, being a View of the Rise, Progress, and Fall of Italian Freedom. 12mo, Muslin, 60 cents.

Hallam's Constitutional History of England, from the Accession of Henry VII. to the Death of George II. 8vo, Sheep extra, $1 75.

Hallam's Introduction to the Literature of Europe, during the Fifteenth, Sixteenth, and Seventeenth Centuries. 2 vols. 8vo, Sheep extra, $3 50.

Hallam's State of Europe during the Middle Ages. 8vo, Sheep extra, $1 75.

Ripley's War with Mexico. With Maps, Plans of Battles, &c. 2 vols. 8vo, Muslin, $4 00; half Calf, $4 50.

Carleton's Battle of Buena Vista, with the Operations of the "Army of Occupation" for one Month. 12mo, Muslin, 70 cents.

Henry's Campaign Sketches of the War with Mexico. Engravings. 12mo, Muslin, $1 00.

Abbott's Illustrated Histories: comprising Nero, Romulus, Cleopatra, Josephine, Madame Roland, Xerxes the Great, Cyrus the Great, Darius the Great, Alexander the Great, Hannibal the Carthaginian, Julius Cæsar, Alfred the Great, William the Conqueror, Queen Elizabeth, Mary Queen of Scots, Charles the First, Charles the Second, Maria Antoinette. 16mo, Muslin, 60 cents each; Muslin, gilt edges, 75 cents each.

The Conquest of Canada. By the Author of "Hochelaga." 2 vols. 12mo, Muslin, $1 70.

James's Dark Scenes of History. 12mo, Paper, 75 cents; Muslin, $1 00.

James's Lectures on Modern Civilization. 8vo.

James's History of Chivalry and the Crusades. Engravings. 18mo, Muslin, 45 cents.

Thirlwall's History of Greece. 2 vols. 8vo, Sheep extra, $3 00; Muslin, $2 75.

Sir E. Bulwer Lytton's Athens, its Rise and Fall; with Views of the Literature, Philosophy, and Social Life of the Athenians. 2 vols. 12mo, Muslin, $1 20.

Sir E. Bulwer Lytton's England and the English. 2 vols. 12mo, Muslin, 85 cents.

Sir Henry Bulwer's France, Social, Literary, and Political. 2 vols. 12mo, Muslin, 90 cents.

Robertson's History of the Emperor Charles V.; with a View of the Progress of Society in Europe, to the Beginning of the Sixteenth Century. With Questions for the Examination of Students, by JOHN FROST, A.M. Engravings. 8vo, Sheep extra, $1 50.

Robertson's History of Scotland and Ancient India. A History of Scotland during the Reigns of Queen Mary and King James VI., till his Accession to the Crown of England. With a Review of the Scottish History previous to that Period. Included in the same Volume is a Dissertation concerning Ancient India. 8vo, Sheep extra, $1 50.

Robertson's History of the Discovery of America. With an Account of his Life and Writings. With Questions for the Examination of Students, by JOHN FROST, A.M. Engravings. 8vo, Sheep extra, $1 50.

Muller's History of the World; from the earliest Period to the Year of our Lord 1783, with particular Reference to the Affairs of Europe and her Colonies. Compared throughout with the Original, revised, corrected, and Illustrated by a Notice of the Life and Writings of the Author, by ALEXANDER EVERETT. 4 vols. 12mo, Muslin, $3 00.

Russell's History of Modern Europe, with a View of the Progress of Society, from the Rise of Modern Kingdoms to the Peace of Paris in 1763. With a Continuance of the History, by WM. JONES. Engravings. 3 vols. 8vo, Sheep, $4 50.

History of Silk, Cotton, Linen, Wool, and other Fibrous Substances; including Observations on Spinning, Dyeing, and Weaving. Also, an Account of the Pastoral Life of the Ancients, their Social State and Attainments in the Domestic Arts. With Appendices on Pliny's Natural History; on the Origin and Manufacture of Linen and Cotton Paper; on Felting, Netting, &c. Deduced from copious and authentic Sources. Steel Engravings. 8vo, Muslin, $3 00.

Lieber's Great Events described by distinguished Historians, Chroniclers, and other Writers. A new Edition. 12mo, Muslin, 75 cents.

Miss E. Robins's Tales from American History. Engravings. 3 vols. 18mo, Muslin, $1 00.

Hopkins's History of the Confessional. 12mo, Muslin, $1 00.

Strickland's History of the American Bible Society, from its Organization in 1816 to the Present Time. With an Introduction by Rev. N. L. Rice, and a Portrait of Hon. Elias Boudinot, first President of the Society. 8vo, Cloth, $1 50; Sheep, $1 75.

Gieseler's Compendium of Ecclesiastical History. From the Fourth Edition, revised and amended. Translated from the German, by Samuel Davidson, LL.D. Vols. I. and II., 8vo, Muslin, $3 00.

Neal's History of the Puritans, or Protestant Non-conformists; from the Reformation in 1518 to the Revolution in 1688; comprising an Account of their Principles, Sufferings, and the Lives and Characters of their most considerable Divines. With Notes, by J. O. Choules, D.D. With Portraits. 2 vols. 8vo, Muslin, $2 75; Sheep, $3 00.

Mosheim's Ecclesiastical History, Ancient and Modern; in which the Rise, Progress, and Variation of Church Power are considered in their Connection with the State of Learning and Philosophy, and the Political History of Europe during that Period. Translated, with Notes, &c., by A Maclaine, D.D. A new Edition, continued to 1826, by C. Coote, LL.D. 2 vols. 8vo, Sheep, $3 00

Grant's History of the Nestorians; or, the Lost Tribes. Containing Evidence of their Identity, an Account of their Manners, Customs, and Ceremonies, together with Sketches of Travel in Ancient Assyria, Armenia, Media, and Mesopotamia, and Illustrations of Scripture Prophecy. Map. 12mo, Muslin, $1 00.

Howitt's History of Priestcraft in all Ages and Countries. 12mo, Muslin, 60 cents.

Waddington's History of the Church. from the earliest Ages to the Reformation. 8vo, Muslin, $1 75.

Jarvis's Chronological Introduction to Church History. Being a new Inquiry into the true Dates of the Birth and Death of our Lord and Savior Jesus Christ; and containing an original Harmony of the Four Gospels, now first arranged in the Order of Time. 8vo, Muslin, $3 00.

Milman's History of Christianity, from the Birth of Christ to the Abolition of Paganism in the Roman Empire. With Notes, &c., by James Murdock, D.D. 8vo, Muslin, $1 50.

Milman's History of the Jews, from the earliest Period to the the Present Time. With Maps and Engravings. 3 vols. 18mo, Muslin, $1 20.

Bonnechose's Reformers before the Reformation. The Fifteenth Century. John Huss and the Council of Constance. Being an Introduction to D'Aubigné's History of the Reformation. Translated from the French, by Campbell Mackenzie, B.A. 8vo, Paper, 50 cents.

Gleig's History of the Bible. Map. 2 vols. 12mo, Muslin, 80 cents.

Prideaux's Connection of the Old and New Testaments, in the History of the Jews and neighboring Nations, from the Declension of the Kingdoms of Israel and Judah to the Time of Christ. 2 vols. 8vo, Sheep, $3 00.

Turner's Sacred History of the World attempted to be Philosophically considered in a Series of Letters to a Son. 3 vols. 18mo, Muslin, $1 35.

Smedley's History of the Reformation in France. Portrait. 3 vols. 18mo, Muslin, $1 40.

Stone's Border Wars of the American Revolution. Including the Life of Joseph Brant, the Indian Chief. 2 vols. 18mo, Muslin, 90 cents.

Keightley's History of England, from the earliest Period to 1839. With Notes, &c., by an American. 5 vols. 18mo, Muslin, $2 25.

Smith's History of Education. Part I.—History of Education, Ancient and Modern. Part II.—A Plan of Culture and Instruction, based on Christian Principles, and designed to Aid in the right Education of Youth, Physically, Intellectually, and Morally. 18mo, Muslin, 45 cents.

*** For a full and complete List of Historical, and other valuable Works in every department of Literature, see Harper & Brothers' Catalogue.

www.ingramcontent.com/pod-product-compliance
Lightning Source LLC
LaVergne TN
LVHW021301110826
845150LV00003B/456

* 9 7 8 1 4 2 5 5 5 9 6 1 8 *